Lecture Notes in Computer Science 6981

Commenced Publication in 1973
Founding and Former Series Editors:
Gerhard Goos, Juris Hartmanis, and Jan van Leeuwen

Editorial Board

David Hutchison
  Lancaster University, UK
Takeo Kanade
  Carnegie Mellon University, Pittsburgh, PA, USA
Josef Kittler
  University of Surrey, Guildford, UK
Jon M. Kleinberg
  Cornell University, Ithaca, NY, USA
Alfred Kobsa
  University of California, Irvine, CA, USA
Friedemann Mattern
  ETH Zurich, Switzerland
John C. Mitchell
  Stanford University, CA, USA
Moni Naor
  Weizmann Institute of Science, Rehovot, Israel
Oscar Nierstrasz
  University of Bern, Switzerland
C. Pandu Rangan
  Indian Institute of Technology, Madras, India
Bernhard Steffen
  TU Dortmund University, Germany
Madhu Sudan
  Microsoft Research, Cambridge, MA, USA
Demetri Terzopoulos
  University of California, Los Angeles, CA, USA
Doug Tygar
  University of California, Berkeley, CA, USA
Gerhard Weikum
  Max Planck Institute for Informatics, Saarbruecken, Germany

Jon Whittle Tony Clark Thomas Kühne (Eds.)

Model Driven Engineering Languages and Systems

14th International Conference, MODELS 2011
Wellington, New Zealand, October 16-21, 2011
Proceedings

 Springer

Volume Editors

Jon Whittle
Lancaster University, School of Computing and Communications
InfoLab21, South Drive, Lancaster LA1 4WA, UK
E-mail: j.n.whittle@lancaster.ac.uk

Tony Clark
Middlesex University, School of Engineering and Information Sciences
The Burroughs, Hendon, London NW4 4BT, UK
E-mail: t.n.clark@mdx.ac.uk

Thomas Kühne
Victoria University, School of Engineering and Computer Science
P.O. Box 600, Wellington 6140, New Zealand
E-mail: thomas.kuehne@ecs.vuw.ac.nz

ISSN 0302-9743   e-ISSN 1611-3349
ISBN 978-3-642-24484-1   ISBN 978-3-642-24485-8 (eBook)
DOI 10.1007/978-3-642-24485-8
Springer Heidelberg Dordrecht London New York

Library of Congress Control Number: 2011937287

CR Subject Classification (1998): D.2, D.3, K.6.3, D.2.9, F.3.3, D.1, D.2.2

LNCS Sublibrary: SL 2 – Programming and Software Engineering

© Springer-Verlag Berlin Heidelberg 2011
This work is subject to copyright. All rights are reserved, whether the whole or part of the material is concerned, specifically the rights of translation, reprinting, re-use of illustrations, recitation, broadcasting, reproduction on microfilms or in any other way, and storage in data banks. Duplication of this publication or parts thereof is permitted only under the provisions of the German Copyright Law of September 9, 1965, in its current version, and permission for use must always be obtained from Springer. Violations are liable to prosecution under the German Copyright Law.
The use of general descriptive names, registered names, trademarks, etc. in this publication does not imply, even in the absence of a specific statement, that such names are exempt from the relevant protective laws and regulations and therefore free for general use.

Typesetting: Camera-ready by author, data conversion by Scientific Publishing Services, Chennai, India

Printed on acid-free paper

Springer is part of Springer Science+Business Media (www.springer.com)

Preface

For the past 14 years, the MODELS conference has been the premier venue for the exchange of innovative ideas and experiences of model-based approaches in the development of complex systems. MODELS is universally recognized as one of the top conferences in software engineering research and is a highly selective conference, with an acceptance rate averaging 20% in recent years. The conference series covers all aspects of model-based development for software and systems engineering, including modeling languages, methods, tools, and their applications.

Research in software and system modeling is now a relatively mature field. Like any mature field, however, it can be a good idea to encourage fresh thinking. Whilst not wishing to reduce the importance of solid incremental research, the conference this year asked participants to think ahead to what modeling would be like a decade hence. For this reason, the Program Chairs selected *Modeling in 2020* as the theme for MODELS 2011. The theme was chosen to encourage new perspectives about the future role of modeling in complex systems engineering. As part of this effort, the conference solicited, for the first time, a new category of research papers—vision papers—that presented "outside the box" thinking. This category was introduced to encourage the submission of papers with new ideas that would take the community beyond its normal boundaries.

As part of the effort to encourage fresh perspectives, the conference invited three outstanding keynote speakers this year, two of which were from outside the software modeling domain.

Marian Petre is a Professor of Computing at the Open University in the UK. She is well known for her work considering software from a 'design studies' perspective and describes her role to 'pick the brains of experts' in studying how leading professional software developers reason about, represent, and communicate designs. Marian's keynote reported on insights from many years of empirical studies of expert software designers.

The conference welcomed its first ever Academy Award winning speaker this year. Mark Sagar is Special Projects Supervisor at Weta Digital. He has developed technologies for interactive applications and for feature films and has won two consecutive Scientific & Engineering Academy Awards for his pioneering work in facial motion capture and realistic relighting of computer generated faces. He has specialized in bringing computer generated faces to life in some of Hollywood's biggest blockbusters including "Avatar" and "King Kong". Mark's fascinating talk focused on creating models for simulating the face.

MODELS was also very lucky to welcome Wolfram Schulte as a keynote speaker. Wolfram is a principal researcher and the founding manager of Microsoft's Research in Software Engineering (RiSE) team in Redmond,

Washington. In his talk, Wolfram presented Formula, a new formal specification language and toolset for describing, transforming and analyzing meta-models and instance models.

MODELS 2011 continued its strong tradition of soliciting both research-oriented papers (the Foundations Track) and practice-oriented papers (the Applications Track). The Foundations Track received 167 full paper submissions, of which 34 were finally selected for presentation by the program committee, giving an acceptance rate of 20%. Out of these, 3 papers were vision papers, selected out of a total of 20 vision paper submissions (15% acceptance rate). The Applications Track was particularly healthy this year: the program committee chose 13 out of 27 paper submissions (48% acceptance rate). In addition, two papers that were originally submitted to the Foundations Track were transferred and accepted into the Applications Track.

The Program Chairs would like to thank all those who submitted papers, as well as those who submitted proposals for workshops and tutorials. We would also like to express our gratitude to the many volunteers who contributed to the success of the conference, including organizers of the Educators' Symposium and Doctoral Symposium. Special thanks are due to Richard van de Stadt for his support of CyberChairPRO, the conference management system used for MODELS 2011. We thank our sponsors, ACM and IEEE, and host, the Victoria University of Wellington. Last, but certainly not least, we give special thanks to the Program Committee and other external reviewers for all their hard work in reviewing and discussing papers.

October 2011

Jon Whittle
Tony Clark
Thomas Kühne

Organization

General Chair

Thomas Kühne — Victoria University of Wellington, New Zealand

Local Chairs

Stuart Marshall — Victoria University of Wellington, New Zealand
Hui Ma — Victoria University of Wellington, New Zealand

Program Chairs

Jon Whittle (Foundations Track) — Lancaster University, UK
Tony Clark (Applications Track) — Middlesex University, UK

Publicity Chair

Werner Heijstek — Leiden University, The Netherlands

Workshop Chair

Jörg Kienzle — McGill University, Canada

Tutorial Chair

Vasco Amaral — Universidade Nova de Lisboa, Portugal

Panel Chair

Colin Atkinson — Universität Mannheim, Germany

Doctoral Symposium Chairs

Jörg Evermann — Memorial University, Canada
Ivan Porres — Åbo Akademi University, Finland

Educators' Symposium Chairs

Marion Brandsteidl — Technische Universität Wien, Austria
Andreas Winter — Carl von Ossietzky University Oldenburg, Germany

Program Committee: Foundations Track

Daniel Amyot — University of Ottawa, Canada
Colin Atkinson — University of Mannheim, Germany
Joanne M. Atlee — University of Waterloo, Canada
Don Batory — UT Austin, USA
Benoit Baudry — INRIA, France
Paulo Borba — Federal University of Pernambuco, Brazil
Ruth Breu — University of Innsbruck, Austria
Lionel Briand — Simula Research Laboratory and University of Oslo, Norway
Jean-Michel Bruel — University of Toulouse, France
Jordi Cabot — INRIA / Ecole des Mines de Nantes, France
Michel Chaudron — Leiden University, The Netherlands
Marsha Chechik — University of Toronto, Canada
Jane Cleland-Huang — DePaul University, USA
Krzysztof Czarnecki — University of Waterloo, Canada
Juergen Dingel — Queens University, Canada
Alexander Egyed — Johannes Kepler University, Austria
Gregor Engels — University of Paderborn, Germany
Rik Eshuis — Eindhoven University of Technology, The Netherlands
Robert France — Colorado State University, USA
Sébastien Gérard — CEA LIST, France
Holger Giese — Hasso Plattner Institute, University of Potsdam, Germany
Martin Glinz — Universität Zürich, Switzerland
Martin Gogolla — University of Bremen, Germany
Aniruddha Gokhale — Vanderbilt University, USA
Jeff Gray — University of Alabama, USA
John Grundy — Swinburne University of Technology, Australia
Mark Harman — CREST Centre, University College London, UK
Øystein Haugen — SINTEF, Norway
Mats Heimdahl — University of Minnesota, USA
Patrick Heymans — University of Namur, Belgium
John Howse — University of Brighton, UK
Zhenjiang Hu — National Institute of Informatics, Japan
Heinrich Hußmann — Ludwig-Maximilians-Universität München, Germany

Paola Inverardi	University of L'Aquila, Italy
Jan Jürjens	TU Dortmund and Fraunhofer ISST, Germany
Shmuel Katz	Technion - Israel Institute of Technology, Israel
Gerti Kappel	Vienna University of Technology, Austria
Gabor Karsai	Vanderbilt University, USA
Jörg Kienzle	McGill University, Canada
Ingolf Krüger	UCSD, USA
Thomas Kühne	Victoria University of Wellington, New Zealand
Jochen Küster	IBM Research - Zurich, Switzerland
Michael Lawley	CSIRO, Australia
Timothy C. Lethbridge	University of Ottawa, Canada
Hong Mei	Peking University, China
Tom Mens	Université de Mons, Belgium
Ana Moreira	Universidade Nova de Lisboa, Portugal
Pierre-Alain Muller	Université de Haute-Alsace, France
Richard Paige	University of York, UK
Mauro Pezzè	University of Lugano, Switzerland and Università degli Studi di Milano Bicocca, Italy
Dorina C. Petriu	Carleton University, Canada
Alfonso Pierantonio	University of L'Aquila, Italy
Ivan Porres	Åbo Akademi University, Finland
Nicolas Rouquette	NASA JPL, USA
Bernhard Rumpe	RWTH Aachen University, Germany
Andy Schürr	Technische Universität Darmstadt, Germany
Bran Selic	Malina Software Corp., Canada
Miroslaw Staron	University of Gothenburg and Chalmers, Sweden
Perdita Stevens	University of Edinburgh, UK
Paul Strooper	University of Queensland, Australia
Kevin Sullivan	University of Virginia, USA
Dániel Varró	Budapest University of Technology and Economics, Hungary
Eelco Visser	Delft University of Technology, The Netherlands
Liming Zhu	NICTA, Australia
Steffen Zschaler	King's College, London, UK

Program Committee: Applications Track

Patrick Albert	IBM CAS France, France
Robert Baillargeon	Sodius, USA
Edward J. Barkmeyer	National Institute of Standards & Technology, USA
Balbir Barn	University of Middlesex, UK
Jorn Bettin	Sofismo, Switzerland
Mariano Belaunde	Orange Labs, France
Rao Bhaskar	Motorola, India
Behzad Bordbar	University of Birmingham, UK
William Cook	University of Texas at Austin, USA
Diarmuid Corcoran	Ericsson Software Research, Sweden
Huascar Espinoza	TECNALIA-European Software Institute, Spain
Geri Georg	Colorado State University, USA
Jack Greenfield	Microsoft Corporation, USA
Pavel Hruby	CSC, Denmark
Narendra Jussien	Ecole des Mines de Nantes, France
Vinay Kulkarni	Tata Consultancy Services, India
Stephen J. Mellor	UK
Dragan Milicev	University of Belgrade, Serbia
Hiroshi Miyazaki	Fujitsu, Japan
Juan Carlos Molina Udaeta	CARE Technologies, S.A., Spain
Syed Salman Qadri	The Mathworks, Inc., USA
Ina Schieferdecker	TU Berlin/Fraunhofer FOKUS, Germany
Bran Selic	Malina Software Corp., Canada
Richard Soley	Object Management Group, USA
Ingo Stürmer	Model Engineering Solutions GmbH, Germany
Jun Sun	Singapore University of Technology and Design, Singapore
François Terrier	CEA-LIST, France
Laurence Tratt	Middlesex University, UK
Michael von der Beeck	BMW Group, Germany
Thomas Weigert	Missouri University of Science and Technology, USA
Frank Weil	UniqueSoft, USA
Ed Willink	Eclipse Modeling Project, UK

Steering Committee

Geri Georg (Chair) Thomas Baar
Gregor Engels (Vice Chair) Jean Bézivin

Lionel Briand
Jean-Michel Bruel
Krzysztof Czarnecki
Matthew Dwyer (ACM SIGSOFT)
Øystein Haugen
Heinrich Hussmann
Stuart Kent
Thomas Kühne
Pierre-Alain Muller

Oscar Nierstrasz
Dorina Petriu
Rob Pettit
Gianna Reggio
Doug Schmidt
Andy Schürr
Steve Seidman (IEEE)
Jon Whittle

Sponsors

ACM (http://www.acm.org)
IEEE (http://www.ieee.org)
Victoria University of Wellington

Additional Reviewers

Ebrahim Abbasi
Mauricio Alferez
Shaukat Ali
Mohamed Almorsy
Anthony Anjorin
Michal Antkiewicz
Kazuyuki Asada
Marco Autili
Iman Avazpour
Fabian Büttner
Omar Badreddin
Prateek Bahri
Kacper Bak
Jan-Christopher Bals
Olivier Barais
Jorge Barreiros
Saeed Ahmadi Behnam
Gábor Bergmann
Jason Biatek
Dénes Bisztray
Quentin Boucher
John Brondum
Petra Brosch
Jens Brüning
Jim Burton
Peter Chapman

Eya Ben Charrada
Hyun Cho
Fabian Christ
Antonio Cicchetti
Harald Cichos
Robert Clariso
Andreas Classen
Benoit Combemale
Arnaud Cuccuru
Duc-Hanh Dang
Sylvain Degrandsart
Barry Demchak
Zinovy Diskin
Didier Donsez
Dirk Draheim
Sophie Ebersold
Eban Escott
Ramin Etemaadi
Claudiu Farcas
Emilia Farcas
Andrew Fish
Franck Fleurey
Frédéric Fondement
François Fouquet
Miguel Garzón
Gregory Gay

Nicolas Genon
Christian Gerth
Achraf Ghabi
Sepideh Ghanavati
Javier Gonzalez-Huerta
Danny Groenewegen
Tim Gülke
Lars Hamann
Brahim Hamid
Ali Hamie
Stefan Hanenberg
Ábel Hegedüs
Werner Heijstek
Zef Hemel
Soichiro Hidaka
Stephan Hildebrandt
Ákos Horváth
Arnaud Hubaux
Javier Gonzalez Huerta
Ferosh Jacob
Cédric Jeanneret
Adam Jensen
Rim Jnidi
Martin Johansen
Maartje de Jonge
Lennart C.L. Kats
Ali Hanzala Khan
Felix Klar
Natallia Kokash
Dimitrios S. Kolovos
Jens Krinke
Amber Krug
Mirco Kuhlmann
Thomas Kurpick
Jan-Christoph Küster
Leen Lambers
Philip Langer
Marius Lauder
Hervé Leblanc
Jaejoon Lee
Philipp Liegl
Qichao Liu
Roberto Lopez-Herrejon
Alexander De Luca
Torbjorn Lundkvist

Martin Mahaux
Nikos Matragkas
Kazutaka Matsuda
Max-Emanuel Maurer
Dieter Mayrhofer
Massimiliano Menarini
Marjan Mernik
Gunter Mussbacher
Benjamin Nagel
Stefan Neumann
Florian Noyrit
Hafees Osman
Sebastian Pape
Lars Patzina
Cedric Peeters
Christian Percebois
Gilles Perrouin
Hung Tuan Pham
Claas Pinkernell
Niusha Hakimi Pour
Alireza Pourshahid
Jorge Pinna Puissant
István Ráth
Alek Radjenovic
Shekoufeh Kolahdouz Rahimi
Irum Rauf
Ruth Raventos
Alexander Reder
Holger Rendel
Márcio Ribeiro
Louis Rose
Rick Salay
Hendrik Schreiber
Andreas Seibel
Ed Seidewitz
Sagar Sen
Cristina Gómez Seoane
Filippo Seracini
Norbert Seyff
Azalia Shamsaei
Steven She
Christian Soltenborn
Gem Stapleton
Jim Steel
Reinhard Stoiber

Ragnhild Van Der Straeten
Espen Suenson
Andreas Svendsen
Jörn Guy Süß
Robert Tairas
Leopoldo Teixeira
Laurent Thiry
Massimo Tisi
Társis Toledo
Dragos Truscan
Hagen Völzer
Gergely Varró
Sander Vermolen
Thomas Vogel
Steven Völkel
Guido Wachsmuth
Fernando Wanderley
Bo Wang

Andrzej Wasowski
Ingo Weisemöller
Sven Wenzel
Magdalena Widl
Konrad Wieland
James R. Williams
Manuel Wimmer
Dustin Wüest
Sebastian Wätzoldt
Yingfei Xiong
Xiwei Xu
Eran Yahav
Li Yi
Tao Yue
Xiang Zhang
Xiaorui Zhang
Celal Ziftci
Olaf Zimmermann

Table of Contents

Keynote 1

The Value in Muddling Around Modelling (Abstract) 1
  Marian Petre

Model Transformations 1

Towards Quality Driven Exploration of Model Transformation Spaces . . . 2
  Mauro Luigi Drago, Carlo Ghezzi, and Raffaela Mirandola

Automated Model-to-Metamodel Transformations Based on the
Concepts of Deep Instantiation 17
  Gerd Kainz, Christian Buckl, and Alois Knoll

Lazy Execution of Model-to-Model Transformations 32
  Massimo Tisi, Salvador Martínez, Frédéric Jouault, and Jordi Cabot

Model Complexity

Measuring UML Models Using Metrics Defined in OCL within the
SQUAM Framework 47
  Joanna Chimiak–Opoka

Modeling Model Slicers 62
  *Arnaud Blouin, Benoît Combemale, Benoit Baudry, and
  Olivier Beaudoux*

Morsa: A Scalable Approach for Persisting and Accessing Large
Models 77
  *Javier Espinazo Pagán, Jesús Sánchez Cuadrado, and
  Jesús García Molina*

Aspect-Oriented Modeling

Expressing Aspectual Interactions in Design: Experiences in the Slot
Machine Domain 93
  Johan Fabry, Arturo Zambrano, and Silvia Gordillo

An Industrial Application of Robustness Testing Using Aspect-Oriented
Modeling, UML/MARTE, and Search Algorithms 108
  Shaukat Ali, Lionel C. Briand, Andrea Arcuri, and Suneth Walawege

Aspect-Oriented Modelling for Distributed Systems 123
  Wisam Al Abed and Jörg Kienzle

Analysis and Comprehension of Models

A Precise Style for Business Process Modelling: Results from Two
Controlled Experiments... 138
  *Gianna Reggio, Filippo Ricca, Giuseppe Scanniello,
  Francesco Di Cerbo, and Gabriella Dodero*

Semantically Configurable Consistency Analysis for Class and Object
Diagrams 153
  Shahar Maoz, Jan Oliver Ringert, and Bernhard Rumpe

Identifying the Weaknesses of UML Class Diagrams during Data Model
Comprehension 168
  *Gabriele Bavota, Carmine Gravino, Rocco Oliveto,
  Andrea De Lucia, Genoveffa Tortora, Marcela Genero, and
  José Antonio Cruz-Lemus*

Domain-Specific Modeling

Engineering Android Applications Based on UML Activities 183
  Frank Alexander Kraemer

Domain-Specific Model Transformation in Building Quantity
Take-Off 198
  Jim Steel and Robin Drogemuller

Improving Scalability and Maintenance of Software for
High-Performance Scientific Computing by Combining MDE
and Frameworks 213
  Marc Palyart, David Lugato, Ileana Ober, and Jean-Michel Bruel

Models for Embedded Systems

A Critical Review of Applied MDA for Embedded Devices: Identification
of Problem Classes and Discussing Porting Efforts in Practice 228
  Michael Lettner, Michael Tschernuth, and Rene Mayrhofer

Designing Heterogeneous Component Based Systems: Evaluation of
MARTE Standard and Enhancement Proposal......................... 243
  Ali Koudri, Arnaud Cuccuru, Sebastien Gerard, and François Terrier

Semantic Clone Detection for Model-Based Development of Embedded
Systems 258
  Bakr Al-Batran, Bernhard Schätz, and Benjamin Hummel

Model Synchronization

Instant and Incremental QVT Transformation for Runtime Models 273
  Hui Song, Gang Huang, Franck Chauvel, Wei Zhang, Yanchun Sun,
  Weizhong Shao, and Hong Mei

Service–Oriented Architecture Modeling: Bridging the Gap between
Structure and Behavior 289
  Mickael Clavreul, Sébastien Mosser, Mireille Blay–Fornarino, and
  Robert B. France

From State- to Delta-Based Bidirectional Model Transformations:
The Symmetric Case 304
  Zinovy Diskin, Yingfei Xiong, Krzysztof Czarnecki, Hartmut Ehrig,
  Frank Hermann, and Fernando Orejas

Model-Based Resource Management

Enforcing S&D Pattern Design in RCES with Modeling and Formal
Approaches 319
  Brahim Hamid, Sigrid Gürgens, Christophe Jouvray, and
  Nicolas Desnos

A Model-Based and Automated Approach to Size Estimation of
Embedded Software Components. 334
  Kenneth Lind and Rogardt Heldal

MDE to Manage Communications with and between
Resource-Constrained Systems 349
  Franck Fleurey, Brice Morin, Arnor Solberg, and Olivier Barais

Analysis of Class Diagrams

Diagram Definition: A Case Study with the UML Class Diagram 364
  Maged Elaasar and Yvan Labiche

Reducing Multiplicities in Class Diagrams 379
  Ingo Feinerer, Gernot Salzer, and Tanja Sisel

Keynote 2

Creating Models for Simulating the Face (Abstract) 394
  Mark Sagar

Verification and Validation 1

EUnit: A Unit Testing Framework for Model Management Tasks 395
  Antonio García-Domínguez, Dimitrios S. Kolovos, Louis M. Rose, Richard F. Paige, and Inmaculada Medina-Bulo

Verifying UML-RT Protocol Conformance Using Model Checking 410
  Yann Moffett, Alain Beaulieu, and Juergen Dingel

Model-Based Coverage-Driven Test Suite Generation for Software Product Lines 425
  Harald Cichos, Sebastian Oster, Malte Lochau, and Andy Schürr

Refactoring Models

Constraint-Based Model Refactoring 440
  Friedrich Steimann

Supporting Design Model Refactoring for Improving Class Responsibility Assignment 455
  Motohiro Akiyama, Shinpei Hayashi, Takashi Kobayashi, and Motoshi Saeki

Modeling Visions

Vision Paper: The Essence of Structural Models 470
  Dmitrijs Zaparanuks and Matthias Hauswirth

Vision Paper: Towards Model-Based Energy Testing 480
  Claas Wilke, Sebastian Götz, Jan Reimann, and Uwe Aßmann

Vision Paper: Make a Difference! (Semantically) 490
  Uli Fahrenberg, Axel Legay, and Andrzej Wąsowski

Logics and Modeling

Automatic Derivation of Utility Functions for Monitoring Software Requirements 501
  Andres J. Ramirez and Betty H.C. Cheng

Logic-Based Model-Level Software Development with F-OML 517
  Mira Balaban and Michael Kifer

Formal Verification of QVT Transformations for Code Generation 533
  Kurt Stenzel, Nina Moebius, and Wolfgang Reif

Development Methods

Model-Based (Mechanical) Product Design 548
    Mehdi Iraqi-Houssaini, Mathias Kleiner, and Lionel Roucoules

Applying a Model-Based Approach to IT Systems Development Using
SysML Extension 563
    Sayaka Izukura, Kazuo Yanoo, Takao Osaki, Hiroshi Sakaki,
    Daichi Kimura, and Jianwen Xiang

Early Experience with Agile Methodology in a Model-Driven
Approach 578
    Vinay Kulkarni, Souvik Barat, and Uday Ramteerthkar

Keynote 3

Finding Models in Model-Based Development (Abstract) 591
    Wolfram Schulte and Ethan K. Jackson

Model Transformations 2

CD2Alloy: Class Diagrams Analysis Using Alloy Revisited 592
    Shahar Maoz, Jan Oliver Ringert, and Bernhard Rumpe

Model-Driven Engineering and Optimizing Compilers: A Bridge Too
Far? 608
    Antoine Floch, Tomofumi Yuki, Clement Guy, Steven Derrien,
    Benoit Combemale, Sanjay Rajopadhye, and Robert B. France

Towards a General Composition Semantics for Rule-Based Model
Transformation 623
    Dennis Wagelaar, Massimo Tisi, Jordi Cabot, and Frédéric Jouault

Verification and Validation 2

Properties of Realistic Feature Models Make Combinatorial Testing of
Product Lines Feasible... 638
    Martin Fagereng Johansen, Øystein Haugen, and Franck Fleurey

Reasoning about Metamodeling with Formal Specifications and
Automatic Proofs 653
    Ethan K. Jackson, Tihamér Levendovszky, and
    Daniel Balasubramanian

Correctness of Model Synchronization Based on Triple Graph
Grammars 668
    Frank Hermann, Hartmut Ehrig, Fernando Orejas,
    Krzysztof Czarnecki, Zinovy Diskin, and Yingfei Xiong

Model Integration and Collaboration

A Toolchain for the Detection of Structural and Behavioral Latent
System Properties.. 683
    Adam C. Jensen, Betty H.C. Cheng, Heather J. Goldsby, and
    Edward C. Nelson

Defining MARTE's VSL as an Extension of Alf 699
    Arnaud Cuccuru, Sébastien Gérard, and François Terrier

Using Delta Model for Collaborative Work of Industrial Large-Scaled
E/E Architecture Models 714
    Rixin Zhang and Ajay Krishnan

Author Index 729

The Value in Muddling Around Modelling

Marian Petre

Centre for Research in Computing, The Open University, UK
m.petre@open.ac.uk

Abstract. Software is a designed artifact. In other design disciplines, such as building architecture, there is a well-established tradition of design studies which inform not only the discipline itself but also tool design, processes, and collaborative work. This talk considers software from such a 'design studies' perspective. The talk will present a series of observations from empirical studies of expert software designers, and will draw on examples from actual professional practice. It will consider what experts' mental imagery, software visualisations, and sketches suggest about software design thinking. It will discuss which representations designers use when allowed to choose freely, how designers' informal representations relate to the formal representations from their discipline, how the character of their informal representations facilitates design discussions, and why many of the functions afforded by their sketching are not well supported by existing CAD systems. It will consider what the observations and sketches reveal about requirements for an idea-capture tool that supports collaborative design. The talk will also discuss some of the deliberate practices experts use to promote innovation. Finally, it will open discussion on the tensions between observed software design practices and received methodology in software engineering.

Keywords: empirical studies, expert design, software design, flexible modeling, software engineering practice.

Towards Quality Driven Exploration of Model Transformation Spaces*

Mauro Luigi Drago, Carlo Ghezzi, and Raffaela Mirandola

Politecnico di Milano
DeepSE Group - Dipartimento di Elettronica e Informazione
Piazza Leonardo Da Vinci, 32 - 20133 Milano, Italy
{drago,ghezzi,mirandola}@elet.polimi.it
http://deepse.dei.polimi.it

Abstract. Verifying that a software system has certain non-functional properties is a primary concern in many engineering fields. Although several model-driven approaches exist to predict quality attributes from system models, they still lack the proper level of automation envisioned by Model Driven Software Development. When a potential issue concerning non-functional properties is discovered, the identification of a solution is still entirely up to the engineer and to his/her experience. This paper presents QVT-Rational, our multi-modeling solution to automate the detection-solution loop. We leverage and extend existing model transformation techniques with constructs to elicit the space of the alternative solutions and to bind quality properties to them. Our framework is highly customizable, it supports the definition of non-functional requirements and provides an engine to automatically explore the solution space. We evaluate our approach by applying it to two well-known software engineering problems — Object-Relational Mapping and components allocation — and by showing how several solutions that satisfy given performance requirements can be automatically identified.

Keywords: Feedback Provisioning, Model Transformations.

1 Introduction

Verifying that a software system exhibits certain non-functional properties is a primary concern in many application areas. Two very different examples are embedded systems and Web-based applications, where the limited computation resources and the possible large number of users may pose serious engineering problems, respectively. Anticipating the discovery of potential issues concerning the non-functional characteristics of a system, before it is implemented, is crucial for the success of the development process and for cost mitigation.

In this direction, *model-based quality prediction* techniques hold a lot of promise. System models may be used to verify certain relevant properties of the

---

* This research was partially founded by the European Commission IDEAS-ERC Project 227977-SMScom.

system being developed — such as performance, reliability, or schedulability — and prevent defects discoverable only after an implementation is available. Several approaches have been proposed in literature to perform model-based quality prediction [6,3,23,4]. However, despite the advances in this research area, the current status of the available methodologies is far from an ideal situation. Current methodologies perform well in the discovery of potential issues, but lack adequate support when it comes to interpretation of results and identification of solutions. These two tasks are usually left entirely up on the engineers, who have to rely on their individual skills and experience.

Developing high-quality software systems is however complex. The experience to identify solutions to quality-related issues is hard to achieve: it is domain specific, requires a lot of time, and few experts possess it. Methodologies to formalize and share this knowledge so that also non-experienced engineers are able to cope with non-functional concerns should be provided by modern Model Driven Software Development (MDSD) environments. This challenging problem — on which our research concentrates — is known as *feedback provisioning*: how to propose solutions to non-experienced engineers and guide them in the selection of an appropriate one when issues concerning quality attributes are detected. The kind of feedback to provide and the way to provide it depend however on the adopted methodology, and some approaches have been already proposed in literature. Examples are *rule-based* approaches [19,24,7], *meta-heuristic* approaches [14,5,1], and *Design Space Exploration (DSE)* frameworks [21,10,17].

Rule-based methodologies rely on a set of domain specific predefined rules to identify potential quality-related problems and to suggest modifications to the system models. These approaches, however, present several drawbacks: human intervention is required, every approach defines its own language to specify rules, and rules propose solutions only for simple issues and at the level of quality prediction models (i.e., manual intervention is required to translate the suggested changes to the abstraction level of design models). Meta-heuristic approaches leverage instead specific algorithms to explore the alternatives space and to propose solutions. Although the implementations of these approaches are rather efficient, the price to pay for this is high: implementations are usually optimized for the specific domains, quality metrics, and exploration directions for which heuristics where thought. Extensions to new metrics and directions may be thus difficult, may require knowing the details of the implementation, and may lead to inefficiencies. DSE works similarly to meta-heuristic approaches, but the alternatives space is explored by encoding the problem as a Constraint Satisfaction Problem (CSP). Although DSE approaches are extremely efficient, they suffer from the same kind of problems outlined for meta-heuristic techniques.

In [8] we showed how the QVT-Relations [18] language may be extended with constructs to support *quality-driven model transformations* [16,11,9,8] and how this constitutes a valid semi-automatic rule-based solution to the feedback provisioning problem. Quality-driven model transformations extend model transformation languages with constructs to promote non-functional attributes to first class citizens that drive the execution of the transformation. In this paper, we extend our approach also to the QVT-Operational language, which is much faster than its declarative counterpart and is thus suitable for efficient design space exploration. We also describe QVT-Rational, the main contribution of this paper. QVT-Rational is a customizable multi-modeling framework, which provides a model to define quality properties, a language to define non-functional requirements, and provides an engine to automatically explore solutions and provide guidance to engineers. The advantages of QVT-Rational with respect to the existing approaches are several:

- **Language Uniformity:** by using widely-adopted model transformation languages to define solutions to quality issues, domain experts may reuse their knowledge and do not need to master new approaches and specific languages.
- **Quality Metrics Support:** our approach is not limited to specific metrics.
- **Environments and Tool-chains Reuse:** existing modeling environment and quality prediction tools may be plugged in as-is into our framework.
- **Automation:** the availability of an automatic, requirements-driven, exploration engine can bypass the engineer in the feedback loop.
- **High Abstraction Level:** feedback is generated and presented at the abstraction level at which the engineer works. End users are not required to know all the details of the underlying quality prediction methodologies.

The rest of this paper is organized as follows. In Section 2 we describe related work. Section 3 gives an overview of QVT-Rational. Section 4 and Section 5 show how the framework can be programmed and the runtime support, respectively. In Section 6 we show QVT-Rational in action by running two case studies, while Section 7 presents final remarks and future research directions.

2 Related Work

QVT-Rational is a rule-based approach to provide feedback to engineers, based on an extended model transformation language to specify how system variants can be generated and how they are bound to the system quality attributes. It is worth citing some of the related approaches existing in two research areas: the feedback provisioning area — classified according to the taxonomy introduced in Section 1 — and the quality-driven model transformations area.

Rule-based Approaches. Xu in [24] describes a semi-automatic approach for the PUMA framework [23] and proposes the JESS scripting language to specify feedback rules. The main disadvantage of this approach is the abstraction level at which rules work. The PUMA framework leverages the Layered Queuing Network (LQN) performance formalism to analyze some quality attributes of the system being designed. Feedback rules identify issues and propose solutions — only for rather simple performance problems — at this level; it is thus left to the engineer to decide which modifications should be applied at the system abstraction level. Another approach is presented by Parsons in [19], where feedback rules are derived from well-known performance anti-patterns [22]. This approach is however tailored to the JavaEE environment and requires the existence of a complete implementation. Finally, McGregor et al. present in [15] ArchE, a programmable framework based on feedback rules to interactively and iteratively guide engineers in the generation of software architectures compliant with certain non-functional requirements.

Meta-heuristic Approaches. Aleti et al. in [1] present a framework for embedded systems, where architectural models are optimized by using evolutionary algorithms. The system, however, only considers component allocation to propose different solutions, and the supported quality attributes are limited to communication reliability and overhead. Canfora et al. in [5] present a similar work for service-oriented architectures which suffers from the same kind of problems: only service selection and few fixed quality metrics are considered. More recent work is proposed by Martens et al. in [14] where the authors describe PerOpterix, a framework to automatically improve component based systems with genetic algorithms. PerOpterix is one of the most complete solutions in this category. It supports several quality attributes and types of reconfigurations to generate candidate solutions. It is however tailored to the Palladio component model [3] and, as the authors say, both quality metrics and exploration dimensions are fixed.

Generic DSE Approaches. In the context of DSE, it is worth citing some of the existing generic approaches, i.e., approaches not tailored to specific engineering domains. The DESERT framework [17] is a notable example; it supports exploration of design alternatives at an architectural level by organizing the system variants as a tree with boolean constraints to prune the set of viable solutions. More recent work is the GDSE framework [21], a meta-programmable system to define and solve domain-specific DSE problems. GDSE is application domain-agnostic, provides its own language to express boolean, arithmetic, and set constraints, and supports different underlying solvers to generate candidate solutions. Another interesting approach is the Formula framework proposed by Jackson et al. in [10], which uses logic programs to specify models, meta-models, quality attributes, and non-functional requirements in order to explore the solutions space. Despite being fast and efficient in exploring the set of viable solutions, all these approaches are limited in their applicability range: the set of supported quality attributes is in fact limited to those that may be expressed in the logic supported by underlying solvers.

Quality-driven Model Transformations. Merillinna describes in [16] a model transformation based methodology to guide engineers in developing architectures compliant with specified non-functional attributes. The approach requires the availability of two knowledge repositories: *Stylebase*, containing the set of known architectural patterns and quality information, and *Rulebase*, a catalog of model-transformations to evolve system architectures. This approach, however, requires complete system designs and is limited only to horizontal transformations, i.e., transformation happening at the same abstraction level. Kurtev in [11] addresses adaptability of model transformation and proposes a general framework to represent transformations with alternatives and to use quality attributes to decide among alternatives. This, however, is only a proposal; no runtime support is provided to automate the exploration process and no constructs are provided to specify how quality attributes may be computed. More recent work is also presented by Insfrán et al. in [9], where authors propose a multi-modeling approach to select among viable alternatives (represented by different transformation rules) according to quality attributes. After the engineer has selected the desired alternatives, the final transformation is derived and system models can be generated. Although in principle this approach is similar to QVT-Rational, it presents several limitations. Human intervention is required in the process, alternatives affect the solution globally (i.e., the same alternative will be selected across the whole system model), alternatives are selected a priori (i.e., before the quality attributes of the system are concretely evaluated), and it is not clear how existing model-based quality prediction techniques can be plugged in.

3 Overview of QVT-Rational

Figure 1 gives an overview of our multi-modeling approach for feedback provisioning. QVT-Rational makes heavy use of MDSD techniques to provide its functionalities. The framework provides the meta-models to define quality metrics and requirements, textual editors to create instances of these models, and leverages High-Order Transformations (HOTs) to generate system variants.

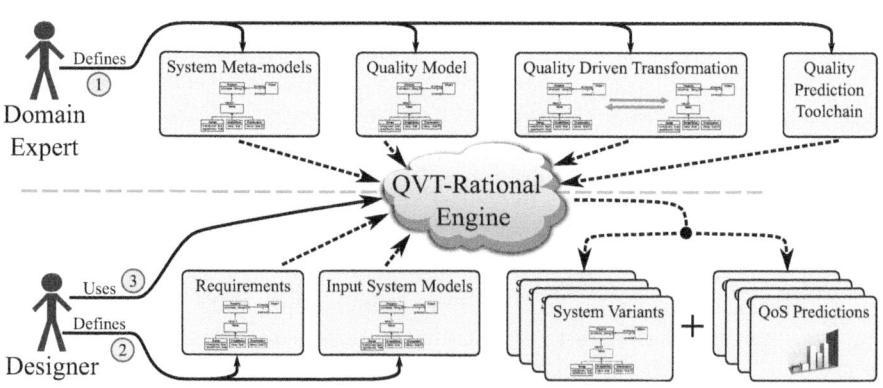

Fig. 1. Overview of the QVT-Rational framework

As the two parts of Figure 1 suggest, QVT-Rational requires the participation of two very different actors: the *domain expert* and the *designer*. The core idea is to partially shift the responsibility of finding solutions from the less-experienced designer to the more-experienced domain expert. The domain expert sets up the MDSD environment for the designer by *programming* the framework. This step is mandatory since every engineering domain has its own best practices, design meta-models, and strategies to deal with quality-related issues. The domain expert specifies the meta-models necessary to design a particular class of software systems, the quality metrics of interest, and packages the quality prediction tools necessary to assess the system non-functional attributes. The domain expert is also in charge of sharing his/her knowledge about the engineering domain (i.e., knowledge about how quality-related issues may be solved) by specifying how design feedback can be generated. This information, which is crucial for our framework, can be elicited through a quality-driven model transformation as we will explain later in Section 4.1.

Once the modeling environment is ready and the framework is *programmed*, QVT-Rational is ready to provide guidance. If system models do not exhibit a satisfactory level of quality, designers can formalize the desired values for the non-functional attributes via our requirements language (presented in Section 5.1), and can ask our framework to generate compliant system variants. It is also worth noticing here that the designer is not required to be aware of all the several methods available to cope with quality-related issues, which only domain experts have. As shown in Figure 1, the designer never sees the underlying quality models used by prediction tools. He/she interacts with the framework, gets feedback, and obtains solutions only at the same abstraction level of the system models.

3.1 A Clarifying Example

In order to better understand how QVT-Rational works, in the following we contextualize the previous description with a well-known engineering problem for embedded systems: component allocation. We use this problem throughout the rest of this paper. As the name suggests, component allocation deals with the allocation of a set of components over a set of limited hardware resources. Different possible allocations are usually viable but they have different non-functional properties. For example, allocation affects schedulability of component operations, system reliability, performance, and manufacturing cost.

QVT-Rational can help solving this kind of problem, by suggesting to designers allocations that show satisfactory quality attributes. In order to do so, the domain engineer first has to populate the framework with domain-specific entities, by specifying the components, the hardware, and the allocation meta-models, by packaging or creating the analysis tools to predict the quality metrics of interest, and by writing a quality-driven model transformation that takes components and hardware models as input, and generates all the possible allocation models as output. Once the components that should be deployed and the available hardware resources have been modeled, the designer can specify the required quality — for example reliability must be greater than 0.999 — and can ask QVT-Rational to provide the viable solutions. Alternatively, the designer may manually generate an initial allocation model and, if quality attributes are not satisfactory, may ask to QVT-Rational to evolve existing models and to find compliant solutions.

4 Programming the Framework

In this section we provide more details about the steps outlined before in the context of the reference component allocation case study.

4.1 Specifying Feedback Rules

Our framework provides feedback in the form of complete alternative design solutions and, as we anticipated in Section 3, the information to identify solutions is embedded into a quality-driven model transformation. The core idea that lies behind our approach is to represent solutions as different rules in a transformation; QVT-Rational will then take care of executing the transformation, selecting the right rules, generating the viable designs, and identifying the satisfactory ones.

To elicit the space of viable system variants and bind them to quality attributes (i.e., to specify the feedback rules), we extend the QVT-Operational [18] transformation language with specific annotations as we proposed in [8] for its declarative counterpart. The annotation language we propose is centered on the concepts of *variability, variation point*, and *variant* which have already been defined in the literature about Software Product Lines (SPLs) [20]. In the context of feedback provisioning, a variability defines the strategy to solve a quality-related issue, a variation point identifies the model entities involved in the solution, while variants specify the different solutions. When these concepts are contextualized to quality-driven model transformations and, in the specific case, to QVT-Operational based quality-driven model transformations, a variant translates to a mapping definition — the unit which specifies in a QVT-O transformation how model entities relate to each other — while a variation point translates to a mapping definition specifying its variants through a *disjunct* clause.

The following example may serve the purpose of clarifying these abstract definitions. Component allocation is a rather simple problem from a conceptual point of view: deployment is the only aspect that can vary. If we denote with C the set of components and with H the set of hardware resources, to generate all the possible deployments we could proceed by iterating over the tuple set $T = C \times H$ and by finding all the possible subsets of T that map every component $c \in C$ on exactly one resource. Specifying this kind of problem in QVT-Rational is rather straightforward and simple. Listing 1.1 shows a fragment[1] of the QVT-Operational quality-driven transformation that represents the allocation problem within our framework. The mapping on lines *10-11* defines the variation point which declares that, given a component and a hardware resource (i.e., a tuple $t \in T$), deployment may take place or not. The variant *allocate* defined by the mapping on line 17 implements the former case, the variant defined on line 20 defines instead the latter. In order to embed feedback-related information, variation points and variants must be tagged with special marker annotations. Annotations enable the specification of bindings to quality

---

[1] Irrelevant details and mapping bodies have been omitted for the sake of clarity.

attributes — which we describe later in Section 4.2 —, the choice of the tool to be used to predict their values, and enable the definition of constraints between variants. We support arbitrarily complex *requires* and *excludes* constraints: OCL queries accessing the model entities involved in a variation point may be used for their definition. An example is the *clustering* constraint defined on line 15: if a component is allocated onto a hardware resource, then every component belonging to the module to which the component belongs must be deployed onto the same hardware resource.

Listing 1.1. The Allocation Variability

```
@varpoint {
  name := ComponentAllocation ,
  analyzer := modeling.allocation.Analyzer () ,
  impact := {
    Schedulability($"comp") ,
    ComponentReliability($"comp") ,
    OperationReliability($"comp", $"comp.operations") ,
    Cost() }
}
mapping allocateOn_VP(in comp:Component, in host:Resource)
disjuncts allocate, dontAllocate;

@variant {
  name := Allocate ,
  requires := Allocate($"comp.module.components", $"host")
}
mapping allocate(in comp:Component, in host:Resource) { ... }

@variant { name := DontAllocate }
mapping dontAllocate(in comp:Component, in host:Resource) { }
```

4.2 Binding to Quality

In order to drive feedback provisioning, transformation rules must be bound to quality attributes. The domain expert performs this task by *i)* defining the set of quality metrics of interest and *ii)* declaring the impact the variation points have on them. QVT-Rational adopts the three-layered solution described in [8] and provides a specific Domain Specific Language (DSL) to accomplish the first sub-task. Quality metrics are usually relative to particular system artifacts. For example, reliability can be measured with respect to a component or with respect to a specific operation. This feature is supported by our DSL through the concept of *context*. Listing 1.2 shows the definition of two quality metrics used in the component allocation example. Lines 1-3 define the *ComponentReliability* metric which is computed with respect to a single component — the name enclosed between the two brackets refers to the meta-class of the context entity — while lines 4-7 define the *OperationReliability* metric which is computed with respect to a component and to an operation.

Listing 1.2. The Definition of Quality Metrics

```
1  template ComponentReliability {
2    context comp[Component];
3  }
4  template OperationReliability {
5    context comp[Component];
6    context op[Operation];
7  }
```

Once quality metrics have been defined, they can be referenced in requirements — as we will see later in Section 5.1 — and in the transformation annotations through the *impact* list. The impact list serves the purposes of identifying which alternatives provide a solution for an issue impacting a specific quality metric, and defining how concrete values for contexts can be retrieved. As we did for constraints, arbitrary complex OCL queries accessing the model entities involved in a variation point may be used for this purpose. For example, the impact defined on line 6 of Listing 1.1 declares that the *ComponentAllocation* variation point has an impact on the reliability of the component being allocated; while line 7 defines an impact on the *OperationReliability* for each operation defined for the component being allocated.

5 Providing Feedback

In this section we describe the steps a designer has to perform to use QVT-Rational to concretely obtain feedback while developing a software system. We concentrate on two of the new features of our framework: the language to express requirements and the automatic exploration engine.

5.1 Specifying Requirements

An important feature missing in our initial proposal [8] was the ability to automatically explore the space of the viable solutions. Only an interactive execution mode was supported; interpretation of quality predictions and decisions about which of the variants proposed by our framework should be selected were left to the designer. To overcome this limitation and bypass human involvement in the process, QVT-Rational provides a meta-model to express requirements about the quality of system designs, a textual notation and textual editors to ease its use, and an evaluation engine to check validity of solutions.

Listing 1.3 shows an excerpt of the requirements we specified for the reference allocation example and outlines the shape of the language. Requirements are specified as boolean expressions over the quality metrics previously defined by the domain expert: standard boolean and arithmetic comparison operators are supported, expressions over quality attributes can be defined with the *dollar* notation, and composition is supported by referencing other requirements via the *at* notation. The *isReliable* requirement on lines 1-4 shows all these features: it constrains the predicted average reliability of every operation to be greater than 0.85, the predicted minimum reliability of every component to be in the (0.8, 1] interval, and references the *isFFTReliable* requirement. As we mentioned in Section 4.2 contexts may be defined for quality metrics. This is reflected in the requirements language and references to quality metrics can be bound either via the *underscore* operator — i.e., a catch all operator capturing all the modeling entities that conform with the context meta-class — or via direct referencing. The former case is shown on lines 2 and 3, while direct referencing is used on line 6 for the *isFFTReliable* requirement which constrains the reliability of the *ComputeFFT* operation of the *NumericComp* component. To handle tradeoffs between properties, we also distinguish between hard and soft requirements: hard requirements are required to hold to consider a design solution valid, soft requirements are not and provide a way to express preferences between valid solutions. The *isCheap* requirement on line 8 is an example of a soft requirement: it tells to QVT-Rational to prefer solutions with a limited manufacturing cost.

Listing 1.3. The Definition of Quality Metrics.

```
1  req isReliable {
2    $OperationReliability (_,_)[avg] >= 0.85 and
3    $ComponentReliability (_)[min] in (0.8,1] and @isFFTReliable
4  }
5  req isFFTReliable {
6    $OperationReliability (NumericComp,ComputeFFT)[min] >= 0.9
7  }
8  soft req isCheap { $Cost <= 10 }
```

5.2 Design Space Exploration

Obtaining feedback requires the ability to execute the model transformations that specify feedback rules. In [8] we described how quality-driven transformations based on QVT-Relations could be executed and used to generate feedback; QVT-Rational extends the execution model also to its operational counterpart. From an abstract point of view, a quality-driven model transformation is a non-injective High-Order Transformation, which produces all the injective transformations to generate viable outputs. The execution model we propose follows exactly this schema: by using novel techniques — such as HOTs and black-box mappings — the occurrence of variation points is intercepted during execution, the space of the possible transformations is explored, the viable outputs are generated, evaluated, checked, and proposed as alternative designs to the engineer. To clarify these concepts, let us consider the allocation example. Figure 2 outlines the process by representing the space of the viable transformations (i.e., variants) as a tree. Each node represents an occurrence of the variation point we defined in Listing 1.1. For example, node *A-H1* corresponds to deciding about the allocation of component *A* on the resource *H1*. Executing a quality-driven transformation amounts to traversing this tree, until some or all the viable solutions — corresponding to paths from the root to the leaves of the tree — are identified, evaluated, and possibly proposed as feedback.

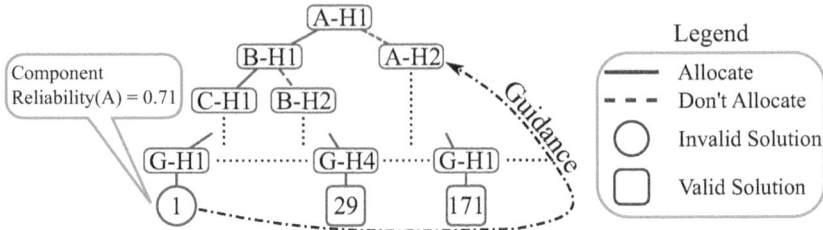

Fig. 2. The execution process

To increase the automation level, our framework provides an automatic exploration mode in addition to interactive execution. Interactive execution requires manual intervention whenever a variation point is intercepted and until a final solution is identified, i.e., for every node encountered along the path to reach a leaf of the tree. When models are large and several strategies are available to solve quality-related issues, the exploration tree may become huge and manual intervention is not feasible anymore. Automatic exploration of the design space overcomes these two problems by removing the engineer from the execution process and by implementing an heuristic to guide the exploration and to reduce the time to generate feedback. In detail, the guidance algorithm works as shown in Figure 2. Whenever an invalid solution is found — a solution for which quality attributes are not satisfactory — the algorithm selects the failed requirements, identifies the *interesting decisions* — the decisions taken to reach the invalid solution which had an impact on the failed requirements — and schedules the visiting of the exploration branches corresponding to the *interesting decisions* with higher priority. This is akin to preferring the exploration branches which may solve immediately a quality issue, by taking different strategies only for decisions which impact quality issues and by leaving unmodified everything else.

To clarify the approach, let us consider again the allocation example and Figure 2. Solution 1 is not valid: the estimated reliability of component A is less than 0.85, only the decision taken at node *A-H1* has an impact on this quality attribute, hence changing only the allocation of such component may suffice to find a valid solution. The guidance algorithm marks thus node *A-H1* as interesting and schedules exploration of branch *A-H2* with higher priority.

6 Evaluation

This section describes two case studies we use to demonstrate QVT-Rational in action. The goals here are to show that we can handle non-trivial modeling situations, that we can do more than existing approaches, and that the framework is able to produce feedback in an acceptable amount of time. All the experiments have been executed on a high-end workstation, equipped with a four core Intel i7 processor and 6 GB of memory. For space reasons, we provide a brief description of the case studies and of their results; their full specification is available on the QVT-Rational website (http://qvtr2.googlecode.com) for reproducibility.

6.1 The Object-Relational Mapping Case Study

Object-Relational Mapping (ORM) deals with the mismatch between the entity models used at the application abstraction level and the representation used by storage technologies. This case study is interesting for several reasons: it is a well-understood engineering problem, real-world examples are publicly available [2,12], other model transformations publications adopt it [18,9], and it fits well our feedback and quality-prediction needs. Indeed, we used it (and detailed it) also in [8] to show how interactive execution works.

Framework Programming by the Domain Expert. Different database schemas with different quality may represent the same entity model. For example, how generalizations are flattened impacts the space required to store data and the time required to execute queries. In this example, we consider two quality metrics: response time of queries and wasted space (i.e., storage space allocated but not used to store data). The quality-driven model transformation that takes a domain model and produces viable database schemas implements three strategies to provide feedback, which concern flattening of generalizations, generation of values for primary keys, and use of data partitioning. Ad-hoc analyzers have been developed to predict quality and, for the response time, we provided two implementations: one based on queuing network simulation and one based on Mean Value Analysis (MVA) [13].

Supporting the Designer. The input model we used to feed our framework defines the domain entities of a real *ecommerce* application and has been extracted from [12]. The model consists of 15 classes connected by 9 associations, presents 3 generalizations, and considers 4 query profiles accessing the various entities with different demands. We asked QVT-Rational to generate the first 5 database schemas exhibiting a maximum 0.2 wasted space factor and a response time for each query not exceeding the 30ms threshold. Table 1 shows some statistics about the performance of QVT-Rational. The T_i columns show the time required to produce the first i alternatives. Although the number of valid solutions is high, i.e., 1944 solutions out of 5836 viable alternatives, QVT-Rational is able to find variants and produce feedback in a reasonable amount of time. Results are even better when the MVA solver is used instead of the queuing network simulator. The time required to analyze the quality of found solutions drops to the 17% of the total execution time, and QVT-Rational produces feedback in 18 s.

Table 1. ORM case study performance statistics

Experiment	Solver	Solutions(Valid)	T_1 [s]	T_5 [s]	Analysis Time
1	Simulator	5836(1944)	112.46	486.86	76%
2	MVA		7.21	18.53	17%

6.2 The Component Allocation Case Study

The second case study concerns component allocation. As we mentioned throughout the paper, component allocation deals with the allocation of a set of

Table 2. Allocation case study performance statistics

Experiment	Modules	Components	Resources	T_1 [s]	T_5 [s]	Analysis Time
1	2	5	5	8.17	34.79	6%
2	2	5	5	0.75	5.68	4.25%
3	3	10	10	2.36	40.29	4.39%
4	5	15	5	159.44	251.55	9.87%

components over a set of limited hardware resources. This example has been extracted from [10], where authors use the Formula framework and compare their results with respect to other approaches (Alloy and SModels). In order to show that we are not limited only to certain quality metrics and that we can reuse existing quality prediction tool-chains — some of the advantages of QVT-Rational — the case study has been extended to support also reliability by plugging in the Recursive Markov Chain (RMC) analyzer available in the KlaperSuite [6].

Framework Programming by the Domain Expert. We programmed QVT-Rational for this case study as we described before throughout the paper. The transformation defining feedback rules specifies only one strategy to generate system variants, i.e., the allocation variability outlined in Listing 1.1. In addition to the metrics defined in Listing 1.2, we considered also schedulability of operations and manufacturing cost. Schedulability depends on three factors specified in the usage profile of the system — worst case execution time (*wcet*) of each operation, frequency, and period with which components invoke operations — and is estimated by performing simple arithmetic. Cost is estimated by counting the resources used to deploy components, while reliability is computed by the RMC analyzer developed for the KlaperSuite [6] framework.

Supporting the Designer. We asked QVT-Rational to generate the first 5 schedulable deployments, exhibiting a limited cost and all reliability predictions greater than 0.85. We have run 4 experiments with different input models: experiment 1 has been manually developed, while remaining experiments have been generated randomly by specifying number of components, modules, and resources. Table 2 shows some statistics about the performance of QVT-Rational. QVT-Rational is rather fast for small and medium-sized case studies (i.e., experiments 1-3), while for the largest case study (experiment 4) the time to generate feedback increases but still remains reasonable. This is even more encouraging if we consider that component allocation is an NP-Hard problem and if we compare with the results described in [10]. Formula is much faster in solving the same problem (given the logic program encoding) but, similarly to our results, shows exponential growth for little larger models. Indeed, it must be noted that the example has been extended with reliability, which is not possible in logic-based frameworks without the extra-effort to encode analysis tools as logic programs.

6.3 Discussion

These experiments show that QVT-Rational is able to handle also non-trivial modeling situations and that it may scale also to large systems. We have also shown that tools reuse is concretely feasible, that we are not limited to specific quality metrics, and that encoding feedback rules does not require mastering specific approaches or new languages. All this features, however, have a cost:

- **Non-Guaranteed Optimality.** Although possible, exploring the whole space of solutions may not be feasible when models are large. If the designer asks for the first i solutions, there is no guarantee that the found solutions are the best in terms of exhibited quality. This problem is however not specific to QVT-Rational, also other methodologies suffer from it.
- **Efficiency.** When analysis tools require a lot of time to be executed, asking for feedback can be a time-consuming operation. This makes not practical an online usage of our system — i.e., while the designer is developing — in such situations. However, QVT-Rational may still be used by running it in parallel with the designer or during moon-light hours.
- **Impact of the Domain Expert.** The quality of the feedback we provide depends much on the quality of the feedback rules specified by the domain expert. This is especially true for the binding between variabilities and quality metrics (i.e., the impact list), on which we rely, for example, to handle interdependent decisions. Identifying in a precise manner such information may be hard also for the most experienced domain experts, and this negatively impacts the efficiency of our approach.

7 Conclusions and Future Work

In this paper we presented QVT-Rational, our proposal to tackle feedback provisioning. QVT-Rational leverages QVT-based quality-driven model transformation to specify how feedback and system variants can be generated, and supports the designer with models and languages to specify quality attributes and requirements. We described the new automatic exploration engine which bypasses the engineer, and we showed that our approach scales also to non-trivial modeling situations by running two case studies. Concerning future work, we are currently working on improving the guidance heuristic, especially for boolean quality metrics, and on using alternative exploration methodologies, such as exploration based on genetic algorithms.

References

1. Aleti, A., Bjornander, S., Grunske, L., Meedeniya, I.: Archeopterix: An extendable tool for architecture optimization of aadl models. In: MOMPES. IEEE, Los Alamitos (2009)
2. Alur, D., Crupi, J., Malks, D.: Core J2EE patterns: best practices and design strategies. Sun Microsystems Press (2003)
3. Becker, S., Koziolek, H., Reussner, R.: Model-based performance prediction with the palladio component model. In: WOSP. ACM, New York (2007)
4. Bures, T., Carlson, J., Crnkovic, J., Sentilles, S., Vulgarakis, A.: Procom - the progress component model reference manual, version 1.0. Tech. Rep. MHD-MRTC-230/2008-1-SE, Malardalen University (June 2008)

5. Canfora, G., Penta, M.D., Esposito, R., Villani, M.L.: An approach for qos-aware service composition based on genetic algorithms. In: GECCO. ACM, New York (2005)
6. Ciancone, A., Filieri, A., Drago, M.L., Mirandola, R., Grassi, V.: KlaperSuite: An integrated model-driven environment for reliability and performance analysis of component-based systems. In: Bishop, J., Vallecillo, A. (eds.) TOOLS 2011. LNCS, vol. 6705, pp. 99–114. Springer, Heidelberg (2011)
7. Cortellessa, V., Martens, A., Reussner, R., Trubiani, C.: A process to effectively identify "Guilty" performance antipatterns. In: Rosenblum, D.S., Taentzer, G. (eds.) FASE 2010. LNCS, vol. 6013, pp. 368–382. Springer, Heidelberg (2010)
8. Drago, M.L., Ghezzi, C., Mirandola, R.: A quality driven extension to the qvt-relations transformation language. In: CSRD. Springer, Heidelberg (2011) (submitted to), http://home.dei.polimi.it/drago/qvtrr.pdf
9. Insfrán, E., Gonzalez-Huerta, J., Abrahão, S.: Design guidelines for the development of quality-driven model transformations. In: Petriu, D.C., Rouquette, N., Haugen, Ø. (eds.) MODELS 2010. LNCS, vol. 6395, pp. 288–302. Springer, Heidelberg (2010)
10. Jackson, E.K., Kang, E., Dahlweid, M., Seifert, D., Santen, T.: Components, platforms and possibilities: Towards generic automation for mda. In: EMSOFT. ACM, New York (2010)
11. Kurtev, I.: Adaptability of Model Transformations. Ph.D. thesis, Unversity of Twente, Twente, Netherlands (2005)
12. Lau, S.Q., Czarnecki, K.: Domain Analysis of E-Commerce Systems Using Feature-Based Model Templates. Master's thesis, University of Waterloo, Canada (2006)
13. Lazowska, E.D., Zahorjan, J., Graham, G.S., Sevcik, K.C.: Quantitative System Performance: Computer System Analysis Using Queueing Network Models. Prentice Hall, Englewood Cliffs (1984)
14. Martens, A., Koziolek, H., Becker, S., Reussner, R.: Automatically improve software architecture models for performance, reliability, and cost using evolutionary algorithms. In: WOSP/SIPEW (2010)
15. McGregor, J.D., Bachmann, F., Bass, L., Bianco, P., Klein, M.: Using arche in the classroom: One experience. Tech. Rep. SEI-2007-TN-001, CMU (2007)
16. Merilinna, J.: A Tool for Quality-Driven Architecture Model Transformation. Ph.D. thesis, VVT Technical Research Centre of Finland, Vuoriemihentie, Finland (2005)
17. Neema, S., Sztipanovits, J., Karsai, G., Butts, K.: Constraint-based design-space exploration and model synthesis. In: Alur, R., Lee, I. (eds.) EMSOFT 2003. LNCS, vol. 2855, pp. 290–305. Springer, Heidelberg (2003)
18. Object Management Group (OMG): Mof qvt specification 1.0 (April 2008), http://www.omg.org/spec/QVT/1.0
19. Parsons, T.: A framework for detecting performance design and deployment antipatterns in component based enterprise systems. In: DSM. ACM, New York (2005)
20. Pohl, K., Böckle, G., van der Linden, F.J.: Software Product Line Engineering: Foundations, Principles and Techniques. Springer, Heidelberg (2005)
21. Saxena, T., Karsai, G.: MDE-based approach for generalizing design space exploration. In: Petriu, D.C., Rouquette, N., Haugen, Ø. (eds.) MODELS 2010. LNCS, vol. 6394, pp. 46–60. Springer, Heidelberg (2010)
22. Smith, C.U., Williams, L.G.: Performance solutions: a practical guide to creating responsive, scalable software. Addison Wesley, Reading (2002)
23. Woodside, M., Petriu, D.C., Petriu, D.B., Shen, H., Israr, T., Merseguer, J.: Performance by unified model analysis (puma). In: WOSP. ACM, New York (2005)
24. Xu, J.: Rule-based automatic software performance diagnosis and improvement. In: WOSP. ACM, New York (2008)

Automated Model-to-Metamodel Transformations Based on the Concepts of Deep Instantiation

Gerd Kainz[1], Christian Buckl[1], and Alois Knoll[2]

[1] fortiss, Cyber-Physical Systems
Guerickestr. 25, 80805 Munich, Germany
{kainz,buckl}@fortiss.org
[2] Faculty of Informatics, Technische Universität München
Boltzmannstr. 3, 85748 Garching, Germany
knoll@in.tum.de

Abstract. Numerous systems, especially component-based systems, are based on a multi-phase development process where an ontological hierarchy is established. Solutions based on modeling / metamodeling can be used for such systems, but all of them are afflicted with different drawbacks. The main problem is that elements representing both CLAsses and oBJECTs (clabjects), which are needed to specify an ontological hierarchy, are not supported by standard metamodeling frameworks. This paper presents the combination of two approaches, namely deep instantiation and model-to-metamodel transformations. The resulting approach combines the clean and compact specification of deep instantiation with the easy applicability of model-to-metamodel transformations in an automated way. Along with this a set of generic operators to specify these transformations is identified.

Keywords: Model-to-Metamodel (M2MM), Model-to-Model (M2M), Model Transformation, Deep Instantiation, Transformation Operator, Clabject, Model-Driven Software Development (MDSD).

1 Introduction

Nowadays model-driven software development (MDSD) is widely used for the development of applications. Relevant tools are in general based on the modeling hierarchy as defined by the Object Management Group (OMG)[1]. The modeling hierarchy is shown in figure 1. It consists of four layers: M3 represents the meta-metamodel layer and describes the concepts used to define application specific metamodels. M3 contains very basic concepts such as classes and attributes. Hence, M3 is generic enough to describe itself and to terminate the modeling hierarchy. M2 defines application specific metamodels defining the application concepts and their related data. Based on the metamodels of M2, the application

---

[1] OMG: http://www.omg.org/

developer can define models in M1, which conform to metamodels of M2 and are used to specify the application. M0 can be interpreted as the real world, which is represented by the models of M1.

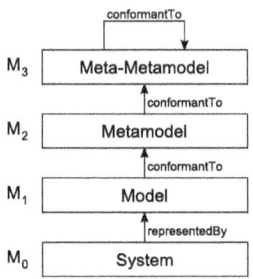

Fig. 1. Model Hierarchy [1] as Specified by OMG

The model hierarchy is well suited if an application can be described by using only the two modeling levels M2 and M1. However, for many systems, this assumption is not true. Examples are the UML specification [2] and the description of hardware components [3]. Here, some system elements have a dual role: in their first role they represent instances of a metamodel element; in their second role they constitute metamodel elements for other system objects. Elements with this dual role have been named clabjects (CLAsses and oBJECTs) by Atkinson [4].

Clabjects have been investigated intensively under various circumstances. The research resulted in many different solutions. Most of them try to find an adequate mapping of the problem to the existing modeling hierarchy. A totally different approach has been proposed by Atkinson and Kühne. In [2] they suggested to change the current instantiation model from shallow instantiation to deep instantiation. Deep instantiation allows that elements of a modeling level have an object and a class facet at the same time. Such a realization requires a fundamental change of the underlying modeling theory, leading to a clean way of describing this and other problems. Another approach based on model-to-metamodel (M2MM) transformations was presented in our previous work [3]. M2MM transformations are based on an iterative development process, where models of one phase (object facet) are transformed into metamodels (class facet) describing the models of the next phase. In our previous work, these M2MM transformations had to be implemented manually without any further support. The implementation complexity and therefore the effort increases drastically with each additional M2MM transformation phase.

This paper presents a combination of deep instantiation and M2MM transformations. The resulting approach combines the clean and compact description of deep instantiation with the easy applicability of M2MM transformations without having to change the underlying metamodeling framework. The automation of the M2MM transformations approach helps in applying this approach to similar problems and reduces the time and effort for implementation. In addition, a set of generic M2MM transformation operators has been identified.

The remainder is structured as follows: Section 2 gives an overview of the problem. Related work is discussed in section 3. Section 4 contains a small motivating example. A detailed description of the suggested approach and the set of generic operators is the content of section 5. Details about the implementation and an evaluated based on a real-world use case is given in section 6. The content of the paper is summarized in section 7.

2 Problem Statement

Modeling languages are described in two orthogonal dimensions: a linguistic and an ontological dimension. The linguistic dimension specifies how a language is constructed and is typically represented by the different modeling levels (metaclass ← class ← object). The ontological dimension represents elements and their instance-of-relationship of a certain domain (e.g. $Component \leftarrow C : Component \leftarrow CI : C$), the so-called ontological hierarchy [5]. Since state-of-the-art modeling frameworks are based on the one-dimensional modeling hierarchy, these two dimensions cannot be represented adequately. This problem becomes obvious as soon as the ontological hierarchy spans more than two levels or can be changed / extended by the user [2]. Examples, where this problem arises, are component based systems where the user is able to define components and store them in a generic library. By doing so the user specifies a new component type which can be instantiated / copied later for use. Ptolemy II [6] and MATLAB/Simulink[2] include for example a library mechanism as described. Since they have no direct support for an ontological hierarchy integrated into their underlying programming model, it requires an enormous effort to emulate ontological support on top of their underlying programming model. Many other examples exist. A simple instance of that kind of problem is presented in figure 2.

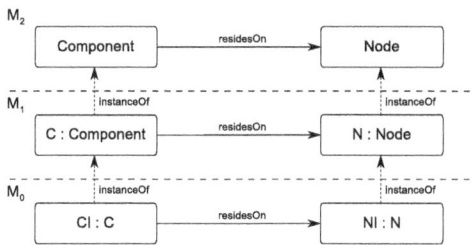

Fig. 2. Ontological Hierarchy Example Based on Components and Nodes [2]

The fundamental problem of expressing ontological hierarchies with current modeling systems is based on the duality of model elements, which is not supported by most metamodeling frameworks. Duality means that model elements

---

[2] MATLAB/Simulink: http://www.mathworks.com/

represent objects and classes at the same time. For example: in figure 2 C is an object of type *Component*, furthermore it represents the type of *CI*. This duality of model elements has been named clabject by Atkinson.

As model elements can represent types of other model elements, they construct their own ontological hierarchy introducing additional levels to the model hierarchy. Since these additional levels are not supported by standard metamodeling frameworks, the ontological hierarchy has to be folded into one level of the linguistic hierarchy. This leads to the problems of ambiguous classification and replication of concepts [2].

- Ambiguous classification: Model elements can be seen as both instances of their linguistic and ontological type, e.g. C has the linguistic type *Class* and the ontological type *Component*.
- Replication of concepts: As it is not possible to propagate attributes and associations over instantiation relations of the ontological hierarchy, the workaround is to replicate concepts, e.g. define class *Component* to represent C, *ComponentInstance* to represent *CI* and for both of them a separate *residesOn* association.

The goal of this paper is to propose an approach for a clean and compact description, which can easily be applied using state-of-the-art metamodeling frameworks. We start with a survey of existing solutions for the above mentioned problems and discuss of their strengths and weaknesses.

3 Related Work

The most promising approach in the context of the problem statement is deep instantiation introduced by Atkinson and Kühne [2, 7–9]. As the name says, the approach is based on a deep instead of a shallow instantiation mechanism, which is used in classical metamodeling frameworks. This enables the specification of model elements (classes, attributes, associations ...), which cannot only affect the direct underlying model level, but also other model levels underneath. To control the behavior of the deep instantiation mechanism, the concepts of *level* and *potency* are added to every model element. *Level* defines for each element at which model level in the hierarchy it resides. *Potency* on the other hand determines the number of times a model element can be instantiated. These extensions allow a compact specification of multi-level metamodeling. A first implementation of the deep instantiation mechanism called DEEPJAVA[3] is available in the context of JAVA programming [7]. One major drawback of DEEPJAVA is the missing support by integrated development environments (IDEs) supporting it. Furthermore, the definition of new ontological types requires that JAVA code has to be written by the developer. Therefore, this approach is only suited for software developers and cannot be directly applied by application users themselves. An advantage is that the whole ontological hierarchy is available and can be accessed at any time in the runtime system.

---

[3] DEEPJAVA: http://homepages.mcs.vuw.ac.nz/~tk/dj/

To avoid the problem of missing IDE and metamodeling framework support, we previously suggested an approach based on M2MM transformations [3]. M2MM transformations are based on multi-phase metamodeling, where models of one phase are transformed into the metamodels of the next phase. This allows users to define new types, e.g. *ControlMotor : Component*, in a model. The subsequent M2MM transformation takes care that the corresponding type is created in the metamodel of the next phase. Each phase constitutes a modeling tool on its own. This means that by generating the metamodel of the next phase also the modeling tool of the next phase is altered to reflect the change of the underlying metamodel. As M2MM transformations are used to regenerate parts of the metamodels of the system based on the input data of the previous model, they do not need additional levels in the metamodeling hierarchy. This is both a strength and a weakness: on the one hand the metamodel only contains the information required in the specific phase, but on the other hand it is hard to determine the relationship between classes / objects at the different levels. Another drawback is the manual specification of M2MM transformations. The transformations must be encoded by the developer, who has to take care that all needed data is transformed according to the requirements of the succeeding phases. This can also imply that data has to be copied to guarantee that it is available in the following phases. If more than one M2MM transformations are executed in a row, it is very hard for the developers to implement those. With each additional M2MM transformation step, it gets harder to deal with the arising complexity of the transformations. The reason for the increasing complexity originates from the additional variability introduced with each new M2MM transformation. While the first M2MM transformation is based completely on a static metamodel, the dynamic part of the subsequent metamodels increases. The increasing complexity and the time consuming implementation of M2MM transformations make this approach very hard to apply. Furthermore, the transformation descriptions are encoded using a program language. This makes it hard to identify how the input model is transformed into the succeeding metamodel.

The power types concept of Odell [10, 11] constitutes another solution to integrate ontological hierarchies into the modeling hierarchy. A power type is defined to be a type whose instances are subtypes of another type. The relation between the power type and its instances is defined by a normal association. When working with power types this fact has to be considered. Furthermore, power types merely describe how to model an ontological hierarchy but offer no additional support for their handling.

Like power types, the prototypical concept pattern presented by Atkinson and Kühne [8] tries to solve the problem of ontological hierarchies within the modeling hierarchy by combining inheritance and instantiation. Compared to power types the prototypical concept pattern uses no normal association to connect the power type with the other type. Instead of the association, the instantiation mechanism of the modeling hierarchy is used. By doing so the number of levels in the modeling hierarchy is extended, which results in the already mentioned problems regarding implementation using current metamodeling frameworks. Moreover the prototypical concept pattern offers no support for the handling of the introduced ontological hierarchy. Hence, it possesses no advantage compared to the deep instantiation approach and can be neglected.

Bragança and Machado [12] describe a similar approach to M2MM transformations supporting multi-phase modeling. In their work they use the term model promotion instead of M2MM transformation. Compared to the M2MM transformations approach where flexibility is provided in each transformation step, they can only specialize their initial metamodel by annotating models with information utilized for M2MM transformations. This restricts the power of their M2MM transformations to the predefined set of transformations offered through annotations. It also limits the usable domain concepts to the concepts introduced in their first metamodel and requires the specification of metamodel information in the model. An advantage is that the number of possible M2MM transformations is unbounded.

4 Motivating Example

As outlined in the previous section each of the presented solutions has different strengths and weaknesses. Therefore, we propose an approach combining the clean and compact description of deep instantiation with the easy applicability of M2MM transformations.

In this section we give a small motivating example based on figure 2. This shall help to better understand the automated M2MM transformations approach. The example is concerned with the definition of components residing on nodes containing various devices. Figure 3 shows the metamodel of the example at $M2^4$. The superscript of the model elements presents the value of potency. The level is depicted at the model elements as subscript. The metamodel defines three classes *Component*, *Node* and *Device* and two associations between them. Additionally three instantiation operators (notes attached to classes) and one split field operator (note attached to association) are specified.

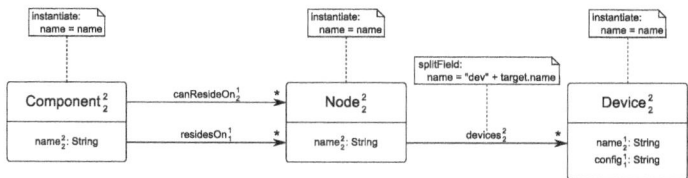

Fig. 3. Model Level 2 of Components-Nodes Example

Based on the metamodel shown in figure 3 the user is able to define the model presented on the upper part of figure 4. Applying an automated M2MM

---

[4] When we talk about metamodel, we mean the class facet of a clabject. We refer to the object facet by talking about the model.

transformation to the model results in the metamodel that is shown at the bottom of figure 4. As is visible in the metamodel the *ReadSensor*, *PC*, *CPU* and *Sensor* objects are transformed into classes. Furthermore, the *devices* association has been refined into a *devCPU* and *devSensor* association for the *PC* class.

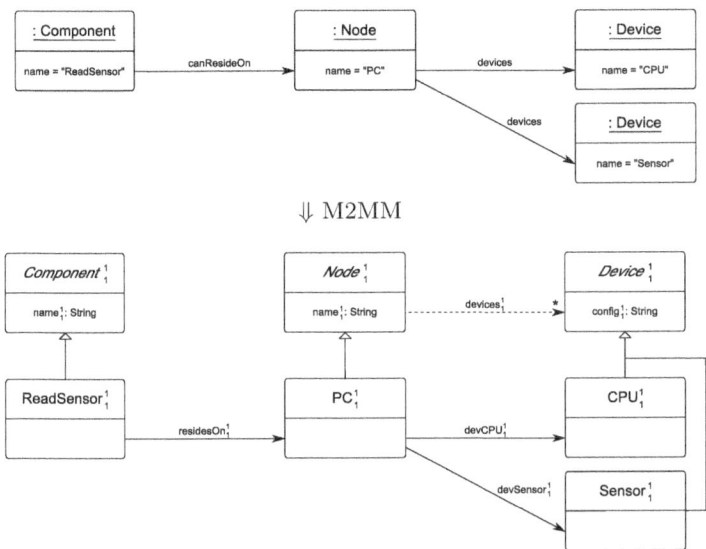

Fig. 4. Model Level 1 of Components-Nodes Example

The user can afterwards use the generated metamodel of figure 4 to define a model at modeling level 0. Such a model is displayed in figure 5, defining the component instance *ReadSensor1* and the node instance *Node1* with its *CPU* and *Sensor* devices.

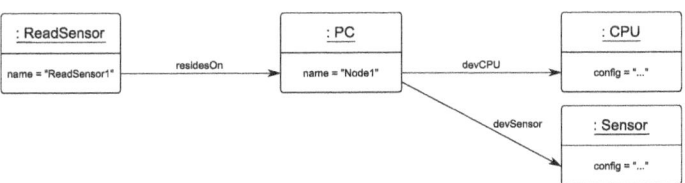

Fig. 5. Model Level 0 of Components-Nodes Example

5 Approach

The idea of this work is to integrate the concepts of deep instantiation in current metamodeling frameworks. To avoid a reimplementation of the metamodeling frameworks for a full support of deep instantiation automated M2MM transformations are used.

For simplification reasons, we will focus on *classes*, *attributes*, *references* (representing associations) and *operations* of the Essential Meta Object Facility (EMOF) [13]. As these are the main concepts, this presents no serious restriction.

Deep instantiation uses level and potency to define at which level a model element exists and how many times it can be instantiated. As this is a very clean and compact description to establish an ontological hierarchy, we adopted these concepts and extended the linguistic metamodel elements *classes*, *attributes*, *references* and *operations* with these attributes. This allows the definition of the basic properties to semi-automatically establish an ontological hierarchy. Additional to level and potency, operations are specified, which are applied during transformation. This information is used by the automated M2MM transformation to generate a metamodel out of an input model. During a M2MM transformation the model data is converted into a new metamodel predominantly by transforming objects into classes. Additional operations allow to steer the automated M2MM transformation and provide the missing information, e.g. the name of a new created class. All the available modification operators are defined later in this section.

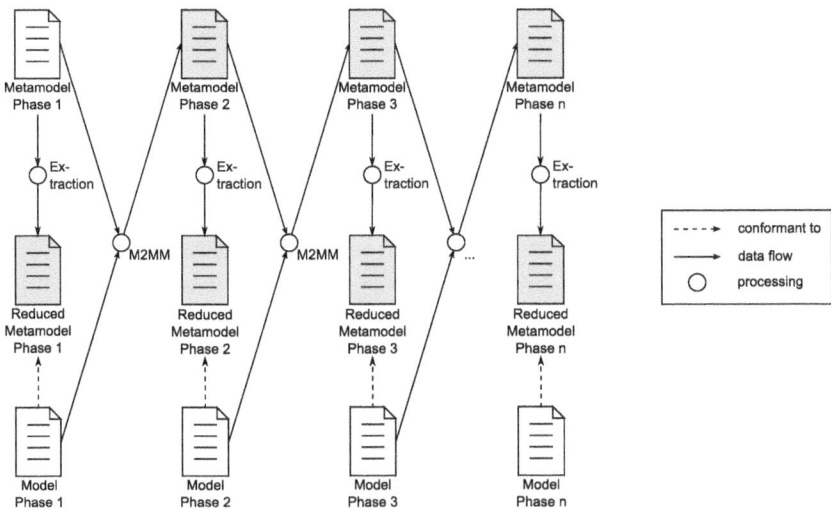

Fig. 6. Principle of the Automated M2MM Transformations Approach (All the Gray Metamodels are Generated)

Figure 6 shows how automated M2MM transformations work. The developer specifies the metamodel of the first phase including all the information needed for the automatic application of all following M2MM transformations. Afterwards a fully automated extraction step is conducted. During the extraction all model elements, which have no effect on the current model level, are eliminated. In short, these are all model elements with a level different to the current model level. This step is only included to ensure that existing metamodeling tools with no support of level, potency and the additional specified operations are still able to handle the new kind of metamodels. If eventually all used metamodeling tools are able to cope with the additional information this step can be skipped. The models can then be defined based on a reduced metamodel of the current phase. Based on the specified model and the complete metamodel (not the reduced metamodel) the M2MM transformation is executed resulting in the complete metamodel of the next phase. A M2MM transformation affects mainly the model elements of the current model level with a potency value greater than 1. These model elements are converted into their corresponding model elements with level and potency reduced by 1^5.

Before going into details on how the algorithm of the automated M2MM transformation works, we will explain all available operators, which can be applied to model elements during a M2MM transformation.

5.1 M2MM Transformation Operators

To reuse common functionality between M2MM transformations we identified a set of various operators by analyzing the use case described in section 6. Since this use case is rather complex, we are quite confident that additional operators are not required. The set of M2MM transformation operators currently supported is: *instantiation*, *change property*, *split field*, *generate enumeration* and *execute*. Typically the operators work on model elements of the current model level with a potency greater than 1. These model elements are converted according to the operator specification into their corresponding model elements with level and potency reduced by 1.

To incorporate the user input during the application of the operators, the operators have access to the model data. By providing the operators with descriptions of how to process the model data to extract needed information, each operator can be adapted to concrete use cases. This makes the operators more flexible and generic. The descriptions are needed to automate the execution of the M2MM transformations.

In the following a comprehensive description of all operators is given. To facilitate the understanding of the M2MM transformation operators, examples for their application are given according to the motivating example of section 4.

Instantiation. The instantiation operator constitutes the main M2MM transformation operator. It is responsible for the transformation of objects into their own classes. Hence it implements the connection between the two facets of clabjects. Since M2MM transformations are based on an iterative definition process of the ontological hierarchy, which means that in each phase only one specific level of the hierarchy can be defined / manipulated, during the application of the instantiation operator the old class is transformed into the new metamodel

---

[5] Decrementing of level and potency logically happens when instantiating new model elements. As level and potency are not directly present during modeling this is done in the M2MM transformation afterwards.

representing the super class of its newly created sub classes. To prevent further manipulation of the super class it is automatically converted into an abstract class. For the fully automatic application of the instantiation operator a description of how to construct the names of the new sub classes out of the object data is needed. For example the component object *ReadSensor* is transformed into a component type *ReadSensor*, which is sub class of an abstract *Component* class.

Additionally the instantiation operator takes care of the transformation of all attributes, references and operations of the class. In cases where sub classes define different values for properties of a contained model element, the model element is moved into the sub classes. To prevent unnecessary type casts to access these elements when working directly with the object model an additional access operation is added to the super class.

Following is the operator definition. It takes as input a class specification, all instances of that class and a description for the calculation of the new sub class names and returns the transformed class and all new created sub classes.

```
instantiation (in class: Class, in instances: Set<Object>,
               in name: Description): Set<Class>
```

Change Property. The change property operator allows the adaption of model element properties. For example a new default value for the attribute *name* of class *PC* can be specified with "PC" + *Counter.getNextID()*, where the function returns the number of a running counter. Even the refinement of the data type of an attribute is possible. This operator is very generic and allows to adapt the next metamodel in a flexible way. As already mentioned at the instantiation operator, special attention has to be taken when properties of elements in sub classes are set to different values. In such cases the elements have to be dragged from the super class into all sub classes. To further support access to those elements based on the super type, access operations must be installed. Sometimes it makes sense to apply this operator on model elements which are not transformed by the M2MM transformation but are coming into life for the first time, e.g. if the value of an attribute can be changed depends on previous model data.

As can be seen from the definition below, the operator takes an identification of the property which shall be changed and a calculation description for the new value as input. To consider the model data for the new property value the corresponding object is given to the operator. The result of the operator is the adaption of the given model element according to the specification.

```
changeProperty (in property: PropertyKind, in value: Description,
                in instance: Object, inout element: ModelElement)
```

Split Field. A very interesting operator is the split field operator. Its task is to allow the refinement of associations between super class and sub classes. Imagine the following example: after specifying that nodes of type *PC* can have the devices *CPU* and *Sensor*, it should only be allowed to link nodes of type *PC* with devices of type *CPU* and *Sensor* but nothing else. As can be seen from the example, this operator can establish very strong constraints on sub types. The additional constrains help preventing a lot of careless mistakes during model handling. Access to referenced object via the previous relation can still be ensured trough the definition of an access operation instead of the relation in the base type. The M2MM transformation can additionally take care of providing an appropriate realization for the access operation for each sub type.

The split field operator is realized in two separate parts. The first part is responsible for transforming the original reference of the super class into an appropriate operation. The second part takes as input the reference, a description of how to define the names of the new references, and a list of all the objects referenced by the object, which is going to be transformed in a sub class. A list containing all new references and the access operation including an appropriate implementation is returned.

```
splitFieldSuperClass (in reference: Reference): Operation

splitFieldSubClass (in reference: Reference, in name: Description,
                    in referencedObjects: List<Object>)
    : List<ModelElement>
```

Backtrack. Since M2MM transformations introduce a cut between two succeeding phases, a backtrack operator is offered to get full access to the model data of previous phases. This operator is able to return the object belonging to a class, so it can be used to traverse the M2MM transformations in reverse order. It is not only available during M2MM transformations but can also be used when working directly with the object model of a phase. In the context of our example the backtrack operator applied to the type *PC* of *Node1* at M0 would result in the object defining *PC* at M1.

The definition of the backtrack operator takes a class as input and returns the related object in the model of the previous phase. The operator is only defined in the context of classes representing the class facet of a clabject with both object and class facet. The behavior for clabjects without any object facet or any other object is undefined.

```
backtrack (in class: Class): Object
```

Generate Enumeration. Generate enumeration is used to create new enumerations. It has been shown during the application of automated M2MM transformations that sometimes the user defines a list of allowed values for a type in one phase and wants to use the generated enumeration for an attribute in the next phase. This helps to assure that only valid values are assigned to the attribute. For example at M1 it could be possible to specify the valid operating systems for the node type *PC* in an additional field *os*. This list is then transformed into a new enumeration. The operating system running on node instance *Node1* can then be only selected among those values.

To create a new enumeration the operator takes a description of the enumeration name and all literals as input and returns the generated enumeration. The literals of the enumeration consist of a name value pair.

```
generateEnumeration (in name: Description,
                     in literals: Description): Enumeration
```

Execute. There will always be special cases, which are not foreseen. To support such situations an execute operator is available in automated M2MM transformations. This operator offers the highest flexibility to transform data according to special needs. In general all presented operators can be emulated using the execute operator. Through its high flexibility this operator can be used to implement highly specialized transformations in a M2MM transformation.

To offer its high degree of flexibility the execute operator gets as input the current class, the complete model and a description of the transformation to execute.

```
execute (in class: Class, in model: Object,
         in modification: Description,
         inout metamodel: List<Object>)
```

Operator Application Specification. The MOF has been designed with expandability in mind. For extensions annotations exists. They can be attached to all model elements. We make extensive use of annotations to specify all the operators with their corresponding data. The operator specifications are attached to the model elements, on which they shall be applied. As it is important to apply the operator during the right M2MM transformation, all the annotations specify the transformation to which they belong.

5.2 Automated M2MM Transformations Algorithm

After the introduction of the different transformation operators the M2MM transformation algorithm is explained in detail. The algorithm is parameterized with the metamodel containing all operator specifications and the model of a phase and returns the metamodel of the next phase. To simplify the transformation the algorithm consists of two parts.

During the first part all types are created. Therefore the *instantiation*, *generate enumeration* and *execute* operators are executed for model elements, whose level is equal to the model level of the next phase plus 1 and have a potency greater than 1. Additionally, all types belonging to a model level lower than or equals to the model level of the next phase are copied. In this process the effect of *change property* operators are incorporated. This part is only responsible for defining all types, but does not take care of their internal structure. By doing so problems of referencing not yet created types is effectively prevented.

The second part is responsible for the completion of the created and copied types. This includes the transformation and copy of all attributes, references and operations. While transforming those model elements special cares have to be taken if for a model element different values are assigned to properties of sub classes created by the *instantiation* operator. In those cases the model elements are moved into the sub classes and an additional access operation is added to the super class. Additionally, the *execute* operators are processed again to finish their tasks.

After the completion of both steps the metamodel of the next phase is completely constructed. It contains a complete definition of the structure of the current and all following model levels. Model elements and specifications belonging to the previous model levels are completely removed.

5.3 Differences between Automated M2MM Transformations and the Two Original Approaches

Beside the transformation of models into metamodels, the specification of additional operations to provide the missing information for the automated M2MM transformations is a big difference compared to deep instantiation. In contrast to the deep instantiation approach, automated M2MM transformations rely on fully automatic creation of new types. Therefore the model data is taken and all needed information is extracted through specified operations. Thus the user does not need to know how to define new types in the metamodel or programming language. The only knowledge needed is how to insert correct model data. The creation of new types is then automatically conducted during M2MM transformations. This relieves the user from knowing how to modify a metamodel or program and helps him to concentrate on the ontology specification via modeling.

Compared to deep instantiation, potency has a slightly different meaning in the context of automated M2MM transformations. In the context of deep instantiation, potency specifies how many times a model element can be instantiated. This fact can be utilized to define abstract elements at the metamodel level with a potency value of 0, which makes the abstract flag obsolete. For automated M2MM transformations this additional utilization is not allowed, because M2MM transformations rely on potency for defining how many times a model element can be instantiated or copied, if it is abstract. Copying model elements is necessary as in contrast to deep instantiation not the complete ontological hierarchy is available for direct access at a specific model level. This requires that parts of the ontological hierarchy are copied to succeeding model levels as needed.

Deep instantiation also defines the concept of simple and dual fields. Field is the generalized term unifying attributes and references on the metamodel level and slots on the model level. A simple field is defined to be a field, which takes only a value when its potency is 0. In contrast a dual field can have a value for each model level. In the context of M2MM transformations it has been shown that the explicit distinction between simple and dual field makes no sense. The distinction is implicitly achieved through the specification of level and potency. Level defines the model level in which the field exits. In cases where the level number is lower than the number of the current model level, the field can be treated as nonexistent. Potency on the other hand specifies how many times the field shall get a value. Through the assumption that an existing field can get a value, the distinction between simple and dual fields is no longer needed. In cases where the assignment of values shall be delayed to a later model level the level can be set accordingly.

As automated M2MM transformations can be seen as an improvement of the M2MM transformations approach the only difference between those two approaches lies in the automation of the transformations. Through the definition of transformation operators the developer is relieved from programming the whole transformation. By using automated M2MM transformations large parts of the transformation can be executed automatically based on the specification of level, potency and the operators to apply.

6 Implementation and Evaluation

A first implementation of the presented approach is available based on the Eclipse Modeling Framework (EMF) [14]. This implementation has been used to demonstrate the usefulness of the approach on the example presented in our previous work [3][6]. The application of the automated M2MM transformations approach on this example resulted in a much simpler and more compact system description. Furthermore, the original three phase approach could be enhanced with an additional fourth phase, to define the different capability types. It also turned out that the new approach simplified the M2MM transformations. Most of the M2MM transformations are described using 43 standard operators (*instantiation* 9, *change property* 29, *split field* 2, *backtrack* 1 and *generate enumeration* 2). Only a special transformation had to be implemented with an *execute* operator.

7 Conclusion

In this paper we presented a combination of the deep instantiation and the M2MM transformations approach. The resulting approach uses the clean and compact description of the deep instantiation to automate the M2MM transformations approach. By combining these approaches main drawbacks of the original approaches are eliminated. The automated M2MM transformations approach does not require a fundamental change of the underlying metamodeling framework. All known and used modeling tools are further utilizable. In addition, the time consuming manual implementation of M2MM transformations is replaced by a clean and compact specification of transformation operators. The M2MM transformation operators support the developer in all transformation cases. For unsupported transformations a generic execute operator exists.

---

[6] Due to space limitations it is not possible to go into details about the example. Interested readers can refer to [3] for more information.

Furthermore, we introduced and presented a set of generic M2MM transformation operators. The operators are used to guide the M2MM transformations and provide the transformation with all needed information to ensure an automatic execution.

Finally a prototype of the automated M2MM transformations approach has been implemented for EMF and its usefulness has been demonstrated in the context of a real world example.

References

1. Bézivin, J.: In search of a basic principle for model driven engineering. UPGRADE-The European Journal for the Informatics Professional 5(2), 21–24 (2004)
2. Atkinson, C., Kühne, T.: The essence of multilevel metamodeling. In: Gogolla, M., Kobryn, C. (eds.) UML 2001. LNCS, vol. 2185, pp. 19–33. Springer, Heidelberg (2001)
3. Kainz, G., Buckl, C., Sommer, S., Knoll, A.: Model-to-metamodel transformation for the development of component-based systems. In: Petriu, D.C., Rouquette, N., Haugen, Ø. (eds.) MODELS 2010. LNCS, vol. 6395, pp. 391–405. Springer, Heidelberg (2010)
4. Atkinson, C.: Meta-modeling for distributed object environments. In: Proceedings of the 1st International Conference on Enterprise Distributed Object Computing, EDOC 1997, Washington, USA, pp. 90–101 (1997)
5. Atkinson, C., Kühne, T.: Model-driven development: A metamodeling foundation. IEEE Software 20(5), 36–41 (2003)
6. Eker, J., Janneck, J., Lee, E.A., Liu, J., Liu, X., Ludvig, J., Sachs, S., Xiong, Y.: Taming heterogeneity - the ptolemy approach. Proceedings of the IEEE 91(1), 127–144 (2003)
7. Kühne, T., Schreiber, D.: Can programming be liberated from the two-level style: multi-level programming with deepjava. In: Proceedings of the 22nd Annual ACM SIGPLAN Conference on Object-Oriented Programming Systems and Applications. OOPSLA 2007, Montreal, Canada, pp. 229–244 (2007)
8. Atkinson, C., Kühne, T.: Processes and products in a multi-level metamodeling architecture. International Journal of Software Engineering and Knowledge Engineering 11(6), 761–783 (2001)
9. Gutheil, M., Kennel, B., Atkinson, C.: A systematic approach to connectors in a multi-level modeling environment. In: Busch, C., Ober, I., Bruel, J.-M., Uhl, A., Völter, M. (eds.) MODELS 2008. LNCS, vol. 5301, pp. 843–857. Springer, Heidelberg (2008)
10. Odell, J.: Power types. Journal of Object-Oriented Programming 7(2), 8–12 (1994)
11. Martin, J., Odell, J.J.: Object-oriented methods: a foundation, UMLed, 2nd edn. Prentice-Hall, Englewood Cliffs (1998)
12. Bragança, A., Machado, R.J.: Transformation patterns for multi-staged model driven software development. In: Proceedings of the 12th International Software Product Line Conference, SPLC 2008, Washington, USA, pp. 329–338 (2008)
13. Object Management Group (OMG): Meta Object Facility (MOF) Core Specification Version 2.0 (January 2006)
14. Steinberg, D., Budinsky, F., Paternostro, M., Merks, E.: EMF: Eclipse Modeling Framework. Addison-Wesley, Reading (2009)

Lazy Execution of Model-to-Model Transformations

Massimo Tisi, Salvador Martínez, Frédéric Jouault, and Jordi Cabot

AtlanMod, INRIA & École des Mines de Nantes, France
{massimo.tisi,salvador.martinez_perez,frederic.jouault,
jordi.cabot}@inria.fr

Abstract. The increasing adoption of Model-Driven Engineering in industrial contexts highlights scalability as a critical limitation of several MDE tools. Most of the current model-to-model transformation engines have been designed for one-shot translation of input models to output models, and present efficiency issues when applied to very large models. In this paper, we study the application of a lazy-evaluation approach to model transformations. We present a lazy execution algorithm for ATL, and we empirically evaluate a prototype implementation. With it, the elements of the target model are generated only when (and if) they are accessed, enabling also transformations that generate infinite target models. We achieve our goal on a significant subset of ATL by extending the ATL compiler.

1 Introduction

Several Model-Driven Engineering (MDE) tools, when adopted in industrial contexts, show critical effeciency limitations in handling very large models (VLMs). When these tools are built around model-to-model (M2M) transformations, the efficiency of the transformation engine risks to become a performance bottleneck for the whole MDE environment. While specific M2M transformation languages and engines have been developed since several years [12,8,3], optimizing the transformation of VLMs is just becoming a compelling research task.

Lazy evaluation is one of the classical approaches that can provide, under specific conditions, a significant speed-up in program execution, especially when manipulating large data structures. When a programming language performs lazy evaluation, the value of an expression is calculated only when it is needed for a following computation (in contrast with *eager evaluation*, where expressions are evaluated as soon as they occur). This avoids the computation of unnecessary intermediate values. The useful part of large data structures is only calculated on-demand, even allowing for infinite-size data structures. For this reason lazy evaluation is a commonly used technique in several programming paradigms (for instance functional programming languages are classified in *lazy* or *eager*, depending on their evaluation strategy).

Lazy evaluation would significantly speed-up the execution of MDE tools based on M2M transformations, e.g., in cases where only part of the VLMs involved in the transformations is actually used. Unfortunately, all the M2M transformation engines we are aware of support only eager computation of the target models. Models are always completely generated according to the transformation logic and it is not possible to automatically avoid the computation of model elements that will not be consumed afterwards.

This paper wants to provide the following contributions: 1) the study of the application of lazy evaluation to M2M transformation languages as a twofold problem, encompassing lazy navigation of the source model and lazy generation of the target model; 2) the implementation of an engine for lazy generation of the target model; 3) a practical evaluation of the lazy approach to model generation.

Our approach has been implemented in a prototype of a lazy transformation engine for the ATL [8] language, obtained by adapting the standard ATL engine. Our experimentation shows that M2M transformation languages like ATL, with an explicit representation of the transformation logic, can be naturally provided with an efficient lazy evaluation strategy.

Moreover, our approach to lazy generation allows the construction of an engine that can be plugged into existing tools consuming EMF models, without requiring modifications to the tools. The output model of the transformation is accessed like a normal EMF model, but its elements are computed on demand.

Finally the lazy generation approach can be naturally applied to transformations that generate an unbounded target model. Only the part of the model explicitly requested by the consumer is generated. In this way finite computations can make use of infinite intermediate models generated by transformation. This represents a significant extension of the application space of existing transformation languages.

The paper is structured as follows: Section 2 introduces the problems motivating the paper, by providing two running examples. Section 3 describes our approach to lazy execution of model transformations, in Section 4 we describe the implementation of a lazy engine for ATL and in Section 5 we experimentally evaluate its behavior; Section 6 discusses related work and, finally, in Section 7 we conclude the paper and propose further challenges.

2 Motivating Scenarios

In this section we provide two application scenarios that are the motivation for our work, running examples of the paper and subject of our experimental evaluation.

2.1 Scenario 1: Large Models

To illustrate how laziness addresses the performance problems of handling VLMs, we introduce an ideal database schema editor based on M2M transformations, whose structure is shown is Fig 1. This tool provides the user with an editor of the conceptual model of the database (in the form of a UML Class Diagram) and with a transformation that generates a corresponding relational model. The user can check the relational model by using a read-only model browser.

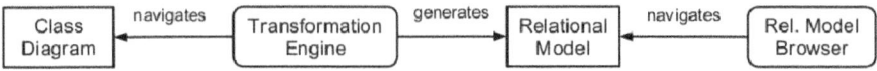

Fig. 1. A model-driven database schema editor

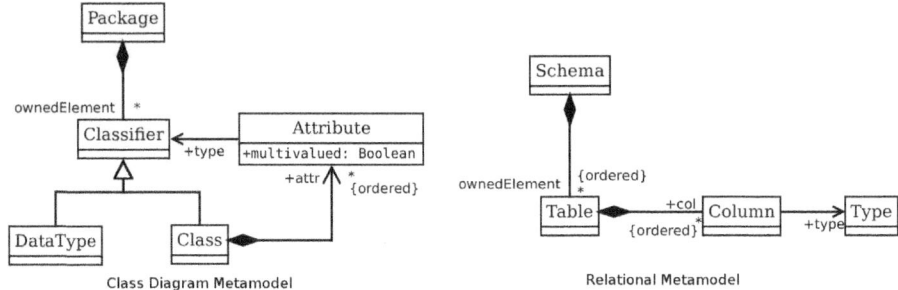

Fig. 2. Class and Relational metamodels

The tool uses a M2M transformation to generate the relational model from the Class diagram (the well-known Class2Relational transformation). In Fig. 2 we show the source and target metamodels of the transformation. The *Class-Diagram* metamodel represents a very simplified UML Class diagram. In this metamodel, *Packages* are containers of *Classifiers* that are either *Datatypes* or *Classes*. *Classes* can, in turn, be containers of *Attributes*, which can be multi-valued. The *Relational* metamodel describes simple relational schemas. *Schema* contains *Tables* that are composed of *Columns*. Finally, *Columns* have a type that characterizes the kind of elements they can hold.

Listing 1.1 shows the main rules of the *Class2Relational* ATL transformation.

Listing 1.1. ATL Class2Relational transformation

```
rule Package2Schema{
  from
    p: ClassDiagram!Package
  to
    out: Relational!Schema (
      ownedElements <- p.ownedElement->
        select(e | e.oclIsTypeOf(ClassDiagram!Class))
    )
}

rule Class2Table {
  from
    c : ClassDiagram!Class
  to
    out : Relational!Table (
      name <- c.name,
      col <- Sequence {key}->
          union(c.attr->select(e | not e.multiValued)),
      key <- Set {key}
```

```
21          ),
22          key : Relational!Column (
23              name <- 'objectId'
24          )
25  }
26
27  rule DataType2Type {
28      from
29          dt : ClassDiagram!DataType
30      to
31          out : Relational!Type (
32              name <- dt.name
33          )
34  }
35
36  rule DataTypeAttribute2Column {
37      from
38          a : ClassDiagram!Attribute (
39              a.type.oclIsKindOf(ClassDiagram!DataType) and not a.multiValued
40          )
41      to
42              out : Relational!Column (
43                  name <- a.name,
44                  type <- a.type
45              )
46  }
47
48  rule ClassAttribute2Column {
49      from
50          a : ClassDiagram!Attribute (
51              a.type.oclIsKindOf(ClassDiagram!Class) and
52                  not a.multiValued
53          )
54      to
55          foreignKey : Relational!Column (
56              name <- a.name + 'Id',
57          )
58  }
```

The ATL transformation constitutes a set of rules that describe how parts of the input model generate parts of the target model. These rules must have an *input pattern* and an *output pattern*. E.g., in the rule *ClassAttribute2Column* input model elements of type Attribute are selected to be transformed into output elements of type Column. Rules can have filters and bindings. Filters are used to impose conditions on the input elements selected by the input pattern and bindings are used to initialize values of the elements created by the output pattern. In the rule *ClassAttribute2Column*, a filter is introduced to select only Attributes that are not multivalued and whose type is *Class*. Two bindings are then used to initialize the name and type of the created Column. The rule *Class2Table* creates a Table for each Class, adds a *key* Column and initializes the list of columns with the respectively transformed Attributes. Finally, rule *Package2Schema* transforms a Package into a relational Schema and initializes the list of Tables.

The ATL transformation is executed in two steps. In the first step all the rules are matched creating all the corresponding target elements. Additionally, matching a rule creates, in the internal structures of the transformation engine, a traceability link that relates three components: the rule, the match (i.e. source

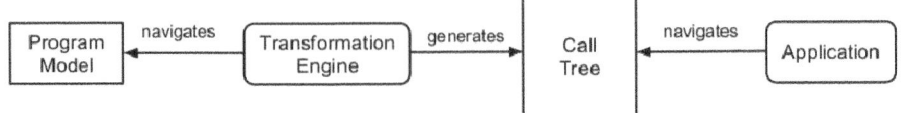

Fig. 3. A model-driven visualizator for method-call trees

elements) and the newly created target elements. In the second step, the created elements are initialized as described in the rule bindings. To perform the inizialization, ATL relies on a resolution algorithm that has been explained in details in [8].

Even with the very simple mapping of this scenario, when the Class diagram is large enough the transformation execution time can be significant. If the transformation engine has no support for change propagation (like the standard ATL engine), after each update to the Class Diagram, the user will have to wait the whole transformation processing, to see the corresponding element update in the relational model. Even a support for change propagation does not avoid the computation time for the whole initial target model.

In the following we propose a solution in which the tool offers a lazy exploration of the relational model. Transformation rules are activated only when the user requests to analyze a table, and only the necessary rules are executed. This delays the computation to the moment it is needed (at data consumption instead of data production) and strongly reduces the computation time.

2.2 Scenario 2: Infinite Models

As a second scenario we introduce a method-call hierarchy browser (similar to the one included in the Eclipse distribution) that computes this hierarchy in a model-driven way. The tool (Fig. 3) represents source code as a model conforming to the *Program* metamodel and uses a M2M transformation to generate the method-call hierarchy as a graph. Source and target metamodels are shown in Fig. 4, while Fig. 5 contains two example models. In the source model, *Programs* contain *Methods* that hold references to the other *Methods* they call. The target model is a simple tree, where *Nodes* represent method calls.

In Listing 1.2 we show an ATL transformation that performs the generation of the method-call hierarchy. Rule *Program2Root* translates the *Program* element into the root of the target tree. Then Program2Root activates the rule *Method2Node*[1] to generate a first-level node for each method. Finally *Method2Node* is a recursive rule that creates new children *Nodes* for each method call. In the

---

[1] *Method2Node*, in the ATL jargon is a *lazy rule*, i.e. a special kind of declarative rule that is only fired when directly called from other rules. We will omit discussing lazy ATL rules in the following sections, to avoid confusion with the concept of laziness we are promoting in this paper (i.e. the rules are not activated until their target element is needed). However our prototype engine includes support for ATL lazy rules.

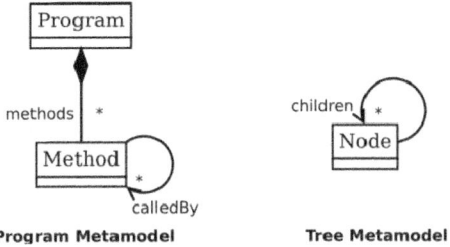

Fig. 4. Program and Tree metamodels

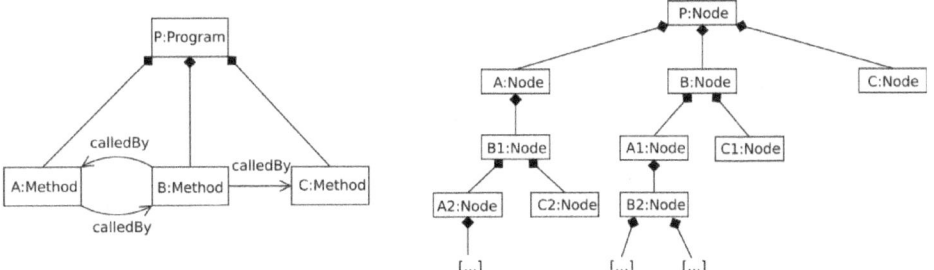

Fig. 5. A recursive program and its corresponding method-call hierarchy

common case in which two methods call each other (as in Fig. 5), the source model will contain a loop and the target method-call tree will become infinite (the *Method2Node* rule will continue to recur).

Listing 1.2. ATL infinite transformation

```
rule Program2Root {
    from
        s : Program
    to
        t : Node (
            children <- s.methods->collect(e | thisModule.Method2Node(e))
        )
}

lazy rule Method2Node {
    from
        s : Method
    to
        t : Node (
            children <- s.calledBy->collect(e | thisModule.Method2Node(e))
        )
}
```

Contrarily to the example in Listing 1.1, this transformation cannot be executed in the current ATL engine, since its computation will not terminate. On the contrary, the lazy engine we propose can launch the transformation, and generate nodes on demand, when the user browses the tree. Moreover the consumer

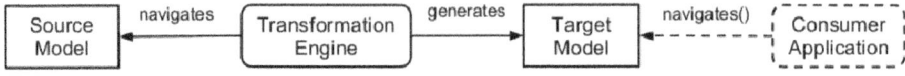

Fig. 6. Transformation and consumer

tool could compute in a finite time expressions on infinite method-call models (e.g., reachability of method C from method A in a given number of steps).

3 Lazy Model Transformation

Since every M2M transformation is both a producer and a consumer of models, a lazy approach to model transformation has to address both the aspects of lazy production and lazy consumption.

1) Model production (or *model generation*) by model transformation is based on an execution strategy that is built-in in the transformation engine or user-controllable as part of the transformation language. Lazy generation requires the introduction of a lazy execution strategy, driven by external model-consumption events.

2) Independently from the execution strategy, transformation engines need to analyze input models, to obtain the necessary information for controlling their execution or computing output values. In MDE we usually refer to this phase with the term *model navigation*. A lazy transformation approach involves lazy navigation of source models, possibly performed by a navigation language with lazy evaluation.

In this section we study the two aspects of lazy model generation and navigation and we argue that they are separated and orthogonal to each other. We will refer to a general schema in which the transformation is connected to a consumer application, as in Fig. 6.

3.1 Lazy Model Generation

With *lazy model generation* we indicate on-demand activation of the computation for generating a data element of the target model. No assumption is made on the strategy for extracting and evaluating data from the source model, i.e. lazy generation is independent from the navigation mechanism. Since only the required subset of the target model is computed, lazy generation can be used to address the problem of VLMs (or infinite models) when they are the *target* of the transformation.

Eager transformation languages activate rules according to internal execution strategies. *Source-driven* transformation languages base their execution strategy on the structure of the source model. For instance ATL has a source-driven execution algorithm that associates source elements to matching rules and fires the rules in non-deterministic order [8]. *Target-driven* languages in contrast follow a predetermined production order for target elements (e.g., sequential or template-based). Lazy generation can be seen as an alternative execution strategy that differentiates from the previous ones for being driven by a special kind of external events, i.e. the consumption requests.

With respect to an eager system, a transformation system with lazy generation has to provide some additional features:

1. To initiate the lazy generation process, consumption requests on the target model have to be tracked. This requires extending the model navigation mechanism the consumer uses, to intercept the requests and activate a corresponding generation in the transformation engine. If this adaptation can be performed in a transparent way, the client system will not notice that the model is lazily built. For instance, several transformation languages use EMF [15] as their model management system. A naturally transparent extension mechanism in this case would be to re-implement the EMF API, so to provide the same interface of a standard EMF model. For performing lazy access by the EMF API, we only need to override the *eGet()* method in the implementation of model elements, in order to trigger a call to the engine operations.
2. The transformation engine has to provide the means to launch the computation of a single model element or a single property of the target model. The degree of laziness in computing the target elements is strongly dependent on the modularity of the transformation algorithm. E.g., in a transformation language natively designed to maximize independent computation of target elements, the performance of a lazy system would be optimal.
3. Finally, the lazy engine can keep track of the status of the partial transformation, and use it as a context for the execution of new computations. The stored context is exploited by the lazy system to avoid recomputations. In transformation systems this context usually includes trace links that map elements in the target model with their corresponding sources. E.g., the trace links in the current state can be used to avoid recomputing previous matches when a new value is requested. Lazy transformation engines that keep extra state information can be *live systems*, and keep their state information constantly in memory, or *offline systems*, and provide a way to freeze and restore their state.

Once the engine provides this infrastructure, a generic lazy generation algorithm works in three corresponding steps:

1. the consumer requests a new target element, and the call gets intercepted by the navigation interface of the target model;
2. the navigation interface (e.g., the lazy model) requests the engine to generate the single requested property or element;
3. the engine determines the computations to activate, based on the current status of the transformation.

In Section 4 we describe an implementation of this approach for the ATL language.

3.2 Lazy Model Navigation

Model navigation can be a more or less clearly separated phase in the transformation execution. In several M2M approaches a different language is used specifically for model navigation. For instance, popular languages like QVT/R [12], ATL [8] and Kermeta [3] use OCL [13] to write expressions on the source models.

Adding a lazy evaluation strategy to the model navigation mechanism allows the engine to 1) delay the access to source model elements to the moment in which this access is needed by the transformation logic and, by consequence, 2) reduce the number of source model elements accessed during navigation, by skipping the unnecessary model elements. For this reason, lazy model navigation can be used to address the problem of VLMs when they are the *source* of transformation. For instance, in Scenario 1, lazy navigation would speed-up the evaluation of expressions on big Class diagrams.

On the other hand, the problem of lazy navigation does not only exist in transformation systems, as navigation mechanisms and languages are commonly used outside of transformations. Fig. 6 shows that the consumer application needs to navigate the generated target model. Lazy target navigation by the consumer is in principle not different from lazy source navigation by the transformation engine. In the case in which transformation and consumer use the same navigation language, a lazy implementation can be re-used for both phases.

Navigation languages can be generally augmented with a certain degree of laziness. For instance, in the case of functional navigation languages, the research problem of implementing a lazy strategy for an existing language is already deeply studied (e.g., in [6]). In the task of adding laziness to OCL some work has already been carried out in [1] and in [2]. Hence, our prototype engine only focuses on lazy generation. However, in building our implementation we maintain a clear decoupling among navigation and generation to allow for independent development of both parts.

Finally, an issue tightly coupled to lazy navigation, is on-demand physical access to the source model elements, i.e. lazy loading. For lazy loading of models for transformation we refer the reader to [9].

4 A Lazy Engine for ATL

To demonstrate the feasibility and performance of lazy generation we implemented a prototype engine that activates ATL rules on demand.[2]

4.1 Transformation Engine

Our implementation consists of an extension of the standard ATL compiler[3] and an adaptation of the EMF *EObject* class. We don't modify the syntax of the ATL language and we reuse the standard ATL Virtual Machine.

---

[2] The full code of the prototype is available at the following address:
http://www.emn.fr/z-info/atlanmod/index.php/Lazy_ATL
[3] On the Eclipse CVS: /modeling/org.eclipse.m2m/atl/dsls/ATL/Compiler/ATL.acg

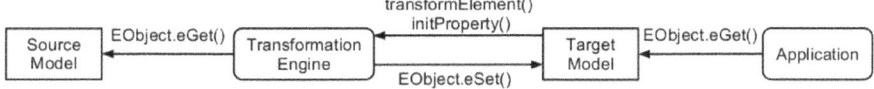

Fig. 7. Adapted lazy transformation engine

The prototype implements the three features discussed in Section 3.

1. To intercept consumption requests we provide an adaptation of EMF *EObject*, called *LazyEObject*. *LazyEObject* implements the EMF interface and overrides only the method *eGet(EStructuralFeature eFeature)* used to request for a model feature from normal EMF model elements. In the new implementation, *eGet()*: a) checks that the requested feature is still not initialized and b) calls the *initProperty* operation of the compiler. The computation of the requested property and its physical storage in the target model for future reuse is delegated to the transformation engine.
2. On-demand computation of model elements and attributes is implemented by refactoring the standard ATL execution algorithm described in Section 2. Once new elements or properties have been computed, the transformation engine explicitly stores their value in the target model by calling a standard *EObject.eSet()* (i.e., data is *pushed* by the transformation engine, and not *pulled* by the lazy model). The fact that the client system leaves to the transformation engine the responsibility to explicitly fill the target model, allows us to keep an execution semantics for atomic initialization as similar as possible to the standard ATL engine. This simplifies the lazy engine implementation, as well as the subsequent maintenance in parallel with the standard engine. Practically, the lazy engine has been refactored to expose two new operations, additional to the standard ones:

    transformElement(source: EObject). The operation *transformElement* performs on-demand transformation of single elements, by activating the ATL rule that matches a given source element and creating the corresponding target. The properties of the newly created elements are not computed in this phase, but they have to be explicitly filled by subsequent calls to the operation *initProperty*. In ATL, once a rule is matched, more elements are generated at once (output pattern). The matching phase has a much higher cost than the creation of new empty elements in the target. For this reason in our implementation *transformElement*, together with the target element that has been requested, generates all the output pattern at once. This optimization is invisible to the user, and can be easily disabled.

    initProperty(target: EObject, propertyName: String). The operation *initProperty* performs on-demand generation of target properties by computing the corresponding ATL bindings. If the property is an attribute its value is computed and stored in the target model. If the property is a reference, the ATL binding is into a set of source elements, the trace links of these elements are navigated to retrieve the corresponding targets (as it happens for the standard ATL resolution algorithm). If a source element has no associated traceability links (which means that it has not been transformed), a transformation on that element is launched by a call to *transformElement*.

3. As in standard ATL, the state of the current transformation is stored as trace links that relate source elements with target elements and their connecting rule. The set of traces in the lazy engine is initially empty, it gets initialized when the lazy transformation is started by a call to *transformElement*, and then it grows monotonically while the user navigates the target model (activating calls to *initProperty* and *transformElement*). For simplicity we implemented our system as a *live transformation system* that keeps its state information in memory, but we plan in future to exploit the serialization of the trace link information provided by the ATL engine to implement an offline behavior.

4.2 Considered ATL Subset

Our prototype supports a well-defined and fully functional subset of the ATL language. While the following advanced features are not supported yet, they do not pose a significant research problem and are included in our future plans:

- **Resolution of specific target elements (resoveTemp operation)** should be extended to launch the correct rule in case the element to be resolved has not been created yet.
- **Rule inheritance** could be natively handled in a future version of the lazy engine. However the inheritance tree in ATL can always be eliminated by copying the inherited features.
- **Multiple source pattern elements** would require to extend the logic to get, using trace links, source elements from target ones.

Adding laziness to other aspects of ATL instead would not be trivial:

- **Reverse bindings** are a means to set the incoming references of the target element. To detect if a reference is modified by reverse bindings, all of them have to be computed in an eager way.
- **Refining mode**: the engine for in-place transformations in ATL first computes the set of changes to apply and then executes them on the source model. Lazy generation and application of changes in ATL has yet to be studied.
- **Imperative constructs**, whose use should be avoided in ATL whenever possible, create and modify target elements without producing corresponding traces: this is not compatible with our approach in its current state.

5 Approach Evaluation

For the experimentation phase, we built a consumer program that performs controlled sequences of accesses to the target model and records the evaluation times, both in lazy and eager modes.

When executed in lazy mode, the consumer uses the Eclipse infrastructure to initiate the process. An extended Eclipse EMF editor allows the user to visualize the source model, select a starting source element and launch the lazy transformations from the source element. The rule matching the selected source element is immediately activated, initial target elements are generated, and the consumer starts browsing the output model by navigating the references of the target model elements. In eager mode the consumer simply launches programmatically an ATL transformation and then performs the same sequence of accesses as in the lazy mode. We implemented different navigation strategies for the target model (e.g. depth-first, random), and the experimentation results do not show significant variations in this respect.

To evaluate the behavior in Scenario 2, the transformation in Listing 1.2 is launched and a constraint is programmatically checked (e.g., reachability of method C from method A in a given number of steps). The computation does not terminate in eager mode and generates an immediate result in lazy mode.

The performance hit of the lazy approach in Scenario 1, is illustrated in Fig. 8. Four sets of tests have been executed, each one characterized by a different source model. The four source models, ordered by increasing model size (respectively of 8020, 16020, 25220 and 50420 elements), originated the four graphs in figure. In all the tests, we applied the transformation of Listing 1.1 in lazy and eager mode, and we navigated a fixed number of target elements[4]. The graphs in Fig. 8 are obtained by varying the length of the navigation and marking the correspondent computation time.

To reduce perturbations, each test has been repeated ten times, with exactly the same conditions. Each point in the graphs of Fig. 8 represents the average value of ten identical tests (actually the first iteration was discarded, to avoid any initialization overhead).

As expected, for a small number of accesses to VLMs, the lazy approach results much faster than the eager one. However, when the number of accesses is close to the size of the model the lazy approach is notably slower. This performance drawback is due to the overhead introduced by the lazy execution, as extra operations have to be performed everytime an element is generated (to find the source model from the trace link, check guards, etc). Nevertheless, it's interesting to observe that the lazy approach keeps better performance than the eager one until a significant percentage of target model navigation (from 48% in the smallest case to 58% in the biggest). Moreover, the evident similarity among the plots, with a nearly linear increase of computation time in the lazy case, shows that we have an approximately constant speed-up with the increase of model size.

---

[4] The experimentation has been performed in the following hardware and software setting: Eclipse 3.5.2, Ubuntu 10.04, Linux kernel v2.6.32, Dell Latitude E6410, Intel Core i7 processor (2,67 GHz).

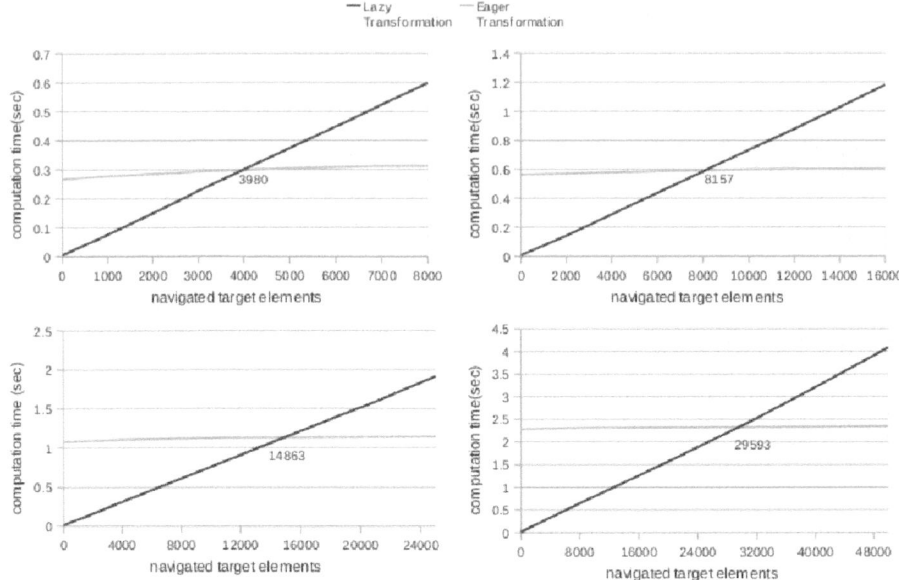

Fig. 8. Experimental results

The performance gap would be much wider for models big enough to exceed the computer memory. In this cases a lazy approach avoids, for limited navigations, the performance drop caused by memory management mechanisms.

6 Related Work

As we said, we are not aware of any transformation tool with a lazy generation strategy in MDE. The Stratego [18] system allows user-defined execution strategies for transformation rules. While user-defined strategies have been used to implement target-driven approaches [19], the activation of rules as answer to external consumption has not been addressed. VIATRA, despite not implementing on-demand transformation, evaluates lazily the matchings of connected rules to avoid unnecessary computation, as described in [16].

Outside the MDE domain, [14] follows an approach similar to ours. The authors provide an interpreter for XSLT that allows random access to the transformation result. They also show how their implementation enables efficient pipelining of XSLT transformations. The implementation of a lazy evaluator for functional (navigation) languages is a subject with a long tradition [7]. We refer the reader to [6] for an example based on Lisp. This subject has been explored in [1] and in [2] where performance measures are presented.

Other optimization techniques have been explored in model transformation engines. Lazy loading [9] is a complementary subject to lazy navigation, when dealing with models that do not fit into the memory of the transformation engine. [11] presents methods to evaluate pattern matches of different rules in an overlapped way, to increase performance. In [5] transformation context is preserved to efficiently perform incremental updates whereas in [17] and [4] strategies for the problem of graph pattern matching optimization are investigated. Finally this paper follows the opposite direction of [10], that adds forward change propagation to ATL. The study of the possible combination of laziness and incrementality in ATL and other M2M languages is part of our future work.

7 Conclusions and Future Work

Our experimentation shows that adding lazy execution of transformation rules to existing transformation languages can provide a remarkable performance gain and extend the application space of transformation languages to infinite data structures.

Complete coverage of ATL. The implementation presented here covers a significant and functional subset of ATL but in the future we plan to extend the support to the complete declarative part of the ATL language.
Optimization of the lazy engine. As in other lazy approaches, we want to evaluate the possibility to store intermediate expression values to avoid intermediate recomputations in target generation. We plan to add a lazy OCL evaluator to address the sub-problem of lazy source navigation (which is especially relevant when working with big source models).
Incrementality. We plan to study the interaction between forward change propagation and laziness in M2M languages and provide a combined engine for ATL.
Transformation chains. Finally we want to study the concatenation of lazy transformations and the possibilities of pipelining.

References

1. Beaudoux, O., Blouin, A., Barais, O., Jézéquel, J.-M.: Active operations on collections. In: Petriu, D.C., Rouquette, N., Haugen, Ø. (eds.) MODELS 2010. LNCS, vol. 6394, pp. 91–105. Springer, Heidelberg (2010)
2. Clavel, M., Egea, M., de Dios, M.A.G.: Building an efficient component for OCL evaluation. ECEASST 15 (2008)
3. Drey, Z., Fleurey, F., Vojtisek, D., Faucher, C., Mahé, V.: Kermeta Language, Reference Manual (2009)
4. Geiß, R., Batz, G.V., Grund, D., Hack, S., Szalkowski, A.: GrGen: A fast SPO-based graph rewriting tool. In: Corradini, A., Ehrig, H., Montanari, U., Ribeiro, L., Rozenberg, G. (eds.) ICGT 2006. LNCS, vol. 4178, pp. 383–397. Springer, Heidelberg (2006)
5. Hearnden, D., Lawley, M., Raymond, K.: Incremental model transformation for the evolution of model-driven systems. In: Wang, J., Whittle, J., Harel, D., Reggio, G. (eds.) MoDELS 2006. LNCS, vol. 4199, pp. 321–335. Springer, Heidelberg (2006)
6. Henderson, P., Morris Jr., J.H.: A lazy evaluator. In: Proceedings of the 3rd ACM SIGACT-SIGPLAN Symposium on Principles on Programming Languages, POPL 1976, pp. 95–103. ACM, New York (1976)

7. Hudak, P., Hughes, J., Jones, S.L.P., Wadler, P.: A history of Haskell: being lazy with class. In: HOPL, pp. 1–55. ACM, New York (2007)
8. Jouault, F., Kurtev, I.: Transforming models with ATL. In: Bruel, J.-M. (ed.) MoDELS 2005. LNCS, vol. 3844, pp. 128–138. Springer, Heidelberg (2006)
9. Jouault, F., Sottet, J.S.: An AmmA/ATL Solution for the GraBaTs 2009 Reverse Engineering Case Study. In: 5th International Workshop on Graph-Based Tools, Grabats (2009)
10. Jouault, F., Tisi, M.: Towards incremental execution of ATL transformations. In: Tratt, L., Gogolla, M. (eds.) ICMT 2010. LNCS, vol. 6142, pp. 123–137. Springer, Heidelberg (2010)
11. Mészáros, T., Mezei, G., Levendovszky, T., Asztalos, M.: Manual and automated performance optimization of model transformation systems. STTT 12, 231–243 (2010)
12. OMG. MOF QVT Final Adopted Specification. Object Management Group (2005)
13. OMG. Object Constraint Language Specification, version 2.0. Object Management Group (June 2005)
14. Schott, S., Noga, M.L.: Lazy XSL transformations. In: ACM Symposium on Document Engineering, pp. 9–18. ACM, New York (2003)
15. Steinberg, D., Budinsky, F., Paternostro, M., Merks, E.: EMF: Eclipse Modeling Framework, 2nd edn. The Eclipse Series. Addison-Wesley Professional, Reading (2008)
16. Taentzer, G., Ehrig, K., Guerra, E., de Lara, J., Lengyel, L., Levendovszky, T., Prange, U., Varró, D., Varró-Gyapay, S.: Model transformation by graph transformation: A comparative study. In: Proc. Workshop Model Transformation in Practice (2005)
17. Varró, G., Friedl, K., Varró, D.: Adaptive graph pattern matching for model transformations using model-sensitive search plans. Electr. Notes Theor. Comput. Sci. 152, 191–205 (2006)
18. Visser, E.: Program transformation with Stratego/XT: Rules, strategies, tools, and systems in Stratego/XT 0.9. In: Lengauer, C., Batory, D., Blum, A., Vetta, A. (eds.) Domain-Specific Program Generation. LNCS, vol. 3016, pp. 216–238. Springer, Heidelberg (2004)
19. Wijngaarden, J.V., Visser, E.: Program transformation mechanics: A classification of mechanisms for program transformation with a survey of existing transformation systems. Technical report, UU-CS (2003)

Measuring UML Models Using Metrics Defined in OCL within the SQUAM Framework

Joanna Chimiak–Opoka

Institute of Computer Science, University of Innsbruck, Austria
joanna.opoka@uibk.ac.at

Abstract. In software engineering practice, measurements may reduce development costs by improving processes and products at early stages. In model driven approaches, measurements can be conducted right from the start of a project. For UML models, a collection of metrics has been empirically validated, however, these need to be precisely defined in order to be useful. Definition of UML metrics in OCL offers a high degree of precision and portability, but due to shortcomings of this language this approach is not widespread. We propose the SQUAM framework, a tool–supported methodology to develop OCL specifications, which incorporates best practices in software development, such as libraries, testing and documentation. As a proof of concept we have developed 26 metrics for UML class diagrams in the academic context. This demonstrated the high effectiveness of our approach: quick learning, high satisfaction of developers, low imposed complexity and potential time reduction through reuse.

Keywords: model analysis, UML metrics, OCL specification, OCL pragmatic extensions, OCL development process.

1 Introduction

Measurement is important in the software engineering domain. Measures can help address some of the most critical issues in software development and provide support for planning, monitoring, controlling, and evaluating the software engineering process [1]. Reliable metrics provide evidence of improvements, allow cost–benefit analysis, and provide the basis for decision making [2]. Metrics are good at summarizing particular aspects of things and detecting outliers in large amounts of data [3].

In *model driven approaches* measurements can be conducted at the very beginning of the software development process. A subset of software metrics was successfully transferred from the code level to the model level. Metrics can be used to measure and evaluate models and to give early feedback in the software development process.

In *our project* we focused on the de facto standard for model driven development: Unified Modeling Language (UML, [4]). We selected UML class diagram metrics from a theoretically defined and empirically validated set [5]. According to [6] four classes of UML metrics can be distinguished: quantity, complexity, quality and size metrics. Most of selected metrics are from the first two classes.

Related Work and Discussion. In the subsequent paragraphs we describe the context of our research, related issues and complementary approaches.

Quality model. Our approach has to be seen as a supporting solution in a larger context of model quality analysis, where a quality model needs to be defined. Most quality models are based on the Goal–Question–Metric approach [7,1,2]. At the conceptual level, a goal of measurement should be established. Next, at the operational level, questions that can help to check if the goal is fulfilled should be defined. And finally, at the quantitative level, metrics supporting answering these questions should be specified. Our approach provides support for the quantitative level. Additionally, it can be used to aggregate information to the upper levels, if an aggregation mechanism is known. Discussion of issues related to the purpose of metrics and their validation [1] is out of scope of this paper.

Variety of specification languages. Different formal or programming languages were used to specify metrics. In academic approaches the following different notations were used, e.g. Z notation [8], XQuery [9], and SQL+Java [10]. The same diversity can be observed in existing modeling tools. For example, in MagicDraw UML[1] metrics are hard–coded in Java, in SDMetrics[2], a proprietary language is used, and in UMLAudit[3], models are converted into database tables. Even though preciseness can be guaranteed when using these approaches, in our opinion they can not guarantee portability. Moreover, metrics definitions are hard to maintain and keep up to date with evolving UML specification.

Advantages of OCL usage. Object Constraint Language (OCL, [11]) 2.x is a query language, i.e. it has the *expressiveness* required by relational algebra. Thus, it enables precise selection of required elements or properties. OCL can express all mathematical operations required for metrics definitions (e.g. sum, average, and even square root, e.g. defined based on Babylonian method). The scalability of the approach is the question of capabilities and performance of used OCL tools. And currently OCL tools provide quite good performance of OCL evaluation after model loading and an initial parsing [12]. The tool support enables metrics evaluation and testing for their correctness. Defining metrics in a *standard language* enables their usage in any UML tool with an OCL interpreter (for the appropriate version of the standard). Another advantage is that metrics are defined at the same *abstraction level* as models. Alternatively to OCL, the Query/View/Transformation (QVT) standard can be considered. This would not significantly differ from usage of OCL, as QVT is based on OCL. The disadvantage of QVT is weaker tool support for this language.

Formalisation of metrics in OCL. As the first attempt [13] metrics were created as additional operations in the UML 1.3 metamodel and expressed as OCL conditions. As OCL 2.0 was published, another approach [14,15] was proposed where metric definitions were decoupled from the metamodel. For this approach a

---

[1] MagicDraw—UML Designing Tool from No Magic, http://www.magicdraw.com/
[2] SDMetrics—Software Design Metrics tool for UML, http://www.sdmetrics.com/
[3] UMLAudit—Auditing a UML Model, http://www.softeam.com/

prototypic implementation was made based on Octopus[4]. Another tool, MOVA[5], provides a collection of predefined metrics and users can additionally write and execute their own metrics using the OCL editor [16]. OCL is used to define metrics in a commercial UML tool, Borland Together[6]. There are several more approaches successfully using OCL to define metrics[7]. All of them are complementary to our work and we plan their successive integration into our project.

Disadvantages of OCL usage. The *low social acceptance* of OCL is a critical issue. It is believed that OCL is hard to use, learn and teach. It has been shown, e.g. [17], that in general, it is a *difficult, error–prone and time–consuming task* for practitioners to define OCL expressions. Moreover, *OCL expressions are often unnecessarily hard to read* [18], UML/OCL models may be *difficult to understand and evolve, particularly when constraints containing complex or duplicate expressions are present* [19]. Additionally, difficulties with teaching OCL were reported in [20]: *the professional programmers usually do not like it: it looks like a programming language, but it is not; it has first order logic semantics, but it does not look like it.*

Problem Statement. UML metrics should be defined at the same abstraction level as models, in a non–ambiguous manner that enables their exchange via a standardised language. In our opinion, the best candidate fulfilling these criteria is OCL. It has been successfully used in several approaches, e.g. [13,14,15,16]. Unfortunately, the usage of UML metrics defined in OCL did not reach a broader acceptance in practice. We suppose that this is due to the low social acceptance of OCL. As the intention of the project was to analyze the development method available in our tool, but not the tool itself, we do not provide any comparison with existing OCL engines. For a comparison we refer to [21].

Proposed Solution. In this paper, we propose a method for systematic development of precise and portable metrics using OCL. To increase acceptance of OCL we use our extensions for modularisation, testing and documentation [22]. With our extensions integrated into a tool–supported systematic development process [23], even OCL novice users may achieve good results. Moreover, it is important that metrics are portable and available[8] to assist evolution of metrics involving multiple contributors.

Structure. To illustrate our approach we will start with a presentation of an example metric (Section 2). Next, we will present the project with 26 UML metrics developed as a proof of concept (Section 3). Finally, we will give conclusions and present our future work (Section 4).

---

[4] Octopus—OCL Tool for Precise Uml Specifications,
http://octopus.sourceforge.net/
[5] MOVA—A Tool for Modeling, Measuring and Validating UML Class Diagrams,
http://maude.sip.ucm.es/mova/
[6] Borland Together—http://conferences.embarcadero.com/article/33187/
[7] A comprehensive list of papers related to metrics can be found at
http://www.monperrus.net/martin/bibtexbrowser.php?bib=metrics.bib
[8] Currently our project is available on request, as we want to keep track of its users.

2 Example Metric: Number of Local Methods (NOM)

Below we will present our idea on an example of Number Of local Methods (NOM) metric. At first we will discuss its original definition, next how it is defined in OCL, and finally how it can be used in model analysis.

Original Definition of NOM. In [24] a set of metrics was proposed to measure different internal attributes such as coupling, complexity and size. These metrics were used to measure Classic–Ada designs and source code. They found that the maintenance effort could be predicted from the values of these metrics. We will take one of them as a running example to explain our approach.

Definition 1 (NOM). *Number Of local Methods provides the number of methods defined in a class. [24]*

Definition 1 seems to be precise, but it states nothing about the visibility of the methods. When taking a closer look at the intention of this metric in [24], it was proposed as *a class interface increment metric to indicate the operation property of a class*. From this usage intention it could be deduced that only public methods should be taken into account. On the other hand, in later work [25], another metric for number of local methods metric (NLM) was proposed, where only public methods were taken into account. For our running example we will assume NOM to count all the methods, as opposed to NLM with public methods only. As Definition 1 mentions methods *defined* in the class (as opposed to the declared ones), we will take overwritten methods into account, too. For the sake of simplification, we treat overloaded methods as same.

It can be seen that even on this simple example informal definition may lead to impreciseness. In general, selection of appropriate elements or properties of a considered element is a weak point of informal definitions. Below we will provide an OCL definition of NOM that overcomes this weakness.

OCL Definition of NOM. In our approach we follow the principle of modularization and split more complex definitions into functionality chunks that are reused by other definitions. Following this principle we obtained four definitions leading to the NOM metric specification.

A: getInheritedMemberOperations returns the set of all inherited members of the context class which are of type operation.

B: getAllInheritedOperations returns the subset of A excluding operations which are locally defined (overwritten).

C: getLocalMethods returns the set of all operations excluding elements of B, i.e. only locally defined operations.

D: NOM returns the size of C, i.e. number of locally defined methods.

Listing 1.1 shows all required OCL definitions and Fig. 1 depicts dependencies between them. Additionally, it is shown where the definitions were reused in the whole project (Section 3). As can be seen all four OCL definitions related to NOM are at least twice directly called. Their reuse is even higher, as neither indirect calls nor potential usages, described below, are shown in the diagram.

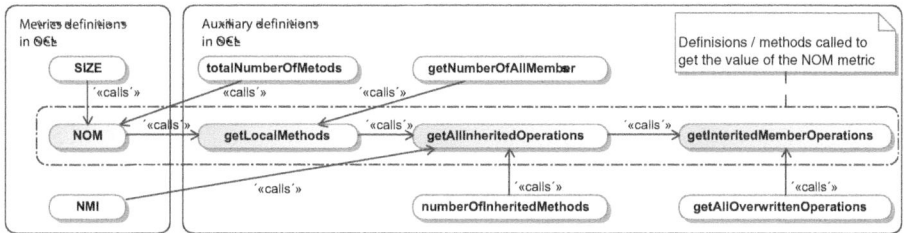

Fig. 1. OCL definitions used to specify the NOM metric (in the middle, in dark) and their direct calls by OCL definitions related to other metrics (in white)

```
1   context Class
    /* ---- DEFINITION A ---------------------------------------- */
3   def getInheritedMemberOperations:
        getInheritedMemberOperations() : Set(NamedElement) =
5           self.inheritedMember-> select(ne: NamedElement |
                ne.oclIsTypeOf(Operation))
7   /* ---- DEFINITION B ---------------------------------------- */
    def getAllInheritedOperations:
9       getAllInheritedOperations() : Set(NamedElement) =
            getInheritedMemberOperations()
11          -> select(op: Operation |
                not self.getOperations().name->includes(op.name))
13          -> asSet()
    /* ---- DEFINITION C ---------------------------------------- */
15  def getLocalMethods:
        getLocalMethods() : Set(String) =
17          self.getAllOperations().name->asSet()
            - (getAllInheritedOperations().name->asSet())
19  /* ---- DEFINITION D ---------------------------------------- */
    def NOM:
21      NOM() : Integer = getLocalMethods()->size()
```

Listing 1.1. Definitions required to formalise NOM. In the listing, the following formatting is used: italic font for user definitions, sans serif font for UML metamodel operations and properties, bold and normal fonts for OCL keywords and operations.

Use of NOM in Model Analysis. The metrics usage scenario is as follows. Initially, a metric is formalised in OCL. For the metric, a method, optionally with auxiliary methods, is defined in a given context, usually a class or a model, and returning a number. Before methods are used, they have to be tested [22].

In Fig. 2, we show related concepts from two perspectives: linguistic and ontological. From the linguistic point of view we have elements from the standards (constraints [4] and definitions [11]) and the extended OCL (queries and tests [22]). From the ontological point of view, in the domain of measurement, we have metrics, thresholds, collections and model queries. We will explain them using a series of examples.

From the calculation point of view metrics can be classified into *basic metrics* directly calculated based on a given model (e.g. NOM) and *derived metrics* calculated based on other metrics. For calculating simple ratios, used metrics should have the same context. A derived metric can have either the same context

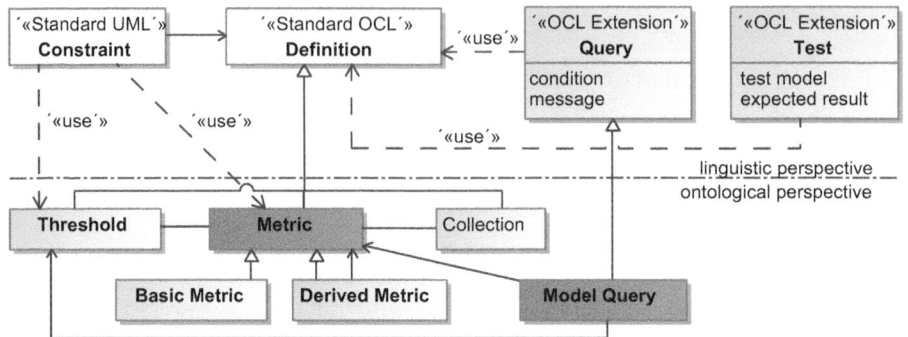

Fig. 2. Overview of specification concepts. Elements stereotyped with ≪Standard OCL≫ and ≪Standard UML≫ are from the OMG standards [11,4] whereas elements stereotyped with ≪OCL Extension≫ are our pragmatic extensions [22]. Elements without stereotypes are used to explain concepts related to the measurement domain.

as a basic metric or a broader context, for example extended from class to package. Metrics with enlarged scope can be used to investigate balance between larger system components.

Example 1. NOM is calculated in the class context, in the package context we can calculate package total NOM (PTNOM) as the sum of NOM for all classes in the package. Next, we can calculate package average NOM as $PANOM = PTNOM/NC$, where NC is the number of classes in the context package.

For a metric, upper and lower *thresholds* can be defined. These thresholds may be set based on statistical data from previous projects, from the current project or arbitrarily set by a chief designer. A metric together with its threshold(s) can be used in a constraint.

Example 2. The lower threshold for NOM[9] can be set to 4 and the upper one to 15 resulting in the following constraint: $NOM \geq 4\ and\ NOM \leq 15$.

Different threshold settings can be specific for particular design phases and used as warnings and errors indicators. Configurations of thresholds can be saved as OCL libraries [22], therefore no definitions need to be rewritten.

Example 3. In the design phase, the lower threshold for NOM can be ignored (i.e. set to 0) and the upper one set to 25. In the code generation phase, they can be set to 4 and 10, respectively. A parametrised constraint can be expressed as $NOM \geq NOMmin\ and\ NCM \leq NOMmax$, where $NOMmin$ and $NOMmax$ are thresholds for an appropriate configuration library. Moreover, 10 can define a warning threshold and 15 an error one, where for the warning a query can be used and for the error a constraint.

---

[9] This and following thresholds are taken from [3].

Having a set of metrics, it is easy to build more complex expressions on top of them. We can define *collections* with model elements filtered based on metrics and thresholds. Next, we can present either information about single elements or aggregated information on a collection. We can use collections to build filters identifying design disharmonies [3] or to obtain statistics.

Example 4. We can detect packages with classes containing too few or too many methods. We can identify a package with the highest number of classes with NOM outside the desired range. We can also define statistics on classes and methods to obtain a set of tuples with a class and its NOM metric value.

Finally, definitions can be used in informative and conditional *model queries*. Using thresholds, conditional queries can be defined. If and only if a class does satisfy the constraint within a query an appropriate message is shown.

Example 5. NOM can be used in an informative query, to show a human readable message, e.g. *Class C1 has 3 methods*. A conditional query for NOM can be defined to show a message only if the value of NOM is not in the range defined by the thresholds.

Model queries can incorporate all types of definitions. A text message in a query is the simplest example of result presentation. If an aggregation algorithm is known, metrics results can be propagated to the upper levels of a GQM model. Based on metrics and model queries, evaluation result reports with charts can be generated. In the next section, we will present our OCL project with a series of metrics.

3 OCL Project with UML Metrics

In this section we will present the OCL project we developed as a proof of concept to show that OCL metrics can be written by semi–skilled OCL developers, OCL expressions can be reused and to see how our method and tool is perceived by users. We start with a description of project settings. Next we present the development process and the environment that were used. And finally we show selected project statistics and feedback from participants.

Project Settings. The OCL project with UML metrics was developed in the Model Engineering (ME) course that took place in the summer semester 2009 at the University of Innsbruck. The course was in the **master program**, thus the participating students were already skilled developers. And as the course was optional, the participants were ambitious and interested in deepening their knowledge in the model engineering domain.

Each of the **12 students** enrolled in ME and **one teacher** (the author) developed two metrics. Students were novices to OCL. In the previous courses they were taught example OCL expressions but they had no hands–on experience in writing OCL, especially at the metamodel level. In ME, prior to the project, they had 3 hours of lectures with practical exercises at the user model level.

Table 1. UML class diagram metrics defined within the project and references to their definition sources taken from [5] ([Li93b] is [24] of this paper)

type	abr.	name / description	source
quantity	NCM	Number of class methods in a class	[Loren94]
	NCV	Number of class variables in a class	[Loren94]
	NIM	Number of methods defined for class' instances	[Loren94]
	NMA	Number of methods defined in a subclass	[Loren94]
	NMI	Number of methods inherited	[Loren94]
	NMO	Number of methods overridden	[Loren94]
	NOM	Number of local methods	[Li93b]
	PIM	Public instance methods	[Loren94]
	SIZE2	Number of attributes + number of local methods	[Li93b]
size	DSC	Total number of classes in the design	[Bansi02]
complexity	AAPM	Average parameters per method	[Loren94]
	AIF	Attribute inheritance factor	[Brito94]
	ANA	Average number of ancestors	[Bansi02]
	DAC	Number of attributes of type defined by another class	[Li93b]
	DAC'	Number of different classes used as types of attributes	[Li93b]
	DAM	Data access metric	[Bansi02]
	DCC	Direct class coupling	[Bansi02]
	DIT	Depth of inheritance tree	[Chida94]
	MAM	Member access metric	[Bansi02]
	MaxDIT	Maximum depth of inheritance tree	[Chida94]
	MIF	Method inheritance factor	[Brito96a]
	NOC	Number of children	[Chida94]
	NOH	Number of hierarchies	[Bansi02]
	OA5	Average of the number of class's direct dependencies	[March98]
	OA6	Standard deviation for OA5	[March98]
	SIX	Specialization index	[Loren94]

The project had two **iterations** and students could work in **teams**. Working versions of metrics were stored in a subversion repository and available to all developers. After the first iteration, 13 metrics were released, i.e. all developers could use or modify them. Students were encouraged to test, bug fix and reuse their own and other students' released definitions and libraries. Moreover, working in teams enabled cooperation before official releases.

We developed OCL libraries with **26 UML class diagram metrics** self–selected from [5]. Self–selection of metrics might lead to selection of apparently easy metrics, but it promoted cooperation of students who selected related ones. These were mostly quantity and complexity metrics (Table 1).

Within the project, we used the following **standards**: UML 2.2 [4] and OCL 2.0 [11]. Moreover, we used the systematic development process and the SQUAM OCL tool described below.

Development Process. To increase the quality of the metrics' formalisation we used a systematic development process for OCL expressions. Within the process we used practices inspired by software development: user–defined OCL libraries, OCL unit tests and documentation. User–defined **OCL libraries** enable modularisation and reuse of expressions, as well as support of configuration settings. Usage of **OCL unit tests** increases semantic quality of OCL expressions. And finally, in–line **documentation** comments increase comprehension of OCL expressions, and thus make team work and maintenance easier. Additionally, HTML documentation was generated out of these comments. For more details about our extensions we refer to [22].

In the project we followed an **iterative process**. It started with selection of a metric, understanding its definition, as well as specifying and documenting required OCL expressions. In addition to the specification, test models have been defined and tests performed. Specification and testing was conducted iteratively, until a developer was convinced of the correctness of the metric and released it. For a detailed description of the process we refer to our prior work [23,26].

Development Environment. The SQUAM framework supports the OCL development process and generation of documentation. When the development process is finished our OCL extensions can be purged and a specification in standard OCL is available.

Fig. 3 depicts a screen shot from the OCL development process of the OCL project. An OCL project consists of the following folders:

- doc documentation generated out of self–documented libraries, it is organised in similar way to the analogous approaches (like JavaDoc);
- html additional documentation files used in doc;
- model in case of this project it consists of test models for metrics; and
- UMLmetrics OCL libraries with metrics definitions at the top level and auxiliary definitions in the helperLibrary folder.

More information about the tool can be found on–line at http://squam.info/. For technical information we refer to the feature model[10], manual[11] and a series of demonstration screen casts[12].

Project Statistics. In the subsequent paragraphs we describe size, time effort, reuse degree and observations in the context of the metrics project.

Project Size. In the project, **51 libraries** were developed: 26 with metrics and 25 with auxiliary operations. The number of tests was 178, with an average of 3.5 tests per library and 2.7 tests per definition. Some definitions were not tested directly as they were intensively used by other definitions. Some tests were complex tests covering multiple test data sets. After release of a library by a developer, students could test it. In this process 4 errors were found and fixed. Moreover, defined tests were enormously useful in later manual conversion of the libraries from Ecore–based expressions into UML–based ones (to use UML metamodel methods only and no Ecore metamodel ones) and in restructuring of the project. The detailed project statistics are presented in Fig. 4.

---

[10] Feature models for selected OCL tools: http://ide4ocl.opoki.com/
[11] SQUAM manual: http://squam.info/ocleditor/manual/
[12] Flash demonstrations are available at http://squam.info/?cat=22

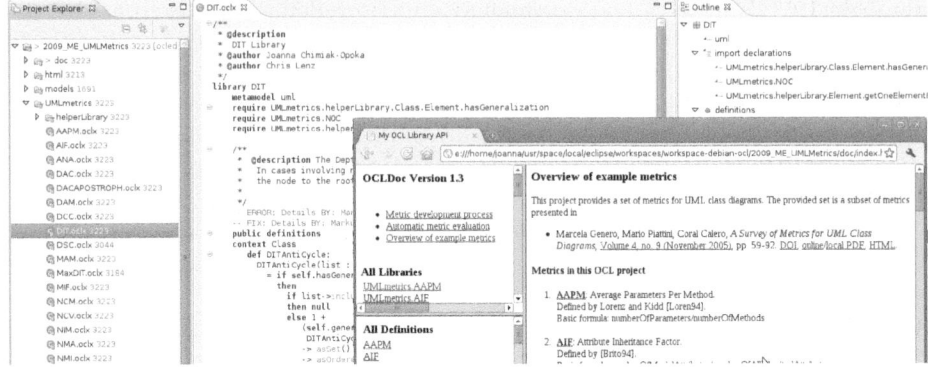

Fig. 3. OCL library development in the SQUAM framework (the background window) and generated documentation (the foreground window). In the background window, the following components can be seen (from left to right): the project explorer, an example library, and the overview of its structure. In the foreground window, the generated documentation can be seen: a list of additional pages (from html) and all libraries in the project (at the top–left corner), a list of definitions, queries and tests (at the bottom–left corner), and an additional page (on the right).

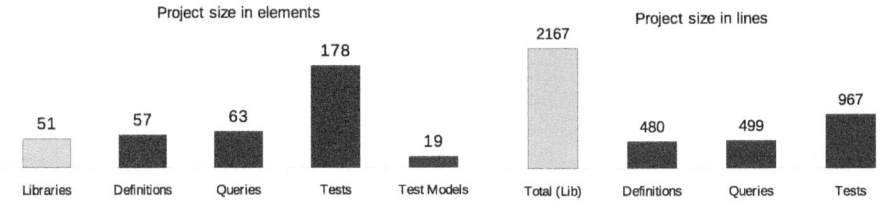

Fig. 4. Project statistics showing number and total size of artefacts in lines of OCL expressions (without comments)

Time Effort. Within the project the time effort was monitored by manual logging by developers. Our estimates may be artificially low because students tended to underestimate the time they spent on learning and development. The whole project took **8.6 person–days** including learning of the development environment and understanding informal definitions of metrics. In total 27% of the time was spent on learning. For a metric, on average 2:38h was required to learn the process and tool, to understand the metric, and to implement it. Development of definitions, queries, tests and test models took on average 1:56h per metric. The statistical analysis of definition specification time showed the median time equal to 0:15h in values ranging from 0:02h to 3:50h. The broad range can be explained by significant differences between complexity of definitions, skills of students and possible reuse. Details of time effort are presented in Fig. 5.

Reuse Degree. For 51 libraries, there were on average 1.4 imports per library, whereas for 26 metric libraries 1.7 imports. The most frequently used definition

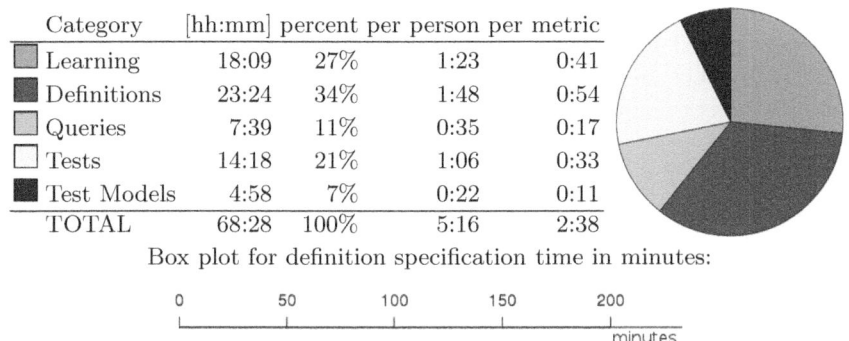

Fig. 5. Time effort measurement statistics

was a method to get one element by name. The library was directly imported by 11 other libraries and the method was called 21 times (in tests). Based on logged data, we estimated the benefit of reuse by comparison of time required to develop a set of all definitions with and without reuse. Our estimation was that the development time could decrease by over half (43% of time without reuse).

Observations. During the project we observed two critical issues related to preciseness and complexity.

The first one was related to *impreciseness of the original definition of metrics*. In a few cases, developers had to arbitrarily decide how to formalise a metric. This observation confirms the need for metrics formalisation, e.g. in OCL. In general, metrics described in the literature can be classified according to a number of possible semantically equivalent implementation in OCL: zero, one or many. If a metric can't be realized as OCL, then it is too ambiguous to be useful, if it realizes as exactly one OCL implementation, then it is useful, and if there is more than one possible OCL implementation, then it is ambiguous. Further the ambiguous metrics could be analysed from the natural language point of view to identify the areas where ambiguity creeps in. Next, a set of language patterns of the sources of ambiguity can be defined similarly to [27].

The second issue was related to *complexity of OCL expressions*. We can consider several sources of complexity. Some complexity is inherited from the underlying UML metamodel. In non–trivial cases the navigation via the metamodel structure is long and not intuitive. It was necessary to look up the semantics of properties of an inspected element in the UML specification to find out the correct navigation paths. This complexity is related to any object–oriented query language, where the original model structure is preserved. An example exception could be transformation to a relational data base and usage of the standard query language. The second type of complexity is caused by the necessity of type casting to access particular properties. For example, to access name of an Element it should be of type or subtype of NamedElement. This complexity is related to any (strongly) typed object–oriented query language. Additionally, there is also complexity related to OCL. In OCL 2.0, which was used in the project, there is no transitive closure implemented. Thus we had to use recursive calls of user defined methods to collect all possible navigation paths. For example, in Depth of the Inheritance Tree (DIT, Fig. 3) metric, to navigate to the bottom of the inheritance tree via generalisation relations we used recursive method calls. In OCL 2.3, the closure is provided, which enables simplification of expressions. And as tests are available, the conversion should be a feasible task.

Feedback from Participants. After completion of the project, students were asked to give their feedback in anonymous surveys on perceived knowledge gain, usability of OCL extensions and the SQUAM framework. Percentages presented in the subsequent paragraphs are based on the answers of 10 students who completed the survey.

Perceived knowledge gain. The students self–estimation was that they **learned a lot** about OCL ($3/10$ strongly agree + $5/10$ agree) and metrics they developed ($4/10$ + $5/10$). Moreover, $8/10$ believed that the gained knowledge has a practical character and they may capitalize on it in the future. The aforementioned statistics were also reflected in the free comments, such as: *Learned much about OCL, I hardly knew OCL before*; *I learned a lot of OCL and the metrics we used during defining them*; *I got a better understanding on how to build OCL statements, how to use them and actually how to work with OCL and UML*.

Perceived usability of the OCL extensions. Most of the students found the extensions for the OCL standard **useful and very useful**. The usefulness of libraries was positively evaluated by $9/10$ of students (very useful by $4/10$ + useful by $5/10$). Even a better score was obtained for queries ($7/10$ + $2/10$). Moreover, all the students found tests ($9/10$ + $1/10$) useful. There was no explicit question on documentation. Students also appreciated possibility of sharing expressions within the same team ($6/10$ + $2/10$) and with other teams ($4/10$ + $5/10$). Additionally, most of the students found the possibility of reusing/importing expressions important, e.g. *in my opinion this is a great idea /.../ in a bigger project this could be very useful*; *a great way to split complexity*.

Feedback on the SQUAM framework. In general there was a positive feedback on the tool, too. $7/10$ of students voted for the **positive overall impression**, satisfying performance and stability of the tool. During the project a few bugs were detected and some improvement ideas were suggested, like debugging or refactoring support. Several improvements are included in the current version.

4 Conclusions and Future Work

We proposed a methodology and a tool to define UML metrics in OCL. To obtain high quality metric specifications we used an iterative development process based on software development best practices. In this process we organised OCL expressions into libraries, tested OCL definitions for semantic correctness and documented them for better comprehension and maintenance.

As a proof of concept we developed 26 UML class diagram metrics with novice OCL users in relatively short time and with positive feedback from them. Within this project, reuse of definitions provides a potential of a significant reduction in OCL development time. Moreover, there was low imposed complexity of OCL expressions. Despite our observations may be project–specific and need to be supported by further empirical studies, they cast a positive light on efficient development of UML metrics in OCL.

It is worth noticing that OCL usage is not restricted to UML, thus in general, our approach can be used to develop metrics for arbitrary models from the Meta Object Facility (MOF, [28]) family. To apply our approach to an arbitrary model, appropriate metric definitions should be formalised in OCL in the context of the underlying metamodel. We used our approach in industrial projects in the business process [23] and model driven testing [26] domains. In these projects we developed OCL expressions for completeness, consistency and coverage criteria in the context of domain specific languages defined as UML profiles.

Recently, within the model engineering course we developed more metrics, including ones for state diagrams, too. We plan to extend and make the project public and to involve other contributors to build a useful public domain resource. The collection of metrics can be used in model reporting, visualisation and static analysis.

Acknowledgement. The contributors and owners of SQUAM framework are the University of Innsbruck and the arctis Softwaretechnologie GmbH. My gratitude goes to Hannes Moesl, Ekrem Arslan and Cornelia Haisjackl for their dedicated work in the SQUAM team and to all students who developed presented metrics. I would like to thank Birgit Demuth, Robert France, Jim Arlow, Ila Neustadt, Gunnar Schulze and Philipp Kalb for their reviews, ideas, constructive feedback and support.

References

1. Briand, L.C., Morasca, S., Basili, V.R.: An Operational Process for Goal-Driven Definition of Measures. IEEE Trans. Softw. Eng. 28, 1106–1125 (2002)
2. Fuggetta, A., Lavazza, L., Morasca, S., Cinti, S., Oldano, G., Orazi, E.: Applying GQM in an Industrial Software Factory. ACM Trans. Softw. Eng. Methodol. 7, 411–448 (1998)
3. Lanza, M., Marinescu, R., Ducasse, S.: Object-Oriented Metrics in Practice. Springer-Verlag New York, Inc., Secaucus (2005)
4. OMG: OMG Unified Modeling LanguageTM (OMG UML), Superstructure. version 2.2 (2009) http://www.omg.org/spec/UML/2.2/Superstructure/PDF
5. Genero, M., Piattini, M., Calero, C.: A survey of Metrics for UML Class Diagrams. Journal of Object Technology 4(9), 59–92 (2005), http://www.jot.fm/contents/issue_2005_11/article1.html
6. Seidl, R., Sneed, H.: Modeling Metrics for UML Diagrams. The Magazine for Professional Testers, 12–20 (September 2010), http://www.testingexperience.com/

7. Basili, V.R., Caldiera, G., Rombach, H.D.: The Goal Question Metric Approach. In: Encyclopedia of Software Engineering, pp. 528–532. John Wiley and Sons, Chichester (1994)
8. Misic, V.B., Moser, S.: From Formal Metamodels to Metrics: An Object-Oriented Approach. In: Marie, R., Plateau, B., Calzarossa, M.C., Rubino, G.J. (eds.) TOOLS 1997. LNCS, vol. 1245, pp. 330–339. Springer, Heidelberg (1997)
9. El-Wakil, M., El-Bastawisi, A., Riad, M., Fahmy, A.: A Novel Approach to Formalize Object-Oriented Design Metrics. In: Proc. Conf. Evaluation and Assessment in Software Eng., EASE 2005 (2005)
10. Harmer, T.J., Wilkie, F.G.: An Extensible Metrics Extraction Environment for Object-Oriented Programming Languages. In: Proc. of the Int. Conf. on Software Maintenance (2002)
11. OMG: Object Constraint Language. OMG Available Spec. Version 2.0 (May 2006), http://www.omg.org/spec/OCL/2.0/
12. Chimiak-Opoka, J., Felderer, M., Lenz, C., Lange, C.: Querying UML Models using OCL and Prolog: A Performance Study. In: Model Driven Engineering, Verification, and Validation, Lillehammer, Norway (April 2008) (presented at MoDeVVa)
13. Baroni, A.L., Braz, S., Abreu, F.B.E., Portugal, N.L.: Using OCL to Formalize Object-Oriented Design Metrics Definitions (July 15, 2002)
14. McQuillan, J.A., Power, J.F.: Towards the Re-usability of Software Metric Definitions at the Meta Level. In: PhD Workshop of the 20th European Conf. on Object-Oriented Programming (2006) (position paper)
15. McQuillan, J., Power, J.: A Definition of the Chidamber and Kemerer Metrics suite for UML. Technical report, National University of Ireland (2006)
16. Clavel, M., Egea, M., Silva, V.T.D.: Model Metrication in MOVA: A Metamodel-Based Approach using OCL (2007) (manuscript published on-line)
17. Ackermann, J.: Fallstudie zur Spezifikation von Fachkomponenten. In: Turowski, K. (ed.) Workshop Modellierung und Spezifikation von Fachkomponenten, Bamberg, Deutschland, pp. 1–66 (2001)
18. Vaziri, M., Jackson, D.: Some Shortcomings of OCL, the Object Constraint Language of UML. In: Li, Q., et al. (eds.) TOOLS (34), pp. 555–562. IEEE Computer Society, Los Alamitos (2000)
19. Correa, A.L., Werner, C., de Oliveira Barros, M.: An empirical study of the impact of OCL smells and refactorings on the understandability of OCL specifications. In: Engels, G., Opdyke, B., Schmidt, D.C., Weil, F. (eds.) MODELS 2007. LNCS, vol. 4735, pp. 76–90. Springer, Heidelberg (2007)
20. Moisan, S., Rigault, J.-P.: Teaching object-oriented modeling and UML to various audiences. In: Ghosh, S. (ed.) MODELS 2009. LNCS, vol. 6002, pp. 40–54. Springer, Heidelberg (2010)
21. Chimiak-Opoka, J., Demuth, B., Awenius, A., Chiorean, D., Gabel, S., Hamann, L., Willink, E.: Ocl tools report based on the ide4ocl feature model (2011) (presented at OCL Workshop, to appear in ECEASST)
22. Chimiak-Opoka, J.: OCLLib, OCLUnit, OCLDoc: Pragmatic Extensions for the Object Constraint Language. In: Schürr, A., Selic, B. (eds.) MODELS 2009. LNCS, vol. 5795, pp. 665–669. Springer, Heidelberg (2009)
23. Chimiak-Opoka, J., Agreiter, B., Breu, R.: Bringing Models into Practice: Design and Usage of UML Profiles and OCL Queries in a showcase. In: Targamadze, A., et al. (eds.) Proc. of the 16th Int. Conf. on Information and Software Technologies, IT 2010, Kaunas, Lithuania, Technologija, April 2010, pp. 265–273 (2010)

24. Li, W., Henry, S.: Object–Oriented Metrics that Predict Maintainability. Journal of Systems and Software 23(2), 111–122 (1993)
25. Li, W.: Another Metric Suite for Object-Oriented Programming. J. Syst. Softw. 44, 155–162 (1998)
26. Felderer, M., Chimiak-Opoka, J., Zech, P., Haisjackl, C., Fiedler, F., Breu, R.: Model Validation in a Tool–based Methodology for System Testing of Service–oriented Systems. Int. Journal On Advances in Software (to appear, 2011)
27. Arlow, J., Neustadt, I.: Secrets of Object Oriented Analysis. John Wiley & Sons, Inc., New York (2009)
28. OMG: Meta-Object Facility (MOF)—Spec. of version 2.0 (January 2006), http://www.omg.org/

Modeling Model Slicers*

Arnaud Blouin[1], Benoît Combemale[1], Benoit Baudry[1], and Olivier Beaudoux[2]

[1] IRISA/INRIA, Triskell Team, Rennes, France
{ablouin,bcombemale}@irisa.fr, benoit.baudry@inria.fr
[2] GRI-ESEO, Angers, France
olivier.beaudoux@eseo.fr

Abstract. Among model comprehension tools, model slicers are tools that extract a subset from a model, for a specific purpose. Model slicers are tools that let modelers rapidly gather relevant knowledge from large models. However, existing slicers are dedicated to one modeling language. This is an issue when we observe that new domain specific modeling languages (DSMLs), for which we want slicing abilities, are created almost on a daily basis. This paper proposes the Kompren language to model and generate model slicers for any DSL (*e.g.* software development and building architecture) and for different purposes (*e.g.* monitoring and model comprehension). Kompren's abilities for model slicers construction is based on case studies from various domains.

1 Introduction

Model slicing is a model comprehension technique inspired by program slicing [16]. This consists in extracting a subset of a model, called a *slice*. A slice has different forms depending on its purpose. For example, when trying to understand a large class diagram, it can help to extract the smallest strongly connected graph that is the subset of the class diagram that represents all dependencies of a particular class of interest. On the other hand for another comprehension purpose, one might want a slice that is closer to what a semantic zoom could provide [4], *e.g.* provide a flat view of all references and attributes inherited by a class of interest.

There has been previous work on the definition of model slicers. For example, [10] proposed model slicers for UML class and state diagrams. However, all existing model slicers are dedicated to extracting one form of slice from models that conform to a specific metamodel. In times when new domain specific modeling languages (DSMLs) appear regularly to improve productivity and increase the adoption of model-driven engineering, this becomes an issue: on one hand it is not convenient to develop slicers from scratch for every new DSML; on the other hand these DSMLs will provide full expected benefits for productivity only if they are supported by the same analysis and comprehension tools as general purpose languages. Thus, it is necessary to develop a generative approach that will automatically build model slicers for new metamodels.

---

* This work is partially supported by the EU FP7-ICT-2009.1.4 Project N°256980, NESSoS: Network of Excellence on Engineering Secure Future Internet Software Services and Systems.

In this paper we propose Kompren[1], a DSML to model model slicers for a particular domain (captured in a metamodel). We learn from existing model slicers, as well as from practical experiences that require the extraction of sub parts out of models. This learning phase leads to the different features of the Kompren language. Kompren mainly allows the selection of classes and properties in an input metamodel. By default, the model slicer generated out of these elements will be such that it builds slices that contain all instances of the selected classes and properties, plus all necessary elements to make the slice a valid instance of the input metamodel. Kompren also offers a set of language features to generate model slicers that can still be parameterized in order to process the model slice for a specific purpose. These different characteristics of Kompren aim at achieving two goals for our generative approach: automatically build model slicers for any DSML; have model slicers that can extract different forms of slices, depending on the purpose of the slice.

The contributions of this paper are the following:

- a language to model model slicers for any metamodel
- a compiler that automatically generates model slicers
- demonstrations of the language expressiveness over three illustrative cases.

In section 2 we introduce several motivating scenarios that illustrate the various forms of model slices that must be generated when analyzing models in various languages. Section 3 introduces the overview of building model slicers with the Kompren language. Section 4 presents the Kompren language: its metamodel, compiler and concrete syntax. Section 5 demonstrates the expressiveness of Kompren on three illustrative cases. Section 6 discusses related work and section 7 concludes this work.

2 Heterogeneous Use Cases of Model Slicing

The classical use of model slicing consists in extracting sub-models from models by keeping conformance rules. However, as shown in the motivating use cases below model comprehension also requires extracting models which do not satisfy conformance. Still, this extraction can rely on model slicing mechanism.

Use case 1: Model operation analysis. Given a model operation on a large metamodel MM_1, developers want to get the *effective* metamodel MM_2 used by the operation such that $MM_2 \subset MM_1$. For instance, when defining a state machine flattening operation over the UML metamodel, only the UML class diagram and the UML state machine elements are used. This model operation must be analyzed to select MM_1 elements it uses and to get the effective metamodel MM_2 [12].

Use case 2: Semantic zooming on models. Understanding and manipulating large models require visualization techniques to provide meaningful navigation capabilities [15]. Semantic zooming is a Human-Computer Interaction (HCI) that can be applied for this purpose. In contrast to physical zooming that changes the size of objects, semantic zooming changes the type and meaning of information displayed by objects [4].

---

[1] https://www.irisa.fr/triskell/Softwares/protos/kompren/

For instance, as shown in Fig. 1a, semantically zooming on class inheritance extracts super-classes of a given class. We can notice that semantic zooming is different from model slicing for two reasons: the extracted slice does not necessarily conform to the metamodel and is not saved as a new model but used by HCI to perform semantic zooming.

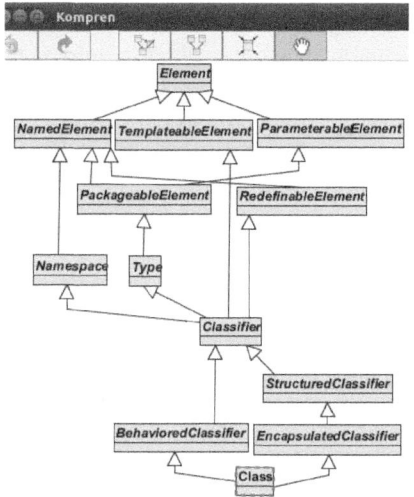
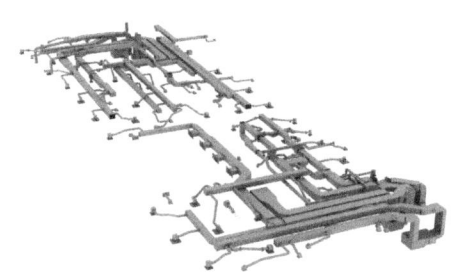

(a) Viewing Super-classes of the UML Class *Class*

(b) Complex Mechanical Model of a Building, extracted from [14]

Fig. 1. Examples of Semantic Zooms

Model slicing and semantic zooming are not limited to the computer science domain. In the design and construction industry, recent works proposed a model-driven approach for the interoperability of building models [14]. Such models are complex and need tools to extract information relevant to a particular concern and stakeholder. For example, Fig. 1b shows the mechanical model of a building. Mechanical model stakeholders may want to focus on the details of a given location or mechanism of the building.

Use case 3: Model Monitoring at runtime. Monitoring models at runtime is an important feature to control their evolution. For example, component-based model stakeholders may want to monitor only component activations among all the different possible modifications. Thus, dedicated tools need to extract only information relevant to component activation. Such information must be incrementally extracted to improve performance on large models.

3 Overview

Figure 2 provides an overview of the proposed approach to model model slicers. The core contribution of this paper is a modeling language dedicated to the construction of model slicers. The language is called *Kompren*. All the concepts and relations of *Kompren* are captured in a model slicer metamodel (MSMM at the top of figure 2). A model slicer model (MSM) expressed with *Kompren* refers to a set of classes and relations from the input *metamodel*. Instances of the referenced classes and relations will be selected for slicing in the input model. Consequently, MSMM points to elements Ecore to enable *Kompren* models to use elements from an *input metamodel*. MSMM also points to Kermeta, an action language used to specify the behavior of a slicer. *Kompren*'s compiler processes a *Kompren* model defined for an *input metamodel*, and automatically generates an actual *model slicer function* (MSF).

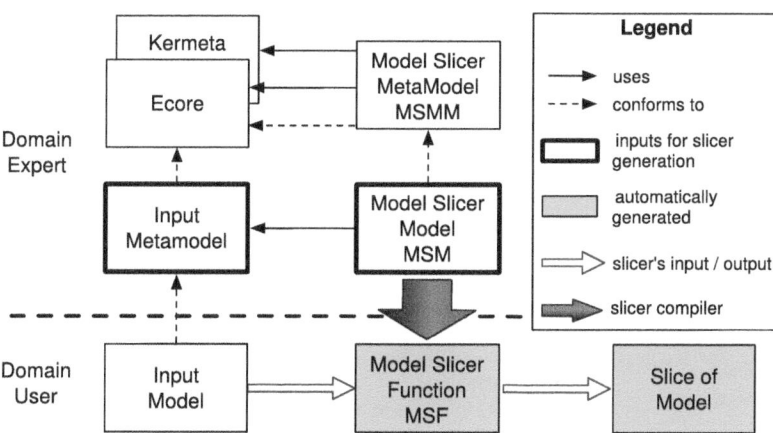

Fig. 2. Overview for Modeling Model Slicers with Kompren

The *Kompren* model can defined elements that are generated as parameters for the *model slicer function*. These parameters allow adjusting the slicing process to an actual instance of the *input metamodel*. Once the function's parameters are set, the *model slicer function* processes an *input model* to automatically extract a model slice from it.

This global approach is a two-level generation process: *Kompren*'s compiler generates a *model slicer function*, which in turn generates a model slice. From a methodological perspective, we also distinguish two roles for *Kompren* users:

- **Domain expert**. The domain expert knows the domain captured in the *input metamodel* and knows its concepts and relationships. This person is thus in charge of leveraging this domain in order to model one or several model slicers that are relevant for this domain. The *domain expert selects the elements in the metamodel* that will be processed by the model slicer.
- **Domain users** create models in the domain. These users, through their modeling activities can create large instances of the *input metamodel*. At some point they need to extract slices thanks to the *model slicer function*. These *users parameterize the model slicer according to their need and according to the values in the instance*.

4 Model-Driven Specification of Slicers

4.1 Expected Features for a Model Slicer

Basically a *Model Slicer Model* (MSM) enables the specification of classes and properties whose instances must be selected from a given *input model*. Input models can be either structural or behavioral. In both cases, their slicing consists in slicing the structure of their metamodel. We distinguish two generation modes of a *model slicing function* (MSF) from a MSM. Below, we detail and illustrate these two modes through examples based on the class diagram *input metamodel* (Fig. 3a) and the *input model* shown in Fig. 3b.

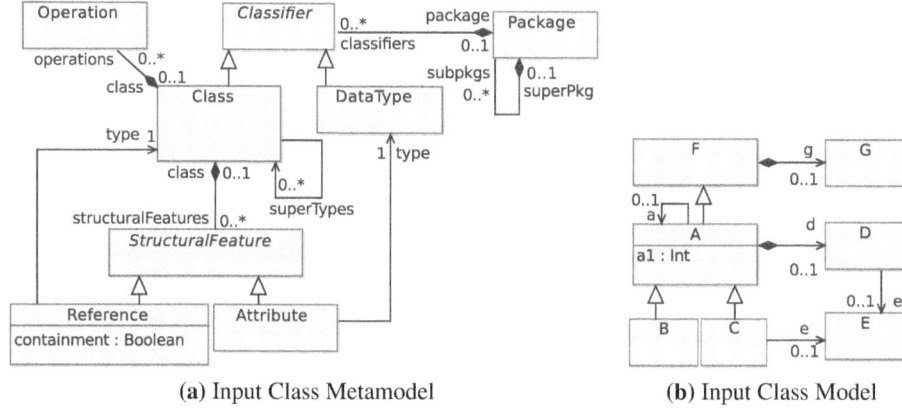

(a) Input Class Metamodel   (b) Input Class Model

Fig. 3. Class Model Example

- The *strict* mode (by default) generates a MSF that extracts model slices that satisfy all the structural constraints imposed by the input metamodel. Thus, by default a slice is a valid instance of the *input metamodel*.

  For example, Fig. 4a is a strict slice of Fig. 3b that conforms to the class diagram *input metamodel*.

- The *soft* mode relaxes the conformity constraint over model slices (ensured by the strict mode) in exchange of additional features for model slicer modeling. This mode is an answer to the usages illustrated in the motivating examples where slices are not instances of the *input metamodel*. In particular, the previous examples have motivated the need for the following features in the soft mode:
  - **Add an opposite property in the input metamodel.** For example, Fig. 4b is a slice of 3b that selects A and its subclasses. To ease the slicing of the *input model*, the MSM requires the opposite of the superTypes property in the *input metamodel*.
  - **Add constraints to filter the sliced elements.** For example, Fig. 4c is a slice of 3b that selects A and only its composite references. Similarly, Fig. 4d is a slice of 3b that selects B and its supertypes within a radius of 1.

- **Enlarge the slicing output format.** For example, instead of saving the sliced elements, they could be used to print their relative information. Other usages such as the notification of external tools must be also considered.
- **Automatically update slices.** On input model changes, the MSF automatically updates the slice.

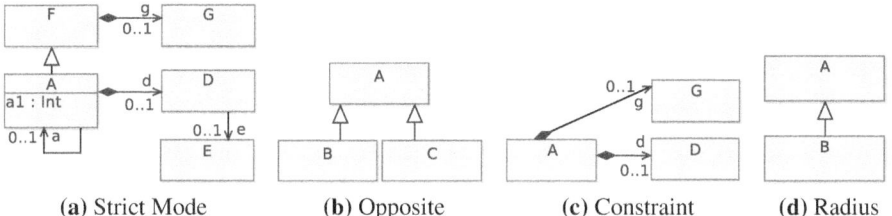

Fig. 4. Class Model Slices

4.2 Kompren Abstract Syntax

The metamodel shown in Fig. 5 describes the abstract syntax of Kompren. An instance of this metamodel is a *Model Slicer Model* (MSM). The main package is *slicer*. In this package, a *Slicer* is mainly composed of *SlicedElements*. These sliced elements correspond to the classes (*SlicedClass*) and the properties (*SlicedProperty*) of interest in the *Model Slicing Function* (MSF). All sliced elements belong to the *input metamodel* identified in the slicer by its URI (*uriMetamodel*). Optional *SlicedElements* (*i.e. isOption* is true) are options of the generated MSF. This lets the domain user choose whether an element is selected or not.

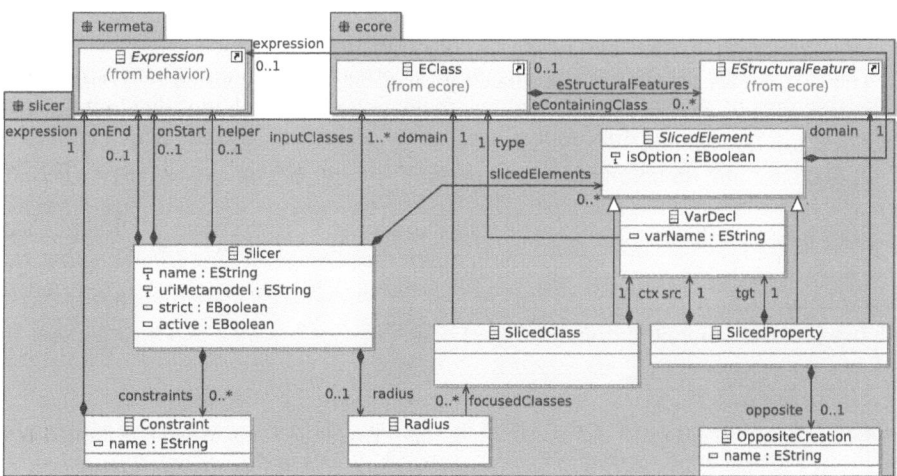

Fig. 5. Model Slicer metamodel

A *SlicedClass* refers to a class (*EClass*) in the *input metamodel* (*domain*). All instances of a referenced class in a given *input model* are selected by the MSF. Then *ctx* (contained in *SlicedClass*) serves as a temporary variable to successively manipulate each instance (*i.e.* an iterator). The type of this iterator (*type* in *VarDecl*) must correspond to the sliced class. This constraint can be formalized using OCL as follows:

```
1  context SlicedClass inv:
2    self.domain = self.ctx.type
```

Similarly, a *SlicedProperty* refers to a property (*EStructuralFeature*) in the *input metamodel*. All instances of a referenced property in an *input model* are selected by the MSF. The *src* and *tgt* iterators allow the manipulation of the property's source and target. The types of these iterators correspond to the source and the target class of the property:

```
1  context SlicedProperty inv:
2    (self.domain.eContainingClass = self.src.type) &&
3    (self.domain.eType = self.tgt.type)
```

In addition, a sliced property may define an *OppositeCreation* to precise the creation of an opposite property whose the role is given by the *name*.

We assume in this paper an *input metamodel* defined with an existing object-oriented metamodeling language. We use in our experiments the Ecore metamodeling language provided by the *Eclipse Modeling Framework*[2] whose elements are imported in the package *ecore*. In Ecore, a class and a property are identified by respectively an *EClass* and an *EStructuralFeature*. Another object-oriented metamodeling language could be easily considered in Kompren.

Moreover, the iterators on sliced elements (instances of the specified *SlicedClass* and *SlicedProperty*) allow the domain expert to express the expected behavior for each selected instance. The effect of the MSF on each selected instance is described as an expression using an action language. In our experiments, we use the action language of Kermeta [11] whose the corresponding metamodel is imported in the package *kermeta*. Another action language could be easily considered in Kompren.

The two modes previously introduced in Section 3 are supported by Kompren. By default, a MSF is generated according to the *strict* mode. By setting the attribute *strict* (in *Slicer*) to false, the MSF is generated according to the *soft* mode.

In that case, the remaining concepts in the Kompren metamodel are used to specify specific behaviors of the generated MSF. The expressions *onStart* and *onEnd* are used to add a particular behavior in the MSF, which are respectively applied before and after the visit of the *input model*. Expressions defined to bring executability to slicers may require classes provided by third party libraries, attributes or operations needed to the slicing process. Thus, the domain expert can specify an *helper* that will contain this information.

The *radius* and the *constraints* can be used to filter the sliced element in the *input model*. The *radius* precises in the MSM the *focusedClasses* for which the MSF should be limited to a selection within a given radius. The focused classes must be included in the sliced classes that can be formalized as follows:

---

[2] http://www.eclipse.org/modeling/

```
1  context Slicer inv:
2    not self.radius.oclIsUndefined() implies
3    self.slicedElements->select{c | c.isTypeOf(SlicedClass)
4    }->includeAll(self.radius.focusedClasses)
```

The value of the radius must be specified by the domain user as a parameter of the MSF. The *constraints* allow the domain expert to define a condition that must be respected to trigger the slicing of the element targeted by the condition.

The *inputClasses* precise the type of instances that the MSF will take as input to start the slicing.

Finally, the attribute *active* permits to specify if the MSF must be executed as a batch or an active process. By default, the generated MSF is a batch process executed a single time on the input model. By settings the attribute *active* to true, the generated MSF is executed a first time and then observes modifications applied on the input model in order to incrementally update the slice.

4.3 Concrete Syntax

A textual concrete syntax has been defined for Kompren allowing the domain expert to define a *Model Slicer Model* (MSM). As an example, the following listing shows the *active* and *soft* MSM *ClassModelSlicer* (*cf.* line 1), for the metamodel in Fig. 3a (*cf.* line 2). The classes of the instances used to launch the *Model Slicing Function* (MSF) are declared line 3.

Thereafter, line 4 specifies a sliced class while lines 5 to 8 specify sliced properties. An expression defined for the sliced class Class is described line 4 where *cl* refers to the context of the sliced class. An optional property is illustrated line 5 thanks to the keyword option. An opposite to a property is defined thanks to the keyword opposite as shown line 6 where *lowerTypes* is the name of the opposite.

Line 9 illustrates how to declare a radius based on Class to limit the selection in the *input model* by the MSF. The definition of a constraint consists in specifying a Kermeta boolean expression as shown line 10. Lines 11 to 13 illustrate the definition of the preprocessing, the post-processing and the helper of the slicer.

```
1  slicer active soft ClassModelSlicer {
2    domain: platform:/resource/classModel.ecore
3    input: Class
4    slicedClass: Class cl{ stdio.writeln(cl.name) }
5    slicedProperty: Class.superTypes option
6    slicedProperty: Class.superTypes opposite(lowerTypes)
7    slicedProperty: Class.structuralFeatures
8    slicedProperty: Reference.type
9    radius: Class
10   constraint: Reference.containment
11   onStart { stdio.writeln("Starting slicing") }
12   onEnd   { stdio.writeln("Ending slicing") }
13   helper  { /* Definition of the helper */ }
14 }
```

4.4 Semantic

As defined in Fig. 2, model slicer models (MSM) are compiled into model slicer functions (MSF). This compilation produces Kermeta programs composed of two parts. The first part augments the input metamodel with required information. These information are the opposites specified in MSMs and methods used to explore the input model. These methods are generated for the metamodel elements selected in MSMs. If the slicer is defined as strict, these methods are also generated for elements not selected in MSMs but required to assure the semantic properties.

The second part generates the slicer function. The preprocessing (*onStart*) and the post-processing (*onEnd*) methods and the Kermeta code corresponding to the helper are created. From the input classes, the radius and the constraints defined in MSMs are generated as parameters of the slicer function. For instance, the following Kermeta code illustrates such generation where: *launch* is the operation that starts the slicing; *inputClass:Class[0..*]* defines the *Class* instances used to launch the slicing; *radius:Integer* specifies the slicing radius; *composition:Boolean* is a constraint that declares if only composition references must be sliced.

```
operation launch(inputClass:Class[0..*], radius:Integer,
                composition:Boolean)
```

Once generated, the slicer function can be executed by calling the launch operation with its required parameters. The preprocessing is first executed. Then begins the exploration of the input model using the input instances given as parameter. Each of these instances is visited. Visiting an instance or a property consists in executing the associated behavior: for strict slicers, adding the sliced instance to a new model; for soft slicers, executing the corresponding Kermeta expression defined by the developer. Each selected property of the current visited class instance are then explored (if they satisfy the constraints defined in MSMs) to recursively explore their target class instance.

Starting at 0, a value is incremented on each visited class instance concerned by the radius. The slicing process thus stops when no elements can be sliced anymore or when this value is greater than the radius given as parameter. When the slicing has stopped, the post-processing is executed.

About *active* slicers, because Kermeta does not manage observability of Ecore models, we use the *ActiveKermeta* toolkit [3]. ActiveKermeta replaces Kermeta batch operations, such as *c.each{e|...}* that visits each element *e* of collection *c*, by active operations, such as *c.eachAdded{e | ...}* supplemented by *c.eachRemoved{e | ...}* that are respectively called when *e* is added or removed from *c*.

5 Validation

In this section, we apply our model slicing approach to three heterogeneous case studies illustrating the main usages that can be done using our approach.

5.1 Model Operation Analysis

Extracting static metamodel footprint for a model operation defined over a metamodel MM_1 (in our case the Kermeta metamodel) consists in extracting the elements of MM_1

used by the operations [5]. In this section, we use Kompren to model the footprint generator proposed by Jeanneret *et al.* [5] and the metamodel pruner proposed by Sen *et al.* [12]. The Kompren model is smaller than the initial model slicers: around 70 LoC have been needed (see details below) while the static metamodel footprinting and the metamodel pruner both required around 1200 Kermeta LoC. This use case illustrates the ability of Kompren to ease the slicer definition process.

The effective metamodel extraction is performed through two model slicers: a first slicer analyzes the model operation to extract the metamodel footprint, *i.e.* the list of MM_1 elements used by the operation; a second slicer uses this footprint to extract the effective metamodel from MM_1. The effective metamodel extraction could have been defined using a single slicer. We divided this operation into two slicers to separate the concerns and be modular.

The first slicer extracts the list of MM_1 elements used by the operation. Since this slice does not conform to MM_1, we model the slicer in *soft* mode (line 1). The model operation is implemented in Kermeta. Thus, it is an instance of the Kermeta metamodel MM_{op} and the slicer explores classes and properties of MM_{op} (lines 5 to 15). The result of the slicing function will be the list of classes used in the operation (line 4). This list is defined in the helper (line 17). By default all the classes, that can come from either MM_1 or MM_{op}, are explored. Because only the classes from MM_1 must be stored, a helper is defined to select them (lines 18 to 22).

```
1  slicer soft OperationStaticAnalysis {
2    domain: platform:/resource/kermeta.language.model/src/main/ecore/kermeta.ecore
3    input : kermeta.structure.ModelingUnit // The model operation to analyse.
4    slicedClass: kermeta.structure.ClassDefinition cd { addClassDefinition(cd) }
5    slicedProperty: kermeta.structure.ModelingUnit.packages
6    slicedProperty: kermeta.structure.Package.ownedTypeDefinition
7    slicedProperty: kermeta.structure.ClassDefinition.ownedOperation
8    slicedProperty: kermeta.structure.ClassDefinition.ownedAttribute
9    slicedProperty: kermeta.structure.Operation.ownedParameter
10   slicedProperty: kermeta.structure.TypedElement.type
11   slicedProperty: kermeta.structure.ParameterizedType.typeDefinition
12   slicedProperty: kermeta.structure.Operation.body
13   slicedProperty: kermeta.behavior.VariableDecl.type
14   slicedProperty: kermeta.behavior.Block.statement
15   //... 29 properties of MM_op are sliced.
16   helper {
17     reference metamodelClassesUsed : ClassDefinition[0..*]
18     reference inputMetamodel : ModelingUnit
19     //... Load of the input metamodel.
20     operation addClassDefinition(cd : ClassDefinition) : Void is do
21       if(inputMetamodel.contains(cd)) then metamodelClassesUsed.add(cd) end
22     end
23  }}
```

The second slicer, modeled as follows, uses the footprint computed by the first one. This slicer is modeled in *strict* mode (line 1) to create an output model that is a strict slice of the input metamodel MM_1 (specified line 2). This slicer slices all the classes (line 4) linked to the input classes by inheritance or properties (lines 10 to 12). All properties and operations of the class sliced are included (lines 5 to 9). Because *ClassDefinition* is linked to *Package* by a 1..1 reference, this relation and its target class must be sliced to extract a strict slice. Since we model in strict mode, the packages containing sliced elements are sliced even if *Package* is not modeled as a *slicedClass*. This mode also includes 1..*n* attributes of classes *ClassDefinition*, *Property* and *Operation*.

```
1  slicer strict MetamodelFootprintExtraction {
2    domain: platform:/resource/kermeta.language.model/src/main/ecore/kermeta.ecore
3    input : kermeta.structure.ClassDefinition
4    slicedClass: kermeta.structure.ClassDefinition
5    slicedClass: kermeta.structure.Property
6    slicedClass: kermeta.structure.Operation
7    slicedProperty: kermeta.structure.ClassDefinition.ownedAttribute
8    slicedProperty: kermeta.structure.ClassDefinition.ownedOperation
9    slicedProperty: kermeta.structure.Operation.ownedParameter
10   slicedProperty: kermeta.structure.TypedElement.type
11   slicedProperty: kermeta.structure.TypedDefinition.superType
12   slicedProperty: kermeta.structure.ParameterizedType.typeDefinition
13 }
```

5.2 Bringing Semantic Zoom to Model Visualization

Model slicing can be used to bring semantic zooming to model visualization. In this case, the slicer defines which classes and relations of the visualized model must be displayed in the user interface (UI). For example, the following code defines a slicer that slices Kermeta models. Because the goal of this slicer is to notify the UI about sliced elements, it is defined as *soft* (line 1). It takes as input instances of *ClassDefinition* (line 3) selected by users using the UI. As shown in Fig. 6, the UI displays classes, inheritances and properties. At the beginning of the slicing all these model elements are hidden (line 6). Then, when model elements are sliced, the UI is notified that they must be shown (lines 9, 11 and 14). At the end of the slicing, the UI is updated to perform the graphical changes (line 7). Some properties must be explored to access the instances to slice (lines 13 to 17). All these properties to slice are defined as optional. Thus, for each feature of the model visualizer (*e.g.* showing the inheritance tree of a selected class), developers can define which properties must be explored.

```
1  slicer soft kermetaSemanticZoom {
2    domain: platform:/resource/kermeta.language.model/src/main/ecore/kermeta.ecore
3    input: kermeta.language.structure.ClassDefinition
4    radius: kermeta.language.structure.ClassDefinition
5    constraint: kermeta.language.structure.Property.lower>0
6    onStart { extern ClassDiagramView.hideAllElements() }
7    onEnd   { extern ClassDiagramView.updateView()     }
8    slicedClass: kermeta.structure.ClassDefinition cd{
9      extern EntityView.showClass(cd) }
10   slicedClass: kermeta.structure.Property prop {
11     extern ReferenceView.showReference(prop.name, prop.owningClass,
12                                        prop.type.asType(Class).typeDefinition) }
13   slicedProperty: kermeta.structure.TypeDefinition.superType option src tar{
14     extern InheritanceView.showInheritance(src, tar.asType(Class).typeDefinition) }
15   slicedProperty: kermeta.structure.ParameterizedType.typeDefinition option
16   slicedProperty: kermeta.structure.ClassDefinition.ownedAttribute option
17   slicedProperty: kermeta.structure.TypedElement.type option
18 }
```

The UI shown in Fig. 6 provides a spinner that permits to define the radius effect of the slicing (defined line 4). The UI also provides a check-box called "With card 0".

This check-box permits to set if properties which lower cardinality equals 0 must be sliced or not (line 5). The graphical representation of the model and the widgets of the UI are defined separately from the slicer.

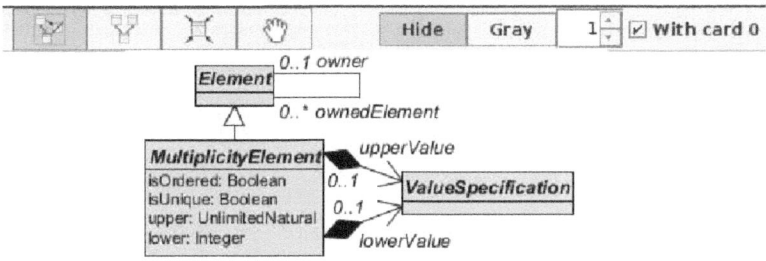

Fig. 6. Class Diagram Visualizer Providing Semantic Zooming Features

5.3 Monitoring Component-Based Models at Runtime

Our model slicing approach can also be used to slice models at runtime, *i.e.* the slicing process is no more a batch process but is sustained at runtime to re-evaluate model elements that change. For example, Kevoree is a component-based model that manages addition and removal of components at runtime[3]. These changes can be monitored to provide stakeholders with such information.

```
1  slicer active soft KevoreeComponentMonitoring {
2    domain: platform:/resource/kevoree/kevoree.ecore
3    input : kevoree.ContainerRoot
4    slicedClass: kevoree.ContainerNode
5    slicedClass: kevoree.ComponentInstance ci
6      { table.addComponent(ci) }
7      { table.removeComponent(ci) }
8    slicedProperty: kevoree.ContainerRoot.nodes
9    slicedProperty: kevoree.ContainerNode.components
10   helper {
11     require "platform:/resource/kermeta/ComponentTable.km"
12     attribute table: ComponentTable
13 }}
```

(a) Excerpt of the Kevoree Metamodel (b) The slicer model

Fig. 7. Model Slicer Model for Monitoring Kevoree Component Additions and Removals

Fig. 7a is the excerpt of the Kevoree metamodel related to component additions and removals. Fig. 7b gives the model slicer model (MSM) dedicated to the slicing at runtime of component additions and removals. In the Kevoree metamodel, activated components are contained into the composition *components* of class *ContainerNode*. The component model can contains several node containers (composition *nodes*). Thus,

---
[3] http://dist.kevoree.org/

these two compositions *components* and *nodes* are selected by the slicer (lines 8 and 9). Classes *ContainerNode* and *ComponentInstance* are defined as the classes to slice (lines 4 and 5). The input instances given to the active slicer are *ContainerRoot* instances (line 3). This MSM differs from the previous "batch" slicers in two points. Firstly line 1, the keyword *active* means that the generated slicer function must remain active by updating the sliced output model whenever the input model changes. Secondly, the attribute *table* (defined in the helper line 12) is managed throughout two subsequent blocks: similarly to batch slicers the first block defines how to update the table whenever a new component instance ci appears (line 6); the second block defines how to update the table whenever ci is removed (line 7).

6 Related Work

Although model slicing has been studied in literature, most of the inventoried approaches focus on a particular DSML. For instance, [6,2,10,9,13] focus on the slicing of UML models whereas [8] proposes the slicing of state-based models. Because of the diversity of DSMLs, our approach aims at being more generic to allow the specification of slicers for any DSML. Our generative approach aims at reducing the programmatic effort spent for the development of model slicers, while giving domain users the ability to customize the application of the MSF (*e.g.* radius).

We identified two kinds of output produced by the slicers of the current approaches. In the first case, the output is a model that conforms to the input metamodel, such as in [12,10,7]. In the second case, the output is a model that may be not conform to the input metamodel, such as in [5]. A key concern that our slicing proposal insists on is the ability for developers to define the kind of output they want. For example, a strict slicer will produce models that conform the input metamodel with respect to the model slicing definition. But we also identified several use cases, such as semantic zooming or model operation analysis, where the expected output is neither a model that conforms to the input metamodel nor even a model. Thus our slicing proposal permits developers to define soft slicers which output is customizable.

Androutsopoulos *et al.* [1] propose different finite state machine slicing algorithms. Their basic slicer removes a set of transitions to ignore and useless states from finite state machines. This algorithm can be performed using our approach by defining parameters that state the slicer not to slice transitions having given names. Their other algorithms extend the first one by removing untriggerable transitions and merging states having identical semantics. Our approach does not permit to define such slicers.

Kelsen *et al.* [7] propose an approach for decomposing models into sub-models to tame the complexity of large models. This approach has similarities with ours since they are both not dedicated to a unique DSML and they can extract sub-models of interest that still conforms to the input metamodel. However, their approach does not permit developers to specify the slicing process, *i.e.* to select which elements of the input models must be sliced, and is restricted to the strict model slicing usage.

Shaikh *et al.* [13] use model slicing for verification purpose. The goal of this approach is to check if an input UML model supplemented by OCL constraints has legal instances. OCL constraints are thus analyzed and interpreted to identify which model elements are constrained. If their application is dedicated to one of our use case (model operation analysis), such OCL analyzes and interpretation is much more complex than extracting types.

Lallchandani *et al.* [9] propose a slicing technique for UML architectural models. Even if the proposed approach is limited to UML architectural models, it uses slicing for different purposes such as regression testing and understanding large architectures.

Obeo Designer[4] offers the possibility to easily create graphical viewpoints on large models. The representation of a slice can be seen as a viewpoint. However, the tool is limited to visualization and does not address manipulation or serialization of the slices.

7 Conclusion

A number of recent work inspired by program slicing [16] have proposed operations that extract sub parts of models for different purposes [13,10,7,5]. These operations are extremely helpful to assist comprehension when building large models. With the growing adoption of domain-specific modeling, these model comprehension abilities should be available for any domain-specific modeling language. However, all existing model slicing approaches are dedicated to one modeling language and one form of slice.

In this work we analyze needs for model slicing to precisely identify expected features for domain-specific model slicers. The major contribution of this paper is the *Kompren* language to model a model slicer for a domain-specific metamodel. We develop a two-level generative approach on the basis of Kompren: Kompren's compiler processes Kompren models to automatically generate an actual model slicer; this slicer can in turn automatically extract model slices from domain-specific models.

This paper presents the details of Kompren's features, abstract and concrete syntax and compiler. We also demonstrate Kompren's expressiveness through three different cases that aim at slicing three different forms of slices in three different domains. In particular we model the slicers defined by Jeanneret *et al.* [5] and by Sen *et al.* [12] and show that the Kompren models (*a.k.a.* model slicer models) are much smaller and easier to understand and evolve than the original slicers.

Following our evaluation on the expressiveness of our language, we plan to experiment the scalability of our approach. It could be interesting to explore MSM debugging as well.

References

1. Androutsopoulos, K., Binkley, D., Clark, D., Gold, N., Harman, M., Lano, K., Li, Z.: Model projection: Simplifying models in response to restricting the environment. In: International Conference on Software Engineering, ICSE 2011 (2011)
2. Bae, J.H., Lee, K., Chae, H.S.: Modularization of the UML metamodel using model slicing. In: Proc. of the IEEE Inter. Conference on Information Technology, pp. 1253–1254 (2008)
3. Beaudoux, O., Blouin, A., Barais, O., Jézéquel, J.-M.: Active operations on collections. In: Petriu, D.C., Rouquette, N., Haugen, Ø. (eds.) MODELS 2010. LNCS, vol. 6394, pp. 91–105. Springer, Heidelberg (2010)

---
[4] http://obeo.fr/pages/obeo-designer

4. Herman, I., Melançon, G., Marshall, M.S.: Graph visualization and navigation in information visualization: A survey. IEEE Trans. on Visual Comput Graph 6, 24–43 (2000)
5. Jeanneret, C., Glinz, M., Baudry, B.: Estimating footprints of model operations. In: International Conference on Software Engineering, ICSE 2011 (2011)
6. Kagdi, H., Maletic, J.I., Sutton, A.: Context-free slicing of uml class models. In: Proc. of the IEEE International Conference on Software Maintenance, pp. 635–638 (2005)
7. Kelsen, P., Ma, Q., Glodt, C.: Models within models: Taming model complexity using the sub-model lattice. In: Giannakopoulou, D., Orejas, F. (eds.) FASE 2011. LNCS, vol. 6603, pp. 171–185. Springer, Heidelberg (2011)
8. Korel, B., Singh, I., Tahat, L., Vaysburg, B.: Slicing of state-based models. In: Proc. of the IEEE International Conference on Software Maintenance, ICSM 2003 (2003)
9. Lallchandani, J.T., Mall, R.: A dynamic slicing technique for uml architectural models. IEEE Transactions on Software Engineering 99 (2010)
10. Lano, K., Kolahdouz-Rahimi, S.: Slicing of UML models using model transformations. In: Petriu, D.C., Rouquette, N., Haugen, Ø. (eds.) MODELS 2010. LNCS, vol. 6395, pp. 228–242. Springer, Heidelberg (2010)
11. Muller, P.-A., Fleurey, F., Jézéquel, J.-M.: Weaving executability into object-oriented meta-languages. In: Briand, L.C., Williams, C. (eds.) MoDELS 2005. LNCS, vol. 3713, pp. 264–278. Springer, Heidelberg (2005)
12. Sen, S., Moha, N., Baudry, B., Jézéquel, J.-M.: Meta-model pruning. In: Schürr, A., Selic, B. (eds.) MODELS 2009. LNCS, vol. 5795, pp. 32–46. Springer, Heidelberg (2009)
13. Shaikh, A., Clarisó, R., Wiil, U.K., Memon, N.: Verification-driven slicing of uml/ocl models. In: Proceedings of the IEEE/ACM International Conference on Automated Software Engineering, pp. 185–194. ACM, New York (2010)
14. Steel, J., Drogemuller, R., Toth, B.: Model interoperability in building information modelling. Software and Systems Modeling, 1–11 (2010)
15. Storey, M.A.D., Fracchia, F.D., Müller, H.A.: Cognitive design elements to support the construction of a mental model during software exploration. Journal of Systems and Software 44(3), 171–185 (1999)
16. Weiser, M.: Program slicing. In: Proceedings of the 5th International Conference on Software Engineering, pp. 439–449. IEEE Press, Los Alamitos (1981)

Morsa: A Scalable Approach for Persisting and Accessing Large Models*

Javier Espinazo Pagán, Jesús Sánchez Cuadrado, and Jesús García Molina

University of Murcia, Spain
{jespinazo,jesusc,jmolina}@um.es

Abstract. Applying Model-Driven Engineering (MDE) in industrial-scale systems requires managing complex models which may be very large. These models must be persisted in a scalable way that allows their manipulation by client applications without fully loading them.

In this paper we propose Morsa, an approach that provides scalable access to large models through load on demand; model persistence is supported by a NoSQL database. We discuss some load on demand algorithms and database design alternatives. A prototype that integrates transparently with EMF is presented and its evaluation demonstrates that it is capable of fully loading large models with a limited amount of memory. Moreover, a benchmark has been executed, exhibiting better performance than the EMF XMI file-based persistence and the most representative model repository, CDO.

Keywords: model persistence, scalability, large models.

1 Introduction

During the last decade, the growing maturity of Model-Driven Engineering (MDE) technologies is promoting their adoption by large companies [1][2], taking advantage of their benefits in terms of productivity, quality and reuse. However, applying MDE in this context requires industry-scale tools that operate with very large and complex models. One such relevant operation is model persistence and the corresponding access, which is typically supported by modeling frameworks. A well-known example of a modeling framework is EMF[3].

One critical concern for the industrial adoption of MDE is the *scalability* of tools when accessing large models. As noted by [4], *"scalability is what is holding back a number of potential adopters"*. Scalability may be tackled in different ways. One approach is the *modularization* of modeling languages [4] to keep models at a reasonable size. However, the complexity of large models makes it difficult to automatically divide them into parts that are easily accessible [5]. For example, code models extracted from a legacy system being modernized may not be properly modularizable because of the complexity

---

* This work is funded by the Spanish Ministry of Science (project TIN2009-11555) and Fundación Séneca (grant 14954/BPS/10).

of their interconnections, hence having a scalable model persistence solution would be mandatory [6]. In EMF models are usually stored in XMI files, which have to be parsed in order to build models in memory. The usual EMF approach consists of a SAX parser that fully reads an XMI file and builds the entire model in memory at once. This solution does not scale since large models may not be fully kept in memory, causing the parser to overflow the client. Therefore handling large models requires some mechanism that allows the client to load only the objects that it will use [5]. Model repositories are emerging as persistence solutions for large models, providing remote model access with advanced features such as concurrent access, transaction support and versioning; model repositories are discussed in Section 7. Currently, CDO is the most mature repository for EMF; however, it does not scale properly as shown in Section 8.

Another concern that arises when client applications access persisted models is *tool integration*. The integration between a persistence solution and any client must be transparent, that is, it must conform to the standard model access interface defined by the modeling framework (e.g. the Resource interface of EMF). Moreover, it would be convenient for a persistence solution not to require any preprocessing on the (meta)models in order to load or store them, e.g. requiring source code generation for the persisted (meta)models [8][9] .

In this paper we present Morsa, a model persistence solution aimed at achieving scalability in large model access. While other approaches use object-relational mappings [8], Morsa relies on a document-based NoSQL database to achieve server scalability; moreover, document-based NoSQL provides a more natural model persistence backend than object-relational mappings since, for example, many-to-many relationships are represented just as any other kind of feature, while object-relational-mappings require intermediate tables. Morsa handles client scalability using a load on demand mechanism supported by an object cache which is configurable with different policies. We discuss how these policies fit for common model traversals such as depth-first order and breadth-first order. We contribute a prototype implementation for EMF [10] that integrates transparently with client tools such as model transformation languages. Its evaluation demonstrates that it is capable of fully loading large models with a limited amount of memory. Moreover, a benchmark has been executed, exhibiting better performance than the EMF XMI file-based persistence and CDO. In this paper we focus only on accessing models. Our implementation supports storing models into the repository, but the details are out of the scope of this paper.

The rest of the paper is structured as follows: Section 2 introduces the NoSQL movement and some terminology about models; Section 3 gives an overview of our approach; Sections 4, 5 and 6 discuss the database and loading algorithm design, and the integration and implementation of our approach, respectively; Sections 7 and 8 comment the related work and the evaluation of Morsa and finally Section 9 shows our conclusions and further work.

2 Background

As introduced in the previous section, this paper deals with the problem of persisting and accessing large models. In this section, the basic concepts regarding models and model persistence that will be used in the rest of the paper are explained. Moreover, the NoSQL paradigm is introduced as an alternative to relational databases and object-relational mappings for model persistence.

2.1 Metamodeling

A model is an instance of a metamodel which defines the metaclasses and relationships that the model elements conform to. It can also be seen as a directed labeled graph, where each node represents an object (i.e., a model element) and each edge represents a relationship between objects, which may be containment or non-containment relationships. A containment relationship specifies a hierarchical transitive link between a parent object (source) and a child object (target), defining tree-like structures. Given this graph nature, the concepts of ascendant, descendant, sibling, breadth, depth, etc. common to this mathematical structure can also be used for models. An object that has no ascendants is called a *root object*.

Non-containment relationships define graph-like structures where objects may refer to non-directly related objects (i.e. non-sibling model elements sharing at least one ancestor). A special kind of non-containment relationship is *instanceOf*, which links a model element to the metamodel element that it conforms to. Since a metamodel is also an instance of a meta-metamodel (i.e. a metamodeling language such as Ecore), it may also be seen as a labeled directed graph containing objects that refer to each other, allowing for a homogeneous management of both models and metamodels.

2.2 Model Persistence

Models can be stored into persistence solutions for permanent storage using different approaches. These persistence solutions may be regular files (e.g. XMI), relational databases through object-relational mappings and, at a higher abstraction level, model repositories [8]. Modeling frameworks usually define persistence interfaces that allow client applications to access persisted models, e.g. the EMF Resource interface. These interfaces provide methods for fully loading, unloading and storing models and in some cases, loading single objects (e.g. EMF Resource's *getEObject* method). Storing a model consists in representing the object graph in the persistence solution and loading a model consists in rebuilding that graph at the client application. If the whole object graph is rebuilt, the model is fully loaded; otherwise, if only a subgraph (i.e. model partition) is loaded, the model is partially loaded. Client applications use these basic functions to access models and traverse them for different purposes. For example: a model-to-model transformation may search for a particular object that satisfies a given condition and then traverse all its descedants; a model-to-code transformation may simply traverse a whole model, processing each object once or twice, etc.

A persistence solution provides *transparent integration* when client applications may access it using the persistence interface defined by the corresponding modeling framework without changing the models or metamodels, generating persistence-specific source code for metamodels, or any other form of specific pre or post-processing. For example, the XMI file-based persistence solution for EMF does not require generating metamodel-specific Java classes because it may use dynamic objects, which can be generically built at runtime.

2.3 The NoSQL Movement

The NoSQL [16] movement is composed of several specialized database paradigms that are used in very large web application scenarios such as Facebook, Google, Amazon, etc. In NoSQL, performance and scalability are more important than the ACID properties (Atomicity, Consistency, Isolation, Durability), proposing the BASE properties (Basically Available, Soft-state, Eventual consistency). Given the objectual structure of the data that are stored in some web applications, object-relational mappings have become an expensive solution that reduces their performance, while the different NoSQL databases are best suited for representing object models. There are also implementation differences between traditional relational databases and NoSQL databases, such as memory-based data storage instead of disk-based storage, logging and locking. [11].

The most used NoSQL database paradigms are key-value stores and document databases. *Key-value stores* have a simple data model in common: a map/dictionary allowing users to put and request values by key. They favor scalability over consistency and most of them omit rich querying and analytics features. A well-known key-value store is Amazon's Dynamo [12]. *Document databases* also use keys and values, but they are encapsulated into top-level structures called documents, which are schemaless. CouchDB [13] and MongoDB [14] are the major representatives of document databases. There is no standard query language in NoSQL; querying capabilities vary from one product to another. For example, CouchDB uses static view functions that implement the map/reduce data processing scheme [15], requiring a view function for each possible query; MongoDB uses a query-by-example approach through JSON documents and Dynamo queries consist simply in requesting values by their keys. The NoSQL movement has some features that are beneficial to our approach:

i. *Scalable*: as explained before, many MDE applications involve large models. Applications involving large amounts of data representing object models scale better in NoSQL than in relational databases [16].
ii. *Schemaless*: having no schemas means having no restrictions to co-evolve metamodels and models. Relational repositories usually create database schemas for each stored metamodel, difficulting their evolution and the conformance of existent models to the newer versions of their metamodels [8].

iii. *Accessible*: many NoSQL databases offer their data as JSON objects [17] through APIs that can be accessed via HTTP calls. This provides additional opportunities to access models from web browsers, web services, etc.

3 Overview

We propose Morsa, a persistence solution for managing large models. It relies on a document-based NoSQL database and integrates transparently with modeling frameworks. The architecture of our approach is shown in Figure 1. Morsa consists of a client and a NoSQL-based persistence backend.

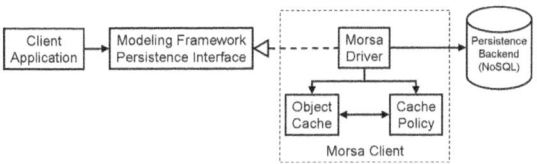

Fig. 1. Architecture of Morsa

The *client* side of Morsa supports tool integration through a driver that implements the modeling framework persistence interface, allowing client applications to access models in a standard way. Since Morsa is aimed at accessing large models, a *load on demand* mechanism has been designed to provide clients with efficient partial load of large models, achieving scalability [5]. This mechanism relies on an *object cache* that holds loaded model objects in order to reduce database queries and manage memory usage; it is managed by a configurable *cache replacement policy* that decides whether the cache is full or not and which objects must be unloaded from the client memory if needed. Section 5 discusses the model loading algorithm and the different cache replacement policies. On the *server* side, a NoSQL document database provides model persistence. We have chosen this kind of database because it provides a simple and natural way to map model elements (objects) to database elements (documents). Moreover, its schemaless architecture is beneficial for model persistence as stated above.

A running example is used to illustrate the design of our approach. It is based on the Grabats 2009 [18] reverse engineering case study, which is aimed at managing large models representing Java source code. A simplification of the JavaMetamodel metamodel provided by the contest is shown in Figure 2, representing Java projects, packages and types, and the source code declarations that are defined inside compilation units (i.e., .java files). The proposed test case was to retrieve every TypeDeclaration which contains a MethodDeclaration for a static and public method with the declared type as its returning type.

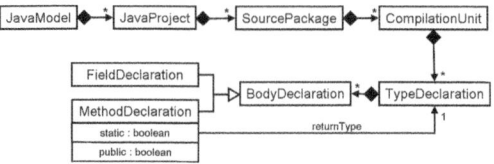

Fig. 2. Grabats 2009 contest JavaMetamodel metamodel simplification

4 Persistence Backend Design

Morsa relies on a document-based NoSQL database persistence backend. The main decision in its design was to choose the *granularity* of the documents, that is, how many documents are needed to represent a model. We have considered three alternatives of model granularity: one document per model, one document per object and one document per model partition.

i. A model can be represented as a *single document*. This is possible since the document-based NoSQL paradigm allows documents to store any number of objects, representing the structure of the model. However, this architecture may not scale for large models because it implies loading an entire model at once; it also has issues related to the maximum document size that some databases like MongoDB impose. Besides, querying single objects or partitions is cumbersome because nested objects are not globally visible.
ii. The opposite design, that is, *one document per object*, does not exploit the nesting capabilities of document-based NoSQL databases, but supports querying individual objects. However, object relationships have to be implemented using database references, that is, values that represent document identifiers, which are less efficient in time than nested objects. The resulting architecture would somehow resemble a relational schema, but it must be kept in mind that NoSQL is schemaless, so foreign keys between documents are far more flexible than the ones of the relational paradigm, since they may refer to any kind of model object.
iii. An intermediate solution would be to represent a model as a *set of documents* representing model partitions. Each model partition would be composed of objects that are always accessed together. Using partitions would speed up model loading because less database connections would be needed to load an entire model. Building these partitions requires access pattern analysis like the one explained in [7]; however, since the database partition is static, no optimal solution for every access pattern could be achieved.

Considering the previous discussion, we have designed Morsa using the second choice, that is, *a document per object*. A Morsa document is composed of a <*ID, value, payload*> tuple that where *ID* is the identifier of the object (object URI for EMF), *value* cointains the values of the object's features in a key-value format, where the *key* is the name of the feature and the *value* is the serialization of

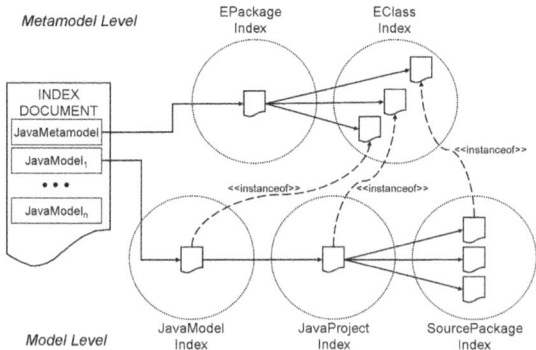

Fig. 3. Persistence backend structure excerpt for the running example

its value as a string; finally, *payload* specifies persistence-related metadata, such as references to the object's metaclass, the model's root object, etc. References to other objects are serialized as document references to their IDs. An index is created for every concrete metaclass, grouping their instances logically for faster queries, both for the meta-metamodel (e.g. an index for each metaclass of the Ecore meta-metamodel) and the metamodels (an index for each metaclass). Metamodels and models are represented homogeneously: documents representing model objects have references to the documents representing their corresponding metaclasses.

A (meta)model is represented as an entry in an *index document* that maps each (meta)model URI to an array of references to the documents that represent its root objects. This design is particulary useful for metamodeling languages like Ecore, where every object except the root ones must be contained by other objects, thus saving space in the index document.

Figure 3 shows an excerpt of the persistence backend structure for the running example. At the metamodel-level, the index for EPackage holds the document that corresponds to the root package of the JavaMetamodel (shown in Figure 2); this document references the documents that correspond to each metaclass (JavaModel, JavaProject, SourcePackage, etc.), which are held by the EClass index. At the model level, there is an index for each metaclass. The index document references a document representing a JavaModel, which is held by the JavaModel index; this document references a document that represents a JavaProject in its corresponding index and so on.

5 Model Loading

Our approach is intented to manipulate large models. In this paper we focus on the task of model loading, which involves three scenarios that require different approaches and algorithms: *full load*, *single load on demand* and *partial load on demand*. The load on demand scenarios have been tackled using an *object cache* managed by a *cache replacement policy*. Metamodels are always fully loaded and kept in memory for efficiency reasons: they are relatively small compared to models and it is worth loading them once instead of accessing the database every time a metaclass is needed. Each object is identified in the database by a global ID attribute (object URI in EMF). A mapping between loaded objects and their IDs is held by the object cache in order to know which objects have been loaded, preventing the driver to load them again.

Consider a model that is small or medium-sized, hence it can be kept in memory by a client application. If the whole model is going to be traversed, it would be a good idea to load the model once, saving communication time with the persistence backend. We call this scenario *full load* and this is the way EMF works when loading XMI files. We aim at supporting full load with the least memory and time overhead possible. The Morsa full load algorithm works as the one for load on demand, which will be explained below, but considering an unlimited object cache, breadth and depth.

5.1 Load on Demand

Consider a model that is too large to be kept in memory by a client application; consider also a model that can be kept in memory but only a part of it is going to be traversed. A solution for both cases would be to load only the necessary objects as they are needed and then unload them to save client memory. We call this scenario *load on demand*. We define two kinds of load on demand: single load on demand and partial load on demand.

A *single load on demand* algorithm fetches objects from the database one by one. This behavior is preferred when the objects that need to be accessed are not closely related (i.e, they are not directly referenced by relationships) and memory efficiency is more important than network performance, that is, when the round-trip time of fetching objects from the database is not relevant. The resultant cache will be populated only with the traversed objects.

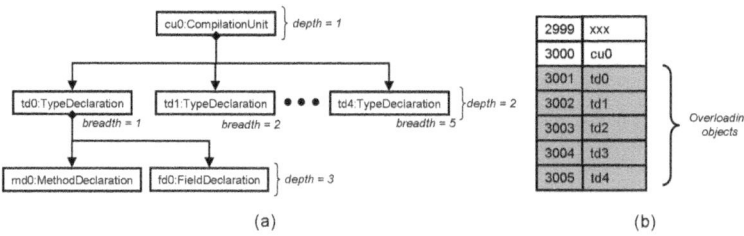

Fig. 4. Object loading in the running example: a) object model b) object cache

On the other hand, a *partial load on demand* algorithm fetches object clusters from the database. The structure of a cluster is customizable: given a requested object, its cluster may contain all its referenced objects, both directly and indirectly within a certain depth and breadth values. For example, when loading the model shown in Figure 4(a), a partial load on demand algorithm configured with a maximum depth and breadth of 2 would load *cu0* (depth 1) and its two first contained TypeDeclaration objects, *td0* and *td1* (depth 2, breadth 2), but not *md0* nor *fd0* (depth 3). This behavior is preferred when all the objects that are related to an object will be traversed soon and memory efficiency is less important than network performance, that is, when the round-trip time of fetching objects from the database is critical. The resultant cache will be populated with the objects that have been traversed and those expected to be traversed in the near future. This is a simple form of prefetching that tries to take advantage of spatial locality. Our load on demand algorithm works as follows:

1. The client application requests an object by its ID
2. The Morsa driver fetches the document identified by that ID
3. A new object is created, filling its attributes with the values stored in the document and its references with proxies whose URIs refer to the referenced documents. A *proxy* is a special object that does not hold any feature value but an URI (containing the object ID and some persistence metadata such as database URL) that allows it to be resolved, i.e., filled with its actual values. In EMF, the idea of proxy is used to represent cross-resource references
4. The new object and its proxies are stored in the object cache, mapping them to their IDs
   (a) If single load on demand is being used, go to step 5
   (b) If partial load on demand is being used, the documents that correspond to the proxies are fetched all at once, saving networking time. The Morsa driver resolves these documents recursively following the two previous steps. This process stops if the cache becomes full or if the maximum depth and breadth is reached
5. If the cache becomes overloaded, some objects of the cache are unloaded
6. The new object is returned to the client application, which can use it as a regular object. When a reference is navigated and its value is a proxy, the resolution of that proxy is automatically requested, executing this algorithm

The size limit of the cache is configurable in terms of object counting, but this limit is soft because some modeling frameworks such as EMF require objects to have their references filled, that is, their values must be fetched in the form of proxies or actual objects. For example, consider Figure 4: an object cache containing 2999 elements is shown (b); its size limit is 3000 objects. Because the modeling framework requires an object to be fully filled, when *cu0* is loaded its 5 contained TypeDeclaration objects (*td0..td4*) must also be fetched as proxies, causing the cache to be overloaded with 3005 objects.

Whenever the cache becomes overloaded, the exceeding objects must be *unloaded*. A *cache replacement policy* algorithm selects the objects to be unloaded. Unloading an object also implies downgrading it to a proxy, i.e. unsetting all its features. A proxy requires less memory than a resolved object and it may be freed by the underlying language if it is not referenced by any other object.

5.2 Cache Replacement Policies

As introduced in the previous section, when the object cache becomes overloaded, a *cache replacement policy* algorithm selects which objects will be unloaded to free the client memory. We have considered four cache replacement policies:

 i. A FIFO (First In-First Out) policy would unload the oldest objects in the cache. This policy is useful when a model is traversed in depth-first order, but only if the cache can hold the average depth of the model. On the contrary, it would cause objects to be unloaded after being traversed and then loaded again when requested for traversal.
 ii. A LIFO (Last In-First Out) policy would unload the newest objects in the cache. This policy is useful when a model is traversed in breadth-first order, but only if the cache can hold the average breadth of the model. Both this and the FIFO policies calculate the size of the partition directly contained by the object that caused the cache overload and unloads that many objects. In the example of Figure 4, a LIFO policy would unload the objects in positions 3001 to 3005, while a FIFO policy would unload first 5 objects in positions 1 to 5.
 iii. A LRU (Less Recently Used) policy would unload the least used objects in the cache. This policy is well known in the area of operating systems. It would be equivalent to a FIFO policy for depth-first and breadh-first orders.
 iv. A LPF (Largest Partition First) policy would unload all the objects that conform the largest model partition contained in the cache. This is a conservative solution that is useful when a model is traversed in no specific order. It does not consider if the selected elements are going to be traversed so it may lead to multiple loads of the same objects. This policy unloads at least an amount of objects proportional to the maximum size of the cache.

The choice of which cache replacement policy is used is currently made by the end-user. However, this choice could be automatically made by the Morsa driver by analysis of (meta)models and access patterns (i.e. prefetching).

6 Integration and Implementation

Morsa is intented to be integrated with modeling frameworks and their applications. Our current prototype is integrated with EMF [3]. A transparent way of achieving this integration is to design the Morsa driver as an implementation of the persistence interface of the modeling framework (EMF Resource for EMF). Persisting a model in Morsa is done without any preprocessing, since there is no need of generating model-specific classes, modifying metamodels or registering them into the persistence solution, as opposed to other approaches [8][9][19]. Metamodels are seamlessly persisted if they are not already in the database. Additional information for persistence configuration can optionally be passed to the driver; Morsa uses the standard parameters of the EMF load and save methods to pass this configuration information.

Morsa supports both *dynamic* and *generated* EMF. A dynamic model object is generated at runtime using EMF dynamic objects (instances of DynamicEObjectImpl) which use reflection to generically instantiate metaclasses. On the other hand, a generated model object is an instance of a metamodel-specific class that has been explicitly generated through an EMF generator model. Dynamic objects are preferred for tool integration since they do not require code generation. Other approaches [8] support only generated model objects reimplementing part of the EMF framework to handle persistency.

We have developed a prototype that exhibits some of the features described previously: EMF integration, single and partial load on demand, FIFO, LIFO and LPF cache replacement policies and full store. Its integration in EMF includes all the methods defined in the Resource interface and also methods for parent resolution (i.e., obtaining the container object of a given object) and special partial loading methods such as loading every instance of a metaclass.

We have chosen MongoDB [14] as the NoSQL database engine for our prototype; however, its architecture could be easily implemented in other engines. MongoDB has JSON access, dynamic queries (as opposed to the static views of CouchDB), server-side Javascript programming and uses BSON [17] objects for communication which provide fast and bandwith-efficient object transfer between the client and the database. MongoDB uses collections to logically organize documents, like the indexes introduced in Section 4. A collection is a set of documents which can be indexed by one or several attributes, allowing faster document access.

7 Related Work

Model persistence is not a novel research field. As the interest in MDE has grown many approaches have been proposed to solve this problem. The standard EMF solution is to persist models in XMI resources, but there are other alternatives. One approach is using binary indexed files [21]. Another approach is to use model repositories. A *repository* is a persistence solution remotely accesible by users and tools. Repositories usually rely on databases and provide additional features such as transactions and versioning. There are many EMF model repositories available today, being the most mature ones CDO [8], ModelBus [19] and EMFStore [9].

The *ModelBus* repository is a web service application that manages an embedded Subversion engine which implements the actual repository; however, Subversion is not designed to be integrated in client applications that access to parts of persisted elements, i.e., it does not support partial access to models. There have been attempts to make model access scalable in ModelBus [22]; however, the official release does not implement them. *EMFStore* implements a different architecture but shares the same philosophy as Subversion: models are fully loaded and stored by human clients using a GUI. This solution does not scale and it is best suited for design environments.

Currently *Connected Data Objects* (CDO) is the only model repository that is capable of managing large models using load on demand. CDO also provides a rough version control system and EMF integration through its EMF Resource implementation, CDOResource. However, CDO is not application-transparent. First of all, we haven't been able to make it work with dynamic model objects, which is a severe drawback for its integration with EMF. Moreover, CDO requires metamodels to be pre-processed in order to persist their instances. One kind of pre-processing is to generate the Java model classes of a metamodel. This allows CDO to work with *legacy objects*. The other kind is to generate CDO-aware model classes from a generator model. This allows CDO to work with *native objects*. The main difference between legacy and native objects is that legacy objects cannot be demand-loaded or unloaded, having a huge impact on performance as will be shown in the next section. Native objects are unloaded from a CDO client when its memory becomes full using a *soft reference* approach, i.e. an object is removed by garbage collector when no other object refers to it with a reference that is not soft.

There are other domains where large and complex data needs to be accessed; for example, ontologies may be very large and complex and many solutions have been proposed, such as creating higher-level descriptions [23], which may be seen as a form of building views. Client scalability has been also tackled in the field of object-relational mappings, proposing prefetching mechanisms that load clusters of objects that will be used by the client application [24][25]. Object caching has also been a subject of study in the field of object databases, with mathematical approaches to optimizing cache coherence, replacement and invalidation [27][28]. Our approach could benefit from this reasearch to improve caching and prefetching with adaptive mechanisms. Finally, as far as we know, little or no research has been published on applying NoSQL to model persistence.

8 Evaluation

As stated in the previous section, CDO is the main alternative to our approach, so the evaluation consisted in executing a set of test cases with Morsa, CDO and the standard EMF XMI parser, comparing their performance results. We have considered the models proposed in the Grabats 2009 contest [18]. They conform to the JavaMetamodel metamodel that is shown simplified in Figure 2. There are five models, from Set0 to Set4, each one larger than its predecessor (from a 8.8MB XMI file with 70447 model elements representing 14 Java classes to a 646MB file with 4961779 model elements representing 5984 Java classes).

Two benchmarks have been executed: model access and model query. The model access benchmark consists in traversing models in depth-first order and breadth-first order. The model query benchmark executes the query proposed in the Grabats contest, which searches for every class that declares a public static method whose returning type is that same class. Each benchmark has been executed using the EMF XMI loading facility, a CDO repository configured for best speed and least memory footprint in legacy mode and native mode and Morsa for least memory footprint and best speed using single and partial load on demand. All tests have been executed under a Intel CoreI5 760 PC at 2.80GHz with 8GB of physical RAM running 64-bit Linux 2.6.35 and JVM 1.6.0. CDO 4.0 is configured using DBStore over a dedicated MySQL database and is used in read-only mode in order to avoid versioning overhead.

8.1 Results

Table 1 shows the results for the model access test cases. Memory footprint is shown in Megabytes and time is shown in seconds. The *Opt* column specifies whether the configuration optimizes speed or memory. As expected, CDO Native mode is more efficient than CDO Legacy mode, but still Morsa is faster and uses less memory for all the models. Note that the minimum memory used by CDO for the Set1 breadth-first order doubles the memory needed by XMI, while Morsa uses 20% less memory than XMI. We haven't been able to load the Set2 model (271MB XMI file, containing 2082481 model elements representing 1605 Java classes) with CDO within a reasonable time (less than 45 minutes). The cache replacement policies used for least memory footprint in Morsa were a LIFO policy for breadth-first order and a FIFO policy for depth-first order. Cache size was 900 objects for load on demand and unlimited for full load (best speed). CDO was configured with a maximum available memory of 70MB for the Set0 model and 30MB and 100MB for the Set1 in depth-first order and breadth-first order, respectively, for the least memory footprint and unlimited memory for the best speed. These configurations have been obtained empirically.

For all models (including Set3 and Set4, which are not shown), Morsa is much slower than XMI, but still can load and traverse them entirely. In the best case for the Set2 model, Morsa uses 17 times less memory than XMI spending 20 times more time. Note that with an unlimited cache, Morsa spends a similar time than the best speed case with a small one (1.5% time difference). This is due to the fact that with an unlimited cache, our prototype holds references to every model object, difficulting garbage collection. On the other hand, a cache with limited size unloads objects more often, facilitating the garbage collection. Since we haven't been able to store the Set3 and Set4 models in CDO, despite assigning it the maximum available memory (Set2 could be stored, but causing an exception on commit), the model access test cases for these models are not shown. For these models, XMI is faster than Morsa but needs much more memory.

The potential of Morsa shows up not only with a limited amount of memory, but also when models do not have to be completely traversed. For example, the Grabats 2009 contest query, whose execution results are shown in Table 2, shows that Morsa is more efficient in memory and time than CDO and XMI for this particular task. These results illustrate that our approach can be very beneficial for applications that do not need to process an entire model, such as certain model transformations. An application can query Morsa for specific objects, consuming less time and memory and achieving scalability. The query has been implemented using dynamic EMF for Morsa and generated model classes for CDO and XMI. CDO and Morsa allow querying the database for all instances of a given metaclass and then traversing the results to check the query condition, while XMI requires loading the entire model prior to its traversal.

Table 1. Performance results for the model access test cases

Order	Opt	Solution	Mode	Set0 Mem	Set0 Time	Set1 Mem	Set1 Time	Set2 Mem	Set2 Time
-	-	XMI	-	63	1.313	113	2.265	1257	15.632
Depth	-	CDO	Legacy	162	32.156	516	91.136	-	-
Breadth	-	CDO	Legacy	172	31.609	444	92.160	-	-
Depth	Speed	CDO	Native	289	21.783	435	59.188	-	-
Breadth	Speed	CDO	Native	308	21.046	467	56.017	-	-
-	Speed	Morsa	Full	113	8.762	363	26.671	1300	317.331
Depth	Mem	CDO	Native	59	31.218	87	80.594	-	-
Depth	Mem	Morsa	Single	25	12.130	32	32.348	92	313.027
Depth	Mem	Morsa	Partial	30	14.163	29	39.197	98	410.829
Breadth	Mem	CDO	Native	59	30.010	250	78.204	-	-
Breadth	Mem	Morsa	Single	32	18.889	90	31.530	400	322.045
Breadth	Mem	Morsa	Partial	40	29.239	96	85.197	460	761.692

Table 2. Performance results for the query test case

Opt	Solution	Mode	Set0 Mem	Set0 Time	Set1 Mem	Set1 Time	Set2 Mem	Set2 Time	Set3 Mem	Set3 Time	Set4 Mem	Set4 Time
-	XMI	-	70	1.513	121	2.465	1265	16.023	2940	81.340	3512	141.752
Speed	CDO	Native	7	0.445	23	0.968	129	18.149	-	-	-	-
Speed	Morsa	Single	5	0.706	8	0.985	168	9.724	205	26.760	254	29.339
Mem	CDO	Native	4	0.545	6	1.731	61	25.798	-	-	-	-
Mem	Morsa	Single	5	0.706	5	1.518	36	14.822	96	36.944	59	40.129

9 Conclusions and Further Work

We have presented Morsa, a persistence solution aimed at achieving scalability for client applications that access large models. Morsa uses load on demand mechanisms to allow large models to be accessed without overflowing the client application memory. We have developed several cache replacement policies that cover different model access patterns. Server scalability is achieved using a document-based NoSQL database, which is a novel feature since model repositories usually work with object-relational mappings. As far as we know, applying document-based NoSQL databases to MDE has not been proposed before, and is a promising approach to build industrial-scale model persistence solutions.

We have implemented a prototype for EMF that in its early development stage shows promising performance results. An evaluation of our prototype is shown, executing two benchmarks against large models and comparing its results with the ones of XMI and the well-stablished CDO repository. This comparison shows that Morsa suits better for partial model access and model querying than XMI and CDO, and that it handles larger models than CDO does.

Our future work is to continue optimizing Morsa while implementing new features. Among others, these features include: *incremental store*, that will allow the client to store changes done to objects that are going to be unloaded, an advanced *query API*, support for *query languages* such as OCL and making our load on demand algorithms and cache replacement policies more adaptative by *collecting metadata information* about the structure of the persisted models.

References

1. Mohagheghi, P., Fernandez, M.A., Martell, J.A., Fritzsche, M., Gilani, W.: MDE Adoption in Industry: Challenges and Success Criteria. In: Chaudron, M.R.V. (ed.) MODELS 2008. LNCS, vol. 5421, pp. 54–59. Springer, Heidelberg (2009)
2. Baker, P., Loh, S.C., Weil, F.: Model-Driven Engineering in a Large Industrial Context — Motorola Case Study. In: Briand, L.C., Williams, C. (eds.) MoDELS 2005. LNCS, vol. 3713, pp. 476–491. Springer, Heidelberg (2005)
3. The Eclipse Modeling Framework, http://www.eclipse.org/emf
4. Kolovos, D., Paige, R., Polack, F.: Scalability: The Holy Grail of Model-Driven Engineering. In: Chaudron, M.R.V. (ed.) MODELS 2008. LNCS, vol. 5421, pp. 35–47. Springer, Heidelberg (2009)
5. Selic, B.: Personal Reflections on Automation, Programming, Culture and Model-based Software Engineering. Automated Software Engineering 15(3-4), 379–391 (2008)
6. Canovas, J., Garca, J.: An architecture-driven modernization tool for calculating metrics. IEEE Software 27(4), 37–43 (2010)
7. Varro, G., Friedl, K., Varro, D.: Adaptive Graph Pattern Matching for MOdel Transformations using Mode-sensitive Search Plans. ENTCS 152, 191–205 (2006)
8. The CDO Model Repository, http://www.eclipse.org/cdo
9. EMFStore: A model repository for EMF models. In: Proceedings of the 32nd ACM/IEEE International Conference on Software Engineering, Cape Town (South Africa) vol. 2, pp. 307–308 (2010), http://www.emfstore.org
10. Morsa prototype, http://www.modelum.es/morsa
11. Stonebraker, M.: SQL Databases vs NoSQL Databases. Communications of the ACM 53(4), 10–11 (2010)
12. DeCandia, G., Hastorun, D., et al.: Dynamo: Amazon's Higly-Available Key-value Store. In: Proceedings of Twenty-First ACM SIGOPS Symposium on Operating Systems Principles, pp. 205–220. ACM, New York (2007)
13. CouchDB: couchdb.apache.org
14. MongoDB, http://www.mongodb.org
15. Dean, J., Ghemawat, S.: MapReduce: simplified data processing on large clusters (2004), http://labs.google.com/papers/mapreduce-osdi04
16. Strauch, C.: NoSQL Databases. Stuttgart Media University (2011), http://www.christof-strauch.de/nosqldbs.pdf
17. JavaScript Object Notation, http://www.json.org
18. Grabats 2009 5th International Workshop on Graph-Based Tools: a reverse engineering case study, Zurich (Switzerland) (July 2009), http://is.tm.tue.nl/staff/pvgorp/events/grabats2009/
19. Blanc, X., Gervais, M.-P., Sriplakich, P.: Model Bus: Towards the Interoperability of Modelling Tools. In: Aßmann, U., Aksit, M., Rensink, A. (eds.) MDAFA 2003. LNCS, vol. 3599, pp. 17–32. Springer, Heidelberg (2005), http://www.modelbus.org
20. Binary JSON, http://www.bsonspec.org
21. Jouault, F., Sottet, J.: An AmmA/ATL Solution for the Grabats 2009 Reverse Engineering Case Study. In: Grabats 2009 5th International Workshop on Graph-Based Tools, Zurich, Switzerland (July 2009)
22. Sriplakich, P., Blanc, X., Gervais, M.: Collaborative Software Engineering on Large-scale models: Requirements and Experience in ModelBus. In: Proceedings on the 2008 ACM Symposium on Applied Computing, pp. 674–681. ACM, New York (2008)

23. Bhm, C., Lorey, J., Fenz, D., Kny, E., Pohl, M., Naumann, F.: Creating voiD Descriptions for Web-scale Data. Winner of the 2010 Billion Triple Track Semantic Web Challenge (2010)
24. Ibrahim, A., Cook, W.: Automatic by Traversal Profiling in Object Persistence Architectures. In: Hu, Q. (ed.) ECOOP 2006. LNCS, vol. 4067, pp. 50–73. Springer, Heidelberg (2006)
25. Han, W., Whang, K., Moon, Y.: A Formal Framework for Prefetching Based on the Type-Level Access Pattern in Object-Relational DBMSs. IEEE Transactions on Knowledge and Data Engineering 17, 1436–1448 (2005)
26. Chang, F., Dean, J., et al.: Bigtable: A Distributed Storage System for Structured Data (2006)
27. Leong, H., Si, A.: On Adaptive Caching in Mobile Databases. In: Proceedings of the 1997 ACM Symposium on Applied Computing, pp. 302–309. ACM, New York (1997)
28. Rathore, R., Prinja, R.: An Overview of Mobile Database Caching (2008), http://www-users.cs.umn.edu/ rohinip/Rohini_Prinja/Research_files/ 8701Project.pdf

Expressing Aspectual Interactions in Design: Experiences in the Slot Machine Domain

Johan Fabry[1,*], Arturo Zambrano[2], and Silvia Gordillo[2]

[1] PLEIAD Laboratory
Computer Science Department (DCC)
University of Chile – Santiago, Chile
http://pleiad.cl

[2] LIFIA, Facultad de Informática, Universidad Nacional de La Plata
La Plata, Argentina

Abstract. In the context of an industrial project we are implementing the software of a casino slot machine. This software has a significant amount of cross-cutting concerns that depend on, and interact with each other, as well as with the modular concerns. We therefore wish to express our design using an appropriate Aspect-Oriented Modeling methodology and notation. We evaluated two of the most mature methodologies: Theme/UML and WEAVR, to establish their suitability. Remarkably, neither of these allow us to express any of the dependencies and interactions to our satisfaction. In both cases, half of the interaction types cannot be expressed at all while the other half need to be expressed using a workaround that hides the intention of the design. As a result, we consider both methodologies and notations unsuitable for expressing the dependencies and interactions present in the slot machine domain. In this paper we describe our evaluation experience.

1 Introduction

A slot machine (SM) is a casino gambling device that has five *reels* which spin when a *play* button is pressed. An SM includes some means for entering money, which is mapped to *credits*. The player bets an amount of credits on each play, the SM randomly selects the displayed symbol for each reel, and pays the corresponding prize, if any. Credits can be extracted (called a *cashout*) by different mechanisms such as coins, tickets or electronic transfers.

In the context of an industrial project we were required to re-implement the software for a particular SM. Previous experience had taught us that, beyond the main functionality sketched above, there are a significant amount of crosscutting concerns present in such applications. For example: counters need to be maintained throughout the application to be able to audit the SM, and the complete working of the SM needs to be accessible over the network. Moreover, these concerns depend on, and interact with each other as well as with

---
* Partially funded by FONDECYT project 1090083.

the modularized concerns. We therefore opted to use Aspect-Oriented Software Development in this implementation, taking special care of dependencies and interactions between the different aspects and modules. In a previous step, we analyzed the different concerns that define the behavior of SMs, with a specific focus on concern interactions at the requirements level [13].

The second step in our development process is modeling the software using an adequate approach for *Aspect Oriented Modeling* (AOM). However, to the best of our knowledge there has been no work published that evaluates AOM approaches in an industrial setting, with a focus on interactions between the different concerns. We therefore undertook an evaluation of two mature AOM approaches to establish their applicability in our context. Somewhat surprisingly, neither of these two is adequate in our setting, as we report in this article.

As basis for our selection we used surveys on AOM [2,12], complemented by a study of more recent literature. The chosen approaches are Theme/UML [4] and WEAVR [6,5]. Beyond their maturity, acceptance in the AOM community, and claimed support for interactions, both methodologies have specific advantages. Theme/UML integrates with Theme/Doc: an aspect-oriented requirements methodology for requirements specification [13]. WEAVR is arguably the best-known industrial application of AOM, and the only methodology that we are aware of that is used in industry to develop complex applications.

We now give an overview of the requirements we have for the design document, before giving a high-level overview of the design and the different interactions that need to be specified. Section 4 then proceeds with an evaluation of Theme/UML, and Sect. 5 follows up with an evaluation of WEAVR. We present related work in Sect. 6, and conclusions and future work in Sect. 7.

2 Requirements for the Design

In the design phase our goal is to refine the requirement specification documents into a model of the software artifacts that will form the final system. This model, written down in a design document, will be passed to the developers for implementation. Hence, it should be sufficiently complete to allow for the implementation to be produced relatively independently. As we are performing Aspect-Oriented Software Development, the choice of an AOM approach for creating this document is a given. We expect that we will be able to produce the complete design documents, *i.e.*, not having to resort to a significant additional documents with an ad-hoc notation to complement for omissions in the methodology. In the latter case the advantages of using a standard AOM are small and we would consider rolling our own AOM. We furthermore have two, related, expectations of the design document: maintenance support and explicit interactions.

In subsequent maintenance or evolution phases the changes made in the requirements will trigger subsequent changes in the design, and the developers will modify the implementation accordingly. Such later modifications may not break the system because they violate constraints of the original design or go against the original design decisions. If the change is significant enough to warrant modifying the design constraints or assumptions, the original intentions should be maintained as much as possible. Hence the design document must be clear on which are the the critical design decisions that were made and what assumptions were taken. Furthermore, it is known that the presence of aspects in a software system that is being evolved can be problematic [9]. Such issues should be mitigated by the information that is explicitly available in the design document. When evolving the software the implementers must be able to use the document as a guide, seeing what assumptions taken by the aspects no longer hold, or what new code now also falls within the realm of an aspect.

As we have said above, our experience is that there is a significant amount of non-trivial interactions between the different aspects of the system. This is also confirmed by the results of the requirements analysis we have performed previously [13]. Even though aspects are intended to provide advanced modularity and decoupling, they do not exist in isolation. As any module in software, their presence impacts other modules and their functionality may depend on other modules. Documented design decisions should therefore include not only which modules will be aspects and where they crosscut, but also how they *interact* with each other. This information must be made explicit so that critical information is correctly passed to the implementation phase, and is present when maintaining or evolving the software.

3 Design Overview

Considering the results of the requirements analysis phase we previously performed, we now give an outline of how we envision the design of the SM software. This provides us with a concrete basis for evaluation of the AOM, as it must allow us to expand and refine this overview into a complete design document.

3.1 Aspects in the Design

A class diagram that shows the outline of the design is given in Fig. 1. It uses an ad-hoc extension of UML to indicate crosscutting, showing that we model the following crosscutting concerns as aspects: Metering, Demo, Program Resumption, Error Conditions, S Communications Protocol, G2S Protocol. We give an overview of these aspects next.

Metering. The Metering aspect crosscuts Game and other base entities in order to keep meters data up to date. Meters are essentially a set of counters that keep information about past plays, *e.g.* the total amount bet. This information is used, among other things, to create reports.

Demo. For legal certification the SM must have a 'Demo' mode, where all possible outcomes for a play can be simulated. The Demo concern therefore needs to control the outcome produced by the Game class. It furthermore crosscuts Metering to avoid polluting accounting meters when it is active.

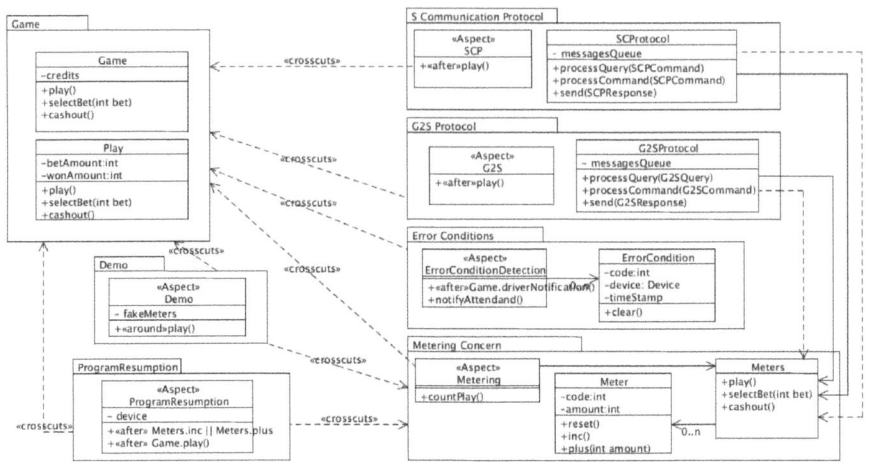

Fig. 1. Overview of the class structure of the design

Program Resumption. Program Resumption is a persistence and recovery requirement. The system should recover the last state after a power outage. Information to be saved includes the status of the current play and the values of the meters.

Error Conditions. Error conditions detected by the game such as: tilt, out of paper, ... are detected by the Error Condition Detection aspect. Once an error condition is detected some actions need to be performed, *e.g.* in case of a tilt illuminating the tower lamp and sounding an alarm to call the casino attendant.

Communication Protocols. The S Communications Protocol[1] (SCP) and G2S Protocol are communications protocols frequently used in the gaming industry. Their corresponding aspects crosscut the Game modules to add behavior such as multiple SMs vying for the same jackpot. Moreover, both protocols need to report metering information and hence crosscut the Meters aspect.

Figure 1 shows that a simple extension of UML already suffices to provide the outlines of the aspectual design. Not surprisingly most, if not all, of the AOM approaches we studied allow us to produce a model similar to this diagram. What is however lacking in the above diagram is the information of how the various aspects interact with each other, as well as with the base application. For example, when in Demo mode network communication must be disabled, as queries from the server may only receive values corresponding to normal play conditions. This information should also be present in the design document, but we find no immediately obvious way in which this can be diagrammed. Hence the lack of this information in Fig. 1.

---

[1] A pseudonym, licensing restrictions prohibit us from using the real name.

3.2 Interactions between Concerns

Our resulting design document not only needs to contain the information of the aspects present in the system, but also how they crosscut. It is also necessary that the interactions which were identified in the requirements analysis phase be present in the design document. To better understand what our needs are for this part of the design document, we now give an overview of the different interactions in the SM, and how we want this to be reflected in the document.

We structure this discussion and the evaluations of the AOM approaches later in the text using the AOSD-Europe technical report on interactions [11]. It classifies interactions in four different types: *dependency*, *conflict*, *mutex* and *reinforcement*, and the SM software contains an instance of each of these types.

Conflict: Demo versus Multiple Concerns. The aspects of Meters, Communication Protocols and Program Resumption are present to comply with legal accounting requirements regarding plays performed on a SM. The Demo aspect, also a legal requirement, conflicts with all of the above aspects. This is as the legislation states that a play in Demo mode must not alter the meters nor that its activity is visible over the network. Hence, after a Demo session the Game must recover its original status and any event or state change while in Demo must not be reported by the communication protocols.

In order to cope with this conflicting behavior the design and implementation must provide support for:

- Avoiding simultaneous activation of Demo and other conflicting aspects.
- While being in Demo a fake set of meters should be used. This ensures that actions in demo mode do not alter the meter values of normal operations.

Communication Protocols: Mutex, Reinforcement and Dependency. Both communication protocols provide similar functionality: allowing the server to query information and set some configuration values and state on the SM. For read-only behavior, such as reporting the value of a meter, there is no problem with having them active at the same time as no interference will result. On the other hand, for operations that alter the state of the machine, mutual exclusion must be ensured during a single program execution. If not, inconsistencies in the SM may arise. For example, consider setting the time of the SM, an operation performed by the casino server. With both communication protocols enabled, two different servers with different clock values may set the time on the SM to either of both clock values. As a result the timing of events on the SM is ambiguous. To document this *mutex* what we need is the ability to express that certain object interactions may not occur during the programs' execution.

There is a *reinforcement* from Error Conditions to Communication Protocols. Not all the Error Conditions specified in the legislation are mandatory, however when an optional error condition is present in the game, *e.g.* because a driver allows for these errors to be detected, the communication protocols must be able to report this to the server. This means that during development of new versions of the Game, when new error conditions are present, the associated behavior in the Communication Protocols should be revisited to ensure that the new information is properly reported. Hence we need to document that a change in a different part of the application enables optional or extended behavior of a given concern.

The last interaction regarding Communication Protocols is a *dependency* of them on Meters. The protocols access the meters in order to report their values to the server. Consequently, if for some reason metering is not present, the communication protocols cannot operate. When a communication protocol is enabled, meters must be present, and must be properly fed. We need to document this dependency to ensure the consistent behavior of the system.

4 Evaluation of Theme/UML

Theme/UML is the second half of the Theme approach for Aspect-Oriented requirements analysis and design. The first half is called Theme/Doc and is a methodology for AO requirements analysis. Theme provides for a process for transforming requirements in Theme/Doc into a design in Theme/UML, and moreover claims to have support for conflict resolution. We therefore chose to evaluate Theme for our development effort. In the requirements engineering phase [13] we have evaluated Theme/Doc, and now continue with an evaluation of Theme/UML.

The Theme/UML approach [4] is an extension of UML that provides both a notation and a methodology for modeling AO systems. In Theme/UML, a *theme* refers to a concern. A theme can consist of class diagrams, sequence diagrams and state diagrams, each of which is extended with the required notation to be able to express Aspect-Oriented concepts. Each theme is designed separately, and subsequently the themes are composed with each other. This is performed using composition relationships that detail how this is performed.

Themes are divided into two classes: base and crosscutting themes. Base themes describe a concern of the system that has no crosscutting behavior. Base themes are composed, both structurally and behaviorally, to form the base model. If a given concept appears in multiple themes, the composition can merge the various occurrences into one entity. Crosscutting themes describe behavior that should be triggered as the result of the execution of some behavior in the base model. They are designed similarly to base themes, and are parameterizable. Parameters provide a point for the attachment of the crosscutting behavior to the base model. By binding them to values of the base themes the crosscutting themes are composed with the base model. Crosscutting themes are composed one by one with the base themes until the complete design is produced.

In accordance to Fig. 1, we modeled Game as a base theme and Demo, G2S, Meters, and SCP as crosscutting themes. We found it is straightforward to express where to attach the crosscutting behavior, both on the base themes and on other crosscutting themes. However, when considering interactions we find that Theme/UML does not perform as well. We now discuss the obstacles we encountered classified in the four different kinds of interactions we discussed in Sect. 3.2: Conflict, Mutex, Reinforcement and Dependency.

4.1 Conflict

Theme/UML provides support for conflict resolution when composing different themes. These composition conflicts arise when the same diagram element in different themes has an attribute with different values. An example of this is an instance variable with different visibility specifications. Conflict resolution then consists of choosing which of the conflicting attributes to use in the composition.

The conflicts we are facing are however of a different nature. For example, consider the Demo aspect. As mentioned in 3.2, when it is active all conflicting aspects must be somehow deactivated. We therefore need to model the predominant nature of this aspect in some way. There is however no explicit means in Theme/UML to declare this kind of predominance. Instead we are required to design a conflict management strategy, making the conflict implicit.

We therefore model conflict management as follows: the Demo theme crosscuts the Game theme, capturing the execution of play() for the Game class. When active, Demo skips the execution of the original play() and instead generates a predetermined outcome (which is the main responsibility of the Demo mode). In order to keep the meters unharmed, parts of the Metering theme behavior are captured and skipped. Considering the communication protocols, their original behavior is altered: instead of responding to queries, failure responses are returned.

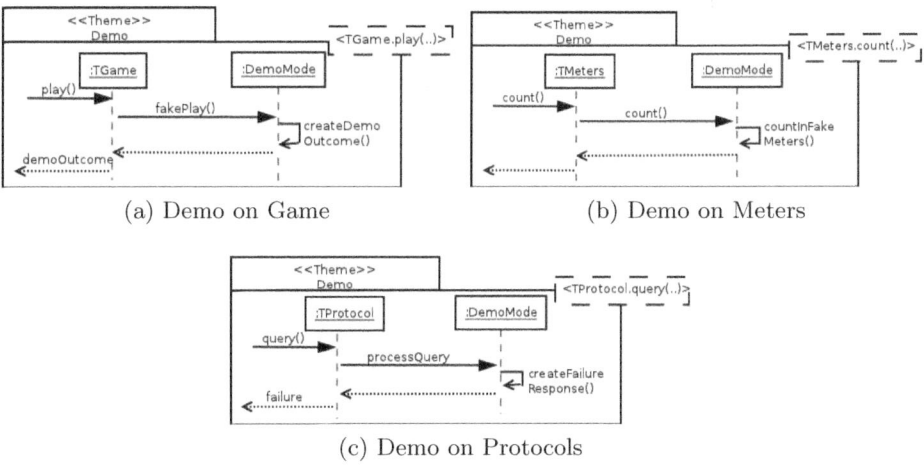

Fig. 2. The Demo theme affecting the behavior defined in Game, Metering and Protocols

Our model is shown in Fig. 2. We use Theme/UML sequence diagrams, a straightforward extension of UML sequence diagrams. The figure shows three Themes, each of which has a template parameter in the top right corner, corresponding to the message send that starts the sequence. At composition time, this parameter is bound to a specific message send in the base theme, *i.e.*, the join point in the base code is identified. Also, within a sequence diagram, the behavior of the join point which is matched can be invoked, put differently, Theme has an equivalent of the AspectJ proceed construct. The syntax to express this call is _do_*templateOperation*. Note that absence of such a call implies that the original behavior never occurs. For instance, in Fig. 2 there are no _do_play, _do_count or _do_query calls, which means the join point behavior is skipped.

The above solution has the major downside that design does not explicitly reveal the intention: the conflict between Demo and Meters, and Demo and the communication protocols. Instead it must be deduced from the implementation proposed in the diagrams. As we require that the design intent is explicit, we do not consider this a feasible solution.

4.2 Mutex

Part of the behavior of the communication protocols is configuration command processing, as these game parameters can be set by the servers. Both protocols implement this feature, but it is not permitted that multiple protocols set the same value during a run of the program. The interaction we thus want to model is mutual exclusion between configuration actions: two protocols cannot configure the same item during a given program execution.

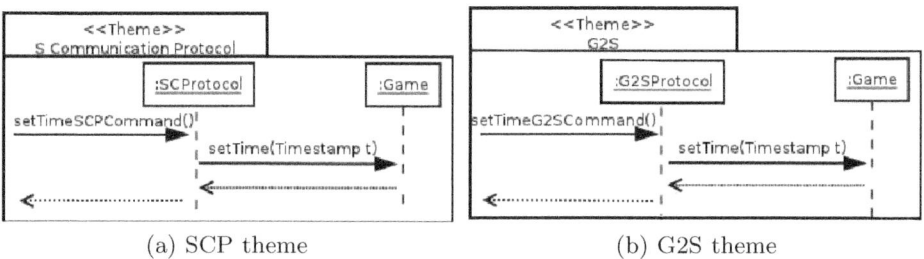

(a) SCP theme (b) G2S theme

Fig. 3. Two themes configuring the same item in the Game

Concretely, the protocols are each modeled as a theme, where each theme defines the behavior through a set of sequence diagrams. Considering the sequence diagrams in Fig. 3 for the two different protocols, what we need to document is that the behavior in diagrams a) and b) cannot happen in the same program execution. However, to the best of our knowledge, Theme does not provide any way in which we can express this mutex relationship between both sequence diagrams. Neither do we see an alternative solution in the same spirit as the design of the conflict interaction. Consequently, we are not able to express this mutex in the design.

4.3 Reinforcement

The error condition aspect reinforces the behavior of the communication protocols, reporting all error conditions to the remote servers. Considering this interaction, we have a situation similar to mutex: We model the communication protocol concern as a theme, and the error conditions concern as a theme but we are unaware of a way in which to explicitly state the reinforcement semantics. In this particular case we are able to integrate the reinforcement into the design, but at the cost of making the reinforcement implicit. We show this next.

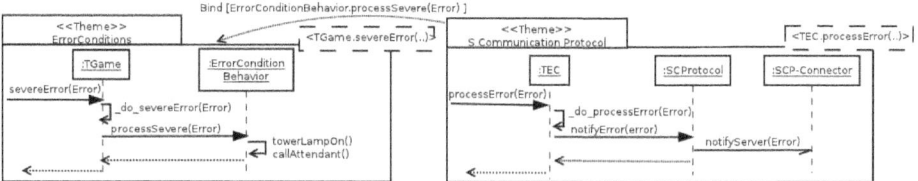

Fig. 4. SCP Theme reinforced by Error Conditions theme

The left hand side of Fig. 4 shows a sequence diagram for the most severe type of error condition. It specifies how the error event occurring causes the tower lamp to be lit and the attendant to be called. Reporting the error to the server is specified in the right hand side of Fig. 4 using a theme for the communication protocol. By binding both themes using the arrow construct, we define a crosscutting behavior of the communication protocol, specifying that it intercepts all calls of ErrorConditionBehavior.processSevere(Error).

However, as this states that the relationship between them is a typical crosscutting relationship, the reinforcement semantics is lost. Even though the generic behavior of the communication protocols captures all error conditions of this type, it is not clear that we know there may be new types of error conditions in the future, and each of them needs to trigger protocol behavior. This information is crucial to check the consistency of the system during maintenance and evolution. As the reinforcement semantics remains implicit here, this verification step might be omitted.

4.4 Dependency

The metering theme maintains track of given events in the game by changing the values of meters objects. Complementary to this, the communication protocols themes specify that to respond to queries sent by the remote server, the information stored in the meters objects are used. It is clear that the latter behavior requires the former, hence the communication theme depends on the meters theme.

The Theme/UML methodology however states that each theme defines all structure and behavior needed to provide the desired functionality, *i.e.*, in a standalone fashion. Furthermore, the designer may choose a subset of all themes to compose a system [4]. In our case this will lead to errors, as selecting the theme of a communication protocol without adding the theme of meters leads to an inconsistent design of the system.

What we need is a way to express that the meters themes are necessary whenever the communication protocol themes are composed into the system, but we have found no way to specify this in Theme/UML. Hence we are unable to include the dependency in the design.

4.5 Conclusion: Theme/UML

We found that Theme/UML does **not** allow us to express **any** of the four types of interactions in an explicit way. At the most, we are able to integrate support for conflict resolution and reinforcement into the design. However this comes at the cost of obscuring the explicit relationship between different aspects, which is likely to lead to errors during maintenance or evolution. As a result, we consider Theme/UML inappropriate to specify the design of a SM.

5 Evaluation of WEAVR

WEAVR is an add-in extension to the MDE tool suite used by Motorola, adding support for AOM to their process of building telecom software [6,5]. As WEAVR is arguably the best-known industrial application of AOM, with claimed support for interactions, we chose it as the second candidate for evaluation.

Next to a UML notation, the Motorola tool suite also uses SDL [7] transition oriented state machines as the graphical formalism to define behavior. These state machines are unambiguous and allow for introducing pieces of code. This enables code generation of the complete application in C and C++.

The WEAVR pointcut notation is based on state machines, permitting the capture of *action* and *transition* joinpoints. Wildcards are allowed to refer to multiple states or actions. Advice are also expressed as state machines, and are related to the pointcuts using the `bind` relationship. WEAVR is an aspect weaver: it combines an aspectual state machine with a base state machine when there is a join point match. The tool allows to visualize the new composed state machine, so that engineers can verify the composition for correctness before actual code generation.

Note that although WEAVR can be used to generate the code of the application, we do not require this, we only want to specify the design. Also, due to licensing issues we were not able to use the tool for our evaluation, instead relying on published work [6,5]. Lastly, even though SDL is a standard, the notation of its usage by WEAVR is not consistent among all the publications. The diagrams in this text are our best effort to produce a consistent notation, but we are not able to guarantee their notational correctness.

5.1 Conflicts

Support for conflict resolution in WEAVR is realized by the hidden_by stereotype that is used in the deployment diagrams, where aspects are applied to classes. The hidden_by stereotype relates two different aspects that intercept the same join point. The relationship states that the aspect that is hidden does not apply in those cases. For example, specifying AspectA hidden_by AspectB denotes that at a join point captured by both aspects, only the behavior of AspectB will be executed. In other words, we can state that the presence of one aspect implies the absence of another aspect, but only at the level of join points.

In our case such conflict resolution is however not sufficient as we are faced with aspects that conflict when active on different join points. For example, consider Demo: when it is active the different protocols must return a failure message upon a query of the server, which is a different join point than starting a play. We require instead of a hidden_by semantics that works at join point level, a similar semantics at the system or aspect level. That is, the activity of Demo should imply the inactivity of G2S and SProtocol.

Similar to the workaround for Theme we proposed in Sect. 4.1, we can provide a design that incorporates the required conflict resolution behavior. Advice in WEAVR are always around advice, and use a proceed call. As in Fig. 2, we can specify an around advice that intercepts Meters and the communication protocols, without performing the original behavior of the intercepted call. This workaround consequently suffers from the same drawbacks as in Sect. 4.1, most importantly the loss of the explicit conflict specification.

5.2 Mutex

Recall that our mutual exclusion consists of the prohibition that, in a single run of the game, the same configuration item is configured by multiple protocols. As an example, Fig. 5 shows the design of the setTime functionality for both protocols in WEAVR . The mutual exclusion in this case boils down to preventing that the state machine of Fig. 5a executes if the state machine of Fig. 5b was previously run, and vice-versa. However, WEAVR does not provide for any way in which this can be specified.

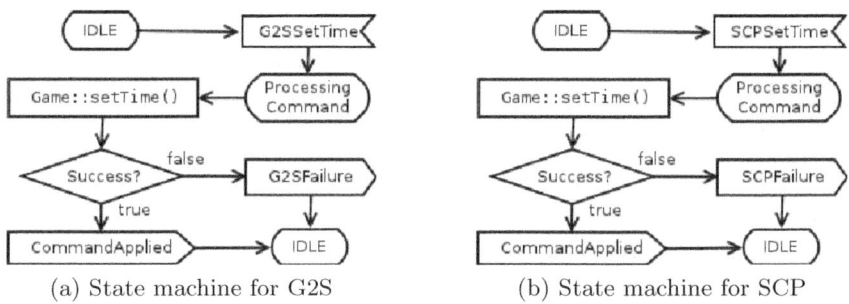

(a) State machine for G2S (b) State machine for SCP

Fig. 5. Mutually exclusive state machines for the setTime command

It is feasible to produce a design document that implements the mutex, but at the cost of making the explicit information of the mutex implicit. We can manually combine the different state machines for the different protocols such that the mutex relation is implemented. Briefly put, for each configuration action we combine the two state machines of the different protocols into one state machine. This combined machine contains the functionality of both protocols together with the logic that ensures that once the item has been configured by one protocol it cannot be configured by the other.

The downside of this solution are that it adds a considerable amount of tedious work, combining the state machines for all configuration settings, and obscures the intent of the design. Moreover it produces a design where both protocols are tightly coupled. Consequently, we consider this option unfeasible and discard it.

5.3 Reinforcement

The design of the reinforcement from error conditions to communication protocols is similar to the design in Theme/UML discussed in Sect. 4.3. We have an error conditions aspect that handles the different types of errors that occur, and the communications protocols report these errors by intercepting this. They define a pointcut that matches on the processing of the error, and the advice then sends the corresponding notification to the server. We have however not found a means to denote the reinforcement relationship as such.

As in Sect. 4.3, the downside of this is that the explicit reinforcement relationship has become implicit, which may lead to inconsistencies during maintenance and evolution, *e.g.* when new types of errors are added to the system. An upside of using WEAVR is that its model simulation capabilities allow for consistency checking of the composed models. This could corroborate the whole execution path from the occurrence of a new error condition to the final notification to the server. However the need for such a verification for all types of error conditions still has to be specified in the design document, and we are unaware of a means to express this in WEAVR .

5.4 Dependency

Similar to the design in Theme, shown in Sect. 4.4, we have an interplay between the metering concern and the communication concerns. The metering concern capturing events regarding game activity and updating the meters, while the communication protocols consult data contained in these meters when processing server requests. In Fig. 6, we show the latter, for the G2S protocol. The action code response := Meters::GetCurrent() refers to data previously stored in the Meters object by the Metering aspect (which is not included in the figure due to lack of space). The communication protocols thus depend on the meters to provide correct functionality. Put differently, if the Meters object is available but for some reason the behavior of the metering aspect is not executed, the data returned will be inconsistent.

To declare dependency relationships, WEAVR provides for the depends_on relationship. It states that one aspect depends on another to be able to provide the required functionality. As in the hidden_by stereotype relationship this however only applies at the join point level. If AspectA depends_on AspectB, for

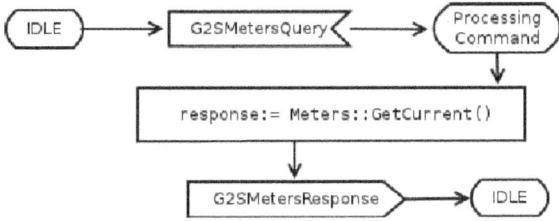

Fig. 6. Part of the G2S Protocol state machine depending on meters

each shared join point the advice of AspectB will be executed before the advice of AspectA. Additionally, if AspectB does not match a join point matched by AspectA, an error is produced.

In our case however, the contact point between two aspects is the existence of the Meters object, not a shared join point. As a consequence, the depends_on relationship does not allow us to express the required dependency. This is as the semantics of the depends_on relationship is too fine grained. In our case we need to be able to express this relation at the level of aspect deployment, *e.g.* state that the deployment of AspectA implies the deployment of AspectB. WEAVR does not provide any other dependency construct, and we are not aware of an alternative option to relate the state diagrams above. We are therefore unable to include the dependency specification in the design.

5.5 Conclusion: WEAVR

We have seen that WEAVR does **not** allow us to explicitly express **any** of the four interaction types. If we allow making the explicit relations implicit, we can include support for conflict resolution and mutual exclusion in the design, the latter of which would be a large amount of tedious work. Such implicit relations however come at a cost of probable errors during maintenance or evolution. Consequently, we consider WEAVR unsuited to specify the design of a SM.

6 Related Work

Schauerhuber *et al.* authored a survey of AOM approaches [12] where concern interactions are part of the evaluation framework. It shows that most of the surveyed approaches do not provide for interaction support. Of those that do, most focus on detection of syntactic and semantic interactions. A representative approach is to transform UML models into graphs which are then analyzed to look for interactions. This approach is also advocated by Ciraci *et al.* [3] and Mehner *et al.* [10].

Similarly, detection of interactions in the design phase has been considered in the feature oriented programming community, *e.g.* the work of Apel *et al.* on FeatureAlloy [1] detects structural (syntactic) and semantic dependencies as well.

The basic assumption in all the above is that interactions are unintended and arise during aspect composition. This however does not hold in our case as interactions may be planned and moreover already have been detected during the requirements phase [13]. Instead of detection, we need for the design to effectively document the decisions made to manage them.

Other authors purely focus on avoiding interactions. For example, Katz and Katz describe how to build an interference-free aspect library [8]. In our case however some interactions are required to obtain the desired behavior, and other interactions cannot be removed but should be controlled instead.

It is interesting to note that the vast majority of AOM work on interactions refer to dependencies and conflicts, but neglect or minimize reinforcement or mutex. This may indicate that these types of interactions are considered less frequent. However they nonetheless occur in our context, and we see no reason why it would be an exceptional case.

7 Conclusions and Future Work

The AOSD-Europe technical report on interactions [11] classifies interactions in four types: dependency, conflict, mutex and reinforcement. In our software for a Slot Machine all four types are present, and we evaluated the abilities of two mature AOM approaches: Theme/UML and WEAVR, to explicitly communicate these in the design.

The somewhat surprising result of our study is that neither Theme/UML nor WEAVR allow us to satisfactorily express any of the four types of dependency. This although both approaches are considered mature, are accepted by the community, and furthermore claim to have support for specific kinds of interactions. In our experience their support is however at the wrong level of granularity and scope to be useful to us. In both methodologies the support is too fine-grained and the scope is too restricted.

As an alternative approach, instead of explicitly specifying the interactions, we have been able to include ad hoc, implicit support for interactions in the design. In Theme/UML we were able to incorporate conflict and reinforcement in the design, while in WEAVR we could include conflict and mutex. However having these relations implicit instead of explicit makes it likely for errors to arise in later maintenance and evolution phases. As a consequence, we need to discard these solutions as well.

The key question for future work is how we would be able to satisfactorily express the interactions in our design. The most straightforward solution would be to extend one of the above methodologies such that it includes the support we are lacking. We consider this therefore as the main avenue for future work.

References

1. Apel, S., Scholz, W., Lengauer, C., Kästner, C.: Detecting dependences and interactions in feature-oriented design. In: ISSRE, pp. 161–170. IEEE Computer Society, Los Alamitos (2010)

2. Chitchyan, R., Rashid, A., Sawyer, P., Garcia, A., Alarcon, M.P., Bakker, J., Tekinerdogan, B., Clarke, S., Jackson, A.: Survey of analysis and design approaches. Tech. Rep. AOSD-Europe Deliverable D11, AOSD-Europe-ULANC-9, University of Lancaster (2005)
3. Ciraci, S., Havinga, W., Aksit, M., Bockisch, C., van den Broek, P.: A graph-based aspect interference detection approach for uml-based aspect-oriented models. T. Aspect-Oriented Software Development 7, 321–374 (2010)
4. Clarke, S., Baniassad, E.: Aspect-Oriented Analysis and Design. The Theme Approach. Object Technology Series. Addison-Wesley, Boston (2005), http://fparreiras/books/AspectOrientedAnalysisAndDesign.chm
5. Cottenier, T., van den Berg, A., Elrad, T.: Motorola weavr: Aspect and model-driven engineering. Journal of Object Technology 6(7), 51–88 (2007)
6. Cottenier, T., Berg, A.V., Elrad, T.: The Motorola WEAVR: Model Weaving in a Large Industrial Context. In: Proceedings of the International Conference on AspectOriented Software Development, Industry Track (2006)
7. ITU, Z.: Specification and description language (sdl). In: International Telecommunication Union (2000)
8. Katz, E., Katz, S.: Incremental analysis of interference among aspects. In: Clifton, C. (ed.) FOAL, pp. 29–38. ACM, New York (2008)
9. Kellens, A., Mens, K., Brichau, J., Gybels, K.: Managing the evolution of aspect-oriented software with model-based pointcuts. In: Hu, Q. (ed.) ECOOP 2006. LNCS, vol. 4067, pp. 501–525. Springer, Heidelberg (2006)
10. Mehner, K., Monga, M., Taentzer, G.: Interaction analysis in aspect-oriented models. In: RE, pp. 66–75. IEEE Computer Society, Los Alamitos (2006)
11. Sanen, F., Truyen, E., Win, B.D., Joosen, W., Loughran, N., Coulson, G., Rashid, A., Nedos, A., Jackson, A., Clarke, S.: Study on interaction issues. Tech. Rep. AOSD-Europe Deliverable D44, AOSD-Europe-KUL-7, Katholieke Universiteit Leuven (2006)
12. Schauerhuber, A., Schwinger, W., Kapsammer, E., Retschitzegger, W., Wimmer, M.: A survey on aspect-oriented modeling approaches. Tech. rep., Vienna University of Technology (2007)
13. Zambrano, A., Fabry, J., Jacobson, G., Gordillo, S.: Expressing aspectual interactions in requirements engineering: experiences in the slot machine domain. In: Proceedings of the 2010 ACM Symposium on Applied Computing (SAC 2010), pp. 2161–2168. ACM Press, New York (2010)

An Industrial Application of Robustness Testing Using Aspect-Oriented Modeling, UML/MARTE, and Search Algorithms

Shaukat Ali[1,2], Lionel C. Briand[1,2], Andrea Arcuri[1], and Suneth Walawege[3]

[1] Simula Research Laboratory, Norway
[2] The University of Oslo, Norway
[3] Cisco Systems Inc, Norway
{shaukat,briand,arcuri}@simula.no,
sunwalaw@cisco.com

Abstract. Systematic and rigorous robustness testing is very critical for embedded systems, as for example communication and control systems. Robustness testing aims at testing the behavior of a system in the presence of faulty situations in its operating environment (e.g., sensors and actuators). In such situations, the system should gracefully degrade its performance instead of abruptly stopping execution. To systematically perform robustness testing, one option is to resort to model-based robustness testing (MBRT), based for example on UML/MARTE models. However, to successfully apply MBRT in industrial contexts, new technology needs to be developed to scale to the complexity of real industrial systems. In this paper, we report on our experience of performing MBRT on video conferencing systems developed by Cisco Systems, Norway. We discuss how we developed and integrated various techniques and tools to achieve a fully automated MBRT that is able to detect previously uncaught software faults in those systems. We provide an overview of how we achieved scalable modeling of robustness behavior using aspect-oriented modeling, test case generation using search algorithms, and environment emulation for test case execution. Our experience and lessons learned identify challenges and open research questions for the industrial application of MBRT.

Keywords: Model-based testing, aspect-oriented modeling, search algorithms, MARTE, UML, robustness.

1 Introduction

Model-based robustness testing (MBRT) is concerned with testing the behavior of a system in the presence of faulty situations in its operating environment. An IEEE Standard [1] defines robustness as *"the degree to which a system or component can function correctly in the presence of invalid inputs or stressful environment conditions"*. A system should be robust enough to handle the possible abnormal situations that can occur in its operating environment and invalid inputs. For example, in our industrial application of MBRT for Video Conferencing Systems (VCS) developed by Cisco Systems, Norway, we model the robustness behavior of a VCS in the presence of hostile environment conditions (regarding the network and other communicating VCSs), such as a high percentage of packet loss and corrupt packets. The VCS should not crash, halt, or restart in the presence of such problems. Furthermore, the VCS should continue to work in a degraded mode, such as continuing the videoconference with low audio and video quality. In the worst case, the VCS should return to the most recent safe state instead of bluntly stopping execution. Such behavior is very important for a commercial VCS, and so it must be accurately tested.

MBRT is considered very critical for embedded systems, for example communication and control systems as is the case of our industrial case study. Such robustness is also considered very critical in many standards such as in the IEEE Standard Dictionary of Measures of the Software Aspects of Dependability [2], the ISO's Software Quality Characteristics standard [3], and the Software Assurance Standard [4] by NASA. Systematic and rigorous robustness testing however requires integration of many tools and techniques in an efficient way.

In this paper, we report on our experience of applying MBRT for VCSs developed by Cisco. Note that such industrial applications of MBRT and even more generally of model-based testing (MBT) are very rare in the literature [5]. These applications are very much needed to evaluate the applicability of MBT in realistic settings. The main contribution of this paper is the integration of the following techniques and tools to achieve the ultimate goal of systematic and rigorous MBRT: 1) Use UML and the MARTE profile to model properties of the environment, whose violations lead to faulty situations the VCS must be robust to; 2) Use aspect-oriented modeling (AOM) to achieve scalable robustness modeling that improves readability of models, reduces modeling complexity, supports enhanced separation of concerns (SOC), and helps in model evolution; 3) Use search algorithms to solve complex OCL constraints on properties of the environment to introduce faulty situations; 4) Integration of the tool support for all of the above with our extensible model-based testing tool (TRUST) [6]. Robustness test case execution requires a special setup to emulate the operating environment. We discuss how we emulate the environment for the MBRT of Cisco's VCS. A preliminary experiment of MBRT in Cisco revealed a critical robustness fault in an already tested VCS. Finally, we discuss our experiences and lessons learned while performing MBRT in Cisco.

The rest of the paper is organized as follows: Section 2 provides a brief description of our case study, Section 3 provides an overview on scalable robustness modeling using AOM and UML/MARTE, and Section 4 discusses test case generation using the TRUST tool. In Section 5, we discuss about robustness test case execution and results from our preliminary experiment with MBRT. Section 6 provides lessons learned and our experiences regarding MBRT in Cisco. Section 7 compares our work with the existing works in the literature. Finally, Section 8 concludes the paper.

2 Case Study

Our case study is part of a project aiming at supporting automated, model-based robustness testing of a core subsystem of a video conference system (VCS) called Saturn. The core functionality to be modeled manages the sending and receiving of multimedia streams. Audio and video signals are sent through separate channels and there is also a possibility of transmitting presentations in parallel with audio and video. Presentations can be sent by only one conference participant at a time and all others receive it. In this paper, we focused on this particularly important subsystem (Saturn) and left out the other functionalities of Saturn. We selected this subsystem because robustness testing is concerned with testing the behavior of Saturn in the presence of faulty environment situations, which can only be tested when Saturn is in a conference call with other systems. Saturn is complex enough to investigate the applicability and usefulness of MBRT in realistic conditions, while still remaining manageable in the context of a case study.

To test the robustness of Saturn, we modeled its behavior in the presence of faulty situations in the network. The behavior of the network can be very unpredictable due to busy routers, high bandwidth demanding traffic (audio and video streaming) and low speed connections. Hence, Saturn is supposed to work even under the presence of faulty situations in a degraded mode. By degraded mode, we mean that the system should continue to behave as in the non-faulty situation, except that the quality (such as audio and video) or the performance is degraded by running applications at a lower speed. The system must try to recover from the degraded mode and go back to a normal mode of operation. In the worst case, the system must return to the most recent safe state. An example of a safe state of a VCS is the idle state, in which the VCS is not in a videoconference with any VCS.

3 Scalable Robustness Modeling

In this section, we discuss our scalable robustness modeling approach. In Section 3.1, we provide and briefly present partial models for the functional behavior of Saturn. In Section 3.2 we discuss how we model robustness behavior with aspect state machines using our proposed AspectSM profile.

3.1 Functional Behavior of Saturn

The functional behavior of Saturn consists of a set of class diagrams and a set of UML state machines. An excerpt of class diagram for the Saturn subsystem described in Section 2 is shown in Fig. 1.

The UML class diagram is meant to capture information about APIs and system (state) variables, which are required to generate executable test cases in our application context. Saturn's API is modeled as a set of methods in the *Saturn* class such as *dial()* and *callDisconnect()*. The state variables of the system are modeled as instance variables of classes. For example, two system variables in the *SystemUnit* class are *NumberOfActiveCalls* and *MaximumNumberOfCalls*. *NumberOfActiveCalls* is an *Integer*, which determines the number of VCS that are currently in a Saturn videoconference, whereas *MaximumNumberOfCalls* determines the maximum number of simultaneous calls supported by Saturn.

The functional behavior of Saturn is modeled as four submachine states. The first submachine state contains three simple states, whereas the second contains two additional submachine states, each having three simple states. This gives in total eleven simple states and 41 transitions in three levels. The flattened state machine consists of 70 transitions and 11 states. The complete models are provided in [7].

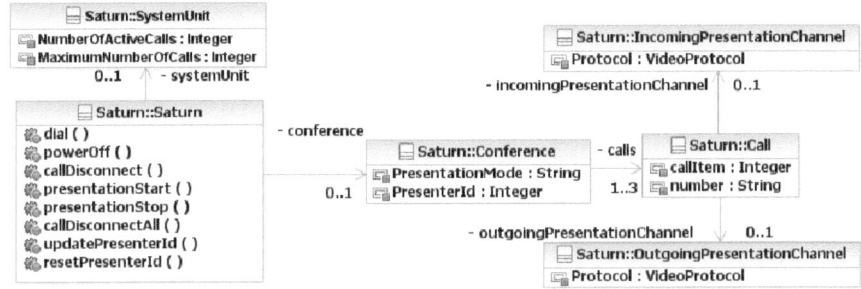

Fig. 1. Class diagram for Saturn

3.2 Robustness Modeling Using RUMM

Previously, we defined a RobUstness Modeling Methodology (RUMM) to model robustness behavior using AOM [7]. Our goal was to devise a solution to model robustness behavior, which (1) is complete in terms of aspect and state machine features, (2) minimizes the learning curve over standard modeling skills, and (3) enable automated, model-based testing. RUMM consists of a series of systematic activities to model robustness behavior. We do not present here details of these activities, however, interested readers may find them in [7]. In this paper, we on modeling robustness behavior using the AspectSM profile. Using the AspectSM profile, we model each aspect as a UML state machine with stereotypes (aspect state machine). The modeling of aspect state machines is systematically derived from a fault taxonomy [7] categorizing different types of faults (faults in the environment such as communication medium and media streams that lead to faulty situations in the environment). Each aspect state machine has a corresponding aspect class diagram modeling different properties of the environment using the MARTE profile, whose violations lead to faulty situations in the environment.

Modeling aspect class diagram. For the robustness behavior presented in Section 2, we were interested in modeling the behavior of Saturn in the presence of faulty situations in the network. For this purpose, we decided to model the following network properties: packet loss, packet delay, duplicate packet, corrupt packet, and reorder packet. These properties are modeled in a class diagram as shown in Fig. 2. All of these properties are modeled using the MARTE profile [8]. For instance, the packet loss property introduces packet loss during communication and is measured in terms of percentage. This property is defined to be of the MARTE type *NFP_Percentage*, which is defined in the MARTE profile for this purpose. Another property we defined is packet delay. This property is defined as a new, non-functional property (NFP) data type stereotyped as *<<NfpType>>* defined in MARTE (Fig. 2). The new NFP type includes other properties such as *unit* of type *TimeUnitKind*. *TimeUnitKind* in MARTE defines units for time values such as millisecond and microsecond. We chose this data type so that a modeler can choose an appropriate time unit.

112   S. Ali et al.

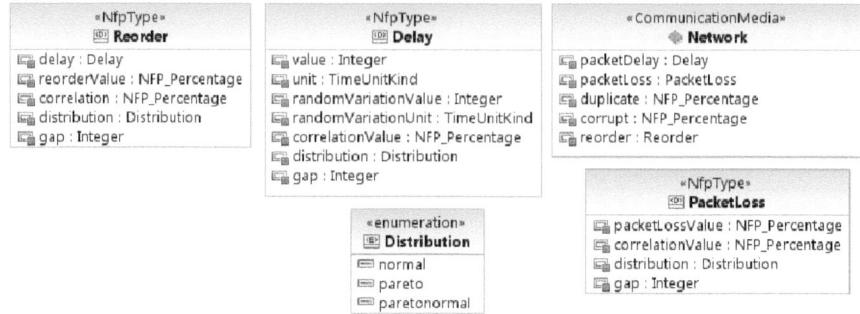

Fig. 2. Aspect class diagram for network communication

Modeling aspect state machine. The aspect state machine for *NetworkCommunication* is shown in Fig. 3. The *'NetworkCommunication'* state machine is stereotyped as *'Aspect'* from the AspectSM profile and the attributes associated with the stereotype are shown in the note labeled 1. The first attribute *name* specifies the name of the aspect, which is *NetworkCommunicationAspect* in this case. The second attribute *baseStateMachine* specifies the base state machine on which the aspect will be woven, which is Saturn in this case.

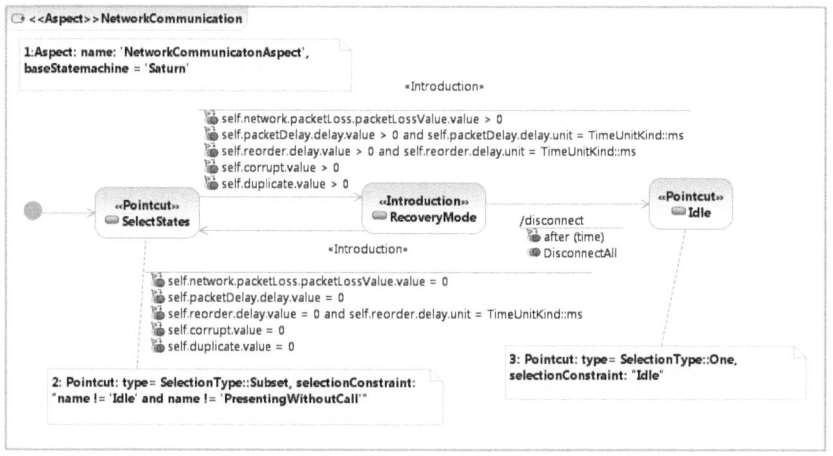

Fig. 3. Aspect state machine for network communication

A pointcut named *'SelectStatesPointcut'* on the state *'SelectedStates'* is shown in Fig. 3 (see note 2), which selects all states of the base state machine except for the *Idle* and *PresentingWithoutCall* states. New transitions modeling robustness behavior of the system from all states selected by the *'SelectStatesPointcut'* pointcut to a new state *'RecoveryMode'* stereotyped with the <<*Introduction*>> stereotype are introduced. These transitions are modeled as UML change events. For instance, when *self.corrupt.value>0* in any of the states selected by the pointcut, the system goes to

'*RecoveryMode*', which is stereotyped as <<*Introduction*>> indicating that this state will be introduced in the base state machine. In this state, the system tries to recover the corrupt packets. If the system is successful, the transition with the change event '*self.corrupt.value =0*' takes the system back to the original state, which is one of the states selected by the *SelectedStates* state. If the system cannot recover within time t, then the system disconnects all the systems and goes to the '*Idle*' state, stereotyped as <<*Pointcut*>> (see Fig. 3). This is modeled as a new transition from the '*RecoveryMode*' state to the '*Idle*' state, with a time event *after(t)*, and a new effect '*DisconnectAll*' with opaque behavior *disconnect*, which disconnects all the connected systems to the system.

4 Test Case Generation

In this section, we discuss how we extended our MBT tool, TRansformation-based tool for Uml-baSed Testing (TRUST) [6] for robustness testing.

4.1 An Overview of TRUST

In our previous work [6], we developed TRUST, whose software architecture and implementation strategy facilitate its customization to different contexts by supporting extensible features such as input models, test models, coverage criteria, test data generation strategies, and test script languages. For example, the tool is extensible with respect to coverage criteria and it lets the user implement and integrate new coverage criteria with minimum changes to the tool [9]. The tool takes as input a UML class diagram and one or more UML state machines and outputs test scripts.

4.2 Integration of the AspectSM Weaver with TRUST

A weaver is a tool that takes as input a base model and one or more aspects and produces a woven model [10]. We developed a weaver for AspectSM using a set of transformation rules in Kermeta [11]. Fig. 4 shows the architecture diagram for the weaver. The aspect weaver works in two steps. First it weaves aspect class diagram into the UML class diagram (e.g., Fig. 1) corresponding to the base state machine using the transformation rules written in Kermeta [11]. These rules take as input an aspect class diagram (e.g., Fig. 2) corresponding to an aspect state machine to be woven, a class diagram (e.g., Fig. 1) corresponding to the base state machine, and output a class diagram which is the class diagram corresponding to the base state machine augmented with the aspect class diagram. In the second step, one or more aspect state machines (e.g., Fig. 3) are woven into the base state machine. Since our queries (Pointcuts [7]) are in OCL, which need to be evaluated during the weaving process, we need to convert OCL expressions into Kermeta expressions. This is achieved through the *OCLToKermeta* component. Finally, *AspectStateMachineWeaver* produces a woven state machine which is a standard UML state machine. This state machine is then provided to the TRUST tool for test case generation.

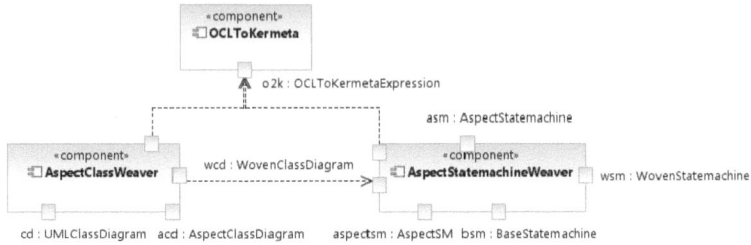

Fig. 4. Architecture diagram for the weaver

4.3 Integration of Search-Based Constraint Solver with TRUST

Emulating faulty situations in the operating environment of a VCS requires solving complex OCL constraints on the properties of the environment. These constraints must be solved during test case generation to emulate the faulty situations (i.e., to set the environment properties in a way for which such faulty situations occur). To efficiently solve these constraints, we developed a search-based OCL constraint solver [12], since current OCL solvers were not able to handle the complexity of our model's constraints within reasonable time. Fig. 5 shows the architecture diagram for our Search-based Constraint solver. We developed a tool in Java that interacts with an existing library, an OCL evaluator called the EyeOCL Software (EOS) [13]. EOS is a Java component that provides APIs to parse and evaluate an OCL expression based on an object model. Our tool implements the calculation of branch distance (*DistanceCalculator*) [12] for various expressions in OCL, which aims at calculating how far are environment properties from satisfying constraints. The search algorithms employed are implemented in Java as well and includes Genetic Algorithms and (1+1) Evolutionary Algorithm [12].

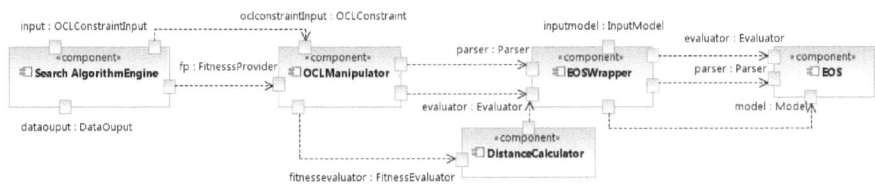

Fig. 5. Architecture diagram for search-based constraint solver

5 Test Case Execution

In this section, we provide details on robustness test case execution. Section 5.1 describes our setup required for test case execution and Section 5.2 provides results of test case execution corresponding to the case study provided in Section 2.

5.1 Setup for Test Case Execution

Fig. 6 shows our test execution setup for executing robustness test cases generated by TRUST. The current setup involves *Saturn*, which is the system under test (SUT) and three video conferences systems (*VCSs*). Since the execution of test cases requires emulating faulty situations in the environment, we needed a network emulator. For this purpose, we relied on software-based emulation facility (*netem* [14]). The setup of network emulator requires setting up a *PC* with three network interface cards (*NICs*). All communication to/from *Saturn* (*SUT* in Fig. 4) passes through *NetworkEmulator*. *Saturn* is connected to *NIC3* of *NetworkEmulator* and all incoming and outgoing traffic from *Network* comes through *NIC1*. *NIC1* is bridged to *NIC3* and hence all the traffic goes to *Saturn* via *NIC3*. Our test case execution system is directly connected to *NIC2* of network emulator and through this *NIC* all faulty situations in the network are introduced by test scripts. All other communication from the test execution system to *SUT* and *VCSs* takes place through *NIC2* of *NetworkEmulator*. We separated them because if the faulty situations are introduced via the same NIC as other communication flows, we might end up affecting the commands that introduce faulty situations. Thus, we may end up not introducing faulty situations at all.

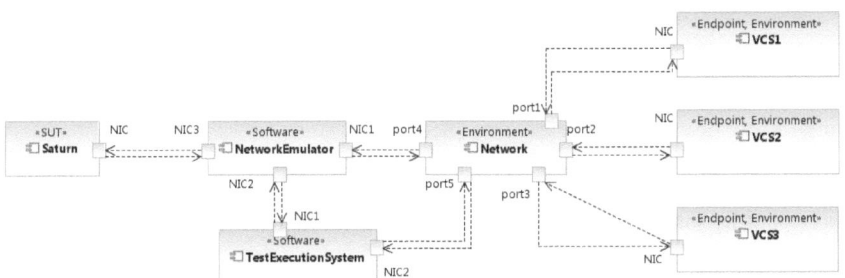

Fig. 6. Setup for robustness test case execution

5.2 Preliminary Test Case Execution Results

For our current case study (Section 2), we used our weaver (Section 4.2) to produce a woven state machine. The woven state machine was given as input to TRUST (Section 4.1), which was configured to generate test cases using *All Transition Coverage* implemented by depth first search. In total 72 test cases were generated by TRUST. OCL constraints (change events in Fig. 3) were solved using our search-based constraint solver (Section 4.3) to generate test data and introduce faulty situations in the environment. We executed test cases using the setup presented in Section 5.1. The execution of test cases found one robustness fault (halt and restart) in *Saturn*, when more than 10% duplicate packets were introduced in network communication. Our approach had more chances to catch this fault compared to existing practices in Cisco. MBT is more systematic and is in our case specifically tailored to catch robustness faults. Our approach indeed focuses on automatically testing the robustness of Saturn over various functional scenarios in the presence of several faulty situations in the network. In contrast, current robustness testing at Cisco is based on scripts written manually by testers to test a few network properties over a few of functional scenarios.

6 Experience and Lessons Learned

This section reports our experience of performing model-based robustness testing (MBRT) at Cisco. As often with many control and communication systems in industry, robustness testing is very critical for Cisco's Video Conferencing Systems (VCS). Currently, robustness testing at Cisco is driven by manually written test scripts, which is a common scenario in many industries. Due to time and resource constraints (e.g., system-level test cases are run with hardware-in-the-loop), only a limited number of test scripts can be written and only a limited number of faulty situations can be emulated. In these constrained cases, it is hence essential to carry out robustness testing in an automated and systematic way.

In order to support scalable modeling, aspect-oriented modeling (AOM) is adapted to support robustness modeling in the context of embedded systems and UML state machines (Section 3). Test cases are then generated based on system models including robustness behavior, using coverage criteria such as all round trip paths and all transitions criteria [9] (Section 4). Such an approach guarantees to cover important test scenarios that could be missed by manual testing, and thus leading to more systematic and comprehensive testing. Furthermore, the models can be used to generate effective, automated oracles (e.g., state invariants). Test cases are then executed using environment emulators (Section 5).

In the section below, we report on our experience of performing MBRT in Cisco. Since such reports are very rare in the literature (see Section 7), we believe that such section would provide useful insights in terms of the challenges we faced and the effectiveness of the solutions adopted in practice.

6.1 Robustness Modeling

In this section, we describe our experience and provide lessons learned obtained from modeling robustness behavior of Saturn, a VCS developed by Cisco. Details on our experience with functional modeling can be found in [6].

Experiences with AOM. Modeling the robustness behavior was performed by the authors with the help of testers in Cisco, who are currently involved in robustness testing. The modeling was done as part of a research project regarding the application of model-based testing technology in industry.

Before modeling, it was important to have meetings with software engineers at Cisco to understand the specifications of the robustness behavior implemented in Saturn. When the specifications were sufficiently understood, the modeling process started. The testers themselves were involved in the modeling of the robustness and functional behavior. The models were discussed and revised several times during the modeling, to ensure that the behavior is modeled completely and correctly. The robustness modeling took around seven hours. Understanding the specification took approximately four hours, whereas the actual modeling took approximately three hours. All the modeling was done with IBM Rational Software Architect (RSA) 7.5 as our UML profile (AspectSM) is also implemented in RSA. Note that this time accounts only for modeling the robustness behavior of Saturn in the presence of faulty situations in the network.

As we discussed in Section 3, robustness behavior crosscuts functional behavior. When robustness behavior is modeled directly with the functional model, the complexity of the resulting model increases enormously due to redundant modeling elements, which are scattered across the model (e.g., repeated in each state of the functional model). Modeling such redundant behavior requires substantial modeling effort if not modeled using an AOM methodology as the same behavior has to be modeled in several places in the model. As we discussed in Section 3, we employed AOM, and more specifically the AspectSM profile to reduce this accidental modeling complexity. Based on our experience with the Saturn VCS, we saved more than 95% of the modeling effort when measured by the number of modeled elements involved in the VCS robustness behaviors [7]. Of course, this effort is saved at the expense of learning and applying various stereotypes defined in AspectSM. We will further investigate the effort required to learn and apply AspectSM with more industrial case studies and controlled experiments in the future. However, the percentage of saving is so large that we consider these results to be very promising. In addition, modeling robustness behavior using AspectSM significantly improves the readability of the models as suggested from the results of a controlled experiment reported in [15].

Modeling crosscutting behavior in UML state machines provides enhanced separation of concerns. This means that a modeler/tester, or several of them with possibly different expertise, can focus on each crosscutting concern separately. They can model these crosscutting concerns separately from the core functionality and other crosscutting concerns (aspects). Our tool [7] can then be used to automatically weave these aspects with the behavioral models.

Experiences with MARTE. As we discussed in Section 3.2, we used a small subset of the MARTE profile to model properties of environment, whose violations lead to the faulty situations in the environment. The MARTE profile has a package dedicated to modeling non-functional properties (NFP). It provides different data types such as *NFP_Percentage* and *NFP_DataTxRate*, which are helpful to model properties of the environment, for instance jitter and packet loss in networks. When the built-in data types of MARTE are not sufficient, the open modeling framework of MARTE can be used to define new NFP types by either extending the existing NFPs or by defining completely new NFPs. For instance, we extended MARTE's NFPs and define several properties of the environment when modeling *echo* in audio streams and modeling *miss-synchronization* between audio and video streams coming to a VCS [7]. From our experience in using MARTE, we can conclude that the MARTE profile and its open modeling framework were sufficient to model relevant properties of the Saturn operating environment. In addition, the fact that MARTE is a standard UML profile by OMG and hence is supported by many modeling tools [8] facilitates the adoption of modeling in industrial contexts since models are assets to be reused and modified over many years.

6.2 Test Case Generation

In this section, we discuss our experiences regarding the generation of robustness test cases.

Experiences with the TRUST tool. We have previously reported [6] the successful application of the TRUST tool in two companies to support functional test case generation. In our current application, we extended TRUST for robustness testing. For this purpose, we only needed to change the transformation rules in MOFScript [14] that generate the concrete test scripts. The modified transformation rules generate appropriate commands in the test scripts that emulate faulty situations in the environment. Generally, the transformation rules written in, e.g., Kermeta [11], MOFScript [14], or Query/View/Transformation (QVT) [16] are relatively compact and easy to read, write, and change as opposed to manipulating models using programming languages such as Java and C++. For the current implementation, we used MOFScript as Model-to-Text (M2T) transformation language, because it was the only M2T transformation language with good enough tool support (at the time of writing this paper).

Experiences with environment fault emulation. The most challenging part for test case generation was emulating faulty situations in the environment to test a system's robustness against them. A faulty situation in the operating environment is emulated when the properties of the environment are violated (Section 3.2). These violations are specified as change events (OCL constraints) on aspect state machines that lead to faulty states. To obtain a test suite that covers all the states in such UML models, it is hence important to find environment configurations for which these OCL constraints are evaluated to be true. Unfortunately, some of these constraints are complex, comprising of up to eight conjuncted clauses and hence are very difficult to solve using existing OCL solvers. For instance, we experimented with one well-known, downloadable OCL solver (UMLtoCSP) [17]. The results showed that, even after running that tool for 10 hours, no solutions could be found for most of the constraints. The reason is that the existing OCL solvers require the conversion of OCL to lower-level languages such as a Satisfiability (SAT) formula [18] or a Constraint Solving Problem (CSP) [17] instance and hence can easily result in combinatorial explosion as the complexity of the model and constraints increase (as discussed in [17]). For industrial scale systems, as in our case, this is a major limitation, since the models and constraints are generally quite complex. Hence, existing techniques based on conversion to lower-level languages seem impractical in the context of large scale, real-world systems. To solve this issue, we developed a new OCL solver based on search algorithms and managed to solve the same constraints in 3.8 minutes on average [12] on a regular PC. This gives empirical evidence that it is possible to quickly and directly solve complex industrial constraints written in a high-level language such as OCL, and hence efficiently emulates faulty situations in the operating environment for robustness testing purposes.

As we discuss in Section 6.2, we developed an OCL constraint solver in Java that interacts with an existing library, an OCL evaluator called EyeOCL Software (EOS) [17]. Our tool implements a set of heuristics as discussed in [12] for various expressions in OCL using EOS's API, which are then used by search algorithms to guide the search for input data that satisfy such constraints. We used EOS for both parsing and evaluating OCL expressions. We experienced that EOS is one of the most efficient OCL evaluators and provides a very simple API to evaluate and parse OCL expressions. In our experience, the only major downside of EOS is that, to evaluate/parse OCL expressions, EOS requires class and/or object diagrams to be loaded into its memory in a specific format. To facilitate this, we wrote a MOFScript transformation that takes the UML class diagram (modeling state variables, method calls, and signal receptions of the SUT) as input and generates a Java wrapper class that includes a set of EOS method calls for making class and object diagrams. During test case generation, we solve the constraints on the environment properties to emulate faulty situations in the environment using EOS and search algorithms. Another issue when solving an OCL constraint using a search algorithm is that it requires evaluating the OCL expression many times, and hence the speed of constraint solving is dependent on the efficiency of the selected OCL evaluator. Recall from Section 4.3 that we developed our TRUST testing tool with an open architecture such that any other OCL evaluator and parser (more efficient) can be easily replaced with EOS if required.

6.3 Test Case Execution

This section discusses our experience with test case execution at Cisco.

Experiences with setting up environment emulators. Executing robustness test cases is expensive because it requires setting up special equipment (hardware and/or software-based emulators) to emulate faulty situations in the environment. The emulators required in our current industrial case study are targeting networks, media streams and VCS. In our case, we only experimented with the network emulator because all communications between VCSs takes place via the network. It is hence important to test a VCS's behavior in the presence of faulty situations in the network. In our current application, we setup network emulator (*netem* [14]) once and then used it for testing without any additional settings for executing each test case.

Experiences with test case execution. Applying standard MBT criteria on UML state machines modeling the VCS results in test suites that are often to expensive or time-consuming to fit available test resources. For instance, in our current experiment, using a very simple coverage criterion on our (partial) case study (Section 5.2) resulted in 72 test cases, which would a take a long time to run in the test lab at Cisco Norway. This is expected to be a problem on most industrial systems, especially when modeling robustness along with the functional behavior. Executing large test suites is not practically feasible in many industrial contexts due to limited time and resources. For instance, running one robustness test case requires booking a specialized testing lab and takes on average 15 minutes on a Cisco's VCS. To cope with this practical problem, and in general to apply MBT in industry, there is the need of smart techniques to automatically select smaller subsets of test cases that can be run within testing budgets [19].

6.4 Current Limitations

As we discussed in Section 3, we need to model the faulty situations in the network, media streams, and VCSs communicating with a VCS under test (VUT). To date, we experimented only with emulating faulty situations in the network, which is just one aspect of the environment. Although we have already modeled the faulty situations in media streams (e.g., echo in audio and miss-synchronization between audio and video) [7], we do not have an appropriate media stream emulator yet. In addition to the media streams emulator, we also need to update our test script generator to generate test scripts that will control the media streams emulator during test case execution. For emulating faulty situations in other VCSs communicating with the VUT, we have not yet modeled the VCSs from that perspective. But we do expect that the models of the VCSs should be quite similar to the models of VUT, except for the need to select test paths from the models that will trigger faulty situations. For this purpose, we do have software-based emulators for VCSs, which can be utilized to emulate faulty situations during test case execution.

7 Related Work

Most of the work related to MBRT focuses on modeling and testing the behavior of a system when invalid inputs are given to the system, or in cases when exceptions (similar to exceptions in a programming language) are thrown in the SUT. For instance, Pintér and Majzik [20] report on the modeling of exceptions in statecharts in a similar fashion to Java mechanisms for writing exceptions (*try/catch* blocks). Exceptions are modeled as events on transitions in statecharts. Such statecharts are subsequently used for model checking. Lei et al. [21] provide a methodology to check the robustness of component-based systems in the case of invalid inputs. Test cases are then generated for invalid inputs at various states and the robustness of the system is checked. Nebut et al. [22] provide an automatic test generation approach based on use cases extended with contracts, after transforming them into a transition system. Their approach supports both functional and robustness test generation. Robustness test cases are generated by calling use cases when their preconditions are false.

The work presented in this paper is different from the existing work in MBRT in one or more of the following ways: 1) It focuses on modeling and testing system robustness in the presence of faults in its environment; this aspect has received little attention in the literature. In contrast, most of the existing work focus only on the behavior of a system when receiving invalid inputs [20] [21]. In contrast to the work presented in [22], our work is based on UML state machines, which is the main notation currently used for model-based test case generation [5]; 2) It uses AOM to model robustness behavior separately from the core, functional behavior, hence decreasing modeling effort by avoiding clutter in models, making them easier to read and decreasing chances of modeling errors; 3) It relies on modeling standards, in this case UML state machines and the MARTE profile [8], to model faulty situations of the environment. Using standards eliminate the need to adopt new notations and consequently facilitates the technology transfer to industry, as there are commercial modeling tools supporting UML and its extensions.

Other related works are the ones which employ search algorithms for non-functional testing. A recent systematic review [23] on the application of search algorithms for non-functional testing reveals that existing works focused on performance, quality of service, security, usability, and safety testing. None targeted robustness testing using search algorithms, as in our work.

8 Conclusion and Future Work

Model-based robustness testing (MBRT) is a solution for systematic and rigorous robustness testing for industrial embedded systems, as for example communication and control systems. MBRT involves testing the behavior of a system in the presence of faulty situations in its operating environment.

In this paper, we reported our experience of applying MBRT to video conferencing systems (VCSs) developed by Cisco Systems, Norway. Such industrial applications of MBRT and even more generally of model-based testing (MBT) are very rare in the literature. They are however very important to evaluate the scalability and applicability of MBT in realistic settings. We discussed how we integrated different tools and techniques to achieve the ultimate goal of automated and systematic MBRT. First, we discussed how we achieved scalable modeling of robustness behavior using Aspect-oriented Modeling (AOM) and more specifically using the AspectSM profile. AspectSM is a UML profile specifically designed to model robustness behavior with minimum extensions to UML to ease practical adoption. We also provided details on the weaver for AspectSM. Second, we provided details on the use of search algorithms (e.g., Genetic Algorithms) to solve complex constraints on environmental properties to emulate faulty situations. Third, we described the integration of the abovementioned tools with our model-based testing tool TRUST to achieve fully automated MBRT. Finally, we discussed the setup required to execute the test cases generated by TRUST and preliminary results when running the case studies on the VCS under test. The execution of test cases revealed a robustness fault in the VCS that had remained undetected by previous testing, in the presence of duplicate packets in the network during a videoconference. We then summarized our experiences and lessons learned while applying MBRT at Cisco.

This paper reports on a successful application of modeling to support testing in a real industrial setting. The results reported in this paper provide useful insights into the challenges and benefits of applying MBRT in a typical embedded system environment. One key success factor is to be able to address serious scalability issues (e.g., in constraint solving), which usually are not faced when dealing with small/artificial problem instances. However, there are still many research questions that need to be addressed. In the future, we are planning to extend the TRUST tool with more sophisticated test strategies specifically tailored to discovering robustness faults in a VCS. We also plan to perform robustness testing in the presence of faulty situations in other aspects of the environment such as in media streams and VCSs.

References

1. IEEE Standard Glossary of Software Engineering Terminology. IEEE, IEEE Std 610.12-1990, p. 1 (1990)
2. IEEE Standard Dictionary of Measures of the Software Aspects of Dependability. IEEE Std 982.1-2005 (Revision of IEEE Std 982.1-1988), pp. 1–34 (2006)
3. Standard for Software Quality Characteristics. International Organization for Standardization, ISO-9126-3 (2003)
4. Software Assurance Standard. NASA Technical Standard, NASA-STD-8739.8 (2005)

5. Shafique, M., Labiche, Y.: A Systematic Review of Model Based Testing Tools. Carleton University, Department of Systems and Computer Engineering, Technical Report, SCE-10-04 (2010)
6. Ali, S., Hemmati, H., Holt, N.E., Arisholm, E., Briand, L.C.: Model Transformations as a Strategy to Automate Model-Based Testing - A Tool and Industrial Case Studies. Simula Research Laboratory, Technical Report (2010-01) (2010)
7. Ali, S., Briand, L.C., Hemmati, H.: Modeling Robustness Behavior Using Aspect-Oriented Modeling to Support Robustness Testing of Industrial Systems. Simula Research Laboratory, Technical Report (2010-03) (2010)
8. Modeling and Analysis of Real-time and Embedded systems, MARTE (2010), http://www.omgmarte.org/
9. Binder, R.V.: Testing object-oriented systems: models, patterns, and tools. Addison-Wesley Longman Publishing Co., Inc., Amsterdam (1999)
10. Yedduladoddi, R.: Aspect Oriented Software Development: An Approach to Composing UML Design Models. VDM Verlag Dr. Müller (2009)
11. Kermeta - Breathe Life into Your Metamodels (2010), http://www.kermeta.org/
12. Ali, S., Iqbal, M.Z., Arcuri, A., Briand, L.C.: A Search-based OCL Constraint Solver for Model-based Test Data Generation. In: Proceedings of the 11th International Conference On Quality Software, QSIC 2011 (2011)
13. Egea, M.: EyeOCL Software (2010), http://maude.sip.ucm.es/eos/
14. netem (2011), http://www.linuxfoundation.org/collaborate/workgroups/networking/netem
15. Ali, S., Yue, T., Briand, L.C., Malik, Z.I.: Does Aspect-Oriented Modeling Help Improve the Readability of UML State Machines? (2010)
16. Query/View/Transformation QVT (2011), http://www.omg.org/spec/QVT/1.0/
17. Cabot, J., Claris, R., Riera, D.: Verification of UML/OCL Class Diagrams using Constraint Programming. In: Proceedings of the 2008 IEEE International Conference on Software Testing Verification and Validation Workshop. IEEE Computer Society, Los Alamitos (2008)
18. Krieger, M., Knapp, A.: Executing Underspecified OCL Operation Contracts with a SAT Solver. In: 8th International Workshop on OCL Concepts and Tools. ECEASST, vol. 15 (2008)
19. Hemmati, H., Briand, L., Arcuri, A., Ali, S.: An Enhanced Test Case Selection Approach for Model-Based Testing: An Industrial Case Study. In: 18th ACM SIGSOFT International Symposium on Foundations of Software Engineering (FSE). ACM, New York (2010)
20. Pintér, G., Majzik, I.: Modeling and Analysis of Exception Handling by Using UML Statecharts. Scientific Engineering of Distributed Java Applications, 58–67 (2005)
21. Lei, B., Liu, Z., Morisset, C., Li, X.: State Based Robustness Testing for Components. Electronic Notes of Theoretical Computer Science 260, 173–188
22. Nebut, C., Fleurey, F., Traon, Y.L., Jezequel, J.-M.: Automatic Test Generation: A Use Case Driven Approach. IEEE Transactions of Software Engineering 32, 140–155 (2006)
23. Afzal, W., Torkar, R., Feldt, R.: A Systematic Review of Search-based Testing for Non-functional System Properties. Information and Software Technology 51, 957–976 (2009)

Aspect-Oriented Modelling for Distributed Systems

Wisam Al Abed and Jörg Kienzle

School of Computer Science, McGill University, Montreal, Canada
Wisam.Alabed@mail.mcgill.ca, Joerg.Kienzle@mcgill.ca

Abstract. *Aspect-Oriented Modelling* techniques allow a modeller to describe within a single aspect model all model elements that define the structural and/or behavioural properties of a concern. When applied to a base model, the model weaver ensures that the entire aspect is reflected in the woven model. While this is essential for centralized systems, it is not the case when model elements of a concern are scattered over nodes in a distributed system. We propose an extension to our *Reusable Aspect Models* that allows the modeller to augment an aspect model of a concern that can crosscut the nodes of a distributed system with *distribution role definitions*. A *distributed system configuration file* specifies the different node types of the distributed system, and which roles of a distributed aspect are assigned to which nodes. The weaver makes sure that every role of a distributed aspect is assigned to at least one node in the system to ensure consistent aspect use. The weaver then generates for each node a final application model that only contains the model elements pertaining to the distribution roles the node plays.

1 Introduction

Aspect-Oriented Modelling (AOM) techniques allow a modeller to describe within a single aspect model all model elements that define the structural and/or behavioural properties of a concern. AOM approaches that emphasize reuse provide features that allow an aspect model to clearly specify its interface, i.e. expose the structure and behaviour provided by the aspect, while hiding unnecessary details about how the functionality is provided. When a concern is needed within a specific application model, the aspect model is simply applied to the application model by matching elements declared in the aspect interface with application model elements. The aspect weaver then combines both models to yield a woven model of the application. In the woven model, the model elements of the aspect crosscut the structure and behaviour of the application model.

The fact that *all* model elements related to a specific concern are grouped together is of major importance for the following reasons:

- It *prevents scattering of model elements* related to the concern over a big application model. Having all model elements pertaining to the concern in one place is useful for reasoning about the concern itself. It also simplifies

making changes to the way a concern provides its functionality, because the modeller is guaranteed not to overlook anything important.
- It *prevents tangling of model elements* related to several concerns within a big application model. This is useful for reasoning about the application model itself, because the modeller is not distracted by any model elements related to the aspect. As a result, the application model is easier to evolve.
- It *ensures consistent use of the aspect model*. Since the aspect model contains all relevant model elements of the concern, the weaver can ensure that the entire structure and behaviour of the aspect is indeed composed with the application model. It would be incorrect to only weave some of the aspect model elements, since they all logically belong together.

While the last point mentioned above is highly desirable for centralized systems, the situation changes in the context of a distributed system composed of many processing nodes. Often, the individual nodes play different roles in the system, contributing in different ways to fulfill the purpose of the system. Typical examples of distributed systems with different kinds of nodes are client-server systems, or systems that use the publish-subscribe paradigm. Unless the distributed architecture is perfectly symmetrical, the implementations of the different nodes vary considerably. For instance, in most client-server systems, the client node typically knows how to send requests to the server and provides an elaborate user interface, whereas the server usually waits for requests from clients and executes them on business objects. When modelling the design of such a distributed system, a separate design model must ultimately be created for each kind of node, since in the end each kind of node is implemented by means of a different executable.

When aspect-oriented modelling techniques are applied in the context of a distributed system, it is possible that the structure and behaviour defined by an aspect model crosscuts the different nodes. The distributed system as a whole still needs all the structural elements and still exhibits the complete behaviour described in the aspect, but the model for each individual node in the system does not need to contain all aspect model elements, but just the ones that are used on that node. For example, in a wireless sensor network, the application running on the resource-constrained sensor nodes might only send sensor information to the backend and never receive any messages. Likewise, for confidentiality reasons, the sensor nodes only need to encrypt the data, whereas the backend application needs to decrypt it. In order to save resources and reduce application complexity, the sensor node application should not contain structure and behaviour related to receiving and decrypting.

In this paper we show how to extend aspect-oriented modelling techniques, and in particular the *Reusable Aspect Models* (RAM) [1,2] approach, to model distributed systems with aspects that crosscut the different kinds of nodes. The outline of the paper is as follows. Section 2 presents the key concepts of RAM by showing the design of an *Observer* aspect that implements the *observer design pattern*. Section 3 shows how we introduced the concept of *distribution roles* into our aspect models, and illustrates their use by showing a simple

SocketCommunication aspect that uses sockets to establish a communication between two nodes. We then proceed to build a *RemoteObserver* aspect based on the centralized *Observer* aspect and the distributable *Communication* aspect. Section 4 presents how we envision the RAM tool and aspect weaver to allow a modeller to configure a distributed system composed of several nodes. Section 5 presents related work, and the last section draws some conclusions.

2 Background on RAM

In [1,2] we have proposed *Reusable Aspect Models* (RAM), an aspect-oriented multi-view modelling approach that 1) integrates class diagram, sequence diagram and state diagram AOM techniques into one coherent approach; 2) provides aspect models with well-defined interfaces for easy and flexible reuse; 3) supports the creation of complex aspect dependency chains; 4) performs elaborate consistency checks to verify correct aspect composition and reuse; 5) defines a detailed weaving algorithm that resolves aspect dependencies to generate independent aspect models and ultimately the final application model.

The section introduces the core concepts of RAM that are relevant for this paper by modelling the structure and behaviour of the *Observer* aspect. The classic *Observer Design Pattern* [3] is a software design pattern in which an object, called the *subject*, maintains a list of dependents, called *observers*. Whenever the subject's state changes, it notifies all observers by calling an *update* operation. The observer design pattern has been used in many publications to demonstrate different aspect-oriented programming and aspect-oriented modelling techniques.

2.1 Designing the Aspect Interface

When designing an aspect model with RAM, the designer usually starts by designing the *aspect interface*, which contains the structural and behavioural model elements that are important in order to apply the aspect to some base model. The interface for the *Observer* aspect is shown in Fig. 1.

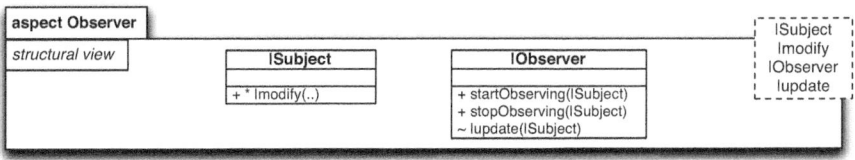

Fig. 1. The *Observer* Aspect Interface

The most important elements of the interface are the mandatory instantiation parameters. They are depicted as UML template parameters in the upper right corner of the structural view of the aspect model. Mandatory instantiation parameters designate aspect model elements that a modeller must map to model elements within the base model in order to make use of an aspect. Another way of looking at this is that the base model must provide model elements for all the mandatory instantiation parameters of an aspect model in order to use it. In case of the *Observer* aspect, the mandatory instantiation parameters are the */Subject* class, which also defines at least one */modify* operation, and the */Observer* class, which must provide an */update* operation. The aspect interface also declares two public operations for the */Observer* class, namely `startObserving` and `stopObserving` that allow an observer instance to register, rsp. deregister, with a subject instance.

2.2 Designing the Aspect Structure

The next step in the design of an aspect model is to complete the internal details of the aspect, i.e. add the structure and behaviour necessary to be able to fulfill the purpose of the aspect. Structurally, in the case of the *Observer* aspect, an association needs to be established between the one subject instance and its observers. Luckily, this is a very common design concern, and there are several RAM models that have already been developed that can be used in this context. Here we are going to use the *ZeroToManyAssociation (ZOM)* aspect, the interface of which is shown in Fig. 2. As expected, the aspect provides operations to *add* an object to the association, *remove* an object from the association or query the current state of the association (*getAssociated*).

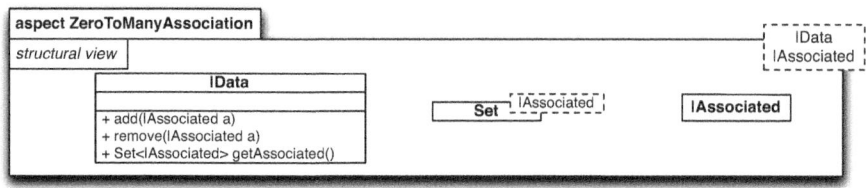

Fig. 2. The *ZeroToManyAssociation* Aspect Interface

To use *ZOM* within the *Observer* aspect, all mandatory instantiation parameters of *ZOM* must be mapped to model elements of the *Observer* aspect. This is done by providing instantiation directives as shown in the second compartment of the complete *Observer* aspect model illustrated in Fig. 3. The directive specifies that */Data* is mapped to */Subject*, and */Associated* to */Observer*. In addition, *getAssociated*, the operation provided by */Data*, is renamed to *getObservers* to better reflect the semantics of the operation in the context of the *Observer* aspect.

2.3 Designing the Aspect Behaviour

Now that we have the necessary structural properties in place, it is time to define the behaviour of the *Observer* aspect. In RAM, aspect behaviour is specified

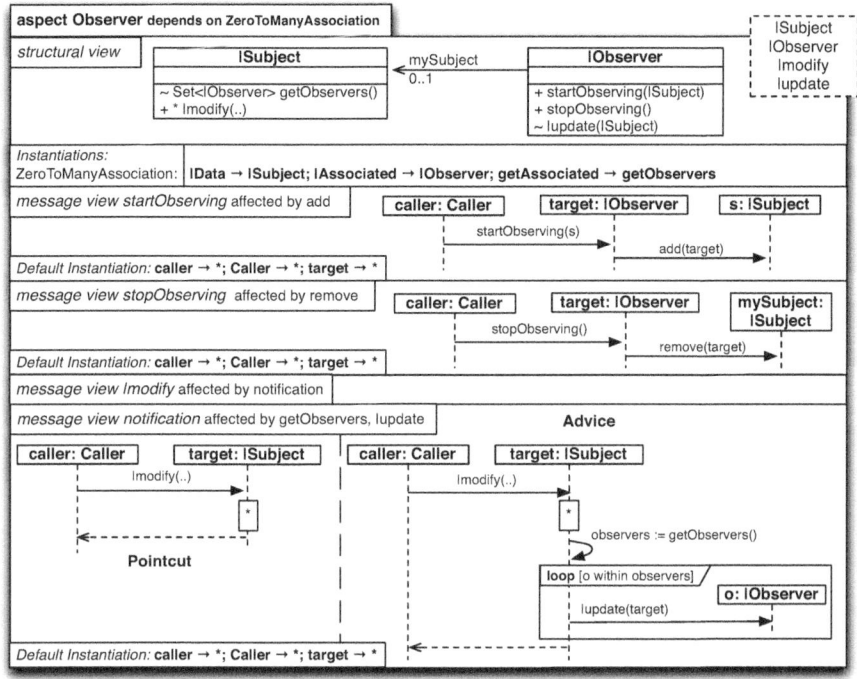

Fig. 3. The Complete *Observer* Aspect

using sequence diagrams and state diagrams. Sequence diagrams are mandatory: for each public operation specified in the interface, an aspect model must specify a message view that shows using a sequence diagram the synchronous message calls that are exchanged between objects as a result of an invocation of the operation. The state diagrams are optional: for each class defined in the structural view, the aspect model can declare a state view that is used to define the operation invocation protocol for instances of the class. The state views are used by the aspect weaver to model check the woven model for consistency. For space reasons, the state views have been omitted in the aspect examples of this paper. The interested reader is referred to [2] for details on state views and verification of composition using model checking.

Since the *Observer* aspect specifies 3 public operations, Fig. 3 defines 3 message views. The message view *startObserving* shows that the *add* operation provided by *ZOM* is used to associate the observer with the subject. Similarly, *stopObserving* uses *remove* to deassociate the observer from the subject. The most interesting message view is /*modify*, which represents operations that modify the state of the subject instance. It specifies that every call to /*modify* is affected by the *notification* message view. Notification states that after any call to /*modify*, *getObservers* provided by *ZOM* is called to obtain the set of currently registered observers. After that, the update operations of each of the observers

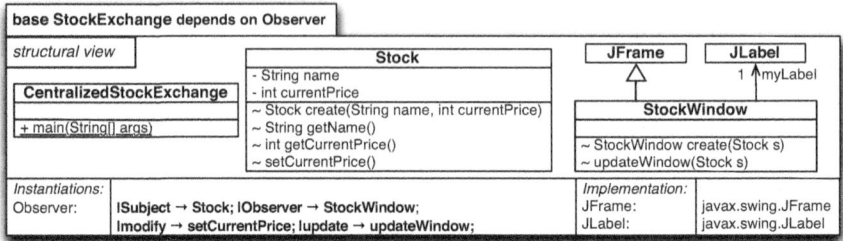

Fig. 4. The Centralized Stock Exchange Base Model

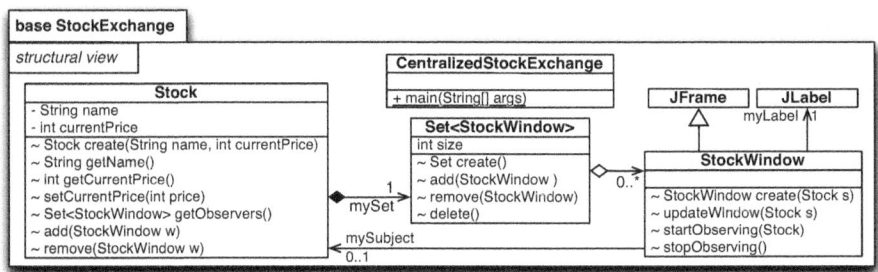

Fig. 5. The Woven Centralized Stock Exchange Structural View

is called. The default instantiation in the message view states that *all* calls to /*modify* made to instances of the class /*Subject* are to be observed, regardless of who the caller is. When the *Observer* aspect is used, this default instantiation can be overridden, if only calls made by specific callers are to be observed.

2.4 Weaving

The simple *StockExchange* base model shown in Fig. 4 applies the *Observer* aspect to update the graphical user interface whenever the price of the visualized stock changes by mapping /*Subject* to *Stock* and /*Observer* to *StockWindow*. To generate the final application model, the aspect weaver recursively weaves all lower-level aspects into the higher level aspects according to the instantiation directives. For illustration purpose, the final woven structural view of the centralized *StockExchange* application is presented in Fig. 5. It shows that the entire structure of *Observer* and indirectly also of *ZOM* is included in the final model. Based on our experience it is always the case in centralized systems that all model elements of a reused aspect model need to be woven with the base model. We believe that if for some reason it would make sense to use only a subset of the model elements of an aspect, then the aspect model itself was not designed correctly. It should have been split into several aspects, with potential dependencies among each other.

3 Modelling Distributed Concerns

While it is essential for centralized systems that all the structure and behaviour of a used concern is woven into the base model, the situation changes in the context of a distributed system composed of many processing nodes. Often, the individual nodes play different roles in the system, contributing in different ways to fulfill the purpose of the system. Unless the distributed architecture is perfectly symmetrical, the implementations of the different types of nodes differ considerably.

To illustrate this point, Fig. 6 presents the model of a very simple *Communication* aspect that is capable of establishing a point to point TCP/IP connection between two nodes using sockets. The design of *SocketCommunication* is closely inspired by how the Java [4] language exposes socket-based communication to the developer. In fact, Java is one of the target languages of RAM, and the *Implementation* compartment of *SocketCommunication* in Fig. 6 specifies how most of the classes of the aspect are mapped to Java classes.

Since Java already provides the behaviour for most of the public operations of *SocketCommunication*, only two message views, i.e. *getSender* and *getReceiver*, are needed to complete the aspect design. Each operation returns the *SocketSender* (*ObjectOutputStream*) resp. *SocketReceiver* (*ObjectInputStream*) associated with the *Socket* to the caller.

The structural and behavioural model elements provided by the *SocketCommunication* aspect clearly belong together: they are all mandatory elements in order to establish a communication between two nodes of a distributed system. However, not all structure and behaviour is used by each of the nodes that want to communicate. The setup protocol is as follows: *one node listens* on a port by creating a server socket; the *other node initiates communication* to that port by creating a socket, passing the hostname and port number of the listening node as a parameter to the constructor. This setup protocol is unavoidably asymmetric. If successful, the thus established bi-directional communication link can be used to *send* or *receive* objects by either one of the nodes, i.e. it can be used in a symmetric way. However, nodes can choose to only send or only receive data, if they wish to.

In order to explicitly support the modelling of distributed systems, we propose to add the notion of *distribution roles* to aspect models. A distribution role is a part of a distributed protocol that a node plays in a distributed system that uses the aspect. Distribution roles allow the designer to partition the model elements of the aspect into classes and operations that need to reside on the same node of a distributed system.

In the *SocketCommunication* aspect there are four distribution roles, i.e. *Listener*, *Initiator*, *Sender* and *Receiver*, as shown in the *Distribution Roles* compartment of Fig. 6. Each role depends on some of the structural and behavioural model elements of the aspect, which are listed as part of the role definition. Finally, since it is only possible to send or receive data after a communication link has been set up, the role definitions specify that a node that plays the *Sender* or *Receiver* role is also required to play either the *Listener* or *Initiator* role.

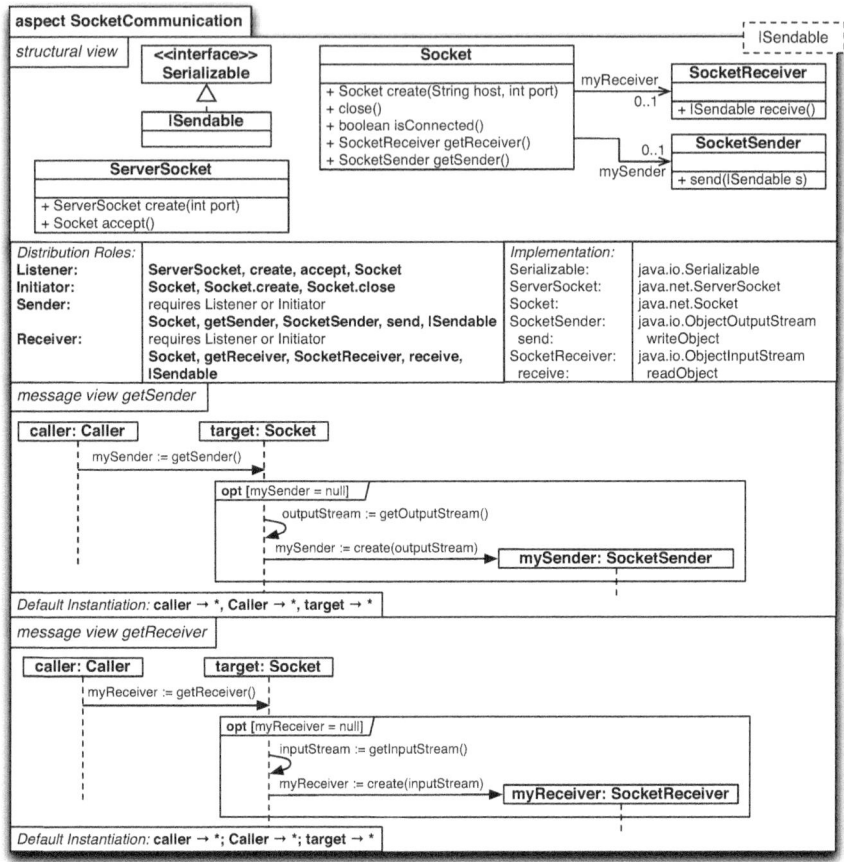

Fig. 6. The *SocketCommunication* Aspect

3.1 Distributing the Observer Design Pattern

This subsection shows that the standard RAM design techniques still apply in the context of modelling of distributed systems. To illustrate how a higher level aspect can implement its functionality based on lower level aspects, we are going to design a simple distributed version of the observer design pattern, in which the subject and the observers are located on different nodes.

The interface of the *DistributedObserver* aspect shown in Fig. 7 is non-surprisingly very similar to the interface of the centralized *Observer* aspect shown in Fig. 1, except that in the distributed design the */Subject* parameter for the operation *startObserving* has been replaced by a host name and port number. This is unavoidable, since standard references do not work across virtual machines. In addition, since this is an aspect for a distributed system, the aspect interface also declares the two distribution roles that the aspect exposes: the *Subject* and the *Observer* role.

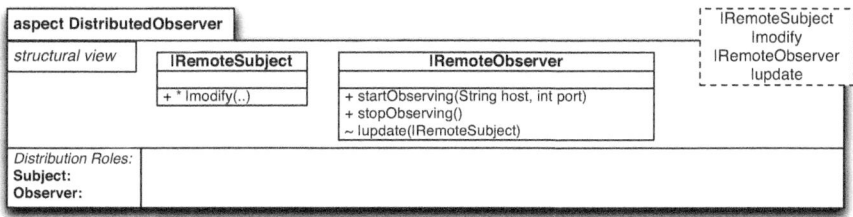

Fig. 7. The *DistributedObserver* Aspect Interface

The idea behind the internal design of the *DistributedObserver* aspect is relatively simple. For every remote observer, a socket-based communication link is established between the subject node and the observer node. To set up this link, on the node with the subject, a thread is listening for incoming connections on the port number associated with the subject. The observer node initiates the connection by connecting to the same port. Once the communication is established, any changes to the state of the subject instance are communicated to the remote observer by sending a copy of the updated subject through the socket. According to this design, the *Subject* role of *DistributedObserver* uses the *Listener* and *Sender* role of *SocketCommunication*, and the *Observer* role uses *Initiator* and *Receiver*.

The complete design of *DistributedObserver* is shown in Figs. 8 and 9. Internally, *DistributeObserver* reuses *SocketCommunication* for communication between the subject and observer nodes. The *Instantiations* compartment shows that /*RemoteSubject* is mapped to /*Sendable* in order to make it possible to send the state of a remote subject over the network. The centralized *Observer* aspect is also reused on the subject node: *ObserverInfo* objects register with the remote subject in order to propagate update notifications to the remote observer node.

The message views shown in Fig. 8 specify the behaviour executed on the *Subject* node. According to the *Distribution Role* compartment, the behaviour involves the classes /*RemoteSubject*, *ObserverInfo* and *Socket*. The *initialization* message view ensures that whenever a /*RemoteSubject* instance is created, a listener thread is started, passing as a reference the remote subject itself. The remote subject implements *Runnable*, and therefore the thread starts executing the behaviour specified in the /*RemoteSubject.run* message view: a server socket is created first, and then the thread waits for incoming connections by observers. For each connecting observer, an *ObserverInfo* instance is created and associated with the socket of the connection, and then registered as an observer with the remote subject by using the *startObserving* operation provided by the centralized *Observer* aspect. It is also the centralized *Observer* aspect that calls *sendUpdate* of all the registered *ObserverInfo* instances when a remote subject is modified. As shown in the *sendUpdate* message view, the *ObserverInfo* subsequently sends the remote subject to the remote observer using the associated socket, if it is still connected. A closed connection on the other hand signals that the corresponding observer is not interested in receiving updates anymore, and hence *stopObserving* is invoked to deregister the *ObserverInfo* instance.

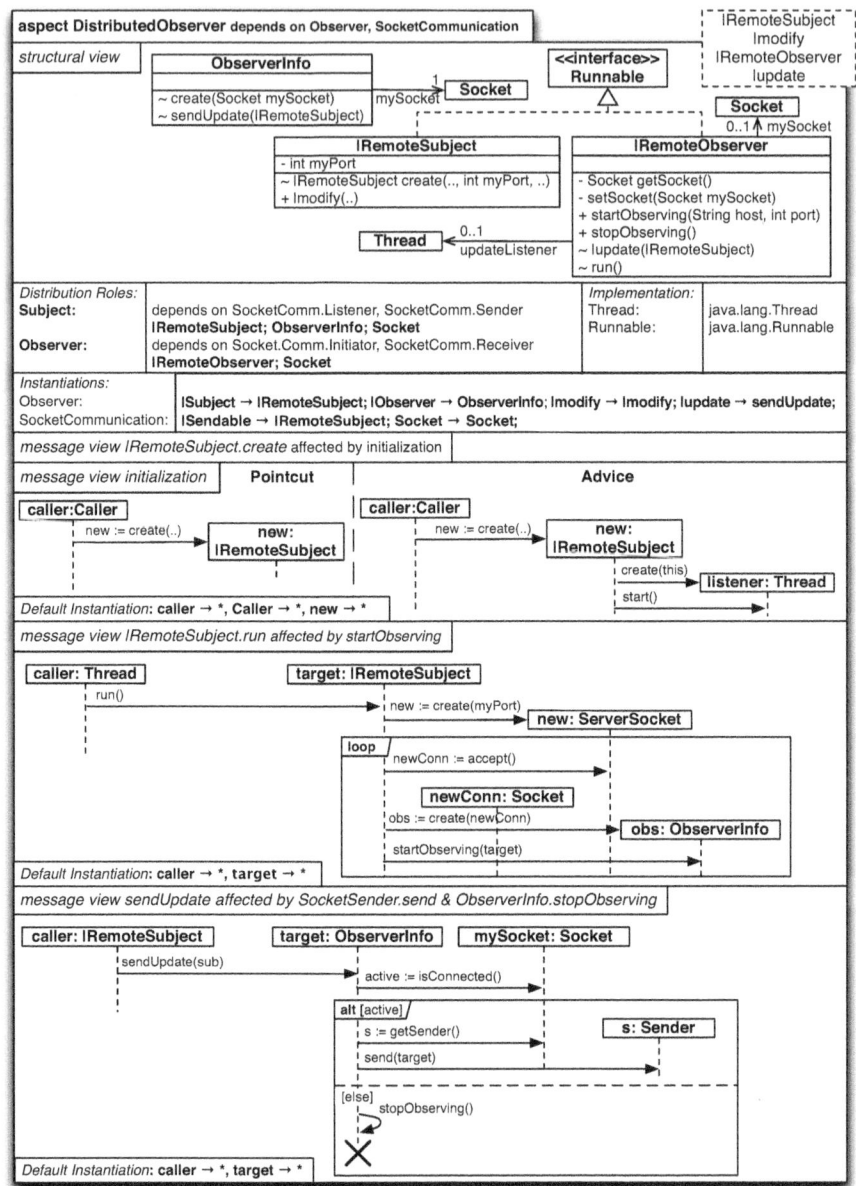

Fig. 8. The Complete *DistributedObserver* Aspect Model – Part 1

The message views shown in Fig. 9 describe the behaviour on the *Observer* node. As shown by the first message view, a call to *startObserving* results in the creation of a socket and attempt to establish a connection with the specified host on the provided port. Then, an *updateListener* thread is started, passing as a parameter the remote observer itself. The */RemoteObserver.run* message view

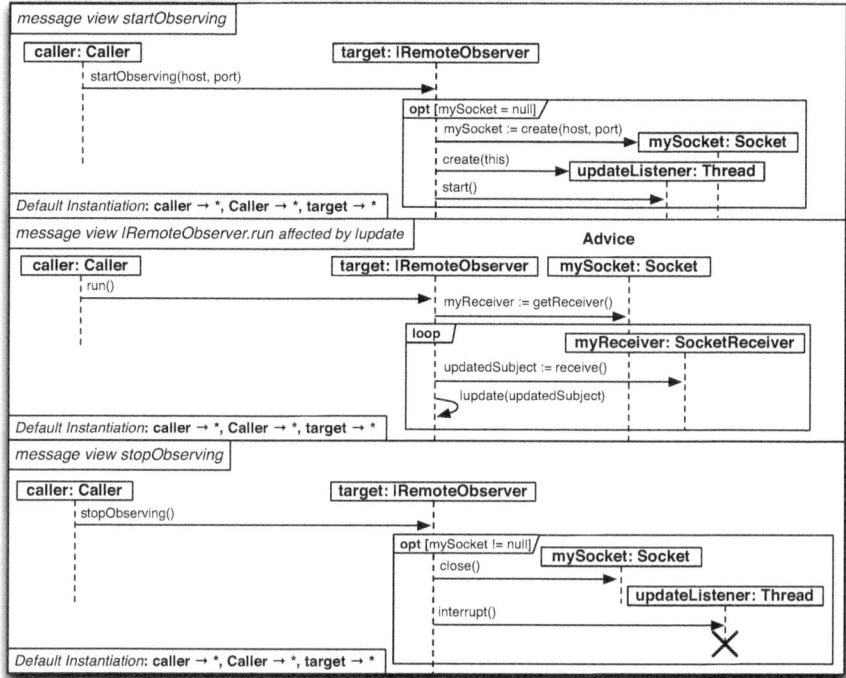

Fig. 9. The Complete *DistributedObserver* Aspect – Part 2

shows that the thread simply waits for incoming subject instances, after which it invokes *!update*. In case *stopObserving* is invoked, the socket to the remote subject node is closed and the *updateListener* thread is interrupted.

4 Generating Models for a Distributed System

The challenge when generating base models for a distributed system is that we want to take advantage of the consistency and completeness checks that the weaver performs just like in the context of centralized systems. This means that we want the weaver to verify that:

- distribution roles are used consistently on each node, i.e. all structure and behaviour associated with a distribution role is woven into the base model of the node, and
- all structure and behaviour of a distributed aspect model is used on some node of the distributed system.

4.1 Instantiating Distribution Roles

In order to ensure consistent use of distribution roles, the instantiation rules of the model weaver need to be relaxed. When modelling centralized systems, the weaver enforces that all the mandatory instantiation parameters of an aspect are mapped to base model elements. In distributed systems, since an individual node does not necessarily play all the distribution roles of an aspect, not all the model elements defined by the aspect are relevant to the node. The distributed aspect clearly lists the defined distribution roles in its interface, together with the model elements associated with each role. In a sense this indirectly defines a (sub) aspect interface for each role. When a distributed aspect model is applied to a base model, the modeller specifies which distribution role(s) should be instantiated. The weaver, using the list of model elements given in the *Distribution Roles* compartment, makes sure that all mandatory parameters that pertain to the distribution roles assigned to the node are instantiated, and that no model elements that are not part of the role are mapped to base model elements.

4.2 Configuring a Distributed System

In order to ensure consistent use of a a distributed aspect model across all nodes of a distributed system, a new notion needs to be added to the modelling environment: a *distributed system configuration*. A distributed system configuration declares a set of *node types*, and then assigns a base model to each node type. Optionally, (centralized) aspect models and distribution roles of distributed aspect models can also be assigned to a node type. The modelling environment then verifies that for each used distributed aspect, all aspect roles have been assigned to at least one node in the configuration before asking the weaver to generate the woven models for each of the nodes.

Currently, our modelling environment does not provide a graphical user interface for specifying distributed system configurations. We envision this to be accomplished with UML deployment diagrams in the future. In the mean time, we propose to use a simple textual configuration file as shown in Listing. 1.1.

Listing 1.1. Stock Exchange Client-Server System Configuration

```
1   configuration StockExchange is
2
3     StockServer : node;
4     StockClient : node;
5
6   begin
7
8     StockServer base is StockBackend;
9     StockServer plays DistributedObserver.Subject
10        (|RemoteSubject -> Stock, |modify -> setCurrentPrice)
11
12    StockClient base is StockGUI;
13    StockClient plays DistributedObserver.Observer
14        (|RemoteObserver ->  StockWindow, |update -> updateWindow)
15
16  end StockExchange;
```

Lines 3 and 4 declare the two node types in the distributed system: the *StockServer* and the *StockClient*. Line 8 assigns the *StockBackend* base model to the

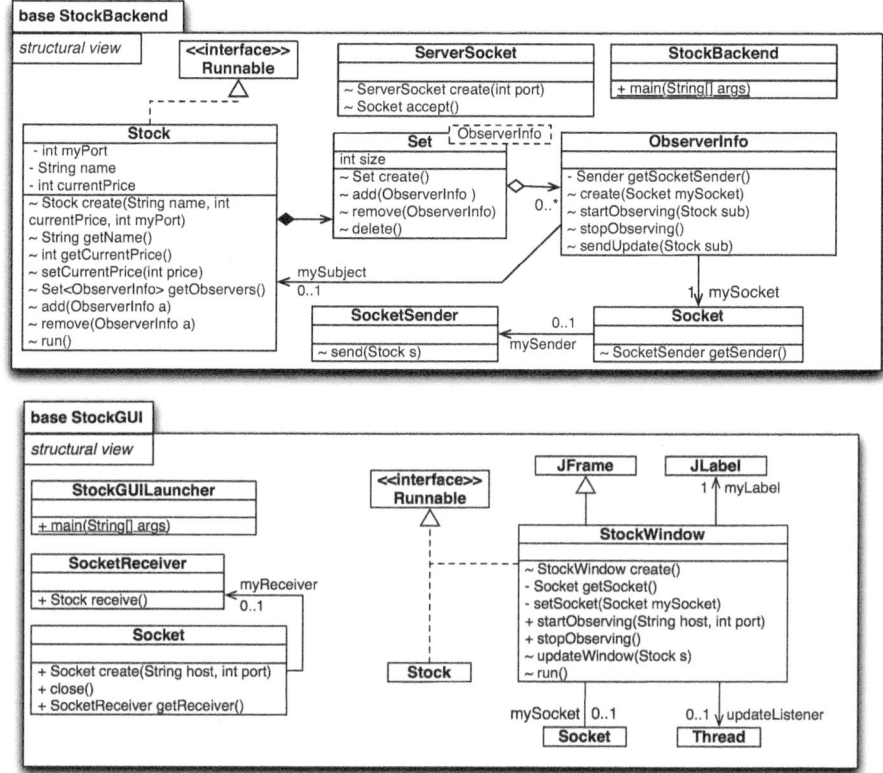

Fig. 10. The Two Woven Base Models of Distributed Stock Exchange

StockServer node. Line 9 declares that the *StockServer* node plays the *Subject* distribution role of the *DistributedObserver* aspect, and the mandatory instantiation parameters of the role are mapped to base model elements of *StockBackend* in line 10. Line 12 assigns the *StockGUI* base model to the *StockClient* node, and lines 13 and 14 declare that the *StockClient* plays the *Observer* role of the *DistributedObserver* aspect and map the mandatory instantiation parameters of the role to *StockGUI* base model elements.

4.3 Generating the Woven Models for Each Node

Based on the configuration file, the weaver then proceeds to generate woven models for each of the defined node types. Fig. 10 shows the two woven models of the *StockExchange* application: one model for the stock backend node, and one for the stock GUI. This example shows how significantly the application models of different node kinds in a distributed system differ from each other. The backend contains the business logic, as well as the association between subjects and observer information. It defines behaviour used for listening on a port for incoming connections, and for sending *Stock* instances over the net. The GUI contains all presentation logic, as well as behaviour for receiving updates over the network.

5 Related Work

To the best of our knowledge, no other extensions to AOM approaches for modelling distributed systems have been proposed in the literature. There are however several papers that apply AOM to model distributed system concerns.

France et al. [5] model client/server systems using aspect-oriented techniques in order to produce logical, aspect-oriented architecture models that describe how concerns such as authentication and role-based access control are expressed in technology-independent modelling terms. The paper mainly focusses on model composition, and not on distribution-specific AOM techniques. Clarke et al. [6] study developing pervasive applications by combining aspect-oriented software development techniques with model driven development techniques using Theme/UML. Subsequently, Clarke et al. [7] studied how Theme/UML can be used to better modularize distributed real-time embedded concerns at the modelling level. They show models of a timing concern for driver information systems and a generic memory management concern. Unlike our proposal, there is no explicit discussion in either paper with regards whether the structure and behaviour of an aspect theme can crosscut several nodes in a distributed system.

At the programming level, Nishizawa et al. [8] modified and extended the existing aspect-oriented programming languages AspectJ to include new constructs that apply to distributed systems. They introduced the notion of a remote pointcut, a programming construct that allows for identifying join points in the execution of a program running on a remote host. This allows a programmer to write simple pointcuts that modularize crosscutting concerns distributed over multiple hosts. Navarro et al. [9] present an aspect-oriented language designed explicitly for distribution called AWED. It proposes 3 key features: *remote pointcuts* with support for remote event sequences, *distributed advice* execution that can be asynchronous or synchronous, and *distributed aspects* with support for deployment, instantiation, and sharing of state.

Finally, many papers have applied aspect-oriented programming to the analysis, design and implementation of middleware. For example, Zhang and Jacobsen [10] study the use of aspect-oriented techniques in middleware, in particular to the design of CORBA-based systems. Cloyer and Clement [11] studied how aspect-orientation may help to separate support for Enterprise Java Beans (EJB) from the rest of the application server. Bouchenak et al. [12] discuss using aspect-orientation to perform caching by treating it as a concern that cuts across the application. They have implemented AutoWebCache which is an AOP based caching middleware system using AspectJ as the AOP language of choice. Fuentes et al. [13] study techniques to integrate heterogeneous event systems in a homogeneous way through the use of an aspect-oriented middleware platform. Truyen et al. [14] present the DyReS framework, which allows coordinated weaving or unweaving of multiple inter-dependent aspects at run-time into a distributed system, while insuring certain safety properties such as global state consistency.

6 Conclusion

In this paper we proposed an extension to aspect-oriented modelling that allows the modeller to augment an aspect model of a concern that can crosscut the nodes of a distributed system with *distribution role definitions*. A *distributed system configuration file* specifies the different node types of the distributed system, and how the roles of a distributed aspect are assigned to the nodes. Based on the role definitions and the configuration, the weaver can then ensure the correct use of the distributed aspect: every role of a distributed aspect must be assigned to at least one node of the distributed system to ensure consistency. Finally, the weaver generates for each node a final application model that only contains the model elements pertaining to the distribution roles the node plays. The presented ideas were illustrated by integrating them into our *Reusable Aspect Models* approach, and by building a model of a distributed version of the observer design pattern.

References

1. Klein, J., Kienzle, J.: Reusable Aspect Models. In: 11th Aspect-Oriented Modeling Workshop, Nashville, TN, USA, September 30 (2007)
2. Kienzle, J., Abed, W.A., Klein, J.: Aspect-Oriented Multi-View Modeling. In: AOSD 2009, March 1-6, pp. 87–98. ACM Press, New York (2009)
3. Gamma, E., Helm, R., Johnson, R., Vlissides, J.: Design Patterns. Addison Wesley, Reading (1995)
4. Gosling, J., Joy, B., Steele, G.L.: The Java Language Specification. The Java Series. Addison Wesley, Reading (1996)
5. France, R., Ray, I., Georg, G., Ghosh, S.: Aspect-oriented approach to early design modelling. IEE Proceedings Software, 173–185 (August 2004)
6. Carton, A., Clarke, S., Senart, A., Cahill, V.: Aspect-oriented model-driven development for mobile context-aware computing. In: SEPCASE 2007, pp. 1–5. IEEE Computer Society, Los Alamitos (2007)
7. Driver, C., Cahill, V.: et al.: Separation of Distributed Real-Time Embedded Concerns with Theme/UML. In: MOMPES 2008, pp. 27–33. IEEE, Los Alamitos (2008)
8. Nishizawa, M., Chiba, S., Tatsubori, M.: Remote pointcut: a language construct for distributed aop. In: AOSD 2004, pp. 7–15. ACM, New York (2004)
9. Navarro, L.D.B., Südholt, M., Vanderperren, W., Fraine, B.D., Suvée, D.: Explicitly distributed AOP using AWED. In: AOSD 2006, pp. 51–62. ACM, New York (2006)
10. Zhang, C., Jacobsen, H.: Refactoring middleware with aspects. IEEE Transactions on Parallel and Distributed Systems 14(11), 1058–1073 (2003)
11. Colyer, A., Clement, A.: Large-scale AOSD for middleware. In: AOSD 2004, pp. 56–65. ACM, New York (2004)
12. Bouchenak, S., Cox, A., Dropsho, S., Mittal, S., Zwaenepoel, W.: Caching dynamic web content: Designing and analysing an aspect-oriented solution. In: van Steen, M., Henning, M. (eds.) Middleware 2006. LNCS, vol. 4290, pp. 1–21. Springer, Heidelberg (2006)
13. Fuentes, L., Jimenez, D., Meier, R.: Modelling Event Systems for AmI Applications Using an Aspect Middleware Platform. In: wUCAmI 2006, pp. 9–18 (2006)
14. Truyen, E., Janssens, N., Sanen, F., Joosen, W.: Support for distributed adaptations in aspect-oriented middleware. In: AOSD 2008, pp. 120–131. ACM, New York (2008)

A Precise Style for Business Process Modelling: Results from Two Controlled Experiments

Gianna Reggio[1], Filippo Ricca[1], Giuseppe Scanniello[2],
Francesco Di Cerbo[3], and Gabriella Dodero[3]

[1] DISI, Università di Genova, Italy
{gianna.reggio,filippo.ricca}@disi.unige.it
[2] Dipartimento di Matematica e Informatica, Università della Basilicata, Italy
giuseppe.scanniello@unibas.it
[3] CASE, Libera Università di Bolzano-Bozen, Italy
{francesco.dicerbo,gabriella.dodero}@unibz.it

Abstract. We present a precise style for the modelling of business processes based on the UML activity diagrams and two controlled experiments to compare this style with a lighter variant. The comparison has been performed with respect to the comprehensibility of business processes and the effort to comprehend them. The first experiment has been conducted at the Free University of Bolzano-Bozen, while the second experiment (i.e., a differentiated replication) at the University of Genova. The participants to the first experiment were Master students and so more experienced than the participants to the replication, who were Bachelor students. The results indicate that: (a) all the participants achieved a significantly better comprehension level with the precise style; (b) the used style did not have any significant impact on the effort; and (c) more experienced participants benefited more from the precise style.

Keywords: Business Process Modelling, UML activity diagrams, Controlled experiment, Precise and Ultra-light styles.

1 Introduction

To be competitive in the global market, many organizations have been changing their business processes [11]. In this context, modelling, management, and enactment of business processes are considered relevant to support organizations in their daily activities.

The UML activity diagrams represent a natural choice for modelling business processes (see, e.g., [10]) since UML has been conceived for the communication among people and then can be easily understood and used by customers, managers, and developers. In favour of UML, there is also its flexibility that allows choosing the preferred degree of precision/abstractiveness to model business processes. For example, processes may be modelled using lighter variants/styles of the activity diagrams, where nodes and arcs are simply decorated by natural language text. Lighter styles could be simpler to use, but they could complicate the communication among stakeholders because of the possible ambiguities they introduce. More precise styles, where for example nodes are expressed in a formal language, could be more complex to use, but they may reduce ambiguities in the modelled processes.

In this paper, we present a precise style for the modelling of business processes based on the UML activity diagrams and two controlled experiments to compare it with a lighter style (*ultra-light* in the following). The participants to the original experiment were students of the Master program in Computer Science at the Free University of Bolzano-Bozen. A preliminary analysis of the experimental data [9] indicated that the participants achieved a significantly better comprehension level when business processes were represented using the precise style, with no significant impact on the effort to accomplish the tasks.

The second experiment was a differentiated replication[1] of the first experiment. It was conducted at the University of Genova with less experienced participants, namely Bachelor students in Computer Science. The data analysis confirmed the results of the original experiment. A further analysis conducted on both the experiments indicated that more experienced participants benefit more from the use of the precise style in the comprehension of business processes.

The work presented here is based on [9] and with respect to that paper, we provide the following further new contributions: (1) a deeper presentation of the visual formalism used to model business processes; (2) a new experiment with less experienced participants; (3) a further analysis to assess the effect of experience on the comprehension of business process models.

The remainder of the paper is organized as follows: Section 2 presents relevant related literature concerning business process modelling with UML and related experiments in comprehension tasks. Section 3 introduces both the precise and the ultra-light styles for business process modelling. Section 4 presents the design of the controlled experiments, while Section 5 shows and discusses the achieved results. Final remarks conclude the paper.

2 Related Work

The UML activity diagrams provide an intuitive and easy way to model business [1] and business process [8,13,10]. For example, Di Nitto *et al.* [10] propose an approach to model business processes by using a subset of UML diagrams, including: (1) UML activity diagrams with object flow to model the control and data flow, (2) class diagrams to model structural properties of the process, and (3) state diagrams to model the behaviour of activities. Subsequently, these models can be translated into executable process descriptions by a UML CASE tool. Several are the differences between our approach and theirs. The most remarkable one is that OCL (Object Constraint Language) is not used.

De Lucia *et al.* [7] present a visual environment, based on an extension of UML activity diagrams, that allows to graphically design a process and to visually monitor its enactment. The main difference with our approach is that

---

[1] This kind of replication introduces variations (e.g., different kinds of participants) in essential aspects of the experimental conditions [3].

participants and objects are not explicitly considered in their proposal. Furthermore, the behavioural conditions are not formally specified.

Differently from us, all the approaches discussed above do not assess the validity of the proposed formalism by means of controlled experiments. To our knowledge, only a few studies perform comparisons among business process formalisms by using empirical evaluations. For instance, Peixoto *et al.* [16] compare UML and BPMN (Business Process Modelling Notation) [15], with respect to their readability in expressing business processes. The authors expected BPMN models to be easier to understand than UML 2.0 activity diagrams, as BPMN is a specialized language, designed for modelling business process and with the primary goal of being understandable by all business stakeholders. However, an experiment with 35 undergraduate students, unskilled in business process modelling, could not confirm their initial hypothesis. A similar result is obtained in [4], where the authors conclude that UML activity diagrams are at least usable as BPMN since neither user effectiveness, efficiency, nor satisfaction differ significantly. Instead, Gross and Doerr [12] conducted two experiments, comparing the UML activity diagrams and Event-driven Process Chains (EPCs). The authors found evidence that activity diagrams performed better than EPCs from a requirements engineer's perspective. When considering end users, no significant difference was identified between the two methods.

3 Business Process Modelling with UML

In this paper, we shall not give a rigorous definition of what a business process is, just assuming the common intuitive meaning, and we shall use the following terminology:

- basic activities in business processes are called *basic tasks* of the process;
- *business process objects* are those entities over which the activities of the process are performed, obviously these entities are passive, i.e., they are unable to do any activity by themselves;
- active entities that perform the various tasks are *business process participants*: whenever relevant, we shall distinguish autonomous participants from those corresponding to software and hardware systems.

Behavioural aspects of business processes may be modelled by using UML activity diagrams, which offer quite a large set of visual constructs to depict the flow of activities. We shall restrict ourselves to use: action nodes, initial, final, decision/merge, fork/join control nodes, control flow edges, time and accept events, and obviously also the rake construct to modularize the activity diagrams. Object nodes and swimlanes may also be optionally used. This holds also for the styles considered in the paper.

Even with such a restricted subset of constructs, a straightforward and unique modelling of a business processes with one UML activity does not exist. Indeed, it is possible to produce complex and unreadable activity diagrams, corresponding to "spaghetti" business processes, or to make mistakes, e.g., using a business object before creating it. To overcome these problems, we proposed a proper discipline for modelling business processes and some notations [17]. The notations mainly differ in the level "of the precision" in using UML to depict the basic ingredients of the activity diagrams (such as actions and guards), or in the way basic tasks are represented.

In the study presented here, we consider the ultra-light and the precise styles. These styles are described in the following through a running example, namely a business process corresponding to order processing in e-commerce systems (EC). More business process examples are available in [17].

The client sends the order. If the client is not already registered, (s)he will be asked to register to the site, if (s)he refuses the order will be cancelled. Then, the order will be sent to the warehouse, which will prepare the package, and in the meantime, to collect the payment, the handler of the credit card, or Paypal will be contacted (depending on client preferences). Then, the package will be sent, and the carrier will inform the company that the package has been delivered. Finally, the order will be archived.

3.1 Ultra-Light Style

In the ultra-light style a business process is modelled by a UML activity diagram, where the action nodes and the guards on the edges leaving the decision nodes are decorated by natural language text; such text does not follow any rules or patterns. Sentences defining the activities may be either in active or passive form (e.g., "Clerk fills the form" or "Form is filled by clerk"), and the entity executing the activity may be precisely determined or be left undefined (e.g., "Form is filled"); in other cases nominal sentences might be used instead of verbal phrases ("Filling the form"). Also the objects over which the business process activities are performed may be described in different ways, for example by a substantive (e.g., "Form", "The form") or by a qualificative sentence (e.g., "Client form", "Filled form", "Sent form").

Fig. 1 shows the ultra-light UML model of the EC business process. It is a simple activity diagram, where various basic tasks are denoted by natural language sentences with different structure (e.g., the first one is active and the subject is explicit, **Order archived** instead is passive and provides no information about who will perform the task, and **Client registration** is just the name of an action). Since the model is prepared in a completely unconstrained way, it is very easy to make mistakes or to introduce ambiguities. For example, the passive sentences in the UML activity diagram do not explicitly mention who will do the last three basic tasks of the process.

3.2 Precise Style

Participants and objects of a business process shall always be explicitly listed and precisely modelled with UML by means of classes; and the behavioural view of business processes shall be given by activity diagrams, with basic activities and conditions written respectively in the language for the actions of UML and OCL, the textual language for boolean expressions, included in UML 2.0. Thus the *UML precise model of a business process* consists of: (1) a class diagram, introducing the classes needed to type its participants and objects, (2) the list of its participants, (3) the list of its objects, and (4) an activity diagram representing its behaviour. All these parts must satisfy the constraints listed below.

- Classes in the class diagram may be stereotyped by ≪object≫ (business process objects), ≪businessWorker≫ and ≪system≫ (business process participants distinguished between: autonomous entities, i.e., human beings or complex entities run by human beings, and hardware/software systems); for readability reasons the stereotype ≪businessWorker≫ will be omitted. Mutual relationships among participants and/or objects are expressed by associations and specializations, whereas the dependency (visually depicted by a dashed arrow) is used to represent the fact that participants from a given class will act over objects from another class.

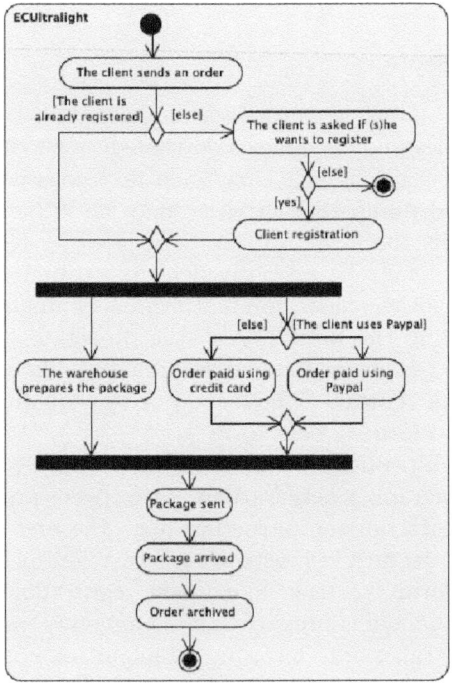

Fig. 1. EC Specified by the Ultra-light Style

- Participants are named, and they are typed by a class with stereotype either ≪businessWorker≫ or ≪system≫. Objects are named and typed by classes stereotyped by ≪object≫. Notice that participants/objects are roles for entities taking part in the business process, and not specific individuals. It is possible to impose some constraints on participants and objects of a business process.

– Basic tasks involving participants and objects are modelled by operations of the various participants/objects classes stereotyped by ≪T≫ (whenever all operations of a class have this stereotype, it shall be omitted to simplify the visual presentation). When defining ≪T≫ operations, it is important to keep in mind that: (1) an operation corresponding to a basic task, part of a class C stereotyped by ≪businessWorker≫ or ≪system≫, describes a task that a participant of type C is responsible to initiate (they should be named using the imperative verbal mode); (2) an operation corresponding to a basic task, part of a class C stereotyped by ≪object≫, describes a task that will be done over an object of type C (they should be named using the past participle).
– Action nodes of an activity diagram are decorated by calls of the the operations corresponding to basic tasks, where participants and objects freely appear as arguments, whereas conditions on edges leaving decision nodes are OCL expressions, where participants and objects shall freely appear.

Fig. 2 shows the models of the the EC business process built using the precise style. The figure shows a class diagram, an activity diagram, and the lists of participants and objects of the process. The class diagram introduces the class defining participants and objects, together with some data-type used to describe them (for example ClientInfo). EC, PAYPAL and CREDITCARD are participants of the process of kind ≪system≫ (they correspond respectively to the software system running the e-commerce site, the Paypal payment service, and the credit card handling system), whereas CLIENT is an human participant, CARRIER and WAREHOUSE are respectively an external transport company, and a department of the e-commerce company. The latter are not classified as systems since they might not be fully automated. The e-commerce system is responsible for four basic tasks, the warehouse for one and the carrier for two.

The model of the process may be made more precise, without modifying the activity diagram, by adding further details to the class diagram. For example, we could model how the class ECommerce handles the list of registered clients, and the effects on it of its operations, e.g., by means of pre-post conditions. More details on this concern can be found in [17].

4 The Controlled Experiments

In this section we present the design of the two controlled experiments following the guidelines proposed by Wohlin *et al.* in [19]. An experimental package, the raw data, and a draft of our previous paper [9] are available on the Web[2].

Applying the Goal Question Metric (GQM) paradigm [2], the goal of our experiments can be defined as follows: "*Analyse* the use of the precise style *for the purpose of* evaluating it *with respect to* the ultra-light style in the comprehension of business processes by two different categories of participants (i.e., High/Low experienced) *from the point of view* of researchers, *in the context of* students in Computer Science, and *from the point of view of* project managers, *in the context of* novice software engineers".

---
[2] www.scienzemfn.unisa.it/scanniello/BPM

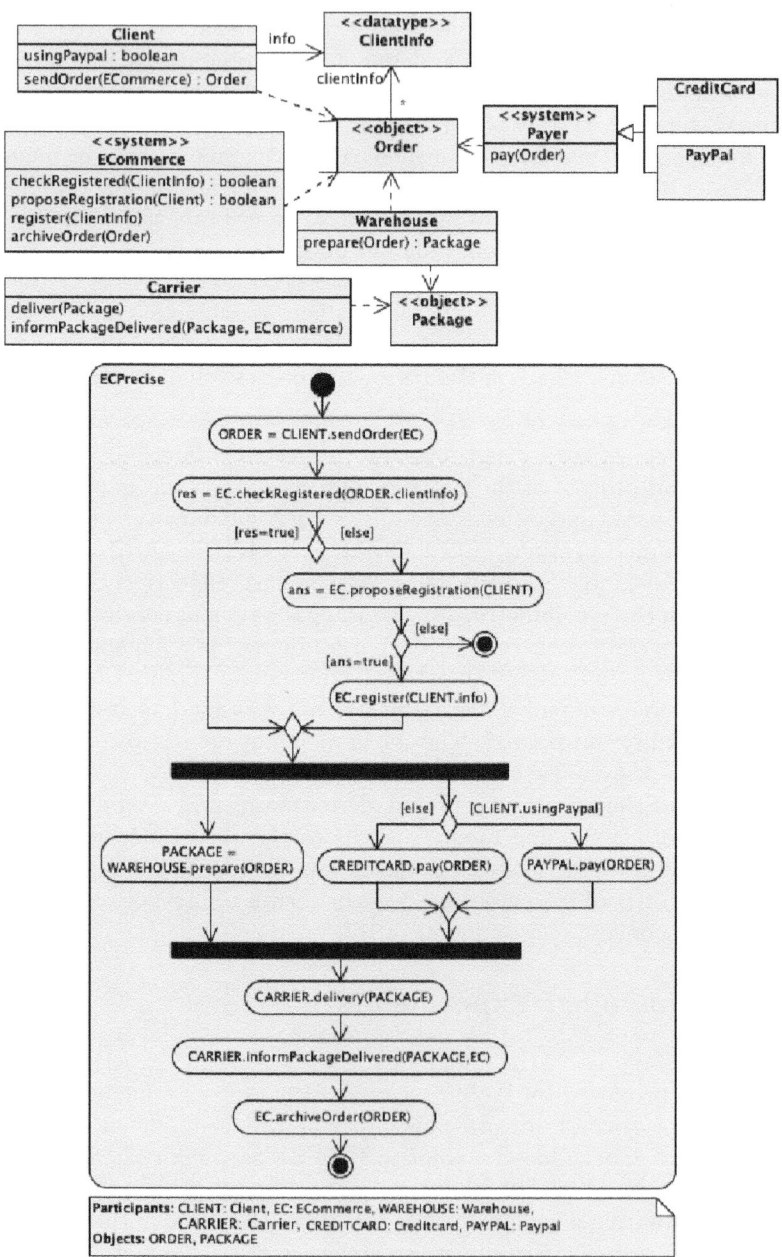

Fig. 2. EC Specified by the Precise Style

4.1 Participants

The two experiments have been conducted with:

- *Master students*. They are enrolled in a Master program in Computer Science at the Free University of Bolzano-Bozen. Some of them are, or were, industry professionals. They can be considered close to young software engineers [5], and in the following we will refer to them as UniBZ.
- *Bachelor students*. They are students of the Bachelor program in Computer Science at the University of Genova (UniGE in the following). They can be considered the next generation of young professional developers [14].

UniGE (62 participants) is a differentiated replication of UniBZ (26 participants). The participants to UniGE are less experienced than UniBZ. For ethic reasons, we informed all the participants that the data of the experiment will be treated anonymously, used only for research purposes, and revealed only in aggregated form.

4.2 Material and Experimental Objects

The prepared experimental material included: two experimental objects, the documentation for the training, and a post-experiment survey questionnaire. The experimental objects are two business processes from application domains on which the participants were familiar with. **Process Order**, shortly **PO**, is in charge of processing orders for an on-line shop. It takes as input an order, then: *(i)* the order is accepted; *(ii)* info is filled; *(iii)* payment processing and shipment are done and, finally; *(iv)* the order is closed. The second business process (i.e., **Document Management Process**, shortly **DPM**) manages the on-line review process of any kind of documents. First a document is created by the author, then it is reviewed by a reviewer, and finally it is approved (if its quality satisfies the imposed constraints). The two business processes are comparable both in complexity and in size. PO comprises 10 nodes (8 activities, 1 decisions and 1 object node) and DPM comprises 12 nodes (6 activities, 2 decisions and 4 object nodes). Furthermore, they both are small enough to fit the time constraints of the experiment and at the same time they are realistic for small/medium sized comprehension tasks. It is worth mentioning that we downloaded the models of the process PO and DPM from http://www.uml-diagrams.org/activity-diagrams-examples.html. In the experiments we used the same descriptions provided in the Website.

The documentation for the training included: *(i)* a set of instructional slides to introduce the precise and the ultra-light style; *(ii)* a training task not related with experimental objects.

Regarding the post-experiment survey questionnaire, we asked the participants to fill it out, so to gain insight and explain the results. This questionnaire contained questions about: the availability of sufficient time to complete the tasks and the clarity of the experimental material and objects. For space reasons, the analysis of the post-experiment questionnaires is not presented.

4.3 Hypotheses Formulation

The following null hypotheses have been defined and tested:

H_{lo}: The use of the precise style **does not significantly improve** the comprehension level of a business process.
H_{to}: There **is no significant difference** in terms of effort when using the precise or ultra-light styles to comprehend a business process.

According to the results of the original experiment [9], the null hypothesis H_{l0} is one-tailed, while H_{t0} is two-tailed. The objective of the statistical analysis is to reject the defined null hypotheses, thus accepting the corresponding alternative ones (i.e., H_{la} and H_{ta}) that can be easily derived from the null ones.

4.4 Design

In the first experiment, we adopted a *counterbalanced design* [19] with four groups: A, B, C, and D. Each participant within these groups worked on two comprehension *Tasks* (i.e., Task 1 and Task 2) on the two experimental *Objects*: PO and DPM. Each time, participants used the precise or ultra-light styles. For example, the participants within the group A started to work in Task 1 on PO using the precise style and then they used the ultra-light style to perform Task 2 on DPM. We randomly assigned the participants to A, B, C, and D.

In the replication a *completely randomized design* [19] was used. This design is simpler than the one used in the first experiment, since each participant used either the precise or the ultra-light styles on only one experimental object (i.e., PO or DPM). We used in the replication a different design for time constraints.

4.5 Dependent and Independent Variables

The *control group* indicates students working with the ultra-light style, while the *treatment group* indicates students working with the precise style. Thus, the only independent variable is *Method* (also named main factor), which is a nominal variable that admits two possible values: *Precise* and *Ultra-light*. To test the null hypotheses, we selected the following dependent variables: *comprehension level* and *comprehension effort*.

The *comprehension level* dependent variable measures the comprehension of the participants on each business process. Similar to previous studies (e.g., [18]), we asked the participants to answer a comprehension questionnaire (it is the same for each object) composed of multiple choice questions. Twelve questions were asked on each business process, each admitting five possible answers, with one or more correct answers. An example of question for the PO object is the following: "*Indicate the participants of the PO business process*". The goal of this question was to investigate whether the experiment participants (subjects) identified the participants to the business process.

We measured the correctness and completeness of the answers the participants provided to the questions of each comprehension questionnaire through an information retrieval based approach [18]. The correctness was measured using the *precision* measure, while we employed the *recall* for the completeness:

$$precision_{s,i} = \frac{|A_{s,i} \cap C_i|}{|A_{s,i}|} \quad recall_{s,i} = \frac{|A_{s,i} \cap C_i|}{|C_i|}$$

where $A_{s,i}$ is the set of answers provided by the participant s on the question i and C_i indicates the correct set of answers of the question i. To get a single value representing a balance between correctness and completeness of a given question, we used the harmonic mean between precision and recall:

$$F\text{-}Measure_{s,i} = \frac{2 \cdot precision_{s,i} \cdot recall_{s,i}}{precision_{s,i} + recall_{s,i}}$$

The overall comprehension level achieved by each participant was computed using the overall average of the F-Measure values on all the questions. This average assumes a value ranging from 0 to 1. Values close to 1 and 0 indicate a very good and very bad understanding, respectively.

The *comprehension effort* dependent variable measures the time, expressed in minutes, that each participant spent to accomplish a task. We got this value using the start and stop times the participants were asked to record.

5 Results

Because of the sample size and mostly non-normality of the data, we adopted non-parametric tests to test the null hypotheses. We used the Mann-Whitney (MW) test for unpaired analysis since it is very robust and sensitive [19]. Further, it has been widely used in the past in studies similar to the one presented in the paper. In all the performed statistical tests, we decided (as it is customary) to accept a probability of 5% of committing Type-I-error [19], i.e., rejecting the null hypothesis when it is actually true.

While the statistical tests check the presence of significant differences, they do not provide any information about the magnitude of such a difference. Therefore, we used the Cohen's "d" standardized difference between two groups [6]. Typically, it is considered negligible for $|d| < 0.2$, small for $0.2 \leq |d| < 0.5$, medium for $0.5 \leq |d| < 0.8$, and large for $|d| \geq 0.8$.

5.1 Comparison between the Experiments

To compare the results of the two experiments, we considered the overall values of comprehension level and effort, without partitioning the observations by Method. For comprehension level we obtained: UniBZ=0.70 and UniGE=0.60. From this preliminary analysis, we observe that the mean value of comprehension level in the first experiment (UniBZ) is 10 points (i.e., 16.6%) higher than in the second experiment (UniGE). This means that the UniBZ participants comprehended better the business process (both represented with the precise and ultra-light styles) than the UniGE participants. The difference is confirmed by the MW test ($p - value = 0.0004$). As far as Comprehension Effort is concerned, the mean effort in the first experiment is about 2 minutes (11.2%) higher than in the first experiment. For the effort, such a difference is not statistically significant as the results of the MW test show ($p - value = 0.48$). Given the observed differences in the results, we cannot simply merge the data from the two experiments. As a consequence, the two data sets ought to be analysed separately and then we can draw joint conclusions from the results.

5.2 Comprehension Level and Effort

Table 1 reports some descriptive statistics (i.e., mean, median, and standard deviation) of comprehension level, and the results of statistical analyses conducted on the data from both experiments with respect to this dependent variable. The comparison for the two experiments, without partitioning the observations by Object, is visually presented in Fig. 3 by means of boxplots. From them, it appears that students with the precise style outperformed in comprehension the students provided with the ultra-light one in both the experiments.

Table 1. Descriptive statistics of comprehension level and the MW p-values

Experiment	Object	Precise			Ultralight			Mann-Whitney p-value	Cohen's "d"
		Mean	Median	SD	Mean	Median	SD		
UniBZ	PO + DPM	0.79	0.84	0.11	0.62	0.66	0.14	**<0.001**	1.35 (large)
	PO	0.80	0.84	0.11	0.58	0.69	0.19	**0.003**	0.56 (medium)
	DPM	0.76	0.74	0.10	0.64	0.64	0.10	**0.005**	1.14 (large)
UniGE	PO + DPM	0.64	0.63	0.14	0.57	0.54	0.13	**0.02**	0.19 (negligible)
	PO	0.66	0.66	0.15	0.52	0.49	0.13	**0.005**	0.24 (small)
	DPM	0.63	0.61	0.14	0.61	0.60	0.11	0.31	0.05 (small)

The MW test provides evidence that the difference in terms of comprehension level between the two styles, and for both experiments ($p - value < 0.001$ for UniBZ and $p - value = 0.02$ for UniGE), is significant. Therefore, we can reject the null hypothesis H_{l0} both for UniBZ and UniGE. As shown in Table 1, the difference is significant for both the objects (PO and DPM) in the first experiment, while only for PO in the replication. The mean comprehension level improvement, achieved with the precise style, is 17 points for UniBZ (see means of the "UniBZ PO + DPM" row in Table 1), i.e., 27.41%[3] and 7 points for UniGE (see means of the "UniGE PO + DPM" row in Table 1), i.e., 12.28%.

Participants with the precise style employed slightly more time than participants with the ultra-light style. Means per experiment are respectively: 22'16" and 22'11 minutes for UniBZ; 20'41" and 19'46" minutes for UniGE. The MW test returned 0.89 for UniBZ and 0.21 for UniGE as $p - values$, respectively. Therefore, we rejected the null hypothesis H_{t0} neither for UniBZ nor for UniGE.

---

[3] The value is computed using the equation: 0.62+0.62*x%=0.79.

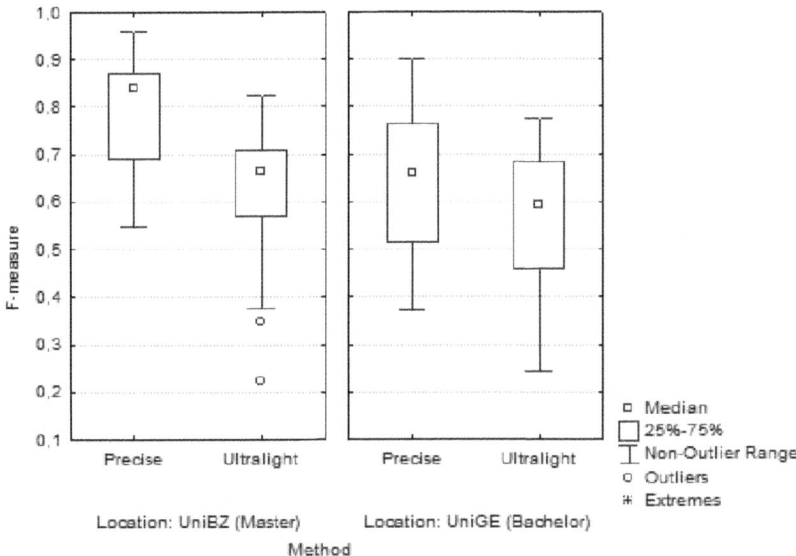

Fig. 3. Boxplots of Comprehension level grouped by Method and Experiment

5.3 Effect of Experience

Fig. 4 shows the interaction plot of method and experience vs. comprehension level. Potential benefits gained with the precise style are represented by the slope of the segments: the slope – and thus the benefit gained with the precise style – is higher for master students from UniBZ than for bachelor students from UniGE. The plot shows a possible trend (to be verified by further experiments): more experienced participants received greater benefits from the precise style than less experienced participants. This could be due to the expertise and level of maturity needed to understand the language for the actions of UML and OCL, used in the precise style.

The effect of experience on the dependent variable has also been analysed using a two-way Analysis of Variance (ANOVA). The results of this further analysis confirm the results shown by the interaction plot. On the overall data set, we found a significant effect of the experience on the comprehension level ($p-value = 0.0002$), already shown by the MW test, and a marginal interaction with the main factor ($p-value = 0.06$).

5.4 Threats to Validity

The threats that could affect the validity of the results for both the experiments belong to the following four categories [19]: *internal*, *external*, *construct*, and *conclusion*.

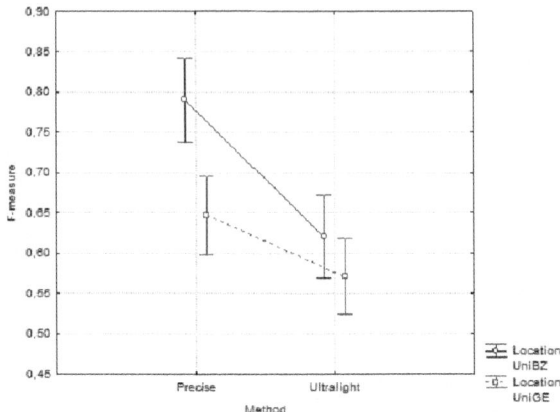

Fig. 4. Interaction of Experience and Method

The experimental designs adopted in these experiments enabled us to mitigate as much as possible *internal validity* threats. The adopted designs mitigated possible learning and fatigue effects as well as the effect of the order of the method. Another threat could be the exchange of information among the participants. This was prevented by monitoring the students while performing the tasks. In addition, students were evaluated neither on the time to accomplish the tasks nor on the their comprehension on the business processes. This reduced possible threats related to the participants' apprehension.

External validity may be threatened when experiments are performed with students and not with software professionals. However, tasks considered in our experiments do not require a high level of industrial experience. Replications with professionals are however needed. To confirm or contradict the achieved results, we also plan to conduct empirical investigations in terms of case studies on larger and more complex tasks.

Construct validity threats are related to the metrics used to quantitatively evaluate the participants' comprehension and effort. We used questionnaires to assess the comprehension of the business processes and the participants' answers to these questionnaires were evaluated using an information retrieval based approach. This design choice avoided as much as possible any subjective evaluation. Furthermore, the comprehension questionnaires were defined to be complex enough without being too obvious. The comprehension effort was measured by means of proper time sheets, and it was validated by researchers. This approach is widely used in the literature.

Conclusion validity concerns data collection, reliability of measurements, and validity of statistical tests. We used a conservative statistical non-parametric test (i.e., Mann-Whitney) to reject the null hypotheses and two-way ANOVA to detect possible effects and interactions between the main factor and the participants' experience. Even if all the assumptions/conditions to use ANOVA were not checked, this test is quite robust and has been extensively used in the past to conduct analyses similar to ours.

6 Conclusion

We have presented a precise style for the modelling of business processes based on the UML activity diagrams. An experiment and a differentiated replication have been conducted to compare it with a lighter variant. The results of these experiments indicate a clear improvement in the comprehension of business models when the precise style is used (UniBZ +27.41% and UniGE +12.26%) with no impact on the effort to accomplish a comprehension task. The analysis of the experiments together showed that more experienced subjects benefited more from the precise style. This result could be due to the needed expertise and level of maturity to understand business processes represented with this style.

Future replications have been planned to investigate: *(i)* the effects of changing the domain of the business processes used in the controlled experiments; *(ii)* whether the observed benefits of the precise style are preserved or improved for subjects with different levels of experience; and *(iii)* whether the additional effort and cost to create models with the precise style is adequately paid back by an improved comprehension of business process models.

Acknowledgements. We would like to thank the participants to the experiments.

References

1. Astesiano, E., Reggio, G., Ricca, F.: Modeling business within a UML-based rigorous software development approach. In: Degano, P., De Nicola, R., Bevilacqua, V. (eds.) Concurrency, Graphs and Models. LNCS, vol. 5065, pp. 261–277. Springer, Heidelberg (2008)
2. Basili, V., Caldiera, G., Rombach, D.H.: The Goal Question Metric Paradigm, Encyclopedia of Software Engineering. John Wiley and Sons, Chichester (1994)
3. Basili, V.R., Shull, F., Lanubile, F.: Building knowledge through families of experiments. IEEE Trans. Softw. Eng., 456–473 (1999)
4. Birkmeier, D., Overhage, S.: Is BPMN really first choice in joint architecture development? An empirical study on the usability of BPMN and UML activity diagrams for business users. In: Heineman, G.T., Kofron, J., Plasil, F. (eds.) QoSA 2010. LNCS, vol. 6093, pp. 119–134. Springer, Heidelberg (2010)
5. Carver, J., Jaccheri, L., Morasca, S., Shull, F.: Issues in using students in empirical studies in software engineering education. In: 9th International Symposium on Software Metrics, pp. 239–249. IEEE CS, Washington, DC (2003)
6. Cohen, J.: Statistical power analysis for the behavioral sciences, 2nd edn. Lawrence Earlbaum Associates, Hillsdale (1988)
7. De Lucia, A., Francese, R., Scanniello, G., Tortora, G.: Distributed workflow management based on UML and web services. In: Encyclopedia of E-Commerce, E-Government, and Mobile Commerce, pp. 217–222. IGI Global (2006)

8. De Lucia, A., Francese, R., Tortora, G.: Deriving workflow enactment rules from UML activity diagrams: a case study. In: Symposium on Human-Centric Computing Languages and Environments, pp. 211–218 (2003)
9. Di Cerbo, F., Dodero, G., Reggio, G., Ricca, F., Scanniello, G.: Precise vs. Ultralight activity diagrams - an experimental assessment in the context of business process modelling. In: Caivano, D., Oivo, M., Baldassarre, M.T., Visaggio, G. (eds.) PROFES 2011. LNCS, vol. 6759, pp. 291–305. Springer, Heidelberg (2011)
10. Di Nitto, E., Lavazza, L., Schiavoni, M., Tracanella, E., Trombetta, M.: Deriving executable process descriptions from UML. In: 22rd International Conference on Software Engineering (ICSE 2002), pp. 155–165 (2002)
11. Eriksson, H.E., Penker, M.: Business Modelling with UML. Wiley Computing Publishing, Chichester (2000)
12. Gross, A., Doerr, J.: EPC vs. UML activity diagram - two experiments examining their usefulness for requirements engineering. In: Proceedings of Requirements Engineering Conference, pp. 47–56. IEEE CS, Washington, DC (2009)
13. Jurack, S., Lambers, L., Mehner, K., Taentzer, G., Wierse, G.: Object flow definition for refined activity diagrams. In: Chechik, M., Wirsing, M. (eds.) FASE 2009. LNCS, vol. 5503, pp. 49–63. Springer, Heidelberg (2009)
14. Kitchenham, B., Pfleeger, S., Pickard, L., Jones, P., Hoaglin, D., El Emam, K., Rosenberg, J.: Preliminary guidelines for empirical research in software engineering. IEEE Trans. Softw. Eng. 28(8), 721–734 (2002)
15. OMG. Business process model and notation (BPMN) Version 2.0. OMG Final Adopted Specification, Object Management Group (2011)
16. Peixoto, D., Batista, V., Atayde, A., Borges, E., Resende, R., Pádua, C.: A Comparison of BPMN and UML 2.0 Activity Diagrams. In: VII Simposio Brasileiro de Qualidade de Software, Florianopolis (2008)
17. Reggio, G., Ricca, F., Astesiano, E., Leotta, M.: On business process modelling with the UML: a discipline and four styles. Technical Report DISI-TR-11-03, DISI - University of Genova, Italy (April 2011),
http://softeng.disi.unige.it/tech-rep/TECDOC.pdf
18. Ricca, F., Di Penta, M., Torchiano, M., Tonella, P., Ceccato, M.: The role of experience and ability in comprehension tasks supported by UML stereotypes. In: 29th International Conference on Software Engineering (ICSE 2007), Minneapolis, MN, USA, May 20-26, pp. 375–384 (2007)
19. Wohlin, C., Runeson, P., Höst, M., Ohlsson, M., Regnell, B., Wesslén, A.: Experimentation in Software Engineering - An Introduction. Kluwer, Dordrecht (2000)

Semantically Configurable Consistency Analysis for Class and Object Diagrams

Shahar Maoz*, Jan Oliver Ringert**, and Bernhard Rumpe

Software Engineering
RWTH Aachen University, Germany
http://www.se-rwth.de/

Abstract. Checking consistency between an object diagram (OD) and a class diagram (CD) is an important analysis problem. However, several variations in the semantics of CDs and ODs, as used in different contexts and for different purposes, create a challenge for analysis tools. To address this challenge in this paper we investigate *semantically configurable model analysis*. We formalize the variability in the languages semantics using a feature model: each configuration that the model permits induces a different semantics. Moreover, we develop a parametrized analysis that can be instantiated to comply with every legal configuration of the feature model. Thus, the analysis is semantically configured and its results change according to the semantics induced by the selected feature configuration. The ideas are implemented using a parametrized transformation to Alloy. The work can be viewed as a case study example for a formal and automated approach to handling semantic variability in modeling languages.

"One man's constant is another man's variable."
Alan Perlis [21]

1 Introduction

A class diagram (CD) specifies a model of an object-oriented system structure. The semantics of a CD, that is, its meaning, consists of the (possibly infinite) set of object models it permits. The related kind of diagram, object diagram (OD), is used to document concrete object models. Thus, when both kinds of diagrams are used in a model-driven design process, e.g., when domain experts and engineers use ODs as a means of communication and the latter are responsible for designing the CDs, checking the consistency between a CD and an OD is an important analysis problem. However, several variations and ambiguities in the semantics of CDs and ODs, as they are used in different contexts and for different purposes, create a challenge for analysis tools.

---

* S. Maoz acknowledges support from a postdoctoral Minerva Fellowship, funded by the German Federal Ministry for Education and Research.
** J.O. Ringert is supported by the DFG GK/1298 AlgoSyn.

To address this challenge in this paper we investigate *semantically configurable model analysis*. First, we formalize the variability in the semantics of the modeling languages at hand using a feature model: each configuration that the feature model permits, induces a different semantics mapping (over the same domain). Second, we develop a parametrized analysis technique that can be instantiated to comply with every legal configuration of the feature model. Thus, the analysis is semantically configured and its results change according to the semantics induced by the selected feature configuration.

Using a feature model to describe semantic variability has several advantages. First, it provides a means to formally structure the various semantic choices; this supports human comprehension of the semantics, allows comparison of different variants, and, significantly, enables the parsing required in order to support an automatically configurable analysis. Second, the use of a feature model provides a formal means to define logical dependencies between the semantic choices, e.g., mutual exclusion, implication etc. This is indeed necessary, because not all theoretically possible combinations induce sound and useful semantics.

As concrete languages we use the CD and OD sublanguages of UML/P [23]. The semantics of CDs and ODs is based on [5,7,10] and is given in terms of sets of objects and relationships between these objects.

Our feature model for the semantics of CD/OD consistency consists of 32 features. One feature, for example, relates to whether empty object models are considered as possible target values in the semantic domain of CDs. Another feature relates to the question of whether incomplete ODs, which describe object models that are missing some attributes or links but can be extended to a complete object model in the semantics of the CD, would be considered consistent with the CD or not. Another feature relates to the semantics of untyped objects in the OD. Each feature is formally defined as part of the CD/OD semantics definition. The feature model organizes the different features so that each of its configurations induces a specific overall semantics.

The consistency analysis itself is realized using a parametrized transformation to an Alloy [13] module. The input for the parametrized transformation consists of a valid configuration of the feature model, a CD, and an OD. The Alloy module is analyzed using a SAT solver and the result shows whether the CD and the OD are consistent given the semantics defined by the configuration. An overview of the architecture of our solution is shown in Fig. 1.

Our work is fully automated and implemented in a prototype Eclipse plug-in, where one can edit CDs and ODs, select a semantic configuration, and check the consistency of a CD and an OD. Feature model definitions and implementation of feature selection use components from FeatureIDE [14]. After the transformation, the Alloy module is analyzed using the APIs of Alloy Analyzer [1].

Sect. 2 discusses related work. Sect. 3 provides a motivating example. Sect. 4 describes the CD and OD languages, their definition of consistency, and the feature models of their semantics. Sect. 5 presents our technique for semantically configurable analysis. Sect. 6 presents the implementation and a discussion. Sect. 7 concludes.

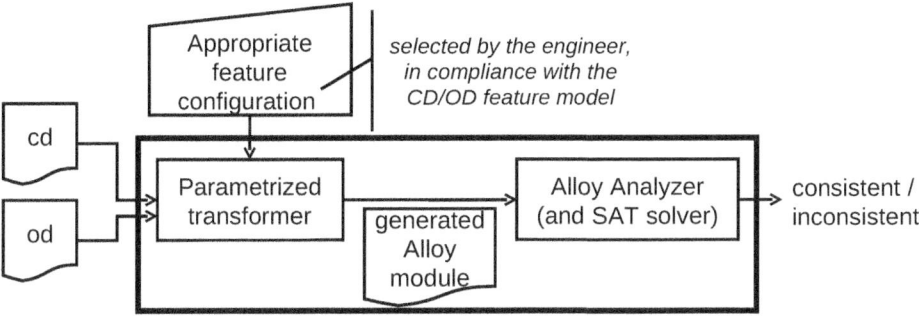

Fig. 1. The architecture of our solution

2 Related Work

The challenge of semantically configurable analysis has been investigated before in a series of works by Atlee et al. [16,20,22,28], which used *template semantics* to configure the semantics of state machines, and demonstrated configured translations of state machines into SMV and into Java code. Different from these works, we use a feature model to model semantic variability. Moreover, these works relate to state-based behavioral models while our present work focuses on structural models. In this sense, our present work may be viewed as complementary to these previous works.

Previous work in our group [8] has presented a taxonomy of variability mechanisms in language definitions syntax and semantics, and demonstrated the use of feature diagrams to model possible variants. The present work builds on these previous ideas while focusing on semantic variability, specifically, semantic mapping variability (rather than syntactic variability) and on its application to semantically configurable analysis, specifically demonstrated and implemented in the context of CDs and ODs.

Some previous works provide various analyses for CDs (often extended with fragments of OCL), using a translation to a constraint satisfaction problem [6], using ad-hoc algorithms or a direct translation to SAT [12,26], using a translation to Description Logic [25,27], or using a translation to Alloy (see, e.g., [2]). We use a transformation to Alloy, but our transformation is very different and much more expressive than the one suggested in [2]. Our transformation extends a basic transformation that we have described in another, more general, paper [17] in two ways: first, it accepts as input not only a CD but also an OD, and second, significantly, it is parametrized based on another input, a feature configuration, so as to support semantically configurable analysis. Finally, to the best of our knowledge, none of the CD analysis works mentioned above support variability-based semantically configurable analysis.

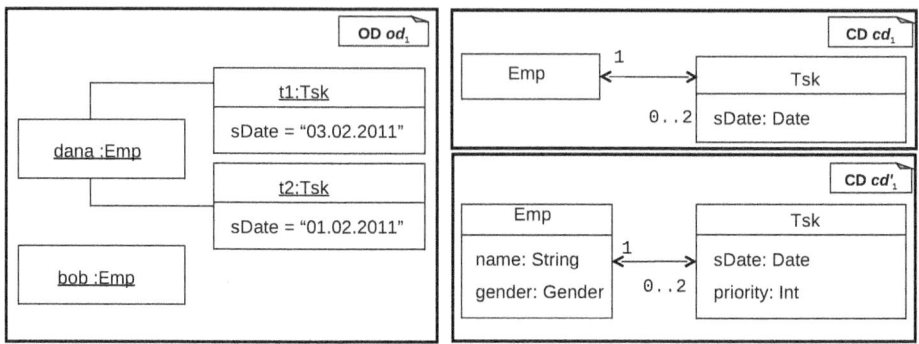

Fig. 2. od_1, cd_1, and cd'_1

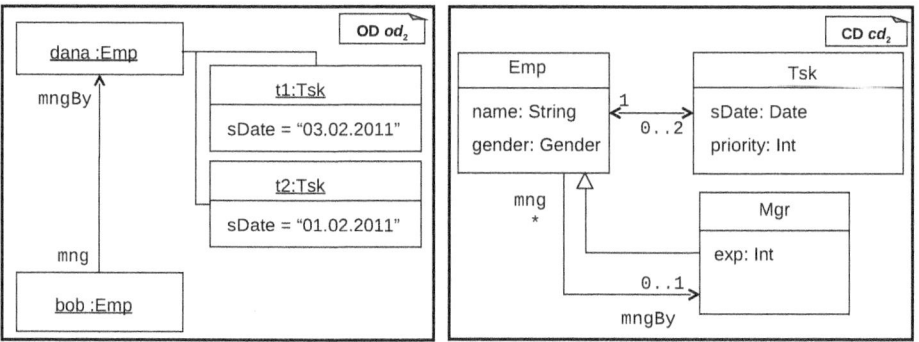

Fig. 3. od_2 and cd_2

3 Motivating Example

We describe a simple example to motivate the need for semantically configurable analysis of CD/OD consistency, when CDs and ODs are used for different activities during the development life cycle and in different contexts. The description is semi-formal. Required definitions are given in the following sections.

Consider od_1, cd_1, and cd'_1, shown in Fig. 2. In early stages of system design, a domain expert suggested several ODs as examples of valid system instances, among them od_1. od_1 consists of employees and tasks: dana and bob are employees, dana has two tasks while bob has no tasks. Dana's tasks have a date attribute. The engineers have designed cd_1 as a CD for the system and wanted to check the pair cd_1 / od_1 for consistency before they continue.

Later in the design process, after more requirements elicitation, additional information became available and the CD cd_1 evolved into a more detailed one, cd'_1, where the same classes include additional attributes. The engineers wanted to check the consistency of cd'_1 not only against some new ODs, where all the new attributes are defined, but also against the older OD od_1, which includes only a partial list of attributes. Although the objects in od_1 did not include all the attributes shown in the new CD, the engineers expected that od_1 would be considered consistent with cd'_1, because it could be extended into a complete valid instance of cd'_1 where more attributes are present.

After a design review, another version of the CD was prepared, cd_2, as shown in Fig. 3. In cd_2 a new class Manager was added as a specialization of Emp, and a related association with roles mngBy and mngs. In turn, the domain expert used od_1 to create od_2, by adding a link between bob and dana, so as to specify that dana manages bob. While in od_2 dana's shown type is Emp, it is understood that dana is also a Manager, because she manages bob. The engineers wanted to check the consistency of cd_2 and od_2 and expected the result to be positive.

A test engineer, responsible for creating test cases that will be executed after a running prototype of the system is created, wanted to specify each test's pre- and post-conditions using ODs. As a sanity check, it was necessary to verify the consistency between each of these ODs and the system's CD. In this case, a much more strict and complete semantics was assumed, i.e., that the instances in the OD include complete lists of attributes and specify their exact type, otherwise the tests may not be accurate or fail (e.g., if dana is constructed as an employee rather than as a manager). Thus, to be useful, CD/OD analysis in the context of testing required a slightly different semantics. Note that based on this semantics, cd_2 and od_2, which have been considered consistent in the context of requirement elicitation, are not considered consistent anymore.

Moreover, the design team noted that the objects in the system may be dynamically constructed and destructed: the system starts with no object instances, and during execution may return to this "no instance" state. Thus, an empty OD, representing the empty OM, should be considered a valid system instance, because, for example, it needs to be used as a pre- or post-condition of some tests. Therefore, despite common standard definitions elsewhere and perhaps against many modelers' intuition, when checking this empty OD against the system's CD for consistency, the team expected a positive result.

Finally, the most complete and detailed version of the system's CD (not shown here) is intended for skeleton code generation of the actual implementation. While in this CD no classes or attributes may be omitted, the team wanted to check it against all ODs used in the design and see that they are consistent.

This example demonstrates that the consistency of a given CD and OD depends on the specific usage of the diagrams and the context in which the question arises; it thus shows the need for more than one definition of semantics for CD/OD consistency. Characterizing and formalizing the required variability, and showing how it can be implemented in a single, configurable analysis solution, are the challenges we address in this paper.

4 CDs and ODs, Consistency, and Semantic Variability

4.1 Class and Object Diagrams Languages

The concrete CD and OD languages we use are sublanguages of UML/P [23], a conceptually refined and simplified variant of UML designed for low-level design and implementation. Our semantics of CDs is based on [5,7,10] and is given in terms of sets of objects and relationships between these objects. More formally, the semantics is defined using three parts: a precise definition of the syntactic domain, i.e., the syntax of the modeling language CD and its context conditions (we use MontiCore [15,19] for this); a semantic domain, for us, a subset of the System Model (see [5,7]) OM, consisting of all finite object models; and a mapping $sem : CD \rightarrow \mathcal{P}(OM)$, which relates each syntactically well-formed CD to a set of constructs in the semantic domain OM. The semantics of ODs is defined over the same semantic domain OM, using a mapping $sem : OD \rightarrow \mathcal{P}(OM)$, which relates each syntactically well-formed OD to a set of constructs in the semantic domain OM, that is, to a set of object models. Note that the semantic domain of CDs is made of OMs, not ODs. For a thorough and formal account of the semantics see [7].

For example, the semantics of cd_1 shown in Fig. 2 includes all object models consisting of tasks and employees where each employee is responsible for up to two tasks, and each task is done by exactly one employee and has an attribute sDate of type date. Note that the empty object model, which is an object model with no objects at all, may or may not be considered in the semantics of this CD. In addition, note that we did not say whether object models whose tasks have additional attributes may be considered in the semantics of this CD or not. As another example, the semantics of od_1 shown in Fig. 2 includes all object models consisting of two employees where one of the employees is linked to two tasks that have certain sDate values. Note that we did not say whether object models that have additional employees, with or without tasks, should be considered in the semantics of this OD or not. These ambiguities and possible variations are examples of the kinds of semantic variability that affect the CD/OD consistency check, as we discuss below.

Finally, we support the following CD language constructs: class attributes, enumerations, uni- and bi-directional associations with multiplicities, aggregation, composition, generalization (inheritance), interface implementation, and abstract and singleton classes. The OD language constructs we support include objects, their attributes, and the links between them.

4.2 Consistency

A set of diagrams is considered *consistent* if the intersection of the semantics of all diagrams in the set is not empty [4]. Formally:

Definition 1 (consistency). *Given a set of diagrams D, we say that D is consistent iff* $\bigcap_{d \in D} sem(d) \neq \emptyset$.

By applying the above definition to the special case of a CD and an OD we get:

Definition 2 (CD/OD consistency). *Given a CD cd and an OD od, we say that the cd and od are consistent iff* $sem(cd) \cap sem(od) \neq \emptyset$.

While the definition of consistency is generally accepted, definitions of the semantic mapping function *sem*, for CDs and ODs, may vary. To formally handle variability in the semantics mapping we use the feature models described next.

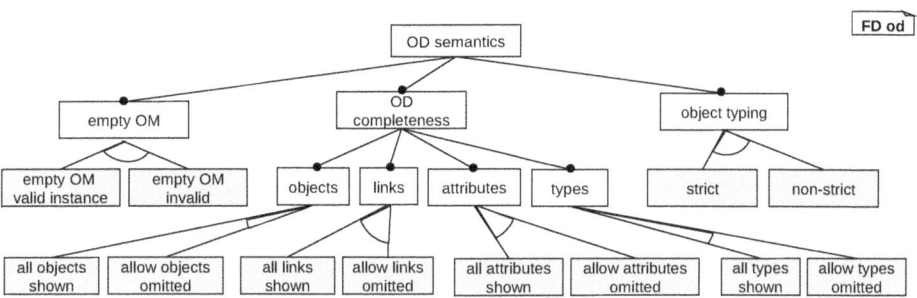

Fig. 4. The OD semantics feature diagram

4.3 The Semantic Variability Feature Models

A feature model describes a structured set of features and their logical dependencies [3,9]. Feature models are commonly used in the area of software product lines. They may be visually represented using feature diagrams, which are basically and-or trees, extended with textual cross-tree logical constraints. Here we use a feature model to formalize variability in the semantics of CDs and ODs. The model is composed of two sub-models, for CD semantics and for OD semantics, and of several cross-tree logical constraints. In the diagrams we use the standard notation: for mandatory features, a line ending with a filled circle; for alternative features of which exactly one must be selected (xor), an empty slice covering the lines leading to the different alternatives.

Our feature model for OD semantics consists of 19 features, as shown in the feature diagram in Fig. 4. Roughly, a valid feature configuration of this model specifies whether the empty object model may be considered a valid OM, whether the objects shown, links shown, attributes shown, and types shown are complete or not, and whether all objects shown in the diagram must be typed with their most specific type, or can use one of their super types.

Our feature model for CD semantics for CD/OD consistency contains 11 features, as shown in the feature diagram in Fig. 5. A valid feature configuration of this model specifies whether the empty object model may be considered a valid instance of a CD, whether the lists of attributes shown are considered complete or not, and whether the set of classes shown is considered complete or not.

The complete feature diagram for CD/OD consistency feature model is built from a CD/OD consistency feature at the root, using the two feature diagrams described above to represent required features, as its sub trees, as shown in Fig. 6. To this composed diagram we add cross-tree logical constraints that define dependencies between the different features, for us, the semantic choices, e.g., mutual exclusion, implication etc. This is indeed necessary, because, as we have found also during evaluation (see Sect. 6), not all theoretically possible combinations (feature configurations) induce sound and useful semantics. Specifically, we add the following 3 constraints:

$$\textbf{not } (\ cd.allowClassesOmitted \textbf{ and } od.allowTypesOmitted\ ) \qquad (1)$$

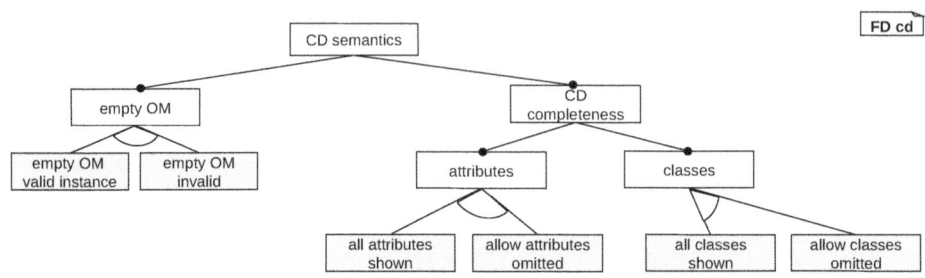

Fig. 5. The CD semantics feature diagram

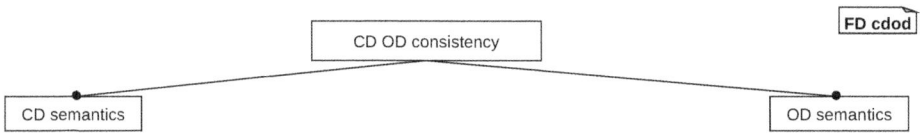

Fig. 6. The composed CD/OD semantics feature diagram

$$od.allowObjectsOmitted \textbf{ implies } od.allowLinksOmitted \qquad (2)$$
$$cd.emptyOMInvalid \textbf{ iff } od.emptyOMInvalid \qquad (3)$$

We add constraint 1 because the combination of allowing classes to be omitted from the CD (which means allowing instances to include objects of classes not shown in the CD) and of allowing the OD to include untyped objects, results in a semantics which is much too permissive and is not useful. We add constraint 2 because if objects are allowed to be omitted, the links they could have been connected with must also be allowed to be omitted. We add constraint 3 because having the empty OM in the semantics of CDs while excluding it from the semantics of ODs (or vice versa) does not make sense.

Overall, our feature model contains 32 features, 14 of which are core features, which are included in all configurations. The model has 144 valid configurations. The complete feature model used in our work is available in [24], also in a format compliant with [18], to allow others to inspect it and use it.

5 Semantically Configurable Consistency Analysis

The key to the semantically configurable consistency analysis is a parametrized transformation to an Alloy [13] module. In addition to a CD and an OD, the input for the parametrized transformation includes one valid configuration of the CD/OD consistency feature model described in the previous section.

We now describe the parametrized transformation to Alloy. A variant of our transformation, which takes only a CD as input and is not semantically configurable, is presented in [17]. Here we give an overview of the generated Alloy module and then focus on the parts related to handling variability. We use the CDs and ODs presented earlier in Sect. 3 as running examples.

5.1 Overview of the Transformation to Alloy

The basic transformation relies on several foundational signatures and facts. These include an abstract signature FName, used to represent association role names and attribute names for all classes; an abstract signature Obj, which serves as the parent of all classes, and whose get Alloy field relates it and an FName to instances of Obj (this allows more flexibility than the built-in Alloy fields); an abstract signature Val as a specialization of Obj, used to represent all predefined types (i.e., primitive types and other types that are not defined as classes in the CD); a signature EnumVal, which extends Obj too, and is used to represent values of enumeration types; and several facts, among them ones that state that enumeration values as well as primitive values can have no further fields and should only appear in an instance if referenced by an object.

A number of parametric predicates are used to specify constraints such as association's multiplicities and directions. These are instantiated with concrete values from within the CD predicate described next. Rather than using Alloy's extends keyword to specify generalization relations, we use generated functions that return the set of sub classes of each class, e.g., if Mgr is a specialization of Emp then the function EmpSubs returns the atoms in {Emp, Mgr}.

The CD and the OD themselves are represented using two predicates, pred cd and pred od. In pred cd the attributes and associations of each class are defined and then restricted using the multiplicity and directionality predicates mentioned above. In pred od the existence of the objects is stated and their attributes and links are defined.

Finally, a predicate pred consistentCDOD is defined, consisting of the single statement cd and od. Checking consistency is done by executing Alloy Analyzer run command for consistentCDOD.

5.2 Handling Semantic Variability

Handling variability is technically realized using generated parametrized Alloy predicates and their instantiation from within pred cd and pred od. Below we show how some of the features are handled.

OD features. List. 1.1 shows several parametrized Alloy predicates corresponding to the different features available for OD semantics. As a concrete example, List. 1.2 shows the predicate that represents an OD, specifically od_2, presented earlier in Sect. 3, Fig. 3, in the context of a specific semantic configuration where the empty OM is not a valid instance, all objects and links are shown but attributes may be omitted, all types are shown but are not strict. We now explain the two listings in detail.

First, the predicate emptyOMNotValidOD (List. 1.1 line 2) specifies that there exists at least one object. It is mentioned in pred od iff the semantic configuration includes the feature *od.emptyOMInvalid* (see List. 1.2 line 18).

Second, the predicates in lines 5-16 are used to specify the three completeness features, for objects, links, and attributes. The predicate allObjectsShownOD

```
1  // Semantic variation feature: empty OM
2  pred emptyOMNotValidOD { some Obj }
3
4  // Semantic variation feature: OD completeness
5  pred allObjectsShownOD[objs: set univ] {
6    univ = (objs + FName + auxilary + Val + EnumVal + Int) }
7
8  pred allLinksShownOD[obj: Obj, roleNames: set FName] {
9    no {obj.get[FName - roleNames] - Val - EnumVal } }
10 pred allLinksShownODCmplt[obj: Obj, roleName: one FName,
11   partners: set Obj] { obj.get[roleName] = partners }
12 pred allLinksShownODIncmplt[obj: Obj, roleName: one FName,
13   partners: set Obj] { partners in obj.get[roleName] }
14
15 pred allAttribShownOD[obj: Obj, definedAttrs: set FName] {
16   obj.get.(Val + EnumVal) = definedAttrs }
17
18 // Semantic variation feature: object typing
19 pred strictTypingOD[obj: univ, type: set univ] {
20   obj in type }
21
22 pred nonStrictTypingOD[obj: univ, subtypes: set univ] {
23   obj in subtypes }
```

Listing 1.1. Parametrized Alloy predicates for OD semantics features

specifies that the set of objects it receives in its parameter (plus some other atoms from utility sets used in our translation) is equal to the module's universe, i.e., that there are no more objects except the ones specified in its parameter. An example instantiation of this predicate appears in line 16 of List. 1.2, specifying that dana, bob, and the two tasks, as shown in the diagram, are all the objects in the object model. The other completeness predicates use the get relation defined in our translation; this special representation of object's attributes and field names allows us to specify their presence or absence. In our example, the semantic configuration requires that all links are shown, and so lines 8-15 of List. 1.2 instantiate the allLinksShownOD and the allLinksShownODCmplt predicates for all the links in od_2.

Third, the last two predicates in List. 1.1 handle strict and non-strict typing: both specify that the set of objects in the first parameter is included in the set of objects assigned to the second parameter. We keep the two predicates separate for better readability when they are used: strict typing is used with a specific signature while non-strict typing is used with our translation's sub classes functions (see above). In our example we chose non-strict typing so we use the sub classes functions EmpSubs, which returns the atoms in {Emp, Mgr}, and TskSubs, which returns the atoms in {Tsk} (lines 5-6 of List. 1.2).

```
 1 pred od2 {
 2   some dana: Obj| some bob: Obj| some t1: Obj| some t2: Obj|
 3   # {dana + bob + t1 + t2} = 4
 4   // Semantic variation feature: object typing
 5   and nonStrictTypingOD[dana + bob, EmpSubs]
 6   and nonStrictTypingOD[t1 + t2, TskSubs]
 7   // Semantic variation feature: OD completeness
 8   and allLinksShownOD[dana, worksOn]
 9   and allLinksShownOD[bob, mngBy]
10   and allLinksShownOD[t1, doneBy]
11   and allLinksShownOD[t2, doneBy]
12   and allLinksShownODCmplt[bob, mngBy, dana]
13   and allLinksShownODCmplt[dana, worksOn, {t1 + t2}]
14   and allLinksShownODCmplt[t1, doneBy, dana]
15   and allLinksShownODCmplt[t2, doneBy, dana]
16   and allObjectsShownOD[dana + bob + t1 + t2]
17   // Semantic variation feature: empty OM
18   and emptyOMNotValidOD }
```

Listing 1.2. Example Alloy predicate for od_2 (shown in Fig. 3)

CD features. List. 1.3 shows the parametrized Alloy predicates related to the different features available for CD semantics. As a concrete example, List. 1.4 shows the predicate that represents a CD, specifically cd_2, presented earlier in Sect. 3, Fig. 3, in the context of a specific semantic configuration where the empty OM is not part of the semantics, all classes are shown and their list of attributes is complete. We now explain the two listings in detail.

The predicate emptyOMNotValidCD (List. 1.3 line 2) specifies that there exists at least one object. It is mentioned in pred cd iff the semantic configuration includes the feature $cd.emptyOMinvalid$ (just like in pred od).

The remaining predicates in List. 1.3 handle completeness. The predicate allAttribShownCD specifies that the get relation of the object does not include any field name outside the set of field names specified in the fNames parameter (see List. 1.4 lines 17-19 for instantiations with all classes and their field names). The predicate allowMoreAttribCD specifies that for the signature given as the objs parameter either there are no more fields than specified in the fNames parameter or there are additional attributes and enumeration values. The predicate allClassesShownCD specifies that the model's universe will only contain object instances of the classes given as a parameter. It is instantiated in List. 1.4 line 20 with all classes shown in cd_2.

6 Implementation and Discussion

Implementation. We have created a prototype implementation of our work, packaged as an Eclipse plug-in. For the representation of the CD/OD semantics feature model and the selection of valid configurations we use components from

```
1  // Semantic variation feature: empty OM
2  pred emptyOMNotValidCD { some Obj }
3
4  // Semantic variation feature: CD completeness
5  pred allAttribShownCD[objs: set Obj, fNames:set FName] {
6    no objs.get[FName - fNames] }
7
8  pred allowMoreAttribCD[objs: set Obj, fNames:set FName] {
9    all f : (FName - fNames) | (
10     (no objs.get[f])
11     or (one v : Val | all o : objs | o.get[f] = v)
12     or attribOfEnumValue[objs, f]  ) }
13
14 pred allClassesShownCD[objs: set Obj] {
15   univ = (objs + FName + auxilary + Val + EnumVal + Int) }
```

Listing 1.3. Parametrized Alloy predicates for CD semantics features

FeatureIDE [14]. For editing CDs and ODs we use parsers and editors (with syntax highlighting etc.) generated by MontiCore [15,19]. The transformation to Alloy uses FreeMarker templates [11]. Analysis is done using Alloy's APIs [1]. The prototype plug-in together with several examples is available from [24].

On semantic variability. One may consider semantic variability in a modeling language definition to be a weakness, as it may create confusion and lead to ambiguities in its comprehension and use. We believe, however, that for general purpose languages such as the sub-languages of the UML, state machines, class diagrams, etc., a certain degree of variability in general, and of semantic variability in particular, is a necessity. The very 'general purpose' nature of the language dictates that it will be used for a variety of tasks and in different contexts, which, in practice, entails a requirement for variability. This is evident also from the works of Atlee et al. [20,22,28]. Still, we do not try to promote the existence of too many semantics; instead, we aim to formally and precisely define the specific points where the semantics should vary and automate the application and use of the possible resulting definitions.

As an alternative to language level semantic variability, one may suggest to enrich the language syntax with keywords that allow the modeler to explicitly choose between variants, e.g., by adding optional keywords such as 'complete' / 'incomplete', 'strict' / 'permissive' etc. as modifiers, at the diagram level or the diagram-element level. The advantage of this is that there is a single semantics to handle. The disadvantages however are (1) that the language syntax becomes more complicated, (2) that questions may arise regarding the default semantics, e.g., if the 'complete' /'incomplete' keywords are omitted, and, significantly, (3) that this solution does not support cases where the same diagram should change its meaning in different phases of the development process (e.g., when the same CD should be considered complete during design but incomplete during

```
pred cd2 {
  // Definition of class attributes
  ObjAttrib[Tsk, priority, type_Int]
  ObjAttrib[Tsk, sDate, type_Date]
  ObjAttrib[Emp, gender, GenderEnum]
  ObjAttrib[Emp, name, type_String]
  ObjAttrib[Mgr, gender, GenderEnum]
  ObjAttrib[Mgr, exp, type_Int]
  ObjAttrib[Mgr, name, type_String]
  // Associations
  ObjLUAttrib[EmpSubs, mngBy, MgrSubs, 0, 1]
  ObjL[MgrSubs, mngBy, EmpSubs, 0]
  BidiAssoc[EmpSubs, worksOn, TskSubs, doneBy]
  ObjLUAttrib[TskSubs, doneBy, EmpSubs, 1, 1]
  ObjLUAttrib[EmpSubs, worksOn, TskSubs, 0, 2]
  // Semantic variation feature: cd completeness
  allAttribShownCD[Tsk, priority+sDate+doneBy]
  allAttribShownCD[Emp, gender+name+mngBy+worksOn]
  allAttribShownCD[Mgr, gender+exp+name+mngBy+worksOn]
  allClassesShownCD[Tsk+Emp+Mgr]
  // Semantic variation feature: empty OM
  emptyOMNotValidCD }
```

Listing 1.4. Example Alloy predicate for cd_2 (shown in Fig. 3)

analysis). It is important to note, though, that our work can easily be adapted to support this solution: the only change is that the 'configuration' would not come from the feature model but from the keywords on the diagrams themselves.

Evaluation of our solution. Our choice of Alloy as the target formalism for analysis was motivated by Alloy's expressive power, its readability, and its readily available automated analysis. Still, it is important to note that Alloy's analysis is generally bounded by a user-defined scope. Interestingly, however, in the context of CD/OD consistency, the scope limitation is relevant to some semantic configurations but is irrelevant to others: specifically, when the CD and OD semantics assume that the diagrams show all classes and all objects, the scope to be used can be calculated from the input and the analysis is sound and complete. That said, our experience with Alloy shows that it does not scale well for large scopes. Alloy was not designed to scale, see the small scope hypothesis discussed in [13].

We have validated our work as follows. First, we created an automated test that generates all 144 legal configurations of our feature model, checks their application to the consistency check of three different CD OD pairs, and verifies that the result is correct. Second, we used FeatureIDE's user interface to manually define 7 different configurations, we used MontiCore's generated CD and OD editors to edit 12 CDs and ODs (including the ones shown in this paper in Sect. 3), we ran the configurable consistency check using our plug-in and observed that the results are correct. Moreover, we have pre-prepared a number of configurations that we believe are most useful for specific task contexts, e.g., for requirements elicitation and for testing. All configurations, CDs, and ODs used in our validation are available with the implemented plug-in from [24]. We encourage the interested reader to check them.

One lesson learned during evaluation was the importance of constraints between features (the second constraint presented in Sect. 4.3, relating object omission with links omission, was discovered in the course of our experiments). Another lesson learned relates to scalability. While our implementation works very fast for small CDs and ODs, it does not scale to handle CDs associations with high multiplicities and ODs with many objects. As mentioned above in the discussion of the use of Alloy, scalability will require the use of abstractions or the development of a different analysis approach. Finally, one may suggest additional CD features we do not yet support (e.g., constrained generalization sets, a fragment of OCL constraints etc.) and additional semantic variation features (e.g., allow role names omitted in the OD). Our work can be extended to support these additions. Each additional feature will require corresponding support in the configurable transformation and possibly logical constraints on its combination with other features. We leave these for future work.

7 Conclusion

In this paper we have investigated the idea of semantically configurable analysis in the context of CD and OD consistency. We formalized semantic variability in these languages using a feature model and presented a semantically configurable fully automated analysis solution based on a parametrized transformation to an Alloy module and its analysis with a SAT solver. The work was implemented in an Eclipse plug-in and demonstrated with examples.

We consider the following possible future work. First, extending our work to support additional CD language features, e.g., constrained generalization sets. Second, defining feature models for semantic variability in other modeling languages and developing related parametric analysis problems, e.g., the model-checking of a statechart against a sequence diagram.

References

1. Alloy Analyzer website, http://alloy.mit.edu/ (accessed July 2011)
2. Anastasakis, K., Bordbar, B., Georg, G., Ray, I.: On challenges of model transformation from UML to Alloy. Software and Systems Modeling 9(1), 69–86 (2010)
3. Batory, D.S.: Feature models, grammars, and propositional formulas. In: Obbink, H., Pohl, K. (eds.) SPLC 2005. LNCS, vol. 3714, pp. 7–20. Springer, Heidelberg (2005)
4. Broy, M., Cengarle, M.V., Grönniger, H., Rumpe, B.: Considerations and Rationale for a UML System Model. In: Lano, K. (ed.) UML 2 Semantics and Applications. Wiley, Chichester (2009)
5. Broy, M., Cengarle, M.V., Grönniger, H., Rumpe, B.: Definition of the System Model. In: Lano, K. (ed.) UML 2 Semantics and Applications. Wiley, Chichester (2009)

6. Cabot, J., Clarisó, R., Riera, D.: UMLtoCSP: a tool for the formal verification of UML/OCL models using constraint programming. In: ASE, pp. 547–548. ACM, New York (2007)
7. Cengarle, M.V., Grönniger, H., Rumpe, B.: System Model Semantics of Class Diagrams. Informatik-Bericht 2008-05, Technische Universität Braunschweig (2008)
8. Cengarle, M.V., Grönniger, H., Rumpe, B.: Variability within modeling language definitions. In: Schürr, A., Selic, B. (eds.) MODELS 2009. LNCS, vol. 5795, pp. 670–684. Springer, Heidelberg (2009)
9. Czarnecki, K., Eisenecker, U.: Generative Programming Methods, Tools, and Applications. Addison-Wesley, Reading (2000)
10. Evans, A., France, R.B., Lano, K., Rumpe, B.: The UML as a Formal Modeling Notation. In: Bézivin, J., Muller, P.-A. (eds.) UML 1998. LNCS, vol. 1618, pp. 336–348. Springer, Heidelberg (1999)
11. FreeMarker, http://freemarker.org/ (accessed July 2011)
12. Gogolla, M., Büttner, F., Richters, M.: USE: A UML-based specification environment for validating UML and OCL. Sci. Comput. Program 69(1-3), 27–34 (2007)
13. Jackson, D.: Software Abstractions: Logic, Language, and Analysis. MIT Press, Cambridge (2006)
14. Kästner, C., Thüm, T., Saake, G., Feigenspan, J., Leich, T., Wielgorz, F., Apel, S.: FeatureIDE: A tool framework for feature-oriented software development. In: ICSE, pp. 611–614 (2009)
15. Krahn, H., Rumpe, B., Völkel, S.: MontiCore: a framework for compositional development of domain specific languages. Int. J. on Software Tools for Technology Transfer (STTT) 12(5), 353–372 (2010)
16. Lu, Y., Atlee, J.M., Day, N.A., Niu, J.: Mapping template semantics to SMV. In: ASE, pp. 320–325. IEEE Computer Society, Los Alamitos (2004)
17. Maoz, S., Ringert, J.O., Rumpe, B.: CD2Alloy: Class diagrams analysis using Alloy revisited. In: Whittle, J., Clark, T., Kühne, T. (eds.) MODELS. LNCS, vol. 6981, pp. 592–607. Springer, Heidelberg (2011)
18. Mendonça, M., Branco, M., Cowan, D.D.: S.P.L.O.T.: software product lines online tools. In: OOPSLA Companion, pp. 761–762 (2009), http://www.splot-research.org/
19. MontiCore project, http://www.monticore.org/
20. Niu, J., Atlee, J.M., Day, N.A.: Template semantics for model-based notations. IEEE Trans. Software Eng. 29(10), 866–882 (2003)
21. Perlis, A.J.: Epigrams on programming. SIGPLAN Notices 17(9), 7–13 (1982)
22. Prout, A., Atlee, J.M., Day, N.A., Shaker, P.: Semantically configurable code generation. In: Busch, C., Ober, I., Bruel, J.-M., Uhl, A., Völter, M. (eds.) MODELS 2008. LNCS, vol. 5301, pp. 705–720. Springer, Heidelberg (2008)
23. Rumpe, B.: Modellierung mit UML. Springer, Heidelberg (2004)
24. Semantic variability project website, http://www.se-rwth.de/materials/semvar/
25. Simmonds, J., Bastarrica, M.C.: A tool for automatic UML model consistency checking. In: ASE, pp. 431–432. ACM, New York (2005)
26. Soeken, M., Wille, R., Kuhlmann, M., Gogolla, M., Drechsler, R.: Verifying UML/OCL models using Boolean satisfiability. In: DATE, pp. 1341–1344. IEEE, Los Alamitos (2010)
27. Van Der Straeten, R., Mens, T., Simmonds, J., Jonckers, V.: Using Description Logic to Maintain Consistency between UML Models. In: Stevens, P., Whittle, J., Booch, G. (eds.) UML 2003. LNCS, vol. 2863, pp. 326–340. Springer, Heidelberg (2003)
28. Taleghani, A., Atlee, J.M.: Semantic variations among UML stateMachines. In: Wang, J., Whittle, J., Harel, D., Reggio, G. (eds.) MoDELS 2006. LNCS, vol. 4199, pp. 245–259. Springer, Heidelberg (2006)

Identifying the Weaknesses of UML Class Diagrams during Data Model Comprehension

Gabriele Bavota[1], Carmine Gravino[1], Rocco Oliveto[2], Andrea De Lucia[1], Genoveffa Tortora[1], Marcela Genero[3], and José Antonio Cruz-Lemus[3]

[1] Software Engineering Lab, University of Salerno, Fisciano (SA), Italy
{gbavota,gravino,adelucia,tortora}@unisa.it
[2] STAT Departement, University of Molise, Pesche (IS), Italy
rocco.oliveto@unimol.it
[3] Dep. of Technologies and Information Systems, University of Castilla, La Mancha
{marcela.genero,joseantonio.cruz}@uclm.es

Abstract. In this paper we present an experiment and two replications aimed at comparing the support provided by ER and UML class diagrams during comprehension activities by focusing on the single building blocks of the two notations. This kind of analysis can be used to identify weakness in a notation and/or justify the need of preferring ER or UML for data modeling. The results reveal that UML class diagrams are generally more comprehensible than ER diagrams, even if the former has some weaknesses related to three building blocks, i.e., multi-value attribute, composite attribute, and weak entity. These findings suggest that a UML class diagram extension should be considered to overcome these weaknesses and improve the comprehensibility of the notation.

1 Introduction

A data model is a set of concepts that can be used to describe both the structure of and the operations on a database [1]. It represents the output of data modeling (or conceptual design), an activity that aims at creating a conceptual schema in a diagrammatic form and facilitating the communication between developers and users [1]. Understanding and interpreting data models represents a fundamental activity from the earliest stages of software development, e.g., requirement analysis. Thus, a comprehensive notation is really desirable to avoid misunderstanding that can lead to the introduction of errors very expensive to remove in the later phases of the software development. A comprehensive notation is also desirable during software maintenance, since it facilitates the comprehension activities that have to be performed to understand the design of the system before the analysis and the implementation of a change request.

Entity-Relationship (ER) and its extensions are the most used notations for database conceptual modeling and still remains the *de facto* standard [1]. The success of the Object-Oriented (OO) approach for software development has encouraged the use of this approach also for database modeling [2]. In particular, UML class diagrams can be used to represent the conceptual schema of the whole software system, so the same notation can be used to model the functionality of the system as well as to represent its data. The structural constructs of the UML class diagram which represents the data structure is somewhat equivalent to Extended ER (EER) representation (e.g., object classes considered equivalent to entity and relationship types). The functionality is represented through "methods" that are attached to the object classes. However, while UML is becoming a *de facto* standard for the analysis and design of software systems, it is not exploited with the same success for modeling databases. Indeed, nowadays ER remains the most used notation to model databases and in some cases it complements UML in the design of software systems. A recent survey also indicated that in some cases both ER and UML class diagrams are employed to represent the same database [3]. Such behaviors might be the trigger for possible problems during the evolution of the data models. More effort is required to maintain the models and their implementation up-to-date, since out-of-data models can generate inconsistency and misunderstanding during software maintenance and evolution. All these considerations lead researchers to empirically compare the ER and UML diagrams to show the actual benefits given by one notation as compared to the other [3,4]. The results achieved in all these studies indicate that the support given by UML class diagrams in comprehension tasks is at least equal (and in some cases higher than) the support given by ER diagrams. However, a qualitative and quantitative analysis concerning the identification of the graphical elements of one notation that are more comprehensible than the corresponding element in the other notation is still missing (this kind of analysis is quantitatively performed in [2] during the comparison of EER and OO models). Such an analysis is vital to provide insight on why UML class diagrams are better than ER diagrams or *vice versa* and highlight strengths and limitations of the two notations. This kind of analysis can be used to (i) justify the need of preferring ER or UML class diagrams for data modeling; or (ii) identify weakness in a notation that could be overcome to improve its comprehensibility.

In this paper we aim at bridging this gap presenting the results of a controlled experiment and two replications to deeply analyze the support given by ER and UML class diagrams during the comprehension of data models. The experiments aimed at performing a fine-grained analysis to (quantitatively and qualitatively) compare the single building blocks, i.e., Entity, Primary Key/ID, Composite Attribute, Multi-value Attribute, Recursive relationship, Relationship cardinality, Ternary relationship, Generalization IS-A, Weak entity, M:N relationship, of the two notations. The experiment and its replications involved 156 students of the university of Salerno (Italy) with different academic background represented by fresher, bachelor, and master students.

The rest of the paper is organized as follows. Section 2 presents the related work. Section 3 provides details of the design of the experiment and presents the results achieved while Section 4 discuss the possible threats to validity. Concluding remarks and directions for future work are given in Section 5.

2 Related Work

In the last two decades some papers have analysed, through controlled experiments, empirical studies, or surveys, graphical notations supporting the software development process.

To the best of our knowledge only four papers compare the ER notation, or its extensions, and Objected-Oriented (OO) models [5], [2], [6], [7]. In particular, Shoval and Shiran [5] compare Extended ER (EER) and OO data models from the point of view of design quality, where quality is measured in terms of correctness of the produced models, time to completely perform the design task, and designers' opinions. The goal of our empirical investigation is different, since we compare ER and UML diagrams from a maintainer perspective in order to verify whether the use of UML diagrams provides better supports during comprehension activities on data models. The comparison performed by Shoval and Shiran reveals that there are no significant differences between Extended ER (EER) and OO data models, except for the use of ternary and unary relationships since in this case EER models provide better results. Furthermore, the designers preferred to work with the EER models.

Shoval and Frumermann [2] also perform a comparison of EER and OO diagrams taking into account the user comprehension. As done by Shoval and Shiran [5], they separately examine the comprehension of various constructs of the analysed models. Their analysis reveals that EER schemas are more comprehensible for ternary relationships while for the other constructs no significant difference is found.

Bock and Ryan [6] also examine the correctness of the design for several constructs of the considered diagram types in an empirical analysis comparing EER and OO models from a designer perspective. The analysis reveals significant difference only in four cases (i.e., representation of attribute identifiers, unary 1:1 and binary m:n relationships) and no difference is found concerning the time to complete the tasks.

A comparison between OO and ER models from an end-user perspective is also carried out by Palvia *et al.* [7], whose aim is to establish which is more comprehensible. Differently from previous reported studies, they measure comprehension on overall terms, not considering specific constructs, and the results of their investigation suggested that OO schemas are superior in this respect.

3 Empirical Evaluation

This section describes in detail the design of the controlled experiment we performed and the analysis and interpretation of the achieved results. A discussion of the threats to validity is also presented at the end of the section.

3.1 Goal, Definition, and Context

The *goal* of our experimentation was to analyse whether UML class diagrams are more comprehensible than ER diagrams during the comprehension of data models. Moreover, we are interested in performing a fine grained analysis to compare the single building blocks B_i of the two notations to identify possible weaknesses of the UML class diagrams with respect to the ER diagrams, where $B_i \in \{$ *Entity, Primary Key/ID, Composite Attribute, Multi-value Attribute, Recursive relationship, Relationship cardinality, Ternary relationship, Generalization IS-A, Weak entity, M:N relationship*$\}$.

The performed experiments involved students of the University of Salerno (Italy) having different academic backgrounds and, consequently, different levels of experience on ER and UML diagrams:

- *fresher students*, i.e., 1st year B.Sc. students that were starting their academic career when the experiment was performed;
- *bachelor students*, i.e., 2nd year B.Sc. students that attended Programming and Databases courses in the past and were attending the Software Engineering course when the experimentation was performed;
- *master students*, i.e., 1st year M.Sc. students that attended advanced courses of Programming and Software Engineering in the past and were attending an advanced Databases course when the experimentation was performed;

Note that in the Software Engineering course the design notation used is UML while for the Databases course the design notation is ER. The number of subjects involved in the original experiment were 37 bachelor students, while the first and second replications involved 52 master students and 67 fresher students subjects, respectively. We employed the data models of the following systems:

- Company, a software system implementing all the operations required to manage the projects conducted by a company;
- EasyClinic, a software system implementing all the operations required to manage a medical doctor's office.

In particular, we exploited two different data models represented in terms of ER and UML class diagrams. Table 1 shows the characteristics of the data models we employed in the experiments. The selection of the objects for each experiment was performed ensuring that the data models had a comparable level of complexity. For this reason, we extracted sub-diagrams of comparable size from the original data models according to the *"the rule of seven"* given by Miller [8] to build comprehensible graphical diagrams[1]. In the context of our experimentation we applied such a rule to select data models easy to comprehend. This was necessary because (i) each experiment was designed to be performed in a limited amount of time and (ii) a simple data model is preferred to a more complex data model since the latter might influence the comprehension activities.

3.2 Design

Each experiment was organised in two laboratory sessions. In particular, in the context of the experiment subjects had to perform two comprehension activities

---

[1] The rule of seven is the generally accepted claim that people can hold approximately seven chunks or units of information in their short-term memory at a time [8].

Table 1. Data models used in each controlled experiment

System	# entities	# attributes	# relationships
Company	7	17	5
EasyClinic-BookingManagement	6	18	5

Table 2. Experimental design

Group	Treatment	
	ER	UML
A	EasyClinic, Lab1	Company, Lab2
B	Company, Lab2	EasyClinic, Lab1
C	Company, Lab1	EasyClinic, Lab2
D	EasyClinic, Lab2	Company, Lab1

on the data models of two different software systems. Each subject analysed the UML diagram (or ER diagram) of one system in one laboratory session and the ER diagram (or UML diagram) of the other system in the other laboratory session. The organisation of each group of subjects[2] in each experimental lab session (*Lab1* and *Lab2*) followed the design shown in Table 2. In particular, the rows represent the four experimental groups, whereas the columns refers to the design notation used to represent the data model (i.e., ER and CD).

3.3 Comprehension Questionnaires

The main outcome observed in the three experiments was the comprehension level. To evaluate it, we asked the subjects to answer a questionnaire (similar to [9]) consisting of 10 multiple choice questions where each question has one or more correct answers. The number of answers is the same for each question (i.e., three answers), while the number of correct answers is different. The questions cover all the building blocks B_i of the two notations exploited to model a database. Figure 1 shows a sample question of the comprehension questionnaire regarding the system Company.

The same building blocks were qualitatively analysed through a questionnaire where subjects specified their preferences between the two considered notations. In particular, for each building block B_i they manifested a preference between ER diagram, No preference, and UML class diagram.

Moreover, at the end of each laboratory session a survey questionnaire was proposed to the subjects. This survey aimed at assessing the overall quality of the provided material as well as the clearness and difficulty of the comprehension tasks. In particular, the subjects provided answers to the following questions (one choice for each question):

S1 : I had enough time to perform the tasks
S2 : The task objectives were perfectly clear to me
S3 : The tasks I performed was perfectly clear to me
S4 : Judging the difficulty of the comprehension task

---

[2] The students were assigned to the four groups in a randomly balanced way.

where S1, S2, and S3 expected closed answers according to the Likert scale [10] from 1 (strongly disagree) to 5 (strongly agree), while S4 from 1 (very low) to 5 (very high).

3.4 Variable Selection

We performed a single factor within-subjects design, where the independent variable (main factor) is represented by the design notation used to represent a data model. This variable is denoted as **Method**, that can be ER diagram (*ER*) or UML class diagram (*CD*).

The dependent variable is **comprehension level**, which denotes the comprehension level achieved by the subjects using the two notations. To measure it we use two well known Information Retrieval metrics, namely recall and precision [11]. Indeed, since the questionnaire is composed of multiple-choice questions, we define recall and precision as follow:

$$recall_s = \frac{\sum_i |answer_{s,i} \cap correct_i|}{\sum_i |correct_i|}\% \quad precision_s = \frac{\sum_i |answer_{s,i} \cap correct_i|}{\sum_i |answer_{s,i}|}\%$$

where $answer_{s,i}$ is the set of answers given by the subjects s to the question i and $correct_i$ is the set of correct answers expected for the question i. Note that the measures defined above represent aggregations of the precision and recall values that have been obtained considering each question of the questionnaire. Differently from aggregate measures based on the mean of precision and recall values the adopted measures also consider the fact that subjects do not provide any answer for a given question [12].

Finally, it is worth noting that recall and precision measure two different concepts. Thus, we decided to use their harmonic mean (i.e., F-measure [11]) to obtain a balance between them and compute the comprehension level.

However, to better assess the effect of **Method** it was necessary to control other factors (called co-factors) that may impact the results achieved by the subjects and be confounded with the effect of the main factor. In the context of our study, we identify the following co-factors:

- **ER and UML experience**: fresher students did not know the ER and UML diagrams, while bachelor and master students had a fairly good knowledge of these notations and master students were more trained than bachelor students on the design methods. We were also interested in analysing the

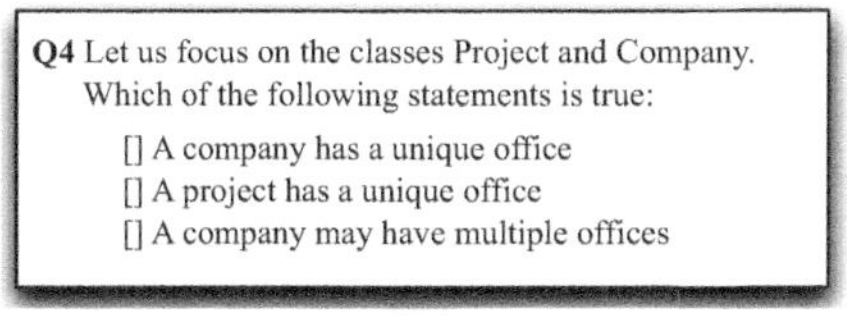

> **Q4** Let us focus on the classes Project and Company.
> Which of the following statements is true:
> [] A company has a unique office
> [] A project has a unique office
> [] A company may have multiple offices

Fig. 1. A question example

effect of the ER and UML experience since the different levels of education (and, consequently, the different levels of UML and ER experience) may impact the results achieved by subjects.
- **System**: even if we tried to select two software systems of a comparable size and tried to balance the complexity of the data models by using as heuristic the Miller's rule, there is still the risk that the system complexity may have a confounding effect with **Method**. For this reason we also considered the modeled system as an experimental co-factor.
- **Lab**: the experiments were organised in two laboratory sessions. In the first session subjects performed the task using UML class diagrams (or ER diagrams) and in the other session they performed the task using ER diagrams (or UML class diagrams). Although the experimental design limits the learning effect, it is still important to analyse whether subjects perform differently across subsequent lab sessions.

3.5 Procedure and Data Analysis

Subjects performed the assigned tasks individually. Before the experiments, subjects were trained on both ER and UML class diagrams. To avoid bias (i) the training was performed on a data model not related to the systems selected for the experimentation and (ii) its duration was exactly the same for the experiment and the replications. Right before the experiments, the students attended a 30 minutes presentation where detailed instructions concerning the tasks to be performed were illustrated. The design, the material[3] and the procedure were exactly the same for the experiment and its replications. Subjects represented the only substantial difference among the experiment and the two replications.

Since in our experiments each subject performed a task on two different models (i.e., *Company*, or *EasyClinic*) with the two possible treatments (i.e., ER, and CD), it was possible to use a paired Wilcoxon one-tailed test [14] to analyse the differences exhibited by each subject for the two treatments. A one-tailed paired t-test [14] can be used as alternative to the Wilcoxon test. However, we decided to use the Wilcoxon test since it is resilient to strong departures from the t-test assumptions [15]. The achieved results were intended as statistically significant at $\alpha = 0.05$. This means that if the derived p-value is less than 0.05, it can be concluded that there is significant difference between the support given by the treatments when performing comprehension tasks on data models. Furthermore, we analysed the students preferences about the single building blocks of the two notations using histograms, while the answers provided by subjects to the survey questionnaire were analysed using boxplots. The chosen design also permitted to analyse the effects of co-factors and their interaction with the main factor. To this aim we used the two-way Analysis of Variance (ANOVA) [14].

---

[3] See [13] for the complete material used in the experiments.

Table 3. Descriptive statistics of comprehension by method and subjects group

Subjects	ER			CD		
	Mean	Median	St. Dev.	Mean	Median	St. Dev.
Fresher	0.801	1.000	0.307	0.816	1.000	0.280
Bachelor	0.849	1.000	0.242	0.845	1.000	0.278
Master	0.849	1.000	0.277	0.838	1.000	0.272

Table 4. Wilcoxon Test results of comprehension by method and subjects group

Subjects	CD$FM - ER$FM			p-value	effect size
	Mean	Median	St. Dev.		
Fresher	0.014	0.000	0.404	0.343	0.037
Bachelor	0.003	0.000	0.330	0.420	-0.011
Master	-0.012	0.000	0.383	0.817	-0.030

3.6 Analysis and Interpretation of the Results

Table 3 reports the descriptive statistics of the F-measure, i.e., comprehension level, achieved by the subjects in our experimentation. The results highlighted that the two notations provided comparable support when performing comprehension activities on data models. In particular, the higher difference between the two notations in terms of F-measure is just 1% (see Table 3). As designed, to analyse if the difference between the results obtained using the two notations is statistically significant, we performed the Wilcoxon test. Table 4 reports the achieved results that highlight no significant difference between the two notations when used to comprehend data models (p-value always higher than 0.05).

Our finding contrasts with the results achieved in [4] where the authors demonstrated the benefits provided by the UML class diagrams with respect to the ER diagrams during the comprehension of data models. To further investigate this discrepancy, we analysed the support given by the two notations at a fine-grained level, i.e., on each building block used in the definitions of data models. Table 5 reports the descriptive statistics of the results achieved in terms of F-measure (considering the subjects answers to questions related to each building block). The achieved results confirmed an overall "performance equilibrium" between the two notations. In particular, there are some building blocks that represent strengths of CD, e.g., Entity and Ternary Relationship, as well as building blocks that represent weaknesses of CD, e.g., Composite and Multi-value attributes. In order to statistically analyse the weaknesses of CD, Table 6 shows the results of the Wilcoxon test executed for each building block to verify where the ER performances are statistically better than those of CD. The achieved results revealed that ER has a comprehension level significantly higher than the comprehension level of CD for three building blocks, i.e., Composite attribute, Multi-value attribute, and Weak entity. These results held for all the subjects involved in the experimentation. The only exception is given by Bachelor students when analysing the Multi-value attribute building block. However, Table 5 shows that Bachelor students also achieved better results in terms of descriptive statistics with ER when answering the questions related to the Multi-value attribute. It

Table 5. Descriptive statistics of the results (F-measure)

Method	Element	Fresher			Bachelor			Master		
		Mean	Median	St. Dev.	Mean	Median	St. Dev.	Mean	Median	St. Dev.
ER	Entity	0.887	1.000	0.260	0.936	1.000	0.125	0.872	1.000	0.281
	Primary Key/ID	0.784	1.000	0.406	0.955	1.000	0.179	0.907	1.000	0.277
	Composite attribute	0.883	1.000	0.159	0.897	1.000	0.146	0.920	1.000	0.140
	Multi-value attribute	0.859	1.000	0.195	0.847	1.000	0.168	0.862	1.000	0.213
	Recursive relationship	0.779	1.000	0.301	0.757	0.667	0.224	0.817	1.000	0.243
	Relationship cardinality	0.875	1.000	0.240	0.892	1.000	0.158	0.929	1.000	0.179
	Ternary relationship	0.741	1.000	0.347	0.828	1.000	0.220	0.804	1.000	0.321
	Generalization IS-A	0.684	0.667	0.369	0.734	1.000	0.363	0.712	1.000	0.379
	Weak entity	0.725	0.800	0.266	0.767	1.000	0.305	0.747	0.900	0.329
	M:N relationship	0.789	1.000	0.368	0.865	1.000	0.319	0.923	1.000	0.244
CD	Entity	0.961	1.000	0.108	0.937	1.000	0.234	0.926	1.000	0.145
	Primary Key/ID	0.875	1.000	0.296	0.937	1.000	0.234	0.926	1.000	0.246
	Composite attribute	0.742	0.667	0.255	0.781	0.800	0.251	0.815	1.000	0.308
	Multi-value attribute	0.775	0.667	0.259	0.788	0.667	0.257	0.801	0.667	0.209
	Recursive relationship	0.767	1.000	0.323	0.856	1.000	0.226	0.806	0.800	0.210
	Relationship cardinality	0.865	1.000	0.261	0.856	1.000	0.320	0.906	1.000	0.150
	Ternary relationship	0.827	1.000	0.265	0.888	1.000	0.150	0.855	1.000	0.162
	Generalization IS-A	0.828	1.000	0.225	0.838	1.000	0.290	0.804	1.000	0.328
	Weak entity	0.629	0.667	0.407	0.611	0.667	0.407	0.608	0.733	0.447
	M:N relationship	0.890	1.000	0.162	0.955	1.000	0.179	0.929	1.000	0.212

Table 6. Wilcoxon Test by Questions

Element	Fresher ER$FM - CD$FM					Bachelor ER$FM - CD$FM					Master ER$FM - CD$FM				
	Mean	Median	St. Dev.	p-value	effect size	Mean	Median	St. Dev.	p-value	effect size	Mean	Median	St. Dev.	p-value	effect size
Entity	-0.059	0.000	0.262	0.983	-0.257	-0.036	0.000	0.153	0.599	-0.032	-0.054	0.000	0.309	0.796	-0.161
Primary Key/ID	-0.091	0.000	0.517	0.927	-0.166	-0.027	0.000	0.198	0.415	0.059	-0.019	0.000	0.388	0.660	-0.049
Composite attribute	0.141	0.000	0.303	**0.000**	0.490	0.116	0.000	0.306	**0.022**	0.380	0.105	0.000	0.304	**0.012**	0.343
Multi-value attribute	0.085	0.000	0.316	**0.014**	0.269	0.059	0.000	0.324	0.141	0.180	0.061	0.000	0.311	**0.080**	0.196
Recursive relationship	0.012	0.000	0.401	0.455	0.024	-0.010	0.000	0.287	0.983	-0.345	0.011	0.000	0.308	0.536	0.037
Relationship cardinality	0.009	0.000	0.358	0.439	0.028	-0.009	0.000	0.200	0.446	0.094	0.023	0.000	0.224	0.258	0.103
Ternary relationship	-0.086	0.000	0.471	0.897	-0.184	-0.042	0.000	0.266	0.869	-0.221	-0.050	0.000	0.368	0.720	-0.135
Generalization IS-A	-0.145	0.000	0.421	0.999	-0.388	-0.104	0.000	0.476	0.905	-0.217	-0.093	0.000	0.526	0.903	-0.177
Weak entity	0.096	0.000	0.457	**0.027**	0.211	0.156	0.000	0.504	**0.045**	0.309	0.139	0.000	0.590	**0.049**	0.234
M:N relationship	-0.105	0.000	0.379	0.972	-0.249	-0.045	0.000	0.334	0.942	-0.252	-0.006	0.000	0.313	0.562	-0.020

bold if ER comprehension level statistically higher than CD comprehension level

is worth noting that the controlled experiments and replications reported in [4] did not consider these three building blocks to determine comprehension level provided by the two notations, i.e., the questionnaires used by the authors did not include questions related to Composite attribute, Multi-value attribute, and Weak entity. To verify whether the different findings between our experimentation and the results achieved in [4] was due to these three building blocks we also performed the comparison between ER and UML class diagrams without considering the answers of the students related to Composite attribute, Multi-value attribute, and Weak entity. In particular, we re-executed the Wilcoxon test to analyse if CD provided a significant higher comprehension level than ER. The results in Table 7 highlight that CD achieved statistically significant higher comprehension level than ER for the Fresher and Bachelor students. Moreover, CD provided better results than ER also for Master students even if this is not statistically significant (p-value 0.096).

Besides a quantitative analysis, we also conducted a qualitative comparison of the support given by the building blocks of the two notations. Figures 2, 3,

Table 7. Wilcoxon Test results of comprehension support by method and subjects' group without the identified weaknesses

Subjects	CD$FM - ER$FM			p-value	effect size
	Mean	Median	St. Dev.		
Fresher	0.066	0.000	0.410	**0.000**	0.161
Bachelor	0.052	0.000	0.290	**0.010**	0.120
Master	0.027	0.000	0.358	0.096	0.074
bold if CD comprehension level statistically higher than ER comprehension level					

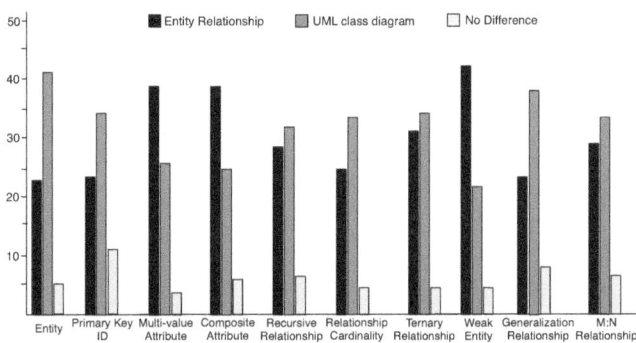

Fig. 2. Subject's preferences - Fresher

and 4 report the preferences expressed by the Fresher, Bachelor, and Master students, respectively. It is worth noting that the results of the quantitative analysis are confirmed by the preferences expressed by the students. In particular, the students preferred ER diagrams to represent the three building blocks identified as weaknesses of the UML class diagrams during the quantitative analysis, i.e., Multi-value attribute, Composite attribute, and Weak entity. Concerning the remaining building blocks, the students preferred UML class diagrams to represent the Entity, the Relationship cardinality, and the Generalization relationship, while they did not provide a clear preference for the Primary key/ID, Recursive relationship, Ternary relationship, and M:N relationship.

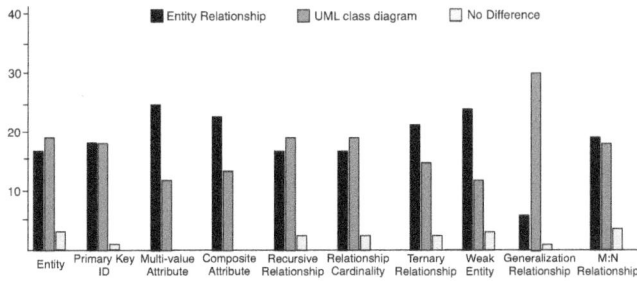

Fig. 3. Subject's preferences - Bachelor

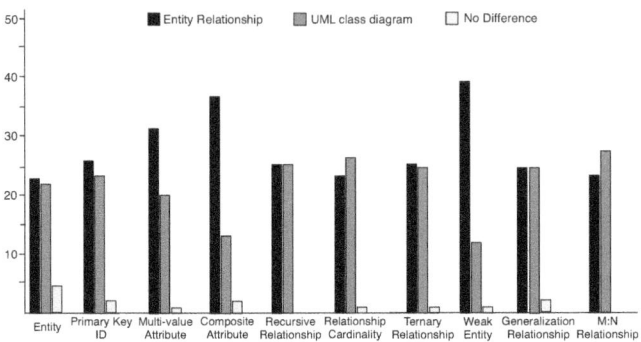

Fig. 4. Subject's preferences - Master

4 Discussion and Threats to Validity

Summarising, the achieved (quantitative and qualitative) results highlighted that the UML notation is characterized by three weaknesses related to the representation of Composite attribute, Multi-value attribute, and Weak entity, with respect to the ER notation, when performing comprehension activity on data models. However, except for the three identified weaknesses, the UML notation is generally more comprehensible than the ER notation, confirming the findings of previous experiments [4]. These findings suggest that a UML class diagram extension focused on these three building blocks should be considered to overcome these weaknesses and improve the comprehensibility of data models given in terms of UML notation. All these findings could be affected by many threats to validity [16] discussed in the following.

Goal, Design, and Statistical analysis. Ease of comprehension was the only criterion examined, because comprehension is a key issue for a graphical notation. However, especially where the design of performance-critical, data-intensive software like databases is concerned, there are other key considerations as well, e.g., analysability. One may choose to sacrifice expressiveness for analysability or other properties. For this reason, future work will be devoted to evaluate other properties of the two notations.

As explained in Section 3 we captured the students' opinion about the quality of the provided material, the clearness of the comprehension tasks and the laboratory goals, and the difficulty in performing the comprehension tasks, to verify if the results of our experimentation could be influenced by these threats. Figure 5 shows boxplots of answers for (a) fresher, (b) bachelor, and (c) master students. The analysis suggested that students had enough time to carry out the tasks (S1) and the objectives and the tasks to perform were clear (S2 and S3), since the median of boxplots of answers was 4 (i.e., I agree). Furthermore, they experienced no particular difficulties when performing the comprehension tasks (S4) since the median of the answers was 3.

Table 8. ANOVA: analysis of the Lab and System co-factors

Factor	Fresher	Bachelor	Master	All
Lab	No (0.787)	No (0.163)	No (0.175)	No (0.216)
System	No (0.793)	No (0.636)	No (0.113)	No (0.229)
Method vs Lab	No (0.817)	No (0.833)	No (0.305)	No (0.439)
Method vs System	No (0.793)	No (0.817)	No (0.618)	No (0.679)

Fig. 5. Answers of subejcts to survey questionnaire

The metric used to assess the subjects' performance (comprehension) is an aggregate measure of precision and recall that well reflects the results achieved by the subjects. We are also confident that the used tool (multiple-choice questions) actually measures the comprehensibility of the data models. This is also confirmed by the fact that previous empirical studies also used similar approaches to measure the same attributes (see for instance [2], [5], [6], [7], [9]).

Even if the chosen design mitigates the learning (or tiring) effect, there is still the risk that, during labs, subjects might have learned how to improve their comprehension performances. We tried to limit this effect by means of a preliminary training phase. In addition, as highlighted in [15], one possible issue related to the chosen experiment design concerns the possible information exchange among the subjects between the laboratories. To mitigate such a threat the experimenters monitored all the students during the experiment execution to avoid collaboration and communication between them. Finally, subjects worked on three different diagrams and, even if we tried to select diagrams having comparable size, there is still the risk that one diagram might be easier than another.

All these considerations suggest to account **Lab** and **System** as co-factors in the analysis of results. Indeed, the chosen design permitted to analyse the effect of co-factors and their interaction with the main factor. Table 8 shows the results of the ANOVA test by **Method** and **Lab**. The analysis did not reveal any significant influence of the two co-factors nor any significant interaction between the main factor and the two co-factors.

Since the assigned task had to be performed in a limited amount of time, the time pressure could represent another threat to validity. However, we decided the duration of each experiment taking into account previous laboratory exercises performed by the students involved in the experimentations during their courses. Furthermore, we also exploited our experience in performing similar controlled experiments in the past [4]. However, all the subjects completed the assigned task and they declared (in the post-experiment questionnaire) that the available time was enough to complete the task. For these reasons we are confident that time pressure did not condition the results and thus we did not consider it as a confounding factor.

Proper tests were performed to statistically analyse the difference in the performance achieved employing the two experimented notations, i.e., ER and UML class diagram. Survey questionnaires, mainly intended to get qualitative insights, were designed using standard ways and scales [10] allowing us to use statistical analysis to analyse differences in the feedback provided by subjects.

Subjects and objects. The three controlled experiments involved students having different backgrounds, i.e., fresher, bachelor, and master students. Concerning the undergraduate and graduate students, they had an acceptable analysis, development, and programming experience. In particular, in the context of the Software Engineering courses, both master and bachelor students had participated to software projects, where they experienced software development and documentation production, including database design documents. Moreover, as highlighted by Arisholm and Sjoberg [17] the difference between students and professionals is not always easy to identify. Nevertheless, there are several differences between industrial and academic contexts. For these reasons, we plan to replicate the experiment with industrial subjects to corroborate our findings. We also plan in the future to conduct a survey involving people from database and software engineering communities aiming at obtaining opinions on why weak entity, multi-value and composite attributes are (or might be) problematic in the UML notation. In this way, we can perform a more notation-oriented discussion about the identified weaknesses.

The different backgrounds of the students involved in the experiments have been accounted as a co-factor to analyse its influence on and interaction with the main factor. As expected the ANOVA test revealed a statistically significant effect of **ER and UML Experience** (p-value < 0.001); bachelor and master students achieved statistically significant better performances than fresher students, while the performances achieved by bachelor and master are almost comparable. In addition, ANOVA did not reveal any interaction between **ER and UML Experience** and the main factor (p-value $= 0.486$).

To avoid social threats due to evaluation apprehension, students were not evaluated on the performances they achieved in the experiments. During the experiment, we monitored the subjects to verify whether they were motivated and paid attention in performing the assigned task. We observed that students performed the required task with dedication and there was no abandonment. Moreover, students were aware that our goal was to evaluate the impact of using ER or UML class diagrams during modelling activities, but they were not aware of the exact hypotheses tested and of the considered dependent variables.

Finally, the size of the data models is small compared to industrial cases, but it is comparable with the size of models used in other related experimentations (see, for instance, [5], [15], [9]). Future work will be devoted to assess the usefulness of the notations on realistically sized artefacts. However, we believe that the comparison of the two notations on small/medium artefacts is still a worthy contribution.

5 Conclusion and Future Work

We have reported on the results of a controlled experiment and two replications aimed at analysing the support given by ER and UML class diagrams during the coprehension of data models. We have also performed a fine-grained analysis to compare the single building blocks of the two notations (e.g., entity, relationships). The results of the empirical analysis have suggested that UML class diagrams are generally more comprehensible than ER diagrams, confirming the results achieved in a previous study [4]. However, the fine-grained analysis has revealed some weakness of UML class diagrams with respect to ER diagrams. In particular, if we take into account the results about the weak entity, multivalue and composite attributes building blocks, the performances achieved with ER diagrams are superior than those obtained with UML class diagrams. Moreover, the performed qualitative analysis has also highlighted that the subjects preferred ER diagrams for specifying weak entities, multivalue and composite attributes. Taking into account these results, in the future we intend to exploit stereotypes, as done in other studies [9], [18], [19], [20], to extend the UML class digrams and bridge the gap with ER diagrams about the specification of weak entity, multivalue and composite attributes building blocks. The aim is to improve the comprehensibility of UML class diagrams and candidate such notation as a new de facto standard also for data modeling.

As it always happens with empirical studies, replications in different contexts, with different subjects and objects, is the only way to corroborate our findings. It would be interesting to consider alternative experimental settings in several respects, but maybe the most important one is the profile of the involved subjects. Replicating this study with students/professionals having a different background would be extremely important to understand how UML class diagrams influence the results of these different sub-populations.

References

1. Navathe, S.B.: Evolution of data modeling for databases. Commun. ACM 35, 112–123 (1992)
2. Shoval, P., Frumermann, I.: OO and EER conceptual schemas: A comparison of user comprehension. Journal of Database Management 5(4), 28–38 (1994)
3. De Lucia, A., Gravino, C., Oliveto, R., Tortora, G.: Assessing the support of ER and UML class diagrams during maintenance activities on data models. In: 2th European Conference on Software Maintenance and Reengineering, CSMR 2008, pp. 173–182 (April 2008)
4. Lucia, A.D., Gravino, C., Oliveto, R., Tortora, G.: An experimental comparison of ER and UML class diagrams for data modelling. Empirical Software Engineering 15(5), 455–492 (2010)

5. Shoval, P., Shiran, S.: Entity-relationship and object-oriented data modeling: an experimental comparison of design quality. Data Knowledge Engineering 21, 297–315 (1997)
6. Bock, D., Ryan, T.: Accuracy in modeling with extended entity relationship and object oriented data models. Journal of Database Management 4, 30–39 (1993)
7. Palvia, P., Lio, C., To, P.: The impact of conceptual data models on end-user performance. Journal of Database Management 3(4), 4–15 (1992)
8. Miller, G.A.: The magical number seven, plus or minus two: Some limits on our capacity for processing information. The Psychological Review 63, 81–97 (1956)
9. Ricca, F., Di Penta, M., Torchiano, M., Tonella, P., Ceccato, M.: How developers experience and ability influence web application comprehension tasks supported by UML stereotypes: A series of four experiments. IEEE Transactions on Software Engineering 36(1), 96–118 (2010)
10. Oppenheim, A.N.: Questionnaire Design, Interviewing and Attitude Measurement. Pinter Publishers (1992)
11. Baeza-Yates, R.A., Ribeiro-Neto, B.: Modern Information Retrieval. Addison-Wesley Longman Publishing Co., Inc., Boston (1999)
12. Antoniol, G., Canfora, G., Casazza, G., De Lucia, A., Merlo, E.: Recovering traceability links between code and documentation. IEEE Transactions on Software Engineering 28(10), 970–983 (2002)
13. Bavota, G., et al.: UML vs ER - experimental material (2011), http://sesa.dmi.unisa.it/UMLvsER.html
14. Conover, W.J.: Practical Nonparametric Statistics, 3rd edn. Wiley, Chichester (1998)
15. Briand, L.C., Labiche, Y., Penta, M.D., Yan-Bondoc, H.D.: An experimental investigation of formality in UML-based development. IEEE Transactions on Software Engineering 31, 833–849 (2005)
16. Wohlin, C., Runeson, P., Host, M., Ohlsson, M.C., Regnell, B., Wesslen, A.: Experimentation in Software Engineering - An Introduction. Kluwer, Dordrecht (2000)
17. Arisholm, E., Sjoberg, D.I.K.: Evaluating the effect of a delegated versus centralized control style on the maintainability of object-oriented software. IEEE Transactions on Software Engineering 30, 521–534 (2004)
18. Cruz-Lemus, J.A., Genero, M., Manso, M.E., Piattini, M.: Evaluating the effect of composite states on the understandability of UML statechart diagrams. In: Briand, L.C., Williams, C. (eds.) MoDELS 2005. LNCS, vol. 3713, pp. 113–125. Springer, Heidelberg (2005)
19. Genero, M., Cruz-Lemus, J.A., Caivano, D., Abrahão, S., Insfran, E., Carsí, J.Á.: Assessing the influence of stereotypes on the comprehension of UML sequence diagrams: A controlled experiment. In: Busch, C., Ober, I., Bruel, J.-M., Uhl, A., Völter, M. (eds.) MODELS 2008. LNCS, vol. 5301, pp. 280–294. Springer, Heidelberg (2008)
20. Staron, M., Kuzniarz, L., Thurn, C.: An empirical assessment of using stereotypes to improve reading techniques in software inspections. In: Proceedings of the Third Workshop on Software Quality, 3-WoSQ, pp. 1–7. ACM, New York (2005)

Engineering Android Applications Based on UML Activities

Frank Alexander Kraemer

Norwegian University of Science and Technology (NTNU),
Department of Telematics, N-7491 Trondheim, Norway
kraemer@item.ntnu.no

Abstract. With the evolving capabilities of devices, mobile applications are emerging towards complex reactive systems. To handle this complexity and shorten development time by increased reuse, we propose an engineering approach based on UML activities, which are used like building blocks to construct applications. Libraries of such building blocks make Android-specific features available. Tool support provides automatic formal analysis for soundness and automatic implementation. Furthermore, the approach is easily extensible, since new features can be provided by new building blocks, without changing the tools or notation. We demonstrate the method by a voice messaging application.

Keywords: Mobile Applications, Android, UML Activities, Model-Driven Engineering.

1 Introduction

A look at the software development kits (SDKs) of Google [1] and Apple [2] quickly reveals that the predominant approach for the development of mobile applications is that of traditional programming. But albeit these SDKs speedup the creation of applications, it still takes a considerable effort to program applications of high quality, especially with respect to responsiveness: Even the official marketplace application, for instance, does at times not react when users want to cancel ongoing downloads, and the popular Spotify music player does not react while logging on. We ask therefore, how modeling techniques can be applied for mobile applications to aid developers by providing better abstraction levels to express also concurrent behavior, higher degrees of reuse, formal analysis of properties as well as a further automation of the implementation.

Although mobile platforms often use system kernels that originate from desktop operating systems, mobile applications are significantly different from their desktop counterparts:

- Mobile applications are event-driven and have to constantly react on input from user interfaces or sensors, as well as on communication via the network.
- Since usually only one application can be operated by a user at a time, the responsiveness of its interface is an important quality criterion.

- Applications are not explicitly terminated by the user, but managed by the operating system, so they have to adhere to strict life cycle protocols.
- Applications need to be programmed efficiently, and avoid polling or busy-waiting to increase battery life.

These differences stress the importance of the behavioral aspect of mobile applications. In fact, we observe that these applications exhibit the typical characteristics of reactive systems [3], and we will later see that also the internal organization resembles that of a distributed system in general. A development approach needs to take this into consideration.

The current SDKs, however, try to handle behavioral complexity by a framework approach, in which applications are constructed by extending given classes, and the operating system takes care of the correct invocation of extended methods upon certain events. The code of an application is therefore mainly shaped by the framework classes; the workflow of the actual application comes second. Further overhead comes from the variety of how application components can be coupled, and the need to introduce synchronization threads to keep the user interface responsive and separated from tasks with high CPU load. This results in the applications being obscured further by technicalities that are not related to the problem domain, which makes it difficult to overlook, understand, maintain and extend them. One can argue further that the obstruction of behavior by coding details also has a direct effect on the functionality of the applications: Programmers may for instance decide to stick to sequential patterns where concurrent ones would be more appropriate, just because they cannot handle the additional complexity.

One way to master reactive behavior and its complexity is by modeling, on an appropriate abstraction level, with a formal foundation to ensure consistency, for instance by means of model checking. This, however, is not incompatible with programming, and a model-based approach should not ignore all aspects that existing SDKs are good at:

- A modeling tool should integrate well with the existing programming tools, and make use of their support for the creation of graphical layouts or detailed API coding support with auto-completion, for example.
- Even though behavior is modeled on idealized levels, there must be a well-defined way how implementations may be derived from it, ideally with refinement semantics, to avoid discontinuities. (See, for instance [4].)
- The entire method must be able to handle the fast-paced evolution of platforms. It must be possible to add new functionality without adjusting the method or tools for each new version of the mobile API.

In this paper, we will describe such an approach and a fully functional model-based SDK that implements it. The method is a specialization of our general method for the development of reactive systems, SPACE [5] and its supporting tool, Arctis [6]. It is based on UML activities which are used as specification building blocks, encapsulated by external contracts to hide their inner details, and which can be connected with each other quite flexibly.

In the following, we will first review existing work in the area of modeling for mobile applications. In Sect. 3, we present an overview of the Arctis/Android SDK and the implied workflow. Section 4 introduces our library of building blocks for Android, and in Sect. 5 we present our case study. Section 6 provides an evaluation of the approach, and we close with some concluding remarks.

2 Related Approaches and Tools

Andromate [7] is an Eclipse GEF-based modeling tool for an early version of Android. It offers specific modeling elements such as menu items, layouts and view elements that can be used to construct applications and generate some part of the code. To define behavior, some actions and triggers are defined that can be added to the model. However, these actions often do not express desired behavior from the view of the problem domain, but the technical details to serve the framework, as mentioned in the introduction.

App Inventor [8] is a web-based tool offered by Google to produce simple Android applications. The tool is based on OpenBlocks [9]. Programming statements as well as elements for functions of the phone are represented by graphical blocks. The resulting diagrams are similar to Nassi-Shneiderman diagrams for structured programming and on such a detailed level that it is probably more correct to talk about "visual programming" instead of "modeling." In consequence, App Inventor may be suitable to make programming easier especially for beginners, but does not provide any specific support to model concurrent behavior.

Thompson et al. [12] developed SPOML, a language to sketch Android applications in order to estimate their power-consumption and reason about design alternatives. This language is, however, neither detailed enough nor intended to generate complete executable code.

Gheis et al. [13] describe an approach to develop context-aware applications. While the work addresses mobile platform in general, they used Android as one specific evaluation platform. Applications are composed of components, from which some can be selected at run-time, based to the evaluation of a utility function that tries to optimize overall quality of service properties depending on the current context. This work is complementary to what we do; we have a focus on detailed concurrent behavior of components, but no adaptation, while they focus with their models on the variability aspect but do not address how the individual components are modeled internally.

Friese and Behrens [10] present a domain specific language (DSL) which is used to compose applications from data views and cells and which are connected by navigation. Code generators produce the necessary code for the provision of content, memory management and navigation for various mobile platforms. In contrast to our approach, their DSL targets data-centric applications, and does not express any concurrent behavior. In contrast, an approach by Dunkel and Bruns [11] uses W3C XForms to describe user interfaces and lets generic clients interpret these, while server logic provides the necessary data. Again, such an approach seems to be suitable only for certain types of data-centric applications.

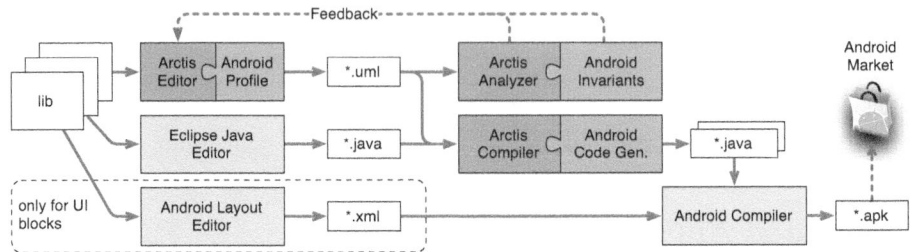

Fig. 1. Combined Arctis/Android SDK and implied workflow

3 The Arctis/Android SDK

Arctis is integrated with the Eclipse-based Android SDK offered by Google. Fig. 1 depicts the tool components and the implied workflow to engineer an Android application using Arctis.

The Arctis Editor: The Arctis Editor is essentially a UML editor for activities with state machines as their external contracts, so-called external state machines (ESM, [14]). We refer to a UML activity with an attached ESM as *building block*. Their formal semantics is an event-driven variant of token flows, defined in [15]. For Android, we add a simple UML profile to mark some elements with stereotypes (shown later). For most applications, a considerable number of building blocks can be taken from our existing libraries (see Sect. 6.2). These blocks are combined in the Arctis editor to form more comprehensive blocks that fulfill certain tasks. For building blocks that represent user interfaces, layout files are created with the Android SDK and linked to the blocks which encapsulate their behavior. Diagrams in this paper are vectorized screenshots taken from the editor.

The Arctis Analyzer: Since building blocks are encapsulated by the ESMs, they can be checked for consistency separately, as further exemplified in Sect. 5.4. For this, the Arctis Analyzer [16] is used, which explores all possible states and checks if the external contracts of all building blocks are obeyed by a composition. In addition, invariants specific for Android are checked, for instance that applications obey some user interface guidelines, as further detailed in Sect. 5.5. Analysis results are provided as feedback annotations into the editor, and consistent blocks may be checked into libraries for later reuse, if desired.

The Arctis Compiler: A complete application (i.e., a hierarchy of composed blocks) can input to the Arctis Compiler which produces all necessary files to obtain an executable application, which is fed to the Android SDK and compiled into an application package that can be deployed in the Android market. The compiler first transforms the UML activities into executable state machines [17], from which efficient code generation is rather simple. An Android-specific code generator adds files needed to wrap the state machines into an executable Android application, for instance a special manifest file.

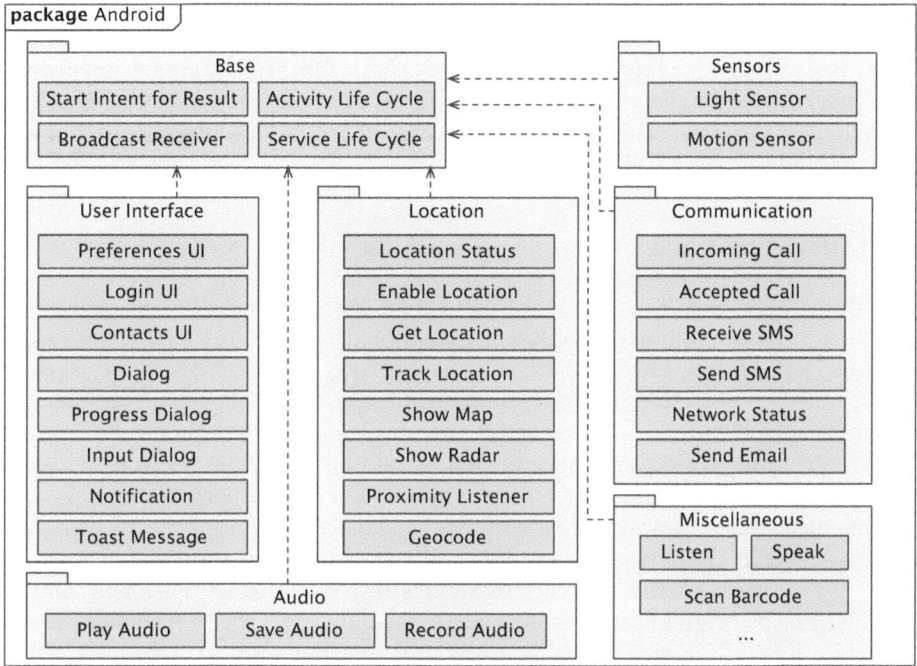

Fig. 2. Libraries of building blocks for Android

4 Library of Android Building Blocks

Figure 2 shows an extract of our libraries for Android. At the time of writing, these libraries contain in total 52 blocks (including variants of blocks for different usage scenarios), and can be accessed via [18]. The base library contains blocks to encapsulate Android-specific mechanisms, described below. The sensor library provides blocks for notifications on ambient light changes, for instance. The user interface library provides dialogs, notifications as well as complete user interfaces that are useful for various applications, such as preferences or login screens. The location library provides access to location features, either to simply query the current location or to periodically receive updates. The communication library lets applications listen for instance for incoming calls or send SMS messages. A miscellaneous library contains blocks providing various other features, such as blocks to easily access the speech recognition API.

4.1 User Interface Blocks for Android Activities

User interface blocks encapsulate an Android activity,[1] a full screen view element that contains other UI elements. The necessary layout files are produced with the

---

[1] To distinguish the activities of Android from UML activities, we refer to the former always as *Android activities*.

Android layout editor. A building block provides the necessary logic to update UI elements and detect user input. Internally, it uses a block to manage the life cycle of an Android activity taken from the base library explained below. We have described a detailed production process of these blocks elsewhere [19]. Since special rules apply to them (which we verify in Sect. 5.5), we mark such blocks with stereotype «activity».

4.2 Blocks to Invoke Other Applications via Intents

Android comes with a coupling mechanism so that applications can utilize capabilities of other applications, like selecting a person from the contact list or scanning a barcode. This coupling is based on asynchronously processed messages, called *intents* [20]. To start an external task, an application can dispatch an intent that contains either a reference to the receiver that should handle the task or a characterization of the task that should be used. The result is delivered back to the application by the system, via a dedicated callback method.

This mechanism, however, disrupts the workflow of the application behavior, as mentioned in the introduction: The callback returns at another place in the code. When we read the callback method later, it is not obvious why and in which state the original intent was started. Second, an intent that yields a result must be started from within the context of an Android activity. This means that when we re-design our UI or workflow, we must move the code to start a task from one Android activity to another.

Instead, our library offers a dedicated, self-contained building block to start intents and listen to their results, shown in Fig. 3 (a). It is started with the intent that describes the task to start. This intent is saved, and an Android activity is started by call operation action *startActivity*.[2] This Android activity provides the necessary context to start an intent and to listen to a result, but is itself invisible. Once it is started by the operating system, it observes the event *CREATED*, upon which the previously saved intent is dispatched by operation *startIntent*. Within the Android activity, we listen for the result, which is either a successful result (event *RESULT*), or a cancellation by the user (event *CANCEL*).

The block from Fig. 3 (a) can be further encapsulated, for instance by *Scan Barcode* (b). It configures an intent to scan barcodes and retrieves the data of the barcode as a String from the returned result. With this block, we can provide the functionality to scan a barcode that can be plugged together with other blocks (Fig. 3 c), without the disruption of workflow, and without needing to reveal the detailed mechanisms.

Other blocks from the base library listen to other events. *Broadcast Receiver* can be configured to continuously listen to specific kinds of intents, so that applications can, for instance, react on incoming calls or changes to the state of the wireless network. In [19], we have described a building block to listen to the life cycle of Android activities, to react on events of the user interfaces.

---

[2] To provide its detailed behavior, the Arctis Editor is integrated with Eclipse's Java editor and keeps a link from a UML operation to a Java method with the same name.

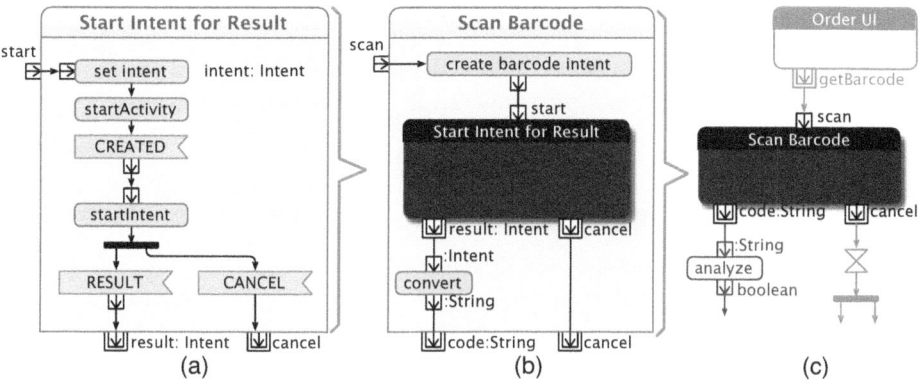

Fig. 3. Block to start an intent for a result and examples of encapsulating blocks

In addition to the Android-specific libraries of Fig. 2, numerous other libraries for the Java Standard Edition are provided, for instance for the HTTP, XMPP and RTP protocols, and others [18], which can also be used for Android.

5 Case Study: Engineering an Instant Voice Messenger

The application originates in a collaboration with TelCage, a provider of a system to monitor and control offshore fish farms. The instant voice messenger enables robust communication via the wireless network present at the fish farm installations. Workers should be able to send short, unidirectional voice messages to each other. In case of connection problems or simultaneous calls, messages should be recorded for later replay.

5.1 Involved Building Blocks

The model for the messenger consists of 28 building blocks in total, including blocks nested within other blocks. Among them are the following ones:

- Blocks *RTP Send* and *RTP Receive* which encapsulate streaming of audio data using the Real-time Transmission Protocol (RTP, [21]).
- Blocks *AudioRecord* and *AudioPlay* that use Android's media API to record, resp. play streaming audio data sent via RTP.
- Block *XMPP* which encapsulates access to the Extensible Messaging and Presence Protocol (XMPP, [22]). It enables to update status information, and send messages that contain the IP address of a user, so that RTP streams may be opened.[3]

---
[3] XMPP was initially called *Jabber* and designed for chat, but it can also transport application-specific data. For our messenger it means that users can participate using their existing XMPP account, for example Google Talk.

– Block *Contacts UI* which is an Android activity that displays a list of all XMPP contacts of a user. From this list, contacts may be selected and a voice message may be sent. Other UI blocks collect credentials to log into XMPP, display information about an incoming message, or show a control while outgoing messages are recorded.

5.2 Separation between Application UI and Background Service

On Android, applications are not terminated by the user. Instead, the operating system decides on its own when application elements are moved into the background and finally terminated. However, the messenger should of course *constantly* listen for incoming messages, even if the user works with other applications in the foreground. For this reason, we separate its model into two parts:

– A *foreground UI application part*, consisting of all functions closely connected to user interactions and related tasks, such as displaying the contacts list, recording a message or adjusting preferences. The foreground part for the messenger is shown in Fig. 4, we will explain it in detail below.
– A *background service part*, hosting all functions not to be interrupted. For the messenger this is the XMPP block, the block to listen for incoming RTP streams, as well as the block to play and save messages, since this could happen while other applications are active.

The two parts are modeled by separate UML activity partitions, to which we apply the stereotypes «foreground» and «background», respectively. Our code generator deploys «background» partitions as Android *services* [20]. The operating system prioritizes such services over inactive foreground activities when resources get sparse, so that they are usually not terminated.

To communicate between foreground and background part, we use dedicated building blocks, *Bridge To Service* in the «foreground» partition in Fig. 4, and *Bridge To UI* in the «background» partition (not shown). Since background services may be executed as separate processes in separate virtual machines (and hence memory spaces) communication between services involves serialization. This can either be done using a remote procedure call (RPC) mechanism offered by Android, or by a manual serialization of objects into bundles of strings, which are sent via Android intents. In both cases, the encapsulation into UML building blocks gives the possibility to describe also the interface behavior of the communication by means of ESMs as contracts, not just their names, types and signatures.

5.3 Foreground Application UI for the Instant Voice Messenger

When the main application starts (via the initial nodes), it activates *Contacts UI*, which shows the initially empty list of contacts. It also activates the background

Engineering Android Applications Based on UML Activities 191

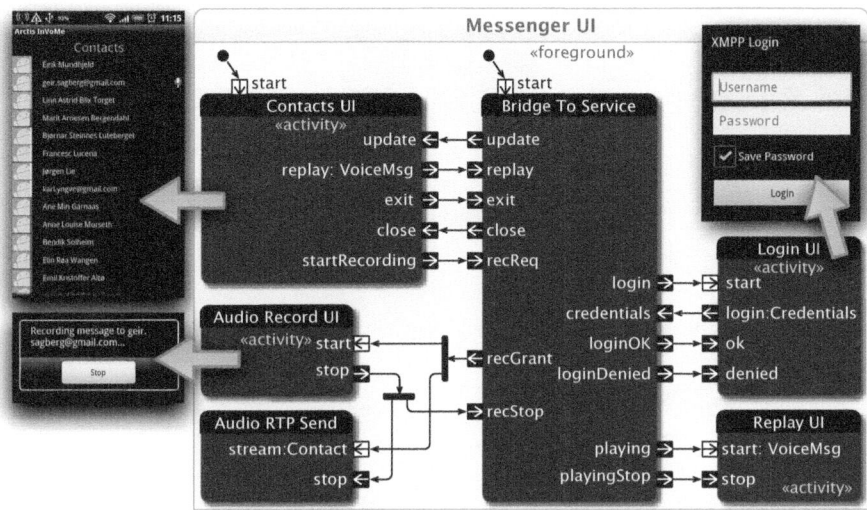

Fig. 4. Foreground application UI part of the voice messenger, with some screenshots

service part, using the bridge block. In case the service needs user credentials to log into XMPP, it requests these credentials via the bridge, which triggers *Login UI*, which is displayed as a dialog over the contact list. Once logged in, the dialog disappears and the contacts list is updated from now on with all contacts and their status. To send an audio message, the user taps one of the contacts. This starts a request to the service, which ensures that no other message is currently received. If the recording is granted, the recording UI is started. A similar workflow handles replay of messages that were previously saved.

The background service (not shown due to space constraints) takes care of the XMPP connection, receiving RTP streams, as well as coordinating all audio functions. It contains the block *Bridge To UI*, which communicates with the foreground UI parts as explained above.

5.4 Formal Analysis of a Building Block

One critical part of the messenger is its ability to coordinate simultaneously incoming audio messages as well as the recording of outbound messages. Obviously, only one message should be played or recorded at a time. This is handled by block *Message Audio*, shown in Fig. 5. Since it needs to be active at all times (playing and storing of messages should not be interrupted), it is hosted in the background service part of the application. It contains block *Play Audio* that can play incoming or previously stored messages. Block *Save Audio* stores incoming messages. Since the messenger should accept several simultaneously incoming

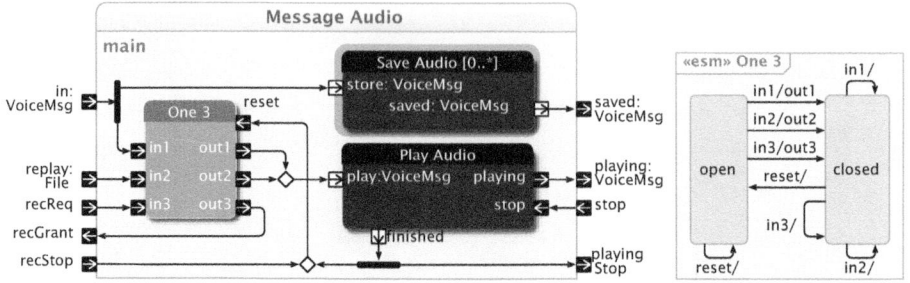

Fig. 5. Audio message block to play and save voice messages

messages at a time, *Save Audio* can be executed with several execution instances at the same time, emphasized by [0..*].[4]

Block *One 3* is responsible for the mutual exclusion. It is completely described by the ESM to the right. In state *open*, any of the incoming flows may pass (for instance from *i1* to *out1*, whereupon the block switches into state *closed*, which ignores further flows until *reset* is invoked. This coordinates the behavior of the message audio block: Incoming voice messages via *in* are stored in any case by forking them towards *Save Audio*, but only played if no other audio task is performed, i.e., *One 3* is in state *open* and *i1* passes to *out1*. The same holds for replay commands, which are simply ignored in case of conflicts. Parameter node *recReq* is used to reserve audio functionality to record a new message, which is allowed to the user interface via parameter node *recGrant*.

Since the *Message Audio* block is encapsulated by an ESM as well (not shown here), it is self-contained and it can be checked for consistency using the Arctis Analyzer via model checking. The analyzer first constructs the state state space of the application based on the formal semantics described in [15]. The state space is then searched for violations of the ESMs. In the example of Fig. 5, the state space has only 7 states. Since no violations are reported, we can be sure that only one message is played or recorded at a time, even though several incoming messages can be accepted at any time.

5.5 Verification of Android-Specific Rules

The building blocks of the base library in Fig. 2 ensure some Android-specific properties, for example by keeping track of the life cycle of Android activities and services. Further, applications as a whole have to adhere to additional rules:

i_1 A «foreground» partition must in its initial step start exactly one «activity» building block. This is the first screen the user will see for this application.

---

[4] UML marks activities that can be executed in several instances with «singleExecution» [23, Sect. 12.3.4]. We observe, however, that the same activity may be used with different execution multiplicities, and that this should therefore rather be a property of the invoking call behavior action, which we annotate here instead.

If several were started, it would be subject to a non-deterministic race which one is shown on top.

i_2 Whenever a «foreground» partition is active, at least one «activity» building block is active. This prevents a foreground application from disappearing visually for the user without terminating correctly.

i_3 A «background» partition is only allowed to start an «activity» building block after the user has been notified in the status bar and tapped on the notification. This rule originates in the guidelines for services [20], which should not interrupt the user's other activities.

These rules are again verified by the Arctis Analyzer. To verify invariant i_3, for instance, all activity steps that start an «activity» building block must be triggered by a parameter *pressed* of the dedicated building block *Notification*, which is part of the user interface library in Fig. 2.

6 Evaluation and Discussion

In this paper, we are interested in how to model Android-specific features appropriately, but do not elaborate on issues of platform-independence.

Concerning the generated code, we have decided to use only the official APIs offered by Android and fit into the Android application framework, in order to stay compatible with future updates. This requires in some cases workarounds in order to obtain the necessary contexts objects, such as for example the creation of the invisible Android activity in Sect. 4.2.

The code generated for the applications makes use of a runtime support system that includes an event-dispatcher, which introduces a slight overhead. However, we have seen that as soon as concurrent problems need to be addressed, proper solutions would introduce similar programming constructs for synchronization anyhow. Using such a runtime support system and generating the necessary synchronization statements automatically relieves the programmer of a complicated and error prone task, so that concurrency problems can be solved appropriately, which by far compensates for the overhead. The introduction of the run-time support system has another benefit: Since all behavior is formulated as event-driven transitions, one can easily monitor the execution time for each transition during debugging. Once the execution duration of a transition takes longer than 100 ms, one may reconsider the design, since a longer reaction may be perceived by the user as a "lack of snappiness" [20].

6.1 Evaluation 1: The Instant Voice Messenger Case Study

The Instant Voice Messenger has been developed within the limited time frame of a student thesis [26], resulting in an application that could be deployed to the Android Market (under the name "NTNU Instant Voice Messenger"), proving the effectiveness of the proposed Arctis/Android SDK.

The separation of the application into foreground UI and background service is necessary due to the way the Android OS automates life cycle management

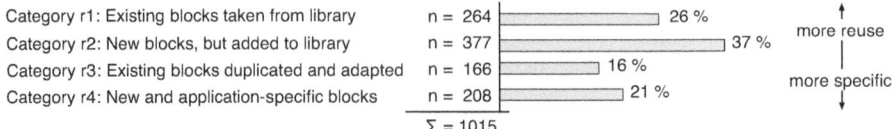

Fig. 6. Reuse profile for the Voice Messenger

of applications. One may argue that the separation leads to a disruption of workflows since communication has to go through the bridge building blocks. For that reason, we are studying how to model this separation by two activity partitions, integrated in the *same* UML activity, and how to use flows that cross partition borders to model communication between foreground and background.

6.2 Evaluation 2: Reuse Profile of the Instant Voice Messenger

As a metric for how much effort may be saved by reusing building blocks, we assign to the UML activity of a block i the number $n_i = v_i + e_i$, where v_i is the number of activity nodes and e_i the number of edges, to estimate the effort spent for its construction. Block *Message Audio* in Fig. 5, for instance, has an estimated effort of $n_{message\ audio} = 40$. The complete model has an estimated effort of $n_{total} = 1015$. To characterize models with a reuse profile, we assign each block to one of the following categories:

r_1 blocks originating from existing libraries, such as Fig. 2
r_2 blocks created for the application but added to libraries for later reuse
r_3 blocks that are duplicated and adapted versions of existing ones
r_4 blocks that are entirely specific for the application

We summarize the numbers n_i of the blocks within the categories and obtain the reuse profile shown in Fig. 6. The graph shows that in total $26+37 = 63\%$ of the modeling effort are reusable, either because blocks already existed or are very likely to be useful in the future. This is consistent with previously reported reuse proportions on smaller, more academic examples from other domains, presented in [14]. We expect that the more blocks we collect over time, the more weight will move from category r_2 to r_1 (since more blocks are initially available for reuse), and we hope to further move weight from category r_3 to r_1 with more advanced parameterization and adaptation techniques.

6.3 Evaluation 3: Rapid Prototyping Experiment

To estimate, how much our approach can accelerate the development of initial prototypes, we created a simple application by two separate developer groups in an experiment [27]. The application should query the user for a target location, verify the address of the location and get its coordinates, and then offer to either navigate to the target via map or a radar-like interface.

– Group A developed the application using the Android SDK by means of traditional programming. The students knew about the main concepts of Android, but had not yet experience with the specific interfaces and Android capabilities and intents that were needed for the application.
– Group B used the Arctis/Android SDK that contained building blocks that encapsulated the needed functionality. The students received introductory training on Arctis, and had similar knowledge about Android as group A.

To complete a running application, group A needed 192 minutes using the traditional SDK with pure programming, while group B only needed 42 minutes using the Arctis SDK. This means the use of Arctis accelerated the development in this case with around a factor of four.

6.4 Evaluation 4: Industrial Case Study with Hrafn

Within an industrial verification project [25], we evaluate the Arctis/Android SDK together with Hrafn AS, a company for tracking and RFID solutions. We currently build an Android application to simplify repair orders in bicycle shops. The phones serve as terminals to capture order data and scan tags using the phone's camera, and interact with a central database to post orders. At the initial meeting, Hrafn represented the domain knowledge of customers, and an expert for user interfaces and a security expert participated as well. Interestingly, we found that all participants their despite different expertise could understand the UML activity diagram capturing the overall workflow quite well:

– The domain experts from Hrafn could see from the UML activity that the business workflow worked as intended, or corrected it where necessary.
– The UI expert could optimize the application workflow so that information is collected from the end-user in a sequence that is intuitive.
– The security expert could recommend necessary authentication and authorization patterns, and adjusted the workflow where necessary.

The result was a model similar to Fig. 4. Each step of the order registration could be modeled by a separate building block, intercepted by blocks to acquire data from various sources. During the discussion, the workflow could be changed simply by re-arranging the blocks. The resulting blocks could be distributed among the developers for further implementation, which is currently ongoing.

7 Concluding Remarks

Our aim was to describe and support a well-balanced method to engineer Android applications. We have covered the design, the analysis and briefly outlined the automated implementation. Several evaluations to cover different aspects of an engineering method have been presented. So let's close with some highlights:

– In addition to general properties for well-formed applications, we can formally analyze Android-specific guidelines, such as the invocation of user interfaces from background tasks.

- Android-specific functions are not built into the language, but encapsulated in model libraries, which can evolve together with the frequent updates of the Android platform. So far, updates of Android could always be taken into account by updating the library.
- The models support the reactive nature of mobile applications, and enable to model and analyze concurrent behavior in detail.
- The method scales well with the complexity of applications. As shown in Sect. 6.3, it is possible to rapidly develop simple applications, but also more complex ones, such as the instant voice messenger.
- The models have compositional semantics [5]. Once engineers have agreed on a set of building blocks, they can be designed and analyzed separately, and the end result will work as intended. Design discontinuities mentioned in the introduction are avoided. The sketch from the development session described in Sect. 6.4, for instance, was taken as a starting point for an initial executable application that was further refined.
- We observed in industrial case studies that the notation based on UML activities not only serves as solid communication medium for engineers, but can also be used to explain solutions to people with a non-technical background.

The theoretical background of the method was treated elsewhere [5,14,15] and we focussed in this paper on more practical issues that need to be taken into consideration in order to improve the development of mobile applications.

Acknowledgements. We would like to thank Geir Sagberg who developed the messenger, as well as Stephan Haugsrud, Hovard Alexander Berg, Kim-Andre Martinsen, Mats Knutsen, Henrik Gundersen and Espen Herseth Halvorsen who contributed to the library of building blocks, as well as Viktor Varan, Geir Vevle and Bjørnar Klein Reinertsen from Hrafn and Songying Lu and Linda Ariani Gunawan for participation in the bicycle repair application development.

References

1. Android SDK (2011), http://developer.android.com/sdk
2. Xcode 4 (2011), http://developer.apple.com/technologies/tools
3. Pnueli, A.: Applications of Temporal Logic to the Specification and Verification of Reactive Systems: A Survey of Current Trends. In: de Bakker, J.W., de Roever, W.P., Rozenberg, G. (eds.) Current Trends in Concurrency. LNCS, vol. 224, pp. 510–584. Springer, Heidelberg (1986)
4. Selic, B., Gullekson, G., Ward, P.T.: Real-Time Object-Oriented Modeling. John Wiley & Sons, New York (1994)
5. Kraemer, F.A.: Engineering Reactive Systems: A Compositional and Model-Driven Method Based on Collaborative Building Blocks. PhD thesis, Norwegian University of Science and Technology (2008)
6. Kraemer, F.A., Bræk, R., Herrmann, P.: Compositional Service Engineering with Arctis. Telektronikk 105, 135–151 (2009)
7. Andromate Website (2011), http://www.lab.telin.nl/~msteen/andromate
8. Google App Inventor Website (2011), http://appinventor.googlelabs.com

9. Roque, R.V.: OpenBlocks: An Extendable Framework for Graphical Block Programming Systems. Master's thesis, Massachusetts Institute of Technology (2007)
10. Friese, P., Behrens, H.: Cross-Platform Mobile Development with Eclipse. In: EclipseCon 2011, Santa Clara, California, USA, March 21-24 (2011)
11. Dunkel, J., Bruns, R.: Model-driven architecture for mobile applications. In: Abramowicz, W. (ed.) BIS 2007. LNCS, vol. 4439, pp. 464–477. Springer, Heidelberg (2007)
12. Thompson, C., Turner, H., White, J., Schmidt, D.C.: Analyzing Mobile Application Software Power Consumption via Model-Driven Engineering. In: Proceedings of the 1st International Conference on Pervasive and Embedded Computing and Communication Systems, Algarve, Portugal, March 5-7 (2011)
13. Geihs, K., Evers, C., Reichle, R., Wagner, M., Khan, M.U.: Development Support for QoS-Aware Service-Adaptation in Ubiquitous Computing Applications. In: Proceedings of the ACM Symposium on Applied Computing (SAC). ACM, New York (2011)
14. Kraemer, F.A., Herrmann, P.: Automated encapsulation of UML activities for incremental development and verification. In: Schürr, A., Selic, B. (eds.) MODELS 2009. LNCS, vol. 5795, pp. 571–585. Springer, Heidelberg (2009)
15. Kraemer, F.A., Herrmann, P.: Reactive Semantics for Distributed UML Activities. In: Hatcliff, J., Zucca, E. (eds.) FMOODS 2010. LNCS, vol. 6117, pp. 17–31. Springer, Heidelberg (2010)
16. Kraemer, F.A., Slåtten, V., Herrmann, P.: Tool Support for the Rapid Composition, Analysis and Implementation of Reactive Services. Journal of Systems and Software 82, 2068–2080 (2009)
17. Kraemer, F.A., Herrmann, P.: Transforming Collaborative Service Specifications into Efficiently Executable State Machines. In: Ehrig, K., Giese, H. (eds.) Graph Transformation and Visual Modeling Techniques 2007, Electronic Communications of the EASST, vol. 6 (2007)
18. Arctis Website (2011), http://arctis.item.ntnu.no
19. Kraemer, F.A., Kathayat, S.B., Bræk, R.: Unified Modeling of Service Logic with User Interfaces. International Journal of Cooperative Information Systems (IJCIS) 20, 177–200 (2011)
20. Android Developer Guide (2011), http://www.developer.android.com
21. Schulzrinne, H., Casner, S., Frederick, R., Jacobson, V.: RTP: A Transport Protocol for Real-Time Applications. RFC 3550 (2003)
22. Saint-Andre, P.: Extensible Messaging and Presence Protocol (XMPP): Core. RFC 6120 (2011)
23. Object Management Group: Unified Modeling Language: Superstructure, version 2.3, formal/2010-05-05 (2010)
24. Yu, Y., Manolios, P., Lamport, L.: Model Checking TLA$^+$ Specifications. In: Pierre, L., Kropf, T. (eds.) CHARME 1999. LNCS, vol. 1703, pp. 54–66. Springer, Heidelberg (1999)
25. Arctis Verification Project. Norwegian Research Council, Project no. 199644
26. Sagberg, G.: Engineering Responsive Mobile Applications for Android from Reusable Building Blocks. Master's Thesis, Norwegian University of Science and Technology (2011)
27. Knutsen, M.: Towards Model-Driven Engineering of Android Applications. Project Thesis, Norwegian University of Science and Technology (2009)

Domain-Specific Model Transformation in Building Quantity Take-Off

Jim Steel[1] and Robin Drogemuller[2]

[1] University of Queensland, Brisbane, Australia
j.steel@uq.edu.au
[2] Queensland University of Technology, Brisbane, Australia
robin.drogemuller@qut.edu.au

Abstract. The two core concepts of model-driven engineering are models and model transformations. Domain-Specific Modelling has become accepted as a powerful means of providing domain experts and end users with the ability to create and manipulate models within the systems that they use. In this paper we argue that there are domains for which it is appropriate to also provide domain experts with the ability to modify and develop model transformations. One such domain is that of quantity surveying, and specifically the taking-off of quantities from a building design. We describe a language for expressing transformations between building models and bills of quantities, and its implementation within an automated quantity take-off tool, reflecting on the commonalities and differences between this language and a general-purpose model transformation language/tool.

1 Introduction

The core components of model-driven engineering are models and model transformations. Models provide a means for a formal expression of the concepts and structures that are used in the description of some system, and model transformations allow for a formal description of the way in which the different models of the system are interrelated.

A complementary area of research to model-driven engineering is that of domain-specific modelling. In domain-specific modelling, the language or system designer is encouraged to provide the end-user, or domain expert, with a modelling language that reflects the vocabulary of concepts that they use in describing their domain. This allows them a stronger sense of ownership of the system, in that they can manipulate these models to reflect their understanding of the system.

Domain-specific modelling encourages system designers to provide modelling languages that are usable by domain experts, but this is less common for model transformations. There is a wide variety of model transformation languages and tools currently available or under development, and these differ quite dramatically in the way that they allow designers to express their transformations. However, these tend to be general purpose solutions, that can be used for any and all domains. This generality can have the effect of making them less approachable, and their learning curve steeper, for non-expert users, as is often the case for the domain experts targeted by domain-specific modelling techniques.

In this paper we present the example of a model-driven system in the quantity surveying discipline of the building design space. The quantity surveyor is responsible for the estimation of the cost of a building design, based on the quantities of different materials or tasks required for the building's construction. The first phase of this calculation is the extraction, or take-off, of these quantities, which might include the surface area of walls to be painted, the tonnage of steel beams of different lengths and profiles, the cubic metres of concrete required either for ground slabs or suspended slabs, or the different surfaces of suspended slabs that need to be smoothed.

The rules for describing the mapping between building elements in a design and their representation in the bill of quantities vary from country to country, from company to company, and from project to project. Because of this, it is important that a user of the quantity take-off system be able to modify the rules, or create new ones, to capture these specific requirements. In order to do this, we have developed a transformation language and tool specific to this transformation task.

Being a transformation language, there are many design elements in common with general-purpose transformation languages. For example, the use of traceability models is similar to what one might expect in a general purpose tool. However, because the language is restricted to specific metamodels, it has been simplified and customised to them, which makes for a language in which the rules are simpler, and that is more approachable for quantity surveyors to whom a general-purpose solution might be intimidating.

The rest of the paper is structured as follows. The next section describes the role of the quantity surveyor, the bill of quantities and the quantity take-off process in the digital building design process. Section 3 presents the Automated Estimator system, and the Intelligent Building Model and Bill of Quantities metamodels, between which the domain-specific transformations are defined. Section 4 presents the domain-specific transformation language and its implementation. Section 5 reflects on the differences and commonalities between this language and general-purpose languages, and what lessons can be learnt for the definition of domain-specific transformation languages.

2 Building Information Models and the Quantity Take-Off Process

Designing and constructing buildings shows many similarities to software development. Both can be considered as "wicked" problems [8] where a part of the process is in defining the scope and requirements of the project. Since both building and software projects can consume large amounts of resources and take long periods to complete, controlling the costs of the project is important. Two roles have emerged within the building industry to assist in controlling project costs.

The quantity surveyor (in UK/Australian practice) works for the project client and provides advice to the building design team on the expected cost to complete the project as the building is being designed. This is an iterative process where cost plans (predictions) are developed several times through the design/documentation process to minimise the risk of cost overruns. On completion of the design, the contract documents will be handed over to an estimator within a building contracting company. The estimator needs to prepare an accurate estimate of the cost of the building within a short period (normally 4–6 weeks).

The fundamental operation underlying cost planning and estimation is the preparation of a Bill of Quantities (BoQ). This consists of an itemised list of the components required to construct a building, prepared at a level of detail enabled by the state of project documentation at the time the BoQ is prepared (top right panel in Figure 1). Once the BoQ is prepared the quantity surveyor/estimator will examine the building components referenced by each item in the BoQ and will apply a "unit rate" from the company or personal database to calculate the estimated cost of the item. A weighting factor may be applied if there are unusual circumstances regarding the buildings element(s). The unit rates are built up statistically over a long period of time and are the major intellectual property of the quantity surveyor/estimator.

Traditionally, the quantity surveyor/estimator reads the plans, sections, elevations, details and specifications of the building project to identify all of the building elements, infer information that was not explicit and then select the items needed for the project from a standard BoQ. The type, structure and units of measurement used are defined in industry standards (i.e. [1]) or in company standards. One organisation does not always use the same measurement rules.

Measurement against the unit rates is not trivial. For some trades, such as masonry wall construction, openings in walls less than $1m^2$ are ignored since the extra work of forming the opening makes up for the reduction in wall material. Other items, such as areas of formwork underneath or around concrete need to be inferred as these are not explicitly represented. Of the two distinct stages within the quantity surveyors/estimators work processes, the extraction of building elements does not require significant levels of intelligence if the source information contains appropriate semantic content. This is also the most time consuming stage, requiring several man-months for a complex building. The addition and modification of unit rates does require a considerable amount of background knowledge and intelligence. Consequently, the extraction stage was identified as the most promising for automation.

The semantic content referred to above is provided by using BIM (Building Information Modelling), which can be considered as second-generation technology in the storage of building information in computer systems. The first generation transferred the traditional geometric primitives (lines, arcs, cubes, spheres, etc) from paper-based hand-drawing methods to virtual paper within CAD (computer aided drafting) systems. This provided only very low levels of semantics. For example, did two parallel lines represent a wall or furniture? A BIM file or database stores objects that describe both the geometric and non-geometric information about a building element. A wall and a piece of furniture have distinguishing labels.

The Industry Foundation Classes (IFC)[2] is an open BIM format that supports semantic content as required above. This was selected as the standard input format for Automated Estimator when development started in 2001.

3 Automated Estimator: Buildings and Bills

The Automated Estimator (Estimator) is a program developed by the Cooperative Research Centre (CRC) for Construction Innovation which aims to automate much of the quantity take-off process by:

1. Reading an IFC file;
2. Identifying the building elements in the model against a predefined method of measurement;
3. Matching the elements against item descriptions in the generic BoQ;
4. Adding information that can be inferred from the model (e.g. areas of formwork);
5. Extracting the relevant quantities and adding them to the BoQ items; and
6. Presenting the BoQ and model information in a variety of views that support the estimating process (Figure 1).

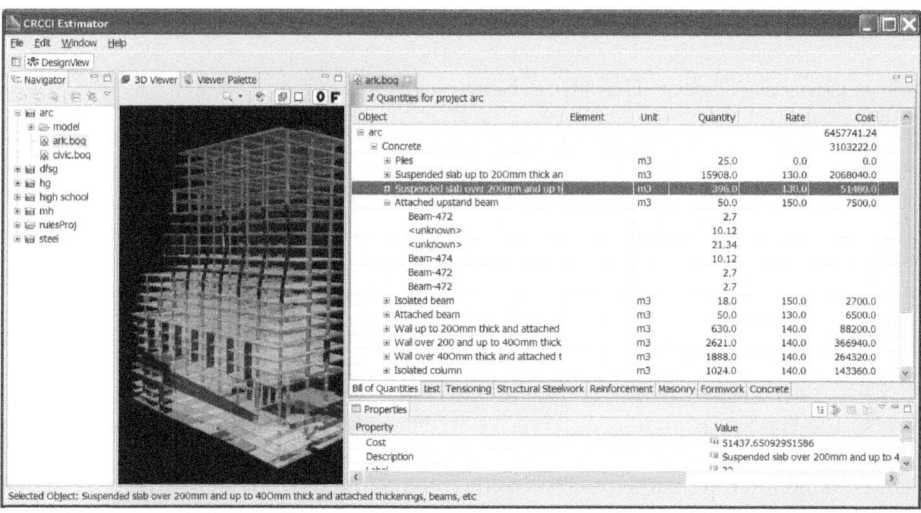

Fig. 1. The Bill of Quantities Editor

Estimator is built on a generalised framework for BIM-based analysis of design models called DesignView. DesignView provides features for the import of IFC files, as well as for the querying, inspecting and visualising the imported models in hierarchical and 3-dimensional views (these views are described in more detail in Section 3.1).

Estimator is able to handle most quantity take-off tasks. A range of take-off rules can be used depending on need and level of detail of information in the BIM. Implicit information, such as formwork and surface finishes can be automated through defining rules that add such items to the BoQ together with the geometric queries necessary to calculate the results. Errors in the original BIM can be identified through built in queries that select all objects measured within a trade package and also all items not measured. Building designers will always come up with new building components that do not fit established types. Additional rules can be added to Estimator to support the gradual evolution of the standard item set. Since BoQs are often prepared by a team, additional rules should be added by a single expert so that the implications can be supported across all trade packages within the project. The major constraint on improved functionality and performance of Estimator is the level of detail and consistency of models currently provided by BIM generating software. These are being addressed both through research projects (by the authors and others) and also developments by the commercial software vendors.

One important aspect of traditional practice that is perhaps threatened by automating quantity take-off in Estimator and similar software is the identification of errors by the quantity surveyor/estimator. The ability to browse the model through the geometric and textual panels provides an alternative method for identifying errors. Additionally, this supports filtering of outputs by element, by material, by type and by storey.

3.1 The Intelligent Building Model Language

Because of the imposing size of the IFC language, the DesignView platform (and, by implication, Automated Estimator) uses a simplified language for representing design models, called the Intelligent Building Model (IntBM). IFC models are converted into the IntBM language through an import wizard. An extract of the IntBM metamodel is shown in Figure 2. As can be seen, this language includes only about 30 classes, as opposed to more than 600 in IFC – a reduction aimed at simplifying the development of design analysis tools, and achieved through a few significant language design decisions.

The first economy is that a lot of elements are not considered during import. Discipline-specific information such as structural moment models, property sets containing metadata for lifecycle or performance data, or information about organisational responsibility for building elements, are not interesting for many design analyses, so these are stripped out during import.

Rather than including classes for all the possible building element types, the IntBM language uses a flattened type hierarchy in which elements and element types are included within the same model. This is facilitated by a standard library of common building element types which are populated during import, and a standardised mapping for IFC building element types outside this set.

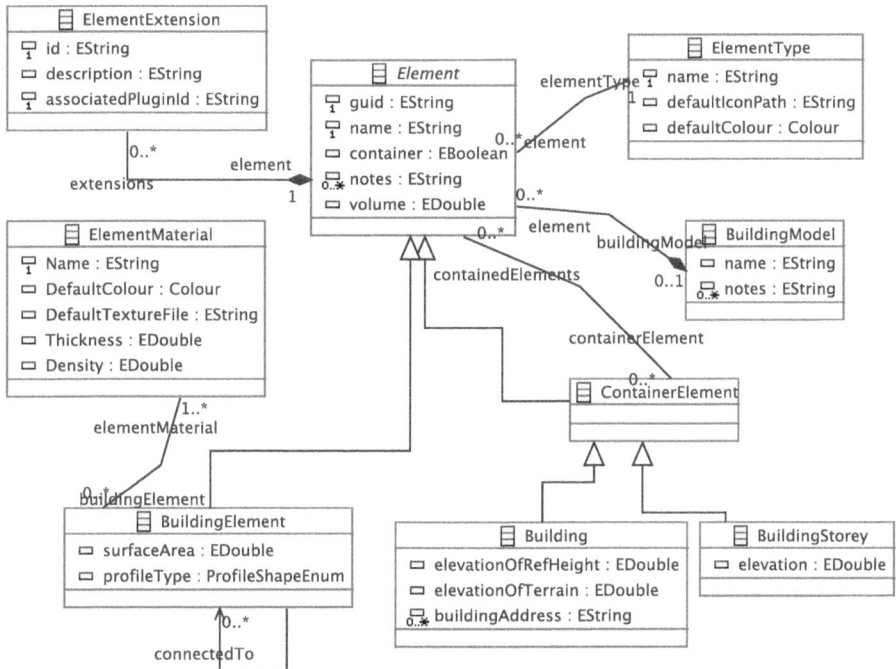

Fig. 2. The intelligent building model metamodel

Because the focus of DesignView is on analysis and visualisation of models rather than creation or modification, it uses triangles for the surface geometry rather than IFC's wide variety of 3D geometry modelling constructs. Conversion from the richer IFC geometry constructs to triangles is done during import. Triangularisation can lead to variation in calculation of geometrical properties, particularly volumes, so some of this calculation is also performed during import and stored in the model.

The IntBM language also includes a facility for extension of model elements with extra information. This is used for two purposes within Automated Estimator. Quantity take-off sometimes requires elements to be classified at a finer grain than normal. For example, most building models will use the Slab element type, but for quantity take-off it is important to distinguish between ground slabs, suspended slabs, or thickening slabs. These extra classifications are included as tags through the *ElementExtension* mechanism. The other use of extensions is for the area-height information for suspended slabs, which are taken off differently based on their height above the slab immediately below them. For this purpose, each suspended slab is annotated with a set of values to show what proportions of its under-surface areas are at what heights. These Estimator-specific extensions are populated using registered processes that run at the end of IFC model import.

Within the DesignView platform, the user can inspect the model using a number of different views. The model browser provides a tree-view of the model elements in the style common to the EMF framework, with separate tabs to see elements arranged according to the physical object hierarchy (element within space within story within building within site), by material, or by element type. The 3D view uses the triangle representations of the building elements to present a graphical presentation of the design. Since the chief purpose is typically per-element analysis of the model, colouring of the 3D model is typically done by element-type in order to distinguish, e.g. walls from beams from columns from slabs, etc. The hierarchy and 3D viewers use two levels of selection sharing in order to facilitate inspection of the models. Clicking on an element or a set of elements in either view will highlight these elements in the other view. Dragging a container element or a set of elements from the hierarchy view to the 3D view will restrict the 3D visualisation to just those elements that are dragged. This is particularly useful for inspecting a single floor.

3.2 The Bill of Quantities Language

The language used for describing bills of quantities is based on an analysis of the existing documents used by quantity surveyors. The result is the metamodel shown in Figure 3.

The BoQ is broken down into a series of trade sections, each of which can in turn have hierarchical structure within them. At the bottom of these hierarchies are *TradeItems*, each of which has a description, a quantity, a unit of measurement for the quantity, and a cost per unit. These trade sections and the trade items within them are not hard-coded in the metamodel; they are created

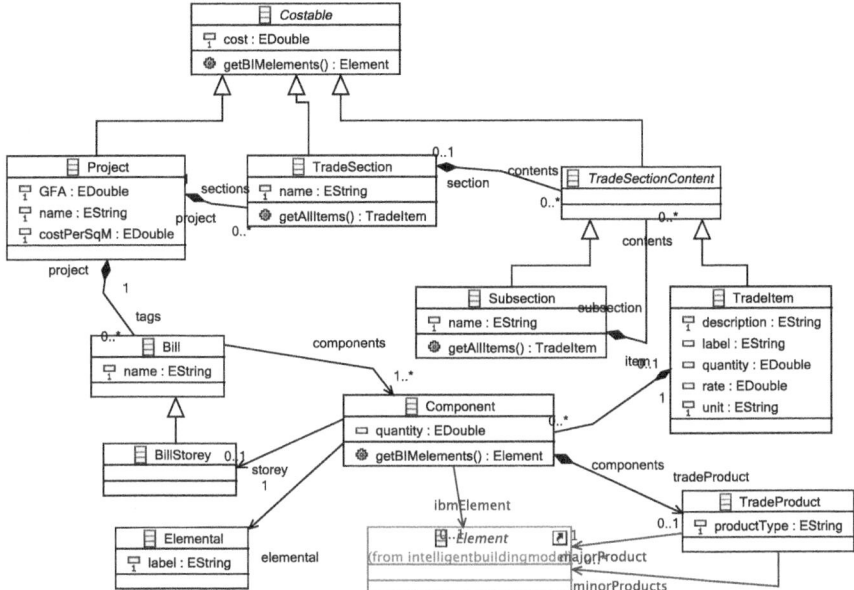

Fig. 3. The Bill of Quantities metamodel

by the take-off rules that populate the model, in order to provide flexibility in the structure of the bills being generated. The default rules shipped with Automated Estimator correspond to the trade sections and items from the Australian Standard Method of Measurement [1].

In some cases, elements are considered as aggregated units called *Trade Products*. For example, in-situ (as opposed to precast) concrete elements such as slabs with attached thickenings or support beams, are constructed in a single pour, and calculations for their surface areas or volumes must be done as an aggregate, not separately for each element. Within the quantities model defined in Automated Estimator, we further allow *TradeItems* to be broken down into *Components*, to show the contribution made to the item's quantity by each building element or trade product. In addition to being defined within a certain *TradeItem*, *Components* can also be tagged, for example by storey, which allows for breakdowns of the BoQ by other characteristics than the dominant hierarchy of *TradeSections*.

BoQ models are accessed using the table-based Bill of Quantities Editor, shown in Figure 1. This editor supports selection sharing in a similar way to that used between DesignView's 3D and Hierarchy views. Selecting building elements in the 3D or Hierarchy views will highlight the BoQ items that are contributed to by the selected elements. Similarly, selecting a *TradeSection*, *Subsection* or *Item* in the Bill of Quantities Editor will highlight the building elements that contribute to the selection. Furthermore, if the user drags a selection of elements into the 3D view, the BoQ will be narrowed to show only the totals for the selected elements.

4 The Take-Off Rules Language and Tool Support

The rules that govern the generation of a bill of quantities from an IntBM model are expressed using the Take-off Rules language. The design of this domain-specific transformation language and its implementation in the take-off rules engine were based on consultation with quantity surveyors and cost engineers, in an effort to ensure that the resultant language would be usable by its target users. These users are already familiar with the idea of using rules in order to populate a bill of quantities, and the take-off rules language within Automated Estimator has been designed to reflect this and provide a familiar formalism.

The next sections describe the Take-off Rules language and the implementation of its engine within Automated Estimator. We also discuss the mechanism for storing the trace information between the building model and the generated BoQ, and the facilities for inspecting/debugging the generated bill.

4.1 Take-Off Rules

Figure 4 shows the metamodel of the rule-based Take-off Rules language used within Automated Estimator. There are two parts to this language – the structural part and the expression part. The high-level structures in the Take-off language are based on those from the Bill of Quantities metamodel. The *RuleModule*, *Subsection* and *TakeoffRule* concepts correspond to, and result in the instantiation/population of, the *TradeSection*, *Subsection* and *TradeItem/Component* concepts, respectively, from the Bill of Quantities metamodel. Unlike bills of quantity, however, Take-off Rule modules are stored with one *RuleModule* per file – the collection of rule modules is not modelled.

The expression language used in the Take-off Rules language is a simplified variant of the expression language from the Tefkat model transformation language[7]. It includes negation, conjunction, and disjunction, literals for strings and numbers, and binary relation operators for value comparison ($=, <, >$, etc). There are also unary operators for checking a building element's type or classification – these include IFC-style element types such as wall, beam or column, as well as Estimator-specific classifications, as outlined in Section 3.1, such as *plinth*, *pile_cap* or *upstand_beam*. Lastly, the expression language also includes *PropertyExpressions*, which allow the retrieval of 16 different string-, number- or boolean-valued properties of elements – either simple properties such as *length*, *height*, or *material*, or take-off-specific "view" properties such as *height_from_floor* or *isCambered*.

The description for each *RuleModule*, *Subsection* and *TakeoffRule* element in the hierarchical structure of a Take-off Rules model is expressed using a *StringExpression*. In the majority of cases this is a *StringLiteral*, but

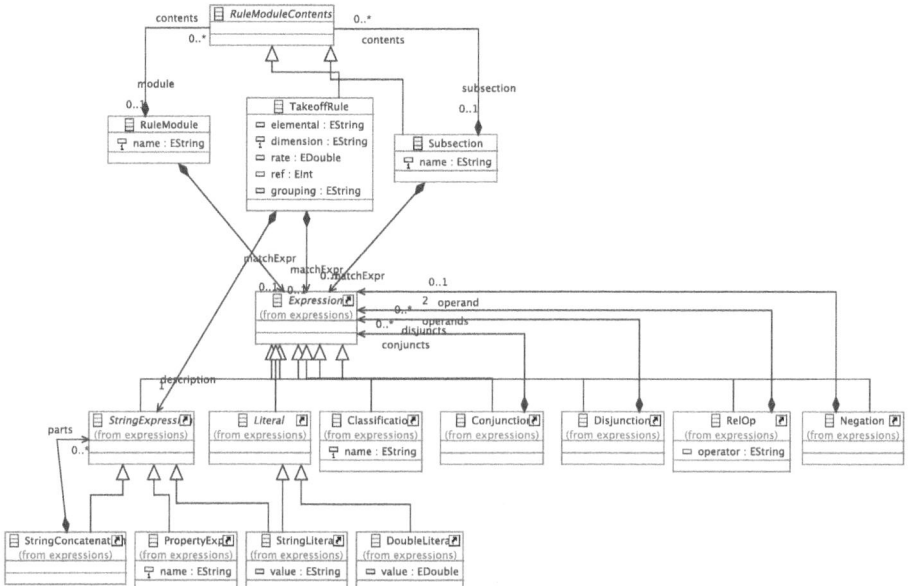

Fig. 4. The Take-off Rules metamodel

some rules include variable elements, which result in the generation of multiple *TradeItems* for a single *TakeoffRule*, each with a different description. One of the motivating cases for this was structural steel members, which must be grouped based on their lengths. The structural elements also include a match expression – a boolean-valued expression which determines whether the section or rule matches in the context of a given element or, if specified in the rule, a certain *TradeProduct* grouping. For *RuleModules* and *Subsections*, this narrows the range of objects that can be matched by the contained *TakeoffRules*. For example, the concrete *RuleModule* might have a match expression such as *material = "concrete"*, which ensures that all the *TakeoffRules* in that *RuleModule* will only match concrete elements.

Most of the work in the take-off process is, unsurprisingly, involved in the evaluation of *TakeoffRule* objects. When the rules engine finds a *BuildingElement* which satisfies the rule's *matchExpr*, it will create a *TradeItem* (if it doesn't already exist), then populate (if it already exists) it with a *Component*, as the element's contribution to the quantity. The main link between the a *TakeoffRule* and the *TradeItem* that is either created or modified is the *description*, which uniquely identifies the trade item within its *TradeSection*. The rule also contains information for the population of a *TradeItem*, including a reference number, default rate, and elemental classification, and these are copied across into the new or modified *TradeItem*. It also includes the dimension to be taken off, a string value taken from a list of 12 dimensions understood by the engine: *No* (a count of matching elements), *Item* (for bill items that appear only once, regardless of how many elements they match, such as requirement for a crane), *volume*, *height*, *tonnes* (for structural steel elements), and various area measures for total, top, bottom, side or specific face areas. These dictate how the engine calculates a quantify from the *BuildingElement* for inclusion in the *TradeItem*.

4.2 Tool Support for Quantity Take-Off

Take-off Rules models are created and modified in a tabular editor, shown in Figure 5. This shows the structure of the rules (corresponding to the structure of the bill to be generated) in the left-most column, with further columns for the reference number of the target *TradeItem*, the rate, the dimension, elemental classification, the *TradeProduct* grouping, and the match expression. Of these, only the first and last columns are required.

Both the description of the *TradeItem*, and the match expression, in the left-most and right-most columns respectively, are handled using an expression parser implemented using the Emfatic[5] framework. Using a tabular view emphasises the relationship between the structure of the take-off rules and the bills that they will generate. Mixing tabular and textual representations is also done to seek a tradeoff between the accessibility of tabular presentation and the expressive power of a textual syntax. The example match expression in Figure 5, : *slab and isCambered*, will match elements classified as *slab* and which satisfy the *isCambered* test (defined as a boolean-valued *PropertyExpression*).

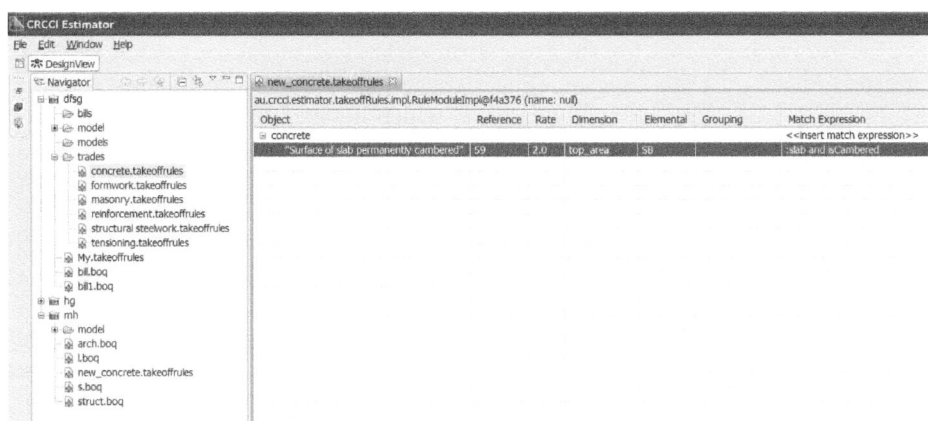

Fig. 5. The Take-off Rules editor

The take-off process is initiated using a contextual command on a building model, which prompts the user to nominate a target bill of quantities, and invokes the engine. The engine then evaluates a registered set of take-off rule modules, managed by the user in a preferences dialog, and populates the new bill.

The matching phase of the engine is largely based on the EMF Query[1] framework, and the target model population is done in Java/EMF.

4.3 Traceability and Debugging

The issue of traceability is very important within Automated Estimator. Much of the time spent by a quantity surveyor within the tool will be spent inspecting an automatically generated bill to check whether the correct quantities have been taken off the building model. Of course, this does not negate the benefit of automating the bill's generation, reproducing several man-weeks of manual effort in less than an hour – much repetitive work is alleviated, and over time, a user will gain a deeper understanding of how a rule works, and gain more confidence in its operation. There are a number of typical questions that the QS will ask:

- What building elements have contributed to this cost item?
- To which cost items have this/these element/s contributed?
- Are there building elements that are not represented in this bill, or within this part of a bill?

The first two questions are primarily answered using the selection sharing mechanism between the bill of quantities editor, and the 3D and Hierarchy views on the building model. Selecting a cost item (including sections or subsections) will highlight all building elements that contribute to it, i.e. that are referenced by a *Component* object within the bill. Similarly, selecting a building element or set of building elements will highlight the cost items to which the element/s contribute, i.e. those *TradeItems* containing a *Component* which refers to one of the selected elements, or to a *TradeProduct* that contains them. These *Component* objects effectively function as in-situ traceability relations within the bill of quantities model.

To address the third question, the Bill of Quantities Editor provides a command for detecting unmatched elements, which can be run either relative to the whole bill, or to some subsection of the bill. This command will highlight any elements in the currently visible selection that are not matched by the bill or part-of-bill. Once again, this is done by consulting the Component objects within TradeItems.

The currently-visible selection is an important factor in the task of inspecting and debugging a bill generated from a building model. The building model will frequently be very large, containing many thousands of building elements. Particularly using a 3D view, it is frequently the case that highlighted building elements will be partially or totally hidden from view behind other elements. This is partly addressed using transparency, but a more powerful technique is by reducing the set of objects shown in the view. A popular use observed has been to inspect the bill storey-by-storey, which allows for a "roof-off" view of a

---

[1] http://www.eclipse.org/modeling/emf/?project=query

more manageable subset of the building, and a more manageable size of bill. Another approach is to inspect one trade at a time, e.g. considering only concrete or only structural steelwork.

At present, the selection-sharing approach to debugging the quantity take-off process has not been extended to take-off rules. That is, it is not currently possible to select a take-off rule and show the building elements and cost items that the rule has matched and generated, respectively. Doing so would not be complicated, but at this point it is felt that because there is such a strong correlation between the rules and the bills that they generate, it is not necessary to provide selection sharing for rules, since selecting the cost item that the rule generates has a similar result.

5 Reflection on Building a Domain-Specific Transformation Language

Analysis of the domain indicated that a transformation language was necessary in order to allow quantity surveyors to modify take-off rules or to define their own. This was particularly appropriate as the target users were comfortable with the paradigm of starting with a model and evaluating rules against it in order to produce another document.

However, it was felt that a general-purpose transformation language would not be appropriate for the situation, since the users do not have the programming or software modelling background of the typical user of a general-purpose model transformation language. The expectation was that a domain-specific approach would yield better results in terms of usability and adoption. We do not suggest that domain-specific transformation languages are universally, or even widely, appropriate. The relative comfort with a transformation-based approach amongst the target users was both a motivation for pursuing the approach, and a strong input to the design of the language itself.

In designing a domain-specific transformation language, it is important to first consider the manner in which the targeted domain users are used to thinking about transformations. It is also important to consider the specifics of the source and target languages, and how these influence the way that one writes transformations between them. Keeping these considerations in mind, one can then evaluate the alternatives available when building a transformation language and/or tool. An excellent discussion of these alternatives is presented by Czarnecki and Helsen in [4]. The feature model presented in that paper could be used, in combination with the domain-specific considerations, to aid in deciding upon an approach to design and build the language.

One of the distinctive characteristics of the Take-off Rules transformation language is the structural similarity between it and the target language. In [6], the authors identify three styles of model transformation – source-driven, target-driven and aspect-driven – distinguished by whether the transformation rules are structured according to the source or target models, or based on aspects of the transformation that potentially cover multiple source and target model elements. In a general transformation language, it is important to support all of these styles, which tends to lead to an aspect-driven style of language design. However, in the case of quantity take-off, it was found that the dominant method of working is by iterating through the trade sections and items, then finding the building elements which match. This is strongly target-driven, which has a strong influence on the design of the Take-off Rules language. Specifically, the high-level structure of a Take-off Rules model corresponds closely to that of the BoQ to be generated, and this structure is then used to generate the corresponding structure in the BoQ.

Another advantage of taking a domain-specific approach to the language is that it allows for presentation of a number of problem-specific elements as first-class syntactic elements. In the Take-off Rules language, the different element types and classifications, property expressions and dimensions are encoded as first-class concepts. In a general-purpose transformation language these would have had to be included as "standard library" elements.

One alternative that was considered for the implementation of the language was to define a mapping between the domain-specific transformation language and a general-purpose language. This would allow the definition of a custom syntax in the style of the present implementation, but for the evaluation of the rules by an exiting rules engine. It was decided not to pursue this approach, on the basis that the semantics of the language were simple enough to be quickly implemented using traditional programming techniques, and that having a custom-built engine would simplify the deployed product. For a language with a more complex semantics, mapping to a general-purpose transformation language might be a more viable option.

The Take-off Rules language was designed keeping in mind the prevailing method by which domain experts think about the quantity take-off process, in the hope that this would lead to a less steep learning curve. At this point, the limited deployment of the tool has made it difficult to assess this claim. The tool has been used by selected users within a large cost engineering firm, and there has been positive feedback on the general approach of automatically generating bills of quantity, but to date there has been little formal evaluation of the take-off rules editing feature and its use.

6 Conclusion

We feel that for some domains there is a case for domain-specific model transformation languages, as illustrated by this example from the field of cost estimation/quantity surveying. Providing domain experts with a transformation language in addition to their domain-specific modelling languages can potentially increase their ability to control and manipulate the way that their models behave, and for a high degree of control and customisation regarding the presentation of the language to users.

Some aspects of the transformation language we have developed, notably traceability, are very similar to the sorts of traceability capabilities from general-purpose transformation languages. Others, such as the close structural similarity between the transformation language and target language, and customised presentation of the transformations in a specific editor, are less typical of general approaches.

By considering the specific requirements of the source and target languages, the users, the nature of the transformations to be expressed, and the points of variability available across transformation languages, a domain-specific transformation language and toolset can be customised to the task. If this practice became more commonplace, it would be interesting to investigate the formalisation of these considerations using a product-family style approach, in order to streamline the development of transformation editors and/or engines. One can envisage using an approach such as that of RubyTL [3] which allows the creation of tool support for variant transformation languages based on feature selection.

Acknowledgements. This paper was developed from research funded by the Cooperative Research Centre (CRC) for Construction Innovation, through the Australian Federal Government's CRC Programme (Department of Innovation, Industry, Science and Research).

References

1. Australian Institute of Quantity Surveyors: Australian standard method of measurement of building works. 5th edn. Australian Institute of Quantity Surveyors (1990)
2. buildingSMART Consortium: Industry foundation classes, ifc2x edition 3, technical corrigendum 1 (2007), http://buildingsmart-tech.org/ifc/IFC2x3/TC1/html/index.htm (accessed April 30, 2011)
3. Cuadrado, J.S., Molina, J.G., Tortosa, M.M.: RubyTL: A practical, extensible transformation language. In: Rensink, A., Warmer, J. (eds.) ECMDA-FA 2006. LNCS, vol. 4066, pp. 158–172. Springer, Heidelberg (2006)
4. Czarnecki, K., Helsen, S.: Feature-based survey of model transformation approaches. IBM Systems Journal 45(3), 621–646 (2006)
5. Daly, C.: Emfatic language for emf development. IBM alphaWorks (November 2004), http://www.alphaworks.ibm.com/tech/emfatic
6. Duddy, K., Gerber, A., Lawley, M., Raymond, K., Steel, J.: Model transformation: A declarative, reusable patterns approach. In: EDOC, pp. 174–185. IEEE Computer Society, Los Alamitos (2003)
7. Lawley, M., Steel, J.: Practical declarative model transformation with tefkat. In: Bruel, J.-M. (ed.) MoDELS 2005. LNCS, vol. 3844, pp. 139–150. Springer, Heidelberg (2006)
8. Rittel, H., Webber, M.: Dilemmas in a general theory of planning. Policy sciences 4(2), 155–169 (1973)

Improving Scalability and Maintenance of Software for High-Performance Scientific Computing by Combining MDE and Frameworks

Marc Palyart[1,2], David Lugato[1], Ileana Ober[2], and Jean-Michel Bruel[2]

[1] CEA / CESTA
33114 Le Barp - France
{marc.palyart,david.lugato}@cea.fr
[2] IRIT – Université de Toulouse
118, route de Narbonne, 31062 Toulouse - France
{ober,bruel}@irit.fr

Abstract. In recent years, numerical simulation has attracted increasing interest within industry and among academics. Paradoxically, the development and maintenance of high performance scientific computing software has become more complex due to the diversification of hardware architectures and their related programming languages and libraries.

In this paper, we share our experience in using model-driven development for numerical simulation software. Our approach called MDE4HPC proposes to tackle development complexity by using a domain specific modeling language to describe abstract views of the software. We present and analyse the results obtained with its implementation when deriving this abstract model to target Arcane, a development framework for 2D and 3D numerical simulation software.

1 Introduction

Thirty-five years ago, Gordon Moore, in one of the most visionary computer-related predictions [1], said that computer performance would increase by 40% per year. That prediction still stands. While for about 30 years that increase in performance was achieved by keeping the traditional sequential programming model, the performance increase has more recently occurred through parallel computer architectures. Such a shift has led to the need to rethink traditional software development in terms of how best to exploit these new architectures.

One of the main concerns of the high-performance scientific computing developer community is to produce efficient code for numerical simulation. Due to their thirst for computational power, this shift had to be initiated a long time ago in order to exploit the architectures of supercomputers. Unfortunately, in current practice mainstream parallel programming models, and in particular those addressing HPC, are low level and machine specific.

Even though good performance levels can be achieved with these approaches, drawbacks in terms of architecture dependency, mix-up of concerns and programming complexity occur:

- *Applications vs. supercomputers lifetime cycle.* In our application domain, the life cycle of supercomputers is five to seven times shorter than the life cycle of scientific applications[2]. CEA's experience has in fact shown that the simulation models and numerical analysis methods associated with our professional problems have a life expectancy of 20 to 30 years and must therefore be maintained over that period, with all the additional problems that come with software maintenance over such a period of time (e.g. team turnover).

  In parallel, through its TERA program [3], the CEA has decided that its main supercomputer has to be replaced every four years in order to increase its computation power by a factor superior to ten (Tera-1: 2002, Tera-10: 2006, Tera-100: 2010). At a pace faster than Moore´s law [1] hardware technological breakthroughs in hardware inevitably appear and software migration problems become an important issue.
- *The lack of separation of concerns.* The problem to be solved - the scientific knowledge of the physics - is entirely mixed with numerical schemes and target dependent information, added to manage the parallelism. Once a complex system has been built, it is difficult to extract the physical models. As a result, maintenance and upgrading become even more complicated.
- *Inaccessibility to domain experts.* The complexity of software programming restricts the use of these workstations and supercomputers to a few scientists who are willing to spend a significant amount of time learning the specificities of a particular set of machines.

Furthermore, the situation is getting worse with the new emerging generation of machines: hybrid machines. They are built by mixing heterogeneous hardware resources such as CPUs with many cores, Graphics Processing Units or CELLs[4]. GPUs are usually found within graphics cards, where they compute the rendering of massive 2D and 3D scenes. However, hardware manufacturers of supercomputers have started to integrate GPUs, since they are particularly well suited to specific operations such as matrix computations and thus linear algebra solving. GPUs contain a large number (in the range of hundreds) of stream processors which increase the computation power of supercomputers. To exploit them, however, developers have to depend on hardware manufacturer specific instructions (NVIDIA Cuda [5], or in the best case, on libraries which attempt to be more generic such as the OpenCL API[6]).

We think that model-based development techniques such as MDA [7] can help us deal with this complexity. In accordance with this opinion, we described in [8] the characteristics and possibilities of such a development approach. In this paper we present results of experiments conducted using this approach.

The rest of this paper is organised as follows: in Section 2 we complete the presentation of the MDE4HPC approach introduced in our previous paper. In Section 3 we introduce ArchiMDE, an implementation of the MDE4HPC approach as well as results obtained using this tool for the development of a numerical simulation software. Finally in Section 4 we discuss the contributions of our research and give directions for future work.

2 MDE4HPC

The Model-Driven Engineering for High Performance Computing (MDE4HPC) approach aims to offer solutions for the development of scientific computing software. The foundations of this approach were presented in [8]. This section aims to complete this broad description by detailing concepts required for the understanding of the results presented in Section 3.

2.1 Collaborative Approach

The development of a numerical simulation software requires the completion of a variety of tasks. Several skills are involved in this process, of course depending on the size of the project and hence the team, while certain tasks might be assigned to only one person.

We think that model sharing between persons from different areas of expertise is a key feature in faster development as it enables enabling reuse, traceability and consistency of the information. The different expertise profiles involved in the development of numerical simulation software and their viewpoint on the global model are presented in Figure 1. This Figure shows that the user point of view on the model of the simulation software is different according to the task he has to perform.

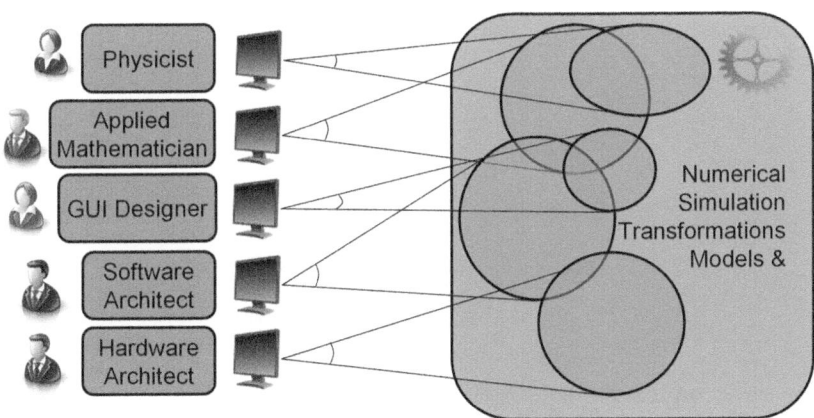

Fig. 1. Viewpoints in scientific computing

2.2 HPCML

High Performance Computing Modeling Language (HPCML) is a domain specific modeling language designed for the description of numerical simulation software. Its specification is part of the MDE4HPC approach. Figure 2 presents a simplified view of the concepts available in the HPCML metamodel for PIM (Platform Independent Model) modeling of the static aspects. Some of these concepts are intentionally derived from technologies massively used in the scientific computing community, such as Fortran. In fact, we wanted to raise the level of abstraction during the development process without revolutionizing development habits.

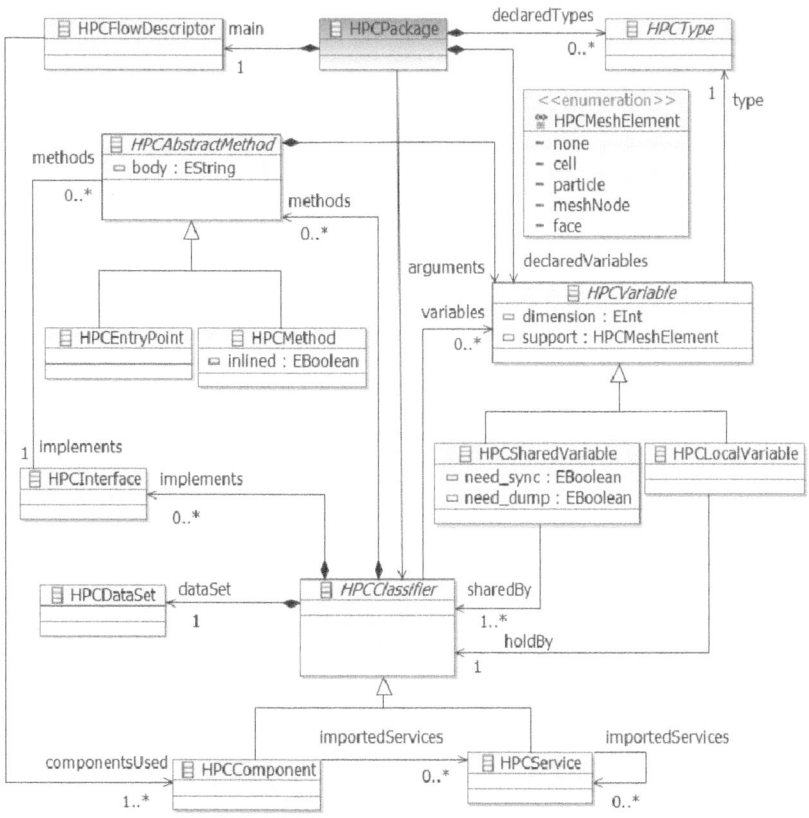

Fig. 2. Simplified view of the HPCML PIM metamodel

The basic building block of HPCML is the *HPCClassifier*. This structural block enables the description of a set of methods which work on a collection of *HPCVariable* that are shared between them. Usually the goal of a numerical simulation is to forecast the evolution in time and space of one or several physical phenomena. In concrete terms, each step of a loop makes the simulation go forward in time which is why this loop is sometimes called a time loop. Computation is performed until the loop stop condition is satisfied (evolution time, physical state reached...). An *HPCFlowDescriptor* describes the sequence of methods which composes the application and thus possesses specific constructs to model this kind of loop.

Within abstract models, we choose to adopt a data parallelism approach based on domain decomposition. Variables can be associated with a mesh element

Improving HPC Software Development by Combining MDE and Frameworks   217

(vertex,face,cell,particle). This information will guide the concrete implementation of data organization. Shared variables (*HPCSharedVariable*) are also an important modeling element as they allow us to express parallelism between different components.

Even though refinement transformations do not take this information into account in the current version of the tool, it is possible to model high level task parallelism within *HPCFlowDescriptor* via fork/join constructs.

3 Experiment Results

This section presents the results of an experiment conducted with the tool *ArchiMDE*, an implementation of the MDE4HPC approach. Before setting out the results, we first introduce projects in relation with *ArchiMDE* and present their integration within the overall development process.

3.1 Paprika Studio

The specification of a complete and coherent dataset from a numerical simulation has always turned out to be a complex task for the end user. For years, human input has been necessary to fulfil this task, usually provided by the developer of the simulation as the person with the best knowledge of the algorithms parametrization. To reduce the degree of involvement of the developers and to expand the community of end users, graphical user interfaces were introduced by specialists.

These specific editors integrate hard coded rules for managing the inputs of the scientific dataset which are specified by the simulation software developer. This co-development method allows the end user—assuming an exhaustive phase of manual validation—to produce complete and coherent datasets for the application. However, the dispersion of knowledge between the HPC application and its user interface is a real challenge for long term maintainability and traceability, especially when the life time of a simulation software—in the order of several decades—is compared to the frequency of renewal of software technologies for user interfaces. Given that a software simulation and its dataset must be upgraded at the same pace, the maintenance of the editor implies the availability of dedicated skills.

At the CEA, the increasing number and diversity of scientific simulation applications are outpacing the renewal of financial and human resources available for GUI development. Both to meet the goal of strengthening the coherence between a simulation software and its dataset editor and to preserve the separation of concerns, a model-driven approach was adopted for the development of these dataset editors.

Paprika is a software suite based on Eclipse for building scientific dataset editors through the use of model-driven engineering techniques. It includes two essential activities: the modeling of a scientific dataset (Numerical metamodel) and the construction of a graphic editor based on dataset and GUI models (GUI metamodel).

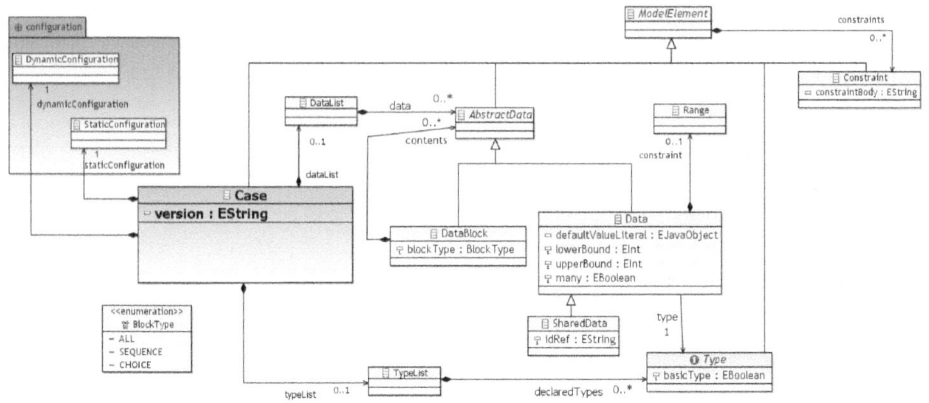

Fig. 3. Simplified view of the Numerical metamodel

In the context of this paper, details about the GUI metamodel are not essential. In consequence we focus our explanation on the Numerical metamodel. A simplified view of its metamodel is presented in Figure 3 and shows that at the highest level, two major concepts are provided:

- the data types, to meet the needs of factorization and reuse of data between several datasets. These types are of three kinds: *predefined*: integer, real, boolean, character string, enumerations; *simple*, i.e. extending a predefined type, for example the "Angle" type by extension of the "real" predefined type; or *structured* to form compound type as from other types. A range value can be specified for a simple data type: default value, minimal and maximal values, increment. It is also possible to associate a simple data type with a physical quantity, for example a frequency, and to set the unit used by default. The structured data types are constructed by the aggregation of predefined and/or simple types. Two structured types can be linked by an inheritance relationship (specialization of a type) or by a reference relationship, with or without containment.
- the data, to define the dataset model. Data are always attached to a predefined, simple or structured type. The supply of predefined types by the *numerical* metamodel makes it possible to define data directly without necessarily defining types beforehand. Data may be isolated or grouped with other data in recursive data blocks.

The choice of Paprika for our experiment was natural for three reasons. Firstly, in our quest for abstraction we needed to model the inputs dataset of the numerical simulation and the Paprika *Numerical* metamodel was already fulfilling that task. Secondly by choosing the *Numerical* metamodel we benefited from the whole generation process to obtain the associated dataset editor. Moreover, as an independent product, Paprika was not capable of generating the persistence management of the dataset and this step was still manual, hence error-prone and time consuming. But with its integration with ArchiMDE, the automation of this step was feasible, allowing easier software maintenance. Finally, Paprika is developed within our laboratory, so it was easier to access information concerning its architecture.

3.2 The Arcane Framework

In line with the TERA program presented in the Section 1, CEA/DAM's main supercomputer is replaced every four years with a growth of its computation power by a factor superior to ten. In order to prepare for these frequent upgrades, in 2000 the CEA-DAM started the development of Arcane [9], a development framework for 2D and 3D numerical simulation software. Several requirements determined the design of Arcane:

- the management of as many technical details (mesh management, memory management, input/output, parallelism) as possible by the framework itself to simplify software development.
- the possibility to obtain high level of performance on clusters of more than 10000 cores.
- to speed up the development phase by providing a set of tools for building, debugging, verifying and validating numerical software.

In addition to mathematical algorithms for solving physics equations, a numerical simulation has to handle several technical aspects such as the mesh management mentioned previously. However for this experiment we wanted to focus on the definition of the high level concepts without having to deal with a too complex generation chain. That is why we chose to rely on the Arcane framework to manage all those technical aspects as it has shown great capabilities on supercomputers and workstations over the last decade.

3.3 Development Process

The MDE4HPC approach presented in Section 2 proposes to offer a tailored perspective of the project for each kind of participant in the development. ArchiMDE follows this recommendation by providing a set of views, each adapted to a specific task. Figure 4 illustrates the different models and transformations which are part of the development process. In this process physicists and applied mathematicians are responsible for modeling what the numerical core of the software must compute(*HPCML PIM*) and its inputs (*Numerical*). Software engineers and hardware architects are in charge of defining *HPCML PDM* and the rules to combine PIM and PDM models, as well as the rules to refine the PSM model until text based generation (numerical software, GUI, test, documentation...). The work of software engineers and hardware architects on this phase of the process is widely reusable between projects while the target machine does not change. The GUI designer has to model the user interface by deriving the *Numerical* model.

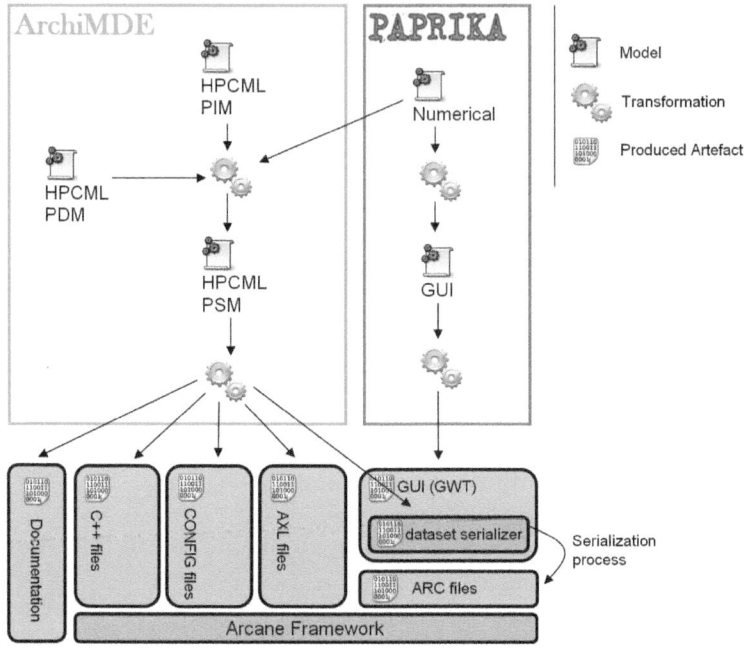

Fig. 4. Development process

All the model transformations are based on Eclipse projects from the *OpenArchitecture Ware* framework. Model-to-Model transformations use the Xtend project and Model-to-Text transformations use the Xpand project. Xpand with its polymorphic template invocation fulfilled most of our needs and its aspect oriented programming possibilities offer a maintenance improvement of M2T transformations. Even though the Xtend syntax and use for M2M transformations is disconcerting at first compared to other M2M framework, it was sufficient for our experiment. Nevertheless the possibility to define functional extensions accessible both from Xpand and Xtend was a powerful and useful feature.

Paprika was not initially designed to be integrated with other modelers such as ArchiMDE. Hence in order to accomplish in ArchiMDE the transformation which takes *Numerical* models as input, we had to define a static mapping between primitive types from Paprika and ArchiMDE. Apart from this point the transformation which integrates the *Numerical* model from Paprika into ArchiMDE is straightforward. *HPCComponents* and their corresponding datasets model are matched together regarding their name.

3.4 Results with an Lagrangian Hydrodynamic Simulation

To assess the validity of the approach, we developed with ArchiMDE a simplified Lagrangian hydrodynamic module introduced in [9] where the mesh nodes are moved according to Newton's law and the thermodynamic values are updated. At each time step this numerical simulation performs the following operations:

- compute pressure force on nodes:
$$\vec{F}_s^n = \sum_q p_q^n \cdot \vec{C}_q^s$$

- apply dynamic principle and compute node speed:
$$\vec{u}_s^{n+\frac{1}{2}} = \vec{u}_s^{n-\frac{1}{2}} + \frac{\Delta t}{M_s} \vec{F}_s^n$$

- apply boundary conditions.
- move nodes:
$$\vec{x}_s^{n+1} = \vec{x}_s^n + \Delta t \cdot \vec{u}_s^{n+\frac{1}{2}}$$

- update geometric values (meshes volume, meshes characteristic length and geometric components required for the pressure gradient calculation)
- update density:
$$\rho_q^{n+1} = \frac{m_q^{n+1}}{\nu_q^{n+1}}$$

- apply equation of state to update internal energy, pressure and sound speed:
$$e^{n+1} = \frac{1 + \frac{(\gamma-1)}{2} \cdot (1 - \frac{\nu^{n+1}}{\nu^n})}{1 + \frac{(\gamma-1)}{2} \cdot (1 - \frac{\nu^n}{\nu^{n+1}})}$$

$$p^{n+1} = (\gamma - 1)\rho^{n+1} e^{n+1}$$

$$c^{n+1} = \sqrt{\frac{\gamma p^{n+1}}{\rho^{n+1}}}$$

- compute the new time step according to the CFL (Courant-Friedrichs-Levy) constraint.

The *HPCFlowDescriptor* describing the sequence of methods is shown in Figure 5. Listing 1.1 shows the body of the *HPCEntryPoint computePressureForce*. It is an Arcane source code, i.e. C++ syntax plus primitives from the Framework. It is interesting to note Arcane primitives for mesh manipulation (ENUMERATE_CELL) which are at a higher level of abstraction than the usual array manipulation.

The graphic user interface of the produced dataset editor is shown in Figure 6. The version presented here is based on GWT (Google Web Toolkit) but Paprika offers also the possibility to generate from the GUI model a version based on SWT.

Regarding the size of the experiment, the generated source code (computational core and dataset editor) is around 12 KLOC, given that the Arcane source code is relatively compact as many aspects of the numerical simulation are handled by the framework (pre-processing, inputs/outputs management, load balancing, post-processing).

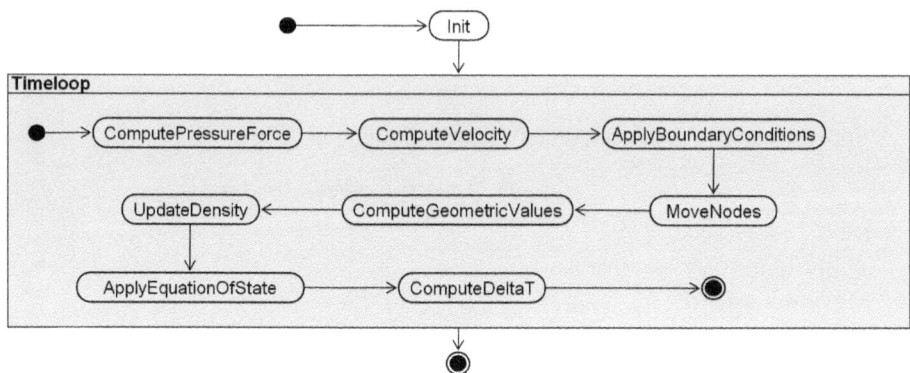

Fig. 5. *HPCFlowDescriptor* of the hydrodynamic simulation

```
// Reset of the force vector
m_force.fill(Real3::null());

// Computation for each vertex of each cell of the
// contribution from the pressure forces
ENUMERATE_CELL(icell, allCells())
{
    const Cell & cell = * icell;
    Real pressure = m_pressure[icell];
    for (NodeEnumerator inode(cell.nodes()); inode.hasNext();
        ++inode)
    {
        m_force[inode] += pressure * m_cell_cqs[icell][inode.
            index()];
    }
}
```

Listing 1.1. Body of the *HPCEntryPoint computePressureForce*

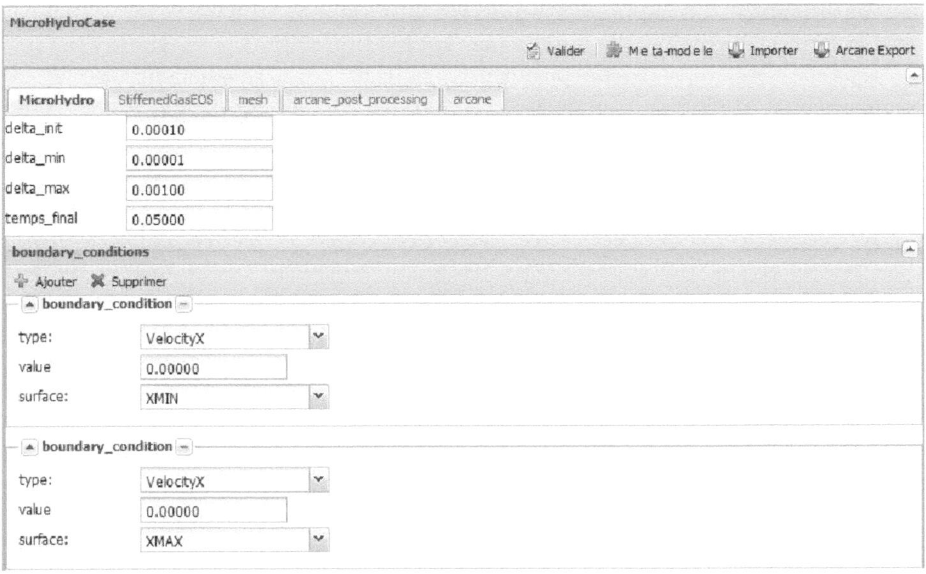

Fig. 6. GUI of the dataset editor generated

We now examine the results of our experiment according to the following points:

- *Performance.* The generated source code of the numerical part (Arcane source code) is similar to the one presented in [9]. Benchmarks of the Arcane framework on the Tera-10 supercomputer are available on this article. Thus from a computational performance point of view both versions would obtain the same results, and benchmarks would only have evaluated the performance of the Arcane framework and not of our approach. However, these results could be improved with the integration of optimization good practice as model transformations.
- *Development Time.* The development time with both approaches —modeling and hand written code— was practically identical. The modeling approach was a little faster thanks to the GUI part. The time taken to develop the different refinement transformations were considered apart from the time required to develop applications. Indeed, as specified in the approach, the transformations rules would be used by several developments, hence their cost could be negligible compared to the application development time. In terms of development productivity, the gain expected by the approach does not appear clearly in this experiment, because the Arcane framework is already at a reasonable level of abstraction and enables developers to avoid certain time-consuming and repetitive tasks. With a low level target generation such as MPI (Message Passing Interface) [10] or Cuda[5], better results would have been obtained.

– *Maintenance.* The approach would reveal its potential with several applications and especially over time when application migrations (adaptive maintenance) will have to be performed. In that case, the benefits would be clearer, as application models could be reused. The gain would therefore be proportional to the number of applications to migrate.

In the case of upgrade maintenance we will take a specific use case to support our explanation. The scenario is the following: to increase the simulation precision of one software, a new parameter must be added. To accomplish this change, several actions have to be performed: the algorithm of the numerical simulation must be updated to profit from this new parameter and this evolution has to be validated, database validation tests datasets must be migrated, the dataset reader of the simulation must be updated to read this new value, tests must be written to ensure that the reading process is correct, the development documentation and user guide must be updated to explain the role of the new parameter, the graphic user interface of the dataset editor must be updated to display the new value and finally the persistence management of this value must be added into the dataset editor. Table 1 gives for each of these activities, the average time in hours required to perform them with four different approaches. It is always a complex task to measure productivity gains in software development, especially when the sample size available for the experiment is small. These measures are based on the experience of two expert engineers and two trainee engineers. Hence we are working in relative and not absolute terms: the aim is only to observe trends.

Table 1. Average upgrade maintenance time in hour with four different approaches

	Fortran Tcl/Tk	Fortran Paprika	Arcane Paprika	ArchiMDE Arcane Paprika
algorithm update	8	8	5	4.5
algorithm validation	4	4	4	4
validation testing migration	1	1	1	1
dataset reader update	0.7	0.7	0.3	0.15
GUI tests	0.3	0.3	0.1	0
documentation	0.25	0.25	0.2	0.15
dataset editor	4	1	1	1
data persistence	2	1	1	0
Productivity improvement	reference	*1.25*	*1.61*	*1.88*

The improvement from using Paprika instead of Tcl/Tk comes from the fact that GUIs usually contain plenty of simple and redundant source code and that thanks to Paprika this GUI is generated and the repetitive tasks are now replaced by a faster modeling phase. The improvement from using Arcane/Paprika instead of Fortran/Paprika can be explained for two reasons: Arcane offers services to reduce the amount of code to produce and

Arcane provides high level concepts to simplify the development. Finally the improvement with the global solution (ArchiMDE/Arcane/Paprika) comes from the integration (more parts can be generated thanks to information sharing via model transformations) and the higher level of abstraction. Sadly the job which globally benefits the most from the productivity increase is the software engineer.

4 Discussion and Perspectives

This experiment is a further step toward the use of model-based techniques for numerical simulation development in an industrial context. Feedback from this experiment and from other projects such as [11] shows that regarding the GUI, model-based development greatly increases the productivity at a low cost. Regarding the computational part, the Arcane framework is capable of providing us with excellent performances and a good scalability which is our primary objective. In this paper we show that on the one hand performance and productivity are provided by the framework and that on the other hand costs reduction and application durability are provided by MDE. Hence this combination of the two allowed us to reach all of our objectives.

As discussed previously, the use of our approach has allowed us to raise the level of abstraction with respect to existing practices. Basing our approach on an existing framework, Arcane, is a pragmatic choice that allowed us to deploy our approach more rapidly. Nevertheless, the drawback of this choice is that we inherit the limitations of this framework, for instance with respect to a new hybrid architecture. This is why the next step of our research is to extend HPCML to cover the full modeling of the numerical code.

Regarding related work, we can mention the High Productivity Computing Systems (HPCS) programme launched in 2002 by the DARPA [12] from emerged novel programming language: Chapel (Cray), Fortress(SUN) and X10 (IBM). The principal drawback of this approach is the need to develop high-performance compiler, debugger and implementation for each existing architecture. Macro-based approaches such as HMPP (Hybrid Multi-core Parallel Programming environment) [13] and OpenMP (Open Multi Processing) [14] offer a respectable solution for improving legacy code. However, as their use is based on compiler directives which limit the separation of concerns, this solution can appear as less attractive for new developments. The step forward embedded DSL techniques such as [15] is language virtualization as defined in the Lizst project [16]. This project shares the same philosophy as ours and represents a good perspective for the modeling of dynamic aspects in the MDE4HPC approach. Globally we can mention that none of these projects are opposed to our approach as they could be used as target technology at various level of our refinement process.

With the adoption of a full model based development, new possibilities will be offered to us. For example, hybrid machines presented in Section 1 would become accessible in order to increase the performance level. Still to fulfil HPC primary objective, low level optimizations could be achieved via model transformations, to achieve better performance levels. Furthermore, with conventional low level hand-written source code, the development of multiple versions of the software to assess which one suits the targeted platform best in terms of performance the targeted platform would be too costly. Even though this feature is not yet implemented, we think that higher-order transformations can make this kind of parametric studies accessible. In the same spirit, projects such as StarPU [17] require the algorithm to be implemented in different languages. StarPU is a unified runtime system that offers support for heterogeneous architectures (CPU, GPUs, IBM Cell) by selecting at runtime the more relevant implementation. With our approach, once the generators for each language have been built, the cost of multi-languages generation is extremely low comparing to the hand-written approach.

The validation phase represents a substantial part of the development time, but for the moment only small productivity gains are offered by our approach on this aspect. We plan to include validation tests in the modeling process in order to automatize the migration of database validation tests datasets.

References

1. Moore, G.E.: Cramming more components onto integrated circuits. Electronics 38(8), 114–117 (1965)
2. Lugato, D.: Model-driven engineering for high-performance computing applications. In: The 19th IASTED International Conference on Modelling and Simulation, Quebec City, Quebec, Canada (May 2008)
3. Gonnord, J., Leca, P., Robin, F.: Au delà de 50 mille milliards d´opérations par seconde! La Recherche (393) (January 2006)
4. Johns, C.R., Brokenshire, D.A.: Introduction to the cell broadband engine architecture. IBM Journal of Research and Development 51(5), 503–520 (2007)
5. Kirk, D.: Nvidia cuda software and gpu parallel computing architecture. In: ISMM, pp. 103–104 (2007)
6. KhronosGroup: The OpenCL specification. Technical report (2009)
7. Miller, J., Mukerji, J.: Mda guide version 1.0.1. omg/2003-06-01. Technical report, OMG (2003)
8. Palyart, M., Lugato, D., Ober, I., Bruel, J.M.: MDE4HPC: An approach for using Model-Driven Engineering in High-Performance Computing. In: 15th System Design Languages Forum, SDL 2011 (2011)
9. Grospellier, G., Lelandais, B.: The Arcane development framework. In: POOSC 2009. ACM, New York (2009)
10. Snir, M., Otto, S.W., Huss-Lederman, S., Walker, D.W., Dongarra, J.: MPI: The complete reference. MIT Press, Cambridge (1996)
11. Schramm, A., Preußner, A., Heinrich, M., Vogel, L.: Rapid UI Development for Enterprise Applications: Combining Manual and Model-Driven Techniques. In: Petriu, D.C., Rouquette, N., Haugen, Ø. (eds.) MODELS 2010. LNCS, vol. 6394, pp. 271–285. Springer, Heidelberg (2010)
12. Weiland, M.: Chapel, Fortress and X10: Novel Languages for HPC. Technical report, The University of Edinburgh (October 2007)
13. Bodin, F.: Keynote: Compilers in the manycore era. In: Seznec, A., Emer, J., O'Boyle, M., Martonosi, M., Ungerer, T. (eds.) HiPEAC 2009. LNCS, vol. 5409, pp. 2–3. Springer, Heidelberg (2009)

14. Dagum, L., Menon, R.: Openmp: An industry-standard api for shared-memory programming. Computing in Science and Engineering 5, 46–55 (1998)
15. Christophe, P.: A domain specific embedded language in c++ for automatic differentiation, projection, integration and variational formulations. Sci. Program (2006)
16. Chafi, H., DeVito, Z., Moors, A., Rompf, T., Sujeeth, A.K., Hanrahan, P., Odersky, M., Olukotun, K.: Language virtualization for heterogeneous parallel computing. In: OOPSLA, pp. 835–847. ACM, New York (2010)
17. Augonnet, C., Thibault, S., Namyst, R., Wacrenier, P.-A.: STARPU: A unified platform for task scheduling on heterogeneous multicore architectures. In: Sips, H., Epema, D., Lin, H.-X. (eds.) Euro-Par 2009. LNCS, vol. 5704, pp. 863–874. Springer, Heidelberg (2009), http://hal.inria.fr/inria-00384363/en/

A Critical Review of Applied MDA for Embedded Devices: Identification of Problem Classes and Discussing Porting Efforts in Practice

Michael Lettner, Michael Tschernuth, and Rene Mayrhofer

Upper Austria University of Applied Sciences
Softwarepark 11
4232 Hagenberg, Austria
{michael.lettner,michael.tschernuth,rene.mayrhofer}@fh-hagenberg.at

Abstract. Model-driven development (MDD) has seen wide application in research, but still has limitations in real world industrial projects. One project which applies such MDD principles is about developing the software of a feature phone. While advantages seem to outweigh any disadvantages in theory, several problems arise when applying the model-driven methodology in practice. Problems when adopting this approach are shown as well as a practical solution to utilize one of the main advantages of MDD—portability. Issues that originate from using a tool which supports a model-driven approach are presented. A conclusion sums up the personal experiences made when applying MDD in a real world project.

1 Introduction

This paper describes the basic idea and architecture behind a project which uses a model-driven development approach and the problems which arise during this process. Our findings are based on personal experience during a case study which led to a successful implementation of a project by means of a tool which supports such an MDD approach. We identify the problems or shortcomings that were observed during the development process, and address what effort was required in practice to port the system to a different platform.

1.1 Case Study Overview

The project is about developing a configurable *Man-Machine Interface (MMI)* and *applications*—such as phonebook or call application—of a low-cost mobile phone. *Low-cost* in that sense refers to rather simple phones being built on *conventional real time operating systems*—as opposed to feature rich smartphones for example.

1.2 Requirements and Aims

Applying MDD in a concrete project—MMI and application layer development of a low-cost mobile phone—is the primary goal of the project behind this paper. The intention of applying MDD was to improve the software development process and subsequently the software quality itself. Two top-level requirements can be distinguished:

- **Platform independent user interface development:** Due to limited hardware resources (screen size, memory constraints), developing user interfaces for cellphones has special requirements, and is conducted by domain experts. As such, these experts often do not have detailed programming skills. The idea is to offer a possibility which allows domain experts to directly specify the MMI structure in a graphical manner (e.g., by means of a WYSIWYG editor).
- **The software should be easily portable to other hardware platforms:** It is important that the program logic—once developed—is portable to different target platforms, hence functionality may be added which is not supported by the current hardware platform. As the main part of the software solution remains the same, the application logic would have to be developed redundantly if a traditional development approach is applied.

The following subsections describe the methodologies suggested to meet these requirements in practice. The platform-independent MMI definition has been realized using a proprietary Domain-Specific Language (DSL) and is not discussed further in this paper (as the focus is on problems experienced when using standard modeling tools).

1.3 Model-Driven Development

The main issue which must be tackled is the platform independence. Thus, MDD fits best because the application logic can be designed using generic software models without having platform-specific elements in it. The generic approach of this development method suits our requirements very well. One way how MDD can be achieved is the *Model-Driven Architecture (MDA)* [1].

1.4 Characteristics of MDA

The Model-Driven Architecture was introduced by the *Object Management Group (OMG)* in 2001 and is one way to achieve the project aims presented above, which primarily are to reduce development time and increase the quality of software for embedded development. The basic idea of MDA is to separate the specification of the operation of a system from how this system is implemented on a specific platform. The three primary goals of MDA are portability, interoperability and reusability through architectural separation of concerns [2]. Strictly speaking, MDA itself is not a standard on its own, but a concept that references a number of related OMG technologies (*Unified Modeling Language (UML)*, *Meta Object Facility (MOF)*, *XML Metadata Interchange (XMI)*, and others) [1]. Our approach relies on UML as the modeling language. This offers a wide range of modeling capabilities with different diagram types [3].

As the benefits promised by MDA meet our requirements very well, the decision was made to apply it to the project. The next section will introduce the key features of the selected MDA tool.

2 MDA Tool Features

There exist a few software tools which support the developer in modeling systems and generating code within the embedded domain which have been evaluated in [4]. As a consequence we decided to use *IBM Rational Rhapsody*[1] due to its focus on embedded development (e.g., reduced memory footprint) and because of the availability of an operating system adaption layer for the platform used in our case study. Rhapsody offers a lot of features for model-driven development which are discussed in the following sections.

2.1 Modeling and Code Generation

Rhapsody supports designing a system by the use of UML diagrams like statecharts or class diagrams for describing the system. Sequence diagrams can be used to analyze the workflow for testing purposes. Rhapsody comes with an *out of the box* code generator for the programming languages C, C++, Java and Ada. It offers possibilities to influence the code generation process by annotating UML elements with *Stereotypes* and *Tagged Values*. The generated code runs in a special framework called *Object eXecution Framework (OXF)* and has to be recompiled for different target operating systems. *IBM Rational Rhapsody* provides an OXF for many of the currently available operating systems [5].

2.2 Action Language

To achieve 100% code generation from a model, actions are required—for instance, in order to invoke operations or to send signals. OMG is currently specifying such an action language for UML[2], which to date is not yet available for every UML tool, since it is a relatively new development. Rhapsody does not support ALF yet and instead has a very practical approach as it uses the syntax of the selected language—and therefore does not provide language-independent action specifications. Rhapsody-specific macros, such as generating an event, are implemented in C syntax. This is very comfortable especially if someone wants to call target-specific APIs which might run besides the Rhapsody code on the target. Integrating the code on the embedded target is easier this way than

---

[1] http://www.ibm.com/software/awdtools/rhapsody/
[2] http://www.omg.org/spec/ALF/

having to translate a proprietary action language syntax to target-specific calls. The big disadvantage of this approach is the lack of flexibility during a platform change. In case you want to switch from C to C++, all action code has to be adapted.

2.3 Product Variants

Rhapsody supports different versions of model elements by specifying product variants. This feature allows you to create different behavior or structure models of one class. The variant for the current build can be set in the run configuration. This way, it is possible to have one basic UML model for different platforms with variations for the platform-specific parts.

2.4 Conclusion

The features of this modeling tool meet our use case as it focuses on the practical applicability of model-driven development. Due to the fact that there is no generic action language implementation, the models are not platform-independent regarding the programming language, thus it is very difficult to port a model developed in C to Java. On the other hand, all features of the target programming language can be utilized.

3 Proposed Solution

Within a case study the software for a mobile phone was developed using a model-driven approach. The basic concepts of the software architecture are described in this section (from [6]):

3.1 System Architecture

The system architecture in Figure 1 shows the layered architecture from a reusability aspect. Reusability is a key criterion in the embedded software domain where product cycles and the time to market are very short. Especially when blocks of well-tested code artifacts should be reused in a product variant, it is essential that these key components are platform-independent and therefore portable.

Three main layers *in terms of reuse* can be distinguished. From bottom to top, these are:

1. *Hardware-related functionality:* On these lower sublayers (Figure 1, illustrated in white) hardware, operating system and abstractions such as drivers, protocol stack, up to middleware, are found. Often these layers are from third-party providers and are *the ones that change* when the underlying platform shall be upgraded or totally replaced.

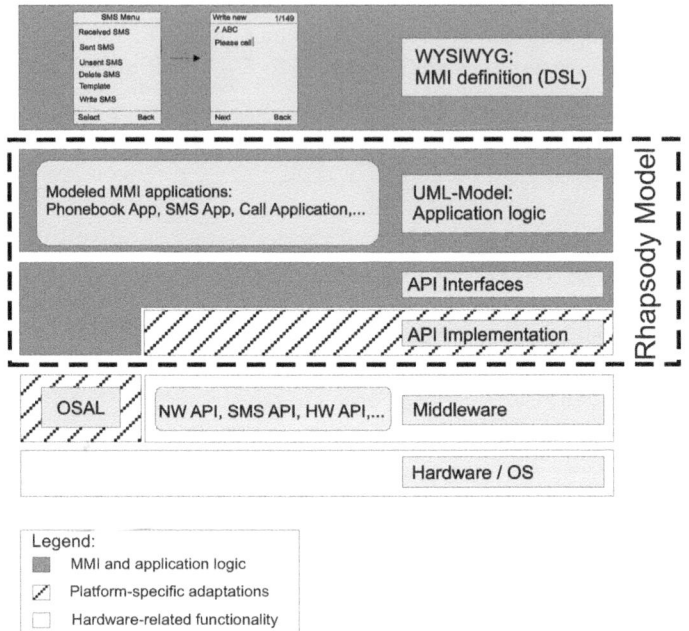

Fig. 1. Simplified system architecture: the different patterns indicate different levels of reuse (according to [6])

2. *Platform-specific adaptations:* The implemented *Operating System Abstraction Layer (OSAL)* is responsible for providing operating system-specific concepts such as tasks, scheduling or memory management in a platform-independent manner to its upper layers—specifically, to *Rhapsody's execution framework OXF* (not illustrated in Figure 1 for sake of simplification). The illustrated *API implementations* realize the platform-independent interfaces by calling platform-specific middleware functions and reacting on callbacks. *When changing to a new platform*, these layers are the crucial parts, as they are the only ones that *need to be adapted* to whatever is provided by the new middleware and operating system.
3. *MMI and application logic:* This layer encapsulates the *user interface*, the *application logic*, and abstractions (illustrated as *API interfaces*) for platform-specific API implementations. One of the big advantages of MDA is that this tier can *remain totally unchanged* during a platform change. The reason is that the user interface structure and application logic are defined in a platform-independent way—the whole model can be reused, thus saving a lot of time and ensuring the same constant high quality products that the previous platform already provided. This argument usually outweighs the drawback of the expected increased time required to create such platform-independent models in the first place (cf. Section 6).

4 Problems

Although the project was successfully realized, a few shortcomings of the modeling approach manifested during the development process. The following section describes several problems related to the model-driven approach in contrast to a traditional code-centric approach. In this section we will discuss tool-related problems as well as issues when working in a team, both from a technical and organizational perspective.

4.1 Tool-Related Problems

Every modeling tool has features to support the developer in their work. For example, a tool which is focused on quick practical applicability could have limitations when it comes to flexibility during a platform change. The usability of the promised modeling features, as well as limitations during practical usage of Rhapsody are pointed out in the following paragraphs. Certain aspects of the problems addressed can be characterized as general problem classes though and thus apply to other modeling tools as well.

- **No action language:** This point has briefly been pointed out before. While writing action code (e.g. calling a method to write something on a display) in the model directly in the target programming language has been considered an advantage due to the fact that developers are already familiar with the syntax, the absence of an action language results in a cumbersome adaptation process if one wants to change the implementation language later on. The target language in Rhapsody must be chosen at the time of creating a new project (either C, C++, Java or Ada). Although changes at a later stage are possible, it may require a lot of changes—especially if action code has been extensively used. For example, all code written into statecharts (e.g. in *entry* or *exit actions*) is *100 % language-specific* and would be required to be rewritten. Only when the target language remains the same, action code can be fully reused.
- **Code generator output:** Regardless of which modeling tool is used, the developer has to be aware of the produced output. For instance, several implementation techniques for statecharts exist. Rhapsody's built-in code generator for C uses a *flat statechart implementation* option (as opposed to a *hierarchical statechart implementation*). The drawback of this implementation is the proliferation of states and transitions, which makes the statechart very cluttered and the resulting code difficult to read [7]. For example, when a statechart contains a state, and there are multiple transitions leading to that state, the action code (e.g., code written into the *entry action* of that state) is generated multiple times—once for each transition. Especially for platforms with scarce memory this might comprise a problem. By reorganizing the statecharts or outsourcing the redundant code part into a function this issue can be circumvented. However, this is only possible if the engineer understands what code is generated from the model. In addition, during

the *debugging phase*, the developer has to be aware of that multiple state generation to *correctly setup breakpoints* in the source code.
- **Round-trip engineering:** The flexibility of both generating code from model, and integrating changes on code level back into the model, is commonly known as *round-tripping*, and has been introduced in many modeling tools. The concept is a big advantage if one favors to work on code level, for instance in one's familiar Integrated Development Environment (IDE)—but based on the experiences made, round-trip *never really worked* as intended[3]: Although it sounds promising, all team members had to experience a similar learning curve: In the beginning, everybody applied round-tripping and wondered how well it actually worked—until a point in time, when something was messed up in generated code, and the project stops building correctly. And while not obvious what caused the problems in the first place, after hours of bug-tracking it almost always could be blamed to round-trip modifying the model (and therefore the code) in a way it shouldn't have (one example was related to altering the #include statements section that led to wrong/corrupt dependencies in the model). Eventually, often reverting the model/code to the last stable revision was the last resort. Bottom line is that every team member came individually to the conclusion that round-trip wastes more time in error cases than it saves when everything works as intended. Future releases of the tool might handle this issue more appropriately which could increase development speed significantly.

    Round-tripping problems are not only inherent to Rhapsody. It is a more sophisticated issue because all constructs of a target language have to be represented somehow in the model after adding them on code level. There are solutions for many use cases—but covering all language features might be too big of a challenge for the current tools [8]. One might argue that round-tripping between models and code should not be done at all[4,5], but it would be supportive for developers who are used to frequently work on code level.
- **Animation:** Another feature offered by Rhapsody is the *animation feature*. During runtime, behavior diagrams like statecharts or sequence diagrams can be animated to analyze if the model behaves as intended. This is a great way of finding design flaws in the system or conceptional errors. As good as this sounds, in our specific case we barely used it for one simple reason: It was too slow! The procedure for rebuilding the whole project with the animation feature enabled took for this case study about 10-15 minutes—one reason for the additional time might have been the integration of the third-party framework. Subsequently, the execution of the solution is delayed as well for a significant time, which leads to a minimal usage of this feature. Every programmer used animation only as a last resort solution as it took most of the time longer to set up the animation than just debugging with standard tools.

---

[3] Project was built using Rhapsody in C, version 7.4, later 7.5.2.
[4] http://vhanniet.wordpress.com/2011/04/20/mdamdd-dont-round-trip/,
[5] http://thinkinmodels.wordpress.com/2011/04/22/transformation-between-models-and-code-can-be-or-not-can-be-that-is-the-question/

- **Abstracting third-party middleware:** A common system modeled using Rhapsody often just consists of a three-layered architecture. On top, there is the UML model. The bottom layer consists of hardware and operating system. In between is the OSAL. Thus, the model is directly situated upon OSAL, and can tap into the abstracted functions from this layer. Whenever the platform changes, it is sufficient to exchange/adapt the OSAL, and the application is good to run on the new hardware. Such a scenario is well supported in Rhapsody, as one simply has to create different *configurations* in the modeling tool for each supported platform.

  Our setup is a little bit different though, as we integrate the platform's middleware (third party) that the application logic can rely on. As Rhapsody doesn't provide a general action language, middleware calls are integrated using plain C language constructs (at specific predefined points within the model)—which is what we call *API Interfaces* in our system architecture (in other words, it is still part of the UML model, but contains language-specific constructs). Thus, just exchanging the OSAL won't be sufficient. The model no longer is situated solely on top of OSAL, but is (in another thread) directly accessing platform-specific middleware, too.

  One way to abstract such platform-specific calls was to use interfaces. As C language does not provide built-in linguistic support for interfaces, it is however possible to simulate interfaces in C (e.g., using function pointers) [9]—Rhapsody even hides this implementation detail when a class is given the *Interface* stereotype.

  Using this approach, in order to support multiple platforms, each interface realization was put into a separate class (that translates into a separate unit), to be maintained by different people. Such an interface-like solution implied two drawbacks in our setup: First, the model needs modification whenever one has to switch between platforms (e.g., for developers working on different platforms), as the assignment of the interface realization in use is done inside the model (e.g., either by modifying a relation in a diagram, or dynamically selecting the proper object in code). Plus, as all interface realizations exist in parallel in the model, this also leads to an increased memory footprint by default, as all platform variations are contained in the generated code.

  Lesson learned: As one can see from Rhapsody's example, an important requirement for a modeling tool is to provide a mechanism to easily switch between different target platforms. Rhapsody has improved on this in a newer version—the new feature called *Variation Points* is discussed in Subsection 5.3.

4.2 Problems When Working in a Team

The support of the tool for collaborative working is another aspect worth discussing because of certain situations that turn out to be problematic when applying model-driven engineering in a software team of two or more people, compared to the traditional code-centric way. The most disturbing ones are:

- **Model granularity:** As soon as more than one person works on the same model, the question of sharing options arise. Rhapsody for that matter allows the user to divide the model in so-called units. A unit may be a whole package, or just a single class. Each unit is stored in a separate file on the file system. Therefore, different users can modify different aspects of a model at the same time. This takes a *very thoroughly designed architecture* which should be reflected by a good package and unit structure. Should such a package structure lack granularity, cooperating on the concerned model elements won't be possible.

  Even if one has a good architecture and a sufficiently detailed unit granularity for cooperation purposes, problems arise as soon as dependencies between different units are created, modified or deleted. Every change of dependencies affects more than a single unit, which could lead to conflicts if not all of the concerned model elements are in control of the developer applying these changes.

- **Merging conflicts in version control systems:** As pointed out above, Rhapsody allows for altering the same model on unit level granularity. When using a version control system with a central repository such as SVN[6], conflicts are inevitably—caused by users having modified the same files at the same time. While it is not too hard to merge code on source file level with traditional programming approaches, mechanisms for merging models are highly tool-dependent.

  In addition to the impractical solution of merging the unit files manually with a file comparison tool, Rhapsody provides a separate model-merge capability [10]. Both approaches turn out to be a very time-consuming and error-prone process, since attention must be paid to identify the intended modifications.

  Lesson learned: There is still potential for improvements on collaboration mechanisms in today's MDA tools, since dividing the model for alteration between different users is a common problem. It is advisable to early investigate a tool's capabilities for identifying differences and merging alternate versions.

- **Problems with tool versions and compatibility:** As long as everyone works with the same version of the modeling tool, sharing is possible without any problems. As soon as different modeling tool versions are used in a project it becomes difficult. A Rhapsody project from a newer version cannot be modified or even opened with an older version once they are converted, since projects are not backwards compatible. This makes upgrades to new tool versions very time consuming because the whole project team has to switch at the same time which is sometimes not that easy considering a development team which works in another country with another IT infrastructure. So every tool version upgrade has to be coordinated and thought through very carefully.

---

[6] Subversion, http://subversion.tigris.org/

- **Difficult sharing of project when OSAL was adapted:** Difficulties arise because the OXF framework files are contained in the Rhapsody installation folder and change with the Rhapsody version. Whenever an update of Rhapsody is released, the custom Operating System Abstraction Layer has to be rebuilt to be compatible with the new version. All changes to the files responsible for the OXF framework have to be exchanged which imposes a problem because the Rhapsody installation is traditionally not under version control, and therefore this process is error-prone.

4.3 Organizational Problems

Introducing model-based engineering approaches promises significant advantages, primarily the increased product quality and higher productivity. However, not always obvious is the resistance that a team that decides to go with such an approach faces during the whole project lifetime. Below, some issues with potential for conflict have been identified—all from the practical standpoint of the experiences made throughout our project.

Resistance from Stakeholders: While technical-savvy stakeholders (technical project manager, employees at the customer's company that we have to cooperate with) are rather easily convinced of the advantages of model-based approaches, resistance may be faced from the stakeholders at the customer's company. Since the client has different interests, its primary focus is on getting a high-quality product, as timely as possible.

We experienced that during the startup phase and the tool research the management was getting impatient due to the lack of presentable results.

Lesson learned: Building a prototype to demonstrate the proof of concept of the model-based approach helps to set more realistic milestone estimates for the project plan, and to convince stakeholders more easily.

Resistance within the Team: While resistance from stakeholders such as the customer or financial partners could be sort of expected, disagreements from within the own team could not. When the project kicked off, we were starting out with a team of two—the founders of the project being convinced of MDA and its advantages. As more developers joined our group and the team grew, not all of those new members were familiar with model-based engineering.

We observed certain skepticism among the team members that have not been familiar with such an approach before. This manifested in co-workers that seemed very doubtful and asked a lot of questions, thus requiring us to repeatedly explain the advantages of model-based versus conventional engineering. Their main arguments would be that traditional software engineering techniques appeared to lead to a result much quicker. The additional abstraction layer seemed to impose a problem, as this can be seen as additional source for errors and thus could increase complexity while debugging. In other words, from their viewpoint it seemed to be a detour to develop a model first and generate the code out of it. They did not foresee the long-term perspective of eased technology or application logic changes, while still preserving high software quality.

Lesson learned: Show the advantages on a practical example that developers have to develop on their own. After experiencing these advantages themselves they were more open minded regarding the new technology.

Especially the reuse of model elements during a platform change is a key advantage of this case study. The following section shows how a platform change was carried out and which additional adaptations had to be made.

5 Porting to Another Platform

While the system was implemented with a specific target in mind, the next logical step was to port it to another platform, to experience the maturity of our MDD approach, the advantages and shortcomings. In correspondence with the system architecture depicted in Figure 1, each of the following subsections concentrates on one of the different levels of reuse and tries to identify whether the promised abstraction level from theory was reached in practice.

5.1 Lower Layers

On the lowest layer, there was a decision to exchange/upgrade the hardware, in particular to allow for more processing power and thus increased performance, more memory, different form factors and/or additional hardware features. With it came the decision to use a new platform that shall enable tapping into all the beforementioned improvements. Therefore, the new hardware and platform were given by the cooperating company—while our software for the to-be-built product was the variable that had to be adaptable.

Implications in Practice: While the previous Real Time Operating System (RTOS) in use was OSE Epsilon[7], the next operating system to be used was Nucleus OS[8]. The currently existing ULC2[9] target platform was to be replaced by the Mediatek (MTK) platform[10]. While the previous hardware was based on a C166 processor by Infineon[11], the next processor was to be an ARM 7[12]. With that, the toolchain for building the target system changed. One such changed element was the need to use an ARM compiler—a target compiler change that would prove to have an influence when trying to compile the generated code for the new environment, as pointed out in Subsection 5.4. All in all, the concerned layers were completely replaced, as decided by company policy. The subsequent subsections will address the required adaptations.

---

[7] http://www.enea.com/
[8] http://www.mentor.com/embedded-software/nucleus/
[9] http://www.intel.com/products/wireless/mobilecommunications/platforms/
[10] http://www.mediatek.com/en/index.php
[11] http://www.infineon.com/
[12] http://www.arm.com/products/processors/classic/arm7/index.php

5.2 Adaptation Layers

As our name for these layers implies, these layers are key to all porting efforts, as they have to mediate between the platform-independent upper tiers and the platform-specific middleware, drivers, protocol stack and hardware. Two different aspects have to be covered:

OSAL: Rhapsody's *Operating System Abstraction Layer (OSAL)* must be adapted to be used with the new Nucleus RTOS. *Rhapsody in C* already comes with an OSAL for Nucleus PLUS, however specifically targeted to PPC CPUs. For this reason, plus the requirement to be compatible with MTK, which already had its own hardware abstraction layer, the OSAL had to be adapted to our specific needs. Specifically, memory management and thread management had to be adjusted (e.g., to prevent delays in controlling the display, as previously experienced).

API Implementations: As the API implementation layer comprises the realization of the API interfaces, all the realization code must be replaced in order to tap into MTK's middleware. The actual function to read the IMEI of the device, the function to set up a call or to perform a manual network search are just a few examples of what had to be adjusted on this level.

5.3 Logic/UI Layers

In theory, as pointed out in Subsection 3.1, none of the layers on this level must be modified on platform change. In our project, this ideal assumption could not completely hold true, as is pointed out below.

API Interfaces: With the recent release of Rhapsody version 7.5.2, a concept called *Variation Points* has been introduced. It allows to model alternative variants of a specific component or class (e.g., to model platform-specific variants of an Audio API). Technically, a variation point is just a stereotype that, once applied to a class, internally generates similar code than the simulated interface solution introduced in Subsection 4.1. The important advantageous difference is however that while all platform variations still exist concurrently in the model, a specific variant can easily be selected (as easy as selecting the proper variant from a dropdown list), thus simplifying working on different API implementations by different users concurrently. As the code generator knows which parts of the model represent a specific variant, it only generates the required code for the currently selected platform, leading to a reduced memory footprint compared to the previous solution (precisely speaking, such behavior could be enforced e.g. using preprocessor conditional blocks in the interface-based solution, too—but only at the cost of increased manual effort). Having the potential of mitigating the problems of a purely simulated interface solution, we decided to change the model on this level and use variation points wherever appropriate. This introduced an additional time delay, but can be considered worth the effort as the model is now cleaner and future-proven for the next platform change.

Application logic: The promise for the application logic of not having to change at all when the underlying platform changes held true. Therefore, the previously modeled application logic could immediately be reused and no porting effort was required.

MMI definition: Similarly, the MMI definition, modeled in a WYSIWYG editor and expressed internally as XML files, would not have to be changed either. Only due to the changed hardware, the MMI required minor adaptations. For example, as the new model would not have a slider, this had to be reflected in the MMI definition. Apart from such direct requirements resulting from hardware change, no further porting effort was required, and the very benefits of a model-driven solution could be experienced.

5.4 Problems Spanning Multiple Layers

Another impact we experienced was that some of the generated code from the UML model—mostly code we have written into Entry/Exit actions—would not build for the new target architecture. Some of the reasons plus lessons learned were:

- **Different compiler warning level:** As the newly used ARM target compiler had a stricter warning level set, some generated statements wouldn't compile. What previously raised a warning was now treated as an error. Thus, errors were detected that were not discovered before. Some examples are *"...different types for formal and actual parameter"* or *"...'xxx' undefined; assuming extern returning int"*. On the previous platform, such inconsistencies would often have resulted in runtime errors during execution.

    Lesson learned: Using a reasonably high compiler warning level right from the start helps to detect issues early, and reduces the porting efforts when changing to a different target compiler.

- **Datatypes:** Rhapsody provides basic C datatypes (e.g., char, int) and language-independent datatypes (such as RhpInteger, a qualifier that could be equally used in Rhapsody for C, C++, Java and Ada, and translates to an integer in each language). However, we had to discover that real platform-independent datatypes were not fully supported. A platform-independent datatype in that sense was a datatype with a specified width in bits, such as `UINT16` for an unsigned integer 16 bits wide—both built-in type classes did not specify a fixed width. In practice, under certain circumstances parameters or return values specified as plain integers for the previous platform resulted in a runtime failure due to a different datatype size on the new platform—which is not a surprise, it's just that support for defining proper types was not satisfying. Of course it is possible to define custom datatypes—but the mapping to the platform (e.g. what native datatype (e.g. `unsigned short` or `unsigned int`) represents an UINT16 on platform X) is *not* in a platform-dependent specification file. As a result, developers must take care of correct specification whenever the OXF layer is built anew

(as opposed to the mapping could ideally be read from a platform-specific file, requiring the user to manually take care of correct specification only once per platform, not once per new OXF building, as the portable files are shared). As datatype sizes vary often between different embedded systems, this is a crucial feature. However, it can be blamed to be a Rhapsody-specific issue (a corresponding change request has been filed and agreed to by IBM).
Lesson learned: Investigate a tool's support for defining platform-independent datatypes early.
- **Wrapper functions:** Another carelessness was to trust that very common C functions would be available on all platforms. Examples are `printf` to put text or certain string functions such as `strcpy`. However, we had to learn that even some of the most basic functions are not guaranteed to be available on every platform (a similar function usually exists, but could have a different name or parameters).
  Lesson learned: Abstracting even very basic functions into wrapper functions saves a lot of effort.

Following best practices [11] such as *strict compilation, segregating platform-dependent files from portable files, abstracting data types, wrapping functions, using various compilers* is highly recommended. Assuming one's model is portable is only valid after it has actually been ported.

6 Conclusion and Future Work

Applying an model-driven approach in a real world project might not always be the best choice but can definitely be a smart one under certain circumstances. It is important that you are aware at the beginning of the project that creating a solution with MDA for the first time is more time consuming—at least that is what we experienced—than traditional ways of development. Important for a successful MDA project are the features provided by the used modeling tool. Especially the support for code generation and code portability are key features a tool has to fulfill. The approach explained in this paper was applied to an actual project and has itself proven successful. Advantages opposed to a conventional development approach can be found in the animation capabilities for model debugging, which encourages correcting bugs early in the design phase, and in the much quicker process of porting the software to a new embedded platform due to the platform-independence inherent to the model. Although these features help during the process they have downsides—e.g., time-consuming animation setup time—and therefore have not been used excessively.

For the case study at hand, quantitative information (e.g., to better compare the model-based approach to a traditional one) has not been included, since no hard facts, but only anecdotal evidence exists: In retrospective, the initial model-based implementation took us about a year for the first platform. Later, when porting the system to a second platform, it only took us about three months for a proof of concept, and three more months for achieving the same functionality. However, future work could focus on the evaluation between a conventional and a model-based solution to derive metrics for more precise quantitative information.

References

1. Object Management Group, MDA Guide Version 1.0.1. Object Management Group, Tech. Rep. (2003)
2. Mellor, S.J., Scott, K., Uhl, A., Weise, D.: MDA Distilled – Principles of Model-Driven Architecture. Addison-Wesley, Reading (2004)
3. Hitz, K., Kappel.: UML @ Work. dpunkt.verlag (2005)
4. Schaetz, B., Rappl, M., Hain, T., Houdek, F., Wisspeintner, A., Houdek, F., Prenninger, W., Romberg, J., Slotosch, O., Strecker, M., Wisspeintner, E., Angerer, C., Glaser, M., Merenda, C., Trimeche, A., Zaouia, A., Jiang, H., Lanthaler, C., Ossipov, P., Fichtner, T.: Case tools for embedded systems (2003)
5. IBM Corporation, Rational Rhapsody User Guide (2009)
6. Lettner, M., Tschernuth, M.: Applied MDA for Embedded Devices: Software Design and Code Generation for a Low-Cost Mobile Phone. In: Computer Software and Applications Conference Workshops, pp. 63–68 (2010)
7. Gomaa, H.: Designing Software Product Lines with UML: From Use Cases to Pattern-Based Software Architectures. Addison-Wesley, Reading (2004)
8. Angyal, L., Lengyel, L., Charaf, H.: A synchronizing technique for syntactic model-code round-trip engineering. In: 15th Annual IEEE International Conference and Workshop on the Engineering of Computer Based Systems, ECBS 2008, 31 2008-April 4 2008, pp. 463–472 (2008)
9. Hanson, D.R.: C Interfaces and Implementations: Techniques for Creating Reusable Software. Addison-Wesley, Reading (1996)
10. IBM Corporation, Rational Rhapsody Team Collaboration Guide (2009)
11. Hook, B.: Write Portable Code: An Introduction to Developing Software for Multiple Platforms. No Starch Press (2005)

Designing Heterogeneous Component Based Systems: Evaluation of MARTE Standard and Enhancement Proposal

Ali Koudri[1], Arnaud Cuccuru[2], Sebastien Gerard[2], and François Terrier[2]

[1] Thales Research and Technology
[2] CEA

Abstract. Building complex real-time embedded systems requires assembly of heterogeneous components, possibly using various computation and communication models. A great challenge is to be able to design such systems using models where these heterogeneity characteristics are described precisely to assist the next step of the development including implementation or analysis. Although the new MARTE standard provides the core concepts to model real-time components using various communication paradigms, we state in this paper that MARTE extensions have still to be made and we propose to extract common features from several component based approaches in order to support finer compositions of heterogeneous sub-systems.

1 Introduction

Building real-time embedded systems through composition of well-defined and well-documented components is a tricky issue. Composition provides means to deal with complexity applying the "divide to conquer" paradigm.

In the field of software engineering, composition issues are addressed by the Component Based Development (CBD) domain. Historically, CBD comes from disciplines of mechanical and electrical engineering where components are intuitively understood. In the field of real-time embedded systems (RTES), composition is difficult to achieve as complexity is increased by sub-systems heterogeneity (analog / digital devices, Globally Asynchronous Locally Synchronous systems – GALS, etc.) and real-time or other QoS issues. Then, a solid alternative is to consider UML models to handle such heterogeneity in a unified way. Unfortunately, current modeling languages lack means to specify rich interfacing and connections between components in both software and hardware domains.

In this paper, we are interested in the "Interface Based Programming" applied to Model Based Engineering (MBE). In particular, we study how assembly can be achieved (interfacing conditions and constraints) and realized (allocation / implementation). We propose then to refine the notions of port, interface and connector of the MARTE GCM (Generic Component Model) sub-profile in order to achieve better composition and substitution capabilities in the context of heterogeneous real-time embedded systems design and analysis.

In the next section, we provide a short survey on component-based approaches from several communities in order to extract key features component models should provide. Then, we list identified issues related to composition in UML, SysML and MARTE. In the third section, we propose a generic solution for composing heterogeneous system models. In conclusion, we provide insights on our future work.

2 Background

In software engineering, a component is defined as "a piece of self-contained, self-deployable computer code with well-defined functionality that can be assembled with other components through its interface" [14]. More precisely, a component model defines "rules for the specification of component properties and mechanisms for component composition, including composition rules of component properties". This definition distinguishes three important parts: the specification of components *internals*, including functional and non-functional properties; the specification of components *interfaces*, e.g. what they provide/require to/from their environment; the specification of *interactions*. While the first and the second parts are usually well addressed by *architectural patterns*, the third part is usually not explicitly specified and is related to implicit *communication patterns*.

In order to provide a better understanding of composition, authors of [2] present a framework for software components that compares interfacing and interaction styles. According to this survey, an interface is mainly characterized by: its type, e.g. operation-based (service invocations) or port-based (data-flow); the distinction between its provided/required parts; the existence of distinctive features (optional modes); its specification language; its contractualisation level (syntactic / semantic / behavioral). Besides, authors characterize interactions by: their interaction type (e.g. request/response, message passing or event-driven); their communication type (e.g. synchronous or asynchronous); their binding type (e.g. connection, hierarchy or both).

In hardware engineering, evolution of technologies has pushed the usage of hardware components as well. Indeed, design of Integrated Circuits (IC) or Very Large Scale Integrated Circuits (VLSI) requires techniques to handle exponential complexity due to Moore's law. Then, hardware engineers can achieve a better productivity assembling reusable and reliable blocks (Intellectual Properties – IP): microprocessor, DSP, memory, bus, etc. Indeed, component-based approaches have been long used with success in hardware engineering and have proven their relevancy to handle complexity and productivity.

Unfortunately, the aforementioned approaches are mainly focused on implementation issues and higher level approaches are required to favor analysis activities. To this end, several Architecture Description Languages (ADL) have been proposed in both software and hardware domains. According to [9], the purpose of an ADL is to shift from lines-of-code to coarser-grained architectural elements (components and connectors). Then, authors define an Architecture Description Language as "a language that provides features for modeling a software system's conceptual architecture distinguished from the system's implementation." Still, there is no consensus on what aspects of architecture should be modeled and interchanged. For instance, among all existing ADLs, some of them are just used to provide a better understanding of the system (global behavior and communications) while other provide full featured language along with analysis tools, checkers, compilers, synthesis tools, etc.

Whatever, an ADL should provide at least a simple and understandable syntax, possibly graphical, to improve the system analysis. This syntax must rely on a clear semantics avoiding ambiguities. In [13], authors elaborate six classes of properties all ADLs should provide: composition, abstraction, reusability, configuration, heterogeneity and analysis. In particular, they argue the *need to consider the connector as a first-class entity to support heterogeneity*. In [9], authors provide a comparison framework for ADLs. In this framework, both component and connector are characterized by their: *Interfaces*, defining a set of interaction points providing/requiring services (messages, operations, variables) to/from external world – Services are related to computations in the case of components and to communications in the case of connectors; *Types*, defining a configurable abstraction allowing re-usability, and extensibility – *Modeling connectors as type makes sense* because interactions are often characterized by complex protocols; *Semantics*, representing a high level behavioral model which is required to perform analysis or to ensure consistent mappings from one level of abstraction to another; *Constraints*, defining assertions whose violation would render the system unacceptable; *Non-functional properties*, e.g. properties that cannot be derived directly from the specification of behaviors (safety, security, performance, etc.). Such properties are required early in the design process to perform relevant analysis or to foster replaceability in context.

3 Motivations

The specification of UML 2.0 [10] introduces several important concepts for supporting composition: Collaboration, Port, Connector, etc. Unfortunately, the semantics of those elements is generally not well defined. The main reason of this lack is because such semantics depends on target domains. Indeed, it is suggested in p.147 of the specification that "profiles based around components will be developed for specific component technologies". In SysML [11], components have been introduced under the notion of "Block" which is defined as "a modular unit of system description" providing general purpose capabilities to model large and heterogeneous systems. SysML refines the UML components in different ways: reusable constraints, multi-level nesting of connector ends, etc. In MARTE [12], the *Generic Component Model* (GCM) sub-profile provides the core concepts to model real-time and embedded system components. Those concepts represent a common denominator among various component models (lightweight-CCM, AADL, EAST-ADL2, etc.) except that no specific execution semantics has been tied. For instance, a structured component is defined as "a self-contained entity of a system which may encapsulate structured data and behaviors".

Regarding UML components, several issues have been raised by the OMG and show inconsistencies in both syntax and semantics:

- Handling of requests by ports (behavioral or not) is not clear (issue 10597),
- Typing a port by a class, behavioral or not, has not a clear semantics (issue 15290),
- Connectors do not provide means for specifying an interaction pattern between involved roles played at connector ends (issue 10474).

Even if SysML proposes refinements of ports, interfaces and connectors, there are still several lacks and semantics issues that have been raised:

- In some situations, it would be useful to be able to attach a protocol state machine to ports (issue 10047),
- Handling of complex ports, mixing services and data-flows, is not well addressed (issues 10059 and 12269),
- Nothing is said about the semantics of binding connector ends with different multiplicities (issue 11333), and particularly in the context of continuous flows (issue 15298),
- Binding connectors should be typed in order to support decomposition (issue 15079),
- There are limitations to represent certain kinds of interfaces (mechanical, electrical, etc.) and ports. For instance, issues 12156 and 15076, propose to introduce the notions of "Junction Port" and "Non-flow property Port". Issue 13179 adds that, in this context, an integration of Modelica concepts should be discussed,
- Issue 13178 suggests that a flow specification should not be a refinement of an interface because port decomposition in that case would not be possible.

Since MARTE reuse definitions of SysML blocks, interfaces and connectors, issues presented above are also applicable in this language. To give insights to those questions, we use the study from section 2 to abstract common denominators so we can propose a flexible way to specify components and composition that takes into account systems heterogeneity. This work is required in order to foster the use of models for design, analysis and implementation of RTES.

4 Contribution

Ideally, the MBE combined with CBD provides a powerful approach as it facilitates design and analysis activities though a clear separation of concerns. In practice, this is another story; and before such approach comes to reality, we have to make efforts to finely characterize components, their interfaces and connectors. To this purpose, we propose to extend the component model of the MARTE GCM sub-profile to tackle issues presented in section 3. This work aims to improve analysis as it contributes to handle emergent behaviors related to implicit choices.

4.1 Core Principles

Today, design methodologies and environments integrating semantically distinct models are in high demand [4]. From study of section 2, we can state that, at some level, hardware and software developments are quite similar: engineers have to think in terms of data, computation, communication and architecture. Then, a system should be conceived as an understandable architecture of cooperating agents which characteristics and interactions should be well understood under a certain Model of Computation (MoC). For instance, the rugby conceptual model [7] states that from specification to implementation, the complexity of a system can be managed through several representations mainly characterized by four axes: *Computation* represents relationship between the inputs and the output of the system: it can be captured for example by an Ordinary Differential Equation at high level or a Netlist at low level; *Communication* represents means for structural elements to exchange data: it can be a functional call at high level or a complex bus at low level; *Data* represents information produced or consumed by structural elements: it can be abstract data types at high level or bit vectors at low level; *Time* represents the causality of the system: it can be causal at high level (succession of events) or clocked at low-level.

Modeling and analysis of complex systems, composing heterogeneous parts, requires taking into account each of those properties. In particular, we need to understand in what circumstances interactions between such heterogeneous parts can occur. According to [6], modeling explicitly MoCs characteristics has several advantages: *Faster specification development* through usage of appropriate primitives and rules; *Optimum simulation speed* using a unified simulation engine instead of using multiple languages / frameworks; *Useful properties*: determinism, protection against deadlocks, introduction of non-determinism only when needed; *Feasible implementation flow* through usage of a syntax which is semantically identifiable by compilation / synthesis tools.

Besides, in [5], authors identify two kinds of specification / integration of MoCs. The first one, called *horizontal heterogeneity*, refers to the ability to integrate a component among others on the same level of abstraction. The second one, called *vertical heterogeneity*, is mainly related to refinements of components between several levels of abstraction and requires transformations.

The next section presents the main concept of our extension to address modeling of heterogeneity for RTES design and analysis.

4.2 Main Concepts

Complex ports. In order to tackle issues related to ports presented in the previous section, we introduce the notion of "complex port" in the GCM MARTE sub-profile. This notion refines the UML port in order to support structural decomposition as well as behavioral specification. A complex port conforms to a "port specification" which defines its structural and behavioral features (figure 1). Its usage serves several purposes.

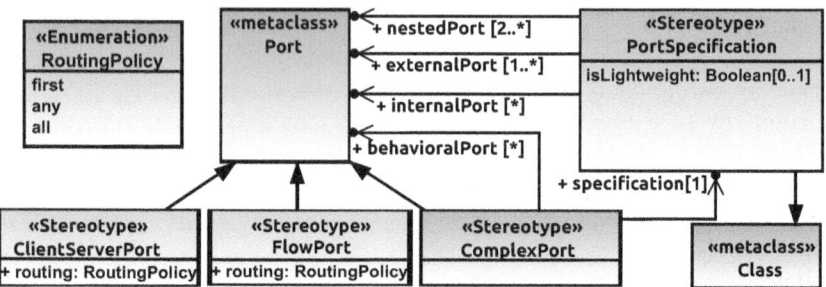

Fig. 1. Refinement of MARTE GCM Port Definition

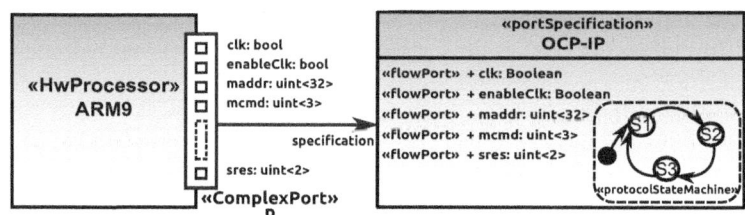

Fig. 2. Ports Group definition

First of all, building large hierarchical systems often requires gathering ports into groups to favor readability and reusability. For instance, figure 2 shows a simple concrete example of complex port usage extracted from OCP/IP specification [1]. We can see in this figure how a complex port can be used to gather a set of ports into a reusable element. We can also notice that such representation improves the readability of the models. Regarding the issues presented above, this first example shows how our proposition contributes to tackle issue 13178.

Another benefit of this proposition is to be able to explicit the way requests / flows must be handled. Indeed, a port specification can contain definition of specific data structures and behaviors required to implement a protocol (using protocol state machines for example) in case of client / server ports, or to specify how received data are transformed in case of flow ports. Then, the property "isLightweight" indicates whether the port has to perform some computation on received data / requests. Setting this property to "false" implies for the port: the specification of discrete or continuous behavior; the specification of both external / internal interfaces, e.g. what is provided / required to / from respectively the context and the nested elements of the component. External and internal interfaces of a port represent two subsets of its nested ports. The first one (external interface) contains ports that are externally visible features (*isService=true*), while the second one are only internally visible features (*isService=false*).

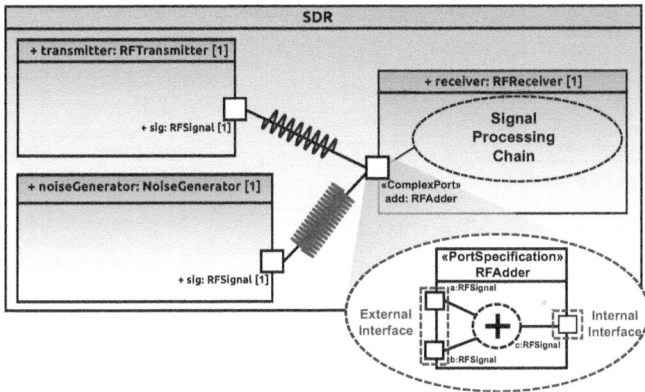

Fig. 3. Specifying junction ports

The figure 3 shows a simple concrete example from a "Software Defined Radio" application where there is a need to specify that incoming signals are mixed before being processed by the signal processing chain. The ports specification of this figure defines actually a junction port where signals mixing occur.

In software domain, one could use for example port specification to store arrival requests (possibly with a timeout) until they are consumed by nested behavior(s). We can see that, in this case, our proposition contributes to give an answer to issues 10597, 15290, 10047, 12156, 13179 and 15076. Additionally, complex ports decomposition allows mixing both services and data-flows ports in an explicit way, which contributes to give an answer to issues 10059 and 12269.

Finally, our proposition addresses also the routing issue, e.g. how a request / flow is propagated to /from the component in case of multiple choices? UML is not clear on that point. We think that such decision is domain dependant and should be explicitly captured in the model. The *Routing Policy* defined by the port tells whether to propagate the request to the first connector (*routing=first*), to any of those connector (*routing=any*) or to all connectors (*routing=all*). For a finer routing decision, one can use a complex connector defining a path between internal and external interfaces.

Complex connectors. Introducing complex ports requires dedicated mechanisms to take into account hierarchy of complex ports. To this purpose, and to clarify inter-connections in UML, we introduce the notion of *complex connector*.

The figure 4 shows the abstract syntax of complex connector which extends the UML connector in order to reinforce its semantic and to provide syntactic facilities to express multi-level nested connections.

In order to better explain introduced concepts, we distinguish three cases in the following paragraphs: the first one clarifies connections in UML; the second one deals with inter-connections of complex ports; the last one discusses usage of typed complex connectors.

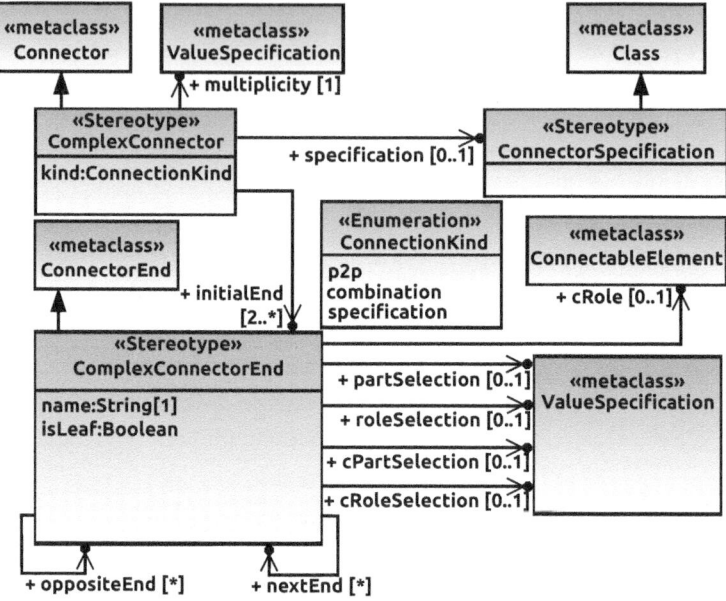

Fig. 4. Refinement of MARTE GCM Connector Definition

To illustrate the first item, we will use an image processing application as example. We consider a piece of the Lucas-Kanade algorithm dedicated to tracking [8] presented in figure 5.

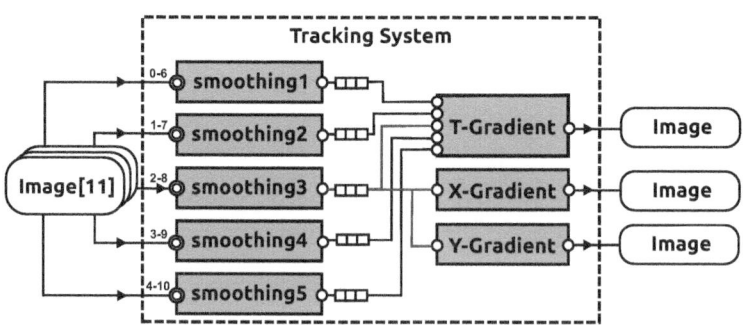

Fig. 5. Tracking System Data-Flow

In this figure, we can see that the algorithm takes as input a set of eleven images which are distributed among 5 Gaussian Smoothing blocks. The resulting images are then passed to 3 different blocks that perform spatial and temporal gradients to produce new images.

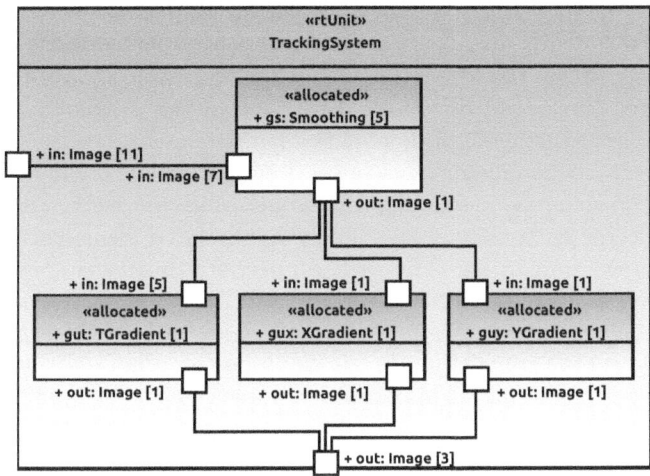

Fig. 6. Tracking System Model

To model this algorithm using UML composite structure and flow ports, we would produce the diagram presented in figure 6. This diagram makes benefits of syntactic facilities of UML to produce a concise model. Unfortunately, because interpretation of cardinalities of both parts and ports between connected elements is not clear in UML, it is quite impossible to infer the architecture presented in figure 5 from the model of the figure 6.

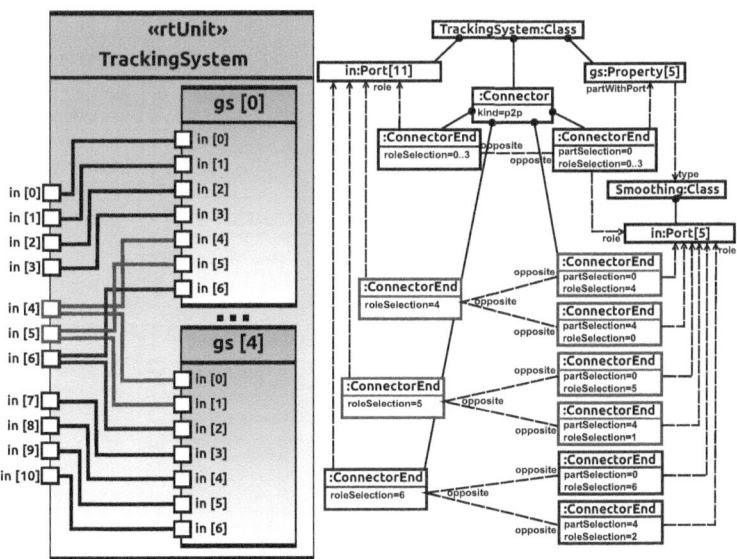

Fig. 7. On richer connection specification

The figure 7 illustrates how our proposition addresses this problem. In the left side of the figure, we can see how the delegation connector set between the input port of the tracking system and the "gs" part should be interpreted. Such interpretation could be achieved in UML at the price of big efforts using OCL constraints. In the right side of the figure, we can see the corresponding repository view. A connector owns several *connector ends* which store relevant information on richer connection specification. More precisely, a connector owns several connector ends that precise finely how related elements are connected. In this example, we can see that each *connector end* selects specific parts and roles from respectively their *partWithPort* and *role* properties using value specification. In this case, we have just used an index to select which parts and roles are involved into the connection, but it could be any other discriminating factor (the best QoS for example). This simple example can also be applied to assembly connector as well as connectors related to service ports. This example shows how our proposition contributes to give an answer to issues 11333 and 15298.

To illustrate the second item, e.g. connection between complex ports, we use the example of the figure 8 which shows a connection between an abstraction of an ARM9 processor and an OCP-IP bus, both complying with OCP-IP standard specification [1].

In this example, we aim to express connections between nested ports defined by ports specification. Using UML, we can connect only the first level of the port hierarchy. Thanks to our extension, it is possible to precise which "sub-ports"

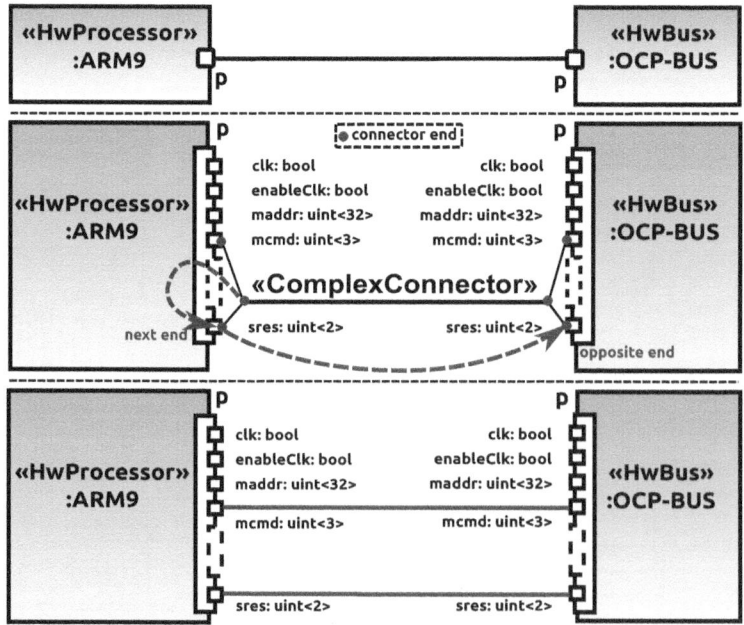

Fig. 8. Connecting Complex Ports

are connected to each other. The upper part of this figure shows the connection between two complex ports of the two parts of the hardware design. Using UML connectors cannot fit the need to specify how the connector is refined through port decomposition. Then, the middle part of the figure shows in more details how a complex connector can be used to achieve such refinement. For instance, we show in this figure that the connector contains two *initial ends* connecting the first level of the ports hierarchy. The connector owns other connector ends that define a path from initial ends. In this example, we can see that *each initial end posses a reference (next end)* to another connector end. Connector ends that are leaf reference one or several opposite ends from which we can infer the refinement of the connector as shown in the lower part of the figure.

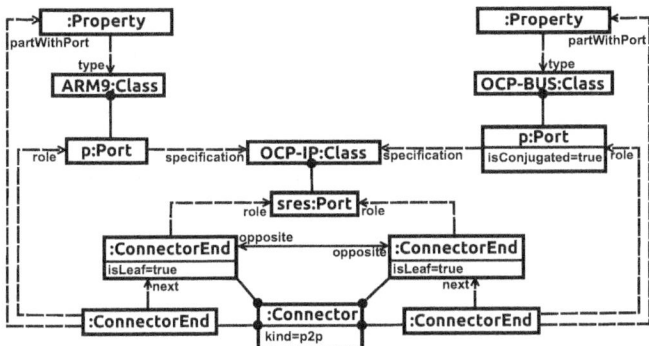

Fig. 9. Repository view

The model repository view presented in figure 9 shows that our proposition clarifies the specification of interconnections between nested ports. This figure focuses on interconnections between sub-ports "sres" of the figure 8. Compared to the RSM sub-profile of MARTE which allows only specification of regular patterns [3] in complex connections, our proposition is complementary as it allows specification of irregular patterns as well. We see through this small example how our proposition contributes to give a partial answer to issues 10474 and 15079.

Regarding the last case, connectors must provide more detailed information to precise finely how messages are conveyed between ports. According to the UML specification, a connector can be realized by a simple pointer as well as a complex network. In the latter case, a connector can be seen as a black box into which several kinds of operation can occur: dispatching, filtering, data corruption, data transformation, etc. Then, in order to achieve realistic analysis, we must be able to specify such features for any complex connector. A UML connector can only be typed by an association, which represents a great limitation to model any behavioral feature required to model and analyze complex communications. That is why we have introduced the notion of *connector specification* to type connectors. A connector specification gathers a set of common features a family of connectors share. For example, the connector between the "Smoothing3" block and the three "Gradient" blocks of the figure 5 illustrates such complex connector. In this example, each image produced by the "Smoothing" block is sent to "X-Gradient" and "Y-Gradient" blocks. Produced images are then queued because the "T-Gradient" block requires 5 images to perform a computation. This kind of model corresponds actually to the Synchronous Data Flow MoC where production and consumption rates are well-known. As we cannot specify such connector using an UML association, the figure 10 shows how our proposition handles this issue.

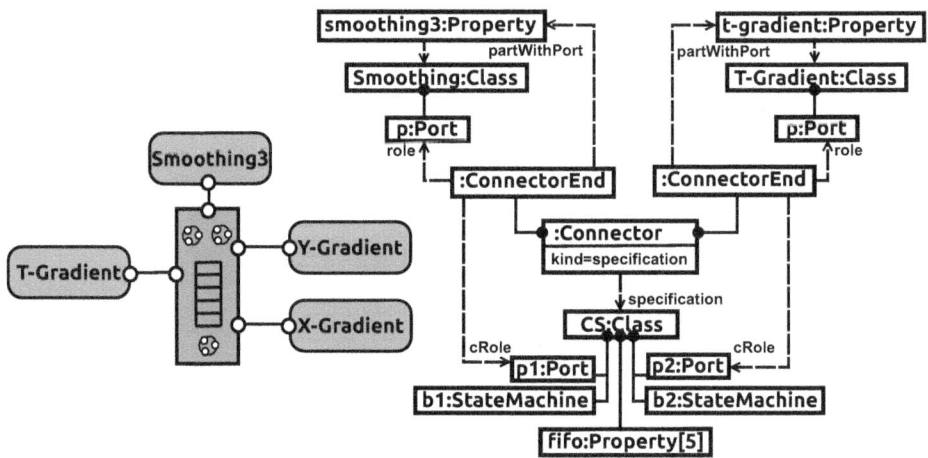

Fig. 10. On richer connection specification

In this example, the specification of the connector is given by the "CS" class which defines one fifo to store incoming images and two behaviors triggered when new images are ready to be processed. The first behavior copies the incoming image into the fifo and the second one sends a block of five images to the "T-Gradient" block when the fifo is full.

Interface realization and usage. We have seen in section 3 that Interface Based Programming is the support of the *replaceability in context*. An interface defines common features a set of components should provide to be used indifferently. This suggests that there exists somehow a matching between the features an interface exposes and the visible features of the implementing component. In current approaches, such matching is implicit and consists usually in name matching. We have seen in section 2 that, among existing CBD approaches, there are several level of conformance between an interface and its implementations (syntactic, structural or behavioral). In this paper, we distinguish between three incremental levels of conformity: *Structural conformity*: a component is replaceable if it has compatible properties; *Behavioral conformity*: a component is replaceable if it has compatible properties and behaviors (example: protocol); *Non-functional conformity*: a component is replaceable if it has compatible properties and behaviors, and it provides the same non-functional properties (example: latency).

Using UML, one can specify that a classifier realizes an interface using the *Interface Realization* direct relationship. This relationship references the contract and the implementing classifier. Thus, the metamodel assumes only a syntactic conformance since no additional information is given about the level of conformance and the way the implementing classifier implements / uses effectively a contract. In RTES, this situation is not acceptable as RTES requires more than a syntactic conformity to allow replacement of a component by one another. We propose then to refine both interface realization and usage.

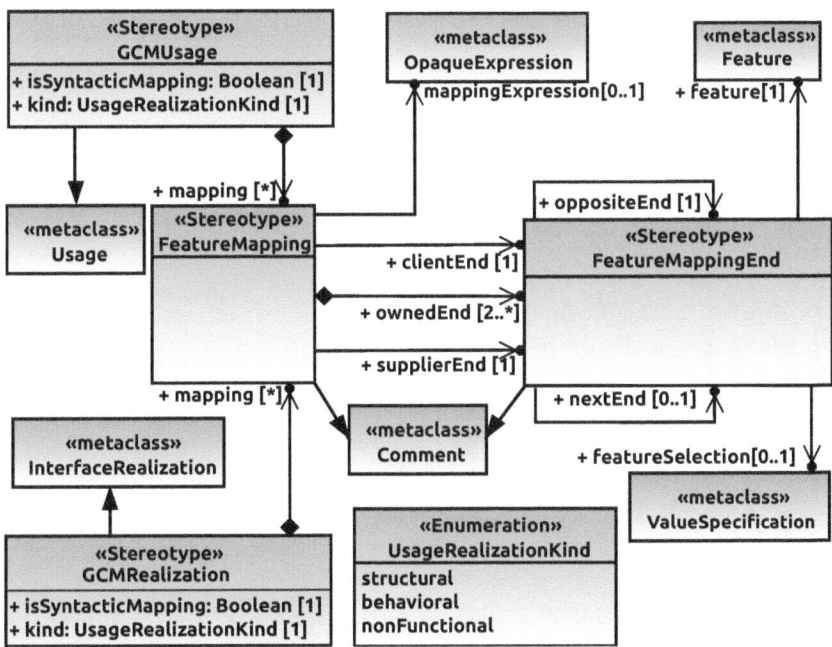

Fig. 11. Refinement of MARTE GCM Interface Definition

Figure 11 presents the abstract syntax of our proposition which is illustrated through the example of the figure 12 taken from the Lucas-Kanade algorithm mentioned above. The left side of the figure 12 tells that the "IMultiplier" block conforms to the "IMultIface" interface, although the signatures of its properties are not the same either in name or in cardinality. In this case, syntactic conformance does not work. Then, we need additional information in the interface realization link to specify how the implementing block actually realizes its interface. We need to express a fine mapping between the properties of the interfaces and the ones of the block. The right side of the figure shows the model repository view focusing on the feature mapping between property "img1" of the interface and the port "itxy[0]" of the block.

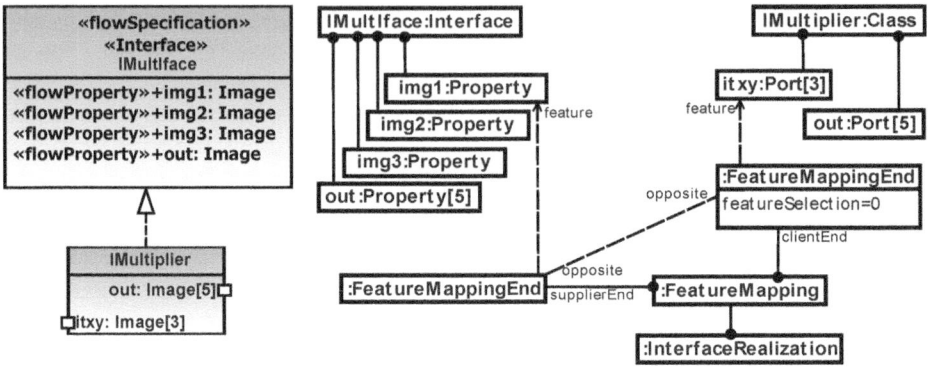

Fig. 12. Example of interface realization

Besides, finer mappings can be expressed using a mapping expression in the feature mapping. For instance, one could split a single property into two distinct properties. For example, we could imagine an unsigned integer property coded into 32 bits ($uint < 32 >$) mapped into two unsigned integer ports coded into 16 bits ($uint < 16 >$) for both Most Significant Bits (MSB) and Least Significant Bits (LSB) parts of the property.

We see through this simple example that our proposition contributes to clarify interfaces usage and realization. Moreover, such specification can be used to automate generation of wrappers or complex connectors facilitating COTS IP integration.

5 Conclusion

Component Oriented Modeling offers several advantages: It is an interface-based approach providing loosely-coupled specifications and favoring better reuse; It provides high level services for NFP (Non-Functional Properties) support; It provides a better support of allocation. Actually, those assumptions are true only if the semantics of components and composition of heterogeneous systems are clearly and unambiguously defined.

In this paper, we have presented a small survey on component based approaches from several domains. From this survey, we have extracted common denominators in order to propose a generic approach that encompasses design and analysis of heterogeneous real-time systems. This proposition aims to give a practical answer to issues raised by the OMG and contributes to reinforce the semantics of real-time components and composition in the UML for MARTE profile.

Beyond UML for MARTE, this work can be generalized to the component model of UML. This work contributes also to explicit the various models of computation and communication of real-time embedded systems. It allows the establishment of libraries of reusable and configurable ports and connectors. Future works will have to take into account system validation through vertical refinements of components as well as support of behavioral and non-functional conformity in order to enable component replaceability in context. This work is partially founded by the VERDE project (http://www.itea-verde.org/).

References

1. Open core protocol specification
2. Crnkovic, I., Chaudron, M., Sentilles, S., Vulgarakis, A.: A classification framework for component models. In: Proceedings of the 7th Conference on Software Engineering and Practice in Sweden (October 2007)
3. Cuccuru, A., Dekeyser, J.-L., Marquet, P., Boulet, P.: Towards UML 2 extensions for compact modeling of regular complex topologies. In: Briand, L.C., Williams, C. (eds.) MoDELS 2005. LNCS, vol. 3713, pp. 445–459. Springer, Heidelberg (2005)
4. Eker, J., Janneck, J., Lee, E.A., Liu, J., Liu, X., Ludvig, J., Sachs, S., Xiong, Y.: Taming heterogeneity - the ptolemy approach. Proceedings of the IEEE 91(1), 127–144 (2003), http://chess.eecs.berkeley.edu/pubs/488.html
5. Herrera, F., Villar, E.: A framework for heterogeneous specification and design of electronic embedded systems in systemc. ACM Trans. Des. Autom. Electron. Syst. 12(3), 1–31 (2007)
6. Jantsch, A.: Modeling Embedded Systems and SoCs. Morgan Kaufmann, San Francisco (2004)
7. Jantsch, A., Kumar, S., Hemani, A.: A metamodel for studying concepts in electronic system design. IEEE Des. Test 17(3), 78–85 (2000)
8. Mahalingam, V., Bhattacharya, K., Ranganathan, N., Chakravarthula, H., Murphy, R.R., Pratt, K.S.: A vlsi architecture and algorithm for lucas-kanade-based optical flow computation. IEEE Trans. Very Large Scale Integr. Syst. 18(1), 29–38 (2010)
9. Medvidovic, N., Taylor, R.N.: A classification and comparison framework for software architecture description languages. IEEE Trans. Softw. Eng. 26(1), 70–93 (2000)
10. OMG: Omg unified modeling languagetm (omg uml) superstructure (v2.3). Tech. rep., OMG (2010)
11. OMG: Sysml 1.1. Tech. rep., OMG (2010)
12. OMG: Uml for marte 1.0. Tech. rep., OMG (2010)
13. Shaw, M., Garlan, D.: Characteristics of higher-level languages for software architecture. Tech. rep., Carnegie Mellon Univ. (1994)
14. Wang, A.J.A., Qian, K.: Component-Oriented Programming. Wiley, Chichester (2005)

Semantic Clone Detection for Model-Based Development of Embedded Systems

Bakr Al-Batran[1], Bernhard Schätz[1], and Benjamin Hummel[2]

[1] fortiss GmbH, München, Germany
{albatran,schaetz}@fortiss.org
[2] Fakultät für Informatik, Technische Universität München, Germany
hummelb@in.tum.de

Abstract. With model-based development becoming an increasingly common development methodology in embedded systems engineering, models have become an important asset of the the software development process. Therefore, techniques for the automatic detection of clones in those models have been developed to improve their maintainability. As these approaches currently only consider syntactic clones, the detection of clones is limited to syntactically equivalent copies. Using the concept of normal forms, these approaches can be extended to also cover semantic clones with identical behavior but different structure. The submission presents a generalized concept of clones for Simulink models, describes a pattern-based normal-form approach, and discusses results of the application of an implementation of this approach.

1 Introduction

Software has become the driving force in many application domains for embedded systems, like the automotive domain. Consequently, software in these domains has reached a substantial size. Furthermore, the developed software systems make use of a high degree of reuse, due to the large number of variants in product-lines, high cost pressure, and decreasing length of innovation cycles. As a result, software maintenance – corrective as well as perfective – has become an important aspect of the current development process. In automotive software development, the use of a model-based approach has become standard, specially in the powertrain, chassis, and body domain. Therefore, the maintenance of those models – with Simulink or TargetLink as the corresponding domain specific language – is becoming an increasingly pressing issue.

In code based development, the existence of clones [12] – duplicate or similar parts of software – is specifically known to often worsen productivity in software maintenance. With the move from code to models in the embedded domain, the question arises how to deal with clones in model-based development.

1.1 Problem and Contribution

As discussed in more detail in Section 2, clones can severely hamper the maintainability of models of embedded systems. However, only few approaches for detection of those clones exist. Furthermore, these approaches are limited to a rather restricted *syntactic* notion of similarity – essentially structural identity. Therefore, an improved technique for model-clone detection is introduced, supporting detection of *semantic clones*, i.e., parts of models with different structure but equivalent behavior. The approach is based on the use of *normal forms* of Simulink models to identify semantic clones with different syntactic structures, and the use of *semantic-preserving graph transformations* to achieve them.

1.2 Outline

Section 2 gives a short introduction on the detection of clones, especially in the context of model-based development of embedded systems. Section 3 provides a description of the core aspects of the approach; furthermore, examples of the normalizing transformations used are given. Section 4 describes the application of the approach to realistic models and discusses the results of the application. Finally, Section 5 discusses related works, while Section 6 concludes with a discussion of the application of the approach and possible future work.

2 Clones in Model-Based Development

Although model-based engineering has become a widespread approach especially in the development of embedded systems, the identification of clones in models has be come only recently a research issue [3]. Investigation on practical application of model-clone detection [2] has shown that it can be successfully applied to industrial-scale models with a low range of false positives.

2.1 Clone Detection

In general, (code) clones are *(code) fragments that are similar w.r.t. to some definition of similarity* [12]. The employed notions of similarity are heavily influenced by the program representation on which clone detection is performed and the task it is used for. The central observation motivating clone detection research is that code clones normally implement a common concept. A change to this concept (e.g., a bug fix) hence typically requires modification of all (code) fragments that implement it, and therefore modifications of all clones.

Clones are introduced for different reasons. Most commonly, they are created by deliberate copy-and-paste from previous solutions, or by explicitly inlining library code. However, clones can also be introduced unintendedly by independently creating similar solutions.

2.2 Model-Based Development for Control Systems

The models used in the development of embedded systems are taken from control engineering. Data-flow diagrams as shown in Figure 1 consisting of blocks and lines are used in this domain as structured description of these systems. Tools like

Matlab/Simulink are used for the construction and simulation of these models. To generate software from these models, these diagrams are interpreted as time- (and value-)discrete control algorithms. By using tools like TargetLink [7], these descriptions are translated into computation tasks, which are then executed by use of a real-time operating system to implement an embedded application.

In the context of Simulink models, [3] defines a model clone to be a connected submodel, which is syntactically equivalent to another one, up to certain edit operations. Syntactical equivalence means that the data-flow networks have essentially the same structure and labeling, allowing for minor modifications of the copied submodel like change of constant parameters. In the following, a model clone is understood as a connected submodel, which is semantically equivalent to another one – which means that it exposes the same behavior, again up to minor adaptions like change of parameters. In contrast to syntactic clones, semantic clones may exhibit a rather different structure.

3 Approach

In this section we introduce our approach for structural normalization of data flow models. Our normalization considers graphs describing computational data-flow. Since structural normalization of these graphs uses graph transformations we briefly introduce directed graphs and graph transformation systems. As we target embedded systems, the approach is illustrated using Simulink data-flow models. However, the approach is applicable on all types of data flow graphs using similar semantics.

Directed Graphs: A directed graph is a triple (V, E, λ) consisting of a set V of nodes, a set E of edges and a function $\lambda : E \to V \times V$ associating each $e \in E$ with an ordered pair $(v_1, v_2) \in V \times V$. Furthermore a labeled directed graph is a graph with an additional labeling function $L : V \cup E \to N$ which maps nodes and edges to labels from a set N.

Graph Transformation Systems: A rewriting rule $p = (L, R) \in P$ is a pair of graphs $L = (V_L, E_L, \lambda_L)$, $R = (V_R, E_R, \lambda_R)$ known respectively as the pattern graph and the replacement graph of p. Applying p to a source graph G resulting in a target graph H implies the existence of the graph morphisms[1] $\alpha : L \to G$ and $\beta : R \to H$ consisting of the two morphisms $\gamma : V_L \to V$ and $\delta : E_L \to E$ such that $H = (G \setminus \alpha(L)) \cup \delta(R)$.

A graph transformation rule p induces a relation $\to_p$ on graphs by $G \to_p H$ iff H results from application of p to G. This relation can be trivially extended to a set P of rules, yielding a relation $\to_P$. Using the transitive and reflexive closure $\to_P^*$ allows to construct chains of transformations from a source to a target graph. $\to_P^*$ is called *confluent* iff for all G, G_1, and G_2 with $G \to_P^* G_1$ and $G \to_P^* G_2$ some G' with $G_1 \to_P^* G'$ and $G_2 \to_P^* G'$ exists. Furthermore,

---
[1] A graph morphism $(V, E, \lambda) \to (V', E', \lambda')$ consists of a pair $\gamma : V \to V'$ and $\delta : E \to E'$ with $\lambda'(\delta(e)) = (\gamma(v), \gamma(v'))$ if $\lambda(e) = (v, v')$.

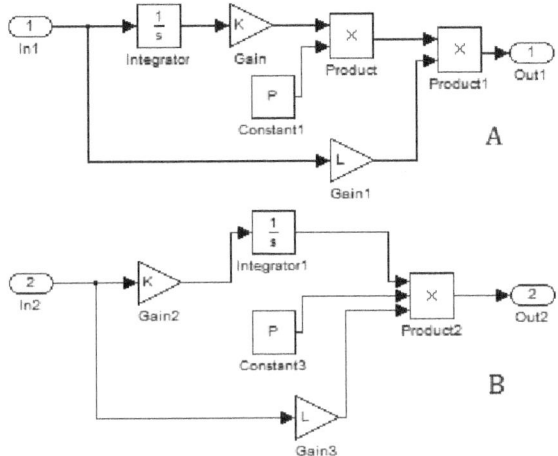

Fig. 1. Two syntactically different but semantically equivalent fragments A and B

$\rightarrow_P^*$ is called *Noetherian* iff for each G a G' exists with $G \rightarrow_P^* G'$ such that $G' \not\rightarrow_P^* G''$ for arbitrary G''. Intuitively, deterministic rule sets yield confluent, terminating rule sets yield Noetherian relations.

3.1 Normal Forms of Data Flow Models

Behaviorally equivalent data-flow (sub-)models can have completely different structures (see Figure 1). Therefore it is difficult to directly establish equivalence of two models using structural comparison techniques. However, if the structures of two equivalent models can be transformed to the same form without changing their behavior, it suffices to check structural equality of the transformed forms to establish their behavioral equivalence. Transforming the data-flow models can be achieved using graph transformation rules. But this approach is only feasible if the transformations yield a unique target model for each source model.

In short, we are therefore looking for *equivalent unique normal forms* of models. For a given set S of elements – in our case data-flow models – and an equivalence relation $\equiv$, a normal form can be achieved by identifying a set $N \subseteq S$ such that for all $s \in S$ exists exactly a unique $n \in N$ with $s \equiv n$. A set of transformation rules P induces an equivalence relation $\equiv_P$ on graphs G and G' via $G \equiv_P G'$ iff $G \rightarrow_P^* H$ and $G' \rightarrow_P^* H$ for some graph H. If the set induces a confluent and Noetherian relation, the required unique normal form can be obtained by selecting graphs for which no applicable transformation rule exists.

3.2 Construction of Normal Forms via Model Transformation

To achieve normal forms, normalization is performed by using a set of transformation rules. The rules are applied iteratively. After no more rules are applicable, the clone detection algorithm proposed in [3] is applied. This strategy allows detecting semantic clones using structural comparison techniques. As the normalization of the syntactically different but semantically equivalent fragments requires *semantically equivalent unique normal forms*, the transformation must be *semantically correct, confluent*, and *terminating*.

Semantic Correctness: The transformation defined by each rule has to preserve the observable behavior of the transformed model fragment, since syntactic modifications that change the behavior will lead to false positives. In our approach all transformations are based on mathematical, logical, or structural equivalence properties of Simulink models.

Rule Confluence: Transformation rules can introduce application conflicts if their matches overlap and thus their application would lead to non-deterministic results. This issue is known as the confluence problem and in generally undecidable [11]. In the approach presented here confluence is approximated by assigning a priority value to each rule in order to solve the overlap conflicts in favor of the rule with the highest priority. Since this however leaves conflicts between applications of the same rule, no complete confluence is assured, potentially leading to non-unique normal forms.

Rule Termination: Apparently, the investigation of the conditions under which the normalization can satisfy the termination criteria is very important for our approach, since a normal form can only be reached if the graph transformation terminates. In our case the set of transformation rules can be subdivided into:

- Rules which reduce the size of the model
- Rules which increase the size of the model or keep it unchanged

Since the first class of rules always reduces the number of the finite model elements, applying these rules always terminates. However the termination of the second type of rules is undecidable in general [10]. A workaround for the problem is to use a layered transformation system [4], grouping rules in deletion and non-deletion layers. All rules belonging to one layer are applied together, and each layer is applied only once. In a deletion layer all member rules must delete at least one element but not a newly created one. In a non-deletion layer each rule must not delete any element or use a newly created element in its pattern. A finite source graph and a finite number of layers guarantee termination. In addition, to reach a normal form using a layered transformation system the following conditions must also be fulfilled:

- The last creation of an element with a certain label should precede the first deletion of an element with the same label.
- The occurrence of an element of a certain label in the pattern of a rule implies that all elements of the same label were already created in previous layers.

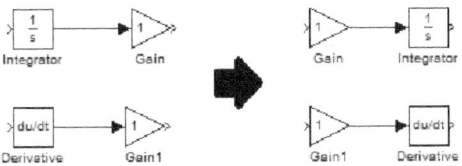

Fig. 2. Placing *Gain* Block before *Integrator* Block

These two conditions imply that no rules are applicable after all layers have been completed. Hence, termination is reached. The grouping of rules into layers is done based on sequential dependency analysis. Furthermore, checking the mentioned termination conditions in each layer can be done automatically [4].

Negative Application Conditions: To avoid transforming a matched fragment changing its behavior, a set of negative application conditions are assigned to rules, which must be fulfilled before applying the transformation. For example, a transformation rule is not applied if matched blocks are involved in feedback cycles as shown in Figure 6.

3.3 Derivation of Transformation Rules

We defined 40 semantic preserving transformation rules which perform structural modifications on Simulink models [1]. The rules are derived using mathematical, logical and structural semantics of Simulink models. In the following, we present some of the transformation rules grouped by the properties they are derived from, discuss their correctness and give examples for clarification.

Rules Derived from Mathematical Properties. The following transformation rules are based on properties of mathematical operations like commutativity, associativity, and distributivity.

Placing Gain Block before Integrator Block: In a model fragment with an *integrator* block followed by a *gain* block, the two blocks are swapped, executing the *gain* before the *integrator*, exploiting the commutativity of the operations. Figure 2 illustrates the rule.

Joining Consecutive Sum/Product Blocks: This rule can be applied on consecutive *sum* or *product* blocks resulting in merging them. The rule is based on the commutativity and associativity of addition and multiplication. In Figure 1 the *product* blocks in fragment A are joined into one *product* block in fragment B .

Trigonometric Functions: These are covered by a set of rules converting a trigonometric function block into its normalized representation using only *sine* blocks. For example, the *tan* block in Figure 3 is replaced by *sine* and *cosine* blocks sharing the original input signal, followed by a *product* block.

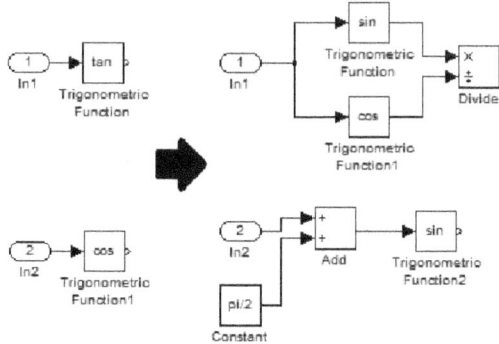

Fig. 3. Normalizing a *tan* block

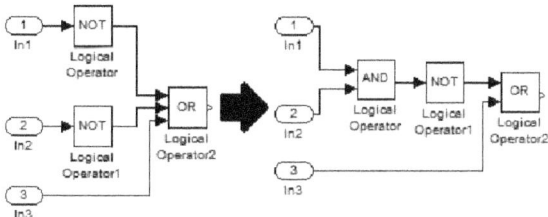

Fig. 4. DeMorgan Law

Rules Derived from Logical Properties. The following transformation rules are used to normalize model fragments of logical blocks. Hence, the rules are based on logical properties such as absorption, negation, distribution and DeMorgan laws.

DeMorgan Law: This rule is executed on two *not* blocks connected to an *or* (*and*) block resulting in replacing them by an *and* (*or*) block followed by a *not* block. The new *and* (*or*) block combines the two original input signals of the mentioned *not* blocks. If the original *or* (*and*) block is connected to other inputs, the original *or* (*and*) block is retained and the output of the newly created fragment is attached to it as a new input (see Figure 4).

Distribution Law: The *or*-form of this rule is executed on a fragment with two *or* blocks, *or*1 and *or*2, both with two input signals whose outputs are combined by an *and* block and their input signals contain the same signal *s*. The rule replaces the fragment by an *or* block combining the signal *s* and a new *and* block whose input signals are those of the blocks *or*1 and *or*2 except for *s*. If an *or* block contains more than two input signals, the rule attaches it as an input signal of the new created *and* block. The other rule is similar to the first one except for swapping the *and* and *or* blocks. The rule uses the distribution property in logic.

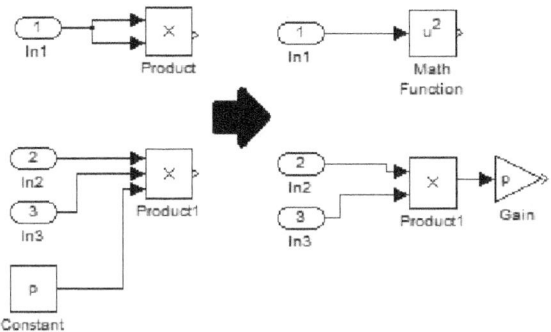

Fig. 5. *Gain* for Multiplying by a Constant

Rules Derived from Structural Properties. The following transformation rules are based on providing alternative structures or model fragments which behave similarly to the original model fragments.

Combining Consecutive Mux Blocks: The rule is applied on two consecutive *mux* blocks resulting in merging them. All original inputs are inputs of the new *mux* block, while its output is the original output of the consecutive *mux* blocks. The rule uses the fact that combining *mux* blocks does not change the resulting signal structure.

Gain for Multiplying by a Constant: This rule is executed on a *product* block with at least one *constant* block as input. In case of a *product* block with two input signals, the rule results in replacing the *product* block by a *gain* block whose value is the value of the *constant* block. In case a *product* block with more than two input signals, only the *constant* block is eliminated and replaced by a *gain* block attached after the original *product* block (see Figure 5).

Execution strategy. Our execution strategy consists of the following steps, described in detail in [1]. First the transformation rules are grouped into rule layers to meet the above-mentioned termination criteria. To construct these layers, each rule p is assigned to the lowest layer L_i respecting the following rules:

1. if L_i is a deletion layer then p must at least delete one element.
2. If L_i is a non deletion layer then p must not delete any element.
3. If L_i is a deletion layer, and p deletes an element e with label l then all rules creating elements of label l belong to layers L_h with $h < i$.
4. If L_i is a non-deletion layer then for each label l of an element e in the left-hand side of p all rules creating elements with label l belong to layers L_h with $h < i$.

Then, the member rules of each group are prioritized in order to solve conflicts of overlapping matches in favor of the rule with the highest priority.

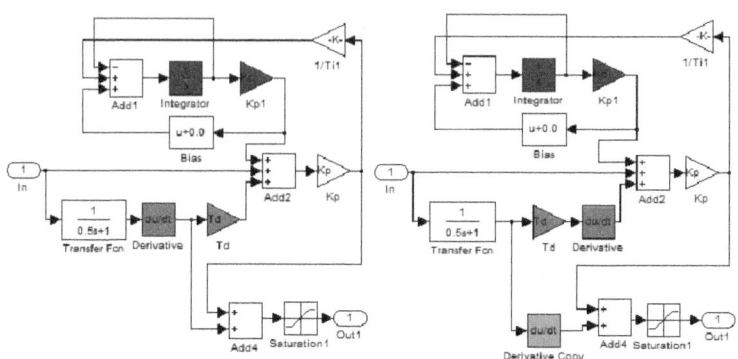

Fig. 6. Context Preparation and Non-Applicability of Transformation Rules

After that, the layers are applied one after another, repeatedly applying the rule with the highest priority as often as possible. Once no more rules can be applied in a layer, the next layer is applied.

Context Preparation: The context preparation is aimed at preserving the overall behavior of the model after a model fragment has been normalized. If a matched block has outgoing lines to other matched blocks as well as to unmatched blocks the latter outgoing lines are called intermediate results. During the normalization the behavior provided by the intermediate results can change, in turn potentially leading a change of the overall behavior of the model outside the fragment. This problem can be solved by defining negative application conditions to forbid rule executions in case of the occurrence of intermediate results. However, this restriction leads to a limitation of further normalization of model fragments.

Therefore, a second possibility has been investigated. This solution is the provision of these intermediate results by copying the parts of the match which generate them. Hence, the intermediate results still are generated in the exact same manner before the normalization and provided to the parts of the model which depend on them. In special cases the context preparation cannot be applied, for example in case of feedback loops between matched and unmatched nodes. Figure 6 illustrates the application of context preparation rules and negative application conditions: The context preparation copies the *derivate* block before applying the transformation rule which swaps the green colored *derivative* and *gain* blocks. The red colored *integrator* and *gain* blocks can not be swapped because of the existence of feedback loops.

4 Case Study

To evaluate the practicability of our approach in enhancing the clone detection algorithm in [3] with the capability of detecting semantic clones, the detection method was implemented and applied to a case study.

4.1 Analyzed Model

We performed our case study on a set of models with more than 1400 Simulink blocks distributed over 8 files. The set consists partly of models which contain several identical fragments and partly of models which implement similar behaviors. The models implement related functionalities of embedded systems in the automotive domain.

4.2 Implementation

To evaluate the normalization approach and its usefulness for clone detection we implemented it as a part of the quality analysis framework ConQAT, performing the normalization as a preprocessing step before applying the clone detection algorithm introduced in [3]. Furthermore, we made use of facilities implemented in [3] for preprocessing the Simulink models used for the case study and for reviewing the results.

4.3 Application

The clone detection algorithm [3] was applied both with and without the normalization step, using 40 transformation rules (see section 3.3). After the clone detection algorithm had been applied, each detected clone class together with its size and the number of its instances was listed. Additionally, for the normalized model the number of the rule executions and the number of the context preparations together with the locations of the rule matches were determined. We removed all clones consisting of less than 4 blocks, since they were considered as irrelevant. Subsequently, we compared the found clones of both cases based on their size and location to detect related and semantic clones. Since clones could be distributed across multiple files, the clone detection algorithm was executed on all models at the same time.

4.4 Results

Our implementation of the normalization algorithm needed 4 seconds and about 6 kB of memory on a 1.7 GHz workstation with 2 GB of main memory for transforming a Simulink model with 1400 blocks into a normal form. The normalization performed 321 applications of 16 defined rules, reducing the size of the model to 1351 blocks. To be able to execute the rules the normalization accomplished 142 context preparations. The execution of the clone detection after performing the model normalization found 127 clone pairs in the models, which resulted in 42 clone classes after clustering. The average clone size was about 14.5 nodes. On the other hand, the execution of the clone detection without performing the model normalization found 113 clone pairs which resulted in 49 clone classes after clustering. The average size of the found clones without performing the normalization was about 12.7 nodes. Table 1 shows how often each transformation rule was applied. The rule with the largest number of executions

Table 1. Number of Executions for each Rule

Rule	# Executions
Gain for Multiplying by Constant	104
Joining Consecutive *Gain* Blocks	58
Bias for Adding a Constant	42
Joining Consecutive *Product* Blocks	40
Joining Consecutive *Sum* Blocks	28
Placing *Gain* Block before *Integrator* Block	16
Sum Rule in Integration	6
Power Rule	5
Distribution of Multiplication over Addition	4
Replacing *Comp. to Const.* by *Comp. to Zero*	4
Placing *Gain* Block before *Derivative* Block	2
Joining Consecutive *Mux* Blocks	2
Joining Consecutive *Bias* Blocks	2
Trigonometric functions	2
Elimination of *Rounding* Blocks	2
Math functions	2
Replacing *Unary Minus* Block by *Gain* Block	2

was the "*gain* for multiplying by constant"-rule followed by the "*bias* for adding a constant"-rule. Furthermore the joining rules were the most frequently applied rules. In contrast, the logical rules were hardly executed. In Table 2 an overview is given of the cardinality of the clone classes found with and without performing the normalization step. In both cases the most commonly reported clone classes were pairs of clones. However, after applying the normalization clone detection reported more clones but the clustering resulted in fewer clone classes and especially fewer pair classes than without normalization. This indicates that the clustering phase was more effective after applying the normalization.

The left half of Table 3 shows the number of found clone classes, while the right half shows the number of reported clones, in each case in relation to the size of the clones for the clone detection with and without applying the normalization. The number of the largest clone classes and their cardinality were similar in both cases. The number of the smallest clone classes detected without the normalization was significantly greater than after applying the normalization. Since the number of the reported clones in both cases was similar we expected that the normalization resulted in detecting semantic clones which led to fewer clone classes after clustering. For the size ranges 7-10 and 16-21, the clone detection reported considerably more clones after applying the normalization which indicated the detection of semantic clones within these size ranges. About 62% of the originally detected clones were recognized again after the normalization. The size of these clones mostly increased or decreased due to the applied rules. In 5 detected clones the cardinality of the detected clone classes increased which indicated the detection of semantic clones. About 17% of the originally detected clones were not recognized after the normalization, since due to the reduction in

Table 2. Number of Clone Classes for Clone Class Cardinality

Cardinality of Clone Class	Number of Clone Classes	
-	Not Normalized	Normalized
2	32	26
3	5	5
4	6	3
5	4	3
6	1	3
7	1	0
8	0	2
9	0	1

Table 3. Number of Clone Classes and Number of Reported Clones for Clone Size

Clone Size	No. of Clone Classes		No. of Reported Clones	
-	Not Normalized	Normalized	Not Normalized	Normalized
4-6	31	17	46	43
7-10	8	13	11	25
11-15	4	4	5	7
16-21	0	4	0	6
21-30	1	0	1	0
>30	4	4	5	5

clone size, they were considered as irrelevant. About 21% of the originally detected clones were destroyed after the normalization, caused by lack of confluence specifically in context preparation.

Detected Semantic Clones: After the reported clone classes had been manually inspected, we found out that 5 clone classes contained substantial semantic clones. One of the found clone classes was very small and of limited functionality. Two pair classes extended syntactic cones by adding more blocks as a result of the normalization. The last two clone classes – one of them shown in Figure 7 – consisted of model fragments of relevant size which had different syntax but similar significant functionalities.

4.5 Discussion

The results – confirmed by additional experiments with models from environment modeling, embedded control, and energy systems – indicate that the normalization approach effectively extends the clone detection algorithm proposed in [3] with the capability of detecting semantic clones. Moreover the manual inspection of the found semantic clones shows that simple rules like replacement (trigonometry rules) or swapping rules can be useful for detecting semantic clones. Such simple rules were useful in our experiment as the syntax of the semantic clones

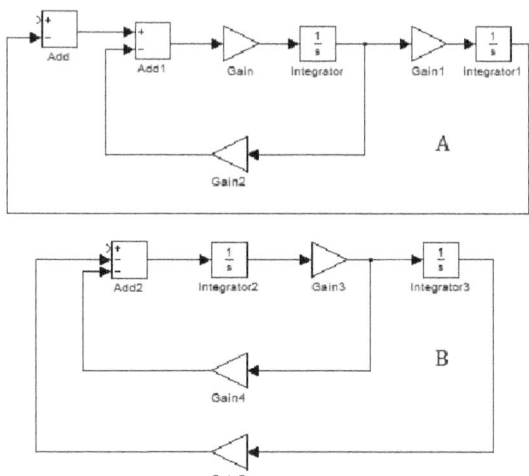

Fig. 7. Two Model Fragments A and B Recognizable as Clones after Normalization

were equal except for slight differences. However, a comparison of the reported clones after applying the normalization with those without applying the normalization shows that the context preparation in our experiment led often to destruction of existing clones or generation of new ones, due to a lack of confluence. Therefore it is favorable to constraint the context preparation using negative application conditions even if this decreases the number of possible rule executions. In addition, the results indicate that normalization often reduced the size of existing clones, making them considered as irrelevant.

The set of transformations used in the case study potentially results in the reduction of the size of clones through the normalization and the lack of confluence, thus leading to a possibility of false negatives, i.e., undetected (syntactic) clones. As semantic clones detection is used *in addition* to the detection of syntactic clones, from a pragmatic point of view this still substantially improves the state of the art via better recall in form of larger and more relevant clones, but requires research to provide a more complete treatment.

5 Related Work

Currently, clone-detection in model-based development has only gained little attention. [3] discusses the use of clone-detection for a Simulink-based development process, however uses a very restricted notion of similarity. [2] gives a more detailed comparison of this syntactic clone detection – forming the second step after the normalization in the semantic clone detection used here – to other related approaches, and discusses means to improve precision.

In [9], Pham et al. presents an approach for detecting approximate clones in Simulink models, allowing slight structural differences in the models. However the approach can not be used to approximate semantic similarity, since small structural modifications can introduce substantial behavior changes.

In [6], a formalism is shown for detecting equivalent business process models based on detecting of semantically equivalent model fragments, transforming a business process model into a term system and using term rewriting to obtain a normal form. However, the approach is very specific to business process models supporting only a more structural notion of similarity. Hence, the approach cannot be directly adapted to data-flow models such as Simulink.

In [5] Program Dependence Graphs (PDG) are used to identify semantic clones in programs independent from their linear syntactic representation. As a dataflow model is similar in nature to a PDG, isomorphic syntactic Simulink-clones already correspond to those kind of semantic clones, while the normalization used here exceeds the aspect of isomorphism. Approaches like [8] are using a more relaxed notion of similarity lifting this limitation, but are not sensitive to topological differences between subgraphs, thus making them unsuitable for data-flow models, as topology plays a crucial role there.

6 Conclusions

In this contribution, an extension to the detection of clones in the development of dataflow models for embedded control systems has been presented. In contrast to previous approaches, mainly relying on the detection of syntactically equivalent model fragments, in the approach presented here the concept of semantic equivalence was used. To that end, normalization of models by means of graph transformations has been used to identify model fragments with equivalent behavior. Although specifically implemented for Simulink, the presented approach is also directly applicable for other data-flow formalisms like ASCET-SD, Esterel, or Lustre. While the basic approach – comparing normal-forms of models obtained by graph transformations – also applies to other specification forms like state machines, the practical usefulness is ongoing research.

The feasibility of the approach has been proven by the successful application of a its implementation to models of practical size. This application lead to the identification of additional clones, not identified by the detection approach relying on structural equivalence alone without the use of normalization. While the basic feasibility of the approach has been shown in the performed case studies, more experiments with larger and more heterogeneous models are needed to finally assess the pragmatic advantages of the approach. As obviously the effectiveness of the detection of semantic clones depends on the notion of similarity used, which depends on the transformations used to obtain the normalizations, the introduction of additional transformations must be investigated for model fragments considered to be equivalent but not detected by the approach.

References

1. Al-Batran, B.: Model-Based Clone Detection Using Normal Forms. Master's thesis, Technische Universität München (2011)
2. Deissenboeck, F., Hummel, B., Jürgens, E., Pfähler, M., Schätz, B.: Model clone detection in practice. In: International Workshop on Software Clones, IWSC 2010, pp. 57–64. ACM, New York (2010), http://doi.acm.org/10.1145/1808901.1808909
3. Deissenboeck, F., Hummel, B., Jürgens, E., Schätz, B., Wagner, S., Girard, J.F., Teuchert, S.: Clone Detection in Automotive Model-Based Development. In: International Conference on Software Engineering (2008)
4. Ehrig, H., Ehrig, K., de Lara, J., Taentzer, G., Varró, D., Varró-Gyapay, S.: Termination criteria for model transformation. In: Cerioli, M. (ed.) FASE 2005. LNCS, vol. 3442, pp. 49–63. Springer, Heidelberg (2005)
5. Gabel, M., Jiang, L., Su, Z.: Scalable detection of semantic clones. In: International Conference on Software Engineering, pp. 321–330 (2008)
6. Gerth, C., Luckey, M., Kuster, J.M., Engels, G.: Detection of Semantically Equivalent Fragments for Business Process Model Change Management. In: International Conference on Services Computing, pp. 57–64. IEEE Computer Society, Los Alamitos (2010)
7. dSpace GmbH: TargetLink Production Code Generation, http://www.dspace.de
8. Krinke, J.: Identifying similar code with program dependence graphs. In: WCRE 2001 (2001)
9. Pham, N.H., Nguyen, H.A., Nguyen, T.T., Al-Kofahi, J.M., Nguyen, T.N.: Complete and accurate clone detection in graph-based models. In: International Conference on Software Engineering, pp. 276–286. IEEE Computer Society, Los Alamitos (2009)
10. Plump, D.: Termination of graph rewriting is undecidable. Fundam. Inf. 33, 201–209 (1998), http://portal.acm.org/citation.cfm?id=294994.294998
11. Plump, D.: Confluence of graph transformation revisited. In: Middeldorp, A., van Oostrom, V., van Raamsdonk, F., de Vrijer, R. (eds.) Processes, Terms and Cycles: Steps on the Road to Infinity. LNCS, vol. 3838, pp. 280–308. Springer, Heidelberg (2005)
12. Roy, C.K., Cordy, J.R.: A survey on software clone detection research. Tech. rep., Queen's University, Canada (2007)

Instant and Incremental QVT Transformation for Runtime Models

Hui Song, Gang Huang*, Franck Chauvel, Wei Zhang, Yanchun Sun,
Weizhong Shao, and Hong Mei

Key Lab of High Confidence Software Technologies (Ministry of Education)
School of Electronic Engineering & Computer Science, Peking University, China
{songhui06,franck.chauvel,zhangwei11,sunyc}@sei.pku.edu.cn,
{hg,wzshao,meih}@pku.edu.cn

Abstract. As a dynamic representation of the running system, a runtime model provides a model-based interface to monitor and control the system. A key issue for runtime models is to maintain their causal connections with the running system. That means when the systems change, the models should change accordingly, and vice versa. However, for the abstract runtime models that are heterogeneous to their target systems, it is challenging to maintain such causal connections. This paper presents a model-transformation-based approach to maintaining causal connections for abstract runtime models. We define a new instant and incremental transformation semantics for the QVT-Relational language, according to the requirements of runtime models, and develop the transformation algorithm following this semantics. We implement this approach on the mediniQVT transformation engine, and apply it to provide the runtime model for an intelligent office system named SmartLab.

1 Introduction

Modern systems provide many kinds of data during runtime, such as their internal states and configurations, the status of their tasks, and even their physical environment. Runtime model is a promising approach towards the manipulation of such runtime system data [1], allowing developers to monitor and control the system in a model-based way. In this paper, we focus on the structural runtime models that can be regarded as dynamic *object diagrams* representing the snapshots of running systems. A key issue for such runtime models is to maintain their *causal connections* with the systems. That means when the systems change, the models should change accordingly and instantly, and vice versa.

Many research approaches provide structural runtime models for different systems [2–5]. These approaches focus on wrapping the low-level management capability of the target systems into model-based interfaces, and thus their runtime models directly reflect the system data. However, for a target system, only one such reflective runtime model is usually not enough. To meet the different

---
* Corresponding author.

requirements and concerns on system monitoring and control, we need to abstract the reflective model again in different concepts and organizations. Such abstract runtime models act as different views of the reflective runtime model. Due to the heterogeneity between the abstract model and the running system, maintaining their causal connection is difficult.

In this paper, we present a model-transformation-based approach to maintaining the causal connection for abstract runtime model, by propagating changes between this abstract model and the existing reflective model of the target system. The change propagation is guided by the relation between the two models, specified in the QVT-Relational language. The challenge here is twofold. First, the changes on the systems and the runtime models are usually small but frequent, and thus the traditional batching QVT transformation that transforms the whole model each time is not efficient. We need an instant (the transformation is triggered instantly after each change) and incremental (the execution is based on the change but not the whole model) transformation appraoch. Second, the relations between models and systems are usually bidirectional rather than bijective. That means for one system change, there may be multiple candidate abstract changes that all obey the relation, and vice versa. Therefore a clear and determinate semantics of the transformation need to be defined.

The contributions of this paper can be summarized as follows.

- We define an instant and incremental transformation semantics for QVT-Relational language, and formulate three properties, namely *consistency*, *stability* and *restorability*, reflecting the requirements of runtime models.
- We develop the transformation algorithm according to the semantics. we analyze the impact of the input change and only re-evaluate the influenced relations and model elements. The impact analysis is based on the QVT rule, the change type, and the trace of previous transformations.
- We implement an instant QVT transformation engine, on the basis of the mediniQVT. We apply this engine to provide the runtime models for an intelligent office system named SmartLab.

The rest of this paper is structured as follows. Section 2 explains the problem based on a running example. Section 3 and Section 4 present the semantics and algorithm of our transformation for runtime models. Section 5 evaluates the approach. Section 6 concludes the paper, with discussions and our future plans.

2 The Running Example

2.1 The SmartLab System

To improve the working condition, the Software Institute of Peking University sets up a smart office system in its office building. We installed sensors in the rooms to measure the physical environment such as temperature, brightness, etc. We also installed an RFID (Radio Frequency Identification) reader in each office or meeting room. Every member in the institute has a unique RFID tag, stuck

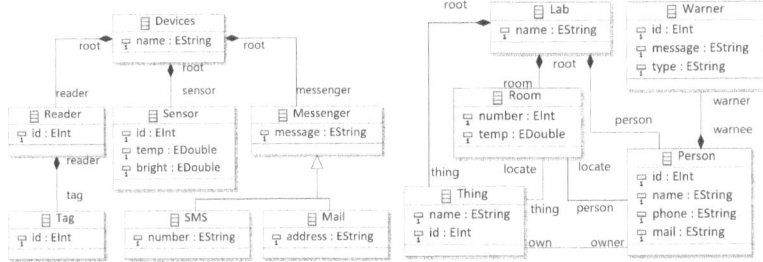

Fig. 1. The reflective and abstract meta-models for SmartLab

on his/her badge card. Some public assets and personal effects also have unique RFID tags bound with them. The tags termly transmit unique radio signals, which can be detected by the reader located in the same room.

Using these devices, SmartLab monitors the status of the whole institute, and interact with the institute members via Email, short message service (SMS), etc. Here are two exemplar monitoring scenarios: 1) **Missing personal effects**. After meetings, people may leave their personal effects in the meeting room, such as mobile phones or keys. SmartLab warns the owners when this happens. 2) **Leaving the air-conditioners on**. People may exit a room without turning off the air-conditioner, wasting electricity. For such situations, SmartLab warns the persons in nearby rooms.

2.2 The Runtime Models for SmartLab

Based on our earlier work [5, 6], we provide a reflective runtime model for Smart-Lab, and an excerpt of its meta-model is shown in the left of Figure 1. The classes directly define the concepts specific to the devices, and the properties define the data that can be retrieved from them. However, this reflective runtime model is still not proper for the above scenarios, because it represents the data in the solution-space which has a gap between the problem-space concepts, such as *persons*, *things*, *rooms*, etc., and cannot carry the problem-specific information such as the ownership relation between persons and things. Therefore, we define an abstract runtime model as shown in the right part of Figure 1. Using this abstract runtime model, the first scenario can be implemented in a straightforward way: If the `locate` values of a `Thing` and its `owner` are not the same, then create a new `Warner`, and add it to the owner's `warner` list.

We need to maintain the *causal connection* between the abstract model and the system, e.g., if a new `tag` is detected by a `Reader`, then the `Person` (or `Thing`) should `locate` in the `Room`, and if a new `Warner` is created, a `Messenger` should be created. The causal connection is guided by the relation between the two models, specified as a QVT-Relational rule in Figure 2. The rule is constituted by a set of `relations`: RR defines that the root elements are mapped if they have the same name. SR defines that a `Sensor` maps to a `Room` with the same `number` and `temp` values, if their roots are mapped. RTRP defines that if there is a pair of

```
1   transformation RFIDLab(sys:RFID,app:Lab){
2       key RFIDRoot{name}; key Sensor{id}; key Room{number};...
3       top relation RR{ name:String;
4           sys rs : Devices{name=name}; abs ra : Lab{name=name}; }
5       top relation SR{
6           id:Integer; temp:Real; rs:Devices; ra:Lab;
7           sys sensor:Sensor{id=id,temp=temp,root=rs};
8           abs room:Room{number=id,temp=temp,root=ra};
9           when{RR(rs,ra);} }
10      top relation RTRP{
11          rid:Integer; tid:Integer; rs:RFIDRoot; ra:LabRoot;
12          sys reader:Reader{id=rid,root=rs}; sys tag:Tag{id=tid,reader=reader};
13          abs room:Room{number=rid,root=ra};
14          abs person:Person{id=tid,root=ra,locate=room};
15          when{RR(rs,ra) and ra.person->collect(id)->includes(tid);} }
16      top relation RTRT{ ... }
17      top relation SMSWarner{
18          phone:String; message:String;rs:Devices;ra:Lab;
19          sys sms:SMS{number=phone,message=message,root=rs};
20          abs person:Person{phone=phone,root=ra};
21          abs warner:Warner{message=message,warnee=person,type='phone'};
22          when{RR(rs,ra);} }
23      top relation MailWarner{ ... } }
```

Fig. 2. Sample QVT relational transformation

Reader and Tag, and the Tag id is one of the Persons ids, then this Person is located in the Room. RTRT is similar. Finally, SMSWarner means that a Person and its Warner in type of "phone" map to an SMS. The relations illustrate the heterogeneity between the two models, e.g., both Sensors and Readers map to Rooms, and the containment association between Readers and Tags map to horizontal association from the Rooms to either Persons or Things. It is not straightforward to infer an abstract change from the system one, and vice versa.

2.3 Model Transformation for Runtime Models

Figure 3 summarizes our approach to supporting abstract runtime models. From the reflective runtime model from our previous work [5, 6], developers define the abstract meta-model according to the problem concepts, and the relation between it and the reflective one, using MOF and QVT-R[7], respectively. Here QVT-R is a natural choice, because it is originally designed for specifying the *relation* between models, rather than the transformation imperatives. Following the provided meta-models and the relation, our transformation engine propagates changes at runtime between the abstract model and the reflective one.

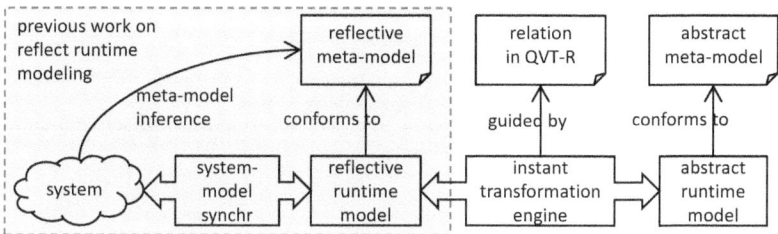

Fig. 3. Model transformation for runtime models

The engine requires a specific semantics and execution of QVT-R, because of the following features of runtime models. 1) The users of runtime models usually require to see the effects of changes and manipulations immediately, and thus we need *instant* transformation that is triggered by each change. Moreover, as the model scale is big and the changes are small but frequent, the transformation should be *incremental*, only considering the part of the model impacted by the change. 2) The users require a clear and determinate expectation about the causal connection between the model and the system. However, since the relations between are bidirectional [8], for a change on one model, there may be multiple candidate changes on the other model that all satisfy the relation. For example, considering RTRP in Figure 2, if a Tag escapes from a Reader, we can either delete a Person or just reset its locate value. Therefore, we need to formulate the semantics for this change-to-change QVT transformation, and this semantics should meet the common requirements of runtime system monitoring and manipulation. 3) The relation is between a model and its view, rather than two totally different models, and thus it will not be extremely complicated. Therefore, we can ignore some sophisticated syntax and usage of QVT-R.

3 The Semantics

This section defines the semantics of our instant and incremental QVT transformation for runtime models, and formulates the properties that must be satisfied.

We first abstract the three inputs: The reflective meta-model S defines the set of all the states of the reflective model, and the abstract meta-model A defines the set for the abstract model. The literal meaning of the transformation is a relation $T \subseteq A \times S$. If $(a, s) \in T$, we say the two models are consistent.

The causal connection between a model and a system has two aspects [2], i.e., *introspection* that propagates the system changes in the abstract model, and *reconfiguration* that propagates the abstract changes back. We use Δ_S and Δ_A to denote all the possible changes on the two models, respectively. The causal connection following a transformation T are two functions on the models and their changes: $\text{Intro}_T : S \times A \times \Delta_S \to S \times A$; $\text{Recon}_T : S \times A \times \Delta_A \to S \times A$. To support the above functions, the instant transformation maintains two live models, and for each time of execution, it takes the change on one model as an input and output the change on the other model.

$$\overrightarrow{T}_{S\times A}: \Delta_S \to \Delta_A;\ \overleftarrow{T}_{S\times A}: \Delta_A \to \Delta_S$$

Using this incremental transformation, we implement Intro_T by calculating the abstract change δ_a from the system change δ_s and then merging δ_a into the original abstract model a: $\text{Intro}_T(s, a, \delta_s) = (s + \delta_s, a + \overrightarrow{T}_{s,a}(\delta_s))$. For Recon_T, we first calculate the system change δ_s, and merge it to s. Since merging changes to the running system does not always lead to the expected effect, we reflect the side-effects back to the abstract model: $\text{Recon}_T(s, a, \delta_a) = (s + \delta_s + \delta'_s, a + \delta'_a)$, here, $\delta_s = \overleftarrow{T}_{s,a}(\delta_a)$, δ'_s is the side-effects of δ_s, and $\delta'_a = \overrightarrow{T}_{s+\delta_s, a+\delta_a}(\delta'_s)$.

Considering the requirements of runtime models, and also referring to the properties of classical QVT transformations [9], we define the following three properties for our incremental transformation, in forms of the post-conditions on the result from any input $(s, a) \in T, \delta_s \in \Delta_S, \delta_a \in \Delta_A$.

Property 1. **Consistency.** First of all, after merging the input and resulted changes, the two models must be consistent.

$$(s + \delta_s, a + \overrightarrow{T}_{s,a}(\delta_s)) \in T;\ (s + \overleftarrow{T}_{s,a}(\delta_a), a + \delta_a) \in T$$

The first part of *consistency* ensures that after Intro or Recon the abstract model correctly represents the system state, and the second part ensures that the changes executed to the system conforms to the intention of abstract changes.

Property 2. **Stability.** If the input change on one model does not violate the relation, it should not cause any change on the other model.

$$(s + \delta_s, a) \in T \Rightarrow a + \overrightarrow{T}_{s,a}(\delta_s) = a;\ (s, a + \delta_a) \in T \Rightarrow s + \overleftarrow{T}_{s,a}(\delta_a) = s$$

For Intro, *stability* ensures that the irrelevant system changes (such as the change of brightness) and intermediate changes (such as detecting a new tag, but having not got its id) do not disturb the monitoring agents. For Recon, it not only ensures that the irrelevant abstract changes (such as changing the ownership relation between persons and things) do not influence the system, but also ensures the relevant abstract changes remain stable: The side-effect of valid system writing is usually just a complement to the original change, e.g., adding a Mail to the Devices.messager will cause the Mail.root set to the root element. Such complementary side-effects should not influence the original abstract change, so that the users can manipulate the model in a coherent way.

Property 3. **Restorability.** After a change δ_s and its propagation result δ_a lead the two models to $s + \delta_s$ and $a + \delta_a$, the opposite change δ_s^{-1} and its propagation result should restore both models back. The other direction is the same.

$$\overrightarrow{T}_{s,a}(\delta_s) = \delta_a \Rightarrow a + \delta_a + \overrightarrow{T}_{s+\delta_s, a+\delta_a}(\delta_s^{-1}) = a$$

$$\overleftarrow{T}_{s,a}(\delta_a) = \delta_s \Rightarrow s + \delta_s + \overleftarrow{T}_{s+\delta_s, a+\delta_a}(\delta_a^{-1}) = s$$

Table 1. The modifications and their inverses

description	μ	μ^{-1}
set the value of $e.p$ from v to v'	$\mathsf{set}(e, p, v, v')$	$\mathsf{set}(e, p, v', v)$
add v to the set $e.p$	$\mathsf{insert}(e, p, v)$	$\mathsf{remove}(e, p, n)$
remove v from the set $e.p$	$\mathsf{remove}(e, p, v)$	$\mathsf{insert}(e, p, v)$
create e of class c, with $id = v$	$e \leftarrow \mathsf{new}(c, id, v)$	$\mathsf{delete}(e, id, v)$
delete the existing element e	$\mathsf{delete}(e, id, v)$	$e \leftarrow \mathsf{new}(c, id, v)$

We require *restorability* based on the following reasons. First, it is a usual case that the users undo their last change on the runtime model, and their intention is to restore the system back. Second, the system changes usually happen in couples, e.g., a person enters a room and then exits, a light is turned on and off again. Coupled changes restore the system state and this should be reflected on the abstract model. Third, for invalid system changes (such as trying to reset the temperature value of a sensor), the side-effect is their inverses, and when propagating them back, the original abstract changes should be clearly rolled back. Finally, *Restorability* and *stability* together allow the abstract model to carry the information that is irrelevant to the system. Since such information does not influence the relation, the transformation could change it any time without violating the relation. These two properties prevent it from changing this information arbitrarily.

4 The Instant and Incremental Transformation Algorithm

Our basic idea is to analyze the impact of the input changes to reduce the scope of execution. The impact analysis is based on the syntactical feature of QVT rules, the type of changes, and the trace recorded from previous executions.

A QVT-R transformation T is constituted by a set of *relations*. A relation has several *domains*, each with a class from the meta-models. The goal of QVT transformation is to *enforce* each of these primitive relations. For each relation, the engine tries to bind model elements to its domains, by *matching* the domain patterns. If no elements can be bound to a domain, the engine creates new elements or updates existing ones. The detailed (but informal) semantics of these `PatternMatching` and `CreateOrUpdate` operations can be found in the QVT standard [7]. For batching transformation, each time the engine checks and enforces all relations, and does pattern matching in the scope of all model elements. Our incremental transformation is also based on the enforcement of primitive relations, but we screen out the irrelevant relations and shrink the scope of model elements according to the input changes.

A *change* is a set of primitive modifications, following Alanen et al.'s definition [10]. Table 1 lists the five kinds of modifications we support. Each modification μ has an inverse μ^{-1}. When propagating a change, we deal with its modifications one by one, in the order of new, insert, set, remove, and delete[10].

Algorithm 1. The Instant and Incremental Transformation

```
1  function InstantTrans: (s, a, μ, tr) → (δ_a, tr')
2    δ_a ← {}, tr' ← tr
3    foreach r ∈ T : ∃d ∈ dom(r), μ.e.class = d.c do
4       if μ = set[e, p, v, v'] ∨ μ = insert[e, p, v] ∨ μ = remove[e, p, v] then
5          if p is mentioned by any patterns in r then
6             (δ_a'', tr'') ← ReEvaluate(r, tr', s, a, μ)
7             tr' ← tr''; δ_a ← δ_a ∪ δ_a''
8       else if μ = e ← new[T, id, v] then
9          if e satisfies the pattern of d then
10            (δ_a'', tr'') ← Construct(τ : {relation ↦ r, d ↦ e}, s, a, μ, tr', φ)
11            tr' ← tr''; δ_a ← δ_a ∪ δ_a''
12      else if μ ∈ delete then
13         foreach τ ∈ tr : rule(τ) = r ∧ μ.e = elem(τ, d) do
14            (δ_a'', tr'') ← Destroy(τ, s, a, μ, tr')
15            tr' ← tr''; δ_a ← δ_a ∪ δ_a''
16   return (δ_a, tr')
```

A *trace* is a set of *relation instances*. An instance records a composition of model elements bound to the domains of the relation, and these elements satisfy the relation. We also record the change on the source model that causes this instance to be established, and the change on the target model calculated by the enforcement. For each transformation, the trace can be accumulated from the previous executions on the changes that create the models from scratch, or can be created at once by a batching transformation.

4.1 The Algorithm

In the rest of this section, we present our algorithm to propagate changes and update the trace step by step. The following algorithm is in the direction from the reflective to the abstract model, and the other direction is the same.

The main algorithm *InstantTrans* takes as input the original models s and a, the modification μ on s, and the previous traces tr. It outputs the change δ_a and the new trace tr'. We initiate δ_a as empty, and tr' as the original tr (Line 2). In the main body, we first screen the relations, and only consider the ones whose domain classes include the class of μ. We handle the left relations according to the type of μ: For a set, insert or remove (Line 4), only if the modified property is mentioned in r, we *ReEvaluate* it. For a new, since there may be new compositions of model elements containing e that satisfies r, we *Construct* new relation instances, starting from a partial relation instant τ with e bound to the proper domain. For a delete, we *Destroy* all the existing instances of r that have been bound with the deleted element. After each iteration on a relation, we update the trace, and unite the resulted changes.

Algorithm 2. Re-Evaluate the QVT Rules

17 **function** ReEvaluate$(r, tr, s, a, \mu) \rightarrow (\delta_a, tr')$
18 $\delta_a \leftarrow \{\}; tr' \leftarrow tr$
19 **foreach** $\tau \in tr : \text{rule}(\tau) = r \wedge \exists d_e \in \text{dom}(r) : \mu.e = \text{elem}(\tau, d_e)$ **do**
20   **if** $\neg \text{check}(r, \tau, s + \mu, a)$ **then**
21      $(\delta_a'', tr'') \leftarrow$ Destroy$(\tau, s + \mu, a, tr')$
22      $tr' \leftarrow tr''; \delta_a \leftarrow \delta_a \cup \delta_a''$
23    $\tau' \leftarrow \{\text{relation} \mapsto r\}$
24   **foreach** $d \in \text{dom}(r) : d = d_e \vee \mu.p$ *is not mentioned by* d **do**
25      $\tau' \leftarrow \tau' \cup \{d \mapsto \text{elem}(\tau, d)\}$
26    $(\delta_a'', tr'') \leftarrow$ Construct$(\tau', s, a, \mu, tr', \phi)$
27    $tr' \leftarrow tr''; \delta_a \leftarrow \delta_a \cup \delta_a''$

28 **if** *no such* τ *is found* **then**
29   **if** *e satisfies the pattern of d* **then**
30      $(\delta_a'', tr'') \leftarrow$ Construct$(\tau : \{\text{relation} \mapsto r, d \mapsto e\}, s, a, \mu, tr', \phi)$
31      $tr' \leftarrow tr''; \delta_a \leftarrow \delta_a \cup \delta_a''$

32 **return** (δ_a, tr')

To *ReEvaluate* a relation r, we first enumerate the instances of r that are bound with the modified element $\mu.e$. For each instance τ, we check the relation again and *Destroy* it if it fails now. The modification may cause new compositions of elements to satisfy the relation, and thus we seek and construct new binding compositions. Here we do not exhaustively enumerate all the possible compositions, but utilize the existing bindings as a reference. Note that the property $\mu.p$ is only mentioned by part of the domain patterns. Take SMSWarner in Figure 2 as an example, the property SMS.message is not mentioned by the person domain, since the pattern does not contain any direct or transitive reference to this property. If there is any new binding compositions emerging to satisfy r, then it must be because the modification makes an element satisfy the pattern that mentions this property. Therefore, we fix the elements bound to irrelevant domains, leaving the other domains as free, and then use this partial binding as a seed to construct new instances. If there is not any existing relation instance as reference, we construct relations just as if this element is newly created.

Construct is similar to the classical enforcement semantics of QVT, but has a partial relation instance as a seed, with some domains bound. The input also includes a δ_a that records the accumulated changes to bind these domains. If the seed τ is already complete, and satisfies the relation, this τ is a successful instance. We return δ_a as the final change, add the new instance τ into the trace, and record the source change $\{\mu\}$ and the target change δ_a under τ. If the input τ is not complete yet, we take one free domain d, perform PatternMatching on it to find all the elements that can satisfy the domain pattern, and store the elements in the set cand (for "candidate"). If no binding is found, we try to create new elements or update existing ones, and regard the result e as a candidate. Finally, we try to bind each element e in *cand*, and invoke *Construct* recursively

Algorithm 3. Construct and Destroy Relation Instances

33 **function** Construct: $(\tau, s, a, \mu, tr, \delta_a) \to (\delta_a, tr')$
34 **if** *every* $d \in \text{dom}(r)$ *is bound in* τ $\wedge \text{check}(\tau, s + \mu, a + \delta_a)$ **then**
35 $\quad$ $tr' \leftarrow tr \cup \{\tau\}$; $\tau.\text{rec}_s \leftarrow \{\mu\}$; $\tau.\text{rec}_a \leftarrow \delta_a$
36 $\quad$ **foreach** $r' \in T : when(r') = r$ **do**
37 $\quad\quad$ $(\delta_a'', tr'') \leftarrow$ Construct $(r', tr', para, s, a, \mu, \delta_a)$
38 $\quad\quad$ $\tau.\text{chd} \leftarrow \tau.\text{chd} \cup (tr'' - tr')$; $\delta_a \leftarrow \delta_a \cup \delta_a''$; $tr' \leftarrow tr''$
39 $\quad$ **return**(tr', δ_a)
40 **else if** $\exists d \in \text{dom}(r) : d \notin \text{dom}(\tau)$ **then**
41 $\quad$ cand$\leftarrow$PatternMatching$(\tau, d, s + \mu, a)$
42 $\quad$ **if** cand $= \phi \wedge$ *d is an enforce app domain* **then**
43 $\quad\quad$ $(\delta_a', e) \leftarrow$ CreateOrUpdate$(\tau, s, a + \delta_a)$; cand$\leftarrow$cand $\cup \{e\}$
44 $\quad$ **foreach** $e \in$ cand **do** Construct$(r, tr, \tau \cup \{d \mapsto e\}, s, a, \delta_a \cup \delta_a')$

45 **function** Destroy: $(\tau, s, a, \mu, tr) \to (\delta_a, tr')$
46 $tr' \leftarrow tr - \{\tau\}$; $\delta_a \leftarrow \tau.\text{rec}_a^{-1}$
47 **foreach** $\tau' \in \tau.\text{chd} : \neg\text{check}(r, \tau', s + \mu, a)$ **do**
48 $\quad$ $(\delta_a', tr'') \leftarrow$ Destroy$(r, tr', \tau', s, a, \mu)$
49 $\quad$ $\delta \leftarrow \delta \cup \delta_a'$; $tr' \leftarrow tr''$
50 **return** (δ_a, tr')

to bind the rest of the free domains. Another thing to consider is the dependency between relations. Due to the establishment of this relation, some other relations that depends on it may be satisfied. Therefore, after constructing a new relation instance, we find the relations depending on it, bind the mentioned elements in this relation to the new ones, and try to construct new instances from this partial seed. The constructed instances $(tr'' - tr')$ are recorded as the children of τ, so that when τ is not satisfied we can destroy them.

Destroy deletes an existing relation instance whose bound elements no longer satisfy r. We delete this relation instance from the trace, and roll back the recorded change on the system side that has made this instance satisfy the relation. Since this relation is no longer satisfied, the relations depending on it cannot be satisfied any longer, and we delete them consequently.

4.2 Examples

We use a set of simplified examples to illustrate how the algorithm works. The original reflective and abstract models (s_0 and a_0, respectively) are shown in Figure 4, without the shaded part. Currently, these two models are consistent, and the trace is: $tr = \{\tau_1 : \langle \text{RR, sr, ar}\rangle, \tau_2 : \langle \text{SR, sn, rm}\rangle, \tau_3 : \langle \text{RTRP, rd, tg}_1\text{, rm, ps}\rangle\}$. For the sake of simplicity, we omit the names of domains. On these two models, we execute the following sample modifications.

For the first example, the sensor detects a change on the brightness, i.e., μ_1 : set$[sn : \text{Sensor}, \text{bright}, 620.0, 150.0]$. Since only SR contains the class Sensor, whereas bright is not mentioned by it, the algorithm stops at Line 5.

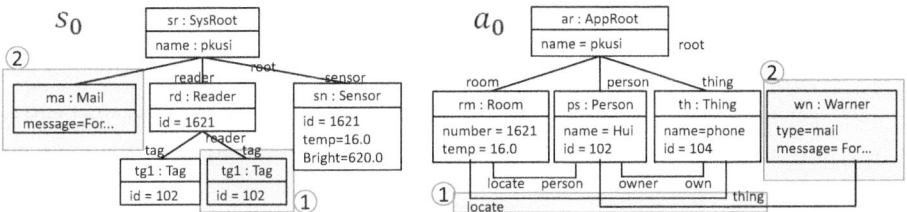

Fig. 4. Sample models for transformation

For the second example, μ_2 : set[sn : Sensor, temp, 16, 15], the algorithm should propagate the new temperature to the abstract side. Following the algorithm, we also find $r = $ SR, and *ReEvaluate* this r. At Line 20, we find the relation instance τ_2, and since it does not satisfy the relation, we destroy it. After that, we instantiate a new τ_4 for r (Line 24), bind sn to its sensor domain, and invoke *Construct*. In this method, since there is one free domain room, we try to bind an element to it (Line 45). The CreateOrUpdate operation find rm and update its temp attribute, and thus finally $\delta_a = $ set[rm : Room, temp, 16, 15].

For a complicated example, we consider the reader detects a new tag, i.e., $\delta_s = \{\mu_3 : \text{tg}_2 \leftarrow \text{new}[\text{Tag}, \text{id}, 104], \mu_4 : \text{set}[\text{tg}_3, \text{reader}, \bot, \text{rd}], \mu_5 : \text{insert}[\text{rd}, \text{tag}, \text{tg}_3]\}$. This time, we expect the thing 104 locate in room 1621. We propagate these modifications one by one. For μ_3, we find two relations, RTRP and RTRT, but for the former, tg_2 does not satisfy its precondition, so we go on with the latter, and invoke *Construct* with τ_5 : $\{\text{relation} \mapsto \text{RTPT}, \text{tag} \mapsto \text{tg}_2\}$ as a seed. In *Construct*, we cannot find any element to be bound to room (because tag_2.reader is not set yet), and stop the propagation on μ_3. When propagating μ_4, we *Construct* τ_5 again, and this time we bind rd to reader, rm to room, th to thing, and update th.locate to rm. So the final result is $\delta_a = \{\text{set}[\text{th}, \text{locate}, \bot, \text{rm}]\}$ and a new τ_5 : $\langle\text{RTRT}, \text{rd}, \text{tg}_2, \text{rm}, \text{th}\rangle$, marked as "1" in Figure 4. If his new tag escapes from rd, the abstract model should be rolled back to a_0. This change also contains three modifications, and for the effective one μ_7 : set[tg_2, reader, rd, $\bot$], we destroy the relation instance τ_5 (Line 6 -> Line 22). And in *Destroy*, we return the inverse of the recorded change under τ_5, i.e., $\{\text{set}[\text{th}, \text{locate}, \text{rm}, \bot]\}$.

Finally, we show a bidirectional example, marked as "2" in Figure 4. SmartLab warns a person by creating a new Warner and adding it to the person's warner list. The last manipulation μ_8 : set[wn, warnee, $\bot$, ps] leads to system changes in the following way. We find the relation MailWarner (Line 3), and invoke *ReEvaluate* (Line 6). Since this relation has no instances yet, we directly invoke *Construct* (Line 27), and it finally creates a new Mail in the system side and set its attributes. After successfully sending the message, the system destroys this new Mail. We finally invoke *Destroy*, and the returned abstract change is the inverse of the recorded modification μ_8, resetting wn.warnee.

5 Evaluation

Implementation. We implemented a prototype engine based on the mediniQVT. The relation instances are extended from the `QvtSemanticTasks`, which are originally used by mediniQVT to store intermediate results during batching transformation. The checking, pattern matching, create-or-update operations in our algorithm are also reused and altered from mediniQVT. The syntactical analysis on QVT rules, such as determining the *mentioned* properties of each domain pattern, is implemented as queries and analysis on the QVT syntax tree.

Feasibility and Effectiveness. We applied this instant transformation engine to provide the runtime model for a medium-scale smart office system, the SmartLab. The reflective meta-model contains 27 classes and 69 properties, and the QVT rule contains 36 relations (471 lines in total). We encouraged all the members in our institute to propose and experiment monitoring scenarios based on the abstract model. Until now, there are totally 41 scenarios proposed within the capability of current SmartLab devices, e.g., turning off the lights when the room is empty, turning on the water boiler in advance before a scheduled meeting, warning nearby persons when a valuable public facility is moving, and so on. Our instant transformation supported all these scenarios: A dedicated group of students implemented all the scenarios as QVT operational scripts, and the execution of these scripts satisfies the expectation of both the scenario proposers and the script developers. To evaluate the approach on a wider scope of runtime models, we also applied it on some small-scaled systems to support different runtime models, such as C2 and Client/Server styled architecture for a JEE middleware named JOnAS and a mobile computing middleware named PLASTIC. We have tried these cases [11] using batching transformation. The reproduction of them still satisfies the requirements stated in the original papers.

Performance. The execution performance of our transformation engine is enough for SmartLab. In peak period there are more than 300 model elements, and for each change, the runtime model environment finishes the execution of monitoring rules between 0.1 to 1 second, including the time spent on device invocation, change collection, instant transformation and script execution. This performance is acceptable for our monitoring scenarios on SmartLab. For the other small-scaled cases, the execution time never exceed 0.1 second.

To evaluate the performance of transformation without the influence of other runtime costs, we made up five pairs of models conforming to the meta-models in SmartLab, and executed the transformation on them. Figure 5 illustrates the experiment results. The horizontal axis lists the total number of model elements, and the vertical axis shows the time spent in millisecond (logarithmic scale). We performed four experiments on each subject. The first three were incremental transformations after the irrelevant changes, changing the properties, and creating new elements. As a contrast, we also executed the batching transformation directly using mediniQVT. All the experiments were executed on a PC with Intel Core 2 Duo 3GHz CPU and 2GB memory. From the curves, we have the

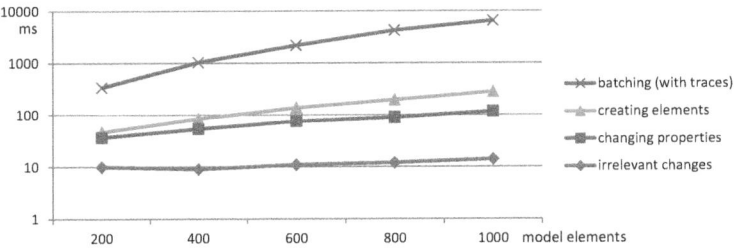

Fig. 5. Performance statistics

following conclusions. 1) the improvement from batching transformation to incremental transformation is significant, and the time increases more gently as the model scale increases. 2) The execution time on irrelevant changes is stable around 10 milliseconds. That means the screening on the relations is independent to the model scales, and adds very little to the total cost. 3) The curve for changing properties is lower and gentler than creating elements. Since the only difference between them is that the former have more fixed domains, this shows that our effort to fix a part of the domain bindings is valuable.

We also performed stress tests to see the extreme change scale and frequency we support, upon the subject models with 1000 elements. For scale, we generate new models and calculate the changes from the original ones to them. When the change contains more than 220 modifications (in average), the time spent to transform these modifications becomes worse than transforming the whole model. For frequency, we continuously generate changes with single modifications, and use them to launch the transformation. The extreme interval between changes is 0.21s. For a smaller interval, there will be a queue of changes blocked.

6 Related Work

Runtime models are widely used on different systems to support self-repair [2], dynamic adaption [4], data manipulation [3], etc. As a direct reflection of the target system, these runtime models are maintained by imperatively mapping the model operations to the system management capabilities. In a previous work [11] we propose the initial idea of using model transformation to maintain the abstract runtime models that are not isomorphic to the low-level systems, but we use batching transformation in that work. Vogel et al. [12] use incremental transformation for runtime models. The difference is that they focus on integrating a general-purpose transformation engine into their runtime model environment, without revising the engine, whereas in this paper, we focus on the semantics and implementation of a new transformation specific to runtime models.

A declarative transformation rule may allow multiple execution effects. The solution is to give unambiguous semantics for transformation languages according to specific usage. Foster et al. formulate three basic properties for the "view-update" transformation between tree-based data [13]. Xiong et al. design and implement their ATL-based model synchronization according to four pre-defined properties [14]. Stevens [9] discusses the semantics of the batching bidirectional QVT transformation. Our properties of instant transformation root in Stevens's work, but are defined on model changes. Diskin et al. [15] formally discuss the semantics and requirements of generic delta-based bidirectional transformation, but in this paper, we employ a more lightweight and easy-to-implement semantics, specific to the requirement of runtime models.

Johann and Egyed [16] implement instant and incremental model transformation approach based on the impact analysis of model changes, but the model relation they support is only the simple mapping between elements. On the basis of incremental pattern evaluation [17], researchers also implement incremental transformation following the trigger-action rules [18] and ATL rules [19]. However, such imperative rules are not natural for specifying the relation between runtime models and systems. Giese and Wagner systematically discuss the definition and requirement of instant and bidirectional transformation, and implement it based on their TGG transformation engine [20]. However, TGG is still heavy-weight for specifying model relations. To the best of our knowledge, there is no work of instant and incremental transformation on QVT-R.

7 Conclusion

This paper presents a model-transformation-based approach to maintaining causal connections between the running systems and their abstract runtime models. We define a new incremental transformation semantics for the QVT-Relational language according to the usage in runtime models, and develop the instant transformation algorithm based on the impact analysis of changes. We implement the approach based on the mediniQVT, and apply it in a pragmatic smart office system named SmartLab.

As an initial attempt, the current target of this approach is not a general-purpose incremental QVT transformation, but the one customized for runtime models. The performance of this approach is not good for too big and too frequent changes. However, these two cases are not common in runtime models. We also have some restrictions on the usage of MOF and QVT. For MOF, we require every class to have a key attribute, and require all the multiple properties to be unordered. For QVT, we require 1) every element mentioned by a relation is explicitly declared as a **domain**, 2) all the relations are defined as **top** ones, and 3) only **when** clauses are used to compose relations. According to our experience, with these restricts, it is still enough to specify the relations in runtime models.

Our main future plan is to evaluate the feasibility and effectiveness of this approach on other transformation contexts rather than merely runtime models, improve the semantics and algorithms, and evaluate the possibility towards wide-scope or even general-purpose instant and increment transformation on QVT-R.

Acknowledgment. This work is sponsored by the National Basic Research Program of China (973) under Grant No. 2009CB320703; the National Natural Science Foundation of China under Grant No. 60873060, 60933003, 60821003;

the EU FP7 under Grant No. 231167; the Program for New Century Excellent Talents in University; the National S&T Major Project under Grant No. 2009ZX01043-002-002.

References

1. Blair, G., Bencomo, N., France, R.: Models@ run.time. Computer 42(10), 22–27 (2009)
2. Sicard, S., Boyer, F., De Palma, N.: Using components for architecture-based management: the self-repair case. In: ICSE, pp. 101–110 (2008)
3. MoDisco Project, http://www.eclipse.org/gmt/modisco/
4. Morin, B., Barais, O., Nain, G., Jézéquel, J.M.: Taming dynamically adaptive systems using models and aspects. In: ICSE, pp. 122–132 (2009)
5. Song, H., Xiong, Y., Chauvel, F., Huang, G., Hu, Z., Mei, H.: Generating synchronization engines between running systems and their model-based views. In: Ghosh, S. (ed.) MODELS 2009. LNCS, vol. 6002, pp. 140–154. Springer, Heidelberg (2010)
6. Song, H., Huang, G., Xiong, Y., Chauvel, F., Sun, Y., Mei, H.: Inferring metamodels for runtime system data from the clients of management aPIs. In: Petriu, D.C., Rouquette, N., Haugen, Ø. (eds.) MODELS 2010. LNCS, vol. 6395, pp. 168–182. Springer, Heidelberg (2010)
7. OMG: MOF/QVT model query, view, transformation, http://www.omg.org/spec/QVT/
8. Czarnecki, K., Foster, J.N., Hu, Z., Lämmel, R., Schürr, A., Terwilliger, J.F.: Bidirectional transformations: A cross-discipline perspective. In: Paige, R.F. (ed.) ICMT 2009. LNCS, vol. 5563, pp. 260–283. Springer, Heidelberg (2009)
9. Stevens, P.: Bidirectional model transformations in QVT: Semantic issues and open questions. In: Engels, G., Opdyke, B., Schmidt, D.C., Weil, F. (eds.) MODELS 2007. LNCS, vol. 4735, pp. 1–15. Springer, Heidelberg (2007)
10. Alanen, M., Porres, I.: Difference and union of models. In: Stevens, P., Whittle, J., Booch, G. (eds.) UML 2003. LNCS, vol. 2863, pp. 2–17. Springer, Heidelberg (2003)
11. Song, H., Huang, G., Chauvel, F., Xiong, Y., Hu, Z., Sun, Y., Mei, H.: Supporting runtime software architecture: A bidirectional-transformation-based approach. Journal of Systems and Software 84(5), 711–723 (2011)
12. Vogel, T., Neumann, S., Hildebrandt, S., Giese, H., Becker, B.: Incremental model synchronization for efficient run-time monitoring. In: Ghosh, S. (ed.) MODELS Workshops 2009. LNCS, vol. 6002, pp. 124–139. Springer, Heidelberg (2010)
13. Foster, J.N., Greenwald, M.B., Moore, J.T., Pierce, B.C., Schmitt, A.: Combinators for bidirectional tree transformations: A linguistic approach to the view-update problem. ACM Trans. Program. Lang. Syst. 29(3), 17 (2007)
14. Xiong, Y., Liu, D., Hu, Z., Zhao, H., Takeichi, M., Mei, H.: Towards automatic model synchronization from model transformations. In: ASE, pp. 164–173 (2007)
15. Diskin, Z., Xiong, Y., Czarnecki, K., Ehrig, H., Hermann, F., Orejas, F.: From state- to delta-based bidirectional model transformations: The symmetric case. In: Whittle, J., Clark, T., Kühne, T. (eds.) MODELS 2011. LNCS, vol. 6981, pp. 304–318. Springer, Heidelberg (2011)
16. Johann, S., Egyed, A.: Instant and incremental transformation of models. In: ASE, pp. 362–365 (2004)

17. Cabot, J., Teniente, E.: Incremental evaluation of OCL constraints. In: Martinez, F.H., Pohl, K. (eds.) CAiSE 2006. LNCS, vol. 4001, pp. 81–95. Springer, Heidelberg (2006)
18. Ráth, I., Bergmann, G., Ökrös, A., Varró, D.: Live model transformations driven by incremental pattern matching. In: Vallecillo, A., Gray, J., Pierantonio, A. (eds.) ICMT 2008. LNCS, vol. 5063, pp. 107–121. Springer, Heidelberg (2008)
19. Jouault, F., Tisi, M.: Towards incremental execution of ATL transformations. In: Tratt, L., Gogolla, M. (eds.) ICMT 2010. LNCS, vol. 6142, pp. 123–137. Springer, Heidelberg (2010)
20. Giese, H., Wagner, R.: From model transformation to incremental bidirectional model synchronization. Software and Systems Modeling 8(1), 21–43 (2009)

Service–Oriented Architecture Modeling: Bridging the Gap between Structure and Behavior

Mickael Clavreul[1], Sébastien Mosser[2],
Mireille Blay–Fornarino[3], and Robert B. France[4]

[1] INRIA, Campus Universitaire de Beaulieu, 35042 Rennes, France
`mickael.clavreul@inria.fr`
[2] INRIA Lille–Nord Europe, LIFL (UMR CNRS 8070), Univ. Lille 1, France
`sebastien.mosser@inria.fr`
[3] I3S (UMR CNRS 6070), Université Nice–Sophia Antipolis, France
`blay@polytech.unice.fr`
[4] Colorado State University, Fort Collins, CO, USA
`france@cs.colostate.edu`

Abstract. Model–driven development of large-scale software systems is highly likely to produce models that describe the systems from many diverse perspectives using a variety of modeling languages. Checking and maintaining consistency of information captured in such multi-modeling environments is known to be challenging. In this paper we describe an approach to systematically synchronize multi–models. The approach specifically addresses the problem of synchronizing business processes and domain models in a Service-oriented Architecture development environment. In the approach, the human effort required to synchronize independently developed models is supplemented with significant automated support. This process is used to identify concept divergences, that is, a concept in one model which cannot be matched with concepts in the other model. We automate the propagation of divergence resolution decisions across the conflicting models. We illustrate the approach using models developed for a Car Crash Crisis Management System (CCCMS), a case study problem used to assess Aspect–oriented Modeling approaches.

1 Introduction

Developing a large–scale software system as a Service–oriented Architecture (SOA) involves the creation and integration of a variety of services. Services must be coordinated to adequately participate in the required behavior of the system. Model–driven development of such systems is highly likely to produce a variety of models capturing the many diverse design concerns that arise during development. The management of models in such multi–modeling environments is known to be challenging. In particular, activities related to checking and maintaining consistency among the multiple views of a system can be complex. There is a need for techniques that developers can use to detect conflicts and divergences across multi-models of systems developed using SOA. Two models diverge when one model consists of elements that do not correspond to elements in the other model.

Our work specifically addresses the problem of synchronizing SOA business process models with domain models. The approach described in this paper provides SOA designers with integrated generative and model composition techniques that can be used to automatically propagate divergence resolution strategies across these models. The core of the iterative synchronization approach consists of four major steps: *(i)* the generation of a structural model based on the data extracted from the business process model, *(ii)* the merge of the generated model with the initial domain model, *(iii)* the identification of formal divergences between these two models and finally *(iv)* the automated propagation of resolution strategies provided by experts.

The remainder of this paper is organized as follows. Section 2 introduces the CC-CMS case study that motivates our approach. Section 3 outlines the challenges and the solution that we propose in this paper. Section 4 presents situations where divergences occur and proposes a formalization of the divergences. Section 5 illustrates how we capture experts knowledge about how to resolve divergences. Section 6 focuses on the fourth step of the process and describes how resolution strategies are automatically propagated across both the domain model and the business processes model. Section 7 discusses related work and Section 8 concludes this paper.

2 Car Crash Crisis Management System (CCCMS)

We illustrate the approach using a case study problem described in a Transactions on Aspect-Oriented Software Development (TAOSD) special issue on Aspect-Oriented Modeling (AOM) [15]. The purpose of the special issue was to compare the application of existing AOM approaches on a common system development problem, namely the development of a Crisis Management System (CMS). In the case study, a CMS is *"a system that facilitates coordination of activities and information flow between all stakeholders and parties that need to work together to handle a crisis"* [11]. Among the multitude of crises handled by CMS, including terrorist attacks, epidemics, or accidents, we focus on car accidents. Car accidents are handled by the Car Crash CMS (CCCMS) which *"includes all the functionalities of general crisis management systems, and some additional features specific to car crashes such as facilitating the rescuing of victims at the crisis scene and the use of tow trucks to remove damaged vehicles"*. The original system includes ten use cases described using textual scenarios.

For ease of understanding, we illustrate our approach on the *Capture Witness Report (CWR)* use case only. The CWR case study (use case #2 in the original document) captures the set of actions that a *Coordinator* takes to create a new *Crisis* based on the information reported by the *Witness* of a car accident. The main success scenario for this use case (extracted from the requirements document) is described in FIG. 1. The subject of the use case is the CCCMS system represented by *System*. Two actors are involved in the sequence of activities needed to report a car crash: *(i) PhoneCompany* is the role played by an external partner that provides phone–related information, and *(ii) Coordinator* is the role played by the person who interacts with the CCCMS system through a graphical user interface to enter information.

We focus on the contribution of two experts in the definition of a solution to this CWR use case: a domain model expert (e_d) designs the structural view of the system

Coordinator requests *Witness* to provide his identification.
1. *Coordinator* provides witness information to *System* as reported by the witness.
2. *Coordinator* informs *System* of location and type of crisis as reported by the witness.
   In parallel to steps 2 – 4:
   2a.1 *System* contacts *PhoneCompany* to verify witness information.
   2a.2 *PhoneCompany* sends address/phone information to *System*.
   2a.3 *System* validates information received from the *PhoneCompany*.
3. *System* provides *Coordinator* with a crisis-focused checklist.
4. *Coordinator* provides crisis information to *System* as reported by the witness.
5. *System* assigns an initial emergency level to the crisis and sets the crisis status to active.

Use case ends in success.

Fig. 1. Textual Scenario of Use Case #2: "Capture Witness Report"

and a business process expert (e_b) designs the behavioral view (*i.e.*, the set of activities and the flow of control between these activities) of the system.

Domain Model Design. FIG. 2(a) is a class diagram that captures problem concepts identified from the requirements and that are relevant to the CWR use case. This domain class diagram (CD_D) is designed by e_d who formalizes his deep understanding of the various concepts manipulated in the CCCMS system. The main concepts with respect to the CWR use case are the following:

Crisis: is the concept shared by any CMS system. A **Crisis** occurs at a given location and at a given time, it has an emergency level, a status and possibly some additional information. A **Crisis** may be reported by a **Witness** and may include **Mission**s.
Witness: is a person who reports a **Crisis**.
Mission: is an action that should be taken when a **Crisis** is reported.
CheckList: is a list of things that should be checked with a **Witness**.
CMSEmployee: is a human resource who is qualified and capable of performing **Mission**s in the context of a **Crisis**.

Business Process Model. The business process model (BPM) associated with the CWR use case is represented in FIG. 2(b). According to SOA principles, e_b designs this business process model with regard to his/her own understanding of the system. For better undestanding, we provide correspondences (black clouds) between the BPM activities and the steps in the textual scenario (see Fig. 1). The business process starts by receiving a crisis coordinator (**coord**) and a crisis identifier (**id**). It contains two branches, executed in parallel. The left branch of the business process deals with the internal logic of the CWR scenario. The context of the current crisis is built by retrieving information from the witness of the crisis: the process requests preliminary information about the crisis and then refines the information it receives through subsequent exchanges between the system and the witness. In parallel (the right branch), the system calls an external partner (**PhoneCompany**) to check the information given by the witness of a crisis and prevent false or erroneous reports. When the two branches join, that is, when the system considers the crisis report to be genuine, the system assigns an emergency level to the crisis and updates the crisis status to **active**.

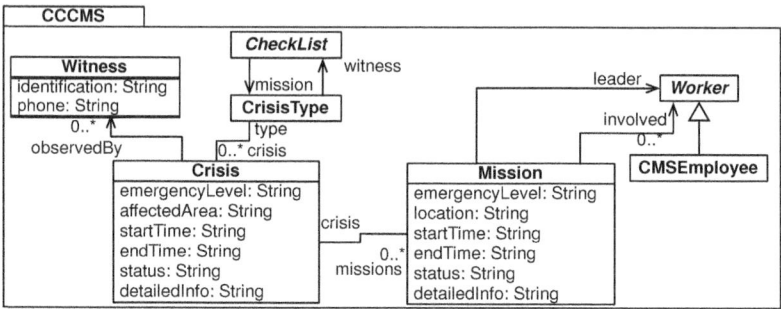

(a) Structural model (CD_D), extract.

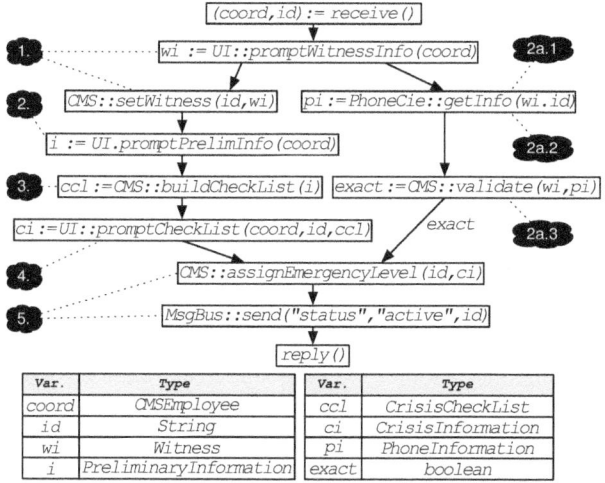

(b) Business process model (BPM), graphical representation

We use here the graphical representation defined by ADORE *[15] to represent business processes. Boxes represent activities (e.g., message reception, service invocation), and arrows represent causality relations (i.e., the associated partial order). A wait relation (a → b) means that b will wait for the end of a to start its own execution. A guard relation (a $\xrightarrow{v}$ b) strengthens the wait semantics, and conditions the start of b to the value of v. Relations are combined using a conjunctive semantics (∧).*

Fig. 2. Initial model artifacts, proposed by experts

3 Challenges and Synchronization Process

The complete CCCMS implementation contains thirteen business processes, describing hundreds of activities and thousands of relations between activities. Manual synchronization of the various views of such a large system can be challenging, time–consuming and error–prone. This section highlights situations in which checking and maintaining consistency across models can benefit from the use of automatic synchronization mechanisms. Since CD_D and BPM are defined by independent experts ($e_d \neq e_b$), one can encounter situations where types from the behavioral model (BPM) and types from the structural model (CD_D) diverge. We illustrate these divergences with examples from Section 2 below:

S_1–**Name Mismatch:** The business expert misspells a concept that already exists in CD_D. In FIG. 2(b), e_d uses a **CheckList** type whereas e_b uses a **CrisisCheckList** type. This situation illustrates naming conflicts that often occur across different views of the same system. For instance, the PROMPT [17] approach for aligning ontologies addresses this kind of conflicts among others.

S_2–**Concept Enforcing:** The business expert uses data collected from an external partner, which are unknown from the domain point of view. In FIG. 2(b), e_b uses information collected from the external agency *PhoneCompany* that is unknown to e_d and thus not modeled in the CD_D. This situation identifies the need to introduce externally defined artefacts (*i.e.*, provided by partner services) to the CD_D.

S_3–**Concept Usages:** The business expert uses his/her own data structure, *i.e.*, uses concepts defined in CD_D in an unforeseen way. In FIG. 2(b), e_b uses a **PreliminaryInformation** concept in Activity 2. Since the original scenario indicates that the **Coordinator** should manipulate the location and type of the **Crisis**, we consider that e_b aggregated several artifacts already defined in CD_D (namely the location of the crisis and its type) in a single object for practical reasons. This situation illustrates how specific usage of data in a BPM can improve the CD_D.

Clearly, the synchronization of both CD_D and BPM is not a trivial problem. We identify two challenges related to these situations: *(i)* the automatic identification of such divergences (C_1) and *(ii)* the capture of resolution strategies and their automated propagation across models in the synchronization process (C_2). FIG. 3 illustrates our approach that tackles these two challenges. The first step of the process extracts data from the set of available BPM to derive a class diagram (CD_I) which contains all the concepts manipulated by this set of processes (1). Then, we use a *divergence detection* algorithm to identify occurrences of the situations (S_i) that we discussed previously (2). The detection of divergences leads to a phase of negotiation between experts from the domain and experts from the business process. Experts should consent on identifying *strategies* to resolve divergences (3) and to ultimately perform an accurate synchronization of CD_D and BPM. The last step of the process (4) propagates the resolution strategies using a dedicated algorithm (*strategies propagation*), which automatically applies changes in both CD_D and BPM.

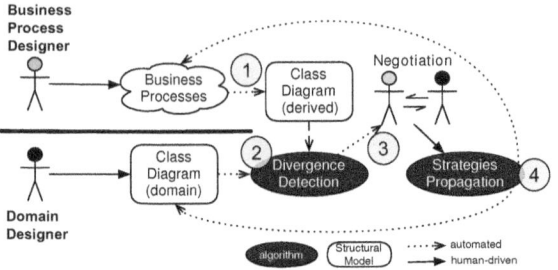

Fig. 3. SOA Models Synchronization: Process Overview

4 Identifying Model Divergences

This section presents the first two steps of the model synchronization process and the formalization of the divergence detection mechanism.

4.1 Naive Synchronization with Merge

The first step of the process extracts data from the BPM to derive a class–diagram (CD_I). The generation procedure visits all available business processes and extracts the types of all the declared variables.

Merging CD_I with CD_D using model composition techniques such as Kompose [8], produces a naive alignment of both models (FIG. 4). Naive alignment relies on an element matching process based on names. Elements with equivalent names are unified into a single element. For instance, the **CMSEmployee** element has been found in both CD_D and CD_I and therefore the merged model contains a single unified **CMSEmployee** element. Though simple, the naive alignment cannot align concepts that have different names. The default behavior of Kompose when such name–mismatches occur is to include the elements that do not match in the merged model. For instance, **PreliminaryInformation** is a concept from CD_I with no candidate match in CD_D.

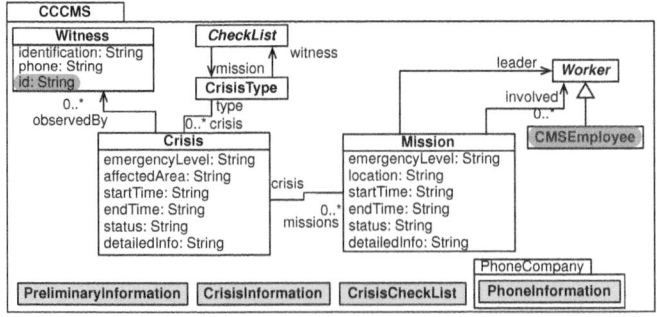

Fig. 4. Merged model: CD_D (white) ⊕ CD_I (gray)

We modified the default behavior of Kompose to record every operation used to produce the merged model. This record is analyzed to (1) validate every element that is automatically merged (*e.g.*, `CMSEmployee`) and to (2) detect divergences between CD_D and CD_I.

4.2 Intuitive Definition of Divergences

The analysis of the recorded operations leads to the detection of two kinds of divergences:

Point-of-view divergences occur when a model element from CD_I has no equivalent counterpart in CD_D (*e.g.*, `PhoneInformation`).

Structural divergences occur when a model element from CD_I has an equivalent counterpart in CD_D but the properties of the model element do not match with the properties of the corresponding model element in CD_D (*e.g.*, a "public" model element in CD_I is "private" in CD_D).

4.3 Divergence Detection Formalization

The divergence detection mechanism uses a matching operator and a set of signatures to compare a model element with another one. Let *match* be the predicate that checks if a model element of CD_I is equivalent to a model element of CD_D. With this match predicate, we formalize the kind of divergences as follows:

- *Point-of-view Divergence* refers to a model element in CD_I that has no equivalent model element in CD_D: $b \in CD_I s.t. \ \nexists d_i \in CD_D, \ match(b,d_i)$.
- *Structural Divergence* refers to a model element in CD_I that has equivalent model element in CD_D but whose properties do not match.

We formalize structural divergences according to the definitions provided by Barais *et al.* [3]. We defined two rules, used to reify the Class signature and the Property signature.

Class Signature. The signature of a Class encompasses its *identifier*, its *modifier*, possible *superclass*es and its *usage*. In the Object–Oriented (OO) paradigm, the *category* and the *visibility* of classes provide additional information on how we may use these classes in a given OO program. A class is *internal* when it participates in calling internal services either as a value or as the type of a parameter of a service. For all other usages, we consider the class as *mixed*.

$$Class^{sig} = (Identifier, Modifier, Superclass, Usage)$$
$$Modifiers \in \{Category, Visibility\}, Category \in \{abstract, concrete, final\}$$
$$Visibility \in \{private, protected, public\}, Usage \in \{internal, mixed\}$$

CD_I reflects the usage of the class definitions at runtime and thus, classes are necessarily *concrete*, *public* with no *Superclass*es. In other words, we detect a divergence (c1) when a class in CD_I has an equivalent class in CD_D that is not *public*:

$$(c1) \ match(C_B, C_D) \wedge Visibility_{C_D} \neq public \tag{1}$$

Usage refers to the class usage in the business processes. This definition has an impact on the process of deriving CD_I: (1) classes that do not participate in calling an internal service are not captured by the data structure extraction process since we cannot modify the definition of a class provided by an external partner for compatibility reasons; (2) classes that are used both within internal and external services are *mixed*. They can only be enriched with additional information that cope with the initial definition of the class. Regarding *Usage*, we detect a divergence (c2) when the usage of a class in CD_D is internal whereas an equivalent class is *mixed* in CD_I:

$$(c2)\ match(C_B, C_D) \wedge Usage_{C_D} = internal \wedge Usage_{C_B} = mixed \qquad (2)$$

Property Signature. The signature of a property encompasses its *Identifier*, its scope of use (*Static*), its *Type* that is either a *Class* or a *Datatype* and its *Access*.

$$Property^{sig} = (Identifier, Static, Type, Access)$$
$$Static \in \{static, nonstatic\},\ Type \in Class \cup Datatype$$
$$Access \in \{read, write, rw, no\}$$

The first divergence (p1) that we may detect is if the two properties that we matched in CD_I and in CD_D have different types:

$$match(P_B, P_D) \wedge (p1)\ Type_{P_D} \neq Type_{P_B} \qquad (3)$$

A property is *static* if it is common to all instances of this property and it is *nonstatic* otherwise. Properties that are used in BPM are necessarily *nonstatic* and thus we may detect the following divergence (p2):

$$match(P_B, P_D) \wedge (p2)\ Static_{P_D} = static \qquad (4)$$

Among these usual OO characteristics, we propose an additional *access* characteristic which determines how a property is accessed in BPM: *read* means that the property is only read by a service; *write* means that the property is only written by a service; *rw* means that the property is read and written by one or more services; *no* is used in other cases. For instance, the property id of a **Witness** in FIG. 2(b) is a *read* property since the property is read in activity 2a.1 and never written in any other activity. From this definition, we may detect two divergences: (p3) a property in CD_D is never accessed (*no*) or (p3') a property in CD_D is not *rw* and an equivalent property in CD_I is accessed differently:

$$(p3)\ Access_{P_D} = no\ \vee\ (p3')\ (Access_{P_D} \neq rw \wedge Access_{P_D} \neq Access_{P_B}) \qquad (5)$$

The formalization of the various kind of divergences allows the definition of generic resolution strategies that we discuss in the next section.

5 Resolution Strategies

This section proposes a formal representation of the resolution strategies (a graphical representation is presented in Fig. 5) to automate their propagation.

In the context of this paper, we focus on Point–of–View divergences, since their resolution requires action from humans and impacts both CD_D and BPM. Resolution of Point-of-View divergences involves a negotiation phase between the experts of the domain and the experts of the business process. Negotiation leads to a consensus on proposing a set of resolution strategies to properly synchronize CD_D with the data structure used in BPM.

To support the negotiation phase and to automate the propagation of resolution strategies, we propose a high-level specification of these resolution strategies, using a mapping language and the graphical tool that supports it. The mapping language and the tool are based on previous work [5]. In this specific case study, we map models of different views of the same system instead of expressing mapping on heterogeneous metamodels. The original definition of a mapping relationship remains: a mapping relationship is a white diamond which has links (dotted lines) to model elements from CD_D and CD_I.

The definition of a mapping strategy is slightly different from [5] since it depends on the types of elements involved in the mapping and the arity of the relationship (*i.e.*, the number of model elements involved in the mapping relationship). The meaning of mapping strategies is to ultimately align CD_I and CD_D data structures and we propose two unidirectional alignment strategies for synchronizing CD_D and BPM:

- *Similarity strategy* addresses the problem of name mismatch (S_1). This strategy allows renaming some classes or properties to allow matching. Experts choose the name of an element that they consider as correct and they expect that each occurrence of the inadequate name is replaced by the chosen name. In FIG. 5, experts chose to keep **CrisisCheckList** from CD_I instead of **CheckList** from CD_D. A similarity strategy must be bound to a mapping between exactly two (arity = 1) model elements of the same type.
- *Replacement strategy* is chosen by experts when they select which model element from CD_I or from CD_D to keep when addressing the two situations of concept enforcing (S_2) and concept usages (S_3). The strategy indicates that one of the model elements is discarded and an additional parameter provides the name of the relation between the initial container and the model element that is kept. In FIG. 5, experts have no choice but to add **PhoneInformation** to CD_D since it is used by an external service. Therefore they indicate the name of the relation between a **Witness** and the new class **PhoneInformation**. Similarly, experts relate **CrisisInformation** with three properties of the class **Crisis**. These properties are replaced by both a new **CrisisInformation** class and a relation between **Crisis** and **CrisisInformation** called **crisisInfo**.

6 Automatic Propagation of the Resolution Strategies

The negotiation phase is important for experts to come to an agreement about how to deal with divergences in views. We capture their decisions in a dedicated language that allows automatic propagation across models. Giving a precise interpretation for

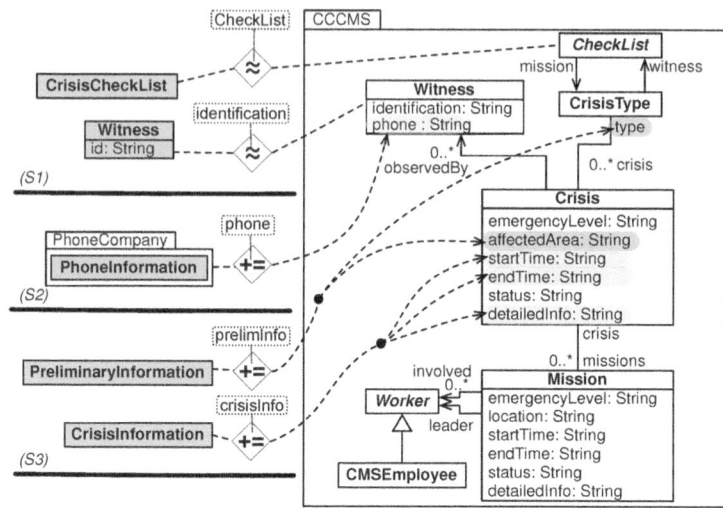

Fig. 5. A mapping model between the extracted model and the domain model is necessary to capture the users expectations

each resolution strategy, we automatically produce a set of operations on both CD_D and BPM to synchronize the views. In the following sections, we illustrate the interpretation of each resolution strategy with examples from the case study.

6.1 Name–Mismatch Strategy

The resolution of name–mismatches is straight-forward. The propagation process identifies every occurrences of a given name and replaces it with the name provided by the experts. The details of the propagation are discussed in the next subsections for both CD_D and BPM.

Domain model synchronization. We use the language of directives provided by the Kompose tool to rename model elements in CD_D. We adapted the Kompose tool to execute directives on a single model. Listing 1.1 lists the directives that the Kompose tool executes for modifying the name of **CheckList** in CD_D.

```
Directives{
   domainmodel :: CheckList.name  :=  "CrisisCheckList"
}
```

Listing 1.1. Kompose directives for renaming the CheckList class of the domain model CD_D

Business Process Synchronization. We use a formal representation of business processes models, based on many-sorted first order logic [14]. Thus, one can use logical substitution ($\theta = \{x \leftarrow x'\}$, [18]) to replace in a given model m all occurrences of x by x'. We denote a $m\theta$ the model obtained after substitution. When several substitutions $\Theta = \{\theta_1, \ldots, \theta_n\}$ need to be performed on the same model, we denote as $m\Theta$

their parallel application on *m*. In the context of name mismatch strategies, the engine will generate the set of substitutions necessary to perform all the expected alignments: $\Theta = \{w.identification \leftarrow w.id\}$. Denoting as $\{bp_1, \ldots, bp_n\}$ the available business processes in the system, the enhanced SOA is therefore defined as $\{bp_1\Theta, \ldots, bp_n\Theta\}$.

6.2 Concept Enforcing and Concept Usage Strategies

The resolution of concept enforcing and concept usages situations may rely on a large number of operations for propagating changes. The details of the propagation are discussed in the next subsections for both CD_D and BPM.

Domain Model Synchronization. Synchronization of CD_D for concept enforcing and concept usages relies on a set of Kompose directives to modify CD_D. We adopt two interpretations that are driven by the arity of the mapping relationship:

– When a mapping relationship relates only two model elements, the model element from CD_D is removed, the model element from CD_I is added to CD_D and a UML relation is created from the container of the initial model element from CD_D to the new model element in CD_D. For instance, experts decided to discard the **phone** property of the class **Witness** and use **PhoneInformation** instead. Property **phone** is removed from the class **Witness** and we create a new containment relation between **Witness** and **PhoneInformation**. This relation is named against the parameter of the replacement strategy.
– When a mapping relationship relates more than two model elements, the synchronization process is almost the same except that the model element from CD_I is considered as the container of the model elements from CD_D. Thus, we *move* the model elements from CD_D into the new model element in CD_D. For instance, experts agreed on using **PreliminaryInformation** instead of the two properties **type** and **affectedArea** from the class **Crisis**. **PreliminaryInformation** is thus enriched with the two properties **type** and **affectedArea** and a new containment relation is created between **Crisis** and **PreliminaryInformation**.

Listing 1.2 lists the directives that are applied on CD_D for replacing the **phone** property of the class **Witness** with **PhoneInformation**.

```
Directives{
  /*Creates a new PhoneInformation class
    and removes existing phone attribute
    in Witness*/
  create Class as $pi
  $pi.name = "PhoneInformation"
  destroy domainmodel::Witness::phone
  //Creates the phone relation
  create Association as $phone
  $phone.name = "phone"
  create Property as $phone_src
  $phone_src.aggregation =
    domainmodel::AggregationKind::
    #composite
  $phone_src.upper = 1
  $phone_src.type = domainmodel::Witness
  create Property as $phone_tgt
  $phone_tgt.upper = 1
  $phone_tgt.type = $pi
  $phone.memberEnd + $phone_src
  $phone.memberEnd + $phone_tgt
  /*Adds the PhoneInformation class and
    the phone relation*/
  domainmodel::packagedElement + $pi
  domainmodel::packagedElement + $phone }
```

Listing 1.2. Kompose directives for integrating PhoneInformation in the domain model CD_D

Business Process Synchronization. The propagation of strategies for the resolution of concept enforcing and concept usage situations relies on logical substitution to propagate the new accesses (*e.g.*, $\{pi \leftarrow wi.phone\}$ to replace the variable *pi* by an access to the attribute *phone* contained in the variable *wi*). However, such replacements impose that we retrieve the "container" variable (*e.g.*, *wi*) that is necessary to access a specific property (*e.g.*, *phone*). Synchronization of **PhoneInformation** and **phone** illustrates the situation where the "container" variable already exists. Thus we use this variable to access to the phone information of a **Witness** and substitutions are propagated. When the "container" variable is not already available, we ask the experts how to initialize this "container" in BPM. After synchronization of **PreliminaryInformation** with **type** and **affectedArea**, **PreliminaryInformation** is contained by a **Crisis** object. Since no **Crisis** object is available in the initial process, experts propose the invocation of the **getCrisis** operation exposed by the **CMS** service. This operation stores a **Crisis** object in a variable *c*. This invocation is automatically inserted into the business process by the ADORE engine (after the **receive** acitivty) and default substitutions are executed.

7 Related Work

Researchers and practitioners recognize the importance of business process modeling in understanding and designing accurate software systems [4]. Service-Oriented Architecture supports composition of standard-based services that can be reused quickly to meet business needs. A common enterprise domain model for integration into a SOA is used for exchanging business information between services. A pragmatic approach to support integration of a SOA is to concurrently design the domain model and business processes.

Model matching and model merging are the key activities in most of the multi–modeling approaches that tackle analysis or design of software systems. The techniques for model matching proposed in [16,1,7] are not incompatible with our approach and we may benefit from them to propose a formal basis for model matching. However, this paper focuses on the automation of the divergence detection and of the synchronization process: we propose to capture divergences resolution strategies between heterogeneous domains in a dedicated model and we provide supporting tools for their automatic propagation.

In [3], authors formalize possible conflicts for classes merging. Predefined *Conflict-Fixers* can then be used to automatically solve conflicts. We extend this approach to provide operations that change the business process when necessary.

In [19], the authors extend the UML metamodel to support consistency maintenance between class diagrams, sequence diagrams and state diagrams. We complement this work, focusing on class diagrams and business processes and proposing strategies for resolving differences. In [6], a component modeling language called MiCo has been defined that supports multi-view modeling. The consistency between different diagrams is automatically achieved by building a unique model, gluing the different view models that the users have built. We provide a similar common model but its purpose is to propagate resolution strategies in multiple business processes models.

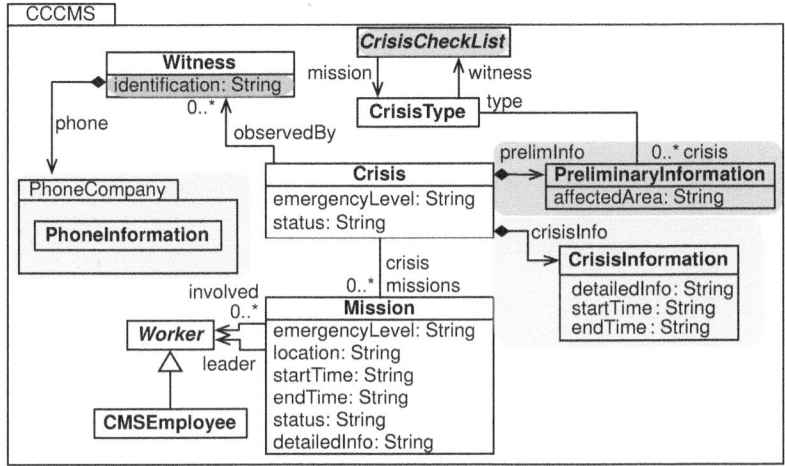

(a) Aligned domain model

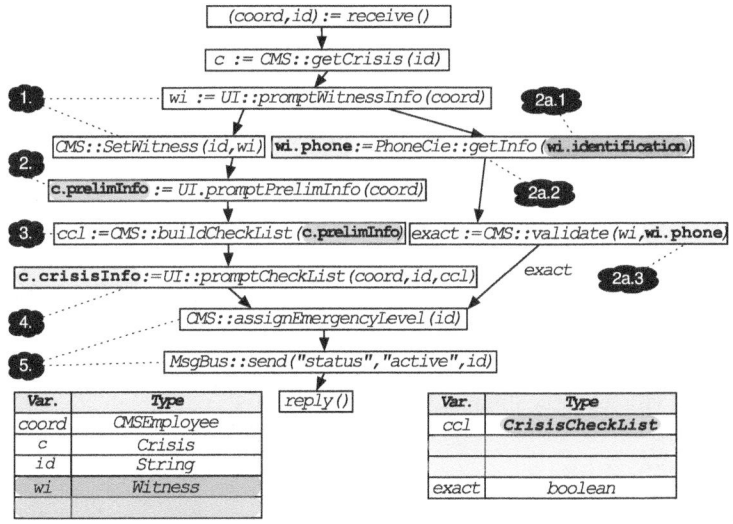

(b) Aligned business process model

Fig. 6. Aligned models, after the synchronization

Among the divergences identified, some require human expertise. Identifying the divergences and proposing changes is similar to refactoring. Kerievsky defines a set of patterns and their corresponding sequences of low-level design transformations, known as refactorings, to improve existing designs [10]. We identify similar patterns for which we propose automatic transformations.

In [13], authors propose the technique of critical pair analysis to detect the implicit dependencies between refactorings. The results of this analysis can help the developer to make an informed decision of which refactoring is most suitable in a given context and why. We are considering integrating this approach with our approach to identifying strategies.

When models of different views are changed, it may be necessary to track these changes. Like [12], we are working to save the changes (synchronization directives) and strategies that have been applied to improve the traceability of the system and automate some particular choice. In the long term we also plan to use this information to allow backtracking and thus support a better management of accidental complexity [2].

8 Conclusion

In this paper we describe an approach for synchronizing business process models with domain models developed by different teams working on the same system. The approach leverages and integrates model composition and generative techniques and tools. While manual intervention is still required, significant aspects of the synchronization process are automated. Manual intervention focuses on activities that require human judgment and experience, for example, on activities concerned with resolving divergences and conflicts across the models. Deciding what to compose and which composition to apply still remains a difficult manual process, due to the many dependencies and interrelationships between relevant compositions.

We plan to dig further for identifying other situations that require specific resolution strategies. Improving the automatic detection of divergences and propose an extensive set of relevant resolution strategies will help managing the global complexity of multi-view synchronization.

Acknowledgments. This work has been partially supported by *(i)* the MOPCOM-I Project from the Images & Réseaux Competitiveness Cluster of Brittany and *(ii)* by the Ministry of Higher Education and Research, Nord–Pas de Calais Regional Council and FEDER through the Contrat de Projets Etat Region Campus Intelligence Ambiante (CPER CIA) 2007-2013.

References

1. Anwar, A., Ebersold, S., Coulette, B., Nassar, M., Kriouile, A.: A Rule-Driven Approach for composing Viewpoint-oriented Models. Journal of Object Technology 9(2), 89–114 (2010)
2. Atkinson, C., Kühne, T.: Reducing accidental complexity in domain models. Software & Systems Modeling 7(3), 345–359 (2007)
3. Barais, O., Klein, J., Baudry, B., Jackson, A., Clarke, S.: Composing Multi-view Aspect Models. In: Seventh International Conference on Composition-Based Software Systems, ICCBSS 2008, pp. 43–52. IEEE, Los Alamitos (2008)

4. Barjis, J.: The importance of business process modeling in software systems design. Science of Computer Programming 71(1), 73–87 (2008)
5. Clavreul, M., Barais, O., Jézéquel, J.M.: Integrating legacy systems with mde. In: ICSE 2010: Proceedings of the 32nd ACM/IEEE International Conference on Software Engineering and ICSE Workshops, Cape Town, South Africa, vol. 2, pp. 69–78 (May 2010)
6. De Lara, J., Guerra, E., Vangheluwe, H., de Lara, J., Guerra, E., Vangheluwe, H.: A Multi-View Component Modelling Language for Systems Design: Checking Consistency and Timing Constrains. In: Proceedings of the VMSIS 2005: 2005 Workshop on Visual Modeling for Software Intensive Systems, pp. 27–34 (2005)
7. Falleri, J.-R., Huchard, M., Lafourcade, M., Nebut, C.: Metamodel Matching for Automatic Model Transformation Generation. In: Busch, C., Ober, I., Bruel, J.-M., Uhl, A., Völter, M. (eds.) MODELS 2008. LNCS, vol. 5301, pp. 326–340. Springer, Heidelberg (2008)
8. France, R., Fleurey, F., Reddy, R., Baudry, B., Ghosh, S.: Providing support for model composition in metamodels. In: 11th IEEE International Enterprise Distributed Object Computing Conference, EDOC 2007, p. 253 (October 2007)
9. Katz, S., Mezini, M., Kienzle, J. (eds.): Transactions on Aspect-Oriented Software Development VII. LNCS, vol. 6210. Springer, Heidelberg (2010)
10. Kerievsky, J.: Refactoring to Patterns. Addison-Wesley, Reading (2004)
11. Kienzle, J., Guelfi, N., Mustafiz, S.: Crisis management systems: A case study for aspect-oriented modeling. In: T. Aspect-Oriented Software Development [9], pp. 1–22
12. Mäder, P., Gotel, O., Philippow, I.: Rule-Based Maintenance of Post-Requirements Traceability Relations. In: 16th IEEE International Requirements Engineering, RE 2008, pp. 23–32. IEEE, Los Alamitos (2008)
13. Mens, T., Taentzer, G., Runge, O.: Analysing Refactoring Dependencies Using Graph Transformation. Software and Systems Modeling 6(3), 269–285 (2007)
14. Mosser, S.: Behavioral Compositions in Service-Oriented Architecture. Ph.D. thesis, Université Nice - Sophia Antipolis, ED STIC, Nice, France (October 2010)
15. Mosser, S., Blay-Fornarino, M., France, R.: Workflow design using fragment composition - crisis management system design through adore. In: T. Aspect-Oriented Software Development [9], pp. 200–233
16. Nejati, S., Sabetzadeh, M., Chechik, M., Easterbrook, S., Zave, P.: Matching and Merging of Statecharts Specifications. In: ICSE 2007: Proceedings of the 29th international conference on Software Engineering, pp. 54–64. IEEE Computer Society, Washington, DC (2007)
17. Noy, N.F., Musen, M.A.: Prompt: Algorithm and tool for automated ontology merging and alignment. In: AAAI/IAAI, pp. 450–455 (2000)
18. Stickel, M.E.: A Unification Algorithm for Associative-Commutative Functions. J. ACM 28, 423–434 (1981)
19. Van Der Straeten, R., Mens, T., Simmonds, J., Jonckers, V.: Using description logic to maintain consistency between UML models. In: Stevens, P., Whittle, J., Booch, G. (eds.) UML 2003. LNCS, vol. 2863, pp. 326–340. Springer, Heidelberg (2003)

From State- to Delta-Based Bidirectional Model Transformations: The Symmetric Case

Zinovy Diskin[1], Yingfei Xiong[1], Krzysztof Czarnecki[1], Hartmut Ehrig[2],
Frank Hermann[2,3], and Fernando Orejas[4]

[1] Generative Software Development Lab, University of Waterloo, Canada
{zdiskin,yingfei,kczarnec}@gsd.uwaterloo.ca
[2] Institut für Softwaretechnik und Theoretische Informatik,
Technische Universität Berlin, Germany
ehrig@cs.tu-berlin.de
[3] Interdisciplinary Center for Security, Reliability and Trust,
Université du Luxembourg
Frank.Hermann@uni.lu
[4] Departament de Llenguatges i Sistemes Informàtics,
Universitat Politècnica de Catalunya, Barcelona, Spain
orejas@lsi.upc.edu

Abstract. A bidirectional transformation (BX) keeps a pair of interrelated models synchronized. Symmetric BXs are those for which neither model in the pair fully determines the other. We build two algebraic frameworks for symmetric BXs, with one correctly implementing the other, and both being delta-based generalizations of known state-based frameworks. We identify two new algebraic laws—weak undoability and weak invertibility, which capture important semantics of BX and are useful for both state- and delta-based settings. Our approach also provides a flexible tool architecture adaptable to different user's needs.

1 Introduction

Keeping a system of models mutually consistent (model synchronization) is vital for model-driven engineering. In a typical scenario, given a pair of inter-related models, changes in either of them are to be propagated to the other to restore consistency. This setting is often referred to as bidirectional model transformation (BX) [3].

As noted by Stevens [15], despite early availability of several BX tools on the market, they did not gain much user appreciation because of semantic issues. Indeed, to avoid surprises, a user should clearly understand the behavior of synchronization procedures implemented by the tool. To formalize the semantics of BX tools and guide their implementation, algebraic frameworks for BX have been studied intensively [8,15,6,19,12].

The majority of algebraic BX frameworks (including all those cited above) are *state-based*. Synchronizing operations take the states of models before and after update as input, and produce new states of models as output. This design assumes that model alignment, i.e., discovering relations (*deltas*) between models, is done by update propagating procedures themselves. Hence, two quite different operations—heuristics-based delta discovery and algebraic delta propagation—are merged, which causes several theoretical and practical problems [2,5]; we will discuss them in Section 2.2 after considering several basic examples.

To separate delta discovery and propagation, several researchers proposed to build *delta-based* frameworks [4,2,5,11], in which propagation operations use deltas as input and output rather than compute them internally. Such frameworks (a general one [5] and a tree-oriented [2]) have been built for the *asymmetric* BX case, in which one model in the pair is a view of the other and hence does not contain any new information. In practice, however, it is often the case that two models share some information but each of them contains something new not present in the other; following [11], we call this case *symmetric* BX. The symmetric case has been considered in the state-based setting [13,15,6,11], yet a precise delta-based symmetric framework has been an open issue.

In this paper, we fill the gap and develop a delta-based framework for symmetric BX. We build two algebraic structures, *symmetric delta lenses* and *(consistency) maintainers*, which comprise delta-based synchronization operations and laws they must satisfy. Lenses are more abstract and specify an interface of a model synchronization tool; maintainers are closer to implementation and allow the tool to reuse an infrastructure for delta composition. We show that 1) a lens can be built from a maintainer, and 2) the lens's laws are derived from the maintainer's laws so that a desirable lens's behavior is guaranteed when the lens is implemented by a suitable maintainer.

The second major contribution of the paper is the introduction of two new algebraic laws: weak invertibility and weak undoability. A long-standing problem in existing symmetric BX frameworks is that the basic laws (correctness and Hippocraticness [13,15]) are not enough to ensure reasonable BX behavior, whereas more advanced laws like undoability [15] and invertibility [6] are known to be too strong and exclude many quite practical BXs. Our new laws solve this problem by reshaping strong laws into a weaker form that allows for reasonable symmetric BXs and yet prohibits BXs with unwanted behavior.

The paper is organized as follows. Section 2 analyzes an example and identifies three problems of state-based BXs that motivate our work on delta-based BXs. We present sd-lenses in Section 3 and maintainers in Section 4. Section 5 discusses related work, and Section 6 concludes the paper. Proofs and examples omitted in the paper can be found in its longer version [7].

2 The Need for Deltas

We begin with an example showing how state-based frameworks work and what their problems are. Then we explain why delta-based frameworks are needed.

2.1 Example

Figure 1 presents two related models A and B. The former specifies a class of Persons with their names and birth years, and the latter specifies Employees

306   Z. Diskin et al.

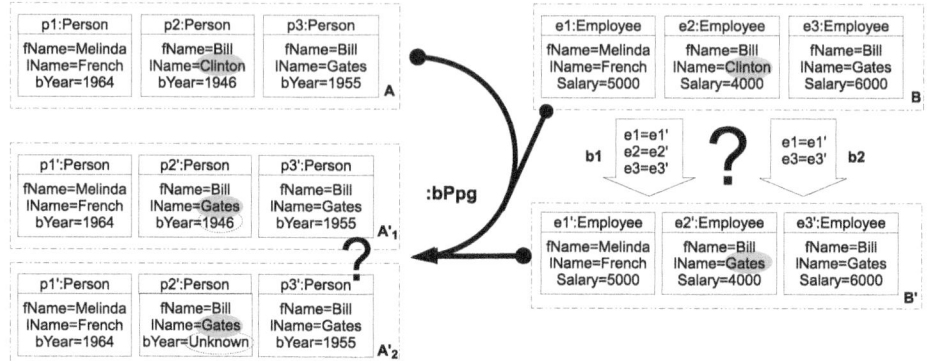

Fig. 1. The need of vertical deltas (updates)

with their names and salaries. Two models are considered consistent if the correspondence between Persons and Employees, inferred from the equality of their full names, is bijective. Initially models A and B are consistent, but then B is modified into B' and we need to propagate the change to the A side.

A suitable state-based BX framework designed for this task is trigonal systems [6]. Changes between the two sides are propagated by two ternary operations: forward propagation fPpg and backward propagation bPpg. When model B changes to B', operation bPpg takes the updated model B' and the original models B, A, and produces an updated model $A' = \mathsf{bPpg}(B', B, A)$. Forward propagation fPpg works similarly: $B' = \mathsf{fPpg}(A', A, B)$.

Figure 1 shows that two reasonable interpretations of the updated model B' are possible. Object $e2'$ may be understood as either a renamed version of $e2$, or a new object inserted into the model while $e2$ is deleted. The difference can be formally captured by specifying sets of pairs $(e, e') \in B \times B'$ with e and e' considered to represent the same object; we call this set $\simeq_v \subset B \times B'$ a *(vertical) sameness* relation. A triple $b = (B, \simeq_v, B')$ is called an *update delta* from B to B' and we write $b \colon B \to B'$. From $\simeq_v$ we can infer which objects were deleted, inserted, or modified. For example, $e2$ is deleted by delta $b2$ because it is not included in $b2$, but it is modified by $b1$ because it is declared to be the same as $e2'$ and the last names in $e2$ and $e2'$ are different.

Now we observe that two different deltas, $b1$ and $b2$, lead to two different synchronization results. To see that, we first define a correspondence between models A and B via full names of objects, i.e., we set a *(horizontal) sameness* relation $\simeq_h \subset A \times B$ between models A and B; in our case, it consists of three pairs (pi, ei), $i = 1, 2, 3$. Propagating delta $b1$ to the A side results in model A'_1: as objects $p2$ and $e2$, $e2$ and $e2'$ are the same, we merely apply modification of $e2$ to $p2$. However, propagation of delta $b2$ leads to model A'_2, which differs from A'_1 in the value of bYear: as object $e2$ is deleted and $e2'$ is inserted, object $p2$ is deleted and A-counterpart of $e2'$ — a new object $p2'$ — is inserted, but

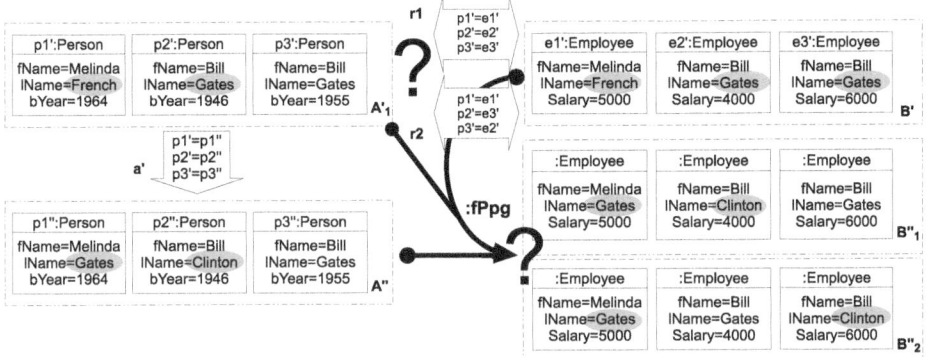

Fig. 2. The need of horizontal delta (correspondence)

its birth date is unknown. Thus, propagation essentially depends on deltas, and propagation operation bPpg has to compute them using some heuristics, and then propagate the change.

To unify terminology and notation, we call a triple $r = (A, \simeq_h, B)$ a *correspondence* or *horizontal* delta from A to B and write $r \colon A \leftrightarrow B$; update deltas are *vertical*. Importantly, the same models A and B may have different correspondence deltas between them. For example, suppose that a user reviews the updated model $A1'$ and discovers that the change is mistaken: it is Melinda French who gets married and changes her last name, but not Bill Clinton. Then the user changes names of objects $p1$ and $p2$ to, respectively, Melinda Gates and Bill Clinton, as shown in Fig. 2 with update delta $a' \colon A'_1 \to A''$. To propagate the update to the B-side, we need to relate models $A1'$ and B' and rename the corresponding Employees. However, because there are two "Bill Gates" in both models, two cases of correspondences, $r1$ and $r2$ in Fig. 2, are possible, which lead to two different results: B''_1 and B''_2. Of course, from the previous propagation we know that the correct delta is $r1$, but since this delta does not explicitly occur in the output of operation bPpg, forward propagation fPpg does not know it and has to infer it from the current states of the models.

2.2 Unweaving Delta Discovery and Propagation

Problems of Merging Delta Discovery into Update Propagation. First, such a merge, as presented in state-based frameworks, essentially complicates propagation operations and their semantics. Delta discovery is an independent operation with its own laws [1,16], and is usually far more complex than propagation as such. Weaving delta discovery into update propagation complicates the laws of the latter and makes its behavior less predictable.

Second, it unnecessarily complicates support of update sequences. Indeed, our example can be specified as shown by the inset diagram above (input nodes are framed and input arrows are solid; output elements are, respectively, non-framed and dashed). It shows that the output horizontal delta r1 produced by bPpg must be the input delta for fPpg. However, in a straightforward state-based implementation, operation fPpg computes the delta afresh, which may result in a different delta $r'_1 \neq r_1$.

Third, our previous work [5] shows that similar problems appear in sequential composition of BX (think of another BX from B- to C-models) if vertical deltas are replaced by pairs of models, as is done in the state-based frameworks.

A solution to these three problems is to encapsulate delta propagation in a special module, which takes the horizontal and vertical deltas as input, and produces new vertical and horizontal deltas as shown in the inset diagram above; we call such a module a delta-based BX. It has a simple algebraic semantics, prevents erroneous composition of updates and BXs, and allows reusing deltas.

Implementation of Deltas. Normally, only small parts of big models are updated, and implementing vertical deltas as sameness relations is very non-economic. A practical solution is to implement them operationally as edit sequences or as overriding deltas [18,5]. Horizontal deltas can be seen as traceability links, which are maintained by many transformation tools. For either representation, deltas can be abstracted as arrows relating two models.

Managing Deltas and Tool Architecture. Having a separate delta-propagating module provides a flexible tool architecture. For example, the state-based framework can be simulated if deltas are first discovered by a model differencing tool and then passed to the propagation module. If the two models are related by a transformation, horizontal deltas can be inferred from it — this architecture is used in SyncATL [17]. Hybrid interfaces (state-based for one dimension and delta-based for the other) are also possible, e.g., two incremental synchronization tools, based on TGG [9] and QVT [14], take vertical deltas as input and store horizontal deltas internally. An additional advantage of separating delta discovery from propagation is that the user may control the result of differencing and correct it if needed. Finally, if the synchronizer can be tightly coupled with the application, deltas can be obtained by recording the user operations within the applications; in this case, model differencing phase is not needed.

Although the tools mentioned above actually use a separated delta propagation module, they lack a precise specification of both their architecture and semantics of propagation procedures they guarantee. Filling the gap needs a precise definition of delta-based symmetric BX and a formal algebraic theory of delta propagation. Developing both of them is our goal for the rest of the paper.

3 Symmetric Delta Lenses

We first specify an algebraic structure modeling the very basic properties of update propagation (Section 3.1). Then we enrich the structure with more advanced laws of undoability and invertibility (Section 3.2).

3.1 The Basic Structure

We begin by defining the space of models and their vertical deltas as a graph with an additional structure representing do-nothing updates and update inversion; this structure makes the graph *reflexive* and *involutive*.

Definition 1 (Model space). A *model space* **A** is a graph $(\mathbf{M_A}, \mathbf{\Delta_A}, \$_\mathbf{A})$, whose nodes $A \in \mathbf{M_A}$ are called **A**-*models*, arrows $a \in \mathbf{\Delta_A}$ are **A**-model *deltas*, and $\$_\mathbf{A}$ is a quadruple of total unary "bookkeeping" functions $(\square_{\mathbf{A}-}, {}_-\square_\mathbf{A}, \mathsf{id}_{\mathbf{A}-}, {}_-{}^{\smile \mathbf{A}})$ (with "_" being the placeholder) providing **A** with the structure of reflexive involutive graph explained below.

Functions $\square_{\mathbf{A}-}, {}_-\square_\mathbf{A} \colon \mathbf{\Delta_A} \to \mathbf{M_A}$ provide deltas with their *source* and *target* models resp., and we write $a\colon A \to A'$ if $\square_\mathbf{A} a = A$ and $a\square_\mathbf{A} = A'$. Intuitively, we understand a as a delta resulting from some update to model A, i.e., as a triple $(A, \simeq_v, A')$ like those considered in Section 2.1. By an abuse of terminology, we will often call delta a an update from A to A' (though different sequences of update operations can result in the same delta).

Function $\mathsf{id}_\mathbf{A}\colon \mathbf{A} \to \mathbf{\Delta_A}$ assign to every model A a special *identity* delta $\mathsf{id}_\mathbf{A} A\colon A \to A$ that identically relates A to itself. Such a delta may be thought of as (the result of) an *idle* update to A, which does nothing. To capture this intuition formally, we need to introduce sequential composition of deltas and require $\mathsf{id}_\mathbf{A}$ to be its neutral unit (see [5] for details), but in this paper we do not consider vertical delta composition. However, we will later capture idleness of $\mathsf{id}_\mathbf{A}$-arrows wrt. their composition with horizontal deltas.

Finally, ${}_-{}^{\smile \mathbf{A}}$ is an unary operation of *delta inversion*: for $a\colon A \to A'$, arrow $a^{\smile \mathbf{A}}\colon A' \to A$ is the same delta traversed in the opposite direction. For example, the inverse of delta $a = (A, \simeq, A')\colon A \to A'$ in Fig. 2 with $\simeq = \{(p1, p1'), (p2, p2'), (p3, p3')\}$ is delta $a^{\smile} = (A', \simeq^{-1}, A)\colon A' \to A$ with $\simeq^{-1} = \{(p1', p1), (p2', p2), (p3', p3)\}$. It can be understood as the delta resulting from undoing update a: changing lNames of $p1'$ and $p2'$ to French and Gates resp.

The following evident laws are required (subscript **A** near ${}^{\smile}$ is omitted):
$$(\mathsf{id}_\mathbf{A} A)^{\smile} = \mathsf{id}_\mathbf{A} A \text{ for all } A \in \mathbf{M_A} \text{ and } (a^{\smile})^{\smile} = a \text{ for all } a \in \mathbf{\Delta_A},$$
which make operation ${}^{\smile}$ an *involution* and the graph *involutive*.

Thus, a model space is a reflexive involutive graph.

Now we introduce horizontal deltas as arrows between models in two model spaces, and come to the notion of *triple spaces*.

Definition 2 (Triple space). A *triple space* $\mathbf{R}\colon \mathbf{A} \leftrightarrow \mathbf{B}$ or $\mathbf{A} \xleftrightarrow{\mathbf{R}} \mathbf{B}$ consists of a pair of models spaces $(\mathbf{A}, \mathbf{B})$, and a set $\mathbf{R}$ of arrows from **A**-nodes to **B**-nodes called *correspondence relations*, or just *corrs*. Formally, $\mathbf{R} = (\mathbf{M_A}, \mathbf{M_B}, \mathbf{\Delta_{AB}}, \$_\mathbf{AB})$ is a graph with $\mathbf{M_A} \cup \mathbf{M_B}$ being the set of nodes, $\mathbf{\Delta_{AB}}$ the set of arrows (corrs), and $\$_\mathbf{AB}$ consists of two functions, $\square_{\mathbf{AB}-}\colon \mathbf{\Delta_{AB}} \to \mathbf{M_A}$ and ${}_-\square_\mathbf{AB}\colon \mathbf{\Delta_{AB}} \to \mathbf{M_B}$, providing corrs with their *source* and *target* models. For $r \in \mathbf{\Delta_{AB}}$, we write $r\colon A \leftrightarrow B$ if $\square_\mathbf{AB} r = A$ and $r\square_\mathbf{AB} = B$.

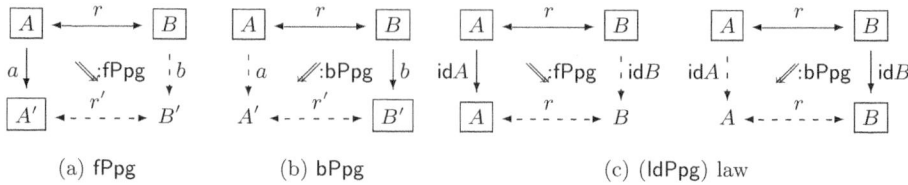

Fig. 3. Stable sd-lens: operations (a,b) and the law (c)

To ease terminology, we will use term 'delta' generically for both updates (*vertical deltas*) and correspondences (*horizontal deltas*). We will also write bookkeeping functions, i.e., components of $\$_\mathbf{A}$, $\$_\mathbf{B}$, and $\$_\mathbf{AB}$ without subscripts.

Now we define operations modeling update propagation.

Definition 3 (sd-lenses). A *symmetric delta lens (sd-lens)* over a triple space $\mathbf{A} \stackrel{\mathbf{R}}{\longleftrightarrow} \mathbf{B}$ is a pair of *forward* and *backward propagation* operations (note that backward propagation arrow goes from right to left)

fPpg: $\Delta_\mathbf{A} \,{}^\square\!\!\times \Delta_\mathbf{AB} \to \Delta_\mathbf{B} \times_\square \Delta_\mathbf{AB}$ and bPpg: $\Delta_\mathbf{A} \,{}_\square\!\!\times \Delta_\mathbf{AB} \leftarrow \Delta_\mathbf{B} \times^\square \Delta_\mathbf{AB}$

of arities shown in Fig. 3(a,b): input nodes are framed, input arrows are solid, and the output elements are non-framed and dashed. Figure 4 shows an example: operation fPpg takes deltas a and r and produces deltas b and r'.

Symbol ${}^\square\!\!\times$ in the formulas above denotes the subset of the respective Cartesian product consisting of all pairs of arrows with the same source: $\Delta_\mathbf{A} \,{}^\square\!\!\times \Delta_\mathbf{AB} = \{(a,r) \in \Delta_\mathbf{A} \times \Delta_\mathbf{AB}: \square_\mathbf{A} a = \square_\mathbf{AB} r\}$, and respectively $\Delta_\mathbf{B} \times_\square \Delta_\mathbf{AB} = \{(b,r) \in \Delta_\mathbf{B} \times \Delta_\mathbf{AB}: b\square_\mathbf{B} = r\square_\mathbf{AB}\}$ is the subset of pairs with the same target. Similarly, the meaning of symbols $\times^\square$ and ${}_\square\!\!\times$ is defined by diagram Fig. 3(b). We must also require right correspondence of the input and output pairs: for fPpg, if $(b,r') = \mathsf{fPpg}(a,r)$, then $\square b = r\square$ and $\square r' = a\square$, and for bPpg, if $(a,r') = \mathsf{bPpg}(b,r)$, then $\square a = \square r$ and $r'\square = b\square$. We call these and similar equations specifying relationships between arrows *incidence conditions*.

Note that the arity diagrams unambiguously specify all required incidence conditions, and their explicit string-based formulation as above can be omitted. In fact, operations like fPpg and bPpg act upon arrow diagrams, and can be accurately formalized in terms of *diagram algebra* [4], which allows one to avoid bulky formulation of incidence conditions. Below we will use the arity diagram of an operation as a part of the definition and write ⊠ for ${}^\square\!\!\times$, $\times_\square$, $\times^\square$, or ${}_\square\!\!\times$.

The small double arrows in the middle labeled by :fPpg, :bPpg indicate that the squares are *application instances* of the operations (other instances are are formed by other arguments). In the same manner we could write also $a{:}\Delta_\mathbf{A}$, $r{:}\Delta_\mathbf{AB}$ *etc*, but we omit these to avoid too heavy notation.

It is convenient to use also the following notation: for the situation in Fig. 3(a), we write $a.\mathsf{fPpg}(r)$ for b and $r.\mathsf{fPpg}(a)$ for r', and similarly for bPpg. To resolve ambiguity, we always use a,b to denote deltas in $\mathbf{A},\mathbf{B}$, and r to denote correspondences.

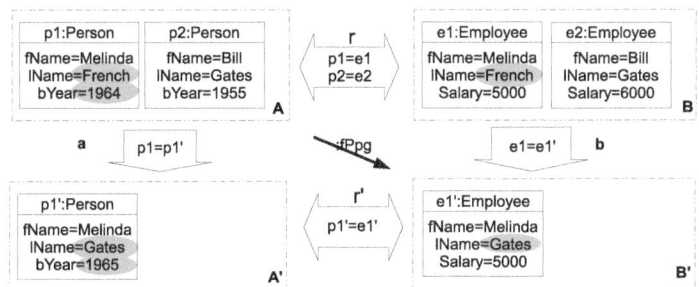

Fig. 4. Example of update propagation

A natural requirement for sd-lenses is that if the input delta changes nothing, the output delta should also change nothing. Formally, we call an sd-lens *stable* if the following law holds for any corr $r: A \to B$ (see Fig. 3c):
(IdPpg)   fPpg(idA,r)=(idB,r) and bPpg(idB,r)=(idA,r).

The rest of the paper assumes this law holds by default unless the otherwise is explicitly specified.

We write an sd-lens over a triple space $\mathbf{A} \stackrel{R}{\longleftrightarrow} \mathbf{B}$ as a double bidirectional arrow $\lambda: \mathbf{A} \stackrel{R}{\Longleftrightarrow} \mathbf{B}$ meaning that the second arrow refers to a pair of operations (fPpg, bPpg) constituting the lens.

3.2 Invertibility and Undoability

A basic requirement for *bidirectional* model synchronization is compatibility of propagation operations between themselves. Given a corr $r: A \leftrightarrow B$, an update $a: A \to A'$ is propagated into update $b = a.\mathsf{fPpg}(r)$, which can be propagated back to update $a' = b.\mathsf{bPpg}(r)$. For an ideal situation of *strong invertibility*, we should require $a' = a$. Unfortunately, it does not hold in general because **A**-specific part of the information is lost in passing from a to b, and cannot be restored. For example, in Fig. 4 **A**-objects have birth years, which are absent on the **B**-side and hence are lost in a'. However, we could still require invertibility for data shared between A and B. In our example, name changes are shared and will be restored in a'; hence, $a \neq a'$ but $a'.\mathsf{fPpg} = a.\mathsf{fPpg}$. We thus come to the notion of *weak invertibility* of update propagation; it is formalized as follows.

Definition 4 (update equivalence). Given an sd-lens $\lambda: \mathbf{A} \stackrel{R}{\Longleftrightarrow} \mathbf{B}$ and a corr $r: A \leftrightarrow B$, two updates of model A, $a_1: A \to A_1'$ and $a_2: A \to A_2'$, are called *r-equivalent* if $a_1.\mathsf{fPpg}(r) = a_2.\mathsf{fPpg}(r)$; we then write $a_1 \sim_r a_2$. Similarly, we introduce *r-equivalence* $b_1 \sim_r b_2$ on **B**-side. (It is easy to see that both relations are indeed equivalence relations.)

Definition 5 (invertible lenses). Operations fPpg and bPpg are *(weakly) invertible* if equations below hold for any $r: A \leftrightarrow B$ and all $a: A \to A'$, $b: B \to B'$:
(fbInv) $a.\mathsf{fPpg}(r).\mathsf{bPpg}(r) \sim_r a$.
(bfInv) $b.\mathsf{bPpg}(r).\mathsf{fPpg}(r) \sim_r b$.

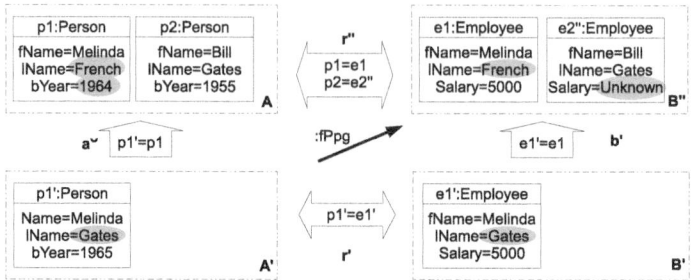

Fig. 5. Undoing update a from Fig. 4

We will call an sd-lens satisfying the laws *invertible*. We show in [10] that invertible sd-lenses can be implemented with triple-graph grammars.

Another important requirement for a reasonable BX is *undoability* discussed by Stevens [15] in the state-based setting. In an ideal situation of *strong undoability*, if update a is first propagated as b and then is cancelled by delta $a^{\smile}\colon A' \to A$, we require a reasonable BX to produce delta $b^{\smile}\colon B' \to B$ to cancel the change on the other side. Unfortunately, it does not hold in general because some information about B may be lost in B' and cannot be restored. For example, Fig. 5 continues the story of Fig. 4 and shows an update $a^{\smile}$ canceling a. According to corr r', a corresponding new object $e2$ (Bill Gates in **B**) should be inserted into model B' and return it back to B. However, since Bill's Salary was lost in B', the propagation of $a^{\smile}$ along r' can only set his Salary to Unknown thus resulting in a new object $e2''$ and a new model B''. It is a vertical-delta analog of the phenomenon we have just discussed for horizontal deltas, and the strong condition should be again relaxed by considering updates up to their equivalence.

Definition 6 (undoable lenses). An sd-lens is called *(weakly) undoable* if the following *forward-undo* and *backward-undo* laws hold:
(fUndo)   Let $(b, r') = \mathsf{fPpg}(a, r)$. Then $a^{\smile}.\mathsf{fPpg}(r') \sim_{r'} b^{\smile}$.
(bUndo)   Let $(a, r') = \mathsf{bPpg}(b, r)$. Then $b^{\smile}.\mathsf{bPpg}(r') \sim_{r'} a^{\smile}$.

In the long version [7], we show that an sd-lens may be (i) invertible but not undoable, (ii) undoable but not invertible, or (iii) invertible and undoable. It means that the two notions are independent and consistent.

To unify terminology, we will call an invertible/undoable lens *horizontally*/resp. *vertically well-behaved (Wb)*. A lens is *well-behaved* if it is both horizontally and vertically Wb. We will also refer to the laws as *horizontal/vertical round-tripping*.

4 Consistency Maintenance and Alignment

We have seen that a well-behaved sd-lens exhibits a truly BX-behavior. An advantage of the framework is its simplicity yet applicability to practical scenarios. However, simplicity of the sd-lens framework comes for a price.

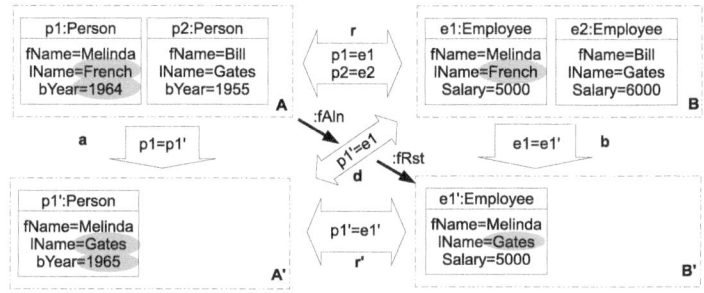

Fig. 6. Two steps in update propagation

First, an update propagation in sd-lenses actually consists of two steps, and their coupling prevents the reuse of operations in the implementation. Consider Fig. 6 that shows the case of propagation in Fig. 4 in more details. The first step is to align models A' and B and compute a new (diagonal) correspondence delta $d \colon A' \leftrightarrow B$ based on the original delta r and update $a \colon A \to A'$. We call this operation *forward (re-)alignment* and denote it as fAln. Note that re-alignment is nothing but composition of two deltas (a simple computation), and should not be confused with delta discovery (requiring heuristics). With this reservation, we will call re-alignment just alignment.

The new correspondence d reveals an inconsistency: objects $p1'$ and $e1$ are declared to be the same yet their lName attributes are different. Hence, in the second step consistency must be restored by updating object $e1$ to $e1'$, and thus we produce an update delta $b \colon B \to B'$ and consistent correspondence delta $r' \colon A' \leftrightarrow B'$ from delta d. We call this operation *forward (consistency) restoration*, fRst. Since different restoration operations can be built on top of the same alignment framework, we could reuse alignment operations. However, their reuse cannot be realized within the sd-lens interface, since (re-)alignment operations are woven into update propagation in sd-lenses.

The second problem of the sd-lens interface is related to an important BX requirement — Hippocraticness law of Meertens/Stevens [13,15]. When model A is updated to A', it may happen that the new diagonal delta d is still consistent and then nothing should be done on the **B**-side. However, since in sd-lenses we have no access to diagonal deltas, we cannot formulate the requirement above.

We call a pair of forward and backward alignment operations an *alignment framework* to stress its basic supporting role for restoration operations built on top of it. We call a pair of forward and backward restoration operations a *maintainer*. Below in this section we formalize the two notions and show that well-behaved maintainers correctly implement well-behaved sd-lenses.

4.1 Alignment Taken Seriously

We define the notion of alignment framework as a triple space enriched with re-alignment operations.

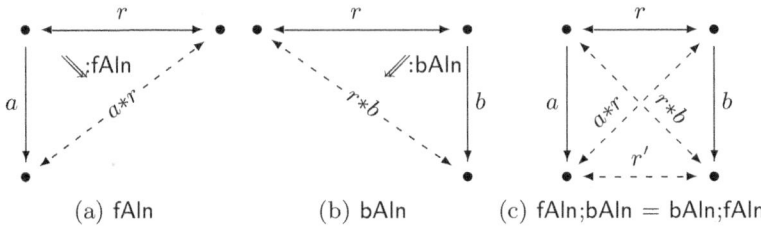

Fig. 7. Alignment operations and their laws

Definition 7 (Alignment framework). An *alignment framework* over a triple space $\mathbf{R}\colon \mathbf{A} \leftrightarrow \mathbf{B}$ is a couple of operations
$$\mathsf{fAln}\colon \Delta_{\mathbf{A}} \boxtimes \Delta_{\mathbf{AB}} \to \Delta_{\mathbf{AB}} \quad \text{and} \quad \mathsf{bAln}\colon \Delta_{\mathbf{AB}} \leftarrow \Delta_{\mathbf{B}} \boxtimes \Delta_{\mathbf{AB}}$$
called *forward* and *backward alignment* resp., where symbols $\boxtimes$ denote subsets of the respective Cartesian products consisting of all incident arrows as specified by Fig. 7(a,b) (see p.310). We will also write $a * r$ for $\mathsf{fAln}(a, r)$ and $r * b$ for $\mathsf{bAln}(b, r)$.

There are two laws. Identity updates do not actually need re-alignment:
(IdAln) $\mathsf{id}A * r = r = r * \mathsf{id}B$
for any corr $r\colon A \to B$.

The result of applying a sequence of interleaving forward and backward alignments does not depend on the order of application as shown in Fig. 7(c):
(AlnAln) $(a * r) * b = a * (r * b)$
for any $a \in \Delta_{\mathbf{A}}, r \in \Delta_{\mathbf{AB}}, b \in \Delta_{\mathbf{B}}$.

We will write an alignment framework as an arrow $\boldsymbol{\alpha}\colon \mathbf{A} \stackrel{\mathbf{R}}{\Longleftrightarrow} \mathbf{B}$.

4.2 Consistency Maintainers: Hippocratic Update Propagation

Definition 8 (maintainers). A *(consistency) maintainer* over an alignment framework $\boldsymbol{\alpha}\colon \mathbf{A} \stackrel{\mathbf{R}}{\Longleftrightarrow} \mathbf{B}$ comprises (i) a subclass $\mathbf{K} \subset \Delta_{\mathbf{AB}}$ of *consistent* corrs and (ii) a couple of *consistency restoration* operations
$$\mathsf{fRst}\colon \Delta_{\mathbf{AB}} \to \Delta_{\mathbf{B}} \boxtimes \Delta_{\mathbf{AB}} \quad \text{and} \quad \mathsf{bRst}\colon \Delta_{\mathbf{A}} \boxtimes \Delta_{\mathbf{AB}} \leftarrow \Delta_{\mathbf{AB}}$$
of arities shown in Fig. 8 (a,b): output nodes and arrows are shown blank and dashed resp.

If $(b, r') = \mathsf{fRst}(r)$, we will also write $r|$ for b and r_- for r'; similarly, if $(a, r') = \mathsf{bRst}(b)$, we write $|r$ and $_-r$ for a and r'. In composed formulas, bars and underscores always have the highest priority.

A maintainer is called *correct* if its output corrs are always consistent, and are compositions of the original corr with output updates:
(Corr) $r * r| = r_- \in \mathbf{K}$ and $|r * r = {_-r} \in \mathbf{K}$
A maintainer is called *Hippocratic* (we borrow Stevens' term [15]) if it does nothing for an originally consistent corr as shown in Fig. 8(c):
(Hipp)   If $r\colon A \to B \in \mathbf{K}$, then $|r = \mathsf{id}A$, $r| = \mathsf{id}B$ and $_-r = r = r_-$.

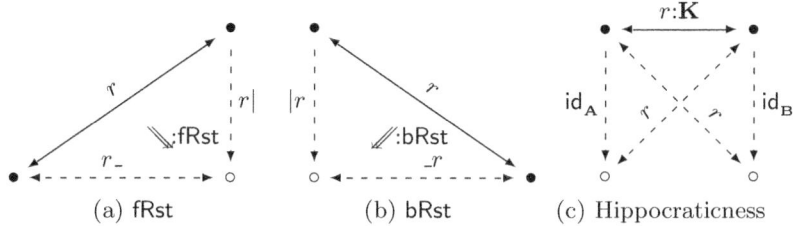

Fig. 8. Consistency restoration operations (a,b) and their laws

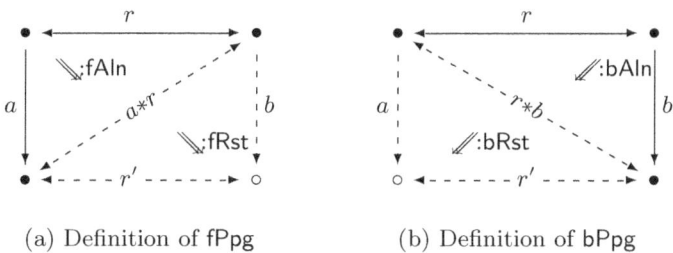

Fig. 9. From maintainers to lenses

We write a maintainer as an arrow $\mu\colon \mathbf{A} \overset{K \subset R}{\Longleftrightarrow} \mathbf{B}$ comprising pairs of operations (fAln,bAln) and (fRst,bRst) over the triple space $\mathbf{A} \overset{R}{\longleftrightarrow} \mathbf{B}$.

4.3 From Maintainers to Lenses: Invertibility and Undoability

Maintainers are designed to implement lenses: update propagation operations can be defined via alignment and restoration operations as shown in Fig. 9(a,b).

Definition 9 (from maintainers to lenses). Given a correct maintainer $\mu\colon \mathbf{A} \overset{K \subset R}{\Longleftrightarrow} \mathbf{B}$, we define a lens $\ulcorner\mu\urcorner\colon \mathbf{A} \overset{K}{\Longleftrightarrow} \mathbf{B}$ by setting
fPpg$(a,r) \overset{\text{def}}{=} (d|, d_{-})$ with $d = a * r$, and bPpg$(b,r) \overset{\text{def}}{=} (|e, {}_{-}e)$ with $e = r * b$.

It is easy to see that lens $\ulcorner\mu\urcorner$ is stable as soon as μ is Hippocratic. That is, a correct and Hippocratic maintainer implements a stable lens.

Now we want to state conditions for μ ensuring that the lens $\ulcorner\mu\urcorner$ is well-behaved. Since the notion of update equivalence is crucial here, we first reformulate it as *corr equivalence* in terms of restoration operations.

Definition 10 (corr equivalence). Two corrs with the same target, $r_i\colon A_i \leftrightarrow B$, $i = 1, 2$ are called *forward equivalent* if $r_1| = r_2|$; we write $r_1 \sim_\bullet r_2$. Dually, two corrs with the same source $r_i\colon A \leftrightarrow B_i$ are *backward equivalent*, $r_1 \bullet\!\!\sim r_2$, if $|r_1 = |r_2$.

The next step is to substitute operations defined in Definition 9 into Definitions 5 and 6 of invertibility and undoability.

Definition 11 (well-behaved maintainer). (a) A correct maintainer is called *invertible* or *horizontally well-behaved (hWb)* if the following two dual conditions hold for any $r\colon A \leftrightarrow B \in \mathbf{K}$:
(fbInv$_m$) For any $a\colon A \to A'$, let $d1 = a*r$, $e1 = r*d1|$. Then $|e1*r \sim_\bullet d1$
(bfInv$_m$) For any $b\colon B \to B'$, let $d1 = r*b$, $e1 = |d1*r$. Then $r*e1| \sim_\bullet d1$

(b) A correct maintainer is called *undoable* or *vertically well-behaved (vWb)* if the following two dual conditions hold for any $r\colon A \leftrightarrow B \in \mathbf{K}$:
(fUndo$_m$) For any $a\colon A \to A'$, let $d1 = a*r$, $b = d1|$, $r' = d1_-$, $d2 = r'*b^\vee$, and $e2 = a^\vee * r'$. Then $d2 \sim_\bullet r' * e2|$
(bUndo$_m$) For any $b\colon B \to B'$, let $d1 = r*b$, $a = |d1$, $r' = \_d1$, $d2 = a^\vee * r'$, and $e2 = r' * b^\vee$. Then $d2 \sim_\bullet |e2 * r'$

Details clarifying the meaning of formulas can be found in the long version. The notion of invertible maintainer is implicit in [10], where alignment and restoration operations are realized by TGG-means.

(c) A correct maintainer is called *well-behaved (Wb)* if it is well-behaved both horizontally and vertically.

Theorem 1. *Let* $\boldsymbol{\mu}\colon \mathbf{A} \overset{K \subset R}{\Longleftrightarrow} \mathbf{B}$ *be a correct maintainer and* $\ulcorner\boldsymbol{\mu}\urcorner\colon \mathbf{A} \overset{K}{\Longleftrightarrow} \mathbf{B}$ *is the sd-lens derived from it. Then the following holds*
(i) $\ulcorner\boldsymbol{\mu}\urcorner$ *is stable iff* $\boldsymbol{\mu}$ *is Hippocratic.*
(ii) $\ulcorner\boldsymbol{\mu}\urcorner$ *is invertible iff* $\boldsymbol{\mu}$ *is invertible.*
(iii) $\ulcorner\boldsymbol{\mu}\urcorner$ *is undoable iff* $\boldsymbol{\mu}$ *is undoable.*
Hence, a correct maintainer $\boldsymbol{\mu}$ *implements a Wb sd-lens* $\ulcorner\boldsymbol{\mu}\urcorner$ *iff* $\boldsymbol{\mu}$ *is itself Wb.*

The proof of the theorem can be found in the long version. The theorem shows that heavy definitions of maintainers' laws can be hidden under the hood of the sd-lens framework. The latter thus demonstrates a reasonable trade-off between concreteness and abstraction: it is abstract enough to free the user from the (re-)alignment concerns, yet provides enough flexibility by explicitly including deltas.

5 Related Work

Algebraic frameworks for symmetric BX did not get as much attention as asymmetric ones, perhaps, because of technical difficulties of working in the symmetric situation. Several closely related state-based frameworks were built by Meertens [13], Stevens [15], and Diskin [6]. In these frameworks, model consistency is a binary relation on model spaces. For us, consistency is a property of the correspondence between models (the idea first proposed in [4]). State-based frameworks mentioned above appear as special cases of our delta-base maintainers, if deltas are merely pairs of models (we call such triple spaces *simple*). Then identity, update inversion and alignment operations are trivial: $\mathrm{id}A = AA$, $(AA')^\vee = A'A$, $AA' * AB = A'B$, $AB * BB' = AB'$, and are uniquely determined by model spaces. Hence, these operations can be removed from the signature and we come to the state-based setting. If undoability of [15] is reshaped to its weak form, then Stevens' coherent transformations are exactly our vertically Wb maintainers over simple triple spaces. If invertibility is also reshaped to its weak form, then undoable and invertible trigonal systems of [6] are exactly our Wb maintainers over simple triple spaces. Precise results can be found in [7].

A different state-based algebraic model of symmetric BX is symmetric lenses with complement by Hofmann *et al* [11] (*ssc-lenses*). They can be seen as our sd-lenses over simple model spaces (update deltas are pairs) but non-simple correspondences, that is, we still consider a *set* $\mathbf{R}(A, B)$ of corrs for a given pair of models (A, B). Given a model A' and a corr $r \colon A \leftrightarrow B$, we can simulate ssc-lens operation $\mathsf{putr}(A, r)$ by computing $\mathsf{fPpg}(AA', r)$; symmetrically for B' and r. Then laws called round-tripping in [11] and our IdPpg laws coincide; however, our invertibility (which we believe is truly about round-tripping) and undoability laws are not considered in [11]. On the other hand, symmetric lenses by Hofmann *et al* have an element *missing* referring to minimal models (empty ones, if permitted by the metamodels), which is omitted in sd-lenses. To fill-in the gap, we need to enrich our model spaces with *initial objects* (a construct well-known in category theory); we leave it for future work.

Mathematical foundations for building delta-based frameworks (called *tile algebra*) are described in [4]. Diagonal synchronizers specified there are basically sd-lenses that distinguish between consistent and inconsistent corrs at the input of propagation operations; in addition, they are equipped with alignment operations called rematching. However, neither update inversion, nor the round-tripping laws are considered in [4].

6 Conclusion

A delta-based symmetric BX is a synchronization module that does nothing but propagating vertical deltas over horizontal ones; how these deltas are computed and passed to the module is a separate concern. This design provides a flexible architecture and fixes compositional problems of the state-based frameworks. In the paper we built two algebraic frameworks for symmetric delta-based BXs: more abstract sd-lenses that screen simple but tedious re-alignment computations from the user, and closer to implementation maintainers. We found new— weaker—versions of important invertibility and undoability laws, which do constrain synchronization behavior, and yet do not exclude many practically interesting BXs incompatible with the strong laws considered previously. Our main result shows that an sd-lens can be implemented by a suitable maintainer, and the former is weakly invertible and undoable iff the latter is such.

The framework still lacks lens and maintainer combinators for specifying complex BX in a compositional way. A well-designed set of combinators would make our frameworks practically applicable to the design of BX languages. We leave it for future work.

Acknowledgment. We are grateful to Michał Antkiewicz, Leo Passos and Arif Wider for discussion and fruitful comments. Financial support was provided by the Ontario Research Fund and NSERC.

References

1. Alanen, M., Porres, I.: Difference and union of models. In: Stevens, P., Whittle, J., Booch, G. (eds.) UML 2003. LNCS, vol. 2863, pp. 2–17. Springer, Heidelberg (2003)
2. Barbosa, D.M.J., Cretin, J., Foster, N., Greenberg, M., Pierce, B.C.: Matching lenses: alignment and view update. In: ICFP, pp. 193–204 (2010)
3. Czarnecki, K., Foster, J.N., Hu, Z., Lämmel, R., Schürr, A., Terwilliger, J.F.: Bidirectional transformations: A cross-discipline perspective. In: Paige, R.F. (ed.) ICMT 2009. LNCS, vol. 5563, pp. 260–283. Springer, Heidelberg (2009)
4. Diskin, Z.: Model synchronization: Mappings, tiles, and categories. In: Fernandes, J.M., Lämmel, R., Visser, J., Saraiva, J. (eds.) Generative and Transformational Techniques in Software Engineering III. LNCS, vol. 6491, pp. 92–165. Springer, Heidelberg (2011)
5. Diskin, Z., Xiong, Y., Czarnecki, K.: From State- to Delta-Based Bidirectional Model Transformations: the Asymmetric Case. Journal of Object technology 10, 6:1–6:25 (2011)
6. Diskin, Z.: Algebraic models for bidirectional model synchronization. In: Busch, C., Ober, I., Bruel, J.-M., Uhl, A., Völter, M. (eds.) MODELS 2008. LNCS, vol. 5301, pp. 21–36. Springer, Heidelberg (2008)
7. Diskin, Z., Xiong, Y., Czarnecki, K., Ehrig, H., Hermann, F., Orejas, F.: From state- to delta-based bidirectional model transformations: the symmetric case. Tech. Rep. GSDLAB-TR 2011-05-03, GSD Lab, University of Waterloo (2011), http://gsd.uwaterloo.ca/node/338
8. Foster, J.N., Greenwald, M., Moore, J., Pierce, B., Schmitt, A.: Combinators for bidirectional tree transformations: A linguistic approach to the view-update problem. ACM Trans. Program. Lang. Syst. 29(3) (2007)
9. Giese, H., Wagner, R.: From model transformation to incremental bidirectional model synchronization. Software and System Modeling 8(1), 21–43 (2009)
10. Hermann, F., Ehrig, H., Orejas, F., Czarnecki, K., Diskin, Z., Xiong, Y.: Correctness of Model Synchronization Based on TGG. In: Whittle, J., Clark, T., Kühne, T. (eds.) MODELS 2011. LNCS, vol. 6981, pp. 662–676. Springer, Heidelberg (2011)
11. Hofmann, M., Pierce, B.C., Wagner, D.: Symmetric lenses. In: POPL (2011)
12. Hu, Z., Mu, S.C., Takeichi, M.: A programmable editor for developing structured documents based on bidirectional transformations. Higher-Order and Symbolic Computation 21(1-2), 89–118 (2008)
13. Meertens, L.: Designing constraint maintainers for user interaction (1998), http://www.kestrel.edu/home/people/meertens/
14. Song, H., Huang, G., Chauvel, F., Zhang, W., Sun, Y., Mei, H.: Instant and incremental QVT transformation for runtime models. In: Whittle, J., Clark, T., Kühne, T. (eds.) MODELS 2011. LNCS, vol. 6981, pp. 273–288. Springer, Heidelberg (2011)
15. Stevens, P.: Bidirectional model transformations in QVT: semantic issues and open questions. Software and System Modeling 9(1), 7–20 (2010)
16. Xing, Z., Stroulia, E.: UMLDiff: an algorithm for object-oriented design differencing. In: ASE, pp. 54–65 (2005)
17. Xiong, Y., Liu, D., Hu, Z., Zhao, H., Takeichi, M., Mei, H.: Towards automatic model synchronization from model transformations. In: ASE, pp. 164–173 (2007)
18. Xiong, Y., Hu, Z., Zhao, H., Song, H., Takeichi, M., Mei, H.: Supporting automatic model inconsistency fixing. In: ESEC/SIGSOFT FSE, pp. 315–324 (2009)
19. Xiong, Y., Song, H., Hu, Z., Takeichi, M.: Synchronizing concurrent model updates based on bidirectional transformation. Software and Systems Modeling (to appear)

Enforcing S&D Pattern Design in RCES with Modeling and Formal Approaches

Brahim Hamid[1], Sigrid Gürgens[2], Christophe Jouvray[3], and Nicolas Desnos[1]

[1] IRIT, University of Toulouse
118 Route de Narbonne, 31062 Toulouse Cedex 9, France
{brahim.hamid,nicolas.desnos}@irit.fr
[2] Fraunhofer Institute for Secure Information Technology SIT
Rheinstrasse 75, 64295 Darmstadt, Germany
sigrid.guergens@sit.fraunhofer.de
[3] TRIALOG
25, rue du Général Foy, 75008 Paris, France
christophe.jouvray@trialog.com

Abstract. The requirement for higher security and dependability of systems is continuously increasing even in domains not traditionally deeply involved in such issues. Yet, evolution of embedded systems towards devices connected via Internet, wireless communication or other interfaces requires a reconsideration of secure and trusted embedded systems engineering processes. In this paper, we propose an approach that associates model driven engineering (MDE) and formal validation to build security and dependability (S&D) patterns for trusted RCES applications. The contribution of this work is twofold. On the one hand, we use model-based techniques to capture a set of artifacts to encode S&D patterns. On the other hand, we introduce a set of artifacts for the formal validation of these patterns in order to guarantee their correctness. The formal validation in turn follows the the MDE process and thus links concrete validation results to the S&D requirements identified at higher levels of abstraction.

Keywords: Resource Constrained Embedded Systems, Trust, Security, Dependability, Pattern, Meta-model, Model Driven Engineering, Formal Modeling.

1 Introduction

An embedded system [32] is a system that is composed of two main parts, software and hardware, which evolves in a real world environment and fulfills a specific function. Such systems come with a large number of common characteristics, including real-time and temperature constraints, security and dependability as well as efficiency requirements. Embedded systems are not classical software which can be built with usual paradigms. In particular, the development of resource constrained embedded systems (RCES) has to address constraints regarding memory, computational processing power and/or limited energy.

Non-functional requirements such as security and dependability (S&D) [25] become more important as well as more difficult to achieve. The integration of S&D features requires the availability of both application domain specific knowledge and S&D expertise at the same time. Currently, the integration of S&D mechanisms is still new in many domains, hence embedded systems developers usually have limited S&D expertise. Thus capturing and providing this expertise by way of S&D patterns can support embedded systems development. Model-Driven Engineering (MDE) provides a very useful contribution for the design of trusted systems, since it bridges the gap between design issues and implementation concerns. It helps the designer to specify in a separate way non-functional requirements such as security and/or dependability needs at a higher level of abstraction. This allows implementation independent validation of models, generally considered an important assurance step.

The question remains at which state of the development process to integrate S&D patterns. As a prerequisite work, we investigate the design process of S&D patterns. In this paper, we propose an approach for S&D pattern development and validation that follows the MDE paradigm. Security and dependability patterns on domain independent (DI) and domain specific level (DS), respectively, that are derived from and associated with domain specific models will help developers to integrate application building blocks with S&D building blocks. Formal pattern validation techniques avoid the integration of badly designed building blocks. As part of pattern development, the validation again follows the levels of system abstraction.

The motivation driving the modeling and formalization of security and dependability of software has typically been the need to amend the principal characteristics of the system targeting several domains with the same set of user requirements. Achieving this goal requires (1) a common representation of patterns for several domains; (2) a pattern flexible structure; (3) unified formal validation of patterns; (4) guidelines for platform specific implementation of the patterns; and (5) guidelines to guarantee the correctness of the pattern integration step.

The rest of this paper is organized as follows. Section 2 briefly reviews related work. Section 3 presents the core of the S&D patterns conceptual modeling. Section 4 provides terminology, techniques, and tools that are required to understand and use the proposed modeling language. Section 5 presents in depth the modeling part and Section 6 deals with the formal and validation concerns. Finally, Section 7 concludes this paper with a short discussion about future works.

2 Related Work

Design patterns are a solution model to generic design problems, applicable in specific contexts. Several tentatives exist in the S&D design pattern literature [30,31,3,28]. They allow to solve very general problems that appear frequently as sub-tasks in the design of systems with security and dependability requirements. These elementary tasks include secure communication, fault tolerance, etc. Particularly, [30] presented a collection of patterns to be used when dealing with application security. [3] described a hybrid set of patterns to be used in the development of fault-tolerant software applications. An extension to the framework [3] for the development of dependable software systems based on a pattern approach is proposed in [28]. The pattern specification consists of service-based architectural design and deployment restrictions in form of UML deployment diagrams for the different architectural services.

To give a flavor of the improvement achievable by using specific languages, we look at the pattern formalization problem. *UMLAUT* [10] is an approach that aims to formally model design patterns by proposing extensions to the UML meta model 1.3. They used OCL language to describe constraints (structural and behavioral) in the form of meta collaboration diagrams. In the same way, *RBML(Role-Based Meta modeling Language)* [18] is able to capture various design perspectives of patterns such as static structure, interactions, and state-based behavior. The framework *LePUS* [9] offers a formal and visual language for specifying design patterns. It defines a pattern in an accurate and complete form of formula with a graphical representation.

With regard to the integration of patterns in software systems, the *DPML (Design Pattern Modeling Language)* [21] allows the incorporation of patterns in UML class models. Recently, [27] explains how pattern integration can be achieved by using a library of precisely described and formally verified S&D solutions.

While many S&D patterns have been designed, still few works propose general techniques for S&D patterns. For the first kind of approaches [8], design patterns are usually represented by diagrams with notations such as UML object, annotated with textual descriptions and examples of code. There are some well-proven approaches [4] based on Gamma et al. However, this kind of techniques does not allow to achieve the high degree of pattern structure flexibility which is required to reach our target. The framework promoted by LePUS [9] is interesting but the degree of expressiveness proposed to design a pattern is too restrictive. The major concern of [22] is how to exploit security analysis patterns during the security engineering analysis, an important issue but out of the scope of our paper. Pattern representation proposed in [5] aims at pattern classification which may be covered by our pattern representation thanks to the properties artifacts. However this work does not address the validation activity which is an important contribution of our paper.

With regard to the modeling of security and dependability in model-driven development, UMLSec [17], SecureUML [19] and [16], to name a few, and our proposal are not in competition but they complement each other by providing different view points to the secure information system. In concept, our modeling framework is similar to the one proposed in [27]. Nevertheless they used a rigid structure (a pattern is defined as quadruplet) and consequently their approach is not usable to capture specific characteristics of S&D patterns for several domains. To summarize, in software engineering, design patterns are considered as effective tools for the reuse of specific knowledge. However to the best of our knowledge there is no approach of pattern development and validation that follows the MDE system development and allows for formal proofs of a domain independant pattern being an abstraction of a domain specific pattern.

Early work on validation discusses the verification of cryptographic protocols and is based on an abstract (term-based) representation of cryptographic primitives that can be automatically verified using model checking and theorem proving tools. One research line in this category is authentication logics, the first of these logics being the BAN Logic [2]. The Inductive Approach by Paulson [24] started another research line. Early work in the area of model checking can be traced back to [20], see [26] for a survey. One of the more recent approaches is AVISPA [1] which provides the High Level Protocol Specification Language (HLPSL [29]) and four different analysis tools. Another approach [14] has been used to find security flaws in a number of key exchange, authentication and non-repudiation protocols and more recently it has been applied to analyze certain scenarios based on Trusted Computing [15]. However, to the best of our knowledge, none of the existing approaches is able to integrate the security solution validation into the MDE refinement process of the application.

3 S&D Patterns Conceptual Framework

One of the major concerns in designing secure and dependable systems is to determine at which level of abstraction security and dependability concerns should be placed. The supporting research includes e.g. specification, modeling, implementation mechanisms, and verification. For example, distributed systems are organized into separate layers following some reference model, e.g. applications, middleware and the operating system services. The framework must cope with S&D, RCES and domain specific properties. For this purpose, the proposition presented in this paper is based on three levels of abstraction: (i) Pattern Fundamental Structure, (ii) Domain Independent Pattern Model (DIPM) and (iii) Domain Specific Pattern Model (DSPM). Firstly this decomposition aims at allowing the design of S&D applications in the context of embedded systems (since combining S&D and domain specific artifacts introduces a high complexity), and secondly it overcomes the lack of formalism of the classical pattern form (e.g. textual). The benefit of this structure is to offer a common modeling language for several domains in the context of trusted embedded systems.

The following two subsections describe an example that will be used throughout the rest of the paper to illustrate our approach, and the Pattern Fundamental Structure metamodel as the first abstraction level.

3.1 Motivating Example: Secure Communication Pattern

The essence of our approach is the separation of general-purpose services from implementations. In our context, this structure highlights the separation of general-purpose of the pattern from its related mechanisms. This is an important issue to understand the use of patterns for security and dependability and, in particular, the notion of *trust*. In which layer security mechanisms are placed depends on the trust a client has in how *secure* the services are in some particular layer. As example of a widely used pattern we choose the Secure Communication Pattern referred to in the following as SCP. Messages passing across any public network can be intercepted. The problem is how to ensure that the data is secure in transit, e.g. how to guarantee data authenticity. This is one of the goals of the SCP.

However, SCP are slightly different with regard to the application domain. A system domain may have its own mechanisms and means, protocols that can be used to implement this pattern. So, the motivation is to handle the modeling of S&D patterns by following abstraction. As a concrete implementation we use the SSL mechanism.

The SSL mechanism is composed of two phases: The *SSL Handshake* that establishes a secure channel, and the *SSL Record* in which this channel can be used to exchange data securely. The client initiates the SSL handshake by providing the server with a random number and information about the cryptographic algorithms it can handle. The server replies by choosing the actual algorithm to use, requiring the client to authenticate itself (this is optional and used in our example) and by sending a random number of its own and its certificate issued by some certificate authorities trusted by both the server and the client. For authenticating itself, in the final handshake message the client includes its own certificate, a signature on all handshake messages generated with its private key, and a third random number encrypted with the server's public key contained in the server's certificate. After having verified the certificates and signature, both client and server use the exchanged random numbers to generate session keys for generating and verifying message authentication codes (MACs) and for encrypting and decrypting messages.

Since the key used by the client for generating a MAC/encrypting a message is used by the server only for MAC verification/decryption and vice versa, and since they are based on a random number confidential for the client and the server, the keys establish a channel that provides authenticity and confidentiality for both client and server.

3.2 Pattern Fundamental Structure

The Pattern Fundamental Structure is a metamodel defining a new formalism for describing S&D patterns, and constitutes the base of our pattern modeling language.

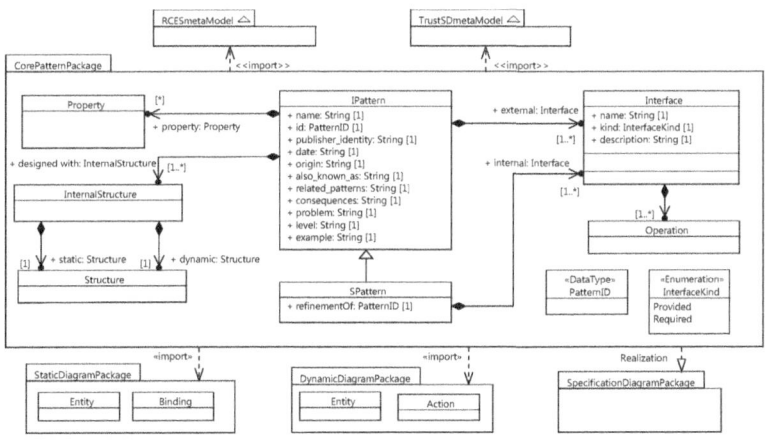

Fig. 1. S&D Pattern Metamodel Dependencies

The metamodel describes all the artifacts (and their relations) needed to represent S&D patterns in the context of trusted embedded systems applications. Here we consider patterns as building blocks that expose services and manage S&D and RCES properties yielding a way to capture meta-information related to patterns and their context of use. These pattern are specified by means of a domain-independent generic representation and a domain-specific representation. The following paragraph details the principle classes of our meta-model, as described with UML notations in Fig. 1.

> **IPattern.** This block represents a modular part of a system that encapsulates a solution of a recurrent problem. An *IPattern* defines its behavior in terms of provided and required interfaces. As such, an *IPattern* serves as a type whose conformance is defined by these provided and required *interfaces*. An *IPattern* may be manifest by one or more artifacts, and in turn, that artifact may be deployed by its execution environment. This is the key entry artifact to model pattern at domain *independent* level.
> **Interface.** *IPattern* interacts with its environment through *Interfaces* which are composed of *Operations*. A provided interface is implemented by the *IPattern* and highlights the services exposed to the environment. A required interface corresponds to services needed by the pattern to work properly. So, larger pieces of a system's functionality may be assembled by reusing patterns as parts in an encompassing pattern or assembly of patterns, and wiring together required and provided interfaces. Finally, we consider two kinds of interfaces:
> - *External interfaces* allow implementing interaction with regard to the integration of a pattern into an application model or to compose patterns.
> - *Internal interfaces* allow implementing interaction with the platform. At a low abstraction level it is e.g. possible to define links with a software or hardware module for the cryptographic key management. These interfaces are realized by the *SPattern*. Note an *IPattern* does not have an *InternalInterface*.
>
> **Property.** Is a particular characteristic of a pattern. A *Property* is either an *S&D Property* or an *RCES Property* (see Section 4). Each property of a pattern will be validated at the time of the pattern validating process and the assumptions used will be compiled as a set of constraints which will have to be satisfied by the domain application.
> **Internal Structure.** Constitutes the implementation of the solution proposed by the pattern. Thus the *InternalStructure* can be considered as a white box which exposes the details of the *IPatterns*. In order to capture all the key elements of the solution, the *Internal Structure* is composed of two kinds of *Structure*: static and dynamic. Note that one pattern can have several possible implementations[a].
> **SPattern.** Inherits from *IPattern*. It is used to build a pattern at DSPM. Furthermore an *SPattern* has *Internal Interfaces* in order to interact with the domain specific platform. This is the key entry artifact to model pattern at domain *specific* level.
>
> ---
> [a] Usually referred to as variants of design patterns.

4 Details on Prerequisites for Using our S&D Patterns

This section describes the external model libraries that are needed to use the proposed modeling language. Specifically, we present the extra-functional properties (*trust and S&D*) and non-functional properties (RCES concerns) applied to S&D patterns metamodel (see Section 3.2). In addition, we provide definitions of the terminology employed as needed.

Resource Constraint Metamodel. The meta-model of resource-constrained embedded systems describes both its hardware and software execution platforms by means of basic elements (e.g. Resource, Service) and their specialization to target the hardware and software platform (e.g. Processor, Memory, Task). In addition the RCES metamodel describes the properties of elements that compose those systems and classify them according to their nature (e.g. Resource Properties, Timing Properties, Computing Properties). Due to space limits, this metamodel is not detailed in this paper. Note, however, that in concept such a modeling part is similar to the one proposed in [23].

Trust and S&D Metamodel. A general definition of trust is: *The term of trust refers to a relation from one entity in the system to another entity with respect to a property, or from an entity directly to a property in the system* [7]. In the context of our work, we restrict this to an entity trusting a property to hold in a system. Fig. 2 presents the class diagram of this metamodel.

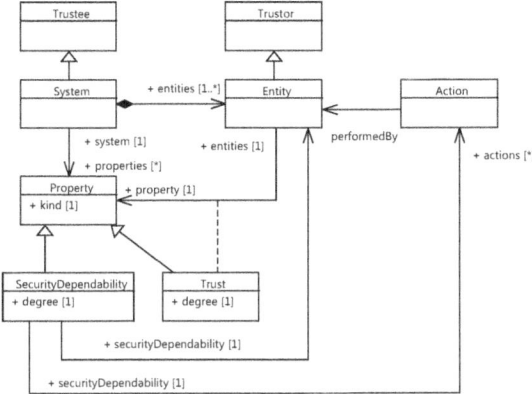

Fig. 2. Properties Metamodel

Trustor. Is an entity who trusts or needs to decide whether to trust one property of the system.
Trustee. Is a system for which trust into a property is evaluated.
Action. Is the activity or behavior that is performed by an entity.
System. Consists of a set of entities acting in the system (i.e. sequences of actions performed by the entities).
Entity. Is an entity acting in a system.
Property. Represents some kind of an extra-functional property of the system (e.g. S&D properties).
Trust. Concretely, the trust relationship is defined between the entity and the property of the system, Trust is itself also a property. In general, a property is characterized with a degree to exhibit the value with which the entity trusts the property to hold in the system. In our context, the entity trusts or does not trust the property to hold.
Security and Dependability. S&D in our metamodel is a class that represents the S&D relationship between the entity and the actions of the system.

5 Modeling S&D Patterns

This section introduces the required artifacts while following the two abstraction levels DIPM and DSPM. These two levels of the Secure Communication Pattern (SCP) presented in Section 3.1 are illustrated. Note, however, that for lack of space we only specify those elements that we need in order to explain our proof.

5.1 Domain Independent Pattern Model (DIPM)

This level focuses on domain independent pattern artifacts. This is an instance of the Pattern Fundamental Structure metamodel. As we shall see, we introduce new concepts through instantiation of the meta-model in order to cover most existing S&D patterns in RCES applications. In our case study, the DIPM of the SCP consists of two entities communicating through a secure channel and is defined as follows:

Properties. At this level, we identify two S&D properties: authenticity and trust.
External Interfaces. The SCP functionalities are exposed through DI external interface function calls:
$Send(P, Q, ch(P, Q), m)$, $Receive(P, Q, ch(P, Q), m)$, with P and Q denoting the client C and server S, respectively, $ch(P, Q)$ their communication channel, and m a message.

Internal Structure. The behavior of SCP can be modeled by a UML Sequence Diagram describing secure date exchange between client and server through the external interface.

5.2 Domain Specific Pattern Model (DSPM)

The objective of this specific design level is to specify the S&D patterns for a specific application domain. This level offers artifacts at a lower level of abstraction with more precise *information* and *constraints* about the target domain. This modeling level is a refinement of the DIPM that considers the specific characteristics and dependencies of the application domain. Different DSPM can refine the same DIPM for different domains. When using SSL as a mechanism related to the application domain to refine the SCP at DSPM, we introduce the following artifacts:

Properties. In addition to the refinement of the trust property identified in the DIPM, at this level we identify some related RCES properties, e.g. the size of the cryptographic key.

External Interfaces. The DS external interface, a refinement of the DI external interface, can be specified as follows:
- $send(C, S, mac_C(m), m)$: The client C sends m and the corresponding MAC (Message Authentication Code) to the server S.
- $recv(S, C, mac_C(m), m)$: The server receives m and corresponding MAC.

Internal Interfaces. The most important functions of the DS internal interface of the SSL pattern can be specified as follows:

$genRand(C, R_C), genRand(S, R_S)$: Client/server generate a random number.

$verifyCert()$: Client/server verify each other's certificate and extract the respective public key.

$encrypt(C, pubKey_S, R_C)$: The client encrypts its random number using the server's public key.

$sign(C, \ldots)$: The client signs the SSL handshake messages.

$verifySig(S, \ldots)$: The server verifies the client's signature.

$genMac(C, macKey_C, m, mac_C(m))$: The client generates the MAC for message m using its own SSL shared secret for MAC generation.

$verifyMac(S, macKey_C, m, mac_C(m))$: The server verifies, using its shared secret for MAC verification (i.e. the client's key for MAC generation), that the MAC for m is correct and thus originates from the client.

$send(), recv()$: Send and receive of the SSL messages by client and server, respectively.

Internal Structure. The behavior of SCP can be modeled by a UML Sequence Diagram following the SSL protocol described in Section 3.1, involving both the DS external and internal interface.

6 The Formalization and Validation Process

In this section we discuss the use of our Security Modeling Framework (SeMF) [13,7] for pattern validation through an application to the secure communication example.

6.1 The Security Modeling Framework SeMF

In SeMF, the specification of any kind of cooperating system is composed of (i) a set of agents (e.g. some clients and a server), (ii) a set of actions (e.g. the DS internal interface actions introduced above, (iii) the system's behavior B, (iv) the agents' local views, and (v) the agents' initial knowledge. The behavior B of a discrete system S can be formally described by the set of its possible sequences of actions. An *agents' initial knowledge* about the system consists of all traces the agent initially considers possible. An agent may assume for example that a message that was received must have been sent before. Finally, an agent's *local view* essentially captures what an agent can see from the system. An agent might see for example only its own actions.

Different formal models of the same application/system are partially ordered with respect to different levels of abstraction. Formally, abstractions are described by so called alphabetic language homomorphisms that map action sequences of a finer abstraction level to action sequences of a more abstract level while respecting concatenation of actions (see Section 6.3.3 for an example).

In SeMF, security properties are defined in terms of such a system specification, i.e. in terms of actions, agents, the agents' initial knowledge and local views. Note that a system specification does not require a particular level of abstraction. The underlying formal semantics then allows to prove that a specific formal model of a system provides specific security properties. In the following section we will introduce our validation artifacts.

6.2 Validation Artifacts

Security properties. One important artifact is the security property (or properties) a system shall provide. In the following we will explain the basic idea of authenticity, precedence and trust that are relevant for the example used in this paper without going into the formal details. For more information about our formal framework and the definitions of security properties we refer the reader to [13] and [7].

We call a particular action a authentic for an agent P (after a sequence of actions ω has happened) if in all sequences that P considers to have possibly happened a must have happened. In many cases we require a particular instantiation of this property to hold:

auth(a, b, P) denotes that whenever a particular action b has happened, it must be authentic for agent P that action a has happened as well.

precede(a, b) holds if all action sequences in the system's behavior that contain an action b also contain an action a.

Finally we introduce our notion of trust which allows to capture basic trust assumptions (like trust in a public key infrastructure) and to reason about these. As illustrated in Fig. 2, trust is a relation between an agent and a property:

trust(P, prop) Agent P trusts a property $prop$ to hold in the system if the property holds in the agent's conception of the system. P's conception of the system may defer from the actual system. P may for example not have all information about the system behavior and believe more sequences of actions to be possible than B actually contains. Note that trust of an agent in a property is again a property of the system S.

Assumptions. Any validation of a security property holding in a system must make use of basic assumptions. In order to prove for example that the SSL handshake results in authentic shared secrets for both the client and the server, we need to assume that they own the authentic public key of the certification authority. In SeMF, these assumptions are again specified as security properties.

SeMF Building Blocks. A SeMF Building Block (SeBB) is essentially a visualization of a proof, concerning either an implication between security properties or a security mechanism. Hence, a SeMF Building Block consists of three different parts:

- The *internal properties* (*assumptions*) that are assumed to be satisfied by the system the SeBB shall be applied to.
- The mechanism or instrument that makes use of the internal properties. There are two different types: F-SeBBs which constitute a formal proof within SeMF, based on the formal definitions of the internal properties, and M-SeBBs which constitute a proof external to SeMF, capturing expert knowledge about security mechanisms like cryptographic protocols and primitives.
- The *external properties* are those that are proven to hold for the overall system, given that the internal properties hold.

An example for an F-SeBB is the transitivity of precedence: $precede(a, b)$ and $precede(b, c)$ imply $precede(a, c)$. An example for an M-SeBB captures the RSA signature mechanism: If the private key is confidential for its owner, then a signature verification action using the respective public key is always preceded by the respective signature generation action by the owner of the private key. See [6] for a set of SeBBs and their respective proofs.

SeBBs can be used to prove that a particular pattern provides a particular property. The assumptions that need to be satisfied in order for the pattern to provide the desired security property represent the internal properties of one or more SeBBs. By consecutively applying appropriate SeBBs we then search for a proof path that ends with the property provided by the pattern as external property. For pattern development we use SeBBs in the reverse way, starting with the property provided by the pattern as external SeBB property and deriving the pattern assumptions as internal SeBB properties by consecutively applying adequate SeBBs. Formally this constitutes a proof that given the assumptions hold, the pattern provides the desired property. Section 6.3 will explain both ways of SeBB application in more detail.

F-SeBBs can be applied on all abstraction levels and are thus domain independent, while M-SeBBs are concerned with particular security mechanisms, hence are considered domain specific.

Security Preserving Homomorphisms. As explained in Section 6.1, a homomorphism is an abstraction that maps a concrete system to an abstract one. For defining a particular homomorphism, we specify which of the concrete actions are mapped onto which of the abstract actions and onto the empty word, respectively. Under certain conditions a homomorphism can preserve specific properties: If the conditions hold, and if the property holds in the abstract system, the respective property also holds in the concrete system. For the formal proof of sufficient conditions for preserving authenticity and confidentiality, we refer the reader to [11] and [12], respectively.

6.3 Validating Secure Communication Patterns

In this section we will explain how the validation artifacts introduced in the previous section can be used for pattern validation. Exemplarily we will apply them to the DIPM and DSPM for the secure communication pattern. We will explain how a proof can be conducted that each time the server receives a message on a channel it shares with the client, it authentically for the server originates from the client.

6.3.1 Applying SeBBs to DIPM

The formal model that corresponds to the DIPM introduced in Section 5.1 has the agents client C and server S and the send and receive actions corresponding to the external DI interface. We further assume that each agent can only see their own actions. According to Section 6.2, the required authenticity property is expressed as:

$$auth(Send(C, S, ch(C, S), m), Receive(S, C, ch(C, S), m), S) \qquad \text{(P-DI)}$$

First, we search for a SeBB whose external property is authenticity. One important SeBB of this type states that the internal properties $trust(P, precede(a, b))$ and $auth(b, c, P)$ imply the external property $auth(a, c, P)$ (see [7] for a proof of this SeBB). Setting $b = c$ and instantiating a, b, P with the concrete send and receive actions and agent of property P-DI, we conclude that P-DI holds if the internal properties (assumptions) $trust(S, precede(Send(C, S, ch(C, S), m), Receive(S, C, ch(C, S), m)))$ and $auth(Receive(S, C, ch(C, S), m), Receive(S, C, ch(C, S), m), S)$ hold. We may assume the latter property to hold: The server sees its own actions, thus they are always authentic for the server.

Regarding the trust of the server into the precedence of its receive action by a client send action, we note that there is no reason that would allow us to just assume this property to hold. So next we need to find another F-SeBB with this property as external property. In a more complex model with for example more actions in between the send and receive action we would certainly be able to apply other F-SeBBs (e.g. the one that captures the transitivity of precede). However, in this simple DIPM setting, no other F-SeBB can be applied. Hence this concludes our proof with respect to the DIPM model. In order for the DIPM model to provide property P-DI, in particular the assumption

$$trust(S, precede(Send(C, S, ch(C, S), m), Receive(S, C, ch(C, S), m))) \qquad \text{(A-DI)}$$

must be assumed to hold. The fact that no more F-SeBBs can be applied shows that we now have to consider the DSPM level, i.e. we have to find and validate a DSPM pattern that provides an equivalent property. This will be discussed in the next paragraph.

6.3.2 Applying SeBBs to DSPM Based on SSL Protocol

The formal model corresponding to the DSPM introduced in Section 5.2 contains the same set of agents, namely client C and server S. Its actions correspond to the external and internal DS interface function calls presented in Section 5.2 and can be considered a refinement of the actions of the DIPM formal model.

The security property that is provided by this SSL pattern and that corresponds to the trust property assumed to hold for the DIPM model (this correspondence will be addressed in the next paragraph) is that the server trusts into the precedence of its own MAC verification action by the MAC generation action of the client:

$$trust(S, precede(genMac(C, macKey_C, m, mac_C(m)),$$
$$verifyMac(S, macKey_C, m, mac_C(m))))$$ (P-DS)

We now identify the assumptions which we need for our proof, i.e. those that the DSPM model needs to satisfy, and then explain the main steps of our proof. An exhaustive proof will be introduced in a forthcoming paper.

ass1 $trust(S, not\text{-}precede(genRand(S, R), genRand(S, R)))$. A random number is only generated once, in particular the server trusts in that its own random number is only generated once.

ass2 $trust(S, conf(privKey_S, \{S\}))$. The server trusts into the confidentiality of its own private RSA key.

ass3 $trust(S, conf(privKey_{CA}, \{CA\}))$. The server trusts into the confidentiality of the certificate authority's (CA) private key.

Assumption ass3 (and ass2) is the internal property of an M-SeBB that captures the nature of RSA signatures. Its application yields the server's trust into the precedence of a certificate verification action performed by the server by a certificate generation action performed by the CA: $trust(S, precede(sign(CA, cert(...)), verify(S, cert(...))))$. This property is the internal property of an M-SeBB that captures the semantics of a certificate: It essentially states that the CA trusts into the confidentiality of the private key which is the counterpart of the public key being certified. Hence the server trusts the CA in this respect: $trust(S, trust(CA, conf(privKey_C, \{C\})))$. The next F-SeBB allows (under certain conditions) to conclude the direct trust of the server into the confidentiality of the client's private key: $trust(S, conf(privKey_C, \{C\}))$. Using again the RSA Signature SeBB, this property implies trust of the server into its own signature verification action being preceded by the client's signature generation action. Applying an RSA encryption SeBB to ass2 allows to conclude that the encrypted random number is only known to client and server. All this together with ass1 and an M-SeBB that captures the SSL session key generation allows to conclude that S trusts in the confidentiality of the shared secrets derived from the SSL handshake, in particular $trust(S, conf(macKey_C, \{C, S\}))$ holds. Applying the M-SeBB that captures the MAC mechanism yields that indeed property P-DS holds.

6.3.3 Correspondence between DIPM and DSPM

We have now achieved proofs that (i) assuming that property A-DI holds, the DIPM model provides property P-DI, and (ii) assuming that assumptions ass1, ass2 and ass3 hold, the DSPM model provides property P-DS. In the final proof step, we have to show that the DIPM model is an abstraction of the DSPM model that preserves property A-DI, and that this property, transfered to the DSPM model, is identical to property P-DS.

Hence we specify an appropriate homomorphism that maps the actions of the DSPM model onto the actions of the DIPM model and then show that this homomorphism preserves trust in precede. We specify h as follows:

$h(genMac(C, macKey_C, m, mac_C(m))) = Send(C, S, ch(C, S), m)$
$h(verifyMac(S, macKey_C, m, mac_C(m))) = Receive(S, C, ch(C, S), m)$
$h(a) = \varepsilon$ for all other actions a

It can be shown that in order for a homomorphism to preserve trust of an agent in a specific precede property, it must be proven that it maps the agent's initial knowledge of the concrete system into the agent's initial knowledge of the abstract system. Since we assume property A-DI to hold in the DIPM model, in the server's abstract initial knowledge all server receive actions are preceded by a client send action. On the other hand, the server's concrete initial knowledge reflects the MAC mechanism, i.e. reflecs that a verifyMac action is always preceded by the respective genMac action. The homomorphism h relates these actions, hence indeed maps the server's concrete initial knowledge onto the abstract one. Hence h preserves trust into precedence and property A-DI transfered to the DSPM model is identical to property P-DS, which concludes our proof.

7 Discussion and Conclusion

Application developers usually do not have expertise in security and dependability. Hence capturing and providing this expertise by way of S&D patterns has become an area of research in the last years. S&D patterns shall enable the development of secure and dependable applications while at the same time liberating the developer from having to deal with the technical details. Model driven engineering (MDE) provides a very useful contribution for the design of secure and trusted systems, since it bridges the gap between design issues and implementation concerns. Hence S&D pattern integration has to be considered at some point in the MDE process.

In this paper, we have proposed an MDE-based approach for S&D pattern development and validation. Defined by a meta-model, S&D patterns can be specified and validated at different abstraction levels. An S&D pattern at domain independent level allows the application developer to identify S&D requirements and select a respective abstract solution without specific knowledge on how the solution is designed and implemented. Thus a DIPM pattern can easily be integrated into the overall abstract system specification. Following the MDE process, the system model is then refined towards a domain specific level, taking into account concrete elements (e.g., mechanisms to use). Pattern validation follows these two abstraction levels (i.e., we validate a DIPM pattern and possible DSPM instantiations independently). However, the additional final validation step proves that the latter is indeed a refinement of the former which in turn proves that the overall application system indeed satisfies the S&D requirements initially specified by the application developer. This process may significantly reduce the cost of system engineering, since it enables to address S&D issues early in the system development process while at the same time relieving the developer from the technical details.

Yet an important task remains to be performed when integrating an S&D pattern into an application: assurance that assumptions used for proving the correctness of a

DSPM pattern are indeed satisfied by the particular application environment. In order to support this task, future work will focus on deriving environment constraints from the assumptions through the external model libraries discussed in Section 4.

Acknowledgements. This work is supported by the European FP7 TERESA project (IST-248410).

References

1. AVISPA. The HLPSL Tutorial, A Beginner's Guide to Modelling and Analysing Internet Security Protocols, http://www.avispa-project.org
2. Burrows, M., Abadi, M., Needham, R.: A Logic of Authentication. ACM Transactions on Computer Systems 8, 18–36 (1990)
3. Daniels, F., Kim, K., Vouk, M.A.: The Reliable Hybrid Pattern: A Generalized Software Fault Tolerant Design Pattern, pp. 1–9 (1997)
4. Douglass, B.P.: Real-time UML: Developing Efficient Objects for Embedded Systems. Addison-Wesley, Reading (1998)
5. Fernandez, E.B., Yoshioka, N., Washizaki, H., Jürjens, J., VanHilst, M., Pernul, G.: Using security patterns to develop secure systems. In: Software Engineering for Secure Systems: Industrial and Research Perspectives. IGI Global (2010)
6. Fuchs, A., Gürgens, S., Rieke, R., Apvrille, L.: 1st Version Architecture and Protocols Verification and Attack Analysis. Technical Report D3.4.1, EVITA Project (2010)
7. Fuchs, A., Gürgens, S., Rudolph, C.: A Formal Notion of Trust – Enabling Reasoning about Security Properties. In: Nishigaki, M., Jøsang, A., Murayama, Y., Marsh, S. (eds.) IFIPTM 2010. IFIP Advances in Information and Communication Technology, vol. 321, pp. 200–215. Springer, Heidelberg (2010)
8. Gamma, E., Helm, R., Johnson, R.E., Vlissides, J.: Design Patterns: Elements of Reusable Object-Oriented Software. Addison-Wesley, Reading (1995)
9. Gasparis, E., Nicholson, J., Eden, A.H.: LePUS3: An Object-Oriented Design Description Language. In: Stapleton, G., Howse, J., Lee, J. (eds.) Diagrams 2008. LNCS (LNAI), vol. 5223, pp. 364–367. Springer, Heidelberg (2008)
10. Guennec, A.L., Sunyé, G., Jézéquel, J.-M.: Precise Modeling of Design Patterns, pp. 482–496. Springer, Heidelberg (2000)
11. Gürgens, S., Ochsenschläger, P., Rudolph, C.: Authenticity and provability - A formal framework. In: Davida, G.I., Frankel, Y., Rees, O. (eds.) InfraSec 2002. LNCS, vol. 2437, pp. 227–245. Springer, Heidelberg (2002)
12. Gürgens, S., Ochsenschläger, P., Rudolph, C.: Abstractions Preserving Parameter Confidentiality. In: di Vimercati, S.d.C., Syverson, P.F., Gollmann, D. (eds.) ESORICS 2005. LNCS, vol. 3679, pp. 418–437. Springer, Heidelberg (2005)
13. Gürgens, S., Ochsenschläger, P., Rudolph, C.: On a Formal Framework for Security Properties. International Computer Standards & Interface Journal (CSI), Special issue on formal methods, techniques and tools for secure and reliable applications 27(5), 457–466 (2005)
14. Gürgens, S., Rudolph, C.: Security Analysis of (Un-) Fair Non-repudiation Protocols. Formal aspects of computing 2629, 229–232 (2004)
15. Gürgens, S., Rudolph, C., Scheuermann, D., Atts, M., Plaga, R.: Security evaluation of scenarios based on the tCG's TPM specification. In: Biskup, J., López, J. (eds.) ESORICS 2007. LNCS, vol. 4734, pp. 438–453. Springer, Heidelberg (2007)
16. Hamid, B., Radermacher, A., Jouvray, C., Gérard, S., Terrier, F.: Designing fault-tolerant component based applications with a model driven approach. In: Brinkschulte, U., Givargis, T., Russo, S. (eds.) SEUS 2008. LNCS, vol. 5287, pp. 9–20. Springer, Heidelberg (2008)

17. Jürjens, J.: UMLsec: Extending UML for Secure Systems Development. In: Jézéquel, J.-M., Hussmann, H., Cook, S. (eds.) UML 2002. LNCS, vol. 2460, pp. 412–425. Springer, Heidelberg (2002)
18. Kim, D.-K., France, R., Ghosh, S., Song, E.: A UML-based Meta-modeling Language to Specify Design Patterns, vol. 30, pp. 193–206 (2004)
19. Lodderstedt, T., Basin, D., Doser, J.: SecureUML: A UML-Based Modeling Language for Model-Driven Security. In: Jézéquel, J.-M., Hussmann, H., Cook, S. (eds.) UML 2002. LNCS, vol. 2460, pp. 426–441. Springer, Heidelberg (2002)
20. Lowe, G.: An Attack on the Needham-Schroeder Public-Key Protocol. Information Processing Letters (1995)
21. Mapelsden, D., Hosking, J., Grundy, J.: Design Pattern Modelling and Instantiation Using DPML. In: CRPIT 2002: Proceedings of the Fortieth International Conference on Tools Pacific, pp. 3–11. Australian Computer Society, Inc. (2002)
22. Nhlabatsi, A., Bandara, A., Hayashi, S., Haley, C.B., Jürjens, J., Kaiya, H., Kubo, A., Laney, R., Mouratidis, H., Nuseibeh, B., Tahara, Y., Tun, T.T., Washizaki, H., Yoshioka, N., Yu, Y.: Security Patterns: Comparing Modeling Approaches. In: Software Engineering for Secure Systems: Industrial and Research Perspectives. IGI Global (2010)
23. OMG. OMG. A UML Profile for MARTE: Modeling and Analysis of Real-Time Embedded Systems,beta 2 (June 2008)
24. Paulson, L.C.: Proving Properties of Security Protocols by Induction. In: 10th Computer Security Foundations Workshop, pp. 70–83. IEEE Computer Society Press, Los Alamitos (1997)
25. Ravi, S., Raghunathan, A., Kocher, P., Hattangady, S.: Security in Embedded Systems: Design challenges. ACM Trans. Embed. Comput. Syst. 3(3), 461–491 (2004)
26. Roscoe, B., Ryan, P., Schneider, S., Goldsmith, M., Lowe, G.: The Modelling and Analysis of Security Protocols. Addison Wesley, Reading (2000)
27. Serrano, D., Maña, A., Sotirious, A.-D.: Towards Precise and Certified Security Patterns. In: Proceedings of 2nd International Workshop on Secure Systems Methodologies Using Patterns (Spattern 2008), pp. 287–291. IEEE Computer Society, Los Alamitos (2008)
28. Tichy, M., Schilling, D., Giese, H.: Design of Self-managing Dependable Systems with UML and Fault Tolerance Patterns, pp. 105–109. ACM, New York (2004)
29. Chevalier, Y., Compagna, L., Cuellar, J., Hankes Drieslma, P., Mantovani, J., Mödersheim, S., Vigneron, L.: A High Level Protocol Specification Language for Industrial Security-Sensitive Protocols. In: Workshop on Specification and Automated Processing of Security Requirements, SAPS 2004 (2004)
30. Yoder, J., Barcalow, J.: Architectural Patterns for Enabling Application Security. In: Conference on Pattern Languages of Programs, PLoP 1997 (1998)
31. Yoshioka, N., Washizaki, H., Maruyama, K.: A survey of Security Patterns. Progress in Informatics (5), 35–47 (2008)
32. Zurawski, R.: Embedded Systems. In: Embedded Systems Handbook. CRC Press Inc., Boca Raton (2005)

A Model-Based and Automated Approach to Size Estimation of Embedded Software Components

Kenneth Lind[1] and Rogardt Heldal[2]

[1] Saab Automobile AB, Electrical Systems Engineering, A1-5 TLEF,
SE-461 80 Trollhättan, Sweden
kenneth.h.lind@saab.com
[2] Chalmers University of Technology, Computer Science and Engineering,
SE-412 96 Göteborg, Sweden
heldal@chalmers.se

Abstract. Accurate estimation of Software Code Size is important for developing cost-efficient embedded systems. The Code Size affects the amount of system resources needed, like ROM and RAM memory, and processing capacity. In our previous work, we have estimated the Code Size based on CFP (COSMIC Function Points) within 15% accuracy, with the purpose of deciding how much ROM memory to fit into products with high cost pressure. Our manual CFP measurement process would require 2,5 man years to estimate the ROM size required in a typical car. In this paper, we want to investigate how the manual effort involved in estimation of Code Size can be minimized. We define a UML Profile capturing all information needed for estimation of Code Size, and develop a tool for automated estimation of Code Size based on CFP. A case study will show how UML models save manual effort in a realistic case.

Keywords: UML Profile, UML components, software components, functional size measurement, code size estimation.

1 Introduction

Early and accurate estimation of Software Code Size is important for developing cost-efficient embedded systems, such as cars, cell phones, washing machines, etc. The Code Size affects the amount of system resources needed, like ROM and RAM memory, and processing capacity. Systems containing too much memory or processing capacity are more expensive than they need to be. Systems containing too little memory or processing capacity may need a redesign after only a part of its expected lifetime.

In our previous work, we have estimated the Code Size based on CFP (COSMIC Function Points) within 15% accuracy [23],[24],[25],[26],[27],[28]. Our results were obtained using software implementations developed by the automotive companies Saab and GM (General Motors). The accuracy of the estimated values is important because the purpose was to decide how much ROM memory to fit into ECUs (Electronic Control Unit, an embedded computer) in products with high cost pressure. Our manual CFP measurement process used UML components and textual information from requirement specifications, which would require up to 2,5 man years of effort to obtain the CFP value for the application software embedded in a typical Saab car.

In this paper, we want to investigate how the manual effort involved in estimation of Code Size can be minimized. The UML components provide some (but not all) of the information needed for estimation of Code Size. Therefore, we define a UML Profile capturing all information needed for estimation of Code Size, and develop a tool for automated estimation of Code Size based on CFP. Besides the increased efficiency obtained by our model-based and automated estimation approach, we expect to increase repeatability and consistency in the estimation process compared to a manual approach. In addition, our UML Profile contains support for estimation of RAM memory size.

In order to investigate if our approach solves our problem, we formulated the following research questions;

RQ1: "How can UML support in modeling all information needed for automated estimation of Software Code Size?"
RQ2: "How much manual effort can be saved by modeling all information needed for automated estimation of Software Code Size?"

We conduct a case study using requirement specifications and software implementations from the automotive industry to answer the research questions.

This paper is organized as follows: The next section provides background information about the COSMIC method. Section 3 defines the UML Profile, and section 4 briefly presents the tool. Section 5 describes the case study, and section 6 evaluates threats to validity. Sections 7 and 8 contain related work, and conclusions.

2 Background

This section presents enough information about Functional Size Measurement and the COSMIC method to understand the rest of the paper.

Functional Size is defined as "size of the software derived by quantifying the Functional User Requirements" [5]. FUR (Functional User Requirement) describes what the software is expected to do for its users. Examples are data transfer, data transformation, data storage, and data retrieval. Functional Size is independent of software language and development methods.

There are several FSM methods available. The original method was described by Albrecht 1979 [1],[2],[3]. A comprehensive literature survey covering several methods is found in [9]. Some of them are IFPUG FPA (Function Point Analysis) [12], and COSMIC Function Points (CFP) [5],[19] to name a few. The typical usage of FSM is development cost estimation and project planning. In our experiments, CFP is chosen because it is known to be suitable for real-time software, like automotive systems [5], and it is a "second generation" method, complying with the ISO/IEC 14143-1:2007 standard for FSM methods [13],[14],[15],[16],[17],[18].

The COSMIC Method defines a standardized measure of software Functional Size expressed in CFP units. The measurement is carried out in three phases; the strategy phase defines the purpose of the measurement and scope of the software to be measured, the mapping phase maps the FUR of the software to be measured onto functional processes in the software component of the COSMIC Generic Software Model (shown in Fig. 1), and the measurement phase counts the data movements contained in each functional process. By defining the purpose of the measurement and scope of the software to be measured during the strategy phase, we identify the level of decomposition and level of granularity of the software to be measured. The level of decomposition points out a particular level in a software – component – sub-component hierarchy. The level of granularity concerns the amount of details defined about the FUR. Both aspects are important when comparing different CFP values to each-other.

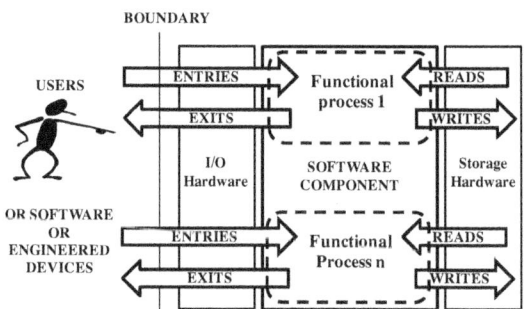

Fig. 1. The Generic Software Model of COSMIC

As can be seen in Fig. 1, there are four different data movement types. Entry types move data across the boundary and into the functional process. Exit types move data across the boundary to a user. Read types move data from persistent storage to the functional process. Write types move data from the functional process to persistent storage. Persistent storage (Storage Hardware in Fig. 1) enables a functional process to store data from one execution cycle to another. Each data movement is equivalent to 1 CFP, and operates on a common set of attributes.

In our previous work [27], we have identified factors to use for categorization of software in our domain. The categorization is important to increase the estimation accuracy, by using historical data from implementations of similar software. This way we can capture algorithmic complexity and manipulation of large amounts of data, although COSMIC cannot measure this directly.

To summarize this section, we conclude that the main concepts we need to consider in COSMIC are the Generic Software Model (containing users, boundary, functional processes, and data movement types), the level of decomposition, and the level of granularity. In addition, categorization of software is important for estimation of Code Size. How these concepts can be modeled in UML will be described in the next section.

3 A UML Profile for Code Size Estimation Based on COSMIC

Our goal is to define how to model the COSMIC Generic Software Model using UML. We have chosen UML because it is commonly used for system architecture and software development, and it was already in use at Saab and GM. UML components [30],[34] have a natural boundary between the software and its users, in a similar way as in COSMIC. If we view the UML component as the COSMIC Generic Software Model (see Fig. 1), then we can view the Entry data movements as operations in required interfaces and Exit data movements as operations in provided interfaces.

The UML components do not capture the Read and Write data movements. Our idea is to capture these data movements by a UML class representing this information within the components. Each attribute of this class represents data that can be read, written, or both to/from memory. To achieve this we extend the Property in the metamodel [31] with the stereotype CompSizeProperty, see Fig. 2. We give the stereotype CompSizeProperty the attribute "direction" to model Read and Write data movements. The value "in" represents Read data movements and the value "out" represents Write data movements. The value "inout" represents a combined Read and Write data movement, which will be counted as 2 CFP.

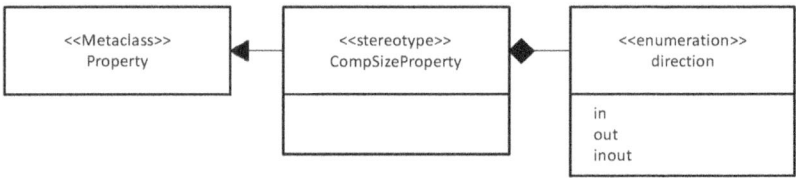

Fig. 2. The CompSizeProperty stereotype

Now we can represent all the data movements of COSMIC using UML components and our extended classes containing attributes with direction. UML components are often used to model complex systems by decomposing a larger software system into smaller parts. In this case we only need to extend the components with a class representing the Read and Write data movements to obtain software models which can be measured by COSMIC.

We can represent the COSMIC Generic Software Model using UML models, and from the models we can obtain CFP values. But how many bytes will 1 CFP represent? This might depend on several factors such as the decomposition level of the component, compilers used, type of functionality, development methods & tools, etc. These factors can be used to categorize the components into groups containing components of similar type. Here we will consider two key factors in some detail: level of decomposition and type of functionality.

In domains where components are used at different levels of decomposition, it has to be clearly marked for each component which level of decomposition the component belongs to. For example, components that describe the top level architecture can contain several other components and will therefore in most cases correspond to more code, compared to components on a lower level only containing classes. In the case study we will present later in this paper, all the components are at the same level of decomposition.

Another factor which might be important is the type of functionality. This factor is of particular importance if the different types of functionality correspond to different byte sizes. This factor gives the possibility to take into account the algorithmic complexity of the components. For the automotive domain we have shown that categorizing the components into groups of similar components is one of the key factors for our good estimation results [27],[28].

To be able to model the categorization information, we extend the Metaclass component with the stereotype CompSizeComponent (see Fig. 3). The stereotype has several attributes to be able to assign values to different factors. Exactly which attributes the stereotype should have may differ between domains, but some factors are probably general such as decomposition_level and functionality. We have included granularity_level which is explained in section 2. Other factors necessary for categorization of components within GM and Saab are identified in [27].

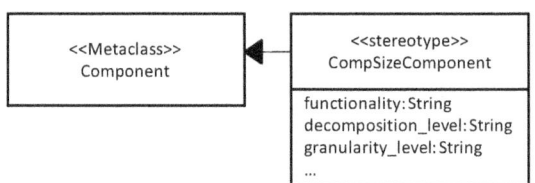

Fig. 3. The CompSizeComponent stereotype

Table 1 summarizes the complete mapping between the main COSMIC concepts and corresponding UML concepts.

Table 1. Mapping rules between main COSMIC concepts and the UML Profile

COSMIC concept	UML concept
Functional process	The functional requirements contained in the component. Must reside completely within one component.
User	Surrounding components.
Boundary	Component boundary.
Level of granularity	Part of categorization.
Level of decomposition	Part of categorization.
Entry data movement	Operation in required interface.
Exit data movement	Operation in provided interface.
Read data movement	CompSizeProperty with direction=in.
Write data movement	CompSizeProperty with direction=out.
Read/Write data movement	CompSizeProperty with direction=inout.

With the UML models described so far, we can capture all information needed for accurate estimation of implemented Code Size in bytes. This bytes value corresponds to the amount of ROM-type memory needed to store the code implementation of the component. But, in addition to ROM, we are interested in estimating the amount of RAM needed to store parameter values, because the RAM size also affects the cost of the embedded system. By extending the Property in the meta-model with the stereotype ByteSizeProperty (as shown in Fig. 4), we can capture the size of each parameter. This is basically the information needed to estimate RAM size.

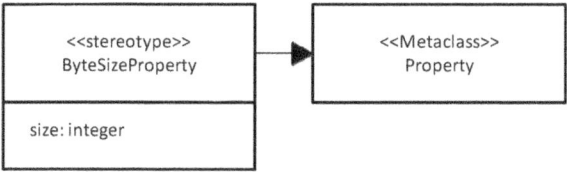

Fig. 4. The ByteSizeProperty stereotype

The UML Profile defined in this section will be evaluated in a case study later in this paper. The case study will show a concrete example on how to use the Profile (see Fig. 9). The mapping rules summarized in Table 1 was implemented in a tool, which will be described in the next section.

4 The CompSize Tool

We have developed a tool based on our results from 3 years of research. The tool can parse information from XMI files exported from the Rhapsody tool [11] containing the information defined in our UML Profile introduced in the previous section. The tool also contains historical data about CFP values and Code Size in bytes from implemented components. Subsets of the data set can be selected using categorization factors (such as the ones described in section 3) to estimate the Code Size of new software.

The tool was implemented in Java resulting in around 1,7 Mbytes of code, and required 6 man months of effort. Further details about the tool are not described in this paper due to page limitations, and because the focus of this paper is the UML Profile and the complete approach rather than the tool itself.

5 Case Study

A case study consisting of several parts was defined, in order to evaluate our model-based and automated approach and to answer the research questions defined in section 1. The case study was conducted at Saab using requirement specifications and software implementations developed by Saab and GM.

5.1 Definition and Planning

Saab and GM use UML Component Diagrams to show how the customer feature is divided into its smallest entities called "distributable components", and the interfaces between them. A distributable component must never be split up into more components, but can be used by several features. The UML Component Diagram is modeled in the Rhapsody tool [11], as part of the system architecture development activities within Saab and GM. This is described further in [4].

The case study will use existing Component Diagrams of the type shown in Fig. 5. In this diagram, we see that the distributable components are modeled as component stereotypes denoted "Distributable" followed by the name of the component. As we can see from the diagram, the Truck Bed Cargo Lamp component has three required interfaces and one provided interface.

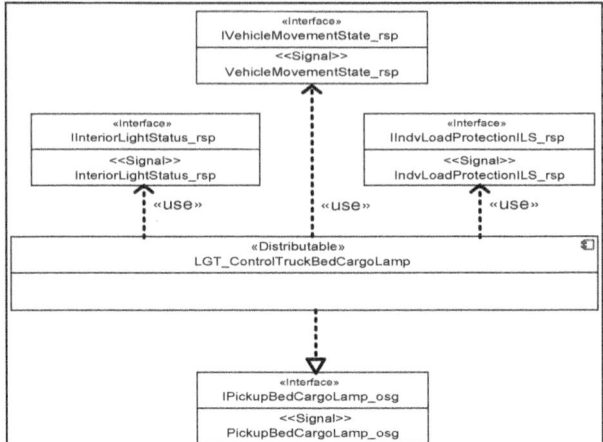

Fig. 5. Component Diagram of the Truck Bed Cargo Lamp component

The Component Diagrams do not contain all the information we need to measure the Functional Size. We also need the requirement specifications related to the components. In the requirement specification we find in textual form the information needed such as: calibration parameters (used for tuning of a general software component to a certain type of product), persistent storage of variables in RAM-type memory, etc. The textual requirements for the software component in Fig. 5 are shown in Fig. 6.

The feature **Shall** be enabled when the calibration CARGO LAMP PRESENT is set true. <END>		
If the vehicle power mode is "OFF", and the cargo lights are illuminated, the SYSTEM **Shall** keep the cargo lamps active as long as Inadvertent Load Control power is active. <END>		
CUSTOMER "ACTION"	CUSTOMER PERCEIVABLE "OUTPUT"	MAXIMUM LATENCY "ACTION" to "OUTPUT"
INTERIOR ILLUMINATION Lamps Switch On and Vehicle Parked.	*Cargo Lamp Illuminates*	100 ms

Fig. 6. Extract from a requirement specification for the Truck Bed Cargo Lamp component

Next we describe the process for estimating the implemented size of software components. The main activities (grey boxes) and artifacts (white boxes) involved in the process for estimation of software component size are shown in Fig. 7. The first activity is the definition of the functional requirements from a user perspective and the non-functional requirements, resulting in a textual specification. This is typically performed by an expert in the particular functional domain, e.g. a door locking expert rather than a software engineer. The textual specification is used by the architect to decompose the functional requirements into distributable components, which are modeled in UML Component Diagrams. The Component Diagrams are used for software design and implementation, as well as for serial data communication definition and implementation. These activities are left out in this description, since they are not important in this work. Instead, we will continue describing the activities performed by the measurement engineer, shown at the bottom of Fig. 7.

The Component Diagram is used to identify the interfaces, and the textual specification is used to identify the calibration parameters and the information needed for categorization of the distributable component. The interfaces, parameters, and categorization constitute the information needed by the COSMIC method. The result from the COSMIC method is a CFP measure. Historical data containing CFP and implemented Code Size in bytes for similar distributable components are used to convert the CFP value into bytes, and thereby estimate the implemented Code Size.

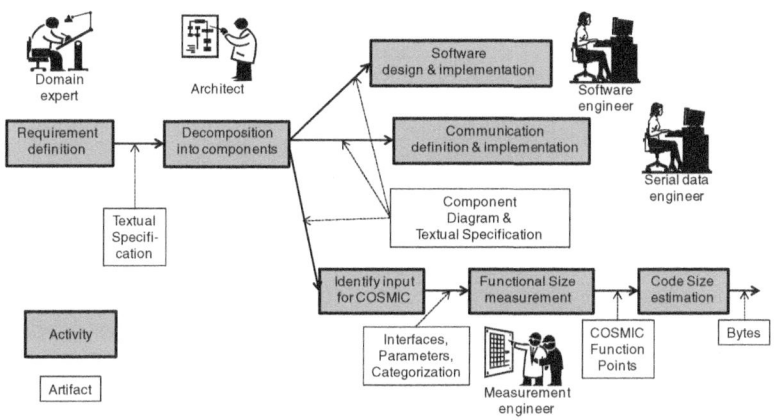

Fig. 7. Main activities and artifacts for estimation of Software Component Size

In our previous work, we have estimated 46 distributable components manually according to this procedure. The main author of this paper acted as measurement engineer, and spent 2-4 hours per distributable component for the activities "Identify input for COSMIC", "Functional Size measurement", and "Code Size estimation". To put this in a practical perspective, we estimate that a typical Saab car contains around 1200 distributable components. This means that it would take up to 4800 man hours (roughly 2,5 man years) to estimate the complete application Code Size of a car. Hence, manual estimation of Code Size is not feasible in this context. Instead we propose a model-based and automated approach, which is described in Fig. 8.

In our proposed approach, the architect adds information about calibration parameters and the information needed for categorization of the distributable component into "Enhanced Component Diagrams". The Enhanced Component Diagrams was defined as a UML Profile in section 3 of this paper. The Enhanced Component Diagrams are exported into an XMI file containing all the information needed for COSMIC. Hence, the activity "Identify input for COSMIC" that was performed manually by reading the textual specification before, is performed by the architect who is already familiar with the requirements. The anticipated saving in manual effort is that the measurement engineer does not have to read the textual specification. The next step in Fig. 8 is that the XMI file is imported to the CompSize tool that automates the "Functional Size measurement" and "Code Size estimation" activities in Fig. 7. The CompSize tool was briefly described in section 4 of this paper.

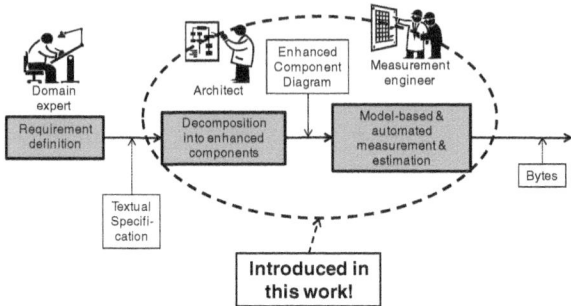

Fig. 8. Main activities and artifacts for the proposed model-based and automated approach to estimation of Software Component Size

The case study was conducted in two steps. The first step of the case study concerns estimation of distributable components with given Component Diagrams. The manual measurements and estimations obtained in our previous work [28] according to Fig. 7 are replicated using the UML Profile and the CompSize tool according to Fig. 8. The purpose is to evaluate the UML Profile and XMI import to the tool, and hence answer RQ1.

The second step of the case study concerns estimation of distributable components with unknown Component Diagrams. The manual measurements and estimations obtained in our previous work [25] according to Fig. 7 are replicated according to the complete process described in Fig. 8. Relative effort data are compared to absolute effort data obtained from interviews with architects. The purpose is to answer RQ2.

5.2 Operation and Data Analysis

The case study was defined, planned, supervised, and analyzed by the authors of this paper, but it was conducted by two Master students with no prior experience from the COSMIC method and with limited knowledge about the automotive domain. The reason that we let students conduct the case study instead of architects is that students are equally inexperienced with each phase of the estimation process as well as with different components. An architect on the other hand, is familiar with the Component Diagrams and can model that faster than the rest of the UML Profile. Therefore we can obtain effort measures that are less biased from the students. The students were given lectures about the COSMIC method, the format and structure of the textual specifications, and the UML Profile. The CompSize tool was implemented by the students, so they were already familiar with the tool before the case study.

Next, we describe the first step of the case study by going through an example. The software component we want to measure is the distributable component, like the one shown in Fig. 5 and Fig. 6. The boundary, the users, the surrounding software, and any engineered devices in Fig. 1 are clearly defined by the component diagram. The distributable components are always defined at the same level of granularity and level of decomposition, which is important to be able to compare CFP values to each-other. To illustrate the usage of the UML Profile we explain how the distributable component in Fig. 5 and Fig. 6 is modeled. The result is shown in Fig. 9.

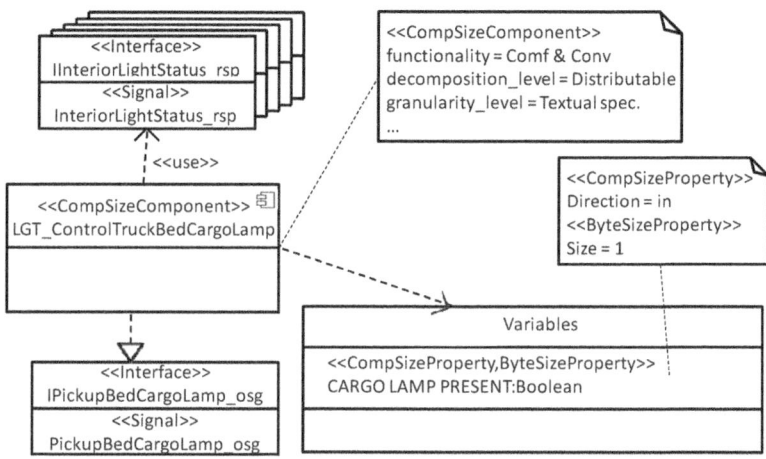

Fig. 9. Mapping of a distributable component onto the UML Profile

The maximum latency requirement in Fig. 6 is modeled as a required interface, because it will be implemented as a periodic invocation of the component with a maximum allowed period time. The vehicle power mode requirement in Fig. 6 is in fact a required interface, and it is modeled accordingly. The other interfaces are modeled as in Fig. 5. The CARGO LAMP PRESENT requirement in Fig. 6 is modeled as a CompSizeProperty with Direction=in. This is the needed information for COSMIC, so we can directly use the mapping rules defined in Table 1 to obtain the CFP value. The result is CFP=7, i.e. 5 Entry data movements + 1 Exit data movement + 1 Read data movement.

The UML Profile in Fig. 9 was modeled in Rhapsody, and an XMI file containing the information in the UML Profile was generated. The CompSize tool imported the information, identified the data movements, calculated the CFP value to 7, and identified the categorization values. The categorization factor values in Fig. 9 are used to select the proper linear regression model to convert the CFP value into bytes, and hence estimate the implemented Code Size of the distributable component. In this case the resulting estimated Code Size is 1441 bytes, exactly as in [28]. Hence, we conclude that the UML Profile can capture the information needed for COSMIC, and that the tool can import this information from an XMI file.

The second step of the case study modeled 10 components based on requirement specifications, as described in Fig. 8. The purpose is to collect timing data. The time was measured for each of the following activities; reading the textual specification to understand the requirements and to identify the distributable component and its interfaces, modeling the distributable component and its interfaces, reading the textual specification to identify the additional information needed for COSMIC, modeling the additional information in the UML Profile, feeding the information into the CompSize tool and obtaining the estimated bytes value.

In addition, the measured CFP values were compared to our previous measurements of the same components. The purpose is to assess whether the students have identified the majority of the data movements, and to make sure that the timing data is relevant. A scatter plot comparing the CFP values obtained in the case study and our previous CFP values from [25], is shown in Fig. 10. As can be seen, the resulting CFP values from the student measurements deviate from ours, but in general the students seem to have identified the majority of the data movements. The R^2 value from the student measurement is high ($R^2=0,80$), which confirms the strong correlation between CFP and bytes we have found in our measurements. We expected some deviation between the measurements performed by the students and our own measurements, because published experiments show good repeatability in CFP measured by experienced engineers, but poor repeatability in CFP measured by inexperienced engineers [7]. Therefore, we concluded that the timing data is realistic.

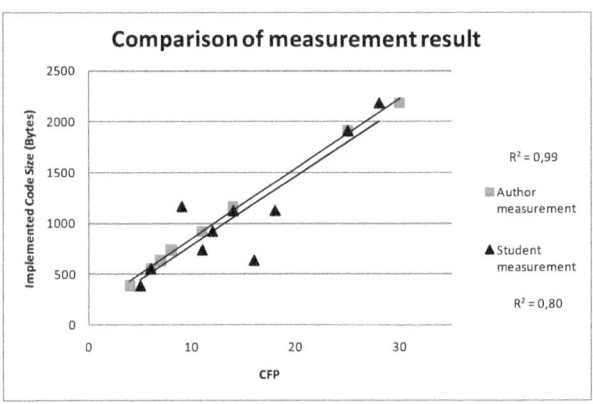

Fig. 10. Scatter plot showing CFP values measured by the main author and the students for the same components

5.3 Interpretation of Results

The time for each step in the estimation process was measured and collected during the case study. The time needed for reading the textual specification to identify the additional information for COSMIC and modeling that in the UML Profile was converted into percentage of the total time.

The time for one of the components was identified as an outlier, because it was significantly larger than for the other components and the student was in fact sick at the time. The statistics of the resulting data for the remaining 9 components is presented in Table 2.

Table 2. Statistics for the amount of added effort for the UML Profile compared to total effort

Mean value (%)	Std deviation (%)	Min value (%)	Max value (%)
13	4,3	5,3	20

From interviews with architects at Saab we have obtained the manual effort involved in creating the standard Component Diagrams according to Fig. 5, to around 6 man hours for a typical distributable component. This effort includes reading of textual specification, modeling the component diagram, having review meetings with the domain expert, etc.

So if we add an additional 13% (mean value from Table 2) of effort to the 6 man hours, we would burden the architect with an additional 47 minutes (0,13*6 hours) for modeling the UML Profile. The additional 47 minutes are much less than the 2-4 hours needed for manual measurement and estimation. For the complete application software of a typical Saab car it would require around 900 man hours (0,5 man years) with our model-based and automated approach, instead of up to 4800 man hours (2,5 man years). In addition, we expect that the effort needed in our approach will decrease even further in a practical case, because an architect will normally read and model everything for a component at once.

A natural question at this point is why the architect would be willing to model the additional information for the purpose of estimating Code Size. The motivating factor is that the architect needs the estimated values as support for allocation decisions, architecture studies in early development phases, etc.

A significant difference in our model-based and automated approach compared to the manual approach, is that much of the COSMIC measurement knowledge is needed when the architect models the UML Profile for the component. This is the step where the actual measurement takes place. Therefore it is crucial that the architect receives COSMIC knowledge support, either directly from a measurement engineer or from written guidelines. Our recommendation is the latter, and that is the way we plan to implement the approach at Saab. The guidelines are important to obtain high repeatability and consistency in the process.

6 Evaluation of Validity Threats

Our case study was conducted by two Master students with no prior experience about the COSMIC method and limited knowledge about the automotive domain. This fact is likely to affect the accuracy of the estimates, as well as the absolute effort to obtain the estimate. However, in this paper we focus on the relative effort required in each phase of the estimation process. Since the students are equally inexperienced in each phase, we expect effort data that are less biased than if an architect who is familiar with parts of the process would conduct the case study. Moreover, the case study was defined, planned, supervised, and analyzed by the authors of this paper. The main author has 15 years of experience from software development activities, of which 6 years were spent managing Architecture teams at Saab and GM. This experience should compensate for the lack of automotive experience of the students.

The UML Profile is tailored to capture the information needed for the COSMIC method. We regard this as a minor limitation, because COSMIC is an approved ISO standard for measuring the Functional Size of software and much of the current publications concerning software size measurement apply COSMIC.

We have only used requirement specifications, Component Diagrams and software implementations from two automotive companies. This means we can only make conclusions that are valid in this particular domain. Therefore we plan to evaluate our approach with data from other domains.

7 Related Work

Marin et al. [29] presents a survey of existing literature related to measurement procedures based on COSMIC FP. Eleven procedures are presented of which two applies to the real-time systems domain. Of these two, the most relevant one [6] uses models developed in the ROOM (Real-time Object Oriented Modeling) language as input to the μcROSE tool [7]. Their work is similar to ours, but they use another modeling language as input for COSMIC measurement. They conduct a case study to validate the tool, but they do not report on the efficiency obtained using the tool compared to manual measurement.

Other works use UML diagrams like use case, class, component, and sequence diagrams as input for COSMIC measurement [20],[21],[22]. The purpose is to improve the practice of COSMIC measurement and to automate the measurement process using a tool, but the tool remains to be developed.

Another group of publications report on how to use UML models as input for IFPUG FPA measurement [8],[35]. In [35], it is shown that UML class diagrams and sequence diagrams can be used as input for a software tool that automatically calculates the IFPUG FP.

Stern [32] reports on lessons learned from using COSMIC FP for effort estimation purposes at Renault automotive company. Very strong correlation ($R^2=0,93$) were found between CFP and supplier effort invoice data. Stern and Gencel [33] investigate the relationship between COSMIC FP and memory size of functions using data from the automotive industry. They found very strong correlation ($R^2=0,99$) in a range of Functional Sizes from CFP=7 to CFP=748. This confirms our own results reported in [23],[24],[25],[26],[27],[28].

8 Conclusion and Future Work

The goal of this paper was to investigate how the manual effort involved in estimation of Code Size can be minimized. We defined a UML Profile capturing all information needed for estimation of Code Size, and developed a tool for automated estimation of Code Size based on CFP.

We conducted a case study using requirement specifications and software implementations from the automotive industry to answer the research questions. The case study showed that the UML Profile can capture all the information needed by the COSMIC method. The case study also showed that the effort for estimating the implemented code size of a component is reduced from 2-4 hours to well below 1 hour. So this work illustrates how the use of UML models can save manual effort (and hence money) in a realistic case.

In addition, our UML Profile contains support for estimation of RAM memory size, which is an extension compared to our previous work. We plan to evaluate this support in future case studies.

As future work we also plan to develop written guidelines to the architects about how they are supposed to model the UML Profile to obtain accurate estimation results. The guidelines and our model-based estimation approach will be further evaluated in a case study conducted by the actual architects.

Acknowledgments. We would like to express our thanks to Tigran Harutyunyan and Tony Heimdahl for implementing and validating the CompSize tool, as well as for conducting parts of the case study in this work.

References

[1] Albrecht, A.: Measuring application development productivity. In: Proc. of the IBM Applications Development Symposium, Monterey, CA, pp. 83–92 (October 1979)
[2] Albrecht, A., Gaffney, J.: Software function, source lines of code, and development effort prediction: A software science validation. IEEE Trans. Softw. Eng. SE-9, 6, 639–648 (1983)
[3] Albrecht, A.: AD/M Productivity Measurement and Estimate Validation. IBM Corporate Information Systems. IBM Corp., Purchase, NY (1984)
[4] Baillargeon, R, Flores, R.: From Algorithms to Software – A Practical Approach to Model-Driven Design. SAE Paper 2007-01-1622
[5] COSMIC, The Common Software Measurement International Consortium Functional Size Measurement Method, Version 3.0, Measurement Manual (2007)
[6] Diab, H., Frappier, M., St-Denis, R.: Formalizing COSMIC-FFP Using ROOM. In: ACS/IEEE Int'l Conf. on Computer Systems and Applications (2001)
[7] Diab, H., Koukane, F., Frappier, M., St-Denis, R.: μcROSE: automated measurement of COSMIC-FFP for Rational Rose RealTime. Information and Software Technology 47(3), 151–166 (2005)
[8] Fornaciari, W., Micheli, P., Salice, F., Zampella, L.: A First Step Towards Hw/Sw Partitioning of UML Specifications. In: Proc. of the Design, Automation and Test in Europe Conf. and Exhibition (DATE 2003), pp. 668–673 (2003)
[9] Gencel, C., Demirors, O.: Functional Size Measurement Revisited. ACM Trans. Softw. Eng. Methodol. 17(3) Article 15 (June 2008)
[10] Gencel, C., Heldal, R., Lind, K.: On the Relationship between Different Size Measures in the Software Life Cycle. In: Proc. of the IEEE Asia-Pacific Software Engineering Conference (APSEC 2009), pp. 19–26 (2009)
[11] IBM Rhapsody, http://www.ibm.com/
[12] IFPUG, Function Point Counting Practices Manual, Release 4.1, IFPUG, Westerville, OH (1999)
[13] ISO/IEC 14143-1:2007, Information Technology - Software Measurement - Functional Size Measurement - Part 1: Definitions of concepts (2007)
[14] ISO/IEC 14143-2:2002, Information Technology - Software Measurement – Functional Size Measurement - Part 2: Conformity Evaluation of Software Size Measurement Methods to ISO/IEC 14143-1 (2002)
[15] ISO/IEC TR 14143-3:2003 Information Technology - Software Measurement – Functional Size Measurement - Part 3: Verification of Functional Size Measurement Methods (2003)
[16] ISO/IEC TR 14143-4:2002, Information Technology - Software Measurement – Functional Size Measurement - Part 4: Reference Model (2002)

[17] ISO/IEC TR 14143-5:2004, Information Technology - Software Measurement – Functional Size Measurement - Part 5: Determination of Functional Domains for Use with Functional Size Measurement (2004)
[18] ISO/IEC 14143-6:2006, Guide for the Use of ISO/IEC 14143 and Related International Standards (2006)
[19] ISO/IEC 19761:2003, Software engineering - COSMIC-FFP - A functional size measurement method (2003)
[20] Lavazza, L., Del Bianco, V.: A Case Study in COSMIC Functional Size Measurement: The Rice Cooker Revisited. In: Abran, A., Braungarten, R., Dumke, R.R., Cuadrado-Gallego, J.J., Brunekreef, J. (eds.) IWSM 2009. LNCS, vol. 5891, pp. 101–121. Springer, Heidelberg (2009)
[21] Lavazza, L., Robiolo, G.: Introducing the Evaluation of Complexity in Functional Size Measurement: a UML-based Approach. In: Int'l Symposium on Empirical Software Engineering and Measurement, ESEM 2010 (2010)
[22] Levesque, G., Bevo, V., Tran Cao, D.: Estimating Software Size with UML Models. In: Canadian Conference on Computer Science & Software Engineering (C3S2E 2008), pp. 81–87 (2008)
[23] Lind, K., Heldal, R.: Estimation of Real-Time System Software Size using Function Points. In: Proc. of the Nordic Workshop on Model Driven En-gineering (NW-MoDE), pp. 15–28 (2008)
[24] Lind, K., Heldal, R.: Estimation of Real-Time Software Code Size using COSMIC FSM. In: Proc. of the IEEE Intl. Symposium on Object/component/service-oriented Real-time distributed Computing (ISORC 2009), pp. 244–248 (2009)
[25] Lind, K., Heldal, R.: Estimation of Real-Time Software Component Size. Nordic Journal of Computing (NJC) (14), 282–300 (2008)
[26] Lind, K., Heldal, R.: On the Relationship between Functional Size and Software Code Size. In: Proc. of the Workshop on Emerging Trends in Software Metrics (WETSoM 2010) Held in Conjunction with the Intl. Conf. of Software Engineering, ICSE 2010 (2010)
[27] Lind, K., Heldal, R.: Categorization of Real-Time Software Components for Code Size Estimation. In: Int'l Symposium on Empirical Software Engineering and Measurement, ESEM 2010 (2010)
[28] Lind, K., Heldal, R.: A Practical Approach to Size Estimation of Embedded Software Components. Approved for publication in IEEE Trans. Softw. Eng. (2011)
[29] Marin, B., Giachetti, G., Pastor, O.: Measurement of Functional Size in Conceptual Models: A Survey of Measurement Procedures Based on COSMIC. In: Int'l Workshop on Software Measurement (IWSM), November 18-19 (2008)
[30] OMG, Unified Modeling Language (UML), Superstructure Specification, V2.3, Object Management Group, http://www.uml.org/.
[31] OMG, Unified Modeling Language (UML), Infrastructure Specification, V2.3, Object Management Group, http://www.uml.org/
[32] Stern, S.: Practical experimentations with the COSMIC method in Automotive embedded software field. In: Int'l Workshop on Software Measurement (IWSM), November 4-6 (2009)
[33] Stern, S., Gencel, C.: Embedded Software Memory Size Estimation Using COSMIC: A Case Study. In: Int'l Workshop on Software Measurement (IWSM), November 10-12 (2010)
[34] Szyperski, C.: Component Software: Beyond Object-Oriented Programming, 2nd edn. Addison-Wesley Professional, Boston (2002) ISBN 0-201-74572-0
[35] Uemura, T., Kusumoto, S., Inoue, K.: Function-point analysis using design specifications based on the Unified Modelling Language. Journal of Software Maintenance and Evolution: Research and Practice 13(4), 223–243 (2001)

MDE to Manage Communications with and between Resource-Constrained Systems

Franck Fleurey[1], Brice Morin[1], Arnor Solberg[1], and Olivier Barais[2]

[1] SINTEF IKT, Oslo, Norway
[2] IRISA, University of Rennes1 and INRIA

Abstract. With the emergence of Internet of Things (IoT), many things which typically used to be isolated or operated in small local networks, will be interconnected through the Internet. One main challenge to tackle in IoT is efficient management of communication between things, since things can be very different in terms of available resources, size and communication protocols. Current Internet-enabled devices are typically powerful enough to rely on common operating systems, standard network protocols and middlewares. In IoT many devices will be too constrained to rely on such resource-consuming infrastructures; they run ad-hoc proprietary protocols. The contribution of this paper is a model-based approach for the efficient provisioning and management of the communication between heterogeneous resource-constrained devices. It includes a DSML which compiles to a set of interoperable communication libraries providing an abstract communication layer that can integrate both powerful and resource-constrained devices. The approach is implemented in an IDE for the development resource-constrained Things.

1 Introduction

We exploit, interact and rely on things in our everyday life (e.g., house-hold appliances, clothing, cars, lights, buildings, mobile phones, etc). Currently, more and more of these things are equipped with sensors, computing power and communication capabilities, leading to the emergence of the Internet of Things (IoT). A vast number of independent or embedded sensors and sensor networks will form the basis of the IoT infrastructure. New innovative applications exploiting the IoT paradigm are already emerging in domains such as Ambient-Assisted Living (AAL), intelligent transport systems and environmental monitoring.

Building advanced services that involve heterogeneous sensors and things that need to communicate and collaborate can be complex and time consuming for the following reasons:

- **Resource Constraints:** While the business logic of each individual thing is often rather simple, the resource constraints (CPU, memory, power, etc) make it challenging to efficiently implement this logic. Typically, these things have to run autonomously for an extended time, which require minimizing their power consumption while still providing quality of service. For example, sensors monitoring the environment are spread in locations not easily

accessible, making such requirements of high importance to maintain the system services.
- **Heterogeneity:** The IoT includes a wide variety of different nodes, ranging from powerful servers to small things operated by micro-controllers. Powerful nodes can run common operating systems and rely on common frameworks and protocols to implement software engineering best practices. However, IoT will include a vast number of resource-constrained things: some can run light operating systems like TinyOS, some can only run C or C-like languages, some can only run low level assembly code. In addition there is a wide range of (wireless) communication technologies (e.g., WiFi, Bluetooth, ZigBee) which provide different trade-offs regarding power-consumption, range, reliability, etc, and which should be combined in a sensor network.
- **Independent development of things and services:** Things (e.g., physical devices operated by a C-based micro-controller) and advanced services (e.g., Java application running on a server) relying on a set of networked things are usually developed concurrently, by different teams having different competencies. This could lead to misalignments and inconsistencies.
- **Interoperability:** Different IoT-related standards have emerged, such as the ones proposed by the Sensor Web Enablement Working Group [3], to provide interoperability support in the context of sensor networks. While these standards address clear needs, their realization (usually verbose XML-based document) cannot fit to the most resource-constrained devices, due to the technical overhead they imply. Instead micro-controllers rely on ad-hoc and highly optimized protocols, which better fits the resource constraints and improve the reliability and speed of wireless communications.

For these reasons, developing and IoT application based on a heterogeneous Wireless Sensor Network (WSN) is challenging. However, solution exists for tackling these issues for the powerful nodes: standards define ways to represent and exchange data in a homogeneous way, some middlewares, software frameworks and networking stacks solve part of the heterogeneity challenges and the business logic can be realized using classic development techniques including MDE. Unfortunately, these solutions cannot directly be applied for the most resource-constrained nodes. As a result, software embedded in the most resource-constrained things are in most cases manually developed in C and ASM. Platforms are too small to embeed OS, middlewares or frameworks so the code is often a tangled mix of business logic, communication and hardware drivers.

This paper presents an innovative Model-Driven approach to support the efficient development IoT applications over heterogeneous WSNs. In particular we have developed a DSML called ThingML, which aims at promoting software engineering best practices for the specific case of resource-constrained systems. ThingML comes with editors and checkers and a set of transformations and code generators which currently target Java and several micro-controller platforms (e.g., TI MSP, Atmel AVR and Arduino). The contribution presented in this paper is a model-driven approach for engineering and managing efficient communications with and between heterogeneous and resource-constrained things within the IoT, with proper support for independent development.

The paper is organized as follows. Section 2 introduces our running example and analyzes the problems related to communication with and between resource-constrained things. Section 3 presents our model-driven approach to tackle these issues. Our approach is validated on two case studies in Section 4. Section 5 presents related work and Section 6 concludes and opens some perspectives.

2 Problem Analysis and Illustrative Example

This section presents a running example used throughout the paper. The example both illustrate our approach and motivates our work by detailing challenges related to development of resource constrained IoT services.

CoffeeSpy is an experimental device that monitors a coffee machine using technologies typically found in wireless sensor network (WSN) applications. The left side of Figure 1 presents an overview of the sensor hardware structure. The core of the device is an 8bits AVR micro-controller with 32ko of flash memory and 2ko of RAM memory connected to 3 sensors: i) a high-resolution infra-red temperature sensor, ii) an infra-red distance sensor, and iii) a light sensor.

The wireless communications are realized via an XBee radio chip which implements the ZigBee protocol (http://www.zigbee.org/). This hardware set-up is rather simple, however, the CoffeeSpy device is representative for devices found in application domains such as environmental sensor networks or industrial process control and monitoring systems, as it uses typical off-the-shelf components. The CoffeeSpy application provides real time information about:

- the temperature and freshness of the coffee using the temperature sensor,
- the number of cups which have been pored since the coffee was made using the distance sensor and the temperature sensor, and
- the activity in the coffee room using the light sensor and the distance sensor.

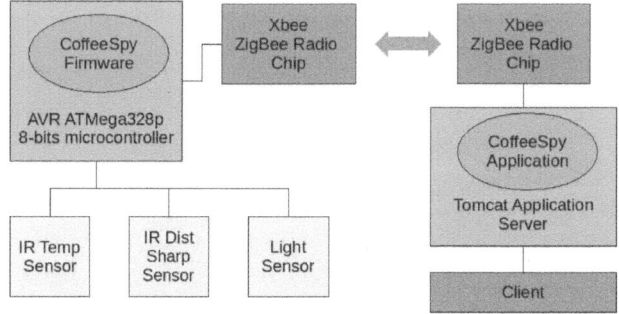

Fig. 1. Architecture of the CoffeeSpy device

As shown in Figure 1, the device communicates with a server equipped with a ZigBee adapter. From a software point of view, the application is composed of two components:

- The server application implemented in Java. The server has a lot of resources available in terms of computing power, memory, software libraries, middlewares, etc. Typical software modeling techniques and development processes can easily be applied in the development of this part of the application.
- The firmware running on the micro-controller, programmed in C. It is constrained in terms of energy, computing power, memory, bandwidth, etc. These constraints make it impossible to rely on standard middlewares and operating systems to implement the device functionalities.

This heterogeneity introduces some accidental complexity for the development of the CoffeeSpy application. Alternatives can be explored to try and avoid this situation, however, they raise other concerns:

- Using a more powerful core for the CoffeSpy which could run a real OS (e.g., embedded Linux) with standard software libraries, network protocols and communication middlewares. This strategy can be applied to some chosen devices but cannot be applied to all the devices of the network: the hardware for such a device would be 50 to 100 times more expensive and its power consumption would be about 1000 times more. Because devices and sensors are deployed in large numbers and often need to be battery-operated and environmentally friendly (green computing), limiting the power consumption is a primary concern.
- Reducing the features of the firmware to the absolute minimum and delegate all the functionalities to large nodes like the server of the CoffeeSpy application. A minimalistic firmware would simply read values from sensors and transmit them periodically. Unfortunately this would not be a good solution for several reasons:
    - It is inefficient. To monitor the coffee, the application can sample the temperature of the coffee every minute, but detecting motion in front of the coffee machine requires more frequent sampling (several times per second). While this can easily be implemented, it is highly inefficient both in terms of power and bandwidth consumption and would thus not scale to any realistic sensor network.
    - It is a threat to reliability. Devices monitoring and controlling equipments, should be able to sustain critical functionalities even if the remote and more powerful nodes are not available. Typically time-critical and safety-critical features should be implemented in the controllers to keep these services available even in case of failure of the other nodes or communication links. The logic of the application should be distributed among all the nodes (including the smallest ones) to avoid critical points of failure.
    - It does not scale. The CoffeeSpy example has only two nodes but real-life sensor networks are typically composed of hundreds or thousands nodes.

The applications running on these nodes need to cope with the sporadic availability of other nodes, the discovery of new nodes and adapt to their environment to provide the best possible services. Such dynamicity cannot be implemented in a centralized way and require each node of the network to implement behavior which contributes to the overall application.

Designing a distributed system which involves resource-constrained nodes is a complex trade-off between maintainability, hardware costs, reliability, power consumption, etc. Once the hardware is selected, the main instrument to adjust this trade-off is the distribution of the features on the different nodes. For example in the CoffeeSpy application, the freshness of the coffee can either be computed on the micro-controller or on the server by analyzing raw data coming from the sensor. As such this would probably be the most convenient solution for our application since many libraries exist in Java to process data. However if we want to extend the CoffeeSpy device with a display (located on the device itself) which shows the age of the coffee, it would be better to have this computation made locally in order to keep the display properly updated and functional even if the server side is down. This would in addition avoid back-and-forth exchange of messages on the wireless network.

The only realistic solution to keep control on this complex trade-off is to provide efficient support for moving functionalities from nodes to nodes both at design-time and during maintenance and evolution. This actually means co-evolving all the nodes contributing to a function in a consistent way. For example, if the freshness of the coffee is computed on the server, then the CoffeeSpy device only needs to provide a service for reading temperature. However if the device does this computation it has to be refactored to also transmit the age of the coffee. There already exist some elegant solutions to seamlessly communicate both with local objects and remote objects in an homogeneous environment. However, when it comes to micro controller-based devices, such an extension means that both the firmware of the device and its driver on the server has to be extended with the appropriate computation and communication functionalities. Even worse, in a realistic setup, the different nodes of an application are typically developed by different teams and have different life-cycles. The goal of the approach proposed in this paper is to allow defining in a simple way the interfaces between devices and to automatically derive APIs to support communications, and stubs to support the development and testing of nodes in isolation.

3 Approach

The approach proposed in this paper is developed as part of an IDE called ThingML[1] for the development of resource-constrained systems. The idea of our approach is to specify protocols in a ThingML model using a concise and comprehensive syntax, as illustrated in Figure 2, and to fully generate code:

---
[1] http://www.thingml.org

- Efficient API for the serialization and de-serialization of messages in/from arrays of bytes, as presented in Section 3.1.
- Handlers for managing message-specific communication features, as presented in Section 3.2.
- Mock-ups and interactive simulators to enable independent development of things and services, as presented in Section 3.3.

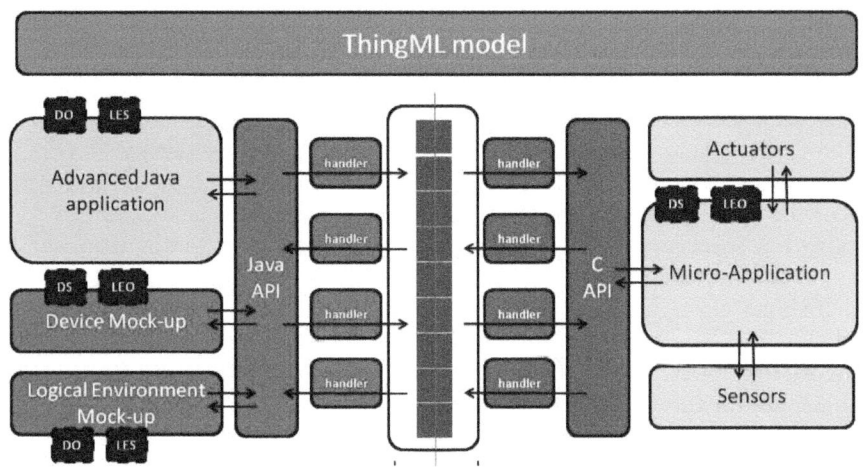

Fig. 2. Overview of the proposed approach

The idea of ThingML is to build a practical development environment and methodology to make typical software engineering good practices available to the development of resource-constrained embedded systems such as micro-controller applications. We believe that model-driven engineering provides the right tools to address this problem because models-based approaches do not need to rely on advanced run-time frameworks, operating systems and middleware to be applicable. Models can be analyzed, tested and verified and exploited to generate optimized code which target resource-constrained platforms. In previous work we have shown how ThingML can be used to produce adaptive firmware using a high-level adaptation DSL and aspect-oriented modeling techniques applied to state machines [7]. In this paper we focus on the generation of interoperable communication APIs to communicate with and between things. To this end, we use a sub-set of the ThingML language to specify messages.

The ThingML metamodel, editors and code generators are available as part of the ThingML open-source project[2].

3.1 Generating Interoperable APIs for Things and Services

An important aspect when setting up an infrastructure for the IoT is the ability to properly connect and interoperate the physical "things" with advanced services relying on standards [3]. Typically, the raw data provided by the sensors

---
[2] https://github.com/ffleurey/ThingML

(e.g., the actual value of a light sensor) is usually not relevant for end-users. Instead, end-users are more interested, for example, by a qualitative estimation of the light in a room.

To ease the integration and interoperability of (C-based) things and (Java-based) services we generate C APIs for the devices and Java APIs for the more powerful nodes. All these APIs are able to communicate together. Fully functional APIs are generated from ThingML models, such as the one illustrated in Figure 3, which define messages with their parameters, and their directions (sent of received) w.r.t. to the physical device: a message sent by the device is a message received by the service, and vice-versa. In the generated code, each message is clearly reified (e.g. by a Java class) and we provide the designers with a factory to create message either by passing parameters, or from a serialized format. The code related to serialization/deserialization is also fully generated.

Our code generators thus alleviate designers from directly manipulating low-level structures, who use the generated APIs instead. The benefits of this approach are:

- **Performance:** Messages are automatically serialized as arrays of bytes, which are the most concise way of representing data, and by consequence the fastest way of transmitting data on (wireless) networks. They are also much faster to parse than XML data. As a comparison [9], this is 3 to 10 times smaller than XML-based data, and 20 to 100 times faster to parse.
- **Interoperability:** Our approach ensures or facilitates different levels of interoperability:
  - **Programming languages:** Relying on the lowest possible abstraction (bytes) ensures the interoperability at the lower level: Java, C, etc can interpret bytes. However, designer only manipulate higher lever representations: Java POJOs, C structures, etc.
  - **Communication links:** Arrays of bytes are common inputs/outputs accepted by most communication stacks: serial port, ZibBee, Bluetooth, etc. This ensures the interoperability among different links, which is an important point in WSN.
  - **Standards:** The generated high-level APIs provides a good support for interoperability with standards. For example, it is straightforward to instantiate XML templates on values of POJOs.

In addition to the API we also generate the interfaces of two Observer patterns. The first Observer aims at managing and facilitating the communications with the device, and the second one for the communications with clients of the device: other devices, heavy applications running on a server, etc. Using these observers, it is rather easy to develop applications that for example log the data of devices, or drive the devices. We also fully generate such an application (an interactive simulator), as described in Section 3.3.

3.2 Generating Light-Weight and Message-Specific Protocols

Networking is a domain where a large number of techniques, standards and tools are available to assist software development. These techniques very often rely on the 7 OSI layers (or similar stacks) to implement networking capabilities and offer high-level and reliable communications. The layers are generic components which require the services of the layer below them and offer a set of services to the layer above. This componentization enables easy deployment and reuse in various contexts, but does not suit well resource-constrained systems:

- The generality implies resource penalties. The different layers typically use different memory buffers to store the incoming an outgoing data and perform their tasks, which multiply the memory usage of the stack. Collapsing the layers together would allow building a more efficient networking component requiring only a fraction of the resources.
- The applications running in a resource-constrained environment typically do not need all the features of a fully fledged protocol stack. In most cases the type of messages can be fixed at design time. Depending on the application, protocol features such as acknowledgments, timeouts, routing, error detection, error correction, assembling and disassembling of packets and so on might not all be required.

```
// Raw Data from the sensors
message subscribeRawData( interval : Integer ) @code "19";
message unsubscribeRawData() @code "22";
message getRawData() @code "20";
message rawData(temp : Integer, dist : Integer, light : Integer) @code "21";
receives subscribeRawData, getRawData, unsubscribeRawData
sends rawData

// Simple Ping
message ping() @code "66"
    @sync_ack "pong" @timeout "1000" @retry "3";
message pong() @code "67";
receives ping
sends pong

// Get the data from individual sensors
message GetTemperature() @code "1"
    @sync_response "TemperatureValue#v" @timeout "500" @retry "0";
message TemperatureValue(v : Integer)
    @code "2";
```

Fig. 3. Messages with communication features

In practice, the networking component embedded in micro-controllers is manually implemented as a single optimized component developed for each specific application [15]. This has great advantages in terms of performance and applicability but comes with a large development, testing and maintenance cost. Our approach leverages models to generate these dedicated networking components. Figure 3 presents part of the protocol model for the CoffeeSpy device. ThingML allows modeling a set of communicating devices and a set of messages they can exchange. By default all messages are considered as asynchronous and are sent with a "send on forget" policy (see messages related to raw data in the Figure). This is the simplest message exchange strategy and it can be implemented at a very low cost on top of any kind of physical link. However, even for applications as simple as the CoffeeSpy, more complex networking features are required:

acknowledgments, synchronous message responses, error detection, messages retransmission, encryption, etc. ThingML relies on a set of predefined annotations to further refine the communication semantics of the messages.

The two messages called *ping* and *pong* can be used to check the communication between the server and the CoffeeSpy device. *Ping* can be sent to the device and the annotations specify that this message has a synchronous acknowledgment called *pong*. This acknowledgment is expected to come within 1 second, and if it does not come, 3 attempts can be made at resending the "ping" message. By processing these annotations, the code generator produces the emission of the acknowledgment message in the device code and an operation in the client API which sends the *ping* message, handles timeouts and retries and return a status information specifying whether or not the acknowledgment was received. By default the operation simply returns a Boolean but several options can be used to throw exceptions when communication failures occur. Similarly, it is possible to manage synchronous calls with a return value in a similar way as illustrated by the messages *GetTemperature* and *TemperatureValue* define a synchronous way of reading the temperature sensor of the CoffeeSpy device. The annotation *sync_response* specifies that the parameter v of the message *TemperatureValue* is the result of the call.

In all cases, the code generator will only include the code required to implement the networking features on the specified messages. The benefits of the approach are two-fold: First it allows for efficient, specific and compact networking components. Second, it provides a fined grained way of defining the specific ways in which different messages should be handled. For example, in a typical sensor network different types of information are exchanged between nodes for collecting sensor data, managing the network, discovering new sensor nodes, etc. Each feature has different needs in terms of synchronization, response time, bandwidth, reliability, etc. With a classical approach this would require using the most advanced protocol stack for all communications or to embed a collection of different protocol stacks. Using the proposed model-based approach, the type of communication and its quality of service properties can be fine tuned for each message in order to fulfill the domain requirement with no accidental overhead.

3.3 Generating Interactive Simulators

In practice, micro-controllers and client software systems are usually developed by two separate teams with different competences. For productivity reasons, it is not reasonable to wait that one end ((Java-based) software or (C-based) things) is fully operational before realizing the second end. Rather, both ends are developed and maintained concurrently, often leading to misalignments and inconsistencies. It is thus very important to provide support early in the development cycle to be able to test the different ends of a WSN-based application.

The fully automated generation of APIs to encapsulate and exchange messages (Section 3.1) is a first step to uncouple the development of advanced services from the development of things. Once messages are specified in ThingML, different teams of developers can rely on the generated API knowing that they will interoperate seamlessly.

Similarly to the development of more classic applications, developing a WSN-based application often requires an iterative process. This is even more important since some constraints are imposed by the low-resource hardware. As motivated in Section 2, it is not always easy to identify a priori the best tradeoff between which part of the application logic should be implemented on the small device, and which part should be executed on more powerful nodes.

To support a more agile development process, we also generate interactive simulators, as illustrated in Figure 4, which respectively mock-up the devices and their logical environment, in order to respectively test the devices or other client devices/services [5].

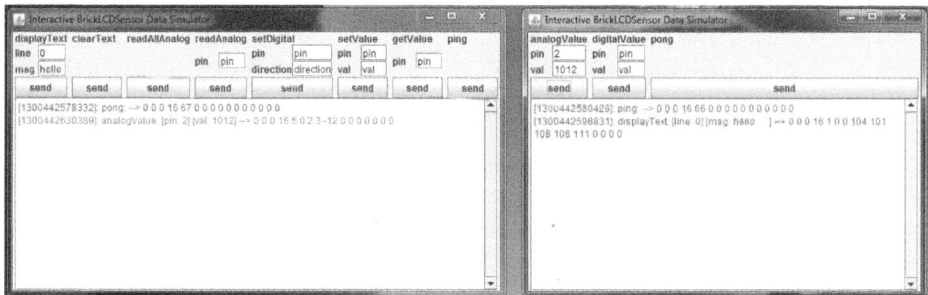

Fig. 4. Interactive simulators to enable independent development

These simulators enables rapid and early testing of the two ends of the system (C-based devices and Java-based services) to identify early in the development cycle potential lacks or mismatches in the set of messages, with no need to wait that one end is fully developed to discover these problems. In the case messages are updated in the ThingML model, API can be re-generated. This would of course imply some refactoring in the client code, facilitated by modern IDEs.

As described in Section 3, ThingML focuses on resource-constrained devices, usually deployed as leaves in a sensor network. However, it is possible to infer some useful information from the ThingML specifications of such devices. Typically, if we reverse the protocol of a given device (i.e, send message that were formerly received, as vice-versa), we can obtain a specification of a client device equivalent to the logical environment of the initial device. Another alternative that we also support is to let the designers specifying other devices (that can potentially run on more powerful nodes, even though ThingML does not specifically address such kind of nodes) that interact with the initial device. These devices partially intersect the logical environment, but might also define other messages. By default we generate an interactive simulator that stubs all the devices specified in the ThingML model, and that also stubs all the logical environment. Both stubs are actually generated using the same code generator, since we consider the logical environment as a "mirror" device. Each stub is composed of a simple (fully generated) GUI and a controller that implements the Observer pattern generated with the API (Section 3.1). By default, we generate a simple test program which connects both stubs together. The utility of this application is simply to check that message are serialized and deserialized in a consistent way by the generated API. However, it is off course straightforward to connect the stubs to other application implementing our Observer pattern, such as the JArduino [6] application presented in Section 4.2.

4 Application

In order to validate our ThingML IDE, we have implemented two case studies in ThingML, on top of the Arduino platforms, and generated the code to actually run these case studies. Arduino [2] is an open-source (both hardware and software) electronics prototyping platform. The Arduino board can be connected to a set of sensors and actuators and programmed in a language close to C/C++.

The first application is a domain-specific application (the coffee spy) based on a precise set of sensors that we used as a running example in this paper. The second case study is a general purpose application to enable the rapid prototyping of sensor networks on top of the Arduino platform, which we have made available as an open-source project on GitHub [6]. The idea is to gather a community (basically, Java developers who wants to try the Arduino platform) around JArduino and collect feedback on the generated code.

We use the Sonar tool (http://www.sonarsource.org/) to compute various metrics and score (based on simple naming convention, anti-pattern detection, etc) on the generated Java code. The metrics of the generated C code (smaller) are provided manually.

4.1 CoffeeSpy: Domain-Specific Application in ThingML

The protocol of the coffee spy is described by 24 messages, in 50 lines of code. From this rather synthetic model, we generate 44 classes for a total of 2702 lines of code for the Java side, and almost 400 LoC for the C side. The expansion factor is thus more than 50. The generated code is fully operational and is of good quality: it obtains a score of 83.7% of rules compliance, using the default Sonar settings.

Based on the generated API, we implemented a simple Java client program (<100 LoC) that monitors the activity around the coffee machine only when this is relevant (i.e., when someone is approaching the machine). This way it reduces the traffic on the wireless network and also reduces the amount of data to log. In more details this program:

1. Subscribes to the motion information,
2. Subscribes to the raw data if it receives an approaching motion message,
3. Logs all the raw data,

4. Un-subscribes to the raw data if it receives a leaving motion message, with no sub-sequent approaching motion message in a given time window. Otherwise it keeps its subscription and continues logging raw data.

This simple Java program has successfully been tested with the generated mock-up device and (with no modification) with the physical device.

4.2 JArduino: Wrapping the Arduino API in ThingML

The goal of this second case study is to easily integrate sensors and actuators in Java, for rapid prototyping and experimentation. To achieve this goal, we wrapped all the standard Arduino API related to Input/Output[3] in ThingML, as well as other commonly used libraries (to interact with LCD, etc). The result is naturally called JArduino [6], for Java for Arduino.

The protocol of this application is described by 40 messages and 8 enumerations to constrain the parameters of the messages, in about 100 lines of code. From this rather synthetic model, we generate 68 classes for a total of 4708 lines of code for the Java side, and close to 500 LoC for the C side embedded in the micro-controller. The expansion factor is thus more than 50. The generated code is fully operational and is of fairly good quality: it obtains a score of 67.9% of rules compliance, using the default Sonar settings. This score is mostly explained by the naming convention used in the ThingML model describing the Arduino, where several messages contain underscores. In order to keep the public part of the generated API aligned with the ThingML specification, we also generate method names, etc with these underscores. This would however be straightforward to generate code complying with Java conventions and we would reach the same score as the Coffee spy case study, but this would slightly change the alignment of the API w.r.t. its specification.

The generated C-code is uploaded on the micro-controller of the Arduino board. This code actually receives messages (arrays of bytes as described in Section 3.1) and dispatches these messages to appropriate handlers, depending on the types of the messages. These handlers simply delegate to the standard Arduino API also located on the micro-controller.

The generated Java code is an API which matches the Arduino APIs. The Arduino API related to control structures, arithmetic, etc is not mapped since this is a direct sub-set of the Java language or Java standard API. When the generated Java API is invoked, it generates a message which is sent to the Arduino board.

This simple yet fully generated case study makes it possible to write Java programs that seamlessly manage sensors and actuators connected to the Arduino board. We have successfully ported most of the standard examples provided by Arduino on JArduino, and provided and extra example which simply connects the stub that simulates the logical environment to the Arduino. It provides a GUI to easily administrate the Arduino and quickly experiment sensors and actuators. More details are available at [6].

---

[3] http://www.arduino.cc/en/Reference/HomePage

5 Related Work

5.1 Remote Procedure Calls for Micro-controllers

Several solutions exist to enable the seamless collaboration of software components written in different languages and running on different platforms. Corba [10], RMI [12], Web Services [14], WCF [13] are well-established alternatives for distributed computing infrastructure. If these technologies differs for some non functional features [8], they provide the same benefits for building distributed applications: Independence from language and OS, Strong Data Typing, High Tune-ability and Compression. CORBA/e [11] sheds the dynamic and high-resource aspects of CORBA but retains full interoperability. Then, CORBA/e Micro Profile shrinks the footprint small enough to fit low-powered microprocessors: only tens of kilobytes. Other researches exist to support Corba on top of micro-controllers [16,4], nevertheless these approaches always use a layer model to hide the communication medium (Bluetooth, RS232, XBee, etc). ThingML use model information to generate the most suitable communication layer for each application depending of the feature required in each of them. In particular, it allows customizing communication features for each specific message.

5.2 Abstractions over Sensors and Micro-controllers

Using higher level of abstraction than the C language is a common approach for building software on top of micro-controller. Then, it is common to find small Java, Processing[4] or Lua[5] implementation for lightweight environment. For example, S4A[6] is a Scratch [1] modification for Arduino, which provides a high level interface to Arduino programmers with functionalities such as interacting with a set of boards through user events. In the same trend, ThingML integrate a language inspired by state machines to define the behavior of devices [7]. In this paper we presented another sub-set of ThingML, which can be seen as an Interface Description Language used to describe the interface of sensors. ThingML describes an interface in a language-neutral way, enabling communication between piece of software written using several programming language. In that sense, ThingML can be combined to high-level micro-controller programming language to manage communication.

Google Protocol Buffer is a DSL which offers abstractions to implement protocols based on efficient serialization/deserialization of structured data [9]. The sub-set of the ThingML metamodel dedicated to protocols is aligned with Protocol Buffer. While Protocol Buffer was formerly designed to handle web protocols, we handle the communication of wireless sensor networks, where nodes communicate via ZigBee, Bluetooth, etc. We also generate the code related to the behavior of the protocols, using synchronous or asynchronous message exchange,

---

[4] http://processing.org/
[5] http://www.tecgraf.puc-rio.br/~maia/oil/
[6] http://seaside.citilab.eu/scratch/arduino

timeout, retries, etc, as well as code which enable independent development of the different ends of a communication protocol.

OGC's Sensor Web Enablement (SWE) framework defines a set of web service interfaces and communication protocols abstracting from the heterogeneity of sensor network communication and enabling their discovery, access, tasking, as well as eventing and alerting [3]. It is an infrastructure enabling access to sensor networks using standard protocols and API. No specific effort is made in SWE to provide the link between the web-services and the real sensor. ThingML provides interoperability at a lower level and the high-level APIs generated from ThingML can be used to bridge the gap with standards like SWE.

5.3 Networking for Micro-controllers

Network library based on Ethernet, IP, ARP, TCP, UDP and HTTP can run on resource-constrained micro-controllers [15]. To provide such a compact library many features of the protocols have been stripped out. For example it does not support assembling and disassembling packets which means that the size of each messages is limited to a few hundred bytes. This is perfectly acceptable on a micro-controller which should just process a set of commands and transmit the data from a few sensors. Thanks to these limitations not only the library fits on micro-controllers but it also outperforms many computer based protocol stacks in terms of response time. Obviously such an approach is very costly in terms of development, testing, maintenance and evolutions. The more specific the protocol component is made, the more optimized it can be but the less reusable it is. ThingML by generating fully functional code to deal with communication can significantly reduces the burden of developing such libraries.

6 Conclusion and Future Work

This paper presented a Model-Driven approach to generate efficient communication APIs to exchange messages with and between resource-constrained devices. Based on a concise ThingML description of the messages sent and received by a device, we fully generate:

- Efficient API for the serialization and deserialization of messages in/from arrays of bytes, as presented in Section 3.1.
- Handlers for managing the communication features (asynchonous/synchronous messages, timeout, retry, etc) specific to each message, as presented in Section 3.2.
- Mock-ups and interactive simulators to enable independent development of things and services, as presented in Section 3.3.

We have validated our approach on two case studies. All the code related to communication has been fully generated. The CoffeeSpy application is a toy example which however relies on standard technologies used in state-of-the-practice wireless sensor networks. JArduino is a medium-sized application that we have made available as an open-source project.

In future works, we plan to extend ThingML both for a technical and a research point of views. From a technical point of view, we will implement a bi-directional bridge between ThingML and Google Protocol Buffer, and extend Protocol Buffer with our C code generator targeting low-resource devices. We will also include the feedback provided by the community on the JArduino project [6] to improve and extend our code-generators, so that all the applications generated from ThingML would benefit from these improvements. From a research point of view, we will continue to investigate how best practices in "classic" software development can be applied to micro-controllers: separation of concerns, self-adaptation [7], variability management and reuse, etc.

References

1. Resnick, M., Maloney, J., Monroy-Hernández, A., Rusk, N., Eastmond, E., Brennan, K., Millner, A., Rosenbaum, E., Silver, J., Silverman, B., Kafai, Y.: Scratch programming for all. Commun. ACM 52(11) (2009)
2. Arduino. Arduino home page, http://www.arduino.cc/
3. Botts, M., Percivall, G., Reed, C., Davidson, J.: OGC® Sensor Web Enablement: Overview and High Level Architecture. In: Nittel, S., Labrinidis, A., Stefanidis, A. (eds.) GSN 2006. LNCS, vol. 4540, pp. 175–190. Springer, Heidelberg (2008)
4. Curino, C., Giani, M., Giorgetta, M., Giusti, R., Murphy, A.L., Picco, G.P.: Tinylime: Bridging mobile and sensor networks through middleware, pp. 61–72 (2005)
5. eviware. Feature overview - soapUI, http://www.eviware.com/soapUI/features.html
6. Fleurey, F., Morin, B.: JArduino Repository on GitHub, https://github.com/ffleurey/JArduino/
7. Fleurey, F., Morin, B., Solberg, A.: A Model-Driven Approach to Develop Adaptive Firmwares. In: SEAMS 2011: 6th International Symposium on Software Engineering for Adaptive and Self-Managing Systems. Waikiki, Honolulu, Hawaii, USA (2011)
8. Gray, N.A.B.: Comparison of web services, java-rmi, and corba service implementation. In: Fifth Australasian Workshop on Software and System Architectures (2004)
9. Google Inc. Protocol buffers, http://code.google.com/apis/protocolbuffers/
10. OMG. Corba / iiop specification 3.1 (January 2008)
11. OMG. Corba for embedded (corbae) specification 1.0. formal/2008-11-06 (November 2008)
12. ORACLE. Java Remote Method Invocation Specification, JDK 1.5. Oracle, Mountain View, Calif. (October 2004)
13. Resnick, S., Crane, R., Bowen, C.: Essential windows communication foundation: for.net framework 3.5, 1st edn. Addison-Wesley Professional, Reading (2008)
14. Snell, J., Tidwell, D., Kulchenko, P.: Programming Web services with SOAP. O'Reilly & Associates, Inc., Sebastopol (2002)
15. tuxgraphics.org. HTTP/TCP with an atmega88 microcontroller (AVR web server), http://www.tuxgraphics.org/electronics/200611/embedded-webserver.shtml
16. Villanueva, F.J., Villa, D., Moya, F., Barba, J., Rincón, F., López, J.C.: Lightweight middleware for seamless HW-SW interoperability, with application to wireless sensor networks. In: DATE 2007: Conference on Design, automation and test in Europe, pp. 1042–1047. EDA Consortium, San Jose (2007)

Diagram Definition: A Case Study with the UML Class Diagram

Maged Elaasar[1,2] and Yvan Labiche[2]

[1] IBM Canada Ltd., Rational Software, Ottawa Lab
770 Palladium Dr., Kanata, ON. K2V 1C8, Canada
melaasar@ca.ibm.com
[2] Carleton University, Department of Systems and Computer Engineering
1125 Colonel By Drive, Ottawa, ON K1S5B6, Canada
labiche@sce.carleton.ca

Abstract. The abstract syntax of a graphical modeling language is typically defined with a metamodel while its concrete syntax (diagram) is informally defined with text and figures. Recently, the Object Management Group (OMG) released a beta specification, called Diagram Definition (DD), to formally define both the interchange syntax and the graphical syntax of diagrams. In this paper, we validate DD by using it to define a subset of the UML class diagram. Specifically, we define the interchange syntax with a MOF-based metamodel and the graphical syntax with a QVT mapping to a graphics metamodel. We then run an experiment where we interchange and render an example diagram. We highlight various design decisions and discuss challenges of using DD in practice. Finally, we conclude that DD is a sound approach for formally defining diagrams that is expected to facilitate the interchange and the consistent rendering of diagrams between tools.

Keywords: Diagram, Definition, Model, MOF, UML, QVT, DD, SVG.

1 Introduction

Model-driven engineering (MDE) is a software methodology that is based on the use of models as a primary form of expression. Models are defined as instances of a metamodel, a higher-level model that describes the abstract syntax of a modeling language. Those languages are either general-purpose like UML [1] or domain-specific (DSML) like BPMN [2]. In fact, metamodels are themselves defined using a DSML called MOF [3]. In addition, models are interchanged between MOF-based tools in XMI [4], a specification that maps MOF to XML.

Moreover, most modeling languages (including the ones aforementioned) have a graphical concrete syntax, i.e., a diagrammatic notation. In fact, some tools (e.g. Microsoft Visio [5]) create models strictly based on the notation. Unfortunately, such a notation and its relation to the language's abstract syntax are often loosely and informally defined using text and figures (showing examples of notation). This lack of precision and formality prevents tools from interchanging modeling diagrams reliably. It also leads to inconsistent rendering of diagrams among tools, which hinders interpretation by users. This led the OMG standards body to issue a request for proposal [6] to address this problem. As a result, a new specification named Diagram Definition (DD) [7] has emerged. The specification, whose formalization is still under way [23], provides an architecture allowing the specification of (1) the diagram interchange (DI) and (2) the diagram graphics (DG) mapping for any modeling language. DI is used to define the graphical aspects that are user controllable whereas DG mapping is used to define the graphical aspects that are specified by the language (and therefore uncontrollable by the user). The role DD plays in specifying the concrete syntax of a modeling language is akin to the role MOF plays in defining the abstract syntax of that language.

In this paper, we report on a case study where we validate the DD architecture by formally specifying the Diagram Definition of a subset of the UML class diagram. First, we define an interchange syntax for this subset with a MOF-based metamodel named UML DI (that is an extension of a more generic DI metamodel provided by DD). This metamodel together with the abstract syntax metamodel represent what is needed to reliably interchange this subset between tools. Second, we define the graphical syntax of the subset by mapping the two interchange metamodels to a generic DG metamodel (provided by DD) with a QVT-based [9] transformation. The mapping rules specify how the chosen subset should be rendered to graphics.

We then carried out an experiment where we exported an example class diagram from the native format of a modeling tool to the standard UML metamodel and to our UML DI metamodel. We also prototyped rendering the exported diagram to graphics based on our specified DG mapping. Results showed that we could effectively interchange the example diagram and render it consistently with the original tool.

The rest of this paper is structured as follows: Section 2 provides an overview of DD and its architecture; a case study of using DD to define a subset of the UML class diagram is presented in Section 3; Section 4 describes an experiment where the definition was used to interchange and render an example diagram; a discussion and reflection on the case study are given in Section 5; Section 6 highlights related works; and finally conclusions and future works are provided in Section 7.

2 Overview of Diagram Definition

2.1 Architecture

The Diagram Definition (DD) specification [7] provides a basis for defining graphical notations, specifically node and arc style diagrams, where the notations are tied to abstract language syntaxes defined with MOF. DD provides an architecture that distinguishes two kinds of graphical information: one that users can control, such as layouts and notational options, is captured for interchange between tools; another that users do not control, such as normative shape and line styles defined by a language specification, is not interchanged because it is the same across all tools conforming to the language. DD defines two metamodels to enable the specification of these two kinds of graphical information: Diagram Interchange (DI) and Diagram Graphics (DG), respectively.

The DD architecture (Figure 2.1) resembles a typical model-view-controller architecture [8], which separates views from underlying models, and provides controllers to keep them consistent. The model part of the architecture is represented by diagram elements and their associated model elements, both of which are created by end users and thus need to be interchanged between tools. Model elements are instances of an abstract syntax (AS) metamodel; while diagram elements are instances of a related diagram interchange metamodel (AS DI). Both metamodels are defined by a language specification (e.g., UML) as instances of MOF. The AS DI metamodel is also defined as a specialization of the more abstract DI metamodel provided by DD. On the other hand, the view part of the architecture is represented by graphical elements that are defined as instances of the MOF-based DG metamodel, provided by DD to represent platform-independent graphics. Finally, the controller part of the architecture is represented by a mapping from the interchanged data (diagrams and models) to the viewable/rendered data (graphics). This mapping, which is part of a language specification, formally encodes the language's concrete syntax (CS) rules and can be expressed using any suitable mapping language (e.g., QVT [9]). The M-levels in Figure 2.1 are layers of the metamodeling architecture described in [10].

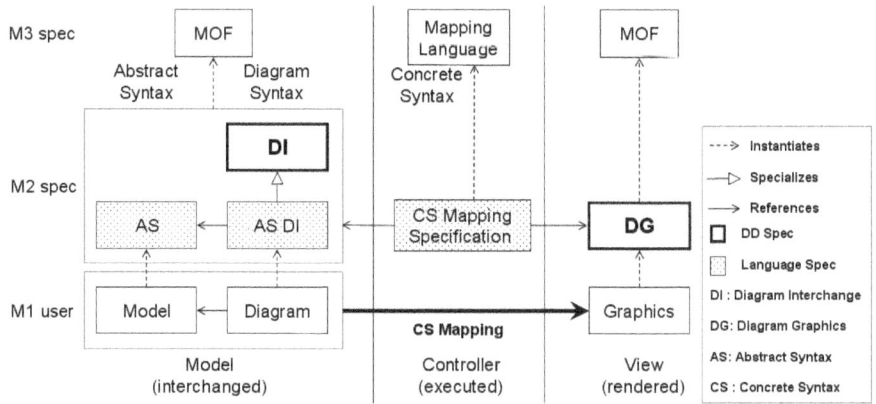

Fig. 2.1. Diagram Definition Architecture [7]

2.2 Diagram Interchange (DI)

DD provides a DI metamodel (shown in Figure 2.2 after incorporating the first official change ballot [23]) that allows defining those aspects of graphics that a language specification chooses to give its users control over and that need to be interchanged. Rather than providing a fit-for-all metamodel, DD provides a high-level metamodel that is intended to be specialized by each language to meet its specific needs while conforming to the same best practices.

The core class in DI is *DiagramElement*, which is the super class of all elements nested recursively (via *ownedElement*) in a diagram. A diagram element can be a depiction of a *modelElement* from an abstract syntax model (e.g., a UML component) or can be purely notational (e.g., an attribute compartment). It can also inherit a style (with visual properties such as colors and fonts) from a nesting element, have a *sharedStyle* with other elements and even have its own *localStyle*. A diagram element is laid out based on being an instance of *Shape* or *Edge*. A shape is laid out within its *bounds* while an edge is laid out as a poly line with a list of *waypoint* going from a *source* element to a *target* element. Also, an element is always rendered on top of its owning element if they overlap. *Diagram* is a special kind of shape that establishes a new coordinate system for its nested elements. The top-left corner of a diagram is the origin and all location and size measurements are in device units (i.e., pixels).

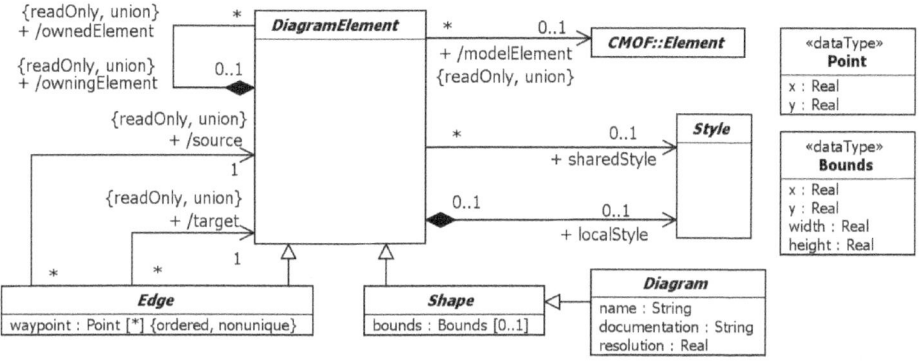

Fig. 2.2. DI Metamodel

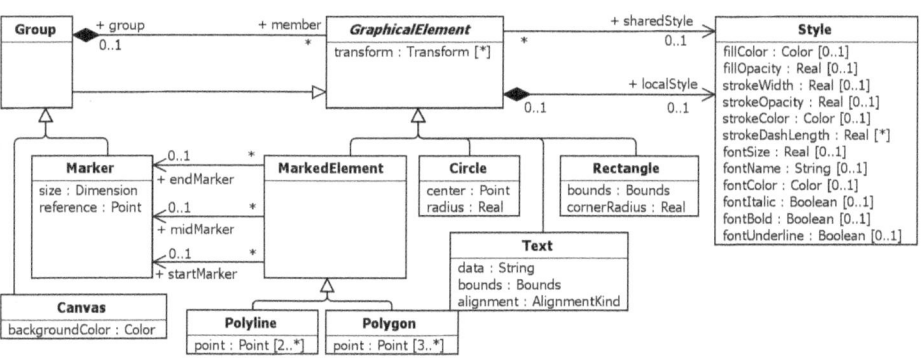

Fig. 2.3. DG Metamodel (excerpt)

2.3 Diagram Graphics (DG)

DD provides a DG metamodel (Figure 2.3) that allows specifying the concrete syntax of languages in a platform-independent way with 2D graphical information. The core class in DG is *GraphicalElement*, which is the super class of all elements nested in a canvas. An element can either be a primitive (e.g., *Rectangle*, *Circle* and *Text*) or a *Group* containing *member* elements. It can inherit a style (with visual properties such as *fillColor* and *fontName*) from a group it belongs to, have a *sharedStyle* with other elements and even have its own *localStyle*. Some primitives are defined as a connected set of points (e.g., *Polygon* and *Polyline*) and may be decorated with markers (groups of elements) at the start, middle and end points. A *Canvas* is a special kind of group used as a root of containment in a graphics model.

3 Case Study: UML Class Diagram Definition

In this section we report on a case study where we used the DD architecture to formally define the UML class diagram, both in terms of interchange and concrete syntax mapping. We choose the class diagram due to its widespread use and familiarity. However, to contain the effort, we limited ourselves to a representative subset consisting of three classifiers (*Class*, *Interface* and *DataType*) and three relations (*Association*, *Generalization* and *InterfaceRealization*). We believe this subset exemplifies the notation (shapes with labels, compartments and alternative graphics—edges with labels, markers and line styles) of the class diagram.

3.1 Diagram Interchange

Before defining the UML DI metamodel, we set some ground rules to govern our design decisions. (1) We avoid interchanging notational information that can be derived from the UML model to minimize redundancy between the DI and UML models. (2) We interchange simple layout constraints (bounds for all shapes/labels and waypoints for all edges) and avoid constraints of more complex layout algorithms to make it easier for tools to map to/from their native layouts. (3) We interchange the overlapping order of sibling diagram elements (which can happen when a diagram is crowded) by making all nested element collections ordered (a higher index implies a higher overlap order). (4) We avoid interchanging purely stylistic properties (e.g., colors/fonts) that tools may give users control over since they may vary dramatically between tools. However, we made an exception to some font properties (e.g., name and size) that we suspected could affect layout. (5) We keep the DI class hierarchy small, thus easier to maintain and evolve, by avoiding extensive sub-classing (resembling the UML class hierarchy). Instead, we allow DI classes to have a mixed bag of optional properties that apply in specific UML contexts only.

Furthermore, we defined the UML DI metamodel (Figure 2.2) by extending the DI metamodel, where appropriate, using MOF's extension semantics (subclassing and property subsetting and redefinition). Specifically, we defined class *UMLDiagram* that composed a collection of elements of type *UMLDiagramElement*. The latter could optionally reference an element from a UML model and could be styled with instances of class *UMLStyle*, which had two properties (*fontName* and *fontSize*).

Then, we defined classes for interchanging the chosen shapes and edges of the class diagram. To do that, we analyzed the relevant notation in the UML specification and identified three cases (shown in Figure 3.2): (a) a shape that has a label and an optional list of compartments, each of which having an optional list of other labels (e.g., the classifier box notation); (b) a shape that has a label only (e.g., the interface ball notation); and (c) an edge that has an optional list of labels (e.g., the association notation). However, (b) is really a special case of (a) when there is no compartment.

Based on that, we defined three shape classes (*UMLShape*, *UMLLabel* and *UMLCompartment*) and one edge class (*UMLEdge*) and related them with the multiplicities in cases (a) and (c). We also defined them (except *UMLCompartment*) as subclasses of *UMLDiagramElement* to allow them to be styled separately, reference their own UML elements, and be connectable (an edge was made to only connect elements of that type). We then added some properties to disambiguate the notation. For example, a *kind* can be set on a label to indicate what aspects of the UML element to show textually. A flag *showClassifierShape* can be set on a classifier's shape to indicate whether to use the *box* notation. Notice that we only added a subset of the possible notational options for brevity.

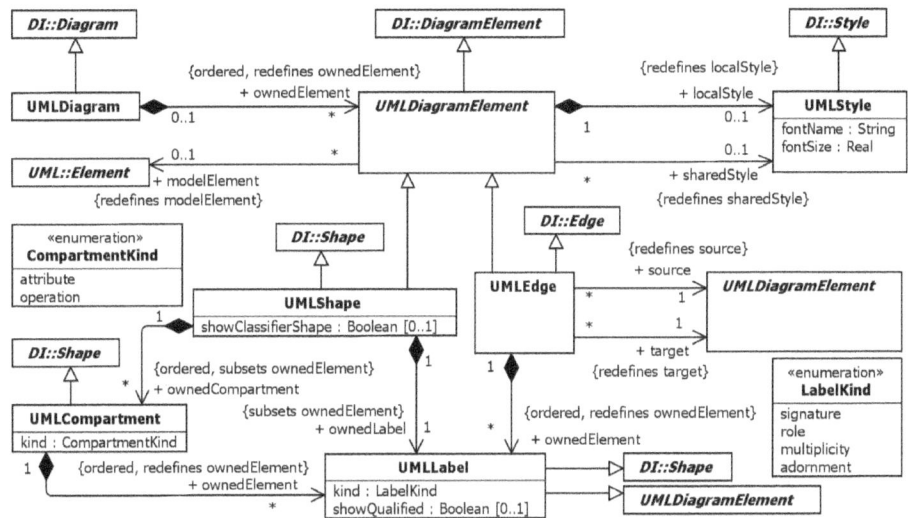

Fig. 3.1. UML DI Metamodel

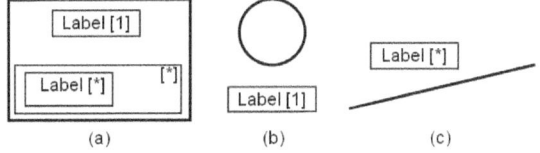

Fig. 3.2. Class Diagram Notational Patterns

3.2 Concrete Syntax Mapping

Recall from Section 2.1, that a language can specify its concrete syntax rules as a mapping from the AS DI metamodel, which references the AS metamodel, to the DG metamodel. The mapping can be expressed using any mapping language. We chose to express it using the QVT Operational (QVTo) [9] transformation language (designed as a thin extension of OCL [11]). The choice was motivated by our previous experience with QVTo, the fact that it is a standard MOF-based language, the fact that it is executable (allowing us to test our mapping), and the availability of a good implementation [12]. Due to space limitation, we only show parts of the transformation we defined. We assume some reader's familiarity with QVTo and OCL. We also assume familiarity with the syntax of the UML metamodel [1].

The class diagram's concrete syntax is defined with a QVTo transformation from a UML DI model to a DG model (Figure 3.3, line 1). The transformation starts by looking for all instances of *UMLDiagram* and initiating the mapping for them (lines 2-4). Mappings (like operations) are defined on UML DI classes and have DG classes as return types. For example, a mapping named *toGraphics* is defined on the *UMLDI::UMLDiagram* and has *DG::Canvas* as a return type (line 5). This maps an instance of *UMLDiagram* to an instance of *Canvas*, and initializes the properties of the latter according to the body of the mapping. In this case, the body iterates on all the owned elements of the diagram, mapping each one in turn to graphics, and adding the resulting graphical elements as members of the canvas (line 6).

```
01  transformation UMLDIToDG(in umldi : UMLDI, out DG);
02  main() {
03      umldi.objectsOfType(UMLDiagram)->map toGraphics();
04  }
05  mapping UMLDiagram::toGraphics() : Canvas {
06      member += self.ownedElement->map toGraphics();
07  }
08  mapping UMLDiagramElement::toGraphics() : Group {
09      localStyle := copyStyle(self.localStyle);
10      sharedStyle := copyStyle(self.sharedStyle);
11  }
12  mapping UMLShape::toGraphics() : Group
13      inherits UMLDiagramElement::toGraphics {
14      member += self.modelElement.map toGraphics(self);
15      member += self.ownedLabel.map toGraphics ();
16      member += self.ownedCompartment->map toGraphics();
17  }
18  mapping UMLEdge::toGraphics() : Group
19      inherits UMLDiagramElement::toGraphics {
20      member += self.modelElement.map toGraphics(self);
21      member += self.ownedElement->map toGraphics ();
22  }
23  mapping UMLCompartment::toGraphics() : Group {
24      member += object Rectangle {bounds := self.bounds};
25      member += self.ownedElement->map toGraphics ();
26  }
27  mapping UMLLabel::toGraphics () : Text
28      inherits UMLDiagramElement::toGraphics {
29      var e := self.modelElement;
30      var q := self.showQualified;
31      bounds := self.bounds;
32      data := switch {
33          case (self.kind = LabelKind::signature)
34              e.oclAsType(NamedElement).getSinature(q);
35          case (self.kind = LabelKind::role)
36              e.oclAsType(Property).getRole();
37          ...
38      };
39      localStyle := e.map toStyle(self); // update style
40  }
```

Fig. 3.3. QVTo Mapping from Class DI to DG

Diagram Definition: A Case Study with the UML Class Diagram   371

Furthermore, a *UMLShape* maps to a *Group* (lines 12-17) consisting of the following: a graphic for the model element (line 14), a graphic for the owned label (line 15) and a graphic for each owned compartment (line 16). These graphics are produced by other nested mappings (shown later). A similar mapping is defined for *UMLEdge* (lines 18-22). However, the mapping for *UMLCompartment* (lines 23-26) is different as the first member graphic is fixed as a *Rectangle* whose bounds are defined by the compartment. The mapping for *UMLLabel* (lines 27-40) is also different as it maps to a *Text* whose bounds are defined by the label and whose data value is defined based on the label kind. For example, if the kind is *signature*, the value is defined by a query *getSignature* defined on *NamedElement* (line 33-34). Also notice how the mapping inherits (line 28) another mapping (lines 8-11) that copies over the local and shared styles. The local style is further updated (line 39) based on the label's model element (e.g., the *fontItalic* property is set to *true* for the *signature* label in the case of an abstract classifier).

Some of the queries used for the label mapping are shown in Figure 3.4. The *getSignature* query (lines 1-3) returns the (simple or qualified) name of an element based on a flag. The query is overridden for different UML types to specify their unique signatures. For example, *Interface* (lines 4-6) overrides it to prefix the name with the «Interface» keyword. *Property* (lines 12-17) overrides it to return the full signature of a property in an attribute compartment (with type, multiplicity, etc.).

```
01   query NamedElement::getSignature(q : Boolean) : String {
02       return self.getName(q);
03   }
04   query Interface::getSignature(q : Boolean) : String {
05       return "«Interface»\n" + self.getName(q);
06   }
07   query Property::getSignature(q : Boolean) : String {
08       var t := if self.type->notEmpty() then ":" +
09                self.type.getSignature(q) else "" endif;
10       return self.getRole()+ t + self.getAdornment();
11   }
12   query Property::getRole() : String {
13       var d := if self.isDerived then "/" else "" endif;
14       var v := if self.visibility = VisibilityKind::public
15            then "+" else ... endif;
16       return d + v + self.getName(false);
17   }
18   query NamedElement::getName(q : Boolean) : String {
19       return if q then self.qualifiedName
20              else self.name endif;
21   }
22   query Property::getAdornment() : String {
23       return "{" + ... + "}";
24   }
```

Fig. 3.4. Queries Used by the UML Label Mapping

Figure 3.5 shows mappings between UML classifiers and their corresponding graphical elements (e.g., box or ball notation). The first mapping (lines 1-3), defined on UML *Element*, delegates to other mappings depending on the type of the element. Notice that both *Class* (lines 4-6) and *DataType* (lines 7-9) have one mapping each creating a rectangle, while *Interface* has two mappings, one creating a rectangle (lines 10-13) and the other creating a circle (lines 14-20), based on the flag *showClassifierShape* (lines 11, 15) on *UMLShape*.

```
01   mapping Element::toGraphics(s:UMLShape):GraphicalElement
02      disjuncts Interface::toRectangle, Interface::toCircle,
03               Class::toRectangle, DataType:toRectangle {}
04   mapping Class::toRectangle (s:UMLShape) : Rectangle {
05      bounds := s.bounds;
06   }
07   mapping DataType::toRectangle (s:UMLShape) : Rectangle {
08      bounds := s.bounds;
09   }
10   mapping Interface::toRectangle (s:UMLShape) : Rectangle
11      when { s.showClassifierShape=true } {
12      bounds := s.bounds;
13   }
14   mapping Interface::toCircle (s:UMLShape) : Circle
15      when { s.showClassifierShape=false } {
16      var b := s.bounds;
17      center := object Point{b.x+b.width/2;b.y+b.height/2};
18      radius := if b.width<b.height then b.width/2
19               else b.height/2 endif;
20   }
```

Fig. 3.5. UML Classifier Mappings to Graphics

Figure 3.6 shows mappings between UML relations and poly lines. The first mapping (lines 10-13), defined on UML *Element*, delegates to other mappings depending on the type of the element. The mapping of relation *InterfaceRealization* (lines 14-19) copies the edge's waypoints to the poly line'a points (line 15). As the notation of this relation depends on whether the interface shape was shown as a box or a ball, this is checked first (line 16). If it is shown as a box, a shared style with a dash pattern (lines 1-2) and a closed arrow marker (lines 3-9) are used (lines 17-18).

```
01   Property interfaceRealStyle = object DG::Style {
02      strokeDashLength := Sequence {2, 2} };
03   property interfaceRealMarker = object Marker {
04      size := object Dimension {width := 10; height := 10};
05      reference := object Point {x := 10; y := 5};
06      member += object Polylgon {
07         point += object Point{ x:=0; y:=0 };
08         point += object Point{ x:=10; y:=5 };
09         point += object Point{ x:=0; y:=10 }; }; };
10   mapping Element::toGraphics(e:UMLEdge):GraphicalElement
11      disjuncts Association::toPolyline,
12               Generalization::toPolyline,
13               InterfaceRealization::toPolyline {}
14   mapping InterfaceRealization::toPolyline(e:UMLEdge):Polyline{
15      point := e.waypoint;
16      var s = e.target.showClassifierShape;
17      sharedStyle := if s then interfaceRealStyle endif;
18      endMarker := if s then interfaceRealMarker endif;
19   }
```

Fig. 3.6. UML Relations Mappings to Graphics

4 Experiment: Interchange and Rendering a Diagram

In this section, we report on an experiment where we used the UML DI metamodel (Section 3.1) and the concrete syntax mapping (Section 3.2) we defined for the UML class diagram to interchange and render an example class diagram (Figure 4.1). The diagram was created using the Rational Software Architect (RSA) v8.0 modeling tool [13] and included model elements for the notational subset we defined. The objective of the experiment was to test the newly defined UML DD architecture in terms of its ability to interchange and consistently render diagrams between tools.

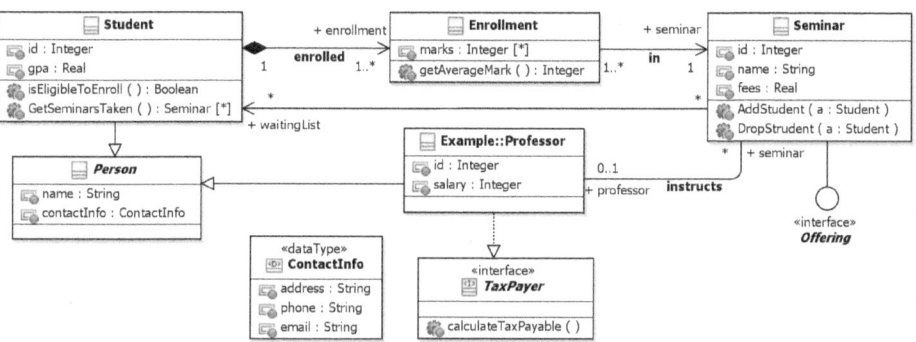

Fig. 4.1. Example Class Diagram Defined in RSA

4.1 Experiment Setup

In order to satisfy our objective, we needed to export the example diagram from tool "A" in UML DI, import it into tool "B" and visually compare the diagram rendered in both tools. Since RSA played the role of tool "A" in this execution chain, we implemented a UML DI exporter for RSA. Moreover, instead of implementing an importer for another UML CASE tool "B", we decided to implement a simple UML DI visualization tool (Section 4.2), which leveraged the UML DI to DG mapping we had specified. This allowed us to test both the effectiveness of the UML DI metamodel and the accuracy of the mapping in the same time. Additionally, such a tool can be used by other UML CASE tools to verify their own UML DI exporters.

We used the open-source Eclipse Modeling Framework (EMF) [14] project, which is packaged and used by RSA, as our MOF-based modeling tool infrastructure. We used EMF to import the two standard metamodels (DI and DG) provided by DD. We also used EMF to define our UML DI metamodel as an extension of DI. Moreover, RSA comes packaged with the open-source M2M/QVTo [12] project, which provides a QVTo editor and execution environment. We used this project to author and execute our concrete syntax mapping between UML DI and DG.

4.2 Experiment Execution

The first step of the experiment was to export the diagram into UML DI. To do that, we defined an exporter from RSA's native diagram format into UML DI. RSA's native format is based on a notation metamodel provided by the Graphical Editing Framework (GMF) [15]. GMF's metamodel is in fact close in many aspects to the standard DI metamodel, so we implemented an exporter as a QVTo transformation between the two metamodels. However, we did not find all needed layout data represented in the example GMF diagram (the bounds of some labels and shapes are derived). We worked around that by doing some pre-processing of the diagram (we rendered it using RSA, obtained the missing layout data from graphics and added them as annotations to the diagram). Support for DD in RSA should facilitate this procedure in future versions of the tool.

The second step was to render the exported diagram in another tool and visually compare it with the original RSA diagram. Our strategy for implementing such a tool consisted of two steps: (1) executing the concrete syntax mapping from UML DI to DG to obtain a resulting DG model (fortunately, since our mapping was done with QVTo, we simply executed the transformation to get a DG model); (2) rendering the DG model to graphics. For that step, we defined a model-to-text transformation to map the (used subset of the) DG metamodel to SVG [17] (DG's design is close to SVG's). We used the JET framework [25] that is packaged with RSA to define the model-to-text transformation. We then used a web browser to view the resulting SVG image. The experiment's complete execution chain is depicted in Figure 4.2.

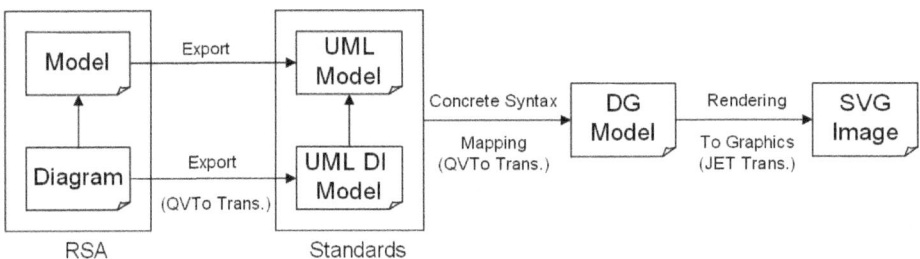

Fig. 4.2. The Execution Chain of the Experiment

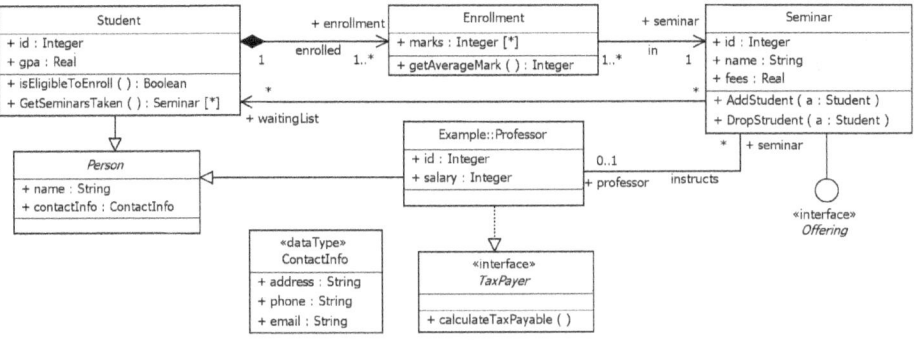

Fig. 4.3. Example Class Diagram Exported and Rendered as SVG

4.3 Experiment Result

We executed the experiment on the example diagram and the resulting SVG image is shown in Figure 4.3. This image resembles to a large extent the original diagram in RSA, indicating an overall successful interchange. However, the two diagrams were not identical due to RSA's own variations on the original notation (e.g., shapes have drop shadows, bold names, metaclass icons and list item visibility icons—edges have round edges at the corners). These variations caused some small differences in the diagram layout. Obviously, bugs in the last two links of the execution chain (Figure 4.2) could have also caused the diagrams to differ. In order for this chain to be an effective way for tool vendors, or for an interchange testing group similar to [16], to test diagram exporters, the last two links must be carefully tested first. This would make tool vendors focus on testing their exporters only. Obviously, this chain does not test each tool's own importer, which needs to be tested separately. Such importer would need to implement the QVT mapping rules in two steps: (1) mapping a UML DI diagram to a tool's native DI format, and (2) rendering the latter to graphics. Using a generic DI visualization tool in an import testing chain can also simplify the testing process for multiple tools. Specifically, it would allow rendering a UML DI diagram and comparing it visually to an imported version by each tool.

5 Discussion

The case study and experiment show that DD is a promising approach for formally defining diagrams of MOF-based languages. By defining a language-specific DI metamodel, tools of that language can precisely interchange modeling diagrams. Also, by formally specifying a mapping from language-specific DI and AS models to DG, vendors can build tools more accurately and with less cost. Users can also reliably interpret diagrams produced by different tools.

Nevertheless, there are a number of current limitations that need to be addressed before DD is finalized. One of those limitations is a need for a normative mapping from DG, which is basically a platform-independent graphics metamodel, to at least one standard vector-based graphics format (e.g., SVG [17]). This would help the testing process as discussed earlier, but it would also help bootstrap the DD architecture by providing a concrete syntax mapping for DG (without requiring the use of DD for that). Another limitation exists when a graphical syntax is specified using a textual mapping language (like QVTo). While it is very formal and flexible, it is also less readable (compared to the current way of defining diagrams that is more readable but less formal). One alternative could be to use a mapping language that has a graphical notation like QVT Relations (QVTr) [9] or GReAT [26]. Another alternative is to define a DD-specific graphical mapping language (e.g., a BNF grammar that incorporates graphical symbols). Such language can make a mapping more readable while still being formal. Moreover, another limitation with DD is the lack of reusable standard libraries to jumpstart a new DD-based specification. One library could provide a set of pre-defined DG types (e.g., styles and markers) that are commonly used in modeling notations. Another could be a general-purpose DI metamodel for annotations (e.g., notes and their attachments) that can integrate with any language-specific DI metamodel. Such metamodel would have its pre-defined mapping to DG. Finally, it would also help if the DD specification highlighted common design options and best practices for DD users to benefit from.

In fact, one of the most important design decisions when defining a language-specific DI metamodel is how far you go in using the MOF extension mechanisms to precisely define the DI syntax. One extreme is to go all the way such that every AS class maps to a unique DI class with applicable properties. This option makes it easier to create valid DI models (as the metamodel becomes very restrictive) but harder to maintain the metamodel (as it becomes very sensitive to changes in the AS metamodel). The other extreme is to settle with a very small hierarchy of DI classes with properties applicable to many AS classes and provide constraints for their applicability. With this option, it becomes more difficult to create valid DI models (since constraints are checked only after creation) but the metamodels become easy to maintain and less sensitive to changes in the AS metamodels. A more pragmatic option is always somewhere in between these two extremes.

Another subtle but interesting point with using QVTo to express a concrete syntax mapping is the fact that QVTo is a unidirectional language. Therefore, what is expressed is how the abstract and diagram syntaxes map to graphics, but not the other way around. While a unidirectional mapping will still help a user interpret a diagram (i.e., relate it back to the AS syntax), it may not always work especially when the notation is ambiguous. In this case, a bidirectional mapping (e.g., with QVTr) is more preferable. However, we believe that removing ambiguity from a graphical notation (if possible) goes further than trying to address it with a bidirectional mapping.

6 Related Works

Two categories of works are discussed here: those related to diagram interchange and those related to concrete syntax mapping. One early work in the first category is the DI v1.0 specification [18], which has been deprecated by the new DD specification. One issue with that specification is that, unlike DD, it provides a fixed interchange metamodel that is not meant for extension. This forces language-specific syntax rules (called nesting rules) and constraints to be provided informally. It also forces language-specific properties to be added through a key-value string map.

Another relevant work in this category is the notation metamodel provided by GMF [15], which is used by a number of tools including RSA and Papyrus [19]. This metamodel is similar to the one discussed above in that it is not meant for extension for a given language (although its diagram elements can have multiple styles and thus new style classes can be defined). Additionally, the diagram syntax is defined by language-specific creation factories (implemented in java). Once created, there is no metadata to help generically interpret or validate the syntax of a given diagram.

Another related work is the BPMN 2.0 specification [2], which uses (an alpha version of) DD to define a BPMN-specific DI metamodel. The metamodel is designed with minimum extension to the higher level DI metamodel. In other words, it has a small number of DI classes with properties applicable to many BPMN classes. The metamodel also represents a departure from XPDL [20], a format that has historically been used to interchange BPMN diagrams. Unlike DD, XPDL uses one schema for both AS and DI data (i.e., does not separate model from notation). Moreover, BPMN specification does not specify a concrete syntax mapping from BPMN DI to DG.

Related works in the second category also exist. The first one is GMF [15], which provides two models to map diagrams to graphics. The first one is called a Graphical Definition model, where one defines graphical elements (called figures) and associate them with notational patterns (called canvas elements) like: nodes, connections, labels and compartments. Unlike DD, these notational patterns are predefined; hence one is restricted to specify a language's notation using them only, which is inflexible. The second one is a Mapping model, where one defines mappings from AS classes to notational patterns (defined in the first model). Mappings are defined in a containment hierarchy starting from a canvas mapping, down to node and connections mappings, then label and compartment mapping. The mapping details are expressed with OCL. This strict containment hierarchy prevents mappings from being reused in other places in the hierarchy. On the other hand, DD allows mapping rules to be reused by flexibly calling them from other rules.

Another related work in this category is contributed by Palies [21], where a transformation is defined using ATL [22] (a non-standard declarative language) between the old DI metamodel [18] and a graphics metamodel (resembling SVG). The DI metamodel in this case is used to interchange UML class diagrams even though, as mentioned earlier, it is not UML-specific. Hence, the author had to make some assumptions regarding the correct DI syntax for UML. In contrast, we captured the UML DI syntax formally with a metamodel.

7 Conclusion and Future Work

Formal diagram definition has been missing in the MOF-based modeling architecture for many years. The OMG recently released a new specification called DD with an architecture that allows for formally defining diagrams of graphical modeling languages. DD allows a modeling language to define an interchange metamodel for its diagrams and precisely map the diagrams' concrete syntax to graphics. In this paper, we verified DD by using it to formally define a subset of the UML class diagram. Specifically, we extended the DI metamodel (provided by DD) to define a UML DI metamodel used for interchanging this subset between tools. We also defined the concrete syntax of the subset by mapping its UML DI metamodel to DG (a graphics metamodel provided by DD) using a QVTo transformation. We then carried an experiment where we used those definitions to interchange an example class diagram. We designed a testing chain where a diagram is exported from a modeling tool to UML DI, transformed to DG and then rendered to SVG. The exported diagram resembled to a large extent the original diagram indicating a successful interchange. We also highlighted a number of issues with DD including a need for a normative mapping to a standard graphics format (e.g., SVG), a need for a more readable mapping to DG and a need for standard libraries to jumpstart a new DD specification.

Going forward, we plan to use DD to define a bigger and more complex subset of the UML metamodel, especially the sequence diagram. We also plan to use it to specify the notation of a UML profile (e.g., SysML [24]) as an extension to that of UML. Other possibilities include defining the concrete syntax of UML with a bidirectional mapping (e.g., with QVTr) to ease the interpretation of diagrams, defining a graphical mapping language specific for DD and investigating other ways to jumpstart the DD definition for modeling languages.

References

1. Unified Modeling Language (UML), Superstructure v2.4. ptc/2010-11-14
2. Business Process Model and Notation (BPMN) v2.0, dtc/2010-06-05
3. Meta Object Facility (MOF) Core v2.4. OMG ptc/2010-12-08
4. MOF 2 XMI Mapping v2.4. OMG ptc/2010-12-06
5. Microsoft Visio (2010), http://office.microsoft.com/en-ca/visio/
6. Diagram Definition Request for Proposal ad/2007-09-02
7. Diagram Definition v1.0 FTF Beta 1. ptc/2010-12-18
8. Booch, G.: Handbook of Software Architecture, http://handbookofsoftwarearchitecture.com
9. Query/View/Transformation (QVT) v1.0. OMG formal/2008-04-03
10. Unified Modeling Language (UML), Infrastructure v2.4. OMG ptc/2010-11-03
11. Object Constraint Language (OCL) v2.2. OMG formal/2010-02-01
12. Dvorak, R.: Model Transformation with Operational QVT – M2M component, http://www.eclipse.org/m2m/qvto/doc/M2M-QVTO.pdf
13. Rational Software Architect v8.0 (RSA) Open Beta, https://www14.software.ibm.com/iwm/web/cc/earlyprograms/rational/rsaob/index.shtml
14. Steinberg, D., Budinsky, F., Paternostro, M., Merks, E.: EMF: Eclipse Modeling Framework, 2nd edn (2009)
15. Graphical Modeling Framework (GMF), http://www.eclipse.org/gmf/
16. Model Interchange Wiki, http://www.omgwiki.org/model-interchange/doku.php
17. Scalable Vector Graphics (SVG) 1.1, http://www.w3.org/TR/SVG/
18. Diagram Interchange v1.0. formal/06-04-04
19. MDT Papyrus, http://www.eclipse.org/modeling/mdt/papyrus/
20. XML Process Definition Language (XPDL), http://www.wfmc.org/xpdl.html
21. Palies, J.: ATL Transformation Example: UMLDI to SVG (2005), http://www.eclipse.org/m2m/atl/atlTransformations/UMLDI2SVG/UMLDI2SVG[0.04].pdf
22. Atlas Transformation Language (ATL), http://wiki.eclipse.org/M2M/Atlas_Transformation_Language_(ATL)
23. DD FTF Wiki, http://www.omgwiki.org/dd/doku.php?id=start
24. Systems Modeling Language (SysML), v1.2. formal/2010-06-02
25. Java Emitter Templates (JET), http://www.eclipse.org/modeling/m2t/?project=jet#jet
26. Balasubramanian, D., Narayanan, A., Buskirk, C., Karsai, G.: The Graph Rewriting and Transformation Language: GReAT. Electronic Comm. of the EASST 1, 1–8 (2006)

Reducing Multiplicities in Class Diagrams

Ingo Feinerer[1], Gernot Salzer[2], and Tanja Sisel[2]

[1] Technische Universität Wien, Vienna, Austria
Institut für Informationssysteme
Ingo.Feinerer@tuwien.ac.at

[2] Technische Universität Wien, Vienna, Austria
Institut für Computersprachen
{salzer,sisel}@logic.at

Abstract. In class diagrams, so-called multiplicities are integer ranges attached to association ends. They constrain the number of instances of the associated class that an instance may be linked to, or in an alternative reading, the number of links to instances of the associated class. In complex diagrams with several chains of associations between two classes (arising e.g. in configuration management) it may happen that the lower or upper bound of a range can never be attained because of restrictions imposed by a parallel chain.

In this paper we investigate how multiplicities behave when chaining associations together, and we characterise situations where intervals can be tightened due to information from other chains. Detecting and eliminating such redundancies provides valuable feedback to the user, as redundancies may hint at some underlying misconception.

1 Introduction

The Unified Modeling Language (UML) [23] nowadays belongs to the repertoire of every software engineer. A wide range of tools allows him/her to model situations by one or the other type of diagrams from the UML standard, to specify constraints, to derive program fragments automatically, thus facilitating model driven development. The familiarity with UML and the ubiquity of tools have also led to the application of UML outside of its core areas in software engineering. [11,14]

In this paper we concentrate on UML class diagrams with associations and multiplicities (sometimes also called cardinalities) in the context of configuration management. The term *configuration* as used in this paper refers to an arrangement of functional units according to their nature, number, and chief characteristics [27]. Functional units may be software or hardware components like computer programs, electronic circuits, or parts of a machine. A major issue is to specify admissible arrangements in a natural way, to set them up according to certain criteria of optimality, and to maintain them when requirements change. These activities are called *configuration management*. In this context, a class diagram is a *specification* (of the component types, their properties and interrelations), and the collection of concrete instances together with their relations is a *configuration*.

Using class diagrams for configuration management emphasises aspects and questions, which are hardly an issue in mainstream software engineering. The main difference probably is the status of instances. In software engineering, instances are second- or rather third-class citizens: First comes the model, second the program as a refinement of the model, and only at runtime, instances are created and destroyed dynamically; in many cases instances do not exist independently of programs and models. In contrast, configurations have a life of their own. A train station and its components remain even if the specification of the components and the construction processes cease to exist. A question like "Given a model, what is its smallest instantiation satisfying all constraints?" is rarely asked in software engineering, while using fewer components for some purpose clearly is more efficient than using more. Similarly, the problem of adapting a configuration with a minimal number of modifications to a changed specification is usually not an issue in software engineering.

Another difference is the characteristic form that multiplicities take in class diagrams. Multiplicities are pairs of numbers, $m..n$, specifying that any instance of a particular class has to be linked to at least m and at most n distinct instances of some other class (corresponding to the multiplicity attribute *unique*), or in another interpretation (attribute *non-unique*), needs that many links to instances of the other class (not requiring distinctness). Apart from textbook examples, such multiplicities are of a simple form in everyday software engineering: 0..∗ (unrestricted), 1..∗ (at least one), 0..1 (at most one, optional), and 1..1 (exactly one). These are also sufficient to express 1-1, 1-M, and M-N relationships typical of database schemes. In contrast, multiplicities in specifications show a higher degree of variability. E.g., a specification may state that a computer in a failsafe environment should be connected to an array of 2..3 power supplies and that each of the latter may serve 1..4 computers.

These differences are reflected in the functionality offered by (or missing from) current UML tools. They allow the user to create and maintain various kinds of UML diagrams (=specifications) as well as to generate code, but it is not possible to handle instances (=configurations) in a similar fashion, checking them against specifications, checking the specifications themselves for inconsistencies arising from the elaborate use of multiplicities, repairing configurations when specifications change, and so on.

Our work was originally motivated by the problems one of our industrial partners experienced when using standard UML tools for configuration management, with all their limitations. Our aim throughout the last years has been to investigate the theoretical foundations of class diagrams in this particular setting; to develop algorithms for checking the consistency of class diagrams, generating minimal instances, repairing instances in the face of specification changes, etc.; and to implement a prototype that hides the complexity behind an intuitive user interface and gives the user instantaneous feedback about specification or configuration errors. [13, 12]

As a running example, consider the specification in Fig. 1. It uses the following basic features of UML class diagrams: *Classes* represent the types of available components; *associations* relate classes; *multiplicities* constrain the number of

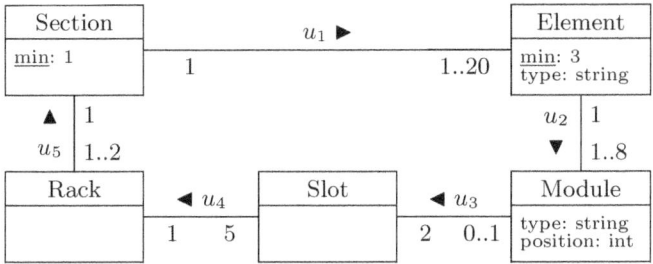

Fig. 1. Specification of hardware components

links between objects; and *multiplicity attributes* label the ends of associations as *unique* (default) or *non-unique*. Moreover, *lower bounds* define the minimal number of objects instantiating a particular class in a valid configuration (modelled in Fig. 1 by the static class attribute min). Classes may have further attributes or methods, but these do not affect our discussion here.

In this paper we deal with the problem of redundant multiplicities, which was identified in [11] as one of the open challenges when using class diagrams in the context of configuration management. Consider the situation in Fig. 1, where a section houses one or two racks with five slots each. Elements containing up to eight modules may be placed into such sections, with each module consuming two slots of a rack. With this intuition in mind it is apparent that the upper bound of 20 elements per section is overly optimistic: A section offers at most two racks with a total of ten slots, which may be connected to five modules, which in turn correspond to at most five elements. Pointing out this discrepancy as an immediate feedback to the person working on the specification helps to weed out misconceptions at an early stage.

The paper is structured as follows. The next two sections explain why we need equations over association chains to model the intended semantics of the associations within class diagrams and how to specify them. After setting up the formal framework in section 4, we investigate the composition of associations with multiplicities tagged *non-unique* (section 5) and *unique* (section 6). Based on these results section 7 solves the initial problem: Given optimised bounds for the whole association chain, these bounds are propagated inwards to tighten the multiplicities of the individual associations. The final two sections discuss related and future work.

2 The Necessity of Additional Constraints

Using the ideas of Lenzerini and Nobili [20], we may represent associations by inequalities. E.g., the relationship between sections and elements in Fig. 1 can be characterised by the linear inequalities

$$1 \cdot |\text{Section}| \leq 1 \cdot |\text{Element}|$$
$$1 \cdot |\text{Element}| \leq 20 \cdot |\text{Section}|$$

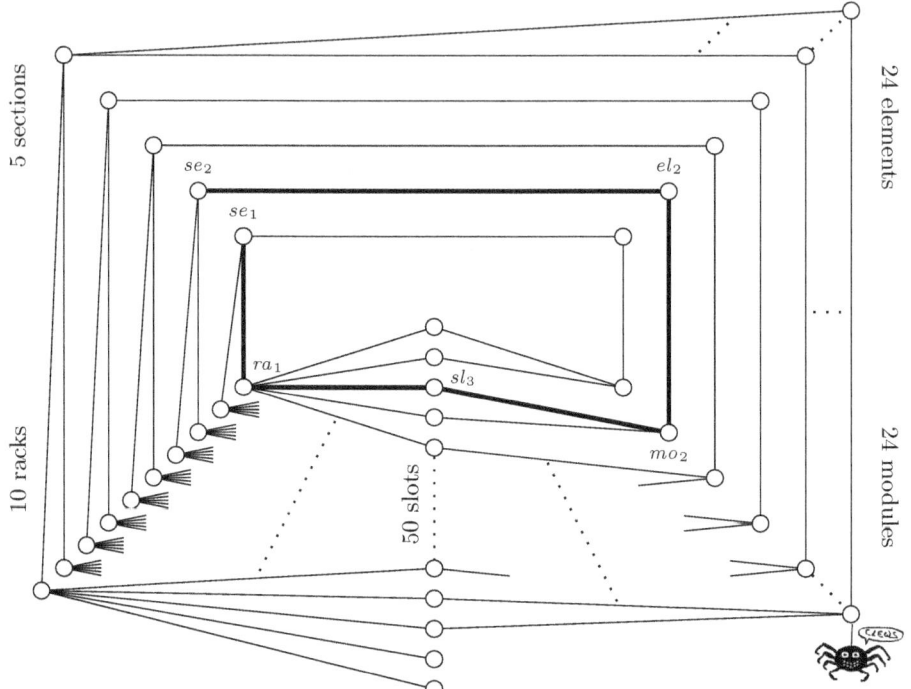

Fig. 2. Instance of the class diagram in Fig. 1 with a section linked to 20 elements and a slot connected to two different sections (bold lines)

where |Section| and |Element| denote the number of sections and elements, respectively, in an admissible instantiation. With small extensions, this approach allows us to check the consistency of specifications and to compute minimal configurations using ILP[1] solvers. And it also solves our problem, as it seems. From the diagram we obtain the inequalities

$$1 \cdot |\text{Element}| \leq 1 \cdot |\text{Module}|$$
$$2 \cdot |\text{Module}| \leq 1 \cdot |\text{Slot}|$$
$$1 \cdot |\text{Slot}| \leq 5 \cdot |\text{Rack}|$$
$$1 \cdot |\text{Rack}| \leq 2 \cdot |\text{Section}| \ .$$

If we multiply the first inequality by 2 and the last one by 5, we obtain $2 \cdot |\text{Element}| \leq 10 \cdot |\text{Section}|$ or equivalently $1 \cdot |\text{Element}| \leq 5 \cdot |\text{Section}|$, which makes the original inequality $1 \cdot |\text{Element}| \leq 20 \cdot |\text{Section}|$ redundant. One might be tempted to conclude that the multiplicity $[1, 20]$ can indeed be reduced to $[1, 5]$. This would be wrong, however. There is a valid configuration with five sections and 24 elements, where one of the sections is connected to 20 elements and the other four to just one (Fig. 2).

---

[1] Integer Linear Programming.

This configuration, however, contradicts our intuition, since it contains slots, where the section reachable via the rack is different from the section reachable via module and element. This possibility is not ruled out by the class diagram in Fig. 1, as it does not restrict the configurations to those associating a unique section with each slot. The inequalities mirror this semantics and only constrain the total number of objects for each class, but not the number of objects related to single instances of a class. Note that the configuration in Fig. 2 satisfies the inequality $1 \cdot |\text{Element}| \leq 5 \cdot |\text{Section}|$ (since $1 \cdot 24 \leq 5 \cdot 5$), even though there is a single section connected to 20 elements. We conclude that we need additional constraints to capture our intuitions, since they are not adequately represented by the class diagram alone.

3 Equating Association Chains

The requirement missing from the class diagram in Fig. 1 is a constraint stating that the relation instantiating the composed association a_1 = Section-Rack-Slot has to be the same as the one instantiating the composition a_2 = Section-Element-Module-Slot. Such a constraint excludes configurations like the one in Fig. 2, since the tuple (se_1, sl_3) (via ra_1) is not contained in the relation corresponding to a_2, whereas (se_2, sl_3) (via el_2 and mo_2) is not contained in the relation corresponding to a_1. The constraint can be expressed in the object constraint language (OCL) [22] as

```
context Section:
   inv: self->collect(s: Section | s.element)
           ->collect(e: Element | e.module)->flatten()
           ->collect(m: Module  | m.slot)->flatten()->asSet()
      = self->collect(s: Section | s.rack)
           ->collect(r: Rack    | r.slot)->flatten()->asSet()
```

or, using the dot notation as shorthand for `collect()`,[2] more compactly as

```
context Section:
   inv: self.element.module->flatten().slot->flatten()->asSet()
      = self.rack.slot->flatten()->asSet()
```

The key element of this OCL constraint is `collect()`, which generates a new bag (multiset). Successive applications (corresponding to the navigation along the chain of associations) yield bags of bags, hence intermediate flattening is necessary. The final equality check on sets models our desired semantics.

In the remainder of the paper we will refrain from using OCL. On the one hand, we are only interested in a tiny fragment of OCL and do not want to purport that our approach handles OCL constraints to any reasonable extent.

---

[2] There are subtle differences, though. `collect` yields a bag, whereas `self.element` is a set. As the final comparison is made `asSet`, this difference does not matter here, but it may be an issue when dealing with the multiplicity attribute *non-unique*.

On the other hand, even in their abbreviated form the OCL constraints are rather bulky. We prefer an abstract notation and represent the constraint above as $u_1 u_2 u_3 = u_5^{-1} u_4^{-1}$, where the u_i denote the five associations in our example and u_i^{-1} denotes their inverse.

4 Formal Definitions

In this section we make precise what we mean by specifications, configurations, and compositions of associations. This formal approach is necessary to reason about class diagrams in a rigorous manner. Our formalisation of class diagrams strictly adheres to the UML standard, hence our results carry over to any framework handling class diagrams according to this standard.

A *specification* is a triple $\langle \mathcal{C}, \mathcal{A}, \mathcal{E} \rangle$, where $\mathcal{C}$ is a set of *classes*, $\mathcal{A}$ is a set of *associations*, and $\mathcal{E}$ is a set of *equations* over $\mathcal{A}$. Classes, associations, and objects (see below) are assumed to be represented by unique symbols.

Each association u has a type, $type(u)$, of the form $C\{a..A\} \to D\{b..B\}$ or $C[a..A] \to D[b..B]$, where C and D are classes and a, A, b, and B are natural numbers; A and B may also be the symbol $*$ denoting infinity. Expressions of the form $\{a..A\}$ or $[a..A]$ are called multiplicities and will be interpreted as intervals. The choice of brackets encodes the multiplicity attribute *(non-)unique*: $\{a..A\}$ marks the association end as *unique* and $[a..A]$ as *non-unique*. The multiplicities $\{0..*\}$ and $[0..*]$ may be omitted.

For an association u of type $C\{a..A\} \to D\{b..B\}$ or $C[a..A] \to D[b..B]$ the inverse association u^{-1} has type $D\{b..B\} \to C\{a..A\}$ or $D[b..B] \to C[a..A]$, respectively. In UML this corresponds to navigating along the association in the opposite direction.

An *equation* over $\mathcal{A}$ is of the form $x_1 \cdots x_m = y_1 \cdots y_n$, where each x_i and y_i is of the form u or u^{-1} for some association u.

Example 1. The specification in Fig. 1 with the constraint discussed above can be formalised as $S = \langle \mathcal{C}, \mathcal{A}, \mathcal{E} \rangle$, where $\mathcal{C} = \{\text{Section}, \text{Element}, \text{Module}, \text{Slot}, \text{Rack}\}$, $\mathcal{E} = \{u_1 u_2 u_3 = u_5^{-1} u_4^{-1}\}$, and

$\mathcal{A} = \{\, u_1\colon \text{Section}\{1..1\} \to \text{Element}\{1..20\},\ u_4\colon \text{Slot}\{5..5\} \to \text{Rack}\{1..1\},$
$\qquad u_2\colon \text{Element}\{1..1\} \to \text{Module}\{1..8\},\ u_5\colon \text{Rack}\{1..2\} \to \text{Section}\{1..1\}\,\}\ .$
$\qquad u_3\colon \text{Module}\{0..1\} \to \text{Slot}\{2..2\},$

A *configuration* is a pair $\langle \mathcal{O}, \mathcal{R} \rangle$, where $\mathcal{O}$ is a set of objects and $\mathcal{R}$ is a set of finite, binary *relations* over $\mathcal{O}$. In our context a relation is a *multiset* of pairs of objects, i.e., it may contain duplicate pairs; the pairs are called *links*. We enclose multisets in square brackets, [ ], and sets in braces, { }. The inverse of a relation r, denoted by r^{-1}, is the multiset $[(o,p) \mid (p,o) \in r]$, i.e. the multiset containing an occurrence of (o,p) for every occurrence of (p,o) in r. The composition of two relations r_1 and r_2, denoted by $r_1 \circ r_2$, is the multiset $[(o,p) \mid (o,q) \in r_1, (q,p) \in r_2]$. More formally, multisets can be regarded as maps from elements to natural numbers that specify how often an element occurs in the multiset. Then r^{-1} and $r_1 \circ r_2$ can be defined by the equations $r^{-1}((o,p)) = r((p,o))$ and $r_1 \circ r_2((o,p)) = \sum_{q \in \mathcal{O}} r_1((o,q)) \cdot r_2((q,p))$ for all objects o and p.

Example 2. As an example, consider the configuration $C = \langle \mathcal{O}, \mathcal{R} \rangle$, where

$$\mathcal{O} = \{se_1, ra_1, ra_2, sl_1, \ldots, sl_{10}, mo_1, \ldots, mo_5, el_1, \ldots, el_5\} \text{ and}$$
$$\mathcal{R} = \{r_1 = [(se_1, el_1), \ldots, (se_1, el_5)],$$
$$r_2 = [(el_1, mo_1), (el_2, mo_2), \ldots, (el_5, mo_5)],$$
$$r_3 = [(mo_1, sl_1), (mo_1, sl_2), (mo_2, sl_3), (mo_2, sl_4), \ldots, (mo_5, sl_{10})],$$
$$r_4 = [(sl_1, ra_1), \ldots, (sl_5, ra_1), (sl_6, ra_2), \ldots, (sl_{10}, ra_2)],$$
$$r_5 = [(ra_1, se_1), (ra_2, se_1)] \} \ .$$

It relates five elements to the single section se_1 (relation r_1), a unique module mo_i to each element el_i (relation r_2), and two slots sl_{2i-1} and sl_{2i} to each module mo_i (relation r_3). Moreover, the section is connected to two racks (relation r_5) each owning five slots (relation r_4).

Given a relation $r \in \mathcal{R}$ and an object $o \in \mathcal{O}$, let $\gamma_r(o) = \{p \mid (o,p) \in r\}$ and $\delta_r(o) = [p \mid (o,p) \in r]$ be the set and multiset, respectively, of objects linked to o. A configuration is an *instance* of a specification, if the following conditions are satisfied.

- There is a mapping $\mathit{class}\colon \mathcal{O} \mapsto \mathcal{C}$ associating a unique class with each object. We say that object o is of class c if $\mathit{class}(o) = c$. The inverse mapping $\mathit{obj}\colon \mathcal{C} \mapsto 2^{\mathcal{O}}$ yields the set of all objects for a given class.
- There is a one-to-one mapping $\mathit{rel}\colon \mathcal{A} \mapsto \mathcal{R}$ from associations to relations such that each association u and its relation $r = \mathit{rel}(u)$ have the following properties.
  - If u is of type $C\{a..A\} \to D\{b..B\}$, then $b \leq |\gamma_r(o)| \leq B$ and $a \leq |\gamma_{r^{-1}}(p)| \leq A$ hold for all $o \in \mathit{obj}(C)$ and all $p \in \mathit{obj}(D)$.
    (This corresponds to the multiplicity attribute *unique* in UML and is the default for class diagrams.)
  - If u is of type $C[a..A] \to D[b..B]$, then $b \leq |\delta_r(o)| \leq B$ and $a \leq |\delta_{r^{-1}}(p)| \leq A$ hold for all $o \in \mathit{obj}(C)$ and all $p \in \mathit{obj}(D)$.
    (This corresponds to the multiplicity attribute *non-unique* in UML.)
  - Relation r is well-typed, i.e., $r \subseteq \mathit{obj}(C) \times \mathit{obj}(D)$.
- All equations in $\mathcal{E}$ have to be satisfied, i.e., for each $x_1 \cdots x_m = y_1 \cdots y_n \in \mathcal{E}$ the composed relations $\mathit{rel}(x_1) \circ \cdots \circ \mathit{rel}(x_m)$ and $\mathit{rel}(y_1) \circ \cdots \circ \mathit{rel}(y_n)$ have to be equal as sets, where $\mathit{rel}(u^{-1})$ is understood as $(\mathit{rel}(u))^{-1}$.

We say that r is of type T, denoted as $r\colon T$, if r instantiates an association of type T. Note the notational correspondence between multiplicities enclosed in braces/brackets and their semantics: Multiplicities of the form $\{a..A\}$ bound the function γ that yields the *set* of partner objects, whereas $[a..A]$ bounds the function δ that yields the *multiset* of partner objects.

A type T is weaker than or equal to a type T' (T' is stronger than or equal to T), if every relation of type T' is also of type T. Since we do not consider

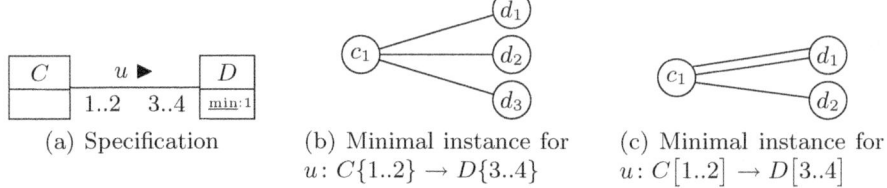

Fig. 3. Binary association with minimal solutions for unique and non-unique ends

hierarchies on classes in this paper, type T is weaker if its intervals contain those of T'. This leads us to the following fact, which is used implicitly throughout the paper.

Lemma 3. *Let r be of type $C\{a..A\} \to D\{b..B\}$ (or $C[a..A] \to D[b..B]$). Then r is also of type $C\{a'..A'\} \to D\{b'..B'\}$ (or $C[a'..A'] \to D[b'..B']$) for all $a' \leq a$, $b' \leq b$, $A' \geq A$, and $B' \geq B$.*

Example 4. For the configuration C in example 2 and the specification S in example 1 we define $class(se_1) = $ Section, $class(ra_i) = $ Rack, $class(sl_i) = $ Slot, $class(mo_i) = $ Module, $class(el_i) = $ Element, and $rel(u_i) = r_i$. Obviously the relations are well-typed. Moreover, they satisfy the multiplicities, since for all objects and all relations the number of unique partner objects is within the range of the multiplicities. E.g., we have $1 \leq |\gamma_{r_1}(se_1)| = |\{el_1, \ldots, el_5\}| = 5 \leq 20$ and $1 \leq |\gamma_{r_5^{-1}}(se_1)| = |\{ra_1, ra_2\}| = 2 \leq 2$. Regarding the equation $u_1 u_2 u_3 = u_5^{-1} u_4^{-1}$ we note that

$$r_1 \circ r_2 \circ r_3 = [(se_1, sl_1), (se_1, sl_2), \ldots, (se_1, sl_9), (se_1, sl_{10})] = r_5^{-1} \circ r_4^{-1} .$$

Therefore configuration C satisfies specification S.

Example 5. Fig. 3 illustrates the effect of the multiplicity attribute *unique*. The specification in Fig. 3(a) requires that there is at least one D-object, as stated by the static class attribute min.[3]

In Fig. 3(b) multiplicities carry the attribute *unique*. Starting with d_1, we need at least one C-object, c_1, because of multiplicity 1..2, which in turn needs at least three D-objects, d_1, d_2, and d_3. The configuration is an instance of the specification, since the relation $[(c_1, d_1), (c_1, d_2), (c_1, d_3)]$ is of type $C\{1..2\} \to D\{3..4\}$, and it is minimal by construction.

In Fig. 3(c), multiplicities are *non-unique*. Starting again with the required object d_1, we need at least one link to a C-object, c_1, which in turn needs at least three links to D-objects. Since d_1 can take another link, it suffices to add a second D-object. The relation $[(c_1, d_1), (c_1, d_1), (c_1, d_2)]$ is of type $C[1..2] \to D[3..4]$, hence the configuration is a minimal instance of the specification.

---

[3] Specifying the lower bound on the number of D-objects by a static class attribute min is pure convention and could e.g. also be expressed by an OCL constraint.

5 Composing Relations under Non-uniqueness

In order to detect redundant multiplicities that result from equating association chains, we first have to understand the effect of composition on relation types. We start with the attribute *non-unique*, where multiplicities bound links. The following proposition shows that in this case the composed relation is bounded by the product of the individual bounds.

Proposition 6. *Let r_i be a relation of type $C_{i-1}[a_i..A_i] \to C_i[b_i..B_i]$, for $i = 1, \ldots, n$. Then the composition $r_1 \circ \cdots \circ r_n$ is of type*

$$C_0\left[\prod_{i=1}^n a_i \: .. \: \prod_{i=1}^n A_i\right] \to C_n\left[\prod_{i=1}^n b_i \: .. \: \prod_{i=1}^n B_i\right] \:.$$

Proof. It suffices to show that the composition of $r_1 \colon C_0 \to C_1[b_1..B_1]$ and $r_2 \colon C_1 \to C_2[b_2..B_2]$ is of type $C_0 \to C_2[b_1b_2..B_1B_2]$, which amounts to showing $b_1b_2 \le |\delta_{r_1 \circ r_2}(o)| \le B_1B_2$ for all objects o. The general statement is obtained by induction on n and by observing that the reverse direction regarding the multiplicities $[a_i..A_i]$ is symmetric.

By the definition of composition and by reordering the terms, we obtain $|\delta_{r_1 \circ r_2}(o)| = |[p \mid (o,p) \in r_1 \circ r_2]| = \sum_p r_1 \circ r_2((o,p)) = \sum_p \sum_q r_1(o,q) r_2(q,p) = \sum_q r_1(o,q) \cdot \left(\sum_p r_2(q,p)\right) = \sum_q r_1(o,q) \cdot |\delta_{r_2}(q)|$. The expression $|\delta_{r_2}(q)|$ is bounded by b_2 and B_2, hence $\sum_q r_1(o,q)|\delta_{r_2}(q)|$ is bounded by $\sum_q r_1(o,q)b_2$ and $\sum_q r_1(o,q)B_2$. Since $\sum_q r_1(o,q) = |\delta_{r_1}(o)|$ is bounded by b_1 and B_1, we obtain that $|\delta_{r_1 \circ r_2}(o)|$ is bounded by b_1b_2 and B_1B_2. □

The bounds of the composed type are tight: For all values of a_i, A_i, b_i, and B_i there are corresponding relations such that their composition is of the type given by the proposition, but of no weaker type. The following example illustrates the case $n = 2$, but can be generalised easily to arbitrary n.

Example 7. Let i, j, k, and l be index variables such that $1 \le i \le a_1$, $1 \le j \le a_2$, $1 \le k \le b_1$, and $1 \le l \le b_2$. In the following we omit these ranges from (multi)set definitions, writing e.g. just $\{c_{ij}\}$ instead of $\{\, c_{ij} \mid 1 \le i \le a_1,\, 1 \le j \le a_2 \,\}$.

Let C, D, and E be classes such that $obj(C) = \{c_{ij}\}$, $obj(D) = \{d_{jk}\}$, and $obj(E) = \{e_{kl}\}$. Consider the relations $cd = [(c_{ij}, d_{jk})]$ and $de = [(d_{jk}, e_{kl})]$ as well as their composition $ce = cd \circ de = [(c_{ij}, e_{kl})]$. For the types of the three relations we obtain $cd \colon C[a_1..a_1] \to D[b_1..b_1]$, $de \colon D[a_2..a_2] \to E[b_2..b_2]$, and $ce \colon C[a_1a_2..a_1a_2] \to E[b_1b_2..b_1b_2]$.

Moreover, let the index variables i', j', k', and l' range from 1 to A_1, A_2, B_1, and B_2, respectively, and let C', D', E', cd', de', and ce' be classes and relations defined as above, but with primed index variables and primed object names. Then the types of the three relations are $cd' \colon C'[A_1..A_1] \to D'[B_1..B_1]$, $de' \colon D'[A_2..A_2] \to E'[B_2..B_2]$, and $ce' \colon C'[A_1A_2..A_1A_2] \to E'[B_1B_2..B_1B_2]$.

Now consider the union of the primed and unprimed classes and relations. Let $obj(C_0) = obj(C) \cup obj(C')$, $obj(C_1) = obj(D) \cup obj(D')$, $obj(C_2) = obj(E) \cup obj(E')$, $r_1 = cd \cup cd'$, $r_2 = de \cup de'$, and $r_1 \circ r_2 = ce \cup ce'$. Then the strongest types characterising the relations are $C_0[a_1..A_1] \to C_1[b_1..B_1]$, $C_1[a_2..A_2] \to C_2[b_2..B_2]$, and $C_0[a_1a_2..A_1A_2] \to C_2[b_1b_2..B_1B_2]$, respectively.

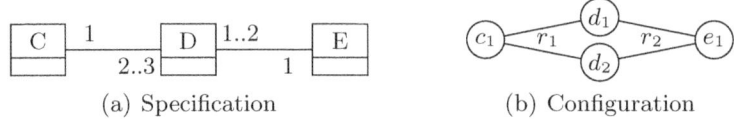

Fig. 4. Lower bounds do not multiply in the case of unique multiplicities

6 Composing Relations under Uniqueness

Regarding upper bounds, multiplicities tagged *unique* behave the same as those tagged *non-unique*. For the lower bounds this is not the case, however.

Example 8. Consider the specification and configuration in Fig. 4. The relations $r_1 = [(c_1, d_1), (c_1, d_2)]$ and $r_2 = [(d_1, e_1), (d_2, e_1)]$ are of type $C\{1..1\} \to D\{2..3\}$ and $D\{1..2\} \to E\{1..1\}$, respectively. Their composition $r_1 \circ r_2 = [(c_1, e_1), (c_1, e_1)]$ is of type $C[1..2] \to E[2..3]$, but not of type $C\{1..2\} \to E\{2..3\}$ since there is only one E-object, e_1, related to c_1. The reason for the diverging behaviour is that the D-objects each contribute a link to the count, but they share the same E-object, which is counted only once.

Let $\Delta_{b,A}(x)$ denote the expression $\max(\lceil \frac{b \cdot x}{A} \rceil, b \cdot \text{sgn}(x))$.[4] The following lemma states that x objects of some class are linked to at least $\Delta_{b,A}(x)$ and at most Bx objects of the associated class.

Lemma 9. *Let r be a relation of type $C\{a..A\} \to D\{b..B\}$. Let $O \subseteq obj(C)$ be a set of some C-objects, and let $r(O) := \{p \mid o \in O, (o,p) \in r\} = \bigcup_{o \in O} \gamma_r(o)$ be the set of related D-objects. Then we have $\Delta_{b,A}(|O|) \leq |r(O)| \leq B \cdot |O|$.*

Proof. Regarding the upper bound we observe that a single C-object is linked to at most B objects of class D. In the maximal case, the D-objects linked to distinct objects in O are pairwise different, hence $|r(O)|$ is bounded from above by $B \cdot |O|$.

Regarding the lower bound we observe that a single C-object is linked to at least b objects of class D. In the minimal case, the objects in O maximally share their D-objects. This sharing is limited by two constraints:

- Due to uniqueness, the D-objects linked to a single C-object have to be pairwise different, hence $r(O)$ contains at least b elements, provided O is not empty. This translates to the lower bound $b \cdot \text{sgn}(|O|)$.
- The number of C-objects linked to a single D-object is limited by the multiplicity $\{a..A\}$. In total, $|O|$ objects of class C need links to at least $b \cdot |O|$ objects of class D. Since at most A objects of class C may be linked to each D-object, we obtain the lower bound $\lceil \frac{b \cdot |O|}{A} \rceil$.

---

[4] The signum (or sign) function is defined by $\text{sgn}(x) = 1$ for $x > 0$, $\text{sgn}(0) = 0$, and $\text{sgn}(x) = -1$ for $x < 0$.

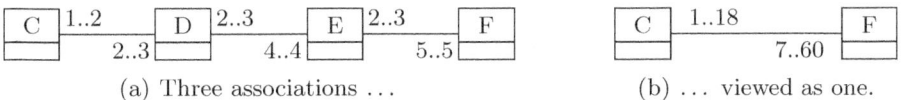

Fig. 5. Example for the composition of associations with the attribute *unique*

The number of D-objects has to satisfy both constraints, hence it is bounded by the maximum of the two expressions. □

Proposition 10. *Let r_i be a relation of type $C_{i-1}\{a_i..A_i\} \to C_i\{b_i..B_i\}$, for $i = 1, \ldots, n$. Then the composition $r_1 \circ \cdots \circ r_n$ is of type*

$$C_0\left[y_n \,.. \prod_{i=1}^n A_i\right] \to C_n\left[x_n \,.. \prod_{i=1}^n B_i\right] ,$$

where the lower bounds are defined by $x_0 = y_0 = 1$, $x_i = \Delta_{b_i,A_i}(x_{i-1})$, and $y_i = \Delta_{a_{n-i+1},B_{n-i+1}}(y_{i-1})$ for $i = 1, \ldots, n$.

Proof. By induction on n: accumulate the bounds given by lemma 9, starting with one C_0- and one C_n-object, respectively. □

The upper bound in this proposition is again tight: Observe that in example 7 the E-objects related to a single C-object are all different. Hence the given upper bounds also apply to the unique case.

Example 11. Consider the chain of associations in Fig. 5(a). For the lower bounds we obtain:

$$x_0 = 1 \qquad\qquad y_0 = 1$$
$$x_1 = \max(\lceil \tfrac{b_1 x_0}{A_1} \rceil, b_1 \operatorname{sgn}(x_0)) \qquad y_1 = \max(\lceil \tfrac{a_3 y_0}{B_3} \rceil, a_3 \operatorname{sgn}(x_0))$$
$$ = \max(\lceil \tfrac{2 \cdot 1}{2} \rceil, 2 \cdot \operatorname{sgn}(1)) = 2 \qquad = \max(\lceil \tfrac{2 \cdot 1}{5} \rceil, 2 \cdot \operatorname{sgn}(1)) = 2$$
$$x_2 = \max(\lceil \tfrac{4 \cdot 2}{3} \rceil, 4 \cdot \operatorname{sgn}(2)) = 4 \qquad y_2 = \max(\lceil \tfrac{2 \cdot 2}{4} \rceil, 2 \cdot \operatorname{sgn}(2)) = 2$$
$$x_3 = \max(\lceil \tfrac{5 \cdot 4}{3} \rceil, 5 \cdot \operatorname{sgn}(4)) = 7 \qquad y_3 = \max(\lceil \tfrac{1 \cdot 2}{3} \rceil, 1 \cdot \operatorname{sgn}(2)) = 1$$

The composed association is depicted in Fig. 5(b).

Example 12. Consider one-to-many associations, i.e., let the relations $r_1, \ldots, r_n$ be given as in proposition 10, but with $A_2, \ldots, A_n$ all set to one and with all b_i greater than zero. In this case we regain the lower bounds of the non-unique case, since $x_i = \max(\lceil \tfrac{b_i x_{i-1}}{A_i} \rceil, b_i \operatorname{sgn}(x_{i-1})) = \max(b_i x_{i-1}, b_i) = b_i x_{i-1}$ and therefore $x_n = \prod_{i=1}^n b_i$.

As an even more restricted sub-case consider one-to-one associations. Intuitively, relations instantiating them should act as neutral elements in compositions, not influencing the multiplicities of the partner relation. More precisely, if we have two relations $r_1 \colon C_0\{a..A\} \to C_1\{b..B\}$ and $r_2 \colon C_1\{1..1\} \to C_2\{1..1\}$, then the composition $r_1 \circ r_2$ should be of type $C_0\{a..A\} \to C_2\{b..B\}$. This is confirmed by proposition 10: We have $y_1 = 1$ and $y_2 = \max(\lceil \tfrac{a_1 y_1}{B_1} \rceil, a_1 \operatorname{sgn}(y_1)) = \max(\lceil \tfrac{a}{B} \rceil, a \cdot 1) = a$.

7 Detecting and Eliminating Redundancies

Our goal is to exploit the information encoded in equations like $u_1 u_2 u_3 = u_5^{-1} u_4^{-1}$ from example 1 to tighten multiplicity bounds. In the previous sections we investigated how bounds evolve when composing associations. In general we obtain two different types, one for each side of the equation, which by the semantics of equations both characterise the relation instantiating the chains. Obviously a relation satisfies both types if it satisfies the intersection type, as formally stated below. If the intersection is empty, then the equation (and the specification) is unsatisfiable.

Lemma 13. *If r is both of type $C\{a..A\} \to D\{b..B\}$ and $C\{a'..A'\} \to D\{b'..B'\}$, then r is also of type $C\{\max(a,a')..\min(A,A')\} \to D\{\max(b,b')..\min(B,B')\}$.*

Bounds like $\min(A, A')$ and $\min(B, B')$ obtained for the whole chain can now be propagated to the constituents of the association chains to tighten the individual multiplicities, based on the following result.

Proposition 14. *Let r_i be a relation of type $C_{i-1}\{a_i..A_i\} \to C_i\{b_i..B_i\}$ for $i = 1, \ldots, n$. Suppose $r_1 \circ \cdots \circ r_n$ is known to be of type $C_0 \to C_n\{m..M\}$, i.e., each object of class C_0 is known to be related to at least m and at most M objects of class C_n. Then each relation r_i is of type $C_{i-1} \to C_i\{b'_i..B'_i\}$, where $b'_i = \min\{\, b \geq b_i \mid f_n(i,b) \geq m\,\}$, $B'_i = \max\{\, B \leq B_i \mid g_n(i,B) \leq M\,\}$, and f_n and g_n are defined recursively as*

$$f_0(i,b) = 1 \qquad\qquad g_0(i,B) = 1$$

$$f_j(i,b) = \begin{cases} B_j \cdot f_{j-1}(i,b) \\ \Delta_{b,A_i}(f_{j-1}(i,b)) \end{cases} \qquad g_j(i,B) = \begin{cases} \Delta_{b_j,A_j}(g_{j-1}(i,b)) & \text{for } j \neq i \\ B \cdot g_{j-1}(i,B) & \text{for } j = i \end{cases}$$

for $j = 1, \ldots, n$.

Proof. First of all, note that even though b'_i is defined as a minimum, it is in fact *larger* than or equal to b_i. Likewise, B'_i is *smaller* than or equal to B_i. Therefore $\{b'_i..B'_i\}$ potentially is a tighter multiplicity than $\{b_i..B_i\}$.

Second, observe that $f_n(i,b)$ essentially is the product of the upper bounds B_j, with the only exception that instead of B_i the potential *lower* bound Δ_{b,A_i} is used (note the occurrence of b instead of b_i). Likewise, $g_n(i,B)$ is the composition of the lower bounds Δ_{b_j,A_j}, with the only exception that instead of Δ_{b_i,A_i} the potential *upper* bound B is used.

The key insight is that we may increase the lower bounds of multiplicities as long as the composed lower bound is smaller than m for all combinations of admissible relations. Suppose we want to find a tighter bound $b'_i \geq b_i$ for relation r_i. We assume the worst bounds for all other relations r_j, which is the case if some C_{j-1}-object is linked to B_j objects of class C_j. For the new bound b'_i we take the smallest value b such that the composed bound does not fall below m.

Likewise we may reduce the upper bounds of multiplicities as long as the composed upper bound is greater than M for all combinations of admissible relations. Suppose we want to find a tighter bound $B'_i \leq B_i$ for relation r_i. We assume the worst bounds for all other relations r_j, which is the case if some C_{j-1}-object is linked to Δ_{b_j,A_j} objects of class C_j. For the new bound B'_i we take the biggest value B such that the composed bound does not exceed M. □

Example 15. Consider Example 1 with its constraint $u_1 u_2 u_3 = u_5^{-1} u_4^{-1}$. Applying proposition 10 to the right-hand side of the equation, we see that relations instantiating $u_5^{-1} u_4^{-1}$ are of type Section{1..1} → Slot{1..10}.

Now consider the types of the associations

$$u_1: \text{Section}\{1..1\} \to \text{Element}\{1..20\}$$
$$u_2: \text{Element}\{1..1\} \to \text{Module}\{1..8\}$$
$$u_3: \text{Module}\{0..1\} \to \text{Slot}\{2..2\} \ .$$

We optimise the multiplicities using proposition 14 with $\{m..M\} = \{1..10\}$ from above. E.g., to check whether the upper bound $B_1 = 20$ can indeed be reduced, we have to compute $B'_1 = \max\{\, B \leq 20 \mid g_3(1, B) \leq 10\, \}$. We obtain

$$g_3(1, B) = \Delta_{b_3, A_3}(\Delta_{b_2, A_2}(B \cdot 1)) = \max(\lceil \tfrac{2\Delta_{b_2, A_2}(B)}{1} \rceil, 2) = \max(2\Delta_{b_2, A_2}(B), 2)$$
$$= \max(2 \max(\tfrac{1 \cdot B}{1}, 1), 2) = \max(2 \max(B, 1), 2) = 2B$$

and thus $B'_1 = \max\{\, B \leq 20 \mid 2B \leq 10\, \} = 5$. Similarly, we find a tighter bound $B'_2 = \max\{\, B \leq 8 \mid g_3(2, B) \leq 10\, \}$:

$$g_3(2, B) = \Delta_{b_3, A_3}(B\Delta_{b_1, A_1}(1)) = \max(\lceil \tfrac{2B\Delta_{b_1, A_1}(1)}{1} \rceil, 2) = \max(2B\Delta_{b_1, A_1}(1), 2)$$
$$= \max(2B \max(\lceil \tfrac{1 \cdot 1}{1} \rceil, 1), 2) = \max(2B \max(1, 1), 2) = 2B$$

and thus $B'_2 = \max\{\, B \leq 8 \mid 2B \leq 10\, \} = 5$. Therefore the multiplicities {1..20} and {1..8} of the associations u_1 and u_2 can be both replaced by {1..5} in the presence of the equation $u_1 u_2 u_3 = u_5^{-1} u_4^{-1}$.

8 Related Work

There are several approaches for expressing the semantics of UML in a rigorous language as needed for formal reasoning on multiplicities. Felfernig et al. [14] translate class diagrams with is-a relationships (i.e., specialisation and generalisation) to OIL, a precursor of the ontology language OWL. Other authors use formal languages like Object-Z [18], Z [10], B [26], Pvs [19], first-order logic [5, 24], Alloy [1], or description logic [6]. Embedding class diagrams into an expressive formal language has the advantage that different formalisms can be translated to the same basic logic and therefore can be mixed in the specification. For instance, it is possible to express the semantics of constraints written in OCL in the same first-order logic. Moreover, well-developed reasoning techniques and theorem provers for these logics can be used to show satisfiability and consistency. Calvanese et al. show that frame languages, semantic data models and object-oriented data models can be translated to a description logic called $\mathcal{ALUNI}$ and that satisfiability and subsumption of models can be checked in this framework. [7] This flexibility and generality comes at a price, however.

Reasoning tasks in expressive logics are of a high computational complexity. E.g., checking the consistency of $\mathcal{ALUNI}$-specifications is ExpTime-complete. [4] Recently *DL-Lite* [2,3] was introduced to address these complexity issues, with an emphasis on finite models. [25]

Dullea and Song analyse cardinality constraints in redundant relationships in the entity-relationship model. [9] This approach takes into consideration minimum and maximum cardinality constraints for one-to-one, one-to-many, and many-to-many multiplicity types. They perform an exhaustive case study for combinations of these multiplicity types with a focus on binary associations. Extensions also deal with n-ary associations but mainly concentrate on the combination of binary and ternary relationships. [17] Our work differs considerably from these approaches since we investigate multiplicities specified by concrete intervals $[a..A]$, where both a and A may be any integers satisfying $A \geq a \geq 0$, instead of generic one-to-one (1:1), one-to-many (1:N), and many-to-many (M:N) multiplicities as originally introduced by Chen for ER diagrams. [8] The second main difference are uniqueness attributes as defined by the UML standard.

Hartmann considers the consistency of so-called int-cardinality constraints [15], i.e. of multiplicities with gaps, as well as the interaction of cardinality constraints with key and functional dependencies [16]. This approach allows one to solve consistency and implication problems, but it does not seem to offer a method for tightening cardinalities.

9 Conclusion

This paper presented an in-depth analysis of redundant multiplicities for unique and non-unique associations. We extended UML class diagrams by equations over association chains to specify additional properties of relations, and described how to derive tighter bounds for individual multiplicities. Currently we are in the process of integrating our theoretical results into an environment capable of manipulating UML class diagrams. This implementation will allow us to perform consistency checks on real-world examples provided by industrial partners. The prototype is available from [21]. The system has the flavour of a spreadsheet program, since it re-checks the consistency of specifications and configurations as well as the redundancy of multiplicities with every change, highlighting inconsistencies and redundancies as an immediate feedback.

References

1. Anastasakis, K., Bordbar, B., Georg, G., Ray, I.: On challenges of model transformation from UML to Alloy. Software and System Modeling 9(1), 69–86 (2010)
2. Artale, A., Calvanese, D., Kontchakov, R., Ryzhikov, V., Zakharyaschev, M.: Reasoning over extended ER models. In: Parent, C., Schewe, K.-D., Storey, V.C., Thalheim, B. (eds.) ER 2007. LNCS, vol. 4801, pp. 277–292. Springer, Heidelberg (2007)
3. Artale, A., Calvanese, D., Kontchakov, R., Zakharyaschev, M.: Adding weight to DL-Lite. In: Grau, B.C., et al. (eds.) DL 2009. CEUR Workshop, vol. 477 (2008)
4. Baader, F., et al. (eds.): The Description Logic Handbook: Theory, Implementation, and Applications. Cambridge University Press, Cambridge (2003)

5. Beckert, B., Keller, U., Schmitt, P.: Translating the Object Constraint Language into first-order predicate logic. In: VERIFY, FLoC Workshop (2002)
6. Berardi, D., Calvanese, D., De Giacomo, G.: Reasoning on UML class diagrams. Artificial Intelligence 168(1–2), 70–118 (2005)
7. Calvanese, D., Lenzerini, M., Nardi, D.: Unifying class-based representation formalisms. Journal of Artificial Intelligence Research 11, 199–240 (1999)
8. Chen, P.P.S.: The entity-relationship model: toward a unified view of data. ACM Transactions on Database Systems 1(1), 9–36 (1976)
9. Dullea, J., Song, I.Y.: An analysis of cardinality constraints in redundant relationships. In: Proceedings of CIKM 1997, pp. 270–277. ACM, New York (1997)
10. Dupuy, S., Ledru, Y., Chabre-Peccoud, M.: An overview of roZ: A tool for integrating UML and Z specifications. In: Wangler, B., Bergman, L.D. (eds.) CAiSE 2000. LNCS, vol. 1789, pp. 417–430. Springer, Heidelberg (2000)
11. Falkner, A., Feinerer, I., Salzer, G., Schenner, G.: Computing product configurations via UML and integer linear programming. Int. J. Mass Cust. 3(4) (2010)
12. Feinerer, I.: A Formal Treatment of UML Class Diagrams as an Efficient Method for Configuration Management. Dissertation, Vienna University of Technology (2007)
13. Feinerer, I., Salzer, G.: Consistency and minimality of UML class specifications with multiplicities and uniqueness constraints. In: Proceedings of TASE 2007, pp. 411–420. IEEE Computer Society Press, Los Alamitos (2007)
14. Felfernig, A., Friedrich, G., Jannach, D., Stumptner, M., Zanker, M.: UML as knowledge acquisition frontend for semantic web configuration knowledge bases. In: Proceedings of RuleML 2002. CEUR Workshop Proceedings, vol. 60 (2002)
15. Hartmann, S.: On the consistency of int-cardinality constraints. In: Ling, T.-W., Ram, S., Li Lee, M. (eds.) ER 1998. LNCS, vol. 1507, pp. 150–163. Springer, Heidelberg (1998)
16. Hartmann, S.: On interactions of cardinality constraints,key, and functional dependencies. In: Schewe, K.-D., Thalheim, B. (eds.) FoIKS 2000. LNCS, vol. 1762, pp. 136–155. Springer, Heidelberg (2000)
17. Jones, T.H., Song, I.Y.: Analysis of binary/ternary cardinality combinations in entity-relationship modeling. Data & Knowledge Engineering 19(1), 39–64 (1996)
18. Kim, S.-K., Carrington, D.: Formalizing the UML class diagram using object-Z. In: France, R.B. (ed.) UML 1999. LNCS, vol. 1723, pp. 83–98. Springer, Heidelberg (1999)
19. Krishnan, P.: Consistency checks for UML. In: Proceedings of APSEC 2000, p. 162. IEEE Computer Society, Washington, DC (2000)
20. Lenzerini, M., Nobili, P.: On the satisfiability of dependency constraints in entity-relationship schemata. Information Systems 15(4), 453–461 (1990)
21. Niederbrucker, G., Sisel, T.: Clews Website (2011), http://www.logic.at/clews
22. Object Management Group: Object Constraint Language 2.3 (2011), www.omg.org
23. Object Management Group: Unified Modeling Language 2.4 (2011), www.omg.org
24. Queralt, A., Teniente, E.: Reasoning on UML class diagrams with OCL constraints. In: Embley, D.W., Olivé, A., Ram, S. (eds.) ER 2006. LNCS, vol. 4215, pp. 497–512. Springer, Heidelberg (2006)
25. Rosati, R.: Finite model reasoning in *DL-lite*. In: Bechhofer, S., Hauswirth, M., Hoffmann, J., Koubarakis, M. (eds.) ESWC 2008. LNCS, vol. 5021, pp. 215–229. Springer, Heidelberg (2008)
26. Snook, C.F., Butler, M.J.: UML-B: Formal modeling and design aided by UML. ACM Trans. Softw. Eng. Methodol. 15(1), 92–122 (2006)
27. The Alliance for Telecommunications Industry Solutions: ATIS telecom glossary 2000 (2000), www.atis.org (approved February 28, 2001 by ANSI)

Creating Models for Simulating the Face

Mark Sagar

Weta Digital,
9-11 Manuka St, Miramar,
Wellington, New Zealand

Abstract. Creating animated computer generated faces which can withstand scrutiny on the large screen is a daunting task. How does the face move? How does it reflect light? What information is relevant? How can it be captured and then transformed to convincingly breathe life into a digital human or fantastic creature? The talk will give examples of new technologies and methodologies developed to achieve this in blockbuster films including "Avatar" and will point the way to the next generation of computer generated characters by showing the increasing importance of computational simulation and discovering and modeling what is really going on underneath the skin.

Keywords: computer animation, computer generated characters, computational simulation.

EUnit: A Unit Testing Framework for Model Management Tasks

Antonio García-Domínguez[1], Dimitrios S. Kolovos[2], Louis M. Rose[2],
Richard F. Paige[2], and Inmaculada Medina-Bulo[1]

[1] University of Cádiz, Department of Computer Languages and Systems,
C/Chile 1, 11002, Cádiz, Spain
{antonio.garciadominguez,inmaculada.medina}@uca.es
[2] University of York, Department of Computer Science,
Deramore Lane, YO10 5GH, York, United Kingdom
{dkolovos,louis,paige}@cs.york.ac.uk

Abstract. Validating and transforming models are essential steps in model-driven engineering. These tasks are often implemented as operations in general purpose programming languages or task-specific model management languages. Just like other software artefacts, these tasks must be tested to reduce the risk of defects. Testing model management tasks requires testers to select and manage the relevant combinations of input models, tasks and expected outputs. This is complicated by the fact that many technologies may be used in the same system, each with their own integration challenges. In addition, advanced test oracles are required: tests may need to compare entire models or directory trees.

To tackle these issues, we propose creating an integrated unit testing framework for model management operations. We have developed the EUnit unit testing framework to validate our approach. EUnit tests specify how models and tasks are to be combined, while staying decoupled from the specific technologies used.

Keywords: Software testing, unit testing, model management, test frameworks, model validation, model transformation.

1 Introduction

Model-driven approaches are being adopted in a wide range of demanding environments, such as finance, health care or telecommunications [10]. In this context, validation and verification is identified as one of the many challenges of model-driven software engineering (MDSE) [21].

MDSE in practice involves creating models, and thereafter *managing* them, via various tasks, such as model transformation, validation and merging. The validation and verification of each type of model management task has its own specific challenges. Kolovos et al. list testing concerns for model-to-model (M2M) and model-to-text (M2T) transformations, model validations, model comparisons and model compositions in [13]. Baudry et al. identify three main issues when testing model transformations [2]: the complexity of the input and output models, the immaturity of the model management environments and the large number of different transformation languages and techniques.

While each type of model management task does have specific complexity, some of the concerns raised by Baudry can be generalized to apply to all model management tasks:

- There is usually a large number of models to be handled. Some may be created by hand, some may be generated using hand-written programs, and some may be generated automatically following certain coverage criteria.
- A single model or set of models may be used in several tasks. For instance, a model may be validated before performing an in-place transformation to assist the user, and later on it may be transformed to another model or merged with a different model. This requires having at least one test for each valid combination of models and sets of tasks.
- Test oracles are more complex than in traditional unit testing [17]: instead of checking scalar values or simple lists, we may need to compare entire graphs of model objects or file trees. In some cases, we might only want to check specific properties in the generated artifacts.
- Models and model management tasks may use a wide range of technologies. Models may be based on Ecore [20], XML files or Java object graphs, among many others. At the same time, tasks may use technologies from different platforms, such as Epsilon [15], oAW [11] or AMMA [6]. Many of these technologies offer high-level tools for running and debugging the different tasks using several models. However, users wishing to do automated unit testing need to learn low-level implementation details about their modelling and model management technologies. This increases the initial cost of testing these tasks and hampers the adoption of new technologies.
- Existing testing tools tend to focus on the testing technique itself, and lack integration with external systems. Some tools provide graphical user interfaces, but most do not generate reports which can be consumed by a continuous integration server, for instance.

In this work, we propose addressing these issues through an integrated test framework for model management tasks. We illustrate this approach with an improved version of the EUnit framework initially presented in [13]. EUnit has been extended with a richer data model, implicit test setup and improved facilities for testing model transformations and validations, among other new features.

The rest of this work is structured as follows. Section 2 illustrates our previous points with a JUnit test case for a model-to-model transformation. Section 3 describes how EUnit test suites are organized, and Section 4 shows how they are written, with an example. Section 5 outlines how EUnit can be extended to accommodate other technologies. Section 6 shows how we used EUnit to test a model-driven workflow to generate GMF editors. Finally, Section 7 presents related works and Section 8 lists the conclusions for this paper and our future lines of work.

2 Testing a Model Transformation with JUnit

In this section we will illustrate the abstract issues listed in Section 1 using a unit testing framework for a general-purpose programming language to test a model management task. We will test a simple model-to-model transformation in the Epsilon Transformation Language (ETL) using JUnit 4 [3]. The input and output models are based on the Eclipse Modeling Framework (EMF) [20].

ETL is one of the languages implemented in the Epsilon platform [15], which provides an infrastructure for implementing uniform, integrated and interoperable model management languages that can be used to manage models of diverse metamodels and technologies. Like all Epsilon languages, ETL is based on the Epsilon Object Language (EOL). EOL is a reworking and extension of OCL that includes the ability to update models, conditional and loop statements, statement sequencing, and access to standard I/O streams.

Definition of the test suite. For the sake of brevity, we will only outline the contents of the JUnit test suite. It is a Java class with three public methods:

1. The test setup method (marked with the @Before JUnit annotation) loads the required models by creating and configuring instances of EMFMODEL. After that, it prepares the transformation by creating and configuring an instance of ETLMODULE, adding the models to its model repository.
2. The test case itself (marked with @Test) runs the ETL transformation and uses the generic comparison algorithm implemented by EMF Compare to perform the model comparison.
3. The test teardown method (marked with @After) disposes of the models.

Issues. We can identify several issues in each part of the test suite. First, test setup is tightly bound to the technologies used: it depends on the API of the EMFMODEL and ETLMODULE classes, which are both part of Epsilon. Later refactorings in these classes may break existing tests.

The test case can only be used for a single combination of input and output models. Testing several combinations requires either repeating the same code and therefore making the suite less maintainable, or using parametric testing, which may be wasteful if not all tests need the same combinations of models.

Model comparison requires the user to manually select a model comparison engine and integrate it with the test. For comparing EMF models, EMF Compare is easy to use and readily available. However, generic model comparison engines may not be readily available for some modelling technologies.

Finally, instead of comparing the obtained and expected models, we could have checked several properties in the obtained model. However, querying models through Java code can be quite verbose.

Possible solutions. We could follow several approaches to address these issues. Our first instinct would be to extend JUnit and reuse all the tooling available for it. A custom test runner would simplify setup and teardown, and modelling platforms would integrate their technologies into it. Since Java is very verbose when querying models, the custom runner should run tests in a higher-level language, such as EOL. However, JUnit is very tightly coupled to Java, and this would impose limits on the level of integration we could obtain. For instance, errors in the model management tasks or the EOL tests could not be reported from their original source, but rather from the Java code which invoked them. Another problem with this approach is that new integration code would need to be written for each of the existing platforms.

Alternatively, we could add a new language exclusively dedicated to testing to the Epsilon family [15]. Being based on EOL, model querying would be very concise, and with a test runner written from scratch, test execution would be very flexible. However, this would still require all platforms to write new code to integrate with it, and this code would be tightly coupled to Epsilon.

As a middle ground, we could decorate EOL to guide its execution through a new test runner, while reusing the Apache Ant [1] tasks already provided by several of the existing platforms, such as AMMA or Epsilon. Like Make, Ant is a tool focused on automating the execution of processes such as program builds. Unlike Make, Ant defines processes using XML *buildfiles* with sets of interrelated *targets*. Each target contains in turn a sequence of *tasks*. Many Ant tasks and Ant-based tools already exist, and it is easy to create a new Ant task.

Among these three approaches, EUnit follows the last one. Ant tasks take care of model setup and management, and tests are written in EOL and executed by a new test runner, written from the ground up.

3 Test Organization

In the previous section, we listed some of the issues when testing M2M transformations with a general-purpose framework. In this section, we will describe how the internal structure of EUnit test suites and test cases helps flexibly combine models, tasks and tests.

3.1 Test Suites

EUnit test suites are organized as trees: inner nodes group related test cases and define *data* bindings. Leaf nodes define *model* bindings and run the test cases.

Data bindings repeat all test cases with different values in one or more variables. They can implement parametric testing, as in JUnit 4. EUnit can nest several data bindings, running all test cases once for each combination. Model bindings are specific to EUnit: they allow developers to repeat a single test case with different subsets of models. Data and model bindings can be combined.

Figure 1 shows an example of an EUnit test tree: nodes with data bindings are marked with `data`, and nodes with model bindings are marked with `model`. EUnit will perform a preorder traversal of this tree, running the following tests: A with $x = 1$ and model X, A with $x = 1$ and model Y, B with $x = 1$ and both models, A with $x = 2$ and model X, A with $x = 2$ and model Y and finally, B with $x = 2$ and both models.

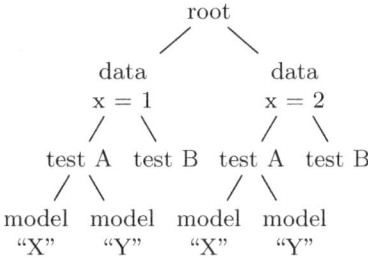

Fig. 1. Example of an EUnit test tree

3.2 Test Cases

The execution of a test case is divided into the following steps:

1. Apply the data bindings of its ancestors.
2. Run the model setup sections defined by the user.
3. Apply the model bindings of this node.
4. Run the regular setup sections defined by the user.
5. Run the test case itself.
6. Run the teardown sections defined by the user.
7. Tear down the data bindings and models for this test.

An important difference between JUnit and EUnit is that setup is split into two parts: model setup and regular setup. This split allows users to add code before and after model bindings are applied. Normally, the model setup sections will load all the models needed by the test suite, and the regular setup sections will further prepare the models selected by the model binding. Explicit teardown sections are usually not needed, as models are disposed automatically by EUnit. EUnit includes them for consistency with the xUnit frameworks.

Due to its focus on model management, model setup in EUnit is very flexible. Developers can combine several ways to set up models, such as model references, individual Apache Ant [1] tasks, Apache Ant targets or Human-Usable Text Notation (HUTN) [18] fragments. This is detailed in Section 4.

A test case may produce one among several results. SUCCESS is obtained if all assertions passed and no exceptions were thrown. FAILURE is obtained if an assertion failed. ERROR is obtained if an unexpected exception was thrown while running the test. Finally, tests may be SKIPPED by the user.

4 Test Specification

In the previous section, we described how test suites and test cases are organized. In this section, we will show how to write them.

As discussed in Section 2, after evaluating several approaches, we decided to combine the expressive power of EOL and the extensibility of Apache Ant. For

Listing 1. Example invocation of the EUnit Ant task

```
<epsilon.eunit src="..." failOnErrors="...">
  <model     ref="OldName" as="NewName"/>
  <uses      ref="x" as="y" />
  <exports   ref="z" as="w" />
  <parameter name="myparam" value="myvalue" />
  <modelTasks><!-- Zero or more Ant tasks --></modelTasks>
</epsilon.eunit>
```

this reason, EUnit test suites are split into two files: an Ant buildfile and an EOL script with some special-purpose annotations. The next subsections describe the contents of these two files and revisit the example in Section 2 with EUnit.

4.1 Ant Buildfile

EUnit uses standard Ant buildfiles: running EUnit is as simple as using its Ant task. Users may run EUnit more than once in a single Ant launch: the graphical user interface will automatically aggregate the results of all test suites.

EUnit Invocations. An example invocation of the EUnit Ant task using the most common features is shown in Listing 1. Users will normally only use some of these features at a time, though.

The EUnit Ant task is based on the Epsilon workflow tasks, inheriting some useful features. The attribute *src* points to the path of the EOL file, and the optional attribute *failOnErrors* can be set to `false` to prevent EUnit from aborting the Ant launch if a test case fails. EUnit also inherits support for importing and exporting global variables through the <*uses*> and <*exports*> elements: the original name is set in *ref*, and the optional *as* attribute allows for using a different name. For receiving parameters as name-value pairs, the <*parameter*> element can be used.

Model references (using the <*model*> nested element) are also inherited from the regular Epsilon workflow tasks. These allow model management tasks to refer by name to models previously loaded in the Ant buildfile. However, EUnit implicitly reloads the models after each test case. This ensures that test cases are isolated from each other.

The EUnit Ant task adds several new features to customize the test result reports and perform more advanced model setup. EUnit generates reports in the XML format of the Ant <*junit*> task. This format is also used by many other tools, such as the TestNG unit testing framework [4], the Jenkins continuous integration server [12] or the JUnit Eclipse plug-ins.

The optional <*modelTasks*> nested element contains a sequence of Ant tasks which will be run after reloading the model references and before running the model setup sections in the EOL file. This allows users to run workflows more advanced than simply reloading model references, such as the one in Listing 4.

Listing 2. Example of a 2-level data binding

```
@data x
operation firstLevel()  { return 1.to(2); }

@data y
operation secondLevel() { return 1.to(2); }

@setup
operation generateModel() { -* generate model using x and y *- }

@test
operation mytest() { -* test with the generated model *- }
```

Helper Targets. Ant buildfiles for EUnit may include *helper targets*. These targets can be invoked using `runTarget("targetName")` from anywhere in the EOL script. Helper targets are quite versatile: called from an EOL model setup section, they allow for reusing model loading fragments between different EUnit test suites. They can also be used to invoke the model management tasks under test.

4.2 EOL Script

The Epsilon Object Language script is the second half of the EUnit test suite. EOL annotations are used to tag some of the operations as data binding definitions (`@data`), additional model setup sections (`@model`), test setup and teardown sections (`@setup` and `@teardown`) and test cases (`@test`).

Data bindings. Data bindings repeat all test cases with different values in some variables. To define a data binding, users must define an operation which returns a sequence of elements and is marked with `@data variable`. All test cases will be repeated once for each element of the returned sequence, setting the specified variable to the corresponding element. Listing 2 shows two nested data bindings and a test case which will be run four times: with $x=1$ and $y=1$, $x=1$ and $y=2$, $x=2$ and $y=1$ and finally $x=2$ and $y=2$. The example shows how x and y could be used by the setup section to generate an input model for the test. This can be useful if the intent of the test is ensuring that a certain property holds in a class of models, rather than a single model.

Model bindings. Model bindings repeat a test case with different subsets of models. They can be defined by annotating a test case with `$with Map {elements}`, where `elements` is a list of key-value pairs. For each key-value pair *dst* → *src*, EUnit will rename the model named *src* to *dst*. Listing 3 shows a test which will be run twice: the first time, model "A" will be the default model and model "B" will be the "Other" model, and the second time, model "B" will be the default model and model "A" will be the "Other" model.

Additional variables and built-in operations. EUnit provides several variables and operations which are useful for testing. For example, supporting Ant

Listing 3. Example of a model binding

```
$with Map {"" = "A", "Other" = "B"}
$with Map {"" = "B", "Other" = "A"}
@test
operation mytest() { -* use the default and Other models *- }
```

targets can be invoked with `runTarget("targetName")`. Models written in HUTN [18] can be loaded with `loadHutn("modelName", "hutnSource")`. Ant tasks can be set up from the EOL script using `antProject`, a new global variable which refers to the Ant PROJECT object being executed.

Assertions. In addition to the usual assertions available in most unit testing frameworks, EUnit implements several assertions which are useful for testing model transformations: `assertEqualModels` and `assertNotEqualModels` compare entire models, `assertEqualFiles` and `assertNotEqualFiles` compare files, and file trees can be compared with `assertEqualDirectories` and `assertNotEqualDirectories`.

Model comparison is not implemented by the assertions themselves. We extended the Epsilon Model Connectivity abstraction layer [15] to provide model comparison as an optional service of its model drivers, in order to decouple tests from the model comparison engine in use. Additionally, model, file and directory comparisons take a snapshot of their operands before comparing them, so EUnit can show the differences right at the moment when the comparison was performed. This is especially important when some of the models are generated on the fly by the EUnit test suite, or when a test case for code generation may overwrite the results of the previous one.

Figure 2 shows a screenshot of the EUnit graphical user interface. On the left, an Eclipse view shows the results of several EUnit test suites. We can see that the `load-models-with-hutn` suite failed. Users can press the Compare button to the right of "Failure Trace" to show the differences between the expected and obtained models, as shown on the right. EUnit implements a pluggable architecture where *difference viewers* are automatically selected based on the types of the operands. There are difference viewers for EMF models and file trees and a fallback viewer which converts both operands to strings.

4.3 Example: Testing a Model Transformation with EUnit

After describing the basic syntax, we will show how to use EUnit to test the transformation in Section 2.

The Ant buildfile is shown in Listing 4. It has two targets: *run-tests* (lines 2–16) invokes the EUnit suite, and *tree2graph* (lines 17–22) is a helper target which transforms model "Tree" into model "Graph" using ETL. The <*modelTasks*> nested element is used to load the input, expected output and output EMF models. "Graph" is loaded with *read* set to `false`: the model will be initially empty, and will be populated by the ETL transformation.

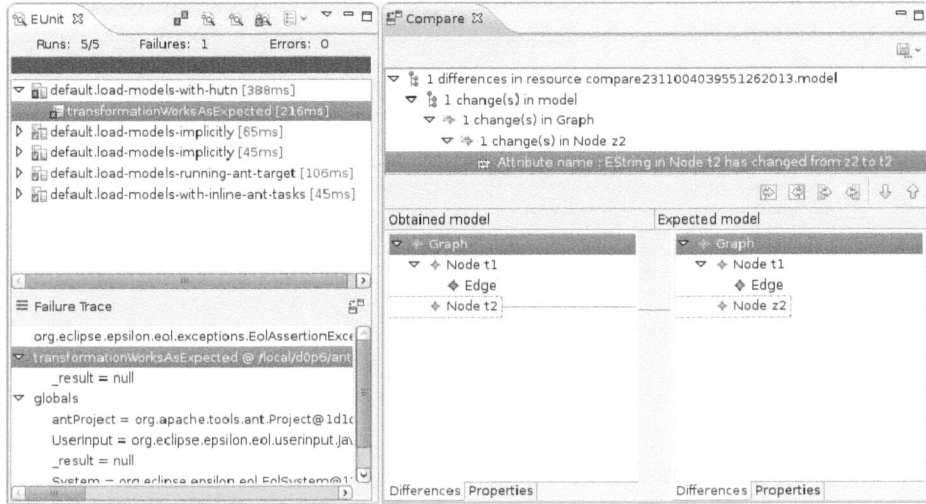

Fig. 2. Screenshot of the EUnit graphical user interface

The EOL script is shown in Listing 5: it invokes the helper task (line 3) and checks that the obtained model is equal to the expected model (line 4). Internally, EMC will perform the comparison using EMF Compare.

5 Extending EUnit

EUnit is based on the Epsilon platform, but it is designed to accommodate other technologies. In this section we will explain several strategies to add support for these technologies to EUnit.

5.1 Adding Modelling Technologies

EUnit uses the Epsilon Model Connectivity abstraction layer [15] to handle different modelling technologies. EMC has support for EMF models, Java object graphs and plain XML files. Drivers for MDR and Z models are also available.

Adding support for a different modelling technology only requires implementing another driver for EMC. Depending on the modelling technology, the driver can provide optional services such as model comparison, caching or reflection.

5.2 Adding Model Management Tasks

As mentioned in Section 3, EUnit uses Ant as a workflow language. Therefore, the basic requirement to test any model management task with EUnit is that it is exposed through an Ant task. It is highly encouraged, however, that the Ant task is aware of the EMC model repository linked to the Ant project. Otherwise,

Listing 4. Ant buildfile for EUnit with <*modelTasks*> and a helper target

```
1  <project>
2    <target name="run-tests">
3      <epsilon.eunit src="test-external.eunit">
4        <modelTasks>
5          <epsilon.emf.loadModel name="Tree" modelfile="tree.model"
6             metamodelfile="tree.ecore" read="true" store="false"/>
7          <epsilon.emf.loadModel name="GraphExpected" modelfile="graph.model"
8             metamodelfile="graph.ecore" read="true" store="false"/>
9          <epsilon.emf.loadModel name="Graph" modelfile="transformed.model"
10            metamodelfile="graph.ecore" read="false" store="false"/>
11       </modelTasks>
12     </epsilon.eunit>
13   </target>
14   <target name="tree2graph">
15     <epsilon.etl src="${basedir}/resources/Tree2Graph.etl">
16       <model ref="Tree"/>
17       <model ref="Graph"/>
18     </epsilon.etl>
19   </target>
20 </project>
```

Listing 5. EOL script using `runTarget` to run ETL

```
@test
operation transformationWorksAsExpected() {
  runTarget("tree2graph");
  assertEqualModels("GraphExpected", "Graph");
}
```

users will have to shuffle the models out from and back into the repository between model management tasks. As an example, a helper target for an ATL [6] transformation with the existing Ant tasks would need to:

1. Save the input model in the EMC model repository to a file, by invoking the <*epsilon.storeModel*> task.
2. Load the metamodels and the input model with <*atl.loadModel*>.
3. Run the ATL transformation with <*atl.launch*>.
4. Save the result of the ATL transformation with <*atl.saveModel*>.
5. Load it into the EMC model repository with <*epsilon.emf.loadModel*>.

This does not prevent EUnit from testing ATL transformations, but it makes the helper task quite longer than the one in Listing 4. Ideally, Ant tasks should be adapted or wrapped to use models directly from the EMC model repository.

Another advantage in making model management tasks EMC-aware is that they can easily "export" their results as models, making them easier to test. To illustrate this point, we extended the Ant task for the Epsilon Validation Language for model validation with the attribute *exportAsModel*: when set, the task exports its validation results as an EMC Java object graph model. This way, EOL can query the results as any regular model (see Listing 6). This is simpler than transforming the validated model to a problem metamodel, as suggested in [5]. The example in Listing 6 checks that a single warning was produced due to the expected rule (`LabelsStartWithT`) and the expected model element.

Listing 6. Testing an EVL model validation with EUnit

```
@test
operation valid() {
  var tree := new Tree!Tree;
  tree.label := '1n';
  runTarget('validate-tree');
  var errors := EVL!EvlUnsatisfiedConstraint.allInstances;
  assertEquals(1, errors.size);
  var error := errors.first;
  assertEquals(tree, error.instance);
  assertEquals(false, error.constraint.isCritique);
  assertEquals('LabelsStartWithT', error.constraint.name);
}
```

5.3 Integrating Model Generators

By design, EUnit does not implement any model generation technique, as we consider that running the tests is orthogonal to generating them. Several model generation tools already exist, such as OMOGEN [7] or Cartier [19]. To EUnit, model generation is just another kind of model management task. There are basically two ways in which models can be generated: *batch* model generation generates all models before repeating every test through them, and *inline* model generation invokes the generator in every test, producing the required models.

Batch model generation can be implemented by calling the Ant task of the model generator before invoking EUnit, and then using a data binding to repeat the tests over every generated model. The Ant tasks required to load these models can be set up by EUnit on the fly in a @model operation, using the *antProject* built-in variable. Inline model generation uses data bindings to set the parameters for generating each model, and then invokes the Ant task of the model generation tool in a @model operation.

Listing 7 shows a simple example of inline model generation, using EOL code instead of invoking the Ant task of a model generation tool. Several Tree models are generated by combining data and model bindings. The data variable *nlevels* indicates the number of levels the generated binary tree should have. The @model operation loads an empty model and populates it as needed. All tests will be repeated 5 times, with complete binary trees of 0 to 4 levels.

6 Case Study: Regression Tests for Eugenia

In this section, we will show a more advanced case study for the EUnit test framework. This case study is a set of regression tests for the Eugenia [14] tool, which simplifies the creation of graphical model editors based on the Eclipse Graphical Modeling Framework (GMF) [8]. The transformations in Eugenia are non-trivial: some of them are implemented in ETL, and some of them are implemented in EOL. Before conducting this case study, testing Eugenia was an entirely manual process, as it was deemed too difficult to automate.

Listing 7. Inline model generation in EUnit

```
@data nlevels
operation levels() { return 0.to(4); }
@model
operation generate() {
  // Load an empty model and populate it
  loadHutn('Tree', '@Spec { Metamodel { nsUri: "Tree" }} Model {}');
  generateBinaryTree(new Tree!Node, nlevels);
}

operation generateBinaryTree(root, nlevels) {
  if (nlevels > 0) {
    for (n in Sequence { new Tree!Node, new Tree!Node }) {
      n.parent := root;
      generateBinaryTree(n, nlevels - 1);
    }
  }
}

/* ... tests ... */
```

After developing EUnit, we decided to use it to add regression tests for the Eugenia model transformations. We created a new Ant task for Eugenia, and defined the EUnit test suite as follows:

- The Ant buildfile contains a single target which prepares a test environment, runs Eugenia on the test environment and invokes EUnit.
- The EUnit test suite uses a data binding to repeat the tests over each of the six models produced by Eugenia: .ecore, .genmodel, .gmfgraph, .gmftool, .gmfmap and .gmfgen.
- Test setup creates, configures and runs <epsilon.emf.loadModel> Ant tasks to load the expected and obtained models.
- Test execution compares the expected and obtained models.

Using regular Ant tasks to integrate external tools has the added benefit that the same Ant tasks used for testing can also help end-users in automating their own workflows. If we had defined our own extension framework for EUnit, end-users would not be able to take advantage of these improvements.

EUnit has reduced the amount of code required to do the tests, by repeating tests implicitly through data bindings. The *antProject* variable supplied by EUnit helped simplify the Ant buildfile as well: instead of specifying everything in it, part of the required Ant tasks are created on the fly inside the EOL script.

Overall, our experience using EUnit in this case study has been positive. Still, we have identified several features which would be useful in EUnit. The EOL script could have run Eugenia by itself if EUnit had support for running a specific operation once before or after all test cases, like the @BeforeClass and @AfterClass annotations in JUnit. With this, the EOL script could do all the work, but users would still need to explicitly write and run an Ant buildfile. It would be convenient to have a launcher which generated and ran a minimal Ant buildfile on the fly, further reducing the learning curve required to use EUnit.

7 Related Work

Initial work on EUnit was presented in [13]. This paper presented the basic testing issues in several common types of model management tasks and showed how model-to-model and model-to-text transformations could be tested with an early prototype of EUnit. The present version of EUnit supports data and model bindings, implicitly reloads models, integrates Ant tasks for model setup and provides a graphical user interface for Eclipse, among other new features. Our current focus in EUnit is to allow users to test efficiently when confronted with the large number of combinations of models, tasks and technologies present in a typical system developed with Model-Driven Engineering.

Lin et al. presented a testing framework for model transformations in [16], identifying three main challenges: automatic comparison, visualization of differences and debugging transformation specifications. Their framework uses the C-SAW model transformation engine, which runs on top of the Generic Modeling Environment platform. Tests are written manually using a textual notation which binds transformations with input and output models. EUnit can be regarded as a more general framework, as it can be used for testing other categories of model management tasks, such as model validations or model-to-text transformations. EUnit delegates comparisons to external engines (such as EMF Compare) and visualizes model, file and directory differences through the Eclipse Compare component. As for the third challenge, interactive debugging was recently added to several Epsilon languages: it could be integrated into EUnit as well by extending the Ant tasks for those languages.

Most of the literature in validation of model management tasks focuses on specific techniques for model transformations, rather than on frameworks to organize them. Baudry et al. show in [7] the OMOGEN tool, which automatically generates input models based on a set of coverage criteria and manually defined *model fragments*. Sen et al. use the Cartier tool to generate models using partition-based testing [19]. Ehrig et al. generate models using graph grammars [9]. These techniques could be integrated in EUnit as model setup tasks.

Mottu et al. identify several test oracles for model transformations [17]: reference transformations, inverse transformations, expected output models, generic contracts, OCL assertions and model snippets. The first three can be implemented using the helper tasks and generic model and file comparison assertions in EUnit. Generic contracts can be checked by repeating a test with data and model bindings. OCL assertions can be emulated with EOL, which is inspired on it. EUnit does not have explicit support for checking if a model snippet is included in the output model, but it can be approximated using EOL.

8 Conclusions and Future Work

Testing any type of model management task involves dealing with several challenges. There are many input and output models, tasks and technologies involved. Models may need to be generated in different ways and tested against several tasks, and a single task may need to be tested against many models. Test oracles are harder to write. The technologies used present additional integration problems when performing automated testing. Existing testing tools do not integrate well with other systems, such as continuous integration servers.

To tackle these issues, we have proposed in this work creating an integrated unit testing framework for model management tasks. To illustrate our ideas, we have developed EUnit, an unit testing framework based on the Epsilon platform:

- EUnit can reuse the same test for many models with suite-wide parametric testing and test-specific model bindings. Parametric testing can integrate hand-written model generation programs into the test suite definition.
- Tests in EUnit are written in the Epsilon Object Language, a high-level imperative language inspired on OCL which is especially well suited for model management. EUnit integrates assertions for comparing models and file trees.
- Modelling technologies are unified by the Epsilon Model Connectivity layer, and model management tasks are wrapped in high-level Apache Ant tasks.
- Ant tasks can be extended to make model management tasks easier to test. For example, the Ant task for the Epsilon Validation Language can now provide EUnit with models of the validation results.
- EUnit provides a graphical user interface for the Eclipse integrated development environment, and generates test reports in the widely used XML format of the JUnit Ant task.

At the same time, there are many ways in which EUnit could be improved. In the near future, we intend to study how EUnit can help test model comparisons and model compositions, while staying decoupled from specific technologies. We also plan to integrate with EUnit the interactive debugging facilities which were recently added to most of the Epsilon languages.

Custom comparison rules could be integrated into the model comparison assertions provided by EUnit. Ant tasks for simplified integration with other platforms (such as AMMA or oAW) could be developed. It would be very interesting to expose model generation tools (such as Cartier) as Ant tasks and use them for model setup. Test specification and organization in EUnit could also be improved with support for running code before and after all test cases and with test groups, theories and assumptions. A test launcher which generated and ran minimal Ant buildfiles on the fly could be useful.

Acknowledgments. This work was partly funded by the research scholarship PU-EPIF-FPI-C 2010-065 of the University of Cádiz. It was also partly supported by the European Commission through the INESS project (Contract #218575).

References

1. Apache Foundation: Ant 1.8.2 (December 2010), http://ant.apache.org/
2. Baudry, B., Ghosh, S., Fleurey, F., France, R., Le Traon, Y., Mottu, J.: Barriers to systematic model transformation testing. Communications of the ACM 53, 139–143 (2010)

3. Beck, K.: JUnit.org (April 2011), http://www.junit.org/
4. Beust, C.: TestNG (March 2011), http://testng.org/
5. Bézivin, J., Jouault, F.: Using ATL for checking models. Electronic Notes in Theoretical Computer Science 152, 69–81 (2006)
6. Bézivin, J., Jouault, F., Rosenthal, P., Valduriez, P.: The AMMA platform support for modeling in the large and modeling in the small. Research Report 04.09, LINA, University of Nantes, Nantes, France (Feburary 2005)
7. Brottier, E., Fleurey, F., Steel, J., Baudry, B., Le Traon, Y.: Metamodel-based test generation for model transformations: an algorithm and a tool. In: Proc. of the 17th Int. Symposium on Software Reliability Engineering, pp. 85–94. IEEE Computer Society, Los Alamitos (2006)
8. Eclipse Foundation: Graphical Modeling Project (2011), http://eclipse.org/modeling/gmf/
9. Ehrig, K., Küster, J.M., Taentzer, G.: Generating instance models from meta models. Software & Systems Modeling 8(4), 479–500 (2008)
10. Guttman, M., Parodi, J.: Real-Life MDA: Solving Business Problems with Model Driven Architecture, 1st edn. Morgan Kaufmann, San Francisco (2006)
11. Haase, A., Völter, M., Efftinge, S., Kolb, B.: Introduction to openArchitectureWare 4.1.2. In: Proc. of the MDD Tool Implementers Forum, TOOLS Europe 2007 (2007)
12. Kawaguchi, K.: Jenkins CI (April 2011), http://jenkins-ci.org/
13. Kolovos, D.S., Paige, R.F., Rose, L.M., Polack, F.A.: Unit testing model management operations. In: Proc. of the 2008 IEEE Int. Conf. on Software Testing Verification and Validation, Lillehammer, Norway, pp. 97–104 (April 2008)
14. Kolovos, D.S., Rose, L.M., Abid, S.B., Paige, R.F., Polack, F.A.C., Botterweck, G.: Taming EMF and GMF using model transformation. In: Petriu, D.C., Rouquette, N., Haugen, Ø. (eds.) MODELS 2010. LNCS, vol. 6394, pp. 211–225. Springer, Heidelberg (2010)
15. Kolovos, D.S., Rose, L.M., Paige, R.F.: The Epsilon Book (March 2011), http://www.eclipse.org/gmt/epsilon
16. Lin, Y., Zhang, J., Gray, J.: A testing framework for model transformations. In: Beydeda, S., Book, M., Gruhn, V. (eds.) Model-Driven Software Development, pp. 219–236. Springer, Berlin (2005)
17. Mottu, J., Baudry, B., Le Traon, Y.: Model transformation testing: oracle issue. In: Proc. of the 2008 IEEE Int. Conf. on Software Testing Verification and Validation, Lillehammer, Norway, pp. 105–112 (April 2008)
18. Object Management Group: Human-Usable Textual Notation (HUTN) 1.0 (August 2004), http://www.omg.org/technology/documents/formal/hutn.htm
19. Sen, S., Baudry, B., Mottu, J.-M.: Automatic model generation strategies for model transformation testing. In: Paige, R.F. (ed.) ICMT 2009. LNCS, vol. 5563, pp. 148–164. Springer, Heidelberg (2009)
20. Steinberg, D., Budinsky, F., Paternostro, M., Merks, E.: EMF: Eclipse Modeling Framework, 2nd edn. Addison-Wesley Professional, Reading (2008)
21. Van Der Straeten, R., Mens, T., Van Baelen, S.: Challenges in model-driven software engineering. In: Chaudron, M.R.V. (ed.) MODELS 2008. LNCS, vol. 5421, pp. 35–47. Springer, Heidelberg (2009)

Verifying UML-RT Protocol Conformance Using Model Checking*

Yann Moffett[1], Alain Beaulieu[2], and Juergen Dingel[3]

[1] CF 18 Avionics System Eng., Dept. of National Defense, Ottawa, Ontario, Canada
yann.moffett@forces.gc.ca
[2] Elec. and Comp. Engineering, Royal Military College, Kingston, Ontario, Canada
alain.beaulieu@rmc.ca
[3] School of Computing, Queen's University, Kingston, Ontario, Canada
dingel@cs.queensu.ca

Abstract. In UML-RT, capsules communicate via protocols which connect capsule ports. Protocol State Machines (PSMs) allow the description of the legal message sequences of a port and are potentially very useful for the modular development and verification of systems. However, it is unclear how exactly conformance of a capsule to its PSMs should be defined and how this can be checked automatically. In this paper, we provide a definition of protocol conformance and show how software model checking can be used to check protocol conformance automatically. We describe the design and implementation of a tool that checks the conformance of a capsule with Java action code with respect to the PSMs of all its ports. The results of the validation of the tool on three case studies are summarized.

1 Introduction

In general, the interface of an entity represents an abstraction that facilitates correct use of the entity by listing the operations that the entity makes available and separating its externally visible parts from the internal ones. Arguably, this notion is one of the great success stories in computer science. It has become indispensable to modern software development, because it, e.g., enables modular development and analysis and facilitates maintenance and evolution. To further increase the utility of interfaces, numerous proposals have been made to enrich them with more specific information about how the externally visible parts are to be used. Examples include contracts in the Java Modeling Language (JML), session types, and Singularity channel contracts [8,4]. In ROOM [18], UML-RT [16], and UML 2 [12] communication between components (called *capsules* in ROOM and UML-RT) is achieved via protocols that connect ports. Protocol State Machines (PSMs) are used to describe the message sequences that the protocol allows and that the components connected via the protocol are supposed to be able to respond to. The idea is that if all components in the system conform

---
* Work supported by NSERC, IBM Canada and Malina Software.

to the PSM on all their ports, i.e., the communication behaviour of each component is consistent with each of its PSMs, then no component will ever receive an "unexpected" message and the system communication will not deadlock.

Current UML-RT tools, such as IBM Rational®Rose RealTime (RoseRT)[1] and its successor IBM Rational®Software Architect, RealTime Edition (RSA-RTE), offer only very rudimentary support for PSMs. PSMs can be drawn and associated with ports, but they are not leveraged for analysis and do not influence code generation at all. In particular, whether a message sequence sent by a capsule over a port is actually allowed by (conforms to) the PSM on that port is not checked at all, relegating PSMs to a documentary role. In this paper, we address this issue. In short, our work leverages software model checking to improve the component-based construction of embedded systems using model-driven development. We define what it means for a capsule state machine to conform to its PSMs, and present a technique that checks this conformance. The technique is based on the observation that under some assumptions (called *Autonomy* and *Finiteness* in Section 2) conformance checking can be reduced to an exhaustive exploration of all the executions of the capsule state machine composed with all its PSMs (Section 3). We present a prototype implementation of the technique. The prototype takes as input a capsule and its PSMs created with IBM RoseRT and checks its conformance fully automatically using RoseRT's code generation and Java Pathfinder, a leading software model checker. We discuss three case studies to illustrate the capabilities of our prototype and the utility of the approach overall (Section 4).

2 Background

2.1 MDD Using UML-RT

Several development methodologies for real-time software have been developed. One of the first approaches to gain popularity was the ROOM methodology [18] which later evolved into a modeling language called UML-RT [16] and now is a proper profile of UML 2. We provide a very short overview of UML-RT. For more information the reader is referred to, e.g., [16].

Capsules, ports, and capsule state machines. In UML-RT, the structure of a system is expressed using capsules, ports, and connectors. The behaviour is described using state machines and sequence diagrams. A system is composed using *capsules* which are specialized classes which communicate with each other exclusively via synchronous or asynchronous message passing through one or more boundary objects called *ports*. Capsules may contain subcapsules, messages can carry data, and several instances of a capsule or a port can be created using *multiplicity*. Each capsule has a *capsule state machine* (CSM) which describes its (top-level) behaviour. A CSM is a special case of UML 2 state machines with some added constraints (e.g., CSMs cannot contain orthogonal regions)

---

[1] IBM and Rational are trademarks of International Business Machines Corporation, registered in many jurisdictions worldwide.

and some refinements (for executability). The services offered by the UML-RT library framework allow, e.g., the creation of a timer, the logging of a message, or the instantiation of a capsule. Services have a port associated with them. For instance, after creation, a timer "goes off" after a user-specified time which causes a timeout message to be sent to the timing port.

Protocols and protocol state machines. The UML-RT stereotype *Protocol* defines the interface between capsules. Ports are part of capsule structure and function as the realization of a so-called *base* or *conjugate protocol role*. UML-RT tools use protocols only to define input messages and output messages along with the types of any data included in these messages. Connectors can only be drawn between *compatible* ports, i.e., the protocol roles must use the same messages and any data types included in those messages must be compatible in the Java or C++ sense. A protocol state machine (PSM) can be used to specify the message sequences that a protocol permits. PSMs in UML 2 [12] are quite rich and allow, e.g., the use of composite states, history, and concurrent regions. While UML-RT itself puts no constraints on PSMs, IBM RoseRT limits PSMs to non-hierarchical state machines without attributes, variables, or branching, and with transitions containing only send and receive actions. We adopt these restrictions and support for the omitted features is left for future work. Examples for the PSMs supported by IBM RoseRT are shown in Fig. 1a where each of the ports *p1*, *p2*, and *p3* has a PSM associated with it.

2.2 Conditions Imposed on PSMs

In [20], an *autonomy condition* is used to guarantee that the contract is *realizable*, i.e., that it is possible to find client and server implementations that satisfy their respective channel contracts and will never deadlock. Slightly rephrased to fit our UML-RT context, autonomy means that *in every state of a PSM, at most one message can be output* and ensures that during the message exchange between two roles of a protocol it can never happen that two output messages "cross" each other and leave the PSMs in inconsistent states.

Asynchronous communication is typically implemented using message queues which store delivered messages until they are received. In general, it is not possible to bound the size of these queues. To force the size of channel queues to be finite, Singularity enforces a *finiteness condition* on contract state machines (its equivalent to PSMs): *Every cycle in a contract state machine must contain at least one output message and at least one input message*. We note that some useful protocols may violate finiteness (e.g., certain polling protocols) [17]. However, it appears that it should be possible to modify these protocols slightly such that finiteness is satisfied, although we have not proved this.

2.3 Java Pathfinder

The implementation of our approach relies on the use of a software model checker [9], that is, a tool that exhaustively explores the state space of a non-deterministic program written in some standard programming language. The use of a software model checker is necessitated by the fact that, transitions in the CSM may contain unrestricted code blocks in Java or C++. So, instead of checking conformance on the model-level, it must be checked at the code-level which also has the advantage that the deployed code is verified. Since existing UML-RT tools are capable of generating Java or C++ code from the models, we require a model checker for one of these two languages. We will use the Java software model checker Java Pathfinder (JPF) [22] together with the extension for LTL verification described in [21].

3 UML-RT Protocol Conformance Checking

Intuitively, protocol conformance is supposed to capture that a CSM and the PSMs on its ports "fit together". However, a more formal definition is needed. Our definition will be based on two safety properties and one liveness property:

(1) **Input Safety:** *None of the inputs received on a port is in conflict with the capsule's CSM.*
(2) **Output Safety:** *None of the outputs generated by the capsule's CSM is in conflict with the PSMs on the ports that these outputs go through.*
(3) **Progress:** *Assuming that the environment of the capsule always eventually provides any expected inputs to the ports, the CSM should allow the ports to make progress, that is, an output enabled at a port will eventually be generated by the CSM.* In some situations, enforcement of Progress may be unrealistic (e.g., in certain protocols that use message priorities) [17]; therefore, in our tool described in Section 3.3 the check for Progress is optional.

Formally, our approach to verify the conformance of a CSM to the PSMs on its ports is based on the exhaustive exploration of the state space of a *Verification Finite State Automaton* (VFSA), or *verification automaton*, for short. The VFSA consists of the composition of the CSM with all its PSMs. Conformance holds if and only if the exploration of the VFSA does not find any violations to the three conformance properties described above.

3.1 Example

A non-conformant capsule C_1 is shown in Fig. 1a. C_1 has three ports *p1*, *p2*, and *p3*. The CSM of C_1 is shown below the PSMs of each of the ports. The state space of the VFSA corresponding to C_1 is shown in Fig. 1b. A state in the VFSA shows which states the CSM and each of the PSMs are in. (C0, P10, P20, P30) is the initial state of the VFSA and corresponds to the initial states of all state machines on the left. In general, a transition in the VFSA is labeled with $?m/\overline{a}$ where $?m$ is the input message that causes (triggers) the transition and $\overline{a} = a_1 \ldots a_n$ is a possibly empty sequence of actions a_i each of which either is an output message $p_i!m_i$ or some other action language statement (such as an assignment) that the capsule executes in response to the input message. In other words, $?m$ is a message that the capsule C_1 receives on one of its ports

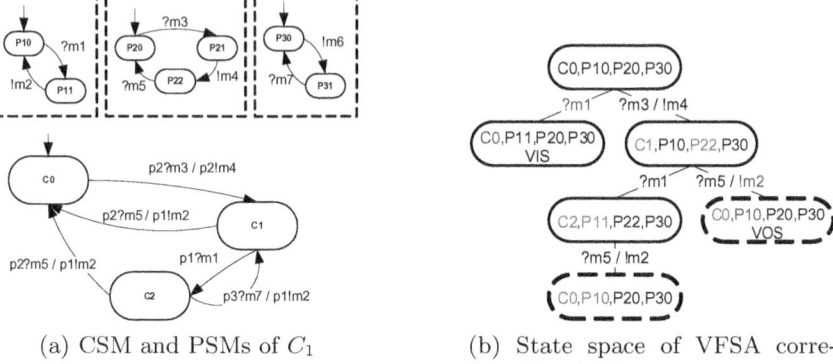

(a) CSM and PSMs of C_1

(b) State space of VFSA corresponding to C_1

Fig. 1. Example of nonconforming capsule C_1 violating Input and Output Safety

from another capsule and each $p_i!m_i$ is a message sent by C_1 to the capsule that is connected to port p_i on C_1. Each transition represents a single "run-to-completion" step and thus may change the state not only of the PSM associated with the port that $?m$ came in on and of the CSM, but also of the PSM of port p_i for each output message $p_i!m_i$. Note that in the examples used in this section, the action sequence $\bar{a}$ is either empty or consists of a single output message $\bar{a} = p!m$. Our case studies in Section 4, however, will consider models with transitions containing action sequences with Java statements.

A violation of Input Safety (VIS) occurs when the input message $?m$ is not enabled in the current state of the CSM. In other words, a port accepts a message that the CSM is currently not able to handle. A violation of Output Safety (VOS) occurs when an output message $p_i!m_i$ destined for port p_i is not enabled in the current state of the PSM associated with p_i. In other words, the CSM intends to send an output message over a port that the port's PSM is currently not able to handle.

For instance, in the initial state (C0, P10, P20, P30), port $p1$ can receive message $?m1$ or port $p2$ can receive $?m3$. In the case of $?m1$, a violation of Input Safety occurs since the capsule does not have a transition defined for that message in location C0. In the case of $?m3$, a transition is triggered which sends message $!m4$ on port $p2$. The VFSA is in state (C1, P10, P22, P30). In this state, the reception of input message $?m5$ on port $p2$ would create a violation of Output Safety, because the capsule would send output message $p1!m2$ which it is not allowed by the PSM of port $p1$.

Fig. 1b shows the result of the exhaustive exploration of the state space of the VFSA corresponding to C_1. VIS and VOS are atomic propositions which indicate, respectively, a violation of Input and Output Safety. A dashed state boundary indicates that the state has already been visited and therefore the subtree rooted at this state does not need to be explored again.

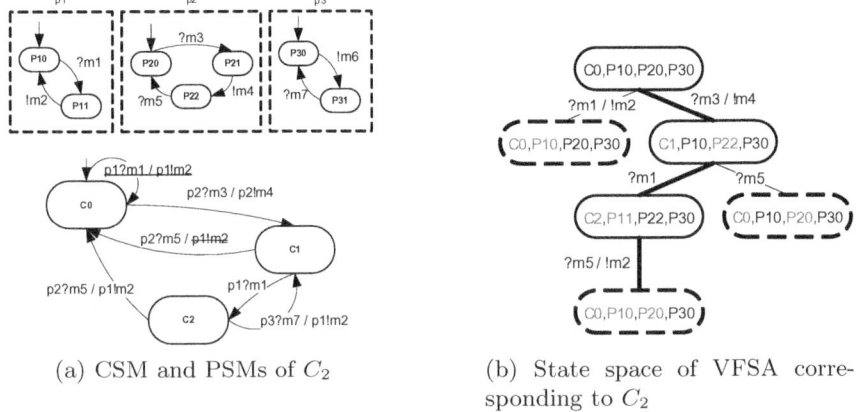

Fig. 2. Example of nonconforming capsule C_2 violating Progress

In Fig. 2, the identified problems have been fixed by adding a transition (label is underlined) and removing an output message. The resulting CSM of C_2 satisfies Input and Output Safety. However, consider the execution indicated by the bold transitions in Fig. 2b. The CSM never sends a message on port $p3$ (i.e., the PSM of $p3$ remains forever in state P30 in which the sending of !$m6$ is enabled), even though the capsule input is *fair* (i.e., all ports eventually receive the input they are expecting). Such executions violate Progress. The final, completely corrected and conformant CSM is shown in Fig. 3.

3.2 Formalization of Conformance Check

We start by formalizing CSMs and PSMs. To avoid confusion, their formal counterparts will be called capsule finite state automata (CFSA) and protocol finite state automata (PFSA), respectively. The formalization of CSMs does not assume a specific action language, but rather leaves the syntax and semantics of actions (i.e., how actions impact the capsule state) unspecified. Moreover, the formalization of CSMs will also ignore many features that our tool readily supports such as nested states, exit and entry actions, and history states, because their inclusion would complicate the explanation of our approach unnecessarily.

Definition 1. *(Capsule Finite State Automaton wrt PN) Given a set of port names PN, a* Capsule Finite State Automaton with respect to PN *($CFSA_{PN}$, also called* Capsule Automaton *for short) is a 4-tuple $(S, s^0, Act_{PN}, \delta)$ where*

1) S is a finite set of capsule states. *A capsule state records the location (active state) that the capsule state machine currently is in and which values the capsule's attributes and variables currently have, that is, $S = Loc \times Val$ where Loc is a finite set of locations and Val is the finite set of valuations.*
2) $s^0 \in S$ is the initial state *of the capsule.*

3) Act_{PN} is a set of actions *consisting of* messages M *and* statements $Stmt$; messages comprise a set of* input messages $M_?$ *of the form* $p?m$ *and* output messages $M_!$ *of the form* $p!m$ *where* $p \in PN$ *and* $m \in MN$ *are port and message names respectively. The message name of an input message may contain variables, while the message name of an output messages may contain action language expressions. Statements are action language statements that are not related to communication such as assignments to attributes and if-then-else statements.*
4) $\delta \subseteq S \times (M_? \times (M_! \cup Stmt)^*) \times S$ is the transition relation. *We assume that transitions containing input actions with variables correctly update the variables using the values provided. Also, for each statement in Stmt, we assume that the transition relation correctly captures the effect of the execution of the statement on the capsule state. For instance, the transition*

$$\big((loc, val), (p?m, x := x + 3), (loc', val')\big)$$

would be triggered by input message ?m received on port p in state (loc, val) and would lead to the value of variable x to be incremented by 3. □

Note that the examples discussed in this section do not contain any statements. Moreover, input messages do not contain variables and output messages do not contain attributes or variables. However, in the case studies to be discussed in Section 4 a subset of Java is used as action language.

Protocol finite state automata formalize Protocol State Machines. To facilitate the definition of conformance, our definition equips them with appropriate atomic propositions and a labeling function.

Definition 2. *(Protocol Finite State Automaton) A Protocol Finite State Automaton (PFSA, or Protocol Automaton for short) is a 6-tuple* $(S, s^0, M, \delta, AP, L)$ *where*

1) S is a finite set of protocol states.
2) $s^0 \in S$ is the initial state.
3) M is the set of messages. M *consists of a set of* input messages $M_?$ *of the form ?m and* output messages $M_!$ *of the form !m where* $m \in MN$ *is the message name. The message name of a message may contain variables.*
4) $\delta \subseteq S \times M \times S$ is the transition relation. δ *is assumed to be deterministic.*
5) $AP = \{enabled_m \mid m \in M_! \cup M_?\}$ is the set of atomic propositions *marking states in which a particular message can be sent or received.*
6) $L \in S \to 2^{AP}$ is a labeling function. *Given a protocol state $s \in S$, $enabled_m \in L(s)$ if and only if $(s, m, s') \in \delta$ for some $s' \in S$.* □

A capsule has ports, a capsule automaton, and attributes.

Definition 3. *(Capsule) A capsule is a triple* (P, CA, A) *where*
1) $P \subseteq Port$ is the capsule's set of ports *where each port has a name and a protocol automaton associated with it, that is, $Port = PN \times PFSA$. Given a port $p \in Port$ with $p = (pn, PA)$, we will use the notation $p.pn = pn$ and $p.PA = PA$ to refer to the port's components.*

2) $CA \in CFSA_{PN}$ is a capsule automaton wrt. the capsule's port names PN.
3) $A \subseteq$ Attribute is the capsule's set of attributes and variables[2]. □

Notation. Given a capsule automaton $CA = (S, s^0, Act_{PN}, \delta) \in CFSA_{PN}$, we will use the following projection notation to refer to the parts of CA: $CA.S = S$, $CA.s^0 = s^0$, $CA.Act_{PN} = Act_{PN}$, and $CA.\delta = \delta$. This notation will also be assumed for protocol automata and capsules.

We can now define the Verification Finite State Automaton corresponding to a capsule. However, due to space limitations, the definition can only be given in an abbreviated form here. Informally, the VFSA is obtained by forming the synchronous composition of the capsule's capsule automaton with the protocol automata on all its ports.

Definition 4. *(Verification Finite State Automaton, abbreviated) Given a capsule $C = (P, CA, A)$, the* Verification Finite State Automaton *(VFSA, also called Verification Automaton for short) corresponding to C is defined to be the automaton $(S, s^0, Act, \delta, AP, L)$ where*

1) the set of verification automaton states *(also called verification states for short)S is given by $S = C.CA.S \times p_1.PA.S \times \ldots \times p_n.PA.S$ for $C.P = \{p_1, \ldots, p_n\}$,*
2) the set of actions *Act is given by the set of actions of the capsule automaton, that is, $Act = C.CA.Act = M_? \cup M_! \cup Stmt$,*
3) the transition relation *$\delta \subseteq S \times (M_? \times (M_! \cup Stmt)^*) \times S$ consists of conforming transitions (δ_{ok}) and nonconforming transitions ($\delta_{\neg ok}$),*
4) the set of atomic propositions *AP is given by $AP = \{VIS, VOS, enabled_{pn,m} \mid pn \in PN \land m \in M_! \cup M_?\}$ where PN is the set of port names used in the capsule automaton $C.CA$.*
5) the labeling function *$L : S \to 2^{AP}$ is used to flag non-conforming states using δ, δ_{ok} and $\delta_{\neg ok}$.* □

Our three conformance properties can now be formalized in Linear Temporal Logic (LTL).

Definition 5. *(Conformance) The capsule automaton of a capsule C is said to conform to the protocol automata of its ports if and only if the verification automaton corresponding to C satisfies the following three LTL formulas:*

1) Input Safety: $\Box(\neg VIS)$
2) Output Safety: $\Box(\neg VOS)$
3) Progress:

$$(\forall p \in C.P \mid \forall ?m \in C.M_? \mid \Box fair(p, ?m)) \Rightarrow$$
$$\forall p \in C.P \mid \forall !m \in C.M_! \mid \Box progress(p, !m)$$

where $fair(p, ?m)$ and $progress(p, !m)$ abbreviate
a) $enabled_{p.name,?m} \Rightarrow \Diamond \neg enabled_{p.name,?m}$, and
b) $enabled_{p.name,!m} \Rightarrow \Diamond \neg enabled_{p.name,!m}$, respectively. □

---

[2] For our purposes, a distinction between variables and attributes is not necessary.

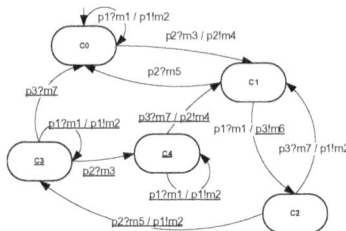
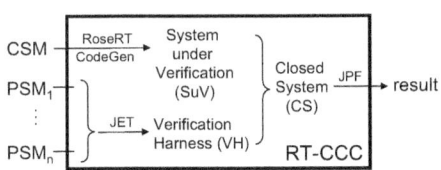

Fig. 3. Final, conformant CSM

Fig. 4. Artifact flow in RT-CCC tool

Progress ensures that whenever a port p is able to send an output message $!m$, then the capsule must eventually send $!m$ over p, i.e., that the execution does not get stuck with respect to $!m$ and p. However, since the occurrence of outputs will in general depend on the prior occurrence of inputs, the formalization requires that an assumption be made about the inputs supplied to the capsule. More precisely, to determine if a capsule can get stuck with respect to $!m$ and p, the verification must only consider *fair* executions, that is, executions along which an input $?m$ enabled at some port q is eventually received on q.

On first glance, it appears that the definition of Progress has an unpleasant side effect: ports with infinite receive cycles (i.e., infinite execution paths in which a message $?m$ can be received continually) will give rise to executions that will not be analyzed for Progress, because $enabled_{p.name,?m}$ never becomes false and these executions will be unconsidered unfair. Also, ports with infinite send cycles (i.e., infinite execution paths in which an output message $!m$ is sent continually) will give rise to executions that will be flagged as violating Progress, because $enabled_{p.name,!m}$ never becomes false. However, these kinds of PSMs are impossible due to the finiteness assumption described in Section 2.2.

Finally, we note that an alternative formalization of input safety would have checked that an input $?m$ enabled at a port p is also enabled at the CSM: $\Box(enabled_{p.name,?m} \Rightarrow enabled_{CSM,?m})$; similarly for output safety.

3.3 Implementation

The conformance check of a UML-RT model created using IBM RoseRT proceeds as follows (see Fig. 4): 1) The user selects a capsule C in this model to be analyzed and selectively enables checks for Input Safety, Output Safety, or Progress as desired. 2) Java code implementing the capsule C and its ports and PSMs is generated and both pieces are combined to form the *System under Verification (SuV)*, i.e., a Java program which captures the behaviours of C's capsule state machine and all its protocol state machines. 3) The SuV is combined with a *Verification Harness (VH)* which executes the SuV non-deterministically using JPF's **choose** statement and checks for safety violations. The resulting Java code, called *Closed System (CS)*, is fed into JPF. The CS is designed in such a way that its reachable state space coincides with that of the VFSA representing C.

```
1   input: Capsule C = (P, CA, A)
2   global
3     variable cState  : C.CA.S;
4     variable pState  : array of C.P.S;
5     variable VIS, VOS ← false : Boolean;
6     variable enabled ← false : array of array of Boolean;
7   begin verificationHarness
8     cState ← C.CA.s⁰;                                          % initialize capsule state
9     for all p ∈ C.P do pState[p] ← p.PA.s⁰;                    % initialize protocol states
10    update(enabled);
11    while (true) do
12      port ← choose({p ∈ C.P | ∃(pState[p], m, s') ∈ C.p.PA.δ_?}); % choose port
13      m_? ← choose({m | (pState[port], m, s') ∈ C.port.PA.δ_?});    % choose input message
14      executeTransition(port, m_?)                                   % take transition
15
16  proc executeTransition(port, m_?)
17    pState[port] ← s' such that (pState[port], m_?, s') ∈ C.port.PA.δ_?;
18    if ∄s' ∈ C.CA.S such that (cState, (m_?, a), s') ∈ C.CA.δ then VIS ← true;
19    acts ← ā such that ∃s' ∈ C.CA.S | (cState, (m_?, ā), s') ∈ C.CA.δ;
20    for all output messages m_i in acts = ⟨m_1,...,m_k⟩ do
21      p_i ← getPort(m_i);                                      % find port m_i is sent over
22      if ∄s' ∈ C.p_i.S such that (pState[p_i], m_i, s') ∈ C.p_i.PA.δ then VOS ← true;
23      pState[p_i] ← s' such that (pState[p_i], m_i, s') ∈ C.p_i.δ_!;
24      cState ← s' such that (cState, (m_?, ā), s') ∈ C.CA.δ    % update capsule state
25    update(enabled)
26  end proc
```

Fig. 5. Pseudo code for Verification Harness (indentation indicates nesting)

4) JPF analyzes the CS. In all our experiments (with one exception), the state space of the CS was small enough to allow exhaustive analysis. If JPF observes a safety or liveness violation, verification stops and an appropriate error message including a detailed execution trace is output.

We describe some of the artifacts and steps in more detail.

Verification Harness. The process described above relies on the correctness of the Closed System, that is, the exploration of the Closed System is tantamount to exploring the VFSA corresponding to C such that C is conformant if and only if an exhaustive search with JPF does not find any violations. We will not formally prove correctness of the CS. Instead, the verification harness of the CS will be described in terms of the formalization as much as possible. Pseudocode for the harness is shown in Fig. 5. Lines 8-10 initialize the harness where $update(enabled)$ is assumed to update $enabled$ correctly to the messages enabled in this state. After nondeterministically choosing a port which has an enabled input message in its current state (line 12), we also choose a message for that port (line 13). The notation $\delta_?$ and $\delta_!$ refers to input transitions and output transitions respectively, i.e., $\delta_? = \{(s, m, s') \in \delta \mid m \in M_?\}$, and $\delta_! = \{(s, m, s') \in \delta \mid m \in M_!\}$. If the input message contains variables (i.e., the capsule expects the environment to also provide data), the choice is extended to range not only over the enabled input messages, but also over finite sets of possible input data values. After updating the port state (line 17), we check Input Safety (line 18) and for all output messages generated by the CSM, Output Safety is checked (line 22) and the port and capsule states are updated appropriately (lines 23 and 24).

Closed System. The Verification Harness (VH) is combined with the System under Verification (SuV) to form the Closed System (CS). Since the action code within the capsule may use RoseRT framework services, JPF must be enabled to handle these services. To this end, a separate verification framework has been implemented since the original cannot be used directly. Also, the framework had to be instrumented for JPF to provide meaningful error traces. Sometimes, our implementation only makes a partial, abstract version of a service available. E.g., the concrete value of a timer is ignored, but care is taken that timeout messages respect timer values, i.e., if two timers t_1 and t_2 are set within the same transition and t_1 has a smaller value than t_2 (i.e., times out sooner), then only the sequence in which t_1's timeout occurs before that of t_2 is considered.

IBM RoseRT ports allow messages to be deferred and recalled. Multiplicity is used to support this functionality. More precisely, every port is given a special instance which has a defer and a recall queue and which is used to defer and recall messages on that port.

Data in input messages is allowed to range over booleans and finite, user-specified ranges of integers only. Alternatively, the CS supports a mode in which variables in choice points in the CSM are left uninterpreted and both choices are explored by JPF. This feature is useful, if, e.g., the message data cannot be encoded as integers or when the exhaustive consideration of all possible input data is not feasible. However, spurious conformance violations now become possible, because the error trace produced may not be feasible.

JPF analysis. The CS is fed into JPF. To implement the check for Input and Output Safety in JPF, simple assertions suffice. However, to implement the check for Progress, we use JPF's *ltl2buchi* package and generate a Büchi automaton from the negated progress formula. If the state space of the CS is finite (only infinitely many possible data values can cause it to be infinite), JPF's analysis of the state space of the CS will terminate. JPF will exhaustively explore all non-deterministic choices in the CS and thus decide conformance.

RT-CCC tool. We have implemented our approach in a publicly available tool called RT-CCC (*UML-RT Capsule Conformance Checker*)[3]. RT-CCC uses JPF as a component and can directly open IBM RoseRT model files. RoseRT's code generation is used to obtain code from the capsule. Since RoseRT's code generation currently does not support PSMs, a model-to-text transformation implemented by us in JET[4] is used to generate Protocol classes which define the ports and the PSMs.

Supported features. RT-CCC supports most UML-RT features. There are no restrictions on PSMs. In the context of CSMs, most features are supported including arbitrary Java action code (in exit points, transitions, and entry points), nested states ("or states"), choice points (branching), deep and shallow history states, and input and output messages with data (as long as it is boolean or

---

[3] Code and case studies available at sourceforge.net/projects/rtccc
[4] Java Emitter Templates; available at www.eclipse.org/modeling/m2t

numerical). In the context of UML-RT, multiplicities on ports and capsules, timers (as long as not more than two are used at any time) and message defer and recall are supported. Currently unsupported are plugin capsules, optional capsules, and message priorities.

4 Case Studies

We report on the use of RT-CCC on three different models with increasing levels of complexity. In each model, a capsule with multiple ports is analyzed and we use RT-CCC iteratively to identify bugs and validate fixes. Each analysis was performed truly compositionally using only the capsule's CSM and PSMs. Performance numbers were obtained using a ThinkPad T61P with 2.5GHz Duo and 2GB RAM. The last two examples are complex enough that RT-CCC repeatedly uncovered new, unexpected violations and proved to be a truly valuable tool for the design of a conforming CSM. Space limitations prevent us for providing more details such as UML-RT artifacts (CSMs or PSMs) or RT-CCC artifacts (e.g., error traces or screen shots); for these and other details, see [10].

ProductionLine example: Our simplest model simulates a basic production line and consists of a *Controller* capsule and a *ProductionLine* capsule which contains a *Robot* and a *WorkStation*. The *Workstation* manufactures "widgets" which are delivered by the *Robot*. The *Controller* has four ports: two connecting it with the *WorkStation* and the *Robot*, respectively, together with a *Timer* and a *Logging* port. The analysis with RT-CCC gives rise to six corrections to the CSM of the *Controller*. All violations were found in less than a second. The state space of this example was trivial: each of the CSM and the two PSMs had five locations, the amount of action code was minimal.

Internet device driver example: Our second model is inspired by the contract for a network device driver (*NicDevice*) used in [4]. The model uses a fairly complex protocol that allows a system to interact with a device. The device capsule has three user-defined ports which are used to communicate with (1) three sensors (the associated port thus has multiplicity three), (2) a monitor, and (3) a controller. A total of nine different input messages (two with integer data) and four output messages are used. The three PSMs have between three and six locations and the CSM is hierarchical with a total of 13 locations distributed over two levels of nesting. Nine analyze-and-edit iterations were necessary to make the initial CSM conformant. The performance of the exhaustive check of the final model are given in Table 1.

ATM example: The last case study models an ATM. The checked capsule has six ports over which 17 different input messages (four with numerical input) and 13 different output messages flow. The CSM has 32 locations distributed over five levels of nesting. Ten analyze-and-edit iterations were necessary. A safety violation is found in less than a minute in each of the first eight. The performance of the exhaustive check of the final model are given in Table 1. Due to the use of data and the large size of the Büchi automaton encoding

Table 1. JPF performance metrics for exhaustive conformance checks of last two examples (dnf = "did not finish")

Example	Type of check	Memory (MB)	Visited states	Time (h:mm:ss)
NicDevice	Safety	51	1776	0:00:15
NicDevice	Progress	1039	799354	2:18:44
ATM	Safety	1488	288064	1:16:25
ATM	Progress	dnf	dnf	dnf

the progress property, the progress check did not complete. However, checks involving progress properties specialized to individual ports did complete and allowed us to identify progress violations.

5 Related Work

No approach has been found that allows protocol conformance verification of UML-RT models that have been created with an UML-RT tool and that have the kind of features found in industrial models such as Java action code, timers, defer and recall of messages, and multiple instantiation of ports and protocols. A large number of related papers either do not go far enough (e.g., [23,13,14]), or are sufficiently different (e.g., [11,7,15,1,24]), that a more detailed comparison does not appear productive. Instead, we will focus on the following four groups of work which we deem most closely related:

(1) Formal definitions of CSMs, PSMs, and conformance are presented in [19] and inspired our safety properties. However, conformance checking of an existing CSM is not discussed. The formalization of conformance in [6] contains a rule similar to our progress property. An algorithm for conformance checking is presented, however, data is not supported and no implementation is mentioned.
(2) The two papers by Engels et al. [2,3] are concerned with the formal analysis of UML-RT models using CSP. In [3], a pair of CSMs connected via a protocol is translated into a CSP process which is then checked for deadlock using the FDR tool. In [2], a methodology is presented for checking the consistency of the communication between two capsules where consistency is defined as deadlock freedom and a CSP-based formalization similar to the one in [3] is used. The definition of protocol conformance is thus based on the communication behaviour between two capsules, and neither paper analyzes a single capsule in isolation. While the use of the FDR tool is described, no implementation is mentioned that allows the direct analysis of UML-RT models.
(3) The work by Giese et al. in [5] brings modular development and analysis to timed state machines via the assume/guarantee paradigm. Development proceeds by (a) identifying composition patterns, (b) verifying them with respect to the guarantees that they are supposed to make, (c) designing components and assigning them to the ports in the pattern, and then (d) verifying the components with respect to the assumptions that the pattern makes. Theoretical machinery is presented that ensures that the resulting system satisfies the pattern constraints and component invariants. The work is more broadly scoped due

to its support of communication patterns and pattern refinement. The various artifacts are described using mathematical notation (e.g., automata, RT-OCL) only, rather than UML-RT as in our case. Nonetheless, similarities exist, e.g., role automata correspond to PSMs and protocol conformance arises as refinement which is checked in step (d) above.

(4) The Singularity OS has already been mentioned [4]. Channels are used exclusively to implement communication between processes written in Sing#, an extension of C#. Channel contracts are used to define acceptable message sequences in form of finite state machines. In contrast to our work, static analysis is used to check processes expressed in an entirely textual language (the potential for false positives is not discussed, though); moreover, only an informal definition of conformance is given which does not seem to include Progress ("the sequence of messages observed on channels correspond to the channel contract" [4, 184]).

6 Conclusion

We have presented an approach and a publicly available tool to check the conformance of a UML-RT capsule state machine to the PSMs of its ports. The approach defines conformance as two safety properties and a liveness property and reduces the conformance verification to the analysis of the synchronous composition of the capsule state machine with all its PSMs. To implement the analysis we have taken advantage of JPF and of the code generation facilities of IBM RoseRT which allows the direct analysis of the code generated by an MDD tool from the model. Our approach requires that the PSMs satisfy certain conditions (autonomy and finiteness) which had already been proposed for the analysis of the channel contracts in Microsoft's Singularity operating system. The approach works on a large enough subset of UML-RT that makes it interesting for industrial UML-RT models.

Our case studies confirmed that the design of protocol-conformant capsule state machines is not trivial and benefits substantially from the availability of an automatic conformance analysis such as the one offered by our tool. Overall, the performance of the analysis was promising with, not surprisingly, the check of the liveness property dominating the costs of checking the safety properties. More work on optimizing the liveness check may improve its performance. We conclude that automatic protocol conformance verification via software model checking is realistic and represents a promising avenue to increase the utility and adoption of interface specifications enriched with PSMs.

References

1. Ball, T., Cook, B., Levin, V., Rajamani, S.K.: SLAM and Static Driver Verifier: Technology Transfer of Formal Methods inside Microsoft. In: Boiten, E.A., Derrick, J., Smith, G.P. (eds.) IFM 2004. LNCS, vol. 2999, pp. 1–20. Springer, Heidelberg (2004)
2. Engels, G., Küster, J.M., Heckel, R., Groenewegen, L.: A Methodology for Specifying and Analyzing Consistency of Object-Oriented Behavioral Models. In: ESEC/FSE 2001, Vienna, Austria, pp. 186–195 (2001)

3. Engels, G., Küster, J., Heckel, R., Lohmann, M.: Model-Based Verification and Validation of Properties. ENTCS 82(7), 133–150 (2003)
4. Fähndrich, M., Aiken, M., Hawblitzel, C., Hodson, O., Hunt, G., Larus, J., Levi, S.: Language Support for Fast and Reliable Message-Based Communication in Singularity OS. In: EuroSys, pp. 177–190 (2006)
5. Giese, H., Tichy, M., Burmester, S., Flake, S.: Towards the Compositional Verification of Real-Time UML Designs. In: ESEC/FSE 2003, pp. 38–47 (2003)
6. Giordano, L., Martelli, A.: Verifying Agent Conformance with Protocols Specified in a Temporal Action Logic. In: Artif. Intelligence and Human-Oriented Computing, pp. 145–156 (2007)
7. Honda, K., Vasconcelos, V., Kubo, M.: Language Primitives and Type Discipline for Structured Communication-Based Programming. In: Programming Languages and Systems, pp. 33–37 (1998)
8. Hunt, G., Larus, J.: Singularity: Rethinking the Software Stack. SIGOPS Oper. Syst. Rev. 41(2), 37–49 (2007)
9. Jhala, R., Majumdar, R.: Software model checking. ACM Comput. Surv. 41(4), 1–54 (2009)
10. Moffett, Y.: UML-RT Protocol Conformance Verification through Exhaustive Exploration - From Theory to Implementation. MSc thesis, Royal Military College of Canada (2010), http://www.cs.queensu.ca/~dingel/moffettMSc.pdf
11. Nierstrasz, O.: Regular Types for Active Objects. SIGPLAN Not. 28(10), 1–15 (1993)
12. Object Management Group. UML 2.0 Superstructure Specification. Technical report, OMG (August 2005)
13. Saaltink, M.: Using SPIN to analyse ROOM models. Technical Report TR-99-5537-02, ORA Canada (1999)
14. Saaltink, M., Meisels, I.: Using SPIN to analyse RoseRT models. Technical Report TR-99-5537-03, ORA Canada (October 1999)
15. Schäfer, T., Knapp, A., Merz, S.: Model Checking UML State Machines and Collaborations. ENTCS 55, 1–13 (2004)
16. Selic, B.: Using UML for Modeling Complex Real-Time Systems. In: Languages, Compilers, and Tools for Embedded Systems, pp. 250–260 (1998)
17. Selic, B.: Personal communication (January 2011)
18. Selic, B., Gullekson, G., Ward, P.: Real-Time Object-Oriented Modeling. Wiley, Chichester (1994)
19. Shigo, O., Okawa, A., Kato, D.: Constructing Behavioral State Machine using Interface Protocol Specification. In: APSEC 2006, pp. 191–198 (2006)
20. Stengel, A., Bultan, T.: Analyzing Singularity Channel Contracts. In: 18th Intern. Symp. on Softw. Testing and Analysis (ISSTA 2008). ACM, New York (2009)
21. Tran, V., Hashimoto, H., Tanabe, Y., Hagiya, M.: Verification of Java Programs under Fairness Assumption. In: 25th Conf. of Japan Society for Softw. Sci. and Techn. (2008)
22. Visser, W., Havelund, K., Brat, G., Park, S., Lerda, F.: Model Checking Programs. Autom. Softw. Eng. 10(2), 203–232 (2003)
23. Whittaker, P., Goldsmith, M., Macolini, K., Teitelbaum, T.: Model checking UML-RT protocols. In: Workshop on Formal Design Techniques for Real-Time UML, York, UK (November 2000)
24. Witkowski, T., Blanc, N., Kroening, D., Weissenbacher, G.: Model Checking Concurrent Linux Device Drivers. In: Intern. Conf. on Autom. Soft. Eng. (ASE 2007). ACM, New York (2007)

Model-Based Coverage-Driven Test Suite Generation for Software Product Lines

Harald Cichos[1], Sebastian Oster[1], Malte Lochau[2], and Andy Schürr[1]

[1] TU Darmstadt
Real-Time Systems Lab
{cichos,oster,schuerr}@es.tu-darmstadt.de
[2] TU Braunschweig
Institute for Programming and Reactive Systems
lochau@ips.cs.tu-bs.de

Abstract. Software Product Line (SPL) engineering is a popular approach for the systematic reuse of software artifacts across a large number of similar products. Unfortunately, testing each product of an SPL separately is often unfeasible. Consequently, SPL engineering is in conflict with standards like ISO 26262, which require each installed software configuration of safety-critical SPLs to be tested using a model-based approach with well-defined coverage criteria.

In this paper we address this dilemma and present a new SPL test suite generation algorithm that uses model-based testing techniques to derive a small test suite from one variable 150% test model of the SPL such that a given coverage criterion is satisfied for the test model of every product. Furthermore, our algorithm simplifies the subsequent selection of a small, representative set of products (w.r.t. the given coverage criterion) on which the generated test suite can be executed.

1 Introduction

Software Product Line (SPL) engineering is a popular approach for the systematic reuse of software artifacts across a large number of similar products [1]. Unfortunately, engineers of different domains are nowadays developing SPLs for embedded, safety-critical systems without knowing how to test the large number of their product configurations systematically and efficiently in strict accordance with new software development standards. For example the new standard ISO 26262 [2] for safety-critical automotive software recommends that each software configurations has been tested thoroughly using model-based techniques and guaranteeing degrees of coverage according to certain criteria. But, nowadays, in the automotive industry almost every car of a certain brand has its individual software configuration, so it is difficult to comply with this recommendation. So far, SPL testing approaches are not able to efficiently test large SPLs thoroughly for the following reasons: First of all, testing every single product configuration of an SPL individually by using common testing techniques is not acceptable for large SPLs [3]. Furthermore, testing all actually used products only following a *demand-driven approach* is inacceptable, too, due to the still large number of relevant products and the fact that the time available at the end of an assembly line for testing a just instantiated product is limited. Even exploiting *regression-based techniques* on SPLs to reduce the efforts for testing a single product based on the already spent efforts for testing other similar products previously is unfeasible as long as precise definitions of "similarity" w.r.t. a chosen coverage criterion are missing [4]. Finally, successfully used *subset selection heuristics* which generate small sets of products that are assumed to be representative for all SPL products are improper for testing safety-critical software systems as long as there is no proof that this small set is *really* representative.

We address this problem and present a new model-based coverage-criteria-driven approach for safety-critical SPL testing. We can prove that our new SPL test suite generation algorithm efficiently generates a set of test cases (*test suite*) that achieves a *complete* test model coverage for *every* product of an SPL w.r.t. the chosen coverage criterion. For this purpose, our approach makes use of the 150% test model [5] which contains all test models of an SPL as special cases. By using the 150% test model it is possible to determine if a created a test case is executable on more than one product. Additionally, our approach utilizes the Quine-McCluskey algorithm [6] (a method used for minimization of boolean functions) that helps to efficiently keep a record of all product configurations which are left to be processed. This makes it possible to create a test suite that achieves a *complete* test model coverage for *every* product of an SPL without processing each product individually. Furthermore, during test suite generation our algorithm gathers information that simplifies the subsequent selection of a small, representative set of products on which this test suite can be executed. To identify a small, representative set of products of an SPL, for every test-model-driven approach it is necessary to assume that products with similar behaviors specified in their test models have similar implementations, i.e. produce the same verdicts for a test case that has identical traces in their related test models.

The remainder of the paper is organized as follows: In the following section we introduce domain specific terms. After that, we present our approach in detail in Section 3 and discuss it in Section 4. In the subsequent Section 5, we show how our work stands out from related work. Finally, in Section 6 we conclude the paper and present our plans for future work.

2 Basic Terms of SPL Testing

In the following we explain basic terms from the domain of SPL testing and model-based testing. A *software product line* (SPL) defines a set of features $F = \{f_1, f_2, \ldots f_n\}$. *Features* are increments of functionality explicitly stating commonality and variability parameters for *product configurations* of the SPL [7]. Theses features are combined into one software product which is interacting with components of the environment, i.e. sensors and actuators.

In this paper we use an embedded Alarm System (AS) SPL as running example. This SPL provides nine features $F_{AS} = \{AS, C, O, P, W, S, V, M, U\}$

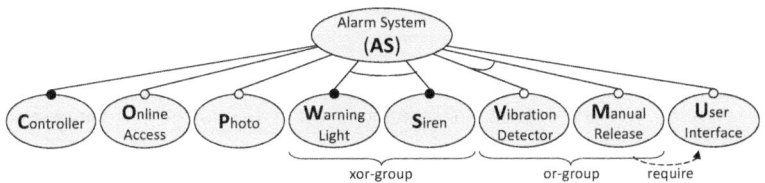

Fig. 1. Feature Model of the AS SPL

(cf. Figure 1). Depending on which features are integrated the functionality of a product in the AS SPL varies. The AS SPL contains products with up to two alarm levels. The alarm is set off if it is released manually (req. M) or the vibration detector detects a vibration over a certain time (req. V). By entering the first level, an alarm signal is sent out by a siren (req. S) or warning light (req. W). When the vibration did not stop after a certain time, the system enters level two. Entering this level the system may call the police (req. O) and/or send an evidence photo to the police (req. P). Additionally, the SPL offers the feature that a photo will be taken as security measure when a user interacts with the environment of the system (req. U).

In Figure 1 the features of the AS SPL are arranged in a FODA *feature model* [7]. The root node of a feature model is a special mandatory feature denoting the name of the whole SPL. Subnodes introduce further variabilities to their parent feature nodes: singleton subfeatures can be either *mandatory* or *optional* variabilities for their parent features, and groups of subfeatures define either or or xor (i.e. *alternative*) subset constraints among features in that group. Consequently, feature models introduce dependencies and constraints on feature combinations, thus limiting the set $\mathcal{P}(F)$ of potential combinations to a subset of *valid product configurations* $PC = \{pc_1, pc_2, \ldots, pc_k\} \subseteq \mathcal{P}(F)$ where each $pc_i \in PC$ corresponds to exactly one subset of selected features of F. Due to the constraints in the feature model of the AS SPL 32 valid product configurations exist, e.g. $pc_i = \{AS, C, P, S, U, V\}$.

In model-based testing, *test models* are used to specify the abstract behavior of one corresponding system-under-test. A test model tm is used to derive a set of test cases (*test suite*) that satisfy certain *coverage criteria*. The derivation happens either manually or automatically by using a test case generator. In this paper, we use deterministic *state machines* as test models, simply consisting of sets of states and transitions.

In SPL testing, each valid product configuration has its own test model. This results in a large number of test models $TM = \{tm_1, \ldots, tm_k\}$. A function $map : PC \rightarrow TM$ maps any valid product configuration $pc_i \in PC$ onto its defined test model $tm_i = map(pc_i)$. We require map to be a bijection, thus every product configuration $pc_i \in PC$ owns a unique behavioral specification tm_i.

To achieve a better maintainability and a better overall view in SPL testing it makes sense to combine all test models of an SPL, which usually are rather similar, into one "super" test model stm, a so-called *150% test model*. For the

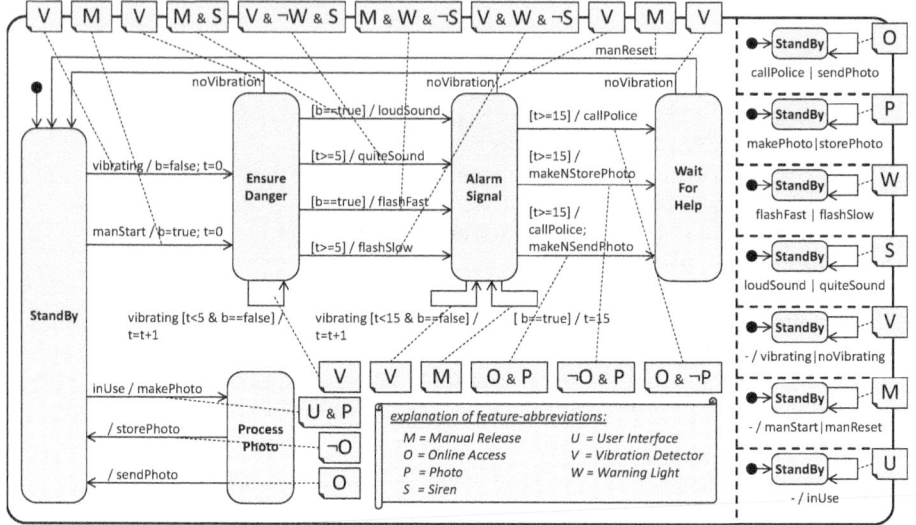

Fig. 2. 150% Test Model of the AS SPL with Annotated Selection Conditions

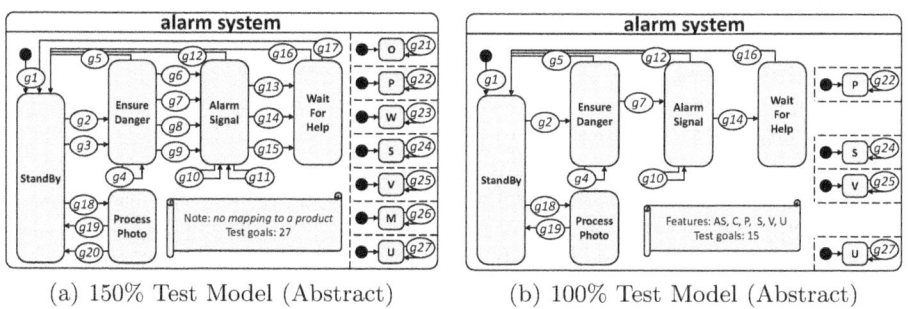

(a) 150% Test Model (Abstract)   (b) 100% Test Model (Abstract)

Fig. 3. Abstract Test Models of the AS SPL with Annotated Test Goals (Transitions)

sake of a better discriminability, in the following, we call a test model for one specific product a *100% test model*. Each 100% test model $tm \in TM$ consists of a subset of states and transitions of the 150% test model stm, which is usually not an element of TM [5]. In our 150% test model, map is implemented by annotating states and transitions with logical formulas as *selection conditions* defined over features in F, which is exemplarily depicted in Figure 2. The 100% test model $tm_i = map(pc_i)$ for product configuration $pc_i \in PC$ can be derived by removing those states and transitions from the 150% model stm whose selection conditions are *not* satisfied for the feature combination in pc_i. For example, in Figure 3(b) the 100% test model of a product of the AS SPL is depicted.

Usually, in a testing process it is hard to know when to stop testing, thus a test end criterion must be selected. In model-based testing such test end criteria are usually defined by means of *coverage criteria*, concerning fragments of a test model to be traversed in test case executions. Therefore, coverage criteria impose requirements for test suite generation from test models. Applied to test model tm, a criterion C selects sets of model fragments, so-called *test goals* $G = \{g_1, g_2, \ldots, g_l\}$, that refer to state machine artifacts, e.g., *all-states*, *all-transitions*, *all-transition-pairs*, etc. [8]. In this paper the set of test goals G is selected using the 150% test model stm as input. This set of test goals G is a superset of all test goals of all 100% test models of the SPL. For instance, considering *all-transitions-coverage* criterion applied to the 150% test model of the AS SPL selects all transitions as test goals, thus leading to 27 test goals $G = \{g_1, g_2, \ldots, g_{27}\}$ as shown in Fig. 3(a). Correspondingly, each 100% test model $tm_i \in TM$ contains a subset $G_i \subseteq G$ of these test goals depending on the transitions selected from stm via map. For instance, the 100% test model in Figure 3(b) owns 15 goals.

A *test case* consists of a sequence of inputs and expected outputs. A *test suite* $T = \{t_1, t_2, \ldots, t_m\}$ is a set of test cases $t_i \in T$. For a test suite T generated from a 150% test model stm, each test case $t_i \in T$ corresponds to a unique execution path of transitions in stm. We consider the following relations:

- $exec \subseteq T \times TM$, where $exec(t, tm) :\Leftrightarrow$ test case t is *executable* on the 100% test model tm, i.e., the execution path of t is contained in tm as it only consists of transitions of stm mapped into tm via map,
- $satisfy \subseteq T \times G$, where $satisfy(t, g) :\Leftrightarrow$ the execution of test case t *satisfies* test goal g selected for some coverage criterion C on stm, and
- $valid \subseteq T \times G \times PC$, where $valid(t, g, pc) :\Leftrightarrow satisfy(t, g) \wedge exec(t, map(pc))$, i.e., test case t is *valid* for test goal g on product pc if it is executable on the test model of product configuration pc and satisfies test goal g.

3 Complete SPL Test Suites

An *SPL test suite* $TS = (T', PC')$ contains test cases $t' \in T'$ for a set of products $PC' \subseteq PC$ of the SPL. We denote the set of all SPL test suites by $TS_{SPL} = \mathcal{P}(T) \times \mathcal{P}(PC)$, where T refers to the set of all test cases executable on stm. A *complete* SPL test suite TS_C achieves a *complete* test model coverage for every product of the SPL w.r.t. a certain coverage criterion C which defines a set of test goals G.

Definition 1. *(Complete SPL Test Suite)*
SPL test suite $TS_C = (T_C, PC') \in TS_{SPL}$ with a set of test cases $T_C \subseteq T$ and valid product configurations $PC' \subseteq PC$ is complete *for a set of test goals G, iff*

$$\forall g \in G, pc \in PC : (\exists t \in T : valid(t, g, pc) \Rightarrow (\exists t_g \in T_C : valid(t_g, g, pc))$$

The easiest way to obtain *complete* test model coverage for every product of the SPL is to compute for each 100% test model of an SPL a test suite that achieves complete coverage, and, afterwards, combine all test suites to TS_C.

This procedure follows a product-by-product approach and is inefficient for large SPLs. Instead, our algorithm avoids the iteration over every single PC. Our algorithm analyzes each created test case and if this test case is valid for more than one PC, all the PCs in this set are processed at once. For this purpose, our approach computes TS_C by deriving test cases from the 150% test model of an SPL and not from each 100% test model.

An SPL test suite derived from the 150% test model is *complete* if for all products of an SPL and for each test goal g in the 150% test model, this SPL test suite contains at least one test case $t_g \in T_C$ such that $valid(t_g, g, pc)$ is true for every product configuration $pc \in PC$ whose 100% test model contains the respective test goal g. It is important to recognize that a complete SPL test suite derived from a 150% test model is a superset of a test suite that achieves a complete 150% test model coverage under the assumption that both test suites use the same coverage criterion.

During test suite generation, our approach already associates each test case with a set of PCs for which this test case is valid. After the test suite generation is finished, these associated sets make it easier to select a small, representative set of products $PC_R \subseteq PC$ for the complete SPL test suite.

Definition 2. *(Representative Set of Products)*
A set of products $PC_R \subseteq PC$ of a complete SPL test suite $TS_C = (T_C, PC_R) \in TS_{SPL}$ is representative *for all product configurations PC, iff*

$$\forall g \in G, pc \in PC, t_g \in T_C : valid(t_g, g, pc) \Rightarrow (\exists pc_R \in PC_R : valid(t_g, g, pc_R))$$

3.1 Complete SPL Test Suite Generation – An Example

In this section, we explain our *complete SPL test suite generation* algorithm by applying it to the 150% test model of the AS SPL. The following explanation refers to the pseudo code of the algorithm in Figure 4. Additionally, we use Figure 5 to illustrate each step in the pseudo code.

Our algorithm iterates over all test goals and repeats each time the same steps (cf. line 7 of Figure 4). Consequently, it is sufficient to focus on one test goal. We chose test goal 14 (cf. Figure 3(a)). Out of all 32 valid PCs only 10 PCs have a corresponding 100% test model that contains test goal 14. For each of these 10 PCs at least one valid test case has to be created. Using a common product-by-product approach, it would be necessary to create 10 test cases - one for each PC. Applying our algorithm, only 4 instead of 10 test cases are created.

At the beginning (cf. first iteration in Figure 5), the test suite is empty and does not contain any test cases that satisfy test goal 14 for any PC, respectively. Before test case generation starts, the set of not yet processed PCs (*processPCset*) is reduced from 512 PCs to 32 valid PCs due to the constraints of the feature model (cf. line 9). The resulting formula is minimized to a DNF-formula by applying the well-known Quine-McCluskey algorithm [6]. This is necessary to efficiently keep a record of all PCs which are left to be processed. This minimized DNF-formula is depicted in *processPCset* of the first iteration

```
1   SuperTestModel stm;                    // 150% test model
2   dnfFormula processPCset := empty;      // DNF formula that describes set of not yet processed product configurations
3   cFormula inputPCset, outputPCset;      // conjunctions describing subsets of (un-)processed product configurations
4   List<TestCase> testsuite := empty;     // generated representative set of all product configurations plus test cases
5
6   // create for each test goal in G a representative set of test products plus test cases
7   for each g in G do {
8       // translate feature model with all constraints into DNF formula
9       processPCset := QMC.minimizeDNF( FeatureModel.getConstraintsAsPropositionalLogicFormula() );
10      do {
11          // select conjunction in DNF formula that references the smallest number of features
12          inputPCset := processPCset.getTermWithSmallestNumberOfLiterals();
13          // try to create a test case for selected subset inputPCset
14          testcase := TestCaseGenerator.create( g, inputPCset , stm );
15
16          if testcase was created then {
17              // find set of PCs for which testcase is valid by analyzing its feature-flags
18              outputPCset := FlagAnalyzer.findPCset( testcase );
19              testsuite.add( testcase , outputPCset );
20              // remove successfully processed subset of product configurations from DNF description
21              processPCset := QMC.minimizeDNF( processPCset ∧ ¬outputPCset );
22          } else {
23              // removes subset for which no test case was found from the set of all not yet processed PCs
24              processPCset := QMC.minimizeDNF( processPCset ∧ ¬inputPCset );
25          }
26      } while ( processPCset ≠ empty )
27  }
```

Fig. 4. Algorithm to Generate a Complete SPL Test Suite

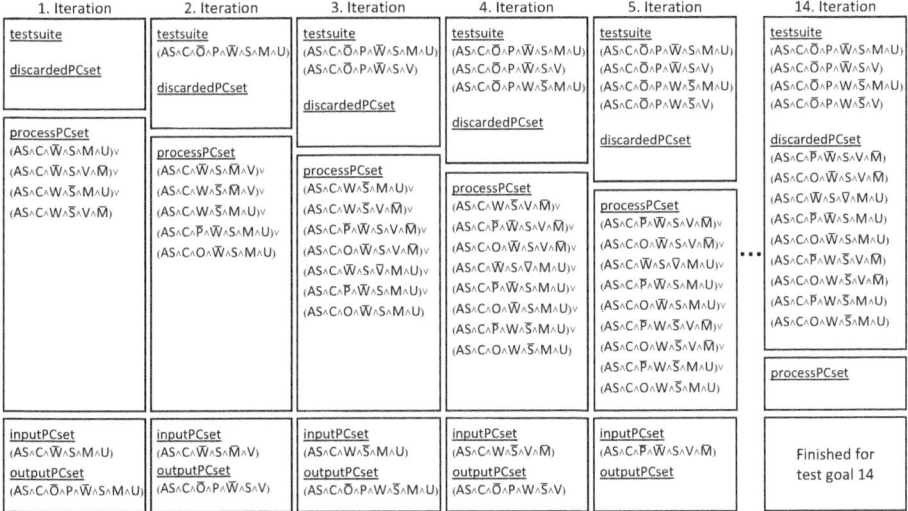

Fig. 5. Generating Test Cases for Test Goal 14 from the AS SPL 150% Test Model

in Figure 5. After that, for efficiency reasons a subformula $inputPCset$ of the formula $processPCset$ is selected which references the smallest number of features of the SPL (one of the conjunctions of $processPCset$ which has a DNF representation). The subformula $inputPCset$ represents the set of all PCs that contain features AS, C, S, M, and U, but not W. This subformula is passed to the test case generator combined with the 150% test model and test goal 14 (cf. line 14). The test case generator creates a test case for any appropriate PC in this passed set of PCs, represented by the subformula $inputPCset$. Due to some preparations in the 150% test model of the AS SPL (see Sections 3.2 and 3.3) it is possible to identify all PCs for which the generated test case is also valid (cf. line 18). These PCs are described by $outputPCset$. In the first iteration $outputPCset$ describes two PCs ($AS \land C \land \neg O \land P \land \neg W \land S \land M \land U \land (V \lor \neg V)$). Next, the generated test case and its associated PCs ($outputPCset$), for which the test case is valid, is added to the test suite (cf. line 19). Finally, due to the fact that a valid test case was created that satisfies test goal 14 for the two PCs described by $outputPCset$, these two PCs are excluded from the unprocessed PCs in $processPCset$ (cf. line 21). In the second iteration, the test suite contains the previously generated test case. From the 2nd to 4th iteration, three additional test cases are created. In the 5th iteration, four test cases that satisfies test goal 14 were generated. For each of these 10 PCs, one of these four test cases is valid owing to their different execution paths in the 150% test model. That means for any of these 10 PCs at least one test case is executable on the corresponding 100% test model and satisfies test goal 14. From the 5th to 14th iteration the test case generator cannot create any more test cases for the remaining 22 PCs in $processPCset$ because there exists no test case satisfying test goal 14. The number of iterations needed from the 5th iteration to the end can be shortened by selecting more than one conjunction in line 12. Summarizing, our algorithm generated not more than 4 test cases satisfying test goal 14 for 10 PCs of the AS SPL compared to 10 test cases generated by an product-by-product approach.

3.2 150% Test Model Preparation

The derivation of a *complete SPL test suite* TS_C from a 150% test model stm requires an appropriate *test case generator*. So far, common test case generators support interfaces to pass the test goal g and the test model tm, i.e. `createTestCase(g,tm)`. But this is insufficient for the generation of test cases from a 150% test model stm. It is necessary to pass a valid product configuration $pc \in PC$ as well, such that the test case generator can instantiate the corresponding 100% test model from stm. Consequently, an appropriate test case generator must support at least the interface `createTestCase(g,stm,pc)`.

Prior to test case generation, an embedding of the mapping function map (see Section 2) into the 150% test model is to be provided. More precisely, each transition which is annotated by a selection condition now includes this condition as additional clause in its transition guard (cf. Figure 6). After that, only *valid* test cases for a valid product configuration pc are generated from 150% test model stm by internally instantiating it to the 100% test model $tm = map(pc)$.

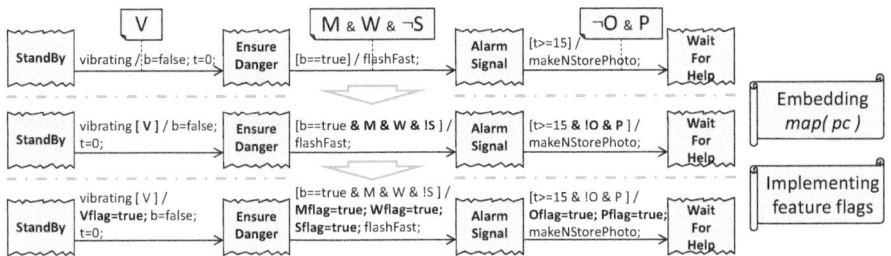

Fig. 6. 150% Test Model Preparation for SPL Test Suite Generation

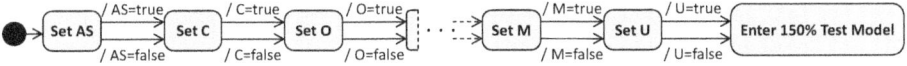

Fig. 7. Setup Section for the 150% Test Model of the AS SPL

We use the model-based testing framework Azmun [9] as test case generator, which is based on the model checker NuSMV. We extended Azmun by implementing a plug-in that supports the interface createTestCase(g,stm,PC_I). As third input parameter we use a *set* of product configurations $PC_I \subseteq PC$ instead of a single product configuration $pc \in PC$. The advantage is that the test case generator has the possibility to search in this set PC_I of product configurations for any product configuration $pc \in PC_I$ for which a *valid* test case t for test goal g exists in the corresponding test model $tm = map(pc)$. If no test case for test goal g can be found, then there exists no test case for test goal g for any of these product configurations in PC_I. In this case, all $pc \in PC_I$ were processed in one go and discarded (as irrelevant) for this specific test goal (cf. *discardedPCset* in Figure 5). In our algorithm, we specify the input set of product configurations PC_I in an implicit way using a propositional formula *inputPCset* (cf. line 14 in Figure 4). Examples for such formulas *inputPCset* are depicted in Figure 5. *inputPCset* assigns conditional values to some features in F, denoting either presence (*true*) or absence (*false*) constraints on those features to hold for all product configurations in PC_I. The formula then conjuncts all predicates over features for which a constraint is given.

In the usual case, PC_I contains more than one product configuration. To ensure that a created test case is *valid* for at least one $pc \in PC_I$, it must be guaranteed that the variable 150% test model is instantiated to exactly one 100% test model before the test case generator starts searching for the test case. This is achieved by determining the product configuration beforehand. Therefore, we add a *setup section* to the 150% test model consisting of a chain of transitions for setting the *feature variable* of each feature, depending on whether this feature should be *present* (true) or *absent* (false). In Figure 7, the setup section of the AS SPL 150% test model is depicted. The test case generator arbitrarily decides the presence/absence for each feature provided that the resultant product configuration pc is in PC_I.

By initially running through some path of this setup section, the test case generator configures the subsequent 100% test model to be $tm = map(pc)$. When this setup is completed, the values of the feature variables cannot be changed afterwards in the 150% test model. For considering another $pc' \in PC$, the setup section has to be traversed again.

Owing to these arrangements it is guaranteed that a valid test case will be derived from the 150% test model if a valid set of product configurations will be passed to the test case generator.

3.3 Valid Test Case for a Set of Product Configurations

As described previously, the test case generator creates (if possible) a test case t for test goal g from the 150% test model for *some* appropriate product configuration $pc \in PC_I$. Usually, the created test case t is valid for many PCs. By $PC_O \subseteq PC$, we refer to the set of *output* product configurations for which the generated test case t is valid. There exists at least one $pc \in PC_O \cap PC_I$. To derive the whole set PC_O, it is necessary to know which features must be present and which features must be absent in the product configuration of each $pc' \in PC_O$ to traverse the transitions of the execution path of the test case. For that reason, we keep a record which features' presence or absence is necessary for the execution of the generated test case.

This is done using a flag variable for each feature. These flags are implemented in the action part of transitions in stm. As a result, a flag is set to true if exactly this value of the corresponding feature variable is necessary to traverse at least one transition in the execution path of the test case. If this flag remains false (default value) then the presence or absence of the corresponding feature has no impact on whether the generated test case is executable on $pc' \in PC_O$.

For example, consider Figure 6: to traverse the second transition the feature M and W must be present, but feature S must be absent. For that reason, the corresponding flags Mflag, Wflag, and Sflag are set to *true* in the action part. By analyzing the values of the feature variable and the feature flag of each corresponding feature $f \in F$, it is possible to determine for which PCs the test case t is valid. In our algorithm, PC_O is specified by a formula *outputPCset* (cf. line 18 in Figure 4) which is constructed by conjunction of values of feature variables whose corresponding flags are set to true.

3.4 Complete SPL Test Suite Generation

The following descriptions relate to the algorithm presented in Figure 4 as well as to Definition 1 and 2. A full execution of the presented algorithm generates an SPL test suite $TS_C = (T_C, PC_R) \in TS_{SPL}$ from a given 150% test model of the SPL for coverage criterion C.

Theorem 1. *SPL test suite $TS_C = (T_C, PC_R)$, $T_C \subseteq T$, is complete and the set $PC_R \subseteq PC$ of products is representative w.r.t. to coverage criterion C.*

Sketch of Proof: For each test goal g in the 150% test model the outer loop (cf. line 7-27) generates a formula *processPCset* that describes all the valid PCs that have not yet been processed and for which a valid test case has to be generated. Afterwards, the inner loop (cf. line 10-26) generates a subformula *inputPCset* of the formula *processPCset* (cf. line 12) that describes a subset of those PCs for which a test case that satisfies g is still missing. Then, the algorithm generates (if possible) for one product configuration in the set of PCs described by *inputPCset* a new test case t for test goal g (cf. line 14). If such a test case t does not exist then the formula *inputPCset* describes a set of PCs for which no test case exists such that test goal g is satisfied. Otherwise, the test case t is added to the test suite combined with the associated set of PCs described by *outputPCset* (cf. line 19). The formula *outputPCset* characterizes a nonempty subset of *processPCset* for which the created test case t is valid (cf. line 18 or see Section 3.3). The inner loop ends by computing a new formula that describes the *new* set of not yet processed PCs by concatenating the old formula stored in *processPCset* with the negation of either *outputPCset* (cf. line 21) or *inputPCset* (cf. line 24).

In each iteration, either (*inputPCset* ∩ *outputPCset*) or at least *inputPCset* describe nonempty subsets of the set of not yet processed PCs described by *processPCset*. Therefore, the inner loop (cf. line 10-26) reduces the number of unprocessed PCs with each iteration. As a consequence the inner loop of the algorithm always terminates and generates for the just regarded test goal g a set of test cases such that for each PC, that contains test goal g, at least one valid test case is in this set. Furthermore, the outer loop (cf. line 7-27) repeats the process for all test goals. This loop terminates due to the fact that G is a finite set. In the end, our algorithm creates a TS_C (cf. Definition 1) which contains for each test case t the associated set of PCs for which t is valid.

To derive an explicitly defined representative set of products PC_R for the complete SPL test suite TS_C it is necessary to select for each test case t at least one PC for which test case t is valid (cf. Definition 2). This can be easily ensured by selecting one PC from the set of products that was associated with test case t during test case generation (cf. line 19). In the end, the number of products in the representative set PC_R depends on the heuristics which is used to select the PCs. A small, representative set of products is achievable by selecting only those products that were already selected for other test cases. The development of a sophisticated algorithm, which searches for a minimal, representative set of products, is subject of our future research activities.

4 Discussion

In our running example, the AS SPL, there exist 32 valid products. If these 32 products are tested individually by using a brute-force "product-by-product" approach (which does not select a representative set of products) it would be necessary to create 432 test cases in total to achieve a full test model coverage w.r.t. the all-transitions coverage criterion for all 32 products. For comparison, by applying our *complete SPL test suite generation* approach to the 150% test model of the AS SPL it is possible to achieve the same full test model coverage by only creating 43 test cases. In addition to this, it was possible to select a representative set of 6 products from 32 possible products by selecting suitable products from those sets that are associated with the test cases in the complete SPL test suite. As a first step we only used a brute-force approach for the selection, although we are planning to do research for suitable heuristics. If these 6 products are tested individually then 120 test cases in total have to be created. Using our new approach it is sufficient to create only 43 test cases to achieve the same complete coverage. Detailed data about our evaluation experiments are published in [10].

We also applied our approach successfully to a *body comfort system* (BCS) SPL, a real-world SPL from the automotive domain. The BCS SPL consists of 12 features and, due to the constraints in its feature model, 312 valid PCs exist. Its corresponding 150% test model contains 152 transitions and 55 states. We applied our algorithm on the BCS SPL and created a complete SPL test suite w.r.t the all-transitions coverage criterion. The generated complete SPL test suite contains not more than 283 test cases and the corresponding representative set contains not more than two products. This very small number of products in the representative set is caused by the small number of exclusion-constraints between the features. These remarkable results for both SPLs, AS SPL and BCS SPL, show how efficiently our new approach generates complete SPL test suites, leading to a considerable reduction of costs for SPL testing.

It is important to note that in this paper we ignored redundant test cases, i.e. it may happen that generated test cases satisfy more than one test goal (accidently). Hence, for our running example, the AS SPL, the number of test cases is rather large and contains quite a number of redundant test cases. In such a case the generated set of test cases may be reduced as, e.g., shown in [11].

4.1 Threats to Validity

A *complete SPL test suite* created by our algorithm allows the subsequent selection of a small, representative set of products. To ensure that this representative set is really representative, it is necessary to require a strong correlation between the similarity of product implementations and the similarity of their related test models. In other words, we assume that two products with similar test models have similar implementations and behavior. Consequently, when the execution path of a test case that is derived from the test model of product $p1$ is also valid for the test model of product $p2$, then our approach implies that the test case will always produce identical verdicts (pass, fail, ...) when executed on both products, $p1$ and $p2$, in practice. However, if the assumption is dropped then any test-model-driven attempt is doomed to fail that tries to identify a small, representative set of products of a large SPL.

In real-world automotive SPLs the size of used models is usually rather large. Our approach scales very well with large SPLs, because our algorithm avoids the iteration over every single PC to create a new test case. Instead, our algorithm analyzes each created test case and if this test case is valid for more than one PC, all the PCs in this set are processed at once. For test case generation purposes we use the model-based testing framework Azmun [9], which integrates the model checker NuSMV. Testing with model checkers is still a field of research and the testing community has different opinions concerning its feasibility and the state space explosion problem [12]. For our research work a model checker is suitable due to its flexibility and great capabilities for model queries. For real-world SPLs with large models, we recommend more efficient model-based testing tools like Conformiq ATD or Rhapsody ATG. However, currently these tools do not support an appropriate interface that is needed for our approach (see Section 3.2).

5 Related Work

Studying related research we have identified three categories for SPL testing approaches. Approaches in these categories are more or less effective and efficient to achieve complete test model coverage for all products of an SPL.

Due to the fact that we pay particular attention to the automotive domain with large SPLs, we skip the first category "Contra-SPL-philosophy". Approaches in this category ignore the SPL-philosophy of reuse and, thus, are only appropriate for small SPLs [3].

The second category "Reuse-Techniques" includes techniques that are applied to reuse test artifacts (e.g. test cases and data) to reduce the test effort for SPLs. Typically, these approaches either make use of *regression testing techniques* to incrementally test products or *reuse and adapt domain tests* during application testing. The former ones are used in [4] to incrementally test products of an SPL treating the different variants of products as changes that have to be retested. This approach struggles with the challenging tasks to (1) identify a suitable product to start with and (2) to find out what needs to be retested. The latter ones, reusing and adapting domain tests, are created during domain engineering for product tests. Especially, model-based test approaches are used for that purpose. Model-based testing approaches provide the basis for SPL testing, due to their reusability and suitability to describe variability. A summary of model-based testing approaches for SPLs can be found in [1]. Frequently, statecharts, activity diagrams, and sequence diagrams are used to specify the behavior of software systems for model-based testing. CADeT [13], ScenTED [14] and Hartmann et al. [15] utilize reusable test models by means of activity diagrams. Instead of activity diagrams, we make use of state machines to derive test cases. In [16] a single state machine is used as test model that describes the functionality of an entire SPL. We also make use of one single test model, called a 150% test model, to derive test cases, according to the idea of [5]. The commercial variant management tool pure::variants [17] in interaction with the modeling tool IBM Rhapsody and ATG supports the modeling and trimming of a 150% model. One major drawback of this whole category is that all approaches still aim at deriving test cases for individual products. The test effort may be reduced because of reuse-techniques, but being confronted with millions of derivable products, these approaches might still not be sufficient. Strategies for the selection of representative sets of products are also out-of-scope.

In the third category "Subset-Heuristics" a subset of products of the SPL for testing is created, instead of testing every possible product. The subsets are generated on the basis of a certain coverage criterion. Scheidemann introduced a heuristics to generate a representative subset of products covering all SPL requirements [3]. Unfortunately, her approach does not scale for large SPLs and does not give any guarantees concerning model/code-based coverage criteria. Kim et al. [18] use static analysis to determine for an existing test case, which features have to be mandatory present or absent for it to be executed. Thus, they are able to determine a set of products to execute all test cases for the entire SPL. In our approach we use a similar concept to generate a complete SPL test suite very efficiently. In [19] and [20] combinatorial feature combination is used to generate a set of products covering all t-wise feature combinations. The corresponding algorithms take all constraints and hierarchies of the feature model into account and generate small (representative) sets of products efficiently. Unfortunately, no guarantees are given concerning required model/requirements-based coverage criteria. Furthermore, generating test cases for the computed sets of products is usually done on a product-by-product basis even in the case of [19], where a 150% test model is used to generate test cases for selected SPL products.

6 Conclusion and Future Work

The SPL test suite generation approach presented in this paper is - as far as we know - the first published approach that uses a 150% test model of the whole SPL as a starting point and generates a *complete* SPL test suite in such a way that (1) the created test cases satisfy required model-based coverage criteria for *every* product of the SPL and (2) the selection of a representative subset of all products is supported that allows for the execution of *all* test cases. To ensure that the selected representative set is really representative, a strong correlation between the similarity of product implementations and the similarity of their related 100% test models is required. Nevertheless, various publications with case studies from the automotive domain show that our SPL testing approach would be very useful in practice despite of the just mentioned restriction.

Our new approach was exemplary applied to a small SPL and additionally to a larger SPL from the automotive industry. It could be shown that our approach is efficient in complete SPL test suite generation for the test models of all products and still achieves full test model coverage. Additionally, the subsequent process for selecting a representative set of products is simplified by associating each generated test case with a set of products on which this test case is executable. Based on the promising results, in future research activities we will develop a more sophisticated algorithm for the minimization of the representative set of products and adapt our test suite reduction approach to a complete SPL test suite.

References

1. Oster, S., Wübbeke, A., Engels, G., Schürr, A.: Model-Based Software Product Lines Testing Survey. In: Zander, J., Schieferdecker, I., Mosterman, P. (eds.) Model-based Testing for Embedded Systems. CRC Press/Taylor&Francis (2011)
2. ISO: ISO - International Organization for Standardization. Website (2011), http://www.iso.org/iso/ (visited on May 2, 2011)
3. Scheidemann, K.: Verifying Families of System Configurations. PhD thesis, TU Munich (2007)
4. Engström, E., Skoglund, M., Runeson, P.: Empirical evaluations of regression test selection techniques. In: Rombach, H.D., Elbaum, S.G., Münch, J. (eds.) Proc. of ESEM 2008, pp. 22–31 (2008)
5. Grönniger, H., Krahn, H., Pinkernell, C., Rumpe, B.: Modeling Variants of Automotive Systems using Views. In: Modellierung (2008)
6. Jain, T.K., Kushwaha, D.S., Misra, A.K.: Optimization of the Quine-McCluskey Method for the Minimization of the Boolean Expressions. In: Proc. of the ICAS 2008, pp. 165–168. IEEE, Los Alamitos (2008)
7. Kang, K.C., Cohen, S.G., Hess, J.A., Novak, W.E., Peterson, A.S.: Feature-Oriented Domain Analysis (FODA) Feasibility Study. Technical report, Carnegie-Mellon University Software Engineering Institute (1990)
8. Souza, S., Maldonado, J., Fabbri, S., Masiero, P.: Statecharts Specifications: A Family of Coverage Testing Criteria. In: CLEI 2000 (2000)
9. Haschemi, S.: Azmun - The Model-Based Testing Framework. Website (2011), http://www.azmun.de (visited on May 2, 2011)
10. Cichos, H., Oster, S., Lochau, M., Schürr, A.: Extended Version of Model-based Coverage-Driven Test Suite Generation for Software Product Lines. Technical Report 07, TU Braunschweig (2011)
11. Cichos, H., Heinze, T.S.: Efficient Test Suite Reduction by Merging Pairs of Suitable Test Cases. In: Dingel, J., Solberg, A. (eds.) MODELS 2010. LNCS, vol. 6627, pp. 244–258. Springer, Heidelberg (2011)
12. Fraser, G., Wotawa, F., Ammann, P.: Testing with Model Checkers: A Survey. Software Testing, Verification and Reliability 19, 215–261 (2009)
13. Olimpiew, E.M.: Model-Based Testing for Software Product Lines. PhD thesis, George Mason University (2008)
14. Reuys, A., Kamsties, E., Pohl, K., Reis, S.: Model-Based System Testing of Software Product Families. In: Pastor, Ó., Falcão e Cunha, J. (eds.) CAiSE 2005. LNCS, vol. 3520, pp. 519–534. Springer, Heidelberg (2005)
15. Hartmann, J., Vieira, M., Ruder, A.: A UML-based Approach for Validating Product Lines. In: Geppert, B., Krueger, C. (eds.) Proc. of the SPLiT 2004, pp. 58–65 (2004)
16. Weißleder, S., Sokenou, D., Schlingloff, H.: Reusing State Machines for Automatic Test Generation in ProductLines. In: Proc. of the MoTiP 2008 (2008)
17. Pure-Systems: pure-systems GmBH. Website (2011), http://www.pure-systems.com (visited on May 2, 2011)
18. Kim, C.H.P., Batory, D.S., Khurshid, S.: Reducing Combinatorics in Testing Product Lines. In: Proc. of the AOSD 2011, pp. 57–68. ACM, New York (2011)
19. Oster, S., Markert, F., Ritter, P.: Automated Incremental Pairwise Testing of Software Product Lines. In: Bosch, J., Lee, J. (eds.) SPLC 2010. LNCS, vol. 6287, pp. 196–210. Springer, Heidelberg (2010)
20. Perrouin, G., Sen, S., Klein, J., Traon, B.B.Y.L.: Automated and Scalable T-wise Test Case Generation Strategies forSoftware Product Lines. In: ICST 2010, pp. 459–468 (2010)

Constraint-Based Model Refactoring

Friedrich Steimann

Lehrgebiet Programmiersysteme
Fernuniversität in Hagen
D-58084 Hagen
steimann@acm.org

Abstract. The UML standard specifies well-formedness rules as constraints on UML models. To be correct, refactoring of a model must take these constraints into account and check that they are still satisfied after a refactoring has been performed — if not, the refactoring must be refused. With constraint-based refactoring, *constraint checking* is replaced by *constraint solving*, lifting the role of constraints from permitting or denying a tentative refactoring to computing additional model changes required for the refactoring to be executable. Thus, to the degree that the semantics of a modelling language is specified using constraints, refactorings based on these constraints are guaranteed to be meaning preserving. To enable the reuse of pre-existing constraints for refactoring, we present a mapping from well-formedness rules as provided by the UML standard to constraint rules as required by constraint-based refactoring. Using these mappings, models can be refactored at no extra cost; if refactorings fail, the lack of meaning preservation points us to how the constraint-based semantic specifications of the modelling language can be improved.

1 Introduction

Refactoring is the discipline of modifying a piece of software so as to improve one or more of its non-functional properties (such as readability, changeability, etc.) whilst maintaining its external behaviour [5]. While originally conceived as program restructuring [7], refactoring is today applied to all kinds of software artefacts, including models [3, 6, 8, 13, 14, 15, 16, 21].

Constraint-based refactoring is a refactoring technique that builds on constraints for the specification of invariants that a refactoring must regard [18, 19, 22, 23]. In constraint-based refactoring, a refactoring problem is translated to a constraint satisfaction problem (CSP) whose solutions represent all legal refactorings of the artefact to be refactored. For this, the syntactic and semantic rules of the language of the artefact must be transcribed to so-called constraint rules which, when applied to the artefact to be refactored, generate the constraints expressing all relevant invariants. Constraint-based refactoring has so far exclusively been applied in programming, a field in which it has however proven highly successful (see, e.g., [18, 19, 22, 23]).

In this paper, we apply — to the best of our knowledge for the first time — the technique of constraint-based refactoring to modelling. Doing this, we are able to exploit that the semantics of modelling languages such as the Unified Modelling Language (UML) is partly specified in terms of so-called well-formedness rules, which

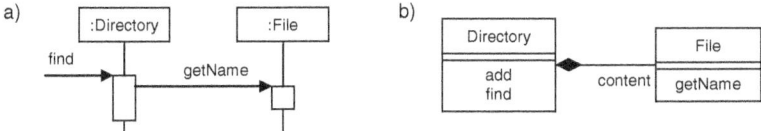

Fig. 1. UML model of a flat file system: a) a Sequence Diagram and b) a Class Diagram

are largely constraints rejecting syntactically correct, but meaningless (malformed) models. In fact, as we will see, well-formedness rules such as the ones found in the UML standard [10] can readily be transformed into constraint rules that can serve as the basis of constraint-based model refactoring; thus, to the degree that the semantics of the UML (or any modelling language for that matter) is specified in terms of well-formedness rules and other constraints, we are able to guarantee that our refactorings are meaning preserving. Furthermore, where the semantics is underspecified, constraint-based refactoring may let us detect this, and guide us in filling the gaps.

The remainder of this paper is organized as follows. In Section 2, we present an instructive example explaining the idea of model refactoring based on well-formedness rules, here expressed using first-order predicate logic (FOPL) with predicates as constraints, extended with path expressions that are required for navigating the associations of the UML metamodel. In Section 3, we briefly recapitulate constraint-based refactoring, explaining how it works for programs. Section 4 specifies how well-formedness rules are transformed to the constraint rules underlying constraint-based refactoring, with emphasis on dealing with the mismatches between what is required for expressing model invariants and what can be processed by a standard constraint solver. Section 5 applies this procedure to a number of real examples from the UML standard expressed in OCL. A brief comparison of related work with ours concludes.

The two main contributions of this paper are

1. the discovery that pre-existing constraints (e.g., existing well-formedness rules) can be used as the basis for constraint-based refactoring of models, and
2. the specification of the necessary transformation of well-formedness rules to the constraint rules that are required for constraint-based refactoring.

2 An Instructive Example

Consider the simple model of a flat file system shown in Figure 1. Files are found in a directory by sending the latter a message named "find", which in turn leads to a message "getName" being sent to a file (from an operating system perspective, this is certainly overly simplistic; however, it will serve our purpose well).

2.1 A Simple Well-Formedness Rule

Following a common language pattern which allows only those elements to be referenced (or used) that have been declared (or defined) elsewhere, we assume that for a Sequence Diagram such as that of Figure 1 a) to be well-formed, the names of the messages must correspond to names of operations defined by the classifiers

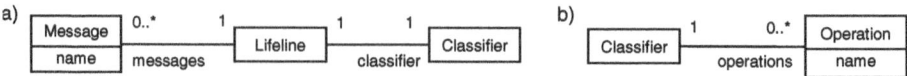

Fig. 2. Metamodels for the diagrams of Figure 1

(as in Figure 1 b) associated with the lifelines of the objects to which the messages are sent.[1] This is expressed by a well-formedness rule

$$\forall l \in \textit{lifelines}\ \forall m \in l.\textit{messages}\ \exists o \in l.\textit{classifier.operations}: m.\textit{name} = o.\textit{name} \quad (1)$$

which is specified relative to the metamodel shown in Figure 2 and in which *lifelines* is the set of lifelines of the Sequence Diagram to be checked (the *context* in OCL terms). The reader can easily verify that, with respect to well-formedness rule (1), the model of Figure 1 is well-formed.

2.2 Name Refactoring

Now suppose that the message labelled "getName" in the Sequence Diagram of Figure 1 a) is to be renamed, say to "x" (a variation of the RENAME METHOD refactoring [5], in which the refactoring is initiated by the renaming of a use rather than that of a definition). Re-evaluating well-formedness rule (1) immediately tells us that this renaming is not acceptable, since the rule now evaluates to *false*: for the message renamed to "x" and the classifier File, there exists no operation defined by File that has the same name "x". Quite obviously, the problem can be fixed by renaming the operation labelled "getName" to "x" also; the question that remains, however, is, can this necessary secondary change be computed, from the given model and well-formedness rule?

As it turns out, it can, simply be replacing the constraint *checker* used for probing well-formedness (evaluating the constraint expression to *true* or *false*) with a constraint *solver*, which can adapt the constrained properties[2] of the model so that the constraint is satisfied (and the model is well-formed). For this, application of the well-formedness rule (1) to the model of Figure 1 must be transformed into a constraint satisfaction problem (CSP), i.e., a set of constraint variables and constraints suitable for submission to a constraint solver such as MiniZinc [9]. In case of (1), this is done by unrolling the quantifiers, instantiating the quantified variables with the elements of the model the rule is applied to. For the model of Figure 1, this leads to the constraint set

$$\{m_{\textit{find}}.\textit{name} = o_{\textit{add}}.\textit{name} \lor m_{\textit{find}}.\textit{name} = o_{\textit{find}}.\textit{name},\ m_{\textit{getName}}.\textit{name} = o_{\textit{getName}}.\textit{name}\}$$

in which $m_{\textit{find}}$ is an object literal denoting the message originally named "find" a.s.f., and in which $m_{\textit{find}}.\textit{name}$ denotes the *name* property of $m_{\textit{find}}$ (a.s.f.) which, for the time being, we equate with a constraint variable. Thus, when the *name* property of $m_{\textit{getName}}$

---

[1] For the sake of simplicity, we assume here that all operations of a classifier are defined in the same Class Diagram. In practice, different operations may be introduced in different Class Diagrams, showing different views on the model; yet, for a Sequence Diagram to be checkable for well-formedness, it cannot introduce the required operations itself.

[2] We use the term *property* here to collectively denote attributes and association ends associated with an object ([11], §7.5.1 and §7.5.3). Conforming to [11], we use the dot notation *o.p* to denote the value of a property *p* of an object *o*, where *o* may be an object literal or a variable (including another property).

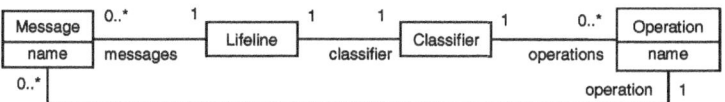

Fig. 3. Integration of the metamodels of Figure 2, extended by an association between messages and the operations they bind to

is set to "x", the solver will force a change of the *name* property of $o_{getName}$ to "x" also, making the model well-formed again. Since it has also kept its original meaning (the message binds to the same operation as before), it is a refactoring.

The situation is somewhat different, however, if m_{find} is renamed, say to "y": in that case, renaming *either* of the operations defined by the classifier Directory associated with the lifeline to which "y" is sent, to "y" also, would *equally* satisfy the above constraint set, and thus restore well-formedness of the diagram. However, *not both* possible renamings maintain the original meaning: if o_{add} is renamed to "y", the model is well-formed with respect to (1), but has a different meaning, since now m_{find} binds to a different operation.

Obviously, the well-formedness rule (1) is insufficient for refactoring, since it is indifferent to the operation a method binds to. Given that (1) is about well-formedness, not about meaning, this is not surprising: (1) and the metamodel of Figure 2 express a necessary condition for the binding of a message to an operation, namely that an operation exists that has the same name as the message, but they do not express which operation a method binds to, or that the notion of binding does at all exist — this is not required for well-formedness.

As it turns out, however, the semantic underspecification in (1) can be easily fixed by replacing the existential quantification with a Skolem function [17]

$$binding: Lifeline \times Message \rightarrow Operation \quad (2)$$

mapping a lifeline and a message to the operation the method (should) bind to. Since the lifeline is functionally dependent on the message (meaning that for any given message, a lifeline is uniquely determined; cf. Figure 2), (2) can be projected to

$$binding: Message \rightarrow Operation \quad (3)$$

which lets us Skolemize (1) to

$$\forall l \in lifelines \ \forall m \in l.messages : m.name = binding(m).name \quad (4)$$

In modelling, the introduction of the binding (or lookup) function represented by (3) translates to adding a metamodel association between Message and Operation as shown in Figure 3. This added association allows us to rewrite (4) to

$$\forall l \in lifelines \ \forall m \in l.messages : m.name = m.operation.name \quad (5)$$

whose application to the model of Figure 1 gives us the constraint set

$$\{m_{find}.name = m_{find}.operation.name, \ m_{getName}.name = m_{getName}.operation.name\}$$

which lacks the disjunction of the previous set. Instead, it has three different kinds of properties (constraint variables): the names of messages and operations (as before), and additionally the operation of a message (the one it binds to). However, considering that to preserve meaning, the binding of messages to operations must not change

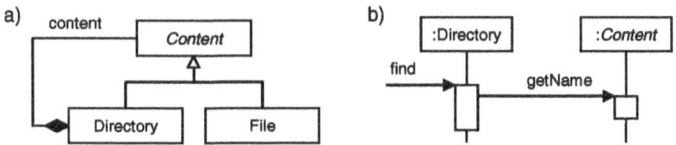

Fig. 4. Model of Figure 1 refactored to nested directories: a) new superclass Content extracted from File and Directory, and change of association end content to target that class; b) generalization of classifier File to Content.

(it is an invariant of the RENAME refactoring), the value of $m.operation$ is *fixed*, meaning that the constraint solver cannot change it. Therefore, if the message m_{find} is renamed from "find" to "y", the solver must rename the operation bound to, o_{find}, with it.

One might contend that RENAME refactorings are particularly simple and that it is pure coincidence that renaming can be done using existing well-formedness rules (enhanced with some additional semantics). To counter this objection, we take a look at another, somewhat more complex refactoring.

2.3 Type Refactoring

Suppose that the model of Figure 1 is to be refactored to allow nested directories. For this purpose, the refactoring EXTRACT SUPERCLASS [5] is applied to classes Directory and File. Besides creating a new superclass, Content, that generalizes both Directory and File, this refactoring suggests that the new generalization be used in place of Directory or File wherever the generalization is deemed useful [5]. In our example, this is the case for the composition of directories, which can now be composed of files *and* directories, as reflected in Figure 4 (note that for this, not only the composition, but also the target of the message labelled "getName" changes). What must be made sure by the refactoring, then, is that the operations required from Content are defined by Content, so that the changed model is well-formed and keeps its meaning. In the given example, this means that Content must define $o_{getName}$.

Contrary to the above RENAME refactoring, applying (5) to the model of Figure 4 does not help to compute the required change: the constraints generated are the same as before but in this case, since no name has changed, are satisfied for the model as is. Interestingly, the same does not hold for applying (1) to Figure 4: (1) requires that the operation a message binds to is defined by the classifier associated with the lifeline the message is sent to. Where did this constraint get lost?

As it turns out, replacing the existential quantification with the Skolem function *binding* in (4) ignored the restriction of the range over which was quantified, namely $l.classifier.operations$, a slip that did not affect the RENAME refactoring (since this refactoring does not change classifiers associated with lifelines or move operations between classifiers), but that shows for EXTRACT SUPERCLASS. In fact, before Skolemization in (4), the subexpression

$$\exists o \in l.classifier.operations : m.name = o.name$$

of (1) must be rewritten to

$$\exists o : o \in l.classifier.operations \wedge m.name = o.name$$

so that Skolemization leads to the well-formedness rule

$$\forall\, l \in \textit{lifelines } \forall\, m \in \textit{l.messages}: \qquad\qquad\qquad\qquad (6)$$
$$m.\textit{operation} \in l.\textit{classifier.operations} \,\wedge\, m.\textit{name} = m.\textit{operation.name}$$

which replaces (5). The constraints generated by applying this rule to the model of Figure 4 are

$$m_{\textit{find}}.\textit{operation} \in l_{\textit{left}}.\textit{classifier.operations} \,\wedge\, m_{\textit{find}}.\textit{name} = m_{\textit{find}}.\textit{operation.name}$$

and

$$m_{\textit{getName}}.\textit{operation} \in l_{\textit{right}}.\textit{classifier.operations}$$
$$\wedge\, m_{\textit{getName}}.\textit{name} = m_{\textit{getName}}.\textit{operation.name}$$

in which $l_{\textit{left}}$ and $l_{\textit{right}}$ denote the left and right lifeline, respectively. Considering

- that the *operation* properties are again fixed, thus maintaining binding,
- that the *name* properties are also fixed for this refactoring, and
- that the *classifier* property of $l_{\textit{left}}$ has remained unchanged, whereas that of $l_{\textit{right}}$ has been given a new, fixed value $C_{\textit{Content}}$ (the class literal representing Content),

the above two constraints can be reduced to

$$o_{\textit{find}} \in C_{\textit{Directory}}.\textit{operations} \,\wedge\, \text{``find''} = \text{``find''}$$

and

$$o_{\textit{getName}} \in C_{\textit{Content}}.\textit{operations} \,\wedge\, \text{``getName''} = \text{``getName''}$$

which, taken as a CSP, are solved by making $o_{\textit{getName}}$ a member of $C_{\textit{Content}}.\textit{operations}$.[3] Note how this change does not necessarily amount to pulling up $o_{\textit{getName}}$ from $C_{\textit{File}}$ to $C_{\textit{Content}}$: in absence of a constraint requiring that an operation can be defined in only one classifier, it could also amount to defining $o_{\textit{getName}}$ in both $C_{\textit{Content}}$ and $C_{\textit{File}}$. If that is not acceptable, the missing constraint must be added.

Thus, we have that the well-formedness rule (1) enhanced and rewritten as in (6) is not only sufficient for performing name refactoring, it also supports a type refactoring of the kind described in [22]. Admittedly, the typing constraint expressed in (6) is somewhat simplistic in that it does not consider inheritance or subtyping; however, we do not delve into the technicalities necessary for this here, because they complicate matters unduly (and have been addressed in great detail elsewhere; see, e.g., [12, 22]).

2.4 Interpreting Diagrams

It is instructive to see that the Skolemized well-formedness rule (6) is not only sufficient for the RENAME and EXTRACT SUPERCLASS refactorings, it also allows the automatic mapping of a Sequence Diagram to an instance of the metamodel of Figure 3, in particular the correct setting of the *operation* property of messages: if the *name* properties of messages and operations, as well as the classifier associated with a lifeline and the operations defined by the classifier of a lifeline are fixed (which they are during interpretation of a given model), a constraint solver applied to the constraints generated from (6) as above sets the values of *m.operation* to those operations that are

---

[3] Note that the class literal $C_{\textit{Content}}$ is both the owner of the property $C_{\textit{Content}}.\textit{operations}$ and the value of the property $l_{\textit{right}}.\textit{classifier}$. This is so because the property *classifier* has reference semantics, a notion foreign to standard constraint solvers; we will return to this in Section 4.2.

defined by the target classifiers and whose names equal those of the messages m.[4] Note that, that a message should bind to the operation of the same name is not formally specified elsewhere: if anything, it reflects our intuitive interpretation of Sequence Diagrams, or how a tool that accepts a Sequence Diagram and maps it to an instance of the metamodel interprets it. Thus, there appears to be a mutual dependency between the ability to refactor, and specifying the semantics of, models using constraints.

2.5 Summary

To summarize, we have that the same constraint (here defined as a well-formedness rule) serves the interpretation of the diagrams it constrains, and their refactoring. The only adaptation necessary for the different uses of the constraint is to specify which properties are fixed and which are non-fixed (and thus can be adapted by the constraint solver). This distinction will play an important role below.

3 Constraint-Based Program Refactoring

The technique of constraint-based model refactoring that we are presenting in this paper is based on constraint-based program refactoring as described in some detail in [18, 19, 22, 23]. In constraint-based program refactoring, a program to be refactored is transformed to a CSP by application of so-called *constraint rules*, which are generally of the form

$$\frac{query}{constraints}$$

Here, *query* represents a logical expression searching for elements of the program to be refactored, and *constraints* represents the set of constraints to be generated (added to the CSP) for the program elements selected by the query. Both the queries and the constraints contain variables that are placeholders for the program elements the rule is applied to; these variables (which are not constraint variables!) are implicitly universally quantified. For instance, application of the constraint rule

$$\frac{binds(r, d)}{r.name = d.name} \quad (7)$$

to a program to be refactored searches the program for occurrences of all pairs of references r and declared entities d such that r binds to d, and generates for each found pair a constraint requiring that *name* properties of r and d equal. This constraint rule expresses a binding invariant of the underlying programming language: for r to bind to d, r and d must have the same names. Taken alone, this constraint allows it that a reference r or a declared entity d be given a new name by a refactoring as long as the

---

[4] Actually, this is not quite correct: for computing the binding of a message to an operation based on names and classifiers, operation names must be unique within each classifier. However, since this does not affect our discourse on refactoring (in which binding is predetermined and only needs to be maintained), we can ignore this constraint here.

name of the other changes to that name as well; however, constraints generated by the same or other constraint rules may constrain the properties (constraint variables) *r.name* and *d.name* further. Note that when applied to a well-formed program, the generated constraints are always satisfied with the properties set to the values reflecting the program as is before the refactoring (the *initial values*).

Once the constraints have been generated from a program to be refactored, the refactoring may commence. For this, one or more of the constrained properties (constraint variables) are assigned new values, reflecting the *refactoring intent*. If the constraints are still satisfied with the new assignments, the refactoring is finished. Else, a constraint solver may attempt to assign other constraint variables new values, until a solution is found. The assignments constituting the solution represent the additional (secondary) changes to the program required to make the refactoring work; if no solution is found, the refactoring must be rejected.

It is instructive to note that to a certain extent, the queries (expressions above the bar) and the constraints (expressions below the bar) of a constraint rule are exchangeable for each other. In fact, as we have noted elsewhere [19, 20], the main difference between constraints and queries is that while a query is evaluated at rule application time, a constraint (generated by rule application) is evaluated at constraint solving time. This means that for constraints whose constrained properties are all fixed (so that they can be evaluated at rule application time), constraint rules can be rewritten to save the generation of these fixed constraints. For instance, in the constraint rule

$$\frac{binds(r, d)}{d \in r.receiver.type.members \quad r.name = d.name}$$

if the receiver of a reference, its type, and the set of members of the type are all fixed, the constraint $d \in r.receiver.type.members$ can be dropped from the rule consequent: it always holds if $binds(r, d)$ holds and therefore does not constrain the solution (if $binds(r, d)$ does not hold, the rule is not triggered and the constraint is not generated, anyway). On the other hand, assuming that names are non-fixed means that the constraint *r.name* = *d.name* is needed for refactoring, since otherwise, one may be changed without the other.

The possible rewriting of constraints rules due to fixed properties is central to our transformation of well-formedness rules to constraint rules.

4 From Well-Formedness Rules to Constraint Rules

Well-formedness rule checking can be viewed as a special case of constraint-based refactoring (constraint generation and subsequent constraint solving) in which all constrained properties (constraint variables) are fixed and set to their initial values. For instance, the constraint rule (7) directly translates to the well-formedness rule

$$\forall r, d, binds(r, d) : r.name = d.name$$

However, the opposite mapping, from a well-formedness rule to a constraint rule, is more difficult, since it must separate the fixed from the non-fixed properties (and therefore depends on the concrete refactoring).

Table 1. Fixed and non-fixed properties for three important refactorings (cf. Figure 3)

REFACTORING PROPERTY	RENAME MESSAGE/OPERATION	EXTRACT SUPERCLASS	MOVE MESSAGE/OPERATION
messages	fixed	fixed	non-fixed
operation	fixed	fixed	fixed
classifier	fixed	non-fixed	fixed
operations	fixed	non-fixed	non-fixed
name	non-fixed	fixed	fixed

4.1 Separation into Queries and Constraints

Generally, a constraint rule has the form of a universally quantified implication, with the additional restriction that, as noted in Section 3, the premise must contain only constraints whose properties are fixed for all model elements quantified over (so that they can be evaluated at rule application time). Thus, the first step in transforming the well-formedness rule (6) into a constraint rule is rewriting it to

$$\forall\, l, m : l \in \textit{lifelines} \wedge m \in l.\textit{messages} \rightarrow \\ m.\textit{operation} \in l.\textit{classifier}.\textit{operations} \wedge m.\textit{name} = m.\textit{operation}.\textit{name} \quad (8)$$

The remainder of the transformation depends on which properties are fixed and which are non-fixed for a given refactoring, as shown in Table 1 for three sample refactorings.

For RENAME, *name* is the only non-fixed property so that (8) can be transformed to

$$\frac{l \in \textit{lifelines} \quad m \in l.\textit{messages}}{m.\textit{name} = m.\textit{operation}.\textit{name}} \quad (9)$$

This is so because *l.messages* never changes so that the constraint $m \in l.\textit{messages}$ can be evaluated at rule application time, after m and l have been bound to concrete model elements (recall that both m and l are implicitly universally quantified), and because neither of *m.operation*, *l.classifier*, and *l.classifier.operations* can change their values, so that $m.\textit{operation} \in l.\textit{classifier}.\textit{operations}$ must remain satisfied and can be dropped[5] (as stated in Section 3, all constraints are satisfied with their initial assignments).

For EXTRACT SUPERCLASS, the transformation is analogous, yielding

$$\frac{l \in \textit{lifelines} \quad m \in l.\textit{messages}}{m.\textit{operation} \in l.\textit{classifier}.\textit{operations}} \quad (10)$$

which, applied to the example of Section 2.3, produces exactly the constraints necessary to force that $o_{\textit{getName}}$ is an operation of $C_{\textit{Content}}$. Finally, for MOVE METHOD [5] (which, depending on which kind of model element or diagram it is applied to, should be called MOVE OPERATION or MOVE MESSAGE), (8) transforms to

$$\frac{l \in \textit{lifelines} \quad m}{m \in l.\textit{messages} \rightarrow m.\textit{operation} \in l.\textit{classifier}.\textit{operations}}$$

---

[5] Note how (9) corresponds to the incomplete well-formedness rule (5) that turned out to be sufficient for the RENAME refactoring of Section 2.2.

in which the constraint $m \in l.messages$ cannot be promoted to a query, since *l.messages* may be changed by the refactoring (it is changed for the source and target lifelines of the message to be moved, and may be changed for other messages that may have to move with it; cf. [5] for why this may be the case).

For well-formedness rules with quantifiers nested inside expressions, these must be moved to the left prior to the transformation [17]. Existential quantifiers that cannot be removed using Skolemization have to be unrolled during constraint rule application (as was done in Section 2.1, before Skolemization was brought into play; note that, since the number of model elements is always finite, unrolling is always possible).

4.2 Mapping Properties to Constraint Variables

In the previous sections, we pretended that the properties involved in well-formedness rules can be directly mapped to constraint variables that can be handled by a constraint solver. Generally, however, this is not the case. Instead, we have to deal with the following mismatches:

- *Properties may have reference semantics.* Properties representing certain attributes and all association ends have reference semantics, i.e., they point to other objects. By contrast, constraint variables generally have value semantics, and their values (except for set values; see below) are unstructured.

  Solution: Map properties with reference semantics to constraint variables with value semantics, and emulate dereferencing of such variables as shown below.

- *Properties may have other than {1} multiplicities.* Many properties are optional, which in UML is represented by a {0..1} multiplicity. Others model links to arbitrary numbers of objects at the same time, which is represented by a {0..*} multiplicity. By contrast, constraint variables always have a single value, which may however be a set.

  Solution: Map properties to constraint variables with set domains, and transform multiplicities to constraints on the cardinalities of the values of these variables.

- *Properties may be chained.* Properties with reference semantics (cf. above) may be chained, which amounts to a navigation of properties, involving dereferencing of intermediate properties. By contrast, constraint variables cannot be dereferenced: the value of a constraint variable cannot be, or have, a constraint variable. This is particularly a problem if the properties through which is being navigated are non-fixed (meaning that their values can be changed by a constraint solver).

  Solution: Let $C(x.p_1.\cdots.p_n.p)$ be a constraint constraining property p accessed via navigation through properties $p_1, \ldots, p_n$ (all with reference semantics and, for uniformity of presentation, all assumed to be set-valued) starting from the object represented by variable x (so that $x.p_1.\cdots.p_n$ evaluates to the set of objects that can be reached from x by navigating through $p_1, \ldots, p_n$; note that C may — and usually will — constrain other properties as well). Without loss of generality, we assume x to be universally quantified and restricted by a predicate (constraint) P involving only fixed properties, so that we have

$$\forall x : P(x) \rightarrow C(x.p_1.\cdots.p_n.p) \qquad (11)$$

To be able to map $C(x.p_1.\cdots.p_n.p)$ to a constraint of a constraint rule, we first have to replace $x.p_1.\cdots.p_n$ with a variable y representing the model elements reached from x via $p_1, \ldots, p_n$ so that we can rewrite (11) to the intermediate form

$$\frac{P(x) \quad y}{y \in x.p_1.\cdots.p_n \to C(y.p)} \tag{12}$$

which is implicitly quantified over x and y and in which $y.p$ is a constraint variable not involving dereferencing. If the $p_1, \ldots, p_n$ are fixed properties (i.e., if their values cannot be changed by the refactoring), (12) translates to

$$\frac{P(x) \quad y \in x.p_1.\cdots.p_n}{C(y.p)}$$

in which $y \in x.p_1.\cdots.p_n$ is evaluated as a query so that the involved properties p_1 through p_n need not be mapped to constraint variables. For instance, the constraint rule for RENAME, (9), translates to

$$\frac{l \in \text{lifelines} \quad m \in l.\text{messages} \quad o \in m.\text{operation}}{m.\text{name} = o.\text{name}}$$

whose generated constraints contain only properties that map directly to constraint variables (cf. Table 1 to see that only fixed properties appear above the bar; note that, conforming to the above, $m.\text{operation}$ is assumed to be set-valued, i.e., a singleton). If a single p_i is non-fixed, (12) translates to

$$\frac{P(x) \quad x_{i-1} \in x.p_1.\cdots.p_{i-1} \quad x_i \quad y \in x_i.p_{i+1}.\cdots.p_n}{x_i \in x_{i-1}.p_i \to C(y.p)}$$

which (implicitly) quantifies over x, x_{i-1}, x_i, and y, and in which the constraint $C(y.p)$ is guarded by the condition that whatever the values assigned (by the solver) to p_i, y is reached from x via $x.p_1.\cdots.p_n$.[6] For instance, the constraint rule for EXTRACT SUPERCLASS, (10), is rewritten to

$$\frac{l \in \text{lifelines} \quad m \in l.\text{messages} \quad c}{c \in l.\text{classifier} \to m.\text{operation} \in c.\text{operations}}$$

in which $l.\text{classifier}$ is a singleton for all l (see Table 1 for fixed and non-fixed properties). If two properties p_i and p_j with $i < j$ are variable, (12) translates to

$$\frac{P(x) \quad x_{i-1} \in x.p_1.\cdots.p_{i-1} \quad x_i \quad x_{j-1} \in x_i.p_{i+1}.\cdots.p_{j-1} \quad x_j \quad y \in x_j.p_{j+1}.\cdots.p_n}{x_i \in x_{i-1}.p_i \wedge x_j \in x_{j-1}.p_j \to C(y.p)}$$

and so forth. Note that in all cases, the queries involve only fixed properties so that they can be evaluated at rule application time, and the generated constraints contain no chained properties so that no dereferencing is required.

Thus, together with the transformations of Section 4.1, we are able to rewrite any well-formedness rule expressed in terms of FOPL with path expressions into a constraint rule that produces only constraints amenable to a standard constraint solver.

---

[6] Note that $x_0 \equiv x$ and $x_n \equiv y$, and that queries involving p_0 (for $i = 1$) or p_{n+1} (for $i = n$) are dropped.

5 Real Examples from the UML Standard

To demonstrate the generality of our approach, we have applied it to three OCL well-formedness rules directly taken from the UML Superstructure specification [10]. We do not delve into the details of translating the various OCL iterators to solver constraints here; this has been dealt with, for instance, in [2].

- From the *Constraints* section of §7.3.22, "InstanceSpecification":

    The defining feature of each slot is a structural feature (directly or inherited) of a classifier of the instance specification.

    slot->forAll(s | classifier->exists (c | c.allFeatures()->includes (s.definingFeature)))

    This is a typing rule, expressing that the defining feature associated with a slot of an instance specification must be a feature of at least one classifier the specified instance is an instance of. Assuming that typing must be preserved, but that the classifier(s) associated with an instance may be changed (e.g., EXTRACT SUPERCLASS [5] or GENERALIZE DECLARED TYPE [22] applied to a Communication Diagram), this translates to the constraint rule

    $$\frac{s \in self.slot}{\exists c : c \in self.classifier \wedge s.definingFeature \in c.allFeatures()} \quad (13)$$

    in which *self* represents the context [11], the Instance Specification the rule is applied to, and in which the existential quantification must be unrolled upon rule application. Skolemization is also possible, but requires a slight adaptation: the derived property *featuringClassifier* of features ([10], §7.3.19) corresponds to a set-valued Skolem function *featuringClassifier*: *Feature* → $\wp(Classifier)$, allowing us to rewrite the above rule to

    $$\frac{s \in self.slot \quad f = s.definingFeature}{f.featuringClassifier \cap self.classifier \neq \varnothing}$$

    in which the second conjunct from the consequent of (13),

    $s.definingFeature \in s.definingFeature.featuringClassifier.allFeatures()$

    has been dropped (because it is tautological).

- From the *Constraints* section of §7.3.44, "Property":

    Subsetting may only occur when the context of the subsetting property conforms to the context of the subsetted property.

    subsettedProperty->notEmpty() implies
        (subsettingContext()->notEmpty() and subsettingContext()->forAll (sc |
          subsettedProperty->forAll(sp |
            sp.subsettingContext()->exists(c | sc.conformsTo(c)))))

    This rule is to express that in case a set-valued property (attribute or association end) is to subset one or more other properties, the context of the property, the owning or, in case of an end of a more than binary association, all owning classifiers, must conform to the classifier(s) of the properties that are being subset. For a PULL UP PROPERTY refactoring, it translates to the constraint rule

$$\frac{|\,self.subsettedProperty\,|>0 \quad sp \in self.subsettedProperty \quad sc}{|\,self.subsettingContext()\,|>0}$$
$$sc \in self.subsettingContext() \rightarrow \exists c \in sp.subsettingContext(): sc.conformsTo(c)$$

which is however ambiguous with respect to which subsetting context should conform to which, in case there is more than one. At least, [10] hints at a suitable Skolemization, by requiring conformance with the "*corresponding* element in the context of the subsetted property" (albeit without formalizing correspondence).

- From the *Constraints* section of §15.3.12, "StateMachine":

    The context classifier of the method state machine of a behavioral feature must be the classifier that owns the behavioural feature.

    specification->notEmpty() implies (context->notEmpty() and
        specification->featuringClassifier->exists (c | c = context))

This is to express that a state machine specifying a behavioural feature (method) of a classifier must have that classifier as its context; it could be violated by a MOVE BEHAVIOURAL FEATURE refactoring, changing the featuringClassifier and context properties. The derived constraint rule for this refactoring is

$$\frac{|\,self.specification\,|>0 \quad s \in self.specification}{|\,self.context\,|>0 \land \exists c \in s.featuringClassifier : c \in self.context}$$

whose existential quantifier must be unrolled upon application. Note that, since *featuringClassifier* has multiplicity {0..*} (cf. above), it is not clear to which classifier the *context* property of a state machine should be set, not even intuitively — in absence of a sensible Skolem function correcting this, *context* should be given multiplicity {0..*}, too, and the constraint should be changed to

   specification->notEmpty() implies context = specification->featuringClassifier

6 Related Work

By presenting an initial set of model refactorings, and by providing formal (OCL) pre- and postconditions for some of them, Sunyé et al. set an early landmark [21]. Philipps and Rumpe subsequently showed how state machine refactorings can be viewed as refinements that can be proven meaning preserving [13], but it is unclear how their approach generalizes to other refactorings. Pretschner and Prenninger let the user specify predicates that partition the state space of state machines, from which refactorings can then be computed [15]; their approach also appears to be specialized to one kind of models. Porres specified a refactoring as a set of transformation rules relying on an action language for query and updating models, where correctness of the refactored model is guaranteed by checking conformance with the metamodel and satisfaction of applicable OCL constraints [14]. By contrast, we use metamodel and constraints as specifications of the refactorings. Gheyi et al. presented an approach for proving structural model refactorings for Alloy [6]; however, the technical scaffolding required for correct refactoring is significant, especially when compared to our approach, which re-uses pre-existing semantic specifications.

Not dealing with model refactoring, but nevertheless related to our work, Cabot et al. investigated how UML/OCL models can be transformed to CSPs that can be submitted to a constraint solver, to verify stated correctness properties of models by generating instances [2]. Our work is different in that we always start with a correct (meta)model instance (the model to be refactored) that is then temporarily invalidated by a refactoring, so that a similar (neighbouring) instance needs to be found. As has been shown elsewhere [19], this allows us to use an algorithm for constraint generation that avoids the complexity problems from which the unbounded translation of [2] suffers. Ali et al. [1] also employ OCL constraint solving, for (UML) model-based test case generation, but to address the combinatorial complexity encountered in [2], resort to a search-based approach; their search heuristics could be integrated in our approach to make constraint solving even faster. Also methodically related to ours is Egyed's work on fixing inconsistencies in models, as detected by the violation of constraints [4]: in fact, fixing inconsistencies can be seen as solving an unsatisfied CSP (with the set of solutions representing all possible repairs). With the Beanbag language [24], OCL-like consistency relations can be extended with fixing behaviour specifying how changes leading to model inconsistencies are to be compensated with other, repairing changes; however, the compensated changes are not necessarily meaning-preserving, and thus not refactorings. Even if certain refactorings could be specified as fixes in Beanbag, different refactorings would still need different fixing operations. This is in contrast to the approach presented here, for which a single set of well-formedness rules suffices for different refactorings. Finally, Correa and Werner extended the notion of model refactoring to the (co-)refactoring of OCL constraints [3]. Since OCL has well-formedness rules specified in OCL [11], our approach should be extendible to OCL refactoring also; however, we have not investigated this further.

7 Conclusion

For a modelling language without semantics, every change to a model is a refactoring. The more of the semantics of a modelling language has been specified, the fewer changes to a model result in models with the same meaning, i.e., in refactorings. By taking semantic specifications pre-existing in the form of well-formedness rules expressed in a constraint language as a starting point, we are able to transform refactoring problems as diverse as renaming, generalizing, or moving model elements, to CSPs that are amenable to a standard constraint solver, which can thus be used to compute the additional changes required for a specific intended model refactoring. Using our approach, semantic underspecification is unveiled by refactored models that do not mean the same to the user; in such cases, the pre-existing constraints may be complemented with the missing semantics, for instance by extending the metamodel and adapting the constraints accordingly.

Acknowledgments. This work has been made possible by the Deutsche Forschungsgemeinschaft (DFG) under grant STE 906/4-1. The author wishes to thank Thomas Kühne and Jens von Pilgrim for supplying valuable comments on a draft version of this paper.

References

1. Ali, S., Iqbal, M.Z., Arcuri, A., Briand, L.: A search-based OCL constraint solver for model-based test data generation. In: Proc. of QSIC, pp. 41–50 (2011)
2. Cabot, J., Clarisó, R., Riera, D.: UMLtoCSP: A tool for the formal verification of UML/OCL models using constraint programming. In: Proc. of ASE, pp. 547–548 (2007)

3. Correa, A.L., Werner, C.M.L.: Applying refactoring techniques to UML/OCL models. In: Baar, T., Strohmeier, A., Moreira, A., Mellor, S.J. (eds.) UML 2004. LNCS, vol. 3273, pp. 173–187. Springer, Heidelberg (2004)
4. Egyed, A.: Fixing inconsistencies in UML design models. In: Proc. of ICSE, pp. 292–301 (2007)
5. Fowler, M.: Refactoring: Improving the Design of Existing Code. Addison-Wesley, Reading (1999)
6. Gheyi, R., Massoni, T., Borba, P.: A rigorous approach for proving model refactorings. In: Proc. of ASE, pp. 372–375 (2005)
7. WG Griswold Program Restructuring as an Aid to Software Maintenance (PhD Dissertation, University of Washington (1992)
8. Moha, N., Mahé, V., Barais, O., Jézéquel, J.-M.: Generic model refactorings. In: Schürr, A., Selic, B. (eds.) MODELS 2009. LNCS, vol. 5795, pp. 628–643. Springer, Heidelberg (2009)
9. Nethercote, N., Stuckey, P.J., Becket, R., Brand, S., Duck, G.J., Tack, G.R.: MiniZinc: Towards a standard CP modelling language. In: Bessière, C. (ed.) CP 2007. LNCS, vol. 4741, pp. 529–543. Springer, Heidelberg (2007)
10. OMG Unified Modeling Language Superstructure Version 2.3 (May 2010), http://www.omg.org/spec/UML/2.3/Superstructure
11. Object Management Group Object Constraint Language Version 2.2, http://www.omg.org/spec/OCL/2.2
12. Palsberg, J., Schwartzbach, M.I.: Object-Oriented Type. Wiley, Chichester (1994)
13. Philipps, J., Rumpe, B.: Refactoring of programs and specifications. In: Practical Foundations of Business and System Specifications, pp. 281–297. Kluwer Academic Publishers, Dordrecht (2003)
14. Porres, I.: Model refactorings as rule-based update transformations. In: Stevens, P., Whittle, J., Booch, G. (eds.) UML 2003. LNCS, vol. 2863, pp. 159–174. Springer, Heidelberg (2003)
15. Pretschner, A., Prenninger, W.: Computing refactorings of state machines. Software and System Modeling 6(4), 381–399 (2007)
16. Reimann, J., Seifert, M., Aßmann, U.: Role-based generic model refactoring. In: Petriu, D.C., Rouquette, N., Haugen, Ø. (eds.) MODELS 2010. LNCS, vol. 6395, pp. 78–92. Springer, Heidelberg (2010)
17. Russell, S., Norvel, P.: Artificial Intelligence: A Modern Approach, 2nd edn. Prentice Hall, Englewood Cliffs (2003)
18. Steimann, F., Thies, A.: From public to private to absent: Refactoring JAVA programs under constrained accessibility. In: Drossopoulou, S. (ed.) ECOOP 2009. LNCS, vol. 5653, pp. 419–443. Springer, Heidelberg (2009)
19. Steimann, F., Kollee, C., von Pilgrim, J.: A refactoring constraint language and its application to eiffel. In: Mezini, M. (ed.) ECOOP 2011. LNCS, vol. 6813, pp. 255–280. Springer, Heidelberg (2011)
20. Steimann, F., von Pilgrim, J.: Constraint-based refactoring with foresight (unpublished manuscript), http://www.feu.de/ps/docs/Foresight.pdf
21. Sunyé, G., Pollet, D., Le Traon, Y., Jézéquel, J.-M.: Refactoring UML models. In: Gogolla, M., Kobryn, C. (eds.) UML 2001. LNCS, vol. 2185, pp. 134–148. Springer, Heidelberg (2001)
22. Tip, F., Kiezun, A., Bäumer, D.: Refactoring for generalization using type constraints. In: Proc. of OOPSLA, pp. 13–26 (2003)
23. Tip, F.: Refactoring using type constraints. In: Riis Nielson, H., Filé, G. (eds.) SAS 2007. LNCS, vol. 4634, pp. 1–17. Springer, Heidelberg (2007)
24. Xiong, Y., Hu, Z., Zhao, H., Song, H., Takeichi, M., Mei, H.: Supporting automatic model incon-sistency fixing. In: Proc. of ESEC/SIGSOFT FSE, pp. 315–324 (2009)

Supporting Design Model Refactoring
for Improving Class Responsibility Assignment

Motohiro Akiyama[1], Shinpei Hayashi[1],
Takashi Kobayashi[2], and Motoshi Saeki[1]

[1] Department of Computer Science, Tokyo Institute of Technology
[2] Department of Information Engineering, Nagoya University
{akiyama,hayashi,saeki}@se.cs.titech.ac.jp, tkobaya@is.nagoya-u.ac.jp

Abstract. Although a responsibility driven approach in object oriented analysis and design methodologies is promising, the assignment of the identified responsibilities to classes (simply, class responsibility assignment: CRA) is a crucial issue to achieve design of higher quality. The GRASP by Larman is a guideline for CRA and is being put into practice. However, since it is described in an informal way using a natural language, its successful usage greatly relies on designers' skills. This paper proposes a technique to represent GRASP formally and to automate appropriate CRA based on them. Our computerized tool automatically detects inappropriate CRA and suggests alternatives of appropriate CRAs to designers so that they can improve a CRA based on the suggested alternatives. We made preliminary experiments to show the usefulness of our tool.

Keywords: object-oriented design, class responsibility assignment, GRASP.

1 Introduction

Maintainability of final products greatly relies on the quality of their design and their design processes. There are many object-oriented analysis and design methodologies, and in particular a family of the methodologies focusing on responsibility of class, so called responsibility-driven methods, is promising. In this family, after identifying responsibilities from a requirements specification, we assign them into the identified classes that fulfill them. We can also re-design classes considering which responsibilities the classes should fulfill. Responsibility Driven Approach [26] and Class-Responsibility-Collaborator (CRC) cards [3] are examples of the methodologies to design classes based on responsibilities and being put into practice [2,21]. Although these approaches allow us to identify classes and their responsibilities, the identified results may be insufficient for the quality of design, e.g., design quality metrics such as coupling and cohesion, and it may be difficult to adopt them as a complete design as they are. For example, in CRC card methodology the quality of the resulting products greatly relies on human cognitive ability, and the methodology may produce the results that human can easily and intuitively understand. However, the results may be less changeability or maintainability, which are very significant for software design of high quality.

It is reasonable to *refactor* classes and responsibilities that have been produced using these methodologies such as CRC cards so that we can obtain a design model of higher quality, i.e., *design model refactoring* on the identified classes and responsibilities. In this framework, the assignment of responsibilities to classes (class responsibility assignment: CRA) is a crucial issue. Therefore, its automated support is necessary for human designers to develop design models of stable quality. There are several techniques to provide guidelines of CRA such as [25] or GRASP (General Responsibility Assignment Software Pattern (or Principle)) [14]. In particular, GRASP aims at the improvement of design quality metrics and is being to achieve satisfactory results. However, since GRASP is described in informal way and a large number of classes, responsibilities, and their combinations frequently emerge in real designs, it is difficult for human designers to apply GRASP by hand and the support of a computerized tool is necessary. In addition, a design process is a series of trial-and-errors, and the designers frequently redo design including CRA during their design processes. Thus the computerized support is preferable to contain the functions of undoing and redoing of CRA. We consider that design model refactoring based on GRASP and its automated support is useful to solve the above issues. We present the formal description technique of GRASP and a computerized tool in this paper. Our formal description of GRASP consists of the followings:

1. the definitions of predicates to detect the parts where GRASP should be applied, so called *bad smells* and
2. refactoring operations as graph transformations on an extended class diagram.

We show the benefits by developing the support tool and making a comparative experiment using this tool.

The rest of the paper is organized as follows. In the next section, we clarify the details of the issues to be solved. Section 3 presents the description technique of GRASP including responsibility description. We respectively present the developed tool and the experiment in Sects. 4 and 5. Section 6 is for related work and we conclude with Sect. 7.

2 Issues in Class Responsibility Assignment

To clarify the issues in CRA, consider the following example shown in Fig. 1(a). Suppose that we design an online shop system like Amazon. This system has two types of users: an administrator and normal users who buy goods. After login to the system, it displays either of a menu for the administrator (admin-menu) or for normal users (user-menu). The administrator can update Web pages of goods, manage the accounts of normal users, etc. using the admin-menu, while normal users can buy goods and specify a payment method, etc. using the user-menu. The class *Menu* in Fig. 1(a) has the two responsibilities r_1 "Display admin menu" and r_2 "Display user menu", which are represented as notes in the figure, and they are fulfilled by the method *displayMenu*.

However, it includes several problems from the view of changeability. For example, since the method *displayMenu* uses many conditional branches for the alternatives of normal users (user-menu) and the administrator (admin-menu) to implement these responsibilities, the body of the method becomes difficult to be changed. Secondly, if we employ a new type of users in the next version of this system, we should add some methods of their new authority and functions to the other classes that implement user account

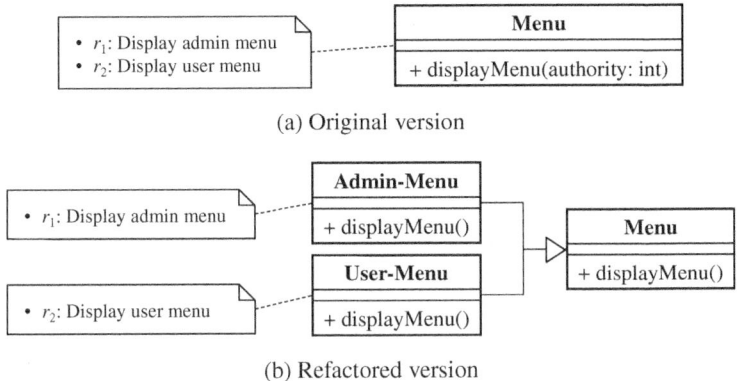

Fig. 1. Motivating example

management and that execute user functions. This addition leads to the changes of the method body of *displayMenu*, i.e., changes are propagated from a class to another class. Change propagation between classes is an obstacle against to design of higher quality.

Figure 1(b) is a refactored version to solve this problem and in this version, we employ two subclasses *Admin-Menu* and *User-Menu* of the class *Menu*. Each of the responsibilities is assigned to the subclass individually. As a result, *displayMenu* is implemented with these subclasses separately. Thus, the function of displaying admin-menu is implemented in the class *Admin-Menu* without any conditional branches for alternatives of users and the administrator; these conditional branches are realized by means of polymorphism of *displayMenu* in the subclasses. This refactoring can be suggested by two patterns of GRASP: **Polymorphism** and **Protected Variations**. In [14], these two patterns are defined as follows.

Polymorphism —When related alternatives or behaviors vary by class, assign responsibility for the behavior using polymorphic operations to the classes for which the behavior varies.

Protected Variations —Identify points of predicted variation or instability; assign responsibilities to create a stable "interface" around them.

GRASP is a set of guidelines or principles that should be kept when assigning responsibilities to classes and includes totally nine patterns, in order to improve object-oriented design, e.g., decreasing coupling between classes and increasing cohesion within a class. The other patterns that appear in this paper are **Information Expert**, **Pure Fabrication**, **Indirection**, and **Creator**. Their details can be found in [14].

Turn back to our example of Fig. 1. First of all, to apply GRASP, we have to detect parts to be improved. The detection is a time-consuming and error-prone task for human designers because of large size of design and of informal descriptions of GRASP. In fact, "when related alternatives or behaviors vary by class" mentioned above specifies the parts that **Polymorphism** should be applied to, but this description is not so concrete and it is difficult to detect the applicable parts of a real design. In our example, the designer could notice that r_1 and r_2 have the potential of alternatives by the reason of the lexical similarity of their description sentences. The designer apply **Polymorphism** to the class *Menu* so that the designer has obtained two subclasses to which each of the responsibilities is assigned individually, as shown in Fig. 1(b).

In the refactoring process, there are two problems; one results from the description of GRASP, and the other does from the description of responsibilities. The former is related to the way of recognizing that responsibility assignment to the class *Menu* was a *bad smell*, i.e., how to recognize the current CRA is the situation where "alternatives or behaviors vary by class". We have to define this situation formally from class structure and CRA in order to find alternatives or behavior by class. The latter is how to capture the contents of a responsibility from its description. In our example, the lexical similarity of the descriptions, i.e., sentence pattern "Display *** menu" allows us to find the potential of alternatives based on the type of menus. However, can we find this potential of the alternative if a designer describes "Show a list of commands (for administrators)" instead of "Display admin menu"? The problem is that we can specify responsibilities in free form with natural language and it may cause the difficulties in identifying the relationship between responsibilities such as this case.

We can summarize the obstacles against the automated support for CRA and their solutions as follows:

1. **Formal definition of GRASP.** To detect bad smells in a class diagram with CRA, we have defined GRASP formally in machine-understandable way. Some of GRASP descriptions consist of the descriptions of bad smells and those of solutions to improve them. We define bad smells as structural properties on a class diagram including CRA and use predicate logic. In the above example, the bad smell can be the property that two or more responsibilities are assigned to the same class and all of them have the *coordinate* relationship to each other. We define it using logical formulas. As for descriptions of the solutions, we use the technique of graph transformation. In the example, we write the sequence of operations on the diagram, e.g., create a subclass for each responsibility and then put in the class a method fulfilling the responsibility.

2. **Description of responsibilities.** To detect the relationships between responsibilities, we propose the technique to make a designer describe responsibilities separating them into finer-grained elements so that their relationships, e.g., *coordinate*, can be automatically detected. This technique is similar to the idea of CASE Grammar [9] that a natural language sentence can be semantically represented with a set of deep cases specific to verbs. In the above example of *coordinate* relationship, the responsibility "Display admin menu" is separated to the verb "Display", the modifier "admin", and target case "menu", when the designer specifies it. "Display user menu" is described in the same way. The only different elements between these two responsibilities are their modifiers: "admin" and "user". Thus we identify the alternatives when there are two responsibilities which are the same except modifier parts. In our technique, we use a *responsibility form* to describe a responsibility separately into its elements like the case frame approach in Case Grammer.

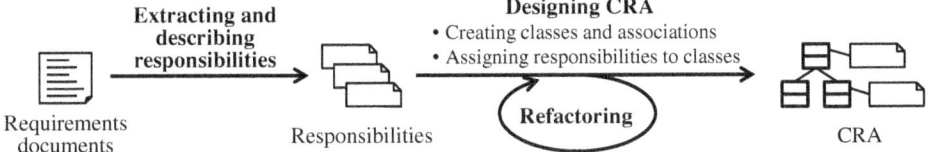

Fig. 2. Overview of our technique

Table 1. Form of responsibility description

ID	(*id*) A unique number to identify the responsibility.
Action	(*action*) The verb of the responsibility.
Target	(*target*) The target of the action.
Possessive	(*pos*) If a noun denoting a target of the action has a modifier of a possessive case, the modifier is assigned to this item. In the example that the target is "name of customer", "customer" is assigned to this item.
Modifier	(*mod*) Otherwise, the modifier to a noun is assigned to this item.
Condition	(*cond*) The condition whether the action of the responsibility is executed or not. For example, the following sentences are the candidates of conditions. "edit mode", "input mode", the phases including "mode", "when the button was pushed".
Dependency	(*dep*) The responsibilities to which are referred by this responsibility. They can be collaborated with this responsibility.

3 Our Approach

3.1 Overview

Figure 2 shows an overview of our proposed technique. First, designers extract responsibilities from requirements documents such as use case descriptions. In this process, they can use existing techniques of responsibility extraction such as CRC card [3] and/or robustness analysis [20]. The extracted responsibilities are described according to our *responsibility form*. Next, they design CRA, i.e., creating new classes and assigning the extracted responsibilities to the classes using a special editor. For every step in CRA, the editor automatically detects bad smells of the current CRA and suggests refactored CRAs as alternatives. Designers can accept or reject the suggested CRAs. By repeating the steps of the responsibility assignment and refactoring, designers explore the most appropriate CRA.

3.2 Describing Responsibilities

Since coordination and dependency relationships among responsibilities are a key factor to detect bad smells, the technique to describe responsibilities should enable us to identify these relationships from responsibility descriptions. Thus it is necessary to describe responsibilities in a finer grain level rather than in one sentence level. More concretely, we separately describe the information of a responsibility into several items as shown

Table 2. Examples of responsibility description

Responsibility	action	target	pos	mod	cond	dep
r_1: "Display admin menu"	Display	menu	–	admin	–	–
r_2: "Display user menu"	Display	menu	–	user	–	–

in Table 1. Some of these items can compose a sentence of the form "an *owner* does an *action* to a *target* under a *condition* (who does what to what when)", and it allows us to extract these items from the sentences expressing responsibilities. In addition, we can paraphrase these items into a sentence easy for a human designer to read. A target can be divided into three finer-grained items, *possessive*, *modifier* and body (*target*), based on the types of modifiers to a noun denoting the target. Note that the last item *dependency* is for specifying explicitly the responsibilities dependent on this responsibility.

The example of Fig. 1 can be described as shown in Table 2. In this example, we had very short phrases as the sentences expressing the responsibilities only. However, by analyzing syntactically their phrase structures we can identify the items to be assigned. If we have more detailed sentences of responsibilities such as use case descriptions and CRC card descriptions, we can use them. To detect coordination relationships, we should focus on the items action and body (of target). In this example, since the responsibilities r_1 and r_2 have the same value in these two items, we detect a coordination relationship between them. This is generally specified as the rules to detect the bad smells that a certain GRASP, e.g., Polymorphism, should be applied to. In addition, the types of actions such as *create* (responsibility related to creating an object) are also used for detecting other types of bad smells. The beneficial point of our technique mentioned in this section is the possibility of lightweight semantic processing of responsibilities by means of separating responsibility descriptions into semantical components such as action and target.

3.3 CRA Refactorings

In our approach, we define the detection rules of bad smells and the transformation rules of CRA refactorings based on GRASP. In the detection rules of bad smells in CRA, we can use facts of the class structure (the name of classes and the types of connections on classes such as inheritances or associations, including the information of stereotypes such as ≪create≫) and given responsibility descriptions on a predicate logic.

List of Refactorings. We have defined the following five refactorings including smell detection rules of their smells and transformation rules of CRAs.

Move Responsibility —It moves a responsibility to more appropriate class using the coordinate relationship among responsibilities. This refactoring is based on Information Expert.
Introduce Simple Factory —When a class is instantiated in multiple parts, this refactoring unifies them using Pure Fabrication and Indirection.
Introduce Creator —It moves responsibilities of instantiating a class to an appropriate class using Creator.

Introduce Polymorphism —It separately assigns coordinate responsibilities to individual classes having a common parent class. This refactoring is based on **Polymorphism** and **Protected Variations** patterns.

Introduce Facade —It reorganizes a CRA having complex dependencies among owners (classes) of the responsibilities by introducing an indirect responsibility among the owner classes. This refactoring is based on **Pure Fabrication** and **Indirection**.

Smell detection rules of each refactoring are defined as predicate logic and based on the descriptions of GRASP. Because of the space limitation, we only picks up **Introduce Polymorphism** and illustrate its detection rules and transformation mechanism.

Example. Introduce Polymorphism refactoring is based on **Polymorphism** and **Protected Variations** patterns. As mentioned in Sect. 2, **Polymorphism** and **Protected Variations** respectively focus on the situations "when related alternatives or behaviors vary by class" and "identify points of predicted variation or instability". These conditions can be substituted to detect *coordinate* relationships. We can detect the coordinates of responsibilities by checking whether (1) both the actions and bodies of the responsibilities are the same and (2) the responsibilities differs in only one of the modifiers and possessives, or in the case that both of the modifiers and possessives are the same but they differ in conditions. More formally, the predicate $coordinate(r, r')$ holds if

$$r.action = r'.action \land r.target = r'.target \land$$
$$((r.pos \neq r'.pos \land r.mod = r'.mod) \lor$$
$$(r.pos = r'.pos \land r.mod \neq r'.mod) \lor$$
$$(r.pos = r'.pos \land r.mod = r'.mod \land r.cond \neq r'.cond)).$$

Here, $r.*$ denotes the property $*$ in the form of responsibility r.

We find a maximal coordinate set R, i.e., $\forall r, r' \in R \cdot coordinate(r, r')$ as the input of **Introduce Polymorphism**. The mechanism how to apply **Introduce Polymorphism** is as follows:

0. Check pre-conditions. Here, we check that **Polymorphism** have not introduced in the current CRA yet. More concretely, we guarantee that there is no common parent class for every owner class of the given responsibilities by checking ($\nexists c \cdot \forall c' \in owners(R) \cdot c \in parents(c')) \lor (\exists r, r' \in R \cdot owner(r) = owner(r'))$. Here, $owner(r)$ denotes the owner class of given responsibility, and $owners(R) := \{ owner(r) \mid r \in R \}$. Also, $parents(c')$ denotes a set of the classes that c' inherits or implements.
1. Create new classes $Class_i$ ($1 \leq i \leq |R| - |owners(R)|$).
2. Move responsibilities $r \in R$ to newly added classes $Class_i$.
3. Create a class *Base*, and make each owner class of R inherit *Base*.
4. Rename each class properly.

For example, consider applying **Introduce Polymorphism** refactoring to the CRA shown in Fig. 1(a). As mentioned above, r_1 and r_2 have a coordination relationship, i.e., $coordinate(r_1, r_2)$. Moreover, they are assigned to a common class *Menu*. Thus, $R = \{r_1, r_2\}$ satisfies the smell detection rules and the precondition of this refactoring. By applying **Introduce Polymorphism**, we obtain the resulting CRA shown in Fig. 1(b).

First, a new class $Class_1$ is created, and the responsibility r_1 is moved to the new class. Second, another new class *Base* is also created. Third, we make both *Menu* and $Class_1$ inherit *Base*. Finally, we respectively rename *Menu*, $Class_1$, and *Base* to *User-Menu*, *Admin-Menu*, and *Menu* according to their meanings.

4 Support Tool

We have implemented RAST, a support tool for automating our approach. RAST is an extended version of an existing CASE tool named AmaterasUML [1].

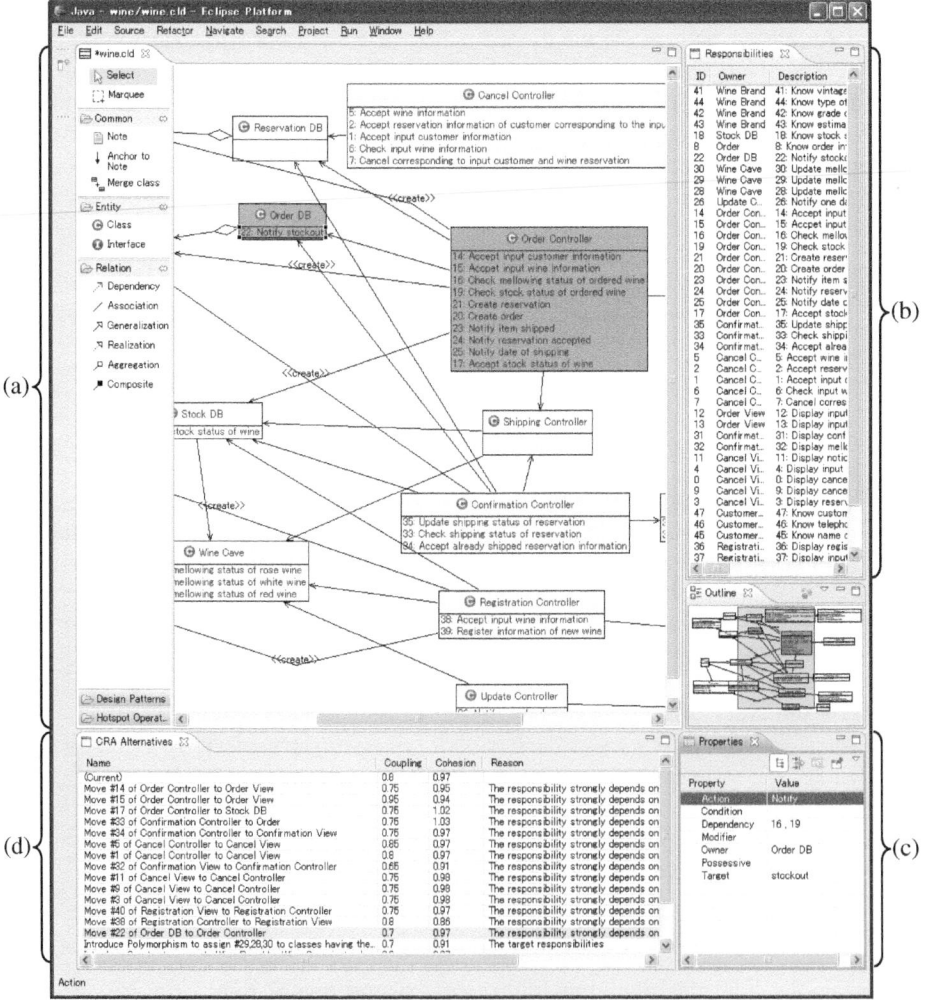

Fig. 3. Snapshot of RAST

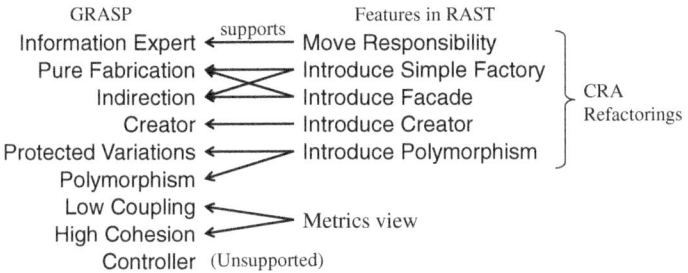

Fig. 4. How many GRASP patterns does RAST supports?

Figure 3 is a snapshot when we develop CRA using RAST. The view (a) is an editor for designing class structure and responsibilities. In RAST, each rectangle box expressing a class in the diagram has extra fourth area in the bottom representing the assigned responsibilities[1]. For example, the class *Order Controller* has 10 responsibilities including "Create order". When we select a class, the responsibilities corresponding with it will be shown in the view (b). All responsibilities for all classes can be shown when we click the background of the editor. We can describe responsibilities in the form proposed in Sect. 3.2 and edit them using the properties view (c). After editing responsibilities, possible refactorings (alternative CRAs) will be suggested in the view (d), and we can accept a suggested CRA by double-clicking it. In the figure, the suggested refactorings include **Move Responsibility** #22: "Notify stockout" in the class *Order DB* to the class *Order Controller*. This refactoring is suggested because the responsibility "Notify stockout" in *Order DB* depends on the responsibilities #16: "Check mellowing status of ordered wine" and #19: "Check stock status of ordered wine", but they are in another class *Order Controller*. When a user single-clicks an alternative, the classes related to the refactoring will be highlighted for confirmation of the refactoring effects. In the case shown in the figure, the user can understand that the above refactoring will affect two classes *Order DB* and *Order Controller*. Additionally, we can undo already-applied refactorings and redo them so that we tend to design our CRA by trial-and-error step by step. This view is also useful because it shows the averages of coupling and cohesion metric values as additional information for each alternative and the current CRA. Although designers are needed to coordinate metric conflicts, i.e., trade-off relationship between cohesions and couplings, listing the suggestions with their metric values after performing the suggested refactoring enables the desingers to understand which refactoring improves which metric values easily.

Figure 4 illustrates how RAST supports GRASP. RAST supports eight patterns of GRASP out of nine. In particular, six patterns are supported by our CRA refactorings. Additionally, **Low Coupling** and **High Cohesion** are indirectly supported by the metric view of RAST. Currently, **Controller** is not supported by RAST. This is because **Controller** is more implementation-side pattern instead of upstream design, dealing with the

---

[1] The reason why there are only two areas in every class in Fig. 3 is that the user did not input any attributes and methods.

flow of events. The current responsibility form does not have the ability to represent the flow of events. It is a candidate of future work to support **Controller** by representing the flow of events in the responsibility form.

5 Preliminary Evaluation

In order to evaluate our method described in Sect. 3, controlled experiments with four subjects are conducted. In particular, we are interested in answering the following research questions (RQs):

RQ1 —Does our method improve the design quality of CRA?
RQ2 —Do CRA alternatives suggested by our tool support designers appropriately?

5.1 Experimental Design

Two students (Subjects S_1 and S_2) and two design experts (Subjects E_1 and E_2 respectively in academia and industry) participated after receiving an explanation about the purpose of this experiment and usage of RAST. Each subject was assigned to the same design task based on responsibility driven design [25]. They designed classes and their CRA of a target system. In the task, at most two hours were spent for each subject. The target system was specified with use case descriptions and with a list of responsibilities extracted from the use case descriptions. These designing tasks were limited to class identification processes only. The details of class features such as attributes and methods were not defined. The target system is a part of a supply chain management system for a virtual winery. The system has five use cases such as "Order a wine", "Update an order", or "Register new wine". We analyzed these use case descriptions and identified 46 responsibilities of the target system. All of the subjects were provided with the use case descriptions and the extracted responsibilities to identify classes and CRA. They could use our tool, but for two of them, i.e., Subjects S_1 and E_1, a part of the tool functions were disabled so that they could not be suggested the CRA alternatives which were displayed in the view (d) of Fig. 3. That is to say, they only used RAST as a tool for input and management of CRA. In contrast, Subjects S_2 and E_2 utilized a function of CRA. They considered the advantages and disadvantages of all the suggested CRAs and selected a CRA which they decided as the best.

We assessed final CRAs of each subject by using following three metrics. A principle of appropriate CRA is low coupling and high cohesion [14]. We used CLC_r and NC_r to measure the strength of coupling based on Class-Responsibility and Class-Class relationships respectively. We also used $LCOM_r^*$ to measure the lack of cohesion. The lower values of all metrics on a CRA indicate the more appropriate CRA. In the following definitions of metrics, $C := \{c_1, \ldots, c_N\}$ and $R(c) := \{r \mid owner(r) = c\}$ respectively denote the set of all classes included in the class diagram and the set of responsibilities assigned to the class c.

CLC_r is a modified CLC (Class Level Coupling) [6,12] which measures the coupling of a class design to adapt for the assessment of CRA. We focus on the relationships between responsibilities instead of ones between methods and/or attributes which are counted in original CLC:

$$CLC_r := \frac{1}{|C|} \sum_{c \in C} \sum_{r \in R(c)} (depend(r) + create(r)).$$

Here, $depend(r)$ and $create(r)$ will be 1 if and only if r is a responsibility depending on another responsibility and r creates an object respectively, and otherwise 0.

NC_r is the average of number of relationships between classes. We refer to metrics [10,15] for assessment of a design model based on the number of relationships such as aggregation, composition, or generalization in a class diagram:

$$NC_r := \frac{1}{|C|} \sum_{c \in C} CO(c)$$

where $CO(c)$ is a number of classes which have relationships with the class c.

$LCOM_r^*$ is a modified $LCOM^*$ (Lack of Cohesion Of Method) [11] to adapt for the assessment of CRA. We use a number of responsibilities which are specified in Dependency column of responsibility descriptions instead of one of attribute references in methods:

$$LCOM_r^* := \frac{1}{|C|} \sum_{c \in C} \frac{\sum_{r \in R(c)} \mu(r,c)/|R(c)| - |R(c)|}{1 - |R(c)|}$$

where $\mu(r, c)$ is the number of responsibilities of the class c which depend on the responsibility r.

In order to evaluate the quality of suggested design alternative, we also conducted a survey in the form of a questionnaire to Subjects S_2 and E_2 who utilized a function of CRA alternative suggestion of RAST. The questionnaire includes questions about a reason why they accept or reject suggestions.

Note that the subjects include one of the authors of this paper. In order to minimize the bias, we carefully set up the experiment; he is independent of the example preparation and did not utilized the function of CRA.

Table 3. Experimental results

Subject		S_1	E_1	S_2	E_2	Average
# accepted suggestions[2]		–	–	6	7	–
# created classes		15	20	27	28	–
CLC_r	w/ suggestions	–	–	0.67	1.04	0.86
	w/o suggestions	2.53	1.30	–	–	1.92
NC_r	w/ suggestions	–	–	0.85	1.07	0.96
	w/o suggestions	1.27	1.60	–	–	1.43
$LCOM_r^*$	w/ suggestions	–	–	0.72	0.79	0.76
	w/o suggestions	0.80	0.97	–	–	0.89

---

[2] Exclude suggestions whose application was canceled.

Table 4. A survey of questionnaire on quality of suggestion by our proposed refactoring

---
Move Responsibility
   (+) Tool suggested just what I intend to move.
   (+/−) Reasonable suggestions. However many unnecessary suggestions included.
Introduce Facade
   (−) The suggestion makes my design more complicated rather than reduce complexity.
Introduce Creator
   (+) Reasonable and useful suggestions.
Introduce Polymorphism
   (+) I just realized coordinate responsibilities when tool suggested this refactoring.
   (+) Tool suggested a responsibility split just what I intend to.

5.2 Experimental Result and Discussion

In this subsection, we show our experimental results and discuss the answer to the research questions mentioned in Sect. 5.1.

Table 3 shows the values of three metrics for a final CRA, the number of accepted suggestions, and the number of created classes of each subject. A summary of questionnaire answers[3] is shown in Table 4. In the table, the symbols '+' and '−' respectively indicate positive and negative answer.

RQ1: Based on differences of average values of CLC_r, NC_r and $LCOM_r^*$, it could be noted that the final design of Subjects S_2 and E_2, who utilized a suggestion function of RAST, had lower coupling and higher cohesion values than Subjects S_1 and E_1. From the viewpoint of a coupling and cohesion principle, the suggestion of CRA alternative based on our approach allowed them to derive more appropriate CRA.

RQ2: As shown in Table 4, the answers for suggestions based on the three CRA refactoring are mostly positive. In the case of **Introduce Polymorphism** and **Move Responsibility**, our subjects obtained the suggestions of CRAs which they just intended to apply and could save time-consuming tasks. In particular, the former found a better CRA rather than one designed by a subject. There were negative answers for unnecessary suggestions of **Move Responsibility** and **Introduce Facade**. Since the target of this experiment is an interactive application such as Web application, some subjects applied the MVC architecture and separately assigned related responsibilities to models and controllers. Our tool suggested that a responsibility for a model/controller must be moved to the other even if it causes architecture violations because these responsibilities often have dependencies. We can reduce unnecessary suggestions by tuning detection rules based on analyses of more case studies. It is quite important in a design task to find many design candidates and choose the best design under various design trade-offs. Therefore, we answer for this research question that our proposed method can help developers to find better CRA appropriately.

---
[3] Since any CRA alternative based on **Introduce Simple Factory** was not suggested in this experiment, there is no answer related this refactoring.

6 Related Work

There are several works for supporting design model refactoring to improve a design. Bowman et al. used genetic algorithm to calculate the assignment of methods and attributes to classes so as to optimize coupling and cohesion values of a class diagram [4,5]. However, their approach is based on coupling and cohesion calculated only from the syntactical relationships among methods and attributes such as caller-callee relationships between methods and referential relationships between methods and attributes. It does not consider any semantical information of responsibilities, differently from ours.

Tsantails et al. focused on source code, not object-oriented design [24]. Their approach is to detect method assignment so that cohesion values become higher preventing coupling values from rising. It also provides a refactoring technique of method movement for designers. Kerievsky also proposed patterns for refactoring, but they are mainly applied to source code [13]. It is preferable to improve method assignment as early as possible, not in the step of source code level but design because of avoiding rework of development activities in later steps.

We can find several metric-based approaches to detect bad smells [16,18,19]. Marinescu [16] defined detection strategies with metrics-based rules to capture deviations from good design principles and heuristics. Oliveto et al. [19] proposed a method to identify occurrences of antipatterns [7] based on numerical analysis of metric values. Moha et al. proposed DECOR method and DETEX technique [18] to specify and automatically generate identification algorithms for code/design smells based on metrics and structural characteristics. They showed the detection performance of 19 automatic generated algorithms by DETEX. However, these approaches have no features to suggest design alternatives against detected bad smells.

Zamani et al. proposed a method to analyze a UML model using the information on stereotypes and checks whether enterprise architectural patterns (EAA patterns) are applied correctly to the model or not [27]. The conditions to decide the correct application of EAA pattern are defined with Object Constraint Language (OCL). However, this approach is for the case where a designer has used specific patterns dealing with relationships among several classes, and it is difficult to apply CRA as it is because CRA requires more general principles for its improvement in the level of finer granularity. In [22], model refactoring on UML class and state diagrams is formalized as a sequence of transformation operations defined in OCL. However, it did not discuss how to define and detect bad smells in diagrams. In addition, it dealt with simple refactoring such as removal, renaming and additions of elements including generalization.

Trifu et al. discussed relationship between a design flaw and the number of directly observable indicators [23]. They defined specifications of the design flaw including context and indicators, and a diagnosis strategy using indicators and correction strategies written in a natural language. They also presented a tool to identify design flaws. Their indicators for design flaw identification are defined as a combination of design metrics and structural information. ClassCompass [8], which is an automated software design critique system, has a feature to suggest design correction based on rules written in a natural language. However, they have no information related to responsibilities of systems.

Some of the principles proposed in [17] can be used for CRA. For example, Dependency Inversion Principle says that modules in a higher level should not be dependent on those in lower level, etc. We can apply our approach to some of them and use them as guidelines of CRA together with GRASP.

7 Conclusion

This paper presented a technique for the automated support of design model refactoring, more specifically improving class responsibility assignment (CRA). In this technique, we describe responsibilities in the form similar to case frames of Case Grammar, and define bad smells and refactoring operations based on GRASP. Our supporting tool called RAST automatically detects bad smells in a class diagram with CRA information and suggests candidates of applicable refactoring operations. A designer can remove the bad smells by performing one of the suggested refactorings. Furthermore, we made a preliminary experiment and it showed a tendency to realize CRA of higher quality from object oriented design view.

We can summarize agenda for future work as follows:

- In the experiment of this paper, our subject did not think that some of the suggestions of refactoring were useful so much. We will analyze its reasons and improve our rules.
- More experiments, including usability evaluations of RAST, are necessary to obtain more meaningful and significant findings.
- We will leverage design constraints and architecture information. For example, a suggestion filtering feature based on such information will effectively reduce unnecessary suggestions.
- The other types of patterns or principles except GRASP such as Dependency Inversion Principle [17] should be considered to make the applicability of our tool wider.
- We did not assess the efforts for designers to describe responsibilities following our approach during their design activities. Based on this assessment, we will explore the improvement of our description technique if any issues are found.

References

1. Project Amateras, http://amateras.sourceforge.jp/
2. Beck, K., Cunningham, W.: A laboratory for teaching object-oriented thinking. In: Proc. Conference on Object-Oriented Programming Systems, Languages and Applications, pp. 1–6 (1989)
3. Bellin, D., Simone, S.S.: The CRC Card Book. Addison-Wesley Professional, Reading (1997)
4. Bowman, M., Briand, L.C., Labiche, Y.: Multi-objective genetic algorithms to support class responsibility assignment. In: Proc. 23rd IEEE International Conference on Software Maintenance, pp. 124–133 (2007)
5. Bowman, M., Briand, L.C., Labiche, Y.: Solving the class responsibility assignment problem in object-oriented analysis with multi-objective genetic algorithms. IEEE Transactions on Software Engineering 36(6), 817–837 (2010)

6. Briand, L.C., Daly, J.W., Wüst, J.K.: A unified framework for coupling measurement in object-oriented systems. IEEE Transactions on Software Engineering 25(1), 91–121 (1999)
7. Brown, W.J., Malveau, R.C., McCormick, H.W., Mowbray, T.J.: AntiPatterns: Refactoring Software, Architectures, and Projects in Crisis. John Wiley and Sons, Chichester (1998)
8. Coelho, W., Murphy, G.: ClassCompass: A software design mentoring system. Educational Resources in Computing 7, 1–18 (2007)
9. Fillmore, C.J.: Lexical entries for verbs. Foundations of Language 4(4), 373–393 (1968)
10. Genero, M., Piattini, M., Calero, C.: Empirical validation of class diagram metrics. In: Proc. International Symposium on Empirical Software Engineering, pp. 195–203 (2002)
11. Henderson-Sellers, B.: Object-Oriented Metrics: Measures of Complexity. Prentice Hall, Englewood Cliffs (1995)
12. Hitz, M., Montazeri, B.: Measuring coupling and cohesion in object-oriented systems. In: Proc. International Symposium on Applied Corporate Computing (1995)
13. Kerievsky, J.: Refactoring to Patterns. Addison Wesley, Reading (2004)
14. Larman, C.: Applying UML and Patterns: An Introduction to Object-Oriented Analysis and Design and Iterative Development, 3rd edn. Prentice Hall, Englewood Cliffs (2005)
15. Manso, M.E., Genero, M., Piattini, M.: No-redundant metrics for UML class diagram structural complexity. In: Eder, J., Missikoff, M. (eds.) CAiSE 2003. LNCS, vol. 2681, pp. 127–142. Springer, Heidelberg (2003)
16. Marinescu, R.: Detection strategies: Metrics-based rules for detecting design flaws. In: Proc. 20th International Conference on Software Maintenance, pp. 350–359 (2004)
17. Martin, R.C.: Agile Software Development: Principles, Patterns, and Practices. Prentice Hall, Englewood Cliffs (2002)
18. Moha, N., Gueheneuc, Y.G., Duchien, L., Meur, A.F.L.: DECOR: A method for the specification and detection of code and design smells. IEEE Transactions on Software Engineering 36(1), 20–36 (2010)
19. Oliveto, R., Khomh, F., Antoniol, G., Gueheneuc, Y.G.: Numerical signatures of antipatterns: An approach based on B-Splines. In: Proc. 14th European Conference on Software Maintenance and Reengineering, pp. 248–251 (2010)
20. Rosenberg, D., Scott, K.: Use Case Driven Object Modeling with UML: A Practical Approach. Addison-Wesley, Reading (1999)
21. Sharble, R.C., Cohen, S.: The object-oriented brewery: A comparison of two object-oriented development methods. ACM SIGSOFT Software Engineering Notes 18(2), 60–73 (1993)
22. Sunyé, G., Pollet, D., Le Traon, Y., Jézéquel, J.-M.: Refactoring UML models. In: Gogolla, M., Kobryn, C. (eds.) UML 2001. LNCS, vol. 2185, pp. 134–148. Springer, Heidelberg (2001)
23. Trifu, A., Reupke, U.: Towards automated restructuring of object oriented systems. In: Proc. 12th Working Conference on Reverse Engineering, pp. 39–48 (2007)
24. Tsantalis, N., Chatzigeorgiou, A.: Identification of move method refactoring opportunities. IEEE Transactions on Software Engineering 35(3), 347–367 (2009)
25. Wirfs-Brock, R., McKean, A.: Object Design: Roles, Responsibilities, and Collaborations. Addison-Wesley, Reading (2002)
26. Wirfs-Brock, R., Wilkerson, B., Wiener, L.: Designing Object-Oriented Software. Prentice Hall, Englewood Cliffs (1990)
27. Zamani, B., Butler, G.: Smell detection in UML designs which utilize pattern languages. Iranian Journal of Electrical and Computer Engineering 8(1), 47–52 (2009)

Vision Paper: The Essence of Structural Models

Dmitrijs Zaparanuks and Matthias Hauswirth

University of Lugano
{zaparand,Matthias.Hauswirth}@usi.ch

Abstract. Models should represent the essential aspects of a system and leave out the inessential details. In this paper we propose an automatic approach to determine whether a model indeed focuses on the essential aspects. We define a new metric, structural essence, that quantifies the fraction of essential elements in a model. Our approach targets structural models, such as the prevalent UML class diagrams. It is inspired by the idea of algorithmic essence – the amount of repetitive constructs in a program – and the duality between behavior and structure. We present a framework for computing the essence of a structural model based on a transformation of that model into a "distilled model" and on an existing graph algorithm operating on that distilled model. We discuss the meaning of our concept of structural essence based on a set of example models. We hope that our notion of structural essence will spark discussions on the purpose and the essence of models.

1 Introduction

Given a structural model of a system, can we help a designer to answer the question whether a given model element is essential, or whether that element could be omitted without affecting the functionality of the system? Models with lots of inessential elements can be considered bloated. From an extreme perspective, one could even argue that models should not contain any inessential elements at all: Models are abstractions of a system, they describe *essential* aspects of the system and leave out the *inessential* details. Brook's "No Silver Bullet – Essence and Accident in Software Engineering" [2] makes a clear distinction between the *essential* and *accidental* artifacts in software construction. Brooks deems essential the "complex conceptual structures that compose the abstract software entity", while he classifies as accidental the "*representation* of these abstract entities in programming languages". Moreover, he writes "The essence of a software entity is a construct of interlocking concepts: data sets, relationships among data items, algorithms, and invocations of functions. The essence is abstract, in that the conceptual construct is the same under many different representations."

Recent work [10] introduced an approach to determine the essence of object-oriented programs by analyzing the implementation of those programs. In this paper we propose to lift that idea from the level of binary code, where complete details are available, to the more abstract level of structural models.

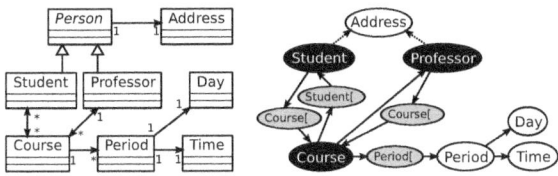

Fig. 1. Example UML Model (Left) and Corresponding Distilled Model (Right)

Figure 1 shows a structural model in the form of a UML class diagram. Our goal is to determine the essential aspects in that model. Following the idea of algorithmic essence [10], we focus on artifacts representing *repetitions*. Our model is *structural*, not behavioral, so it does not directly represent repetitive behavior. Nevertheless, some structural artifacts will *lead* to repetitive behaviors. These are (1) multiplicity on associations, and (2) navigable cycles in the model. The distilled model on the right of the figure brings out these essential aspects. Association ends with unbounded (*) multiplicity are reified as gray nodes (e.g., Period[]). Public concrete classes participating in navigable cycles are represented as black nodes. Other concrete classes are represented as white nodes. The gray and black nodes constitute the essence of the model. The other (white) classes could be considered inessential, because they do not lead to repetitive computations or data structures. Those inessential classes could theoretically be inlined into the essential classes, without affecting the functionality of the model.

We now define our approach for transforming a UML model into a distilled model to identify its essential elements, and for computing our essence metric. Then we present our implementation of that approach, and we discuss how our notion of structural essence can affect research on models.

2 Approach

Our approach to compute structural essence is based on two steps. First, we transform the UML class diagram into a *distilled model*, and second we compute the structural essence on the distilled model.

A distilled model is a directed graph. It represents an abstract view of a UML class diagram. The distilled model is a static structural model of the system. It *describes all possible runtime object graphs*. Most nodes in the distilled model correspond to a class in the UML model, and most edges in the distilled model correspond to an association in the UML model. However, some nodes in the distilled model (the multiplicity nodes) do not correspond to a UML class, and some edges in the distilled model (the inferred edges) do not correspond directly to a UML association.

2.1 Model Transformation

Our model transformation consists of four steps: (1) All non-abstract classes in the UML model are converted into nodes in the distilled model. (2) In the UML model, attributes of classes are converted into equivalent associations between classes. (3) Associations in the UML model are converted into edges in the distilled model. (4) Generalizations in the UML model are used to generate additional implicit association edges in the distilled model. We now define this transformation in more detail.

Classes. For each non-abstract Class in the UML model we create a corresponding node in the distilled model. We do not create nodes for Interfaces and abstract Classes, because the dynamic type of an object in the runtime object graph must correspond to a concrete class.

Properties. In a UML model, a class can have attributes (Properties). An attribute p of type B in a class A often is a manifestation of an association between class A and class B. In particular, it manifests an association that is navigable from A to B. The attribute p also can have a multiplicity, which corresponds to the multiplicity of the association end at class B. Figure 2 shows how, for every property of every class, we infer the corresponding association, if that association does not already exist. The top half of the figure shows the original UML model containing classes with attributes, and the bottom half shows the resulting UML model where attributes have been transformed into associations. Note that each attribute leads to exactly one unidirectional association, navigable from the class containing the attribute to the class representing the type of the attribute. The source end (tail) of the association always has a multiplicity of "1". The multiplicity of the target end (head) corresponds to the multiplicity of the attribute.

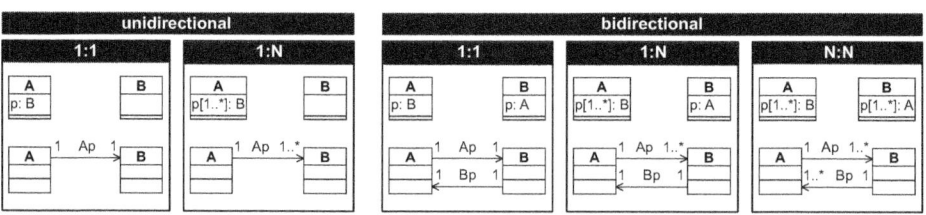

Fig. 2. Transforming UML Properties to UML Associations

Associations. The transformation of *associations* in the UML model into the distilled model depends on the multiplicity and navigability of those associations. Figure 3 shows the seven variants of a binary association and their transformations into the distilled model. The two parts of the figure (unidirectional vs. bidirectional) differ in terms of navigability. The columns within a part differ in terms of multiplicity: they represent 1-to-1, 1-to-many, many-to-1, and many-to-many relationships. For each column in the figure, the top shows the UML class diagram, the middle shows the corresponding distilled model, and the bottom shows the structural essence (number of multiplicity nodes plus cycle header nodes).

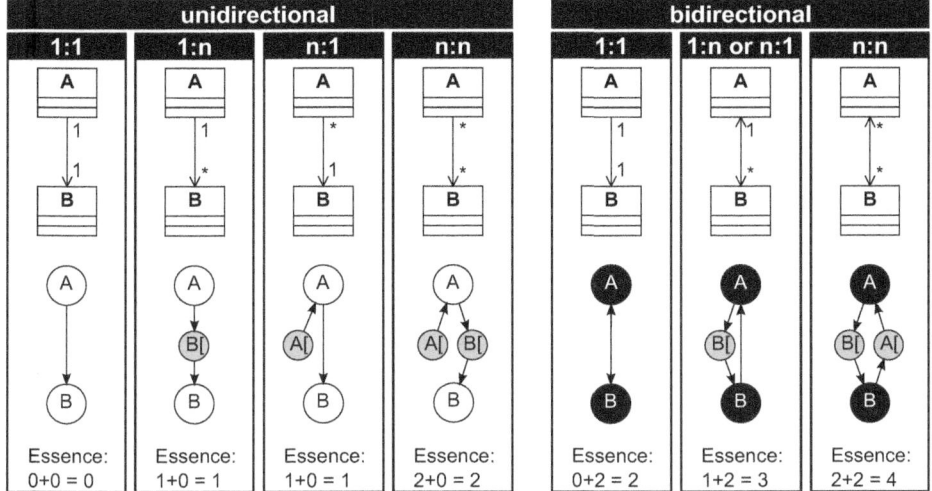

Fig. 3. Transforming UML Associations to Distilled Model

For each association end with a multiplicity involving a "*" (i.e., "0..*" or "1..*"), we create a multiplicity node (grey) in the distilled model. The multiplicity node can be seen as an array (e.g., of type B[]). The reason for creating multiplicity nodes is that an unbounded multiplicity implies repetition: there could be an arbitrary number of objects on that end, and an implementation of the system will need to traverse that association using either a loop or a recursion. Our idea of structural essence is directly tied to the notion of repetition: the repetitions represent the essential aspects of the system.

If the "*" occurs at a navigable end (the arrow head), we add an edge from the origin (e.g., A) to the multiplicity node, and a second edge from the multiplicity node to the target (e.g., B). However, a "*" occurring at the non-navigable (tail) end of an unidirectional association has to be treated specially: We want to create a multiplicity node to represent the importance of such a N:1 relationship, but we do not want to introduce a cycle into the distilled model, because the UML model does not contain a cycle. Thus, we create the multiplicity node, and we add an edge from the multiplicity node to the class at its association end. This almost introduces a cycle: it only leaves one edge out (the one from the opposite class to the multiplicity node).

The figure shows that bidirectional associations introduce cycles into the distilled model. This is desired. Like multiplicity nodes, cycles contribute to essence because they imply repetition: there could be an arbitrary number of objects represented by such a cyclic model (e.g., a linked list), and an implementation of the system will need to traverse that cycle using either a loop or a recursion.

Generalizations. Generalizations can introduce cycles into an otherwise acyclic distilled model. Thus, generalizations can affect structural essence. Figure 4

shows the transformation of generalizations into the distilled model. It contains five cases, and for each case, it shows the original UML class diagram (top) and the resulting distilled model (bottom). The figure explains the effects of two basic principles: *field polymorphism* and *field inheritance*.

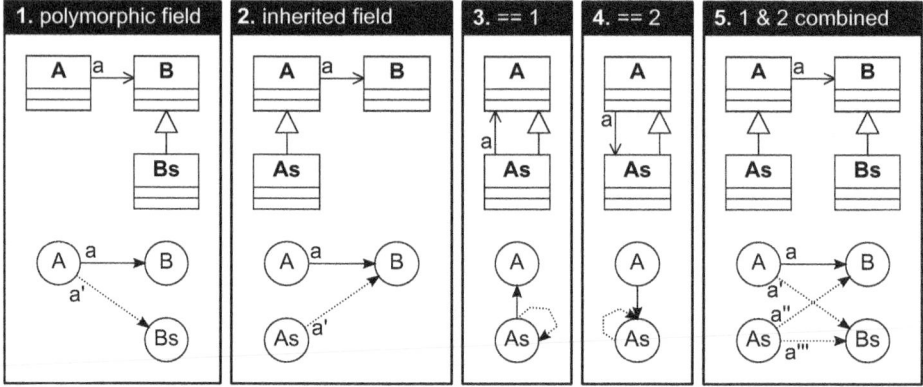

Fig. 4. Transforming UML Generalizations to Distilled Model

Field polymorphism means that a field of a given type may refer to an object of that type *or of any subtype of that type*. Case 1 in the figure shows the effect of field polymorhism on the distilled model. The UML class diagram shows one uni-directional binary association. That association a from A to B implies two possible kinds of links at runtime: links of an instance of A to an instance of B, and links of an instance of A to an instance of Bs. We thus make that second link explicit as the inferred edge a' from A to Bs in the distilled model[1].

Field inheritance means that a field in a superclass *is inherited by that superclass' subclasses*. Case 2 in the figure shows the effect of field inheritance on the distilled model. The UML class diagram shows one uni-directional binary association. That association a from A to B implies two possible kinds of links at runtime: links of an instance of A to an instance of B, and links of an instance of As to an instance of B. We thus make that second link explicit as the inferred edge a' from As to B in the distilled model.

Cases 3 and 4 are special cases of field polymorphism and field inheritance where the field refers to a superclass (case 3) or a subclass (case 4).

Case 5 combines field polymorphism and field inheritance. It shows that this leads to more than one implicit edge in the distilled model: for each subtype of A (incl. A) we need to create an edge to each subtype of B (incl. B).

---

[1] Such implicit associations due to field polymorphism are the structural equivalent to the behavioral idea of inferred call edges due to method polymorphism in static call graphs. In a call graph involving a method A.m(), and a method B.x() that is overridden in subclass Bs, a call site in A.m() with the static call target B.x() would imply that at runtime, A.m() might call Bs.x().

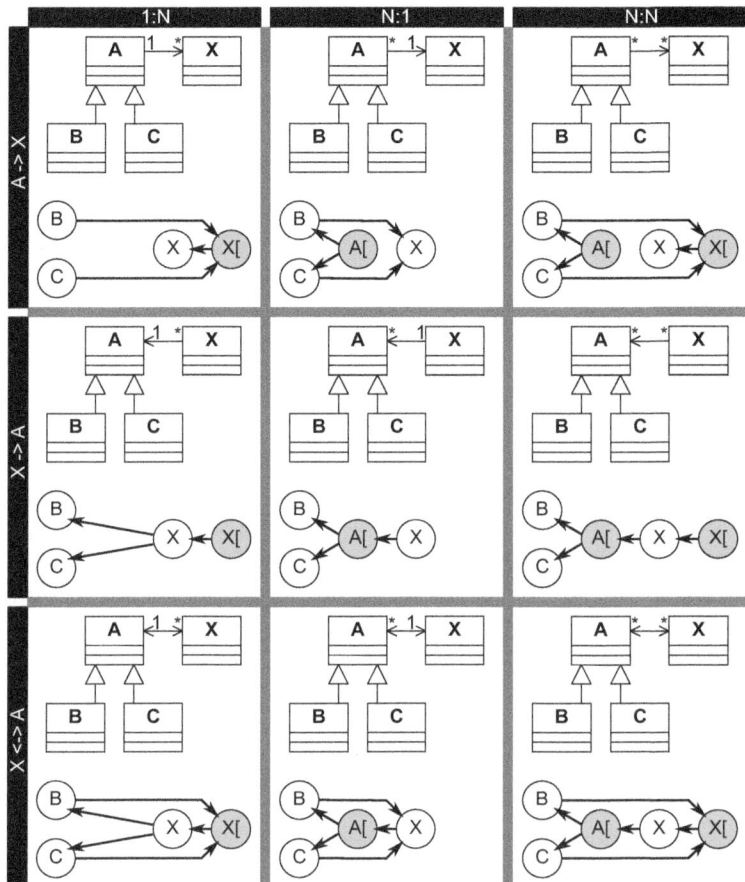

Fig. 5. Interaction of Generalization and Multiplicity

Generalization and Multiplicity. Above we have shown how generalization affects the transformation of associations with a bounded multiplicity (e.g., "1"). We also have seen that associations with unbounded multiplicity lead to multiplicity nodes in the distilled model. Here we combine the two aspects to define the transformation for associations with unbounded multiplicity that refer to a superclass. Figure 5 shows the nine possible cases. The main design decision in this aspect of the transformation is that we create only one multiplicity node for each unbounded association end (e.g., "A[" and "X["), and that we do not create additional multiplicity nodes for inferred associations[2].

---

[2] The online appendix for this paper discusses design alternatives for this and other aspects of our approach: http://sape.inf.usi.ch/essence/structural

2.2 Essence Computation

The distilled model constitutes the minimal representation necessary to compute essence. It consists of multiplicity nodes that represent 1-to-many relationships and class nodes that represent classes[3].

Essence quantifies the amount of repetition (multiplicity and cycles). To compute essence, we thus count the number of multiplicity nodes and the number of "cycle header" nodes. To detect cycles in the graph and to identify the header nodes of those cycles, we use an algorithm that detects nested strongly connected components [10]. Because that algorithm requires an "entry" node from which all other nodes are reachable, we introduce an artificial entry node, and we create an edge from that entry node to all public class nodes. We also add edges from the entry node to those multiplicity nodes that are otherwise unreachable.

The cycle header detection algorithm proceeds iteratively: First, it finds strongly connected components (SCC). Second, it identifies all nodes in an SCC reachable from outside that SCC as "cycle header" nodes. Third, it removes all back-edges (edges from nodes within the SCC to its cycle headers). It repeats these three steps until all SCCs are trivial (single nodes).

The *absolute structural essence* of a model corresponds to the number of cycle header nodes plus the number of multiplicity nodes. The *relative structural essence* of a model corresponds to the absolute structural essence divided by the number of class nodes.

3 Implementation

Figure 6 presents our implementation of the above approach. The "XMI Structure Transformer" represents the approach described in Section 2.1. We implemented this transformation as an extension[4] of the SDMetrics framework [9]. The "Essence Metric Analysis" corresponds to the approach described in Section 2.2. It is based on the implementation of the cycle detection algorithm for computing *algorithmic* essence of Java bytecode [10]. The "Distilled Model Visualizer" transforms the distilled model into GraphViz dot visualizations similar to the ones used throughout this paper.

The "XMI Structure Transformer" represents just one possibility to derive a distilled model. Given the relative scarcity of publicly available example UML models, we also implemented a second transformer, the "Java Bytecode Structure Transformer", which transforms the structural aspects of a *Java implementation* of a system into a distilled model. That transformer reads Java class files instead

---

[3] The distilled model is logically equivalent to the loop call graph used when computing behavioral essence [10]. The multiplicity nodes in the distilled model correspond to the loop nodes in the loop call graph, and the class nodes in the distilled model correspond to the method nodes in the loop call graph.

[4] We slightly changed SDMetrics to gather information about multiplicities and static vs. instance members.

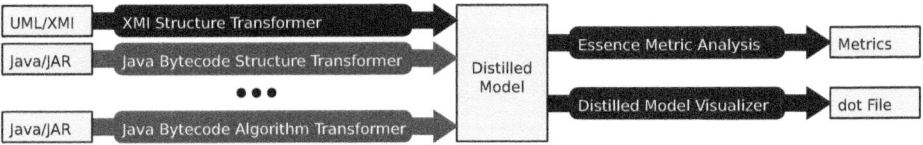

Fig. 6. Extensible Framework for Computing Essence

of UML/XMI structural models. For the cases where Java classes are created 1:1 from UML models, the resulting distilled model is equivalent to the one produced from UML.

Our implementation is extensible and allows the addition of new kinds of transformers. For example, we recast the computation of a loop call graph [10] (which represents the behavioral, or algorithmic, aspects of a Java application) as a transformer for our new framework ("Java Bytecode Algorithm Transformer"). We could also envision a transformer that transforms the *behavioral* aspects of a UML model (e.g., the call graph and loop information available in UML interaction diagrams) into a distilled model.

4 Discussion

We now discuss how the concept of structural essence may affect work on models.

Essence of model vs. essence of implementation. Models are abstract representations of systems. They abstract away the inessential details and describe the essential aspects of a system. Structural essence represents an automatically computable and (we believe) intuitive measure of the essential aspects of a system. Should an (abstract) model have a higher relative essence than a (concrete) implementation, because the model omits inessential artifacts? Could one also claim that the higher the relative essence of a model, the "better" (more essential) that model?

Matching models and implementations. Could structural essence and our distilled model help in establishing the correspondence between a model and its implementation? Could our distilled models, which include multiplicity nodes and highlight cycle headers, be effective as a basis for building software reflexion models [6]? Could our idea improve correspondence matching approaches such as those introduced by van Opzeeland et al. [8]?

Structural essence of recursive data types. We computed the essence of UML models of different designs of lists, trees, and graphs[5]. We found that the absolute structural essence of all directly-recursive design variants is constant, and that essence increases from lists to trees to graphs (all directly-recursive list designs have structural essence 1, all trees 2, all graphs 3).

---

[5] Details on http://sape.inf.usi.ch/essence/structural/recursive-datatypes

Structural essence of design patterns. We computed the structural essence of UML class diagrams of the 23 GoF design patterns [4][6]. 15 patterns have an essence of 0; they represent artifacts of modularization. Composite and Decorator have essence 2; they introduce tree structures. Flyweight, Memento, and Chain of Responsibility have essence 1; they introduce new lists. Observer and Mediator have essence 3; they decouple cyclic relationships.

Essence of other structural models. In this paper we focused on computing essence based on structural models in the form of class diagrams. The reason for this is the prevalence of this kind of model. How could one best compute essence based on other structural models such as component diagrams?

Structural vs. behavioral essence. Prior work introduced the notion of *algorithmic* (behavioral) essence of Java code [10]. Given the duality between behavior and structure, between loops and association multiplicities, between recursions and cyclic associations, between the inlining of methods and the inlining of objects, does structural essence correlate with algorithmic essence? We performed a preliminary experiment, where, due to the lack of a large suite of complete UML models, we analyzed the structural and behavioral essence of Java code. We measured 81 realistic open-source applications consisting of 73246 classes (a subset of the Qualitas Corpus [7]) and found Pearson's correlation coefficient between structural and behavioral essence to be only 0.2, with a 95% confidence interval of $[-0.017, 0.402]$. It remains to be seen whether this low correlation would also apply to structural and behavioral essence computed on real-world UML models.

Behavioral essence of models. The original measure of algorithmic essence is based on a *behavioral* view of the *implementation* of a system (the bytecode instructions in Java code) [10]. How could we best compute essence based on more abstract behavioral *models*? Assuming the availability of a complete set of interaction diagrams, one could construct the system's call graph (and count the number of recursions) based on the messages, and one could count the number of loops based on the loop combined fragments. Alternatively, one could use activity diagrams (with loop nodes) or state machine diagrams (through cycles involving states and transitions) to determine analogous ways to determine repetitive behavior.

Practical use: quality prediction. Briand and Wüst [1] review prior empirical results on modeling external system qualities based on internal properties. Most of the surveyed work uses the measures proposed by Chidamber and Kemerer [3] to characterize structure. The most prevalent of the C&K measures are *coupling* and *cohesion*. They help in deciding which parts of a model to *move* where. Our measure of *essence* may help in deciding which parts of a model to *keep* and which parts to *remove*. NAS, number of associations [5], is a metric that looks similar to essence. However, essence focuses on repetition, and thus it excludes associations with bounded multiplicities, and it also counts cycle headers in the model. Given the difference between structural

---

[6] Details on http://sape.inf.usi.ch/essence/structural/design-patterns

essence and existing metrics, would structural essence, an internal structural property, improve quality prediction models based on existing metrics?

Evaluation on benchmark models. We have created the essentializer[7], a web site that allows developers to analyze the essence of their model and to compare their model to a corpus of public models in terms of essence. We have populated the essentializer's database with a set of artificial "micro-benchmark" models. We would like to study the structural essence of representative real-world models, based on a future corpus of application models similar to the Qualitas Corpus [7] of Java application implementations.

In this paper we introduce the notion of "structural essence", and we describe an approach to compute that metric on UML class diagrams. Unlike the traditional view that navigability and multiplicity are details of associations that may be omitted from higher-level models, our view is that multiplicities (and the cycles due to the navigability of associations) are essential. We hope that this idea will spark discussions on the purpose and the essence of models.

References

1. Briand, L., Wüst, J.: Empirical studies of quality models in object-oriented systems. Advances in Computers 59, 97–166 (2002)
2. Brooks Jr, F.P.: The mythical man-month. anniversary ed.. Addison-Wesley Longman Publishing Co., Inc., Boston (1995)
3. Chidamber, S.R., Kemerer, C.F.: A metrics suite for object oriented design. IEEE Trans. Softw. Eng. 20(6), 476–493 (1994)
4. Gamma, E., Helm, R., Johnson, R., Vlissides, J.: Design Patterns: Elements of Reusable Object-Oriented Software. Addison-Wesley, Boston (1995)
5. Harrison, R., Counsell, S., Nithi, R.: Coupling metrics for object-oriented design. In: Proceedings of the 5th International Symposium on Software Metrics, METRICS 1998, pp. 150–156. IEEE Computer Society, Washington, DC (1998)
6. Murphy, G.C., Notkin, D., Sullivan, K.J.: Software reflexion models: Bridging the gap between design and implementation. IEEE Trans. Softw. Eng. 27, 364–380 (2001)
7. Tempero, E., Anslow, C., Dietrich, J., Han, T., Li, J., Lumpe, M., Melton, H., Noble, J.: Qualitas corpus: A curated collection of java code for empirical studies. In: 2010 Asia Pacific Software Engineering Conference (APSEC 2010) (December 2010)
8. van Opzeeland, D.J.A., Lange, C.F.J., Chaudron, M.R.V.: Quantitative techniques for the assessment of correspondence between UML designs and implementations. In: Proceedings of the 9th QAOOSE (July 2005)
9. Wüst, J.: SDMetrics: UML software design metrics, http://www.sdmetrics.com/
10. Zaparanuks, D., Hauswirth, M.: The beauty and the beast: Separating design from algorithm. In: Mezini, M. (ed.) ECOOP 2011. LNCS, vol. 6813, pp. 27–51. Springer, Heidelberg (2011)

---

[7] The essentializer is available at http://essentializer.org

Vision Paper:
Towards Model-Based Energy Testing

Claas Wilke, Sebastian Götz, Jan Reimann, and Uwe Aßmann

Institut für Software- und Multimediatechnik
Technische Universität Dresden
D-01062, Dresden, Germany
{claas.wilke,jan.reimann,uwe.assmann}@tu-dresden.de,
sebastian.goetz@acm.org

Abstract. Today, energy consumption is one of the major challenges for optimisation of future software applications and ICT infrastructures. To develop software w.r.t. its energy consumption, testing is an essential activity, since testing allows quality assurance and thus, energy consumption reduction during the software's development. Although first approaches measuring and predicting software's energy consumption for its execution on a specific hardware platform exist, no model-based testing approach has been developed, yet. In this paper we present our vision of a model-based energy testing approach that uses a combination of abstract interpretation and run-time profiling to predict the energy consumption of software applications and to derive energy consumption test cases.

Keywords: Energy consumption testing, abstract interpretation, profiling, unit testing, model-based testing.

1 Introduction

Today, energy consumption of software systems is gaining more and more importance. The energy demand of information and communication technology (ICT) infrastructures is growing rapidly and has become a significant factor of worldwide carbon dioxide emissions. In 2007, Gartner, Inc. estimated an amount of 2% of world-wide CO2 emissions for ICT [1]. The SMART2020 report confirmed that estimation and predicted an annual growth of 6% of the ICT's emissions until 2020 [2]. For hardware, first approaches for energy-saving operation modes have been developed [3, 4]. In the domain of wireless sensor networks (WSNs) first solutions for energy-optimised operation and energy testing exist [5–7]. However, classical software is optimised w.r.t. its functional and specific non-functional requirements like real-time or performance constraints only. For an energy-optimal ICT application, software must be optimised w.r.t. energy consumption as well, since software is executed on (i.e., CPU) and uses (e.g., network devices) hardware and thus influences the hardware's utilisation and energy consumption. We argue that an application's energy consumption must be tested to ensure that it can be reduced during development in an easy manner such as today's testing frameworks allow quality assurance for real-time and functional requirements.

Our vision is a *model-based energy testing (MBET)* approach that allows not only testing the energy consumption of software artefacts but deriving such test cases from the software's implementation code or a behavior model. MBET allows developers predicting and analysing the energy consumption bounds of their software w.r.t. input parameters (i.e., data) and the software's execution context (i.e., hardware). The envisioned solution predicts the energy consumption in a generic way that allows the use of same test cases on different execution platforms, consuming different amounts of energy (as they are built of different hardware devices). The major idea of MBET is to interpret the application's behavior model in an abstract manner to derive formulas for its best, worst and average case energy consumption. The basis for these predictions is data obtained from energy consumption profiling of atomic building blocks (e.g., single Java bytecode instructions). This allows the prediction of a program's energy consumption based on static analysis and the derivation of test cases comparing these estimations with real values profiled during runtime. Although some approaches for resource and energy consumption analysis of software systems exist [8-11], this is—to the best of our knowledge—the first model-based approach for energy consumption testing of software applications.

The remainder of this paper is structured as follows. In Section 2 we introduce model-based testing (MBT), energy consumption analysis of Java applications, and abstract interpretation. Further we present some related work w.r.t. energy testing. Afterwards, our MBET approach is described in Section 3. Since the approach is still in an early development phase, we present our plan to achieve a fully-implemented realisation of MBET and conclude this paper in Section 4.

2 Background and Related Work

In this section we introduce the three domains related to our MBET approach. These are: MBT, energy consumption prediction of Java programs and abstract interpretation. Finally, we present related work in the domain of energy testing.

Model-Based Testing. Utting et al. define MBT as the "automatable derivation of concrete test cases from abstract formal models, and their execution" [12]. Furthermore, they provide a taxonomy for MBT and a classification of several MBT approaches. Another definition is given by Roßner et al. They define MBT as a process including either (1) utilisation of models for automation of testing activities, (2) the modelling of artefacts within a testing process, or (3) both [13]. Our MBET approach uses a behavior model (e.g., program code, pseudocode, state charts, or sequence diagrams) as input for energy test case generation. Thus, it can be considered as a white-box MBT approach.

Energy Consumption of Java Applications. Lafond et al. [8] developed a framework that allows measuring the average energy consumption of Java bytecode instructions executed on a specific Java virtual machine (JVM). They used their framework to estimate the energy consumption for a large subset of all Java bytecode instructions and evaluated their measurements using several benchmarks. A similar framework was implemented by Seo et al. [9, 10] who profiled Java bytecode to predict the average energy consumption for the execution on a specific platform. Navas et al. [11] designed a framework that allows analysing the resource usage of Java bytecode instructions. Furthermore, they used formal methods to compute mathematical expressions describing the upper bounds for a program's resource utilisation w.r.t. its input parameters. Similar work has been done by Süttner who developed a framework to predict a Java program's *resource* (e.g., CPU, harddrive, or network device) utilisation [14]—which is a prerequisite to predict its energy consumption. He developed an invasive profiling approach that can be used to profile a method's resource utilisation and to derive mathematical expressions approximating resource consumption w.r.t. input data.

Abstract Interpretation. As defined by Cousot and Cousot, "Abstract Interpretation of programs consists in using [a program's computational denotation] to describe computations in another universe of abstract objects, so that the results of abstract execution give some information on the actual computations" [15]. It can be used to derive constraints or equations from the program's static semantics to prove general properties of a program's behavior for every possible execution. For example, abstract interpretation can be used to check whether a mathematical expression always results in a negative value, to predict the bounds of a specific variable's possible values or for static semantics such as type analysis. In our MBET approach we plan to use abstract interpretation to compute bounds for energy consumption of programs based on their control flow graphs (CFGs) and input data.

Energy Testing Approaches. As stated above, energy testing is a rather new research domain in software engineering. Existing approaches focus on hardware's energy optimisation or on embedded systems such as WSNs. Chan et al. [6] proposed a power-aware testing approach for WSNs that is based on metamorphic testing. Energy consumption test cases are created by tracing the energy consumption of functional test cases. Although they propose an approach for energy consumption testing, they focus on WSNs. Similar work has been done by Woerhle et al. [7] who developed a testing architecture for WSNs that is based on so-called *power unit tests*. The tests are associated to regular functional test cases and use a temporal function that predicts lower and upper bounds for the test case's energy consumption during execution.

3 Model-Based Energy Testing

In this section we present our MBET approach that shall allow testing software w.r.t. its energy consumption in a model-based manner. Our MBET approach can be described as a process consisting of six steps which are (cf. Fig. 1):

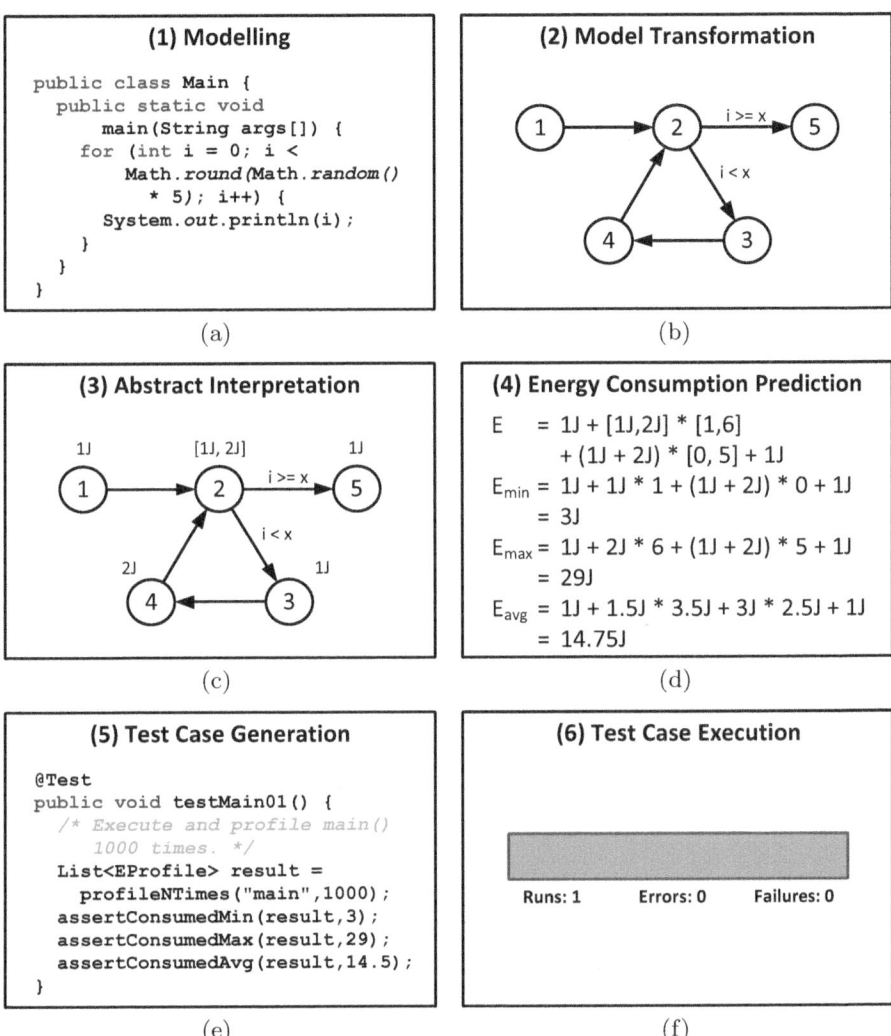

Fig. 1. The MBET Approach

1. Modelling
2. Model Transformation
3. Abstract Interpretation
4. Energy Consumption Prediction
5. Test Case Generation
6. Test Case Execution

These six steps form our testing process which can of course consist of multiple iterations. For example, test cases can be regenerated after the behavior model changed during development. All six steps are shortly explained in the following using the example program[1] given in Figure 1. Possible solutions and approaches to achieve these steps are given as well.

3.1 Modelling

Our vision of an energy testing approach targets to support energy testing for different platforms and hardware. We envision an MBET approach that allows deriving energy test cases from models. Thus, modelling of the system under test (SUT) is its first step. As a model we consider either executable code (e.g., a Java program) or a behavior model (e.g., pseudocode, a UML state chart or a UML sequence diagram). The major requirement for the model used for MBET is a description of the software's behavior on a level of detail that allows deriving a control flow graph (CFG). Figure 1(a) shows a simple Java program that contains a `for` loop that is executed for 0 to 5 times depending on a random value. This program can be considered as an example input model for MBET.

3.2 Model Transformation

In a second step, the model must be transformed into a data structure that can be used for abstract interpretation. In MBET we plan to use a CFG as the basis for abstract interpretation. This leads to a data structure where each statement or state from the behavior model corresponds to a node in the CFG with transitions probably having guards (i.e., Boolean expressions) to represent loops and `if` statements. As can be seen in Figure 1(b), the example input model has been transformed into a CFG consisting of five nodes. Furthermore, the graph contains a cycle which represents the `for` loop from the input program.

3.3 Abstract Interpretation

During abstract interpretation, the CFG is interpreted in an abstract manner. For example, abstract interpretation can be used to predict bounds for the values that variables of a program can have at runtime [15]. For example, one might prove that a specific integer variable can never reach a negative value during a program's execution and thus, the variable has a lower bound of 0. In our case the result of abstract interpretation shall be a set of formulas that allow to compute the lower and upper bounds of a program's energy consumption (cf. Fig. 1(d)). Each node of the graph—representing an instruction of the program—has to be associated with its average energy consumption. These values can be measured or predicted during benchmarking and profiling, e.g., for Java bytecode instructions as done by Lafond et al. [8] and Seo et al. [9, 10]. Once each node has a predicted energy consumption (cf. Fig. 1(c)), formulas can be derived that express the program's best, worst and average case energy consumption. In the

---
[1] For simplicity, all energy consumption rates of the presented example are specified in simple Joule values. We did not try to use realistic values but simple and clarifying values instead.

given example, all nodes have a constant energy consumption. Only node (2) has a consumption that can vary between $1J$ and $2J$. However, its imaginable that nodes may have a more complex energy consumption rate. For example, the rate may depend on the data structure handled by the instruction represented by the node or the times the instruction has been executed before. In such cases nodes may have energy consumption rates expressed by mathematical expressions instead of constant values.

3.4 Energy Consumption Prediction

Once the formulas are derived from abstract interpretation, they can be used to predict a program's energy consumption. As shown in Figure 1(d), we have derived formulas for the program's minimal, maximum, and average energy consumption, based on a general formula for the program's energy consumption:[2]

$$E = 1J + [1J, 2J] * [1, 6] + (1J + 2J) * [0, 5] + 1J \tag{1}$$

The minimal and best case is an execution where the program's **for** loop is not executed at all. The initial node (1) is executed; afterwards, the loop's condition (2) is checked and results in **false**. Finally, node (5) is executed. This results in a minimal execution of $1J + 1J + 1J = 3J$. The maximum energy consumption is the worst case where the loop is executed five times (nodes (3) and (4)) and its loop condition (node (2)) is executed six times, each time consuming its worst case energy ($2J$). This results in a maximum energy consumption of $1J + 2J * 6 + (1J + 2J) * 5 + 1J = 29J$. The average energy consumption rate can be computed in a similar way as illustrated in Figure 1(d). Besides best, worst, and average case energy consumption, other predictions are imaginable as well. For example, it is possible to combine the formulas from abstract interpretation with concrete input values of a program to predict specific energy consumptions for test cases using specific input values as their test data.[3]

An interesting research question for energy consumption prediction is which energy consumption cases can be predicted for which programs. According to Seo et al., three different types of programs exist [9]: Programs having constant energy consumption (1), programs whose energy consumption depends on the data they are processing (2) (e.g., a sort algorithm's energy consumption depends on the size of the data to sort) and (3), programs whose energy consumption is unpredictable (e.g., a program requesting an external database whose consumption depends on the size of the data within the database and the network's response time). Whereas the energy consumption of type (1) and (2) programs can be predicted using abstract interpretation, the prediction of type (3) programs can be complicated if not impossible. Furthermore, some programs do not allow to predict worst case energy consumptions as, e.g., loops may not have

---

[2] Square brackets denote intervals with lower and upper bounds. For example, $[0, 5]$ means values between 0 and 5 inclusively.
[3] Of course, this would require another example program using input parameters.

```
1  /* Simple example to test main(). */
2  @Test
3  public void testMain() {
4    // Execute and profile main() a 1000 times.
5    EProfiler profiler = new EProfiler();
6    List<EProfile> result = EProfilerUtil
7      .profileNTimes(this, "main", new Object[0], profiler, 1000);
8    // Test best and worst case consumption.
9    EAssert.assertConsumedMin(result, 3);
10   EAssert.assertConsumedMax(result, 29);
11   // Test average consumption (delta is +/-1.5).
12   EAssert.assertConsumedAvg(result, 14.75, 1.5);
13 }
```

Listing 1. A JouleUnit Example

upper bounds w.r.t. their number of iterations. A possible solution would be to predict probabilistic values or quantiles for these cases (e.g., a program that consumes a maximum amount of $10J$ with a probability of 99%).

3.5 Test Case Generation

Once a program's energy consumption has been predicted, test cases can be generated that execute the program, measure its real energy consumption and check the measured consumption against the predicted values. Our vision is to develop a testing framework *JouleUnit* for energy consumption profiling and testing (cf. Fig. 1(e)). Similar to other non-functional optimisation problems, energy consumption should not be tested in isolation but altogether with other functional and non-functional requirements of the SUT. Thus, JouleUnit extends the functional testing capabilities of JUnit[4] for energy consumption profiling and testing.[5] As shown in Listing 1, JouleUnit supports energy consumption profiling as well as assertions for best, worst and average case energy consumption including the specification of deltas for allowed variances between expected and measured values. Furthermore, we plan to support a construct that allows executing a method under test multiple times to measure its average energy consumption in an appropriate way (cf. Listing 1, lines 7–8). As JouleUnit is still in an early development phase, the proposed syntax may change and further constructs for profiling and energy consumption testing may be introduced.

3.6 Test Case Execution

Finally, of course, the derived test cases have to be executed and their assertions have to be checked. Our vision is that we are able to implement MBET platform-independently such that it is possible to execute the same test cases on different

---
[4] http://www.junit.org/
[5] Of course, extending JUnit is just one possibility. Developing similar unit testing framework extensions for other programming languages is possible as well.

machines (and even different operating systems) in a way that they lead to the same deterministic results although the program consumes different amounts of energy on different platforms. Therefore, we plan to generate energy test cases that can be configured or calibrated for each execution platform. A possible solution for this problem would be to generate the test cases in a way that they use abstract energy consumption values instead of concrete Joule values (e.g., abstract formulas derived from the abstract interpretation that were not calibrated to a specific platform using profiling results). A setup phase could benchmark and profile the execution platform and transform the generic test cases into platform-specific ones. However, such a solution is only a first idea and implementation details of the soultion are the target of future work.

Another challenge is the question how to monitor the SUT during test execution to retrieve real energy consumption rates of the program during testing. We are planning to build a specific JouleUnit component that is responsible to monitor the energy consumption at runtime. First work in this direction has been done by Süttner [14], but a sufficient solution will be another task of future work. As monitoring a SUT introduces a probe effect that influences the monitoring results, another challenging question for future work will be to estimate or avoid the probe effect of energy consumption testing.

4 Conclusion

In this paper we have presented our vision of an MBET approach. To the best of our knowledge this is the first approach for model-based energy testing. As the major basis for MBET we proposed a six-step testing process using combination of abstract interpretation and statement-based energy consumption profiling to predict a program's best, worst, and average case energy consumption. Further we have presented our vision of a JouleUnit framework that extends JUnit for energy consumption profiling and testing. As stated above, MBET has not been implemented nor evaluated completely, yet. Thus, we identified many open issues that have to be realised until we obtain a realisation of our complete MBET process.

At first we focus on the development and improvement of our JouleUnit extension for JUnit. JouleUnit will provide the required energy consumption profiling and testing statements and will also provide methods to execute and profile a Java program multiple times for its best, worst, and average case energy consumption testing. The first JouleUnit prototype is currently under development and shows promising results for energy consumption testing of Java applications on desktop PCs as well as for Java applications controlling embedded systems (e.g., Nao humanoid robots). Once JouleUnit is working, we plan to implement a test case generator that generates JouleUnit code from the formulas for a program's energy consumption derived from static program analysis.

Thus, we need an abstract interpreter that allows deriving these formulas from a program's CFG or a similar behavior model. We plan to either implement a specific abstract interpreter for energy consumption predictions of Java CFGs or to realise a more generic solution by implementing a program analysis generator that is able to generate energy consumption analysers for different programming languages and behavior models. Earlier work in the domain of abstract interpretation has shown that it is possible to develop such analyser generators for static program analysis [16]. Whether a similar solution is possible for energy consumption analysis and which kind of statements, languages and maybe even which kinds of applications do allow static energy consumption analysis based on abstract interpretation remains a challenging task of future work. First investigations showed that this is possible for small domain-specific languages (DSL) (e.g., a simple DSL controlling a Nao humanoid robot), but whether the same appraoch is appropriate for complex programming languages remains a research question for future work. For energy consumption analysis we further need a model that associates different nodes from CFGs to their average energy consumption. We have started first work that analyses the CPU and memory utilisation of Java programs [14], but further work is necessary that allows deriving energy consumption of Java instructions from their hardware utilisation. Alternatively, results presented by Lafond et al. [8] could be used as a basis for instruction-wise energy consumption prediction. The profiling capabilities of JouleUnit could help here by benchmarking and profiling specific Java instruction w.r.t. their energy consumption. For modelling software applications we have developed the cool component model (CCM) that can be used to model software and hardware components w.r.t. their behavior and their demands of non-functional properties (i.e., qualities) as well as hardware dependencies [17]. Besides Java source code, we plan to investigate the usability of the CCM for input models of MBET. Furthermore, other behavior models like UML state machines and sequence diagrams are further options for MBET input models.

Finally, evaluation plays a major role to develop a reasonable MBET implementation. Thus, we plan to evaluate both the JouleUnit framework and the energy consumption prediction using several case studies to ensure that our test framework evaluates the programs in an appropriate and realistic way.

As this paper is entitled as a vision paper it presented our vision of MBET and not our final solution. Some parts of the MBET concepts may evolve or be even removed during our research, as it remains open whether or not it is possible to statically predict a program's energy consumption by using abstract interpretation. However, we are sure that the general idea of MBET can help to reduce the energy consumption of future software applications.

Acknowledgement. This research has been funded by the European Social Fund and Federal State of Saxony within the project ZESSY #080951806 and by the Federal Ministry of Education and Research within the project CoolSoftware #FKZ13N10782. We would like to thank the reviewers of this paper who did an excellent job and helped to improve the paper's quality.

References

1. Gartner, Inc.: Gartner Estimates ICT Industry Accounts for 2 Percent of Global CO_2 Emissions. Gartner Press Release (April 2007)
2. The Climate Group: SMART 2020: Enabling the low carbon economy in the information age. Report on behalf of the Global eSustainability Initiative (GeSI) (2008)
3. Intel Corporation, Microsoft Corporation: Advanced Power Management (APM) BIOS Interface Specification. Revision 1.2 (February 1996)
4. Hewlett-Packard, Intel, Microsoft, Phoenix Technologies, Toshiba: Advanced Configuration and Power Interface Specification, Revision 4.0a (2010)
5. Lachenmann, A., Marrón, P., Minder, D., Rothermel, K.: Meeting lifetime goals with energy levels. In: Proceedings of the 5th International Conference on Embedded Networked Sensor Systems, pp. 131–144. ACM, New York (2007)
6. Chan, W.K., Chen, T.Y., Cheung, S.C., Tse, T.H., Zhang, Z.: Towards the Testing of Power-Aware Software Applications for Wireless Sensor Networks. In: Abdennahder, N., Kordon, F. (eds.) Ada-Europe 2007. LNCS, vol. 4498, pp. 84–99. Springer, Heidelberg (2007)
7. Woehrle, M., Beutel, J., Lim, R., Yuecel, M., Thiele, L.: Power monitoring and testing in wireless sensor network development. In: Workshop on Energy in Wireless Sensor Networks (WEWSN), Citeseer (2008)
8. Lafond, S., Lilius, J.: An Energy Consumption Model for an Embedded Java Virtual Machine. In: Grass, W., Sick, B., Waldschmidt, K. (eds.) ARCS 2006. LNCS, vol. 3894, pp. 311–325. Springer, Heidelberg (2006)
9. Seo, C., Malek, S., Medvidovic, N.: An Energy Consumption Framework for Distributed Java-Based Systems. In: Proceedings of the 22nd IEEE/ACM Intl. Conference on Automated Software Engineering, Atlanta, Georgia, USA. ACM, New York (2007)
10. Seo, C., Edwards, G., Malek, S., Medvidovic, N.: A Framework for Estimating the Impact of a Distributed Software System's Architectural Style on its Energy Consumption. In: WICSA 2008: Proceedings of the Seventh Working IEEE/IFIP Conference on Software Architecture, pp. 277–280. IEEE Computer Society, Los Alamitos (2008)
11. Navas, J., Méndez-Lojo, M., Hermenegildo, M.: Safe Upper-bounds Inference of Energy Consumption for Java Bytecode Applications. In: Proceedings of The Sixth NASA Langley Formal Methods Workshop, pp. 29–32 (2008)
12. Utting, M., Pretschner, A., Legeard, B.: A Taxonomy of Model-Based Testing. Technical Report 04/2006, University of Waikato, Department of Computer Science, Hamilton, NZ (April 2006)
13. Roßner, T., Brandes, C., Götz, H., Winter, M.: Basiswissen Modellbasierter Test. dpunkt Verlag, Heidelberg (2010)
14. Süttner, P.: Abstract Behavior Description of CCM Software Components (Abstrakte Verhaltensbeschreibung von CCM Softwarekomponenten). Diploma Thesis, Technische Universität Dresden (March 2011)
15. Cousot, P., Cousot, R.: Abstract interpretation: a unified lattice model for static analysis of programs by construction or approximation of fixpoints. In: Proceedings of the 4th ACM SIGACT-SIGPLAN Symposium on Principles of Programming Languages, pp. 238–252. ACM, New York (1977)
16. Martin, F.: Generating Program Analyzers. PhD thesis, Universität des Saarlandes (1999)
17. Götz, S., Wilke, C., Schmidt, M., Cech, S., Aßmann, U.: Towards Energy Auto Tuning. In: Proceedings of First Annual International Conference on Green Information Technology, GREEN IT (2010)

Vision Paper: Make a Difference! (Semantically)*

Uli Fahrenberg[1], Axel Legay[1], and Andrzej Wąsowski[2]

[1] INRIA / Irisa Rennes, France
{ulrich.fahrenberg,axel.legay}@irisa.fr
[2] IT University of Copenhagen, Denmark
wasowski@itu.dk

Abstract. Syntactic difference between models is a wide research area with applications in tools for model evolution, model synchronization and version control. On the other hand, semantic difference between models is rarely discussed. We point out to main use cases of semantic difference between models, and then propose a framework for defining well-formed difference operators on model semantics as adjoints of model combinators such as conjunction, disjunction and structural composition. The framework is defined by properties other then constructively. We instantiate the framework for two rather different modeling languages: feature models and automata specifications. We believe that the algebraic theory of semantic difference will allow to define practical model differencing tools in the future.

1 Introduction

The notion of syntactic difference is well established in software engineering. Textual and graphical algorithms are used to identify differences between text files (source code) and models, and then employed to construct versioning systems, which support comparison and merging of files. *Semantic* difference between models is rarely discussed in the modeling community. This is surprising given the wide recognition of importance of software evolution; semantic difference can support evolution scenarios like bug localization, or incremental verification, and enable model merging that does not fail on ad-hoc syntactic conflicts.

While working on specification theories, within the realm of concurrency and verification, we have observed that many familiar operators on specifications also apply to other models: conjunction – superposition of requirements; parallel composition – structural composition of models; refinement – subtyping, just to mention the most important ones. However the notion of *difference*, as a form of (partial) inverse to the above operators, does not attract nearly as much interest in software engineering.

Our objective is to define and present semantic difference between models in a general fashion. We propose an unambiguous definition of difference which emphasizes its algebraic properties. We instantiate it both for a very simple modeling language, *feature models* [13], and also for the mode complicated language of *automata specifications* [14].

---

* Supported by MT-LAB: a VKR Centre of Excellence in Modeling of IT Systems.

Finally, we also try to explain how difference operators can be used to make formal software development more iterative. It is a common belief that development by stepwise refinement, or use of component algebras, requires using a highly planned and waterfall-like development process. See for example the following quote:

> An important variant of the waterfall model is formal system development, where a mathematical model of a system specification is created. This model is then refined, using mathematical transformations that preserve its consistency, into executable code. Based on the assumption that your mathematical transformations are correct, you can therefore make a strong argument that a program generated in this way is consistent with its specification. [22, p.32]

We will point out uses of difference between models involving flow of information between the stages of the development process and abstraction layers in either way. This allows to run the formal development process in a more agile and iterative manner.

Let us give a teaser of our approach to difference with an extremely simple example: the difference operator for integer numbers. Observe that given two integers t and s, the difference $t - s$ can be defined as the maximum integer x for which $s + x \leq t$. More succinctly: x is a difference of t by s if it holds that for any other integer y:

$$s + y \leq t \quad \text{iff} \quad y \leq x.$$

It is then easy to see that this defines a unique notion of difference. Now observe that we have here defined $t - s$ by *property* rather than *construction*. To show that such a difference actually exists, one has to do more work; but if it does, we already know that it is unique. We will repeatedly use constructions like the above for defining differences with respect to other binary operators and for other objects than integers.

A similar algebraic structure can be uncovered in the area of *software verification*: In programming languages, there is a long established notion of weakest precondition, as the proof obligation on the context of a piece of code which suffices to conclude a given goal [8,11]. Let P be a fragment of imperative code consisting of a number of sequentially composed statements $s_1, \ldots, s_k$. Let the axiomatic semantics for each statement be expressed by a Hoare triple $\{\varphi_i\} s_i \{\psi_i\}$, where φ_i is a precondition and ψ_i is a postcondition, and let ψ be a desired property of the state after executing P. Proving that P is correct, i.e. that $\{\text{true}\} P \{\psi\}$ describes P, amounts to showing that $\text{true} \to \varphi_1, \varphi_1 \to \psi_1, \psi_1 \to \varphi_2, \ldots, \psi_k \to \psi$.

However this may not always be possible, since it enforces correctness regardless of the initial state. Instead it is more reasonable to *synthesize* an assumption X for which $X \to \varphi_1, \varphi_1 \to \psi_1, \psi_1 \to \varphi_2, \ldots, \psi_k \to \psi$. The property X is called a sufficient precondition for P to guarantee ψ. We say that X is the *weakest precondition* if it is also necessary, i.e. if it holds for all formulae Y that

$$Y \to \varphi_1, \varphi_1 \to \psi_1, \psi_1 \to \varphi_2, \ldots, \psi_k \to \psi \quad \text{iff} \quad X \to Y.$$

The precondition X informs the *user* of P on what conditions she has to meet. Dually if the precondition φ for P is fixed by the users of the program, the strongest postcondition shows the developer what can be guaranteed with P. If this conclusion is unsatisfactory, the *developer* can use it to improve P, to give stronger guarantees.

In the following section we will see that this weakest precondition structure, will also appear in differencing feature models.

2 Case Study: Difference for Feature Models

We will now define difference for the language of feature models [13]. To the best of our knowledge, semantic differences for feature models have not been studied before.

Definition 1. *A feature model is a tuple* $M = (F, H, G, \varphi)$. *F is a finite set of features,* $H \subseteq F \times F$ *is a set of directed edges,* $G \subseteq 2^F$ *is a set of or-groups, and φ is a Boolean formula over F expressing so-called* cross-tree constraints. *We demand that i)* (F, H) *is a forest[1] and write parent(f), for $f \in F$, for the unique $p \in F$ for which $(p, f) \in H$, and that ii) all states in an or-group share the same parent, so for all $e, f \in g \in G$, parent(e) = parent(f).*

Fig. 1 presents feature models of two applets (in the spirit of [1]) which we will use as examples. We will use single letter names for features (underlined in the diagram). In applet$_1$, the root feature is a and represents the concept of an applet itself. The diagram says that the applet is decomposed into three smaller features (m, d, t). The empty circles above the names of d and t mean that implementing these two features is optional: an applet *may*, but does not *have to* override d and t. However, each applet *must* override (m) at least one of the methods p, s, and i; this necessity is denoted by the filled circle above the feature m and the filled arc in the concrete syntax. In the abstract syntax, this is expressed by or-groups {m}, {p, s, i} $\in G$. Moreover the cross-tree constraint (placed under the diagram) requires that any applet overriding d or s must also override i.

The variant of feature models presented above is among the simplest (and perhaps most popular) in use. The semantics of the language is defined in terms of translation to Boolean logics, see [2]. Let $M = (F, H, G, \varphi)$ be a feature model, then

$$[\![M]\!] = \varphi \wedge \big(\bigwedge_{(p,c) \in H} c \to p \big) \wedge \bigwedge_{\{f_1,\ldots,f_k\} \in G} (parent(f_1) \to \bigvee_{i=1}^{k} f_i).$$

The generated formula describes the configurations allowed by M. All of them need to satisfy the cross-tree constraint φ. Also, whenever a feature f is included in a configuration, its parent must be included, too. Finally, for each group at least one of its members must be present as soon as its (unique) parent is present. The semantics of our example is hence

$$((\mathsf{d} \to \mathsf{i}) \wedge (\mathsf{t} \to \mathsf{i})) \wedge ((\mathsf{m} \to \mathsf{a}) \wedge (\mathsf{d} \to \mathsf{a}) \wedge (\mathsf{t} \to \mathsf{a})$$
$$\wedge (\mathsf{p} \to \mathsf{m}) \wedge (\mathsf{s} \to \mathsf{m}) \wedge (\mathsf{i} \to \mathsf{m})) \wedge ((\mathsf{a} \to \mathsf{m}) \wedge (\mathsf{m} \to (\mathsf{p} \vee \mathsf{s} \vee \mathsf{i}))).$$

Analysis techniques for feature models often rely on SAT solving or BDDs [23,16,24,17].

Consider now the feature model applet$_2$ of Fig. 1, which could emerge as a result of the same concept being modeled by another engineer. To focus attention we will

---
[1] A forest is a finite disjunction of rooted trees, so technically we capture sets of feature models.

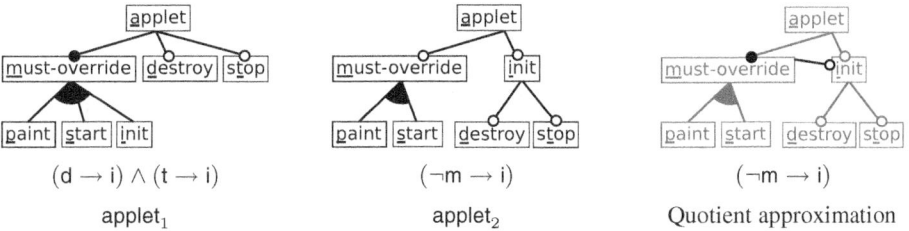

Fig. 1. The two example feature models and an over-approximation of their quotient

assume that this model has been created by a designer of a component that needs to satisfy model applet$_1$ as a requirement. A few questions arise: How do these two models differ? Are they equivalent? If not, what is the actual difference?

Syntactic difference algorithms cannot address these questions. A textual difference algorithm applied to the cross-tree constraint would just say that they differ, being unable to qualitatively explain the difference. An edit-distance based algorithm applied to the tree diagram could likely discover that i has been moved to become a parent of d and t, but not more – tree difference algorithms inform about the editing steps, but they cannot explain their impact. Admittedly, syntactic difference has a proven record of usefulness in many situations. However a modeler trying to understand the difference between the two diagrams, would likely ask a non-syntactic question: *What does this change mean?* Such question is best addressed semantically.

Following the pattern of the examples in the introduction, we will define the semantic difference of formulae φ and ψ as the "weakest" solution X to the implication $\varphi \wedge X \to \psi$. Hence:

Definition 2. *Given two formulae φ and ψ, a formula X is an* adjoint to the conjunction $\varphi \wedge \psi$ *if it holds for all formulae Y that*

$$\varphi \wedge Y \to \psi \quad \text{iff} \quad Y \to X.$$

Thus X satisfies $\varphi \wedge X \to \psi$ and is implied by any Y which also solves this "equation". The next lemma shows that adjoints to conjunction are defined uniquely up to bi-implication, hence we may speak of *the* adjoint to a conjunction $\varphi \wedge \psi$ and denote it $X = \psi \setminus^{\wedge} \varphi$ (provided that it exists, which we shall show below):

Lemma 1. *If X_1 and X_2 are adjoints to the conjunction $\varphi \wedge \psi$, then $X_1 \leftrightarrow X_2$.*

Proof. $X_1 \to X_1$ entails $\varphi \wedge X_1 \to \psi$ and hence $X_1 \to X_2$. Similarly for $X_2 \to X_1$. □

Existence of adjoints to conjunction is settled by the following lemma, whose proof is a routine verification of the property in the definition.

Lemma 2. *For formulae φ, ψ, we have $\psi \setminus^{\wedge} \varphi \equiv \varphi \to \psi$.*

Coming back to our example, a routine computation shows that $[\![\mathsf{applet}_1]\!] \setminus^{\wedge} [\![\mathsf{applet}_2]\!] = m \vee p \vee s \vee \neg a \vee \neg i$. We have computed the weakest cross-tree constraint which needs to be added to applet$_2$ for it to act like applet$_1$. In other cases it might not be useful just to compute a cross-tree constraint as the difference of two feature models; instead one might want a representation which is closer to the concrete feature-model syntax.

For this the algorithm displayed on the right can be used. It takes as input two formulae φ and ψ in conjunctive normal form (note that semantics of feature models are easily converted to CNF) and then finds for the quotient all clauses in ψ which are not entailed by φ (through the satisfiability check of $\varphi \wedge \neg c$ in line 3). This is clearly an over-approximation of the quotient, but might fail

QUOTIENT-AND

Input: φ, ψ : formulae in CNF
Output: an over-approx. to $\psi \setminus\!\!\setminus \varphi$
1 Let $X = \emptyset$
2 **for each** clause $c \in \psi$ **do**
3   **if** SAT($\varphi \wedge \neg c$) **then** add c to X
4 **return** X

at maximality. It can still be useful in the software development process as a more syntactic representation.

As an example, the approximation computed for the quotient of applet$_1$ by applet$_2$ is $(\neg a \vee m) \wedge (\neg i \vee m) = (a \rightarrow m) \wedge (i \rightarrow m)$, and this can easily be added to the syntactic representation of applet$_2$ to signal the changes necessary, see Fig. 1 (rightmost).

In [6] we have presented a general feature model synthesis algorithm. The concrete syntax for the difference in the example above could be automatically computed by this algorithm. In general the algorithm could be used in a modeling tool visualizing semantic differences between feature models.

3 A Categorical Intermezzo

We will now generalize the considerations on adjoints and difference.

Definition 3. *A* preorder category *is a class C of* objects *and a* morphism *relation $\rightarrow_C \; \subseteq C \times C$ which is reflexive and transitive. A* functor *of preorder categories C, D is a mapping $F : C \rightarrow D$ which respects the morphisms: if $x \rightarrow_C y$ then $F(x) \rightarrow_D F(y)$.*

A preorder category is just a usual preorder, and a functor is a preorder homomorphism. We use categorical language here because *adjoints* are categorical concepts:

Definition 4. *Let C, D be preorder categories and $L : C \rightarrow D$, $R : D \rightarrow C$ functors. Then (L, R) is called an* adjoint pair *if it holds for all $x \in C$, $y \in D$ that*

$$L(x) \rightarrow_D y \quad \textit{iff} \quad x \rightarrow_C R(y).$$

In an adjoint pair (L, R), L is called the *left* and R the *right* adjoint. The notion of adjoints is important in category theory; note that we have simplified things here by only working in preorder categories, see e.g. [15, Ch. 4] for the full story. We can generalize the proof of Lemma 1 to show that up to isomorphism, one half of an adjoint pair determines the other:

Lemma 3. *If (L_1, R_1), (L_1, R_2), and (L_2, R_1) are adjoint pairs between preorder categories C, D, then $R_1(y) \leftrightarrow_C R_2(y)$ and $L_1(x) \leftrightarrow_D L_2(x)$ for all $x \in C, y \in D$.*

To apply these considerations to the setting of Section 2, we need only notice that we are working there in the category $\mathcal{F}$ with logical formulae as objects and implications as morphisms. If we denote by A_φ and I_φ, for $\varphi \in \mathcal{F}$, the mappings $\mathcal{F} \rightarrow \mathcal{F}$ given by $A_\varphi(\psi) = \varphi \wedge \psi$, $I_\varphi(\psi) = \psi \setminus\!\!\setminus \varphi$, then the biimplication of Definition 2 reads

$$A_\varphi(Y) \rightarrow \psi \quad \text{iff} \quad Y \rightarrow I_\varphi(\psi),$$

hence we are defining an adjoint pair (A_φ, I_φ) for all formulae φ. Lemma 2 then says that such an adjoint pair exists for each formula φ. Another way to state this is that with tensor product $\wedge$, the category $\mathcal{F}$ is (strict symmetric) *closed monoidal*; in this context, the adjoint $\setminus^\wedge$ is also called the *exponential* to $\wedge$.

4 Difference and Development Processes

The adjoint to conjunction is useful in a top-down development scenario, when a general requirements model is given (applet$_1$) and a refinement is developed by a component designer (applet$_2$). By visualizing the difference $[\![\text{applet}_1]\!] \setminus^\wedge [\![\text{applet}_2]\!]$, the designer can monitor his refinement, and see how to constrain it to meet the general requirements.

In this scenario, *information flows top-down* – as in the quote in the introduction. The difference is used to refine models at lower abstraction levels. As much as this is useful, this is not fully satisfactory. In software engineering processes, *information flows both ways*. Especially in iterative processes the implementations are continuously adjusted to meet requirements, while requirements themselves are also continuously adjusted as a result of changing business conditions, and learning from experience in implementing the previous iterations. So we need to not only have ways for communicating model changes top-down in the refinement hierarchy, but *also* bottom-up.

Let us link these observations to differencing feature models. Observe that $\varphi \wedge X \to \psi$ is equivalent to $\varphi \to \neg X \vee \psi$. Moreover, if X is the weakest constraint that makes the former valid, then $\neg X$ is the strongest constraint that makes the latter valid. If interpreted in modeling terms, $\neg X$ represents the least amount of weakening that needs to be added to the model whose semantics is given by ψ (in the example applet$_1$) in order for the requirements to be possible to meet with components satisfying φ (applet$_2$). So $\neg X$ represents the information that *flows upwards* in the refinement hierarchy whenever it is not the component that needs to be 'fixed', but the requirements that need to be relaxed.

In our example, the negation of the difference formula is $\neg \text{m} \wedge \neg \text{p} \wedge \neg \text{s} \wedge \text{a} \wedge \text{i}$. It directly describes a configuration of applet$_2$ that needs to be admitted by applet$_1$ in order to make the two models equivalent. In general this negation encodes all configurations of applet$_2$ that need to be admitted by applet$_1$ in order to make the two models equivalent.

We define the adjoint to disjunction using a universal property as in Def˙ 2: Given formulae φ, ψ, say that a formula X is an adjoint to the disjunction $\varphi \vee \psi$ if it holds that

$$\varphi \to Y \vee \psi \quad \text{iff} \quad X \to Y$$

for all formulae Y; hence X is now to be the "strongest" (with respect to implication ordering) solution to the implication $\varphi \to X \vee \psi$.

If we denote by O_ψ the mapping $O_\psi(\varphi) = \varphi \vee \psi$, the above bi-implication defines a *left adjoint* J_ψ to O_ψ, i.e. an adjoint pair (J_ψ, O_ψ). By the considerations of Section 3 we know that such left adjoint, if it exists, is unique; using Lemma 2 and self-duality of the category $\mathcal{F}$ we can conclude that $\psi \setminus^\vee \varphi := J_\psi(\varphi) = \neg(\psi \setminus^\wedge \varphi) = \neg(\varphi \to \psi)$, hence the adjoint to disjunction always exists.

Use Cases for Semantic Difference of Feature Models. Let us conclude the feature modeling example with a list of concrete applications for the difference of feature models, seen as a difference of their semantics (some of them already suggested above):

- Visualizing and explaining difference between models as specifications.
- The difference is a *debugging information*. Instances satisfying applet$_2$ but not the adjoint, are examples of configurations that are illegal in the requirements model.
- Dually they can be shown to the designer of applet$_1$ as examples of possible configurations, which might be used to expand requirements.
- If system configurations in $[\![\text{applet}_2]\!] \wedge \neg([\![\text{applet}_1]\!] \mathbin{\backslash\!\!\wedge} [\![\text{applet}_2]\!])$ pass correctness tests then the modeler should consider communicating them upward, to negotiate relaxation of these (otherwise reuse may be hindered).

5 Difference for Automata Specifications

We will now briefly show that the same construction of adjoint is applicable (and in fact known) for automata specifications. Assume a fixed alphabet of actions Σ.

Definition 5 ([14]). *A modal specification (MS) is a tuple $\mathcal{R} = (P, \lambda^0, \Delta^m, \Delta^M)$ where P is a set of states, $\lambda^0 \in P$ is the initial state and $\Delta^M \subseteq \Delta^m \subseteq P \times \Sigma \times P$. Δ^M and Δ^m are respectively* must- *and* may-transitions, *both deterministic and total: for every state $p \in P$ and action $a \in \Sigma$, there is exactly one $\lambda \in P$ such that $(p, a, \lambda) \in \Delta^m$.*

An automaton is a MS where $\Delta^M = \Delta^m$. An *instance* of a MS is an automaton that is obtained by unfolding the modal specification and cutting some may transitions while ensuring that all the must transitions stay present. Formally, let $R = (P, \lambda^0, \Delta^m, \Delta^M)$ be a MS and $A = (M, m^0, \Delta)$ an automaton. A is an instance of R, written $A \models R$, if there exists a binary relation $\rho \subseteq M \times P$ such that $(m^0, \lambda^0) \in \rho$, and for all $(m, p) \in \rho$:

(1) for every $(p, a, \lambda) \in \Delta^M$ there is a transition $(m, a, m') \in \Delta$ with $(m', \lambda) \in \rho$
(2) for every $(m, a, m') \in \Delta$ there is a transition $(p, a, \lambda) \in \Delta^m$ with $(m', \lambda) \in \rho$.

We write $[\![R]\!]$ for the set of instances of a MS R and say that a MS S refines another MS T, written $S \leq T$, iff $[\![S]\!] \subseteq [\![T]\!]$.

Two modal specifications over the same alphabet can be composed by synchronizing on common actions, similarly to composition for regular transition systems, but with the provision that the composition of two may-transitions is again a may-transition, and the composition of two must-transitions is a must-transition. The composition $M_1 \parallel M_2$ accepts all compositions between models of M_1 and of M_2, so $[\![M_1 \parallel M_2]\!] = \{(m_1 \parallel m_2) \mid m_1 \in [\![M_1]\!], m_2 \in [\![M_2]\!]\}$.

Given specifications S and T, the *quotient* operation $\backslash\!\!\parallel$ computes the greatest specification X (with respect to the refinement order) such that $S \parallel X \leq T$. So $T \backslash\!\!\parallel S$ is essentially the difference between S and T with respect to structural composition – it describes the component that is missing in order to provide T. In a more succinct way we can say that X is a quotient of T by S if it holds that

$$S \parallel Y \leq T \quad \text{iff} \quad Y \leq X$$

for all specifications Y. In the spirit of Section 3, we can note that modal specifications and refinements form a preorder category $\mathcal{M}$, and then the bi-implication above means that quotient is the *right adjoint* to structural composition, i.e. that for any specification S, the functors $P_S(T) = S \parallel T$ and $Q_S(T) = T \backslash\!\!\parallel S$ form an adjoint pair (P_S, Q_S).

Algorithms for computing these quotients are known for many behavioral component algebras [7,4,19,3,10].

6   Discussion: Towards Difference between Languages

We have characterized semantic distance as an adjoint of a composition operator, and exemplified it for conjunction, disjunction, and parallel composition. In this section we want to illustrate an interesting direction into discussing semantic difference, namely characterizing distance between an instance of a modeling language and a subclass of this language.

This problem appears often in practice. For instance model-checkers for automata-like models may assume that models are deterministic to improve efficiency. Similarly, analysis tools for class diagrams may assume use of a subset of OCL, in order to make the validity (or consistency) problem decidable. For feature models, it is sometimes interesting to look at a class of models that are possible to represent purely diagrammatically (i.e. without cross-tree constraints). However modeling using the full power of the language is usually easier. It is efficient to abstract behaviors with nondeterminism; it is easier to write constraints in full OCL; and it is often natural to express some cross-tree constraints in propositional logics. So the problem arises, whether the full-featured instance of the language is far, or not far, from the subclass of models which are easy to analyse. Is it easy to translate into this subclass? How much expressivity is lost (if any)?

Such translation is usually performed by an abstraction operation. Automata can be determinized; OCL (and propositional) constraints can be weakened to approximate their semantics within the sublanguage. Interestingly such an abstraction is also an adjoint, manifesting the same abstract structure as the instance-to-instance differences. Below we detail this for the example of determinization of modal automata.

The essence of a *determinization* operator det for (non-deterministic) modal specifications is that for any specification S, $\det(S)$ is the *smallest deterministic over-approximation* of S. Hence $\det(S)$ is deterministic, $S \leq \det(S)$, and for any deterministic specification D, $S \leq D$ implies $\det(S) \leq D$. Now the last two properties can be combined by demanding that

$$S \leq D \quad \text{iff} \quad \det(S) \leq D$$

for all deterministic D, which is almost the property we have encountered earlier.

Now let $\mathcal{M}$ be the preorder category of deterministic modal specifications as before, and let $\mathcal{N}$ be the larger category of non-deterministic specifications. We have a functor $I : \mathcal{M} \to \mathcal{N}$ (which "forgets" that the specification is deterministic; hence called a *forgetful* functor), and det is a functor $\mathcal{N} \to \mathcal{M}$. The equation above then becomes

$$\det(S) \leq_{\mathcal{M}} D \quad \text{iff} \quad S \leq_{\mathcal{N}} I(D)$$

for all $S \in \mathcal{N}$, $D \in \mathcal{M}$. Hence the determinization functor det is *left adjoint* to the forgetful functor I; this type of functors is usually called *free*.

We see in this example that existence of a faithful abstraction to the subclass of our modeling language, which maps a model to an abstraction which is "not too far" away, is the same as a *free* functor from the language to the subclass, left adjoint to the forgetful functor. This is indeed characteristic of a number of other examples, and motivates the search for free functors also in other areas.

7 Final Remarks and Related Work

We have described a formal approach to defining semantic difference between models. Perhaps somewhat unexpectedly, our proposal relies on using a preorder on models, instead of using equality (equivalence) and attempting to construct some sort of counterpart of subtraction. Our difference is an operator that is defined as an adjoint. In modeling it makes sense to consider differencing with respect to various composition operators, with conjunction and structural composition being the two main contenders.

Let us briefly summarize the process of defining a semantic difference:

1. Identify a set of models $\mathbf{S}$ and a preorder $\leq$ on $\mathbf{S} \times \mathbf{S}$ (here this was a refinement on automata, or implication of formulae; in other contexts it could be subtyping).
2. Choose a binary composition operator (merge) $\otimes : \mathbf{S} \times \mathbf{S} \to \mathbf{S}$. We have used entailment, parallel composition, conjunction and disjunction in this role.
3. The semantics of models is given as a mapping $[\![\cdot]\!] : \mathbf{S} \to \mathbf{D}$ to a semantic domain.
4. Usually the semantic domain $\mathbf{D}$ has better algebraic structure than the syntactic domain $\mathbf{S}$. Thus it is easier to define the difference, as an operator $\backslash^\otimes$ on the semantic domain: $\backslash^\otimes : \mathbf{D} \times \mathbf{D} \to \mathbf{D}$. By definition $T \backslash^\otimes S$ returns the maximum X for which $S \otimes X \leq T$, or (as for disjunction) the minimum X for which $S \leq X \otimes T$. Not in all semantic domains such a maximum, or minimum, may exist, but if it does, it is unique (up to the equivalence relation induced by the preorder $\leq$).

In the future we intend to work on semantic differences for other modeling languages, including UML class diagrams. Providing a difference for this language requires that we are able to compute differences for a substantial fragment of first order logics.

Related Work. Semantic difference is discussed in [21], which defines the difference operator between models $T - S$ as a set of *witnesses*, which are instances of T but not instances of S. While this definition is natural, and can be useful in many practical cases (for example it directly allows providing counterexamples for non-emptiness of difference), it also has drawbacks. Unlike our proposal, such definition of difference defines an operator which has a different co-domain than the domains of operands. A difference between models is no longer a model. Secondly, in most practical cases, the set of witnesses is infinite and cannot easily be enumerated.

Model merging [5] is composing overlapping models, typically, without prior computation of differences between them. In [18] a semantics oriented merge operation is discussed for statecharts. It would be interesting to see whether this work could be extended to provide visualization of semantic differences for statecharts.

Gerth and co-authors [9] present a semantic-based notion between change operations in a version control scenario. Two operations are equivalent if they lead to equivalent business process models (in the sense of trace inclusion). They are not concerned with synthesizing difference models, but with detecting and avoiding merge conflicts. Our operator, could potentially be used in conflict resolution or visualizing changelogs.

Segura et al. [20] define a syntactic merge operator for feature models using graph transformations. Closer to semantics, Thüm et al. [23] discuss semantic differences of edits to feature models. They do not compute differences but simply classify them as strengthening, weakening, refactoring, and incomparable.

Semantic difference for programs is understood better than for models. For instance, in [12] differences between procedures are approximated by dependence relations.

Acknowledgments. We thank Krzysztof Czarnecki for indicating the semantic difference problem to us, and Jose Fiadeiro for an encouraging discussion on the subject.

References

1. Antkiewicz, M., Busch, C.: Framework-specific modeling languages with round-trip engineering. In: Wang, J., Whittle, J., Harel, D., Reggio, G. (eds.) MoDELS 2006. LNCS, vol. 4199, pp. 692–706. Springer, Heidelberg (2006)
2. Batory, D.: Feature models, grammars, and propositional formulas. In: Obbink, H., Pohl, K. (eds.) SPLC 2005. LNCS, vol. 3714, pp. 7–20. Springer, Heidelberg (2005)
3. Bertrand, N., Legay, A., Pinchinat, S., Raclet, J.-B.: A compositional approach on modal specifications for timed systems. In: Breitman, K., Cavalcanti, A. (eds.) ICFEM 2009. LNCS, vol. 5885, pp. 679–697. Springer, Heidelberg (2009)
4. Bhaduri, P., Ramesh, S.: Synthesis of synchronous interfaces. In: ACSD. IEEE, Los Alamitos (2006)
5. Brunet, G., Chechik, M., Easterbrook, S., Nejati, S., Niu, N., Sabetzadeh, M.: A manifesto for model merging. In: GaMMa. ACM, New York (2006)
6. Czarnecki, K., Wąsowski, A.: Feature diagrams and logics: There and back again. In: SPLC, pp. 23–34. IEEE Computer Society, Los Alamitos (2007)
7. David, A., Larsen, K.G., Legay, A., Nyman, U., Wąsowski, A.: Timed I/O automata: a complete specification theory for real-time systems. In: HSCC. ACM, New York (2010)
8. Dijkstra, E.W., Scholten, C.S.: Predicate calculus and program semantics. Springer, Heidelberg (1990)
9. Gerth, C., Küster, J.M., Luckey, M., Engels, G.: Precise detection of conflicting change operations using process model terms. In: Petriu, D.C., Rouquette, N., Haugen, Ø. (eds.) MODELS 2010. LNCS, vol. 6395, pp. 93–107. Springer, Heidelberg (2010)
10. Goessler, G., Raclet, J.-B.: Modal contracts for component-based design. In: Hung, D.V., Krishnan, P. (eds.) SEFM. IEEE Computer Society, Los Alamitos (2009)
11. Hoare, C.A.R.: An axiomatic basis for computer programming. Commun. ACM 12(10) (1969)
12. Jackson, D., Ladd, D.A.: Semantic diff: A tool for summarizing the effects of modifications. In: Müller, H.A., Georges, M. (eds.) ICSM. IEEE Computer Society, Los Alamitos (1994)
13. Kang, K., Cohen, S., Hess, J., Nowak, W., Peterson, S.: Feature-oriented domain analysis (FODA) feasibility study. Technical Report CMU/SEI-90-TR-21 (1990)
14. Larsen, K.G.: Modal specifications. In: Sifakis, J. (ed.) AVMS 1989. LNCS, vol. 407, pp. 232–246. Springer, Heidelberg (1990)
15. Mac Lane, S.: Categories for the Working Mathematician, 2nd edn. Graduate Texts in Mathematics. Springer, Heidelberg (1998)
16. Mendonca, M., Wąsowski, A., Czarnecki, K.: SAT-based analysis of feature models is easy. In: SPLC 2009, IEEE Computer Society, Los Alamitos (2009)
17. Mendonça, M., Wąsowski, A., Czarnecki, K., Cowan, D.D.: Efficient compilation techniques for large scale feature models. In: GPCE (2008)
18. Nejati, S., Sabetzadeh, M., Chechik, M., Easterbrook, S.M., Zave, P.: Matching and merging of statecharts specifications. In: ICSE. IEEE Computer Society, Los Alamitos (2007)
19. Raclet, J.-B.: Residual for component specifications. ENTCS 215, 93–110 (2008)
20. Segura, S., Benavides, D., Ruiz-Cortés, A., Trinidad, P.: Automated merging of feature models using graph transformations. In: Lämmel, R., Visser, J., Saraiva, J. (eds.) Generative and Transformational Techniques in Software Engineering II. LNCS, vol. 5235, pp. 489–505. Springer, Heidelberg (2008)

21. Shahar Maoz, J.R., Rumpe, B.: A manifesto for semantic model differencing. In: International Workshop on Models and Evolution (2010)
22. Sommerville, I.: Software Engineering, 9/E. Addison-Wesley, Reading (2011)
23. Thüm, T., Batory, D.S., Kästner, C.: Reasoning about edits to feature models. In: ICSE, pp. 254–264. IEEE Computer Society, Los Alamitos (2009)
24. Trinidad, P., Benavides, D., Cortés, A.R., Segura, S., Jimenez, A.: FAMA framework. In: SPLC, p. 359. IEEE Computer Society, Los Alamitos (2008)

Automatic Derivation of Utility Functions for Monitoring Software Requirements*

Andres J. Ramirez and Betty H.C. Cheng

Michigan State University
Department of Computer Science and Engineering
3115 Engineering Building
East Lansing, MI 48824
{ramir105,chengb}@cse.msu.edu

Abstract. Utility functions can be used to monitor requirements of a dynamically adaptive system (DAS). More specifically, a utility function maps monitoring information to a scalar value proportional to how well a requirement is satisfied. Utility functions may be manually elicited by requirements engineers, or indirectly inferred through statistical regression techniques. This paper presents a goal-based requirements model-driven approach for automatically deriving state-, metric-, and fuzzy logic-based utility functions for RELAXed goal models. State- and fuzzy logic-based utility functions are responsible for detecting requirements violations, and metric-based utility functions are used to detect conditions conducive to a requirements violation. We demonstrate the proposed approach by applying it to the goal model of an intelligent vehicle system (IVS) and use the derived utility functions to monitor the IVS under different environmental conditions at run time.

1 Introduction

A dynamically adaptive system (DAS) monitors itself and its execution environment to assess how well it satisfies requirements at run time. This monitoring information enables a DAS to detect both requirements violations, as well as conditions conducive to their occurrence [7,8,16]. Utility functions have been successfully applied for self-assessment purposes in DASs [3,9,15,17]. Within the context of a DAS, a utility function maps monitoring data to a scalar value, typically within the ranges of zero and one, that is proportional to how well the DAS satisfies its requirements at run time. This paper presents a goal-based model-driven approach for automatically deriving utility functions during the requirements engineering phase. The set of derived utility functions enable a

---

* This work has been supported in part by NSF grants CCF-0541131, IIP-0700329, CCF-0750787, CCF-0820220, DBI-0939454, CNS-0854931, Army Research Office grant W911NF-08-1-0495, Ford Motor Company, and a Quality Fund Program grant from Michigan State University. Any opinions, findings, and conclusions or recommendations expressed in this material are those of the author(s) and do not necessarily reflect the views of the National Science Foundation, Army, Ford, or other research sponsors.

DAS to monitor the satisfaction of requirements at run time, as well as identify potential sources of obstacles that may impede a goal's satisfaction.

Utility functions provide a light-weight technique for associating the actions taken by a decision-making process with a DAS's high-level goals, concerns, and requirements [9,17]. As such, utility functions can be used to monitor both functional and non-functional requirements of a DAS. Utility functions for monitoring the functional behavior of a DAS are often derived manually by requirements engineers with the aid of domain experts. In contrast, utility functions for monitoring the non-functional requirements (e.g., performance) of a DAS may be indirectly inferred at run time through statistical regression-based techniques [1,9]. These *performance-based* utility functions often generate a single, application-level utility value representative of the overall system's performance. Deviations from this utility value suggests an anomalous behavior that may require an adaptation. While these approaches facilitate the derivation of performance-based utility functions, they tend to postpone their integration until deployment when real execution data becomes available to drive the regression process.

This paper presents Athena, an approach that leverages goal-based models to facilitate the automatic derivation of utility functions at the requirements level. Currently, Athena supports the automatic derivation of state-, metric-, and fuzzy logic-based utility functions for KAOS models [5,12] that include RELAXed goals [2,18]. State-based utility functions assess whether a DAS satisfies functional invariant goals. Metric-based utility functions, on the other hand, detect conditions conducive to a requirements violation, ideally enabling a DAS to mitigate such conditions before an invariant goal becomes violated. Lastly, fuzzy logic-based utility functions compute the satisfaction of non-invariant goals that have been RELAXed in order to explicitly account for the effects of environmental uncertainty. Derived utility functions enable a DAS not only to monitor requirements at run time, but also identify candidate sets of system and environmental agents that may be responsible for a requirements violation.

Athena accepts as input a goal model and a mapping between environmental conditions and the monitoring elements responsible for observing them, and generates utility functions to be used for requirements monitoring. To generate a utility function, Athena uses these mappings to identify observable conditions of the system-to-be and its execution environment specified in a goal's definition. Next, Athena maps keywords in a goal's definition to different types of utility function templates. For each invariant goal, Athena generates a state-based utility function that returns true or false depending on the satisfaction of the goal. For a non-invariant goal, Athena generates a metric-based utility function to measure the degree to which some observable condition in the goal's definition is minimized or maximized with regards to a given threshold. Lastly, for a RELAXed goal, Athena generates a fuzzy logic-based utility function by mapping RELAX operators to their corresponding fuzzy logic-based mathematical functions [18]. At run time, derived utility functions accept monitoring data from the environmental agents (i.e., sensors) in order to detect requirements violations and conditions conducive to their occurrence.

We demonstrate Athena by applying it to a goal model we constructed to capture the objectives, constraints, and requirements of an Intelligent Vehicle System (IVS) application that must perform adaptive cruise control and lane keeping while avoiding collisions with other vehicles on the road. Based on this goal model, Athena generated utility functions to assess how well the IVS satisfies its requirements at run time. Lastly, we implemented the set of derived utility functions within a prototype of the IVS in the Webots simulation platform [14] to enable the monitoring of requirements during simulation runs. The remainder of this paper is organized as follows. In Section 2 we present background material on goal-oriented requirements modeling and the RELAX language. Next, in Section 3, we introduce the IVS application domain and use it to present the proposed approach. Section 4 presents our case study. We then provide an overview of related work in Section 5. Lastly, Section 6 discusses Athena, summarizes main findings, and presents future directions.

2 Background

This section presents background material on goal-based requirements modeling, and the RELAX requirements specification language.

2.1 Goal-Based Requirements Modeling

From the perspective of a stakeholder, a goal specifies the objectives that the system-to-be and its execution environment must satisfy at run time [12]. While the system-to-be must always satisfy invariant goals, it may temporarily allow the dissatisfaction of non-invariant goals. In general, goals may be classified across two orthogonal dimensions. A goal may be classified either as functional or non-functional depending on whether it specifies *what* services the system-to-be must provide or whether it constrains *how* such services must be provided, respectively. In addition, a goal may also be classified either as a hard or soft goal. The satisfaction of a *hard* goal can be determined in a crisp manner, usually through state-based predicates. In contrast, a *soft* goal may be measured, to some degree, through user-defined metrics, though their ultimate satisfaction may not be precisely determined due to subjective, and potentially conflicting, preferences by various stakeholders. Since the satisfaction of a soft goal cannot be absolutely determined, it is often said that a soft goal is *satisficed* [4]. Jureta *et al.* [11] extended these concepts of achieving a hard goal and satisficing a soft goal with the notion of *excelling*, where a goal may be constantly improved upon some measurable dimension (e.g., minimize vehicle acceleration rate).

A key objective in goal-based analysis is to systematically decompose high-level goals into finer-grained goals. To this end, goals are graphically represented in an acyclic directed graph where a goal may be decomposed into subgoals through AND/OR refinements. While a goal that has been AND-decomposed may only be satisfied if all of its subgoals are satisfied, a goal that has been OR-decomposed is satisfied if at least one of its subgoals is satisfied. This goal decomposition process terminates once each goal is assigned to a single system or environmental agent. Whereas a goal under the assignment of an agent in the system-to-be is a requirement, a goal under the assignment of an environmental agent is an *expectation* of the environment [12]. Darimont and van Lamsweerde [6] developed a set of goal refinement patterns to guide requirements engineers through the process of decomposing higher-level goals into finer-grained goals. Each refinement pattern is proven correct, thereby enabling a requirements engineer to instantiate them and leverage the underlying theoretical framework without having to prove their correctness again.

2.2 RELAX Specification Language

RELAX [2,18] is a requirements specification language for identifying, evaluating, and mitigating sources of environmental uncertainty in a DAS. RELAX focuses on declaratively specifying the sources and impacts of uncertainty at the shared boundary between the system-to-be and its execution environment [10]. This information is organized into ENV, MON, and REL elements. In particular, ENV specifies environmental properties that may or may not be directly observable by a DAS; MON specifies the elements that make up the DAS's monitoring infrastructure; and REL defines how to compute the values of ENV properties from MON elements. The semantics of RELAX operators have been defined in terms of fuzzy logic to constrain the extent to which a non-invariant requirement may become temporarily unsatisfied [18]. For example, the RELAXed goal "*Achieve [VehicleSpeed AS CLOSE AS POSSIBLE TO DesiredSpeed]*" specifies that while the value of *VehicleSpeed* should approximate the *DesiredSpeed* threshold value, minor deviations between the two values, as specified by a corresponding fuzzy logic operator, are tolerable at run time.

Previously, Cheng *et al.* [2] presented an approach for applying the RELAX process to non-invariant goals in a KAOS model [5,12] where uncertainty may cause a goal to become temporarily unsatisfied. To apply their approach, a requirements engineer informally specifies ENV, MON, and REL elements. This paper automates the derivation of utility functions for KAOS models with RELAXed goals where the definition of ENV, MON, and REL are specified more formally and amenable to automated processing.

3 Athena Approach

This section presents a goal-based, requirements model-driven approach for automatically deriving utility functions. First, we introduce the intelligent vehicle system (IVS) application domain and present a goal model that captures its requirements, including several goals that have been RELAXed when environmental uncertainty is an issue. We then use the IVS goal model as an example to present and describe the steps of Athena in detail.

3.1 Intelligent Vehicle System

Intelligent transportation systems (ITS) will provide safe and efficient transportation of passengers across roadways. Within the ITS domain, an intelligent vehicle system (IVS) provides autonomous vehicle control through a combination of adaptive cruise control (ACC), lane keeping, and collision avoidance features. As Figure 1 illustrates, the ACC module is responsible for maintaining a *SafeDistance* between the IVS and obstacles in front of the IVS, such as Lead Vehicle. Specifically, the ACC module commands the vehicle's engine to maintain a *SafeSpeed* and keep the IVS within the *CoastingZone*. The lane keeping module, on the other hand, detects roadway markings and keeps the IVS within the center of the driving lane. Lastly, the collision avoidance module uses cameras and distance sensors to detect obstacles and adjust the vehicle's engine and steering mechanisms in response.

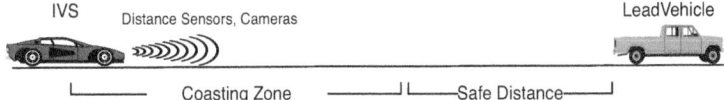

Fig. 1. Intelligent Vehicle System

The Webots simulation platform [14] provides a generic implementation of an IVS capable of cruise control and lane keeping. This generic IVS model comprises a GPS unit for computing the vehicle's velocity, a camera for detecting roadway markings, and an accelerometer to compute acceleration and deceleration rates. For this study, we extended the basic Webots IVS implementation with a monitoring infrastructure that supports ACC, lane keeping, and collision avoidance. The extended IVS also includes a compass and a gyroscope to compute changes in vehicle heading and velocity, three additional cameras to detect roadway markings and obstacles, and ten laser- and sonar-based distance sensors that measure the distance between the IVS and nearby obstacles. For the remainder of this paper, IVS refers to the extended IVS implementation.

Figure 2 shows an elided RELAX goal model for the IVS application. This model captures goals for computing the current speed of the IVS, as well as its distance to nearby obstacles. The IVS can use either a GPS unit or wheel sensors to compute its velocity, and either cameras or distance sensors to compute its distance to nearby obstacles. These alternative refinements enable the IVS to change how it senses its environment at run time. Several non-invariant goals were RELAXed in this goal model, where the RELAX operators are in uppercase, to explicitly account for the effects of uncertainty in achieving a goal. For instance, goal (C) was RELAXed since the IVS can tolerate minor differences between *VehicleSpeed* and *DesiredSpeed*. However, goal (D) was not RELAXed as deviations between *VehicleSpeed* and *SafeSpeed* may cause a collision. Lastly, to capture the interactions between system and environmental agents (denoted by a stick figure in an agent hexagon), we applied the *unmonitorability* refinement pattern [6] to goals (I,L,M) (J,N,O), and (K,P,Q). This refinement pattern was applied because system agents alone were not capable of monitoring the conditions formulated in goals (I,J,K). Instead, by applying this refinement, system

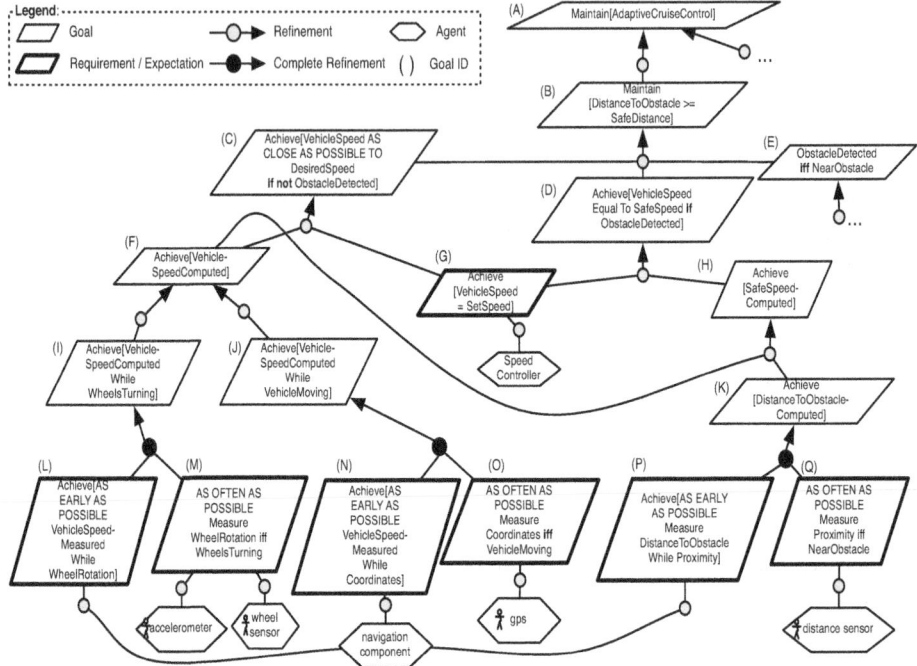

Fig. 2. Goal model for adaptive cruise control in IVS, including RELAXed goals

agents process the environmental conditions measured by an environmental agent. Due to space constraints we only show the ACC goal model and not its lane keeping counterpart.

3.2 Description of Athena Approach

To use Athena, a requirements engineer must first follow the RELAX goal modeling approach [2] and construct a goal model, specify invariant goals, and ENV, MON, and REL elements for each requirement. ENV specifies environmental conditions observable by the DAS; MON specifies environmental agents (i.e., sensors) that make up the DAS's monitoring infrastructure; and REL specifies how to compute the values of ENV properties from MON elements. Table 1 presents a subset of ENV, MON, and REL elements for the IVS application. For example, row (1) specifies that the IVS obtains the value of the *WheelRotation* ENV property directly from its *WheelSensor* MON element. In contrast, row (2) specifies that the IVS is unable to directly compute the value of the ENV property *VehicleSpeed*. Instead, the IVS computes the value of this property from the wheel's dimensions and rotation rate, as specified in the REL relationship for that row.

Athena accepts as input a goal model and set of ENV, MON, and REL elements, and produces as output a set of state-, metric-, and fuzzy logic-based utility functions by instantiating functions templates based on the goal's type. As with

Table 1. Table with ENV, MON, and REL elements for IVS application

Row	Goal	ENV	MON	REL
1	M	WheelRotation	WheelSensor	WheelSensor.value
2	L	VehicleSpeed		VehicleSpeed = IVS.wheel_diameter * 3.1415 * WheelRotation
3	O	Coordinates	GPS	Coordinates = GPS.value
4	N	VehicleSpeed		VehicleSpeed = (NavigationComponent.prev_pos - Coordinates) / GPS.time_unit
5	Q	Proximity	DistanceSensor	Proximity = DistanceSensor.value
6	P	DistanceToObstacle		DistanceToObstacle = Proximity * DistanceSensor.max_range
7	H	SafeSpeed	WheelSensor, GPS, DistanceSensor	SafeSpeed = VehicleSpeed - 0.1 * VehicleSpeed * (1.0 - SafeDistance / DistanceToObstacle)
8	E	ObstacleDetected	DistanceSensor	ObstacleDetected = Proximity > 0.95
9	B	SafeDistance	WheelSensor, GPS	SafeDistance = 2.5 * VehicleSpeed * 1000 / 3600

traditional requirements monitoring approaches, Athena generates state-based functions to monitor functional invariant goals since their *satisfaction* can be absolutely determined. In contrast, Athena generates metric- and fuzzy logic-based utility functions to monitor the *satisficement* [4] of non-invariant goals whose satisfaction may not be precisely determined, ideally enabling a DAS to detect and mitigate conditions that would otherwise lead to the violation of an invariant goal. Once implemented within a DAS, these utility functions compute utility values at run time based on available monitoring data, thereby enabling a DAS to monitor requirements, detect conditions conducive to a requirements violation, and facilitate the identification of potential goal obstructions.

The data flow diagram in Figure 3 illustrates the bottom-up approach that Athena applies to *automatically* generate utility functions starting at the leaf goals and progressing towards the root goal. We now describe each of the key steps that Athena automatically applies:

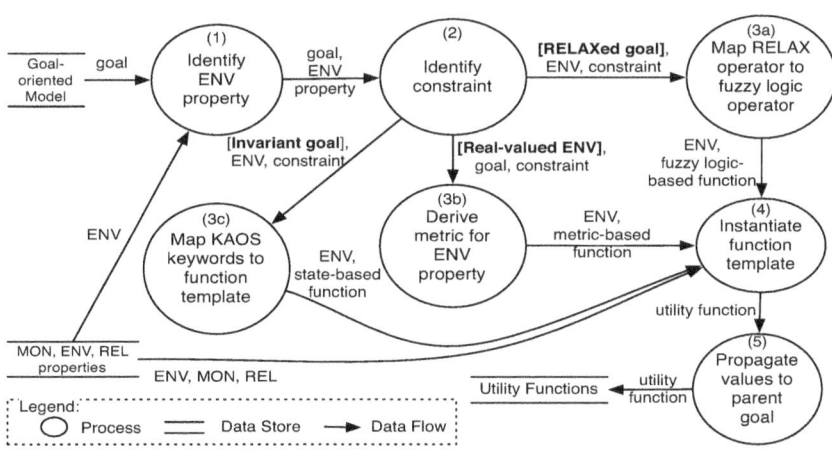

Fig. 3. Data flow diagram describing the approach

(1) Identify ENV Property. ENV specifies observable conditions of the execution environment, and can thus be observed by the DAS through its monitoring infrastructure. Athena matches text elements in a goal's specification with the set of ENV properties (see Table 1). For example, goal (B) refers to the ENV property *DistanceToObstacle* specified in row 6 of Table 1. Not all goals, however, refer to an ENV property. For instance, goal (F) does not refer to an ENV property (i.e., *VehicleSpeedComputed* is not specified in Table 1). If a goal does not refer to an ENV property, then Athena proceeds to step (5).

(2) Identify Constraints on the Goal. Constraints are often logical conditions or thresholds that can be evaluated in a crisp fashion (i.e., true or false). A goal may specify either an *absolute* constraint (i.e., a fixed threshold), or a *relative* constraint that specifies a relationship between properties whose value may change, such as an ENV property. For instance, goal (B) specifies a relative constraint/threshold, *SafeDistance*, whose value depends upon the IVS's current speed that is observable and controllable by the system. If a goal does not specify a constraint or threshold, then Athena proceeds to step (5).

(3a) Map RELAX Operator to Fuzzy Logic-Based Utility Function. RELAX defines a set of operators to constrain how a non-invariant goal may become temporarily unsatisfied due to environmental uncertainty [2,18]. Each operator is associated with a fuzzy logic-based function that evaluates the degree to which a non-invariant goal is satisfied. Athena generates a fuzzy logic-based utility function by mapping a RELAX operator to its corresponding fuzzy logic operator. For instance, Figure 4(A) presents a triangle-shaped function template for the RELAX operator *MeasuredQuantity AS CLOSE AS POSSIBLE TO DesiredQuantity*. This utility function returns a value between 0 and 1 proportional to how much *MeasuredQuantity* approaches *DesiredQuantity*.

Continuing with this example, Figure 4(B) illustrates how this fuzzy logic-based utility function template was applied to goal (C). In particular, the measured ENV property, *VehicleSpeed*, is mapped to a triangular shape that is centered at the ENV property's constraint (i.e., *DesiredSpeed*). This RELAXed goal specifies that the IVS tolerates temporary deviations between *VehicleSpeed* and *DesiredSpeed* within the minimum and maximum bounds allowed.

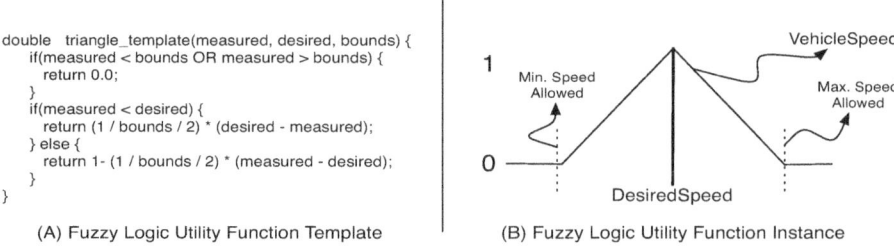

(A) Fuzzy Logic Utility Function Template (B) Fuzzy Logic Utility Function Instance

Fig. 4. Example function template for RELAX operator

(3b) Derive a Metric for a Real-Valued ENV Property. Athena generates a metric-based utility function for measuring the *satisficement* of invariant and non-invariant goals. While it is possible to determine whether an invariant goal is *satisfied*, Athena *also* evaluates the degree to which an invariant goal is satisficed or *excelled* [11], thereby enabling a DAS to detect and mitigate conditions conducive to a requirements violation. To this end, Athena leverages a goal's fitness criterion, which is an annotation often associated with soft goals to quantify the extent to which a goal should be met [12]. Specifically, Athena maps keywords in this annotation (i.e., minimize/maximize some condition) to a function template that either minimizes or maximizes the divergence between an ENV property and its constraint or threshold. For instance, the following function template measures the degree to which an ENV property approaches a given constraint, $Val_{constraint}$:

$$UT_{minimize} = 1 - \min \left\{ \frac{|Val_{ENV} - Val_{Constraint}|}{Val_{ENV}}, 1 \right\} \quad (1)$$

As such, Athena generates a utility function that measures the degree to which the IVS minimizes the difference between *VehicleSpeed* and *SafeSpeed*. Function template (1) can be instantiated as follows:

$$UT_{SafeSpeed} = 1 - \min \left\{ \frac{|VehicleSpeed - SafeSpeed|}{VehicleSpeed}, 1 \right\} \quad (2)$$

This utility function produces a utility value inversely proportional to the difference between *VehicleSpeed* and *SafeSpeed*. A sharp drop in the utility values produced by this utility function may suggest the IVS is exceeding its *SafeSpeed* constraint, which may lead to a collision with an obstacle.

(3c) Derive State-Based Function for an Invariant Goal. An invariant goal describes a functionality that the system-to-be must *always* provide. To specify an invariant goal, a requirements engineer uses a set of KAOS [5,12] keywords (i.e., *Maintain, Achieve, Avoid*) that can be mapped to precise semantics in temporal state-based logic [12]. Athena maps these keywords to a state-based utility function template that returns true or false depending on whether the constraint is satisfied. For instance, Figure 5(A) presents a state-based utility function template that is used to monitor the satisfaction of *Maintain* goals, where *ENV* refers to the environmental condition identified in step (1), *Op* refers to a logical operator (i.e., <, =, etc.), and *Constraint* refers to the goal's constraint identified in step (2). This template uses a *satisfied* guard to preserve the semantics of a *Maintain* goal and thus returns true only if the constraint has always been satisfied. As an example, Figure 5(B) shows how this template was instantiated for goal (B), where the utility function returns true as long as the IVS has never crossed the *SafeDistance* threshold.

```
boolean  maintain_template(ENV, Op, Constraint) {
    if(satisfied) {
        return (satisfied = Op(Env, Constrain));
    }
    return false;
}
```

(A) general state-based utility function

```
boolean  maintain_template(DistanceToObstacle, <=, SafeDistance) {
    if(satisfied) {
        return (satisfied = DistanceToObstacle <= SafeDistance);
    }
    return false;
}
```

(B) instance of state-based utility function

Fig. 5. Example state-based function template for *Maintain* goals

(4) Instantiate Function Template. Athena leverages the set of ENV properties, MON elements, and REL relationships (See Table 1) to express each utility function solely in terms of MON elements. These MON elements provide the monitoring information that each utility function needs to assess the satisfaction of a goal at run time. For example, Athena replaces the ENV property term *VehicleSpeed* in the utility functions derived for goal (D) with the following expression:

$$\text{VehicleSpeed} = \text{IVS.wheel\_diameter} * 3.1415 * \text{WheelSensor.value} \quad (3)$$

This expression, shown in row (2) of Table 1, specifies that the value of *VehicleSpeed* can be computed based on the wheel's geometry and its rotation rate, which is measured by *WheelSensor*.

(5) Propagate Utility Values to Parent Goals. Athena propagates the utility values associated with a goal (if any) to its parent goal in order to detect conditions conducive to a requirements violation. To a parent goal, this propagated utility value measures how well its subgoals are satisfied. The utility values of multiple subgoals are combined in different ways depending on the type of goal refinement applied. For an AND-decomposition, Athena computes the product of each utility value reported by the subgoals in the refinement. For instance, if the utility value associated with goals (L) and (M) are 0.8 and 1.0, respectively, then from the perspective of goal (I), its subgoals are satisfied to a degree of 0.8. In contrast, for an OR-decomposition, Athena selects the *maximum* value of each utility value produced by the subgoals in the OR-refinement. For example, if the utility value associated with goals (I) and (J) are 0.8 and 0.9, respectively, then from the perspective of goal (F), its subgoals are satisfied to a degree of 0.9. These semantics capture the notion that to satisfy a goal that has been AND-decomposed all subgoals must be satisfied, whereas to satisfy a goal that has been OR-decomposed, at least one subgoal must be satisfied.

(6) Repeat Steps (1) through (5) Until the Root Goal is Reached.

4 Case Study

This case study presents two different scenarios, each implemented in the Webots simulation platform [14], to illustrate how the set of derived utility functions enable a DAS to perform self-assessment in response to changing system and environmental conditions. The following scenarios involve a single IVS placed 400 meters behind a Lead Vehicle in the same lane. During each simulation, both vehicles accelerate in order to achieve their desired velocities. While the IVS sets its desired speed to 60 km/h, the Lead Vehicle sets its desired speed to 40 km/h. This speed differential makes it necessary for the ACC module in the IVS to readjust its speed to prevent a collision with the Lead Vehicle.

4.1 No Requirements Violations

In this scenario, the utility functions derived by Athena enable the IVS to satisfy its requirements by mitigating conditions conducive to a requirements violation, such as a collision, via dynamic adaptive behavior. Figure 6 shows an excerpt of the values produced by four different utility functions during this simulation, as they relate to the high-level goal (B) in Figure 2. As this plot illustrates, in order to satisfice RELAXed goal (C), the IVS gradually increases its *VehicleSpeed* until it is equivalent to *DesiredSpeed* (at approximately time step 400). The IVS maintains its *DesiredSpeed* until its distance sensors detect the Lead Vehicle, at approximately time step 840 in Figure 6(A). At this point, the metric-based utility function measuring the satisficement of goal (B) reports lower values as the distance between the IVS and the Lead Vehicle decreases. Simultaneously, the IVS switches from satisficing goal (C) to satisfying goal (D). Figure 6(A) illustrates this transition as the utility function that measures the satisficement of goal (D) drops to 0 (time step 860) and then progressively increases to 1 as the IVS achieves its *SafeSpeed*. Lastly, the IVS continues to maintain its *SafeSpeed* until the end of the simulation, at which point the IVS has not violated any invariant goals, as shown by Figure 6(B).

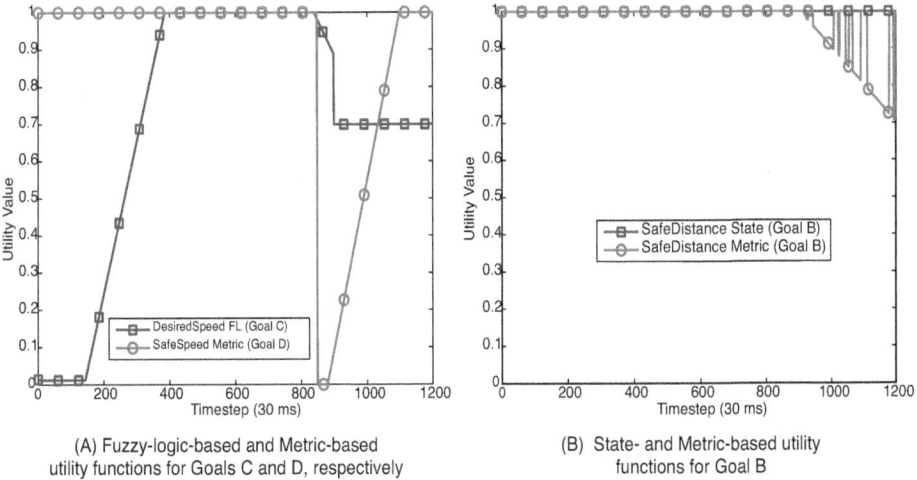

(A) Fuzzy-logic-based and Metric-based utility functions for Goals C and D, respectively

(B) State- and Metric-based utility functions for Goal B

Fig. 6. Plot of recorded utility functions for adaptive cruise control in IVS application

4.2 Sensor Noise Leads to Requirements Violation

In this scenario, the utility functions derived by Athena enable the IVS to detect the violation of an invariant requirement and diagnose potential causes for such a violation. To produce such a requirement violation, we introduced intermittent noise in the forward-bearing sensors of the IVS, which are responsible for detecting and computing the distance between the IVS and the Lead Vehicle. Due to the severe levels of noise applied to these sensors, the IVS is unable to accurately measure the distance to the Lead Vehicle and thus violates several requirements.

Figure 7 shows an excerpt of the values produced by utility functions during this simulation as they relate to the high-level goal (B) in Figure 2. Initially, the

IVS satisfies all invariant goals and satisfices its RELAXed goal (C) by achieving its *DesiredSpeed*, at timestep 450 in Figure 7(A). Shortly thereafter, the IVS distance sensors detect the Lead Vehicle. Due to environmental uncertainty, however, the computed value of *DistanceToObstacle* is unreliable. In particular, forward-bearing distance sensors intermittently report noisy data that suggests no obstacle is present. As a result, the IVS begins to alternate between satisficing goal (C), when distance sensors do not report an obstacle, and satisfying goal (D), when distance sensors report an obstacle. Alternating between these two goals impedes the IVS from successfully achieving its *SafeSpeed* objective.

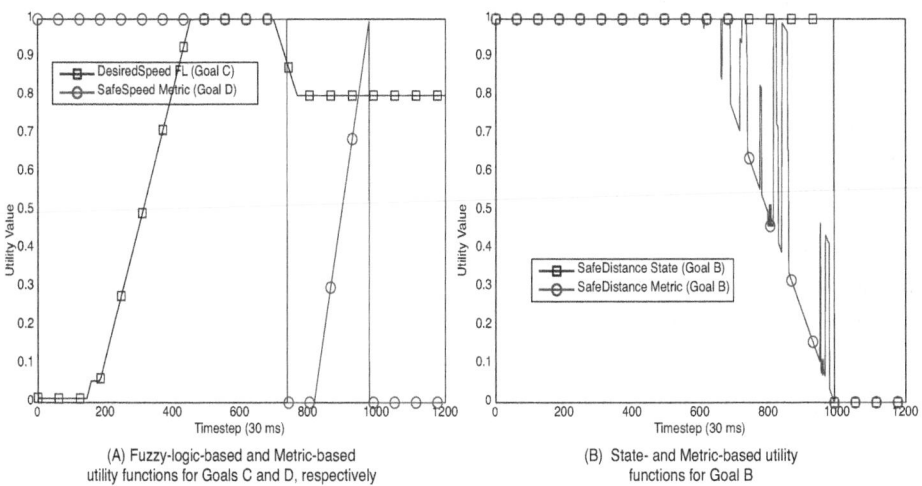

Fig. 7. Plot of recorded utility functions for adaptive cruise control in IVS application

Given the failure to accurately compute the value of *DistanceToObstacle*, the IVS crossed the *SafeDistance* threshold (at approximately time step 1000) and violated the invariant goal (B). The state-based utility function for this invariant goal successfully detected this requirement violation, as can be observed in Figure 7(B), where the *SafeDistance State* utility curve dropped from 1 to 0 for the remainder of the experiment. As the *SafeDistance Metric* utility curve shows, the metric-based utility function for this invariant goal suggested an imminent violation of goal (B) by gradually reporting values closer to 0 as the IVS approached the *SafeDistance* threshold. By leveraging the entire set of utility functions, the DAS is able to partially detect a set of agents involved in the goal's violation. In particular, plotted utility curves indicate goals (B) and (D) were violated during the simulation. Moreover, by examining the utility values produced by (D)'s subgoals, the DAS is able to further pinpoint that goals (H), (K), and (P) were not satisfied multiple times between time steps 700 and 1000, thus suggesting the *NavigationComponent* and *DistanceSensor* agents as root causes for the invariant goal's violation. This information enables requirements engineers to either revise the interactions between the *NavigationComponent* and the *DistanceSensors*, or alternatively, add new refinements to mitigate the obstacle that caused this requirement violation.

5 Related Work

This section overviews related work in specifying partial satisfaction of goals, requirements monitoring, and the use of utility functions for self-assessment in a DAS.

5.1 Partial Satisfaction of Goals

Letier and van Lamsweerde [13] introduced a probabilistic framework for specifying and analyzing the partial satisfaction of goals. Their approach leveraged probability theory to model how requirements may become obstructed, as well as how the obstruction of such goals impact the satisfaction of other goals in the goal-oriented model. In addition, Letier and van Lamsweerde also presented various heuristics to identify probabilistic functions that measure the likelihood of goals becoming unsatisfied. While similar in objective, Athena uses utility functions to measure requirements satisfaction instead of probability theory. As a result, a requirements engineer can apply Athena without requiring data from which goal satisfaction probabilities may be derived.

5.2 Requirements Monitoring

Requirements monitoring focuses on detecting and mitigating both requirements violations and conditions conducive to a requirements violation. Feather, Fickas, and Robinson [7,8,16] developed frameworks for run-time monitoring of software requirements that support the instrumentation, diagnosis, and reconfiguration of the system. To leverage these frameworks, a requirements engineer must first model the system's requirements through a goal-based modeling language, such as KAOS [5], and identify assumptions and constraints that could become violated. At run time, a requirements monitoring framework observes traces of the executing system, logs violations of assumptions and constraints, and then reconciles the system with its goals. Athena shares similar objectives as these requirements monitoring frameworks. However, Athena supports the automatic derivation of utility functions from goal models. Furthermore, Athena supports state-, metric-, and fuzzy logic-based utility functions for measuring the satisfaction and satisficement of goals at run time.

5.3 Utility Functions for Self-adaptive Systems

Utility functions have been applied for self-assessment purposes in DASs. For instance, Walsh *et al.* [17] used utility functions to map monitoring data to a scalar value representative of how well the system was executing, akin to the concept of a *health* value. In this manner, utility functions provide not only an objective and quantitative basis for automated decision-making, but also facilitate the mapping of those decisions to higher-level goals, requirements and concerns. Similarly, utility functions have been applied within a DAS to guide the selection of self-optimizing strategies. For instance, Garlan *et al.* [3] applied utility functions to evaluate and select among different reconfiguration strategies depending on how each satisfied architectural and performance-based constraints. Even though utility functions provide numerous benefits for decision-making within a DAS, these are usually elicited either from domain experts or application users [9].

Statistical regression techniques enable a DAS to infer utility values that capture their overall performance at run time [1,9]. For instance, Valetto *et al.* [9] proposed a statistical correlation-based approach for generating, at run time, a single application-level utility value that measured the most salient properties of that system. These approaches automate the task of deriving utility functions, but their success depends on the quality of monitoring data gathered from the executing DAS. Specifically, regressed utility functions may inadvertently miss the detection of anomalous behaviors if this behavioral data is incomplete or contains undesirable behaviors. Athena does not suffer from such drawbacks as it derives utility functions directly from a goal model. Athena could, however, leverage these techniques to further refine derived utility functions at run time.

6 Conclusions

This paper presented Athena, a goal-based requirements model-driven approach for automatically deriving utility functions from a KAOS or RELAX goal model. In particular, Athena leverages the information contained in a KAOS goal model, as well as its RELAXed goals, corresponding fuzzy logic-based constraints, and MON, ENV, and REL elements to derive utility functions that can be used at run time to monitor the requirements of a DAS. As such, the primary benefit of Athena is that it leverages artifacts already produced by a requirements engineer that applied either a KAOS or RELAX goal modeling approach, thereby enabling a requirements engineer to focus on other aspects of the design rather than on manually deriving utility functions via ad-hoc manual approaches.

These utility functions enable a DAS to assess requirements satisfaction and satisficement at run time. In particular, state- and fuzzy logic-based utility functions enable a DAS to determine whether an invariant or a RELAXed goal has been violated, respectively. Metric-based utility functions enable a DAS to detect conditions conducive to a requirements violation, thereby facilitating the mitigation of such conditions before a goal violation occurs. Experimental results show that utility functions generated by Athena are not only successful at requirements monitoring, but also at identifying a candidate set of agents responsible for the violation of a goal.

Future directions for this work include applying evolutionary computation techniques in order to optimize the set of utility functions generated by Athena. In addition, we are also exploring the use of generated utility functions for adaptive requirements monitoring [15].

References

1. Chajewska, U., Koller, D., Ormoneit, D.: Learning an agent's utility function by observing behavior. In: Proceedings of the Eighteenth International Conference on Machine Learning, ICML, pp. 35–42. Morgan Kaufmann Publishers Inc., San Francisco (2001)
2. Cheng, B.H.C., Sawyer, P., Bencomo, N., Whittle, J.: A goal-based modeling approach to develop requirements of an adaptive system with environmental uncertainty. In: Schürr, A., Selic, B. (eds.) MODELS 2009. LNCS, vol. 5795, pp. 468–483. Springer, Heidelberg (2009)
3. Cheng, S.W., Garlan, D., Schmerl, B.: Architecture-based self-adaptation in the presence of multiple objectives. In: Proceedings of the 2006 International Workshop on Self-adaptation and Self-Managing Systems, pp. 2–8. ACM, Shanghai (2006)
4. Chung, L., Nixon, B., Yu, E., Mylopoulos, J.: Non-Functional Requirements in Software Engineering. Kluwer Academic Publishers, Dordrecht (2000)
5. Dardenne, A., van Lamsweerde, A., Fickas, S.: Goal-directed requirements acquisition. Science of Computer Programming 20(1-2), 3–50 (1993)
6. Darimont, R., van Lamsweerde, A.: Formal refinement patterns for goal-driven requirements elaboration. SIGSOFT Software Engineering Notes 21(6), 179–190 (1996)
7. Feather, M.S., Fickas, S., van Lamsweerde, A., Ponsard, C.: Reconciling system requirements and runtime behavior. In: IWSSD 1998: Proceedings of the 8th International Workshop on Software Specification and Design, pp. 50–59. IEEE Computer Society, Washington, DC (1998)
8. Fickas, S., Feather, M.S.: Requirements monitoring in dynamic environments. In: RE 1995: Proceedings of the Second IEEE International Symposium on Requirements Engineering, pp. 140–147. IEEE Computer Society, Washington, DC (1995)
9. de Grandis, P., Valetto, G.: Elicitation and utilization of application-level utility functions. In: The Proceedings of the Sixth International Conference on Autonomic Computing (ICAC 2009), pp. 107–116. ACM, Barcelona (2009)
10. Jackson, M., Zave, P.: Deriving specifications from requirements: an example. In: Proceedings of the 17th International Conference on Software Engineering, ICSE, pp. 15–24. ACM, Seattle (1995)
11. Jureta, I.J., Faulkner, S., Schobbens, P.Y.: Achieving, satisficing, and excelling. In: Parent, C., Schewe, K.-D., Storey, V.C., Thalheim, B. (eds.) ER 2007. LNCS, vol. 4801, pp. 286–295. Springer, Heidelberg (2007)
12. van Lamsweerde, A.: Requirements Engineering: From System Goals to UML Models to Software Specifications. Wiley, Chichester (2009)
13. Letier, E., van Lamsweerde, A.: Reasoning about partial goal satisfaction for requirements and design engineering. In: Proceedings of the 12th ACM SIGSOFT International Symposium on Foundations of Software Engineering, pp. 53–62. ACM, Newport Beach (2004)
14. Michel, O.: Webots: Professional mobile robot simulation. Journal of Advanced Robotics Systems 1(1), 39–42 (2004)
15. Ramirez, A.J., Cheng, B.H.C.: Adaptive monitoring of software requirements. In: Proceedings of the 2010 Workshop on Requirements at Run Time, RE@RunTime, pp. 41–50. IEEE Computer Society, Sydney (2010)

16. Robinson, W.N.: Monitoring software requirements using instrumented code. In: HICSS 2002: Proceedings of the 35th Annual Hawaii International Conference on System Sciences, pp. 276–285. IEEE Computer Society, Hawaii (2002)
17. Walsh, W.E., Tesauro, G., Kephart, J.O., Das, R.: Utility functions in autonomic systems. In: Proceedings of the First IEEE International Conference on Autonomic Computing, pp. 70–77. IEEE Computer Society, New York (2004)
18. Whittle, J., Sawyer, P., Bencomo, N., Cheng, B.H.C., Bruel, J.M.: RELAX: Incorporating uncertainty into the specification of self-adaptive systems. In: The Proceedings of the 17th International Requirements Engineering Conference (RE 2009), pp. 79–88. IEEE Computer Society, Atlanta (2009)

Logic-Based Model-Level Software Development with F-OML

Mira Balaban[1,*] and Michael Kifer[2,**]

[1] Ben-Gurion University, Israel
mira@cs.bgu.ac.il
[2] Stony Brook University, USA
kifer@cs.sunysb.edu

Abstract. Models are at the heart of the emerging *Model-driven Engineering* (*MDE*) approach in which software is developed by repeated transformations of models. Intensive efforts in the modeling community in the past two decades have produced an impressive variety of tool support for models. Nonetheless, models are still not widely used throughout the software evolution life cycle and, in many cases, they are neglected in later stages of software development. To make models more useful, one needs a powerful model-level IDE that supports a wide range of object modeling tasks. Such IDEs must have a consistent formal foundation.

This paper introduces *F-OML*, a language intended as an expressive, executable formal basis for model-level IDEs. F-OML supports a wide variety of model-level activities, such as *extending* UML diagrams, defining *design patterns*, *reasoning* about UML diagrams, *testing* UML diagrams, specification of *Domain Specific Modeling Languages*, and *meta-modeling*. F-OML is a semantic layer on top of an elegant logic programming language of *guarded path expressions*, called *PathLP*. We believe that a combination of current object technology with F-OML as an underlying language can lay the basis for a powerful model-level IDE.

1 Introduction

Models are at the heart of the emerging *Model-driven Engineering* (*MDE*) approach in which software is developed by repeated transformations of models. The MDE approach is motivated by the understanding that the growing complexity of software requires multiple levels of abstraction that programming languages do not usually support [1].

Intensive efforts in the modeling community in the last two decades have produced an impressive variety of tool support for models. Nevertheless, models are still not widely used throughout the software evolution life cycle and, in many cases, they are neglected in later stages of software development. Moreover, users neglect specification of essential constraints, since they are not supported by the software tools that implement the models. To make models more useful, one

---

* Supported in part by the Paul Ivanir Center for Robotics and Production Management at Ben-Gurion University of the Negev.
** Supported in part by the NSF grant 0964196.

needs a powerful model-level IDE that supports a wide range of object modeling tasks. Such IDEs must have a consistent formal foundation.

This paper[1] introduces *F-OML*, a language intended as an expressive, executable formal basis for model-level IDEs. F-OML can support a wide variety of model-level activities, such as *extending* UML diagrams, defining *design patterns*, *reasoning* about UML diagrams, *testing* UML diagrams, specification of *Domain Specific Modeling Languages* (*DSMLs*), and *meta-modeling*. F-OML provides a formal API for object modeling, supported by a well-defined semantics and a provably correct execution methods. The visual models (e.g., UML) provide concrete syntax on top of the language abstract syntax.

F-OML is a semantic layer on top of an elegant formal language of *guarded path expressions*, called *PathLP*, which is used to define objects and their types. PathLP is a logic programming language, inspired by F-logic [3]. It supports *path expressions*, *rules*, *constraints*, and *queries*, and can be easily implemented in a tabling Prolog engine, such as XSB. PathLP has three distinctive features that make it a particularly powerful tool for object modeling: (1) polymorphism of language expressions and of class hierarchies; (2) multilevel object modeling; (3) executable model instantiation. F-OML consists of the two first-class object concepts of *Class* and *Property*, and a library of parameterized constructors and features. The paper defines PathLP and F-OML, and illustrates them with examples of various model-level tasks.

Section 2 describes F-OML by example, and Section 3 formally introduces the PathLP language. The F-OML layer is described in Section 4, and its usage is demonstrated in Section 5. Section 6 briefly describes related work and Section 7 concludes the paper.

2 F-OML by Example

2.1 PathLP Introduction

PathLP consists of *path expressions, facts, rules, queries* and *constraints*.

Path Expressions: The key syntactic element of PathLP, which generalizes path expressions in traditional object-oriented languages is *path expression*. They extend a similar notion in XSQL [4], an F-logic [3] based language for querying object-oriented databases, in the direction of the more general path expressions in the F-logic systems [5]. PathLP also generalizes many aspects of XPath.

The building blocks of path expressions are *terms, guards, cardinalities*, and two *operators*: ".". and "!". Terms are constructed from *constant symbols* and *variables* (which are denoted by symbols prefixed with "?"). Guards are path expressions written within square brackets. Examples of PathLP path expressions are shown in Table 1. In these path expressions, Mary, spouse, ageAt(2010), and ?C are terms, [?S] and [Person] are guards, and {0..1} is a cardinality. ?C:Student and ?C.ageAt(2010)<20 are query formulas.

---
[1] A preliminary overview on this work appeared in [2].

Intuitively, the "." operator provides navigation along *value paths*. Therefore, in a path expression $n.e_1. \ldots .e_k$ (ignoring guards), we refer to n as a *node* and to the e_i-s as edges. The "." in $n.e$ yields a "value" that results from navigation along an "edge" e whose origin is n. There can be multiple such edges as, for example, in John.childOf.

Table 1. Examples of path expressions

Expression	Informal meaning
Mary.spouse.ageAt(2010)	the age at 2010 of the spouse of Mary
?C.student[?S].name	given a binding c for the variable ?C, binds ?S to an object who is a student of C, and returns its name
John.childWith(Mary)[?C].name, ?C:Student, ?C.ageAt(2010)<20	the name of a child of John and Mary, who is a student, whose age in 2010 is less than 20
Person!spouse[Person]{0..1}	restricts the type of the spouse property of Person to be Person, and to have cardinality 0..1

The intuition behind the operator "!" is similar to ".", but "!" yields a *type* of an edge, rather than its value. For instance, Person!spouse denotes the possible types of a spouse edge of a person, Person!spouse[Person] checks that Person is one of these types (implying that so are also all of its super types), and Student!thesis[Document]!length[NaturalNumber] checks that the type of a Student thesis is Document, and the type of the length edge from Document is NaturalNumber. Type path expressions can also have constrained cardinalities of the form {low..high}, which specify the minimum and maximum cardinality for member nodes (precise definition in Section 3). Altogether, the semantic domain of PathLP can be viewed as directed *value graphs* and directed *type graphs* sharing the same set of nodes.

Guards play the role of *selectors*. They are usually variables or constants. For instance, John.childOf[?X].name binds the variable ?X to the object that represents one of John's children, and denotes the value of the edge labeled name of that object. Similarly, John.childOf[Mary].height checks that Mary is one of the children of John and denotes her height. Guards can be followed by query formulas that act like tests on the intermediate values of path expressions. For instance, John.childOf[?X].name,?X:Student,?X.ageAt(2009)<10, binds ?X to an object that represents one of Johns children who is a student and is under 10 years old, and denotes the name of that child.

Facts, Rules, Queries, and Constraints: Facts specify assertions, rules specify implications, and constraints restrict the legal states, by specifying forbidden states. Queries trigger reasoning.

Fact Examples

1. John.spouse[Mary]. John.childOf[Bob]. John.childOf[Bill].
   John has a spouse Mary, and children Bob and Bill (and possibly others).
2. Inclusion and membership assertions: Nodes are related by two relations "::" and ":" that have properties of set inclusion and membership, respectively.

Bob:CS_committee. CS_committee::Academic_committee.
Academic_committee:Committee. Committee::Group.

The intuition behind these facts is
Bob ∈ CS_committee ⊆ Academic_committee ∈ Committee ⊆ Group.

3. A type assertion: Person!spouse[Person]{0..1}.
Person is one of the types of the spouse edge of Person, and its cardinality constraint is {0..1}.

Rule and Constraint Examples

1. ?S.studentOf[?Prof] :- ?S:Student, ?S.takes.teaches[?Prof].
A rule stating that if ?S is a member of the Student node and ?S takes a course taught by ?Prof then ?Prof is a value of a studentOf edge from ?S.
2. ?A:advisor :- ?T:Thesis, ?T.author.advisor[?A].read[?T], ?A:Professor.
This rule states that ?A is an advisor if ?A has read a thesis ?T of an author that ?A advises.
3. !- ?P:Professor, not ?P.degree[PhD].
A constraint that forbids states where a professor ?P has no PhD degree.

2.2 Introduction to F-OML

F-OML uses PathLP for formulating the two fundamental object oriented concepts of *Class* and *Property*. This approach is close to meta-modeling semantics [6], since the two model levels are expressed in PathLP, which defines the abstract syntax and semantics of models. F-OML specifications are executable since they are expressed in PathLP. The library of constructors and properties is a major source of expressivity for F-OML.

The following examples use model-level constructors for expressing class invariants and for generalizing a concrete invariant into an invariant pattern. We use UML class diagrams for visualizing (as concrete syntax) F-OML expressions that specify classes, properties and cardinality constraints.

Example 1. Figure 1 describes a User-Table class diagram. A table has a single user as its owner, and a user might own multiple tables. The tableDependency association is not constrained by multiplicity constraints.

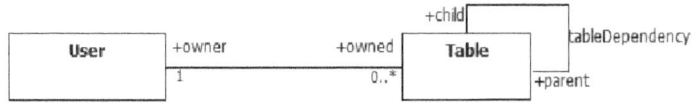

Fig. 1. User-Table ownership Class Diagram

Assume that the model requires the constraint: "Tables with a common owner are directly or indirectly linked via the tableDependency association." In order to express this constraint there is a need to relate a table to all of its indirect parent tables and all of its indirect child tables. The property constructor

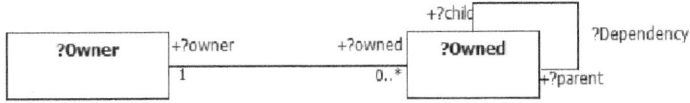

Fig. 2. Single ownership Class Diagram pattern

closure is used to define the new *parameterized properties* closure(parent) and closure(child) that provide the necessary mappings. The or-constructor defines a parameterized property which is the union mapping of its arguments. Therefore, the property or(closure(parent),closure(child)) maps a table to all of its direct and indirect parent and child tables. The required constraint is captured by a rule stating that a table ?s is a direct or indirect parent or child table of a table ?t if ?t and ?s have the same user owner:

?t.or(closure(parent),closure(child))[?s] :-
                    ?t:Table,?s:Table,?t.owner=?s.owner.

Example 2. Suppose that the above constraint is identified by domain experts as a typical ownership situation that can serve as a *reference model*. They define the following design pattern: *A single owner of multiple objects of the same class requires mutual relationships between its owned objects.* A solution is to instantiate the reference model given by the *class diagram pattern* in Figure 2 and the associated constraint pattern.

?o1.or(closure(?parent),closure(?child))[?o2] :-
                    ?o1:?Owned,?o2:?Owned,?o1.?owner=?o2.?owner.

Instantiation is performed by replacing class and property variables (?Owned and ?owner) with concrete classes and properties (Table and owner) in Figure 1.

The reference model formulation exploits the expression polymorphism and the multi-level features of PathLP. Due to the executable nature of PathLP at the foundation, we can further manipulate the reference model and its instantiation.

3   PathLP — The Underlying Logic of F-OML

3.1   Syntax

The ***alphabet*** of the PathLP language includes countably many constant symbols, (e.g., Foo_123) and variables (designated with the "?" prefix, e.g., $?x$), plus the auxiliary symbols "!", ".", "..", "[", "]", "(", ")", ":-", ">", "=", and so on.

A ***term*** is defined recursively as either a variable, a constant, or an expression of the form $c(t_1, ..., t_n)$, where c is a constant and $t_1, ..., t_n, n \geq 0$, are terms. The latter kind of a term is called a ***compound term***.

Path Expressions: The following BNF productions define path expressions where Var, Term, NonNegInt denote variables, terms, and non-negative integers.

```
PathExpr         := ObjectPathExpr | TypePathExpr
ObjectPathExpr   := (Expr '.')* Expr
TypePathExpr     := (Expr '!')+ Expr [ '{' Cardinality '}' ]
Expr             := GuardedExpr | UnguardedExpr
UnguardedExpr    := Term
GuardedExpr      := UnguardedExpr '[' Guard ']'
Guard            := UnguardedPathExpr (',' UnguardedPathExpr)*
Cardinality      := (Var|NonNegInt) '..' (Var|NonNegInt|'*')
```

where UnguardedPathExpr is a PathExpr ending with UnguardedExpr (it is not defined explicitly to simplify the presentation).

PathLP expressions resemble those of XPath.[2] Examples include John.spouse, Person!name[String], and Person!spouse[Person]{0..1}. The last two of these are *guarded* path expressions. The definition of query formulas, below, uses GuardedPathExpr as a syntactic category for guarded path expressions.

Queries and constraints: PathLP uses *query formulas* as selectors in path expressions and as bodies of PathLP inference rules and constraints.

```
Query             := '?-' QueryFormula '.'
Constraint        := '!-' QueryFormula '.'
QueryFormula      := ElementaryFormula
                   | 'not' QueryFormula | '(' QueryFormula ')'
                   | (QueryFormula ('and'|'or') QueryFormula)
ElementaryFormula := Membership|Subset|GuardedPathExpr|Comparison
Membership        := Term ':' Term
Subset            := Term '::' Term
Comparison        := Term Op Term
Op                := '=' | '!=' | '>' | '<' | '>=' | '=<'
```

The **and** connective in query formulas can be replaced by a comma.

Facts and Rules: We introduce a new syntactic category Consequent, that represents formulas that are allowed as facts or rule consequences. Such formulas are considerably simpler than query formulas and even than elementary formulas – the usual restriction in logic programming languages. Consequents are ElementaryFormulas that are subject to the following restrictions:

- Comparison formulas can be only of the form Term = Term. That is, we are not allowed to infer facts like a > b.
- Path expressions can have only one operator "." or "!" and only terms as guards. That is, they can take one of the following forms: Term.Term[Term], Term!Term[Term], or Term!Term[Term]{Cardinality}.

These restrictions make PathLP reducible to Logic Programming and provide a way for an efficient implementation. Finally, the definition of facts and rules:

```
Fact := Consequent '.'
Rule := Consequent ':-' QueryFormula '.'
```

---

[2] Apart from the differences in the underlying models, PathLP variables turn it more expressive than XPath. Although PathLP expressions have no descendant-or-self wildcards of XPath, these can be defined recursively by rules.

PathLP has three language features that make it a powerful foundation for supporting object modeling:

1. **Polymorphism:** PathLP has two forms of polymorphism: *expression polymorphism*, which enables the specification of patterns and reference models as in or(closure(?parent),closure(?child))[?o2] – see Example 2, and the standard *class hierarchy polymorphism* of object-oriented modeling.
2. **Multi-level object modeling:** This feature enables full meta-modeling, defining the abstract syntax on the meta-model level, and the semantics on the model level, as in:

   ```
   intersection(?C1,?C2):Class :- ?C1:Class, ?C2:Class.
   ?o:intersection(?C1,?C2) :- ?o:?C1, ?o:?C2.
   ```

   The first rule specifies the class constructor intersection on the meta-model level, and the second rule partially specifies its semantics, on the model level. Section 4 provides further explanations.
3. **Executable language:** PathLP is an executable standalone language (unlike OCL). It supports model instantiation (*i.e.*, population of objects and links) which enables testing and querying on various modeling levels.

3.2 Semantics

The semantic domain of PathLP is a set of entities, over which various structures (value graphs, type graphs, membership and inclusion relations, and cardinality constraints) are defined. The domain does not differentiate entities by their role: node, edge, or type: the same entity can play different roles depending on the syntactic context. Formally, *up to an isomorphism*, the **domain** is a set of all *ground* (i.e., variable-free) terms, which includes the values of standard data types (strings, numbers, etc.).

A PathLP **interpretation**, $\mathcal{I}$, is a tuple of the form $\langle U, I_C, I_V, I_F, I_{val}, I_{type}, I_{min}, I_{max}, \in_\mathcal{I}, \prec_\mathcal{I} \rangle$, where U is the *domain*, I_C is a mapping from constant symbols to U; I_V is a variable assignment mapping, which is a total function $Vars \longrightarrow U$; I_F is a function $U \longrightarrow (\cup_{n=0}^\infty U \longrightarrow U)$, which associated to every element in U a polyadic function $\cup_{n=1}^\infty U \longrightarrow U$; and I_{val}, I_{type} are both ternary relations over U. $I_{min}, I_{max} : U \times U \longrightarrow (Integers \cup \{*\})$ are mappings such that $0 \le I_{min}(x,y) \le I_{max}(x,y)$ for all $x, y \in U$. $\in_\mathcal{I}$ and $\prec_\mathcal{I}$ are binary relations over U: $\in_\mathcal{I}$ represents the **membership relation**, and $\prec_\mathcal{I}$ is a partial order that represents the **subset relation**.

The mapping I_{val} determines the values of edges. A triple $(n, e, v) \in I_{val}$ defines v as the value of the edge e of node n. For a given node n and edge e, there can be multiple such triples, since the value graph structure allows multiple edges with the same label for a node. The mapping I_{type} determines the types of edge values. A triple $(n, e, t) \in I_{type}$ defines t as the type of the edge e of node n. Typing should satisfy *closure properties* with respect to the subset relation, and *well-typing properties* with respect to the value mapping.

Closure Properties:
- *Upward-closure*: if $(n,e,t) \in I_{type}$ and $t \prec_\mathcal{I} t'$ then also $(n,e,t') \in I_{type}$ (if e has type t then every supertype of t is also a type of e).
- *Inheritance*: if $n \prec_\mathcal{I} n'$ and $(n',e,t) \in I_{type}$ then $(n,e,t) \in I_{type}$ (if e has type t for a node n' then it has type t for every subset-related node of n'; i.e., e is inherited).

Well-typed Interpretations: *Well-typed* interpretations, first introduced in [3], enforce well-typing of edge values of member nodes. Well typing has two aspects: A typing restriction for each value, and obeying the cardinality restrictions. Namely, for every value-triple $(n,e,v) \in I_{val}$, there is a type-triple $(n',e,t) \in I_{type}$ such that
- $n \in_\mathcal{I} n'$ and $v \in_\mathcal{I} t$
- $I_{min}(n',e) \leq$ `cardinality`$(\{v \mid (n,e,v) \in I_{val}\}) \leq I_{max}(n',e)$

The membership and subset relations are required to satisfy these properties: $n \in_\mathcal{I} n'$ and $n' \prec_\mathcal{I} n''$ imply $n \in_\mathcal{I} n''$. This implies that the set of all the members of n' is a subset of the set of the members of n''. Note that the opposite does not have to hold.

The Meaning of PathLP Constructs

Given an interpretation $\mathcal{I}$, we define the notion of *satisfaction by interpretation* for PathLP query formulas, facts, rules, and constraints. We first define the *denotation mapping* associated with $\mathcal{I}$. The purpose of that mapping is to interpret path expressions as subsets of the domain of $\mathcal{I}$. It is common to use the same symbol $\mathcal{I}$ both for the interpretation and for its associated denotation mapping. The definitions of the denotation mapping and of satisfaction are inductive on the structure of the formulas and are mutually dependent.

Denotation of Path Expressions
- *Constant*: If c is a constant then $\mathcal{I}(c) = \{I_C(c)\}$.
- *Variable*: If $?x$ is variable then $\mathcal{I}(?x) = \{I_V(?x)\}$.
- *Unguarded expression*: If τ is a compound term $c(t_1, ..., t_n)$ (an unguarded expression) with zero or more arguments then:
  $\mathcal{I}(\tau) = \{I_F(I_C(c))(t'_1, ..., t'_n)\}$, where $t'_i \in \mathcal{I}(t_i)$ for $i = 1, ..., n$.

The previous three cases form the basis for the inductive definition of $\mathcal{I}(\tau)$, where τ is a path expression. The inductive part of the definition now follows.

- *Unguarded object path expression*: If τ is $objpathexp.expr$, where $objpathexp$ is an object path expression and $expr$ is a term then:

  $\mathcal{I}(\tau) = \{v \mid \exists n \in \mathcal{I}(objectpathexp), \exists e \in \mathcal{I}(expr), \text{ such that } (n,e,v) \in I_{val}\}$.

  Note that $\mathcal{I}(\tau)$ can be empty.
- *Guarded object path expression*: If τ is $ungobjpathexp[grd]$, where $ungobjpathexp$ is an unguarded object path expression and grd is a guard of the form $ungpathexp_1, ..., ungpathexp_n$ then:

  $\mathcal{I}(\tau) = \mathcal{I}(ungobjpathexp) \cap \mathcal{I}(ungpathexp_1) \cap \cdots \cap \mathcal{I}(ungpathexp_n)$

- *Type path expression*:
    - *Unguarded without cardinality constraint*: If τ is *tpathexp!expr*, where *tpathexp* is a type path expression and *expr* is an expression then:
    $\mathcal{I}(\tau) = \{v \mid \exists n \in \mathcal{I}(tpathexp), \exists e \in \mathcal{I}(expr), \text{ such that } (n, e, v) \in I_{type}\}$.
    - *Unguarded with cardinality constraint*: If τ is *tpathexp!expr{lo..hi}*, where *tpathexp* is a type path expression and *expr* is an expression then:
    $\mathcal{I}(\tau) = \{v \mid \exists n \in \mathcal{I}(tpathexp), \exists e \in \mathcal{I}(expr), \text{ such that }$
    $(n, e, v) \in I_{type} \text{ and } I_{min}(n, e) = I(lo), I_{max}(n, e) = I(hi)\}$.
    - *Guarded*: Similarly to guarded object path expressions.

Built-in size Terms: PathLP assigns special meaning to the properties size() and size(prop), used for counting the number of objects in a class and the range size of a property. Thus, the denotation of these properties must satisfy:
- size(): $(n, \mathcal{I}(\text{size}()), N) \in I_{val}$, where $n \in U$ and $N \geq 0$ is an integer, if and only if the set $\{v \mid v \in_{\mathcal{I}} n\}$ is finite and has cardinality N.
- size(e): $(n, \mathcal{I}(\text{size}(e)), N) \in I_{val}$, where $n \in U$ and $N \geq 0$ is an integer, if and only if the set $\{v \mid (n, \text{e}, v) \in I_{val}\}$ is finite and has cardinality N.

Satisfaction by Interpretations
1. *Elementary formulas*
    - *Membership*: $\mathcal{I} \models t : s$, where t, s are terms, if and only if $\mathcal{I}(t) \in_{\mathcal{I}} \mathcal{I}(s)$.
    - *Subset*: $\mathcal{I} \models t :: s$, where t, s are terms, if and only if $\mathcal{I}(t) \prec_{\mathcal{I}} \mathcal{I}(s)$.
    - *Guarded path expression with and without cardinality constraints*: $\mathcal{I} \models p$, where p is a guarded path expression, if and only if $\mathcal{I}(p)$ is non-empty.
    - *Comparison formulas* $\mathcal{I} \models (t = s)$, where t, s are terms, iff $\mathcal{I}(t) = \mathcal{I}(s)$. Likewise, $\mathcal{I} \models t < s$, iff $\mathcal{I}(t) < \mathcal{I}(s)$. The definition of satisfaction for the remaining comparisons is similar.
2. *Query formulas:*
    - *And*: $\mathcal{I} \models t$ and s iff $\mathcal{I} \models t$ and $\mathcal{I} \models s$.
    - *Or*: $\mathcal{I} \models t$ or s iff either $\mathcal{I} \models t$ or $\mathcal{I} \models s$.
    - *Not*: $\mathcal{I} \models$ not t iff it is not the case that $\mathcal{I} \models t$.
3. *Rules and facts*: $\mathcal{I} \models (t :\text{-} s)$ if and only if either $\mathcal{I} \models t$ or $\mathcal{I} \not\models s$. This also covers the case of satisfaction for PathLP facts, since we can view any fact t as a rule of the form $t :\text{-} true$.
4. *Constraints*: $\mathcal{I} \models (!\text{-} queryformula)$ iff $\mathcal{I} \not\models queryformula$.

A PathLP interpretation that satisfies the facts, rules, and constraints of a PathLP specification is a ***model*** of that specification. As usual in logic programming, we focus on ***canonical*** models. Without negation (not), there is a unique least model, which is the canonical model. With negation, the semantics is defined using so-called *well-founded* models [7]. A PathLP specification is *satisfiable* if it has a canonical model. An ***answer*** to a query ?- *queryformula* is the set of all instantiations of *queryformula* satisfied by the canonical model.

With no negation, PathLP reduces to classical logic analogously to the reduction of F-logic to classical logic [3] and is semi-decidable. With negation, it reduces to logic programs with the well-founded semantics and can be implemented on top of a tabling deductive engine, like XSB, similarly to the FLORA-2 implementation of F-logic [5]. Without function symbols, PathLP is decidable and has polynomial data complexity even with negation.

4 F-OML – The Semantic Layer over PathLP

F-OML uses PathLP to define axioms for two basic notions of object modeling, *classes*, and *properties*, along with their *interrelationships*. Class characterizes objects that function as collections of objects. Property defines objects that function as mappings among classes. The definition covers three modeling levels: the *Meta Model* level (OMG's M2 level) that specifies the abstract syntax of F-OML models, and *Model* and *Data* levels (OMG's M1 and M0 levels), that specify the semantics of F-OML specifications.

F-OML Syntax: Figure 3 presents the meta-model of F-OML notions.

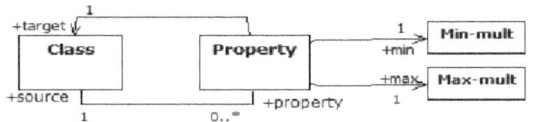

Fig. 3. Meta-model of F-OML

This meta-model is defined by the following PathLP specification:

1. *F-OML classes*, i.e., members of Class, have multiple properties which are members of Property: Class!property[Property].
2. F-OML *properties*, i.e., members of Property, have a unique source class, target class, and minimum and maximum multiplicities:
   Property!source[Class]{1..1}.   Property!target[Class]{1..1}.
   Property!min[Min_mult]{1..1}.   Property!max[Max_mult]{1..1}.
3. *Class-Property inter-relationships*: Property is a member of Class, and the source of a property is a class with that property:
   Property:Class.
   ?C.property[?p] :- ?p:Property,?p.?ST[?C],(?ST=source or ?ST=target).
   ?p.source[?C] :- ?C:Class, ?S.property[?p].
4. Class and Property properties are not defined on other objects:
   !- ?C.property[?p], not ?C:Class.
   !- ?p.target[?C], not?p:Property.
   Similarly for other Property properties.

An **F-OML specification** is a collection of class and property facts:
1. *Class definitions*: $\{t_i : \text{Class}\}_{i=1...n}$, where $t_1, \ldots, t_n$ are ground (i.e., variable-free) terms. These are the *classes* of the model.
2. *Property definition*: $\{\langle p_i.source[t_j], p_i.target[t_k], p_i.min[n_i], p_i.max[x_i]\rangle\}_{i=1...m}$, where $p_1 \ldots p_m$ are all different ground terms; t_j, t_k are classes of the model; and $n_i \leq x_i$ are natural numbers, where x_i can also be $*$. The p_is are the *properties* of the model.
3. *Additional constraints*: PathLP specification imposing inter-relationships among the classes or the properties.

An *atomic F-OML specification* is one whose classes and properties are constants. A *non-atomic F-OML specification* might have classes such as intersection(User,

Guest) or properties such as inverse(owner). Example 3 presents a (non-atomic)
F-OML specification that describes the class diagram in Figure 1.

Example 3. An F-OML specification for Figure 1.
User:Class. Table:Class. owned=inverse(owner). parent=inverse(child).
owner.source[User]. owner.target[Table]. owner.min[1]. owner.max[1].
owned.source[Table]. owned.target[User]. owned.min[1]. owned.max[1].
parent.source[Table]. parent.target[Table]. parent.min[0]. parent.max[*].
child.source[Table]. child.target[Table]. child.min[0]. child.max[*].

An **F-OML pattern** is an F-OML specification with non-ground classes or
properties. F-OML patterns function as reference models for typical problems.
F-OML semantics: An **F-OML state** is a PathLP canonical model that satisfies axioms that define the intended meaning of F-OML classes and properties:

1. Semantics of properties of classes:
   ?C!?p[?T]{?low .. ?hi} :-
     ?p:Property,?p.source[?C],?p.target[?T],?p.min[?low],?p.max[?hi].
2. Classes must not have undeclared properties:
   !- ?C:Class, ?C!?p[?T]{?low .. ?hi},
       not(?p:Property, ?p.source[?C], ?p.target[?T],
         ?p.min[?low], ?p.max[?hi]).
3. Members of classes can have only the properties declared for their classes:
   !- ?o:?C, ?C:Class, ?o.?p[?v], not ?C!?p[?x].

The set of *members of a class* C in an F-OML state $\mathcal{I}$ is the set of objects
that relate to it under the membership relation: $\{e | e \in_\mathcal{I} \mathcal{I}(C)\}$. Due to space
limitations we omit the notions of *satisfiability* and *finite-satisfiability* in F-OML.

F-OML Specifications and Class Diagrams: An atomic F-OML specification is equivalent to a class diagram that has the same classes, properties, and multiplicity constraints. A non-atomic F-OML specification can enforce inter-relationships among classes or properties, as in GuestUser:Class; GuestUser = difference(User, RegisteredUser). Such inter-relationships are inexpressible by class diagrams.

The correspondence between F-OML specifications and class diagrams has several important consequences. First, F-OML specifications can be **visualized** by class diagrams. Second, F-OML state can be used for formulating and implementing object modeling tasks. Third, results on satisfiability [8] and finite satisfiability [9] can be used for static analysis.

Parameterized Construction and Characterization

F-OML provides specification for a wide variety of library *constructors* and *predicates* that enable definition of non-atomic F-OML specifications and F-OML patterns. Due to space restrictions, we present just a few, and provide only object-level axioms, and omit meta-level characterization.

1. **Class construction using *Set operations*:**
   ?o:intersection(?C1,?C2):- ?o:?C1, ?o:?C2.

2. **Finite class construction:** Defined by the classOf class constructor, e.g.,
   Color = ClassOf([red, blue, yellow]).
   ?o:ClassOf(?List) :- ?List.members[?o].
   !- ?o:ClassOf(?List), not ?List.members[?o].
3. **Property construction using logic-based constructors:**
   Property disjunction: ?o.or(?p1,?p2)[?v] :- ?o.?p1[?v] or ?o.?p2[?v].
4. **Property inversion:** ?o1.inverse(?p)[?o2] :- ?o2.?p[?o1].
5. **Property composition:**
   Binary: ?o.compose(?p1,?p2)[?v] :- ?o.?p1.?p2[?v].
   N-ary: ?o.path([?p])[?v] :- ?o.?p[?v].
                 ?o.path([?p|?path])[?v] :- ?o.?p.path(?path)[?v].
                 where [?p|?path] is Prolog List notation
   Transitive closure: ?o.closure(?p)[?v] :- ?o.?p[?v].
                         ?o.closure(?p)[?v] :- ?o.?p.closure(?p)[?v].

F-OML provides a variety of library definitions that characterize classes and properties e.g., *injective, surjective, bijective* [10], *acyclic* and *unary* properties, a *subproperty* relation, and *disjoint* and *singleton classes*. For example,

1. *Injective properties*:
   ?p.kind[injective]:-?p:Property,inverse(?p).min[0],inverse(?p).max[1].
   Assuming that the Property class has a kind property.
2. *The subproperty relation*: All p-mappings are also q-mappings:
   ?s.?q[?t]:- ?p:Property, ?q:Property, ?p.subproperty[?q], ?s.?p[?t].
3. *An acyclic property*: !- ?p:Property,?p.circularity[false],?o.closure(?p)[?o].
4. *Disjoint classes*:
   !- ?C1:Class, ?C2:Class, ?C1!=?C2, ?C1.disjointfrom[?C2], ?o:?C1, ?o:?C2.

5 Using F-OML

This section illustrates various uses of F-OML for modeling objects.

I. Static Invariant Language: Figure 4 presents a class diagram that models User-Table access permissions in a database. A user that has an access permission to a table (its **grantor**), can grant access permission to another user (the **grantee**). Assume that the following invariant requirements are given:

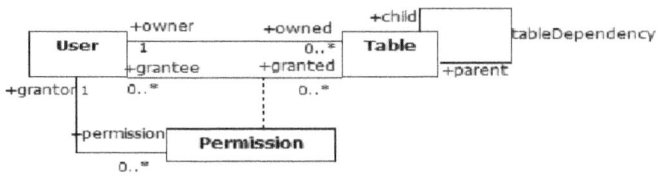

Fig. 4. User-Table permission Class Diagram

Requirement 1. The owner of a table is automatically granted an access permission and is the grantor for that permission.

Requirement 2. A non-owner user cannot grant himself a permission to a table, directly or indirectly.

These requirements cannot be captured by class diagram constraints, and require a constraint language. In UML, this is provided by the *Object Constraint Language (OCL)* [11]. The F-OML class invariants that capture these requirements rely on the F-OML *class diagram module* (not presented in this paper) that formulates class diagram constraints. For the association class constraint, the class diagram module defines parametrized navigation properties to and from an association class to its related classes. For Figure 4, the navigation properties from a Permission object to its associated User and Table objects are grantee(Permission) and granted(Permission). Requirement 1 is captured by a class diagram invariant that consists of 2 rules:

```
?t.grantee[?u]  :-  ?t:Table, ?t.owner[?u].
?p.grantor[?u]  :-  ?p:Permission, ?p.grantee(Permission)[?u],
                    ?p.granted(Permission).owner[?u].
```

Requirement 2 is captured by the following rule and constraint:

```
?u.permissionGrantor(?t)[?v]  :-
     ?u:User, ?u.Permission(grantee)[?p].granted(Permission)[?t],
     ?p.grantor[?v].
!- ?u:User,?t:Table,not ?u.owner[?t],?u.closure(permissionGrantor(?t))[?u].
```

The rule defines an auxiliary parametrized property permissionGrantor(?t) that, for a table ?t, maps a grantee user ?u to the grantor of his/her permission to ?t. The rule uses the inverse navigation property Permission(grantee) that maps a User-object to the associated Permission-objects (this property is provided by the association class formulation in the F-OML class diagram module). The guarded path expression ?u.Permission(grantee)[?p] selects a permission ?p for a user ?u and ?u.Permission(grantee)[?p].Table(Permission)[?t] further selects the table ?t of that permission ?p. This constraint denies circular access granting to prevent non-owners from granting mutual access permissions.

The OCL formulation of requirement 2 is not straightforward. The rule can be captured by a similar query. However, the acyclicity constraint requires computation of a closure, which is rather complex in OCL (due to the need to compute navigation paths whose length cannot be bound a priori).

II. Design Pattern Formulation: F-OML provides natural support for formulating design patterns, including specification of their semantics. We show a design pattern generalization of the User-Table access permission model.

Access-permission-granting **Pattern**

Problem: An access policy of *readers* to *objects* allows: (1) owner access to the owned object, (2) authorized readers granting access to object to other readers, (3) disallows granting cycles.

Solution: (1) Instantiate the class diagram pattern (a visualization of an F-OML pattern) in Figure 5. *Instantiation* means replacement of the class variables ?Reader, ?Object, ?Access and the property variables ?owner, ?owned, ?grantee, ?granted, ?grantor, ?permission by constants.

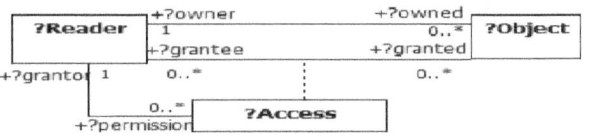

Fig. 5. Access permission Class Diagram pattern

(2) Apply the same instantiation of Class and Property typed variables to the following F-OML specification:

```
?r.accessGrantor(?o)[?q] :- ?r:?Reader,
    ?r.?Access(?grantee)[?a].?granted(?Access)[?o],?a.?grantor[?q].
!- ?r:?Reader, ?o:?Object, not ?r.?owner[?t],
        ?r.closure(?AccessGrantor(?o))[?r].
```

III. Meta-Modeling: The PathLP features of polymorphic expressions and multi-level specification enable full meta-modeling.

A *key* **Property:**

```
!- ?C:Class, ?C.key[?p], ?p:Property, ?o1:?C, ?o2:?C,
    ?o1.?p[?val1], ?o2.?p[?val2], ?val1 != ?val2.
```

One can postulate that a property named ID is a key property as follows:
`?C.key[?p] :- ?C:Class, ?C.property[?p].name[ID].`

IV. Model Query and Reasoning: Model-level reasoning has an essential role in the process of software development, explanation, understanding, and validation. F-OML supports such reasoning with PathLP queries and rules.

***Class reachability*:** In Figure 4, find all classes accessible from User, and the sequence of properties in the access path.

```
?C.path([?p])[?C1] :- ?C.property[?p].target[?C1].
?C.path([?p|?path])[?C1] :- ?C.property[?p].target.path(?path)[?C1].
```

The reachability query can be `?- User.path(?path)[?C]`. The answer includes `?path=[owned,grantee,permission], ?C=Permission`.

V. Model Testing: Model testing involves checking *mandatory* and *possible* characterizations of F-OML specifications (like object diagrams). Mandatory properties should hold in every state, and can be tested by posting F-OML queries. For example, in Figure 4, if class Table is restricted to be non-empty then in every state there is a Permission object whose grantee is also the owner of the table of the permission. This can be verified as follows:

```
?- ?p:Permission, ?p.grantee(Permission).owned[?T],
    ?p.granted(Permission)[?T].
```

Negative examples, that present illegal instantiations, are also helpful in model testing. A negative example can be tested by posing their negation as queries.

6 Related Work

The Object Constraint Language (OCL) [11] is the UML 2.0 language for specification of invariants, queries, and pre/post conditions on operations. It is not a standalone language; its expressions must be associated with UML diagrams. In general, the OCL handling of nested collections, unbounded data structures and recursive constraints is quite cumbersome. For example, suppose that the class Table in Figure 1 has two subclasses, SystemTable and UserTable, and we wish to add the invariant: "A user cannot be an owner of a system table and of a user table at the same time." The OCL formulation is:

```
Context User
inv: self.owned->select(oclIsTypeOf(SystemTable))->
    intersection(self.owned->select(oclIsTypeOf(UserTable)))->isEmpty()
```

For comparison, the F-OML 1-line formulation is:

```
!- ?u:User, ?u.owned[?st], ?st:SystemTable, ?u.owned[?ut], ?ut:UserTable.
```

F-OML has a number of advantages over OCL, including wider applicability, simplicity, full support for meta-modeling, patterns, simple management of unbounded data structures and recursion, model querying, analysis, and testing. The model analysis and the testing features rely on the status of F-OML as a standalone executable language.

Alloy [12] has been used recently for analysis, validation, and testing of UML models. Alloy is a standalone model checker, and it appears to support part of the functionality of F-OML. Yet, as a modeling language it resides at a lower level. Also, Alloy's handling of recursion and unbounded data structures like paths, cycles and tree is quite complex.

Another related work is that of [13], which extends the standard *instance diagram* language to support positive or negative examples as well as invariants. As illustrated earlier in the paper, F-OML provides an underlying logic support for the language of mandatory, possible, and negative instance diagrams.

7 Conclusion and Future Work

We presented *F-OML*, an expressive, executable modeling language, that can provide a formal basis for model-level IDEs. It is a semantic layer on top of the *PathLP* path expression language. PathLP has three distinctive features: (1) polymorphism of language expressions and of class hierarchies; (2) multilevel object modeling; (3) executable semantics. F-OML supports the basic concepts of *Class* and *Property*, and provides a library of constructors and features that function like modeling patterns.

At present, an implementation of PathLP is underway. We have already accomplished a major part of the Class diagram module. Once PathLP, F-OML and the class diagram module are implemented, we plan to combine it with a UML modeling tool (e.g., http://sourceforge.net/apps/trac/mide-bgu/wiki). Then, we can experiment with F-OML as an underlying language for the IDE, in combination with other IDE applications (http://www.cs.bgu.ac.il/ modeling/?page_id=314). One specifically challenging goal is extending F-OML to support dynamic models, such as statecharts or sequence diagrams.

Acknowledgments. We would like to thank Igal Khitron who implemented PathLP and provided numerous suggestions for improvements. We also thank the referees for the remarks that helped improve the presentation.

References

[1] France, R., Rumpe, B.: Model-driven development of complex software: A research roadmap. In: Intl. Conf. on Software Engineering, pp. 37–54 (2007)
[2] Balaban, M., Kifer, M.: An overview of F-OML: An F-Logic based object modeling language. Electronic Communications of the EASST 36 (2011)
[3] Kifer, M., Lausen, G., Wu, J.: Logical foundations of object-oriented and frame-based languages. Journal of ACM 42, 741–843 (1995)
[4] Kifer, M., Kim, W., Sagiv, Y.: Querying object-oriented databases. In: ACM SIGMOD Conf. on Management of Data, pp. 393–402. ACM, NY (1992)
[5] Kifer, M.: FLORA-2: An object-oriented knowledge base language. The FLORA-2 Web Site (2007), http://flora.sourceforge.net
[6] Lano, K.: UML 2 semantics and applications. Wiley Online Library, Chichester (2009)
[7] Van Gelder, A., Ross, K., Schlipf, J.: The well-founded semantics for general logic programs. Journal of ACM 38, 620–650 (1991)
[8] Berardi, D., Calvanese, D., Giacomo, D.: Reasoning on UML class diagrams. Artificial Intelligence 168, 70–118 (2005)
[9] Maraee, A., Balaban, M.: Efficient reasoning about finite satisfiability of UML class diagrams with constrained generalization sets. In: The 3rd European Conf. on Model-Driven Architecture, pp. 17–31 (2007)
[10] Wahler, M., Basin, D., Brucker, D., Koehler, K.: Efficient analysis of pattern-based constraint specifications. Software and Systems Modeling 9, 225–255 (2010)
[11] Object Management Group: UML 2.0 Object Constraint Language Specification (2006)
[12] Jackson, D.: Alloy: A new technology for software modelling. In: Katoen, J.-P., Stevens, P. (eds.) TACAS 2002. LNCS, vol. 2280, pp. 175–192. Springer, Heidelberg (2002)
[13] Maoz, S., Ringert, J.O., Rumpe, B.: Modal Object Diagrams. In: Mezini, M. (ed.) ECOOP 2011. LNCS, vol. 6813, pp. 281–305. Springer, Heidelberg (2011)

Formal Verification of QVT Transformations for Code Generation

Kurt Stenzel, Nina Moebius, and Wolfgang Reif

Institute for Software and Systems Engineering,
Augsburg University, 86135 Augsburg, Germany
{stenzel,moebius,reif}@informatik.uni-augsburg.de

Abstract. We present a formal calculus for operational QVT. The calculus is implemented in the interactive theorem prover KIV and allows to prove properties of QVT transformations for arbitrary meta models.

Additionally we present a framework for provably correct Java code generation. The framework uses a meta model for a Java abstract syntax tree as the target of QVT transformations. This meta model is mapped to a formal Java semantics in KIV. This makes it possible to formally prove with the QVT calculus that a transformation always generates a Java model (i.e. a program) that is type correct and has certain semantical properties. The Java model can be used to generate source code by a model-to-text transformation or byte code directly.

1 Introduction

Model-driven development holds the promise to create better software in shorter time since the modeler can concentrate on the essential properties of the application under development. Technical details will be filled in by model transformations. In specialized areas the complete source code of an application can be generated from the model.

However, there is the question of the correctness of the generated code, or – more broadly speaking – of the model transformations. This is a largely unsolved problem. First, it can be quite difficult to describe precisely, i.e. formally, what correctness means. Usually a formal semantics of the source and target model is needed, which is definitely not trivial if, for example, UML activity diagrams are transformed into Java code. Second, the transformation must be proved correct. This in turn requires a formal logic and proof support for the transformation language. Third, the transformations itself can be large and complex which makes a formal proof difficult and time-consuming.

In this paper we present a framework that allows to prove properties of generated Java code for transformations written in operational QVT (QVTO [15]). This work is part of our SecureMDD approach [22,23], a model-driven development method for security-critical applications based on cryptographic protocols. The application, e.g. an electronic purse or a ticketing system, is modeled with UML extended with a profile and an abstract programming language MEL. From the model a formal specification can be generated, and the security of the application can be proved [24,25]. Additionally, the complete Java code for the protocols can be generated by model transformations. In this setting it is imperative that the code is correct and secure with respect to the formal specification (i.e. is a refinement that preserves security [13]).

In the next section the framework for correct code generation will be presented with a very simple example that generates Java classes from a UML class diagram. Sect. 3 describes a formal calculus for reasoning about operational QVT transformations, and discusses some experiences. Sect. 4 presents related work, and Sect. 5 concludes.

2 A Framework for Correct Code Generation

We illustrate our approach with a small example. The idea is to generate Java classes with fields, getters, and setters from simple UML class diagrams as shown in Fig. 1. The result are three Java classes A, B, and C. The UML primitive type `Integer` is translated to `int`. Obviously it is possible to generate more methods (e.g. in SecureMDD we generate equals, copy, and de-/serialization methods).

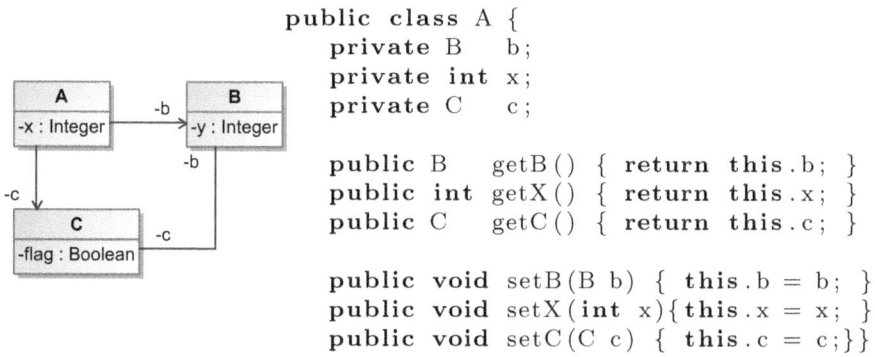

Fig. 1. A simple UML class diagram and the generated Java code for class A

The aim is to formally prove properties about the generated Java code, e.g.:
1. The code is type correct.
2. Correspondence to the UML model: One Java class for every UML class, one Java field for each UML Property etc.
3. Semantic properties of the generated methods: A getter returns the value of a field, calling a setter, then the corresponding getter returns the same reference, etc.

Formal treatments of Java (either formal semantics of Java, e.g. [39,34,37] or Java calculi for program verification, e.g. [18,36,2]) all work on an annotated abstract syntax tree of a Java program. This makes sense since parsing Java text, and annotating an abstract syntax tree are problems of compiler correctness that pose very different challenges, and should be separated from a Java semantics. If we use a model-to-text transformation to generate Java code from the UML class diagram we have a problem: A model-to-text transformation essentially concatenates strings. For example, generating the getter methods in XPand [41] looks like

```
«FOREACH this.ownedAttribute AS a»
   public «a.type.toJavaType()» get«a.name.toFirstUpper()»(){
      return this.«a.name»; }
«ENDFOREACH»
```

Formal reasoning about the text requires parsing this mixture of source text and quoted expressions (and it is not clear how this can be done), annotating the resulting syntax tree, and then reasoning about its semantics, thereby mixing the different problems. Our framework introduces a meta model that represents a Java annotated abstract syntax tree (JAST). This allows a separation of concerns (see also Fig. 2):

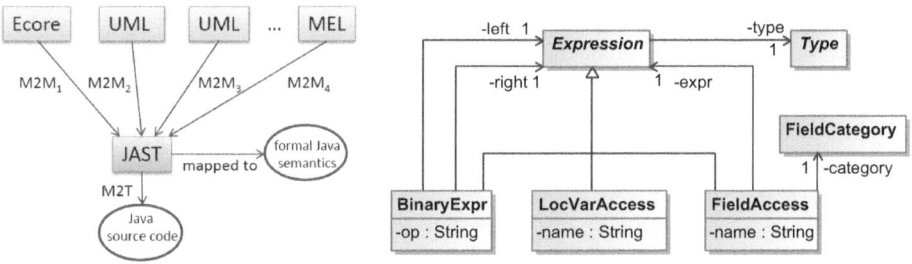

Fig. 2. Generating Java code with an intermediate JAST model (left) and part of the JAST meta model (right)

1. A model-to-model transformation is used to generate an instance of the JAST meta model from an arbitrary source and meta model (MEL is a meta model used in SecureMDD). The transformation is specific for the model-driven application. The JAST model is the basis for formal reasoning.
2. From the JAST model text can be generated by model-to-text transformation. It is also possible to generate byte code directly. (Not supported in our framework, though.) It should be noted that this step depends only on the JAST meta model, and is completely independent of the transformation that created the JAST model.

A small part of the JAST meta model is shown in Fig. 2 as a UML class diagram. The actual model is defined as an Ecore model in Eclipse.

Every Java expression and statement becomes one EClass in the meta model (37 in our case). Other elements represent method and field declarations and class declarations. Every Java expression has a result type (that would be computed by a compiler when annotating the syntax tree); a binary (infix) expression like x + y has a left and right expression and an operation; a local variable access is a separate expression; an instance field access **FieldAccess** has an invoking expression and a reference **FieldCategory** that identifies the accessed field (a Java compiler determines whether x is a local variable or an instance field and treats the latter as this.x).

2.1 Transforming UML to JAST

In our example we use operational QVT to transform the UML class diagram into a JAST model. Operational QVT (chapter 8 in [15]) is essentially a programming language based on OCL [14] and tailored to model transformations. Fig. 4 shows the start of the transformation, and Fig. 5 shows the generation of a getter method for an attribute.

```
1   modeltype UML uses 'http://www.eclipse.org/uml2/3.0.0/UML';
2   modeltype J uses 'http://isse.de/JAST';
3
4   transformation simple(in umlmodel : UML, out res : J);
5   main() {
6     var model : Model := umlmodel.rootObjects()![Model];
7     model.map createModel();
8   }
9   mapping Model::createModel() : JModel {
10    init {
11      var css := self.packagedElement[Class];
12      var jcs := css->map toJavaClass();
13    }
14    name := self.name;
15    ownedElements += object PackageDeclaration
16                            { name := packageName();
17                              typedecls := jcs; }
18  }
19  /* create every class */
20  mapping Class::toJavaClass(): TypeDeclaration {
21    init { var atts := self.ownedAttribute; }
22    modifiers += 'public';
23    name := self.name;
24    classtype := classType(self.name);
25    members += atts->map declareField(self.name);
26    members += atts->map createGetter(self.name);
27    members += atts->map createSetter(self.name);
28  }
```

Fig. 3. Start of the QVTO transformation

Lines 1 and 2 declare UML and J as abbreviations for the meta models, and line 4 declares the transformation **simple** that transforms a UML model into a J(AST) model. Running the transformation will call the main method (line 5) that selects an element of the UML type **Model** from the input (line 6) and calls the mapping **createModel** (line 7). There is no explicit assignment to the output variable **res** because all model elements that are created during the transformation will be collected automatically in the output variable. A mapping (line 9) is one of the central concepts of QVT and creates a correspondence between a source and a target element. The target element is created automatically, and in lines 14–17 its properties are set. In the case a **JModel** has a **name** and **ownedElements**, a list of (Java) packages. In line 11 the classes from the UML model are selected and mapped to Java (JAST) classes in line 12. The mapping **toJavaClass** creates a class by iterating over the attributes and creating the fields, getters, and setters (lines 25–27).

```
1  mapping Property :: createGetter (c: String) : MethodDeclaration{
2      modifiers := Sequence { 'public' };
3      name := 'get' + self.name.firstToUpper();
4      returnType := self.type.toJast();
5      methodbody := object Block {
6          stms += object ReturnStm {
7              expr := self.fa(thisExpr(c), c);
8      }; };
9  }
10 query Property :: fa(e: J :: Expression, c: String) : J :: Expression{
11     return object FieldAccess {
12              expr := e;
13              category := object SimpleFieldCategory {
14                  name := self.name;
15                  classtype := classType(c);
16                  isStatic := false;
17                  type := self.type.toJast();
18              };
19          type := self.type.toJast();
20     };
21 }
22 query thisExpr(c: String) : J :: Expression {
23     return object LocVarAccess {
24          name := 'this'; type := classType(c); };
25 }
```

Fig. 4. Generating a getter method with QVTO

The mapping **createGetter** (line 1 in Fig. 5) is defined for a UML property (the class attributes in this case), has as additional input the name of the class, and creates a JAST method declaration. The body of the method (line 5) is a block containing a return statement that returns a JAST field access (line 7) (i.e. **this.field**). The statements and expressions are not mapped, but generated as new objects (with the keyword `object`), because they have no correspondence to a UML source element. Finally the field access is created by the method `fa` (line 10).

Obviously the QVT code is much more verbose than the actual Java source code, because the JAST model contains much more information explicitly. A programmer needs a good knowledge of the JAST model, but the QVT program in itself is simple (and uses only a fraction of all operational QVT features). The programming style shown in this example is typical for operational QVT, and well suited for the creation of abstract syntax trees.

2.2 Formal Reasoning about Models and Meta Models

We have described the JAST meta model, and we have shown how QVT transformations look like. Now we will show how a JAST model is given a formal semantics in our framework. For the formal part we use the KIV system [19,1,16] that is developed in our group. KIV is an interactive theorem prover based on algebraic specifications with several logical extensions (e.g. Dynamic Logic for imperative programs and Java and temporal logic for parallel programs and state charts).

The calculus for operational QVT presented in the next section is not limited to UML and JAST, but supports arbitrary input and output (meta) models. This means we need an algebraic specification for meta models and models. Basically, we follow the EMF [35] approach: A meta model is defined as an Ecore model. In a slightly simplified version a meta model is an `EPackage` containing `EClassifier`s (that define the model elements) that in turn contain `EAttribute`s for properties with primitive types and `EReference`s for properties containing model elements (i.e. other EClassifiers). This is a standard algebraic specification with freely generated data types.

The formal specification of a model follows its internal representation in EMF. Model elements are `EObject`s with an unique identifier and a list of `EContent` that are either attribute values, contained references (to model elements with `Containment = true`), or external references. Contained references are again `EObject`s, while external references simply contain the identifier of the referenced object. The result is a tree structure that is well suited for algebraic specifications. Meta models and models that are available in Eclipse can be exported with a plugin into a format suitable for the KIV system. Built on these specifications is the formal definition of a *valid* meta model, and a *valid* model *with respect to* a meta model.

There exists a formal Java semantics in KIV [36,37] that was defined several years ago. The formal semantics is based on an algebraic specification of a Java abstract syntax tree. The connection between a JAST model (formally an `EObject` structure) and the existing abstract syntax tree is obtained by a specification `model2sem` mapping a JAST model to the abstract syntax tree. In this manner a formal semantics is provided for a JAST model. Another approach is to specify the Java semantics in terms of a JAST model, but this requires very much effort since a formal Java semantics is huge and complex, especially with a proof of type soundness.

The Java semantics in KIV is a natural big-step operational semantics. A Java expression defines a relation between an initial Java heap and variable binding and a resulting Java heap, variable binding, and result after evaluating the expression: $(v \times h) [\![e]\!]_{tds} (v' \times h' \times \text{result})$ Here v is the variable binding for local variables and method parameters, h is the Java heap, e is the Java expression, tds is the context consisting of the class declarations, v', h' are the resulting binding and heap, and result is the result of evaluating the expression. If the expression does not terminate (e.g. if it is a call to a recursive, non-terminating method) there is no resulting state, i.e. the relation $[\![.]\!]$ is empty. The semantics faithfully models class initialization (first active use), and exceptions.

3 Formal Reasoning about QVT Transformations

3.1 Formulating Properties in Dynamic Logic

Operational QVT is essentially an object-oriented, imperative programming language that operates on input and output models, and keeps track of mappings with the help of a *trace* that contains source object, target object, and applied mapping operation for every executed mapping call. Our calculus for QVTO is a sequent calculus for dynamic logic (DL, [17]). DL extends predicate logic with two modal operators, box $[\,.\,]$ and diamond $\langle\,.\,\rangle$, written as $\langle (\text{in, out, trace})\, \alpha \rangle\, \varphi$. Here α is a QVTO expression, (in, out, trace) are the initial input and output models, and the trace, and φ is again a DL formula. The intuitive meaning is: with initial models and trace (in, out, trace) the QVTO expression α terminates, and afterwards the formula φ holds ($[\,.\,]$ does not include termination). φ usually reasons about the resulting output model. A sequent $\varphi_1, \ldots, \varphi_m \vdash \psi_1, \ldots, \psi_n$ consists of two lists of formulas (often abbreviated by Γ and Δ) divided by $\vdash$ and is equivalent to the formula $\varphi_1 \wedge \ldots \wedge \varphi_m \rightarrow \psi_1 \vee \ldots \vee \psi_n$. $\varphi_1, \ldots \varphi_m$ can be thought of as preconditions, while one of $\psi_1, \ldots, \psi_n$ must be proved. A Hoare triple $\{\varphi\} \alpha \{\psi\}$ can be expressed as $\varphi \vdash [\alpha] \psi$ or $\varphi \vdash \langle \alpha \rangle\, \psi$ if termination is included. An example is the following sequent:

valid(in, UML), suitable(in), out == [], trace == []
$\vdash \langle(\text{in, out, trace})$ `Simple::main()`$\rangle$ typeCorrect(model2sem(out))

`Simple::main()` is a call to the QVTO transformation's `main()` method (see Fig. 4). The `in` model must be a valid UML model `valid(in, UML)`, that is additionally suitable for the transformation `suitable(in)`. The output model `out` and the `trace` are initially empty. Then after running the transformation the resulting output model `out`, converted to the formal Java specification `model2sem(out)` is a type correct Java program `typeCorrect(model2sem(out))`.

It is also possible to prove properties for parts of the transformation. In our example we have one mapping that creates a Java method declaration for a

setter, and one mapping for a getter. We can formulate a property that calling
the setter, and then the getter returns the setter's argument. In Java this would
look like `a.setB(b); b == a.getB();`. Formally (and simplified) this looks like

1. valid(in, UML), suitable(in), isProperty(a), a ∈ in, unmapped(a, trace)
2. ⊢ ⟨(in, out, trace) g := a.map createGetter(c)⟩
3.   ⟨(in, out, trace) s := a.map createSetter(c)⟩
4.   ⟨(in, out, trace) f := a.map declareField(c)⟩
5. ($\forall\, v_1, h_1, a, b, v_2, h_2, v_3, h_3, val, tds.\ \text{valid}(v_1, h_1, a, b)\ \wedge$
6. tds = class c { model2sem(f), model2sem(s), model2sem(g) }
7. $\wedge\ (v_1 \times h_1)[\![a.setB(b)]\!]_{tds}(v_2 \times h_2 \times \bot)$
8. $\wedge\ (v_2 \times h_2)[\![a.getB()]\!]_{tds}(v_3 \times h_3 \times val)$
9. $\rightarrow val == b)$

In lines 2, 3, 4 the mappings from the transformation (see Fig. 4) are called
and each result is assigned to a variable. Since the mappings are defined for
a UML property the invoking variable a must be a property that has not yet
been mapped by any mapping operation (line 1). The postcondition of the three
consecutive diamonds begins in line 5. In line 6 the JAST elements g, s, f, are
converted to their Java semantics counterpart (two Java method declarations
and a field declaration), and a class containing them is constructed. In line 7
the semantics of a setter call is used. This will modify the heap h_2 which is
then used in line 8 as the initial heap for a getter call. Evaluating the expression
will produce a result val which is equal to the setter's argument b (line 9), our
desired property. The proof requires a couple of minutes.

3.2 Two Example Rules of the Calculus

The calculus essentially has one rule for every operational QVT expression. It
works by symbolic execution of the QVT program from its beginning to its end
(i.e. computation of strongest postcondition). This means it follows the natural
execution of the program.

Most QVT expressions return a result. To make this result accessible the calculus introduces assignments if necessary. For example, the rule for a conditional
works like this:

$$\frac{1.\ e = true, \Gamma \vdash \langle(in, out, trace)\ x := \alpha\rangle\ \varphi \qquad 2.\ e \neq true, \Gamma \vdash \langle(in, out, trace)\ x := \beta\rangle\ \varphi}{\Gamma \vdash \langle(in, out, trace)\ x := \textbf{if}\ e\ \textbf{then}\ \alpha\ \textbf{else}\ \beta\ \textbf{endif};\rangle\ \varphi}$$

Γ is an arbitrary list of formulas (other preconditions), α and β are QVT expressions, and φ is a Dynamic logic formula, i.e. it may contain again diamonds
or boxes with QVT expressions. The rule has two premises, one for the case that
the test is true, one for the case that it is not. The conclusion contains the **if**
expression. In case the test is true the **then** part is assigned to x, otherwise the
else part. This captures the standard meaning of an **if** expression. However, the
interesting part is the test e. The rule is only applicable if e is a simple expression, either a literal (like $true$ or $false$) or a variable. In these cases it is possible

to write e = *true* because a literal and a variable have a truth value in our logic. If the test is a more complex expression like `a.map someMap(b.someQuery())` it will be replaced by a new variable that is assigned to the expression:

`y := a.map someMap(b.someQuery()); if y then ...`

Nested expressions are flattened to a sequence of simple expressions that can be executed directly by introducing intermediate assignments. In the above example `y := a.map someMap(b.someQuery());` is flattened to `z := b.someQuery(); y := a.map someMap(z);`.

One of the most interesting rules of the calculus is the rule for a mapping call, i.e. `x := a.map m(args);`. Mapping operations and mapping calls are described in Sect. 8.2.1.5 and 8.2.1.21 in the QVT specification [15]. We describe only a simplified version of the rule. It has three premises:

1. The invoking expression `a` may not be null: $a \neq null \land a \neq invalid$
2. If the invoking object has been mapped before (i.e. is contained in the trace) the result is looked up in the trace:

    $a \in trace \vdash \langle (in, out, trace) x := lookup(a, trace); \rangle \varphi$

    lookup is not a QVT expression, but a logical function. It behaves similar to QVT's `resolveIn` expression. In fact, `resolveIn` is reduced to *lookup*.
3. Otherwise, the mapping call is replaced by the (slightly modified) body of the mapping operation. The body of a mapping operation consists of three (optional) sections: an initialization section (denoted by `init {...}`), a population section where attributes of the result are computed, and a termination section (denoted by `end {...}`). The mappings in our example (Fig. 4,5) contain only an init section and a population section (without any keywords). The QVT specification states that between the init and population section the following happens: If the result is still null an object of the correct result type is created, and the source and result objects are added to the trace.
   In the proof rule a mapping call `x := a.map m();` with declaration `mapping m() {init; population; end;}` is replaced by
   `{init; trace(result); population; end; x := result;}`
   First, the init section is executed. Then, the logical extension `trace(result)` is executed. This extension has its own proof rule that either does nothing or creates the result object, assigns it to `result`, and adds it to the trace. `result` is a predefined variable containing the result. Then population and end sections are executed, and finally the result variable is assigned to `x`.

This finished the description. Fig. 5 shows the rule. Since mappings can be overridden for more specific invokers there can be more premises similar to premise 3 for every possible mapping body. (The QVT specification states that "This follows usual object-oriented virtual call semantics.") Additionally, the formal parameters are bound to the actual arguments by equations, and the predefined QVT variable `self` is bound to the invoker `a`. This may require renaming of variables to avoid conflicts.

$$\frac{\begin{array}{l}1.\ \Gamma \vdash a \neq null\\ 2.\ \Gamma, a \neq null, a \in trace \vdash \langle (in, out, trace)\ x := lookup(a, trace)\rangle\ \varphi\\ 3.\ \Gamma, a \neq null, \neg\ a \in trace, self = a, params = args\\ \quad \vdash \langle (in, out, trace)\ init; trace(result); population; end; x := result;\rangle\ \varphi\end{array}}{\Gamma \vdash \langle (in, out, trace)\ x := a.map\ m(args)\rangle\ \varphi}$$

Fig. 5. The proof rule for mapping calls

3.3 Discussion

OCL has 12 expressions, imperative OCL 21, and QVT 5 additional expressions, most of them with many features (e.g. the ImperativeIterateExp (QVT 8.2.2.7) defines 6 different iterators). The OCL and QVT standard library have about 175 predefined operations. This means that implementing a calculus for full QVT requires a *huge* effort. Therefore we follow a pragmatic approach: Currently the calculus has rules only for a subset of all expressions (18) and operations (30), namely those that occur in the transformations we verified so far. More proof rules will be added in the future.

The OCL and QVT specifications are together 500 pages long. However, the description is often imprecise and leaves many issues open, even for rather central language constructs. This raises the question how a correct proof rule should look like. Here we follow the following strategy:

1. If an issue is not clear from the specification, but is irrelevant for 'normal' QVT transformations, the proof rule will have a precondition that excludes the issue.
2. Otherwise we check what the QVTO implementation in Eclipse [29] and SmartQVT [32] do. If their behavior seems reasonable the proof rule is designed correspondingly. This makes sense because verifying and actually running a transformation should produce the same results (i.e. correct target models).
3. Otherwise we program our transformations around the issue and do not support it. We also make sure that our transformations work in both Eclipse QVTO and SmartQVT. (There are some differences, but they change between versions.)

Some examples of open issues:

- **Mapping operations:** (QVT 8.2.1.15) *"Resolving the mapping call implies finding the operation to call on the basis of the actual type of the source (self variable). This follows usual object-oriented virtual call semantics."*
  This leaves room for interpretation since different object-oriented languages have different call semantics.
- **Mapping operations:** The result object of the mapping operation is (usually) created automatically. But what happens if the result type is abstract? E.g. in `mapping UML::Type::toJastType() : J::Type` the JAST Type is abstract (the subtypes PrimitiveType, ClassType and so one are concrete), so it is not possible to create a result object automatically. The QVT

specification is silent about this. The Eclipse QVTO compiler requires an init section where the result should be instantiated manually. At run time, if the result after the init section is still null the transformation fails with a run time exception, SmartQVT also fails.
- **Assignments:** (QVT 8.2.2.11) *"In addition null values are automatically skipped."* For example, in `modifiers := Sequence { null, "public" };` the result will be a list with one element, `"public"`. This is a nice feature for programming. But what about `OclInvalid`? Older versions of QVTO failed with an EMF error, newer versions also skip `OclInvalid`.

OclInvalid. Essential OCL does not support error handling, but has a generic error element `OclInvalid` that can occur almost everywhere. Programming experience with several thousand lines of QVT transformations shows that this concept has some drawbacks. If a simple programming error (applying `first()` on an empty sequence or casting to the wrong type with `oclAsType`) raises an exception the error is easy to locate. However, if the result is `OclInvalid` it will propagate through the rest of the code and the result of the transformation will be something unexpected. Locating the error can be very time consuming.

Therefore, we feel deliberately programming with `OclInvalid` should be avoided. For this reason, our calculus guarantees that `OclInvalid` does not occur. For `x.first()` it must be proved that `x` is a non-null, non-empty sequence. This simplifies the calculus considerably because a special treatment of `OclInvalid` can be avoided. Otherwise a three valued logic must be used (see e.g. the OCL specification [14] p. 213, Semantics of boolean operations), and every proof rule will have at least one additional premise. Both would make proofs more complex. But there is no theoretical obstacle against supporting invalid values.

Assumption hunting. Often it is not clear what assumptions are made about the input model of a transformation. A standard assumption is that the model is a correct instance of its meta model. We make this assumption for the UML model, but do not assume that the additional constraints mentioned in the UML specification hold. But usually there are more specific assumptions. E.g. in our example it is necessary that all class attributes have types, although a type is optional in UML, i.e. can be null. Otherwise the formal verification that the resulting JAST model is type correct will fail, because the JAST type will also be null. A second assumption is that the type is something expected – many UML elements can be used as a type. A third assumption is that a class type will reference a class that is contained on top level in the `packagedElements` of the model, and not in a sub package. In general, formal verification is very good at finding (hunting for) implicit assumptions. All assumptions must be incorporated explicitly in the preconditions, or the verification will fail. However, not all assumptions are found. For example, generalizations in the class diagram are simply ignored by the transformation (Fig. 4) and the JAST model will have no subclassing. This may not be what a modeler would expect. The assumptions could be checked with another QVTO program, but this is future work.

Proof experiences. Interactive theorem provers require quite a lot of experience to use successfully, because the user must know the logic, the input language, how things are formalized, and how to utilize the strength of the tool.

QVT transformations often use iterators over sequences or sets, e.g. `css->map toJavaClass()` (line 12 in Fig. 4). This avoids loops or recursion, but is similarly difficult for verification. The properties that hold during the iteration must be formulated as invariants. The first elements of the collection have already been mapped, and the output model contains appropriate elements, and the remaining elements are not yet mapped. Quite a lot of work also goes into reasoning about the structure of the models since the specification is quite complex, and UML itself is very complex.

Proving type correctness of the generated Java abstract syntax tree is actually more difficult than the properties about setter and getter methods. The problem is that intermediate results are not type correct, only the final result is. E.g. class A is generated first and has a field of class type B. However, B is created later so A in itself is not type correct. Here some kind of look ahead is needed that the missing parts are eventually generated.

4 Related Work

Related work can be divided into two areas: formal treatment of OCL and QVT, and correctness of model transformations in general. The OCL specification [14] contains a formal semantics on paper (i.e. not tool supported which makes a big difference). A formalization of OCL in Isabelle/HOL is described in [4] on 500 pages, and identifies many problems in the specification. Their goal is to *"provide a semantic representation compliant with the OCL standard semantics definition"*. They define OCL with respect to UML class diagrams (in contrast to Ecore/MOF used in QVT), and faithfully model undefined and invalid values. This means their calculus is based on a three valued logic. Experience shows that a three valued logic creates a considerable technical overhead for concrete proofs. Therefore we designed our calculus without undefined/invalid values as discussed in the previous section. The USE tool [12] supports different techniques for checking OCL constraints for concrete UML models, e.g. with SAT solvers [33]. Other automated approaches are e.g. [20,28]. They all do not aim at the verification of QVT transformations. There is some work on the semantics of different parts of QVT. [5] identifies problems with imperative OCL, [10] formalizes the QVT Core language [7] and [40] map QVT relations to petri nets, thereby providing a formal semantics. [31] show (informally) how QVT relations can be translated into operational QVT. We are not aware of work on the formal verification of QVT transformations.

An overview over model transformation approaches in 2006 [6] concludes that they are *"often ad hoc, that is, without proper theoretical foundation."*. Correctness is mentioned only once as a vague possibility. Early work translates UML models and transformation to B [21], and triple graph grammar transformations to Isabelle/HOL [11]. [27] (and also [38,3,26]) present frameworks for the verification of model transformations. The transformations are based on (triple) graph transformations that have a long tradition and well-defined formal foundation [8]. Rewriting logic can be used to verify relations between input and output models. The results presented in [27] are not yet implemented in a verification tool, and focus on structural models. This means it is not clear if the framework can be used for code generation.

[9] transform activity diagrams to TAAL, a Java-like programming language, with graph transformations, and present a correctness notion based on trace equivalence. They can check the correctness for concrete input and output models, but their *"ultimate aim is a general proof of correctness for the transformation"*. [30] transform state machines to Java code, and add annotations for a model checker to the Java code. The model checker can then be used to prove that the Java code behaves as the state machine for every concrete input and output model. They argue that *"Verifying the generated output in this way is more efficient than formally verifying the transformation's definition."* This may be true, but what if the verification fails because the output is not correct? Only a verification of the transformation itself can guarantee that the output will always be correct.

5 Conclusion

We have presented a framework that allows the formal verification of Java code generation in a model-driven setting. It is based on a meta model for an annotated abstract Java syntax tree (JAST), a formal Java semantics, and operational QVT transformations from arbitrary models into a JAST model. The major ingredient is a calculus for operational QVT that allows formal reasoning about transformations. It is implemented in our theorem prover KIV.

Our target are transformations for security-critical systems, primarily in the context of our SecureMDD project. Here, a UML model extended with our MEL programming language of a security protocol is the basis for a formal specification where the security of the system can be proved, and for generating a Java implementation of the protocols. It is essential that the generated code is correct, i.e. is a correct refinement of the formal specification. Since we generate Java Card code that runs on resource restricted smart cards the generated code is not trivial. Serialization and de-serialization must work correctly, and detect malicious input. Objects must be reused, values copied, the code must never throw run time exceptions, etc.

The transformations are several thousand lines long. In principle, it is now possible to prove these properties though the effort will be considerable. The work presented in this paper is just a starting point. Future work includes adding heuristics to the prover to increase automation, supporting more QVTO operations, incorporating input validation, and proving the correctness of our SecureMDD transformations.

References

1. Balser, M., Reif, W., Schellhorn, G., Stenzel, K., Thums, A.: Formal system development with KIV. In: FASE 2000. LNCS, vol. 1783, p. 363. Springer, Heidelberg (2000)

2. Beckert, B., Hähnle, R., Schmitt, P.H. (eds.): Verification of Object-Oriented Software. LNCS (LNAI), vol. 4334. Springer, Heidelberg (2007)
3. Boronat, A., Heckel, R., Meseguer, J.: Rewriting logic semantics and verification of model transformations. In: Chechik, M., Wirsing, M. (eds.) FASE 2009. LNCS, vol. 5503, pp. 18–33. Springer, Heidelberg (2009)
4. Brucker, A.D., Wolff, B.: The HOL-OCL book. Technical Report 525, ETH Zürich (2006)
5. Büttner, F., Kuhlmann, M.: Shortcomings of the embedding of OCL into QVT imperativeOCL. In: Chaudron, M.R.V. (ed.) MODELS 2008. LNCS, vol. 5421, pp. 263–272. Springer, Heidelberg (2009)
6. Czarnecki, K., Helsen, S.: Feature-based survey of model transformation approaches. IBM Systems Journal 45(3) (2006)
7. de Lara, J., Guerra, E.: Formal support for QVT-relations with coloured petri nets. In: Schürr, A., Selic, B. (eds.) MODELS 2009. LNCS, vol. 5795, pp. 256–270. Springer, Heidelberg (2009)
8. Ehrig, H., Ehrig, K., Prange, U., Taentzer, G.: Fundamentals of algebraic graph transformation. Springer, Heidelberg (2006)
9. Engels, G., Kleppe, A., Rensink, A., Semenyak, M., Soltenborn, C., Wehrheim, H.: From UML activities to TAAL - towards behaviour-preserving model transformations. In: Schieferdecker, I., Hartman, A. (eds.) ECMDA-FA 2008. LNCS, vol. 5095, pp. 94–109. Springer, Heidelberg (2008)
10. Favre, L.: A formal foundation for metamodeling. In: Kordon, F., Kermarrec, Y. (eds.) Ada-Europe 2009. LNCS, vol. 5570, pp. 177–191. Springer, Heidelberg (2009)
11. Giese, H., Glesner, S., Leitner, J., Schäfer, W., Wagner, R.: Towards verified model transformations. In: Proceedings of the MoDeVa Workshop at MoDELS 2006 (2006)
12. Gogolla, M., Büttner, F., Richters, M.: USE: A UML-Based Specification Environment for Validating UML and OCL. Science of Computer Programming 69 (2007)
13. Grandy, H., Stenzel, K., Reif, W.: A refinement method for java programs. In: Bonsangue, M.M., Johnsen, E.B. (eds.) FMOODS 2007. LNCS, vol. 4468, pp. 221–235. Springer, Heidelberg (2007)
14. Object Management Group. Object Constraint Language, Version 2.3 (2010)
15. Object Management Group. Meta Object Facility (MOF) 2.0 Query/View/Transformation Specification, Version 1.1 (2011)
16. Haneberg, D., Bäumler, S., Balser, M., Grandy, H., Ortmeier, F., Reif, W., Schellhorn, G., Schmitt, J., Stenzel, K.: The User Interface of the KIV Verification System — A System Description. Electronic Notes in Theoretical Computer Science UITP Special Issue (2006)
17. Harel, D., Kozen, D., Tiuryn, J.: Dynamic Logic. MIT Press, Cambridge (2000)
18. Huisman, M., Jacobs, B.: Java program verification via a hoare logic with abrupt termination. In: FASE 2000. LNCS, vol. 1783, pp. 284–303. Springer, Heidelberg (2000)
19. KIV homepage, http://www.informatik.uni-augsburg.de/swt/kiv
20. Krieger, M., Knapp, A.: Executing underspecified OCL operation contracts with a SAT solver. In: Proceedings of the 8th International Workshop on OCL Concepts and Tools (OCL 2008) at MoDELS 2008. Electronic Communications of the EASST, vol. 15 (2008)
21. Lano, K.: Using B to verify UML transformations. In: Proceedings of the MoDeVa Workshop at MoDELS 2006 (2006)
22. Moebius, N., Stenzel, K., Grandy, H., Reif, W.: SecureMDD: A Model-Driven Development Method for Secure Smart Card Applications. In: Workshop on Secure Software Engineering, SecSE, at ARES 2009. IEEE Press, Los Alamitos (2009)

23. Moebius, N., Stenzel, K., Reif, W.: Modeling Security-Critical Applications with UML in the SecureMDD Approach. International Journal On Advances in Software 1(1) (2008)
24. Moebius, N., Stenzel, K., Reif, W.: Generating formal specifications for security-critical applications - a model-driven approach. In: ICSE 2009 Workshop: International Workshop on Software Engineering for Secure Systems (SESS 2009), IEEE/ACM Digital Libary (2009)
25. Moebius, N., Stenzel, K., Reif, W.: Formal verification of application-specific security properties in a model-driven approach. In: Massacci, F., Wallach, D., Zannone, N. (eds.) ESSoS 2010. LNCS, vol. 5965, pp. 166–181. Springer, Heidelberg (2010)
26. Orejas, F., Guerra, E., de Lara, J., Ehrig, H.: Correctness, completeness and termination of pattern-based model-to-model transformation. In: Kurz, A., Lenisa, M., Tarlecki, A. (eds.) CALCO 2009. LNCS, vol. 5728, pp. 383–397. Springer, Heidelberg (2009)
27. Orejas, F., Wirsing, M.: On the specification and verification of model transformations. In: Palsberg, J. (ed.) Semantics and Algebraic Specification. LNCS, vol. 5700, pp. 140–161. Springer, Heidelberg (2009)
28. Queralt, A., Rull, G., Teniente, E., Farré, C., Urpí, T.: AuRUS: Automated Reasoning on UML/OCL Schemas. In: Parsons, J., Saeki, M., Shoval, P., Woo, C., Wand, Y. (eds.) ER 2010. LNCS, vol. 6412, pp. 438–444. Springer, Heidelberg (2010)
29. QVT Operational (Eclipse Project), http://www.eclipse.org/projects/project_summary.php?projectid=modeling.m2m.qvt-oml
30. Ab Rahim, L., Whittle, J.: Verifying semantic conformance of state machine-to-java code generators. In: Petriu, D.C., Rouquette, N., Haugen, Ø. (eds.) MODELS 2010. LNCS, vol. 6394, pp. 166–180. Springer, Heidelberg (2010)
31. Romeikat, R., Roser, S., Müllender, P., Bauer, B.: Translation of QVT relations into QVT operational mappings. In: Vallecillo, A., Gray, J., Pierantonio, A. (eds.) ICMT 2008. LNCS, vol. 5063, pp. 137–151. Springer, Heidelberg (2008)
32. SmartQVT, http://sourceforge.net/projects/smartqvt/
33. Soeken, M., Wille, R., Kuhlmann, M., Gogolla, M., Drechsler, R.: Verifying UML/OCL Models Using Boolean Satisfiability. In: Proc. Design, Automation and Test in Europe (DATE 2010). IEEE, Los Alamitos (2010)
34. Stärk, R.F., Schmid, J., Börger, E.: Java and the Java Virtual Machine: Definition, Verification, Validation. Springer, Heidelberg (2001)
35. Steinberg, D., Budensky, F., Paternostro, M., Merks, E.: EMF Eclipse Modeling Framework, 2nd edn. Addison-Wesley, Reading (2009)
36. Stenzel, K.: A formally verified calculus for full java card. In: Rattray, C., Maharaj, S., Shankland, C. (eds.) AMAST 2004. LNCS, vol. 3116, pp. 491–505. Springer, Heidelberg (2004)
37. Stenzel, K.: Verification of Java Card Programs. PhD thesis, Faculty of Informatics, Augsburg University, Germany (2005)
38. Troya, J., Vallecillo, A.: Towards a rewriting logic semantics for ATL. In: Tratt, L., Gogolla, M. (eds.) ICMT 2010. LNCS, vol. 6142, pp. 230–244. Springer, Heidelberg (2010)
39. von Oheimb, D., Nipkow, T.: Machine-checking the java specification: Proving type-safety. In: Alves-Foss, J. (ed.) Formal Syntax and Semantics of Java. LNCS, vol. 1523, pp. 119–156. Springer, Heidelberg (1999)
40. Wimmer, M., Kusel, A., Schoenboeck, J., Kappel, G., Retschitzegger, W., Schwinger, W.: Reviving QVT relations: Model-based debugging using colored petri nets. In: Schürr, A., Selic, B. (eds.) MODELS 2009. LNCS, vol. 5795, pp. 727–732. Springer, Heidelberg (2009)
41. XPand, http://wiki.eclipse.org/Xpand

Model-Based (Mechanical) Product Design

Mehdi Iraqi-Houssaini, Mathias Kleiner, and Lionel Roucoules

Arts et Métiers ParisTech ; CNRS, LSIS, 2 cours des Arts et Métiers, 13697
Aix-en-Provence, France
{mehdi.iraqi-houssaini,mathias.kleiner,lionel.roucoules}@ensam.eu

Abstract. Mechanical product engineering is a research and industrial activity which studies the design of complex mechanical systems. The process, which involves the collaboration of various experts using domain-specific software, raises syntactic and semantic interoperability issues which are not addressed by existing software solutions or their underlying concepts. This article proposes a flexible model-based software architecture that allows for a federation of experts to define and collaborate in innovative design processes. The presented generic approach is backed and validated by its implementation on an academic usecase.

1 Introduction

(Mechanical) product engineering is a domain which studies the entire lifecycle of a complex mechanical system from the customer requirements analysis to its end of life. It involves several phases: design, industrialization, production, exploitation, dismantling, recycling. The design phase is the activity that aims at creating a complete digital mock-up including all information on the product coming from multiple points of view: functions, components, form features, materials, multi-physical behaviors, etc. [30,27,38]. This strongly knowledge-based and collaborative activity involves many partners with different expertises, each of them using very specialized computer tools, in their turn based on different knowledge representations and operational procedures.

Such a complex computer-assisted activity has to be supported by a flexible and efficient software architecture based on rigorous knowledge formalizations. Although it has been the subject of many research over the past 20 years, the current state-of-the-art, mainly centered on extended CAD tools, suffers from many deep limitations such as lack of interoperability [22], lack of flexibility [6], lack of control over the manipulated knowledge [28], etc.

This article proposes a software architecture based on model-driven engineering that aims at overcoming the current scientific and operational issues. The approach, called Model-driven product design, is backed by preceding motivations studies [25,1], operational, and validated through its application to an industrial product.

This paper is organized as follows. In section 2, we briefly introduce the context of product design, model-driven engineering main principles, as well as motivations to this work through a study of current issues and challenges. Section 3 describes the approach and proposes a generic model-driven software architecture. In Section 4, we show its application to a product design scenario. Finally, Section 5, discusses related work and proposes directions for future research.

2 Context

2.1 Introduction to (Mechanical) Product Design

Mechanical product design is part of mechanical product engineering that aims at studying a product from its beginning of life (marketing, value analysis...) to its end of life (dismantling, recycling...). This approach strongly supports the design rational information that assists industry both in innovative or routine product design. Product design has to tackle the path from functions (what the product is designed for) and solutions (what are the technologies to achieve functions). The design process is commonly composed of several phases [15]: requirements specification, conceptual design, embodiment design and detailed design that progressively breakdown the product in multiple bill of material (BOM): as-specified (F-BOM), as-designed (Product-BOM, CAD-BOM...), as-manufactured (CAM-BOM...). In the current industrial context of the extended enterprise, the design activity is composed of collaborative and remote tasks that need to link all the knowledge coming from different experts that define their own BOM (functional analysis, components and material selection, structure analysis, manufacturing process selection...). Nowadays most of those BOM are computer-supported. Three main categories of computer tools can be listed:

- The PLM (Product LifeCycle Management) system which acts as the information backbone by linking BOMs [3]. However, these tools operate at a low-granularity level. Indeed, they mainly consist in a database of files produced by different expert tools (CAD or CAx), with some additional workflow management (files repositories, access restrictions and versioning). As such, they do not provide detailed knowledge management and rely on existing file exchange standards to achieve interoperability.
- The CAx (Computer Aided X) tools that support product's X assessments during the design process (X being related to functional analysis, manufacturability, recyclability, etc.).
- The CAD (Computer Aided Design) software that manages form features and acts as one of the collaborative space for designers since the design process is still CAD-centric. Some CAD tools have been extended over the years to embrace the increasing collaborative aspect of engineering. A perfect example of this approach is the leading CAO tool CATIA [35]. Based on engineering good practices, they have developed additional modules (CAx like) which plug different expertises to the geometrical representation of the product. Limits of such an approach are well known by software developers: lack of modularity (*ad hoc* integration), lack of functionalities (modules are less powerful than specialized tools), lack of efficiency (engineers have to adapt their practices to the tool).

2.2 Introduction to MDE and Model Transformation

Model Driven Engineering considers models, through multiple abstract representation levels, as a unifying software concept. The central notions that have been introduced are terminal model, metamodel, and metametamodel. A terminal model is a representation of a system. It captures some characteristics of the system and provides knowledge about it. MDE tools act on terminal models expressed in precise modeling languages. The abstract syntax of a modeling language, when expressed as a model, is called a metamodel. The relation between a model and the metamodel of its language is called conformsTo. Metamodels are in turn expressed in a modeling language for which conceptual foundations are captured in an auto-descriptive model called metametamodel. This metametamodel language, derived from set-theory and object-languages, usually consists of entities, attributes and relations.

While this originates from an industrial need to have a homogeneous organization where different facets of a software system may be easily separated or combined, the proposed architecture goes beyond software or platform models and reveals itself suited for many other areas where knowledge representation, exchange and reasoning is a central preoccupation, including ontologies [32].

The main way to automate MDE is by executing operations on models. For instance, the production of a model Mb from a model Ma by a transformation Mt is called a model transformation. The OMG's Query View Transform (QVT) specification[26] defines a set of useful model operations, an appropriate descriptive language, and proposes clues on how it should be implemented.

Finally, interoperability with non-MDE enabled technologies (here called technical spaces) is achieved by special projections here called injection (obtaining a model from structured data) and extraction (the opposite operation).

These main MDE principles and technologies are summarized in Figure 1.

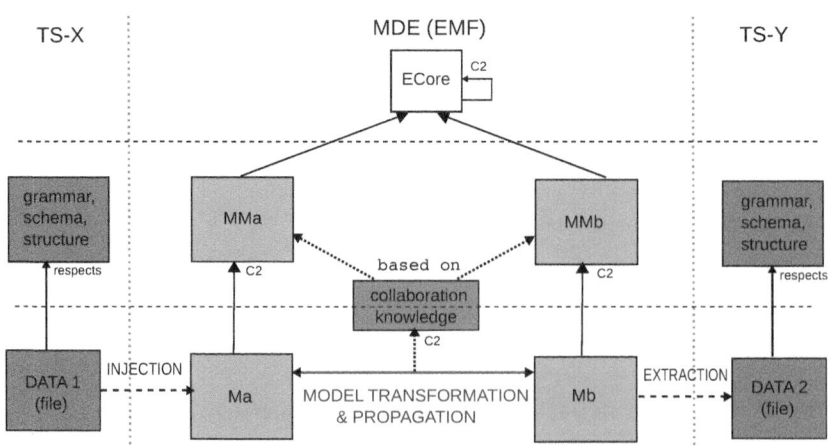

Fig. 1. Model-driven engineering main principles

2.3 Current Issues and Challenges in Product Design Software

In order to support the product design activity, the information system is now recognized as a critical component of collaborative engineering practices [6]. Subsection 2.1 has presented the main categories of current computer tools currently used in industry to support mechanical product modelling. Although those tools have reached a high level of functionalities several issues remain to fully tackle the real complexity of the design process. For 15 years the paradigm of design activity has changed from a sequential process to a concurrent process [31]. This new paradigm increased the involvement of several experts in the solution selection. The design process then has to be centered on shared experts knowledge. New issues are thus related to the complexity of managing that knowledge via computer-supported tools:

Knowledge Synthesis versus form Feature Modelling. For almost 30 years CAD systems have been developed and improved to currently reach powerful features that support product's shape modelling, which makes the design process geometric centric. This approach has shown its great interest in industry to tackle the problem of digitizing hand-done drawing and to improve the CAD-CAM links. Nowadays, the CAD model also finds an interest in improving the digital mock-up used during a decision making process. However current CAD systems are not able to manage all the knowledge related to the product definition. This information has to be related to the whole lifecycle [9] (from requirement specifications to dismantling information). The product, and its CAD model, is now defined, as far as possible, taking into account "X" constraints as assumed in a DFX (Design For X) approach. CAD model (i.e. form feature) then has to be generated from knowledge synthesis approach [24].

Interoperability versus Heterogeneity of Knowledge Modelling. Since the number of experts and product assessments are increasing, knowledge is becoming more and more heterogeneous but has to be linked in order to manage the impact of changes on each other. Each knowledge model is indeed created and can evolve independently. [17] proposes three approaches to afford the interoperability:

- Integration aims at proposing a unique global fused model that integrates every knowledge concept. A consensus has to be found among every concept, and should be changed when a new concept is added.
- Unification aims at proposing a metamodel used to map some knowledge concepts via semantic associations. This metamodel has to evolve or a new one has to be created when a new concept is added.
- Federation aims at creating mappings between knowledge models dynamically. This distributed approach seems to be the more flexible one since only local changes have to be treated when adding new concepts.

We propose to use a model-based architecture to support the federation approach since MDE principles naturally promote its distributed nature. Metamodels will be used to formalize collaborative knowledge, while projections and transformations will be used to support syntactic and semantic interoperability between BOMs (as proposed for instance in [13]). The dynamic creation of mappings remains nevertheless a great difficulty and will not be fully treated in this paper.

3 A Model-Based Software Architecture for Product Design

As seen previously, we believe MDE is fitted to support a federated product design software architecture. In order to map MDE concepts and operations to product engineering, we have compiled design scenarios from academic litterature and industrial usecases. As a result, we identified a set of different concepts, design patterns and requirements. We first give an overview of the proposed architecture, then discuss its different parts and alternatives in details.

3.1 Architecture Overview

Figure 2 presents an overview of the proposed software architecture, illustrated through a fictive scenario involving various components. As outlined by the squares on the side, the symbols may be read equally at two levels with different semantics, corresponding to the M1 and M2 levels of MDE:

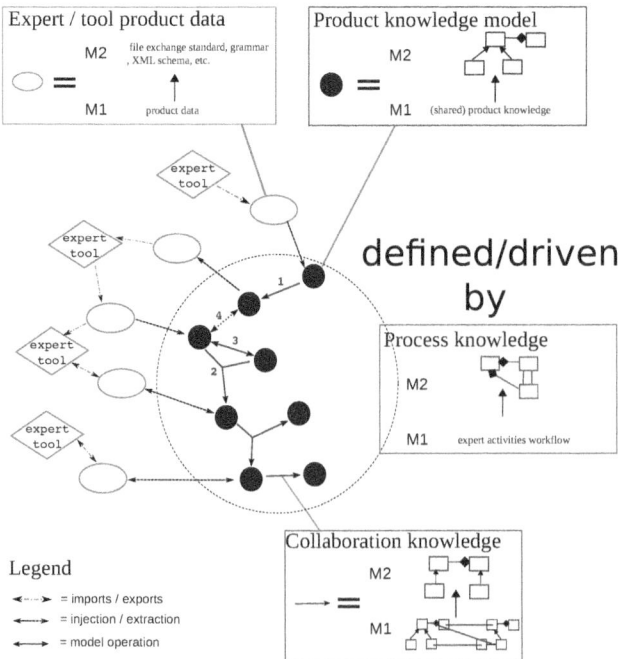

Fig. 2. Architecture overview

– Yellow ellipses represent expert tools data. At level M2, their data structure or grammar. At level M1, the actual file produced (i.e. exported) or used (i.e. imported) by a specialized tool.
 – At both levels, the dotted circle represents the frontier between tools technical spaces and MDE. The dotted arrows represent the injections/extractions required to obtain corresponding knowledge models.
 – At a level M2 lecture, blue-filled circles represent the domain-specific metamodels, whereas at level M1 they are the actual models manipulated during the scenario.
 – Green solid arrows represent (inter-)model operations. At level M2, it is their definition (hopefully a declarative description). At level M1, their execution on the models during the scenario. The different types of operations needed (marked by numbers on the figure) are detailed in a following subsection.
 – The whole process is defined and driven by design process knowledge, expressed as a model of some workflow language (red square).

3.2 Technical Spaces and Connectors

Expert tools use various formats to store and manipulate data. Most, if not all, provide import/export facilities from/to either proprietary formats, or, for interoperability requirements, from/to industry standards (in our industrial context, STEP [33] is largely used). In order to manipulate product data in the MDE environment, we need to obtain corresponding knowledge models.

This operation, here called injection/extraction, has a well-known process in the MDE community: 1) obtain, or define, the data structure of the technical space; 2) define the corresponding metamodel; 3) map both of them using a MDE language/tool that automates the operation.

In practice, we usually fall into two main possibilities:

 – An XML format is provided: the process is then eased by existing work on briding XML schemas to metamodels.
 – A textual file is provided: a grammar of the textual syntax has to be defined (usually in EBNF style), and its concepts mapped to the metamodel.

The obtained metamodel is often syntactically close to the original data structure. However, it is possible to complete the connector with an additional transformation, defining (or reusing) a target metamodel that has a more appropriate structure.

Finally, it is important to note that not all the data manipulated by the expert tool may be of relevance for collaborating with other experts. In that sense, the model-based architecture offers a very flexible approach: the knowledge model can very well be a (reformulated) subset of the original expert data.

In the implementation and usecase sections, we will show the application of these alternatives on a concrete scenario and discuss potential fallbacks.

3.3 Knowledge (Meta) Models

Knowledge metamodels capture a subset of expert data that is relevant for other experts in the design scenario. The architecture does not place any constraint on which metamodels should be used, hence remaining flexible. However, our experience shows that we are mainly dealing with three types of knowledge models:

- Tool models. These counterparts of expert tools data structure, as seen in the previous subsection, may be used as entry-point models to obtain specialized (tool-independant) models, or simply linked to another tool model in order to achieve interoperability.
- Specialized models. Design scenarios literature describe custom knowledge models which aim at defining, checking or enforcing specific properties of the product (such as its energetic integrity).
- Intermediate models. Complex transformations may require intermediate models for technical (simplicity) or conceptual reasons (semantic decomposition).

The flexibility of the approach allows for an easier development of new design scenarios: knowledge models may be reused, extended or created from scratch depending on the scientific analysis rather than tools existing support. Possibilities are however limited by the expressiveness of the metametamodel language.

3.4 Model Operations

From the studied scenarios, we outline a (non-exhaustive) list of different experts collaboration patterns, translate them to knowledge manipulation requirements, and map these to existing MDE concepts and technologies:

- The output of an expert is used, later in the design process, by another expert. This is a typical interoperability problem. To obtain the downstream knowledge model, existing rule-based model transformation techniques [18,7] can be used (mark 1 on Fig 2).
- The output of several expert analysis have to be combined. A classical example is the geometrical mockup of the designed product, which is constrained by several expert analysis (energy flows, materials, technologies, etc.). In order to merge (and/or divide) knowledge, modern MDE tools offer the possibility to specify multi-source (and/or multi-target) transformations (mark 2 on Fig 2).
- Two (or more) experts share some knowledge and have to maintain their data consistent. Typically, different analysis will share product parameters. When activities are held in a back and forth stream, bijective transformations may be used. Since these transformations are not yet mature [34], MDE applications usually simulate this behavior with two injective transformations. When activities are held concurrently, more advanced mechanisms, such as constraint-based propagation of modifications [4], are to be investigated (mark 3 on Fig 2).

– An expert is faced with two or more inconsistent data constraints. It is thus required to calculate the impact of modifications and notify upstream experts. Although a rough impact can be calculated from the activities workflow, the MDE approach may offer more fine-grained possibilities through traceability mechanisms [16]. As the production of knowledge may be achieved through an external tool operation, traceability must also be kept between the models which are not directly transformed (mark 4 on Fig 2).

3.5 Process (Meta) Model

A design scenario is supported by a process which describes the different experts, activities and tools involved, as well as temporal and collaboration constraints. This description may be captured using existing generic *workflow* languages or product engineering specialized languages [14]. The MDE process, which describes the models and model operations involved, may be automatically derived from the expert activities workflow. These are however out of scope of this paper which does not preclude or impose the use of a particular process language.

4 Usecase

In order to further validate the presented architecture, we illustrate its use on an innovative design scenario which is not currently well supported by existing software solutions. The usecase, adapted from [19], deals with the design of a mechanical coupling system between a plane propeller and a diesel engine. The design process aims at obtaining a description of a product assembly from its functional and energetic analysis.

Figure 3 outlines the tools, data files and knowledge models used in the scenario. The following subsections detail each operation.

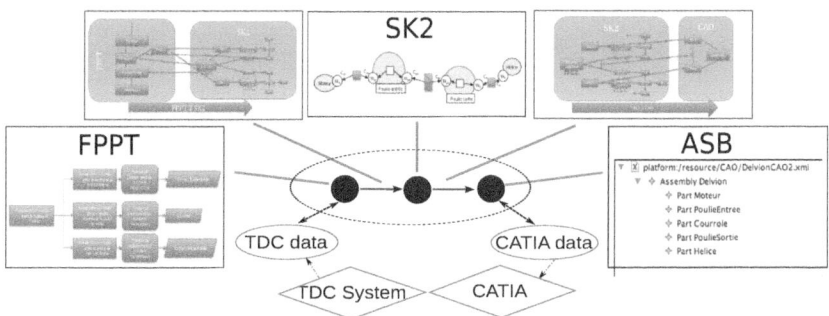

Fig. 3. Usecase scenario

4.1 Architecture Implementation

We have chosen the Eclipse EMF platform [8] as the implementation framework, mainly for its maturity and tools support. ECORE is used as the metametamodel language, and ATL [18] for transformations. The usecase files, models and transformations are open source and can be freely downloaded from a single package [5]. In the following, metamodels will be represented using ECORE diagrams.

4.2 Knowledge Models

Our scenario uses three specialized models which are briefly introduced below.

FPPT. FPPT stands for Function, Physical Principle, Technology. Informally described in [21], we created a metamodel which covers most of its concepts. An excerpt is shown in Figure 4. Functions refer to abstract product functionalities, which may be divided into subfunctions. Terminal functions are realized, through a physical principle, by a specific (known) technology.

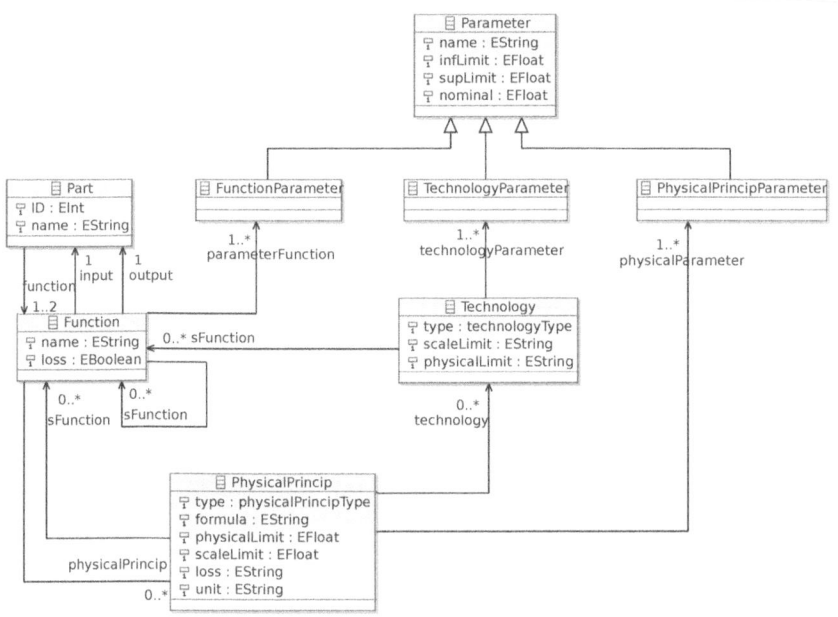

Fig. 4. An excerpt of the FPPT metamodel

SK2. SK2 stands for Skins, Skeletons, informally described in [23]. Figure 5 is an excerpt of the corresponding metamodel. Briefly, product parts have external skins which can be linked to other skins. The product skeleton, which represents the energy flows, is made of external functions between those skins, and internal functions inside the parts. Each function has energetic properties.

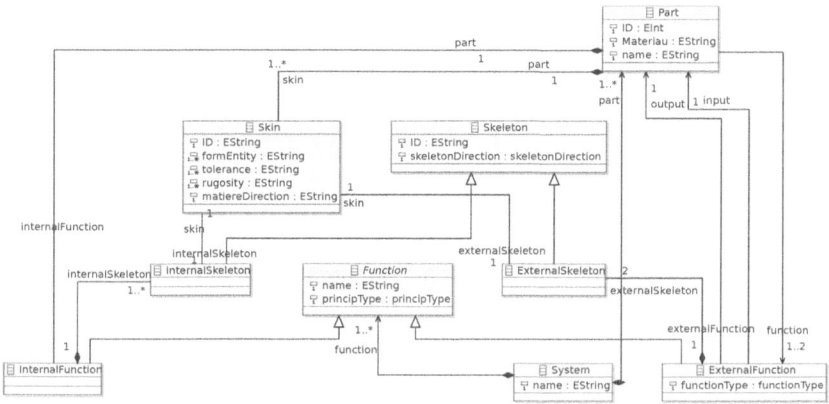

Fig. 5. An excerpt of the SK2 metamodel

ASB. ASB stands for product ASemBly. This very simple metamodel, in which the system is simply viewed as a set of interconnected parts, has been created specifically for this scenario, as an intermediate knowledge model between SK2 and the CAD tool CATIA.

4.3 TDC - FPPT Connector

The functional analysis tool selected for the usecase is TDC [36]. The tool provides an export of its data as an XML file. We used EMF native facilities to obtain the ECORE metamodel from the provided XML schema and the associated injection/extraction operation. However, due to XML arborescent restrictions, the associative references of the schema are simulated through the equivalence of textual properties (IDs). We thus created an additional model transformation, using ATL, to a target metamodel where associative references are restored.

The final step to the connector is an ATL transformation which targets the FPPT metamodel. The transformation involves a loss of knowledge which is not relevant for other experts in the context of our collaborative scenario.

Figure 6 summarizes this chain of transformations.

4.4 FPPT to SK2 Transformation

This ATL transformation mainly consists of two parts:

- a mapping from FPPT's functions and technologies to SK2's external functions and parts.
- a characterization of the skeleton energetic properties obtained from FPPT's physical principles.

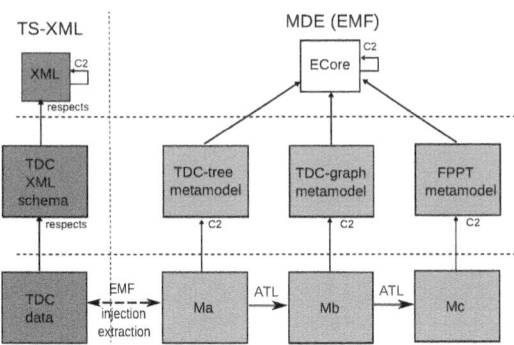

Fig. 6. TDC - FPPT: chain of transformations

4.5 SK2 to ASB Transformation

This very simple ATL transformation uses SK2's knowledge to create an assembly where different product parts are linked according to the skeleton.

4.6 ASB to CATIA Connector

The selected geometrical modelling tool is CATIA [35]. Among the possible formats for importing data, CATIA proposes STEP AP-203 [11], an industry standard for exchanging geometrical information about a mechanical product.

The STEP standard [33] defines textual files which conform to a STEP schema (Application Protocol here AP-203), which in turn is defined using a relational language called EXPRESS [10]. The OMG had already considered the interoperability between STEP files and MOF models in the original XMI proposal. Two alternatives were envisioned:

- a metametamodel mapping between EXPRESS and MOF, if any is possible due to the semantic gap.
- a metamodel mapping between a specific STEP schema and its counterpart metamodel.

To the best of our knowledge, the first option has been worked on by various projects but is not yet mature nor known feasible in the general case. We thus chose the second option.

Technically, we used XTEXT/XPAND [39] to define the STEP grammar and generated the corresponding metamodel. This state-of-the-art technology allows us to inject and extract STEP files to/from STEP models.

For the sake of clarity, we separated the STEP general metamodel from the AP-203 schema metamodel (which contains most fo the product information). An excerpt of the latter is shown in Figure 7.

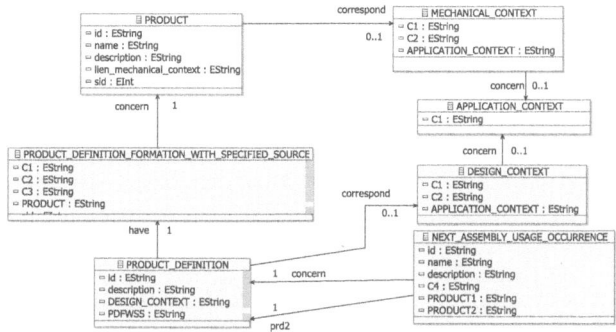

Fig. 7. excerpt of the STEP AP-203 metamodel

A first ATL transformation generates an AP-203 model from our assembly knowledge model (ASB). In order to obtain the general STEP model, a second ATL transformation takes two models as source: the AP-203 model and a custom model which only contains necessary header information for the STEP file (such as author, etc.). Figure 8 shows the whole connector chain of transformations.

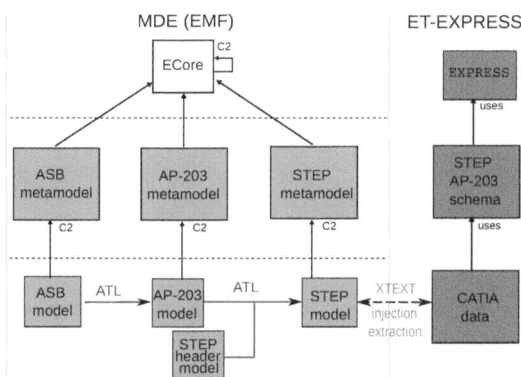

Fig. 8. ASB - CATIA: chain of transformations

5 Related and Future Work

From the product engineering perspective, most of the related work has been carried out using integrated product model approaches [27], often supported by ontology management technologies [20], as opposed to the model-based federation proposed in this article. Recent work have explored the use of meta-modelling [37], but are restricted to specific operations such as tool interoperability [22], design coherency [28], use a unifying metamodel like SysML [29], or focus small parts of the design process such as functional requirements [20]. [12,25] share our requirements for weaving and transformations between federated product models but stay at a conceptual level. Our work generalizes these principles in an flexible federation approach grounded in model-based techniques.

From the model-driven engineering perspective, product design requires complex metamodels and transformation processes. Therefore, while our work makes use of several existing model-based techniques, it also raises new challenges regarding traceability, consistency, bidirectional transformations and metamodels expressiveness. A large share of the work on megamodels, for instance [2], may also be investigated to ease the definition and evolution of the design process.

Future work includes experimentations on various industrial usecases, in order to confirm the viability of the MDE architecture and propose generic methods for the different collaboration patterns. One of the critical issues is incremental change management and its propagation to upstream models. Finally, investigations are currently carried out to tackle the dynamic aspects of creating the information system dynamically with respect to the adequate knowledge used in the product design process. That would provide a great opportunity to support the flexibility of the design process in industry. The expected output is a design process model which will be used to generate and automate the software process.

6 Conclusion

In the context of mechanical product engineering, software systems such as CAx and PLM have provided functionalities to manage product breakdown through organizational access rights and workflows on persistent files generated by specialized expert tools. However the increasing complexity of systems now requires a fine-grained control over collaborative knowledge in order to assess the impact of local changes, as well as flexible software systems which support the creation of innovative scenarios.

This paper describes an original model-based federation approach for the design of mechanical products, complementary to existing solutions (integration, unification). The proposed architecture adapts model techniques such as metamodelling, transformations and projections to the context of collaborative product design software. Based on previous experiences and studied design scenarios, generic model-based solutions are proposed to handle the digital chain of product knowledge at the desired granularity level, while preserving a flexibility that allows for innovative scenarios to be defined and automated. The implementation on an academic usecase validates the viability of the approach. Considering the high complexity and heterogeneity of product design scenarios, a number of original issues and challenges are raised, which lays the path for future investigations on both product engineering and model-based software techniques.

Acknowledgements. This work has been partially funded by the French project *ADN*. The authors would like to thank *S. Roger*, who did his master study on some metamodels and model transformations for the usecase; as well as *TDC Software*, for their help in understanding the concepts of the TDC XML schema.

References

1. Etienne, A., Guyot, E., Cabannes, G., Ducellier, G., Roucoules, L.: Specification and developments of interoperability solutions dedicated to multiple expertise collaboration in a design framework. In: International Conference on Software, Knowledge, Information Management and Applications (2008)
2. Bézivin, J., Jouault, F., Rosenthal, P., Valduriez, P.: Modeling in the large and modeling in the small. In: Aßmann, U., Aksit, M., Rensink, A. (eds.) MDAFA 2003. LNCS, vol. 3599, pp. 33–46. Springer, Heidelberg (2005)
3. PLM Market Growth in 2008, Mid-Year (2009), http://www.cimdata.com
4. Czarnecki, K., Helsen, S.: Feature-based survey of model transformation approaches. IBM Syst. J. 45, 621–645 (2006)
5. Delvion usecase (2011),
http://www.lsis.org/kleinerm/MPD/Delvion_usecase.html
6. Kadiri, S.E., Pernelle, P., Delattre, M., Bouras, A.: Current situation of plm systems in sme/smi: Survey's results and analysis. In: International Conference on Product Lifecycle Management (2009)
7. Ehrig, K., Guerra, E., Lengyel, J.L., Levendovszky, T., Prange, U., Taentzer, G., Varró, D., Varró-Gyapay, S.: Model transformation by graph transformation: A comparative study. In: MTiP 2005, International Workshop on Model Transformations in Practice (Satellite Event of MoDELS 2005) (2005)
8. EMF (2009), http://www.eclipse.org/modeling/emf/
9. Krause, F.-L., et al.: Product modelling. CIRP Annals - Manufacturing Technology 42(2), 695–706 (1993)
10. ISO 10303-11, Industrial automation systems and integration - Product data representation and exchange - Part 11: The EXPRESS language reference (1994)
11. ISO 10303-203, Industrial automation systems and integration - Product data representation and exchange - Part 203: Configuration controlled 3D designs of mechanical parts and assemblies (1994)
12. Maier, F., Mayer, W., Stumptner, M., Muehlenfeld, A.: Ontology-based process modelling for design optimisation support. In: Design Computing and Cognition 2008, pp. 513–532. Springer, Heidelberg (2008)
13. Frey, E., Ostrosi, E., Roucoules, L., Gomes, S.: Multi-domain product modelling: from requirements to cad and simulation tools. In: International Conference on Engineering Design (2009)
14. Booch, G., Rumbaugh, J., Jacobson, I.: Unified Modeling Language User Guide. Addison-Wesley Professional, Reading (2005)
15. Pahl, G., Beitz, W., Feldhusen, J., Grote, K.H.: Engineering design: a systematic approach, 6th edn. Springer, Heidelberg (1996)
16. Galvão, I., Goknil, A.: Survey of traceability approaches in model-driven engineering. In: EDOC, pp. 313–326. IEEE Computer Society, Los Alamitos (2007)
17. ISO 14258, Industrial Automation Systems - Concepts and Rules for Enterprise Models (1994)
18. Jouault, F., Kurtev, I.: Transforming Models with ATL. In: Bruel, J.-M. (ed.) MoDELS 2005. LNCS, vol. 3844, pp. 128–138. Springer, Heidelberg (2006)
19. Klein Meyer, J.S.: Modélisation multi-physique des systémes complexes dans un contexte de DFX. Application á la conception de micro-mécanismes. PhD thesis, Université de Technologie de Troyes (2008)
20. Kitamura, Y., Takafuji, S., Mizoguchi, R.: Towards a reference ontology for functional knowledge interoperability. In: ASME Conference Proceedings, 2007(48078), pp. 111–120 (2007)

21. Klein Meyer, J., Roucoules, L., Grave, A., Chaput, J.: Case study of a mems switch supported by a fbs and dfm framework. In: The Future of Product Development, pp. 377–386. Springer, Heidelberg (2007)
22. Krause, F.-L., Kaufmann, U.: Meta-modelling for interoperability in product design. CIRP Annals - Manufacturing Technology 56(1), 159–162 (2007)
23. Roucoules, L., Skander, A.: Manufacturing process selection and integration in product design. analysis and synthesis approaches. In: CIRP Design Seminar (2003)
24. Roucoules, L., Lafon, P., et al.: Knowledge intensive approach towards multiple product modelling and geometry emergence to foster cooperative design. In: CIRP Design Seminar (2006)
25. Mühlenfeld, A., Maier, F., Mayer, W., Stumptner, M.: Modelling and management of design artefacts in design optimisation. In: Collaborative Product and Service Life Cycle Management for a Sustainable World, Advanced Concurrent Engineering, pp. 513–520. Springer, London (2008)
26. Object Management Group. Meta Object Facility (MOF) 2.0 Query/View/Transformation (QVT) Specification, version 1.0 (2008)
27. Tichkiewitch, S.: Specifications on integrated design methodology using a multi-view product model. In: Biennial Joint Conference on Engineering Systems Design and Analysis, pp. 101–108 (1996)
28. Sadeghi, M., Noel, F., Hadj-Hamou, K.: Development of control mechanisms to support coherency of product model during cooperative design process. Journal of Intelligent Manufacturing 21, 539–554 (2010)
29. Shah, A.A., Schaefer, D., Paredis, C.J.J.: Enabling multi-view modeling with sysml profiles and model transformations. In: International Conference on Product Lifecycle Management, pp. 527–538 (2009)
30. Shah, J.J.: Assessment of features technology. Computer-Aided Design 23(5), 331–343 (1991)
31. Sohlenius, G.: Concurrent engineering. CIRP Annals - Manufacturing Technology 41(2), 645–655 (1992)
32. Staab, S., Walter, T., Gröner, G., Parreiras, F.S.: Model Driven Engineering with Ontology Technologies. In: Aßmann, U., Bartho, A., Wende, C. (eds.) Reasoning Web. LNCS, vol. 6325, pp. 62–98. Springer, Heidelberg (2010)
33. ISO 10303, Industrial automation systems and integration - Product data representation and exchange (1994)
34. Stevens, P.: Bidirectional model transformations in qvt: semantic issues and open questions. Software and System Modeling 9(1), 7–20 (2010)
35. CATIA (Dassault systems) (2011), http://www.3ds.com/products/catia/welcome/
36. TDC system (2011), http://www.tdc.fr/en/products/tdc_system.php
37. Gary Wang, G., Shan, S.: Review of metamodeling techniques in support of engineering design optimization. Mechanical Design 129(4), 370–380 (2007)
38. Yan, X.-T.: A multiple perspective product modeling and simulation approach to engineering design support. Concurrent Engineering Research and Application Journal 11(3), 221–234 (2003)
39. XTEXT (2011), http://www.eclipse.org/Xtext

Applying a Model-Based Approach to IT Systems Development Using SysML Extension

Sayaka Izukura[*], Kazuo Yanoo, Takao Osaki, Hiroshi Sakaki,
Daichi Kimura, and Jianwen Xiang

NEC Corporation, Kawasaki, 211-0068, Japan
s-izukura@az.jp.nec.com

Abstract. Model-based system engineering (MBSE) is regarded as an effective way of developing systems. We are now applying the model-based approach to IT system development/integration (SI) because we urgently need to reduce the cost of SI. However, there are various challenges imposed when applying MBSE to SI. One of these is that reducing the cost to update models is more significant than that in other MBSE domains such as embedded systems. We adopted SysML to handle these issues and extended it to modeling IT systems. We present the details on this SysML extension and how it overcame these issues. We are developing an in-house SI-support tool called "CASSI", which evaluates the non-functional requirements; performance and availability of the IT system's models written in that extended manner and helps these models to be reused. This paper also includes industrial case studies of CASSI, and its effectiveness is discussed.

Keywords: Model-based, IT systems development, system modeling.

1 Introduction

It is urgently needed to suppress cost of enterprise IT system development/integration (SI). Model-based system engineering (MBSE) is regarded as an effective methodology to achieve this. Requirements, specifications, and design in MBSE are written in formal modeling language, and the models can be automatically verified and reused. The main benefits of MBSE are summarized below [1].

1. Improved quality
   More complete, unambiguous, and verifiable requirements
   More rigorous traceability of requirements
   Enhanced design integrity
2. Increased productivity
   Improved impact analysis of requirements and design changes
   Reuse of existing models to support design evolution
3. Reduced development risks
   Ongoing validation of requirements and verification of design
   More accurate cost estimates to develop the system

---
[*] Corresponding author.

However, the model-based approach is less popular for developing enterprise IT systems in our experience, despite the rate at which many frameworks and view models have been proposed. We consider that this is mainly because of cost-benefit conflicts. If the effort of creating and updating models is larger than the benefit brought about by modeling, MBSE will not be practical. We observe that three properties of enterprise IT systems prevent MBSE from being cost effective.

1. Rapidly changing hardware infrastructure
   IT products are shifted and updated too rapidly and models quickly become out of date.
2. Large-scale and heterogeneous components
   IT systems comprise a wide variety of third party application software, libraries, and middleware. Consequently, it is not cost effective to model them all, unless they are repeatedly reused.
3. Comparatively easy bug fixing nature
   Most problems with IT systems are caused by software defects, which can easily be fixed, even after their release. Therefore, very strict modeling at the design phase is less important.

Issues 1 and 2 increase the cost of modeling, and issue 3 decreases benefits. These issues suggest that we should apply *lightweight* MBSE to SI, where lightweight means ease of learning, ease of use, and less modeling effort.

We are now developing an in-house MBSE environment named CASSI (Computer Aided System model-based System Integration environment) [2], which employs SysML [3] as a modeling language. As the name indicates, CASSI is intended to be a Computer Aided Engineering (CAE) tool for SI. Generally, more detailed systems are modeled, better results, such as more accurate evaluation and verification or more cost saving benefit will be obtained. However, we must avoid over-modeling to enable CASSI to be corporate-widely used as a pragmatic tool. Otherwise, the benefits previously listed are ruined by the efforts of modeling. This level of modeling detail largely depends on target domain of modeling and will vary from organization to organization, because the extra effort of applying MBSE heavily depends on skill and knowledge of engineers. Consequently, even if our design choice (the level) is proven to be effective for us, it might not be for other organizations. However, our practice and knowledge will be a good reference for other organizations.

The primary contribution of this paper is to present our implementation in applying MBSE to the practical development of enterprise IT systems. We have defined minimal views for our needs, and extended (specialized) SysML according to this. We also managed some problems attributed to SysML itself. This paper also includes industrial case studies of CASSI, and discusses its effectiveness.

The rest of this paper is structured as follows. Section 2 presents the overall framework for model-based SI using CASSI. Also, details on our SysML extension, which we called PlatForm Modeling Language or PFML, are presented in this section. Section 3 explains case studies of CASSI that were applied to real SI. Then, some related work covering other modeling frameworks for IT systems and comparisons are presented in Section 4. Section 5 concludes this paper and outlines future work.

2 Details on CASSI and PFML

We present the overall framework for model-based SI using CASSI in this section. Also, the definition of PFML, which is used as a modeling language, is explained in detail.

2.1 Framework for Model-Based SI

An enterprise IT system is so complex that its architecture should be described according to the interests (concerns) of all stakeholders such as clients, architects, designers, application programmers, and infrastructure engineers [4]. We assumed that three kinds of stakeholders would interact with CASSI.

- System Engineers (SEs)
  An SE is responsible for providing customers with an IT system with the requirements they demand. For example, in developing an e-commerce site, he/she designs database schema, configures Web applications, and determines the appropriate platform architecture.
- Platform Architects (PAs)
  A PA is responsible for providing modules of platform architecture, which we call *system model*s. A system model is a self-contained unit of reuse that achieves a certain functionality. For example, a Web 2-tier system, composed of Web servers, a load balancer, a database server, and network peripherals is an example of system models.
- Infrastructure Architects (IAs)
  An IA is responsible for providing verified combinations of products. For example, he/she verifies whether a certain type of network card or memory can be mounted on some type of server.

Here, *platform* means hardware and software elements that are not specific to particular projects. For example, computers, routers, and RDBMS software compose a platform. Application code dedicated to a particular project is not part of a platform.

There is an overview of model-based SI flow using CASSI in Figure 1. The PA designs common architecture for various systems as system models and stores them in the repository. In parallel, IA verifies combinations of products, stores them in the product library, and updates them along with the release of products. The SE can utilize them and only need to select an adequate system model from the repository and customize it and adopt an appropriate product for their system design according to user requirements. We call this process as "constructing a *system* from a system model", where the system model is used as a design template.

Basically, we separate the modeling of "system dependent" and rapidly changing parts from that of comparably unchanging parts and attempt to reduce the effort of modeling.

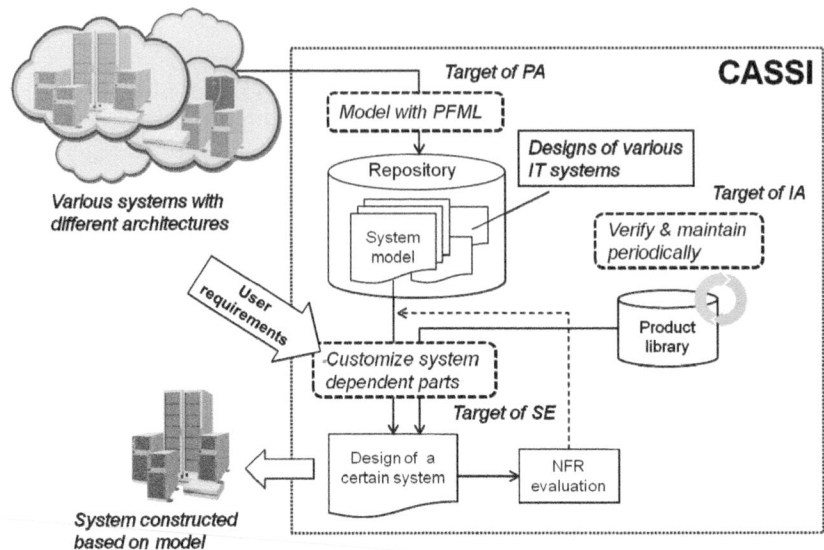

Fig. 1. Model-based SI flow using CASSI

The two primary objectives of CASSI are to reuse system models and evaluate non-functional requirements (NFRs).

1. Reuse and integration of system models
   An SE chooses and integrates existing system models as an execution platform for the project. Reuse reduces the effort and cost of development, and maintains quality. Being model-based, CASSI helps the SE to retrieve appropriate system models and checks the integrity among them.
2. Evaluation of NFRs during whole design process
   An SE needs to adjust the execution platform to meet the NFRs required by the customer (e.g., capacity planning). CASSI can evaluate the performance and availability of the model, and helps the SE's decisions [2].

Currently, we do not pursue other MBSE benefits such as tracing and verification of functional requirements, since CASSI focuses on the platform design phase within the whole system development process and application design or testing phase is out of scope. The reason we omit the application modeling is that application models are less reusable than platform models and require more modeling effort. It is a future task whether we extend our target to the application modeling or not.

2.2 System Model Overview

The definition of system model is outlined in Figure 2.

The system model consists of a logical model, a process model, and physical models. The logical model describes use cases (related to functional requirements) and the functions of the system. Each function has links to a process, which are the

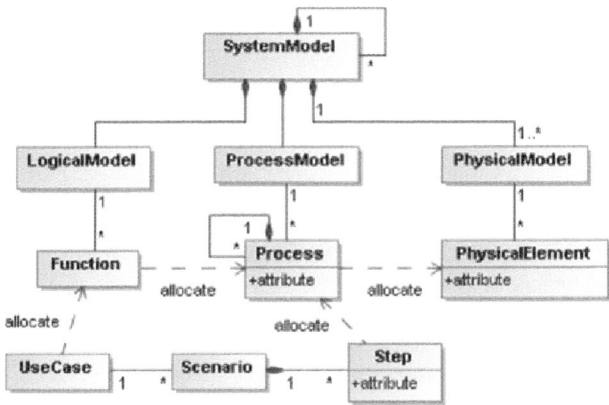

Fig. 2. Definition of system model

components of the process model. Here, function does not mean application-level functions such as "adding items to the user's cart", but platform-level functions such as a "Web server". For example, the "Web server" function can be allocated to the "Apache" or "Tomcat" process. There are various implementation of the same platform-level function and CASSI currently utilizes the logical model for searching adequate system models holding a certain function from various process models. As there are not many differences between logical and process models in our model, the relations between them can be handled by allocations, which are comparatively simple relationships. The process model describes the structure of processes, which comprise the sequence (scenario) performed by the application software. Here, a scenario is constructed of several steps. A physical model describes the structure of physical elements, such as servers, network devices, and their connections. When cloud systems are modeled, we can define two physical models: the first for virtual servers and the second for physical (real) servers.

Note that Figure 2 briefly outlines the structure and more specialized classes are defined in CASSI. For example, the subclass of physical element includes servers, processors, memory, and network peripherals. Also, scenarios can include control flow elements, such as branches, loops, forks, and joins.

Additionally, there are two types of system models, viz., white-box and black-box models [5]. If the details of a system are known, the corresponding system model can be written to be as detailed as possible, i.e., as a white box. Otherwise, we need to treat uncertain parts of systems as a black box and do not go into component details. This is effective for modeling large-scale systems and their multiple components. Thus, we can omit detailed modeling of uncertain components and its behavior.

Also, the system model can include other system models. The included system models behave as components of the including system model, where the allocations of the included system models are preserved.

The relation between a system model and a system is somewhat similar to that of a class and instances in the object-oriented approach. The system model is *instantiated* by fixing user-changeable factors as follows.

- Scaling Factors

Scaling factors indicate user-changeable parameters of system models, such as the number of servers in a cluster and size of thread pools. As such values vary from system to system even if the basic architecture remains the same, they are to be specified separately from the system model. Scaling factors instantiate processes and physical elements by applying specified values to them, through their attributes.

- Application Factors

Application factors mean the values that are specified according to the properties of the user and real behavior of applications, such as count/size of requests arriving at the system and the CPU time for each request. As such values vary for scale and content of the job of each application, they cannot be fixed in the design phase for the platform architecture. As a result, they need to be defined separately from system models and be easily fixed and changed later. Application factors instantiate steps, by applying the specified value to them through their attributes. Many application factors are common with those defined in MARTE-PAM [6], but we have defined more domain-specific factors such as the number of SQL queries.

- Product Allocations

There are many options for selecting products. That means we can use several kinds of servers and network devices for implementation. For example, servers may be exchanged with newly released products with better specifications. Therefore, actual information about products for constructing systems and their specifications should easily be updated as products are exchanged. Information on several products and their possible inner structures, such as the number of CPU cores and mounted memory size, is defined as a library (separate from the system model) in CASSI and is periodically maintained by IA. Physical elements are allocated to these products in the instantiation procedure and the destination for allocation can easily be changed to another product.

We call these factors configuration parameters (CPs), and the instantiated system model in which CPs are fixed is known as an *instance model*. CPs affect the NFRs of the system, and by changing them, we can make models for various system designs with different NFRs, such as performance and availability. Thus, once the basic system model is constructed by the PA, all SEs can utilize it as a template for the design of various systems.

The separation of CPs and system models makes it easy to update and customize parts of the model, and minimize the effort of constructing instance models (the model of various systems) by reusing existing models. Furthermore, we can define the platform and application parts independently, and integrate them later in each development phase. This is also convenient for the platform as a service (PaaS) environment, whose application platforms are provided by the PaaS vendor and application developers do not know the platform's details.

2.3 SysML Representation

We employ SysML to represent the above model (meta-model of PFML). The logical model, process model, and physical model are represented by SysML blocks and the components of each model are represented by part properties and connectors. Their structure is described with internal block diagrams (IBD). We employ a sequence diagram to describe scenarios. Steps are written as messages and execution specifications. A scenario is represented by the first message in the sequence. The use case is naturally represented by a SysML use case, and described by a use case diagram. These extensions are done by stereotypes in a standard way.

We also added some extensions to SysML. One of the advantages of SysML in representing systems architecture is that IBD can present nested parts intuitively. However, because properties cannot be nested in the UML2 meta-model, there is a gap between presentation and internal representation.

For example, we assume that there is a different part "a1" and "a2" with the same type of A in a certain IBD. If A includes a part "b", two parts "a1.b" and "a2.b" are shown in the IBD and they are the identical element, even though they look different elements to the user. Therefore, it is impossible to describe allocations from the element "a1.b" to a different element to that allocated from "a2.b". If done so, two allocations from the block A to the different elements are generated. This is so confusing that we redefined allocation so that it could represent the relation between propertyPath to propertyPath, where propertyPath is the same as the attribute of SysML's NestedConnectorEnd. For the same reason, we avoided using "represents" for the attributes of lifelines but used the redefined allocation to relate lifelines and parts.

CPs are represented by a dedicated data structure and externally related to a path of part properties inside the system model. Although SysML defines a method of representing configurations without the problem stated above (i.e., initialValues), there are few reasons to employ this complex representation, because we implemented a dedicated configuration view to simplify use.

The diagrams and their relationships are outlined in Figure 3. This also shows the CPs editing view used in the instantiation procedure above.

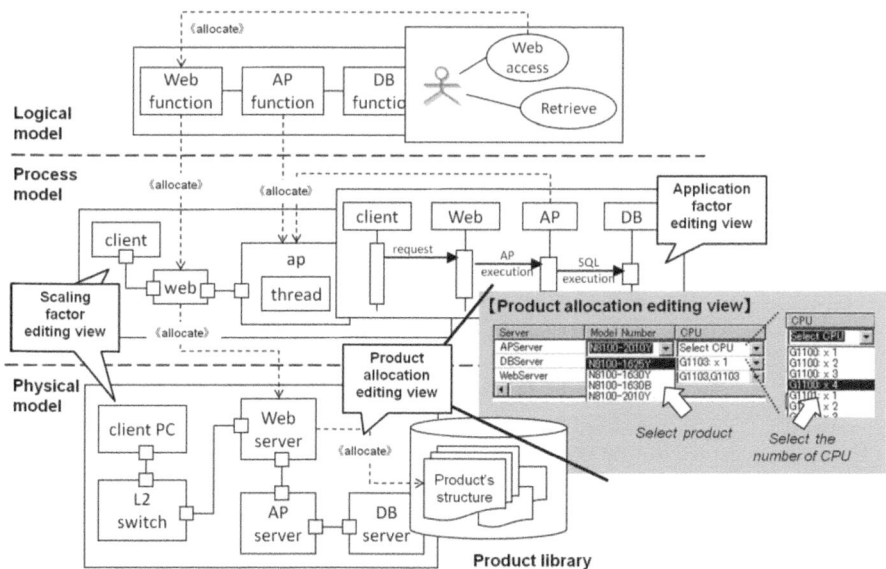

Fig. 3. Relationship between each diagram and example of CPs editing view

2.4 NFR Evaluation

This paper only briefly illustrates the method of evaluating performance (one important property of NFRs) due to space limitations. Details on the evaluation of availability are given in [2] [7]. The module for performance evaluation converts SysML (XMI) files and CPs, which describe an instance model, into a simulation model, and then executes discrete event simulation. The simulation model is comprised of a directed graph, whose semantics is similar to the activities of UML, and its node reference resources [2]. Similar approaches are found in [8].

Figure 4 is an example of conversion. The right side shows translated graphs, where the resource for each node is after a colon. This can be summarized in four steps.

1. Convert a sequence diagram into an equivalent activity graph.
2. Translate the graph according to allocation between a lifeline and a process. The allocated part is established as a resource for the node. If there are other elements between allocated parts, the nodes or edges for them are also generated (e.g., "c:fio").
3. Translate the graph again according to allocation between a process and a physical element. Products are expanded and allocation is inferred by its type (e.g., "b:CPU", "d:DISK"). This step can be repeated if there are multiple physical layers. The performance of a virtual environment is evaluated as such.
4. Calculate the service demand of each node from the application factors of the node and attributes of the resource (e.g., the demand of "a:C1" is a.msgSize * C1.bandWidth).

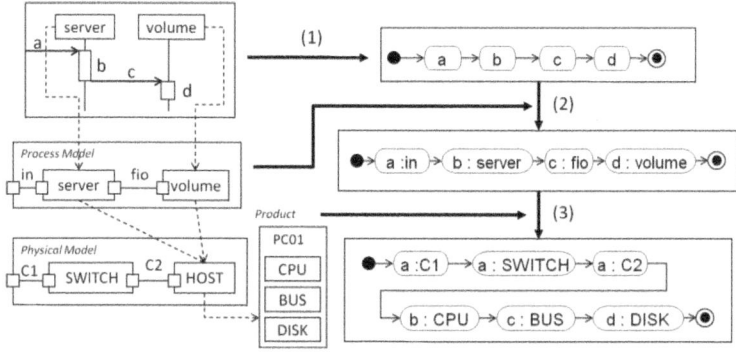

Fig. 4. Conversion from system model to simulation model

Here, the reason we first convert a sequence diagram into a graph like an activity diagram is that its semantics is much clearer. A comprehensive discussion about the semantics of a sequence diagram and its translation into formal language (such as Petri net) is presented in [9]. As explained in the paper, there are so many interpretations for a sequence diagram that we need a less ambiguous data structure for the conversion process. The whole conversion process from system models to simulation models will be addressed in another paper.

Note that the user (SE/PA) does not need to create all allocations, because some allocations such as the ones for SWITCH are inferred automatically. Also, the SE does not need to know details on products, because allocations to inner components are also inferred. Although it was not included in the example, CASSI fills other semantic gaps between the system model and simulation model. For example, if the object in the process model is a thread and its multiplicity is limited, the performance evaluation module generates nodes for allocating/releasing a thread from a thread pool, each time when the thread is used. These features reduce the cost of modeling.

3 Case Studies

We present two case studies in this section. The first is server consolidation: migration from existing systems to virtual environments without changing applications. This is one of the standard patterns in recent SI with the trend in cloud computing. The second one is the evaluation of performance of an integrated system composed of multiple system models (System of Systems: SoS) [5]. As an SoS includes various third-party systems (unknown parts) to achieve functional requirements, the system model includes some black-box parts.

3.1 Server Consolidation

We assumed migration from two Web 3 tier systems to a virtual environment in this case study. The system model for the pre-migrated (two Web 3 tier) systems is illustrated in Figures 5 and 6. Since this model is written by the PA and stored in the repository, the SE only needs to access it using CASSI.

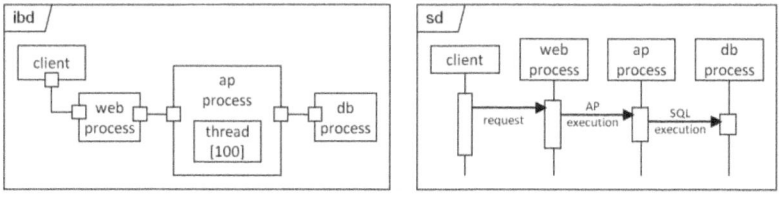

Fig. 5. Process structure of system and its behavior (process model)

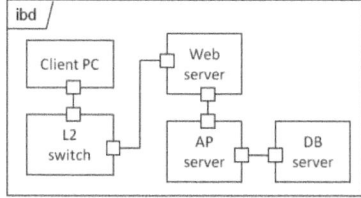

Fig. 6. Physical structure of system (physical model)

Note that each target system of migration (two Web 3 tier systems) is described with the same system model but has different CPs (different instance model). Therefore, we next customize (instantiate) the above system models with the performance data of pre-migration systems. We can edit these parameters with the application factor editing view of CASSI.

Then, the above instance model is migrated onto a post-migrated system model. Here, we assume that the post-migration system has the two host servers in Figure 7, and Web/AP processes will be migrated (allocated) on one server (Host1) and the DB process, on another server (Host2). These allocations can be done with the product allocation editing view.

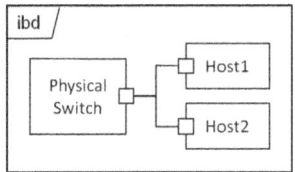

Fig. 7. Physical model of post-migrated system

The SE can now evaluate the performance of the post-integrated system, which is first done with the default configuration (Figure 8). The left indicates the utilization of each resource (here, the CPUs of Host1 and Host2), and the right indicates the response time for the request.

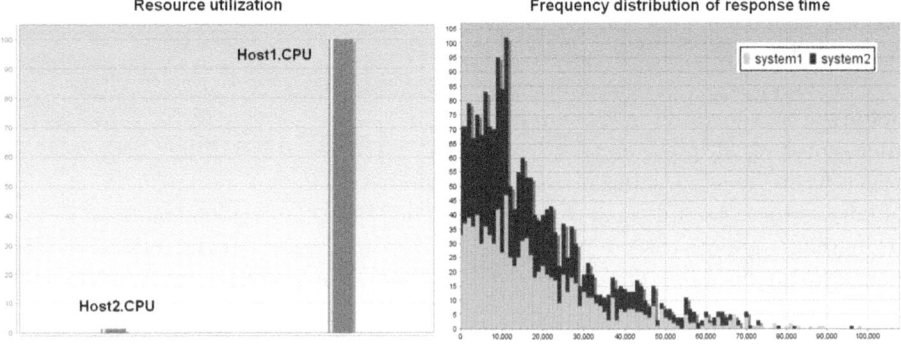

Fig. 8. Resource utilization (left) and response time for request (right) with default setting

These results indicate that the CPU of Host1, on which the APServer is migrated, will be saturated. One solution to this is to increase the number of CPUs of Host1 from 1 to 4. The SE can change this with the product allocation editing view, reevaluate it, and confirm if the performance problem has been resolved.

This case shows the following benefits.

- The SE can estimate the appropriate configuration (e.g., the number of CPU cores and number of servers) without any knowledge of the performance model of the 3 tier Web system, or virtual machine monitors.
- The SE can confirm that the post-migration system satisfies user requirements, such as the "response time for 90% of requests must be within 1 sec".
- SE only needs to modify the CP through the CP editing view on CASSI, and does not need to go into the detailed architecture of the pre/post migrated system.
- CASSI will be effective for developing applications in the PaaS environment.

3.2 System of Systems Evaluation

We dealt with an actual Web system for a network carrier in this case study (the left of Figure 9), which consisted of a reverse proxy, authorization system, and a Web system. Transactions to the reverse proxy are forwarded to the authorization system, and then the reverse proxy forwards these transactions to the Web system if authorization succeeds. The Web system consists of a Web/application server (Web/AP), database server (DB), an enterprise service bus (ESB), and a business logic server (BS). The BS is connected to an external system that provides various Web services (the right of Figure 9). Here, the details on the external system are unknown and are therefore treated as a black box.

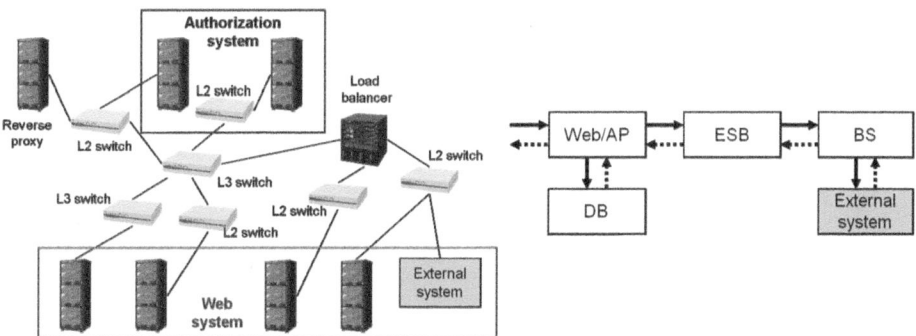

Fig. 9. Schematics of system (left) and Web system (right)

The process construction (process model) of the Web system is outlined in Figure 10. Also, the behavior of each process is modeled in detail except for the external system part. Its sequence diagram is omitted due to space limitations.

This black-box part and other part of the Web system are defined as a separated system model and the SE can combine them. When the SE is analyzing the performance of the Web system, he/she gives a reasonable value to the response time of the external system since the details on the external system are unknown.

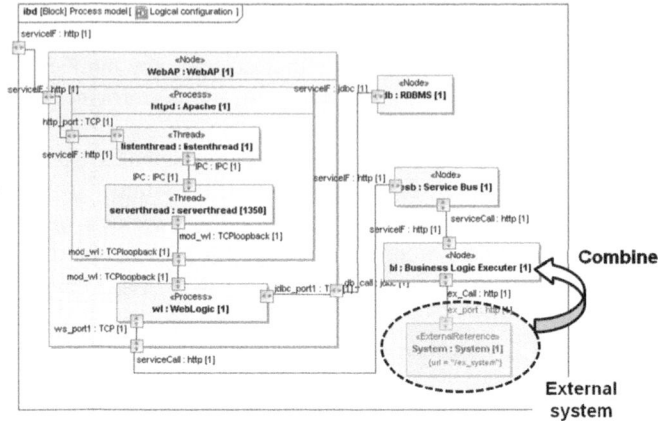

Fig. 10. Process structure of Web system including external system model

Then, CASSI analyzes the performance of this system model and the influence caused by the increase in the number of requests arriving at the external system. In the first case, we applied 1 sec to the response time of the external system. The left of Figure 11 shows the results obtained from the performance simulation. We can see that the utilization of Web/AP's CPU is saturated, i.e., it is the bottleneck in this system. In the second case, we applied a larger response time (4 sec) to the external system than to the first case. The simulation results shifted as seen at the right of Figure 11, and the utilization of thread pool in the Web/AP process is saturated. Namely, the bottleneck of this system shifted from Web/AP's CPU to Web/AP's thread pool.

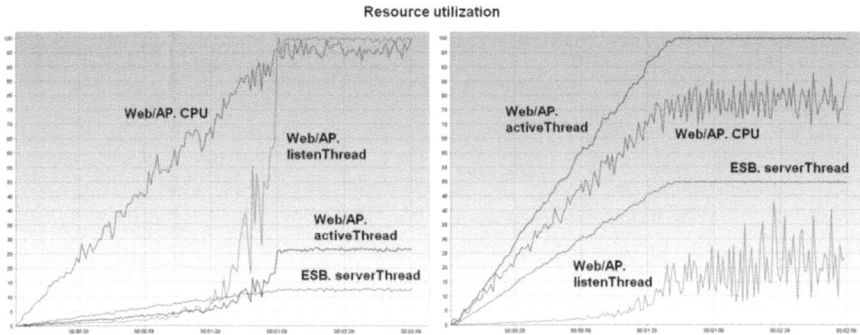

Fig. 11. Resource utilization in first (left) and second cases (right)

It is possible to detect the influence, shift of a bottleneck due to the change in the external system in this way. This bottleneck was detected because CASSI generates a simulation model that includes thread pools from the process structure shown in

Figure 10. Since the details on the external system are unknown, this external system could not be modeled explicitly. CASSI was able to incorporate this external system as a black box by defining the interaction between this black-box part and other independent systems.

This case shows the following benefits.

- CASSI can comprehensively deal with several system models regardless of whether they are white or black boxes, so the system models defined separately can be combined as needed and thus effectively reused.
- If the PA models details on the middleware in a system model, all SEs who use it can evaluate the complex nature of the system with little extra effort. It will make capacity planning much more accurate.

4 Related Work

MBSE is regarded as a promising method of developing real time embedded systems, such as avionics and automotive control systems. AADL [10] has been a successful modeling language target in developing real time embedded systems. Also, the UML profile for Modeling and Analysis of Real Time Embedded Systems (MARTE) has been standardized by OMG [6].

Also, many view models have been proposed for decades to describe enterprise architectures or technical architectures. Enterprise architectures such as [11-14] treat a wide range of enterprises and include many viewpoints. Technical (software and/or system) architectures such as the 4+1 model view [15] include a concise set of views to describe the system architecture. IBM's System Description Standard (SDS) [16] is represented by UML2, and focuses mainly on the technical aspects of an enterprise [17]. The viewpoint model for IT systems can be found in [18].

Some prior work has applied the model-based approach to SI. Balmelli et al. demonstrated practical MBSE based on a Rational Unified Process for Systems Engineering (RUP-SE) [19]. It is a heavyweight approach and requires a great deal of effort for modeling. It is cost efficient if the target system is highly mission critical or its lifetime is long. However, we consider lightweight approaches are more suitable for the majority of modern enterprise IT systems. Tsadimas et al. proposed the model-based design of an enterprise information system architecture [20]. CASSI is similar to their approach; both focus on NFR evaluations and employ a similar view model. However, CASSI takes a more pragmatic approach such as having dedicated configuration views.

Furthermore, there has been much prior work on UML-based analysis of software performance [8] [21-23]. Most of this work has required comprehensive modeling to analyze performance, which requires knowledge of performance engineering. As explained in Section 2.4, CASSI defines a more domain specific model so that the performance evaluation module can efficiently fill semantic gaps and ordinary SEs do not need special knowledge about performance engineering.

5 Conclusion and Future Work

We presented a model-based SI environment CASSI. The benefits of CASSI are summarized as follows and it becomes possible to accelerate the reuse of IT platform architectures (system models).

1. SE can efficiently adjust the configuration of the system model by evaluating NFRs. Configuration parameters can be set with a dedicated view to simplify both use and learning.
2. SE can integrate multiple system models without having to know details on uncertain parts of the system, such as third-party systems or application libraries.
3. SE can easily change the physical infrastructure by selecting a verified combination of products from the library.
4. SE can retrieve appropriate system models from the repository by querying their logical models.

Considering the nature of enterprise IT systems discussed in Section 1, we consider it is cost-efficient and pragmatic approach to accelerate the development of enterprise IT systems with model-based engineering. We are now evaluating the effectiveness of CASSI with real projects on SI, and intend to have the results published in future papers.

References

1. Friedenthal, S., Moore, A., Steiner, R.: A Practical Guide to SysML. The MK/OMG PRESS (2008)
2. Yanoo, K., Izukura, S., Xiang, J., Kimura, D., Sakaki, H., Tani, M., Tajima, S.: Evaluation of Non-functional Requirements based on Model-based System Integration Environment. In: Proceedings of the 5th International Conference on Project Management (2010)
3. OMG Systems Modeling Language (OMG SysML) Version 1.2 (2010)
4. IEEE Std 1471-2000, IEEE Recommended Practice for Architectural Description of Software-Intensive Systems (2000)
5. Kimura, D., Osaki, T., Yanoo, K., Izukura, S., Sakaki, H., Kobayashi, A.: Evaluation of IT Systems Considering Characteristics as System of Systems. In: 6th IEEE International Conference on System of Systems Engineering (2011)
6. UML Profile for MARTE: Modeling and Analysis of Real-Time Embedded Systems, http://www.omg.org/spec/MARTE/1.0
7. Xiang, J., Yanoo, K.: Automatic Static Fault Tree Analysis from System Models. In: 2010 IEEE 16th Pacific Rim International Symposium on Dependable Computing (2010)
8. Marzolla, M.: Simulation-Based Performance Modeling of UML Software Architectures, PhD Thesis TD-2004-1, Dipartimento di Informatica, Universit'a Ca' Foscari di Venezia, Italy (2004)
9. Micskei, A., Waeselynck, H.: The many meanings of UML 2 Sequence Diagrams: a survey, Software and Systems Modeling. Springer, Heidelberg (2010), doi:10.1007/s10270-010-0157-9
10. Feiler, P.H., Gluch, D.P., Hudak, J.J.: The Architecture Analysis & Design Language (AADL): An Introduction (2006)

11. Zachman, J.A.: A Framework for Information Systems Architecture. IBM Systems Journal 26(3) (1987)
12. TOGAF – The Open Group Architecture Framework, http://pubs.opengroup.org/architecture/togaf8-doc/arch/toc.html
13. The DoDAF Architecture Framework Version 2.2, http://cio-nii.defense.gov/sites/dodaf20/index.html
14. RM-ODP – The Reference Model of Open Distributed Processing, http://www.rm-odp.net
15. Kruchten, P.: Architectural Blueprints – The "4+1" View Model of Software Architecture. IEEE Software 12(6) (1995)
16. Spaas, P.: SDS R3: System Description Standard: Semantic Specification, IBM Corp. (2009)
17. Brooch, G., Mitra, T.: A Survey of Enterprise View Models, IBM Research Report, RC25049, (W1009-064) (2010)
18. Cook, D., Cripps, P., Spaas, P.: An introduction to the IBM Views and Viewpoints Framework for IT systems, IBM Corp. (2007)
19. Balmelli, L., Brown, D., Cantor, M., Mott, M.: Model-driven systems development. IBM Systems Journal 45(3) (2006)
20. Tsadimas, A., Nikolaidou, M., Anagnostopoulos, D.: Handling Non-functional Requirements in Information System Architecture Design. In: Fourth International Conference on Software Engineering Advances, ICSEA (2009)
21. Cortellessa, V., Goseva-Popstojanova, K., Appukkutty, K., Guedem, A.R., Hassan, A., Elnaggar, R., Abdelmoez, W., Ammar, H.H.: Model-Based Performance Risk Analysis. IEEE Transactions on Software Engineering 31(1) (2005)
22. Woodside, M., Petriu, D.C., Petriu, D.B., Shen, H., Israr, T., Merseguer, J.: Performance by unified model analysis (PUMA). In: 5th International Workshop on Software and Performance (2005)
23. Lee, S.-Y., Mallet, F., de Simone, R.: Dealing with AADL End-to-End Flow Latency with UML MARTE. Engineering of Complex Computer Systems (2008)

Early Experience with Agile Methodology in a Model-Driven Approach

Vinay Kulkarni, Souvik Barat, and Uday Ramteerthkar

Tata Consultancy Services, 54-B Indusutrial Estate, Hadapsar, Pune, India
{vinay.vkulkarni,souvik.barat,uday.r}@tcs.com

Abstract. We are in the business of delivering software intensive business systems using model-driven techniques. Developing suitable code generators is an important step in model-based development of purpose-specific business applications. Hence, it becomes critical to ensure that code generator development doesn't become a bottleneck for the project delivery. After establishing a sophisticated technology infrastructure to facilitate quick and easy adaptation of model-based code generators, we experimented with agile methodology. In this paper, we discuss why pure agile methodology does not work for model-driven software development. We propose a modification to the agile methodology in the form of meta-sprints as a golden mean between agile method and traditional plan-driven method. Early experience with the proposed development method is shared along with the lessons learnt.

Keywords: model-driven development, agile method, software intensive business systems.

1 Introduction

We are involved in developing business-critical software systems for large enterprises. These systems are characterized by low algorithmic complexity, database intensive operation, large size, and distributed architecture. The large size of a typical business application leads to large development team that needs to work in a coordinated manner. Choice of distributed architecture paradigm necessitates effective management of multiple technologies such as databases, online transaction processing monitors, batch schedulers, and graphical user interface platforms. Moreover, many a time the customer has non-negotiable technology platform preferences. To avail the short opportunity window, the solution needs to be delivered quickly, and being business critical in nature, is expected to be in use for a long time. Given the increasing business and technology dynamics, the latter poses a significant architectural challenge. Our experience is that no two solutions, even for the same business intent such as straight-through-processing of trade orders, back-office automation of a bank, and automation of insurance policies administration, are identical. Though there is a significant overlap across functional requirements for a given business intent, the variations are manifold too. Moreover, the higher management expects delivery of subsequent solutions for the same business intent to be significantly faster, better and cheaper.

Use of the model-driven approach helped us to separate functional concerns from technology platform thus enabling developers to focus solely on specification of business functionality in an intuitive manner closer to the problem domain [13]. Use of a component abstraction designed essentially to facilitate divide-and-conquer helped manage the large size. The application could now be modelled as a set of related components with provider – consumer relationship being made explicit. Use of component as a unit of development led to better coordinated development process wherein components could be implemented in parallel with assurance of integration into a well-formed application later [15]. A set of code generators translated component / application specifications into the desired technology platform thus delivering increased productivity, uniformly high code quality, and platform independence [14]. In our experience, no two solutions shared identical choices for design strategies, architecture, and technology platform. Since code generators encode these details while transforming application specs to implementation, every new project necessitated development of new set of code generators. Therefore, MasterCraft team was becoming a bottleneck in fast delivery of the purpose-specific business application. We devised the building block abstraction to specify the desired code generator as a hierarchical composition from which its implementation can be automatically derived [16]. In spite of these advances in the mechanisms for implementing a model-driven approach, we were still somewhat away from the desired agility and responsiveness. This led to us looking into the process aspect of model-driven development.

Agile development method is gaining industry acceptance. We argue the method cannot be used as is with model-driven approaches. We suggest modifications that need to be introduced into the agile method for delivering purpose-specific software systems at product cost. We begin with an overview of our model-driven approach and toolset. We then describe the proposed agile development methodology. We discuss early experience, benefits and lessons learnt before concluding with a summary.

2 Our Model-Driven Development Approach and Toolset

Model-driven development approach starts with defining an abstract specification that is to be transformed into a concrete implementation on a given target architecture [16]. The target architecture is usually layered with each layer representing one view of the system. Typically, business applications are implemented across three layers – user interface, application functionality and database, where a user interacts with an application through its user interface layer, application layer implements the business functionality in terms of business logic, business rules and business process, and database layer provides persistency of an application. The modeling approach constructs the application specification using different abstract views - each defining a set of properties corresponding to the layer it models. The model captures structural concerns and a high level language or meta-model is used to specify behavioral concerns. View specification in terms of the model and the text is transformed into the desired implementation.

We developed a model-driven development toolset, MasterCraft [19], for developing large database-centric business critical applications. It comprises: i) a meta modeling tool to specify an abstract view, ii) a set of modelers to populate an instance of an abstract view, iii) a set of code generators that transform each view instance to the desired implementation artifacts, iv) several build automation utilities, and v) a repository-centric component-based development method. An application specification, specified using the various modelers, can be targeted to multiple technology platforms and different architectures of choice by using suitable code generators and build automation utilities. In essence, model-based code generator interprets the model in the light of suitable design decisions and architectural strategies in order to generate code for a specific implementation technology platform. For instance, a class model can be transformed into database access layer code for JDBC or ODBC or ProC while incorporating suitable O-R mapping and currency management strategies.

Managing evolution of MasterCraft was fairly simple when target platform and technology choices for the generated application were relatively bounded. But of late, with increased number of users the demand for supporting new technologies and evolving architectures has increased significantly. Moreover, we experienced that no two generated applications made the same choices of design decisions, architectural strategies and technology platform. With MasterCraft tools interpreting the choice in order to generate the desired code, addition of a new choice or a new configuration of choices would result in modifications to these tool implementations. Our standard practice was to identify a closest-match version of the tool, create a copy of its implementation, and modify it suitably. One would expect such jump-started approach to be time and effort saving, but our experience was to the contrary – to say nothing of the increased hassles of versioning and configuration management. To overcome these issues, we re-architected MasterCraft such that a code generator is specified as a hierarchical composition of model-to-text transformation templates with well-defined extension points. A plug-in for an extension point is also a model-to-text transformation template which in turn may have its own extension points and so on [2]. This extensible plug-in architecture is implemented on Eclipse [11]. Though this enabled MasterCraft toolset to be maintained as a code generator product line, the complexities related to changes that are not predicted a priori and hence require exploration remained unaddressed. Based on the ease of evolution, we categorize MasterCraft activities into the following three kinds:

- *Extension*: Adding new extension for a predefined extension point. Impact of this kind of activity is typically localized and low. For instance, supporting a new widget such as new grid control in GUI modeler, supporting a different kind of logging capability in generated application.
- *Mutation*: Changes related to the internal structure / architecture / design of a tool so as to add a new extension point and the related refactoring effort. This impact is typically large and knowledge intensive. For instance, re-architecting a tool for the plug-in architecture, externalizing GUI screen flow.
- *Exploration*: Exploratory work for introducing new concepts into MasterCraft and proving them. For instance, code generation for deployment on public cloud.

Typical characteristics of these kinds of activities with respect to overall MasterCraft development effort are described in table 1.

Table 1. Characteristics of MasterCraft Development effort

	Extensions	Mutations	Explorations
Typical demand/year	~100	~10	3-4
Average invested effort with respect to total invested effort	50%	30%	20%
Success rate (Converted into MasterCraft feature in time)	80%	60%	40-50%
Typical turnaround time	6 months (One release cycle)	6 months – 1 years (1-2 release cycle)	> 1 year
Customer focus	High	Low	High-Low

Even with clear understanding of MasterCraft evolution characteristics, use of abstractions for improved change isolation, and use of software product line techniques, the overall turnaround time for delivering new functionality did not improve to the desired degree. This led us to look into the process aspect of MasterCraft evolution. We were using traditional waterfall method [22] along with traditional team structure for managing evolution of MasterCraft toolset. Development activities were characterized by detailed planning and rigorous review process as prescribed by waterfall model. MasterCraft development team comprised of independent teams one each for a tool catering to a specific architectural layer of the generated application, e.g. GUI team, Server side team, DB team. Each team was reasonably small in size and conformed to the traditional organization structure i.e. a team lead, one or two module leads and team members. All team leads reported to a single group leader responsible for the entire toolset. Typical turnaround time was about 6-12 months.

This mode of operation served well in early development of MasterCraft when more than 70% of activities were either exploratory or mutative and the delivery timeframes were more relaxed. With more than 50% of the development activities today being extensions, MasterCraft users naturally demand a far shorter turnaround time for new enhancement requests. We were unable to meet this demand with existing team structure using the waterfall model of development. We discovered several reasons for these limitations. It was difficult to plan for small and semi-volatile requirements. The low value-add activities such as status reporting, tracking meetings and so on made the operational process sluggish. Rapidly changing requirements and lack of coordination between different sub-teams led to high amount of rework. Fewer and far spaced deliveries meant infrequent and delayed user feedback resulting eventually in low team morale. The waterfall model didn't provide the necessary visibility at the desired frequency to customer about the development artifacts. As a result, work reprioritization suffered. In addition, we found that existing methodology left little scope for partial (and incremental) delivery for quick-win (and continuous improvement), and early demonstration of research ideas for end-users' feedback.

3   Proposed Development Methodology

With the principal objectives of delivering functionality that brings value to the customers, establishing better mechanisms for feedback from all stakeholders, and enabling quick transformation of an idea/requirement into a set of MasterCraft features, we found Agile Manifesto [18] as the best bet for many reasons. Existing approach heavily depended on documentation for communication between the phases that, we felt, could be eliminated to some extent by having more and closer interactions of customer with tool and solution builders – it was always a demand to show some working software than say, a usecase diagram or a design document. In existing approach, one could get to see a working version after a significant time has elapsed after the requirements were communicated. Thus, it was hard to establish quick-wins with the existing approach. Moreover, most certainly the requirements would have undergone a change thus necessitating rework. Agile method puts greater stress on close collaboration with the customer as opposed to a contract. As advised in Agile methodology, we felt that responding to a change requisitioned by the customer should take precedence over following a plan.

However, we found some limitations of using Agile methodology for all kinds of MasterCraft development activities. Agile methods haven't been as useful for large development teams comprised of members having wide variance in expertise levels and operating in a geographically distributed manner [10]. In addition, some characteristics of MasterCraft created hindrances for applying Agile methodology uniformly. We observed that *mutation* and *exploration* kind of changes are not suitable for Agile method. Catering to mutative changes demands in-depth analysis, experimentation and detailed documentation of the results, observations and conclusions. These activities are difficult to achieve in the short sprint cycles advocated by Agile method. Exploratory work demands in-depth study and analysis which is hard to synchronize with sprint timelines. Agile method advocates to keep customer aware of all decisions, however, that may create unnecessary pressure during exploratory stage and also entail significant product testing and quality assurance effort at the exploratory stage itself. Agile method puts greater stress on working software as opposed to documentation, however, low / no documentation of design rationale and far reaching changes may create problems for hassle-free maintenance and smooth induction. Customer visibility into sprint-backlogs and planning means there is little opportunity for long term research activities. Moreover, defining sprint-backlogs based purely on customer requirements is not always possible – as MasterCraft is a set of interrelated tools, sometimes the order of scoping a feature in a sprint-backlog depends on internal factors rather than purely customer needs.

To overcome these concerns, we modified the standard Agile methodology as depicted in Fig. 1. We organized the development process at two levels which execute

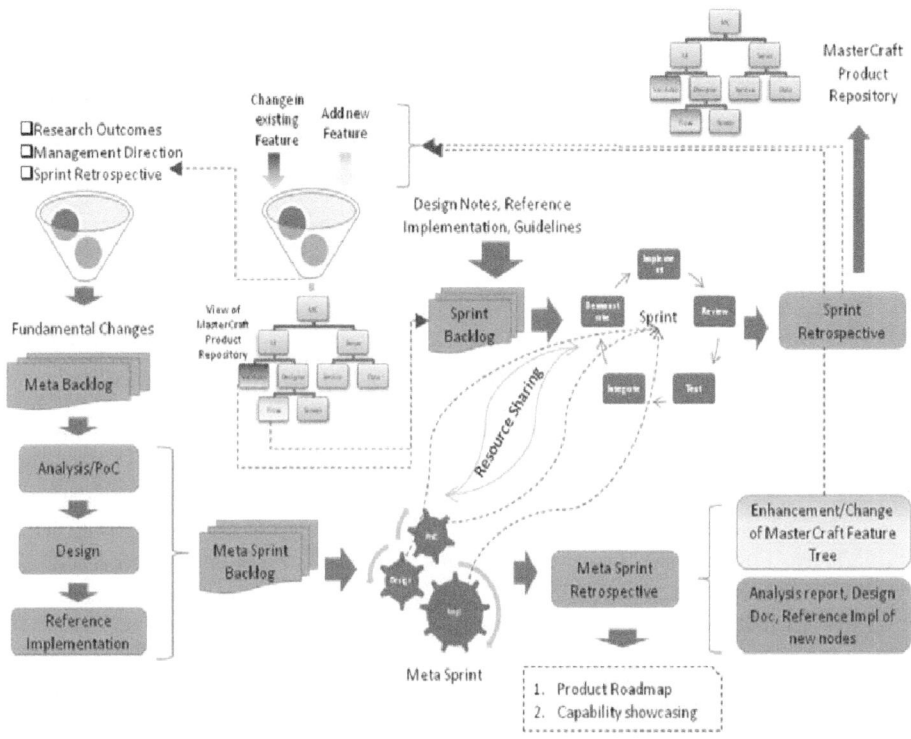

Fig. 1. Adapted Agile Methodology for MasterCraftDevelopment

as parallel threads having periodic synchronization. A feature backlog comprising of new feature requests and change requests drives the development process [7]. Items that are well-understood are prioritized to be taken up for implementation through a series of normal sprints. Changes that are more fundamental in nature and require detailed exploration or even research are prioritized to be taken up for implementation through a series of longer duration sprints that we term as meta-sprints. Meta-sprints differ from normal sprints in that they don't necessarily produce working software as deliverable. Instead, meta-sprints carry out precise investigations the results of which enable product evolution through normal sprints which is similar to SCRUM [24] iteration. Essentially, meta-sprint is to understand the problem statement, to determine the *what* part of the solution, and to break the what part into smaller units of work (work breakdown structures) such that these can be scoped in sprint iteration(s). Meta-sprint also deals with the inherent precedence amongst the units of work. Typically, meta-sprints are of a longer duration than normal sprints. For instance, we are gravitating towards a 12-week meta-sprint whereas normal sprint lasts for 4 weeks. Unlike Agile method, meta-sprint deliverables are not working software but can be a design document, a proof-of-concept implementation, evaluation of a set of design strategies, work breakdown structures, or prioritization preferences for sprints

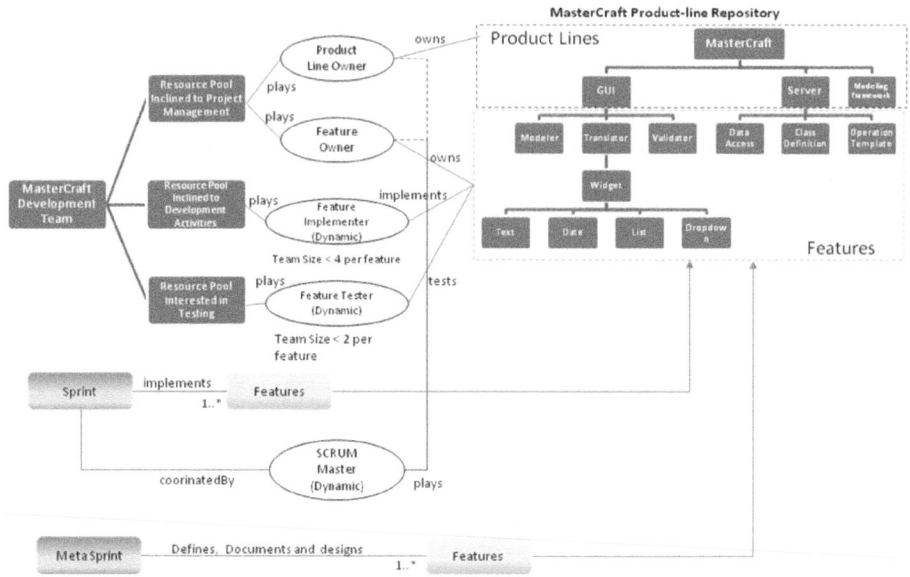

Fig. 2. MasterCraft productline team structure with roles and responsibilities

iteration. Unlike traditional method, meta-sprint puts an upper bound in terms of time (and hence effort) on exploratory and mutative activities. In addition, meta-sprint deliverables facilitate subsequent normal sprints. Thus, development proceeds on two parallel threads namely meta-sprint and sprint with periodic synchronization between the two threads. We use a planning technique, similar to Timeboxing planning technique [12], for synchronizing instances of the two threads. Our planning technique emphasizes on agreed timeline for deliverables instead of the scope of the deliverables i.e. compromise on the scope of the delivery of an iteration to maintain the timeline. Both the threads share a common feature list or sprint-backlog. Theoretically, one can possibly think of meta-meta-sprint, meta-meta-meta-sprint and so on. However, in our experience, so far two levels seem to suffice.

We used feature model notation to declaratively state MasterCraft capabilities. Since MasterCraft code generators themselves are specified declaratively in a model form, establishing traceability from the feature model to code generator specs was relatively straightforward [16 and 17]. Repository-centric model-driven nature of MasterCraft ensured that its feature model can act as the sole driver for the evolution process. Meta sprint delivers working prototypes/concept notes and a proposed feature tree with new feature/option whereas sprint delivers a working MasterCraft with new features/options. We used burn-down charts as an indicator of health and hygiene of overall MasterCraft.

Since developing suitable code generators is an important step in model-based development of purpose-specific business applications, it becomes critical to ensure that code generator development doesn't become a bottleneck for the project delivery. We used meta-sprints primarily to manage evolution of MasterCraft and normal sprints to manage delivery of application using MasterCraft. Therefore, meta-sprints were needed only in the initial stages of the project delivery. However, there were occasions when meta-sprints were resorted to in the light of significant changes requested by customer at a later stage of project delivery. The two level process, and repository-centricity and model-driven nature of both MasterCraft and application development help address such changes in a tractable manner.

Development team was restructured to make everyone accountable and responsible for delivering MasterCraft feature(s). We restructured our development team as shown in Fig. 2. Essentially, we moved the ownership from Project Lead / Module Lead to a feature owner for delivering or exploring a feature, and scrum–master for executing iterations. To improve involvement, we encouraged members to play different roles for different sprints. We encouraged all stakeholders to participate in decision-making. Essentially, sprint flow is a minor adaptation of SCRUM methodology. In addition, we set some rules for smooth execution of sprints. For instance,

- All stakeholders to be involved in scoping the sprint backlog.
- Items exceeding 5% schedule slippage to be automatically dropped from the current sprint-backlog.
- Each sprint to produce an *adequately tested* working version.
- A sprint to last for 4 weeks out of which- 3 weeks to be reserved for development, internal testing and review, and one week for integration and integration testing.
- Stand-up meetings to be conducted as and when required but at least twice a week.

4 Early Results, Benefits and Lessons Learnt

With the proposed development method, we observed slow but steady improvement in delivery of features on time. In first iteration we delivered only 50% of the promised sprint-backlog with a delay of 2 weeks. But results improved significantly in subsequent iterations, and we could achieve our target on time within 3 sprints. We conducted many sprints of duration 4-5 weeks and a few meta-sprints of duration 2-3 months. About 15-20 features were implemented in each sprint and 1-2 research ideas/mutative changes were taken up in each meta-sprint. The usual sprints worked well for *extension* kind of evolution with fairly accurate effort estimation. We tried to use normal sprint for *mutation* and *exploration* kinds of activities, but the result was not very positive. However, those worked well with the proposed approach with improved turn-around as compared to the existing approach. Sprint and meta-sprint bring several tangible and intangible values to the overall development. Those are documented in table 2.

Several literature surveys, case studies and our early experience essentially suggest a limited scope of using Agile methodology, i.e. it is more effective in a context where development infrastructure and development team are matured, development

Table 2. Deliverables and benefits of Sprint and Meta-sprint

	Sprint	Meta-Sprint
Turnaround time from requirement to delivery	4 weeks as compared to 6 months for traditional approach	3 months as compared to minimum 6 months for traditional approach
Productivity	High due to continuous focus on deliverable unit and better issue resolution.	Better as research and exploratory efforts channelize through proper execution path.
Customer Expectation Management	A demonstrable version with latest feature is always available	A demonstrable PoC/Prototype is available
Resource Utilization	High	Not changed from traditional approach.
Team morale	High (nobody, specially juniors, feels left out at any time of development activity)	High due to more frequent interaction with end-users and early feedback.
Rework effort	Low due to early feedback	Low due to early demonstration with a working prototype.

architecture and core design decisions are proven, and requirements are relatively dynamic but less critical in terms of rework for any change. The effective context of Agile methodology with respect to traditional methodology along with the increased scope of the context while adapting meta-sprint flow is depicted in Fig. 3. It worked well for mutative and exploratory activities. However we identified several challenges that need to be addressed for better execution of sprints and meta-sprints,

Team Maturity: Sprint and meta-sprint both work well for teams strong on knowledge and experience. However, inducting new people in the team becomes a challenge as every team member is fully occupied throughout the iteration.

Automated Testing: Lack of automation in integration testing led to longer sprint durations.

Configuration Management: Typically, many parallel teams are working for different sets of features; hence a better configuration management tool is required.

Document Generation: As the method puts more stress on producing working software over documentation, we resorted to generation of minimal documentation from the models. As MasterCraft code generators are also generated from their model specifications, this strategy sufficed for documenting generated applications as well as the code generation toolset.

Migration of Models: Some change requests involved change in the meta models. These changes resulted in a side-effect – earlier models had to be migrated to the new meta model. Here, at times, the short sprint cycles were a challenge.

There were many lessons learnt while moving a large project from traditional development method to the proposed development method. We took time to stabilize into the new method. Initial estimates were off by a large margin and burn charts were always red. Working on smaller chunks with frequent synchronization resulted in on-time and high quality delivery. Non-technical issues like coordination, motivation and

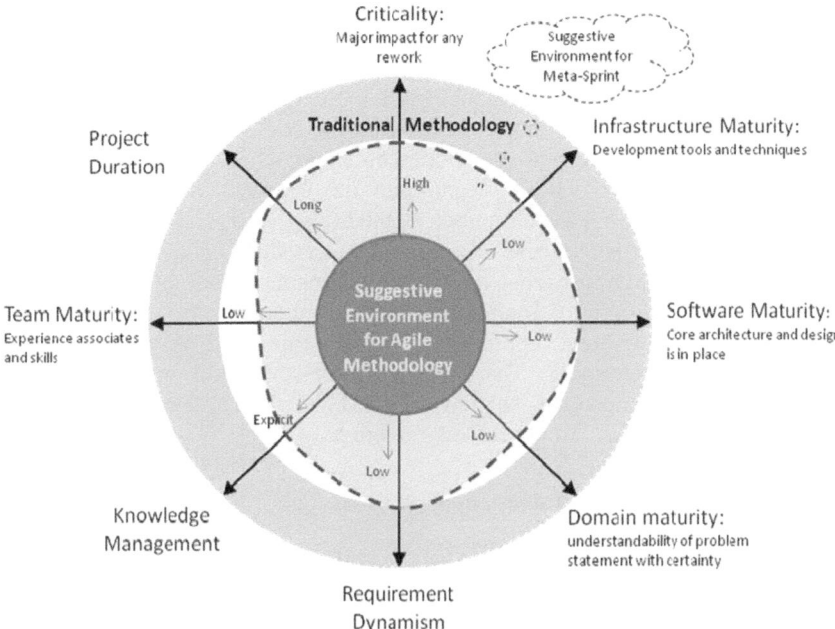

Fig. 3. Environment of different methodologies and fitment of meta-sprint

taking ownership seemed to be the key success factors. We experienced the necessity of a motivated scrum master in the transition phase for bringing an attitude change in the entire team. We learnt not to be particular about the process – whether to use agile, traditional or something in-between like meta-sprint. Letting the requirement decide the development process rather than any organizational diktat seemed to work. For example MasterCraft uses product line architecture to guide product evolution. Thus visualization of requirements in the form of a feature model is very intuitive. Early experience indicates that a hybrid approach is better for projects in incubation stage. Today, MasterCraft is a mature software system with more than 50% work being of extension kind. Therefore, pure Agile methodology works well. It might not have worked in the early stages where core architecture and design were being formulated.

5 Related Work

Numerous development methods and models have been proposed for developing applications in a systematic and efficient manner. Fundamentally, they are categorized into two kinds – Plan-driven approach and Agile approach. The Plan-driven approach, like waterfall model, spiral model, V-model, focuses on stability and higher assurance for a predefined sets of requirements. On the other hand, Agile approach, such as XP [3], Crystal Clear [8], Dynamic System Development Method [23] Feature Driven Development [21], and SCRUM [24], advocates faster development with increased customer satisfaction for dynamic requirements using iterative and incremental development techniques [4]. As argued in [4] we also experienced that there are some home grounds for pure plan-based approach and Agile approach but appropriate balancing of these two approaches provides better handle for managing dynamic requirements with increased stability and assurance. In the literature, several tailored development approaches are recommended for developing applications such as Lean/Agile development methodology [6], and SCRUM and CMMI based development methodology [26]; and few approaches are also presented to systematize these tailoring processes with increased precision [5, 9]. However these tailored approaches address development of one-off application only. The need of delivering a set of applications that vary along multiple dimensions is not met. We presented a tailored approach to address this need of managed evolution using model-based techniques. The proposed meta-sprint follows agile philosophy rather than any specific process, such as SCRUM, XP, FDD. The core differences of sprint and meta-sprint flow are discussed in table 3.

Table 3. Sprint Vs Meta-Sprint

	Sprint	Meta-sprint
Qualifying criteria	No impact on the core architecture/design or concept.	Fundamental changes to MasterCraft
Output	Working MasterCraft with new features	Approach note, reference implementation of features, prospective feature tree
Timeline	4-5 weeks (fixed)	2-3 months (varies)
Communication	Informal	Formal but not in specific format
Knowledge Management	Tacit	Explicit
Visibility	To all stake-holders	Opaque to external stakeholders, e.g. customers.

Essentially, meta-sprint relaxes the criteria of plan-based approach by limiting the planning only for strategic and high-level activities, and monitoring them in terms of observable outcomes instead of recording day-to-day progresses. Similarly, it relaxes some of the mandates of Agile approach such as working software as a deliverable at the end of each cycle, 3-6 weeks cycle time and total visibility to all the stakeholders. With these adaptations in development methodology, we could overcome the limiting factors [10, 20] of both kinds of methodologies while retaining the benefits of both. We adapted Timeboxing technique [12] suitably to synchronize different iterations of meta-sprint and sprint threads. On the other hand, the meta-sprint differs from meta-SCRUM [25] to some extent as meta-sprint details a requirement and analyzes it further to break a larger activity into smaller units that can be accommodated in sprint whereas meta-SCRUM synchronizes and plans several interrelated sprints to manage them flawlessly.

The use of Agile methodology in model-driven development is not very prevalent yet, except tailored Agile approaches, such as Agile model driven development [1]. However these approaches are restricted to modeling activities rather than emphasizing on delivering entire application from the models. On the contrary, we argue that true agility in model-driven development is possible only when code generators can also be adapted as quickly as application models.

6 Summary

We are in the business of delivering software intensive business systems using model-driven techniques. Since developing suitable code generators is an important step in model-based development of purpose-specific business applications, it becomes critical to ensure that code generator development doesn't become a bottleneck for the project delivery. After having put in place sophisticated technology infrastructure in place to facilitate quick and easy adaptation of model-based code generators, we experimented with agile methodology. We discussed why pure Agile methodology does not work for model-driven software development. We proposed modification to the Agile method in the form of meta-sprints as a golden mean between Agile method and traditional plan-driven method. Unlike Agile method, meta-sprint deliverables are not working software but could be a design document, a proof-of-concept implementation, evaluation of a set of design strategies etc. Unlike traditional method, meta-sprint puts an upper bound in terms of time (and hence effort) on exploratory activities. In addition, meta-sprint deliverables facilitate subsequent normal sprints. Thus development proceeds on two parallel threads namely meta-sprint and sprint with periodic synchronization between the two threads.

Early results of using Agile methodology are encouraging with a note that it is not applicable for all kinds of development activities and needs considerable preparedness for deployment in practice. We adapted true agile methodology by introducing meta-sprint concept for mutative and exploratory work; and used this methodology only after plug-in architecture and suitable tools were in place. Though our objective is to channelize more development activity through sprint stream than meta-sprint stream and establish an agile development environment, we would like to continue with a relatively relaxed environment (meta-sprint) for exploratory and knowledge intensive activities. Our early results show that this kind of hybrid development environment is better suited for model-driven software development.

References

1. Ambler, S.W.: Agile Model Driven Development, AMDD (2007), http://www.agilemodeling.com/essays/amdd.htm
2. Barat, S., Kulkarni, V.: Developing configurable extensible code generators for model-driven development approach. In: SEKE, pp. 577–582 (2010)
3. Beck, K.: Extreme Programming Explained: Embrace Change. Addison-Wesley, MA (2000)
4. Boehm, B., Turner, R.: Observations on Balancing Discipline and Agility. In: Proceedings of the Agile Development Conference, ADC 2003. IEEE Computer Society, Los Alamitos (2003)

5. Cao, L., Mohan, K., Xu, P., Ramesh, B.: A framework for adapting agile development methodologies. EJIS 18(4), 332–343 (2009)
6. Cawley, O., Wang, X., Richardson, I.: Lean/Agile Software Development Methodologies in Regulated Environments – State of the Art. In: Abrahamsson, P., Oza, N. (eds.) LESS 2010. LNBIP, vol. 65, pp. 31–36. Springer, Heidelberg (2010)
7. Cockburn, A.: Agile Software Development. Addison-Wesley Professional, Reading (2001) ISBN 0-201-69969-9
8. Cockburn, A.: Crystal Clear, A Human-Powered Methodology for Small Teams. Addison-Wesley Professional, Reading (2004) ISBN 0-201-69947-8
9. Conboy, K., Fitzgerald, B.: Method and developer characteristics for effective agile method tailoring: A study of XP expert opinion. ACM Trans. Softw. Eng. Methodol. 20(1) (2010)
10. Dybå, T., Dingsøyr, T.: Empirical studies of agile software development: A systematic review. Information & Software Technology 50(9-10), 833–859 (2008)
11. Eclipse, http://www.eclipse.org/
12. Jalote, P., Palit, A., Kurien, P., Peethamber, V.T.: Timeboxing: a process model for iterative software development. Journal of Systems and Software 70(1-2), 117–127 (2004)
13. Kulkarni, V., Venkatesh, R., Reddy, S.: Generating enterprise applications from models. In: Bruel, J.-M., Bellahsène, Z. (eds.) OOIS 2002. LNCS, vol. 2426, pp. 270–279. Springer, Heidelberg (2002)
14. Kulkarni, V., Reddy, S.: Model-Driven Development of Enterprise Applications. UML Satellite Activities, 118–128 (2004)
15. Kulkarni, V., Reddy, S.: Introducing MDA in a large IT consultancy organization. APSEC, 419–426 (2006)
16. Kulkarni, V., Reddy, S.: An abstraction for reusable MDD components: model-based generation of model-based code generators. In: GPCE, pp. 181–184 (2008)
17. Kulkarni, V.: Use of SPLE to deliver Custom Solutions at Product Cost - Challenges and Way forward. In: Product LinE Approaches in Software Engineering (PLEASE 2011)Conjunction with the 33nd International Conference on Software Engineering, ICSE 2011 (2011)
18. Manifesto for Agile Software Development - agilemanifesto.org/
19. MasterCraft – Component-based Development Environment. Technical Documents. Tata Research Development and Design Centre, http://www.tata-mastercraft.com
20. Nerur, S., Mahapatra, R., Mangalaraj, G.: Challenges of Migrating to Agile Methodologies. Communications of the ACM 48(5) (May 2005)
21. Palmer, S.R., Felsing, J.M.: A Practical Guide to Feature-Driven Development. Prentice Hall, Englewood Cliffs (ISBN 0-13-067615-2)
22. Royce, W.: Managing the Development of Large Software Systems. In: Proceedings of IEEE WESCON 26, pp. 1–9 (August), http://www.cs.umd.edu/class/spring2003/cmsc838p/Process/waterfall.pdf
23. Salo, A., Warsta, R.: Agile Software Development Methods: Review and Analysis, vol. 478, pp. 61–68. VTT Publications (2002)
24. Schwaber, K., Beedle, M.: Agile Software Development with SCRUM. Prentice Hall, Englewood Cliffs (2001)
25. Sutherland, J.: Future of scrum: parallel pipelining of sprints in complex projects. In: Agile Conference (2005)
26. Sutherland, J., Jakobsen, C.R., Johnson, K.: Scrum and CMMI Level 5: The Magic Potion for Code Warriors, agile. In: AGILE 2007, pp. 272–278 (2007)

Finding Models in Model-Based Development
(Abstract)

Wolfram Schulte and Ethan Jackson

Microsoft Research, Redmond, WA
{schulte,ejackson}@microsoft.com

Model-based development focuses on creating and manipulating domain models. We present the FORMULA language and its tool environment for specifying, documenting, and analyzing models.

The FORMULA language is based on the observation that constraints are ubiquitous. For instance, a real-time system must meet its deadlines, a software deployment must obey resource constraints, a compiler must preserve the meaning of its source language. Each design problem is defined w.r.t. some abstraction; in FORMULA these abstractions are called domains. A domain encapsulates a set of data structures used to formalize key concepts, and *logic programming* is used to describe restrictions on the set of possible solutions. Complex systems have a multitude of facets. Our language provides a rich set of domain composition operators for building new abstractions. Similarly, transforms synthesize other models at the same or different level of abstractions. FORMULA has a standard first-order logic semantics.

The FORMULA solver answers queries under the *open-world-assumption*, which considers that not all facts are known *a priori*. Evaluating a query under this assumption means searching for a finite set of facts where the program satisfies the query. These missing facts are the solutions to our modeling problems, *e.g.* legal instances of schedules, feasible deployments, necessary synchronization constraints. In the end, FORMULA translates to state-of-the-art satisfiability-modulo-theory solvers, which search through complex spaces in the presence of many constraints.

FORMULA draws on methods from type theory, logic programming, and automatic theorem proving. It has successfully been applied to a number of domains from scheduling, meta-modeling and configuration management, to software deployment. More information at: **http://research.microsoft.com/formula**. Joint work with Nikolaj Bjorner, Dirk Seifert, Markus Dahlweid, and Thomas Santen.

References

1. Jackson, E.K., Kang, E., Dahlweid, M., Seifert, D., Santen, T.: Components, Platforms and Possibilities: Towards Generic Automation for MDA. In: EMSOFT, pp. 39–48 (2010)
2. Jackson, E.K., Balasubramanian, D., Levendovszky, T.: Reasoning about Metamodeling with Formal Specifications and Automatic Proofs. In: Whittle, J., Clark, T., Kühne, T. (eds.) MODELS 2011. LNCS, vol. 6981, pp. 647–661. Springer, Heidelberg (2011)
3. Jackson, E.K., Bjørner, N., Schulte, W.: Canonical regular types. In: ICLP (Technical Communications), pp. 73–83 (2011)

CD2Alloy: Class Diagrams Analysis Using Alloy Revisited

Shahar Maoz*, Jan Oliver Ringert**, and Bernhard Rumpe

Software Engineering
RWTH Aachen University, Germany
http://www.se-rwth.de/

Abstract. We present CD2Alloy, a novel, powerful translation of UML class diagrams (CDs) to Alloy. Unlike existing translations, which are based on a shallow embedding strategy, and are thus limited to checking consistency and generating conforming object models of a single CD, and support a limited set of CD language features, CD2Alloy uses a deeper embedding strategy. Rather than mapping each CD construct to a semantically equivalent Alloy construct, CD2Alloy defines (some) CD constructs as new concepts within Alloy. This enables solving several analysis problems that involve more than one CD and could not be solved by earlier works, and supporting an extended list of CD language features. The ideas are implemented in a prototype Eclipse plug-in. The work advances the state-of-the-art in CD analysis, and can also be viewed as an interesting case study for the different possible translations of one modeling language to another, their strengths and weaknesses.

1 Introduction

The analysis of artifacts in one modeling language can, in many cases, be done using a semantics preserving translation to another language, and a reversed translation, back from the analysis results to the concepts of the first language. Often, more than one possible translation may be developed, and so, the definition of alternative translations, their implementation, and a comparative discussion on their strengths and weaknesses is worthwhile.

A UML class diagram (CD) can be analyzed using a translation to Alloy [1,14]. The Alloy module is analyzed using a SAT solver, and the analysis result, an instance of the module, if any, can be translated back to the UML domain, as an object diagram. Existing translations [2,3,18,22], however, are limited to this basic analysis of a single CD and are missing support for several CD language features, e.g., multiple inheritance and interface implementation, mainly because these features of CDs do not have direct, immediate counterparts in Alloy. In other words, they use a shallow embedding strategy.

---

* S. Maoz acknowledges support from a postdoctoral Minerva Fellowship, funded by the German Federal Ministry for Education and Research.
** J.O. Ringert is supported by the DFG GK/1298 AlgoSyn.

In this paper we present CD2Alloy, a new, alternative translation of UML CDs to Alloy, which is based on a deeper embedding strategy. Rather than mapping each CD construct to a semantically equivalent Alloy construct, our translation defines (some of) the CD constructs as new concepts within Alloy. For example, class inheritance is not mapped to its Alloy's counterpart — the `extends` keyword. Instead, it is defined using several of Alloy's language constructs — facts, functions, and predicates, whose semantics reflects the semantics of class inheritance in CDs.

The alternative translation we present has several advantages. First, it allows us to support more CD language features, in particular those features that do not have direct counterparts in Alloy, such as multiple inheritance and interface implementation. Second, significantly, it allows us to solve several analysis problems that go beyond the basic consistency check and instance generation tasks of a single CD, e.g., the analysis of the intersection of two CDs (i.e., generating common object models), the comparison of two CDs (checking if one is a refinement of the other), etc. These would have been very difficult, if not impossible, to support using existing translations from the literature.

Technically, as concrete languages we use the CD and object diagrams (OD) sublanguages of UML/P [20], a conceptually refined and simplified variant of UML designed for low-level design and implementation. Our semantics of CDs and ODs are based on [4,8,10] and are given in terms of sets of objects and relationships between these objects.

We define a transformation that takes one or more CDs and outputs an Alloy module. The Alloy module can then be analyzed with the Alloy Analyzer. Finally, using another transformation, instances of the Alloy module, if any, as found by the SAT solver connected to the Alloy Analyzer, are translated from Alloy back to ODs. The transformations are presented in Sect. 3. As mentioned above, the new translation allows us not only to support an extended list of CD language features but also to solve analysis problems that involve a number of CDs and could not have been solved before. We discuss the extension of the transformation from a single CD to multiple CDs, and some of the analysis problems we solve, in Sect. 4.

Our work is fully implemented in a prototype Eclipse plug-in we call CD2Alloy. CD2Alloy allows the engineer to edit a CD, to analyze it using Alloy, and to view the instances that the SAT solver finds, if any, back in the form of ODs. The analysis is fully automated, so the engineer need not see the generated Alloy code. We discuss the implementation in Sect. 5.

Sect. 2 gives brief background on the CD and OD languages and a short overview of Alloy. Sect. 3 describes our new translation from CDs to Alloy and back to ODs, side by side with the shallow translation described in [3]. Sect. 4 shows how the new transformation can be used to solve several analysis problems involving more than one CD. Sect. 5 presents the CD2Alloy plug-in. Sect. 6 summarises the comparison between the existing shallow translations and the new one, considering their strengths and weaknesses. Sect. 7 discusses related work and Sect. 8 concludes.

2 Preliminaries

2.1 Class and Object Diagrams

As concrete languages we use the CD and OD sublanguages of UML/P [20]. UML/P is a conceptually refined and simplified variant of UML designed for low-level design and implementation. Our semantics of CDs is based on [4,8,10] and is given in terms of sets of objects and relationships between these objects. More formally, the semantics is defined using three parts: (1) a definition of the syntactic domain, i.e., the syntax of the modeling language CD and its context conditions (we use MontiCore [15] for this), (2) a semantic domain, in our case, a subset of the System Model (see [4,8]) OM, consisting of all finite object models, and (3) a mapping $sem : CD \rightarrow \mathcal{P}(OM)$, which relates each syntactically well-formed CD to a set of constructs in the semantic domain OM. A thorough and formal account of the semantics can be found in [8].

2.2 A Brief Overview of Alloy

Alloy [1,14] is a textual modeling language based on relational first-order logic. An Alloy module consists of signature declarations, fields, facts and predicates. Each signature denotes a set of atoms, which are the basic entities in Alloy. Relations between two or more signatures are represented using fields and are interpreted as sets of tuples of atoms. Facts are statements that define constraints on the elements of the model. Predicates are parametrized constraints. A predicate can be included in other predicates or facts.

Alloy modules can be analyzed using Alloy Analyzer, a fully automated constraint solver. This is done by a translation of the module into a Boolean expression, which is analyzed by SAT solvers embedded within the Analyzer. The analysis is based on an exhaustive search for instances of the module, bounded by a user-specified scope, which limits the number of atoms for each signature in an instance of the system that the solver analyzes. The Analyzer can check for the validity of user-specified assertions: if an instance that violates the assertion is found within the given scope, the assertion is not valid, but if no instance is found, the assertion might be invalid in a larger scope. Used in the opposite way, the Analyzer can look for instances of user-specified predicates: if the predicate is satisfiable within the given scope, the Analyzer will find an instance that proves it, but if not, the predicate may be satisfiable in a larger scope. For a complete and detailed account of Alloy see [14].

3 The CD2Alloy Translation

We show our translation from CD to Alloy and from Alloy's instances back to ODs. We present these side by side with the shallow translation, described in [3], and focus on the key technical differences between the two (we chose to compare with [3] because it provides an implementation and appears to be the most advanced work of the shallow embedding approaches). The presentation

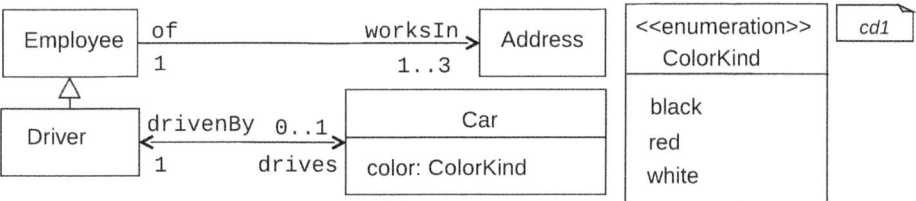

Fig. 1. cd_1, an example class diagram with classes, attributes, enumerations, associations with multiplicities, and inheritance

```
1  // Names of fields/associations in classes of the model
2  abstract sig FName {}
3
4  // Parent of all classes relating fields and values
5  abstract sig Obj { get: FName -> {Obj + Val + EnumVal} }
6
7  // Values of fields
8  abstract sig Val {}
9
10 // No values can exist on their own
11 fact { all v: Val | some f: FName | v in Obj.get[f] }
12
13 // Names of enum values in enums of the model
14 abstract sig EnumVal {}
15
16 // No enum values can exist on their own
17 fact { all v: EnumVal | some f: FName | v in Obj.get[f] }
```

Listing 1.1. Excerpt from the generic part of our translation: FName, Obj, Val, and EnumVal signatures and related facts

uses the CD of Fig. 1 as a running example. We begin with an overview of our approach and continue with specific examples for various features. The complete translation will appear in an extended version of this paper.

3.1 From CD to Alloy

CD2Alloy takes a CD as input and generates an Alloy module. The module consists of a generic part (described below) and a CD specific part, which includes a predicate that describes the CD itself.

The Generic Part. List. 1.1 shows the abstract signature FName used to represent association role names and attribute names for all classes in the module. The abstract signature Obj is the parent of all classes in the module; its get Alloy field relates it and an FName to instances of Obj, Val, and EnumVal. The

```
pred ObjAttrib[objs:set Obj,
        fName:one FName, fType:set {Obj + Val + EnumVal}] {
    objs.get[fName] in fType
    all o: objs| one o.get[fName] }

pred ObjNoFName[objs:set Obj, fName:set FName] {
    no objs.get[fName] }

pred ObjUAttrib[objs:set Obj,
        fName:one FName, fType:set Obj, up: Int] {
    objs.get[fName] in fType
    all o: objs| (#o.get[fName] =< up) }
```

Listing 1.2. Excerpt from the generic part of our translation: parametrized predicates for the relations between objects and their fields, and for their multiplicities

abstract signature `Val`, which we use to represent all predefined types (i.e., primitive types and other types that are not defined as classes in the CD). Values of enumeration types are represented using the signature `EnumVal`. Enumeration values and primitive values should only appear in an instance if they are referenced by an object (as specified by the facts in line 11 and line 17).

List. 1.2 shows some of the generic, parametrized predicates responsible for specifying the relation between objects and fields: `ObjAttrib` limits `objs.get[fName]` to the correct field's type and ensures that there is exactly one object, value, or enumeration value related to the field name by the `get` relation; `ObjFNames` is used to ensure objects do not have field names other than the ones stated in the CD. List. 1.2 also shows one of the generic predicates responsible for specifying association multiplicities: `ObjUAttrib` provides an upper bound for the number of objects in the set represented by the `get` relation for a specified role name.

All the above are generic, that is, they are common to all generated modules, independent of the input CD at hand. We now move to the parts that are specific to the input CD, and present specific examples of various features.

Classes and Attributes. Consider a fragment of the CD shown in Fig. 1 consisting of only the class `Car` and its `color` attribute. With the transformation of [3], this fragment translates to the Alloy code shown in List. 1.3. In our transformation, this fragment translates to the Alloy code shown in List. 1.4.

Associations. We continue with associations, where directions and multiplicity ranges need to be expressed. To support bidirectional associations and custom multiplicity ranges in the shallow translation of [3], engineers are required to manually write the specific OCL constraints that characterize these features, because Alloy does not have a direct counterpart to the concept of association and its signature field definition does not have explicit built-in support for

```
1  sig Car{color:one ColorKind}
2  abstract sig ColorKind{}
3  one sig black extends ColorKind{}
4  one sig red extends ColorKind{}
5  one sig white extends ColorKind{}
```

Listing 1.3. Car with color in the translation of [3]

```
1  one sig color extends FName {}
2
3  lone sig enum_ColorKind_black extends EnumVal {}
4  lone sig enum_ColorKind_red extends EnumVal {}
5  lone sig enum_ColorKind_white extends EnumVal {}
6
7  sig Car extends Obj {}
8
9  fun ColorKindEnum: set EnumVal {
10    enum_ColorKind_black +
11    enum_ColorKind_red +
12    enum_ColorKind_white }
13
14 pred cd {
15    ObjAttrib[Car, color, ColorKindEnum]
16    ObjFNames[Car, color] }
```

Listing 1.4. Car with color in our translation

cardinalities. In our work, however, the semantics of bidirectionality and custom multiplicity ranges is part of the translation itself: there is no need for manual OCL writing to express these standard concepts.

For example, consider a fragment of the CD shown in Fig. 1 consisting of only Employee and Address, and the association worksIn between them. With the transformation of [3], this fragment translates to the Alloy code shown in List. 1.5.[1] It is translated in our transformation to the code shown in List. 1.6.

Single Inheritance, Interfaces, and Multiple Inheritance. We now extend the examples above with inheritance. We show how the two translations handle single inheritance and how our translation can also support interfaces and multiple inheritance.

The translation of [3] takes advantage of Alloy's built-in support for inheritance, and thus directly maps CD class inheritance to Alloy's **extends** keyword. In our translation, in contrast, the semantics of inheritance, that is, the meaning

---

[1] According to our experience, UML2Alloy tool of [3], version 0.5.2, does not support such multiplicity ranges without the manual addition of OCL expressions. The above code shows how the translation of UML2Alloy could have handled multiplicity ranges if it supported this feature.

```
1  sig Address{}
2  sig Employee{worksIn:set Address}
3  fact Asso_Employee_of_worksIn_Address { Employee <:
4     worksIn in ( Employee) one->set ( Address) }
5  fact AssoCustom_Employee_of_worksIn_Address {
6     all var:Employee| #var.worksIn =< 3 && #var.worksIn >= 1}
```

Listing 1.5. Employee works in Address in the translation of [3]

```
1  one sig of,worksIn extends FName {}
2
3  sig Address,Employee extends Obj {}
4
5  fun AddressSubs : set Obj {Address}
6  fun EmployeeSubs : set Obj {Employee}
7
8  pred cd {
9     ObjFNames[Address , of]
10    ObjFNames[Employee , worksIn]
11    ObjLUAttrib[EmployeeSubs , worksIn , AddressSubs , 1,3]
12    ObjLUAttrib[AddressSubs , of, EmployeeSubs , 1,1] }
```

Listing 1.6. Employee works in Address in our translation

of the 'is-a' relation in terms of inclusion between sets, is explicitly expressed using sub class functions. The inheritance hierarchy is flattened and then rebuilt: in particular, as part of flattening, the complete list of attributes and associations of each class is collected from all its super classes. The sub class functions define the set of sub classes of each class.

Listings 1.7 and 1.8 show the parts related to inheritance in the Alloy code for the example CD of Fig. 1 in the two translations. Note the EmployeeSubs function in line 8 of List. 1.8 which returns the set of sub classes of Employee.

Similar functions are used to support interfaces. For every interface we define a function which returns all classes implementing it.

Significantly, consider a different CD where the class Driver does not inherit Employee, but where a new class Chauffeur inherits both Driver and Employee. This multiple inheritance setup is not supported by shallow translations like the one of [3] but it is supported by our translation (see List. 1.9). The use of functions provides the flexibility required to support multiple inheritance.

Composition. Our translation supports a whole/part composition relation. Composition is not supported by shallow translations like the one of [3] because CD's composition has no direct counterpart construct in Alloy.

The semantics of composition requires that a part cannot exist without a whole and that it belongs to exactly one whole. The predicate for composition

```
sig Address{}
sig Employee{worksIn: set Address}
sig Car{drivenBy: one Driver}
sig Driver extends Employee{drives: one Car}
```

Listing 1.7. Driver inherits from Employee in the translation of [3]

```
one sig drivenBy, of, worksIn, drives extends FName {}

sig Driver, Car, Address, Employee extends Obj {}

fun DriverSubs: set Obj {Driver}
fun CarSubs: set Obj {Car}
fun AddressSubs: set Obj {Address}
fun EmployeeSubs: set Obj {Employee + Driver}

pred cd {
    ObjFNames[Driver, drives]
    ObjFNames[Car, drivenBy]
    ObjFNames[Address, of]
    ObjFNames[Employee, worksIn]
    ObjLUAttrib[EmployeeSubs, worksIn, AddressSubs, 1,3]
    ObjLUAttrib[AddressSubs, of, EmployeeSubs, 1,1]
    BidiAssoc[DriverSubs, drives, CarSubs, drivenBy]
    ObjLUAttrib[CarSubs, drivenBy, DriverSubs, 1,1]
    ObjLUAttrib[DriverSubs, drives, CarSubs, 0,1] }
```

Listing 1.8. Driver inherits from Employee in our translation

is shown in List. 1.10. This predicate can be used, e.g., to specify a composition relation between Employee and Address, by adding the statement Composition [EmployeeSubs, worksIn, AddressSubs] to the CD predicate.

3.2 Back to UML Object Diagrams

Finally, we discuss the translation back from Alloy instances to UML ODs. In the translation presented in [3], the translation of an Alloy instance back to a UML OD is an immediate one to one mapping, which, according to [22], can be automatically computed from the first translation. Each atom is transformed, directly, into a UML object.

In contrast, in our translation, object instances are constructed only for the atoms in the Alloy instance that are instances of Obj; for each of these, attributes and their values are computed from the instances of their get relation (see line 5 of List. 1.1). More specifically, an Alloy instance that is found for a module generated by our translation may also include atoms that do not correspond to objects in the object model it represents, e.g., field names and enumeration

```
1  one sig drivenBy, of, worksIn, drives extends FName {}
2
3  sig Driver, Car, Address, Employee, Chauffeur extends Obj {}
4
5  fun DriverSubs: set Obj {Driver + Chauffeur}
6  fun CarSubs: set Obj {Car}
7  fun AddressSubs: set Obj {Address}
8  fun EmployeeSubs: set Obj {Employee + Chauffeur}
9  fun ChauffeurSubs: set Obj {Chauffeur}
10
11 pred cd {
12    ObjFNames[Driver, drives]
13    ObjFNames[Car, drivenBy]
14    ObjFNames[Address, of]
15    ObjFNames[Employee, worksIn]
16    ObjFNames[Chauffeur, worksIn + drives]
17    ObjLUAttrib[EmployeeSubs, worksIn, AddressSubs, 1,3]
18    ObjLUAttrib[AddressSubs, of, EmployeeSubs, 1,1]
19    BidiAssoc[DriverSubs, drives, CarSubs, drivenBy]
20    ObjLUAttrib[CarSubs, drivenBy, DriverSubs, 1,1]
21    ObjLUAttrib[DriverSubs, drives, CarSubs, 0,1] }
```

Listing 1.9. Multiple inheritance: `Chauffeur` inherits both `Driver` and `Employee`, in our translation (note the functions in lines 5 and 8)

```
1  pred Composition[wholes: set Obj,
2            rName: some FName, parts: set Obj] {
3     all p: parts | #{w: wholes, r: rName | p in w.get[r]}=1 }
```

Listing 1.10. A predicate for whole/part composition relation

values. Thus, these should not be translated to objects in the translation back to UML ODs. This makes our transformation from Alloy instances back to UML somewhat complicated. The resulting OD is a valid UML object diagram that indeed describes an instance of the original CD in terms of UML semantics.

4 Multiple CD Analysis

In addition to supporting an extended list of CD language features, the new translation allows us to solve several analysis problems beyond the basic, single CD consistency and instance generation. We show how the translation described in the previous section is generalized to support multiple CDs and continue to present its application to two analysis problems.

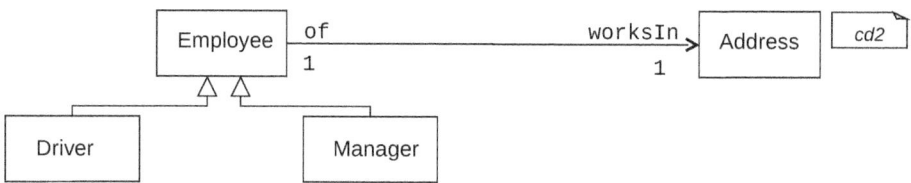

Fig. 2. cd_2, an example CD for the computation of intersection with cd_1 (see Sect. 4.2)

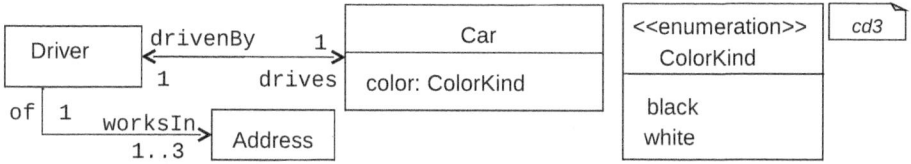

Fig. 3. cd_3, an example CD that refines cd_1 (see Sect. 4.3)

4.1 Handling Multiple CDs

To handle multiple CDs in one Alloy module, we define signatures for the union of classes from all input CDs, and divide the CD specific functions (sub class functions, enumeration value functions) between the CDs by adding a suffix CDi to all functions generated for the i-th CD. Moreover, instead of creating a single predicate cd, we generate several predicates, cd1, cd2, etc., one for each of the input CDs. Each predicate cd$i$ uses the functions with suffix CDi and defines constraints to not include any objects of classes not in cd_i. This is necessary because the predicate is interpreted as part of the module, which contains signatures representing classes from other CDs too.

4.2 Example Analysis Problem: Intersection

As one example application, we show how to use our translation to check the intersection of the semantics of two (or more) CDs. Recall the CD shown in Fig. 1 and consider a second CD, as shown in Fig. 2. Is there a system that satisfies both CDs, i.e, do the two CDs have common object model instances?

To answer this question using our translation we ask Alloy to find instances of the predicate cd1 and cd2. If any exist, we know that the intersection of the two CDs semantics is not empty. List. 1.11 shows snippets from the Alloy module corresponding to checking the intersection of the two CDs in our example, cd_1 of Fig. 1 and cd_2 of Fig. 2. Analyzing the predicate cd1 and cd2 reveals that their intersection is not empty: for example, an object model consisting of two drivers, each with one address, is an instance of both CDs. This object model can be found when executing the analyzer on the predicate cd1 and cd2 with our translation of the two CDs.

```
1  // signatures for the union of classes from the two CDs
2  // ...
3
4  // functions with CD# suffix
5  fun DriverSubsCD1: set Obj {Driver}
6  fun EmployeeSubsCD1: set Obj {Employee + Driver}
7  fun DriverSubsCD2: set Obj {Driver}
8  fun EmployeeSubsCD2: set Obj {Employee + Driver + Manager}
9  // more functions...
10
11 pred cd1 {
12   // use functions with suffix CD1
13   // ...
14   no Manager }
15
16 pred cd2 {
17   // use functions with suffix CD2
18   // ...
19   no Car }
20
21 run {cd1 and cd2} for 10
```

Listing 1.11. Checking the intersection of cd_1 and cd_2 using our translation

4.3 Example Analysis Problem: Refinement

The above technique can be easily generalized to solve the consistency of any Boolean expression over a set of CDs. For example, an analysis of the predicate `cd1 and not cd2` would find instances of the first CD that are not instances of the second, if any.

So, as a second analysis problem, we show that our translation can be used to check for refinement relations between CDs: If the predicate `cd1 and not cd2` is inconsistent (has no instances) and the predicate `cd2 and not cd1` is consistent (has instances), we can conclude that all instances of cd_1 are also instances of cd_2 (but not the other way around), namely, that cd_1 is a (strict) refinement of cd_2. As a concrete example, recall CD cd_1 of Fig. 1 and consider cd_3 shown in Fig. 3. Analyzing `cd1 and not cd3` and `cd3 and not cd1` reveals that all instances of cd_3 are indeed instances of cd_1, but not the other way around. Thus, the analysis shows that cd_3 is a refinement of cd_1.

To the best of our understanding, such analyses are not possible in existing translations.

5 Implementation: The CD2Alloy Plug-In

Our work is implemented in a prototype Eclipse plug-in called CD2Alloy. The input for the implementation is a UML/P CD, textually specified using Monti-Core grammar and generated Eclipse editor [15]. The transformation to Alloy is implemented using templates written in FreeMarker [11] and the execution of the generated module's run commands is done using Alloy's APIs [1]. The analysis is fully automated so the engineer does not need to see the generated Alloy code (viewing the generated Alloy code is optional).

CD2Alloy allows the engineer to edit a CD, to analyze it using Alloy, and to view the instances that the SAT solver finds back in the form of ODs. The plug-in, together with relevant documentation and examples, is available from [7]. We encourage the interested reader to try it out.

6 Discussion

The analysis of artifacts in one modeling language can, in many cases, be done using a semantics preserving translation to another language (and a reversed translation, back from the analysis results to the concepts of the first language). Often, more than one possible translation may be developed, and so, a comparative discussion on the characteristics of such translations and their implementation is worthwhile. Our work may be viewed as an interesting case study example of the differences between two different translations, their strengths and weaknesses, in particular when they are used in the context of mechanized analysis (rather than, say, in the context of a pure theoretical definition of a semantics).

Strengths of the translations of [3,18], and other shallow translations, are readability and relatively simple definition and implementation. The translation of each class requires only a local analysis and the resulting module syntax is linear in the size of the input CD. Weaknesses are the limited list of language features and possible potential analyses supported; these translations do not take full advantage of the expressive power of Alloy to cover the rich features of CDs.

Strengths of the new translation are twofold. First, the powerful possible analyses, such as refinement checking, mounting to evaluating any Boolean expression over CDs. Second, the extended list of features, including multiple inheritance and interface implementation, which have no direct counterparts in Alloy and are thus handled using a deep embedding strategy. Supporting these is important not only for theoretical coverage of language features but also because many CDs in the real world do make significant use of them.

One weakness of the new translation is that it is more difficult to read and understand, because there is no direct explicit mapping between the syntax of the generated module and the syntax of the CD. However, readability may be not so important in our context because the analysis is fully automated and the results are translated back to the UML domain.

Another weakness of the new translation is that it is harder to implement and more computationally complex: the flattening of the inheritance hierarchy requires a global analysis of the CD and in the worst case its reconstruction using functions may result in a module whose size is quadratic in the size of the input CD. This leads to a larger formula for the SAT solver used by Alloy.

As an example for the differences in computation complexity and performance, according to our experience, checking the consistency of the CD of Fig. 1 by generating an instance, with Alloy scope 3, using UML2Alloy (the tool described in [2,3]), resulted in a SAT formula of 618 variables and 1025 clauses. Using our new translation, CD2Alloy, the same problem resulted in a formula of 3354 variables and 5627 clauses. SAT solving time increased too, from 6 to 14 milliseconds (using SAT4J, on a Dell Latitude E6500 laptop running Windows 7). Note, however, that the use of the same scope in this comparison may be misleading: in the translation of [3], the scope defines the maximal number of objects per class in the instance, while in CD2Alloy, the scope defines the maximal number of objects in the instance.

To conclude, our work clearly demonstrates the tradeoff between the readability and intuitiveness of a simple shallow translation on the one hand and the expressiveness of a deeper translation on the other hand. The choice of translation to use depends on the specific needs of the applications at hand.

Finally, it is important to note that all existing translations, our new translation, and any other analysis performed with the Alloy Analyzer, are subject to a scope, which limits the number of atoms per signature (see [14]). In particular, it may be the case that a predicate does not hold in one scope but holds in a larger one. For an unbounded analysis one would need a translation of CDs to other formalisms, e.g., to enable the use of theorem provers, giving up full-automation, as in [5,13].

7 Related Work

In [2,3], the authors present a tool called UML2Alloy and provide a detailed discussion of the challenges of transforming CDs and OCL expressions into Alloy. One strength of this work is that the transformation used is defined and implemented using an MDA technique, that is, by formally defining a metamodel for CDs, a metamodel for Alloy, and transformation rules between the two. However, the shallow nature of the transformation between these metamodels limits the set of UML CD features that the work supports. For example, as multiple inheritance cannot be directly represented in Alloy, it is not supported by this work and is explicitly disallowed by the related profile (see [3, pp. 75]). Following an in-depth discussion of the differences between the languages, the authors of [3] conclude that "Because of these differences, model transformation from UML to Alloy has proved to be very challenging." [3, pp. 70]. Indeed, our work proposes to address this challenge by means of a deeper embedding strategy that bridges some of the differences between the languages: it takes advantage of Alloy's own expressive power to represent CD concepts that cannot be mapped directly to semantically equivalent concepts in Alloy.

A related work by some of the same authors [22] uses the same MDA approach, transformation, and tool, and adds a round trip transformation, from Alloy's instances back to UML ODs, implemented in QVT [19]. As we have shown in Sect. 3, our work supports a backward translation which results in correct ODs, i.e., ones which represent valid instances of the original CD according to the UML semantics. Supporting a translation back to the UML space is of course critical to the usefulness of the entire approach in practice.

In [18], the authors suggest to analyze CDs with Alloy, using a shallow embedding similar to [3]. This work does not present an implementation.

In [9], the authors use Alloy to formalize UML package merge. The work models a fragment of the UML metamodel in Alloy, in order to check various properties of package merge. Unlike our approach, this work does not present a generic transformation to Alloy. Analyses of multiple models are not discussed.

In [21], Sen presents a translation of the UML metamodel to Alloy, formalized and implemented in Kermeta. Similar to our work, this translation is not shallow and handles an extended list of CD features such as multiple inheritance and composition. Different from our work, it does not support analyses of multiple input models such as checking refinement and intersection.

UMLtoCSP [6] verifies UML/OCL models by a translation to a constraint satisfaction problem, solved using a constraint solver within a user-defined bounded search space. The tool checks for various kinds of satisfiability (and other analysis problems), and can generate an example instance (object model). Our work has similar strengths and weaknesses: the analysis is fully automated but is conducted in a bounded scope. We do not know whether UMLtoCSP supports multiple inheritance. It may be possible to extend UMLtoCSP to check for Boolean expressions over CDs, as supported by our work.

The USE tool [12] supports the analysis of CDs and related OCL invariants, checking, e.g., the consistency of a single CD, the independence of an OCL invariant, etc. A more recent work by the same group [23] reports on analyzing UML/OCL models directly using a SAT solver. To the best of our knowledge, applications such as checking refinement between two CDs are not available in [12,23], but it may be possible to extend these works to support such applications.

Finally, in recent work [16] we have defined a semantic differencing operator for CDs (used for semantic model comparison in the context of model evolution), which we have implemented using a translation to Alloy, similar to the one presented here. This work takes two CDs as input and outputs an Alloy module whose instances represent *diff witnesses*, object models in the semantics of one CD that are not in the semantics of the other. Also, in another recent work [17] we use a variant of the translation presented here and extend it to support semantic variability in CD/OD consistency analysis. This work takes three artifacts as input: a CD, an OD, and a feature configuration, which specifies choices over a set of semantic variability points; the analysis is semantically configured and its results change according to the semantics induced by the selected feature configuration. These works are additional examples for the kinds of analyses enabled by our translation.

8 Conclusion

We have presented CD2Alloy, a translation from UML CDs to Alloy, which is deeper and qualitatively different than previously suggested translations. Our translation takes advantage of Alloy's expressive power and advances the state-of-the-art in CD analysis in several ways: (1) support for more CD language features and (2) support for solving additional analysis problems concerning multiple CDs. The ideas are implemented in a prototype Eclipse plug-in and demonstrated with running examples.

Future work includes the investigation of additional possible embeddings of fragments of UML into Alloy, in order to support additional language features and analyses, for example, constrained generalization sets.

References

1. Alloy Analyzer website, http://alloy.mit.edu/ (accessed July 2011)
2. Anastasakis, K., Bordbar, B., Georg, G., Ray, I.: UML2Alloy: A challenging model transformation. In: Engels, G., Opdyke, B., Schmidt, D.C., Weil, F. (eds.) MODELS 2007. LNCS, vol. 4735, pp. 436–450. Springer, Heidelberg (2007)
3. Anastasakis, K., Bordbar, B., Georg, G., Ray, I.: On challenges of model transformation from UML to Alloy. Software and Systems Modeling 9(1), 69–86 (2010)
4. Broy, M., Cengarle, M.V., Grönniger, H., Rumpe, B.: Definition of the System Model. In: Lano, K. (ed.) UML 2 Semantics and Applications. Wiley, Chichester (2009)
5. Brucker, A.D., Wolff, B.: HOL-OCL: A Formal Proof Environment for UML/OCL. In: Fiadeiro, J.L., Inverardi, P. (eds.) FASE 2008. LNCS, vol. 4961, pp. 97–100. Springer, Heidelberg (2008)
6. Cabot, J., Clarisó, R., Riera, D.: UMLtoCSP: a tool for the formal verification of UML/OCL models using constraint programming. In: ASE, pp. 547–548. ACM, New York (2007)
7. CD2Alloy project website, http://www.se-rwth.de/materials/cd2alloy/
8. Cengarle, M.V., Grönniger, H., Rumpe, B.: System Model Semantics of Class Diagrams. Informatik-Bericht 2008-05, Technische Universität Braunschweig (2008)
9. Dingel, J., Diskin, Z., Zito, A.: Understanding and improving UML package merge. Software and Systems Modeling 7(4), 443–467 (2008)
10. Evans, A., France, R.B., Lano, K., Rumpe, B.: The UML as a Formal Modeling Notation. In: Bézivin, J., Muller, P.-A. (eds.) UML 1998. LNCS, vol. 1618, pp. 336–348. Springer, Heidelberg (1999)
11. FreeMarker, http://freemarker.org/ (accessed July 2011)
12. Gogolla, M., Büttner, F., Richters, M.: USE: A UML-based specification environment for validating UML and OCL. Sci. Comput. Program. 69(1-3), 27–34 (2007)
13. Grönniger, H., Ringert, J.O., Rumpe, B.: System model-based definition of modeling language semantics. In: Lee, D., Lopes, A., Poetzsch-Heffter, A. (eds.) FMOODS 2009. LNCS, vol. 5522, pp. 152–166. Springer, Heidelberg (2009)
14. Jackson, D.: Software Abstractions: Logic, Language, and Analysis. MIT Press, Cambridge (2006)
15. Krahn, H., Rumpe, B., Völkel, S.: MontiCore: a framework for compositional development of domain specific languages. Int. J. on Software Tools for Technology Transfer (STTT) 12(5), 353–372 (2010)
16. Maoz, S., Ringert, J.O., Rumpe, B.: CDDiff: Semantic differencing for class diagrams. In: Mezini, M. (ed.) ECOOP 2011. LNCS, vol. 6813, pp. 230–254. Springer, Heidelberg (2011)
17. Maoz, S., Ringert, J.O., Rumpe, B.: Semantically configurable consistency analysis for class and object diagrams. In: Whittle, J., Clark, T., Kühne, T. (eds.) MODELS 2011. LNCS, vol. 6981, pp. 153–167. Springer, Heidelberg (2011)

18. Massoni, T., Gheyi, R., Borba, P.: A UML Class Diagram Analyzer. In: 3rd Int. Work. on Critical Systems Development with UML (CSDUML), Affiliated with UML Conf., pp. 143–153 (2004)
19. Object Management Group. MOF Query View Transformation (QVT) (2008), http://www.omg.org/spec/QVT/1.0/ (accessed, July 2011)
20. Rumpe, B.: Modellierung mit UML. Springer, Heidelberg (2004)
21. Sen, S.: Automatic Effective Model Discovery. PhD thesis, Univ. of Rennes (2010)
22. Shah, S.M.A., Anastasakis, K., Bordbar, B.: From UML to alloy and back again. In: Ghosh, S. (ed.) MODELS 2009. LNCS, vol. 6002, pp. 158–171. Springer, Heidelberg (2010)
23. Soeken, M., Wille, R., Kuhlmann, M., Gogolla, M., Drechsler, R.: Verifying UML/OCL models using Boolean satisfiability. In: DATE, pp. 1341–1344. IEEE, Los Alamitos (2010)

Model-Driven Engineering and Optimizing Compilers: A Bridge Too Far?

Antoine Floch[1], Tomofumi Yuki[2], Clement Guy[1], Steven Derrien[1], Benoit Combemale[1], Sanjay Rajopadhye[2], and Robert B. France[2]

[1] University of Rennes 1, IRISA, INRIA
{antoine.floch,clement.guy,steven.derrien,benoit.combemale}@irisa.fr
[2] Colorado State University
{yuki,svr,france}@cs.colostate.edu

Abstract. A primary goal of Model Driven Engineering (MDE) is to reduce the cost and effort of developing complex software systems using techniques for transforming abstract views of software to concrete implementations. The rich set of tools that have been developed, especially the growing maturity of model transformation technologies, opens the possibility of applying MDE technologies to transformation-based problems in other domains.

In this paper, we present our experience with using MDE technologies to build and evolve compiler infrastructures in the optimizing compiler domain. We illustrate, through our two ongoing research compiler projects for C and a functional language, the challenging aspects of optimizing compiler research and show how mature MDE technologies can be used to address them. We also identify some of the pitfalls that arise from unrealistic expectations of what can be accomplished using MDE and discuss how they can lead to unsuccessful and frustrating application of MDE technologies.

1 Introduction

Model Driven Engineering (MDE) research is primarily concerned with reducing the accidental complexities associated with developing complex software systems [1]. This is accomplished through the use of technologies that support rigorous analysis and transformation of abstract descriptions of software to concrete implementations [2]. At the core of MDE are modeling languages that are typically defined as metamodels. The metamodels are expressed in a metalanguage such as the OMG Meta-Object Facility (MOF). Developers can use these modeling languages to describe complex systems at multiple levels of abstraction and from a variety of perspectives. MDE is essentially concerned with transforming descriptions of software artifacts to other forms that better serve specific purposes. For example, MDE techniques can be used to transform a detailed design model expressed in the Unified Modeling Language (UML) [3] to a Java program that can be compiled and executed, or to transform an abstract description of software to a performance model that can be used to estimate software performance characteristics.

It may seem that researchers in the MDE and optimizing compilers communities tackle vastly different problems. However, some of the more mature MDE technologies can be fruitfully leveraged in research-oriented optimizing compiler infrastructures. The connection between MDE and the optimizing compiler domains stems from the observation that the intermediate representations of optimizing compilers are *abstractions* of input programs that are repeatedly *transformed* to more efficient forms. In addition, researchers in the optimizing compiler domain need tools that enable rapid development and continuous evolution of compiler implementations built specifically to prototype and evaluate research ideas. The preceding concerns makes the application of MDE techniques in the optimizing compiler research domain appealing and useful.

In this paper, we illustrate the role MDE techniques can play in the optimizing compiler research domain using two on-going research compiler projects as case studies. These two compilers accept and optimize significantly different languages, C/C++ and a purely functional language, but they both benefit from the use of MDE techniques in a similar manner. We identify significant tasks in research compiler development, and highlight how MDE techniques can help reduce the cost and effort of performing these tasks. Our experience provides some evidence that bridging the two communities is possible and can yield significant benefits. Unrealistic expectations of what MDE can do may lead to ineffective use of MDE in the optimizing compiler domain, and thus we discuss pitfalls that users should be aware of when using these techniques. Our experience also revealed that the concept of a *transformation* in the optimizing compiler domain is broader than the concept currently supported by MDE tools. It would be interesting to explore how the broader notions of transformation can be leveraged in the MDE community. In this paper we identify some of the broader transformation concepts that may usefully be explored by the MDE community.

The rest of this paper is organized as follows. In Section 2, we briefly characterize optimizing compiler research, and the similarity between compiler intermediate representations and models. Then we describe common challenges that arise in research compiler development in Section 3. Section 4 highlights the benefits of applying MDE techniques to compilers through examples taken from our research compilers being developed with MDE. In Section 5, we present some of the pitfalls that researchers in the optimizing compiler domain need to be aware of in order to use MDE effectively. Finally, we give our conclusions and perspectives in Section 6.

2 Optimizing Compilers

Experimental compiler infrastructures play an important role in compiler research. Such infrastructures are different from production compilers as illustrated by our two example infrastructures, namely GeCoS[1] and AlphaZ[2].

2.1 Optimizing Compiler Research

Optimizing compiler research infrastructures are key elements in many research communities including High Performance Computing [4] and Embedded Systems Design

---

[1] http://gecos.gforge.inria.fr
[2] http://www.cs.colostate.edu/AlphaZ/

Automation [5]. Optimizing compilers aim at obtaining the best possible performance from input programs. Performance is to be understood in its broader sense, and may either correspond to execution time, power/energy consumption, code size or any combination of these metrics. Achieving better performance depends on both the target application and the target architecture.

Indeed, target physical machines can be very different, ranging from general purpose single/multi-core processors to special purpose hardware. Such target machines include, Graphics Processing Units (GPUs), Application Specific Instruction-set Processors (ASIPs) and/or application specific hardware accelerators implemented on either Complex Programmable Logic Devices (CPLD) or dedicated VLSI circuits.

For example, in High Performance Computing, applications (climate modeling, weather prediction, physical simulation, etc.), often run on supercomputers, where the execution time directly affects the cost. In Embedded Systems Design Automation, many applications involve Digital Signal Processing and/or multimedia algorithms, and target machines usually consist of special purpose hardware with a short life cycle. For these targets, the focus is cost (i.e., silicon area), performance/energy trade-off and also design time (because of time to market constraints).

Optimizing compiler research is therefore a collection of efforts to achieve high performance by analysis and optimizations of programs at the compiler level. Individual research usually tackles very specific problems (automatic parallelization, instruction selection, etc.), and can be therefore be seen as developing building blocks of a full compiler. As a consequence, significant effort is spent on prototyping new analysis/transformation passes in a research compiler infrastructure. There is hence a strong need for highly productive compiler infrastructure, where research ideas and prototypes can be quickly validated.

2.2 Optimizing Compiler Infrastructures

Compilers range from industrial strength production compilers to experimental ones that tackle domain specific problems and generally require more user intervention and/or multiple input specifications. However, most compilers share the same structure with three stages:

1. **Parsing** takes some form of input, usually a program written in a textual language, and constructs its Intermediate Representation (IR). The input language can be virtually anything, from complex languages such as C++ to domain specific languages. Similarly, compiler IRs range from Abstract Syntax Trees to complex data structures including additionnal information (typing, control flow, etc.).
2. Program **Optimizations** are repeatedly performed as transformations on the IR. The result of a transformation may stay in the same IR, or it may be another (generally lower level) IR, better suited to support platform specific optimizations. In the context of optimizing compilers, these stages involve complex combinatorial optimizations problems.
3. **Code Generation** translates the transformed IR to either executable binaries or source programs (which may not use the same language). As a matter of fact, Source-to-Source compilers are very common in optimizing compiler research.

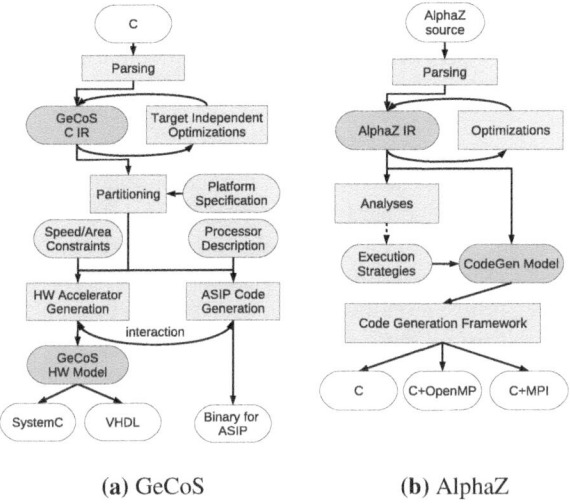

Fig. 1. Basic flow of GeCoS and AlphaZ. Transformations are performed in various places for optimization or lowering the level of abstraction. There are a number of different specifications that are given as additional inputs, and multiple different outputs are produced.

2.3 Role of Compiler Infrastructures

Research on optimizing compiler tries to answer questions such as: what transformations leads to more efficient code, how to define good cost functions to predict performance, how to ensure legality of a transformation, etc.

Whenever a new and/or better answer to one of these questions is found, researchers provide a "proof of concept" implementation of their approach that is used to experimentally validate their claims. The main role of research oriented compiler infrastructures is therefore to facilitate such rapid prototyping. As a consequence, the infrastructure code base tends to evolve very quickly. Fortunately, such compilers are not expected to be as stable and robust as production compilers. Similarly, the performance of the compiler implementation itself is rarely an issue, as long as the compiler output ultimately leads to improved performance.

2.4 GeCoS and AlphaZ

We now present two research compiler infrastructures: GeCoS and AlphaZ that illustrate the diversity of the optimizing compiler infrastructure landscape.

GeCoS is a C compiler infrastructure geared toward embedded system design. It can be used for Application Specific Processors (ASIPs) design and Custom Hardware Accelerator Synthesis. It can be used as a Source-to-Source C compiler or as a standalone flow with a complete retargetable compiler back-end and support for hardware synthesis via back-end to generate hardware descriptions.

AlphaZ is a system for exploring and prototyping analyses, transformations, and code generations for a class of programs that fit a formalism called the Polyhedral model. The system takes programs written in an equational language as inputs, and produces C codes targeting general purpose processors, in particular, multi-core architectures.

It is important to note that these two compilers take very different input languages, C and an equational language, and also produce outputs for diverse set of target platforms, from custom application specific hardware accelerators to general purpose processors. The internal flow of the two compilers are also significantly different as depicted in Figure 1. GeCoS has a number of different IRs being used at different stages of compilation, but AlphaZ performs all optimizing transformations in a single IR.

Interestingly, and despite all these differences, the developers of these compilers face very similar issues and challenges, that we describe in the following section.

3 Challenges in Optimizing Compilers

Research compiler infrastructure developers face many challenges, some of them being quite specific to compiler design, as explained below.

3.1 Maintainable and Sustainable Code

One of the fundamental challenges in our context is sustainability and maintainability of the code. Research-oriented compilers are very complex pieces of software, generally developed by generations of graduate students and interns working on parts of the infrastructure. This high turn over rate raises the need to support incremental development practices, and the seamless homogenization of programming style.

Furthermore, it is difficult to expect that contributors to such compiler infrastructures have a solid software engineering background and/or practice. Worse, many students working in the embedded system design automation community have an electrical/computer engineering background, rather than computer science.

3.2 Structural Validity of Intermediate Representation

When writing an optimizing transformation, one of the most tedious task consists in making sure that the transformed IR remains consistent with respect to the IR data structure. There are many consistency rules that must be enforced by the IR. For example, in many imperative programs, the use of a variable in a statement must be preceded by its declaration somewhere in the program execution flow. Such validations are generally performed on the IR after parsing. In research compiler infrastructures, it may also be desirable to perform these checks after a call to a transformation/optimization so as to spot obvious inconsistencies as early as possible. Writing these static checks is however very time consuming, as it involves a lot of navigation and book keeping operations, which are tedious to write and very error prone.

Moreover, experimental languages are more frequently extended and/or modified than conventional languages. Any non-trivial extensions or modification of the language forces developers to spend significant effort for updating these analysis, making this task even more time consuming.

3.3 Complex Querying of the IR

A compiler optimization is generally only applicable to a narrow subset of constructs of the language, and for which a precise set of preconditions holds. Retrieving the target constructs and checking that the corresponding preconditions are enforced requires a lot of querying within the IR. Many of these queries actually correspond to more or less simple pattern matching operations. As an example, a simple loop unrolling transformation requires to retrieve all the loop constructs from the IR in which the bounds and the step are constant. Then, for each of such loop, the transformation must check that the loop body has no side-effect on the loop iterator.

While navigation can be efficiently handled through the use of visitor design patterns, the code complexity induced by the query implementation quickly makes the code difficult to understand and to maintain.

3.4 Interfacing with External Tools

Experimental research compilers infrastructures make an extensive use of third party libraries that are used for very specific purposes. For example, boolean satisfiability, integer linear programming solvers and/or machine learning libraries are often used to express and solve compiler optimization problems. These libraries may be implemented in various languages, and therefore require custom bindings if the compiler is written in a different language.

Similarly, there also exist powerful tools to ease the implementation of complex pattern matching operations over trees/graphs. For example, Tom/Gom[3] provides a term rewriting engine, particularly well suited to express compiler optimization. However, exposing the IR to the Tom/Gom engine requires a complex mapping specification that has to be written by hand.

3.5 Semantics Preserving Transformations

One of the most fundamental requirements for a compiler is to ensure that the semantics of the original source code are retained by the output. This has led to growing emphasis on provability, as seen in the CompCert [6] project that implemented a verified production compiler, as well as increasing influence of theorem provers in compilers [7]. In the context of an optimizing compiler, where usually only small parts of the code are changed based on specific preconditions, an important challenge is that in addition to proving that a proposed transformation preserves the original semantics, we must also prove that the *implementation* of the transformation correctly preserves the designer's intention. Ideally, every transformation needs a proof of correctness before being implemented, and tools to certify that the implementation preserves this. Such an ability would turn out to be very useful to identify mismatch between theory and practice (unsupported corner cases, flawed algorithm, etc.)

---
[3] http://tom.loria.fr/

3.6 Systematic Approaches for Capturing Domain Specific Knowledge

Optimizing compilers often fail at fully taking advantage of all optimization opportunities because they lack of knowledge about low level details of the target machine.

These limitations have been addressed by proposing language dialects and/or extensions to address the shortcoming of existing general purpose programming languages. This is particularly true for parallel programming where such domain specific knowledge is mandatory to achieve reasonable performance: [8,9,10]. Other approaches advocate the use of alternatives and/or more specific languages, that better fit some purpose. AlphaZ uses an equational language as inputs, where the computation is specified as mathematical equations. One of the motivations for this equational language is the separation of concerns; what to compute should be separated from other choices, such as memory allocation.

Such domain specific knowledge may also be used by the compiler developers themselves. For example, most compiler frameworks rely on a formal description of the processor instruction set and of its micro-architecture. This description is then used to automate the porting of the compiler to that new architecture.

However, the use of DSL in the context of optimizing compiler is hindered by by the fact designing custom languages involves high development and maintenance efforts. In particular, even if existing tools (e.g., ANTLR, Yacc) help addressing parsing issues, they fail at providing facilities for interfacing the parser output to the target IR (and to other components of the compiler). This is a significant problem in compiler research, where domain specific languages are generally designed incrementally, and where adding a new feature in the language has hence significant development cost.

Of course, these problems are even more severe when it comes to extending GPL with embedded DSLs, as the languages that have to be extended are often very complex (e.g., C/C++). As of now, even compiler compilers do not provide enough facilities to help solving this type of problems.

3.7 Code Generation

In a research context, compilers may need to target multiple architectures or languages. In addition, a same input program can lead to several distinct code in the same target language (e.g., sequential C code and MPI parallel C code). This is particularly common in research paralleling compilers that deals with emerging architectures (e.g., IBM/SONY/Toshiba Cell BE, GPGPUs, Intel Larrabee) to explore optimization opportunities. Developing code generators for each target and/or language requires a lot of effort that could be significantly reduced by the use of facilities to reuse and customize code generators.

4 How to Use MDE in Compilers

Since compiler IRs are abstractions used to represent programs, they are by essence models (an instance of IR is an abstraction of the given source code). In this context, the grammar of the source language, or more often the structure of IR, becomes the metamodel. We now report how three kind of MDE uses can answer to the challenges described in Section 3. The description leverages our development experience after we started using these technologies two years ago for both the GeCoS and AlphaZ infrastructures.

4.1 Direct MDE Benefits

The GeCoS and AlphaZ compilers started from a significant legacy code base, and we therefore soon felt a strong need for a formalized and standardized software development process. Because the GeCoS compiler infrastructure was already tightly coupled with the Eclipse environment, it seemed natural for us to use the metamodeling facilities provided by EMF[4].

Model can Serve as a Documentation. An immediate benefit is that all the key information lies in the metamodel specification. It focuses on the problem domain, without excessive implementation details and helps bootstrap new developers into a project, even when documentation is lacking.

Code Generator. Homogenization and good development practices are some of the most immediate benefits of MDE. The use of code generators (e.g., generic EMF Java code generator) providing standardized interfaces and ensuring (structural) model consistency has a direct impact on code quality. The advanced reflexivity (e.g., containments and structural features) of the generated code eases the development of tool functions without requiring tedious instrumentation (that is usually far from the process being modelled) of the metamodel.

Generic Tools. All the generic tools based on the model specification also offer significant added value at zero development cost. These tools can help a lot to increase the robustness of compilers. First, a model enforces its metamodel simple structural properties (arity of references and containments consistency). These properties can be easily verified by using standard serialization process.

Moreover, the EMF Tree editor generated from the metamodel specification also proved to be helpful. During early development stages it helped us in fixing bugs through an understandable visualization of transformation results. Figure 2 shows the slightly customized editors for AlphaZ and GeCoS IRs.

Finally, Object Constraint Language (OCL) can be used to express additional invariant rules (and pre/post-conditions) that are checked at runtime against model instances. This turns out to be particularly useful in the context of an optimizing compiler, as it helps ensure that a given transformation preserves the correctness of transformed IR. For example, many transformations requires the input IR to be in SSA[5] form. A simple OCL query can easily check this property as a post-condition of the SSA transformation and as pre-condition of the optimizations.

---

[4] http://www.eclipse.org/modeling/emf/
[5] Static Single Assignment. All variables within a function are assigned exactly once.

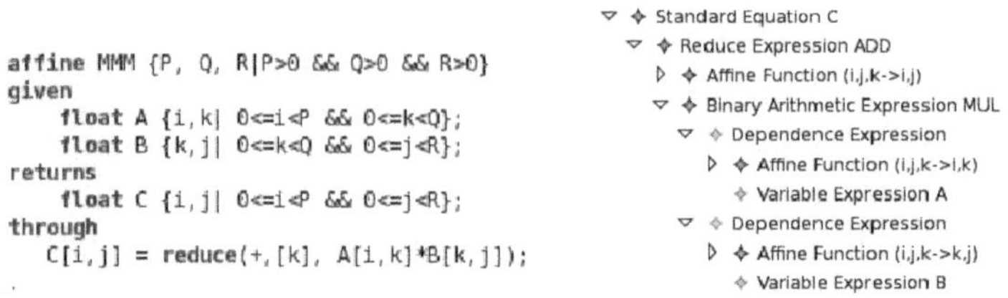

```
affine MMM {P, Q, R|P>0 && Q>0 && R>0}
given
    float A {i,k| 0<=i<P && 0<=k<Q};
    float B {k,j| 0<=k<Q && 0<=j<R};
returns
    float C {i,j| 0<=i<P && 0<=j<R};
through
    C[i,j] = reduce(+, [k], A[i,k]*B[k,j]);
```

(a) AlphaZ source

```
▽ ✦ Standard Equation C
   ▽ ✦ Reduce Expression ADD
      ▷ ✦ Affine Function (i,j,k->i,j)
      ▽ ✦ Binary Arithmetic Expression MUL
         ▽ ✦ Dependence Expression
            ▷ ✦ Affine Function (i,j,k->i,k)
               ✦ Variable Expression A
         ▽ ✦ Dependence Expression
            ▷ ✦ Affine Function (i,j,k->k,j)
               ✦ Variable Expression B
```

(b) AlphaZ IR

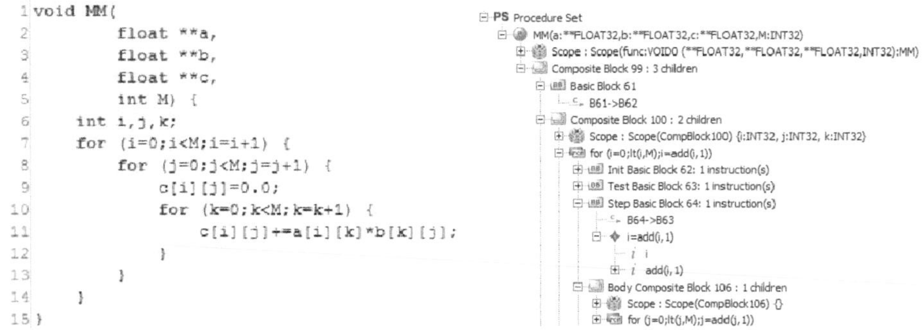

```
1  void MM(
2      float **a,
3      float **b,
4      float **c,
5      int M) {
6      int i,j,k;
7      for (i=0;i<M;i=i+1) {
8          for (j=0;j<M;j=j+1) {
9              c[i][j]=0.0;
10             for (k=0;k<M;k=k+1) {
11                 c[i][j]+=a[i][k]*b[k][j];
12             }
13         }
14     }
15 }
```

(c) C source

```
⊟ PS Procedure Set
  ⊟ ⓜ MM(a:**FLOAT32,b:**FLOAT32,c:**FLOAT32,M:INT32)
     ⊞ ⓢ Scope : Scope(func:VOID0 (**FLOAT32,**FLOAT32,**FLOAT32,INT32):MM)
     ⊟ 🗎 Composite Block 99 : 3 children
        ⊟ 🗎 Basic Block 61
           └─ c- B61->B62
        ⊟ 🗎 Composite Block 100 : 2 children
           ⊞ ⓢ Scope : Scope(CompBlock100) (i:INT32, j:INT32, k:INT32)
           ⊟ 🔁 for (i=0;i<t(i,M);i=add(i,1))
              ⊞ 🗎 Init Basic Block 62: 1 instruction(s)
              ⊞ 🗎 Test Basic Block 63: 1 instruction(s)
              ⊟ 🗎 Step Basic Block 64: 1 instruction(s)
                 └─ c- B64->B63
                 ⊟ ✦ i=add(i,1)
                    ├─ i i
                    ⊞ i add(i, 1)
              ⊟ 🗎 Body Composite Block 106 : 1 children
                 ⊞ ⓢ Scope : Scope(CompBlock106) ()
                 ⊞ 🔁 for (j=0;lt(j,M);j=add(j,1))
```

(d) GeCoS IR

Fig. 2. Matrix multiplication in AlphaZ and C, and its corresponding intermediate representation in AlphaZ and GeCoS

4.2 Using Metatools

MDE can significantly increase efficiency through generic tools targeted at complex and specific development tasks.

Facilities to Define DSLs. As discussed in Section 3, compilers can benefit a lot by capturing domain specific knowledge. Tools such as Xtext[6] or EMFText[7] can provide concrete textual syntax to a DSL, together with an editor with basic syntax highlighting and auto-completion.

For example, the equational language used in AlphaZ is parsed using Xtext generated parser. Because the language is experimental, minor/major language changes or extensions occur frequently, and the use of model based tools makes it easier to maintain the consistency between the parser and other components.

Facilities to Generate Code. Model-to-Text (M2T) tools such as Xpand/Xtend[8] provides a modular and extensible template based specification of the generated text through

---
[6] http://www.eclipse.org/Xtext/
[7] http://www.emftext.org/
[8] http://www.eclipse.org/modeling/m2t/?project=xpand

imports and aspects. In Xpand, each template rule supports parametric polymorphism that simplifies the management of specialized entities (especially useful for compiler IRs described as an abstract syntax tree with specialized nodes).

In both GeCoS and AlphaZ, these facilities are heavily utilized for code generation. In the case of GeCoS, the compiler IR is eventually translated into a model that represents the target hardware to generate, and different templates are used to generate VHDL (hardware description language), or SystemC (C-like language for high-level synthesis). In AlphaZ, the compiler IR corresponding to the functional representation is transformed into another representation that is closer to imperative programs. From the imperative IR, Xpand aspects are used to generate variations such as C code with OpenMP pragmas for loop parallelization, or alternate implementations of multi-dimensional arrays.

4.3 Defining Metatools

All metamodels are described using the same model (metametamodel), and thus we can manipulate/analyze metamodels in a generic fashion, by developing in the metametamodel. One of the benefits, is to bind some generic behaviors to the manipulated metamodels. This can be achieved by a generative approach or even by interpretation for a fast prototyping. In both cases, a dedicated environment based on the common metametamodel provides a language to describe the executable behaviors.

Generative Approaches. The definition of generative metatools allows the developers to automate a task to all or some subset of metamodels comforting to the metametamodel. Some tasks may be fully automated through Model-to-Model (M2M) transformations on the metamodel using tools such as ATL[9] or Kermeta[10]. Others, can be guided by DSLs. The resulting metatools generate codes corresponding to the tasks instantiated for different metamodels.

Structural software design patterns are a perfect example of generic concepts. Expressing them at a metametamodel level gives a powerful toolbox to the developers who can apply or reuse these patterns on all their metamodels. In compilers, we need to query/transform the IR. This is done mostly by using the visitor design pattern and extensively used tree traversal algorithms such as depth first and breadth first. Whereas adding a visitor pattern to an existing code is tedious since it needs to add a function to each visited entity, it can be done automatically using a simple M2M transformation. Behavior codes of the various traversal strategies are inferred by a simple containment analysis and added as annotations to the transformed metamodel.

Using DSLs proves to be especially useful to build generative tools for more complex repeated tasks such as interfacing with external tools. We give here two examples of DSL-based metatools that significantly enhanced our productivity for difficult and time consuming tasks.

Example: Graph Mapper. Compiler optimizations often rely on graph-based IR and thus can benefit from an external, optimized graph library implementation. The key

---

[9] http://www.eclipse.org/atl/
[10] http://www.kermeta.org/

idea of *Graph Mapper* is to map the library graph implementation to the IR instead of defining the IR from this graph (through inheritance). Hence, we designed a DSL that takes any metamodel as input and helps to explicitly describes how to map nodes and edges to this metamodel. The tool then generates an adapter to the external graph implementation.

Example: Tom/Gom bindings. Tom/Gom is a term rewriting system for Java. Both GeCoS and AlphaZ use Tom/Gom for a number of transformations that are pure rewriting of the IR. For example, expressions that occur in programs like $2i + 2i$ can be simplified as $4i$ by applying the rewrite rule expressed as the following:

$$\mathtt{add(term(c1,var),term(c2,var))} \rightarrow \mathtt{term(c1+c2,var)}$$

that simplifies additions of two terms when the variables in the two linear terms are identical.

These rules are much easier to express and to understand than visitor based implementations. However, Tom/Gom requires bindings from expressions in its language to Java objects. We have developed a tool that automates this task using a simple DSL to specify the terms that are manipulated in a model, and the names of the Tom expressions. Binding specifications are then generated using M2T facilities.

Model Mapping. Previous examples of bindings using DSLs can be seen as specific model mappings. Some existing generic mapping languages enable defining such links between metamodels and to use them for M2M transformations. For example the semi-automatic process presented by Clavreul et al. [11] enables defining mappings between two metamodels and generating bidirectional transformations. This kind of approach could be used for external tool interfacing and to pass from one IR to another.

Metamodel Instrumentation. Executable metamodeling languages (i.e., action languages provided by the metametamodel) such as Kermeta provide facilities to express executable behaviors directly on the metamodel. They enable the instrumentation of metamodels through aspect oriented modeling thereby providing a very elegant way to achieve separation of concerns. Thus, complex IR transformations can be efficiently described without the need of visitors. Since the metamodel can be instrumented with new attributes and methods in the intent of the transformation, it significantly reduces the complexity of the algorithm implementation.

A concrete example is an M2M transformation from a IR where an instruction is described as a tree to another one where a sequence of instructions corresponds to a directed acyclic graph (DAG). If M2M tools such as ATL provide an easy way of doing M2M for *one to one* mapping rules, it becomes difficult and nearly intractable for a standard software engineer to express complex *any to any* mappings. In the case of the tree to DAG transformation it is much more convenient to instrument each of the metamodels by tools aspects and to code the transformation using these new helpful attributes and methods. Some subsets of the added features may be useful for other transformations and can be advantageously split into independent layers as depicted

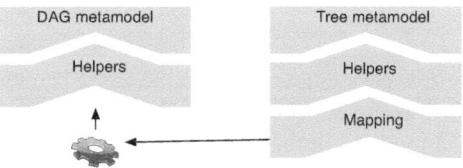

Fig. 3. Tree instructions to DAG instructions transformation through Kermeta. Layers of aspects instrument the metamodels and simplify the transformation code.

in Figure 3. The helpers layers corresponds to utilities aspects that can be reused in multiple other transformations. The mapping layer adds simple references to avoid the need of expensive maps linking DAG/tree elements.

The instrumentation of a metamodel introduces powerful concepts but also an important tooling overhead in terms of memory and speed. Opening/transforming a large model in a framework such as Kermeta can be quite slow or even impracticable in industrial cases containing tens of thousands of model elements. Although we strongly believe that the use of metamodel instrumentation significantly enhances flexibility and maintainability, the scalability issues we currently are facing prevents us from using this facility to our research compilers.

4.4 Summarizing Answers from MDE to Compilers Challenges

MDE provides low-entry-cost advanced solutions for M2M and M2T transformations making it a very attractive technology for developing compiler components. We now briefly summarize how MDE facilities introduced in this Section correspond to the challenges described in Section 3.

The use of generative programming tools based on metamodel specifications leads to well structured and homogeneous code, and forces programmers to follow good software engineering practices addressing the challenge described in Section 3.1. MDE also contribute to the validation of IR and transformations through enforced simple structural properties and more complex OCL queries, corresponding to challenge in Section 3.2, and partially to challenges in Sections 3.3 and 3.5.

Defining metatools, by generation or instrumentation of the metamodels, simplifies the design of complex transformations/queries on the IR also addressing the challenges in Section 3.3. It also enables the automation of time consuming interfacing with external tools described in Section 3.4. Some of these defined metatools benefits from the facilities for describing DSLs and code generation that also give partial answers to challenges in Section 3.6 and 3.7.

5 Applicability of MDE

While it is possible and beneficial to build bridges that put MDE technologies to work in optimizing compiler research infrastructures, it is also important to understand that unrealistic expectations of MDE approaches can lead to frustration and failure. Some of this may also be due to poor software modeling skills needed to effectively apply MDE.

5.1 Scope

MDE is a very attractive solution to many problems in the complex software system development. For such systems, models can be used to describe the software to be built at various levels of abstraction and MDE technologies can be used to manage the creation and manipulation of the models. Here, models are used to describe solutions to problems. It may be tempting to extrapolate this use of models to system software infrastructures, including optimizing compilers. Indeed, compilers can be viewed as a kind of complex information systems. However, a compiler is much more than an information system. Many of the compiler design challenges involve complex combinational optimization problems that are outside the scope of problems targeted by MDE techniques. Furthermore, many parts (e.g., classic data flow analysis and abstract and non-standard interpretation) require deep understanding of the mathematical foundations of lattice theory, fixed points, etc. As an example, modeling the instruction set of a given processor is not enough to efficiently compile a program for that instruction set. In a sense, modeling the problem is not solving the problem.

A key to effective use of MDE techniques is an understanding that models are created to serve specific purposes, and a good model is one that effectively serves its purposes. Developers need to ensure that the models they build are fit for purpose. For example, a good compiler intermediate model is one that describes a program in a format that can be efficiently analyzed as required in particular compilation stages.

Developers also need to be aware that MDE technologies are not intended to create models that are guaranteed to be fit for purpose. Human creativity is needed to create models that are fit for purpose. MDE techniques are designed to *enhance*, not *replace*, the creative abilities of modelers. They allow modelers to describe and analyze their models in order to build confidence that their models effectively serve its purposes. In the optimizing compiler research, this means that MDE technologies will not help produce better models of programs that are fit-for-use in the compilation process.

5.2 Prerequisites

The first requirement is that team members must be able to deal with abstraction, and more precisely must have solid modeling skills. Modeling here is in its broader sense, from mathematical analytical modeling through combinatorial/operational research optimization problem modeling to UML like approaches.

It is also mandatory for developers to be comfortable with OO programming principles. Our experience has shown that even though most young electrical engineers have followed some OO programming courses in their curriculum, few of them have a good understanding of its concepts like polymorphism. A basic understanding of design patterns is also required.

To obtain an executable code, the MDE developer needs first to model the software and then to generate it. These two steps introduce a tooling overhead which may slow down the initial development. Moreover, even if most MDE tools provide a low entry cost for common metamodel-based tools (e.g., primary model editor automatically generated from a default configuration of tools, such as EMF, GMF and TMF), the price of a flexible tool is often high software design complexity. If MDE tools rapidly provide prototypes, reaching an industrial level leads to an extra load of understanding.

Developers with experience in complex software development will quickly find MDE attractive. These developers know from their previous experience that the quality of the design is critical, and time spent on modeling may be greater than that for implementation. This family of users will be easily convinced of the interest of metaness. It is not so obvious for inexperienced developers working on simple softwares projects with a low level of flexibility and reusability. Based on our experience, successful use of MDE in the compiler domain requires an open-minded development team that is willing to try software engineering techniques to tackle their development problems. This is often facilitated by an influential champion who is willing to spend the time and effort learning and experimenting with MDE technologies.

6 Conclusion and Perspectives

In this paper, we described how optimizing compiler research and MDE can be easily bridged due to inherent modeling aspects of compilers. We illustrated the benefits of MDE through our experiences in building research compiler infrastructures.

The most obvious benefit is a seamless systematization/homogenization of development practices, something that is often very difficult to achieve in an academic environment. Metamodels also offer an abstract representation of the software, and documents many important design choices. This is a very valuable benefit in a context where most of the development consist in undocumented prototypes. Additionally, metatools and metatooling greatly help in automating many of the time consuming and error prone development tasks. Finally, we observed that metatools and generative approaches operate as creativity boosters as they enable very fast prototyping and evaluation of many new ideas.

Even though MDE has proved to be well suited for solving many of challenges arising in optimizing compilers development, this new context of utilization also raises many open research directions that we believe to be of high interest to the MDE community. First, the growing use of M2M transformations (e.g., to implement compilation passes) raises the need for that ensuring structural and behavioral properties are preserved during model transformations. As a consequence, we see model transformation verification and testing as a very important research challenge that needs to be tackled by the MDE community.

Moreover, since MDE now offers tools that significantly ease the definition of DSLs, it is becoming urgent to efficiently handle their rapid increase in numbers. In particular, a DSL should not be created from scratch if another DSL exists that can be used to derive the new DSL (e.g., using reutilization and extension), and the DSL tooling (e.g., simulator, checker and generator) should be reused over a family of DSLs. We believe that the ability to capitalize transformations by enabling their application over a family of metamodels rather than on a single metamodel is a very important issue. To address this challenge, we are currently studying a theory leveraging model typing [12] and model mapping [11] so as to be able to manipulate DSLs as first class entities.

Finally, it turns out that applying MDE technologies to the development of optimizing compilers led us to face a scalability barrier. The models manipulated by compilers are indeed generally fairly large (in terms of number of model elements) and are not handled very well by many of the MDE tools. Besides, even if research-oriented optimizing compilers do not suffer from strong constraints on execution time, current MDE technologies renders them unsuitable for industrial strength compilers.

We hope these three topics; semantics preserving transformations, model transformations reuse, and tools scalability; will motivate future work.

References

1. France, R., Rumpe, B.: Model-driven development of complex software: A research roadmap. In: Briand, L., Wolf, A. (eds.) Future of Software Engineering 2007. IEEE-CS Press, Los Alamitos (2007)
2. Schmidt, D.: Guest editor's introduction: Model-driven engineering. Computer 39(2), 25–31 (2006)
3. The Object Management Group: UML 2.0: Superstructure Specification. Version 2.0, OMG, formal/05-07-04 (2005)
4. Hall, M., Padua, D., Pingali, K.: Compiler research: the next 50 years. Communications of the ACM 52(2), 60–67 (2009)
5. Tripp, J.L., Gokhale, M., Peterson, K.D.: Trident: From High-Level Language to Hardware Circuitry. IEEE Computer 40(3), 28–37 (2007)
6. Leroy, X.: Formal certification of a compiler back-end or: programming a compiler with a proof assistant. In: Conference Record of the 33rd ACM SIGPLAN-SIGACT Symposium on Principles of Programming Languages, pp. 42–54. ACM, New York (2006)
7. Arnold, G., Hölzl, J., Köksal, A., Bodík, R., Sagiv, M.: Specifying and verifying sparse matrix codes. In: Proceedings of the 15th ACM SIGPLAN International Conference on Functional Programming, pp. 249–260. ACM, New York (2010)
8. Yelick, K., Semenzato, L., Pike, G., Miyamoto, C., Liblit, B., Krishnamurthy, A., Hilfinger, P., Graham, S., Gay, D., Colella, P., et al.: Titanium: A high-performance Java dialect. Concurrency Practice and Experience 10(11-13), 825–836 (1998)
9. Charles, P., Grothoff, C., Saraswat, V., Donawa, C., Kielstra, A., Ebcioglu, K., Von Praun, C., Sarkar, V.: X10: an object-oriented approach to non-uniform cluster computing. In: ACM SIGPLAN Notices, vol. 40, pp. 519–538. ACM, New York (2005)
10. Chamberlain, B., Callahan, D., Zima, H.: Parallel programmability and the Chapel language. International Journal of High Performance Computing Applications 21(3), 291 (2007)
11. Clavreul, M., Barais, O., Jézéquel, J.M.: Integrating legacy systems with mde. In: ICSE 2010: Proceedings of the 32nd ACM/IEEE International Conference on Software Engineering and ICSE Workshops, Cape Town, South Africa, vol. 2, pp. 69–78. (May 2010)
12. Steel, J., Jézéquel, J.M.: On model typing. Journal of Software and Systems Modeling (SoSyM) 6(4), 401–414 (2007)

Towards a General Composition Semantics for Rule-Based Model Transformation

Dennis Wagelaar[1,*], Massimo Tisi[2], Jordi Cabot[2], and Frédéric Jouault[2]

[1] Vrije Universiteit Brussel, Pleinlaan 2, 1050 Brussels, Belgium
`dennis.wagelaar@vub.ac.be`
[2] École des Mines de Nantes, 4, rue Alfred Kastler, 44307 Nantes, France
`{massimo.tisi,jordi.cabot,frederic.jouault}@inria.fr`

Abstract. As model transformations have become an integral part of the automated software engineering lifecycle, reuse, modularisation, and composition of model transformations becomes important. One way to compose model transformations is to compose modules of transformation rules, and execute the composition as one transformation (internal composition). This kind of composition can provide fine-grained semantics, as it is part of the transformation language. This paper aims to generalise two internal composition mechanisms for rule-based transformation languages, module import and rule inheritance, by providing executable semantics for the composition mechanisms within a virtual machine. The generality of the virtual machine is demonstrated for different rule-based transformation languages by compiling those languages to, and executing them on this virtual machine. We will discuss how ATL and graph transformations can be mapped to modules and rules inside the virtual machine.

Keywords: Model transformation, Model transformation composition, ATL, Graph transformation.

1 Introduction

Model transformations play a central role in MDE, and have become an integral part of the automated software engineering lifecycle, just like build script interpreters and compilers. In order to keep this automated lifecycle maintainable, model transformations will have to be reusable, modular, and composable. We can distinguish between two kinds of composition for model transformation: *external* composition and *internal* composition [1]. External composition refers to a chain of several model transformation executions, where models are passed from one transformation to another. Internal composition refers to the composition of multiple transformation rules and/or modules into one transformation module, which can then be executed as a whole.

---

[*] The author's work is funded by a postdoctoral research grant provided by the Institute for the Promotion of Innovation by Science and Technology in Flanders (IWT-Flanders).

The advantage of external composition is its independence of the transformation language, while internal composition relies on specific transformation language semantics and/or constructs (e.g. modules, rules, operations, etc.). It therefore often applies to one transformation language only, as language semantics generally apply to one language only. The advantage of internal composition is the richer, more fine-grained composition semantics it can provide. It is possible to refine or redefine existing rules, add new rules, etc., as long as there is a common notion of what a rule is.

Different transformation languages have different strengths, which has been demonstrated by the Transformation Tool Contest workshop series[1]. The ability to perform fine-grained composition of transformation rules expressed in different languages is a powerful tool for tackling complex transformation problems, as each language can be used for their strong points.

This paper aims to mitigate the problem of internal composition being specific to one transformation language by defining the composition mechanism within the context of a transformation virtual machine (VM). The VM provides a common, executable semantics for (composition of) transformation modules and rules. Two internal composition mechanisms for rule-based transformation languages are generalised in this way: module import and rule inheritance. The VM, called EMF Transformation Virtual Machine (EMFTVM), is based on the Eclipse Modeling Framework (EMF) [2], which represents a de facto standard for modelling today. As a result, the proposed composition mechanisms are specific to EMF.

The generality of EMFTVM – within the scope of EMF – is demonstrated by compiling more than one rule-based model transformation language to the VM, and by extension provide executable semantics for those languages. As a proof of concept, we discuss how ATL [3] and graph transformations [4] can be mapped to modules and rules in our VM. For this purpose, we've developed SimpleGT, a minimal graph transformation language on top of EMF, based on double pushout (DPO) semantics. The combination of ATL and SimpleGT already provides a non-trivial spectrum of rule-based languages, as ATL is a model *mapping* language, and SimpleGT is a recursive model *rewriting* language. This difference is discussed in detail in the paper.

The generality of EMFTVM also applies to the composition mechanisms implemented in EMFTVM: ATL's and SimpleGT's notion of module import and rule inheritance are mapped to the same implementation, and therefore have common executable semantics. In the long term, EMFTVM may evolve towards a general interoperability solution for model transformation languages that leverages commonalities between languages.

The rest of this paper is organised as follows: in section 2, we discuss related work. In section 3, we briefly explain the EMFTVM language. Then, we discuss how the VM implements rule inheritance in section 4, and module import in section 5. Section 6 discusses how ATL and SimpleGT are mapped to modules and rules in our VM. Section 7 concludes this paper.

---

[1] http://planet-research20.org/ttc2011/

2 Related Work

2.1 Common Semantics and Virtual Machines

In the domain of model transformation, there have been two efforts to provide common executable semantics for multiple transformation languages. One of these concerns the alignment of ATL and QVT Operational [5]. The executable semantics are provided by the ATL VM in this case. Another such effort is the ATC VM[2], which aims to provide a common execution framework for languages such as QVT or RubyTL. In both cases, composition possibilities are limited, because rules are compiled away into low-level primitives. The necessary metadata to perform rule composition, such as what code belongs to what rule, what are the rule's input/output elements, and what are a rule's super-rules, are no longer available.

2.2 Rule Inheritance

Rule inheritance allows a transformation rule to specify one or more super-rules, where structure and behaviour of super-rules is inherited cf. object-oriented inheritance. According to [6], there are currently three model transformation languages that include an explicit notion of rule inheritance: ATL [3], the Epsilon Transformation Language (ETL) [7], and Triple Graph Grammars (TGG) [8]. Each of these languages assumes slightly different semantics for rule inheritance, and conflict with each other at specific points. For example, ETL triggers a super-rule whenever its sub-rule triggers, whereas ATL will only trigger a sub-rule if its super-rule triggers first. TGG in turn requires you to include the entire super-rule as part of each sub-rule, which allows both ETL's and ATL's rule inheritance strategy to be used.

QVT Operational and Relations [9] include "when" and "where" clauses, which allow for triggering other mappings/relations from the context of a mapping/relation. A "when" clause requires the referenced mapping/relation to match first, before the current mapping/relation is applied. This corresponds to the rule inheritance strategy for ATL. A "where" clause enforces the referenced mapping/relation to be applied before the current mapping/relation is applied. This corresponds to the rule inheritance strategy for ETL.

The VIATRA2 language [10] uses reusable patterns to specify rule trigger conditions. Rules can refer to patterns, and patterns may include other patterns. This results in a kind of "inheritance hierarchy" of patterns, where each pattern requires all its included patterns to match first. VIATRA2 also uses the pattern hierarchy to perform optimised matching [11].

2.3 Module Import

Module import allows model transformation languages to separate transformation rules into multiple modules, and allow a module to include the contents

---

[2] http://sourceforge.net/projects/atc/

of one or more other modules. ATL provides a feature called module superimposition [12], which allows for combining multiple transformation modules by loading them on top of each other, redefining rules and helpers with the same signature. ETL supports a built-in module import construct, which loads other modules during the loading of the current module. Elements with the same signature are also redefined in ETL. QVT Operational uses "access" and "extends" to compose modules. "Access" loads another module in its own namespace, and all its mappings must be explicitly triggered. "Extends" loads another module into the current namespace, where the current module redefines any mappings with the same signature in the extended module. VIATRA2 supports a module import construct as well, which enables fine-grained reuse of patterns. It is unclear whether VIATRA2's module import also supports redefinition.

3 Transformation Virtual Machine Language

The EMFTVM is a stack-based VM (i.e. instructions communicate values via a stack), and uses a low-level bytecode language to describe model transformations. The main feature of this bytecode language is that it includes an explicit representation of transformation *modules* and *rules*. This decision allows performing module and rule composition on the bytecode itself, as all necessary meta-data is available as a first-class entity in the bytecode. This section discusses the two main EMFTVM bytecode language features that are relevant for module import and rule inheritance: modules and rules.

3.1 Modules

EMFTVM bytecode is organised into *modules*, which represent self-contained units of execution. Each module consists of a number of *fields*, *operations*, and *rules*. Fields and operations can be static or dynamic, similar to Java fields and methods. Modules may *import* other modules, as is further explained in section 5.

Instructions are organised into *code blocks*. Fig. 1 shows the structure of code blocks. Code blocks are executable lists of instructions, and have a number of local variables and a local stack space. Code blocks are used to represent operation bodies and field initialisers. Code blocks may also have nested code blocks, which effectively represent *closures*. Closures are nameless functions that can be invoked or passed as parameters to other functions. Closures are helpful for the implementation of OCL's higher-order operations, such as `select` and `collect`. Closures are also helpful to simplify compilation of source transformation languages, as each source language AST node can be locally compiled into its own code block, and may be nested into the correct place. Such closures may be inlined after compilation.

EMFTVM supports 47 different instructions[3]. Apart from the general-purpose instructions for control flow, several EMF-specific instructions exist, such as

---

[3] http://soft.vub.ac.be/viewvc/*checkout*/EMFTVM/trunk/emftvm/EMFTVM.html

SET, GET, ADD, REMOVE, and INSERT. While *mapping* style transformation languages typically SET element properties, *rewriting* style languages typically ADD and REMOVE element properties. As EMF properties are ordered lists, an INSERT instruction allows one to insert a property value at a specific index.

Finally, modules specify a number of *input*, *inout*, and *output* models. This distinction allows one to enforce read-only or write-only constraints at run-time: input models are read-only, output models write-only, and inout models can be read and written.

3.2 Rules

Fig. 1 shows the part of the EMFTVM metamodel that defines rules and code blocks. Rules consist of input elements, output elements, a *matcher* code block, *applier* code block, and *post-apply* code block. This distinction between *matcher*, *applier*, and *post-apply* allows one to execute rules in stages: the *matcher* filters potential input element matches, the *applier* assigns element properties and deletes elements, and the *post-apply* block contains code that should be run after a rule has been applied. EMFTVM provides a framework for automatic matching and tracing, which invokes these three different code blocks at specific stages.

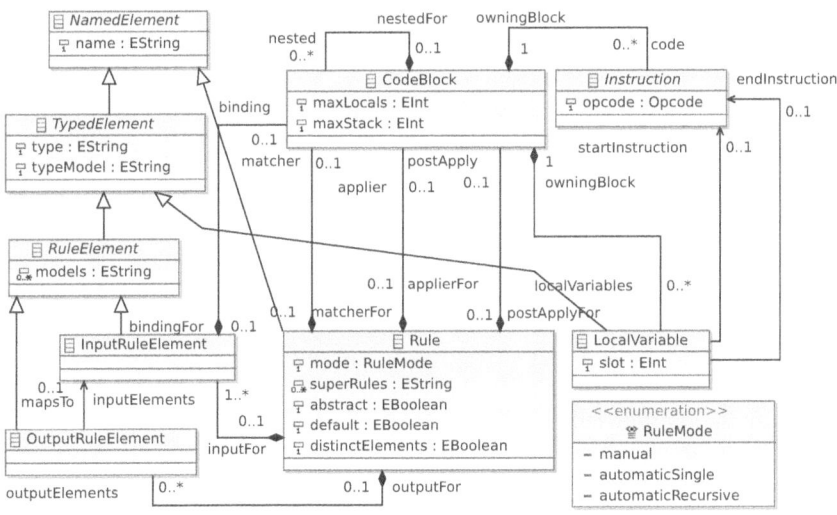

Fig. 1. Structure of EMFTVM rules and code blocks

Input elements can have a *binding* code block. This allows EMFTVM to apply a *search plan* strategy [10] in its automatic matcher. Each *binding* block calculates the valid values for an input element, given the values of the input elements that have already been bound (either by iteration or by another *binding*).

Furthermore, rules have a name that is unique within its module, and can have a number of super-rules. These super-rules are stored as names only, and are resolved at load-time, when rules are composed. This is done to facilitate interaction with the module import mechanism, and is further discussed in section 5. Super-rules and rule inheritance are further explained in section 4.

Rules can be *abstract*, which means that they are only applied in combination with a non-abstract sub-rule. A rule may create *default* traces, which allows the transformation module to *resolve* target elements from a (list of) source element(s). Default traces have as consequence that the same input pattern may not be matched by another rule that creates default traces, as this would result in ambiguous source-target value resolution. Rules may also match against *distinct elements*, which means that no two elements in a single input pattern match can be equal.

Finally, rules have an execution *mode*, which can be either *manual*, *automatic single*, or *automatic recursive*. *Manual* rules have to be explicitly invoked. *Automatic single* rules are matched once, then applied once by the automatic matching framework. *Automatic recursive* rules are matched and applied by the automatic matching framework until there are no more matches.

The next section proposes a common semantics for rule inheritance.

4 Rule Inheritance

Rule inheritance in EMFTVM allows rules to specify a list of super-rules, whereby sub-rules can only match on input that has also matched against their super-rules. As a result, rule inheritance serves as an optimisation strategy that only tries to match sub-rules whenever their super-rules have already matched. This effectively represents a RETE network, such as applied in VIATRA2 [11]. Rule inheritance also serves as a reuse mechanism, whereby sub-rules can reuse and extend the input pattern and output pattern with new elements. Reducing the number of input elements – or output elements – is not possible, and any omitted input/output elements are implicitly inherited from the super-rule. However, super-rule input/output elements must be repeated in the sub-rule in case lexical access to the elements is required (e.g. in the applier or post-apply block).

The EMFTVM rule inheritance mechanism supports multiple inheritance, which requires all super-rules to have matched on the same input before trying to match the sub-rule. Before applying the sub-rule, all super-rules are applied in the order they are specified in the sub-rule. Fig. 2 outlines the semantics for rule matching in the context of rule inheritance. Each rule is represented by a box with compartments. The left compartment contains the input elements, whereas the right compartment contains the output elements. Each input/output element is specified by a label and a type (i.e. `label:Type`).

Rule R3 in the figure only matches against input elements that have also been matched by super-rules R1 and R2. Input/output elements correspond by label: input element `b:B` in rule R1, and `b:D` in rule R2 are the same as input element `b:F` in rule R3 for any match of rule R3. Therefore, R3 only matches b's that are an instance of B, D, and F.

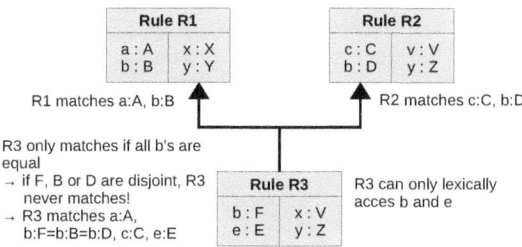

Fig. 2. Matching semantics for rule inheritance

As the number of input/output elements cannot be reduced in sub-rules, R3 is considered to inherit the input elements a:A and c:C from rules R1 and R2, respectively, and output element v:V from rule R2. Rule R3 cannot lexically access those elements, however, as the EMFTVM engine does not pass them as parameters to R3's matcher, applier, and post-apply code blocks.

It is only possible to define super-rule relations between rules of the same kind: manual, automatic, or recursively automatic, and default or non-default. This is because super- and sub-rules are executed together according to the same execution semantics. Taking this into account, the matching semantics of each rule remains sound, even if any of the rules is replaced by an arbitrary other rule (of the same kind). If rules are truly incompatible, they will simply not produce any combined match.

Fig. 3 outlines the semantics for rule application in the context of rule inheritance. Whereas the matching semantics are sound for any change in the rule hierarchy, the application semantics comes with some type safety constraints. The types of all input elements are already guaranteed by the matching algorithm (matches only occur on the specified types). However, the types of the output elements must be compatible between super- and sub-rule. The rule application algorithm creates output elements that are instances of the types specified in the sub-rule. Therefore, those types must be *co-variant* with the types specified for the same elements in the super-rule. For example: an element x : V is created for each match of R3, but is considered as x : X in the application of R1. Therefore, V must be *co-variant* with X: each instance of V must also be an instance of X. Similarly, for the creation of y : Z for R3, and y : Y in R1, Z must be co-variant with Y. These type safety constraints may be checked at load-time by the virtual machine.

The automatic rule matching framework performs optimised matching of rule hierarchies, while being implemented reflectively, i.e. looking up super-rules and input/output elements and their types at run-time. The algorithm is split up into two phases: (1) matching the single automatic rules and (2) matching the recursive automatic rules. The algorithm for single rules works as follows:

1. All rules without super-rules are matched, and their matches (tuple of input elements) are stored.

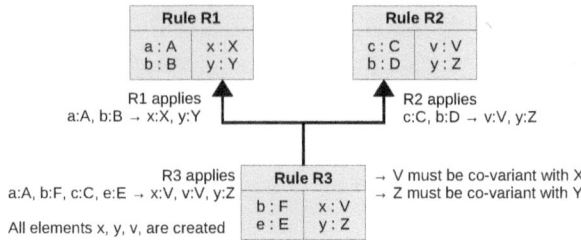

Fig. 3. Application semantics for rule inheritance

2. All rules for which all of their super-rules have matched the same elements are now matched on those elements, and their matches are stored. For all matches, the super-rule matches are removed.
3. The previous step is repeated until all applicable rules are processed.
4. For all matches of non-abstract rules, output elements are created, and the match tuple is converted to a trace tuple that includes the output elements.
5. For all traces, the corresponding rule applier code block is invoked, super-rules first, then the sub-rule.
6. For all traces, the corresponding rule post-apply code block is invoked, super-rules first, then the sub-rule.

Single automatic rules are expected to match on elements from a different model (e.g. an *input* model) than the model in which the rules are applied (e.g. an *output* model). This guarantees that previously found matches are not invalidated by applying rules.

The same cannot be expected for recursive rules, which must be able to match on their own output. Therefore, recursive rules can match on elements from any model (e.g. *inout* models). The algorithm for recursive rules takes this into account, by re-matching after each apply:

1. Rules without super-rules are matched first. For rules with sub-rules, all matches (tuple of input elements) are stored, while only the first match is stored for rules without sub-rules. If a (non-abstract) rule without sub-rules matches, it is applied[4], the recorded matches are cleared, and the algorithm restarts.
2. Rules for which all of their super-rules have matched the same elements are now matched on those elements. Again, for rules with sub-rules, all matches are stored, while only the first match is stored for rules without sub-rules. For all matches, the super-rule matches are removed. If a (non-abstract) rule without sub-rules matches, it is applied, the recorded matches are cleared, and the algorithm restarts.

---

[4] For recursive rules, applying involves converting a match to a trace, creating output elements, and invoking the applier block and post-apply block.

3. When all rules have been processed, and (non-abstract) matches have been recorded, the first of those matches is applied, the recorded matches are cleared, and the algorithm restarts. Otherwise, the algorithm ends.

These algorithms ensure that sub-rules are only matched for the elements that have already been matched by their super-rules, with no unnecessary matching. They also ensure that sub-rules cannot widen the initial input element type constraints and constraints encoded in the matcher code block of the super-rules.

When executing single and recursive automatic rules together, they may operate on the same models in the following way: the single rules transform from an *input* model to an *inout* model, and the recursive rules then further transform the *inout* model.

Even though the different kinds of rules use different matching algorithms, these algorithms share their implementation of rule inheritance. A unified semantics for rule inheritance is enforced in this way.

The following section proposes a common semantics for module import.

5 Module Import

EMFTVM supports module import via the "imports" attribute of each module, which lists a number of module names. These names are resolved at load-time by the VM. Fig. 4 shows how EMFTVM module import works. Each module loads its imported modules before loading itself, in the specified order. For example, module M1 requires that first M2 is loaded, and then M3. The first step is then to start loading M2 (1). Then, M2 requires that M4 and M3 are loaded before itself. Therefore, M4 is loaded (2), and then M3 is loaded (3), which finds that its imported M4 was already loaded (4). Now, M2 can be loaded, and M1 finds that M3 was already loaded (5). Finally, M1 is loaded. Circular imports – and self-imports – are ignored.

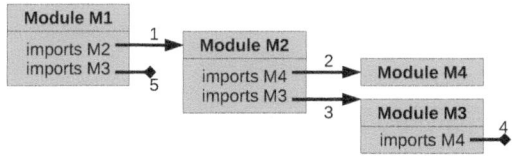

Fig. 4. Module import semantics

Module import supports *redefinition* of fields, operations, and rules that were already specified in an imported module. Whenever a module is imported, its fields, operations, and rules are registered in the VM's lookup table: rules are registered by name, whereas fields and operations are also registered by their context and parameter types[5]. Fields and operations are only *redefined* by an

---
[5] Static fields/operations have a separate lookup table.

importing module if the context and parameter types match. Fields and operations with different context/parameter types are *overloaded* instead. Hence, redefinition of fields and operations is always type-safe. Redefined elements are completely removed, and cannot be accessed by the redefining element.

Because rules are only registered by name, any rule with the same name may redefine an existing rule. That means additional constraint checking is required for rule redefinition. Rules must be of the same kind – manual/automatic single/automatic recursive, and default/non-default – to allow sound redefinition. After all modules are imported, and all rule redefinition has been performed, the super-rules for each rule are resolved. At this time, the type safety checks for rule inheritance are performed (see section 4).

Finally, in case of conflicting specified importing orders, the depth-first loading order, as shown in Fig. 4, is followed. For example, if M1 specified another `imports M4` statement after `imports M3`, the loading algorithm would still load M3 after M4. This is considered correct, because by specifying `imports M4`, M3 states that it wants the opportunity to redefine elements of M4. M1 may still redefine all elements, as it is the last module to be loaded.

Module import is considered transitive: if M1 imports M2, and M2 imports M4, then M1 imports M4, and can redefine elements of M4.

6 Mapping of Rule-Based Model Transformation Languages

To demonstrate the generality of the previously explained composition mechanisms, a mapping from ATL and SimpleGT to the EMFTVM is presented. ATL is an established, *mapping*-style model transformation language, and SimpleGT is a proof-of-concept, *rewriting*-style model transformation language, based on double push-out (DPO) graph transformation semantics. By mapping these two different languages to the same VM, we effectively provide common executable semantics for both languages, including a common semantics for the composition mechanisms discussed before.

6.1 ATL

ATL transformation definitions consist of modules, which can contain different kinds of rules, helper attributes, and helper methods. The mapping of ATL to EMFTVM is straightforward for the most part: Table 1 provides an overview of how ATL constructs are mapped to EMFTVM constructs.

As ATL includes OCL to do its model navigation, OCL support also has to be included in the mapping. EMFTVM forms a symbiosis with the underlying Java run-time environment, and allows the lookup of Java types and invocation of Java methods. OCL support is provided in the form of a natively implemented EMFTVM module of operations, and a set of natively implemented collection types (Sequence, Set, Bag, OrderedSet). Higher-order collection operations, such as `select` and `collect`, take an EMFTVM code block as an argument. The

Table 1. Mapping of ATL constructs to EMFTVM constructs

ATL construct → EMFTVM construct
module → module
uses → imports
input model → input model
output model → output model
metamodel → metamodel
matched rule → automatic single default rule
nodefault matched rule → automatic single rule
lazy rule → manual rule
unique lazy rule → manual default rule
rule input element → input element
rule output element → output element
input pattern filter expression → code in rule matcher block
output pattern bindings → code in rule applier block
code in "**do**" block → code in rule post-apply block
matched rule variables → rule fields
called rule → static operation
called rule variables → local variables in operation code block
entrypoint rule → static operation, called from `main`
endpoint rule → static operation, called from `main`
helper attribute without context → static field
helper attribute with context → field
helper method without context → static operation
helper method with context → operation

complete mapping of ATL to EMFTVM is described in the ATL-to-EMFTVM compiler[6]. This compiler is written in ATL, and compiled by itself to EMFTVM.

6.2 Graph Transformations

Most existing graph transformation languages have already evolved into a fairly complex language (e.g. using implicit NAC expressions [13] and control flow constructs [14]). However, none of them support rule inheritance yet[7], and the transformation language has to be altered to support it. Therefore, we introduce a basic, proof-of-concept graph transformation language with built-in rule inheritance and module import support: SimpleGT. SimpleGT is a textual graph rewriting language, based on *double push-out semantics* (DPO): rules include an input graph, correspondence graph, and output graph, where the input graph is deleted, the correspondence graph is left unchanged, and the output graph is created. The correspondence graph is implicit, and is represented by the

---
[6] http://tinyurl.com/ATLtoEMFTVM-atl
[7] Triple Graph Grammars (TGG) do support rule inheritance, but form a different class of graph transformation.

```
module InlineCodeblocks;
transform M : EMFTVM;
rule RetargetInvoke_cbLocalVariableStart { ... }
rule RetargetInvoke_cbLocalVariableEnd {
    from lv : EMFTVM!LocalVariable (endInstruction =~ invoke_cb),
         invoke_cb : EMFTVM!Invoke_cb (codeBlock =~ nestedCb),
         nestedCb : EMFTVM!CodeBlock (code =~| last),
         last : EMFTVM!Instruction
    to lv : EMFTVM!LocalVariable (endInstruction =~ last),
       invoke_cb : EMFTVM!Invoke_cb (codeBlock =~ nestedCb),
       nestedCb : EMFTVM!CodeBlock (code =~ last),
       last : EMFTVM!Instruction }
abstract rule Invoke_cb {
    from cb : EMFTVM!CodeBlock (code =~ invoke_cb),
         invoke_cb : EMFTVM!Invoke_cb
    to cb : EMFTVM!CodeBlock (code =~ invoke_cb),
       invoke_cb : EMFTVM!Invoke_cb }
rule Invoke_cb_inline_locals extends Invoke_cb {
    from cb : EMFTVM!CodeBlock (code =~ invoke_cb),
         invoke_cb : EMFTVM!Invoke_cb (codeBlock =~ nestedCb),
         nestedCb : EMFTVM!CodeBlock (localVariables =~ lv),
         lv : EMFTVM!LocalVariable (slot =~ lv.slot)
    to cb : EMFTVM!CodeBlock (code =~ invoke_cb,
                localVariables =~ lv),
       invoke_cb : EMFTVM!Invoke_cb (codeBlock =~ nestedCb),
       nestedCb : EMFTVM!CodeBlock,
       lv : EMFTVM!LocalVariable }
rule Invoke_cb_inline extends Invoke_cb {
    from cb : EMFTVM!CodeBlock (code =~ invoke_cb),
         invoke_cb : EMFTVM!Invoke_cb (codeBlock =~ nestedCb),
         nestedCb : EMFTVM!CodeBlock
    not nestedCb : EMFTVM!CodeBlock (localVariables =~ lv),
        lv : EMFTVM!LocalVariable
    to cb : EMFTVM!CodeBlock (code =~ invoke_cb,
            code =~ nestedCb.code before invoke_cb,
            lineNumbers =~ nestedCb.lineNumbers,
            nested =~ nestedCb.nested before nestedCb),
       invoke_cb : EMFTVM!Invoke_cb }
```

Listing 1.1. Excerpt of InlineCodeblocks SimpleGT module

intersection of the input and output graph. SimpleGT uses explicit *negative application condition* graphs (NACs), which specify input patterns that prevent the rule from matching.

Listing 1.1 shows an excerpt of a SimpleGT transformation module, named "InlineCodeblocks". This transformation rewrites INVOKE_CB instructions by inlining the invoked code block into the calling code block. SimpleGT uses `from` to specify the input pattern, and `to` to specify the output pattern. The common elements in the input and output pattern form the correspondence graph, and is not altered by EMFTVM. Nodes map to EMF EObjects and edges map to EMF EReferences. A node is specified using a label and type. An edge is specified using the '=~' matching operator: this operator specifies the existence of an edge (or EReference value). In addition, the '=~' operator can be used to match node attribute values (EAttributes).

The rules `RetargetInvoke_cbLocalVariableStart` and `RetargetInvoke_cb-LocalVariableEnd` re-map the start and end instruction of local variables that refer to INVOKE_CB instructions. Only the latter rule is listed here, as it

Table 2. Mapping of SimpleGT constructs to EMFTVM constructs

SimpleGT construct → EMFTVM construct
module → module
imports → imports
model → inout model
metamodel → metamodel
rule → automatic recursive distinct rule
input nodes → input element
nac nodes → *code in rule matcher block*
output nodes → output element *if new element*
unchanged edges → code in rule matcher block
deleted edges → code in rule matcher block and applier block
new edges → code in rule applier block
deleted nodes → code in rule matcher block and applier block

includes a special feature: EMF models have *ordered* edges; the '=~|' operator allows one to match the *last* edge going out from a node (the regular '=~' operator always matches the *first* edge). In this case, the endInstruction of local variable lv should be re-mapped to the last instruction in the nested code block.

The Invoke_cb rule is an example of an *abstract* rule that is inherited by Invoke_cb_inline_locals and Invoke_cb_inline. An abstract rule is only applied when a non-abstract sub-rule is applied. Conversely, the sub-rules only match when all super-rules have matched. Invoke_cb_inline_locals moves one local variable at a time into the calling code block, while re-setting the assigned local variable slot (the EMFTVM metamodel implementation automatically sets this again on read access). Invoke_cb_inline performs the actual inlining, and moves the code (i.e. instructions), nested code blocks, and line number mappings from each invoked code block into its calling code block. The before keyword is used to enforce *insert* semantics instead of *append* semantics (the default): the code of the nested code block should be inserted *before* the subject INVOKE_CB instruction.

The remainder of the transformation module[8] is omitted, as it does not introduce new SimpleGT constructs. An overview of the mapping of SimpleGT to EMFTVM is provided in Table 2. The complete mapping of SimpleGT to EMFTVM is described in the SimpleGT-to-EMFTVM compiler[9], which is written in ATL, and compiled to/executed in EMFTVM.

SimpleGT rules map to automatic, recursive, non-default rules in EMFTVM. Input nodes map to input elements, output nodes map to output elements *only if* they did not occur in the input pattern. NAC nodes are not explicitly represented by rule elements in EMFTVM: the goal is to *not* match them. Instead, they are represented in the rule matcher code block, to make sure they do not occur as

---

[8] http://tinyurl.com/InlineCodeblocks-simplegt
[9] http://tinyurl.com/SimpleGTtoEMFTVM-atl

part of the input graph. The *binding* code block of EMFTVM rule input elements is used to implement a search plan strategy, where input node values are derived from other input node values. The search plan code for NAC nodes is embedded in the rule matcher code block.

7 Conclusion and Future Work

This paper has presented an approach to achieve a general semantics for two internal composition mechanisms for rule-based model transformation languages: module import and rule inheritance. These general semantics are achieved in three steps: (1) module import and rule inheritance are defined within a virtual machine (VM) for model transformation, named EMFTVM, (2) the generality of the VM is demonstrated by translating two distinct transformation languages, ATL and graph transformations, to the VM, and (3) by translating ATL and graph transformations to the same VM, a common semantics for module import and rule inheritance applies to those languages.

The generality of the presented semantics is limited by two factors: (1) EMFTVM is specific to EMF models, and (2) only two rule-based languages have been translated to EMFTVM. As EMF is a de facto standard for modelling, and many transformation languages target EMF [3,7,9,10,14,15,16], the scope of EMF is considered sufficiently relevant to the modelling community. The fact that only ATL and SimpleGT, a proof-of-concept graph transformation language, have been translated to EMFTVM is mitigated by the nature of both languages. ATL is a model *mapping* language, which uses a single rule matching phase, after which all rules are applied. SimpleGT is a recursive model *rewriting* language, which applies its rules recursively until no more matches can be found. Both are very different in rule matching and application semantics, but are still able to share the semantics for module import and rule inheritance. Any languages with semantics similar to either ATL (i.e. the QVT-like languages) or SimpleGT (i.e. graph transformation languages) can likely be mapped to EMFTVM as well.

As EMFTVM implements the entire ATL and SimpleGT languages, it provides a complete interoperability solution for these languages (including ATL's rule invocation and implicit tracing mechanism). Over time, EMFTVM may evolve as a general interoperability solution, as more languages are mapped to it. It is currently not possible to map *synchronisation*-style languages, such as QVT Relations [9] and Triple Graph Grammars (TGG) [8], to EMFTVM. These languages try to first match output elements, and will create them if not found. Current EMFTVM output elements are always created.

References

1. Kleppe, A.G.: First European Workshop on Composition of Model Transformations - CMT 2006. Technical Report TR-CTIT-06-34, Enschede (2006)
2. Budinsky, F., Steinberg, D., Merks, E., Ellersick, R., Grose, T.J.: Eclipse Modeling Framework. The Eclipse Series. Addison Wesley Professional, Reading (2003)

3. Jouault, F., Kurtev, I.: Transforming Models with ATL. In: Bruel, J.-M. (ed.) MoDELS 2005. LNCS, vol. 3844, pp. 128–138. Springer, Heidelberg (2006)
4. Ehrig, H., Ehrig, K., Prange, U., Taentzer, G.: Fundamentals of Algebraic Graph Transformation, 1st edn. Springer, Heidelberg (2006)
5. Jouault, F., Kurtev, I.: On the Architectural Alignment of ATL and QVT. In: Proceedings SAC 2006 (2006)
6. Wimmer, M., Kappel, G., Kusel, A., Retschitzegger, W., Schönböck, J., Schwinger, W., Kolovos, D., Paige, R., Lauder, M., Schürr, A., Wagelaar, D.: A Comparison of Rule Inheritance in Model-to-Model Transformation Languages. In: Cabot, J., Visser, E. (eds.) ICMT 2011. LNCS, vol. 6707, pp. 31–46. Springer, Heidelberg (2011)
7. Kolovos, D.S., Paige, R.F., Polack, F.A.C.: The Epsilon Transformation Language. In: Vallecillo, A., Gray, J., Pierantonio, A. (eds.) ICMT 2008. LNCS, vol. 5063, pp. 46–60. Springer, Heidelberg (2008)
8. Schürr, A.: Specification of graph translators with triple graph grammars. In: Mayr, E.W., Schmidt, G., Tinhofer, G. (eds.) WG 1994. LNCS, vol. 903, pp. 151–163. Springer, Heidelberg (1995)
9. Object Management Group, Inc.: Meta Object Facility (MOF) 2.0 Query/View/-Transformation Specification, Final Adopted Specification, ptc/05-11-01 (2005)
10. Varró, G., Friedl, K., Varró, D.: Adaptive Graph Pattern Matching for Model Transformations using Model-sensitive Search Plans. Electr. Notes Theor. Comput. Sci. 152, 191–205 (2006)
11. Bergmann, G., Ökrös, A., Ráth, I., Varró, D., Varró, G.: Incremental pattern matching in the viatra model transformation system. In: Proceedings of GRaMoT 2008, pp. 25–32. ACM Press, New York (2008)
12. Wagelaar, D., Van Der Straeten, R., Deridder, D.: Module superimposition: a composition technique for rule-based model transformation languages. Software and Systems Modeling 9, 285–309 (2009)
13. Fischer, T., Niere, J., Torunski, L., Zündorf, A.: Story Diagrams: A New Graph Rewrite Language Based on the Unified Modeling Language and Java. In: Ehrig, H., Engels, G., Kreowski, H.-J., Rozenberg, G. (eds.) TAGT 1998. LNCS, vol. 1764, pp. 296–309. Springer, Heidelberg (2000)
14. Arendt, T., Biermann, E., Jurack, S., Krause, C., Taentzer, G.: Henshin: Advanced Concepts and Tools for In-Place EMF Model Transformations. In: Petriu, D.C., Rouquette, N., Haugen, Ø. (eds.) MODELS 2010. LNCS, vol. 6394, pp. 121–135. Springer, Heidelberg (2010)
15. Lawley, M., Steel, J.: Practical Declarative Model Transformation with Tefkat. In: Bruel, J.-M. (ed.) MoDELS 2005. LNCS, vol. 3844, pp. 139–150. Springer, Heidelberg (2006)
16. Kalnins, A., Barzdins, J., Celms, E.: Model Transformation Language MOLA. In: Aßmann, U., Aksit, M., Rensink, A. (eds.) MDAFA 2003. LNCS, vol. 3599, pp. 62–76. Springer, Heidelberg (2005)

Properties of Realistic Feature Models Make Combinatorial Testing of Product Lines Feasible

Martin Fagereng Johansen[1,2], Øystein Haugen[1], and Franck Fleurey[1]

[1] SINTEF ICT, Pb. 124 Blindern, 0314 Oslo, Norway
{Martin.Fagereng.Johansen,Oystein.Haugen,Franck.Fleurey}@sintef.no
[2] Institute for Informatics, University of Oslo, Pb. 1080 Blindern, 0316 Oslo, Norway

Abstract. Feature models and associated feature diagrams allow modeling and visualizing the constraints leading to the valid products of a product line. In terms of their expressiveness, feature diagrams are equivalent to propositional formulas which makes them theoretically expensive to process and analyze. For example, satisfying propositional formulas, which translates into finding a valid product for a given feature model, is an NP-hard problem, which has no fast, optimal solution. This theoretical complexity could prevent the use of powerful analysis techniques to assist in the development and testing of product lines. However, we have found that satisfying realistic feature models is quick. Thus, we show that combinatorial interaction testing of product lines is feasible in practice. Based on this, we investigate covering array generation time and results for realistic feature models and find where the algorithms can be improved.

Keywords: Software Product Lines, Testing, Feature Models, Practical, Realistic, Combinatorial Interaction Testing.

1 Introduction

A software product line is a collection of systems with a considerable amount of code in common. The commonality and differences between the systems are commonly modeled as a feature model. Testing of software product lines is a challenge since testing all possible products is intractable. Yet, one has to ensure that any valid product will function correctly. There is no consensus on how to efficiently test software product lines, but there are a number of suggested approaches. Each of the approaches still suffers from problems of scalability (Section 2).

Combinatorial interaction testing [4] is a promising approach for performing interaction testing between the features in a product line. Most of the difficulties of combinatorial interaction testing have been sorted out, but there is one part of it that is still considered intractable, namely finding a single valid configuration, an NP-hard problem. This is thus the bottleneck of the approach. In this paper we resolve this bottleneck such that combinatorial interaction testing should not be considered intractable any more (Section 3). We then investigate how a basic covering array generation algorithm performs on realistic feature models (Section 4), and suggest, based on the resolution of the bottleneck and on the empirics, how the algorithm can be improved (Section 5).

2 Background

2.1 Software Product Lines

A software product line (SPL) [19] is a collection of systems with a considerable amount of code in common. The primary motivation for structuring one's systems as a product line is to allow customers to have a system tailored for their purpose and needs, while still avoiding redundancy of code. It is common for customers to have conflicting requirements. In that case, it is not even possible to ship one system for all customers.

The Eclipse products [22] can be seen as a software product line. Today, Eclipse lists 12 products on their download page[1]. These products share many components, but all components are not offered together as one single product. The reason is that the download would be unnecessary large, since, for example, a C++ systems programmer usually does not need to use the PHP-related features. It would also bloat the system by giving the user many unnecessary alternatives when, for example, creating a new project. Some products contain early developer releases of some components, such as Eclipse for modeling. Including these would compromise the stability for the other products. Thus, it should be clear why offering specialized products for different use cases is good.

One way to model the commonalities and differences in a product line is using a feature model [10]. A feature model sets up the commonalities and differences of a product line in a tree such that configuring the product line proceeds from the root of the tree. Please refer to an example of a feature model for a subset of Eclipse in Figure 1. Proceeding from the root, configuring the product line consists of making a decision for each node in the tree. Each node represents a feature of the product line. The nature of this decision is modeled as a decoration on the edges going from a node to another. For example, in Figure 1, one has to choose one windowing system which one wants Eclipse to run under. This is modeled as an empty semi-circle on the outgoing edges. When choosing a team functionality provider, one or all can be chosen. This is modeled as a filled semi circle. The team functionality itself is marked with an empty circle. This means that that feature is optional. A filled circle means that the feature is mandatory. One has to configure the feature model from the root, and one can only include a feature when the preceding feature is selected. For example, supporting CVS over SSH requires that one has CVS.

The parts that can be different in the products of a product line are usually called its *variability*. One particular product in the product line is called a *variant* and is specified by a configuration of the feature model. Such a configuration consists of specifying whether each feature is included or not.

---
[1] http://eclipse.org/downloads/

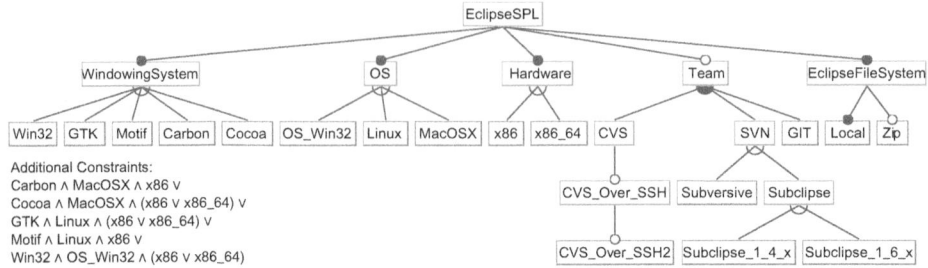

Fig. 1. Feature model for a subset of Eclipse

2.2 Software Product Line Testing

Testing a software product line poses a number of new challenges compared to testing single systems. It has to be ensured that each possible configuration of the product line functions correctly. One way to validate a product line is through testing, but testing is done on a running system. The software product line is simply a collection of many products. One cannot test each possible product, since the number of products in general grows exponentially with the number of features in the product line. For the feature model in Figure 1, the number of possible configurations is 512, and this is a relatively simple product line.

There is no single recommended approach available today for testing product lines efficiently [5], but there are many suggestions. Some of the more promising suggestions are combinatorial interaction testing [4], discussed below; reusable component testing, seen in industry [9], but which does not test for interaction faults in the product line; a technique called ScenTED, where the idea is to express the commonalities and differences on the UML model of the product line and then derive concrete test cases by analyzing it [21]; and incremental testing, where the idea is to automatically adapt a test case from one product to the next using the specification of similarities and differences between the products [25].

2.3 Combinatorial Interaction Testing for Product Lines

Combinatorial interaction testing [4] is one of the most promising approaches. The benefits of this approach is that it deals directly with the feature model to derive a small subset of products which can then be tested using single system testing techniques, of which there are many good ones. The idea is to select a small subset of products where the interaction faults are most likely to occur. For example, we can select the subset of all possible products where each pair of features is present. This includes the cases where both features are present, when one is present, and when none of the two are present. Table 1 shows the 22 products that must be tested to ensure that every pair-wise interaction between the features in the running example functions correctly. Each row represents one feature and every column one product. 'X' means that the feature is included for the product, '-' means that the feature is not included. Some features are included for every product because they are mandatory, and some pairs are not covered since they are invalid according to the feature model.

Table 1. Pair-wise coverage of the feature model in Figure 1 the test suites numbered

Feature\ Product	1	2	3	4	5	6	7	8	9	10	11	12	13	14	15	16	17	18	19	20	21	22
EclipseSPL	X	X	X	X	X	X	X	X	X	X	X	X	X	X	X	X	X	X	X	X	X	X
WindowingSystem	X	X	X	X	X	X	X	X	X	X	X	X	X	X	X	X	X	X	X	X	X	X
Win32	-	-	X	-	-	X	-	-	X	-	-	-	-	-	X	-	-	-	-	-	-	X
GTK	-	X	-	-	-	X	-	X	-	-	X	-	-	X	-	X	-	-	-	-	-	-
Motif	-	-	-	-	X	-	-	X	-	-	-	X	-	-	-	-	-	-	X	-	-	-
Carbon	-	-	-	X	-	-	-	-	-	X	-	-	-	-	X	-	X	-	-	-	-	-
Cocoa	X	-	-	-	-	-	-	-	-	-	X	-	-	-	-	-	-	-	X	X	-
OS	X	X	X	X	X	X	X	X	X	X	X	X	X	X	X	X	X	X	X	X	X	X
OS_Win32	-	-	X	-	-	X	-	-	X	-	-	-	-	-	X	-	-	-	-	-	-	X
Linux	-	X	-	-	X	-	X	X	-	X	-	X	-	X	-	-	X	-	X	-	-	-
MacOSX	X	-	-	X	-	-	-	-	-	X	-	X	-	-	X	-	X	-	X	X	-
Hardware	X	X	X	X	X	X	X	X	X	X	X	X	X	X	X	X	X	X	X	X	X	X
x86	X	-	-	X	X	-	-	X	-	X	X	X	-	-	X	X	-	X	X	-	-	-
x86_64	-	X	X	-	-	X	X	-	X	-	-	-	X	X	-	X	-	-	X	-	X	X
Team	-	-	-	-	-	X	X	X	X	X	X	X	X	X	X	X	X	X	X	X	X	X
CVS	-	-	-	-	-	-	-	-	-	-	-	-	-	-	X	X	X	X	X	X	X	X
CVS_Over_SSH	-	-	-	-	-	-	-	-	-	-	-	-	-	-	-	X	X	X	X	X	X	X
CVS_Over_SSH2	-	-	-	-	-	-	-	-	-	-	-	-	-	-	-	-	X	X	X	X	X	X
SVN	-	-	-	-	-	X	X	X	X	X	X	X	X	X	X	-	X	X	X	X	X	X
Subversive	-	-	-	-	-	-	-	-	-	-	X	X	X	X	X	-	-	-	-	-	-	X
Subclipse	-	-	-	-	-	X	X	X	X	X	-	-	-	-	-	X	-	X	X	X	X	-
Subclipse_1_4_x	-	-	-	-	-	-	-	X	X	X	-	-	-	-	-	X	-	-	-	-	X	-
Subclipse_1_6_x	-	-	-	-	-	X	X	-	-	-	-	-	-	-	-	-	-	X	X	X	-	-
GIT	-	-	-	-	-	-	-	-	X	-	-	-	-	-	-	X	X	-	X	X	-	X
EclipseFileSystem	X	X	X	X	X	X	X	X	X	X	X	X	X	X	X	X	X	X	X	X	X	X
Local	X	X	X	X	X	X	X	X	X	X	X	X	X	X	X	X	X	X	X	X	X	X
Zip	-	-	-	X	X	-	-	-	X	-	-	-	-	X	-	-	-	-	-	X	-	X

Testing every pair is called 2-wise testing, or pair-wise testing. This is a special case of t-wise testing where $t = 2$. 1-wise coverage means that every feature is at least included and excluded in one product, 3-wise coverage means that every combination of three features are present, etc. For our running example, 5, 64 and 150 products is sufficient to achieve 1-wise, 3-wise and 4-wise coverage, respectively.

An important motivation for combinatorial interaction testing is a paper by Kuhn et al. 2004 [11]. They indicated empirically that most bugs are found for 6-wise coverage, and that for 1-wise one is likely to find on average around 50%, for 2-wise on average around 70%, and for 3-wise around 95%, etc.

There are three main stages in the application of combinatorial interaction testing to a product line. First, the feature model of the system must be made. Second, the subset of products must be generated from the feature model for some coverage strength. Such a subset is called a t-wise covering array for a coverage strength t. Last, a single system testing technique must be selected and applied to each product in this covering array. The first and last of these stages are well understood. The second stage, however, is widely regarded as intractable, thereby rendering the approach useless for industrial size software product lines.

3 The Case for Tractable t-wise Covering Array Generation

3.1 Complexity Analysis of Covering Array Generation

The generation of t-wise covering arrays is equivalent to the minimum set cover problem, an NP-complete problem. Given a set of elements, for example $U = \{1,2,3,4,5\}$; we have a set of sets of elements from U, for example $S = \{\{1,2,3\}, \{2,4\}, \{3,4\}, \{4,5\}\}$. The set cover problem is to identify the minimum number of sets, C, from S such that the union contains all elements from U, which is for the example $C = \{\{1,2,3\}, \{4,5\}\}$.

1-wise covering array generation is easily converted to a set cover problem by listing all valid configurations of the product line, and having that as S. Each element of U is a pair with the feature name and a Boolean specifying the inclusion or exclusion of the feature. Solving this set cover problem then yields a 1-wise covering array. This can be done similarly for $t > 1$ by having tuples of assignments in U.

The set cover problem has a known approximation algorithm. (An approximation in this context is not the degree of t-wise coverage, which is 100% for all the discussion in this paper; but how many more products are selected than absolutely necessary.) The approximation algorithm was presented in Chvátal 1979 [3]. It is a greedy algorithm with a defined upper bound for the degree of approximation which grows with the size of the problem, but the degree of approximation remains acceptable. The algorithm is quite simple; it selects the set in S which covers the most uncovered elements until all elements are covered. For t-wise testing, this means selecting the product which covers the most uncovered tuples.

The set cover problem assumes that the sets with which to cover are already available so that one can look at all of them. For feature models, the solution space grows exponentially with respect to the number of features. Thus, it is infeasible to iterate through all the valid configurations.

And it gets worse, even generating a single configuration of a feature model is equivalent to the Boolean satisfiability problem (SAT), an NP-hard problem. SAT is the problem of assigning values to the variables of a propositional formula such that the formula evaluates to true. Batory 2005 [1] showed that ordinary feature models are equivalent to propositional formulas with respect to expressiveness, and that a feature model can easily be converted to a propositional formula.

Approximating the SAT problem is not possible: either we have the solution or we do not. This is also why the literature on combinatorial interaction testing classifies the generation of covering arrays as intractable.

3.2 Quick Satisfiability of Realistic Feature Models

Nie and Leung 2011 [16] is a recent survey of combinatorial testing. They state that their survey is the first complete and systematic survey on this topic. They found 50 papers on the generation of covering arrays. Covering array generation is reported to be NP-hard, but no detailed analysis is given. Such an analysis is given in both Perrouin et al. 2010 [18] and Garvin et al. 2011 [6] which both classify covering array generation as intractable because finding a single configuration of a feature model is equivalent to the Boolean satisfiability problem.

And this is indeed the general case given an arbitrary, grammatically valid feature model, but is it so in practice? It was observed by Mendonca et al. 2009 [15] that SAT-based analysis of realistic feature models with constraints is easy, but they did not identify the theoretical reason for this nor whether it is necessarily so and suggested finding the theoretical explanation as future work.

We propose that the theoretical explanation simply is that realistic feature models must be easily configurable by customers in order for them to efficiently use them. Configuring a feature model is equivalent to solving the Boolean satisfiability problem for the feature model.

The primary role of feature models in software product line engineering is for a potential customer to be able to sit down and configure a product to fit his or her needs. Imagine the opposite case. A company has developed a product line, but finding a single product of the product line takes a million years since there is no tractable solution to NP-hard problems. This situation is absurd. If it is really that difficult to find even a single product in a product line, then the feature model is too difficult for customers to use. If the customers cannot configure a feature model by hand assisted by a computer, is not an important point of the product line approach lost?

The same argument also shows that finding the solution to a partially configured feature model remains quick. If not, a customer might come into the situation that he or she cannot manage to complete the product configuration.

The kind of complexity that gives rise to modern computers being unable to solve a Boolean satisfiability problem in a timely manner would start challenging what is understandable by an engineer maintaining the product line.

Therefore, for the class of feature models intended to be configured by humans assisted by computers, which we think at least is a very large part of the realistic feature models, quick satisfiability is also a property.

3.3 Configuration Space

Even if the satisfiability of a realistic feature model is quick, traversal of the configuration space is still an issue. The configuration space of a feature model grows exponentially with the number of features, so one cannot traverse this space looking for the configuration that covers the most uncovered tuples, as required by Chvátal's greedy approximation algorithm.

Even if one only manages to cover one tuple per iteration, the upper bound for both time and the numbers of products is polynomial, since the number of tuples is $\binom{f}{t}$ (where f is the number of features and t the coverage strength; for example, $\binom{f}{2}$ gives the number of ways we can select a pair out of the configured features where order does not matter.) It is highly likely, however, that one is able to quickly cover many tuples. For pair-wise coverage, finding the first product covers $\binom{f}{2}$ out of $4\binom{f}{2}$ pairs for the worst case scenario. This is at least 25% of the possible pairs.

Covering many tuples at each iteration is still a challenge, but the upper bound of the penalty is polynomial. Since it is not feasible to traverse the configuration space to find the product which covers the most tuples, neither is it possible to guarantee the upper bound for the approximation with Chvátal's greedy algorithm. As we will see in the section on empirics, this does not seem to be a problem as one is usually able to cover many tuples per iteration.

3.4 Tractable Approximation of Covering Arrays

Since finding a covering array consists of two parts, finding valid configurations and solving the set cover problem, and since the former was shown to be tractable and the second is approximable by Chvátal's algorithm, we conclude that finding an approximation of the covering array is also tractable for realistic feature models.

4 Performance of Chvátal's Algorithm for Covering Array Generation

Even if the generation of covering arrays can be shown to be tractable, some improvement of the algorithms still have to be done in order to generate covering arrays from some of the largest known feature models. Let us look at how a basic implementation of Chvátal's algorithm for generating covering arrays performs and then discuss how to improve it.

The following algorithm assumes a feature model, FM, has been loaded, and a strength, t, of the wanted coverage strength has been given. From the set of assignments, (f, i), where f is a feature of FM, and i is a Boolean specifying whether f is included, all combinations of t assignments are generated and placed in a set, U. This set then includes all valid and invalid tuples.

An Adaption of Chvátal's Algorithm for Covering Array Generation.

```
While U is not empty:
  c is a configuration of FM with no variables assigned.
  For each tuple e in U:
    Satisfy FM assuming the assignments in both c and e.
    If satisfiable: Fix the assignments of e in c. Remove e from U.
  Satisfy FM assuming c, add the solution to the covering array C.
  //At some point, decide to remove the invalid tuples from U.
  If the number of newly covered tuples < number of features:
    For each tuple e in U:
      If FM is not satisfiable assuming e, remove e from U.
//C now holds the covering array of FM of strength t.
```

4.1 Models

Sometimes in papers discussing combinatorial interaction testing, experiments are run on randomly generated feature models. The problem with that is that one is assuming things about feature models that might not be realistic. Here, performance measurements will be run on realistic feature models, so that no assumptions are made on the nature of realistic feature models.

Models[2] were gathered from some available sources within software product line engineering research where the models are open and available. All the feature models are either of actual product lines or related to publications. The models are listed in Table 2 together with the product line name and their source.

Table 2. Models and Sources

System name	Model File Name	Source
X86 Linux kernel 2.6.28.6	2.6.28.6-icse11.dimacs	[23]
Part of FreeBSD kernel 8.0.0	freebsd-icse11.dimacs	[23]
eCos 3.0 i386pc	ecos-icse11.dimacs	[23]
e-Shop	Eshop-fm.xml	[12]
Violet, graphical model editor	Violet.m	http://sourceforge.net/projects/violet/
Berkeley DB	Berkeley.m	http://www.oracle.com/us/products/database/berkeley-db/index.html
Arcade Game Maker Pedagogical Product Line	arcade_game_pl_fm.xml	http://www.sei.cmu.edu/productlines/ppl/
Graph Product Line	Graph-product-line-fm.xml	[13]
Graph Product Line Nr. 4	Gg4.m	an extended version of the Graph Product line from [13]
Smart home	smart_home_fm.xml	[27]
TightVNC Remote Desktop Software	TightVNC.m	http://www.tightvnc.com/
AHEAD Tool Suite (ATS) Product Line	Apl.m	[24]
Fame DBMS	fame_dbms_fm.xml	http://fame-dbms.org/
Connector	connector_fm.xml	a tutorial [26]
Simple stack data structure	stack_fm.xml	a tutorial [26]
Simple search engine	REAL-FM-12.xml	[14]
Simple movie system	movies_app_fm.xml	[17]
Simple aircraft	aircraft_fm.xml	a tutorial [26]
Simple automobile	car_fm.xml	[28]

4.2 Tool and Transformations

The models gathered were of many different formats. Software product line engineering is an active field of research, and there are many research tools for different purposes and with various strengths and weaknesses.

In order to measure the performance of covering array generation on the gathered models, integration and some modification of existing tools and libraries were needed to make them cooperate. Figure 2 shows the overview of the tool

---

[2] The models are available at the following URL: http://heim.ifi.uio.no/martifag/models2011/fms/

that was constructed for this purpose[3]. The figure is of no particular graphical modeling notation. The diamonds symbolize files with a certain suffix, the boxes symbolize internal data structures and the arrows symbolize transformations between the formats.

The tool accepts feature models in three different formats: GUI DSL (model names suffixed with '.m'), as shipped with earlier versions of Feature IDE; SXFM, the Simple XML Feature Model format (model names suffixed with '.xml') and dimacs (model names suffixed with '.dimacs'), a file format for storing propositional formulas in conjunctive normal form (CNF).

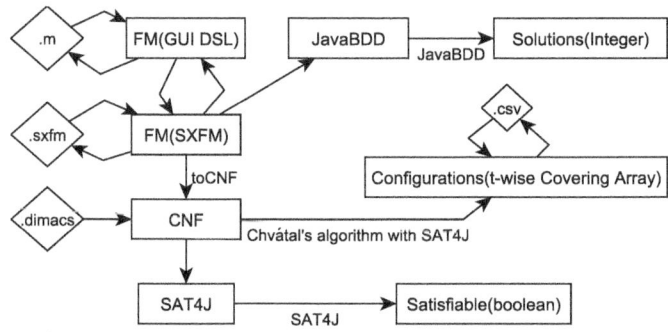

Fig. 2. Transformations in the tool

The GUI DSL files can be loaded using the Feature IDE library. This library allows writing and reading of SXFM files. Thus, they can be loaded into the SPLAR library[4] along with other SXFM files.

The SPLAR library provides an export to conjunctive normal form (CNF), a canonical way of representing general propositional constraints. Thus all the previously loaded models can be converted into CNF formulas, along with other formulas stored in dimacs files.

Once a model is in the form of a CNF formula, it can be given to SAT4J, an open source tool for solving the SAT problem. Thus, all the feature models can be input to the covering array algorithm discussed above. (SAT4J is also used to calculate satisfiability time for the feature models.)

The covering arrays are written to a comma separated values (CSV) file, which can be viewed in Microsoft Excel, Open Office Calc, etc. The covering arrays are then ready to be used to configure products for which single system testing is applied.

(Another interesting thing to know about a feature model is the number of possible configurations. The SPLAR library makes it possible to generate a

---

[3] The tool is available as open source at http://heim.ifi.uio.no/martifag/models2011/spltool/
[4] http://splar.googlecode.com

binary decision tree (BDD) which JavaBDD can work with. It then calculates the number of possible configurations of the feature model.)

4.3 Results

Table 3 shows the results from running[5] our tool on the feature models in Table 2. The feature models are ordered after the number of features. The next column shows the number of unique constraints in the model as the number of clauses of the conjunctive normal form of the constraints. (Constraints implied by the structure of the feature diagrams were not included in the count.) The number of valid products for each feature model is available for some of the smaller models, and as can be seen, quickly increases. The next column shows the time, in milliseconds, for running SAT4J on the feature model to find a single valid solution. The following columns show both the size and time for generating covering array of strengths 1–4. Some of the results are not available because the current implementation of the tools to not scale well to these sizes.

Boolean Satisfiability Times for Feature Models. Satisfiability in general has a worst case of about $O(2^n)$ according to Pătrașcu and Williams 2010 [20]. Table 3 shows the satisfiability times for the feature models. Empirically the satisfiability time of the feature models remains low. Thus, our conclusion regarding the quickness of satisfiability of realistic feature models is consistent with these few observations. Note that this is not meant as a validation, but merely as a demonstration of what we discussed in Section 3; that is, it follows from the fact that the feature models are meant to be configured manually.

Covering Array Generation. The following are the statistically significant relations[6] between the number of features and the sizes of the covering arrays. $CA(P,t)$ is the covering array with strength t for the propositional formula, P, representing a feature model with F features. The size function gives the size of the covering array.

$log(size(CA(P,2))) = 0.37 * log(F) + 1.30$, adjusted R^2: 0.59
$log(size(CA(P,3))) = 1.09 * log(F) + 0.00$, adjusted R^2: 0.63

Covering array sizes of strength 1 and 4 did not allow for a statistical model with a decent fit to be made. The fit for strengths 2 and 3 are poor. The reason is that covering array sizes are not really dependent on the number of features but on the structure of the feature model. For example, for 1-wise coverage, a covering array of size 2 might be sufficient: a certain assignment of optional features and the inverse.

---

[5] The computer on which we did the measurements had an Intel Q9300 CPU @2.53GHz and 8 GB, 400MHz ram. All executions ran in one thread.
[6] Adjusted R^2 is a measure, ranging from 0 to 1, of the goodness of fit of a statistical model. A value of 0.90 means that it is very unlikely a random sample would fit this approximation with the same significance, and a value of 0.20 means that it is very likely.

Table 3. Feature Models, satisfiability times, covering array sizes and generation times

Feature Model \ keys	Features	Constraints	Solutions	SAT time (ms)	1-way size	1-way time (ms)	2-way size	2-way time (ms)	3-way size	3-way times (ms)	4-way size	4-way time (ms)
2.6.28.6-icse11.dimacs	6,888	187,193	n/a	125	n/a	n/a	n/a	n/a	n/a	n/a	n/a	n/a
freebsd-icse11.dimacs	1,396	17,352	n/a	18	7	257,324	n/a	n/a	n/a	n/a	n/a	n/a
ecos-icse11.dimacs	1,244	2,768	n/a	12	6	16,178	n/a	n/a	n/a	n/a	n/a	n/a
Eshop-fm.xml	287	22	n/a	5	4	920	22	364,583	n/a	n/a	n/a	n/a
Violet.m	101	90	1.55E+26	1	4	280	28	21,278	121	3,865,245	n/a	n/a
Berkeley.m	78	47	4.03E+09	1	3	250	23	11,195	96	1,974,741	n/a	n/a
arcade_game_pl_fm.xml	61	35	3.30E+09	3	4	249	17	8,219	63	681,044	n/a	n/a
Gg4.m	38	23	960	1	6	171	22	1,903	63	88,355	156	11,915,393
smart_home_fm.xml	35	1	1,048,576	9	2	141	11	1,046	28	33,010	73	1,995,731
TightVNC.m	30	4	297,252	1	4	109	13	917	46	18,144	124	1,404,756
Apl.m	25	3	4,176	1	3	78	10	583	34	8,865	91	429,207
fame_dbms_fm.xml	21	1	320	3	3	109	9	515	24	5,138	49	121,989
connector_fm.xml	20	1	18	3	6	141	15	485	18	4,147	18	48,086
Graph-product-line-fm.xml	20	15	30	3	5	141	15	512	26	4,390	30	88,022
stack.fm.xml	17	1	432	7	3	109	12	409	41	2,471	96	56,086
REAI-FM-12.xml	14	3	126	7	4	94	13	340	33	1,261	66	18,807
movies_app_fm.xml	13	1	24	3	2	78	6	252	14	963	22	6,065
aircraft.fm.xml	13	1	315	7	3	78	10	286	23	1,131	54	9,597
car_fm.xml	9	3	13	7	3	63	7	200	12	425	13	1,141

The following are the estimated relations between the number of features and the time taken in milliseconds of generating the covering arrays.

$log(time(CA(P,1))) = 1.46 * log(F) + 0.00$, adjusted R^2: 0.84
$log(time(CA(P,2))) = 2.13 * log(F) + 0.00$, adjusted R^2: 0.96
$log(time(CA(P,3))) = 4.03 * log(F) - 3.51$, adjusted R^2: 0.98
$log(time(CA(P,4))) = 6.02 * log(F) - 6.41$, adjusted R^2: 0.97.

5 Discussion

5.1 Memory Requirements

The way our tool deals with the constraints in a feature model is to calculate and store the valid, uncovered tuples in memory. The tuples need to be traversed in order to find the configurations which cover the most uncovered tuples at each iteration. Doing it this way, the number of constraints does not affect the memory requirement significantly, but memory might prove to be a bottle neck.

This effectively sets the memory requirement to $O(F^t)$, where F is the number of features in a feature model and t is the strength of the coverage. For a system with M bytes of memory and assuming each t-tuple requires $t*x$ bytes, the upper bound for t-wise coverage is $F^t = M/(t*x)$.

For pair-wise coverage on a system with 8GB of memory, and assuming that a structure holding the pairs take 20 bytes, the upper bound is $n = \sqrt{8,000,000,000/20}$, $n = 20,000$ features. This is the upper bound of a high-end laptop. More powerful computers are available which can be used for generating covering arrays which increases the upper bound such that even 3-wise coverage of the second largest feature model in our sample is within.

5.2 Accepted Covering Array Size

There is a correspondence between the number of features in a feature model and the size of the team working with it. Thus a team of developers and testers should be able to deal with a covering array of a size around the same size as the number of features. If we look at the data and statistical models for covering array size, we can see that the size of 1–3-wise covering arrays is below or close to the number of features since the coefficient of log(F), and thus the exponent of F, is less than or close to 1.

5.3 Suggested Improvements and Future Work

Given the evaluations up to this point, there are a number of source of improvement for generating covering arrays for software product lines.

Exploiting the Boolean Satisfiability Speed. Nie and Leung 2011 [16] classified handling constraints for covering array generation is an open problem for covering array generation in general. Using SAT-solvers is good way to handle constraints for covering array generation based on feature models. Also, since satisfiability of feature models has been assumed to be intractable up to this point, it might be an unexploited source for improvement of covering array generation speed.

Parallelization. The algorithm that was used to make the measurements in this paper ran in one thread. An algorithm which supports running on several threads will improve the execution time for generating the covering arrays. For example, the step for finding all invalid tuples in the adaption of Chvátal's algorithm above can be run in parallel by splitting the set of tuples in, for example, four and checking each fourth in a separate thread.

Heuristics. Another unexploited source of improvement for covering array generation is knowledge from the domain model. UML-models and annotations on feature models should be taken into account when generating a covering array to make it smaller and its generation time lower. CVL [7] is a variability language with tool support which, in addition to feature diagrams, models the variability of a system on the system model as well. Knowing what a feature refers to in a system model is an unexploited source of improvement for covering array generation.

In a recent publication [8], we show how to exploit one commonly occurring structure in product lines when doing combinatorial interaction testing. Often there are several implementations of the same basic functionality which is used by the other components in the product line through an abstraction layer. These implementations occur as mutual exclusive alternatives in the feature model. Mutual exclusive alternatives are detrimental to combinatorial interaction testing [2], causing a substantial increase in the number of products in the covering arrays. We show that if the increase of products is due to the abstraction layer implementations, then the number of test suites required can be reduced by reusing test suites for several of the products in the array without losing the bug detection capabilities.

6 Conclusion

In this paper we showed that although it is widely held that configuring feature models is intractable, in practice the role of feature models in software product line engineering implies that it is quick. Boolean satisfiability solvers thus provide an efficient way to handle constraints in feature models and should be exploited for doing covering array generation without the fear that the running time will be intractable.

Acknowledgments. We want to thank the anonymous reviewers for their helpful feedback.

The work presented here has been developed within the VERDE project ITEA 2 - ip8020. VERDE is a project within the ITEA 2 - Eureka framework.

References

1. Batory, D.: Feature models, grammars, and propositional formulas. In: Obbink, H., Pohl, K. (eds.) SPLC 2005. LNCS, vol. 3714, pp. 7–20. Springer, Heidelberg (2005)
2. Cabral, I., Cohen, M.B., Rothermel, G.: Improving the testing and testability of software product lines. In: Bosch, J., Lee, J. (eds.) SPLC 2010. LNCS, vol. 6287, pp. 241–255. Springer, Heidelberg (2010)
3. Chvátal, V.: A greedy heuristic for the Set-Covering problem. Mathematics of Operations Research 4(3), 233–235 (1979)
4. Cohen, M.B., Dwyer, M.B., Shi, J.: Constructing interaction test suites for highly-configurable systems in the presence of constraints: A greedy approach. IEEE Transactions on Software Engineering 34, 633–650 (2008)
5. Engström, E., Runeson, P.: Software product line testing - a systematic mapping study. Information and Software Technology 53(1), 2–13 (2011)
6. Garvin, B.J., Cohen, M.B., Dwyer, M.B.: Evaluating improvements to a meta-heuristic search for constrained interaction testing. Empirical Softw. Engg. 16, 61–102 (2011)
7. Haugen, Ø., Møller-Pedersen, B., Oldevik, J., Olsen, G.K., Svendsen, A.: Adding standardized variability to domain specific languages. In: SPLC 2008: Proceedings of the 2008 12th International Software Product Line Conference, pp. 139–148. IEEE Computer Society, Washington, DC (2008)
8. Johansen, M.F., Haugen, Ø., Fleurey, F.: Bow tie testing - a testing pattern for product lines. In: Proceedings of the 16th Annual European Conference on Pattern Languages of Programming (EuroPLoP 2011), Irsee, Germany, July 13-17 (2011)
9. Johansen, M.F., Haugen, Ø., Fleurey, F.: A survey of empirics of strategies for software product line testing. In: 2011 IEEE Fourth International Conference on Software Testing, Verification and Validation Workshops, ICSTW, pp. 266–269 (March 2011)
10. Kang, K.C., Cohen, S.G., Hess, J.A., Novak, W.E., Peterson, A.S.: Feature-oriented domain analysis (foda) feasibility study. Tech. rep., Carnegie-Mellon University Software Engineering Institute (November 1990)
11. Kuhn, D.R., Wallace, D.R., Gallo, A.M.: Software fault interactions and implications for software testing. IEEE Transactions on Software Engineering 30(6), 418–421 (2004)
12. Lau, S.Q.: Domain analysis of e-commerce systems using feature-based model templates. Master's thesis, ECE Department, University of Waterloo, Canada (2006)
13. Lopez-Herrejon, R.E., Batory, D.: A standard problem for evaluating product-line methodologies. In: Dannenberg, R.B. (ed.) GCSE 2001. LNCS, vol. 2186, pp. 10–24. Springer, Heidelberg (2001)
14. Mendonca, M.: Efficient Reasoning Techniques for Large Scale Feature Models. Ph.D. thesis, School of Computer Science, University of Waterloo (January 2009)
15. Mendonca, M., Wasowski, A., Czarnecki, K.: Sat-based analysis of feature models is easy. In: Proceedings of the 13th International Software Product Line Conference, pp. 231–240. Carnegie Mellon University (2009)
16. Nie, C., Leung, H.: A survey of combinatorial testing. ACM Comput. Surv. 43, 11:1–11:29 (2011)
17. Parra, C., Blanc, X., Duchien, L.: Context awareness for dynamic service-oriented product lines. In: Proceedings of the 13th International Software Product Line Conference, SPLC 2009, pp. 131–140. Carnegie Mellon University, Pittsburgh (2009)

18. Perrouin, G., Sen, S., Klein, J., Baudry, B., le Traon, Y.: Automated and scalable t-wise test case generation strategies for software product lines. In: Proceedings of the 2010 Third International Conference on Software Testing, Verification and Validation, ICST 2010, pp. 459–468. IEEE Computer Society, Washington, DC (2010)
19. Pohl, K., Böckle, G., van der Linden, F.J.: Software Product Line Engineering: Foundations, Principles and Techniques. Springer-Verlag New York, Inc., Secaucus (2005)
20. Pătraşcu, M., Williams, R.: On the possibility of faster sat algorithms. In: Proceedings of the Twenty-First Annual ACM-SIAM Symposium on Discrete Algorithms, SODA 2010, pp. 1065–1075. Society for Industrial and Applied Mathematics, Philadelphia (2010)
21. Reuys, A., Reis, S., Kamsties, E., Pohl, K.: The scented method for testing software product lines. In: Käkölä, T., Dueñas, J.C. (eds.) Software Product Lines, pp. 479–520. Springer, Heidelberg (2006)
22. Rivieres, J., Beaton, W.: Eclipse Platform Technical Overview (2006)
23. She, S., Lotufo, R., Berger, T., Wasowski, A., Czarnecki, K.: Reverse engineering feature models. In: Taylor, R.N., Gall, H., Medvidovic, N. (eds.) ICSE, pp. 461–470. ACM, New York (2011)
24. Trujillo, S., Batory, D., Diaz, O.: Feature refactoring a multi-representation program into a product line. In: Proceedings of the 5th International Conference on Generative Programming and Component Engineering, GPCE 2006, pp. 191–200. ACM, New York (2006)
25. Uzuncaova, E., Khurshid, S., Batory, D.: Incremental test generation for software product lines. IEEE Transactions on Software Engineering 36(3), 309–322 (2010)
26. Voelter, M.: Using domain specific languages for product line engineering. In: Proceedings of the 13th International Software Product Line Conference, SPLC 2009, pp. 329–329. Carnegie Mellon University, Pittsburgh (2009)
27. Weston, N., Chitchyan, R., Rashid, A.: A framework for constructing semantically composable feature models from natural language requirements. In: Proceedings of the 13th International Software Product Line Conference, SPLC 2009, pp. 211–220. Carnegie Mellon University, Pittsburgh (2009)
28. White, J., Dougherty, B., Schmidt, D.C., Benavides, D.: Automated reasoning for multi-step feature model configuration problems. In: Proceedings of the 13th International Software Product Line Conference, SPLC 2009, pp. 11–20. Carnegie Mellon University, Pittsburgh (2009)

Reasoning about Metamodeling with Formal Specifications and Automatic Proofs

Ethan K. Jackson[1], Tihamér Levendovszky[2], and Daniel Balasubramanian[2]

[1] Microsoft Research, Redmond, WA
[2] Vanderbilt University, Nashville, TN
ejackson@microsoft.com,
{tihamer,daniel}@isis.vanderbilt.edu

Abstract. *Metamodeling* is foundational to many modeling frameworks, and so it is important to formalize and reason about it. Ideally, correctness proofs and test-case generation on the metamodeling framework should be automatic. However, it has yet to be shown that extensive automated reasoning on metamodeling frameworks can be achieved. In this paper we present one approach to this problem: Metamodeling frameworks are specified modularly using *algebraic data types* and *constraint logic programming* (CLP). Proofs and test-case generation are encoded as CLP satisfiability problems and automatically solved.

1 Introduction

Metamodeling is foundational to many modeling frameworks, and so it is important to formalize it properly. Ideally, a formalization should enable automated reasoning by generating test cases, proving correctness of the meta-interpreter, and proving correctness of editing operations. However, the state-of-the-art is somewhat less than ideal. On one hand, there has been a general consensus that the *Meta-Object Facility* (MOF) standard is under-formalized and deserves careful attention [1,2,3,4,5]. On the other hand, attempts at full formalization of MOF/MOF-alternatives have not yet enabled extensive automated reasoning on metamodeling frameworks. (We give a summary of existing results shortly.)

In this paper we present a new approach to formalizing and reasoning on metamodeling frameworks. The core of our approach uses *algebraic data types* (ADTs) and *constraint logic programming* (CLP) for formal specifications. We modularize these specifications so they mirror the key components of metamodeling frameworks: (1) A *model store* for representing models, metamodels, and conformance. (2) A set of model editing operations. (3) A *meta-interpreter* for promoting model-level elements to meta-level elements. We encode proof goals as instances of *CLP satisfiability* problems, and use our *FORMULA* framework to solve these instances [6]. The result is a concise formal specification whose structure resembles the tool architecture, but allows constructive automated reasoning to perform correctness proofs and test case generation.

Our contributions are: First, we develop a complete specification of a simple metamodeling framework based on *typed graphs* [7]. This gives a blueprint for specifying more complicated frameworks. Second, We prove that our choice of editing operations preserves model conformance. We prove *metacircularity* by automatically constructing a meta-metamodel. These results have the interesting side-effect that it is unnecessary to write a bootstrapping meta-metamodel; it falls out of the proof. Third, we relate these results to a MOF-like metamodeling framework with richer conformance constraints, such as acyclicity and multiplicity constraints. These results are obtained using our FORMULA specification and analysis framework.

2 Related Work

Metamodeling continues to be an extensively researched topic [8] with many approaches to formalization. A few representatives are: The *Metamodeling Language Calculus* (MML) based on ς-calculus [1]. The graph-theoretic approaches of *KM3* [2] and *VPM* [3]. The work of [4] provides a rich set-theoretic setting for metamodeling. *MOMENT2* uses *membership equational logic* and *term rewriting* as a formal foundation [5]. Though formal, many approaches support limited automated reasoning on the metamodeling framework.

In this paper we investigate the power of automated formal methods to reason on metamodeling frameworks. Our tool supports expressive specifications corresponding to *fixpoint logic* (FPL) over theories [9], and provides a *finite model finder* for automated reasoning. Other automated techniques have been applied to metamodeling. The work of [5] uses *MAUDE* [10] to check metamodel/model conformance and *linear temporal logic* (LTL) properties via term rewriting systems. A proof is a reduction of an input term to a term with no further reductions. Model finding is not generally supported by this approach. Related to this, [11] describes translators from *VPM*-style specifications into explicit/symbolic state model checkers, though not necessarily for the purpose of reasoning on metamodeling frameworks.

The work of [12] provides a translation from UML and a subset of OCL into the finite model finder *Alloy* [13]. Alloy is perhaps the closest tool to FORMULA; for an extensive comparison see [6]. Alternative approaches avoid solving altogether, in favor of abstracting to graph grammars [14], or interactive theorem provers [15]. Yet, model finders continue to be effective for automative reasoning, even in areas such as *software product lines* [16].

These results are based on preliminary work we presented in [17]. To our knowledge, this is the first time such automated proofs have been shown for a metamodeling framework.

3 Introduction to CLP and Satisfiability

Constraint Logic programming (CLP) provides a powerful approach to writing formal specifications. First, a logic program Π can be directly (i.e. in polynomial-time) translated into first-order logic (FOL) according to its *Clark Completion*. Following the notation of [18], we refer to this translation as $\Pi^\star$. Second, logic programs are executable, allowing programmatic reasoning to be applied while devising specifications. This form of reasoning is harder to obtain when directly writing FOL. Actually, an even stronger property holds: The execution of a logic program proves theorems about its logical semantics. If g is a quantifier-free formula over the relations computed by Π, then $\widetilde{\exists} g$ can be decided by executing Π. ($\widetilde{\exists} g$ denotes the existential closure of g.) The formula g is called a *goal*.

Consider the following program, which computes paths and cycles occurring in a directed graph.

Example 1 (Cycles)

$$\Pi_{cycles} \doteq \begin{array}{l} \mathsf{path(x, y) :\!\!- e(x, y).} \\ \mathsf{path(x, z) :\!\!- e(x, y), path(y, z).} \\ \mathsf{inCycle(x) :\!\!- path(x, x).} \end{array}$$

The symbols $e()$, $path(,)$, and $inCycle()$ are user defined relations. Each logic programming *rule* behaves like a universally quantified implication. Whenever the relations on the right-hand side of a rule hold for some substitution of the variables, then the left-hand side holds for that same substitution. A logic program is stronger than a set of implications, because it only entails theorems that can be explained by repeated applications of rules. Derivations must begin with *facts*, which are rules whose right-hand side is true. Formally, this means: (1) $\Pi^\star$ contains additional formulas to constrain the implications, and (2) the *intended interpretation* of $\Pi^\star$ is the smallest set of relations satisfying $\Pi^\star$. In this way, Example 1 encodes the transitive closure of a directed graph. (An alternative formalization for CLP is obtained by extending FOL with fixpoint operators [9].)

The program Π_{cycles} is not very interesting because it contains no facts. The least interpretation of this program assigns $e = path = inCycle = \emptyset$; it is called the *least Herbrand model* and denoted $lm(\Pi^\star)$. A goal $\widetilde{\exists} g$ holds for a program Π if g evaluates to true under the least Herbrand model; denoted:

$$lm(\Pi^\star) \models \widetilde{\exists} g.$$

In particular, $lm(\Pi^\star_{cycles}) \not\models \exists x\, inCycle(x)$. Suppose the program is extended with the fact $e(1,1)$, then exactly the additional facts $path(1,1)$ and $inCycle(1)$ are deducible and the goal is satisfied. Most LP languages are concerned with efficient rule application to prove a goal, either by working backwards from a goal to facts or forwards from facts to a goal.

3.1 CLP Satisfiability

We will generate automatic proofs from formal specifications by solving CLP *satisfiability* problems. Satisfiability is different from checking goal satisfaction; it is to determine if a program can be extended by a finite set of facts so that a goal is satisfied. As the previous example shows, this problem cannot be solved by simply running a logic program. It requires searching through (infinitely) many possible extensions, which we achieve by efficient forward *symbolic execution* of a logic program into the state-of-the-art *satisfiability modulo theories* (SMT) solver *Z3* [19]. As a result, specifications can include variables ranging over infinite domains and rich data types. Nonetheless, the method is constructive; it returns extensions of the program witnessing goal satisfaction.

Let U be a (possibly infinite) set called a *universe* and r an n-ary relation symbol. Then a (finite) interpretation of r, written r^I, is a (finite) subset of U^n. We write $r(\vec{t})$ as a shorthand for r applied to elements $t_1, \ldots, t_n$ of U.

Definition 1 (CLP Satisfiability). *Given:*

1. *A program Π with relation symbols $R = \{r_1, r_2, \ldots, r_n\}$,*
2. *$R_p \subseteq R$ a subset of the program relations, called the primitive relations.*
3. *A quantifer-free goal g over the program relations.*

Then find a finite interpretation R_p^I for primitive relations such that:

$$lm((\Pi \cup R_p^I)^\star) \models \widetilde{\exists} g. \tag{1}$$

The program $\Pi \cup R_p^I$ is obtained by extending Π with a fact $r(\vec{t})$ whenever $R_P^I \models r(\vec{t})$.

The program can only be extended by primitive relations R_P. The contents of R_P^I are the facts that, when added to the program, cause the goal to be satisfied. We write $\mathbb{S}(\Pi, R_p, g)$ to denote an instance of CLP satisfiability and $R_P^I \in \mathbb{S}(\Pi, R_p, g)$ to denote an interpretation satisfying the problem. In a very technical sense, we refer to R_P^I as a *model* of $\mathbb{S}$. However, such interpretations can also represent instances of an abstraction, allowing them to serve as models in a more general sense. Thus, we may use the symbol M when more intuitive.

3.2 Blueprint of a Metamodeling Framework

We formalize metamodeling frameworks using CLP and CLP satisfiability according to the following blueprint:

1. **Model Store.** The model store encodes the set of all conforming metamodel/model pairs. It captures the semantics of metamodel conformance. Interesting instances of metamodel/model pairs can be constructed by solving satisfiability problems. We present a two-level model store, though an arbitrary number of meta-layers could be specified.
2. **Editing Operations.** These are transformations for editing model-level elements through creation and deletion. These transformations are also defined over the model store. By formalizing editors we can generate test cases where editing breaks model conformance. For a simple metamodeling framework we can choose model editors so that conformance is always maintained.
3. **Meta-interpreter.** The meta-interpreter is a transformation promoting model-level elements to meta-level elements. This transformation is defined over the model store. We say a framework is *metacircular* if there exists an input model that is promoted to its own metamodel by the meta-interpreter. Again, this property can be rephrased as a satisfiability problem and meta-metamodels are constructed witnessing this property.

4 Metamodeling by Typed Graphs

Typed graphs have been studied extensively as representations for (meta-) models, especially by the model transformation community [7]. For example, they are the basis for *KM3* metamodeling notation employed by the *ATLAS transformation language*, and can be used as a more basic foundation for MOF [2]. They are simple to define and easy to understand, so we use them to illustrate a complete metamodeling framework.

4.1 Typed Graphs and the Model Store

Definition 2 (Directed Graph). *A directed graph is a quadruple* $G = \langle V, E, src, dst \rangle$ *where V and E are sets; $src : E \to V$ and $dst : E \to V$.*

Definition 3 (Typed Graph). *A typed graph is a quadruple $T = \langle G, H, \tau_v, \tau_e \rangle$ where G and H are directed graphs; $\tau_v : V_H \to V_G$ and $\tau_e : E_H \to E_G$.*

The graph G acts like a metamodel providing a set of node types and edge types[1]. Graph H is an instance model referencing these types. The type of each vertex v is $\tau_v(v)$ and edge e is $\tau_e(e)$. A model H *conforms* to the metamodel G if the edges and vertices of H are connected according to their types:

$$conforms(T) \doteq \forall e \in E_H \begin{pmatrix} src_G(\tau_e(e)) = \tau_v(src_H(e)) \land \\ dst_G(\tau_e(e)) = \tau_v(dst_H(e)) \end{pmatrix}. \quad (2)$$

Fixing the universe U of edge/vertex labels yields a set of all possible conforming metamodel/model pairs. We call this set the *model store*:

$$Store(U) \doteq \{T \mid conforms(T) \land V_G, E_G, V_H, E_H \subseteq U\}. \quad (3)$$

4.2 Specifying the Model Store with ADTs and CLP

Figure 1 shows an equivalent specification of the model store in FORMULA. This specification is wrapped in a **domain** block, which delimits a domain-specific abstraction. As mentioned earlier, FORMULA directly supports algebraic data types and these are used to encode user defined relations. For example, Line 3 declares a data type constructor *MetaNode()* for instantiating meta-level nodes (V_G). This constructor produces *MetaNode* records, each of which has a field called *typename* of type *String*. Similarly, *MetaEdge(,,)* constructs elements of E_G using *MetaNodes* as endpoints (Line 5). The *Node* and *Edge* constructors instantiate model-level elements (graph H), and the fields called *type* encode τ_v and τ_e.

Due to the flexibility of ADTs, it is unnecessary to distinguish between data type constructors and user-defined relation symbols. Instead, every program computes two standard unary program relations, r_p and r_d, over records. The primitive relation r_p contains only records built with *primitive constructors*, and

---
[1] Our definition differs from others as we allow edges to also acts as types.

```
1.   domain ModelStore
2.   {
3.     MetaNode  ::= (typename: String).
4.     [Closed(src, dst)][Unique(typename -> src, dst)]
5.     MetaEdge  ::= (typename: String, src: MetaNode, dst: MetaNode).
6.     [Closed(type)][Unique(name -> type)]
7.     Node      ::= (name: String, type: MetaNode).
8.     [Closed(src, dst, type)][Unique(name -> src, dst, type)]
9.     Edge      ::= (name: String, src: Node, dst: Node, type: MetaEdge).
10.
11.    badSrc    := Edge(_, src, dst, t), t.src != src.type.
12.    badDst    := Edge(_, src, dst, t), t.dst != dst.type.
13.    conforms  := !badSrc & !badDst.
14.  }
```

Fig. 1. FORMULA specification of a model store containing typed graphs

the derived relation r_d contains only records built with *derived constructors*. Primitive constructors can be used to extend a program in order to solve a satisfiability problem; derived constructors cannot. Primitive constructors always begin with a capital letter. Every FORMULA domain contains a special nullary derived constructor called **conforms**. The models of a domain D are those extensions of Π by r_p where *conforms* is derivable:

$$models(D) \doteq \{r_p^I \mid r_p^I \in \mathbb{S}(\Pi_D, \{r_p\}, conforms)\}. \quad (4)$$

FORMULA provides special syntax for expressing domain models, as shown in Figure 2. The declaration **model M of D** is a claim that the code-to-follow gives an interpretation $r_P^I \in models(D)$. This claim is checked by the compiler. Recall that r_p^I is just a set of records, thus a *model* block is just a set of records. The *StateDiagram* model in Figure 2 is an instance of the model store representing a small state diagram over the meta-types *State* and *Transition*.

The constraints describing typed graph conformance are expressed in Lines 11 - 13 of Figure 1. FORMULA also provides special syntax for rules where the left-hand side is a nullary constructor. We refer to these as *queries* and use the *query definition* operator (:=) for query definitions. Intuitively, a query behaves like a propositional variable that is true if and only if the right-hand side of the definition is true for some substitution. As a convenience, FORMULA allows queries to be treated like propositional variables when they appear in other query definitions. For example, the *badSrc* query in Line 11 of Figure 1 detects if the source of a model-level edge has been connected improperly. It corresponds to the following formula in Π^*:

$$badSrc \in r_d \Leftrightarrow \exists Edge(n, src, dst, t) \in r_p \; get_{src}(t) \neq get_{type}(src). \quad (5)$$

where $get_x()$ extracts the field named x. Similarly, the *conforms* query is expressed as:

$$conforms \in r_d \Leftrightarrow badSrc \notin r_d \wedge badDst \notin r_d \wedge \varphi_{compiler}. \quad (6)$$

```
1.  model StateDiagram of ModelStore
2.  {
3.      MetaNode("State")
4.      MetaEdge("Transition",
5.              MetaNode("State"),
6.              MetaNode("State"))
7.      Node("S1", MetaNode("State"))
8.      Node("S2", MetaNode("State"))
9.      Edge("T1",
10.             Node("S1", MetaNode("State"))
11.             Node("S2", MetaNode("State"))
12.             MetaEdge("Transition",
13.                     MetaNode("State"),
14.                     MetaNode("State")))
15. }
```

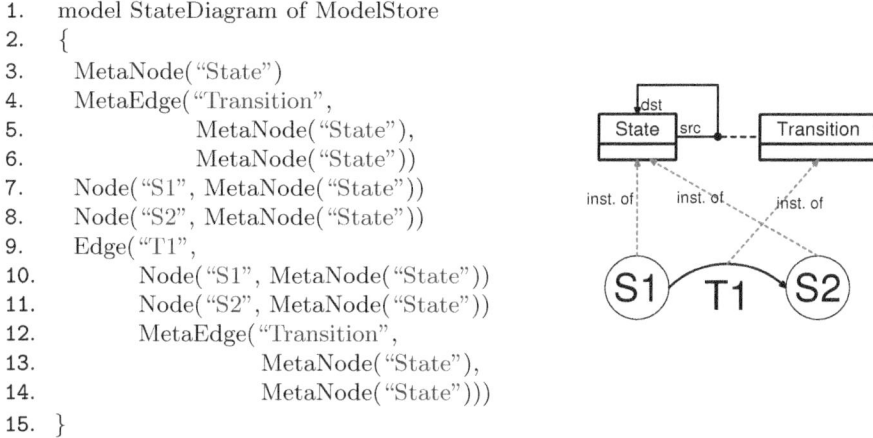

Fig. 2. A FORMULA model from the model store that encodes a state diagram

The sub-formula $\varphi_{compiler}$ holds additional conformance constraints that are automatically added by the compiler. These extra constraints may appear due to inheritance of constraints through the module system or due to shorthands. One such shorthand is the *Closed* annotation (Line 4), which requires the *src/dst* fields of *MetaEdge* to contain only meta-nodes declared at the top level. The *Unique* annotation requires all records with identical fields on the left of the arrow ($->$) to have identical fields on the right of the arrow. These shorthands encompass many common constraints, though it always possible to express the same constraints without using them.

In summary, the FORMULA specification encodes a typed graph model store using ADTs and CLP. The set of all conforming metamodel/models pairs is characterized by the satisfiability problem *models(ModelStore)*. Therefore, we can use automated techniques to prove properties about the model store. We shall illustrate this in the later sections. But first, our typed graph framework requires a few operations for editing models: Delete node, create node, delete edge, and create edge. In the next sections we show how to specify these operations, illustrating that CLP satisfiability can also be used to reason about model transformations.

5 Encoding Model Transformations

Model transformations are encoded as logic programs where data types distinguish the inputs and outputs of the transformation. For example:

Example 2 (Filter MetaNodes)

$$\Pi_{filter} \doteq \mathsf{out.MetaNode(x)\ :\text{-}\ in.MetaNode(x)}.$$

The constructor $in.MetaNode()$ stands for meta-node primitives at the input of the transformation. Similarly, $out.MetaNode()$ stands for meta-node primitives on the output of the transformation. A transformation is executed by providing an interpretation r_p^I for the input primitives, and then computing the output primitives according to the logic program:

$$transform(\Pi, r_p^I) \doteq \{f(\vec{t}) \mid lm((\Pi \cup r_p^I)^\star) \models f(\vec{t}) \land isOut(f)\} \quad (7)$$

where the predicate $isOut(f)$ tests if constructor f is an output primitive.

In order to ease the use of transformations we introduce the *renaming operator* **as**. Let Π **as** X return a new program Π_X obtained by replacing every occurrence of a function symbol f with $X.f$ in Π. This also applies to the type declarations in Π. Similarly, r_p^I **as** X replaces every f-record with an equivalent $X.f$ record. Thus, the program Π_{filter} can be used to transform the model *StateDiagram* in Figure 2 as follows:

$$transform(\Pi_{filter}, StateDiagram \text{ as } in) = \{out.MetaNode(\text{``State''})\}.$$

The *filter* transformation only copies meta-nodes to the output, so it effectively deletes all other information from the output.

Satisfiability can be used to reason about model transformations. The approach is to compose renamed versions of input/output domains with the transformation in order to reason about its impact on domain constraints. For example, we may wish to know if there exists a conforming instance from the model store that is no longer conforming after *filter* is applied.

Example 3 (Property Conformance-Breaking)

$$\Pi_{CB} \doteq \begin{array}{l} \Pi_{filter} \cup (\textit{ModelStore} \text{ as } in) \cup (\textit{ModelStore} \text{ as } out) \cup \\ \text{confBreaking} := \text{in.conforms \& !out.conforms}. \end{array}$$

The problem $\mathbb{S}(\Pi_{CB}, \{r_p\}, confBreaking)$ has a solution if and only if there exists such an input to the transformation. (Note that r_p only contains input primitives; output primitives are placed in r_d). In this case, the problem is unsatisfiable, so there is no such input to the transformation.

5.1 Editing by Transformations

The FORMULA module system simplifies the specification of model transformations, as shown in Figure 3. Line 1 declares the transformation called *CreateNode*, which requires two *parameters* called *newName* and *newType*. Parameters are extra pieces of information provided to the transformation, in addition to the input models. These parameters give the name and type of the node to be added. Line 2 identifies the inputs/outputs of the transformation by two lists of renamed domains. The compiler automatically composes the transformation logic (Lines 4 - 10) with the renamed input/output domains.

Lines 4 - 7 of the transformation copy the input metamodel/model to the output of the transformation. These rules are particularly simple due to renaming inference by the compiler. For example, the right-hand side of the rule in

```
1.   transform CreateNode  <newName : String, newType : in.MetaNode>
2.   from ModelStore as in to ModelStore as out
3.   {
4.     out.MetaNode(typename)           :- in.MetaNode(typename).
5.     out.MetaEdge(typename, src, dst) :- in.MetaEdge(typename, src, dst).
6.     out.Node(name, type)             :- in.Node(name, type).
7.     out.Edge(name, src, dst, type)   :- in.Edge(name, src, dst, type).
8.     out.Node(newName, newType)       :- fail in.Node(newName, _).
9.
10.    confBreaking   := in.conforms & !out.conforms.
11.  }
```

Fig. 3. A *CreateNode* transformation in FORMULA

```
1.   partial model PInst of ModelStore
2.   {
3.     MetaNode(_) MetaNode(_) MetaNode(_)
4.     MetaEdge(_, _, _) MetaEdge(_, _, _) MetaEdge(_, _, _)
5.     Node(_, _) Node(_, _) Node(_, _)
6.     Edge(_, _, _, _) Edge(_, _, _, _) Edge(_, _, _, _)
7.   }
```

Fig. 4. Partial instance of r_p^I to guide the solver

Line 5 has a variable called *src* that must be of type *in.MetaNode*. However, the constructor *out.MetaNode* on the left-hand side expects *src* to be of type *out.MetaNode*. The compiler detects this and applies renaming to *src* on the left-hand side. In addition to copying, Line 8 adds a new node called *newName* to the output if such a node does not already exist. Line 10 specifies the conformance-breaking property.

The *CreateNode* transformation has all the context needed for proving properties about its behavior. The solver can be used to find an instance of the inputs and parameters causing conformance to be broken. Because there are many degrees of freedom in this problem, it is useful to give the solver some guidance. We call this guidance a *partial model*; it is roughly a lower bound on the structure of r_p^I. Figure 4 shows a partial model containing three applications of each primitive constructor to *fresh variables* (denoted _). This partial model requires the solver to return models with at least one (meta-)node/edge each. In addition, the free variables cause the solver to eagerly search for larger models. The size and structure of r_p^I may be further expanded during the search process, beyond the contents of the partial model. In order to check the conformance-breaking property, we issue the following command to FORMULA:

solve CreateNode <_,_> PInst confBreaking

This allows the solver to search for any parameter values that break conformance when applied to some instance of the model store. In this case, the problem is

```
1.  model Proof of ModelStore
2.  {
3.    MetaNode("A")
4.    MetaEdge("B", MetaNode("A"), MetaNode("A"))
5.    Node("C", MetaNode("A"))
6.    Edge("D", Node("C", MetaNode("A")), Node("C", MetaNode("A")),
7.         MetaEdge("B", MetaNode("A"), MetaNode("A")))
8.  }
9.  newName = "E", newType = in.MetaNode("F")
```

Fig. 5. An automatically generated witness that *CreateNode* is conformance breaking

satisfiable because an undeclared meta-node may be provided as the *newType* parameter. (This violates the *Closed* constraint in Figure 1, Line 6.) Figure 5 shows an example of the FORMULA output, which consists of a model and parameter valuations solving the satisfiability problem.

5.2 Conformance-Preserving Edits

The typed graph formalism is simple enough that we can define editing operations which never break conformance. Specifically, *CreateNode* should only create a node if there is no other node with same name and the meta-node exists. Thus, Line 8 is replaced by:

out.Node(newName, newType) :- in.MetaNode(n), n = newType.typename,
                                fail in.Node(newName, _).

Similar rules hold for *CreateEdge*. *DeleteNode* must also delete all incident edges. See http://research.microsoft.com/formula for the complete specification of these transformations.

In general it is undecidable whether or not there exists a finite interpretation satisfying a CLP satisfiability problem. Therefore, the solver can only guarantee the absence of solutions up to some size of r_p^I. This is a well-known problem when using constructive methods to generate proofs. Fortunately, there is a well-known solution: Provide an inductive argument that generalizes the absence of solutions to interpretations of arbitrary size. The advantage of such inductive arguments is that they can be rather generic and reusable across problem instances.

For example, the FORMULA solver can be used to show that for all conforming inputs r_p^I where $|r_p^I| \leq k$, then no editing operation breaks conformance. These results can be paired with a theorem showing that all other cases can be decomposed into these small cases. First, a *term homomorphism* φ is a function from records to records with the property that $\varphi(f(t_1,\ldots,t_n)) = f(\varphi(t_1),\ldots,\varphi(t_n))$. Let the *base cases* $\mathbb{B}$ be a finite set of input interpretations, and $\tau\langle\vec{x}\rangle(M)$ denote an editing operation with parameters $\vec{x}$ applied to model (input interpretation) M.

Theorem 1 (Decomposition Theorem). *The transformation $\tau\langle\vec{x}\rangle(M)$ is equivalent to transforming a relabeled instance of $\mathbb{B}$ and combining it with a subset of M. In symbols:*

$$\forall M, \vec{x} \;\; \exists M', M'', \varphi \quad \tau\langle\vec{x}\rangle(M) = M' \cup \varphi^{-1}\Big(\tau\langle\varphi(\vec{x})\rangle(\varphi(M''))\Big) \tag{8}$$

such that:
$$M = M' \cup M'' \quad \text{and} \quad \exists B \in \mathbb{B} \;\; \varphi(M'') = B. \tag{9}$$

Note, $\varphi(M)$ is φ applied to every term in M. The function φ^{-1} is the inverse image of φ.

This theorem formalizes the fact that an edit operation acts locally on an input. Reasoning on the set of base cases $\mathbb{B}$ is sufficient, because every input can be described as a local edit on a base case. In fact, $\mathbb{B}$ need not be constructed manually; only an upper bound k on the largest interpretation in $\mathbb{B}$ needs to be constructed. While the proof of this theorem is not automatic, its form is not specific to this example so it provides a general proof strategy.

6 The Meta-interpreter

A meta-interpreter is a transformation promoting model-level elements to meta-level elements. When combined with editing operations, it provides a way to build new abstractions using the operations provided by the framework.

Figure 6 shows one such meta-interpreter in FORMULA; there are several noteworthy aspects. First, the promotion is determined by arbitrary and hard-coded type names. Lines 3, 4 promote a model-level node to a meta-node only if the node has type *Class*. Similarly, the promotion of edges to meta-edges only occurs if an edge's type is *Assoc* and its end-points are *Class*es (Lines 5 - 11). Second, the choice of type names is unrelated to the formalization of the model store. The strings "Class" and "Assoc" are convenient, but arbitrary, monikers. Thus, the model store may have a simpler formalization than the concepts exposed by the meta-interpreter (though perhaps less convenient). Certainly, the model store can be insulated from the naming of the concepts, which may vary between standards.

Metamodeling frameworks are said to be bootstrapped by a *meta-metamodel* or are *"described using themselves"* [20]. Informally, a framework is *meta-circular* if there exists a metamodel MM whose conforming models are metamodels and MM is among them. Of course, this terminology has concerned many researchers, as it may lead to circular definitions. We formalize meta-circularity as a simple property of the framework:

Definition 4 (Meta-circularity). *A framework is a meta-circular if there exists a conforming input to the meta-interpreter producing a conforming output with the same metamodel.*

```
1.  transform MetaInterpreter from ModelStore as in to ModelStore as out
2.  {
3.     out.MetaNode(name)        :- in.Node(name, type),
4.                                  type = in.MetaNode("Class").
5.     out.MetaEdge(name,
6.         MetaNode(srcname),
7.         MetaNode(dstname))    :- in.Edge(name, src, dst, type),
8.                                  src = in.Node(srcname, mClass),
9.                                  dst = in.Node(dstname, mClass),
10.                                 type = in.MetaEdge("Assoc", mClass, mClass),
11.                                 mClass = in.MetaNode("Class").
12. }
```

Fig. 6. A simple meta-interpreter that promotes nodes of type *Class* and edges of type *Assoc* to the meta-level

```
1.  metaDiffers    := in.MetaNode(t), fail out.MetaNode(t).
2.  metaDiffers    := out.MetaNode(t), fail in.MetaNode(t).
3.  metaDiffers    := in.MetaEdge(t, MetaNode(st), MetaNode(dt)),
4.                    fail out.MetaEdge(t, MetaNode(st), MetaNode(dt)).
5.  metaDiffers    := out.MetaEdge(t, MetaNode(st), MetaNode(dt)),
6.                    fail in.MetaEdge(t, MetaNode(st), MetaNode(dt)).
7.  metaCircular   := !metaDiffers & in.conforms & out.conforms.
```

Fig. 7. Specification of meta-circularity for the typed graph framework

The input witnessing this property is the meta-metamodel.

In our approach neither meta-circularity is required for bootstrapping nor does a meta-metamodel determine properties of the framework. Instead, the framework is determined by the model store, editing operations, and meta-interpreter. A meta-metamodel, if it exists, is a byproduct of this framework. In fact, it can be constructed automatically as a witness to the meta-circularity property. Figure 7 shows the specification of meta-circularity in FORMULA. The query definitions in Lines 1 - 2 test if there exists a meta-node in the input, which is not in the output, and *vice versa*. Lines 3 - 6 perform the same test for meta-edges. Then meta-circularity is simply the absence of any discrepancies at the meta-level of the input and output, both of which must conform to the model store.

A meta-metamodel is constructed by adding the specification of meta-circularity to the meta-interpreter and invoking the solver as follows:

solve MetaInterpreter PInst metaCircular

The result is the meta-metamodel of Figure 8. There is an additional use for this meta-metamodel; it provides a starting point for building metamodels using only the framework operations. For example, the state diagram abstraction used in Figure 2 can be constructed as follows:

```
1.  model MetaMetaModel of ModelStore
2.  {
3.      MetaNode("Class")
4.      MetaEdge("Assoc", MetaNode("Class"), MetaNode("Class"))
5.      Node("Class", MetaNode("Class"))
6.      Edge("Assoc",
7.           Node("Class", MetaNode("Class")),
8.           Node("Class", MetaNode("Class")),
9.           MetaEdge("Assoc", MetaNode("Class"), MetaNode("Class")))
10. }
```

Fig. 8. An automatically generated meta-metamodel witnessing meta-circularity

$$\left(\tau_{+edge} \left\langle \begin{array}{c} \tau_{mi} \circ \\ \text{``Transition''}, in.Node(\text{``State''}), in.Node(\text{``State''}), \\ in.MetaEdge(\text{``Assoc''}, \ldots) \\ \tau_{+node} \langle \text{``State''}, in.MetaNode(\text{``Class''}) \rangle \circ \\ \tau_{mi} \end{array} \right\rangle \circ \right) MM \quad (10)$$

where MM is the meta-metamodel, τ_{mi} is an application of the meta-interpreter, τ_{+edge} creates an edge, and $\tau_2 \circ \tau_1$ is the application of τ_2 after τ_1. If the semantics of the model store or meta-interpreter are changed, then the starting point MM can be automatically reconstructed. To our knowledge, this is the first time such a technique has been demonstrated.

7 A MOF-Like Framework

Several issues arise when specifying a richer metamodeling framework, such as the *Meta-Object Facility* (MOF). The first issue is the number of additional concepts that must be specified. Naturally, this is handled by introducing more types in the model store and more rules in the meta-interpreter. In the case of MOF, the key concepts at the meta-level are *Classifier*, *Class*, *Association*, *Generalization*, and *Property*. At the instance level there are *InstanceSpecification*, *InstanceValue*, and *Slot* concepts. An instance is related to one or more meta-level *Classifiers*, which include *Classes* and *Associations*. Each instance specification contains *Slots*, which bind *Values* to *Properties*. The endpoints of n-ary associations are expressed using slots and properties.

The second issue is the expressiveness needed to define the model store. Here the primary complications are acyclicity and multiplicity constraints. MOF requires the generalization relationship to be acyclic and strong containment to be tree-structured. These constraints are not first-order definable, as they are equivalent to finite transitive closure. Fortunately, CLP exposes fixpoint operators via recursive rules (see Example 1), so acyclicity constraints are easily captured. Multiplicity constraints require the number of instances related to another to be in an interval $[k_l, k_u]$. FORMULA supports encoding of multiplicity constraints through *aggregation operators*, such as $count()$, which count the number of facts matching some pattern. For example, the following rule:

```
outEdgesInInterval(n)   :- n is Node, Multiplicity(n, kl, ku),
                           count(Edge(_, n, _, _)) >= kl,
                           count(Edge(_, n, _, _)) <= ku.
```

produces an *outEdgesInInterval(n)* fact for every node n whose out-edges number between $k_l(n)$ and $k_u(n)$. The expression n *is Node* is a shorthand for *Node*$(\_,\_)$. Please see http://research.microsoft.com/formula for an example of a MOF-like framework.

8 Discussion and Conclusion

We have provided a modular specification of a complete metamodeling framework using ADTs and CLP. The key components of this specification where: (1) a model store, formalizing the legal metamodel/model pairs, (2) editing operations, formalizing the evolution of the model-level elements within the framework, (3) a meta-interpreter, formalizing the promotion of elements from the model-level to the meta-level. We have illustrated that FORMULA simplifies the presentation through the use of *domains*, *transformations*, and *partial models*. We have shown that proofs can be phrased as CLP satisfiability problems and automatically solved. Using this approach we were able to provably synthesize the meta-metamodel of the specified framework. To our knowledge, this is the first time this has been accomplished. It also shows concretely that meta-metamodels simply fall out of the specification, and are not paradoxical. (Though this fact has long been known.)

Throughout this paper we focused on automatic proofs, though test-case generation is another immediate consequence. This can be accomplished by describing a regime of interesting test-cases using a query definition, and then constructing instances satisfying the query. For example, to generate metamodels we solve for conforming instances of the model store with no model-level elements. To generate models conforming to a metamodel, we solve for conforming instances that share a common fixed meta-level. The FORMULA module system makes it straightforward to add these additional constraints for the purpose of test-case generation.

These results point the way to interesting future work. First, there is the question of how to automatically generalize unsatisfiability results to interpretations of arbitrary size. Positive theoretical results include known fragments of CLP that are decidable and well-behaved. However, we do not know of existing tools that leverage these results to compute an automatic upper-bound on the size of r_p^I. Second, there are other properties of a metamodeling framework that might be of interest. We might want to know a *closure property* that every well-formed instance of the model store can be constructed by starting from the meta-metamodel and applying the framework operations. Automatically deciding such a property may very well require symbolic model checking in addition to the techniques illustrated here.

References

1. Clark, T., Evans, A., Caskurlu, B.: The Meta-modeling Language Calculus: Foundation Semantics for UML. In: Hussmann, H. (ed.) FASE 2001. LNCS, vol. 2029, pp. 17–31. Springer, Heidelberg (2001)
2. Jouault, F., Bézivin, J.: KM3: A DSL for Metamodel Specification. In: Gorrieri, R., Wehrheim, H. (eds.) FMOODS 2006. LNCS, vol. 4037, pp. 171–185. Springer, Heidelberg (2006)
3. Varró, D., Pataricza, A.: VPM: A visual, precise and multilevel metamodeling framework for describing mathematical domains and UML. Journal of Software and Systems Modeling 2(3), 187–210 (2003)
4. Alanen, M., Porres, I.: A Metamodeling Language Supporting Subset and Union Properties. Software and System Modeling 7(1), 103–124 (2008)
5. Boronat, A., Meseguer, J.: An Algebraic Semantics for MOF. Formal Asp. Comput. 22(3-4), 269–296 (2010)
6. Jackson, E.K., Kang, E., Dahlweid, M., Seifert, D., Santen, T.: Components, platforms and possibilities: towards generic automation for MDA. In: EMSOFT, pp. 39–48 (2010)
7. Ehrig, H., Ehrig, K., Prange, U., Taentzer, G.: Fundamentals of Algebraic Graph Transformation (Monographs in Theoretical Computer Science). An EATCS Series. Springer-Verlag New York, Inc., Secaucus (2006)
8. Atkinson, C., Kühne, T.: The Essence of Multilevel Metamodeling. In: Gogolla, M., Kobryn, C. (eds.) UML 2001. LNCS, vol. 2185, pp. 19–33. Springer, Heidelberg (2001)
9. Dantsin, E., Eiter, T., Gottlob, G., Voronkov, A.: Complexity and expressive power of logic programming. ACM Comput. Surv. 33(3), 374–425 (2001)
10. Clavel, M., Durán, F., Eker, S., Lincoln, P., Martí-Oliet, N., Meseguer, J., Quesada, J.F.: Maude: Specification and Programming in Rewriting Logic. Theor. Comput. Sci. 285(2), 187–243 (2002)
11. Varró, D.: Automated Formal Verification of Visual Modeling Languages by Model Checking. Software and System Modeling 3(2), 85–113 (2004)
12. Anastasakis, K., Bordbar, B., Georg, G., Ray, I.: UML2Alloy: A Challenging Model Transformation. In: Engels, G., Opdyke, B., Schmidt, D.C., Weil, F. (eds.) MODELS 2007. LNCS, vol. 4735, pp. 436–450. Springer, Heidelberg (2007)
13. Torlak, E., Jackson, D.: Kodkod: A relational model finder. In: Grumberg, O., Huth, M. (eds.) TACAS 2007. LNCS, vol. 4424, pp. 632–647. Springer, Heidelberg (2007)
14. Ehrig, K., Küster, J.M., Taentzer, G.: Generating Instance Models From Meta Models. Software and System Modeling 8(4), 479–500 (2009)
15. Grönniger, H., Ringert, J.O., Rumpe, B.: System Model-Based Definition of Modeling Language Semantics. In: FMOODS/FORTE, pp. 152–166 (2009)
16. Mendonça, M., Wasowski, A., Czarnecki, K.: SAT-based Analysis of Feature Models is Easy. In: SPLC, pp. 231–240 (2009)
17. Jackson, E.K., Sztipanovits, J.: Constructive Techniques for Meta- and Model-Level Reasoning. In: Engels, G., Opdyke, B., Schmidt, D.C., Weil, F. (eds.) MODELS 2007. LNCS, vol. 4735, pp. 405–419. Springer, Heidelberg (2007)
18. Jaffar, J., Maher, M.J., Marriott, K., Stuckey, P.J.: The Semantics of Constraint Logic Programs. J. Log. Program. 37(1-3), 1–46 (1998)
19. de Moura, L., Bjørner, N.S.: Z3: An efficient SMT solver. In: Ramakrishnan, C.R., Rehof, J. (eds.) TACAS 2008. LNCS, vol. 4963, pp. 337–340. Springer, Heidelberg (2008)
20. Object Management Group: Meta Object Facility (MOF) Core Specification Version 2.4 (2010)

Correctness of Model Synchronization Based on Triple Graph Grammars

Frank Hermann[1,2,*], Hartmut Ehrig[1], Fernando Orejas[3], Krzysztof Czarnecki[4], Zinovy Diskin[4], and Yingfei Xiong[4]

[1] Institut für Softwaretechnik und Theoretische Informatik,
Technische Universität Berlin, Germany
{frank,ehrig}@cs.tu-berlin.de
[2] Interdisciplinary Center for Security, Reliability and Trust, Université du Luxembourg
[3] Departament de Llenguatges i Sistemes Informàtics,
Universitat Politècnica de Catalunya, Barcelona, Spain
orejas@lsi.upc.edu
[4] Generative Software Development Lab, University of Waterloo, Canada
{kczarnec,zdiskin,yingfei}@gsd.uwaterloo.ca

Abstract. Triple graph grammars (TGGs) have been used successfully to analyze correctness and completeness of bidirectional model transformations, but a corresponding formal approach to model synchronization has been missing. This paper closes this gap by providing a formal synchronization framework with bidirectional update propagation operations. They are generated from a TGG, which specifies the language of all consistently integrated source and target models.

As a main result, we show that the generated synchronization framework is correct and complete, provided that forward and backward propagation operations are deterministic. Correctness essentially means that the propagation operations preserve consistency. Moreover, we analyze the conditions under which the operations are inverse to each other. All constructions and results are motivated and explained by a small running example using concrete visual syntax and abstract syntax notation based on typed attributed graphs.

Keywords: Model Synchronization, Correctness, Bidirectional Model Transformation, Triple Graph Grammars.

1 Introduction

Bidirectional model transformations are a key concept for model generation and synchronization within model driven engineering (MDE, see [22,19,1]). Triple graph grammars (TGGs) have been successfully applied in several case studies for bidirectional model transformation, model integration and synchronization [17,21,9,8], and in the implementation of QVT [12]. Inspired by Schürr et al. [20,21], we started to develop a formal theory of TGGs [7,14], which allows us to handle correctness, completeness, termination, and functional behavior of model transformations.

The main goal of this paper is to provide a TGG framework for model synchronization with correctness guarantees, which is based on the theory of TGGs, work

---
* Supported by the National Research Fund, Luxembourg (AM2a).

on incremental synchronization by Giese et al. [9,8], and the replica synchronization framework [3]. The main ideas and results are the following:

1. Models are synchronized by propagating changes from a source model to a corresponding target model using forward and backward propagation operations. The operations are specified by a TGG model framework, inspired by symmetric replica synchronizers [3] and realized by model transformations based on TGGs [7]. The specified TGG also defines consistency of source and target models.
2. Since TGGs define, in general, non-deterministic model transformations, the derived synchronization operations are, in general, non-deterministic. But we are able to provide sufficient static conditions based on TGGs to ensure that the operations are deterministic.
3. The main result shows that a TGG synchronization framework with deterministic synchronization operations is correct, i.e., consistency preserving, and complete. We also give sufficient static conditions for invertability and weak invertability of the framework, where "weak" restricts invertability to a subclass of inputs.

Deriving a synchronization framework from a TGG has the following practical benefits. Consistency of related domains is defined declaritively and in a pattern-based style, using the rules of a TGG. After executing a synchronization operation, consistency of source and target models is always ensured (correctness) and the propagation operations can be performed for all valid inputs (completeness). The required static conditions of a TGG and the additional conditions for invertibility can be checked automatically using the existing tool support of AGG [23].

The next section presents our running example and Sec. 3 introduces the TGG model framework. Therafter, we briefly review model transformations based on TGGs in Sec. 4 and define the general synchronization process in Sec. 5. Section 6 presents the main result on the correctness of model synchronization. Finally, Secs. 7 and 8 discuss related work, conclusions, and future work. The proof of our main result is given in a technical report [15].

2 Running Example

Throughout the paper, we use a simple running example, which is based on previous work [2]. The example considers the synchronization of two organizational diagrams as shown in Fig. 1. Diagrams in the first domain—depicted left—provides details about the salary components and is restricted to persons of the marketing department. The second domain provides additional information about birth dates (marked by "*") and does not show the salary components. Therefore, both domains contain exclusive information and none of them can be interpreted as a view—defined by a query—of the other. Both diagrams together with some correspondence structure build up an integrated model, where we refer by source model to the first and by target model to the second diagram. Such an integrated model is called *consistent*, if the diagrams coincide on names of corresponding persons and the salary values are equal to the sums of the corresponding base and bonus values.

Example 1 (Integrated Model). The fifth row of Fig. 1 shows a consistent integrated model M in visual notation. The source model of M consists of two persons belonging

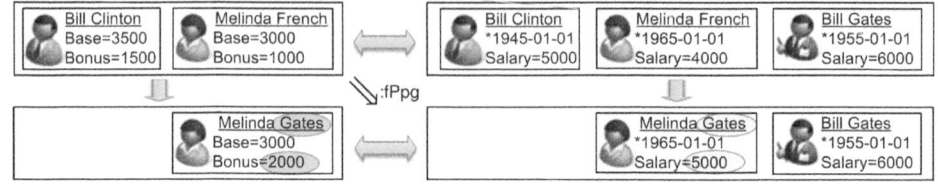

Fig. 1. Forward propagation

to the marketing department (depicted as persons without pencils) and the target model additionally contains the person "Bill Gates" belonging to the technical department (depicted as a person with pencil). The first row of Fig. 7 in Sec. 5 shows the corresponding underlying formal graph representation of the integrated model.

The synchronization problem is to propagate a model update in a way, such that the resulting integrated model is consistent. Looking at Fig. 1, we see a source model update that specifies the removal of person "Bill Clinton" and a change of attributes **LastName** and **Bonus** of person "Melinda French". The executed forward propagation (fPpg) removes person "Bill Clinton" and updates the attribute values of "Melinda French" in the target model, while preserving the unchanged birth date value.

3 Model Synchronization Framework Based on TGGs

Model synchronization aims to achieve consistency among interrelated models. A general way of specifying consistency for models of a source and a target domain is to provide a consistency relation that defines the consistent pairs (M^S, M^T) of source and target models. We argue that triple graph grammars (TGGs) are an adequate technique for this purpose. For this reason, we first review main concepts of TGGs [21,7].

In the framework of TGGs, an integrated model is represented by a triple graph consisting of three graphs G^S, G^C, and G^T, called source, correspondence, and target graphs, respectively, together with two mappings (graph morphisms) $s_G : G^C \to G^S$ and $t_G : G^C \to G^T$. Our triple graphs may also contain attributed nodes and edges [7,6]. The two mappings in G specify a *correspondence* $r : G^S \leftrightarrow G^T$, which relates the elements of G^S with their corresponding elements of G^T and vice versa. However, it is usually sufficient to have explicit correspondences between nodes only. For simplicity, we use double arrows ($\leftrightarrow$) as an equivalent shorter notation for triple graphs, whenever the the explicit correspondence graph can be omitted.

Triple graphs are related by triple graph morphisms $m : G \to H$ consisting of three graph morphisms that preserve the associated correspondences (i.e., the diagrams on the right commute).

$$G = (G^S \xleftarrow{s_G} G^C \xrightarrow{t_G} G^T)$$
$$m \downarrow \quad m^S \downarrow \quad m^C \downarrow \quad m^T \downarrow$$
$$H = (H^S \xleftarrow{s_H} H^C \xrightarrow{t_H} H^T)$$

Our triple graphs are typed. This means that a type triple graph TG is given (playing the role of a metamodel) and, moreover, every triple graph G is typed by a triple graph morphism $type_G : G \to TG$. It is required that morphisms between typed triple graphs preserve the typing. For $TG = (TG^S \leftarrow TG^C \to TG^T)$, we use $VL(TG)$, $VL(TG^S)$, and $VL(TG^T)$ to denote the classes of all graphs typed over TG, TG^S, and TG^T, respectively.

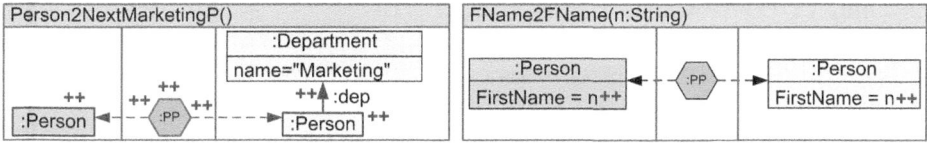

Fig. 2. Some triple rules of the TGG

A TGG specifies a language of triple graphs, which are considered as consistently integrated models. The triple rules of a TGG are used to synchronously build up source and target models, together with the correspondence structures.

A triple rule tr, depicted on the right, is an inclusion of triple graphs, represented $L \hookrightarrow R$. Notice that one or more of the rule components tr^S,
$$L = (L^S \xleftarrow{s_L} L^C \xrightarrow{t_L} L^T) \quad L \xhookrightarrow{tr} R$$
$$tr \downarrow \quad tr^S \downarrow \quad tr^C \downarrow \quad tr^T \downarrow \quad m \downarrow \ (PO) \ \downarrow n$$
$$R = (R^S \xleftarrow{s_R} R^C \xrightarrow{t_R} R^T) \quad G \xhookrightarrow{t} H$$
tr^C, and tr^T may be empty. In the example, this is the case for a rule concerning employees of the technical department within the target model. A triple rule is applied to a triple graph G by matching L to some sub triple graph of G. Technically, a match is a morphism $m : L \to G$. The result of this application is the triple graph H, where L is replaced by R in G. Technically, the result of the transformation is defined by a pushout diagram, as depicted above on the right. This triple graph transformation (TGT) step is denoted by $G \xRightarrow{tr,m} H$. Moreover, triple rules can be extended by negative application conditions (NACs) for restricting their application to specific matches [14]. A triple graph grammar $TGG = (TG, S, TR)$ consists of a triple type graph TG, a triple start graph S and a set TR of triple rules and generates the triple graph language $VL(TGG) \subseteq VL(TG)$.

Example 2 (Triple Rules). Figure 2 shows some triple rules of our running example using short notation, i.e., left- and right-hand side of a rule are depicted in one triple graph and the elements to be created have the label "++". The first rule **Person2NextMarketingP** requires an existing marketing department. It creates a new person in the target component together with its corresponding person in the source component and the explicit correspondence structure. The TGG contains a similar rule (not depicted) for initially creating the marketing department together with one person, where an additional NAC ensures that none of the existing departments is called "Marketing". The second rule in Fig. 2 extends two corresponding persons by their first names. There are further similar rules for the handling of the remaining attributes. In particular, the rule for the attribute birth is the empty rule on the source component.

A TGG model framework specifies the possible correspondences between models and updates of models according to Def. 1 below. The framework is closely related to the abstract framework for diagonal replica synchronizers [3] and triple spaces [4]. In our context, a model update $\delta : G \to G'$ is specified as a *graph modification* $\delta : G \xhookleftarrow{i_1} I \xhookrightarrow{i_2} G'$. The relating morphisms $i_1 : I \hookrightarrow G$ and $i_2 : I \hookrightarrow G'$ are inclusions and specify the elements in the interface I that are preserved by the modification. While graph modifications are also triple graphs by definition, it is conceptually important to distinguish between correspondences and updates δ.

Definition 1 (TGG Model Framework). *Let* $TGG = (TG, \emptyset, TR)$ *be a triple graph grammar with empty start graph. The derived* TGG model framework $MF(TGG) = (VL(TG^S), VL(TG^T), R, C, \Delta_S, \Delta_T)$ *consists of source domain* $VL(TG^S)$, *target domain* $VL(TG^T)$, *the set* R *of correspondence relations given by* $R = VL(TG)$, *the set* C *of consistent correspondence relations* $C \subseteq R$ *given by* $C = VL(TGG)$, *(i.e.,* R *contains all integrated models and* C *all consistently integrated ones), and sets* Δ_S, Δ_T *of graph modifications for the source and target domains, given by* $\Delta_S = \{a : G^S \to G'^S \mid G^S, G'^S \in VL(TG^S), \text{ and } a \text{ is a graph modification}\}$ *and* $\Delta_T = \{b : G^T \to G'^T \mid G^T, G'^T \in VL(TG^T), \text{ and } b \text{ is a graph modification}\}$, *respectively.*

Given a TGG model framework, the synchronization problem is to provide suitable forward and backward propagation operations fPpg and bPpg, which are total and deterministic (see Fig. 3, where we use solid lines for the inputs and dashed lines for the outputs). The required

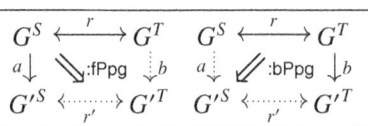

Fig. 3. Synchronization operations

input for fPpg is an integrated model (correspondence relation) $G^S \leftrightarrow G^T$ together with a source model update (graph modification) $a : G^S \to G'^S$. In a common tool environment, both inputs are either available directly or can be obtained. For example, the graph modification of a model update can be derived via standard difference computation and the initial correspondence can be computed based on TGG integration concepts [5,17]. Note that determinism of fPpg means that the resulting correspondence $G'^S \leftrightarrow G'^T$ and target model update $b : G^T \to G'^T$ are uniquely determined. The propagation operations are *correct*, if they additionally preserve consistency as specified by laws (*a*1) – (*b*2) in Fig. 4. Law (*a*2) means that fPpg always produces consistent correspondences from consistent updated source models G'^S. Law (*a*1) means that if the given update is the identity and the given correspondence is consistent, then fPpg changes nothing. Laws (*b*1) and (*b*2) are the dual versions concerning bPpg. Moreover, the sets VL_S and VL_T specify the *consistent source and target models*, which are given by the source and target components of the integrated models in $C = VL(TGG)$.

Definition 2 (Synchronization Problem and Framework). *Let* $MF = (VL(TG^S), VL(TG^T), R, C, \Delta_S, \Delta_T)$ *be a TGG model framework (see Def. 1). The* forward synchronization problem *is to construct an operation* fPpg : $R \otimes \Delta_S \to R \times \Delta_T$ *leading to the left diagram in Fig. 3, called* synchronization tile, *where* $R \otimes \Delta_S = \{(r, a) \in R \times \Delta_S \mid r : G^S \leftrightarrow G^T, a : G^S \to G'^S\}$, *i.e.,* a *and* r *coincide on* G^S. *The pair* $(r, a) \in R \otimes \Delta_S$ *is called* premise *and* $(r', b) \in R \times \Delta_T$ *is called* solution *of the forward synchronization problem, written* fPpg$(r, a) = (r', b)$. *The* backward synchronization problem *is to construct an operation* bPpg *leading to the right diagram in Fig. 3. The operations* fPpg *and* bPpg *are called* correct *with respect to consistency function* C, *if axioms (a1) and (a2) resp. (b1) and (b2) in Fig. 4 are satisfied.*

Given propagation operations fPpg *and* bPpg, *the derived* synchronization framework $Synch(TGG)$ *is given by* $Synch(TGG) = (MF, \mathsf{fPpg}, \mathsf{bPpg})$. *It is called* correct, *if* fPpg *and* bPpg *are correct; it is* weakly invertible *if axioms (c1) and (c2) in Fig. 4 are satisfied; and it is* invertible *if additionally axioms (d1) and (d2) in Fig. 4 are satisfied.*

$(a1):$ $\forall c \in C:$ $\begin{array}{c} G^S \xleftrightarrow{c} G^T \\ 1 \downarrow \searrow_{\text{:fPpg}} \downarrow 1 \\ G^S \xleftrightarrow{c} G^T \end{array}$	$(a2):$ $\forall G'^S \in VL_S:$ $\begin{array}{c} G^S \xleftrightarrow{r} G^T \\ a \downarrow \searrow_{\text{:fPpg}} \downarrow b \\ G'^S \xleftrightarrow{r':C} G'^T \end{array}$	$(b1):$ $\forall c \in C:$ $\begin{array}{c} G^S \xleftrightarrow{c} G^T \\ 1 \downarrow \diagup_{\text{:bPpg}} \downarrow 1 \\ G^S \xleftrightarrow{c} G^T \end{array}$	$(b2):$ $\forall G'^T \in VL_T:$ $\begin{array}{c} G^S \xleftrightarrow{r} G^T \\ a \downarrow \diagup_{\text{:bPpg}} \downarrow b \\ G'^S \xleftrightarrow{r':C} G'^T \end{array}$
$(c1):$ $\begin{array}{c} G^S \xleftrightarrow{r} G^T \xleftrightarrow{r} G^S \xleftrightarrow{r} G^T \\ a_1 \downarrow \searrow_{\text{:fPpg}} \downarrow b \searrow_{\text{:bPpg}} \downarrow a_2 \searrow_{\text{:fPpg}} \downarrow b \\ G_1^S \xleftrightarrow{r_1} G'^T \xleftrightarrow{r_2} G_2^S \xleftrightarrow{r_2} G'^T \end{array}$		$(d1):$ $\begin{array}{c} G^S \xleftrightarrow{r} G^T \xleftrightarrow{r} G^S \\ a_1 \downarrow \searrow_{\text{:fPpg}} \downarrow b \searrow_{\text{:bPpg}} \downarrow a_2 \\ G'^S \xleftrightarrow{r'} G'^T \xleftrightarrow{r'} G'^S \end{array}$	
$(c2):$ $\begin{array}{c} G^T \xleftrightarrow{r} G^S \xleftrightarrow{r} G^T \xleftrightarrow{r} G^S \\ b_1 \downarrow \searrow_{\text{:bPpg}} \downarrow a \searrow_{\text{:fPpg}} \downarrow b_2 \searrow_{\text{:bPpg}} \downarrow a \\ G_1^T \xleftrightarrow{r_1} G'^S \xleftrightarrow{r_2} G_2^T \xleftrightarrow{r_2} G'^S \end{array}$		$(d2):$ $\begin{array}{c} G^T \xleftrightarrow{r} G^S \xleftrightarrow{r} G^T \\ b_1 \downarrow \searrow_{\text{:bPpg}} \downarrow a \searrow_{\text{:fPpg}} \downarrow b_2 \\ G'^T \xleftrightarrow{r'} G'^S \xleftrightarrow{r'} G'^T \end{array}$	

Fig. 4. Laws for correct and (weak) invertible synchronization frameworks

Remark 1 (Correctness and Invertibility). Correctness of fPpg according to $(a1)$ means that for each consistent correspondence $c: G^S \leftrightarrow G^T$ and identity as modification $1: G^S \to G^S$ we have an identical result, i.e., fPpg$(c, 1) = (c, 1)$. According to $(a2)$, we have for each general correspondence $r: G^S \leftrightarrow G^T$ and modification $a: G^S \to G'^S$ with consistent source model $G'^S \in VL_S$ a solution $(r', b) = $ fPpg(r, a), where $r': G'^S \leftrightarrow G'^T$ is consistent, i.e., $r' \in C$. Note that also for non-consistent $r: G^S \leftrightarrow G^T$ the result $r': G'^S \leftrightarrow G'^T$ is consistent, provided that G'^S is consistent.

Weak invertibility (laws $(c1)$ and $(c2)$) imply that the operations are inverse of each other for a restricted set of inputs. Update b in $(c1)$ is assumed to be part of the result of a forward propagation and update a in $(c2)$ is assumed to be derived from a backward propagation. Invertibility $((d1)$ and $(d2))$ means that the operations are essentially inverse of each other, although the interfaces of a_1 and a_2 (resp. b_1 and b_2) may be different. Invertibility requires effectively that all information in one domain is completely reflected in the other domain.

4 Model Transformation Based on TGGs

The *operational rules* for implementing bidirectional model transformations can be generated automatically from a TGG. The sets TR_S and TR_F contain all source and forward rules, respectively, and are derived from the triple rules TR as shown in the diagrams below. The rules are used to implement source-to-target transformations. The sets of target rules TR_T and backward rules TR_B are derived analogously and the generation of operational rules has been extended to triple rules with negative application conditions [7].

$$L = (L^S \xleftarrow{s_L} L^C \xrightarrow{t_L} L^T) \quad (L^S \leftarrow \emptyset \to \emptyset) \quad (R^S \xleftarrow{tr^S \circ s_L} L^C \xrightarrow{t_L} L^T)$$
$$tr \downarrow tr^S \downarrow \quad tr^C \downarrow \quad tr^T \downarrow \quad tr^S \downarrow \quad \downarrow \quad \downarrow \quad id \downarrow \quad tr^C \downarrow \quad \downarrow tr^T$$
$$R = (R^S \xleftarrow{s_R} R^C \xrightarrow{t_R} R^T) \quad (R^S \leftarrow \emptyset \to \emptyset) \quad (R^S \xleftarrow{s_R} R^C \xrightarrow{t_R} R^T)$$

       triple rule tr source rule tr_S forward rule tr_F

Example 3 (Operational Rules). The rules in Fig. 5 are the derived source and forward rules of the triple rule FName2FName in Fig. 2.

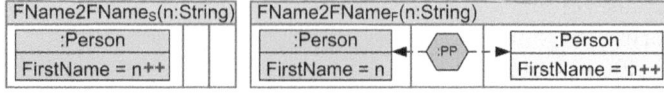

Fig. 5. Derived source and forward rules

The derived operational rules provide the basis for the definition of model transformations based on source-consistent forward transformation sequences [7,11]. *Source consistency* of a forward sequence ($G_0 \xRightarrow{tr_F^*} G_n$) via TR_F is a control condition which requires that there is a corresponding source sequence ($\emptyset \xRightarrow{tr_S^*} G_0$) via TR_S, such that matches of corresponding source and forward steps are compatible ($n_{i,S}^S(x) = m_{i,F}^S(x)$). The source sequence is obtained by parsing the given source model in order to guide the forward transformation. Moreover, source and forward sequences can be constructed simultaneously and backtracking can be reduced in order to derive efficient executions of model transformations [7,14]. Given a source model G^S, a *model transformation sequence* for G^S is given by ($G^S, G_0 \xRightarrow{tr_F^*} G_n, G^T$), where G^T is the resulting target model derived from the source-consistent forward sequence $G_0 \xRightarrow{tr_F^*} G_n$ with $G_0 = (G^S \leftarrow \emptyset \rightarrow \emptyset)$ and $G_n = (G^S \leftarrow G^C \rightarrow G^T)$.

Model transformations based on model transformation sequences are always syntactically correct and complete [7,11,14]. *Correctness* means that for each source model G^S that is transformed into a target model G^T there is a consistent integrated model $G = (G^S \leftarrow G^C \rightarrow G^T)$ in the language of consistent integrated models $VL(TGG)$ defined by the TGG. *Completeness* ensures that for each consistent source model there is a forward transformation sequence transforming it into a consistent target model.

The concept of *forward translation rules* [14] provides a simple way of implementing model transformations such that source consistency is ensured automatically. A forward translation rule tr_{FT} extends the forward rule tr_F by additional Boolean valued translation attributes, which are markers for elements in the source model and specify whether the elements have been translated already. Each forward translation rule tr_{FT} turns the markers of the source elements that are translated by this rule from **F** to **T** (i.e., the elements that are created by tr_S). The model transformation is successfully executed if the source model is completely marked with **T**. We indicate these markers in the examples by checkmarks in the visual notation and by bold font face in the graph representation. Similarly, from the triple rules, we can also create *marking rules* [15], which, given an integrated model ($G^S \leftrightarrow G^T$), simulate the creation of the model by marking its elements. If all elements are marked with **T**, then ($G^S \leftrightarrow G^T$) belongs to $VL(TGG)$.

5 General Synchronization Process Based on TGGs

This section shows how to construct the operation fPpg of a TGG synchronization framework (see Def. 2) as a composition of auxiliary operations ⟨fAln, Del, fAdd⟩. Symmetrically, operations ⟨bAln, Del, bAdd⟩ are used to define the operation bPpg.

Signature	Definition of Components	
$G^S \xleftrightarrow{r=(s,t)} G^T$ $a=(a_1,a_2)\downarrow \searrow{:\text{fAln}} \downarrow 1$ $G'^S \xleftrightarrow{r'=(s',t')} G'^T$	$G^S \xleftarrow{s} G^C \xrightarrow{t} G^T$ $a_1\uparrow \quad (PB) \quad \uparrow a_1^*$ $D^S \xleftarrow{s^*} D^C$	$s' = a_2 \circ s^*$, $t' = t \circ a_1^*$
$G^S \xleftrightarrow{r=(s,t)} G^T$ $a=(f^S,1)\downarrow \Downarrow{:\text{Del}} \downarrow b=(f^T,1)$ $G_k^S \xleftrightarrow{r'=(s_k,t_k):C} G_k^T$	$G = (G^S \xleftarrow{s} G^C \xrightarrow{t} G^T)$ $f\uparrow \quad f^S\uparrow \quad f^C\uparrow \quad f^T\uparrow$ $\emptyset \xRightarrow{tr^*} G_k = (G_k^S \xleftarrow{s_k} G_k^C \xrightarrow{t_k} G_k^T)$	$\emptyset \xRightarrow{tr^*} G_k$ is maximal w.r.t. $G_k \subseteq G$
$\forall G'^S \in VL_S:$ $G^S \xleftrightarrow{r=(s,t):C} G^T$ $a=(1,a_2)\downarrow \searrow{:\text{fAdd}} \downarrow b=(1,b_2)$ $G'^S \xleftrightarrow{r'=(s',t')} G'^T$	$G = (G^S \xleftarrow{s} G^C \xrightarrow{t} G^T)$ $g\uparrow \quad a_2\uparrow \quad 1\uparrow \quad 1\uparrow$ $G_0 = (G'^S \xleftarrow{a_2 \circ s} G^C \xrightarrow{t} G^T)$ $tr_F^*\Downarrow \quad 1\Downarrow \quad \cap \quad b_2\Downarrow \cap$ $G' = (G'^S \xleftarrow{s'} G'^C \xrightarrow{t'} G'^T)$	$G_0 \xRightarrow{tr_F^*} G'$ with $G' \in VL(TGG)$

Fig. 6. Auxiliary operations fAln, Del and fAdd

As a general requirement, the given TGG has to provide *deterministic* sets of operational rules, meaning that the algorithmic execution of the forward translation, backward translation, and marking rules ensures functional behavior (unique results) and does not require backtracking. For this purpose, additional policies can be defined that restrict the matches of operational rules [15], as discussed in Ex. 5 in Sec. 6. Fact 1 in Sec. 6 provides sufficient conditions for deterministic operational rules. We provide additional static conditions and automated checks in the technical report [15].

The general synchronization process is performed as follows (see Fig. 6; we use double arrows ($\leftrightarrow$) for correspondence in the signature of the operations, and the explicit triple graphs for the construction details). Given two corresponding models G^S and G^T and an update of G^S via the graph modification $a = (G^S \xleftarrow{a_1} D^S \xrightarrow{a_2} G'^S)$ with $G'^S \in VL_S$, the forward propagation fPpg of δ_S is performed in three steps via the auxiliary operations fAln, Del, and fAdd. At first, the deletion performed in a is reflected into the correspondence relation between G^S and G^T by calculating the forward alignment remainder via operation fAln. This step deletes all correspondence elements whose elements in G^S have been deleted. In the second step, performed via operation Del, the two maximal subgraphs $G_k^S \subseteq G^S$ and $G_k^T \subseteq G^T$ are computed such that they form a consistent integrated model in $VL(TGG)$ according to the TGG. All elements that are in G^T but not in G_k^T are deleted, i.e., the new target model is given by G_k^T. Finally, in the last step (operation fAdd), the elements in G'^S that extend G_k^S are transformed to corresponding structures in G'^T, i.e., G_k^T is extended by these new structures. The result of fAdd, and hence also fPpg, is a consistent integrated model.

Definition 3 (Auxiliary TGG Operations). *Let $TGG = (TG, \emptyset, TR)$ be a TGG with deterministic sets of operational rules and let further $MF(TGG)$ be the derived TGG model framework.*

1. *The auxiliary operation* fAln *computing the forward alignment remainder is given by* fAln$(r, a) = r'$, *as specified in the upper part of Fig. 6. The square marked by* (PB) *is a pullback, meaning that* D^C *is the intersection of* D^S *and* G^C.
2. *Let* $r = (s, t): G^S \leftrightarrow G^T$ *be a correspondence relation, then the result of the auxiliary operation* Del *is the maximal consistent subgraph* $G^S_k \leftrightarrow G^T_k$ *of* r, *given by* Del$(r) = (a, r', b)$, *which is specified in the middle part of Fig. 6*.
3. *Let* $r = (s, t): G^S \leftrightarrow G^T$ *be a consistent correspondence relation,* $a = (1, a_2)$: $G^S \rightarrow G'^S$ *be a source modification and* $G'^S \in VL_S$. *The result of the auxiliary operation* fAdd, *for propagating the additions of source modification* a, *is a consistent model* $G'^S \leftrightarrow G'^T$ *extending* $G^S \leftrightarrow G^T$, *and is given by* fAdd$(r, a) = (r', b)$, *according to the lower part of Fig. 6*.

Remark 2 (Auxiliary TGG Operations). Intuitively, operation fAln constructs the new correspondence graph D^C from the given G^C by deleting all correspondence elements in G^C whose associated elements in G^S are deleted via update a and, for this reason, do not occur in D^S. Operation Del is executed by applying marking rules (cf. Sec. 4) to the given integrated model until no rule is applicable any more. If, at the end, $G^S \leftrightarrow G^T$ is completely marked, the integrated model is already consistent; otherwise, the result is the largest consistent integrated model included in $G^S \leftrightarrow G^T$. Technically, the application of the marking rules corresponds to a maximal triple rule sequence as shown in the right middle part of Fig. 6 and discussed in more detail in [15]. Finally, fAdd is executed by applying forward translation rules (cf. Sec. 4) to $G'^S \leftrightarrow G^T$ until all the elements in G'^S are marked. That is, these TGT steps build a model transformation of G'^S extending G^T. Technically, the application of the forward translation rules corresponds to a source-consistent forward sequence from G_0 to G', as shown in the right lower part of Fig. 6. By correctness of model transformations [7], the sequence implies consistency of G' as stated above. The constructions for these auxiliary operations are provided in full detail in [15].

Example 4 (Forward Propagation via Operation fPpg*).* Figure 7 shows the application of the three steps of synchronization operation fPpg to the visual models of our running example. After removing the dangling correspondence node of the alignment in the first step (fAln), the maximal consistent subgraph of the integrated model is computed (Del) by stepwise marking the consistent parts: consistent parts are indicated by grey boxes with checkmarks in the visual notation and by bold font faces in the graph representation. Note that node "Bill Gates" is part of the target graph in this maximal consistent subgraph, even though it is not in correspondence with any element of the source graph. In the final step (fAdd), the inconsistent elements in the target model are removed and the remaining new elements of the update are propagated towards the target model by model transformation, such that all elements are finally marked as consistent.

Definition 4 (Derived TGG Synchronization Framework). *Let* $TGG = (TG, \emptyset, TR)$ *be a TGG with deterministic sets of derived operational rules and with derived model framework MF(TGG), then operation* fPpg *of the derived TGG synchronization framework is given according to Def. 2 by the composition of auxiliary operations (*fAln, Del, fAdd*) with construction in Rem. 3. Symmetrically—not shown explicitly—we obtain* bPpg *as composition of auxiliary operations (*bAln, Del, bAdd*)*.

Correctness of Model Synchronization Based on Triple Graph Grammars 677

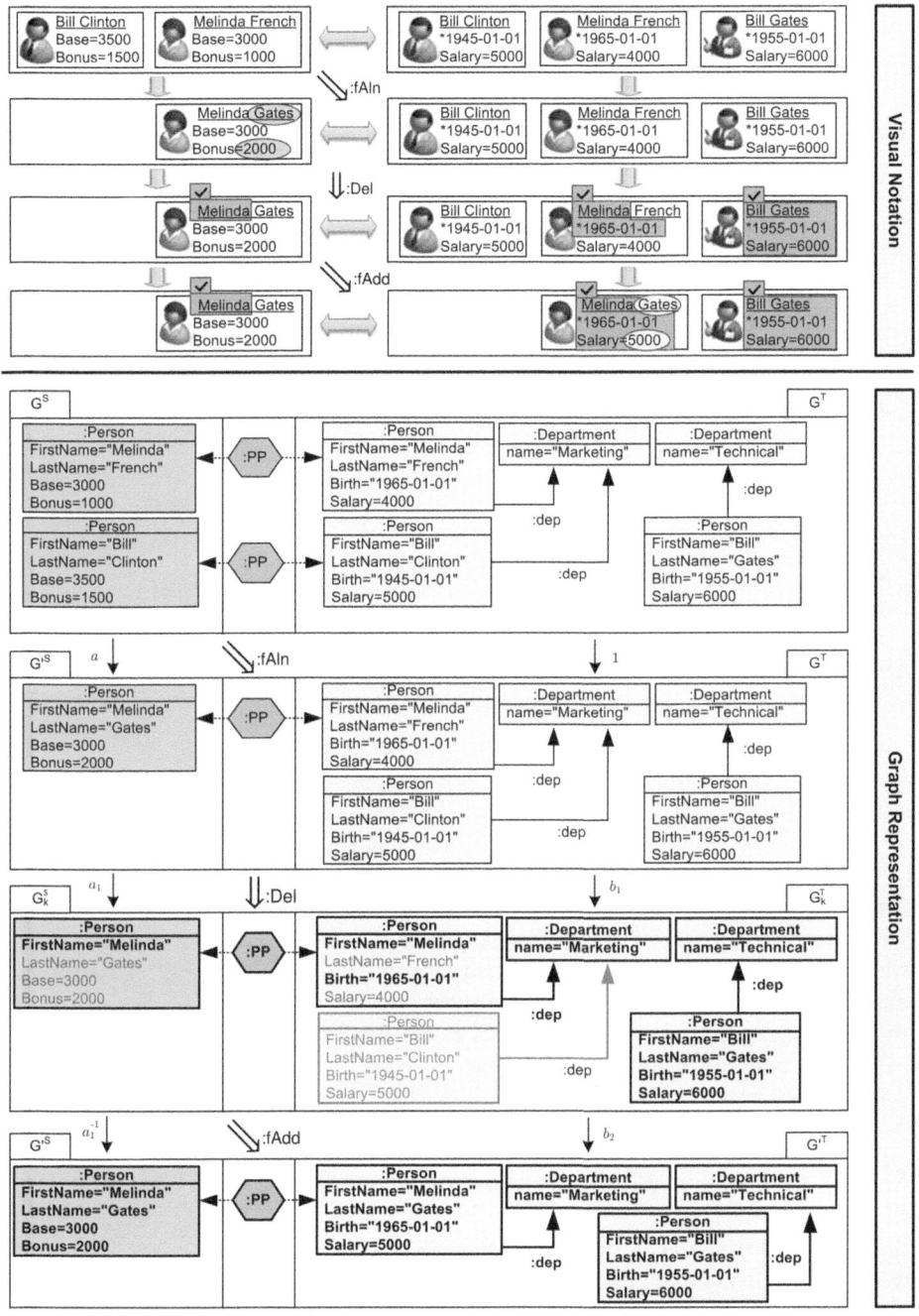

Fig. 7. Forward propagation in detail: visual notation (top) and graph representation (bottom)

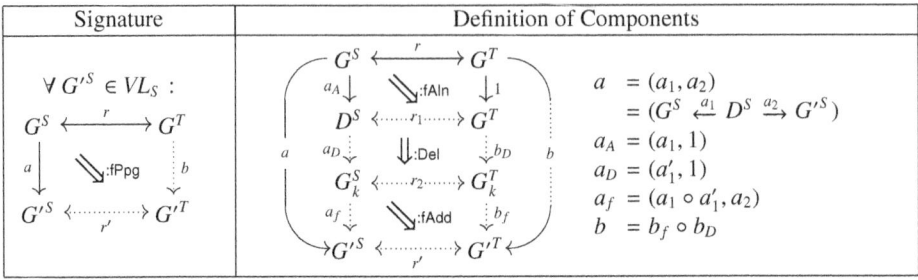

```
1   /* == alignment remainder == */
2   forall(correpondence nodes without image in the source model){
3       delete these elements }
4   /* ==== delete === */
5   while(there is a triple rule p such that R\L is unmarked){
6       apply to G the marking rule corresponding to p }
7   forall(unmarked nodes and edges from the target model){
8       delete these elements }
9   /* ===== add ===== */
10  while(there is a forward translation rule applicable to G){
11      apply to G the forward translation rule }
```

Fig. 8. Synchronization operation fPpg - top: formal definition, bottom: algorithm

Remark 3 (Construction of fPpg *according to Fig. 8).* Given a not necessarily consistent integrated model $r: G^S \leftrightarrow G^T$ and source model update $a: G^S \to G'^S$ with $G'^S \in VL_S$, we compute fPpg(r, a) as follows. First, fAln computes the correspondence ($D^S \leftrightarrow G^T$), where D^S is the part of G^S that is preserved by update a. Then, Del computes its maximal consistent integrated submodel ($G_k^S \leftrightarrow G_k^T$). Finally, fAdd composes the embedding $G_k^S \to G'^S$ with correspondence ($G_k^S \leftrightarrow G_k^T$) leading to ($G'^S \leftrightarrow G_k^T$), which is then extended into the consistent integrated model ($G'^S \leftrightarrow G'^T$) via forward transformation. If $G'^S \notin VL_S$, then the result is given by $b = (1,1): G^T \to G^T$ together with the correspondence relation $r' = (\emptyset, \emptyset)$ and additionally, an error message is provided. The bottom part of Fig. 8 describes this construction algorithmically in pseudo code, leaving out the error handling; marking is explained in Sec. 4.

6 Correctness of Model Synchronization Based on TGGs

Based on the derived TGG synchronization framework (Def. 4), we now state our main result concerning correctness, completeness, and invertibility. The proofs and full technical details are provided in the technical report [15]. According to Def. 2, correctness requires that the synchronization operations are deterministic, i.e., they have functional behaviour and ensure laws (*a*1) - (*b*2). Concerning the first property, Fact 1 below provides a sufficient condition based on the notion of critical pairs [6], which is used in the automated analysis engine of the tool AGG [23]. A critical pair specifies a conflict between two rules in minimal context. Solving a conflict means to find compatible merging transformation steps, which is formalized by the notion of strict confluence [6]. The result is provided for almost injective matches, which means that matches are injective on the graph part and may evaluate different attribute expressions to the same values. *Completeness* requires that operations fPpg and bPpg can be successfully applied to all consistent source models $G'^S \in VL_S$ and target models $G'^T \in VL_T$, respectively. For this reason, additional propagation policies are defined in order to eliminate non-determinism. They can be seen as a kind of application conditions for the rules and are called *conservative*, if they preserve the completeness result. By Fact 2 in [15], we provided a sufficient static condition for checking this property.

Fact 1 (Deterministic Synchronization Operations). *Let TGG be a triple graph grammar and let matches be restricted to almost injective morphisms. If the critical pairs of the sets of operational rules are strictly confluent and the systems of rules are terminating, then the sets of operational rules are deterministic, which implies that the derived synchronization operations* fPpg *and* bPpg *are deterministic as well.*

Remark 4 (Termination). In order to ensure termination of the TGG constructions, we can check that each operational rule is modifying at least one translation attribute (cf. Sec. 4), which is a sufficient condition as shown by Thm. 1 in [14] for model transformation sequences.

Invertibility of propagation operations depends on additional properties of a TGG. For this purpose, we distinguish between different types of triple rules. By TR^{+s} we denote the triple rules of TR that are creating on the source component and by TR^{1s} those that are identical on the source component and analogously for the target component. A TGG is called *pure*, if $TR^{1s} \subseteq TR_T$ and $TR^{1t} \subseteq TR_S$ meaning that the source-identic triple rules are empty rules on the source and correspondence components and analogously for the target-identic triple rules. According to Thm. 1 below, weak invertibility is ensured if the TGG is pure and at most one set of operational rules is restricted by a conservative policy. In the more specific case that all triple rules of a TGG are creating on the source and target components ($TR = TR^{+s} = TR^{+t}$), then the TGG is called *tight*, because the derived forward and backward rules are strongly related. This additional property ensures invertibility meaning that fPpg and bPpg are inverse to each other when considering the resulting models only.

Theorem 1 (Correctness, Completeness, and Invertibility). *Let Synch(TGG) be a derived TGG synchronization framework, such that the sets of operational rules of TGG are deterministic. Then Synch(TGG) is correct and complete. If, additionally, TGG is pure and at most one set of operational rules was extended by a conservative policy, then Synch(TGG) is weakly invertible and if, moreover, TGG is tight and no policy was applied, then Synch(TGG) is also invertible.*

Example 5 (Correctness, Completeness, Invertibility, and Scalability). The initially derived set of backward transformation rules for our running example is not completely deterministic because of the non-deterministic choice of base and bonus values for propagating the change of a salary value. Therefore, we defined a conservative policy for the responsible backward triple rule by fixing the propagated values of modified salary values to *bonus* = *base* = 0.5 × *salary*. By Fact 2 in [15], we provided a sufficient static condition for checking that a policy is conservative; we validated our example and showed that the derived operations fPpg and bPpg are deterministic. For this reason, we can apply Thm. 1 and verify that the derived TGG synchronization framework is correct and complete. Since, moreover, the TGG is pure and we used the conservative policy for the backward direction only, Thm. 1 further ensures that *Synch(TGG)* is weakly invertible. However, it is not invertible in the general sense, as shown by a counter example in [15], which uses the fact that information about birth dates is stored in one domain only. The automated validation for our example TGG with 8 rules was performed in 25 seconds on a standard consumer notebook via the analysis engine of the tool AGG [23]. We are confident that the scalability of this approach can be significantly improved with additional optimizations.

In the case that the specified TGG does not ensure deterministic synchronization operations, there are still two options for synchronization that ensure correctness and completeness. On the one hand, the triple rules can be modified in a suitable way, such that the TGG can be verified to be deterministic. For this purpose, the critical pair analysis engine of the tool AGG [23] can be used to analyze conflicts between the generated operational rules. Moreover, backtracking can be reduced or even eliminated by generating additional application conditions for the operational rules using the automatic generation of filter NACs [14]. On the other hand, the TGG can be used directly, leading to nondeterministic synchronization operations, which may provide several possible synchronization results.

7 Related Work

Triple graph grammars have been successfully applied in multiple case studies for bidirectional model transformation, model integration and synchronization [17,21,9,8], and in the implementation of QVT [12]. Moreover, several formal results are available concerning correctness, completeness, termination [7,10], functional behavior [16,10], and optimization with respect to the efficiency of their execution [14,18,10]. The presented constructions for performing model transformations and model synchronizations are inspired by Schürr et al. [20,21] and Giese et al. [8,9], respectively. The constructions formalize the main ideas of model synchronization based on TGGs in order to show correctness and completeness of the approach based on the results known for TGG model transformations.

Perdita Stevens developed an abstract state-based view on symmetric model synchronization based on the concept of constraint maintainers [22] and Diskin described a more general delta-based view within the *tile algebra* framework [3]. The constructions in the present paper are inspired by tile algebra and follow the general framework presented by Diskin et al. [4], where propagation operations are defined as the composition of two kinds of operations: alignment and consistency restoration. In the current paper, operations fAln and bAln take care of the alignment by removing all correspondence nodes that would be dangling due to deletions via the given model update. Then, operations Del and fAdd resp. bAdd provide the consistency restoration by first marking the consistent parts of the integrated model and then propagating the changes and deleting the remaining inconsistent parts.

Giese et al. introduced incremental synchronization techniques based on TGGs in order to preserve consistent structures of the given models by revoking previously performed forward propagation steps and their dependent ones [9]. This idea is generalized by the auxiliary operation Del in the present framework, which ensures the preservation of maximal consistent substructures and extends the application of synchronization to TGGs that are not tight or contain rules with negative application conditions. Giese et al. [8] and Greenyer et al. [13] proposed to extend the preservation of substructures by allowing for the reuse of any *partial* substructure of a rule causing, however, non-deterministic behavior. Moreover, a partial reuse can cause unintended results. Consider, e.g., the deletion of a person A in the source domain and the addition of a new person with the same name, then the old birth date of person A could be reused.

In order to improve efficiency, Giese et al. [9,8] proposed to avoid the computation of already consistent substructures by encoding the matches and dependencies of rule applications within the correspondences. In the present framework, operation Del can be extended conservatively by storing the matches and dependency information separately, such that the provided correctness and completeness results can be preserved [15].

8 Conclusion and Future Work

Based on our formal framework for correctness, completeness, termination and functional behavior of model transformations using triple graph grammars (TGGs) [7,14], we have presented in this paper a formal TGG framework for model synchronization inspired by [9,8,20,21]. The main result (Thm. 1) shows correctness, completeness and (weak) invertibility, provided that the derived synchronization operations are deterministic. For this property, sufficient static conditions are provided (Fact 1) based on general results for TGGs in [14].

In future work, the tool Henshin based on AGG [23] will be extended to implement the synchronization algorithm for forward propagation in Fig. 8. Moreover, the relationship with lenses [22] and delta based bidirectional transformations [4] will be studied in more detail, especially in view of composition of lenses leading to composition of synchronization operations. Furthermore, we will study synchronization based on non-deterministic forward and backward propagation operations in more detail.

References

1. Czarnecki, K., Foster, J.N., Hu, Z., Lämmel, R., Schürr, A., Terwilliger, J.F.: Bidirectional Transformations: A Cross-Discipline Perspective. In: Paige, R.F. (ed.) ICMT 2009. LNCS, vol. 5563, pp. 260–283. Springer, Heidelberg (2009)
2. Diskin, Z., Xiong, Y., Czarnecki, K.: From State- to Delta-Based Bidirectional Model Transformations: the Asymmetric Case. Journal of Object technology 10, 6:1–6:25 (2011)
3. Diskin, Z.: Model Synchronization: Mappings, Tiles, and Categories. In: Fernandes, J.M., Lämmel, R., Visser, J., Saraiva, J. (eds.) Generative and Transformational Techniques in Software Engineering III. LNCS, vol. 6491, pp. 92–165. Springer, Heidelberg (2011)
4. Diskin, Z., Xiong, Y., Czarnecki, K., Ehrig, H., Hermann, F., Orejas, F.: From State- to Delta-based Bidirectional Model Transformations: The Symmetric Case. In: Whittle, J., Clark, T., Kühne, T. (eds.) MODELS 2011. LNCS, vol. 6981, pp. 304–318. Springer, Heidelberg (2011)

5. Ehrig, H., Ehrig, K., Hermann, F.: From Model Transformation to Model Integration based on the Algebraic Approach to Triple Graph Grammars. EC-EASST 10 (2008)
6. Ehrig, H., Ehrig, K., Prange, U., Taentzer, G.: Fundamentals of Algebraic Graph Transformation. EATCS Monographs in Theor. Comp. Science (2006)
7. Ehrig, H., Ermel, C., Hermann, F., Prange, U.: On-the-Fly Construction, Correctness and Completeness of Model Transformations based on Triple Graph Grammars. In: Schürr, A., Selic, B. (eds.) MODELS 2009. LNCS, vol. 5795, pp. 241–255. Springer, Heidelberg (2009)
8. Giese, H., Hildebrandt, S.: Efficient Model Synchronization of Large-Scale Models. Tech. Rep. 28, Hasso Plattner Institute at the University of Potsdam (2009)
9. Giese, H., Wagner, R.: From model transformation to incremental bidirectional model synchronization. Software and Systems Modeling 8(1), 21–43 (2009)
10. Giese, H., Hildebrandt, S., Lambers, L.: Toward Bridging the Gap Between Formal Semantics and Implementation of Triple Graph Grammars. Tech. Rep. 37, Hasso Plattner Institute at the University of Potsdam (2010)
11. Golas, U., Ehrig, H., Hermann, F.: Formal Specification of Model Transformations by Triple Graph Grammars with Application Conditions. EC-EASST 39 (2011)
12. Greenyer, J., Kindler, E.: Comparing relational model transformation technologies: implementing query/view/transformation with triple graph grammars. Software and Systems Modeling (SoSyM) 9(1), 21–46 (2010)
13. Greenyer, J., Pook, S., Rieke, J.: Preventing information loss in incremental model synchronization by reusing elements. In: France, R.B., Kuester, J.M., Bordbar, B., Paige, R.F. (eds.) ECMFA 2011. LNCS, vol. 6698, pp. 144–159. Springer, Heidelberg (2011)
14. Hermann, F., Ehrig, H., Golas, U., Orejas, F.: Efficient Analysis and Execution of Correct and Complete Model Transformations Based on Triple Graph Grammars. In: Proc. MDI 2010 (2010)
15. Hermann, F., Ehrig, H., Orejas, F., Czarnecki, K., Diskin, Z., Xiong, Y.: Correctness of Model Synchronization Based on Triple Graph Grammars - Extended Version. Tech. Rep. TR 2011-07, TU Berlin, Fak. IV (2011)
16. Hermann, F., Ehrig, H., Orejas, F., Golas, U.: Formal Analysis of Functional Behaviour for Model Transformations Based on Triple Graph Grammars. In: Ehrig, H., Rensink, A., Rozenberg, G., Schürr, A. (eds.) ICGT 2010. LNCS, vol. 6372, pp. 155–170. Springer, Heidelberg (2010)
17. Kindler, E., Wagner, R.: Triple graph grammars: Concepts, extensions, implementations, and application scenarios. Tech. Rep. TR-ri-07-284, Department of Computer Science, University of Paderborn, Germany (2007)
18. Klar, F., Lauder, M., Königs, A., Schürr, A.: Extended Triple Graph Grammars with Efficient and Compatible Graph Translators. In: Engels, G., Lewerentz, C., Schäfer, W., Schürr, A., Westfechtel, B. (eds.) Nagl Festschrift. LNCS, vol. 5765, pp. 141–174. Springer, Heidelberg (2010)
19. Object Management Group: Meta Object Facility (MOF) 2.0 Query/View/Transformation Specification. Version 1.0 formal/08-04-03 (2008), http://www.omg.org/spec/QVT/1.0/
20. Schürr, A.: Specification of Graph Translators with Triple Graph Grammars. In: Mayr, E.W., Schmidt, G., Tinhofer, G. (eds.) WG 1994. LNCS, vol. 903, pp. 151–163. Springer, Heidelberg (1995)
21. Schürr, A., Klar, F.: 15 Years of Triple Graph Grammars. In: Ehrig, H., Heckel, R., Rozenberg, G., Taentzer, G. (eds.) ICGT 2008. LNCS, vol. 5214, pp. 411–425. Springer, Heidelberg (2008)
22. Stevens, P.: Bidirectional Model Transformations in QVT: Semantic Issues and Open Questions. Software and Systems Modeling 9, 7–20 (2010)
23. TFS-Group, TU Berlin: AGG (2011), http://tfs.cs.tu-berlin.de/agg

A Toolchain for the Detection of Structural and Behavioral Latent System Properties[*]

Adam C. Jensen[1], Betty H.C. Cheng[1],
Heather J. Goldsby[1], and Edward C. Nelson[2]

[1] Michigan State University, East Lansing MI 48824, USA
{acj,chengb,hjg}@cse.msu.edu
[2] Ford Research and Advanced Engineering, Dearborn, MI 48121, USA
enelson7@ford.com

Abstract. The cost to repair a requirements-based defect in software-based systems increases substantially with each successive phase of the software lifecycle in which the error is allowed to propagate. While tools exist to facilitate early detection of design flaws, such tools do not detect flaws in system requirements, thus allowing such flaws to propagate into system design and implementation. This paper describes an experience report using a toolchain that supports a novel combination of structural and behavioral analysis of UML state diagrams that is not currently available in commercial UML modeling tools. With the toolchain, models can be incrementally and systematically improved through syntax-based analysis, type checking, and detection of latent behavioral system properties, including feature interactions. This paper demonstrates use of the toolchain on an industry-provided model of onboard electronics for an automotive application.

Keywords: requirements engineering, UML, latent properties, model checking.

1 Introduction

In software development, the cost to repair a defect increases substantially with each successive phase of the software lifecycle [1, 2]. When a defect is allowed to propagate into the design and implementation phases, the number of artifacts (e.g., models and documentation) that are affected by it also increases. Typically, during the requirements phase the system's stakeholders describe the key needs and problems that the system-to-be should address, usually using natural

---

[*] This work has been supported in part by NSF grants CCF-0541131, IIP-0700329, CCF-0750787, CCF-0820220, DBI-0939454, CNS-0854931, Army Research Office grant W911NF-08-1-0495, Ford Motor Company, and a Quality Fund Program grant from Michigan State University. Any opinions, findings, and conclusions or recommendations expressed in this material are those of the author(s) and do not necessarily reflect the views of the National Science Foundation, Army, Ford, or other research sponsors.

language. As a means to clarify and refine requirements that have been expressed in natural language, developers construct *domain models* that identify the key elements of the system and their relationships to one another, as well as their relationships to external elements. In order to better understand the required behavior, developers often create prototypes or state-based representations based on the domain model. While simulations and executable prototypes enable *validation* of requirements, it is equally important to be able to *verify* requirements to identify inconsistencies, (invariant) property violations, etc. Thus, there is a need for tools that identify errors in requirements specifications based on analysis of early prototype models. This paper presents a toolchain that facilitates the detection of syntactic and semantic errors in state-based diagrams and also identifies properties that specify *latent behavior*, the unspecified and potentially unwanted behavior of the model.

Many tools have been developed to support model-driven engineering of software systems. Tools such as ArgoUML, IBM Rational Software Architect, and Microsoft Visio support visual modeling of software designs via the Unified Modeling Language (UML). IBM Rational Rhapsody supports UML modeling as well as code generation and many consistency tests to ensure that the system under development is free of syntax errors. However, none of these tools performs syntax or type checking on state transition expressions in state diagrams. Particularly for applications involving complex logic and system behavior (e.g., embedded systems), transitions may contain complex guards and action statements that often define the core functionality of the system being modeled. Thus, tools that treat the transition expressions as uninterpreted strings allow subtle errors to propagate into the source code that is generated from the model, particularly in the context of model-driven engineering. Furthermore, while tools such as Rhapsody provide traceability from requirements to source code, to the best of the authors' knowledge, no existing commercial or research tools provide the comprehensive automated identification of the collection of different types of errors covered by our toolchain for UML models.

This paper describes an experience report from using a newly-developed toolchain that supports syntax and type checking as well as detection of latent system properties. After requirements have been elicited for an embedded system, developers often build a domain model using class diagram syntax that describes the key elements of the system (including physical elements, such as sensors and actuators, and software elements, such as controllers) and elements in the environment with which the system interacts. A state diagram is created for each key element, resulting in a collection of interacting state diagrams. While such diagrams are useful for refining system requirements and may be used during the design phase, there is limited tool support for detecting errors in syntax and semantics, and to our knowledge there is no tool support for automatically identifying latent properties. The proposed toolchain has two key advantages over current approaches. First, all state transition expressions are parsed and type-checked, thus identifying many errors that existing tools do not address until the code generation phase. Second, automated detection of latent properties enables system developers to identify so-called *blind spots* in system requirements. Blind spots are missing or incomplete requirements that are overlooked by requirements engineers, and they are often discovered only after the system has been partially implemented or, worse yet, deployed to the field. By identifying these errors early in the development process and suggesting potential resolution strategies, the proposed toolchain minimizes the number of subtle design defects and the cost of redesigning the system to correct the defects.

The proposed toolchain comprises three main tools: CYCLOPS, a model preprocessor that identifies common syntax and semantics errors in behavioral models specified in XMI (XML Metadata Interchange) format; HYDRA, a tool for translating UML behavioral models into Promela, the formal language for the SPIN model checker [3]; and MARPLE, a tool for automatically generating properties that are satisfied by the model and may represent latent and potentially erroneous behavior. We apply this toolchain to an industrial software system from the automotive embedded systems domain. The software system was developed using UML version 1.5 and comprises three subsystems: Lighting, Power Management, and Windshield Wipers.[1] The Lighting subsystem handles all functionality related to interior lamps, headlights, and tail lights. The Power Management subsystem monitors and controls the ignition status, vehicle speed, door statuses, battery status, and other electronic features. The Windshield Wipers subsystem controls the movement and speed of the windshield wipers. The subsystems are sophisticated and interact with one another at run time, thus creating the potential for errors in modeling semantics, unintended behavior that spans multiple subsystems, and feature interactions.

Based on feedback from the developer of the model, it is clear that several of the detected errors would have been very difficult and time-consuming to detect and resolve without the use of the toolchain. The remainder of the paper is organized as follows. In Section 2, we discuss background concepts. We present the software model that was studied in this work in Section 3. Next, we describe the process of using the toolchain in Section 4. Section 5 describes related work. Our experience of applying the toolchain to an automotive embedded systems model is presented in Section 6. We discuss the results and implications of applying the toolchain in Section 7. Finally, we present our conclusions and discuss future work in Section 8.

2 Background

In this section, we discuss background concepts and enabling technologies that support the proposed toolchain, including the Unified Modeling Language, the SPIN model checker, evolutionary computation, and novelty search. These enabling technologies are presented according to the tool(s) that leverage their capabilities.

---

[1] Due to organizational constraints and in-house tool support, the industrial collaborator was constrained to use UML 1.5 for its modeling activities.

2.1 CYCLOPS and HYDRA

CYCLOPS and HYDRA have been developed to support the analysis of models in the Unified Modeling Language (UML), the *de facto* standard in object-oriented software modeling. They enable developers to perform extensive error checking on UML models that describe system prototypes and support the translation of UML state diagrams into Promela for analysis with the SPIN model checker.

Unified Modeling Language. The Unified Modeling Language (UML) is a general-purpose visual modeling language that is used for modeling object-oriented software. It comprises several types of diagram notations, including support for class diagrams, interaction diagrams, state machine diagrams, and others. A UML model may contain many different diagrams that describe different views of the same system. For the purposes of this paper, we assume the use of UML version 1.5 and focus on state machine diagrams. A state machine diagram (hereafter, "state diagram") describes the various states in which a system can be and the transitions between the states. Visually, a state diagram comprises rounded rectangles (representing states) and lines with arrows that indicate transitions between states. The lines are annotated with optional guards and trigger events that denote the conditions that enable a transition and the actions that are generated as a result of the transition, respectively. In this study, we use a domain model (expressed in terms of a class diagram notation) to provide the context and vocabulary for the state diagrams.

SPIN Model Checker. The SPIN model checker [3] is a tool for exhaustively verifying state-based models. It takes a model expressed in Promela and produces a model checker in C code. SPIN uses nondeterministic automata to check properties expressed in Linear Temporal Logic (LTL) [4] and performs exhaustive analysis of a system's state space in order to identify undesirable system behaviors. It was originally developed to formally analyze telecommunications protocols, but in recent years it has also been used to analyze distributed systems [5, 6].

2.2 MARPLE

MARPLE is a tool that automatically discovers latent properties in UML state diagrams [7]. It leverages novelty search, an evolutionary search technique, and formal model analysis to generate a list of properties that describe the behavior specified by the model.

Evolutionary Computation. Evolutionary computation (EC) is a biologically-inspired family of techniques for exploring large solution spaces using concepts such as mutation and selection [8]. EC is effective for finding solutions to problems that have large solution spaces that cannot be exhaustively explored in a reasonable amount of time. It begins with a large population of randomly-generated individuals. Each individual is evaluated to determine its fitness for a given task. Next, an EC algorithm probabilistically selects a set of individuals that will represent the next generation. Each selected individual is probabilistically mutated, thus introducing diversity into the population. This process of selection, mutation, and evaluation continues until a fixed number of generations have passed or an optimal solution (if one exists) has been found.

Novelty Search. One EC technique, known as *novelty search* [9], replaces the explicit fitness computation with a novelty function that measures how different each individual is from other individuals in the population and in an archive of previous individuals. Novelty search then selects individuals whose behavior is the most distant (i.e., the most novel), thus increasing the diversity in the population and exploring the solution space more efficiently than a random search. The specific measure of distance between individuals varies with the problem being solved, but a Euclidean distance is typically used when the behavior of an individual can be mapped to a numerical vector.

3 Body Subsystem Model

In this section, we describe the Body Subsystem model that was used in this study. The model describes embedded devices that control the electronic subsystems of a modern passenger automobile and was created for the purposes of requirements elicitation and analysis.[2] The subsystems of the model include interior and exterior lighting, power management, and windshield wiper control. While the onboard electronics involves several more subsystems, these three were selected because they exhibit known, intended interactions. One of our objectives was to investigate whether the subsystems also exhibit unknown interactions. The remainder of this section provides a brief description of each subsystem under study.

3.1 Lighting Subsystem

The Lighting subsystem comprises 16 classes and is responsible for managing interior lights, including map, vanity, trunk, and under-hood lamps; and exterior lights, including head lights (low- and high-beam) and tail lights. The subsystem also contains classes that monitor the intensity of ambient light in order to control day time running lights and activate the vehicle's head lights and tail lights for night time driving.

3.2 Power Management Subsystem

The Power Management subsystem comprises 25 classes and is responsible for monitoring ignition status, sleep mode status, battery voltage, and commands from remote key fobs. The subsystem responds to events such as the insertion of an ignition key, exceeding vehicle speed thresholds, and the firing of timers.

---

[2] The model was developed by the industrial partner as an example of an industrial-strength model with representative system elements and behavior. The model does not contain any proprietary or specific configuration parameters of a deployed vehicle.

3.3 Windshield Wiper Subsystem

The Windshield Wiper subsystem comprises eight classes and is responsible for controlling wiper behavior. The classes represent hardware and software ranging from the low-level motor controller, the washer fluid pump, and a stall sensor that turns off the wiper motor if it detects that the wipers are not moving.

4 Process

In this section, we provide an overview of the process that was used to apply the toolchain to the Body Subsystem model. A data flow diagram for the process is shown in Figure 1. The process begins with a system model in XMI (XML Metadata Interchange) format. In this case, Rhapsody was used by our industrial collaborators to create the system model due to its support for requirements traceability, code generation capabilities, and support for state-based modeling.

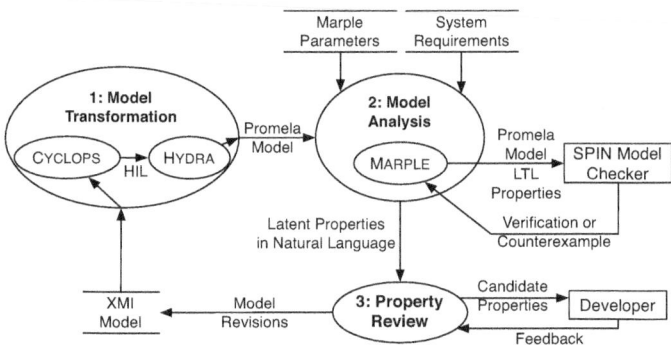

Fig. 1. Data Flow Diagram

4.1 Model Transformation

First, the XMI model is given to step **1: Model Transformation**. The CYCLOPS tool takes the XMI model and checks for common syntax and semantics errors. For example, it parses and checks each state transition expressions to ensure that they are well-formed and do not refer to undeclared classes, attributes, or operations. CYCLOPS produces specific error messages that indicate the nature of any errors that are discovered, and it makes suggestions when appropriate (e.g., when an attribute from another class is referenced as though it were declared in the current class). CYCLOPS supports an iterative process of analysis, detection of errors, and model correction. This incremental error-correction cycle is shorter and more interactive than comparable techniques available in commercial tools. For example, using code generation to detect syntactic and semantic errors in a model would require at least one additional step for compilation and linking compared to our toolchain. Once the errors detected by CYCLOPS are resolved, it translates the XMI model into the Hydra Intermediate Language (HIL) that can then be processed by the HYDRA tool.

HYDRA is a model translator initially developed by McUmber and Cheng [10]. It takes a model in HIL format and produces an equivalent model in Promela (the PROcess MEta Language). Promela is a formal logic language that was developed to support analysis and exhaustive checking of concurrent systems of communicating processes [11]. Promela models are checked using the SPIN model checker [3], a tool that identifies livelocks, deadlocks, error conditions, and other undesirable behavior. It also has support for verifying arbitrary properties specified using LTL.

4.2 Model Analysis

Goldsby and Cheng developed MARPLE [7], a novelty-search tool for automatically discovering properties that represent the behavior of UML models. Specifically, a property may specify a known system requirement or, more interestingly, an unknown latent behavior of the model. As part of the **2: Model Analysis** step, MARPLE accepts the Promela model generated by HYDRA and a set of parameters as input. MARPLE parameters include the number of properties that should be returned, the size of the population that the novelty search algorithm should use, and the number of distinct classes (i.e., domain elements) that are mentioned in each property. The parameters may be tuned by the system developer according to the model being analyzed and the number of results that are desired.

Each property generated by MARPLE is created by instantiating one the five most commonly occurring LTL specification patterns, identified by Dwyer *et al.* [12], with model-specific domain elements provided as parameters. For example, one of the specification patterns is stated as follows: "Globally, it is always the case that P holds". The placeholder P is constructed from an alphabet that includes the set of domain elements in a given model, integer values for those domain elements to take, and operators for conjunction, disjuction, equality, and inequality. The novelty search algorithm creates properties from the specification patterns by filling in the placeholder with varying combinations of items from the alphabet. One such value of P might be "`DriverDoor.Closed`== 1 ∧ `MapLamp.Brightness` == 3". MARPLE could also generate variants of this property, perhaps with different numerical values, that may evaluate differently from the original. The property grammar supports nesting of conjunctions and disjunctions, thus facilitating a rich space of properties to consider.

Once a property has been generated, it is evaluated using the SPIN model checker [3]. A property that is shown to be false is discarded. Properties that hold true are retained for further analysis. To assess the novelty of a property that holds for the model, MARPLE compares the state space of the shortest path that satisfies the property to the state space of other properties. If the property visits a previously unexplored region of the state space, then the property is considered more novel, and thus more fit, than a property that visits states within a well-explored region. New properties are compared to other properties within the current generation and within the archive of previously generated properties. By including the properties in the archive in the comparison process, the novelty search algorithm is able to "remember" the portions of the solution space that it has explored previously, thus ensuring that the algorithm does not stagnate or become "stuck" in a suboptimal portion of the space.

As output, MARPLE produces a set of LTL properties that are presented to the developer in natural language for readability purposes. To enable this natural language property representation, we use a component of SPIDER [13], a specification pattern instantiator and analysis tool to translate between LTL properties and natural language [13].

4.3 Property Review

Finally, in step **3: Property Review**, the latent properties discovered by MARPLE are presented in natural language to the system developer for review. If a given property is desirable, then the developer may consider adding it to the list of explicit system requirements. If the property is undesirable, however, then action must be taken to ensure that the property does not continue to hold. For example, the developer might examine the state diagrams for the classes that are mentioned in the property. If an error is discovered in the diagrams, then the model is revised and the toolchain is restarted at step **1**.

5 Related Work

As stated earlier, many commercial tools support the creation of UML models, syntax checking, simulation, and code generation capabilities. However, they do not support the automated detection of the full suite of syntactic and semantic error checks for state-based diagrams that we describe in this paper. Additionally, they do not support the identification of latent properties satisfied by the model. In this section, we overview research tools that have been created to address these two challenges.

5.1 Consistency Checking among UML Class and State Diagrams

One key challenge that arises as the result of using multiple diagrams to provide different views of the same system is maintaining consistency among these different representations. As a result, researchers have developed a number of approaches to support various aspects of consistency checking among UML models (e.g., [14–19]). The toolchain described by this paper automatically detects inconsistencies in the syntax and semantics of UML class and state diagrams created as part of the late requirements engineering phase of development. Thus, we focus our attention on approaches that examine consistency among these two diagram types. Simmonds *et al.* [18] use rules presented in terms of description logic [20], a subset of first order predicate logic, to identify inconsistencies among UML class, sequence, and state diagrams during the design phase. However, their approach does not check that the transitions within the state diagram use viable elements from the class diagram. Gomaa et al. [16] present an approach to checking the consistency among use case diagrams, class diagrams, sequence diagrams, and state diagrams. Their manual approach involves specifying consistency checking rules among the various types of diagrams, including class and state diagrams. Egyed proposes an automated approach for detecting and resolving inconsistencies that arise within UML models during the design phase [14]. His approach relies upon the specification of consistency rules, which are periodically evaluated. To the best of our knowledge, these consistency rules can detect whether elements of the state diagrams are consistent with those that appear in the class diagram, but do not detect subtle errors, such as assignments that occur within transition guards. Schwarzl and Peischl [17] propose an approach to statically analyzing state diagrams for syntax, existence, data type, communication, non-determinism, and transition hiding errors. As part of this process, the transitions on the state diagrams are checked for well-formedness. The set of syntactical and semantic errors that they detect is a subset of the errors that CYCLOPS detects. However, the behavioral errors that they detect (e.g., deadlock conditions and circular messaging dependencies) are complementary to errors detected by the approach presented in this paper.

5.2 Detection of Latent Properties

Several approaches generate temporal logic properties that specify the behavior of systems [21–25]. Because the objective of our approach is to automatically identify obscure latent properties that might not otherwise be discovered, we focus on how the approaches blend developer knowledge and automation to identify properties. Perracotta [25] is a dynamic inference approach that infers properties from imperfect execution traces, which have been generated by running the program code. To produce these execution traces, the developer must instrument the program to monitor events and states of interest; these are used to form the possible propositions. Perracotta then creates properties by instantiating eight variations of the temporal logic response pattern with the propositions. Weimer and Necula proposed a static inference approach [24], which analyzes program text and generates properties. These properties specify potentially erroneous behavior of the error-handling portions of the source code. Lastly, Chang et al. [22] proposed a dynamic inference approach that generates properties from program event traces. The program traces are created during the execution of the program and track developer-specified events. Chang's approach involves refining the inference templates built using the Propel patterns [26] to eliminate properties that are not satisfied by the program's event traces.

These approaches differ from our toolchain-based approach in two key ways. First, they focus on automatically generating properties that describe the behavior of the *code*, rather than the model. As such, the cost of correcting errors in the later development phase is likely to be more expensive. Second, in general, these approaches rely on the developer to select portions of the code to explore for properties, and this limits the ability of the approaches to discover properties that represent unwanted latent behavior in blind spots. These notable differences mean that our approach can be used in a complementary fashion. Specifically, as part of the model-driven development process our toolchain can be used to automatically discover properties that may represent unwanted latent behavior within the UML model. Once the UML model has been translated to code, the other approaches could be used to ensure that no errors have been introduced.

6 Applying the Toolchain

This section describes our experience of applying the proposed toolchain to the Body Subsystem model that was presented in Section 3. We present the types of errors that were discovered, the mitigation strategy that was used for each error, and the consequences of correcting the error. For clarity, we present the errors according to the stages of the toolchain. That is, we begin with a discussion of syntax and consistency errors that CYCLOPS detected. Next, we discuss the errors in types and semantics that CYCLOPS also detected. Finally, we describe how the model was translated into the Promela language and discuss the latent properties that MARPLE discovered.

6.1 Preliminaries

The model comprises class diagrams, sequence diagrams, and state diagrams, thus providing a rich domain vocabulary (i.e., class, operation, and attribute names) as well as a complete set of states and transitions that represent the behavior of the system-to-be. The Body Subsystem model contains 52 classes, 37 state diagrams, 255 states (including composite states), and 400 state transitions. There are fewer state diagrams than classes because several of the classes are abstract superclasses or static classes that serve as structures. The model generated approximately 38,000 lines of C++ code. This code was intended to provide a means to execute the requirements; it is not intended to be sufficiently detailed to contain platform-specific or implementation details.

6.2 Phase I: Syntax and Consistency Check (CYCLOPS)

We begin by applying CYCLOPS to the model, which comprises class and state diagrams. CYCLOPS performs a battery of checks on the input model before it is passed to HYDRA to be translated into Promela. It examines each class, attribute, and operation reference and verifies that the referenced element exists. CYCLOPS also checks for unmatched or missing parentheses, missing semicolons between action statements, and ensures that attributes and operations do not have the same name as their owning class. It also ensures that each state transition expression is well-formed. CYCLOPS identified a wide range of errors in our model, including references to undeclared variables and typographical mistakes.[3]

---

[3] A complete listing of the categories of errors that were discovered, and their frequency of occurrence, is available as a technical report [27].

Error Mitigation. Defects that are discovered during Phase I are typically inconsistencies that result from typographical errors. Automated tools cannot make reliable suggestions for resolving most defects of this type, and therefore CYCLOPS must rely on software engineers who are familiar with the model to correct the problem. Once each defect has been corrected, the revised model is given again as input to CYCLOPS, and the Phase I analysis is reapplied. It takes less than one second to parse and check the Body Subsystem, thus providing an interactive experience. This incremental defect resolution process proceeds until no further syntax errors are found in the model.

6.3 Phase II: Semantics and Type Check (CYCLOPS)

Next, we used CYCLOPS to check the semantics of each state transition in the model's state diagrams. CYCLOPS ensures, for example, that each reference to an attribute, operation, or class is valid with respect to the model being analyzed, using the domain model as a point of reference. Furthermore, CYCLOPS verifies that boolean comparisons and assignments are between compatible data types.

Error Mitigation. Phase II focuses on discovering defects that are more subtle, and therefore more difficult to detect, than those discovered during Phase I. The primary focus of Phase II is on parsing and verifying the contents of state transition expressions. A state transition expression specifies the conditions under which the modeled system will move from the current state to the next state and what actions (e.g., variable assignments or calls to operations) will be taken as a result of the transition. Each expression comprises an optional triggering event, a set of expressions that form a *guard*, and a set of actions to perform in the following format: `event[guard]/action-list` .

Errors in state transition expressions can be difficult to detect by visual inspection. For example, it is easy to overlook an assignment operator ('=') that was mistyped as an equality operator ('=='). Such an error still produces valid, executable code in many programming languages that are used for embedded systems (e.g., C). However, there is a mismatch between the intent of the code and its actual behavior when the system is executed, thus making this class of subtle defects potentially very serious.

6.4 Phase III: Model Translation

Once the model is free of syntactic and semantic errors, the third phase uses CYCLOPS and HYDRA to translate the model into the formal language Promela. CYCLOPS begins by translating the model into the Hydra Intermediate Language (HIL). This intermediate step enables us to build new front-end translators for successive versions of XMI, whose formats evolve over time, without needing to modify the core translation code in HYDRA. Next, HYDRA translates the HIL code into Promela. By constructing an equivalent model in Promela, we are able to conduct formal analysis of the model and to verify model properties specified in LTL. Each state diagram in the model is treated as a distinct Promela process, thus facilitating the interleaved execution that often reveals unexpected interactions among system components. The translation phase completes within two seconds for the Body Subsystem model.

6.5 Phase IV: Discovery of Latent System Properties (Marple)

In the fourth and final phase, the Promela model that was produced by HYDRA is provided as input to MARPLE, which generates a suite of LTL properties that are presented to the developer in natural language. If a property is deemed desirable, then it is added to the list of system requirements. A property that is undesirable must be addressed by the system's developer. Potential problems created by unwanted properties include incorrect functional behavior, feature interactions, distributed behavior problems, and behavioral inconsistencies. This phase takes on the order of six hours to complete on a 1.8 GHz PC with 16 GB of memory. According to our industrial collaborators, this time frame was well within the acceptable range given the potential severity of errors found. For these experiments, MARPLE was configured to return 25 properties.

Next, we present a sample set of latent properties that were discovered in the Body Subsystem. We provide a natural language representation of each property along with a brief discussion of the property, its consequences, and the mitigation strategy that was used.

Property 1: Globally, `WiperModes.WiperMaster` != RSM eventually holds

Property 1 states that the `WiperMaster` attribute in the `WiperModes` class must eventually have a value that is not RSM (Rain Sensor Mode). The developer determined that one of the state transitions in the `WiperModes` state diagram was missing a guard. Therefore, the transition was always available to be executed. Once the missing guard was added, as part of regression analysis we verified that the property no longer held.

Property 2:
Globally, it is always the case that if `DrvrDrSwitch.Switch` == 1 holds, then `Voltage_Range_Monitor.VBattRaw` != 18 previously held

---

Property 2 states that if the `Switch` attribute in the `DrvrDrSwitch` (Driver Door Switch) class has a value of 1 then the `VBattRaw` attribute of the `Voltage_Range_Monitor` class must not have had a value of 18 in the previous state. Once the property was identified, the model developer was able to identify a missing assignment statement (`battStatus = NORM`) for the INITIAL state in the `VoltageRangeMonitor` state diagram. After the missing assignment statement was added, the property no longer held.

Property 3:
Globally, it is always the case that if `WiperModes.Command` == 5 holds, then `AmbientLightSensorInput.lightLevel` != 4 previously held

---

Property 3 states that if the value of the Command attribute in the WiperModes class is HALT, then the value of the lightLevel attribute in the Ambient LightSensorInput class must not have been TWILIGHT in the previous state. Despite the different set of classes and attributes in this property as opposed to **Property 2**, the model developer discovered that **Property 2** and **Property 3** held because of the same missing assignment statement in the VoltageRange Monitor state diagram. After the statement was added to remedy **Property 2**, **Property 3** no longer held.

> **Property 4**: Globally, it is always the case that WiperModes.Command != HALT

Property 4 states that the value of the Command attribute in the WiperModes class will never be HALT. From this property, the model developer determined that a triggering event in the RelayControl class (part of the Windshield Wipers subsystem) never occurs, and thus the state machine remains in the WAIT state indefinitely. Figure 2 shows partial state diagrams from the RelayControl and WiperModes classes. There was a missing call to the event RlyCtlActive (shown in **bold**) in the transition expression for the initial state in RelayControl (Figure 2(a)). Since the transition expression for WiperModes (Figure 2(b)) is waiting for the event to be fired (also shown in bold), it will wait indefinitely. After adding a call to the missing event in the appropriate state transition in RelayControl, the property no longer held.

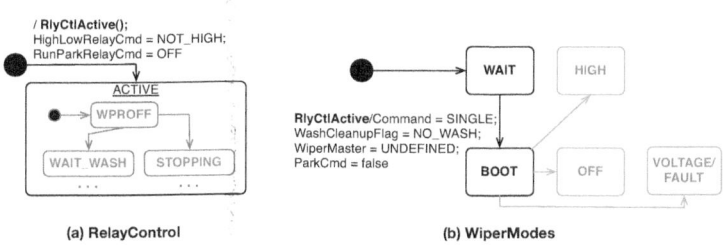

Fig. 2. Partial State Diagrams for Classes Affected by **Property 4**

7 Discussion

In this section, we present a discussion of the results of applying the proposed toolchain and consider the consequences of its use in an industrial development setting. As in previous sections, we present the discussion in terms of each phase of the toolchain.

7.1 Syntax and Semantics Defects

We had access to two major revisions of the Body Subsystem model for this work: an early revision that had not been used to generate source code and thus contained syntax errors and type inconsistencies, and a subsequent revision that had undergone source code generation and compilation. In order to assess CYCLOPS's ability to detect syntax and semantics errors, we applied it to the earlier model revision. CYCLOPS detected all of the errors that the compilers had detected during source code generation and compilation, and it also identified additional errors that were subtle and would be difficult to locate by manual inspection. For example, an assignment statement that was mistyped as a boolean comparison would not be detected by a compiler, but such a mistake may have an adverse effect on system behavior. The developer of the Body Subsystem model stated that without the use of a tool such as CYCLOPS, these subtle errors would have been allowed to propagate into generated source code and, perhaps, into the design and implementation of the system. Since system models are typically small during the late requirements stage of the software lifecycle, such defects are straightforward to resolve once they have been identified. Identifying and resolving these subtle defects in the requirements stage reduces the amount of time spent debugging and reengineering the system at later stages of development.

7.2 Latent Property Detection

While the proposed toolchain detects several types of model errors, the developer of the Body Subsystem told us that the toolchain is most useful for identifying portions of the model or system requirements that are missing. The toolchain identified a set of missing constant initializations, transition guards, and transition action statements. The discovered properties did not always point directly to the missing model components (e.g., properties 2 and 3 in Section 6), but they yielded enough information for a developer with knowledge of the system and model to make inferences about the possible causes of the defect and to revise the model accordingly. In the absence of the proposed toolchain, such defects would most likely be discovered during integration testing after the source code has been completed, thus increasing the cost to repair the defect.

MARPLE uses an evolutionary search technique to explore the space of properties for a given model. Due to inherent randomness in the search process, it is unlikely that MARPLE will revisit the same property in independent executions. However, it is straightforward to make note of any interesting properties and to re-examine them at a later time to monitor for regressions. The ability to track defects over time facilitated a step-wise, iterative model refinement process that enabled us to work remotely with the model developer to incrementally resolve the problems that our toolchain identified.

8 Conclusions

In this paper, we presented an experience report describing the use of a toolchain for detecting syntactic and semantics errors in behavioral system models, as well as detecting latent system properties during the early requirements phase of the software lifecycle. We demonstrated that the proposed toolchain is an effective means for identifying syntax errors, resolving ambiguous references, and discovering unwanted latent system properties.

We are considering several avenues for future work. First, we plan to integrate metamodel-level consistency checking into the CYCLOPS tool, thus enabling flexible and robust error detection that is grounded in a formal semantics for UML state diagrams. Next, we are investigating patterns within the discovered latent properties and to leverage their key features to fine-tune parameters for the MARPLE tool. We are exploring several strategies for reconfiguring the toolchain to detect situations in which two system features interact and lead to system failures or other unexpected behavior. Finally, we are exploring how to apply the principles of this toolchain to other languages and environments, including Simulink.

References

1. Lutz, R.R.: Analyzing software requirements errors in safety-critical, embedded systems. In: Proceedings of IEEE International Symposium on Requirements Engineering, pp. 126–133. IEEE, Los Alamitos (1993)
2. Pressman, R.: Software Engineering: A Practitioner's Approach (2007)
3. Holzmann, G.J.: The model checker SPIN. IEEE Transactions on Software Engineering 23(5), 279–295 (2002)
4. Pnueli, A.: The temporal logic of programs. In: 18th Annual Symposium on Foundations of Computer Science, pp. 46–57. IEEE, Los Alamitos (1977)
5. Kars, P.: The Application of PROMELA and SPIN in the BOS Project. In: The Spin Verification System: The Second Workshop on the SPIN Verification System: Proceedings of a DIMACS Workshop, August 5, page 51. American Mathematical Society, Providence (1997)
6. Havelund, K., Lowry, M., Park, S.J., Pecheur, C., Penix, J., Visser, W., White, J.L., et al.: Formal analysis of the remote agent before and after flight. In: Lfm2000: Fifth NASA Langley Formal Methods Workshop, Citeseer (2000)
7. Goldsby, H.J., Cheng, B.H.C.: Automatically Discovering Properties That Specify the Latent Behavior of UML Models. In: Petriu, D.C., Rouquette, N., Haugen, Ø. (eds.) MODELS 2010. LNCS, vol. 6394, pp. 316–330. Springer, Heidelberg (2010)
8. Bäck, T., Fogel, D.B., Michalewicz, Z.: Handbook of evolutionary computation. Taylor & Francis, Abington (1997)
9. Lehman, J., Stanley, K.O.: Exploiting open-endedness to solve problems through the search for novelty. Artificial Life 11, 329 (2008)
10. McUmber, W.E., Cheng, B.H.C.: A general framework for formalizing UML with formal languages. In: Proceedings of the 23rd International Conference on Software Engineering, pp. 433–442. IEEE Computer Society, Los Alamitos (2001)
11. Holzmann, G.J.: Design and validation of computer protocols, vol. 94. Prentice Hall, New Jersey (1991)
12. Dwyer, M.B., Avrunin, G.S., Corbett, J.C.: Patterns in property specifications for finite-state verification. In: Proceedings of the 21st International Conference on Software Engineering, pp. 411–420. IEEE Computer Society Press, Los Alamitos (1999)
13. Konrad, S., Cheng, B.H.C.: Real-time specification patterns. In: Proceedings of the International Conference on Software Engineering (ICSE 2005), St Louis, MO, USA (2005)
14. Egyed, A.: Automatically detecting and tracking inconsistencies in software design models. IEEE Transactions on Software Engineering (2010)

15. Engels, G., Küster, J.M., Heckel, R., Groenewegen, L.: A methodology for specifying and analyzing consistency of object-oriented behavioral models 26(5):186–195 (2001)
16. Gomaa, H., Wijesekera, D.: Consistency in multiple-view UML models: a case study. In: Workshop on Consistency Problems in UML-based Software Development II, page 1. Citeseer (2003)
17. Schwarzl, C., Peischl, B.: Static- and dynamic consistency analysis of UML state chart models. In: Petriu, D.C., Rouquette, N., Haugen, Ø. (eds.) MODELS 2010. LNCS, vol. 6394, pp. 151–165. Springer, Heidelberg (2010)
18. Simmonds, J., Van Der Straeten, R., Jonckers, V., Mens, T.: Maintaining consistency between UML models using description logic. Série L'objet-logiciel, base de données, réseaux 10(2-3), 231–244 (2004)
19. Wagner, R., Giese, H., Nickel, U.: A plug-in for flexible and incremental consistency management. In: Proc. of the International Conference on the Unified Modeling Language 2003 (Workshop 7: Consistency Problems in UML-based Software Development), San Francisco, USA (2003)
20. Baader, F.: The description logic handbook: theory, implementation, and applications. Cambridge Univ. Pr., Cambridge (2003)
21. Chan, W.: Temporal-logic queries. In: Emerson, E.A., Sistla, A.P. (eds.) CAV 2000. LNCS, vol. 1855, pp. 450–463. Springer, Heidelberg (2000)
22. Chang, R.M., Avrunin, G.S., Clarke, L.A.: Property inference from program executions. Technical Report UM-CS-2006-26, University of Massachusetts (2006)
23. Gurfinkel, A., Chechik, M., Devereux, B.: Temporal logic query checking: A tool for model exploration. IEEE Transactions on Software Engineering 29(10), 898–914 (2003)
24. Weimer, W., Necula, G.C.: Mining temporal specifications for error detection. In: Halbwachs, N., Zuck, L.D. (eds.) TACAS 2005. LNCS, vol. 3440, pp. 461–476. Springer, Heidelberg (2005)
25. Yang, J., Evans, D., Bhardwaj, D., Bhat, T., Das, M.: Perracotta: mining temporal API rules from imperfect traces. In: ICSE 2006: Proceedings of the 28th International Conference on Software Engineering, pp. 282–291. ACM, New York (2006)
26. Smith, R.L., Avrunin, G.S., Clarke, L.A., Osterweil, L.J.: Propel: an approach supporting property elucidation. In: ICSE 2002: Proceedings of the 24th International Conference on Software Engineering, pp. 11–21. ACM, New York (2002)
27. Jensen, A.C., Cheng, B.H.C., Goldsby, H.J.: A toolchain for the detection of structural and behavioral latent system properties. Technical Report MSU-CSE-11-10, Computer Science and Engineering, Michigan State University, East Lansing, Michigan (May 2011)

Defining MARTE's VSL as an Extension of Alf

Arnaud Cuccuru, Sébastien Gérard, and François Terrier

CEA LIST, Boîte 94, Gif-sur-Yvette, F-91191 France
{arnaud.cuccuru,sebastien.gerard,francois.terrier}@cea.fr

Abstract. VSL and Alf are two OMG standards providing a textual notation for complex mathematical expressions and detailed activities respectively. Since these two notations have been designed by separate communities (real-time embedded for VSL and software engineering for Alf), they differ in syntax and semantics. Nevertheless, they clearly exhibit intersections in their form and use cases. The purpose of this article is to demonstrate that an alignment effort between the two languages would be beneficial for both users and tool providers. We show that most of the syntactic constructs introduced in VSL are related to general-purpose concerns (i.e., they are not specific to the real-time domain), most of them being covered by Alf. In this paper, we first identify the subset of VSL which is valuable for the real-time domain, and then propose a way of extending Alf with this subset[1].

1 Introduction

Concrete syntaxes associated with modeling languages must provide abstractions suited to the targeted domains, offering to users the right balance between conciseness and expressiveness. In UML, this balance is found with a mix of graphical and textual notations, some concepts having a straightforward representation in diagrams (classes, state machines, etc.), some others clearly requiring text. Complex mathematical expressions and detailed UML activities are representative examples of model elements for which a textual specification can be preferred. These two cases have been specifically addressed by two recent OMG initiatives: the Value Specification Language (VSL) and the Action language for foundational UML (Alf).

VSL has been standardized in the context of the UML profile for Modeling and Analysis of Real-Time and Embedded systems (MARTE) [1]. The main rationale for VSL was to provide users from the real-time domain with a simple textual syntax for specifying the values of non-functional properties of their system models. VSL has proven successful for this primary objective, as well as for another major concern of real-time systems development and analysis: the specification of time expressions. As a typed expression language, VSL more generally provides users with the ability to express complex mathematical expressions, involving timing aspects and non-functional values.

---

[1] This work is partially supported by the ITEA 2 - 08020VERDE project.

The standardization of Alf [2] is more recent. It can be considered as a logical follow-up to the OMG standard on the Semantics of a Foundational Subset for Executable UML Models (fUML) [3]. fUML identifies a structural and behavioral subset of UML for which it provides a precise execution semantics. Activities are the only kind of UML behavior to be included in this subset. An Activity enables the expression of data and control flow graphs, focusing on sequences and conditions for coordinating lower-level behaviors. While the formalism is precise and expressive enough to describe algorithms at a low abstraction level, the widespread dissemination of Activities as a behavioral formalism is limited by the inadequacy of activity diagrams to capture detailed descriptions. These diagrams often result in specifications too complex to handle and understand. Alf fills the gap by providing a mostly Java-like syntax for Activities which is by far more readable and intuitive for users. With the formal semantics provided by fUML for Activities, Alf moreover benefits from a sound semantic definition.

As explained above, these two textual languages have been designed in different contexts, involving separate communities with distinct concerns. Nevertheless, VSL and Alf clearly exhibit intersections in their form and potential use cases. On the one hand, a significant part of Alf syntactic constructs is dedicated to the specification of typed expressions. This is a common situation for imperative languages where statements rely on expressions. On the other hand, we explain in this paper that VSL rules for producing typed expressions mainly address aspects which are not specific to the real-time domain. They are related to general-purpose concerns which are also considered by Alf. With its Java-like syntax and its precise semantic basis, Alf does have a chance of becoming more widely used, whereas VSL will always remain a niche language. In terms of consolidation of the MARTE profile, it is necessary to clarify the future of VSL with respect to the emergence of Alf. Our proposal consists in properly defining VSL as an extension of Alf, focusing on the aspects of VSL which are valuable for the real-time domain.

Section 2 provides strategic and pragmatic arguments in favor of an alignment of the two languages, and motivates the idea of defining VSL as an extension of Alf. Section 3 establishes a comparison between VSL and Alf type systems, in order to precisely identify aspects of VSL which are not already covered by Alf. From the aspects identified in this section, section 4 describes our concrete proposal: a definition of VSL as an extension of Alf, which is validated by the description of a prototype implementation for our UML modeling tool Papyrus. Section 5 finally concludes this article and sets guidelines for future work.

2 Why VSL Should Be Defined as an Extension of Alf?

As explained in the introduction to this article, both VSL and Alf enable the specification of typed expressions. In the context of a UML model, it basically means that the two languages can be used in any case where an expression is required. For example, this includes: default values for properties of a classifier, lower and upper bound of a multiplicity, tagged-values of a stereotype or specification of constraints. Maintaining two distinct languages for common use cases however implies several disadvantages for users, tool providers and standardization actors. These disadvantages, detailed in the next paragraphs, clearly motivate a definition of VSL as an extension of Alf.

From a user standpoint, learning a new language is not an easy task. Obviously, users will accept learning costs only if they are worthwhile for their activities. Ideally, the new language should address concerns which are as much orthogonal as possible to what they already know and practice. In case of intersections, the syntactic differences between the two languages should be negligible. If one of these two conditions is not satisfied, it is highly probable that the new language will be rejected (A third condition concerns tool support. It is discussed in the next paragraph). This fact has clearly influenced the definition of the Alf syntax, which basically reuses Java syntax. On top of this Java basis, Alf then brings additional syntactic constructs which make sense and are useful in a UML context. Users are, however, free to use these additional facilities or only rely on the Java constructs they already know. In this case, Alf clearly implies a limited learning effort and does have a chance of becoming more widely used. Since VSL mostly addresses concerns which are already covered by Alf (details are given in section 3), it runs the risk of remaining a niche language. A reasonable strategy to favor its adoption is to define it as an extension of Alf, focusing on aspects which are valuable to the real-time domain, while leaving users leverage on their Alf or even Java knowledge.

From a tool provider standpoint, developing an editor for a textual language is costly and error-prone, even if model-based technologies such as Xtext or emfext greatly ease the development task. Using Xtext, we have recently developed a VSL editor for our UML modeling tool Papyrus[2]. We also have an ongoing development effort around an editor for Alf. Regarding VSL, we spent approximately 6 person-months to develop a parser, a type checker and editing facilities such as completion proposals. For Alf, we have also spent 6 person-months, except that the type checker is 70% complete and that 6 extra person-months will probably be necessary to provide user-friendly editing facilities (completion proposals, quickfixes, ...). As a public Research and Technology Organisation, CEA LIST has to promote new technologies and formalisms among industry and can therefore support this kind of efforts. For commercial tool vendors, the situation is quite different. The development cost is worthwhile only if they can secure a return on investment, which at least implies interested users. We have shown in the previous paragraph that having VSL defined as an extension of Alf would greatly improve its potential for adoption by users. On the one hand, it means that if tool providers actually develop tool support around Alf, they will find clients for it. On the other hand, it also means that any VSL-specific tool support could be implemented as an extension of existing tool support for Alf, where reuse would significantly decrease development costs.

From a standardization actor standpoint, there are also pragmatic reasons in favor of having VSL defined as an extension of Alf. VSL has some basic

---

[2] http://www.eclipse.org/modeling/mdt/papyrus/

flaws and limitations for which Alf already provides solutions. The purpose here is not to establish an exhaustive list but rather to provide a few examples illustrating how the VSL specification could benefit from such an alignment. For example, VSL implies that any model element must have a Java compliant name so that it can be referenced in an expression. This is a real issue since UML does not imply any restrictions regarding naming conventions (a name can start with a figure, contain white spaces, exotic characters such as *?* etc.). It means that a UML model not designed with the intent of using VSL could require name refactorings before actually be suited to a VSL usage. In this case, Alf simply proposes to use a delimiter (') to encapsulate the name. Another issue concerns the limitations of VSL for the specification of constraints. VSL does not provide any OCL-like quantifier such as *forAll*, *exist*, *one* or more generally collection operators such as *select* or *reject* (Rationale for this situation can be found in [4], section 3.2.1, which has been used as a basis for the definition of VSL). If a user needs to specify a constraint involving both a collection and a timing aspect (e.g. all the tasks assigned to a processor must have an execution duration lower than a given duration), he simply cannot. Alf provides all these operators (more information about the inclusion of OCL in Alf can be found in [2], section 1). These issues, among others, will require fixes by the MARTE revision task force. Defining VSL as an extension of Alf would give an elegant solution to these issues without having to reinvent the wheel.

We have given arguments in favor of defining VSL as an extension of Alf. The purpose of the next sections is to demonstrate the feasibility of the proposal. Section 3 is meant to clearly identify the aspects of VSL which are valuable to the real-time domain. Taking into account identified aspects, Section 4 proposes a refactoring of VSL in order to properly define it as an extension of Alf.

3 Comparison of VSL and Alf Type Systems

A type system represents the collection of rules specifying the types that can be inferred from syntactic constructs provided by a language [6]. Comparing type systems of VSL and Alf is therefore a good strategy to identify how the two languages overlap, and consequently precisely identify aspects of VSL which need to be considered in a potential extension of Alf. Figure 1 illustrates in an abstract way the relationship between the type systems of VSL (depicted by the small ellipse in the top-left part of the figure) and Alf (depicted by the ellipse in the center).

Figure 1 is horizontally partitioned. The lower part of the figure abstracts syntactic constructs related to the specification of statements. The upper part concerns expressions. Since VSL is not an imperative language (and consequently does not carry any rule for specifying statements), it only appears in the upper part of the figure. Zone 1 depicts the intersection between type systems of VSL and Alf. It represents the subset of VSL type system which clearly addresses general-purpose considerations and for which Alf could be directly used instead. Zones 2 and 3 concern aspects which are not covered by Alf. We however establish

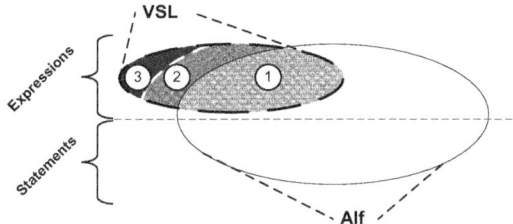

Fig. 1. Overlapping between VSL and Alf type systems

a distinction between zone 2, still addressing general purpose considerations, and zone 3, which covers aspects more directly related to the real-time domain.

The next three sections refer to these zones to provide a more detailed comparison of VSL and Alf type systems. We organize this comparison according to three kinds of syntactic rules that can be found in the VSL grammar: Type-specific rules, metatype-specific rules and generic rules. These categories are relevant with respect to the type system, in the sense that each one implies a particular strategy for determining the type of a syntactic construct. This in turn gives useful inputs for the realization of a type checker that would actually implement the type system.

3.1 Type-Specific Rules

By "Type-Specific" rule, we mean a rule for which the type system statically specifies the exact evaluation type. Syntactic rules for literal specifications usually fall into this category. The table contained in figure 2 identifies all type-specific rules of VSL (column "VSL syntactic rule"), provides usage examples in VSL and equivalent Alf expressions when possible (columns "examples") and finally gives the evaluation type associated with each rule (columns "inferred type"). Note that these types are all defined in model libraries which are intrinsically parts of the two language definitions (see [1] section D.1 for VSL and [2] section 11.2 for Alf).

Overlapping with Alf. The table contained in figure 2 is horizontally partitioned into 3 zones (numbered 1, 2 and 3), where each zone corresponds to a subset identified in figure 1. For rules of category 1, we can notice that VSL and Alf syntaxes are almost the same. The first syntactic difference concerns the additional capability of Alf to specify integer literals using octal form (i.e. 017 in the example) whereas VSL only supports decimal, binary and hexadecimal forms (i.e. 15, 0b1111 and 0xF in the example). Note that in Alf, the type associated with these literals is *Natural*, a datatype part of the standard Alf library which is defined as an extension of Integer and UnlimitedNatural. The second syntactic difference concerns the delimiter symbol used for string literals. VSL uses symbol ' whereas Alf uses symbol ".

	VSL syntactic rule	VSL Example	Alf equivalent Example	Infered VSL type	Infered Alf type
①	Literal Integer	15 0b1111 0xF	15 0b1111 0xF 017	Integer	Natural
①	Literal Unlimited Natural	*	*	Unlimited Natural	Unlimited Natural
①	Literal Boolean	true false	true false	Boolean	Boolean
①	Literal String	'A String'	"A String"	String	String
②	Literal Real	1234.56 1.2E3		Real	
②	Literal DateTime	12:24:00 2006/02/07 Tue		DateTime	
③	Jitter Expression	jitter(t2-t1)		Real	

(Rows ①: General purpose; Rows ②③: Domain specific)

Fig. 2. Type-specific rules of VSL and overlapping with Alf

Complementarity with Alf. Other type-specific rules of VSL evaluate to primitive types Real or DateTime. These rules naturally fall into categories 2 and 3 of figure 1 (i.e. Alf has no equivalent predefined type in its model libraries and therefore no equivalent type-specific rule). Primitive type Real represents the set of real numbers ℝ. The rule LiteralReal enables the literal representation of real values with the usual dot or scientific notations (i.e., in the example, 1234.56 and 1.2E3 respectively). Primitive type DateTime represents the set of time instants. The rule LiteralDateTime enables the literal representation of a time instant using a calendar form.

Finally, the rule JitterExpression addresses a more domain-specific need. It specifies a particular kind of duration observation, which denotes an unwanted variation (i.e. a jitter) between the time instants of two observed events (in the example, these time instants are identified with time observations t1 and t2. See section 3.3 for a definition of TimeObservation).

3.2 Metatype-Specific Rules

The term "Metatype" refers to metaclasses and stereotypes which can be used to define the types actually handled by a language. For example, in the UML metamodel, all the children of metaclass Classifier (such as Class, PrimitiveType or DataType) are metatypes. By metatype-specific rule, we therefore refer to syntactic rules for which the type system statically specifies the metatype that can be derived. However, determining the exact evaluation type typically requires further context analysis. Figure 3 illustrates the various metatype-specific rules considered by VSL. The figure is vertically partitioned in 2 numbered zones. Each zone maps to a subset with corresponding number in figure 1. Note that category 3 is not represented here. It means that VSL do not carry metatype-specific rules which can be considered as specific to the real-time domain.

Overlapping with Alf. VSL mostly provides metatype-specific rules which evaluate to stereotypes defined in MARTE (except Enumeration Specification, which evaluates to an UML Enumeration. VSL and Alf examples provided in figure 3 relate to the enumeration TimeUnitKind in the bottom part of figure 4.

	VSL syntactic rule	VSL Example	Alf equivalent Example	Infered VSL Metatype	Infered Alf Metatype
	Enumeration Specification	ms TimeUnitKind.ms	ms TimeUnitKind.ms TimeUnitKind::ms	UML::Enumeration	UML::Enumeration
	Tuple Specification	(15, ms) (value = 15, unit = ms)	new Duration(15, ms) new Duration(value => 15, unit => ms) new (15,ms) new (value => 15, unit => ms)	<<TupleType>>	UML::DataType
	Collection Specification	{1, 2, 3}	new Collection<Integer>{1,2,3} Collection<Integer>{1,2,3} {1,2,3}	<<CollectionType>>	UML::Class
	Interval Specification	[2..45]		<<IntervalType>>	
	Choice Specification	periodic(value = 15, unit = ms) other(aperiodic)		<<ChoiceType>>	

Fig. 3. Metatype-specific rules of VSL and overlapping with Alf

Note that the definition of this enumeration is the same for VSL and Alf.). These stereotypes, depicted in the top-left part of figure 4, are all defined as extensions of the UML metaclass DataType.

TupleSpecification enables the specification of tuple values, whose evaluation resolves to a TupleType. Property *tupleAttribs* of this stereotype enables to reference the properties which are actually part of the tuple (i.e., it can be a subset of all the properties owned by the TupleType). In the examples *(15,ms)* and *(value=15,unit=ms)* (whose evaluations resolve to TupleType Duration defined in the bottom-left part of figure 4), each element of the tuple specification provides a value for a property of the TupleType. In the first notation option, the reference with the property is established by order: *15* provides a value for property *value*, *ms* for property *unit*. In the second notation option, each property is explicitly named. Note that the equivalent Alf syntax is less concise. It relies on the usage of the instance creation operator *new*, applied to a DataType (in the example, the DataType is Duration, defined in the bottom-right part of figure 4). The arguments of the instance creation provide values for the properties of the DataType. Like in VSL, the relationships between values and properties can be established by order or by explicitly specifying the name of the property. Note that the shorter notation options provided by Alf (i.e., where the name of the datatype is not explicitly specified) can be used only in specific cases.

CollectionSpecification enables the specification of sequence of values, whose evaluation resolves to a CollectionType. A CollectionType is characterized by the type and number of elements that can be contained. This information is derived from the type and multiplicity of the Property referenced via the attribute *collectionAttrib* of this stereotype. The CollectionType *IntegerCollection* depicted in the bottom-left part of figure 4 therefore represents an unbounded collection of integer values. The equivalent Alf expressions do not rely on a specific collection metatype. The standard Alf library rather introduces a template class Collection which is parameterized by the type of elements it can contain (depicted in the bottom-right part of figure 4). Like for tuple values, specifying a sequence of values then comes to write an instance creation expression (where the operator "new" is optional), provide a template binding (e.g., *Collection<Integer>*, or to be more precise, a concrete subclass of Collection) and finally specify the sequence of values. Note that the third notation option of the examples, which is the same as the VSL notation, is available only in very specific cases.

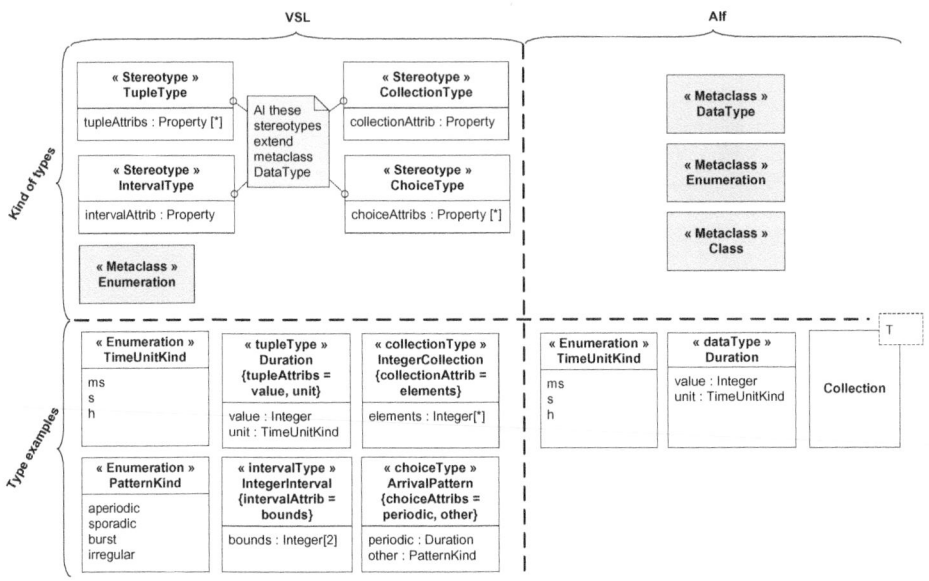

Fig. 4. VSL and Alf metatypes and type definition examples

Complementarity with Alf. VSL introduces two additional metatype-specific rules which have no equivalent in Alf: IntervalSpecification and ChoiceSpecification. An IntervalSpecification represents the specification of an open/closed interval of values, and its evaluation resolves to an IntervalType. Figure 4 (bottom left-part) illustrates the usage of this stereotype for the specification of IntegerInterval. The type of the elements contained in the interval is derived from the Property referenced by the attribute *intervalAttrib* of the stereotype IntervalType (i.e., in the example, the property is *bounds : Integer [2]*). The expression *[2..45]* (depicted in figure 3) therefore specifies a valid IntegerInterval value.

The rule ChoiceSpecification evaluates to ChoiceTypes, a metatype similar to C unions and Ada/Pascal "variant-records". The stereotype ChoiceType enables to combine multiple types into a single data type, where each type represents a kind of alternative. Each alternative is defined by a Property of the ChoiceType (the type of this property determines the type of the alternative) and the set of all alternatives is identified via the attribute *choiceAttribs* of the stereotype (see top-left part of figure 4). With the rule ChoiceSpecification, specifying a value for a ChoiceType implies to identify the chosen alternative, and then specify the corresponding value. As illustrated in figure 3, the chosen alternative is identified by specifying the name of the corresponding property.

3.3 Generic Rules

By "generic" rule, we mean syntactic rules for which the type system does not statically specify the evaluation type or metatype. These rules usually involve the manipulation of names, where each name is used to identify a named element from the context model. Depending on the syntactic construct and the context, the type system determines how to retrieve the corresponding named element and infer a type from it. Figure 5 identifies all the generic rules provided by VSL and determines whether they are covered (zone 1) or not (zone 2 and 3) by the type system of Alf.

VSL syntactic rule	VSL Example	Alf equivalent Example
Literal Null	null	null
Conditional Expression	(a > b) ? a : b	a > b ? a : b
Property Call Expression	size v.size	size v.size
Operation Call Expression	v.get(2)	v.get(2) v.get(index => 2)
Behavior Call Expression	Max(a, b) IntegerFunctions.Max(a,b)	Max(a,b) IntegerFunctions.Max(a, b) Max(y = >b, x => a) IntegerFunctions::Max(a, b)
Literal Default	-	
Instant Expression	t1	
Duration Expression	d1	

Fig. 5. Generic VSL rules and overlapping with Alf

Overlapping with Alf. Even though they do not necessarily imply names, rules LiteralNull and ConditionalExpression fall into the category of generic rules as defined in the introduction to this section. Their evaluation type is indeed completely context dependent. In the case of LiteralNull, the VSL specification states that it should be evaluated to the DataType of the element for which the expression is specifying a value. Note that this interpretation differs from Alf, where the same expression would be considered untyped with multiplicity 0. The rule ConditionalExpression enables the specification of two possible return values, the one to be returned depending on the evaluation of a condition. The expression *(a > b) ? a : b* given as an example in figure 5 will either return *a* if a is greater than b, or *b* otherwise. The evaluation type therefore depends on the type of the two possible return values. The type system of Alf specifies the same evaluation rule.

Rules PropertyCallExpression, OperationCallExpression and BehaviorCall-Expression actually deal with names, which must resolve to properties, operations and behaviors respectively. In figure 5, PropertyCallExpression examples refer to a property called *size*. OperationCallExpression examples refer to an operation called *get*. Finally, BehaviorCallExpression examples refer to a behavior called *Max*, defined in a package called *IntegerFunctions*. Regarding the noteworthy differences between VSL and Alf syntax, we can notice that Alf enables explicit naming of parameters when specifying the arguments of the operation or behavior invocation (e.g. *get(index => 2)*). Alf also enables the usage of delimiter :: in qualified names, whereas . is the only delimiter considered by VSL.

Regarding the overlapping between generic rules, another interesting difference between VSL and Alf (not reported in figure 5 due to the limited size of this article) concerns the management of predefined binary and unary operators in infix and prefix expressions. In VSL, signatures of these operators are defined as operations of predefined data types. Alf rather follows a procedural approach, where each signature is defined as a function. For example, an expression such as $a + b$ will be interpreted as $a.+(b)$ in VSL (i.e., a call to the operation $+$ associated with the datatype of a) whereas in Alf, it will be interpreted as $+(a,b)$ (i.e., a function call).

Complementarity with Alf. In the specification of a tuple value or an operation/behavior call expression, a DefaultLiteral (symbol -) can be used to denote that no specific value is provided for a tuple element or an argument. If a default value exists for this element, it must be used. Otherwise, - is interpreted as *null*. Note that in practice, this symbol appears to be unusable when the number of elements to specify (i.e. tuple elements or arguments) is important. This is a common situation for most of the tuple types defined in the MARTE libraries.

Rules InstantExpression (which Evaluates to DateTime) and DurationExpression (which evaluates to Real) consist in the specification of a (potentially qualified) name identifying a TimeObservation or a DurationObservation respectively. TimeObservation is a UML concept which enables to model the time instant when a particular event occurs (e.g., communication event, start of execution event, etc.). DurationObservation is another UML concept which represents the duration between the occurrences of two events. Rules InstantExpression and DurationExpression are typically useful to specify time constraints, as illustrated in [5].

3.4 Summary of the Comparison

We have reviewed all the syntactic rules provided by VSL and described how they are considered by the VSL type system to evaluate their type. The rules have been categorized according two orthogonal criteria: The potential overlapping with Alf (i.e. categories identified in figure 1) and how they are perceived by the type system of VSL (type-specific, metatype-specific or generic rules). The first criteria provides a global overview of where Alf needs to be extended (i.e. all aspects falling into categories 2 and 3 of figure 1). Note that for some of the rules falling into category 1 (i.e. TupleSpecification and CollectionSpecification), we have shown that the VSL syntax was much more concise. This aspect must be considered in the extension of Alf.

The second criteria provides a more precise idea of how Alf should be extended. Globally, type-specific rules rather require a syntactic extension (i.e. for specific literals and keywords) and a model library extension (i.e. for specific types associated with these literals and keywords). Metatype-specific rules rather require an extension of the metatypes supported by the language (e.g. stereotype «ChoiceType»). Generic rules rather imply an extension of the type system, showing how existing Alf construct (e.g. qualified names) can resolve to named elements considered by VSL (e.g. time and duration observations). The next section takes into account these considerations for a definition of VSL as an extension of Alf.

4 A Definition of VSL as an Extension of Alf

The extension we propose covers 3 aspects: Refactor the VSL types and metatypes, extend Alf syntactic rules and finally extend the type system of Alf. These aspects are detailed in the next sections.

4.1 Refactoring of VSL Types and Metatypes

Figure 6 illustrates our refactoring proposal regarding types and metatypes of VSL. In figure 2 (zones 2 and 3), we have highlighted the fact that Alf does not have predefined types equivalent to Real and DateTime. Integer, UnlimitedNatural, String and Boolean are however considered, since they are imported from UML primitive types. Our proposal, depicted in left part of figure 6, then consists in refactoring library MARTE_PrimitiveTypes by including only Real and DateTime primitive types and importing other primitive types from Alf. In order to be consistent with Alf principles and architecture (see discussion about VSL operations and Alf function behaviors in section 3.3), refactoring also implies removing all PrimitiveType operations defined in the original MARTE library. They are replaced by function behaviors (which are not depicted in the diagram due to size limitations).

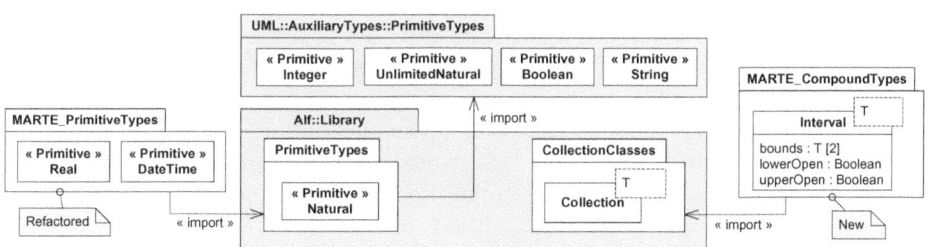

Fig. 6. Modification of MARTE type libraries

In figure 3, we have highlighted the various metatypes considered by VSL: TupleType, CollectionType, IntervalType and ChoiceType. Our proposal consists in reducing the set of VSL-specific metatypes. The purpose is to limit unnecessary complexity and therefore minimize the learning effort for an Alf user. In section 3.2, we have explained the subtle difference between a UML DataType and a MARTE TupleType (a TupleType can identify a subset of its own properties which are actually part of the tuple). In practice, this difference is never exploited, and this stereotype can be safely removed. In section 3.2, we have also explained the similarities between the VSL metatype CollectionType and the predefined Alf class Collection. We propose to remove CollectionType and rely on class Collection instead. We follow a similar approach for the stereotype IntervalType: the stereotype can be removed and replaced by a new template class Interval. Interval is illustrated in the right part of figure 6 with the package MARTE_CompoundTypes (in the MARTE specification, the term Compound-Type designates all the stereotypes discussed in this section).

Finally, since ChoiceType carries a particular semantics (i.e., similar to C unions and Ada/Pascal "variant-records"), we propose to keep it as part of the VSL-specific metatypes. The other metatype to be kept is BoundedSubtype (not discussed so far since it has no syntactic impacts), which can be used to statically specify that a type subsets another type in terms of range of values.

4.2 Extension of Alf Syntactic Rules

Rules LiteralReal, LiteralDateTime and JitterExpression (see figure 2) can be easily integrated in the Alf grammar. Indeed, their implementation can be based on terminals which do not conflict with existing Alf rules. The type system of Alf can be extended consequently to infer primitive types Real or DateTime (as defined in the previous section).

In section 3.2, we have highlighted the fact that the syntax for sequences (e.g. *{1, 2, 3}*) or tuple values (e.g. *(value = 15, unit = ms)*) is much more concise in VSL than in Alf. Our proposal then consists in extending Alf syntax to support corresponding syntactic sugar. Regarding sequences, Alf enables a concise syntax (i.e. *{1, 2, 3}*) only in the case where a sequence is itself composed of sequences (e.g. *new Collection<Collection<Integer> >{{1,2}, {3}}*). The extension then consist in relaxing this constraint by promoting the corresponding rule (i.e. SequenceCreationExpression) as a primary expression of the language. The type system is extended to infer class Collection (as described in the previous section) with appropriate template binding.

Regarding tuple values, the solution is not so straightforward. In the Alf grammar, directly introducing support for expressions like *(value = 15, unit = ms)* raises numerous issues, mainly due to the presence of parentheses. There is basically a conflict with parenthesized and cast expressions. Our pragmatic solution consists in considering a tuple value as a sequence, except that all its elements do not necessarily have the same type, and that in addition, a name (used to denote the property of the tuple) can be specified. The rule SequenceCreationExpression (mentionned above) is extended in this way. Its usage would produce expression such as *{15, ms}* or *{value => 15, unit => ms}*, which are quite near from the original VSL examples depicted in figure 3. Note that symbol => is used instead of =. An expression such as *{value = 15}* would indeed be parsed as an assignment expression. The type system is extended to infer the corresponding DataType. If the exact DataType cannot be inferred from the context, users still have the possibility to specify an Alf instance creation expression with the operator *new*.

Rule IntervalSpecification (depicted in figure 3) also requires some syntactic adaptations before being integrated in Alf. An expression such as *]a..b]* (i.e., an interval where the lower bound a is not included) raises parsing issues. The conflicts are due to the fact that other Alf constructs (which are part of the Statement subset of Alf) also rely on symbols *[* and *]*. Again, our proposal consists in extending rule SequenceCreationExpression mentioned above. When using this rule for instantiating a collection, Alf supports the option of specifying the interval of values to be contained in the collection instance. For example, an expression such as *new Collection<Integer>{0..3}* is equivalent to *new Collection<Integer>{0, 1, 2, 3}* (i.e. the lower and upper bound are implicitly included). According to the extension described in the previous paragraphs (i.e. promoting SequenceCreationExpression as a primary expression), *{0..3}* is already a valid expression, and it is syntactically very near from the original VSL syntax (i.e. *[0..3]*). We simply extend the rule to optionally specify if the lower and/or upper bounds are actually included in the interval. According to this extension, the expression *]a..b]* would become *{]a..b}*. The type system is extended to infer Interval (as defined in figure 6), where the binding for the template parameter is inferred from the type of the lower and upper bound expressions.

Rule ChoiceSpecification, also depicted in figure 3, does not imply any syntactic extensions. We see in the next section that an extension of the Alf type system is sufficient.

4.3 Extension of Alf Type System

Rule ChoiceSpecification (depicted in figure 3) evaluates to metatype ChoiceType. Syntactically, it is however very similar to an operation or behavior invocation (e.g., *other(aperiodic)*, provided as an example in figure 3). There are other cases in Alf where an invocation-like syntax is used, such as for link expressions (which can be used to get all the instances playing a given role in the context of an association). At the parsing level, these rules are not syntactically distinguishable. They are all merged into a single parsing rule, which consists in specifying a (potentially qualified) name, followed by a list of (potentially named) arguments. Depending on the context, the qualified name may resolve to an Operation, a Behavior or an Association, and the arguments may refer to parameters of the operation/behavior or association ends of the Association. To support rule ChoiceSpecification, we simply propose to extend this inference rule, so that the qualified name can refer to a property of a ChoiceType, and arguments may refer to properties of this property's type.

Alf introduces a rule called NameExpression. It enables to specify a reference to a property, a local variable or a formal parameter by giving its (potentially qualified) name. Concerning rules InstantExpression and DurationExpression introduced in figure 5, our proposal simply consists in extending the inference rule associated with NameExpression so that it can also resolve to a TimeObservation or a DurationObservation.

VSL syntactic rule	VSL (original)	VSL (as an extension of Alf)	Libraries	Syntax	Type System
Literal Real	1234.56 1.2E3	1234.56 1.2E3			
Literal DateTime	12:24:00 2006/02/07 Tue	12:24:00 2006/02/07 Tue			
Jitter Expression	jitter(t2 - t1)	jitter(t2 - t1)			
Tuple Specification	(15, ms) (value = 15, unit = ms)	{15, ms} {value => 15, unit => ms}			
Collection Specification	{1, 2, 3}	{1, 2, 3}			
Interval Specification	[2..45]	{2..45}			
Choice Specification	periodic(value = 15, unit = ms) other(aperiodic)	periodic(value => 15, unit => ms) other(aperiodic)			
Literal Default	-	/////////////////////////////////			
Instant Expression	t1	t1			
Duration Expression	d1	d1			

Fig. 7. VSL as an extension of Alf: Synthesis of proposed extensions

Finally, rule LiteralDefault (see figure 5) is simply ignored in this proposal due to the fact that the symbol has proven unusable in practice (see discussion in section 3.3).

Figure 7 summarizes all the extensions we have proposed in order to properly define VSL as an extension of Alf. For each VSL rule implying an extension of Alf (the names depicted in the first column are those used in section 3), it provides examples using the original VSL syntax, the one based on the Alf extension and finally identifies the extension strategy which has been followed (i.e., extending libraries and/or extending the syntax and/or extending the type system).

4.4 Prototype Implementation

The elements described in the proposal above have almost all been validated by a prototype implementation. This prototype consists in an extension of the Alf parser, a refactoring of the MARTE type libraries and a partial implementation of the type system extensions. As explained in section 2, we are developing an Alf editor for Papyrus. This editor is developed with Xtext, which provides an interesting feature called "grammar mixins". This functionality enables grammar designers to reuse and overload existing grammars. In our prototype, the VSL grammar (as described in this section) simply reuses the Alf grammar, extends it with new rules (e.g., LiteralReal, LiteralDateTime), and finally overloads where necessary (e.g., SequenceCreationExpression, described in section 4.2). The syntactic extensions we have proposed have all been implemented. They do not bring any ambiguity in the parsing process.

The extensions of the type system have been implemented for simple cases, such as LiteralReal (which evaluates to primitive type DateTime from the refactored MARTE library) or NameExpression for the cases where it refers to time or duration observations (which requires a simple name analysis). The overloading related to management of ChoiceSpecification has not been implemented yet. Since it relies on principles that we have already implemented for managing operation or behavior invocations, we however have no doubt regarding its technical feasibility.

5 Conclusion

We have proposed a definition of VSL as an extension of Alf. This extension covers three aspects. The first one concerns a refactoring of MARTE libraries (underlying the type system of VSL) so that they properly import and then extend Alf libraries. The second aspect concerns an extension of the Alf syntax, in order to consider the need for new literals or syntactic sugar (e.g. for tuple values or sequences). The last aspect concerns the extension of the Alf type system, where we have extended inference rules of Alf to account for VSL concerns. The technical feasibility of the proposal has been validated with the description of a prototype implementation for our UML modeling tool Papyrus.

The direct follow-up to this work concerns the raising of an official MARTE issue regarding the future of VSL with respect to the emergence of Alf. This issue will of course motivate the need to define VSL as an extension of Alf. All the ideas that we have presented in this article will provide useful material in the context on the ongoing MARTE revision task force 1.2, where CEA LIST is strongly involved.

A more long-term work concerns the impact of the proposed extensions regarding the statement subset of Alf. As explained in the introduction to this article, Alf (via statements, themselves relying on expressions) provides a concrete syntax for UML Activities. fUML in turn provides a precise and executable semantics for this behavioral formalism. Some of the extensions we have proposed are related to Time. Since fUML is time-agnostic, extensions to fUML are clearly required. Defining these extensions in a simple revision task force requires too much work and adds to the current version of MARTE. It will be addressed in a request for proposal (more generally concerning the relationship between MARTE and fUML) which will be raised before the end of 2011.

References

1. OMG: UML Profile for MARTE: Modeling and Analysis of Real-Time Embedded Systems, version 1.1 (2010)
2. OMG: Action Language for Foundational UML (Alf), Beta 1 (2010)
3. OMG: Semantics of a Foundational Subset for Executable UML Models (fUML), version 1.0 (2011)
4. Espinoza, H.: An Integrated Model-Driven Framework for Specifying and Analyzing Non-Functional Properties of Real-Time Systems, PhD Thesis (September 2007)
5. Cuccuru, A., Mraidha, C., Radermacher, A., Gérard, S., Rioux, L., Vergnaud, T., Hachet, O.: Methodological Guidelines on the Usage of MARTE VSL for Specification of Time Constraints. In: 2nd Workshop on Model Based Engineering for Embedded Systems Design (M-BED 2011), Grenoble, France (March 2011)
6. Chattopadhyay, S.: Compiler Design. Prentice Hall of India, Englewood Cliffs (2008)

Using Delta Model for Collaborative Work of Industrial Large-Scaled E/E Architecture Models

Rixin Zhang and Ajay Krishnan

aquintos GmbH, Philipp-Reis-Straße 1, Karlsruhe, 76137, Germany
{rixin.zhang,ajay.krishnan}@aquintos.com

Abstract. Development of model-based Electric/Electronic (E/E) architecture in the automotive industry poses a high demand on the data management of models. The collaborative modeling work involves stakeholders dispersed across various locations and departments, while the models themselves are often extremely large-scaled. In this paper, we present our approach addressing the model data management issue for both asynchronous and synchronous modeling. Compared to asynchronous modeling, which is based on the lock/commit mechanism for cross-department collaboration, synchronous modeling is targeted to assist quick and efficient interaction among small groups of members. We use the delta model for versioning in the database as well as for the synchronous modeling functionality. Furthermore, other versatile uses of the delta model such as the cumulative delta model and the reverse delta model are also introduced.

Keywords: Delta Model, Collaborative Modeling, Real-time Collaboration, Versioning, Groupware, Computer Supported Cooperative Work (CSCW).

1 Introduction

In the last decades, model-based development has been applied in various domains which go beyond just software. Just like other Computer Supported Cooperative Work (CSCW) tools which can be classified as asynchronous and synchronous [14], tools supporting collaborative co-modeling also fall into these two groups. There are two important issues related to data: (1) how to organize the data for model versioning (normally occurs in asynchronous co-modeling environment) and (2) how to minimize the transferred data in a synchronous (real-time) collaborative environment.

Our tool PREEvision is a model-based system engineering solution for complex electric/electronic (E/E) systems design and optimization [10, 12, 17]. As Fig. 1 shows, an E/E model integrates huge amount of engineering data spread across various domains. Members participating in the overall modeling process often involve engineers belonging to diverse functional departments situated at various locations. Hence, the two issues mentioned above become more important here than in the case of other tools. The reasons are: (1) **Large-scaled meta-model and model**: The PREEvision model is based on a highly complex domain specific meta-model supporting various industrial standards such as AUTOSAR, KBL, ELOG, FIBEX etc.

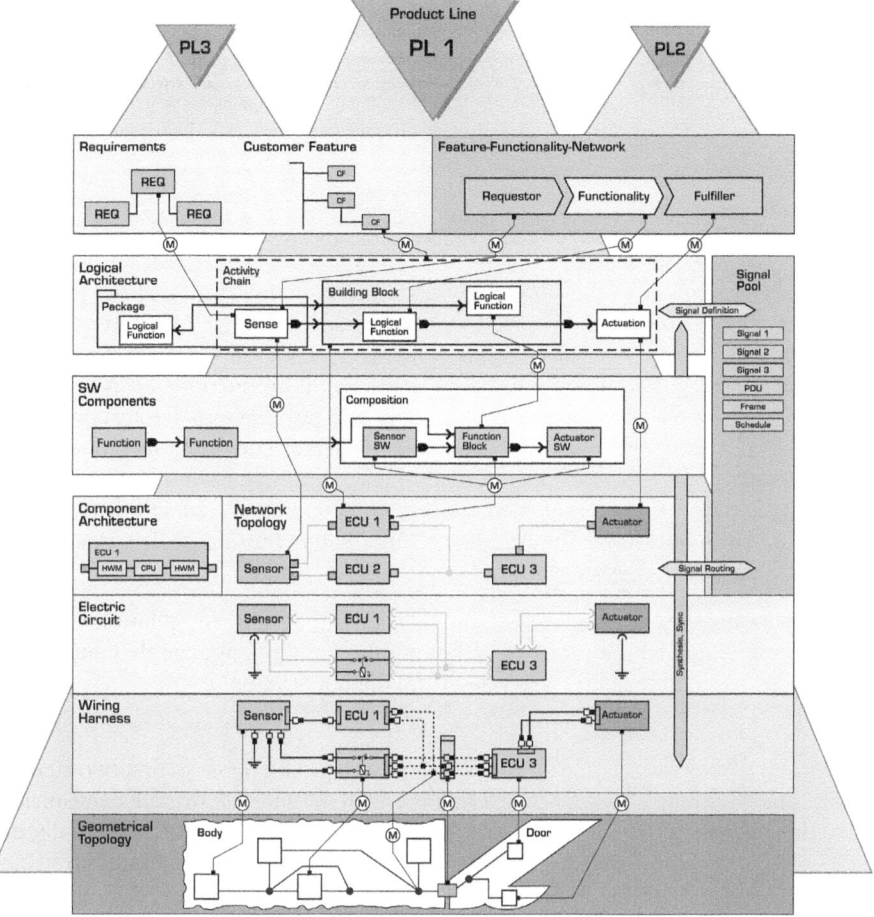

Fig. 1. Modeling layers in the PREEvision Tool [20]

The meta-model contains more than 1000 meta-classes at the time of writing this paper (Fig. 2). The model which the users edit is often extremely large-scaled (more than 500,000 artifacts and the model XMI-file is larger than 200MB). (2) **Supporting flexible collaboration**: Our goal is to support both asynchronous and synchronous collaboration. As Fig. 3 shows, at the organizational level, collaborative modeling is generally asynchronous based on pessimistic locking with version support. Synchronous modeling is typically used among small groups of users to collectively explore, discuss, and brainstorm a solution simultaneously. Here the model changes of all the group members are always synchronized to the same state.

In this paper, we describe our approach addressing these two issues. Our contributions can be summarized in the following two points: (1) Fine-grained delta model is used both in the persistent layer to minimize the data for model versioning and in real-time collaboration to minimize the network traffic. (2) The delta model is used for solving other problems in real-time collaboration such as undo/redo and latecomer support.

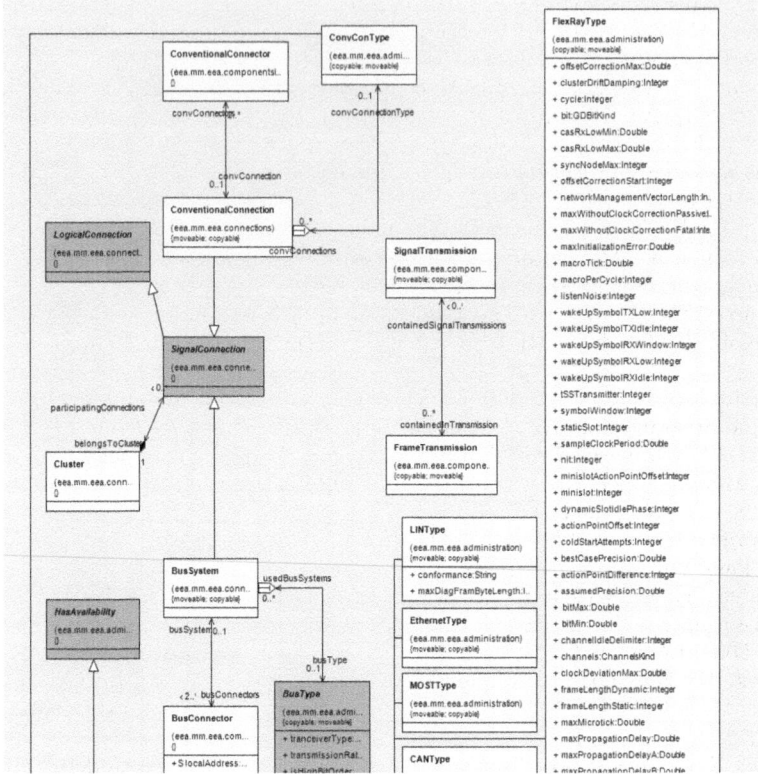

Fig. 2. A part of the PREEvision meta-model

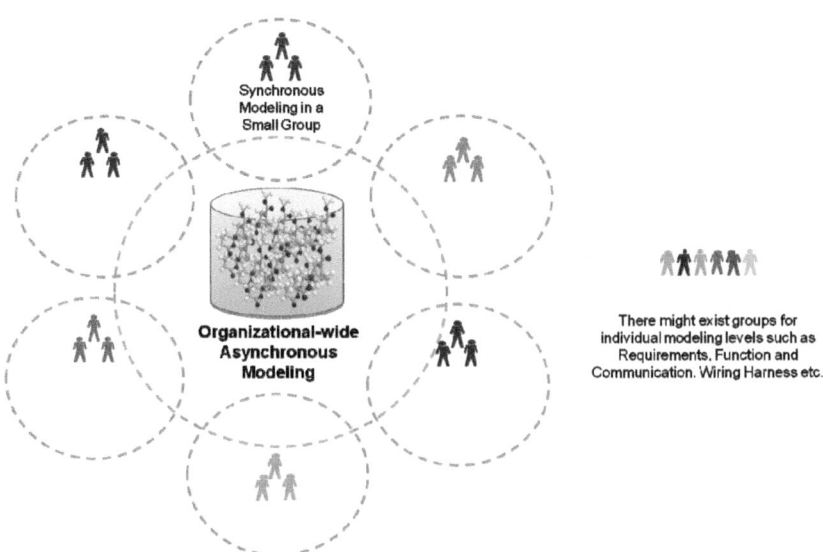

Fig. 3. Asynchronous and Synchronous Modeling in an Organization

The remainder of this paper is structured as follows: related work is discussed in Section 0. Section 0 provides a brief overview of the PREEvision collaboration environment. Section 0 lays down the principle and the concrete usage of the delta model. Finally, Section 0 talks about the state of the current work and briefly discusses the future work that needs to be done in this area.

2 Related Work

For a system with versioning functionality, data volume would be an important topic in the persistent layer in which all different versions of models are stored. The required data volume is dependent on the individual data structure as well as (perhaps more) on the versioning granularity. CVS [2] and SubVersion [7] are examples of extreme coarse versioning. A file is the minimal versioning unit. If the versioning of a complete model is based on the file level, each version of the model is then stored in the persistent layer as a single file. Fine grained versioning could be versioning smaller units such as package, diagram or single artifact. For example, commercial UML tool Poseidon [19] enables versioning a diagram. STEVE is a framework in the research field with a fine-grained versioning mechanism making versioning software artifacts possible [15].

In contrast, a synchronous groupware system is highly interactive, volatile and focused. It requires a short response time (time necessary for the actions of one user to be reflected by his/her own interface) as well as a short notification time (time necessary for one user's action to be propagated to the other users' interface) [9]. Compared to versioning that mainly influences the persistent layer, synchronous modeling demands a harder requirement on "live" data on the network traffic.

Most of the collaborative modeling tools supporting synchronous modeling are UML tools. D-Meeting uses a simple extra layer such as whiteboard which is purely additive to the model layer [3]. The white board is used as a medium to have a quick stretch of ideas. In the work of Chen [5], manual stretch is recognized and transformed to artifacts as integrated part of the model. For the two examples mentioned above, the transferred data might be data streaming representing the shared image. Other tools allow users to directly work on model artifacts. SLIM [22] and ProcessWave [21] are such examples which are lightweight applications and use web browser to do the synchronous collaborative modeling. For these two examples, transferred data might be a simple command object representing the action to be executed.

Obviously, handling data is more complicated in a synchronous collaborative modeling environment as compared to an asynchronous one. Some of the features, which are normally of no concern in asynchronous modeling, can pose real challenges in a synchronous collaborative modeling environment. Undo/redo and latecomer support are two such examples. Undo action removes the past action and allows the user to reverse erroneous operations. Redo is the inverse of undo. A late comer is a user who joins the collaborative synchronous work process after the session has already been established. In other words, there are changes that have already been carried out by other participants. Before starting to work on the shared area, the late comer needs to retrieve all the changes first.

There exist some conceptual works addressing the undo/redo problem [1, 4, 11]. For instance, Chen et al. [4] propose an algorithm enabling the user to undo any operation in history; Göhnert et al. [11] further suggest a multi-mode undo mechanism to provide the participants the flexibility in terms of undo mode and maintain the integrity of the history. In a collaborative modeling tool, undo/redo is typically realized through a command pattern, in which forward and reverse state transitions at the action level is encapsulated in a command object [1]. It works fine in simple cases (e.g. moving an object from a position A to B corresponds to a reverse transition of moving the position from B to A.). However, it is not appropriate for complex operations for which a forecast of reverse action is difficult or even impossible. Furthermore, because it is not suitable for software refactoring, long-term software maintenance would also be a problem if the number of actions is large.

Related work in CSCW uses a different technique to handle the latecomer problem. One sends the entire data over the network for the latecomer, proposed by Illmann et al. [13] and the other sends the missing data in sequential units, suggested by Chiara, et al. [6]. These two mechanisms will work well in small-scaled data, but is not suitable in our case. Transmission of large amount of a complete model data is time consuming. Sequential update of all individual data could consume even more time in an extreme case.

To sum up, in spite of the existence of various applications, there has not been enough work that really addresses the problem of the data itself. The reasons might be that most models in the research area are restricted to small-scaled models. Another reason might be that few tools needed to handle large-scaled models both in asynchronous and synchronous modeling. In fact, this is where our work differs from other existing works in that we focus on the data aspect in the context of asynchronous and synchronous collaborative work of large-scaled models.

3 Overview of the Collaborative Modeling Environment

Fig. 4 shows the PREEvision collaborative modeling environment. All model information is stored in a relational database. A model has different versions with a unique version number for each version as its indicator. With versioning, a user can view an earlier state of the model. Exclusive locking on the sub-model in the database is required before changes at that locked area are allowed. The locked sub-model can be of different granularity. After a commit operation, the local model changes are finalized in the persistence layer and the version number is incremented by one. Moreover, within the locked area, the user has the flexibility to involve other participants to synchronously make model changes. The inclusion of group members in synchronous modeling is through the share/join action. In order to begin a session, the owner of the lock can share the locked sub-model and group members need to explicitly execute the join action to participate (Fig. 5).

Fig. 6 illustrates our overall three tier software architecture. It consists of the PREEvision client, the middleware and the underlying database. Architecture model is replicated in every PREEvision client. The middleware serves as an intermediate layer responsible for data exchange, task coordination, undo/redo as well as latecomer support. The workflow for synchronous modeling is as follows: (1) the client works

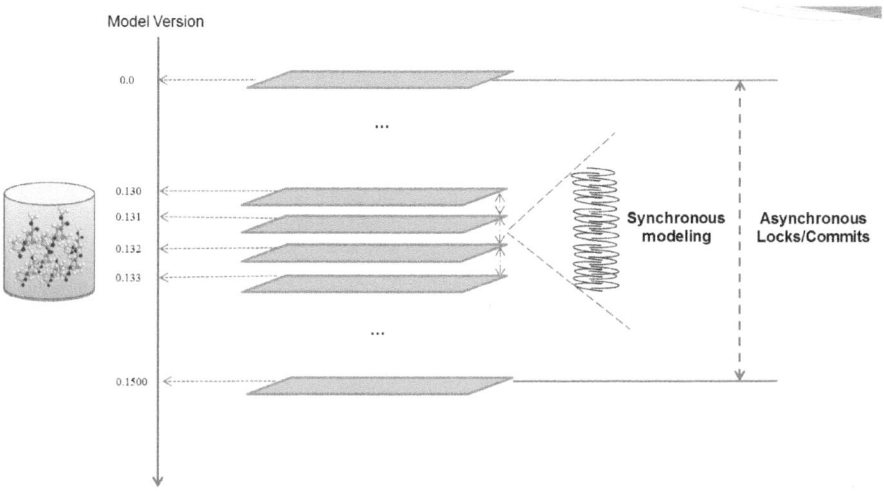

Fig. 4. Asynchronous and Synchronous Collaborative Modeling

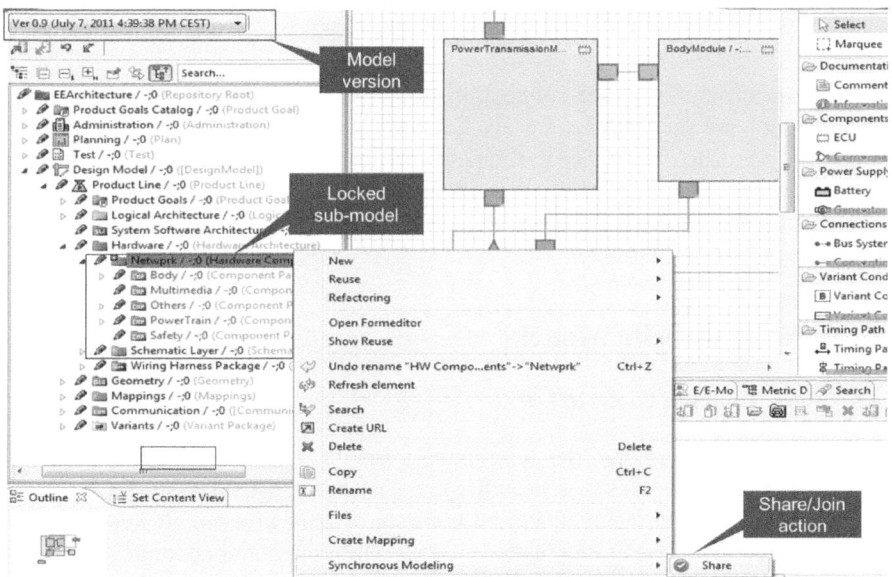

Fig. 5. Screenshot of PREEvision

with the domain specific model based on our complex meta-model. A delta model listener registered in the model repository observes changes at the artifact level. (2) Based on the information provided by the listener, the delta model is serialized to a generic and domain independent binary model format (see Section 0) after every individual model operation. (3) The binary model delta is transferred to the

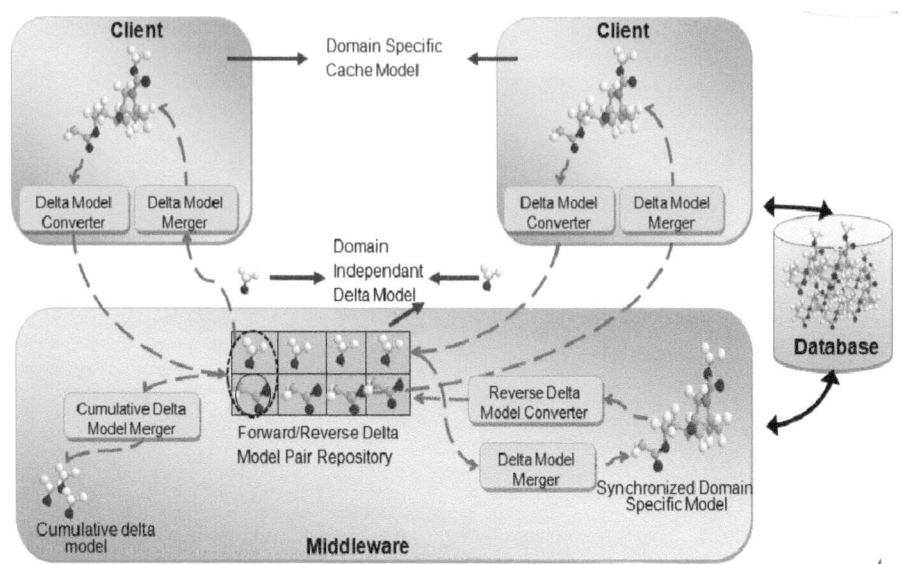

Fig. 6. Software architecture

middleware through a socket connection. In order to ensure that models in participating clients and middleware are always in the same state, every model change is immediately broadcast to other participants. (4) Finally, this received delta model is merged with the cache model in other clients using the delta model merger. After the merging process is finished, the model state of other clients is then updated to the same state as that of the sender.

4 The Use of Delta Model

4.1 Delta Model in Generic Form

It was mentioned before that the delta model format is based on a generic data model (Fig. 7) in order to have better reusability and scalability. This data model is to a large extent compatible with MOF [18] and consists of only objects, attributes and relations. Object corresponds to an instance of the MOF class and contains its attributes. Attribute corresponds to a MOF attribute and has its name and value. Relation corresponds to an association from one to another object. In order to assure the order, relations are saved as a list aggregated to the source object.

In our relational database, the models themselves are also saved as fine-grained objects, attributes and relations. In each model version, only the delta model in terms of objects, attributes and relations compared to the last model version is saved in the database. Switching or updating to a specific model version is also through the fine-grained delta model. Thus, the data storage in the database is reduced.

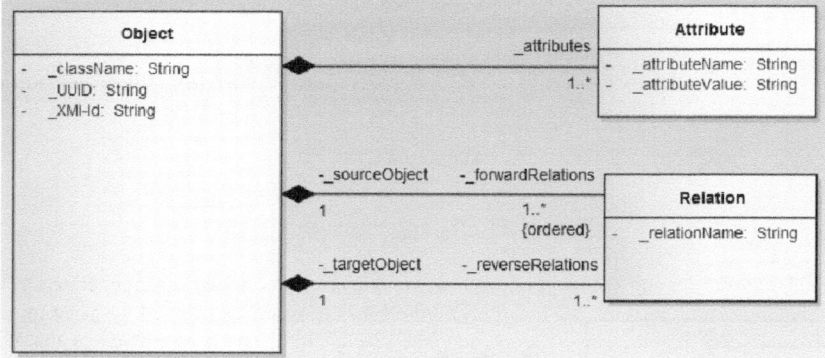

Fig. 7. Generic data model

4.2 Principle of Delta Model

The delta model represents the difference between two model states. In Fig. 8, the generation (upper part) enables the serialization of the delta model. The merging (lower part) enables the model to transit from one state to another through the merging of the delta model into the complete model.

Generally the changes can be classified as addition, deletion and changes of an artifact. Deleting an artifact automatically causes the deletion of artifacts contained directly or indirectly by this artifact. Moreover, changing an artifact can be a result of the changing of its attributes as well as its relations.

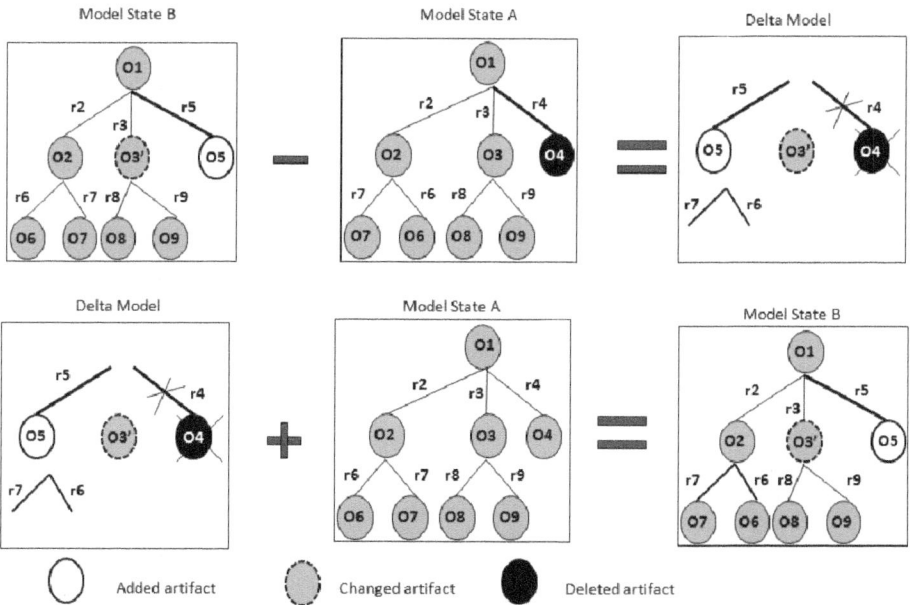

Fig. 8. Principle of delta model

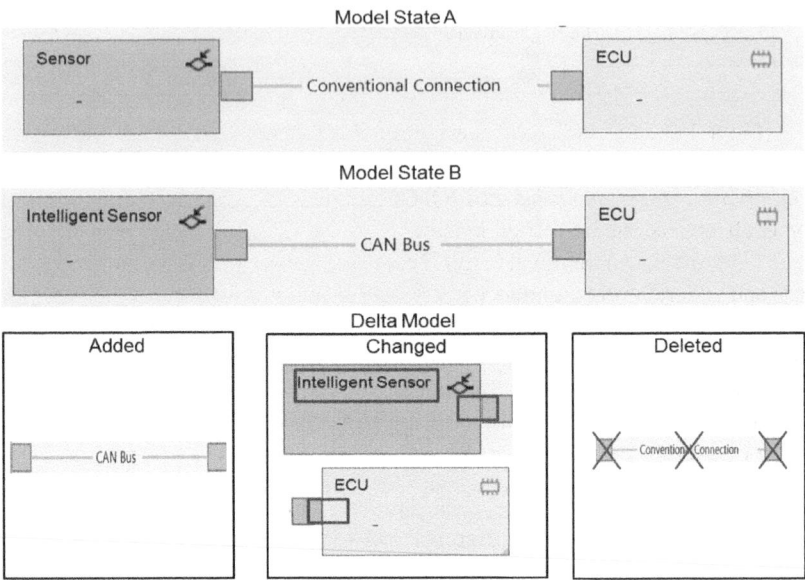

Fig. 9. A simple example of concrete model

As shown in the simple and concrete example in Fig. 9, the name of sensor becomes "intelligent sensor" and the communication medium is also changed from conventional connection to CAN bus system. If we ignore the diagram part of the model, the delta model is: (1) the deletion of objects (two conventional connectors and conventional connection) with the automatic deletion of relations to other objects (sensor and ECU at two sides). (2) The added bus system and two bus connectors. (3) The change of name (attribute) of sensor and the relations of bus connectors with sensor and ECU at each side.

4.3 Model Transition between Different Model States

The model states between which a model can "move" were illustrated earlier in Fig. 4. Our use of delta model is shown in Fig. 10. The model that a user edits is always at a certain model state. The model state can be transformed to forward and backward with the help of forward delta model and reverse delta model. The transition from one model state to another adjacent model state is atomic. Cumulative delta model is the cumulative result of all individual delta models. As explained in Table 1, the above terms have different meanings and use cases in asynchronous and synchronous modeling.

Forward/Reverse Delta Model
Forward/Reverse delta model enables the model transition to forward/backward direction respectively. The format of forward and reverse delta model is the same. For asynchronous modeling, given the specific source and target model versions, delta model can be obtained through SQL-Query in the persistent layer. For synchronous modeling, we currently use forward/reverse delta model for redo/undo action. In

Delta Model for Collaborative Work of Industrial Large-Scaled E/E Architecture Models 723

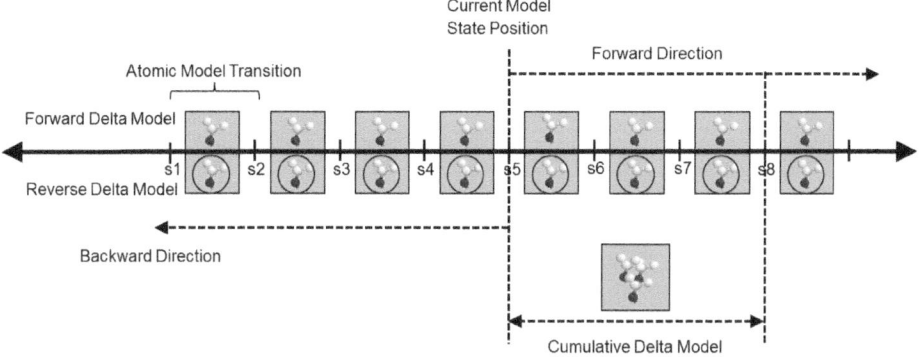

Fig. 10. Model transition between different model versions

Table 1. Different meaning and use cases in asynchronous and synchronous modeling

	Asynchronous modeling	**Synchronous modeling**
Atomic model transition	Delta model between two adjacent model versions	Delta model caused by one model operation
Forward/Backward direction	Forward: switch from an older to a newer model version; Backward: switch from a newer to an older model version	Forward for redo action Backward for undo action
Delta model	Model difference between two model versions in persistent layer	Model difference in cache model caused by model operation(s)
Forward/Reverse delta model	Delta model between model version X and Y depending which value is greater	Delta model in cache enabling model transition for forward/backward direction
Cumulative delta model	Delta model between model version X and Y which are not adjacent	Cumulative cache of all cached delta models addressing the latecomer problem

general, history and selective undo/redo are two kinds of undo/redo modes. History undo/redo mode performs the linear transformation of data state according to the history tree. Selective undo/redo provides the user the possibility to select one or more specific history changes. As Fig. 10 shows, a forward and its reverse delta model form a pair. In the middleware repository, sequential pairs are stored in list. Each new model change from the client will take its place at the foremost position. Middleware knows the current position of the model state. Our tool currently supports only history redo/undo. If the current state is not the foremost position and a user submits model change, the delta model pairs in front of the current position will automatically be removed and replaced by this new change.

Table 2 gives a summary of the relationship of forward and reverse delta models. As the concrete example shown in Fig. 11, added artifact in the delta model will be the deleted artifact in its reverse delta model and vice versa. If it is a changed artifact, then the artifact state including its attributes and relations at the target state is in the delta model.

Table 2. Forward and reverse delta model

	Forward delta model (model state A to B)	**Reverse delta model (model state B to A)**
Added artifact	Added artifact with its attributes and relations	The XMI-ID of deleted artifact
Deleted artifact	The XMI-ID of deleted artifact	Added artifact with its all attributes and relations
Changed artifact	Changed artifact with its attributes and relations at state B	Changed artifact with its all attributes and relations at state A

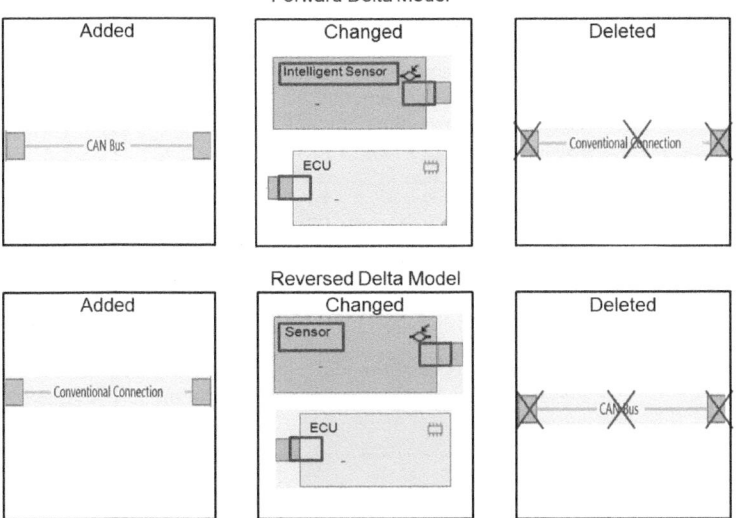

Fig. 11. A simple example of reverse delta model

Cumulative Delta Model. Cumulative delta model enables the switch to a model state which is not adjacent to current model state. Similar to the forward/reverse delta model in asynchronous modeling, cumulative delta model can be obtained through SQL-Query in persistent layer. For synchronous modeling, we currently only support the cumulative delta model corresponding to the sum of all model changes since the start of a session. We use cumulative delta model to resolve the latecomer problem discussed in Section 2. Having identified the problems of other existing mechanisms, our aim is to let the user update the newest model state through minimal data. A cache repository of the cumulative delta model is initialized once the synchronous modeling session is created. It is not a complete model repository because only the changed parts are gathered. Middleware cumulates the received individual delta model in the background upon receiving it from a client. After the merging of the cumulative delta model, the newly joined user can immediately update to the newest state.

Fig. 12 shows exemplarily the principle of the cumulative delta model. Again, the algorithm is based on classification of added/changed/deleted artifacts. If an artifact exists in two delta models, its attributes and relations in later delta model will replace the earlier. A simple concrete example of cumulative delta model can be seen in Fig. 13. The cumulative is a result of four delta models caused by four model operations: (1) deleting the conventional connection, (2) changing the name of sensor to "Sensor Unknown", (3) adding and connecting a bus system and (4) renaming once more the sensor name to "Intelligent Sensor".

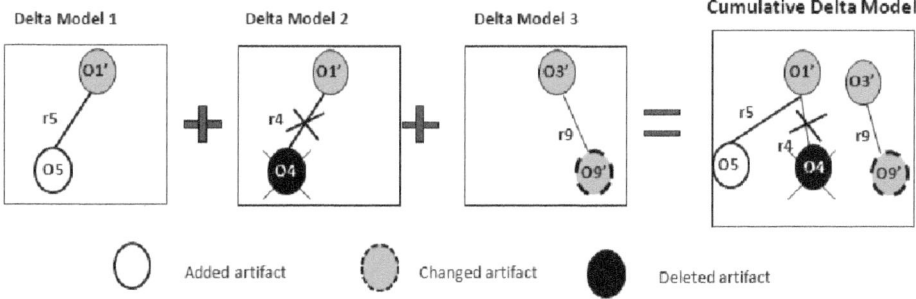

Fig. 12. The principle of cumulative delta model

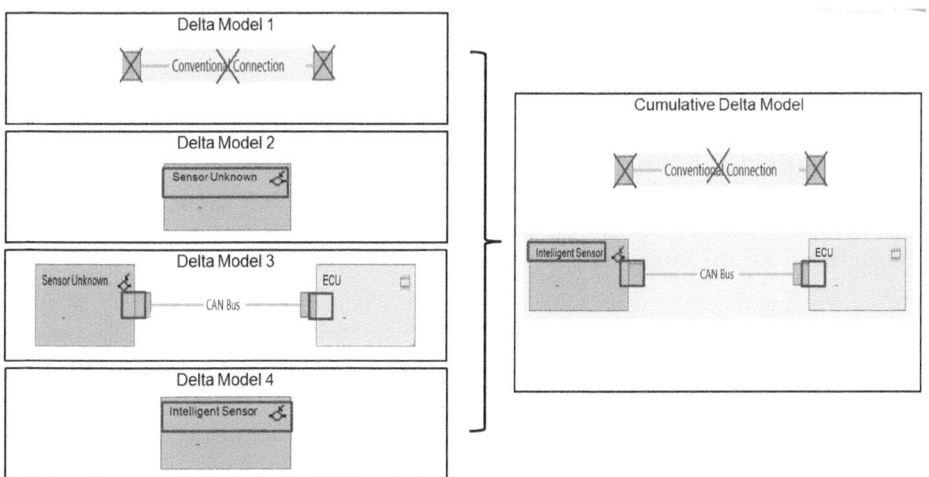

Fig. 13. A simple example of cumulative delta model

5 Discussion and Future Work

This paper presents our approach of using delta model for asynchronous and synchronous collaborative modeling. For both working modes the delta model is crucial. First of all, it reduces the storage in the persistent layer, as only the difference between model versions is saved. Secondly, it reduces the network traffic, which is one of the most important requirements for synchronous work.

Although our approach is targeted for collaborative E/E architecture development, its principle could be used in other areas, as delta model both in the persistent and the cache layers is generic. In other words, we can even resolve the collaborative textual editing in a model-based way, as we need only to generate a corresponding domain specific model for textual editing without reimplementation of business logics related to delta model.

So far, the implementation of asynchronous work with versioning in the database has been productively used for more than two years. Experience shows that it is an efficient concept. Synchronous collaborative modeling is still under development. We have finished implementation of all the work related to data manipulation (delta model generation, serialization, merging, undo/redo support and cumulative delta model). A prototype with the most pessimistic concurrency control has already been developed. However, there is still some way to go, before our mechanism can be put into productive use. The focus of our future work lies in the follows areas:

Extension of delta models: In the future, we need to have a mechanism for selective undo/redo support. The main problem here is how to undertake dependency analysis of the generic delta models which do not bear the real semantics. Furthermore, undo/redo delta model storage opens various new possibilities. For instance, user can use the delta model to have a complete view of model evolvement during the overall synchronous collaborative modeling process. Moreover, the extension of the cumulative delta model would enable a participant to disconnect and reconnect at any time.

"Awareness" support: Dourish and Bellotti [8] define "Awareness" as an "understanding of the activities of others, which provides a context for your own activity". Particularly in synchronous collaborative modeling environment, "awareness" information is critical. "Awareness" is the area where our work needs to intensify. Generally we need to have good UI concepts to let all the participants know what others are doing in order to avoid the users editing the same artifact at the same time.

Concurrency control: Right now we do not have a mature mechanism for concurrency control. It is one of our core future tasks to implement a much more optimistic concurrency control without losing data consistency.

Acknowledgement. We would like to thank Dr. Clemens Reichmann, CTO, aquintos GmbH, and Prof. K.D. Müller-Glaser from the Institute for Information Processing, Karlsruhe Institute of Technology (KIT) for their valuable guidance and support.

References

1. Berlage, T., Genau, A.: From Undo to Multi-User Applications. In: Proceedings of the Vienna Conference on Human-Computer Interaction, Vienna, pp. 213–224 (1993)
2. Berliner, B.: CVS II: Parallelizing Software Development. In: Proceedings of 1990 Winter USENIX Conference, Washington, D.C., pp. 341–352 (1990)

3. Bourlila, N., Dutoit, A.H., Brügge, B.: D-Meeting: an object-oriented framework for supporting distributed modeling of software. In: International Workshop on Global Software Development, International Conference on Software Engineering, Portland, Oregon, pp. 34–38 (2003)
4. Chen, D., Sun, C.: Undoing any operation in collaborative graphics editing systems. In: Proceedings of the 2001 International ACM SIGGROUP Conference on Supporting Group Work, New York, pp. 197–206 (2001)
5. Chen, Q., Grundy, J., Hosking, J.: An e-whiteboard application to support early design-stage sketching of UML diagrams. In: Proceedings of the 2003 IEEE Symposium on Human Centric Computing Languages and Environments, Auckland, pp. 219–226 (2001)
6. Chiara, R.D., Matteo, A.D., Manno, I., Scarano, V.: CoFFEE: cooperative Face2Face educational environment. In: Proceedings of the the 3rd International Conference on Collaborative Computing: Networking, Applications and Worksharing, New York, pp. 243–252 (2007)
7. Collins-Sussman, B., Fitzpatrick, B.W., Pilato, C.M.: Version Control with Subversion. O'Reilly (ed.) (2004)
8. Dourish, P., Bellotti, V.: Awareness and coordination in shared workspaces. In: Proceedings of the 1992 ACM Conference on Computer-supported Cooperative Work, Toronro, pp. 107–114 (1992)
9. Ellis, C.A., Gibbs, S.J.: Concurrency control in groupware systems. ACM SIGMOD Record 18(2), 399–407 (1989)
10. Gebauer, D., Matheis, J., Reichmann, C., Müller-Glaser, K.D.: Ebenenübergreifende, variantengerechten Beschreibung von Elektrik/Elektronik-Architekturen (in German) In: Bäker Bernard (Hrsg.): Moderne Elektronik im Kraftfahrzeug IV, Haus der Technik Fachbuch Band 105, pp. 49–61. Expert Verlag, Renningen (2009)
11. Göhnert, T., Malzahn, N., Hoppe, H.U.: A flexible multi-mode undo mechanism for a collaborative modeling environment. In: Carriço, L., Baloian, N., Fonseca, B. (eds.) CRIWG 2009. LNCS, vol. 5784, pp. 142–157. Springer, Heidelberg (2009)
12. Hillenbrand, M., Heinz, M., Adler, N., Müller-Glaser, K.D., Matheis, J., Reichmann, C.: An Approach for Rapidly Adapting the Demands of ISO/DIS 26262 to Electric/Electronic Architecture Modeling. In: 21th IEEE/IFIP International Symposium on Rapid System Prototyping, Fairfax, pp. 1–7 (2010)
13. Illmann, T., Thol, R., Weber, M.: Transparent latecomer support for web-based collaborative learning environments. In: Proceedings of the Conference on Computer Support for Collaborative Learning: Foundations for a CSCL Community, Colorado, USA, pp. 540–541 (2002)
14. Johansen, R.: Teams for Tomorrow. In: Proceedings of IEEE Hawaii International Conference on System Sciences, pp. 520–534. IEEE Computer Society Press, Los Alamitos
15. Lucia, A.D., Fasano, F., Scanniello, G., Tortora, G.: Enhancing collaborative synchronous UML modeling with fine-grained versioning of software artifacts. Journal of Visual Languages and Computing 18(5), 492–503 (2007)
16. Magicdraw UML, No Magic Inc., http://www.magicdraw.com/ (accessed January 15, 2011)
17. Matheis, J.: Abstraktionsebenenübergreifende Darstellung von Elektrik/Elektronik-Architekturen in Kraftfahrzeugen zur Ableitung von Sicherheitszielen nach ISO 26262 (in German), Ph.D. Dissertation University of Karlsruhe (2009)
18. Object Management Group, http://www.omg.org/mof/(accessed January 15, 2011)

19. Poseidon for UML, Gentleware AG, http://www.gentleware.com/ (accessed January 10, 2011)
20. PREEvision 3.0 User Manual, pp. 62
21. Processwave, http://www.processwave.org/ (accessed January 10, 2011)
22. Thum, C., Schwind, M., Schader, M.: SLIM—A lightweight environment for synchronous collaborative modeling. In: Schürr, A., Selic, B. (eds.) MODELS 2009. LNCS, vol. 5795, pp. 137–151. Springer, Heidelberg (2009)

Author Index

Akiyama, Motohiro 455
Al Abed, Wisam 123
Al-Batran, Bakr 258
Ali, Shaukat 108
Arcuri, Andrea 108
Aßmann, Uwe 480

Balaban, Mira 517
Balasubramanian, Daniel 653
Barais, Olivier 349
Barat, Souvik 578
Baudry, Benoit 62
Bavota, Gabriele 168
Beaudoux, Olivier 62
Beaulieu, Alain 410
Blay–Fornarino, Mireille 289
Blouin, Arnaud 62
Briand, Lionel C. 108
Bruel, Jean-Michel 213
Buckl, Christian 17

Cabot, Jordi 32, 623
Chauvel, Franck 273
Cheng, Betty H.C. 501, 683
Chimiak–Opoka, Joanna 47
Cichos, Harald 425
Clavreul, Mickael 289
Combemale, Benoît 62, 608
Cruz-Lemus, José Antonio 168
Cuccuru, Arnaud 243, 699
Czarnecki, Krzysztof 304, 668

De Lucia, Andrea 168
Derrien, Steven 608
Desnos, Nicolas 319
Di Cerbo, Francesco 138
Dingel, Juergen 410
Diskin, Zinovy 304, 668
Dodero, Gabriella 138
Drago, Mauro Luigi 2
Drogemuller, Robin 198

Ehrig, Hartmut 304, 668
Elaasar, Maged 364
Espinazo Pagán, Javier 77

Fabry, Johan 93
Fahrenberg, Uli 490
Feinerer, Ingo 379
Fleurey, Franck 349, 638
Floch, Antoine 608
France, Robert B. 289, 608

García-Domínguez, Antonio 395
García Molina, Jesús 77
Genero, Marcela 168
Gérard, Sébastien 243, 699
Ghezzi, Carlo 2
Goldsby, Heather J. 683
Gordillo, Silvia 93
Götz, Sebastian 480
Gravino, Carmine 168
Gürgens, Sigrid 319
Guy, Clement 608

Hamid, Brahim 319
Haugen, Øystein 638
Hauswirth, Matthias 470
Hayashi, Shinpei 455
Heldal, Rogardt 334
Hermann, Frank 304, 668
Huang, Gang 273
Hummel, Benjamin 258

Iraqi-Houssaini, Mehdi 548
Izukura, Sayaka 563

Jackson, Ethan K. 591, 653
Jensen, Adam C. 683
Johansen, Martin Fagereng 638
Jouault, Frédéric 32, 623
Jouvray, Christophe 319

Kainz, Gerd 17
Kienzle, Jörg 123
Kifer, Michael 517
Kimura, Daichi 563
Kleiner, Mathias 548
Knoll, Alois 17
Kobayashi, Takashi 455
Kolovos, Dimitrios S. 395

Koudri, Ali 243
Kraemer, Frank Alexander 183
Krishnan, Ajay 714
Kulkarni, Vinay 578

Labiche, Yvan 364
Legay, Axel 490
Lettner, Michael 228
Levendovszky, Tihamér 653
Lind, Kenneth 334
Lochau, Malte 425
Lugato, David 213

Maoz, Shahar 153, 592
Martínez, Salvador 32
Mayrhofer, Rene 228
Medina-Bulo, Inmaculada 395
Mei, Hong 273
Mirandola, Raffaela 2
Moebius, Nina 533
Moffett, Yann 410
Morin, Brice 349
Mosser, Sébastien 289

Nelson, Edward C. 683

Ober, Ileana 213
Oliveto, Rocco 168
Orejas, Fernando 304, 668
Osaki, Takao 563
Oster, Sebastian 425

Paige, Richard F. 395
Palyart, Marc 213
Petre, Marian 1

Rajopadhye, Sanjay 608
Ramirez, Andres J. 501
Ramteerthkar, Uday 578
Reggio, Gianna 138
Reif, Wolfgang 533
Reimann, Jan 480
Ricca, Filippo 138

Ringert, Jan Oliver 153, 592
Rose, Louis M. 395
Roucoules, Lionel 548
Rumpe, Bernhard 153, 592

Saeki, Motoshi 455
Sagar, Mark 394
Sakaki, Hiroshi 563
Salzer, Gernot 379
Sánchez Cuadrado, Jesús 77
Scanniello, Giuseppe 138
Schätz, Bernhard 258
Schulte, Wolfram 591
Schürr, Andy 425
Shao, Weizhong 273
Sisel, Tanja 379
Solberg, Arnor 349
Song, Hui 273
Steel, Jim 198
Steimann, Friedrich 440
Stenzel, Kurt 533
Sun, Yanchun 273

Terrier, François 243, 699
Tisi, Massimo 32, 623
Tortora, Genoveffa 168
Tschernuth, Michael 228

Wagelaar, Dennis 623
Walawege, Suneth 108
Wąsowski, Andrzej 490
Wilke, Claas 480

Xiang, Jianwen 563
Xiong, Yingfei 304, 668

Yanoo, Kazuo 563
Yuki, Tomofumi 608

Zambrano, Arturo 93
Zaparanuks, Dmitrijs 470
Zhang, Rixin 714
Zhang, Wei 273

GPSR Compliance

The European Union's (EU) General Product Safety Regulation (GPSR) is a set of rules that requires consumer products to be safe and our obligations to ensure this.

If you have any concerns about our products, you can contact us on ProductSafety@springernature.com

In case Publisher is established outside the EU, the EU authorized representative is:

Springer Nature Customer Service Center GmbH
Europaplatz 3
69115 Heidelberg, Germany

Batch number: 09478952

Printed by Printforce, the Netherlands

CAMBRIDGE LIBRARY COLLECTION
Books of enduring scholarly value

Mathematics

From its pre-historic roots in simple counting to the algorithms powering modern desktop computers, from the genius of Archimedes to the genius of Einstein, advances in mathematical understanding and numerical techniques have been directly responsible for creating the modern world as we know it. This series will provide a library of the most influential publications and writers on mathematics in its broadest sense. As such, it will show not only the deep roots from which modern science and technology have grown, but also the astonishing breadth of application of mathematical techniques in the humanities and social sciences, and in everyday life.

Popular Instructions on the Calculation of Probabilities

The Belgian polymath Lambert Adolphe Jacques Quetelet (1796–1874) was regarded by John Maynard Keynes as a 'parent of modern statistical method'. Applying his training in mathematics to the physical and psychological dimensions of individuals, his *Treatise on Man* (also reissued in this series) identified the 'average man' in statistical terms. Reissued here is the 1839 English translation of his 1828 work, which appeared at a time when the application of probability was moving away from gaming tables towards more useful areas of life. Quetelet believed that probability had more influence on human affairs than had been accepted, and this work marked his move from a focus on mathematics and the natural sciences to the study of statistics and, eventually, the investigation of social phenomena. Written as a summary of lectures given in Brussels, the work was translated from French by the engineer Richard Beamish (1798–1873).

Cambridge University Press has long been a pioneer in the reissuing of out-of-print titles from its own backlist, producing digital reprints of books that are still sought after by scholars and students but could not be reprinted economically using traditional technology. The Cambridge Library Collection extends this activity to a wider range of books which are still of importance to researchers and professionals, either for the source material they contain, or as landmarks in the history of their academic discipline.

Drawing from the world-renowned collections in the Cambridge University Library and other partner libraries, and guided by the advice of experts in each subject area, Cambridge University Press is using state-of-the-art scanning machines in its own Printing House to capture the content of each book selected for inclusion. The files are processed to give a consistently clear, crisp image, and the books finished to the high quality standard for which the Press is recognised around the world. The latest print-on-demand technology ensures that the books will remain available indefinitely, and that orders for single or multiple copies can quickly be supplied.

The Cambridge Library Collection brings back to life books of enduring scholarly value (including out-of-copyright works originally issued by other publishers) across a wide range of disciplines in the humanities and social sciences and in science and technology.